Authors, Consultants, Partners

[Authors]

Elisabeth Gaynor Ellis

Elisabeth Gaynor Ellis holds a BS from Smith College and an MA and MS from Columbia University. Before she began writing textbooks, Ms. Ellis taught World Cultures, European History, and Russian Studies in Ardsley, New York. Ms. Ellis co-authored Prentice Hall's *World History: Connections to Today* with Dr. Anthony Esler. Ms. Ellis has also written other social studies materials, including *America's Holidays*, individual state histories, and a variety of Teacher's Edition materials.

Anthony Esler

Anthony Esler is an Emeritus Professor of History at the College of William and Mary in Williamsburg, Virginia. His books include several studies of the conflict of generations in world history, half a dozen historical novels, and two other surveys of world and Western history besides this one. He is a member of the American Historical Association, the World History Association, and the Authors Guild. He has received Fulbright, Social Science Research Council, and other research grants, and is listed in the *Directory of American Scholars*, the *Directory of Poets and Fiction Writers*, and *Who's Who in America*. Books by Dr. Esler include *Bombs, Beards, and Barricades, Forbidden City,* and *The Human Venture.*

[Program Consultant]

Dr. Kathy Swan is an Associate Professor of Curriculum and Instruction at the University of Kentucky. Her research focuses on standards-based technology integration, authentic intellectual work, and documentary-making in the social studies classroom. Swan has been a four-time recipient of the National Technology Leadership Award in Social Studies Education. She is also the advisor for the Social Studies Assessment, Curriculum, and Instruction Collaborative (SSACI) at CCSSO.

[Program Partners]

NBC LEARN

NBC Learn, the educational arm of NBC News, develops original stories for use in the classroom and makes archival NBC News stories, images, and primary source documents available on demand to teachers, students, and parents. NBC Learn partnered with Pearson to produce the myStory videos that support this program.

Constitutional Rights Foundation
Educate. Participate.

Constitutional Rights Foundation is a nonprofit, nonpartisan organization focused on educating students about the importance of civic participation in a democratic society. Constitutional Rights Foundation is the lead contributor to the development of the Civic Discussion Topic Inquiries for this program. Constitutional Rights Foundation is also the provider of the Civic Action Project (CAP) for the *Economics* and *Magruder's American Government* programs. CAP is a project-based learning model for civics, government, and economics courses.

Reviewers & Academic Consultants

Pearson World History The Modern Era was developed especially for you and your students. The story of its creation began with a three-day Innovation Lab in which teachers, historians, students, and authors came together to imagine our ideal Social Studies teaching and learning experiences. We refined the plan with a series of teacher roundtables that shaped this new approach to ensure your students' mastery of content and skills. A dedicated team, made up of Pearson authors, content experts, and social studies teachers, worked to bring our collective vision into reality. Kathy Swan, Professor of Education and architect of the new College, Career, and Civic Life (C3) Framework, served as our expert advisor on curriculum and instruction.

Pearson extends a special thank you to all the teachers who helped guide the development of this program. We gratefully acknowledge your efforts to realize Next Generation Social Studies teaching and learning that will prepare American students for college and careers.

[Program Advisors]

Campaign for the Civic Mission of Schools is a coalition of over 70 national civic learning, education, civic engagement, and business groups committed to improving the quality and quantity of civic learning in American schools. The Campaign served as an advisor on this program.

Buck Institute for Education is a nonprofit organization dedicated to helping teachers implement the effective use of Project-Based Learning in their classrooms. Buck Institute staff consulted on the Project-Based Learning Topic Inquiries for this program.

[California Academic Reviewers]

Robert Cleary
Temescal Canyon High School
Lake Elsinore, California

Nina Glassen
Capistrano Unified School District
San Juan Capistrano, California

Robert Hiles
Newport-Mesa Unified School District
Newport Beach, California

Sarah Nauss
Fremont Unified School District
Fremont, California

Michael Ochs
Chaminade High School
West Hills, California

Michelle Ritter
Temescal Canyon High School
Lake Elsinore, California

Gary Roldan
Orosi High School
Orosi, California

[Program Academic Consultants]

Barbara Brown
Director of Outreach
College of Arts and Sciences
African Studies Center
Boston University
Boston, Massachusetts

William Childs
Professor of History Emeritus
The Ohio State University
Columbus, Ohio

Jennifer Giglielmo
Associate Professor of History
Smith College
Northhampton, Massachusetts

Joanne Connor Green
Professor, Department Chair
Political Science
Texas Christian University
Fort Worth, Texas

Ramdas Lamb, Ph.D.
Associate Professor of Religion
University of Hawaii at Manoa
Honolulu, Hawaii

Huping Ling
Changjiang Scholar Chair Professor
Professor of History
Truman State University
Kirksville, Missouri

Jeffery Long, Ph.D.
Professor of Religion and Asian Studies
Elizabethtown College
Elizabethtown, Pennsylvania

Gordon Newby
Professor of Islamic, Jewish and Comparative Studies
Department of Middle Eastern and South Asian Studies
Emory University
Atlanta, Georgia

Mark Peterson
Associate Professor
Department of Asian and Near Eastern Languages
Brigham Young University
Provo, Utah

William Pitts
Professor, Department of Religion
Baylor University
Waco, Texas

Benjamin Ravid
Professor Emeritus of Jewish History
Department of Near Eastern and Judaic Studies
Brandeis University
Waltham, Massachusetts

Harpreet Singh
College Fellow
Department of South Asian Studies
Harvard University
Cambridge, Massachusetts

Christopher E. Smith, J.D., Ph.D.
Professor
Michigan State University
MSU School of Criminal Justice
East Lansing, Michigan

John Voll
Professor of Islamic History
Georgetown University
Washington, D.C.

Michael R. Wolf
Associate Professor
Department of Political Science
Indiana University-Purdue University Fort Wayne
Fort Wayne, Indiana

Social studies is more than dots on a map or dates on a timeline. It's where we've been and where we're going. It's stories from the past and our stories today. And in today's fast-paced, interconnected world, it's essential.

Welcome to the next generation of California social studies!

Pearson's new California social studies program was created in collaboration with California educators, social studies experts, and students. The program is based on Pearson's California History Social-Science Standards and Framework (CAHSS) Mastery. The System uses tested best practices, CAHSS expectations, technology, and a four-part framework—Connect, Investigate, Synthesize, and Demonstrate—to prepare students to be college and career ready—while mastering CAHSS.

The System includes:

- 100% coverage of the California State Standards.
- CAHSS-focused table of contents that will save teachers time and improve pacing. Higher-level content that gives support to access complex text, acquire core content knowledge, and tackle rigorous questions.
- Inquiry-focused Projects, Civic Discussions, and Document Analysis activities that develop content and skills mastery in preparation for real-world challenges.
- Digital content on Pearson Realize that is dynamic, flexible, and uses the power of technology to bring social studies to life.

» Go online to learn more and see the program overview video.

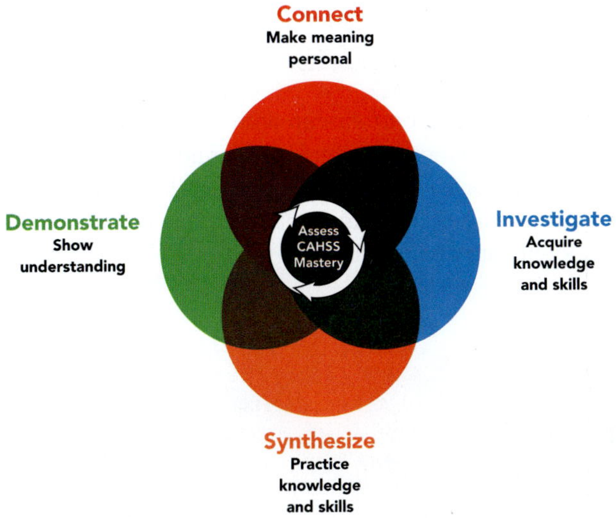

PEARSON realize™

The digital course on Realize!

The program's digital course on Realize puts rich and engaging content, embedded assessments with instant data, and flexible tools at your fingertips.

Connect: Make Meaning Personal

CONNECT! California students will begin the Pearson California CAHSS Mastery System by engaging in the topic story and connecting it to their own lives.

CAHSS Preview—Each Topic opens with CAHSS, allowing students to preview expected learning outcomes. CAHSS analysis skills are closely integrated within the content.

>> Instruction begins with an **Essential Question**. These thought-provoking questions engage students and introduce the Topic.

[ESSENTIAL QUESTION] What are the benefits and risks of interdependence?

>> Developed in partnership with NBCLearn, the **My Story** videos help students connect to the Topic content by hearing the personal story of an individual whose life is related to the content students are about to learn.

INVESTIGATE! Step two of the CAHSS Mastery System allows California students to investigate the topic story through a number of engaging features as you learn the content.

>> **Active Classroom Strategies** integrated in the daily lesson plans help to increase in-class participation, raise energy levels and attentiveness, all while engaging in the story. These 5-15 minute activities have you use what you have learned to draw, write, speak, and decide.

>> **Interactive Primary Source Galleries:** Use primary source image galleries throughout the lesson to see, analyze, and interact with images that tie to the topic story content.

Investigate

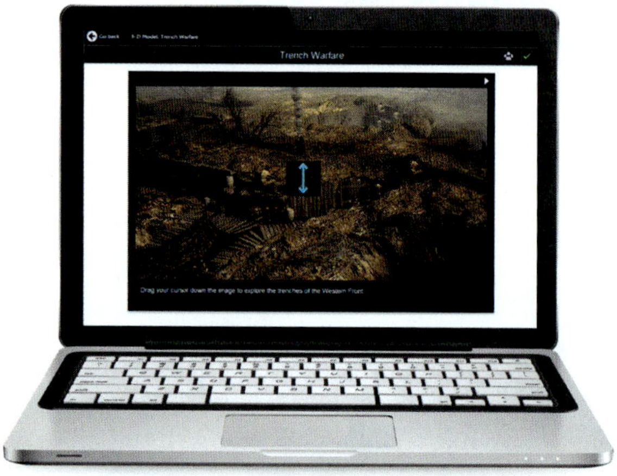

>> Feel like you are a part of the story with **interactive 3-D models**.

>> Continue to investigate the topic story through **dynamic interactive maps**. Build map skills while covering the essential standards.

>> Learn content by reading narrative text online or in a printed Student Edition.

Synthesize: Practice Knowledge and Skills

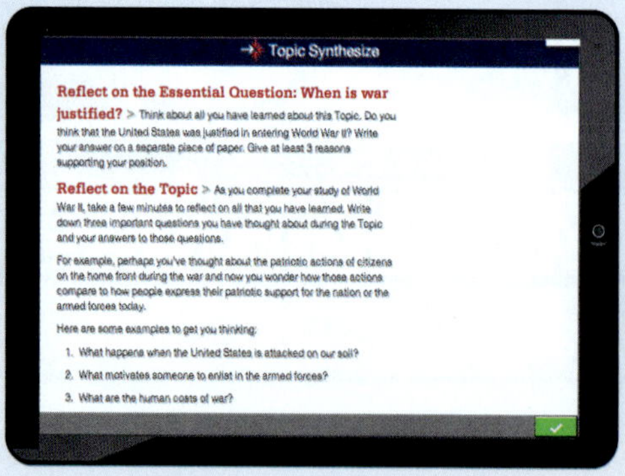

SYNTHESIZE!

In step three of the Mastery System, pause to reflect on what you learn and revisit an essential question.

DEMONSTRATE! The final step of the CAHSS Mastery System is to demonstrate understanding of the CAHSS.

PEARSON realize™

>> The digital course on Realize! The program's digital course on Realize puts engaging content, embedded assessments, instant data, and flexible tools at your fingertips.

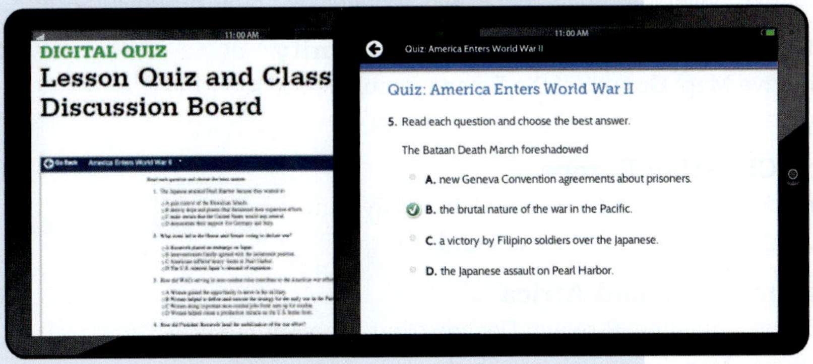

>> CAHSS Assessment. At the end of each lesson and topic, demonstrate understanding through Lesson Quizzes, Topic Tests, and Topic Inquiry performance assessments. The System provides remediation and enrichment recommendations based on your individual performance towards mastery.

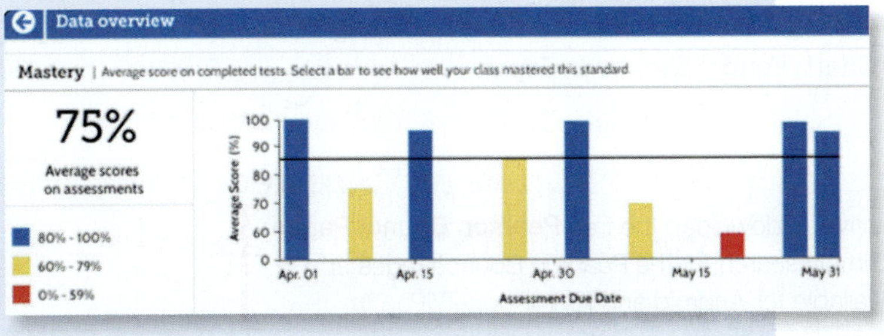

>> Class and Data features on Realize make it easy to use students' CAHSS mastery data to show if time is needed to re-teach or move ahead.

Table of Contents

REVIEW

Connecting with Past Learnings (Prehistory–1700) 2

Content Standards

HSS 10.1.1
HSS 10.2.2
Analysis CST.1
Analysis CST.2
Analysis HRE.4
Analysis HI.1

To activate your digital course interactivities download the free **Pearson BouncePages** app on your smartphone or tablet. Simply search for the Pearson BouncePages app in your mobile app store. The app is available for Android and IOS (iPhone®/iPad®).

TOPIC 1 Absolutism and Revolution (1550–1850) 96

Content Standards

HSS 10.1.1
HSS 10.1.3
HSS 10.2
HSS 10.2.1
HSS 10.2.2
HSS 10.2.3
HSS 10.2.4
HSS 10.2.5
Analysis CST.1
Analysis CST.2
Analysis CST.3
Analysis HRE.4
Analysis HI.1

Table of Contents

TOPIC 3 Nationalism and the Spread of Democracy (1790–1914) 224

Content Standards
HSS 10.3.4
Analysis CST.1
Analysis CST.2
Analysis CST.3
Analysis HRE.4
Analysis HI.1

Table of Contents

TOPIC 4 The Age of Imperialism (1800–1914) 288

Content Standards

HSS 10.4
HSS 10.4.1
HSS 10.4.2
HSS 10.4.3
HSS 10.4.4
Analysis CST.1
Analysis CST.2
Analysis CST.3
Analysis HRE.4
Analysis HI.1

PEARSON realize™ PearsonSchool.com/CASS Access your Digital Lesson

TOPIC 5 World War I and the Russian Revolution (1914–1924) 346

Content Standards

HSS 10.5
HSS 10.5.1
HSS 10.5.2
HSS 10.5.3
HSS 10.5.4
HSS 10.5.5
HSS 10.6
HSS 10.6.1
HSS 10.6.2
HSS 10.7.1
HSS 10.8.1
Analysis CST.1
Analysis CST.2
Analysis HRE.4
Analysis HI.1

Table of Contents

TOPIC 6 The World Between the Wars (1910–1939) 386

Content Standards

HSS 10.6.3
HSS 10.6.4
HSS 10.7
HSS 10.7.2
HSS 10.7.3
HSS 10.8.2
Analysis CST.1
Analysis CST.2
Analysis CST.3
Analysis HRE.4
Analysis HI.1

PEARSON realize
PearsonSchool.com/CASS
Access your Digital Lesson

TOPIC 7 World War II (1930–1945) 452

Table of Contents

TOPIC 8 The Cold War Era (1945–1991) 498

Content Standards

HSS 10.9
HSS 10.9.1
HSS 10.9.2
HSS 10.9.3
HSS 10.9.4
HSS 10.9.5
HSS 10.9.7
HSS 10.9.8
Analysis CST.1
Analysis CST.2
Analysis HRE.4
Analysis HI.1

PearsonSchool.com/CASS
Access your Digital Lesson

TOPIC 9 New Nations Emerge (1945–Present) 544

Content Standards

HSS 10.9.2
HSS 10.9.3
HSS 10.9.6
HSS 10.10
HSS 10.10.1
HSS 10.10.2
Analysis CST.1
Analysis CST.2
Analysis CST.4
Analysis HRE.4
Analysis HI.1

Table of Contents

TOPIC 10 The World Today (1980–Present) 590

Content Standards
HSS 10.9.2
HSS 10.9.4
HSS 10.9.8
HSS 10.10
HSS 10.10.1
HSS 10.10.2
HSS 10.3
HSS 10.11
Analysis CST.1
Analysis CST.2
Analysis CST.4
Analysis HRE.4
Analysis HI.1

PEARSON realize
PearsonSchool.com/CASS
Access your Digital Lesson

Digital Resources

Many types of digital resources help you investigate the topics in this course. You'll find biographies, primary sources, maps, and more. These resources will help bring the topics to life.

Core Concepts

Culture

- What Is Culture?
- Families and Societies
- Language
- Religion
- The Arts
- Cultural Diffusion and Change
- Science and Technology

Economics

- Economics Basics
- Economic Process
- Economic Systems
- Economic Development
- Trade
- Money Management

Geography

- The Study of Earth
- Geography's Five Themes
- Ways to Show Earth's Surface
- Understanding Maps
- Earth in Space
- Time and Earth's Rotation
- Forces on Earth's Surface
- Forces Inside Earth
- Climate and Weather
- Temperature
- Water and Climate
- Air Circulation and Precipitation
- Types of Climate
- Ecosystems
- Environment and Resources
- Land Use
- People's Impact on the Environment
- Population
- Migration
- Urbanization

Government and Civics

- Foundations of Government
- Political Systems
- Political Structures
- Conflict and Cooperation
- Citizenship

History

- How Do Historians Study History?
- Measuring Time
- Historical Sources
- Archaeology and Other Sources
- Historical Maps

Personal Finance

- Your Fiscal Fitness: An Introduction
- Budgeting
- Checking
- Investments
- Savings and Retirement
- Credit and Debt
- Risk Management
- Consumer Smarts
- After High School
- Taxes and Income

Landmark Supreme Court Cases

- *Korematsu* v. *United States*
- *Marbury* v. *Madison*
- *McCulloch* v. *Maryland*
- *Gibbons* v. *Ogden*
- *Worcester* v. *Georgia*
- *Dred Scott* v. *Sandford*
- *Plessy* v. *Ferguson*
- *Schenck* v. *United States*
- *Brown* v. *Board of Education*
- *Engel* v. *Vitale*
- *Sweatt* v. *Painter*
- *Mapp* v. *Ohio*
- *Hernandez* v. *Texas*
- *Gideon* v. *Wainwright*
- *Wisconsin* v. *Yoder*
- *Miranda* v. *Arizona*
- *White* v. *Regester*
- *Tinker* v. *Des Moines School District*
- *Roe* v. *Wade*
- *Baker* v. *Carr*
- *Grutter* v. *Bollinger*
- *Edgewood* v. *Kirby*
- *Texas* v. *Johnson*
- *National Federation of Independent Businesses et al.* v. *Sebelius et al.*
- *Mendez* v. *Westminster* and *Delgado* v. *Bastrop*

Interactive Primary Sources

- Code of Hammurabi
- Psalm 23
- The Republic, Plato
- Politics, Aristotle
- De re publica, Cicero
- Edicts, Asoka
- Analects, Confucius
- First Letter to the Corinthians, Paul
- The Quran
- The Magna Carta
- Travels, Ibn Battuta
- The Prince, Niccolò Machiavelli
- The Destruction of the Indies, Bartolomé de Las Casas
- Mayflower Compact
- English Petition of Right
- English Bill of Rights
- Two Treatises of Government, John Locke
- The Spirit of Laws, Baron de Montesquieu
- The Social Contract, Jean-Jacques Rousseau
- The Interesting Narrative of the Life of Olaudah Equiano
- "Give Me Liberty or Give Me Death," Patrick Henry
- "Remember the Ladies," Abigail Adams
- Common Sense, Thomas Paine
- Declaration of Independence
- Virginia Declaration of Rights
- Virginia Statute for Religious Freedom, Thomas Jefferson
- "To His Excellency, General Washington," Phillis Wheatley
- Articles of Confederation
- Anti-Federalist Papers
- The Federalist No. 10, James Madison
- The Federalist No. 39, James Madison
- The Federalist No. 51
- The Federalist No. 78, Alexander Hamilton
- Northwest Ordinance
- Iroquois Constitution
- Declaration of the Rights of Man and the Citizen
- Farewell Address, George Washington
- Mexican Federal Constitution of 1824
- State Colonization Law of 1825
- Law of April 6, 1830
- Debate Over Nullification, Webster and Calhoun
- Turtle Bayou Resolutions
- Democracy in America, Alexis de Tocqueville
- 1836 Victory or Death Letter from the Alamo, Travis
- Texas Declaration of Independence
- Declaration of Sentiments and Resolutions
- "Ain't I a Woman?," Sojourner Truth
- Uncle Tom's Cabin, Harriet Beecher Stowe
- "A House Divided," Abraham Lincoln
- First Inaugural Address, Abraham Lincoln
- Declaration of Causes: February 2, 1861
- Emancipation Proclamation, Abraham Lincoln
- Gettysburg Address, Abraham Lincoln
- Second Inaugural Address, Abraham Lincoln
- "I Will Fight No More Forever," Chief Joseph
- How the Other Half Lives, Jacob Riis
- The Pledge of Allegiance
- Preamble to the Platform of the Populist Party
- Atlanta Exposition Address, Booker T. Washington
- "The White Man's Burden," Rudyard Kipling
- The Jungle, Upton Sinclair
- Hind Swaraj, Mohandas Gandhi
- The Fourteen Points, Woodrow Wilson
- Two Poems, Langston Hughes
- Four Freedoms, Franklin D. Roosevelt
- Anne Frank: The Diary of a Young Girl, Anne Frank
- Charter of the United Nations
- Universal Declaration of Human Rights
- Autobiography, Kwame Nkrumah
- Inaugural Address, John F. Kennedy
- Silent Spring, Rachel Carson
- "I Have a Dream," Martin Luther King, Jr.
- "Letter From Birmingham Jail," Martin Luther King, Jr.
- State of the Union address, Lyndon Johnson
- State of the Union address, Gerald Ford
- "Tear Down This Wall," Ronald Reagan
- "Freedom From Fear," Aung San Suu Kyi
- State of the Union address, William Jefferson Clinton
- "Glory and Hope," Nelson Mandela
- State of the Union address, George W. Bush

Biographies

- Abigail Adams
- John Adams
- John Quincy Adams
- Samuel Adams
- James Armistead
- Crispus Attucks
- Moses Austin
- Stephen F. Austin
- James A. Baker III
- Emily Greene Balch
- William Blackstone
- Simón Bolívar
- Napoleon Bonaparte
- Chief Bowles
- Omar Bradley
- John C. Calhoun
- César Chávez
- Wentworth Cheswell
- George Childress
- Winston Churchill
- Henry Clay
- Bill Clinton
- Jefferson Davis
- Martin De León
- Green DeWitt
- Dwight Eisenhower
- James Fannin
- James L. Farmer, Jr.
- Benjamin Franklin
- Milton Friedman
- Betty Friedan
- Bernardo de Gálvez
- Hector P. Garcia
- John Nance Garner
- King George III
- William Gladstone
- Henry B. González
- Raul A. Gonzalez, Jr.
- Mikhail Gorbachev
- William Goyens
- Ulysses S. Grant
- José Gutiérrez de Lara
- Alexander Hamilton
- Hammurabi
- Warren Harding
- Vaclav Havel
- Friedrich Hayek
- Jack Coffee Hays
- Patrick Henry
- Adolf Hitler
- Oveta Culp Hobby
- James Hogg
- Sam Houston
- Kay Bailey Hutchison
- Andrew Jackson
- John Jay
- Thomas Jefferson
- Lyndon B. Johnson
- Anson Jones
- Barbara Jordan
- Justinian
- John F. Kennedy
- John Maynard Keynes
- Martin Luther King, Jr.
- Marquis de Lafayette
- Mirabeau B. Lamar
- Robert E. Lee
- Abraham Lincoln
- John Locke
- Niccolò Machiavelli
- James Madison
- John Marshall
- George Marshall
- Karl Marx
- George Mason
- Mary Maverick
- Jane McCallum
- Joseph McCarthy
- James Monroe
- Charles de Montesquieu
- Dwight L. Moody
- Edwin W. Moore
- Moses
- Benito Mussolini
- José Antonio Navarro
- Chester A. Nimitz
- Richard M. Nixon
- Barack Obama
- Sandra Day O'Connor
- Thomas Paine
- Quanah Parker
- Rosa Parks
- George Patton
- John J. Pershing
- John Paul II
- Sam Rayburn
- Ronald Reagan
- Hiram Rhodes Revels
- Franklin D. Roosevelt
- Theodore Roosevelt
- Lawrence Sullivan Ross
- Haym Soloman
- Antonio Lopez de Santa Anna
- Phyllis Schlafly
- Erasmo Seguín
- Juan N. Seguín
- Roger Sherman
- Adam Smith
- Alexander Solzhenitsyn
- Joseph Stalin
- William Graham Sumner
- Billy Sunday
- Raymond L. Telles
- Alexis de Tocqueville
- Hideki Tojo
- William B. Travis
- Harry Truman
- Lech Walesa
- Mercy Otis Warren
- George Washington
- Daniel Webster
- Lulu Belle Madison White
- William Wilberforce
- James Wilson
- Woodrow Wilson
- Lorenzo de Zavala
- Mao Zedong

21st Century Skills

- Identify Main Ideas and Details
- Set a Purpose for Reading
- Use Context Clues
- Analyze Cause and Effect
- Categorize
- Compare and Contrast
- Draw Conclusions
- Draw Inferences
- Generalize
- Make Decisions
- Make Predictions
- Sequence
- Solve Problems
- Summarize
- Analyze Media Content
- Analyze Primary and Secondary Sources
- Compare Viewpoints
- Distinguish Between Fact and Opinion
- Identify Bias
- Analyze Data and Models
- Analyze Images
- Analyze Political Cartoons
- Create Charts and Maps
- Create Databases
- Read Charts, Graphs, and Tables
- Read Physical Maps
- Read Political Maps
- Read Special-Purpose Maps
- Use Parts of a Map
- Ask Questions
- Avoid Plagiarism
- Create a Research Hypothesis
- Evaluate Web Sites
- Identify Evidence
- Identify Trends
- Interpret Sources
- Search for Information on the Internet
- Synthesize
- Take Effective Notes
- Develop a Clear Thesis
- Organize Your Ideas
- Support Ideas With Evidence
- Evaluate Existing Arguments
- Consider & Counter Opposing Arguments
- Give an Effective Presentation
- Participate in a Discussion or Debate
- Publish Your Work
- Write a Journal Entry
- Write an Essay
- Share Responsibility
- Compromise
- Develop Cultural Awareness
- Generate New Ideas
- Innovate
- Make a Difference
- Work in Teams
- Being an Informed Citizen
- Paying Taxes
- Political Participation
- Serving on a Jury
- Voting

Atlas

- United States: Political
- United States: Physical
- California: Political
- California: Physical
- World Political
- World Physical
- World Climate
- World Ecosystems
- World Population Density
- World Land Use
- North Africa and Southwest Asia: Political
- North Africa and Southwest Asia: Physical
- Sub-Saharan Africa: Political
- Sub-Saharan Africa: Physical
- South Asia: Political
- South Asia: Physical
- East Asia: Political
- East Asia: Physical
- Southeast Asia: Political
- Southeast Asia: Physical
- Europe: Political
- Europe: Physical
- Russia, Central Asia, and the Caucasus: Political
- Russia, Central Asia, and the Caucasus: Physical
- North America: Political
- North America: Physical
- Central America and the Caribbean: Political
- Central America and the Caribbean: Physical
- South America: Political
- South America: Physical
- Australia and the Pacific: Political
- Australia and the Pacific: Physical

History-Social Science Content Standards for California Public Schools

World History, Culture, and Geography: The Modern World

10.1 Students relate the moral and ethical principles in ancient Greek and Roman philosophy, in Judaism, and in Christianity to the development of Western political thought.

10.1.1 Analyze the similarities and differences in Judeo-Christian and Greco-Roman views of law, reason and faith, and duties of the individual.

10.1.2 Trace the development of the Western political ideas of the rule of law and illegitimacy of tyranny, using selections from Plato's *Republic* and Aristotle's *Politics*.

10.1.3 Consider the influence of the U.S. Constitution on political systems in the contemporary world.

10.2 Students compare and contrast the Glorious Revolution of England, the American Revolution, and the French Revolution and their enduring effects worldwide on the political expectations for self-government and individual liberty.

10.2.1 Compare the major ideas of philosophers and their effects on the democratic revolutions in England, the United States, France, and Latin America (e.g., John Locke, Charles-Louis Montesquieu, Jean-Jacques Rousseau, Simón Bolívar, Thomas Jefferson, James Madison).

10.2.2 List the principles of the Magna Carta, the English Bill of Rights (1689), the American Declaration of Independence (1776), the French Declaration of the Rights of Man and the Citizen (1789), and the U.S. Bill of Rights (1791).

10.2.3 Understand the unique character of the American Revolution, its spread to other parts of the world, and its continuing significance to other nations.

10.2.4 Explain how the ideology of the French Revolution led France to develop from constitutional monarchy to democratic despotism to the Napoleonic empire.

10.2.5 Discuss how nationalism spread across Europe with Napoleon but was repressed for a generation under the Congress of Vienna and Concert of Europe until the Revolutions of 1848.

10.3 Students analyze the effects of the Industrial Revolution in England, France, Germany, Japan, and the United States.

10.3.1 Analyze why England was the first country to industrialize.

10.3.2 Examine how scientific and technological changes and new forms of energy brought about massive social, economic, and cultural change (e.g., the inventions and discoveries of James Watt, Eli Whitney, Henry Bessemer, Louis Pasteur, Thomas Edison).

10.3.3 Describe the growth of population, rural to urban migration, and growth of cities associated with the Industrial Revolution.

10.3.4 Trace the evolution of work and labor, including the demise of the slave trade and the effects of immigration, mining and manufacturing, division of labor, and the union movement.

10.3.5 Understand the connections among natural resources, entrepreneurship, labor, and capital in an industrial economy.

10.3.6 Analyze the emergence of capitalism as a dominant economic pattern and the responses to it, including Utopianism, Social Democracy, Socialism, and Communism.

10.3.7 Describe the emergence of Romanticism in art and literature (e.g., the poetry of William Blake and William Wordsworth), social criticism (e.g., the novels of Charles Dickens), and the move away from Classicism in Europe.

10.4 Students analyze patterns of global change in the era of New Imperialism in at least two of the following regions or countries: Africa, Southeast Asia, China, India, Latin America, and the Philippines.

10.4.1 Describe the rise of industrial economies and their link to imperialism and colonialism (e.g., the role played by national security and strategic advantage; moral issues raised by the search for national hegemony, Social Darwinism, and the missionary impulse; material issues such as land, resources, and technology).

10.4.2 Discuss the locations of the colonial rule of such nations as England, France, Germany, Italy, Japan, the Netherlands, Russia, Spain, Portugal, and the United States.

10.4.3 Explain imperialism from the perspective of the colonizers and the colonized and the varied immediate and long-term responses by the people under colonial rule.

10.4.4 Describe the independence struggles of the colonized regions of the world, including the roles of leaders, such as Sun Yat-sen in China, and the roles of ideology and religion.

10.5 Students analyze the causes and course of the First World War.

10.5.1 Analyze the arguments for entering into war presented by leaders from all sides of the Great War and the role of political and economic rivalries, ethnic and ideological conflicts, domestic discontent and disorder, and propaganda and nationalism in mobilizing the civilian population in support of "total war."

10.5.2 Examine the principal theaters of battle, major turning points, and the importance of geographic factors in military decisions and outcomes (e.g., topography, waterways, distance, climate).

10.5.3 Explain how the Russian Revolution and the entry of the United States affected the course and outcome of the war.

10.5.4 Understand the nature of the war and its human costs (military and civilian) on all sides of the conflict, including how colonial peoples contributed to the war effort.

10.5.5 Discuss human rights violations and genocide, including the Ottoman government's actions against Armenian citizens.

10.6 Students analyze the effects of the First World War.

10.6.1 Analyze the aims and negotiating roles of world leaders, the terms and influence of the Treaty of Versailles and Woodrow Wilson's Fourteen Points, and the causes and effects of the United States's rejection of the League of Nations on world politics.

10.6.2 Describe the effects of the war and resulting peace treaties on population movement, the international economy, and shifts in the geographic and political borders of Europe and the Middle East.

10.6.3 Understand the widespread disillusionment with prewar institutions, authorities, and values that resulted in a void that was later filled by totalitarians.

10.6.4 Discuss the influence of World War I on literature, art, and intellectual life in the West (e.g., Pablo Picasso, the "lost generation" of Gertrude Stein, Ernest Hemingway).

10.7 Students analyze the rise of totalitarian governments after World War I.

10.7.1 Understand the causes and consequences of the Russian Revolution, including Lenin's use of totalitarian means to seize and maintain control (e.g., the Gulag).

10.7.2 Trace Stalin's rise to power in the Soviet Union and the connection between economic policies, political policies, the absence of a free press, and systematic violations of human rights (e.g., the Terror Famine in Ukraine).

10.7.3 Analyze the rise, aggression, and human costs of totalitarian regimes (Fascist and Communist) in Germany, Italy, and the Soviet Union, noting especially their common and dissimilar traits.

10.8 Students analyze the causes and consequences of World War II.

10.8.1 Compare the German, Italian, and Japanese drives for empire in the 1930s, including the 1937 Rape of Nanking, other atrocities in China, and the Stalin-Hitler Pact of 1939.

10.8.2 Understand the role of appeasement, nonintervention (isolationism), and the domestic distractions in Europe and the United States prior to the outbreak of World War II.

10.8.3 Identify and locate the Allied and Axis powers on a map and discuss the major turning points of the war, the principal theaters of conflict, key strategic decisions, and the resulting war conferences and political resolutions, with emphasis on the importance of geographic factors.

10.8.4 Describe the political, diplomatic, and military leaders during the war (e.g., Winston Churchill, Franklin Delano Roosevelt, Emperor Hirohito, Adolf Hitler, Benito Mussolini, Joseph Stalin, Douglas MacArthur, Dwight Eisenhower).

10.8.5 Analyze the Nazi policy of pursuing racial purity, especially against the European Jews; its transformation into the Final Solution; and the Holocaust that resulted in the murder of six million Jewish civilians.

10.8.6 Discuss the human costs of the war, with particular attention to the civilian and military losses in Russia, Germany, Britain, the United States, China, and Japan.

10.9 Students analyze the international developments in the post-World World War II world.

10.9.1 Compare the economic and military power shifts caused by the war, including the Yalta Pact, the development of nuclear weapons, Soviet control over Eastern European nations, and the economic recoveries of Germany and Japan.

10.9.2 Analyze the causes of the Cold War, with the free world on one side and Soviet client states on the other, including competition for influence in such places as Egypt, the Congo, Vietnam, and Chile.

10.9.3 Understand the importance of the Truman Doctrine and the Marshall Plan, which established the pattern for America's postwar policy of supplying economic and military aid to prevent the spread of Communism and the resulting economic and political competition in arenas such as Southeast Asia (i.e., the Korean War, Vietnam War), Cuba, and Africa.

10.9.4 Analyze the Chinese Civil War, the rise of Mao Tse-tung, and the subsequent political and economic upheavals in China (e.g., the Great Leap Forward, the Cultural Revolution, and the Tiananmen Square uprising).

10.9.5 Describe the uprisings in Poland (1952), Hungary (1956), and Czechoslovakia (1968) and those countries' resurgence in the 1970s and 1980s as people in Soviet satellites sought freedom from Soviet control.

10.9.6 Understand how the forces of nationalism developed in the Middle East, how the Holocaust affected world opinion regarding the need for a Jewish state, and the significance and effects of the location and establishment of Israel on world affairs.

10.9.7 Analyze the reasons for the collapse of the Soviet Union, including the weakness of the command economy, burdens of military commitments, and growing resistance to Soviet rule by dissidents in satellite states and the non-Russian Soviet republics.

10.9.8 Discuss the establishment and work of the United Nations and the purposes and functions of the Warsaw Pact, SEATO, NATO, and the Organization of American States.

10.10 Students analyze instances of nation-building in the contemporary world in at least two of the following regions or countries: the Middle East, Africa, Mexico and other parts of Latin America, and China.

10.10.1 Understand the challenges in the regions, including their geopolitical, cultural, military, and economic significance and the international relationships in which they are involved.

10.10.2 Describe the recent history of the regions, including political divisions and systems, key leaders, religious issues, natural features, resources, and population patterns.

10.10.3 Discuss the important trends in the regions today and whether they appear to serve the cause of individual freedom and democracy.

10.11 Students analyze the integration of countries into the world economy and the information, technological, and communications revolutions (e.g., television, satellites, computers).

Historical and Social Sciences Analysis Skills

Chronological and Spatial Thinking

CST.1 Students compare the present with the past, evaluating the consequences of past events and decisions and determining the lessons that were learned.

CST.2 Students analyze how change happens at different rates at different times; understand that some aspects can change while others remain the same; and understand that change is complicated and affects not only technology and politics but also values and beliefs.

CST.3 Students use a variety of maps and documents to interpret human movement, including major patterns of domestic and international migration, changing environmental preferences and settlement patterns, the frictions that develop between population groups, and the diffusion of ideas, technological innovations, and goods.

CST.4 Students relate current events to the physical and human characteristics of places and regions.

Historical Research, Evidence, and Point of View

HRE.1 Students distinguish valid arguments from fallacious arguments in historical interpretations.

HRE.2 Students identify bias and prejudice in historical interpretations.

HRE.3 Students evaluate major debates among historians concerning alternative interpretations of the past, including an analysis of authors' use of evidence and the distinctions between sound generalizations and misleading oversimplifications.

HRE.4 Students construct and test hypotheses; collect, evaluate, and employ information from multiple primary and secondary sources; and apply it in oral and written presentations.

Historical Interpretation

HI.1 Students show the connections, causal and otherwise, between particular historical events and larger social, economic, and political trends and developments.

HI.2 Students recognize the complexity of historical causes and effects, including the limitations on determining cause and effect.

HI.3 Students interpret past events and issues within the context in which an event unfolded rather than solely in terms of present-day norms and values.

HI.4 Students understand the meaning, implication, and impact of historical events and recognize that events could have taken other directions.

HI.5 Students analyze human modifications of landscapes and examine the resulting environmental policy issues.

HI.6 Students conduct cost-benefit analyses and apply basic economic indicators to analyze the aggregate economic behavior of the U.S. economy.

COURSE INTRODUCTION

Questions from the History–Social Science Framework for California Public Schools to guide your study of World History

The study of world history covers the stories of the people who have lived on all the continents over a span of thousands of years. Though cultures have varied widely, and steady progress has changed the nature of people's struggles, certain themes are universal. The following Guiding Questions will help you focus on some of the major changes that have affected the course of modern history.

GUIDING QUESTION

How did ideas associated with the Enlightenment, the Scientific Revolution, the Age of Reason, and a variety of democratic revolutions develop and impact civil society?

Several periods of revolutionary thought followed the years of the middle ages. During these movements, prominent thinkers, scientists, artists, and leaders questioned traditional social values and traditional ways of doing things. As they developed new philosophies related to the arts, sciences, and government, they affected how people in general viewed the world around them. New ways of thinking forced changes to society.

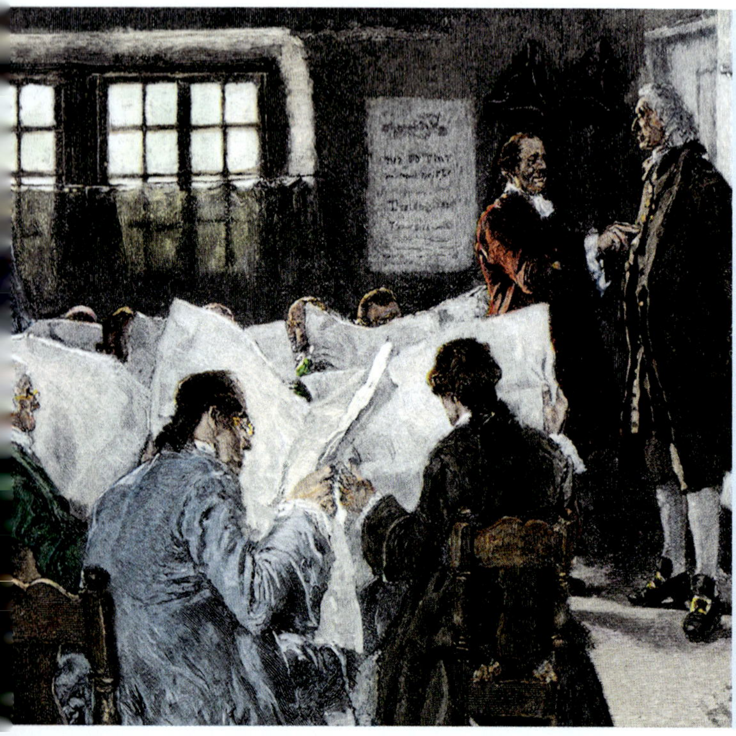

The Enlightenment and the Age of Reason

>> The Enlightenment, sometimes called the Age of Reason, was a period of revolutionary thinking in the 17th and 18th centuries. Philosophers and other writers studied the ideas of the ancient Greeks and Romans as well as advances made during the Renaissance and Reformation in the 14th through 17th centuries. Inspired by these periods, Enlightenment figures refocused society on the value of individual rights and responsibilities. They questioned blind obedience to rulers and thought that the answers to society's problems could be found through reason, the thought process that observes and evaluates evidence.

See Topic 1, Lesson 4, to learn more about the philosophies of the Enlightenment and their impact.

The Scientific Revolution

>> In the 16th and 17th centuries, the practice of modern science was established by scientists using new methods of observing and evaluating the world. Like the philosophers of the Enlightenment, these scientists used reason and logic to come to conclusions. This way of thinking, called the scientific method, relied on careful observation and analysis based on evidence. By using the evidence in front of them instead of being influenced by religious and other cultural pressures, the scientists of the time made revolutionary advances in their fields.

See Topic 1, Lesson 4, to learn more about the Scientific Revolution.

Democratic Revolutions

>> Between the years of 1750–1917, political revolutions upended the ruling governments throughout much of the Americas and Europe. Starting with the American Revolution and French Revolution, these rebellions found inspiration in the concept of democracy formed by ancient Greeks in Athens. Revolutionaries also borrowed on philosophies from the Enlightenment that stressed the importance of reason, individual rights, and citizenship. Replacing monarchs and other authoritarian leaders with democratic and representative forms of governments, these revolutions established the nature of civil society prevalent through much of the world today.

See Topic 1, Lessons 5–7, and Topic 3, Lessons 1 and 2, to learn more about democratic revolutions.

CONNECTING TO THE GUIDING QUESTION

1. How was the history of democratic revolutions linked to the Enlightenment?
2. How did the practices of scientists during the Scientific Revolution break from the teachings of religion?
3. How are modern American values representative of philosophies popularized during the Enlightenment?

GUIDING QUESTION

Why did imperial powers seek to expand their empires? How did colonies respond? What were the legacies of these conquests?

Imperialism is the policy of one country's political, economic, or cultural domination over other lands and territories. In the late 19th and early 20th century, the United States and several European countries expanded their imperial reach in Asia, Africa, and Latin America. Looking to obtain more resources, expand their markets, and spread Western culture, the imperial powers controlled many societies outside of their borders. Most of the people of their colonies resisted and eventually achieved independence, but the history of foreign control has left legacies that exist today.

Causes of Imperialism

>> Countries had four main motivations for extending their imperial power. First, the Industrial Revolution increased the demand for resources to use in the manufacturing of goods. Conquering new lands could tap into new sources of materials. Secondly, the Industrial Revolution also motivated countries to expand the markets that could buy their goods. Thirdly, nations took pride in competing for new territories. Finally, the countries wanted to spread Western values. A belief in cultural superiority and racism fed into this motivation.

See Topic 4, Lesson 1, to learn more about the drive for imperialism.

Responses to Imperialism

>> People living in colonies lived under the crushing power of the imperial giants. Even with this disadvantage, rebels still found ways to resist the influence of the Western governments. Armed rebellions and nonviolent protests chipped away at the hold the imperialists had on them. In addition to protesting the very principle of outside control, these rebels fought against the exploitation of their resources and workforce; the lack of representation and respect given to their people; and the erosion of traditional culture.

See Topic 4 and Topic 6, Lessons 1–4, to learn more about the responses of people living in different colonies, including their resistance, to imperialism.

The Legacy of Imperialism

>> Imperial powers could argue that they helped their colonies in some ways. They usually brought economic expansion to the lands and improved infrastructure, health, and education. However, they introduced alien cultures to lands with differing values and beliefs. In uniting different lands under the colonial banner, they threw together groups with different cultures and needs; some of these groups had been historical rivals. Departing the lands after independence meant that new governments had to be hastily set up in societies that had been disrupted for generations.

See Topic 4 to learn more about the legacy of imperialism.

CONNECTING TO THE GUIDING QUESTION

1. Why did the United States and European nations enter a period of imperialism in the late 19th and early 20th centuries?
2. What kind of harm did imperial powers cause in their colonies?
3. What do you think motivates countries today when they get involved in the governing of other countries?

GUIDING QUESTION

Why was the modern period defined by global conflict and cooperation, economic growth and collapse, and global independence and connection?

In the 20th and into the 21st century, the fortunes of the nations of the world are increasingly connected. Economic gains and losses ripple through many economies, and conflicts between two powers adversely affect many nations that are mostly uninvolved. At the same time, global cooperation and connection have hastened great technological and cultural progress as well as strengthened bonds between people worldwide.

Global Conflict and Cooperation

>> Perhaps no other events illustrate the power of conflicts and cooperation among nations as World War I and World War II. Both started with rivalries among nations and quickly pulled in additional powers as governments stepped up to support established alliances. In both wars, cooperation among allied nations led to victory. In the years after World War II, allegiances shifted as once-allied nations the United States and the Soviet Union entered a decades-long conflict known as the Cold War. Again, additional nations were drawn into the fray because of their alliances with one country or the other.

See Topics 5, 7, and 8 to learn more about how alliances and rivalries caused World War I, World War II, and the Cold War.

Economic Growth and Collapse

>> Increasingly, the economic fortunes of nations are linked. Especially when the world's major economies improve or decline, world markets as a whole follow the lead. In the years after World War I, the United States experienced rapid economic growth, while several European nations, backed by American loans and investments, recovered from the devastation of the Great war. In the 1930s, however, an economic crisis in the United States triggered the Great Depression, the longest and most severe economic downturn to have affected the West. Because of loans and investments among nations, this collapse quickly spread throughout the world.

See Topic 6, Lesson 5 to learn more about how economic growth and collapse affected the world in the period between the world wars.

Global Independence and Connection

>> In the 21st century, the nations of the world struggle with the decision to forge ahead as independent powers or to work together in an interconnected world. Globalization has led to a great deal of economic and technological progress. At the same time, the drive for global connection has forced independent nations to give up some of their national autonomy. Coalitions such as the European Union and the United Nations have formed among nations that want to achieve similar goals. These coalitions are sometimes criticized for making decisions individual countries do not agree with.

See Topic 10 to learn more about the challenges nations face as they strike a balance between independence and global connection.

CONNECTING TO THE GUIDING QUESTION

1. How are the economic fortunes of countries linked in ways they previously were not?
2. How did interdependence lead to the two world wars?
3. What is one argument for nations today to work independently of one another? What is one argument for nations to work cooperatively?

"We hold these truths to be self-evident, that all men are created equal, that they are endowed by their Creator with certain unalienable Rights, that among these are Life, Liberty and the pursuit of Happiness. That to secure these rights, Governments are instituted among Men, deriving their just powers from the consent of the governed…."

Declaration of Independence

Thomas Jefferson and other Founding Fathers wrote the Declaration of Independence in 1776. By issuing this document, some of England's colonies in North America announced to the world that they were separating from England and forming a new, independent nation. Many ideas in the Declaration were inspired by English Enlightenment philosopher John Locke. He believed that all people were born with certain natural rights, including the freedom to oppose oppressive governments. While the ideas of the Declaration affected people in other places, it was not until 1948 that the Enlightenment ideals of universal natural rights were affirmed in the Universal Declaration of Human Rights.

Read this opening section of the Declaration of Independence aloud. As you read, think about the ideas it expresses.

Identify Central Ideas What point is Jefferson making about the rights to life, liberty, and the pursuit of happiness?

Make Inferences Based on this passage, what is a "just," or fair, government?

Apply Information How could the ideas expressed in this section of the Declaration be used to justify a political revolution?

endowed, v., given; provided
unalienable, adj., not to be taken away
deriving, v., getting from a source
consent, n., agreement

Connect to World Events

The Declaration of Independence and the American Revolution inspired people around the world. In 1789, the French Revolution began. French revolutionaries issued the Declaration of the Rights of Man and the Citizen.

> "Men are born and remain free and equal in rights. Social distinctions may be founded only upon the general good.
>
> The aim of all political association is the preservation of the natural and imprescriptible rights of man. These rights are liberty, property, security, and resistance to oppression."

After a slave revolt, the French colony of Haiti became the second independent nation in the Americas. Other Latin American nations soon followed. Haitian leaders issued their own Declaration of Independence in 1804.

> "We must, with one last act of national authority, forever assure the empire of liberty in the country of our birth; we must take any hope of re-enslaving us away from the inhuman government that for so long kept us in the most humiliating torpor. In the end we must live independent or die."

Liberia, on the west coast of Africa, was founded as a colony for freed American slaves. In 1847, Liberia also issued a Declaration of Independence.

> "We recognize in all men certain inalienable rights; among these are life, liberty, and the right to acquire, possess, enjoy, and defend property. By the practice and consent of men in all ages, some system or form of government is proved to be necessary to exercise, enjoy, and secure their rights...."

Compare and Contrast Identify at least three similarities between these documents and the Declaration of Independence. Why do you think the American Revolution and the Declaration had an impact around the world?

>> Toussaint L'Ouverture, leader of the rebellion that led to Haiti's independence

PEARSON realize™ PearsonSchool.com/CASS

Go **ONLINE** for digital resources

VIDEO | AUDIO | ETEXT | ACTIVITY | WRITING | GAMES | PDF | ASSESSMENT

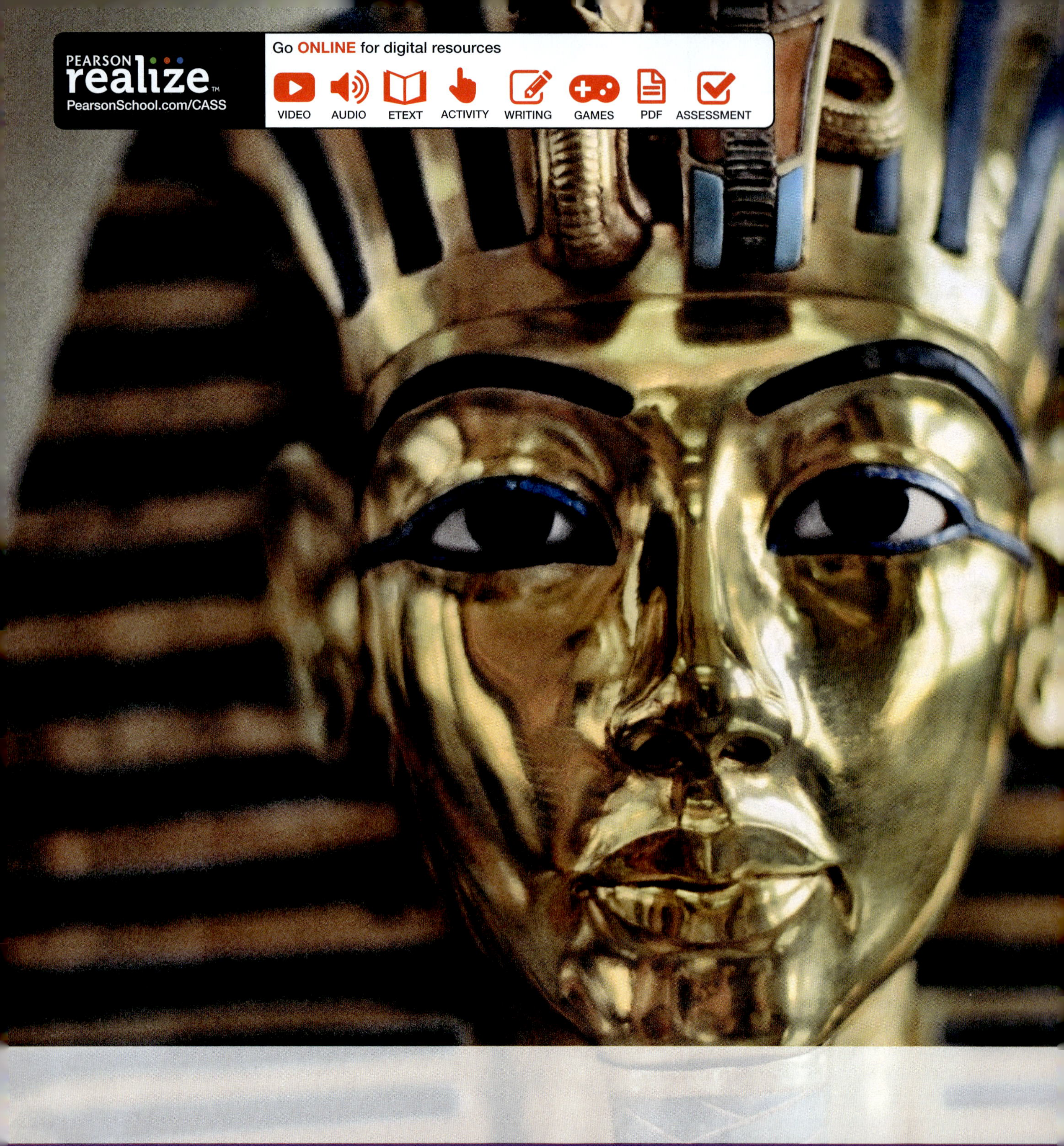

0 Connecting with Past Learnings (Prehistory–1700)

>> Gold burial mask of King Tutankhamen

Enduring Understandings

- The first civilizations took shape in fertile river valleys; they developed complex ways of life with features including governments, religions, social classes, and arts.
- Empires combining many cities and small countries emerged in various parts of the world in ancient times; some of the largest took shape in India, China, Europe, and, later, in the Americas.
- The civilizations of ancient China, India, Greece, Rome, and the Middle East developed ideas in government, religion, philosophy, and the arts and sciences that still influence the world today.
- During the period of roughly one thousand years from 500 to 1500, sprawling regional civilizations came to dominate much of the world, bringing common religious, economic, and cultural characteristics to large regions of Europe, Asia, and Africa.
- New technology and the desire for a wider variety of resources and the land that held them brought changes to various groups of people throughout the world. Beginning in the 1500s, distant cultures came into contact with one another in both positive and negative ways. The world would never be the same as civilizations around the globe exchanged both resources and ideas.
- People began to view the world differently than they had the past. They developed new ideas about learning and focused strongly on the arts. Individuals began sharing new ideas, which brought about changes in religion, scientific knowledge, and society.

California Topic 0 Overview

In this Topic, you will explore ancient civilizations as well as later ones. In doing so, you will learn about the people, places, and events that helped shape our world. Look at the lesson outlines and study the timeline, which shows important events from the period referred to as prehistory to 1700. Timelines are extremely useful because they help historians identify and evaluate patterns of change in historical events. As you study this Topic, you will complete the Quest Team Project.

LESSON OUTLINE

R.1 Origins of Civilization
Analysis CST.1, CST.2, HRE.4, HI.1

R.2 The Ancient Middle East and Egypt
HSS 10.1.1; Analysis CST.1, CST.2, HRE.4, HI.1

R.3 Ancient India and China
Analysis CST.1, CST.2, HRE.4, HI.1

R.4 The Americas
Analysis CST.1, CST.2, HRE.4, HI.1

R.5 Ancient Greece
Analysis CST.1, CST.2, HRE.4, HI.1

R.6 Ancient Rome and the Origins of Christianity
Analysis CST.1, CST.2, HRE.4, HI.1

R.7 Medieval Christian Europe
HSS 10.2.2; Analysis CST.1, CST.2, HRE.4, HI.1

R.8 The Muslim World and Africa
Analysis CST.1, CST.2, HRE.4, HI.1

R.9 Civilizations of Asia
Analysis CST.1, CST.2, HRE.4, HI.1

R.10 The Renaissance and Reformation
Analysis CST.1, CST.2, HRE.4, HI.1

R.11 New Global Connections
Analysis CST.1, CST.2, HRE.4, HI.1

Early Civilizations

3300 B.C. City-states in Sumer

2000 B.C. Chinese civilization

900 Feudalism develops

1500 Atlantic slave trade grows

4000 B.C. | 3000 B.C. | 2000 B.C. | 1000 B.C. | B.C. | A.D. | 1000 | 2000

2600 B.C. Egypt's Old Kingdom

1500 B.C. Olmec civilizaton

1300 The Renaissance

1492 Columbus lands in the Americas

QUEST! TEAM PROJECT

Create an Early World History Video Game

How did civilizations grow and change over time and why is it important to learn about them? In this Quest you will research, plan, and create a video game that will explore important world cultures and events of long ago.

STEP 1
Discuss the civilizations you will study (prehistory to 1700). With your team, brainstorm the features of these civilizations.

STEP 2
Each team will choose a specific civilization to investigate. Begin your research using reliable sources.

STEP 3
Once your team has gathered information, start writing a narrative for your video game. Choose images. Remember, make your video game interactive.

STEP 4
Work with your team to build your video game. Reflect on how civilizations grow and the impact of culture on the development. Are there any factors that have continued to shape today's civilizations?

PEARSON realize™ PearsonSchool.com/CASS
Go ONLINE for complete Quest materials
VIDEO ETEXT WRITING RUBRIC PDF ASSESSMENT

>> Paleolithic cave paintings helps us to understand the lives of Old Stone Age nomadic hunters.

0.1 **The long period before the invention of writing is called prehistory. Then, about 5,000 years ago, humans invented writing and recorded history began.**

Bounce to Activate Flipped Video

>> Objectives

Learn how scholars study the past and what they have learned about early hominids in Africa.

Analyze the skills people developed during the Old Stone Age and the Neolithic Revolution.

Trace the development of the first cities and civilizations.

>> Key Terms

artifact
anthropology
archaeology
cultures
technology
Paleolithic Period
Neolithic Period
Neolithic Revolution
domesticate
civilization
polytheistic
cultural diffusion
city-state
empire

Origins of Civilization

Learning About Our Past

Historians learn details of the past from **artifacts** such as clothing, coins, and artwork. However, most rely on written evidence, such as letters or tax records. Historians must also evaluate evidence to determine if it is reliable. Then they interpret it to explain why an event happened. Historians help us understand what happens today and what may happen in the future. Though historians generally try to give a straightforward account of events, their personal or cultural biases can affect their interpretations.

Anthropologists and Archaeologists **Anthropology** is the study of the development of people and their societies. Some anthropologists study human bones to understand how physical traits have changed. Others study **cultures,** or ways of life, from the past and present.

Archaeology, a specialized branch of anthropology, is the study of past cultures through material remains, including buildings and artifacts. In the past, archaeologists might just choose a likely site and start digging to try to find ancient artifacts. Today, they

work with experts in many fields, such as geology and biology. They also use modern innovations, such as computers and aerial photography. A technique for measuring radioactivity helps these scholars determine the age of objects.

Discoveries in Africa and Beyond Before the 1950s, anthropologists knew little about early humans and their ancestors. Anthropologists Mary and Louis Leakey searched for clues in East Africa at Olduvai Gorge. There they found many ancient stone tools. The tools showed that early hominids had developed the **technology,** or skills and tools, to survive.

Then, in 1959, after two decades of searching, Mary Leakey found a skull embedded in ancient rock. After careful testing, the Leakeys concluded that the skull belonged to an early hominid. Hominids, a group that includes humans and their closest relatives, all walk upright on two feet. Humans are the only hominids that live today.

In 1974, anthropologist Donald Johanson found pieces of a hominid skeleton in Ethiopia. "Lucy" was at least 3 million years old. Discoveries like these helped establish that a number of different groups of hominids, such as *Homo habilis* and *Homo erectus,* lived over the course of several million years. Two groups of *Homo sapiens* arose. One group—the Neanderthals—disappeared between 50,000 and 30,000 years ago. Early modern humans were then the only hominids on Earth.

SUMMARIZE What kinds of evidence do historians use to study the past?

The Neolithic Revolution

The Neolithic Revolution Scholars have divided prehistory into eras called the Old Stone Age, or **Paleolithic Period,** and the New Stone Age, or **Neolithic Period.** During both, people made stone tools. However, during the New Stone Age, people began to develop new skills and technologies that led to dramatic changes.

The Old Stone Age Early modern humans lived toward the end of the Paleolithic Period. They were nomads who moved around in small groups, hunting and gathering food. These people made simple tools and weapons, built fires for cooking, and used animal skins for clothing. They also developed spoken language, which helped them cooperate during the hunt. Some people also began to bury their dead. This suggests belief in a spiritual world or life after death.

Cave paintings around the world depict animals and humans. Many scholars think that our ancestors believed the world was full of spirits and forces that might reside in animals, objects, or dreams. Such beliefs are known as animism.

Attributes of Early Hominids

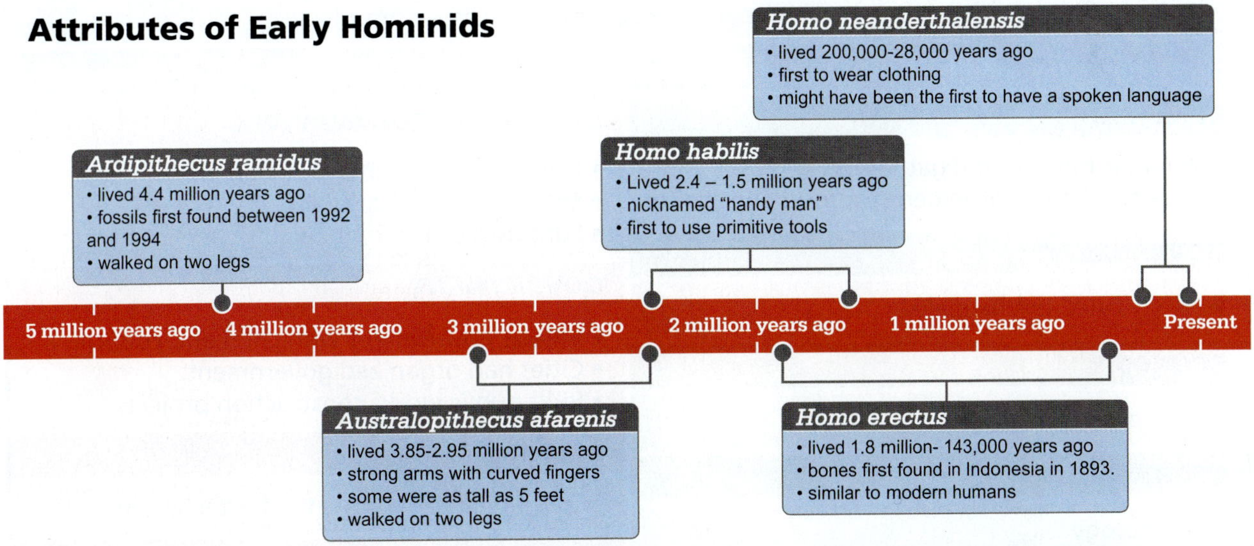

Source: Smithsonian Institution

>> As the centuries passed, hominid groups developed physically and gained new skills.

Bounce to Activate Gallery

The New Stone Age The New Stone Age began about 12,000 years ago (or about 10,000 B.C.), when nomadic people made a great breakthrough—they learned to farm. By producing their own food, people no longer needed to roam in search of it. As a result, early farmers settled the first permanent villages. This transition from nomadic life to settled farming brought about such dramatic changes in way of life that it is often called the **Neolithic Revolution.** No greater change in human history took place until the Industrial Revolution of the late 1700s. These early farmers were the first to **domesticate** plants and animals.

Archaeologists have unearthed the remains of some early Neolithic villages, including Çatalhüyük (chah TAHL hyoo YOOK)in modern-day Turkey, and Jericho (JEHR ih koh), which exists today in the West Bank. In these settled communities, people accumulated personal property. A council of male elders or elite warriors made the important decisions for all the villagers.

To farm successfully, people developed new technologies, such as ways to protect their crops, calendars, and the use of animals for plowing. However, not all technologies were invented everywhere at the same time.

☑ **IDENTIFY MAIN IDEAS** How did farming change the lives of Neolithic people?

Civilization Begins

The earliest **civilizations,**or highly organized and complex societies, developed near major rivers. The earliest of these river valley civilizations arose in Egypt, the Middle East, India, and China. Rivers provided water, transportation, and food. Flood waters made the soil fertile. In such rich conditions, farmers produced surpluses, which allowed them to store food and feed growing populations. As populations grew, villages expanded into cities. Away from these cities, people lived in farming villages or as nomadic herders on grasslands, or steppes.

Features of Civilizations The rise of cities is the main feature of civilization. In addition to this, historians distinguish other basic features of most early civilizations. They include organized governments, complex religions, job specialization, social classes, arts and architecture, public works, and writing.

In these early civilizations, central governments led by chiefs or elders established laws, organized defense, and coordinated large-scale projects such as farming or public works. Public works might include roads, defensive walls, and irrigation systems.

Most people were **polytheistic,** believing in many gods, which they associated with natural forces.

Before and After the Neolithic Revolution

Thousand of years after it began, the Neolithic Revolution still affects our lives.

BEFORE	AFTER
STRATEGIES FOR SURVIVAL	**STRATEGIES FOR SURVIVAL**
• Nomadic hunters and gatherers • Depended on environment for food and shelter	• Domesticated plants and animals • Settled in farming villages • Surpluses of food
GOVERNMENT	**GOVERNMENT**
• Family ruled by the male	• Village government with chief and council • Cities had organized government • Built public works construction projects
ECONOMY	**ECONOMY**
• No real economy	• Traditional economy—the barter system
TECHNOLOGY	**TECHNOLOGIES**
• Technology • Language developed	• Plowing • Weaving • Pottery • Calendars

>> **Analyze Charts** Based on this chart, which statement would be correct? Paleolithic people were more advanced than Neolithic people; or Neolithic people were more advanced than Paleolithic people.

Basic Features of Civilizations

FEATURE	DESCRIPTION
Cities	• Larger and more organized than villages • Cities support the other features of civilization
Governments	• Coordinate public works projects such as bridge and dam construction • Establish laws and organize defense
Complex Religions	• Belief in one or more gods or goddesses • Institution of rituals
Job Specialization	• Different types of jobs that leads workers to specialize on one task
Social Classes	• Ranked groups are based on job or economic standing
Arts and Architecture	• Artwork that expresses a society's talents, beliefs, and values
Public Works	• Large-scale projects for the mutual benefit of a city and its people
Writing	• Structured writing system initially used by governments and religious leaders to record important information

>> **Analyze Charts** Which features do you think most affected the daily lives of average people?

Bounce to Activate Map

People thought gods and goddesses controlled human affairs. People tried to gain the favor of these deities by building temples and performing elaborate rituals.

Also, for the first time, individuals began to specialize in certain jobs. Some became skilled artisans, making the tools and other objects needed by the society. In many civilizations, people's jobs determined their social rank. Priests and nobles usually occupied the top level. Wealthy merchants and artisans were next. Below them were peasants, the majority of people who farmed the surrounding land. In many civilizations, slaves occupied the lowest social level.

Art and architecture developed, reflecting the beliefs and values of the civilization. Skilled workers built large, ornate palaces and temples decorated with paintings and statues.

Many civilizations also developed writing from pictographs. As writing grew more complex, only specially trained people called scribes could read and write.

Civilizations Change Over time, early civilizations changed. Famine, drought, or other disasters sometimes led people to migrate. Migration, as well as trade and warfare, led to **cultural diffusion.** Trade introduced people to new goods or better methods of making them. In warfare, victorious armies forced their ways of life on conquered peoples while they incorporated aspects of the new cultures into their own. Rulers acquired more territory. This brought about the development of **city-states** and, later, the rise of the first **empires.**

IDENTIFY CENTRAL IDEAS What role did religion play in early civilizations?

ASSESSMENT

1. **Apply Concepts** What types of obstacles do historians have to overcome to give a straight-forward account of past events?
2. **Connect** How have anthropologists learned about early hominids?
3. **Predict Consequences** How might the development of spoken language have influenced the religious beliefs of Stone Age people?
4. **Determine Relevance** Why is the beginning of farming considered the beginning of the Neolithic Revolution?
5. **Identify** Name the eight basic features of civilization.

>> The ancient Egyptians believed in many gods and goddesses, each of whom had a role in maintaining peace and prosperity across Egypt.

Bounce to Activate Flipped Video

0.2 **Around 3300 B.C., Sumer, the world's first civilization, arose in southeastern Mesopotamia. Mesopotamia lay within the Fertile Crescent, between the Tigris and Euphrates rivers. The region's geography affected its people. Frequent flooding forced Sumerians to work together to protect homes and control water for irrigating farms. Although the region had rich soil, it lacked natural resources. Yet, Sumerians built some of the world's first great cities using bricks from readily available clay and water. Sumerians also became traders along the rivers.**

The Ancient Middle East and Egypt

>> Objectives

Understand how geography influenced the development of civilization in the Fertile Crescent.

Understand how conquests brought new empires and ideas into the Middle East.

Outline the main events in the early history of the Israelites and the central moral and ethical ideas of Judaism.

Describe the ways in which religion shaped the lives of ancient Egyptians and outline the advances Egyptians made in learning, the arts, science, and literature.

>> Key Terms

Fertile Crescent
Mesopotamia
The Epic of Gilgamesh
Hammurabi
alphabet
monotheistic
Torah
Abraham
Moses
David
Solomon
Diaspora
pharaoh
Amon-Re
mummification
hieroglyphics
Rosetta Stone

A Civilization Emerges in Sumer

Eventually, Sumer had 12 city-states, which often battled over control of land and water. So people turned to war leaders for protection. Over time, this changed when war leadership evolved into hereditary monarchy, in which a king or queen exercises central power.

Sumerian Civilization Develops Sumerian society had a social rank, or hierarchy, including an upper class (rulers, priests, officials), a small middle class (lesser priests, scribes, merchants, artisans), and a vast lower class (peasant farmers). Like most ancient peoples, Sumerians practiced polytheism, the worship of many gods. In ziggurats, stepped platforms topped by a temple, priests led religious ceremonies.

Perhaps the Sumerians' greatest achievement was the invention of writing. Beginning as simple pictographs, by 3200 B.C. writing had developed into wedge-like symbols, called cuneiform. Cuneiform could be used to record complex information. People now had access to knowledge beyond what they could remember. Eventually, conquering Akkadian, Babylonian, and Assyrian armies swept across the region.

Sumer's Legacy However, Sumerians left a lasting legacy. Besides creating a writing system, they developed basic astronomy and early mathematics. They created a number system based on six, setting up 60-minute hours and 360-degree circles. We still use this system today. Akkadians, Babylonians, and Assyrians carried Sumerian learning across the Middle East. They adopted cuneiform for their own use. Babylonians recorded the Sumerian oral poem, ***The Epic of Gilgamesh***, in cuneiform, thus preserving it. They also expanded on Sumerian learning to develop basic algebra and geometry, to create accurate calendars, and to predict eclipses. Later, the Greeks and Romans built on Sumerian knowledge; then they went on to influence all of Western civilization.

IDENTIFY MAIN IDEAS How did geography influence the development of civilizations in the Fertile Crescent?

Empires of Mesopotamia

Many groups rose to power in ancient Mesopotamia and made long-lasting cultural contributions. Some invaders simply destroyed; others created vast empires. The first invader, in 2300 B.C., was the Akkadian leader, Sargon. He conquered Sumer and formed the world's first empire. In 1790 B.C., **Hammurabi**, king of Babylon, unified Mesopotamia. He made the first important attempt to codify, or arrange and record, all laws of a state. Hammurabi's Code was carved on public pillars for all to see. It included civil laws, which covered private matters, like contracts, taxes, marriage, and divorce, and criminal laws, which covered offenses against others, like robbery and murder.

Empires Rise and Fall Other conquerors brought new learning to Mesopotamia. Hittites extracted iron from ore to forge strong weapons. Although their empire collapsed around 1200 B.C., ironsmithing spread to Asia, Africa, and Europe, launching the Iron Age. Next, Assyrians, though warlike, created a well-ordered society and founded one of the world's first libraries.

Later, the ruthless Babylonian king Nebuchadnezzar controlled the region. He rebuilt and restored the city of Babylon to greatness. His empire eventually stretched from the Persian Gulf to the Mediterranean Sea. However, it fell to Persia in 539 B.C. The Persian empire was enormous. It reached from present-day Turkey to India. Emperor Darius I formed provinces ruled by local governors and a bureaucracy, or system of government through

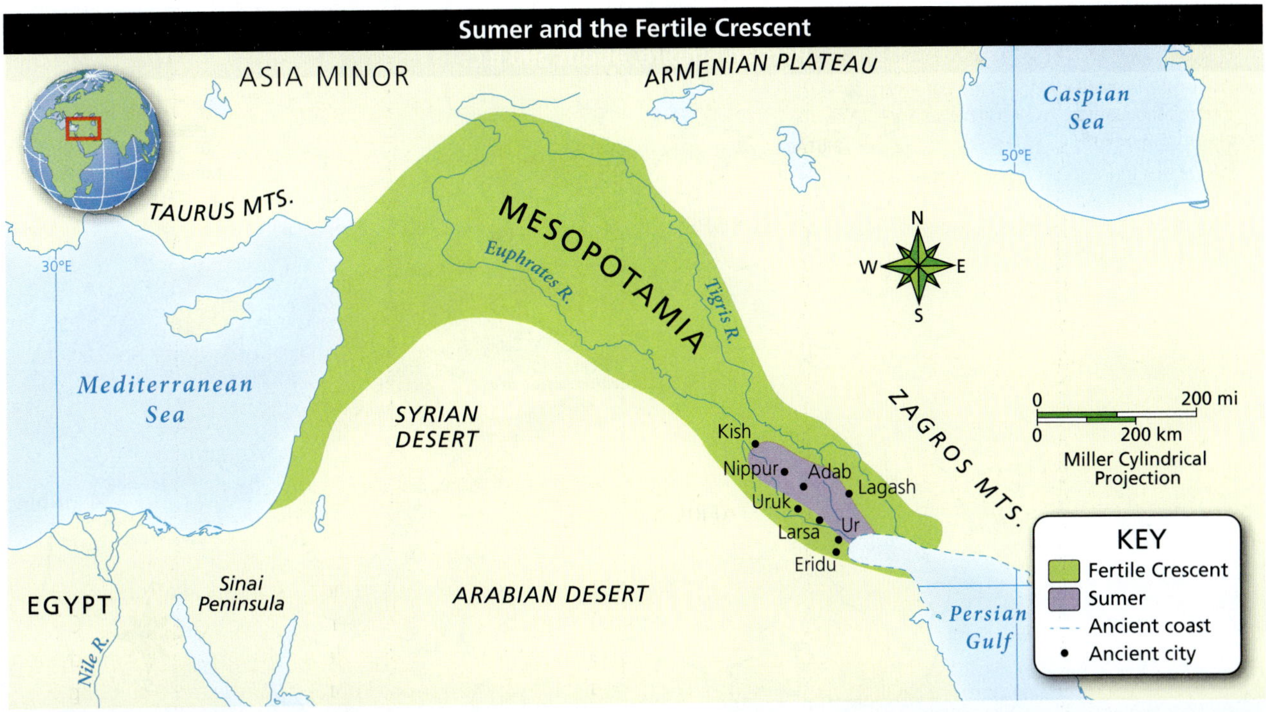

>> Analyze Maps A series of early civilizations arose between the Tigris and Euphrates rivers, called Mesopotamia. What natural features may have limited the expansion of these civilizations?

Bounce to Activate Map

departments and subdivisions administered by officials who follow set rules.

He also encouraged unity by building roads across the empire and establishing a single Persian coinage. This helped people move from a barter economy toward a money economy. Another unifying force came from the Persian prophet Zoroaster, who taught belief in a single god and ideas of heaven, hell, and final judgment day. When both Christianity and Islam emerged, or arose, in the Middle East, these new religions stressed similar beliefs.

Phoenician Contributions Not all achievements came from conquerors, however. The Phoenicians were skilled sea traders from the eastern Mediterranean coast. They formed colonies around the Mediterranean. A colony is a settlement ruled by people from another land. The Phoenicians spread Middle Eastern culture over a large area. However, perhaps their greatest achievement was the creation of an **alphabet**. The Greeks expanded on this letter system, leading to the alphabet we use today.

IDENTIFY Name a significant contribution made by the Hittites, Assyrians, and Babylonians after each group's conquest in the Middle East.

The Hebrews and the Origins of Judaism

About 4,000 years ago, the ancient Israelites developed the religion of Judaism, which became a defining feature of their culture. Today, Judaism is one of the world's major faiths. Unlike neighboring peoples, the Israelites, also called the Hebrews for the first three generations, were **monotheistic**, believing that there was only one god. They believed every event reflected God's plan for the people of Israel. The **Torah**, their most sacred text of the Israelites, or Jews, tells the history of the ancient Israelites and their continuing relationship with God. The Torah includes the first five books of the Hebrew Bible.

Abraham and Moses According to the Torah, about 2000 B.C., **Abraham** and his family migrated to a region called Canaan. Abraham is considered the father of the Israelites. The Israelites believed that God made a covenant, or promise and agreement, with Abraham. This covenant promised a special relationship with God and a homeland in Canaan, which they viewed as their "promised land." However, famine forced the Israelites into Egypt, where they became slaves. Much later, **Moses** led their exodus, or departure, from Egypt back to Canaan.

Persian Empire, about 500 B.C.

>> **Analyze Maps** Study the locations of the Persian capitals. Were they well placed for rule over the entire empire?

The Ten Commandments

The Ten Commandments helped shape American laws and people's ideas about right and wrong.	
COMMANDMENT	**EXPLANATION**
1st "Thou shalt not have strange gods before me."	to recognize God as the one and only God
2nd "Thou shalt not take the name of the Lord thy God in vain."	to speak the truth; seen today in legal oaths
3rd "Remember that you keep Holy the Sabbath Day."	to dedicate one day to worship
4th "Honor thy father and thy mother..."	to respect and love one's parents
5th "Thou shalt not kill."	to avoid killing others; seen today in laws about murder
6th "Thou shalt not commit adultery."	to ensure faithfulness to one's spouse; seen today in divorce laws
7th "Thou shalt not steal."	to prevent taking another person's belongings
8th "Thou shalt not bear false witness against thy neighbor."	to prevent lying; seen today by laws against testifying falsely in a court of law
9th "Thou shalt not covet thy neighbor's goods."	to prevent wanting other people's possessions
10th "Thou shalt not covet they neighbor's wife."	to help ensure that families are not broken up

>> Over time, the ideas in the Ten Commandments have influenced aspects of some modern legal and political systems.

Bounce to Activate Gallery

There, they set up the kingdom of Israel by 1000 B.C. The Torah tells of twelve separate tribes of Israel that were not united before this time. Saul, the first king of Israel, united these tribes into a single nation. The second king, **David**, established Jerusalem as its national capital and led successful military campaigns creating secure borders for Israel. Then, David's son **Solomon** undertook the task of turning Jerusalem into an impressive capital city. However, after his death, the kingdom split and eventually fell to the Assyrians and Babylonians.

Jewish Law and Ethics Like other early civilizations, Israelite society was patriarchal, meaning that men held the greatest legal and moral authority. Also from early times, law was central to Judaism. The Torah contains laws on such subjects as cleanliness, food preparation, and crime. Also in the Torah is a special set of laws called the Ten Commandments, a set of laws that Jews believe God gave to them through Moses. These laws stress moral conduct and religious duty, such as keeping the Sabbath, a holy day of rest and worship. Often in Jewish history, prophets, or spiritual leaders, arose. They urged social justice and taught strong codes of ethics, or moral standards of behavior.

During a 500-year period called the **Diaspora**, the Jews left or were exiled from Israel, and they spread out around the world. Still, they maintained their identity in close-knit communities, following religious laws and traditions. This helped them to survive centuries of persecution. Other values found in Jewish law that have become part of the roots of democracy include the belief that all men are equal before God.

Judaism's Legacy Today, Judaism is numbered among the world's major religions for its contributions to religious thought as well as its strong influence on Christianity and Islam, two other monotheistic faiths that also arose in the Middle East. Jews, Christians, and Muslims alike honor Abraham, Moses, and the prophets, and they all teach the ethical worldview developed by the Israelites. Today, in the West, this shared heritage of Jews and Christians is known as the Judeo-Christian tradition.

IDENTIFY MAIN IDEAS According to the Torah, where did the Israelites go once they left Egypt? What was special to them about their destination?

Egyptian Civilization

Fertile land along the Nile brought early peoples to Egypt, and over time, a powerful Egyptian civilization arose. Farming flourished in the rich soil deposits from annual river floods. People cooperated to build dikes, reservoirs, and irrigation ditches to channel the floods and store water for the dry season.

Two Regions United Egypt was made up of two regions. Upper Egypt began at the Nile's first cataract, or waterfall, in the south. Lower Egypt covered the Nile's delta, the triangular marshland where it emptied into the Mediterranean. According to classical tradition, about 3100 B.C. King Menes united both regions. Though leadership passed from one dynasty, or ruling family, to another, Egypt generally remained united.

During the Old Kingdom, **pharaohs**, or Egyptian kings, organized a strong central government and established a bureaucracy, with different jobs and authority levels. A vizier, or chief minister, was the pharaoh's chief of government business.

The Middle Kingdom saw unpredictable flooding and rebellion, but also growth in farmland and trade. Powerful Egyptian leaders ushered in an age of expansion in the New Kingdom. One of these leaders was Hatshepsut, the first female pharaoh. Her stepson, Thutmose III, a great military leader, stretched Egypt's borders to their greatest extent. Much later, Ramses II pushed north into Syria.

Egyptian Culture Ancient Egyptians made lasting contributions to civilization in many fields. Their religion, written language, art, science, and literature have fascinated people for thousands of years.

During the Old Kingdom, the chief god was the sun god, Re. By the Middle Kingdom, Egyptians called the supreme god **Amon-Re**. Most Egyptians related to the god Osiris, who ruled the dead. They also worshipped the goddess Isis, who promised life after death.

People believed the afterlife was much like life on Earth, so they buried people's possessions with them. The Egyptians also learned to preserve bodies by **mummification**, or embalming and wrapping in cloth, so that the soul could return to the body. During the Old Kingdom, they buried the bodies of their dead rulers in majestic pyramids.

Ancient Egyptians made advances in learning. Their first writing system, **hieroglyphics**, used symbols. Symbols were originally carved in stone. They also developed material to write on, made from papyrus plants.

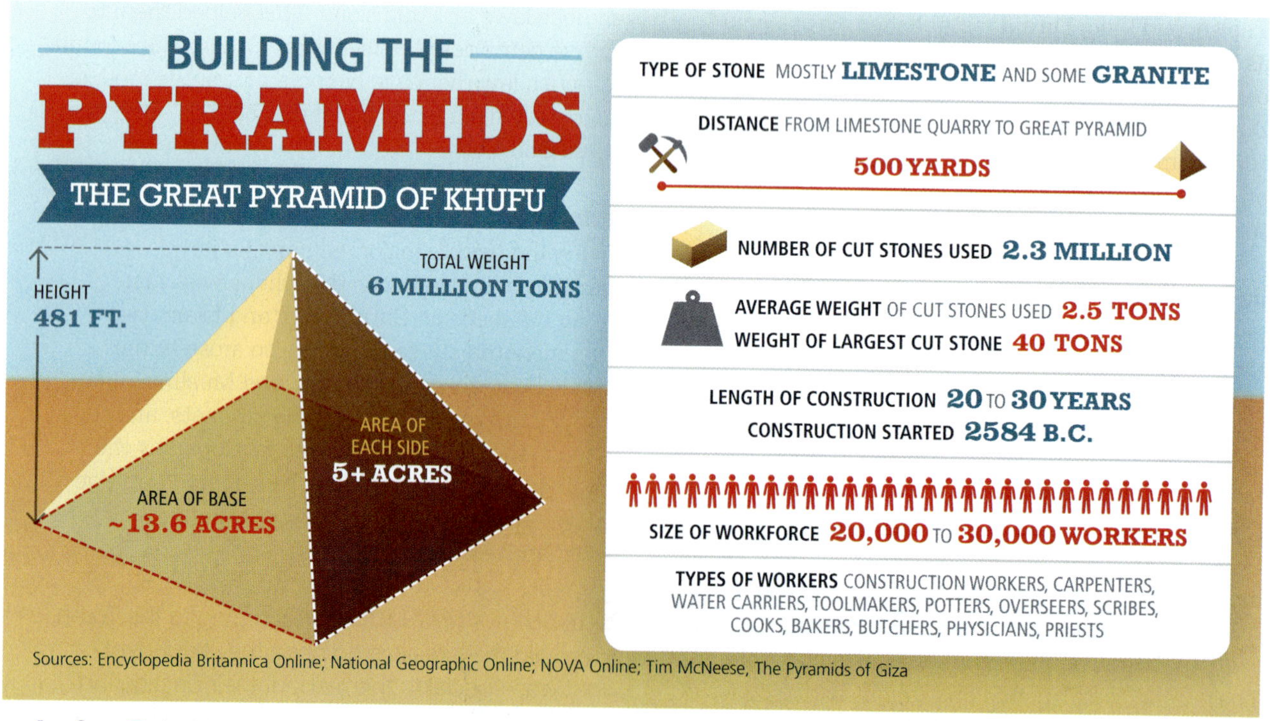

>> **Analyze Data** Pharaohs spent a great deal of resources and time building pyramids. Based on the information here, why do you think Giza pyramids built after Khufu's were not as large as his? How many acres did the Great Pyramid use?

Egyptian civilization eventually declined, yet its written records survived. No one understood them until the early 1800s, when a French scholar, Jean Champollion, deciphered, or figured out meanings for, the carvings on the **Rosetta Stone**.

Egyptians also made advances in medicine, astronomy, and mathematics. Egyptian artwork and literature has endured for thousands of years.

DRAW CONCLUSIONS How did mummification reflect Egyptian beliefs about the afterlife?

ASSESSMENT

1. **Describe** What are some Sumerian inventions and advances in learning that influenced the development of later civilizations?
2. **Synthesize** How did the geography of the Fertile Crescent affect the development of civilizations there?
3. **Compare** How did conquests contribute to the growth of well-organized empires?
4. **Support Ideas with Examples** Name two events from Jewish history that reflect the Israelites' belief that God had a plan for the people of Israel.
5. **Describe** Describe some of the main achievements of the ancient Egyptians.

>> The Maurya emperor Asoka went from warrior to Buddhist, and then ruled by moral example instead of excessive force.

Bounce to Activate Flipped Video

0.3 The Indian subcontinent is a large landmass that juts out from Asia. It is divided into three zones: the Gangetic Plain, with rivers that support farming; the Deccan plateau, a raised area of level land too dry for farming; and the coastal plains, which receive plenty of rain. Monsoons, or seasonal winds, bring dry air from the northeast in winter and rains from the southwest in summer.

Ancient India and China

>> Objectives

Analyze what historians have discovered about early civilizations on the Indian subcontinent.

Trace the origins and development of Hinduism and Buddhism in India.

Explain how strong rulers created powerful empires in India.

Describe the features of early Chinese civilizations and the influence of Confucius.

Understand the causes and effects of the unification of China.

>> Key Terms

monsoon
Vedas
Brahman
moksha
karma
dharma
ahimsa
Siddhartha Gautama
nirvana
Chandragupta Maurya
Asoka
clans
dynastic cycle
feudalism
Confucius
Laozi
Shi Huangdi
Wudi
monopoly
expansionism

Early Civilizations in South Asia

Indus Civilization About 2600 B.C., the earliest South Asian civilization emerged in the valleys of the Indus River and the now dried up Saraswati River in present-day Pakistan and India. Archaeologists believe organized governments helped plan cities such as Harappa and Mohenjo-Daro. Mohenjo-Daro was laid out in an organized pattern, with long, wide main streets and large rectangular blocks. In addition, Indus houses had complex plumbing systems and merchants used a uniform system of weights and measures.

People of the Indus civilization worshipped many gods and regarded certain animals as sacred, perhaps influencing later Indian beliefs such as the veneration of, or special regard for, cattle. The civilization declined by about 1900 B.C., possibly as a result of environmental damage, a major flood, a devastating earthquake, or perhaps a drought.

Aryan Civilization Emerges During the centuries between 2000 B.C. and 1500 B.C., a new civilization developed. A number of the groups that shaped this era spoke Indo-European languages. They intermarried with other groups and eventually called themselves Aryans (noble ones). The early Aryans in India built no cities and left behind very little archaeological evidence. Most of what we know about them comes from the **Vedas,** a collection of hymns, chants, ritual instructions, and other religious teachings.

The Aryans built a civilization after 1000 B.C. Many small independent kingdoms formed in northwestern India, ruled by elected leaders called rajahs.

Aryan Social Structure From the Vedas, we learn that Aryan society was made up of four groups of people. Ancient Indian society was seen as needing four classes of people to function properly. Each of these clases, called varnas, were based on a person's ability and interests. The classifications were Brahmins, those who learn; Kshatriyas (kuh SHAT ree yuhz), those who accumulate power; Vaisyas(VYS yuz), those who produce goods; and Sudras, those who serve. Even though the Brahmins were the highest caste, the Kshatriyas were the rulers.

During the medieval period, these divisions would evolve into a more rigid, hierarchical system known as the caste system. People were rigidly fixed in the class or caste into which they were born.

Religion and Epic Poetry The Aryans worshiped gods and goddesses who embodied natural forces, such as sky, sun, storm, and fire. They viewed these gods and goddesses as manifestations of a single, divine, absolute. Indra, the god of war, was the chief deity and used thunderbolts as weapons.

Epic poems were part of the culture. The *Mahabharata* (muh hah BAH rah tuh) and the *Ramayana* (rah MAH yuh nuh) described Aryan warfare, important religious beliefs, and valued behavior.

Over time, Aryan beliefs changed. There was a move toward the concept of **Brahman,** a single spiritual power beyond the gods of the Vedas and existing in all things. Mystics also sought direct communion with divine forces.

CITE EVIDENCE What evidence shows that the Indus civilization included a well-organized government?

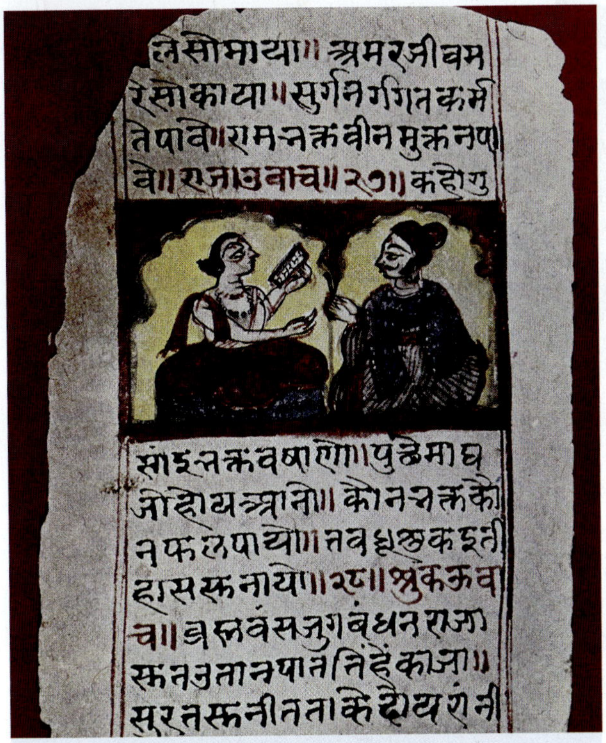

>> The Vedas were recited for many years before they were written down. This page is from the *Rig Veda,* or "Knowledge of the Hymns of Praise," the largest Veda, containing over 1,000 hymns.

>> Artworks depicting scenes from the *Mahabharata* have been created since ancient times. This folk-art painting on cloth shows the god Krishna in a chariot pulled by horses.

>> This painting shows the goddess Durga, or Shakti. Hindus believe that Shakti protects mankind from misery by destroying evil forces.

Bounce to Activate Gallery

>> **Recall** A statue of the wheel of dharma, a Hindu symbol of life, death, and rebirth. In Hinduism, how does one escape the cycle of birth and rebirth?

The Origins of Hinduism and Buddhism

Two major religions, Hinduism and Buddhism, emerged in ancient India. The ethical and spiritual messages of both religions shaped Indian civilization.

Hindu Beliefs Develop Although Hinduism grew out of the overlapping religious ideas of diverse groups, all Hindus share basic beliefs. Hindus believe that all existence, is within Brahman. Animals, plants, and objects like rocks and water are treated with great respect and even venerated.

The ultimate goal of existence, Hindus believe, is achieving **moksha,** or union with Brahman. Most people cannot achieve moksha in one lifetime but Hindus believe in reincarnation, or the rebirth of the soul in another bodily form. Reincarnation allows people to continue working toward moksha through several lifetimes.

In each existence, Hindus believe, a person can come closer to achieving moksha by obeying the law of karma. **Karma** refers to both action and result. Someone's good and moral actions lead to good results either in this lifetime or the next. A life filled with misdeeds will lead to hardship and suffering in either this life or the next.

By following **dharma,** or personal religious and moral duties, Hindus believe they can escape the cycle of birth and rebirth. Another key belief is **ahimsa,** or nonviolence, toward all people and things.

The Caste System Evolves Hinduism was connected to a system of castes, social groups that evolved out of Aryan social divisions. Caste, over time, became closely linked to Hindu notions of a proper society. Each caste had different functions and were set off from one another by specific rules of behavior, such as where people lived, how they earned a living, who they could eat with, and who they could marry. These rules became more rigid as Hindu society moved into the medieval and modern periods.

High-caste people had the strictest rules to separate them from the lower castes. Because they had jobs such as digging graves, cleaning streets, or turning animal hides into leather, some people were considered so impure that they were called "untouchables."

Despite its inequalities, the caste system ensured a stable social order by giving people a sense of identity. Today, untouchability is outlawed and the Indian government has urged its citizens to reject any form of discrimination based on caste.

Central Beliefs of Buddhism

Four Noble Truths

1. All life is full of suffering, pain, and sorrow.
2. The cause of suffering is nonvirtue, or negative deeds and mindsets.
3. The only cure for suffering is to overcome nonvirtue.
4. The way to overcome nonvirtue is to follow the **Eightfold Path.**

The Eightfold Path

1. Right views (which include knowing the **Four Noble Truths**)
2. Right aspirations (which include knowing the **Four Noble Truths**)
3. Right speech
4. Right conduct
5. Right livelihood
6. Right effort
7. Right mindfulness
8. Right contemplation

>> **Analyze Charts** The Buddha shared his knowledge by teaching other people. Choose one of the Eightfold Path steps. Then describe how the Buddha might teach others about following that particular step.

Teachings of the Buddha In the 500s B.C., a Hindu prince named **Siddhartha Gautama** (sih DAHR tuh gow TUH muh) left home to seek the causes of human suffering. Eventually, he believed he understood the answer. He became known as the Buddha, or "the Enlightened One." His teachings became the basis of Buddhism.

The Buddha taught the Four Noble Truths, which explain life as suffering and give ways to overcome it. The fourth truth is to follow the Eightfold Path. The Eightfold Path includes "right aspirations" and directs people in achieving the goals of a moral life and enlightenment. Buddhists strive to achieve **nirvana,** or union with the universe and release from the cycle of death and rebirth.

Buddhism and Hinduism share many beliefs. However, Buddhism teaches people to seek enlightenment personally, rather than through priests or gods. Buddhists also rejected the Indian caste system as practiced at that time. Buddhism offered the hope of nirvana to all regardless of birth.

Spread of Buddhism Buddhism spread throughout Asia but gradually broke into two sects, or subgroups, with differing beliefs. Theravada Buddhism spread to Sri Lanka and Southeast Asia. It taught that only the most dedicated seekers, such as monks and nuns, could hope to reach nirvana.

Mahayana Buddhism made Buddhism easier for ordinary people to follow. It pictured the Buddha and other holy beings as compassionate gods who could help people ahieve salvation. Mahayana Buddhism spread to China, Tibet, Korea, and Japan.

Buddhism remained very popular in Asia but declined in India. Hinduism there absorbed some Buddhist ideas.

SUMMARIZE How do the Hindu gods relate to the concept of Brahman?

Powerful Empires Emerge in India

Northern India was often a battleground where rival rajahs fought for control of the rich Ganges valley. Then, **Chandragupta Maurya** conquered much of the subcontinent and founded the first Indian empire in 321 B.C.

The Maurya Dynasty From 321 B.C. to 185 B.C., the Maurya dynasty ruled over a vast, united empire. Chandragupta and his followers presided over a well-organized bureaucracy. Royal officials supervised the building of roads and harbors to benefit trade. Other officials collected taxes, managed state-owned factories and shipyards, and ran courts of justice.

Maurya rule was efficient but harsh. A secret police force reported on crime and dissent, or ideas opposed to those of the government.

Asoka Spreads Buddhism Chandragupta's grandson, **Asoka,** began ruling in 268 B.C. At first, he continued to expand the empire. After fighting a bloody war, however, he became horrified at the violence. He then became a Buddhist and resolved to rule by moral example.

Asoka had stone pillars set up across India, offering moral advice and promising a just government. To help his people, Asoka built hospitals and roads. He also sent missionaries to spread Buddhism throughout Asia.

Kingdoms of the Deccan The Maurya empire declined after Asoka's death and ended around 185 B.C. Rival princes then held power for about 500 years. Each kingdom had its own government and capital. Dravidians in the Deccan spoke different languages and had different traditions from peoples of northern India.

Golden Age of the Gupta Dynasty The Gupta dynasty united India from A.D. 320 to about 540. Gupta emperors organized a strong central government that promoted peace and prosperity.

Under the Guptas, India enjoyed a period of great cultural achievement called a golden age. Prosperity contributed to a flowering of the arts and learning. Universities attracted students from many parts of Asia. Advances in mathematics included the system of numerals that we use today, the concept of zero, and the decimal system, the number system based on ten that we still use today. Villages had more power than they had under the Mauryas. Eventually, nomadic people from Central Asia overran Gupta India.

Family and Village Life For most Indians, everyday life revolved around the rules and duties associated with caste, family, and village. Villages produced most of the food and goods they needed. People regularly interacted with others from nearby villages while attending weddings, visiting relatives, or going to markets.

Parents, children, and their offspring shared a common dwelling as a joint family. The father or oldest male served as head of the household. Children were trained to do the duties of their caste. Arranging good marriages was important and some families provided a dowry, or payment to the bridegroom. Women had lower status than they had in early Aryan society.

EXPLAIN Why was Chandragupta's government efficient?

>> **Analyze Maps** China's geographic barriers made it difficult for both invaders and traders to make their way to the center of China's emerging civilization. What physical features acted as obstacles to outside contact with China?

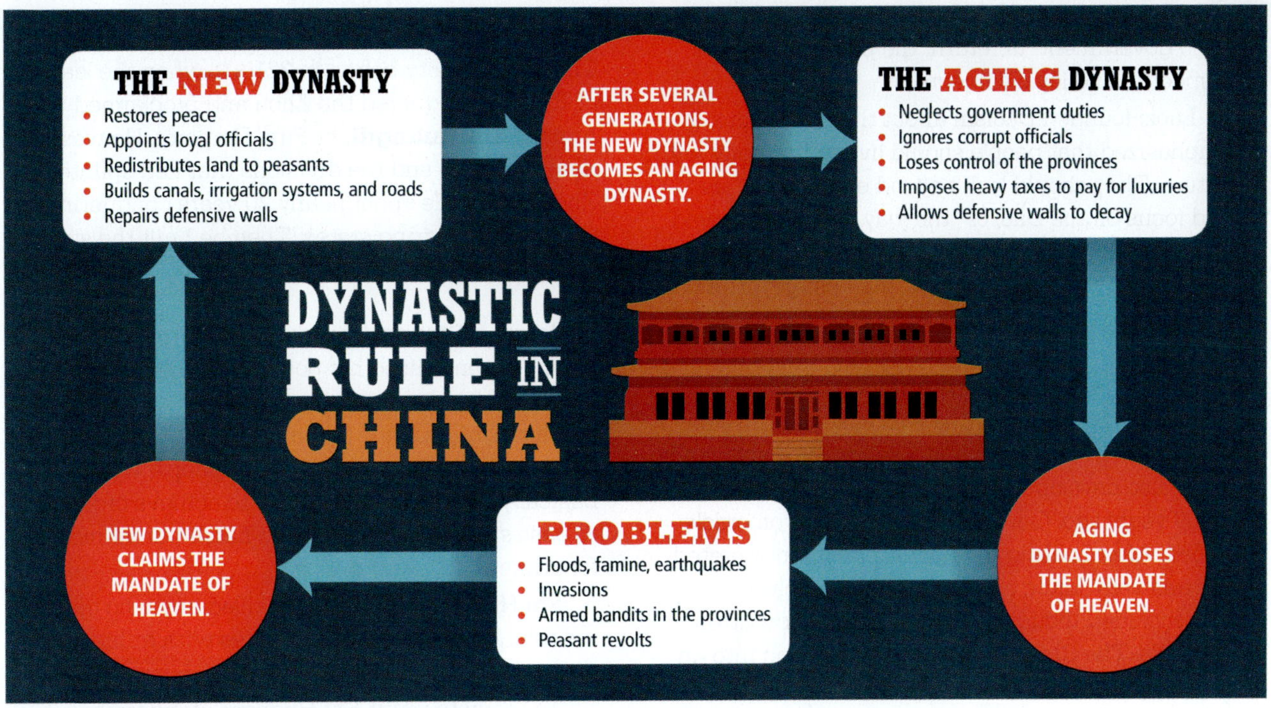

>> Analyze Information What causes a dynasty to lose the Mandate of Heaven?

Ancient Civilizations in China

The earliest civilization in China grew along the Huang River. This river carries loess, or fine windblown yellow soil, which raises the water level. People suffered from the river's frequent floods. The need to control the water likely led to the rise of government.

The Shang, China's First Dynasty About 1766 B.C., the first Chinese dynasty for which scholars have found solid evidence arose in northern China. This dynasty, the Shang, would dominate the region until about 1122 B.C. Shang kings probably controlled only a small area. Loyal princes and local nobles governed most of the land. They were likely the heads of important **clans,** or groups of families who claim a common ancestor.

Shang warriors used leather armor, bronze weapons, and horse-drawn chariots. They may have learned of chariots as they interacted with other Asian peoples.

The Zhou Dynasty The Zhou people overthrew the Shang in 1122 B.C. They promoted the Mandate of Heaven, or divine right to rule. This idea later expanded to explain the **dynastic cycle,** or rise and fall of dynasties. According to this idea, if rulers became corrupt, heaven would withdraw support and dynasties would fail.

The Zhou established **feudalism,** where lords governed their own land but owed military service and support to a ruler. In the 600s B.C., iron tools made farming more productive and the population increased. The Zhou dynasty ended when fighting feudal lords could not be controlled.

Religion in Ancient China During the Shang dynasty, the Chinese prayed to many gods and nature spirits. The king was seen as the link between the people and the chief god.

The Chinese came to believe that the spirits of their ancestors could influence the gods to bring good fortune to the family. To honor their ancestors' spirits, they offered them sacrifices of food and other necessities.

Two Systems of Thought During the Zhou dynasty, two great thinkers emerged: **Confucius** and **Laozi** (LOW dzuh). Confucius developed a philosophy, or system of ideas, that greatly influenced Chinese civilization. Confucius was concerned with social order and good government. He argued that people should accept their station in life and emphasized five key relationships between people. Filial piety, or respect for parents, was everyone's highest duty. Confucius also taught that it was a ruler's responsibility to provide good government. In return, the people would be respectful and loyal subjects.

Laozi founded Daoism about the same time. It emphasized that people should live in harmony with nature. They should look beyond everyday cares and focus on the Dao, or "the way." Daoists viewed government as unnatural and, therefore, the cause of many problems. To Daoists, the best government was one that governed the least.

Early Chinese Achievements One great achievement of early China was silk-making. The Chinese kept the technique a secret for many years. They also developed a system of writing at least 4,000 years ago. Questions were written on oracle bones. After heating the bones, priests interpreted the answers. Later, a writing system evolved that included thousands of characters, or written symbols. The Chinese then turned writing into an art called calligraphy.

SUMMARIZE How did the Shang kings govern China?

Strong Rulers Unite China

The Qin Dynasty began in 221 B.C. when the leader of the Qin conquered the Zhou and proclaimed himself **Shi Huangdi,** or First Emperor. He was determined to end the divisions that had splintered Zhou China. He spent nearly 20 years conquering most of the warring states. Then he built the strong, authoritarian Qin government.

Building a Strong Central Government Shi Huangdi centralized his power by adhering to Legalism. This philosophy was based on the teachings of Hanfeizi (hahn fay dzuh). Unlike Confucius, Hanfeizi insisted that people were basically evil and the only way to achieve order was to pass strict laws and impose harsh punishments for crimes.

Shi Huangdi tortured and killed any who opposed his rule. He replaced feudal states with military districts headed by loyal officials.

To promote unity, Shi Huangdi standardized weights and measures, coins, and Chinese writing. Under his orders, thousands of workers connected shorter walls to form the one Great Wall against invaders from the north.

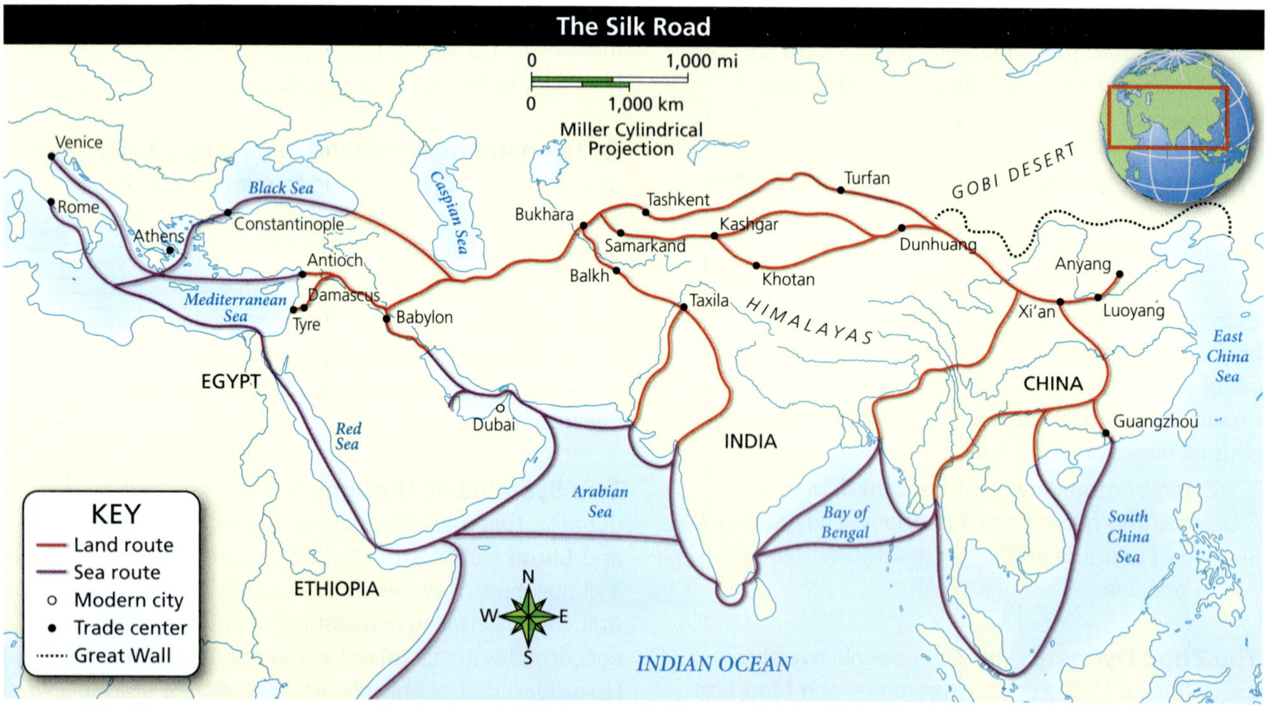

>> Analyze maps The Silk Road stretched from China to the Mediterranean. New ideas, as well as goods, were exchanged along the Silk Road. Describe two possible travel routes for a shipment of silk traveling from Taxila to Babylon.

The Han Dynasty When Shi Huangdi died, anger over heavy taxes, forced labor, and cruel policies exploded into revolts. The Qin dynasty officially collapsed in 206 B.C. Four years later, Gao Zu (gow dzoo) founded the new Han dynasty.

The most famous Han emperor, **Wudi,** ruled from 141 B.C. to 87 B.C. Instead of Legalism, Wudi made Confucianism the official belief system of the state. He improved transportation, controlled prices, and created a government **monopoly** on iron and salt. His policy of **expansionism** increased the land under Chinese rule. He also opened a network of trade routes, later called the Silk Road.

Han rulers chose Confucian scholars as government officials, or civil servants. Young men could advance in government through skill, rather than family influence. They were tested on their knowledge of the Five Classics, a collection of histories, poems, and handbooks compiled from the works of Confucius and others.

The Han dynasty was a golden age for Chinese culture. Han scientists wrote texts on chemistry, zoology, and botany. The Han invented the seismograph, suspension bridge, rudder, and paper from wood pulp. Medical treatment included acupuncture to relieve pain or treat illness. Artisans created products from jade, ceramics, bronze, and silk. Poets and historians wrote about the grandeur of Han cities.

As the Han dynasty aged, emperors could no longer control warlords, or local military rulers. Peasants rebelled. The last emperor was overthrown in A.D. 220, after 400 years of Han rule.

Spread of Buddhism in China Buddhism had spread from India to China by about A.D. 100. It became increasingly popular during the times of crisis that followed the fall of the Han, and by A.D. 400 it had spread throughout China. Buddhist monasteries became important centers of learning and the arts. Buddhism absorbed many Confucian and Daoist traditions. Chinese Buddhist monks stressed filial piety and honored Confucius

COMPARE How does Legalism differ from Confucianism?

>> This giant statue of Buddha was carved directly into a sheer cliff that leads to a Buddhist temple in China.

Bounce to Activate Map

ASSESSMENT

1. **Summarize** How was Aryan society structured? How did this social hierarchy change over time?
2. **Summarize** What is the final goal of Buddhists in their practice of the religion?
3. **Compare and Contrast** Compare and contrast the approaches of Chandragupta and Asoka to ruling the Mauryan empire.
4. **Analyze Information** What aspects of Confucianism and Daoism do you think contributed to their long-lasting influence?
5. **Identify Main Ideas** Why was the Han period considered a Golden Age of Chinese civilization?

>> Maya temples were built in the shape of pyramids using hand-cut limestone blocks. The interior usually consisted of a few narrow rooms, indicating that they were intended for ceremonial purposes rather than for the public.

Bounce to Activate Flipped Video

0.4 **People first came to the Americas from Asia between 60,000 B.C. and 18,000 B.C. They may have walked across a land bridge or come by boat. In Mesoamerica, a cultural region including Mexico and Central America, people grew maize and other crops. They raised animals and settled into villages by about 1500 B.C. As populations grew, some of the villages developed into the early, great cities of the Americas.**

>> Objectives

Describe the major developments of the Maya and Aztec civilizations.

Describe the major developments of Inca civilization.

Examine the cultures that developed in the different geographic regions of North America.

>> Key Terms

Mesoamerica
Olmec
Tenochtitlán
chinampa
adobe
Pachacuti Inca Yupanqui
Sapa Inca
quipu
pueblo
earthwork
Iroquois League
potlatch

The Americas

Civilizations of Middle America

Olmec Civilization Emerges The earliest American civilization, that of the **Olmec**, developed along the Gulf Coast of Mexico. That civilization lasted from about 1500 B.C. to 400 B.C. A class of priests and nobles led it. Later Mesoamerican peoples, including the Maya and Aztec, adopted elements of Olmec culture, such as carved stone, hieroglyphs, and the calendar.

The Maya Around 300 B.C., the Maya were building large cities in present-day Guatemala. By the time the Maya golden age began, about A.D. 250, Maya civilization included large, independent city-states throughout southern Mexico and Central America. The Maya were not united politically as an empire. Instead, cities maintained contact through trade and, sometimes, warfare. Maya cities included temples, palaces, and stelae, which were tall stone monuments decorated with carvings. Scribes carved each stela with historical information, such as the names of rulers and dates. They also wrote about astronomy and religion in books made of bark paper. However, around A.D. 900, the Maya abandoned most of their cities, possibly because of frequent warfare or over-farming.

The Aztec Aztec civilization began in the Valley of Mexico. The Aztec founded **Tenochtitlán**, their capital city, in A.D. 1325. Because it was located on an island in a lake, they found ingenious ways to create more farmland. They built **chinampas**, which were artificial islands made from mud and reeds. They gradually filled in parts of the lake and created canals for transportation. Wide stone causeways linked the city to the mainland.

Unlike the Maya, the Aztec built an empire. They also fought wars continuously. War brought wealth and power. As their empire grew, the Aztec used tribute, or payment from conquered peoples, to make Tenochtitlán magnificent. They also sacrificed war prisoners to the sun god. Among the gods they worshipped were powerful gods from an earlier culture centered at the city of Teotihuacán. Although the city fell, its culture influenced later peoples of Mesoamerica.

EXPLAIN How did the Maya operate politically without a centralized government?

The World of the Incas

The first cultures of South America developed in the Andean region. The earliest was the Chavín culture, named for the ruins at Chavín de Huantar in Peru. Around 900 B.C., the people built a huge temple complex. Chavín's arts and religion influenced later peoples of Peru. Later, between A.D. 100 and 700, the Moche people lived along the north coast of Peru. They improved farming techniques, built roads, and used relay runners to carry messages. They also used **adobe** to build the largest adobe structure in the Americas. Skilled artisans worked in textiles, gold, woodcarving, and ceramics.

The Nazca people lived between 500 B.C. and A.D. 500. They are known for the geoglyphs they etched in the desert of southern Peru. East of the Nazca, the city of Huari controlled mountains and coastal areas in Peru. To the south, Tiahuanaco became a powerful city on Lake Titicaca. The two cities may have been connected through trade or religion because their artistic styles are similar.

The most powerful of the Andean peoples were the Inca. Their civilization began in the 1100s, but greatly expanded its power after 1438. That is when **Pachacuti Inca Yupanqui**, a skilled warrior and leader, declared himself **Sapa Inca**, or emperor. Eventually, the Inca empire controlled 2,500 miles

Civilizations of Mesoamerica

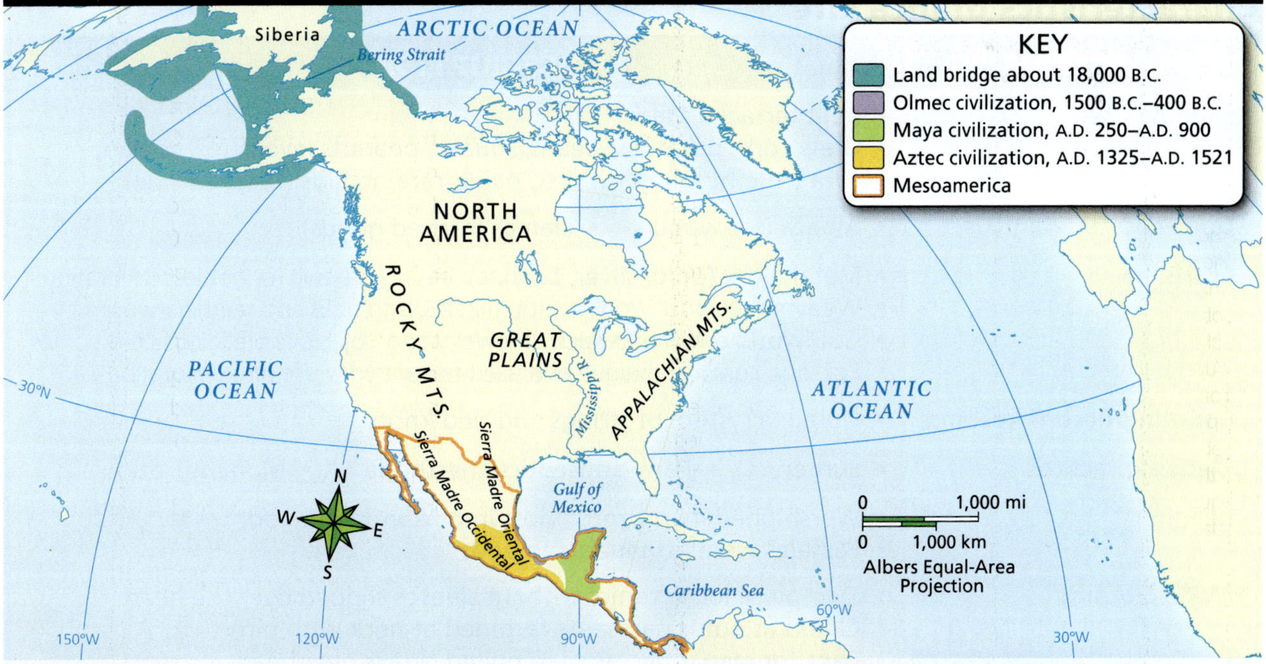

>> Analyze Maps Early people are thought to have crossed the Bering Strait from Asia to the Americas either on foot or in small boats. What might have been one of the biggest geographic influences on Mesoamerican civilizations?

Bounce to Activate Map

along the Andes, from Ecuador to Chile. To unite their empire, the Inca imposed their language, Quechua (KECH wuh) and their religion on the people they conquered.

The Inca built a network of roads of about 14,000 miles, winding through deserts and over mountains. The roads allowed news and armies to travel quickly throughout the empire. All roads led through the capital Cuzco. Various culture groups from all over the empire lived in this city.

The emperor had absolute power and was also the religious leader. The Sapa Inca laid claim over all the land, herds, mines, and people of his empire. As the Inca people had no personal property, there was little demand for items for barter or sale, and trade played a much smaller role in the Inca economy than it had in the earlier Maya economy.

Inca rulers ran an efficient government. Nobles ruled provinces, and local officials handled everyday business. Officials kept records on colored, knotted strings called **quipu**. Everyone had to speak the Inca language and follow the Inca religion. Each village, or ayllu, had a leader who assigned jobs and organized work for the government. Farmers created terraces to farm the steep hillsides. They spent part of the year farming for their village and part working land for the emperor.

The Inca worshipped many gods, but the chief god was Inti, the sun god. Religious festivals occurred each month to celebrate the forces of nature that were important to the Inca.

SYNTHESIZE How did the Sapa Inca consolidate his power and keep control of his large empire?

The Peoples of North America

Before A.D. 1500, there were many Native American culture groups in North America. Scholars have organized early people of North America into culture areas based on where they lived. This section covers the following culture areas: Southwest, Southeast, Arctic, Northwest Coast, and Northeast.

The Desert Southwest In the deserts of the Southwest, around 300 B.C., the Hohokam built canals to carry river water to crops. Between A.D. 1150 and A.D. 1300, the Ancestral Puebloans built homes on cliffs. The largest of these housing complexes, at Mesa Verde in present-day Colorado,

Characteristics of Inca Life

CHARACTERISTIC	DESCRIPTION
Farming	• Built terraced fields • Grew corn, potatoes, beans, squash, peanuts, avocados, cotton, coca (fought hunger, thirst, pain), rare orchids (for medicine)
Domesticated Animals	• Alpaca (for wool) • Llamas (carried goods)
Crafts	• **Metal work (gold, silver, bronze):** eating utensils for nobles, decoration • **Weaving:** colorful wool, cotton textiles with gold and feathers woven in • **Goldwork:** ornaments such as jewelry and objects for religious ceremonies • **Pottery:** coiled technique and used for everyday use and decoration
Counting/Record-keeping	• Quipu: a system of strings and tied knots
Medical practices	• Surgery • Early antiseptics/anesthesia • Mummification
Religion	• Worshipped many gods, most importantly sun god; • Females were attendants to gods
Made Clothing	• Two-piece loose tunics without sleeves slipped over the head • Cloaks as outer garments fastened at neck with pin • Caps for men, only; women pulled cloaks over head

>> **Analyze Information** Inca society was sophisticated, and much of daily life was structured and strictly regulated by government officials. How was their religion similar to many other cultures?

Bounce to Activate Gallery

had more than 200 rooms built with stone blocks. The cliffs offered protection from enemies.

The Ancestral Puebloans also used stone and adobe bricks to build villages on the ground, which they modeled after the cliff dwellings. The Spanish called these villages **pueblos**. Pueblo Bonito was the largest. It still stands in New Mexico. This huge complex was five stories high and had over 800 rooms. In the center was the kiva, a round, underground room used for religious ceremonies and meetings.

The East The Adena and the Hopewell of the Northeast farmed in the Ohio and Mississippi river valleys. They built **earthworks**, which were large piles of earth shaped into burial mounds, bases for structures, and defensive walls. By A.D. 800, these cultures had disappeared. A new people of the Southeast, the Mississippians, began to build large towns and ceremonial centers. They also built mounds. The homes of rulers and nobles sat on top of the mounds. By about A.D. 1100, their great city of Cahokia, in present-day Illinois, had 20,000 people.

Distinct Cultures Develop in Different Geographic Regions The Inuit adapted to the harsh Arctic climate by 2000 B.C. They used seals and other animals for food, tools, and cooking, and used skins and furs for blankets and clothing. They built igloos, or dome-shaped homes made from snow and ice, and used dogs to pull sleds that carried goods across the ice.

The Northwest Coast provided Native Americans there with plentiful fish and game, and trees for building permanent homes. Wealth gained from trading surplus goods was shared in **potlatch** ceremonies. In this ceremony, a high-ranking person gave gifts to a large number of guests.

Many Native American groups of the Northeast were known as the Iroquois. To stop constant warfare, they formed the **Iroquois League**. This was an alliance of five Iroquois groups, known as the Five Nations.

SUMMARIZE How did the Inuit protect themselves from the harsh Arctic cold?

>> The Great Serpent Mound, built by the Adena people, is some 1300 feet long and ranges in width from three to twenty feet. Inside the mound, which is made of yellow clay, are hollow cave-like openings.

ASSESSMENT

1. **Contrast** What is the main difference between the Aztec and Maya regarding the governing of their societies?
2. **Summarize** How was the Aztec skill at engineering demonstrated in Mesoamerica after about 1300?
3. **Explain** What features and policies of the Inca government helped the emperor control his empire?
4. **Draw Conclusions** How did the Ancestral Puebloans adapt their housing to the building materials that were available in the arid Southwest?
5. **Infer** What purposes did the earthwork mounds of the Adena and Hopewell serve? How can archaeologists know that?

>> The ancient Parthenon temple crowns the Acropolis (or "highest city" in Greek) in present-day Athens.

0.5 The island of Crete, located on the Aegean Sea, was home to a successful trading civilization known as the Minoan civilization. Minoan rulers lived in a vast palace at Knossos. This palace housed rooms for the royal family, banquet halls, and work areas for artisans. It also included religious shrines, areas dedicated to the honor of gods and goddesses. The walls were covered with colorful frescoes—watercolor paintings done on wet plaster. The frescoes revealed much about Minoan culture by illustrating scenes from daily life.

Bounce to Activate Flipped Video

>> Objectives

Identify how Minoan civilization prospered and summarize the Mycenaean involvement in the Trojan War.

Explain how democracy and other forms of government developed in Ancient Greece.

Analyze the political and ethical ideas developed by ancient Greek philosophers.

Explain how Alexander the Great built an extensive empire and describe the empire's cultural impact.

>> Key Terms

fresco
Trojan War
Homer
polis
monarchy
aristocracy
oligarchy
Athens
democracy
Pericles
philosopher
Socrates
Plato
Aristotle
Herodotus
Phillip II
Alexander the Great
Pythagoras
Archimedes
Hippocrates

Ancient Greece

Early Greece

By about 1400 B.C., the Minoan civilization vanished. The reasons are unclear, but it is certain that invaders played some role in its destruction. These invaders were the Mycenaeans.

Mycenaean Civilization and the Trojan War The Mycenaeans ruled the Aegean world from about 1400 B.C. to 1200 B.C. They were also sea traders whose civilization reached as far as Sicily, Italy, Egypt, and Mesopotamia. The Mycenaeans learned skills from the Minoans, such as writing. They also absorbed Egyptian and Mesopotamian customs, which they passed on to later Greeks.

The Myceneans are remembered for their part in the **Trojan War**, which began about 1250 B.C. The conflict may have started because of economic rivalry between Mycenae and Troy, a rich trading city that controlled the vital straits, or narrow water passages, connecting the Mediterranean and Black seas. According to Greek legend, the war erupted when the Mycenaeans, or Greeks, sailed to Troy to rescue the kidnapped wife of the king. The war lasted 10 years, until the Mycenaeans finally burned Troy to the ground.

Homer and the Great Greek Legends Much of what we know about the Trojan War and life during this period comes from two epic poems, the *Iliad* and the *Odyssey*. These works are credited to the poet **Homer**, who probably lived about 750 B.C. The *Iliad* and the *Odyssey* reveal much about the values of the ancient Greeks. The poems' heroes display honor, courage, and eloquence.

In about 1100 B.C., invaders from the north known as the Dorians conquered the Mycenaeans. After the Dorian invasions, Greece passed several centuries in obscurity. Over time, a new Greek civilization emerged that would extend its influence across the Western world.

DESCRIBE How did trade shape Mycenaean society?

>> In this scene from the *Illiad,* the water goddess Thetis, mother of Achilles, brings her son new divinely forged armor after his best friend Patroclus dies wearing Achilles's armor.

The Greek City-States

As their world expanded, the Ancient Greeks evolved a unique version of the city-state, called the **polis**. The polis consisted of a major city or town and its surrounding countryside. The acropolis, or high city with its many temples, stood on a hill. Because the population was small for each city-state, the citizens felt a shared sense of responsibility for their polis.

Types of Government Evolve Different forms of government evolved in ancient Greece. At first, there was a **monarchy**. In a monarchy, a hereditary ruler exercises central power. In time, the power shifted to an **aristocracy**—or rule by the landholding elite. As trade expanded and a wealthy middle class emerged, the result was an **oligarchy**—where power is in the hands of a small, wealthy elite.

A new method of fighting also emerged. The phalanx was a massive tactical formation of heavily armed foot soldiers. In the city-state of Sparta, Spartans focused on developing strong military skills.

>> The Spartans put great emphasis on the strength and agility of the human body. This sculpture from 530 B.C. shows a Spartan woman exercising, a task rarely expected of other Greek women.

Reforms and Democracy in Athens In **Athens**, government evolved from a monarchy into an aristocracy, but discontent spread among ordinary citizens. Despite government reforms under Solon around 594 B.C., there was still unrest. This led to the rise of tyrants, or those who gained power by force. They often won support from the merchant class and the poor by imposing reforms to help these groups. In 507 B.C., the reformer Cleisthenes made the assembly a genuine legislature, or lawmaking body. Slowly Athens moved toward a form of limited **democracy**, or government by the people.

Forces for Unity Despite divisions among city-states, Greeks shared a common culture. They spoke the same language, honored the same ancient heroes, participated in common festivals, and prayed to the same gods.

The Greeks were victorious in the Persian Wars, which began in 499 B.C. This victory increased the Greeks' sense of uniqueness. Athens emerged from the wars as the most powerful city-state in Greece. Athens formed an alliance, called the Delian League, with other Greek city-states.

Pericles, Democracy, and War After the Persian Wars, a golden age began in Athens under the skillful leadership of **Pericles**. The Athenian economy and culture thrived and the government became more democratic. The role of the individual in society was important. Periclean Athens was a direct democracy. Under this system, citizens take part directly in the daily affairs of government. In addition, Athenians served on juries. A jury is a panel of citizens who make the final judgment in a trial. Athenian citizens could also vote to banish a public figure they believed was a threat to their democracy. This was called ostracism. Ideas from Athenian democracy became part of Western political thought. Greek philosopher Aristotle's mention of a "mixed government" would become the basis for separation of powers. That idea translated as a way to keep power in check in a democratic government.

Many Greeks outside Athens resented the growing Athenian domination. In 431 B.C., warfare broke out between Athens and Sparta. This conflict, known as the Peloponnesian War, soon engulfed all of Greece. Sparta defeated Athens with the help of Persia. The defeat ended Athenian domination of the Greek world.

DESCRIBE Describe Pericles' influence on Athens.

Greek Thinkers, Artists, and Writers

Ancient Greek thinkers used observation and reason to explain events. These thinkers were called **philosophers**, meaning "lovers of wisdom." Philosophers explored many subjects, from mathematics and music to logic, or rational thinking. They believed that through reason and observation they could discover laws that governed the universe.

Debating Morality and Ethics Some philosophers were interested in ethics and morality. In contrast, the Sophists believed that success was more

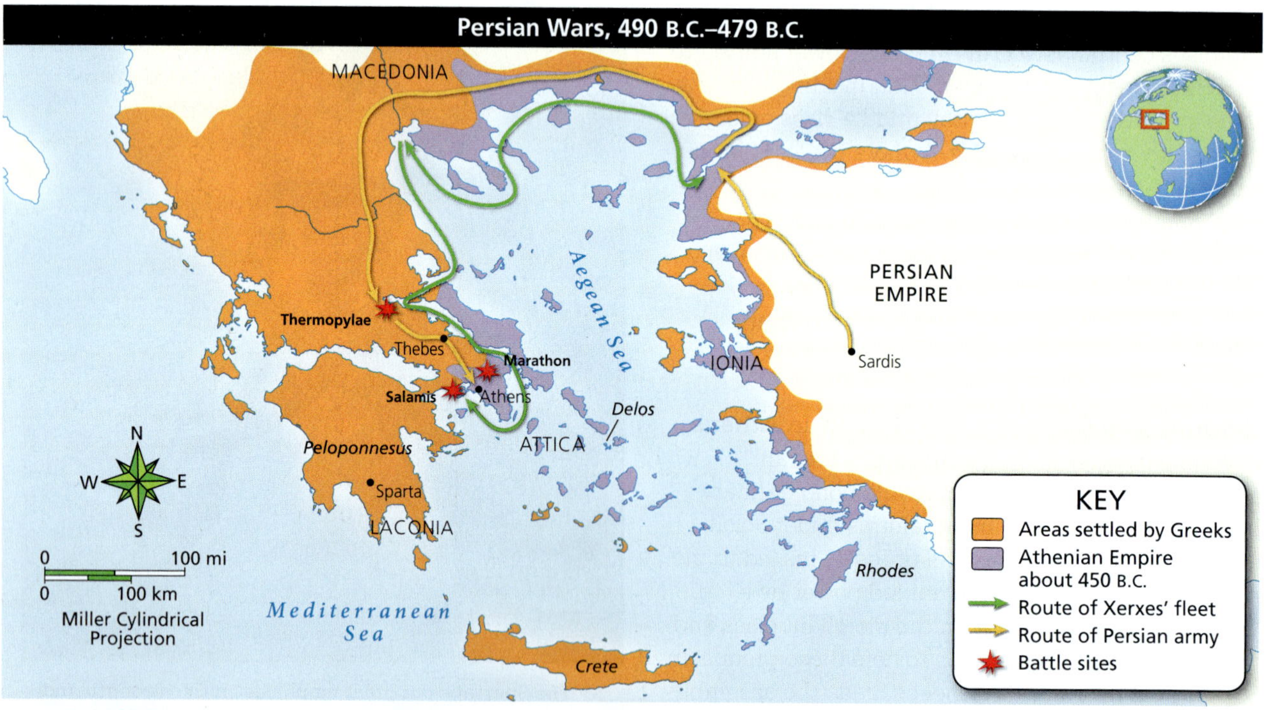

>> Analyze Maps When the Persian empire attacked Greece, the Greek city-states briefly joined forces for defense. Describe the routes of the Persian army and navy toward Athens.

important than moral truth. They developed skills in rhetoric, the art of skillful speaking. Ambitious men could use clever and persuasive rhetoric to advance their careers.

The philosopher **Socrates** was an outspoken critic of the Sophists. He believed in seeking truth and self-knowledge. Most of what we know about Socrates comes from his student **Plato**. Plato set up a school called the Academy where he taught his own ideas. Like Socrates, Plato emphasized the importance of reason.

Plato's most famous student, **Aristotle**, also promoted reason as the guiding force for learning. He set up a school, the Lyceum, for the study of all branches of knowledge.

Conveying Ideals in Architecture and Art While Plato argued that every object on Earth has an ideal form, ancient Greek artists and architects reflected a similar concern with balance, order, and beauty. The most famous example of Greek architecture is the Parthenon. The basic plan of the Parthenon is a simple rectangle with tall columns supporting a gently sloping roof.

Early Greek sculptors carved figures in rigid poses. Later, they emphasized more natural forms. Sculptors carved their subjects in a way that showed human beings in what was considered their most perfect, graceful form.

Literature and the Study of History In literature, the Greeks also developed their own style. Some Greek playwrights wrote tragedies, or plays that tell stories of human suffering, usually ending in disaster. Others wrote comedies, or humorous plays that mock customs or that criticize society.

History was also an important subject for ancient Greeks. **Herodotus**, often called the "Father of History," stressed the importance of research. He visited many lands to collect and chronicle information from witnesses of actual events. Thucydides also recorded events as he experienced them. Both men set standards for future historians.

DRAW CONCLUSIONS Why might some of the philosophers' ideas be a threat to Greek tradition?

Alexander the Great and the Legacy of Greece

Soon after Macedonian king **Phillip II** gained the throne in 359 B.C., he built a powerful army and eventually brought all of Greece under his control.

>> Athena, patroness of Athens and goddess of wisdom, observes citizens fulfilling one of their most important responsibilities in a democracy—voting.

Bounce to Activate Gallery

Philip's next goal was to conquer the Persian empire. However, he was assassinated before he could. Assassination is the murder of a public figure, usually for political reasons.

After Philip's death, his son, who came to be known as **Alexander the Great**, acquired the throne and began organizing forces to conquer Persia. Alexander was victorious. Once much of the Persian empire fell under his control, he advanced into India.

Alexander's Legacy Unexpectedly in 323 B.C., Alexander died at the age of 33 in Persia from a fever. Although his empire collapsed soon after, he is credited with spreading Greek culture from Egypt to the borders of India. Local people assimilated, or absorbed, Greek ideas. In turn, Greek settlers adopted local customs. Gradually, a new Hellenistic culture emerged that blended Greek, Persian, Egyptian, and Indian influences.

Hellenistic Arts At the very heart of the Hellenistic world stood the magnificent city of Alexandria, founded in Egypt by Alexander. Its great library was among the greatest scientific and cultural centers of the age. Like Alexandria, cities of the Hellenistic world employed many architects and artists.

THE GREEK LEGACY

GOVERNMENT

- Written code of laws
- Citizens bring charges of wrongdoing
- Trial by jury
- Citizenship expands to all free adult men, except foreigners
- Athenian assembly makes laws
- Direct democracy: male citizens rule by majority vote

CULTURE

- Greek language: many roots, prefixes, suffixes used in English
- Mythology about gods and goddesses
- Olympic games
- Philosophers searching for truth, apply reason, question tradition

ARTS

- Drama and poetry
- History: encouraging research, unbiased accounts
- Sculpture portraying lifelike human forms and ideal beauty
- Painted pottery with scenes of everyday Greek life and legendary tales
- Classical architecture embodies balance, grace

MATHEMATICS, SCIENCE, AND TECHNOLOGY

- Properties of numbers and proportion studied
- Disagreement whether sun or Earth at center of universe
- Accurate estimate of circumference of Earth
- Development of lever, pulley, pump
- Natural not divine causes and cures of illness sought, code of ethics for physicians

>> Ancient Greece's legacy has been as broad as it is deep, including major concepts, institutions, and inventions in government, culture, the arts, mathematics, the sciences, and technology.

Bounce to Activate Gallery

Temples, palaces, and other public buildings were larger and grander than the buildings of classical Greece. The elaborate new style reflected the desire of Hellenistic rulers to glorify themselves as godlike.

Advances in the Sciences During the Hellenistic age, scholars built on earlier Greek, Babylonian, and Egyptian knowledge. In mathematics, **Pythagoras** derived a formula to calculate the relationship between the sides of a right triangle. The astronomer Aristarchus developed the theory of a heliocentric, or sun-centered, solar system. Another scientist, **Archimedes**, applied the principles of physics to make practical inventions. In the field of medicine, the Greek physician **Hippocrates** studied the causes of illnesses and looked for cures.

Greek works in the arts and sciences set a standard for later Europeans. Greek ideas about law, freedom, justice, and government continue to influence political thinking today.

IDENTIFY In what fields did Hellenistic civilization make advancements?

ASSESSMENT

1. **Hypothesize** Why do you think that for centuries most people thought the Trojan War was just a legend?
2. **Infer** Why do you think the Minoans and Mycenaeans absorbed ideas, customs, and skills from other cultures?
3. **Identify Steps in a Process** Explain how democracy evolved in ancient Greece from earlier forms of government in Greece.
4. **Cite Evidence** How did balance and order govern Greek architecture?
5. **Cite Evidence** How did Alexander and his successors spread Greek culture through the Hellenistic world?

0.6 Rome's location on the Italian peninsula, centrally located in the Mediterranean Sea, benefited the Romans as they expanded. Italy also had wide, fertile plains, which supported a growing population.

>> Praetorian Guards were skilled and loyal bodyguards who protected generals during the time of the late republic. Later, they became an elite guard for Roman emperors.

Bounce to Activate Flipped Video

Ancient Rome and the Origins of Christianity

>> Objectives

Analyze the history and nature of the Roman republic.

Trace the rise and decline of the Roman empire.

Describe the major achievements of Roman civilization.

Understand the origins and teachings of early Christianity.

>> Key Terms

republic	Constantine
patrician	Virgil
consul	aqueduct
dictator	messiah
plebeian	Jesus
tribune	apostle
veto	Paul
imperialism	martyr
Julius Caesar	pope
Augustus	heresy
Hadrian	Augustine
Diocletian	

The Roman Republic

The Founding of Rome By about 800 B.C., the ancestors of the Romans, called the Latins, had migrated into Italy. The Latins settled along the Tiber River in small villages scattered over seven low-lying hills. There, they herded and farmed. Their villages would in time grow together into the city of Rome.

Romans shared the Italian peninsula with Greek colonists and the Etruscans—a people who at one time ruled most of central Italy. The Romans learned from the Etruscans, studying their engineering techniques and adapting their alphabet. The Romans ousted their Etruscan ruler and founded Rome in 509 B.C.

Birth of the Roman Republic The Romans established a new form of government called a **republic,** in which people chose their own officials. This form of government would prevent any individual from obtaining too much power.

The main governing body was the senate. Originally, all 300 members were **patricians,** or members of the landholding upper class. Each year, the senators nominated two **consuls** from the patrician class to supervise the government and command the armies. Also, in the event of war, the senate might choose a temporary **dictator,** or ruler with complete control over the government.

Plebeians, or common people, at first had little influence in the republic. However, the plebeians fought for the right to elect their own officials, called **tribunes.** The tribunes could **veto,** or block, laws that they felt harmed the plebeians. Although the senate still dominated the government, the plebeians had gained access to power and their rights were protected.

Roman Society The family was the basic unit of Roman society. The male head of the household had absolute power in the family. During the early Roman Republic, women had few rights. Later, they were able to own property and run businesses. Girls and boys from the upper and lower classes learned to read and write.

The Romans believed in many gods and goddesses, who resembled those of the Etruscans and Greeks. Numerous festivals were held to honor the gods and goddesses and to ensure divine favor for the city.

>> Julius Caesar dictated his commentaries on war to scribes who recorded his words.

Bounce to Activate Map

Expansion of Rome By 270 B.C., Rome controlled most of the Italian peninsula. This was due mainly to a well-trained army. The basic military unit was the legion. Each legion included about 5,000 citizen-soldiers. As Rome conquered new territories, they treated their defeated enemies well. As long as conquered peoples accepted Roman rule and obeyed certain laws, the Romans allowed them to maintain their own customs and governments.

SUMMARIZE How did the common people gain influence in the Roman republic?

The Roman Empire Rises and Declines

As Rome extended its territory, it encountered Carthage, an empire that stretched across North Africa and the western Mediterranean. These two powers battled in the three Punic Wars, which lasted from 264 B.C. to 146 B.C., when Rome finally destroyed Carthage.

Rome was committed to a policy of **imperialism,** establishing control over foreign lands. Roman power soon spread from Spain to Egypt. Rome soon controlled busy trade routes that brought tremendous riches.

Troubles in the Republic Conquest brought problems to Rome. Wealthy families purchased large estates and forced war captives to work as their slaves. Widespread use of slave labor and declining grain prices hurt small farmers. The gap between rich and poor grew, leading to corruption and riots.

The senate felt threatened when the patrician tribunes Tiberius and Gaius Gracchus attempted reforms. They were killed in street riots staged by the senate, leading to a period of civil wars.

Caesar Takes Power Out of the chaos emerged **Julius Caesar,** a brilliant military commander. By 50 B.C., after nine years of fighting, he completed the conquest of Gaul—the area that is now France and Belgium. Rivalry erupted between him and another general, Pompey. After defeating Pompey, Caesar swept around the Mediterranean, suppressing rebellions.

Victorious, Caesar returned to Rome and forced the senate to make him dictator for life. He pushed

Comparing Structures of Government

ROMAN REPUBLIC		ROMAN EMPIRE
HIGHEST OFFICIALS		**HIGHEST OFFICIALS**
Two Consuls • annually elected • held equal power	**Dictator** • appointed in times of emergency • held office for 6 months only	**Emperor** • inherited power • served for life • if served well, was worshipped as a god after death
GOVERNING BODIES		**GOVERNING BODIES**
Senate • issued advisory decrees to magistrates and people • in practice, held enormous power • had about 300 members	**Popular Assemblies** • two assemblies: centuriate (miltary), tribal (nonmilitary) • elected magistrates, held legislative power, made key decisions	**Senate** • issued binding decrees, acted as a high court, elected magistrates • in practice, held little power as compared to the emperor • had about 600 members

>> Analyze Charts There were significant differences between the governments of the Roman republic and the Roman empire. For a plebeian, which of the two structures of government would be preferable?

through a number of reforms to help solve Rome's many problems.

Fearing Caesar's growing power, his enemies killed him in 44 B.C. Caesar's friend, Marc Antony, and his nephew, Octavian, joined forces to avenge Caesar. However, they soon battled one another for power. In 31 B.C., Octavian defeated Antony.

The Roman Empire With this triumph, the senate gave Octavian the title of **Augustus,** or "Exalted One." Under Augustus, who ruled from 27 B.C. to A.D. 14, the Roman republic came to an end and the Roman empire began. Augustus was its first emperor.

Augustus built a stable government for the empire and undertook economic reforms. He left the senate in place and created an efficient, well-trained civil service to enforce the laws. He cemented the allegiance of cities and provinces to Rome by allowing them a large amount of self-government. To make the tax system more fair, he ordered a census, or population count, of the empire so there would be records of all who should be taxed. He set up a postal service and issued new coins to make trade easier. He put the jobless to work building roads and temples and sent others to farm the land.

Another influential Roman emperor was **Hadrian.** He codified Roman law, making it the same for all provinces. During the golden age of the Pax Romana, or "Roman Peace," Roman rule brought peace, prosperity, and order to the lands it controlled, from the Euphrates River in the east to Britain in the west.

However, social and economic problems hid beneath the general prosperity. In the A.D. 200s, the Roman empire began to weaken. Rome suffered political and economic turmoil and a decline in traditional values. The oppressive government and corrupt upper class generated hostility among the lower classes.

The Empire is Divided In 284, the emperor **Diocletian** set out to restore order. He divided the empire into two parts. He appointed a co-emperor to rule the western provinces, and he controlled the eastern part, known as the Byzantine Empire. To slow inflation, Diocletian fixed the prices of many goods.

When the emperor **Constantine** came into power, he continued Diocletian's reforms. In addition, he granted toleration to Christians and moved the empire's capital to Constantinople, making the eastern empire the center of power.

The Decline of Rome These reforms failed to stop the long-term decline of the empire. Nomadic people from Asia, called Huns, were forcing Germanic peoples into Roman territory. By 410, Rome itself was under attack. By then, the empire had surrendered much of its western territories to invaders.

There were several reasons for Rome's decline, but the primary reason was the many invasions. Rome's legions were not as strong or as loyal as they had been. As Roman citizens suffered the consequences of a declining empire, patriotism diminished. The Roman empire finally "fell" in 476, when Germanic invaders captured Rome and ousted the emperor.

EXPLAIN How did Augustus lay the foundation for stable government in the Roman empire?

The Legacy of Rome

Romans spread their Latin language and Roman civilization to distant lands. At the same time, Roman civilization blended Greek, Hellenistic, and Roman achievements.

Literature, History, and Philosophy The greatest Roman authors wrote in Latin. In his epic poem the *Aeneid,* the Roman poet **Virgil** tried to show that Rome was as heroic as Greece. He hoped this tale of Rome's founding would arouse patriotism and help unite Rome after years of civil wars.

Other writers used poetry to satirize, or make fun of, Roman society. Dramatists wrote many plays, including dramas that built on Roman legends and comedies that portrayed everyday life.

Roman historians recalled Rome's triumphant past in an attempt to renew patriotism. In philosophy, Roman thinkers were impressed with the Hellenistic philosophy of Stoicism. Stoics stressed the importance of duty and acceptance of one's fate.

>> Attending the theater was a popular pastime in Rome. Here, actors don costumes and masks before a performance.

Art and Architecture Like their Greek predecessors, Roman sculptors portrayed their subjects realistically, focusing on every detail. However, the Romans distinguished themselves by also focusing on individual character. Artists depicted scenes from Roman literature and daily life in frescos and mosaics—pictures made from chips of colored stone or glass.

Another distinction that set the Romans apart from the Greeks was their architecture. Unlike the Greeks, the Romans emphasized grandeur. They built immense palaces, temples, and stadiums, which stood as impressive monuments to Roman power. The Romans also improved structures such as columns and arches. Utilizing concrete as a building material, they developed the arched dome as a roof for large spaces.

Engineering and Science Romans excelled in engineering, which is the application of science and mathematics to develop useful structures and machines. Roman engineers built roads, bridges, and harbors throughout the empire. They built **aqueducts,** or bridge-like stone structures that carried water from the hills into Roman cities.

In general, the Romans entrusted the Greeks, who were citizens of the empire, with scientific research. Ptolemy, the astronomer-mathematician, proposed his theory that Earth was at the center of the universe. This mistaken idea was accepted in the Western world for nearly 1,500 years.

The Legacy of Roman Law Rome was committed to the rule of law and to justice. To protect the empire and its citizens, Rome developed civil law. As Rome expanded, the law of nations was established. This law applied to both citizens and non-citizens of Rome. As Rome extended citizenship across the empire, the two systems merged.

As Roman law developed, certain basic principles evolved. Many of these principles are familiar to Americans today. Among the most important was that an accused person is presumed innocent until proven guilty. A second principle ensured that the accused was allowed to face the accuser and mount a defense. A third principle was that guilt must be firmly established using solid evidence. Still another principle was that judges interpret the laws and make fair decisions. The system of laws in the Roman Empire created stability and unity. Some of these laws have become part of today's democracies. Early Roman laws included the ideas that everyone should have equal treatment under the law and that a person is innocent until proven guilty. Needing evidence to establish guilt and setting aside unfair laws are also Roman ideas.

IDENTIFY MAIN IDEAS How did Roman writers promote patriotism?

>> The Pont du Gard in France was a Roman aqueduct built in 19 B.C. The three tiers of arches rise about 155 feet (47 m).

The Origins of Christianity

Early in the Pax Romana, Christianity arose in a distant corner of the Roman empire. It grew from a small sect to become the dominant religion of the empire.

Diverse Religions in the Empire Within the vast Roman empire, numerous religious beliefs thrived. Generally, Rome tolerated these varied religious traditions. As long as citizens showed loyalty by honoring Roman gods and accepting the divinity of the emperor, they were allowed to worship as they pleased.

Jews in the empire were excused from worshipping Roman gods. However, over time, some Jewish conservatives called on Jews to revolt against Rome. Some Jews also believed a **messiah,** or anointed king sent by God, would appear and lead them to freedom. As rebellion grew, the Romans crushed the rebels, and eventually destroyed the Jewish temple. Thousands of Jews were killed in the fighting and others were enslaved. However, teachers called rabbis preserved Jewish law.

Life and Teachings of Jesus Christianity developed as people began to follow the teachings of **Jesus.** Almost all the information we have about the life of Jesus comes from the Gospels, the first four books of the New Testament of the Christian Bible.

According to the Gospels, Jesus was born into a Jewish family in Bethlehem around 4 B.C. At the age of 30, the Gospels relate that Jesus began preaching to large crowds. He recruited 12 **apostles,** or close followers, to help spread his message.

>> The apostles accompanied Jesus and later spread his teachings.

Bounce to Activate Gallery

Spread of Christianity to A.D. 476

>> **Analyze Maps** How did the extent of Christianity in A.D. 325 compare to that in A.D. 476?

Jesus' teachings were firmly rooted in Jewish tradition. Jesus believed in one God, accepted the Ten Commandments, and preached obedience to the laws of Moses. However, Jesus also preached new beliefs. According to his followers, he called himself the Son of God. Many people believed Jesus was the long-anticipated messiah. Jesus proclaimed that his mission was to bring spiritual salvation and eternal life to anyone who believed in him. He emphasized God's love and the need for justice, morality, forgiveness, and service to others.

According to the Gospels, Jesus was betrayed by one of his disciples and condemned to death by crucifixion, a method of execution frequently used by the Romans. The Gospels report that he was resurrected, or raised from the dead. The Gospels go on to say that Jesus, after commanding his disciples to spread his teachings to all people, ascended into heaven.

Spread of Christianity After Jesus' death, the apostles and other followers spread his message. The apostle **Paul** played the most influential role in spreading Christianity. Paul traveled the extensive Roman road network spreading the teachings of Jesus. He explained that Jesus sacrificed his life to atone, or make amends, for the sins of humankind.

However, Rome was not tolerant of Christianity as it was with other religions. Christians often met in secret and, under some Roman rulers, were persecuted. Those that were killed in times of persecution became known as **martyrs.**

Despite these attacks, Christianity continued to spread. In 313, the emperor Constantine issued the Edict of Milan, which granted freedom of worship to all Roman citizens. Soon after, Theodosius made Christianity the official religion of Rome.

The Early Christian Church In time, the scattered Christian communities came together as a structured church. To join the Christian community, a person had to be baptized. Through baptism, a person's sins were forgiven by God.

Each Christian community and its clergy were grouped together as a diocese with a priest. Over the priest presided a bishop, a high Church official. Some bishops of important cities such as Rome, gained greater authority and were given the title of patriarch.

In time, rivalries among the patriarchs grew. In the Latin-speaking west, the bishops of Rome became known as popes. The **popes** claimed authority over all other bishops. The bishops in the Greek-speaking east disagreed. They felt the authority should be shared. The growth of **heresies,** or beliefs said to be contrary to official teachings, also caused divisions in the church.

Early Christians produced many works defining Christian theology. One of the greatest Church scholars was **Augustine,** bishop of Hippo in North Africa. He combined Christian doctrine with Greco-Roman learning, especially the philosophy of Plato.

SUMMARIZE Summarize the main ideas of Jesus' teachings.

>> Augustine was the bishop of Hippo in North Africa. A noted Church scholar, he combined Christian doctrine with the philosophy of Plato.

ASSESSMENT

1. **Explain** How did the republic's structure of government change and develop over time?
2. **Draw Conclusions** What factors caused Rome to plunge into civil wars and how did they weaken the republic?
3. **Identify Main Ideas** Why did Diocletian decide to split the empire?
4. **Analyze Information** Give two examples of American legal principles that had their foundation in Roman law.
5. **Trace** What were the historical origins of Christianity, and how did that affect the development of montheism in the Roman empire?

>> A monarch dubs a kneeling young man a knight. Two knights sponsor and stand by him in this French illustration from the late 1200s.

0.7 In European history, a thousand years passed between the fall of the Roman empire and the Renaissance. This era is known as the medieval period, or Middle Ages.

>> Objectives

Describe the political development of medieval Europe from the time of the Germanic kingdoms through the rise of nation-states.

Explain the role of feudalism, the manor economy, and the expansion of trade on medieval Europe.

>> Key Terms

Justinian
autocrat
Justinian's Code
Charlemagne
vassal
feudal contract
fief
chivalry
manor
serf
secular
sacrament
Benedictine Rule
papal supremacy
excommunication
Francis of Assisi
anti-Semitism
Great Schism
charter
capital
guild
apprentice
Crusades
Reconquista
Ferdinand and Isabella
Inquisition
William the Conqueror
common law
Magna Carta
due process of law
habeas corpus
Gregory VII
lay investiture
Henry IV
Innocent III
scholasticism
Thomas Aquinas
vernacular
Dante Alighieri
Geoffrey Chaucer
Gothic style
Black Death
steppe
Ivan the Great
Ivan the Terrible
ethnic group

Medieval Christian Europe

The Early Middle Ages

The Byzantine Empire As German invaders pounded Rome in the west, the emperor Constantine and his successors shifted their base to the eastern Mediterranean. Constantine rebuilt the city of Byzantium and renamed it Constantinople. Commanding key trade routes linking Europe and Asia, Constantinople grew wealthy from trade. In 330, Constantine made Constantinople the new capital of the Roman empire. In time, the eastern Roman empire became known as the Byzantine empire.

The Byzantine empire reached its peak under the emperor **Justinian.** With the help of his wife, Theodora, Justinian ruled as an **autocrat,** with complete authority. After a fire in 532, Justinian made Constantinople even grander. One of his most important achievements was rebuilding the church of Hagia Sophia.

Under Justinian, Byzantine armies reconquered North Africa and parts of southern Europe. However, these victories were only temporary, as Justinian's successors later lost these lands.

Justinian also had a commission collect and organize the laws of Rome. This collection, which had a strong impact on future monarchs and legal thinkers, became known as **Justinian's Code.** It helped unify the empire.

Germanic Tribes Dominate Western Europe

After the western Roman empire fell, Western Europe was cut off from advanced cultures in Asia, overrun by invaders, and divided. The centralized Roman state and its powerful military were no longer available to maintain the rule of law and keep the peace locally.

In the early Middle Ages, Germanic tribes, such as the Franks, divided Western Europe. In 486, Clovis, king of the Franks, conquered Gaul, later to become France. Clovis followed his own customs but also kept Roman customs and converted to Christianity.

In the 600s, Muslims, or believers in Islam, created a huge and expanding empire. When a Muslim army crossed into France, Charles Martel and his Frankish warriors fought them at the battle of Tours in 732. Muslims ruled in Spain but did not advance farther into Western Europe.

The Age of Charlemagne In 768, Charles Martel's grandson, also named Charles, became king of the Franks. He built an empire covering what are now France, Germany, and part of Italy, and he was known as **Charlemagne,** or Charles the Great. Later, the pope crowned him the new emperor of the Romans.

Charlemagne united his kingdom by fighting off invaders, conquering peoples, spreading Christianity, and further blending Germanic, Roman, and Christian traditions. He set up an orderly government, naming nobles to rule locally. Charlemagne regarded education as another way to unify his kingdom. He revived Latin learning and encouraged the creation of local schools.

After Charlemagne's death in 814, his sons battled for power. In the end, his grandsons split up his empire.

A New Wave of Invasions About 900, nomads called Magyars settled in what is present-day Hungary. They overran Eastern Europe and moved into Germany, France, and Italy, but they were eventually pushed back.

Also, in the late 700s the Vikings from Scandinavia began to invade towns along coasts and rivers in Europe. The Vikings were skilled sailors and explorers. They settled and mixed with local peoples in England, Ireland, northern France, and parts of Russia, bringing their culture with them.

IDENTIFY How did Charlemagne unify Europe?

>> The Byzantine empire reached its greatest size by 565. **Analyze Maps** Describe the Byzantine empire's extent in 1020. **Infer** What does the empire's size in 565 suggest about Justinian's rule?

Feudalism and the Manor Economy

In the face of invasions, a decentralized political and economic structure evolved in medieval Europe. Feudalism was a loosely organized system of rule in which powerful local lords divided their landholdings among lesser lords. In exchange, these lesser lords, or **vassals,** pledged service and loyalty to the greater lord. The same man might be both vassal to a more powerful lord above him and lord to a less powerful vassal below him.

A lords and his vassal would exchange a pledge, known as a **feudal contract.** Lords expected military service, payments, and loyalty from vassals. In return, they granted vassals protection and parcels of land, called **fiefs.** By the 1100s, many nobles lived in castles, which served as fortresses. Wars often centered on seizing castles that commanded strategic river crossings, harbors, or mountain passes. In time of war, peasants from nearby villages might take refuge within the castle walls.

Lives of the Nobility For nobles, war was a way of life. Many trained from boyhood to become knights. They learned to ride horseback, fight, and care for weapons. They competed in mock battles called tournaments.

Noblewomen, too, participated in the warrior society. They took over estates while their husbands were at war and even fought to defend their lands. A few learned to read or write. All were expected to learn spinning, weaving, and the supervising of servants.

In the later Middle Ages, knights were expected to follow a code of ideal conduct, called **chivalry.** It required them to be brave, loyal, and honest, to fight fairly, to treat captured knights well, and to protect the weak. In practice, few knights could live up to the standards of chivalry, but it did provide a standard of behavior.

Troubadours, or wandering musicians, often sang about knights and ladies. Their songs formed the basis for medieval romances, or epic stories and poems.

The Manor System The **manor,** or lord's estate, was central to the feudal economy. Most manors included one or more villages and the surrounding lands. The lord administered justice and provided land and protection to the peasants who lived on his estate. In return, peasants owed their lord labor and goods.

Manors were self-sufficient, producing all that their people needed. A typical manor included a water mill to grind grain, a church, and shops to manufacturer various needed items. Pastures and fields surrounded the village.

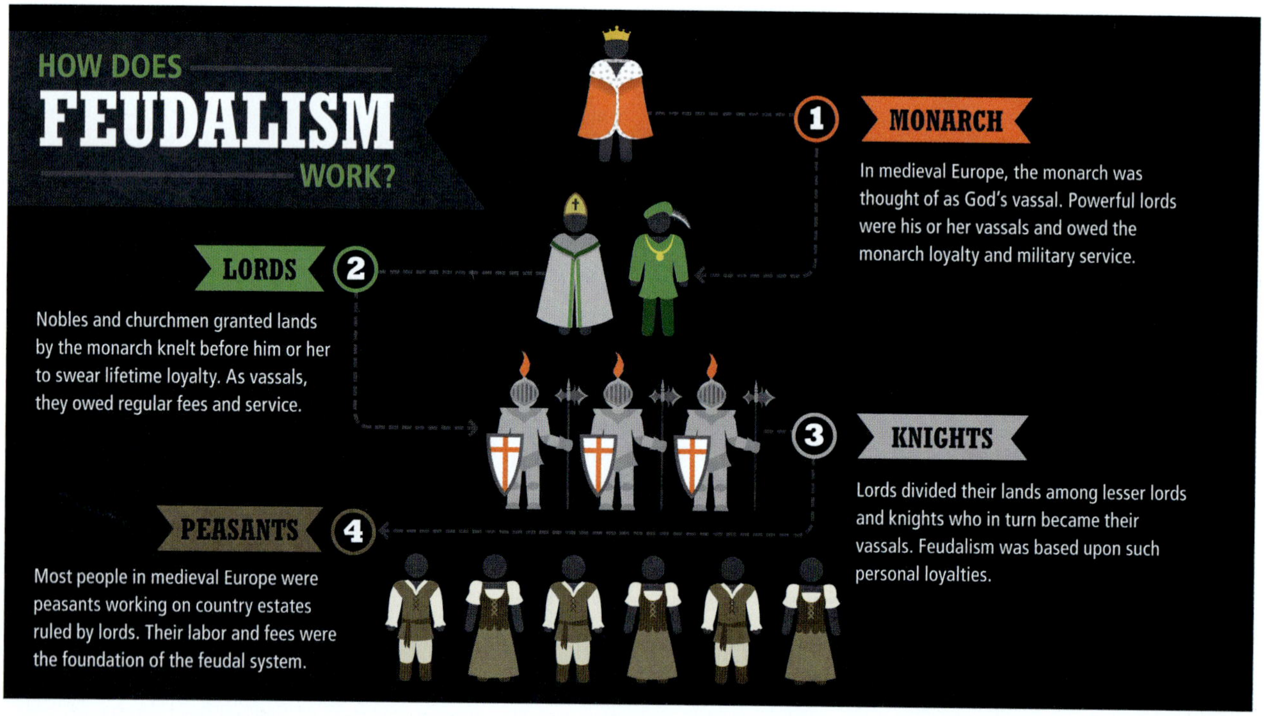

>> Feudalism was based on mutual loyalty and obligations. **Analyze Information** What were some of feudalism's advantages and disadvantages for medieval knights and peasants?

>> A bird's-eye view of a typical medieval manor, which might include a manor house, a village church, a grain mill, storage barns, a blacksmith's shop, clustered peasant huts, and fields for crops and grazing.

Bounce to Activate Chart

Most peasants on manors were **serfs** who were bound to the land. Although they were not slaves, serfs could not leave the manor without permission. They had to work the lord's lands several days a week, pay fees, and get permission to marry. In return, they were allowed to farm some land for themselves and received protection during war.

Their work was harsh, and hunger and disease were common. Yet they found times to celebrate during the year, such as for marriages and births, as well as at Christmas and Easter.

IDENTIFY What was the relationship between lords and vassals?

The Medieval Christian Church

During the Middle Ages, the Roman Catholic Church controlled the spiritual life of Christians in Western Europe but was also the strongest **secular,** or nonreligious force. Church officials were closely linked to secular rulers. Clergy might even be nobles with lands and armies.

The Parish Church For most people, village churches were the center of community life. Their parish priest celebrated mass and administered **sacraments,** or sacred rites. The medieval church taught that the sacraments were needed to achieve salvation. If he could read or write, the local priest served as the only teacher in the village. Priests also collected the tithe, or tax paid each year to the Church.

The Church taught that men and women were equal before God. But on Earth, women were viewed as weak and easily led into sin. Thus, they needed the guidance of men.

Life in Monasteries and Convents Some men and women chose to live a religious life as monks or nuns. About 530, a monk named Benedict created rules governing life in monasteries, or communities of monks. Under the **Benedictine Rule,** monks and nuns took three vows. The first was obedience to the abbot or abbess who headed the monastery or convent. The second was poverty, or giving up worldly goods, and the third was chastity, or purity. Each day was divided into periods for worship, work, and study.

Monasteries and convents often provided basic social services. Monks and nuns looked after the poor and sick and set up schools for children. Travelers could find food and a night's lodging at many monasteries and convents. Monasteries and convents also preserved the writings of the ancient world. Their libraries contained Greek and Roman works, which monks and nuns copied as a form of labor.

Power of the Church Medieval popes eventually claimed that, as God's representatives on Earth, they had **papal supremacy,** or authority over kings and emperors. The Church had its own body of laws and issued its own punishments. One was **excommunication,** the withholding of sacraments and Christian burial. According to Church doctrine, this condemned a sinner to hell.

In addition, a pope could punish rulers with an interdict. This barred entire towns or kingdoms from receiving sacraments and Christian burial. The Church also used its authority to end warfare among nobles by declaring times of peace.

As Church wealth and power grew, so did corruption. Monks and nuns ignored their vows, leading to calls for reform. In the early 900s, Abbot Berno of Cluny brought back the Benedictine Rule. Other reforms came from friars, or monks who traveled and preached to the poor. The first order of friars, the Franciscans, was founded by **Francis of Assisi.** The Franciscans preached poverty, humility, and love of God.

Medieval Jewish Communities Jewish communities existed across medieval Europe. Jewish culture flowered in Muslim Spain, which became a major center of Hebrew scholarship. Jews also found homes in northern Europe. Jewish communities everywhere preserved the oral and written laws that were central to their faith.

During the early Middle Ages, Christians and Jews often lived side by side in relative peace. By the late 1000s, however, **anti-Semitism,** or prejudice against Jews, had increased. The Church eventually issued orders forbidding Jews from owning land or having certain jobs. Because the Church forbade Christians from usury, or lending money at interest, some Jews became moneylenders.

Between 1096 and 1450, Jews were persecuted and expelled from major European cities and states, including England, France, and parts of what is today Germany, Italy, Austria, and Hungary. Many thousands of Jews migrated into Eastern Europe.

Eastern and Western Churches Split

Christianity was practiced differently in the Byzantine empire than in the West. The Byzantine emperor controlled Church affairs and appointed the patriarch, or highest Church official in Constantinople. Byzantine Christians rejected the pope's claim to authority over all Christians.

During the Middle Ages, the eastern and western branches of Christianity grew further apart, partly due to a dispute over the use of icons, or holy images. In 1054, other controversies caused a split known as the **Great Schism.** The pope of the Byzantine patriarch excommunicated one another. The Byzantine Church became known as the Eastern Orthodox Church. The western branch became known as the Roman Catholic Church. Both branches of Christianity continue today.

DRAW CONCLUSIONS How did monks and nuns contribute to their surrounding communities?

A Divided Church

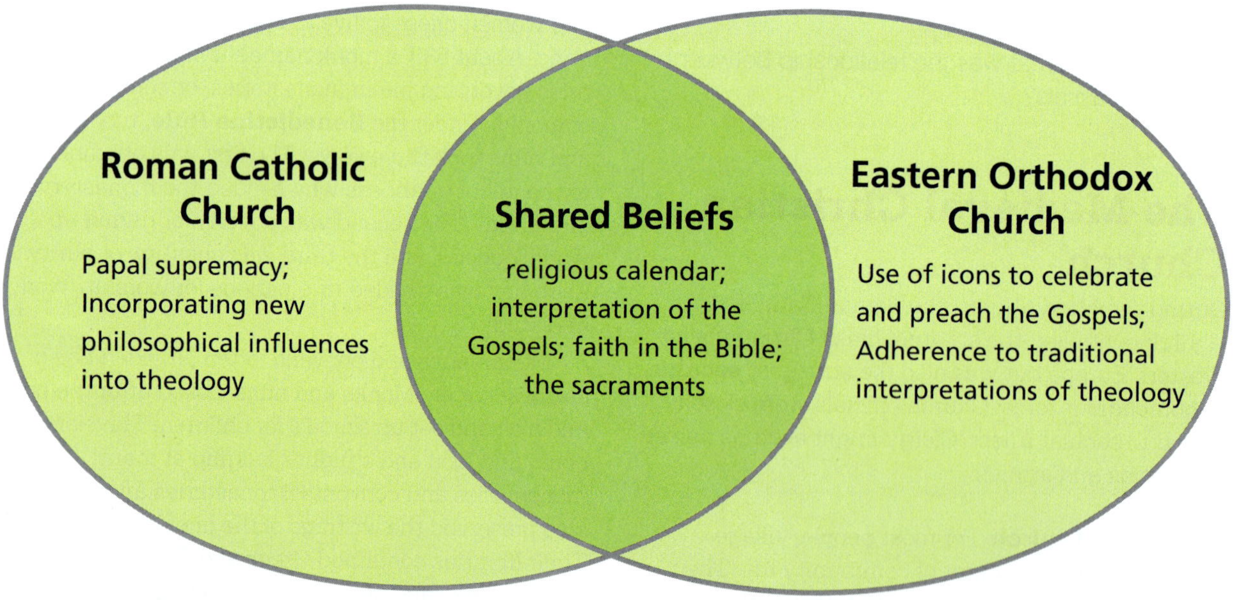

>> **Analyze Charts** Which church branch used icons? Which professed papal supremacy?

Economic Expansion and Change: The Crusades and After

By about 1000, Europe was undergoing an economic revival. Over the next few centuries, remarkable changes greatly strengthened Western Europe.

Improvements in Agriculture By the 800s, farmers were using iron plows instead of wooden ones and horses to pull plows rather than slower oxen. Also, a new crop rotation system improved soil fertility.

These changes helped farmers produce more food. As a result, Europe's population nearly tripled between 1000 and 1300.

Trade and the Growth of Cities As warfare declined in the 1100s, trade improved. Demand for goods increased and trade routes expanded. Annual trade fairs were an early sign of economic revival. Traders from all over Europe met at fairs near navigable rivers or where trade routes met.

Trade centers arose along the routes and slowly grew into the first medieval cities. The richest cities emerged in northern Italy and Flanders—the two ends of the profitable north-south trade route.

To protect their interests, merchants would ask the local lord or king for a **charter.** This was a document establishing rights and privileges for the town in exchange for a large sum of money, a yearly fee, or both.

A typical medieval city was a jumble of narrow streets lined with tall houses. Most towns were filthy, smelly, noisy, and crowded—a perfect breeding ground for disease. Despite the drawbacks of town and city life, people were attracted to the opportunities available there.

New Ways of Doing Business As trade expanded, new business practices arose. The need for **capital,** or money for investment, stimulated the growth of banks. In addition, merchants sometimes joined together in partnerships, pooling their money to finance large-scale ventures.

Other business changes included development of insurance and use of credit rather than cash, allowing merchants to travel without having to carry gold. Overall, however, the use of money increased.

Social Changes Peasants began selling their goods to townspeople for cash. By 1300, most peasants were hired laborers or tenant farmers paying rent for their land, rather than serfs.

>> New farming technologies changed medieval Europe. In the fields, a new type of harness distributed pressure along the shoulders of the horse, which allowed the plowing of heavier soils.

By 1000, merchants, traders, and artisans had become a powerful social class between nobles and peasants, called the middle class. Members of this class formed **guilds,** associations which controlled and protected specific trades or businesses.

To become a guild member, people often began learning a craft or trade in early childhood as **apprentices.** After seven years, an apprentice became a journeyman, or salaried worker. Few became guild masters. Women dominated some trades and even had their own guilds.

The Crusades The **Crusades** were a series of wars in which Christians fought Muslims for control of Middle Eastern lands. The Crusades were destructive but ultimately opened a wider world to Europeans and increased the pace of change.

In 1071, Seljuk Turks conquered Byzantine lands in Asia Minor and then moved into the Holy Land, the lands were Jesus had lived. Pope Urban II launched the Crusade to win control of the Holy Land. Only the First Crusade was a success for European crusaders, who captured Jerusalem in

1099. In the Second Crusade, Jerusalem fell to the Muslim leader Saladin. Crusaders failed to take Jerusalem in the Third Crusade, but Saladin agreed to reopen the city to Christian pilgrims.

By the Fourth Crusade in 1202, knights were fighting other Christians to help Venice against its Byzantine trade rivals. The Byzantines lost control of trade and much of their wealth. In 1453, Ottoman Turks conquered Constantinople, renaming it Istanbul.

Impact of the Crusades The Crusades left a legacy of distrust in the Middle East and Europe. They also produced vast changes in society. In the Middle East, Muslims began to reunify.

In Europe, trade increased. The Crusades encouraged the growth of a money economy, which contributed to the decline of serfdom. Monarchs gained strength as they won the right to collect taxes to support the Crusades. The Crusades also increased the power of the papacy.

The experiences of crusaders in the Muslim world introduced Europeans to new places. In 1271, Venetian Marco Polo headed for China and returned home to write a book. The experiences of both Polo and the crusaders brought new knowledge and a wider worldview to Europe.

The Reconquista in Spain Around 1100, Christian kingdoms in Spain began a struggle called the **Reconquista,** or reconquest. The purpose was to expel Muslims, who had lived there since the 700s. In 1469, **Ferdinand and Isabella** married, unifying Spain. They captured the last Muslim stronghold, Granada, in 1492.

Under Muslim rule, Spanish Christians, Jews, and Muslims had been able to live together. However, Ferdinand and Isabella wanted to impose religious, as well as political, uniformity on their diverse peoples. With the help of the **Inquisition,** they launched a campaign against Muslims and Jews. Those found guilty of heresy were burned at the stake. More than 150,000 people, mostly Muslims and Jews, fled Spain, taking their skills and learning with them.

DRAW CONCLUSIONS Did the Christian kings of Europe achieve their goals during the Crusades?

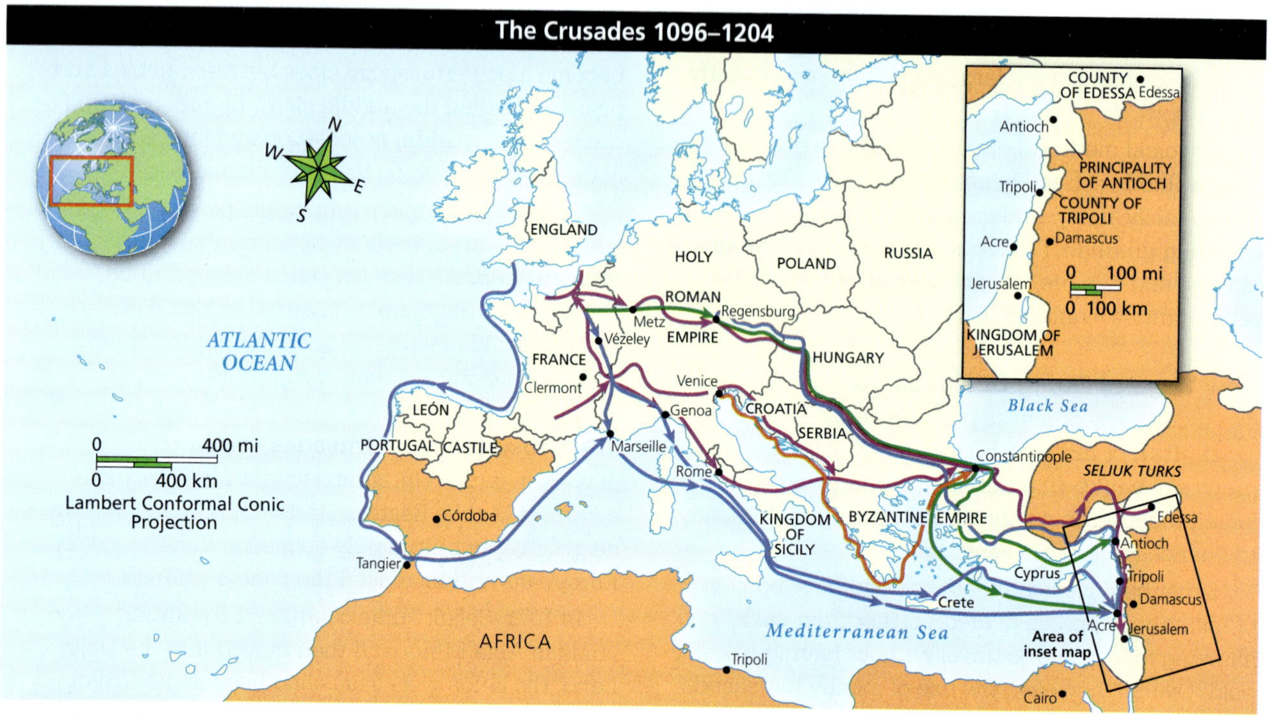

>> **Analyze Maps** Urged on by Pope Urban II, thousands of Europeans joined the Crusades to expel Muslims from the Holy Land. What route did English crusaders take? Why do you think they took that route?

Feudal Monarchs and the Church

During the early feudal period, most lords acknowledged a king or other overlord, but royal rulers had little real power. However, from 1000 to 1300, monarchs took steps to centralize their power. They sought to extend royal law and justice over their kingdoms. They set up government bureaucracies that administered justice and taxation. With a larger income, monarchs could support a standing army, rather than rely on the military service of their nobles.

The rise of towns and the money economy also strengthened royal rulers. The growing middle class often turned to monarchs, rather than nobles, to ensure peace. Increases in royal power gradually established the foundations of modern government.

>> King John signs the Magna Carta under the watchful eyes of the English nobles. The document restricts John's power and the power of all kings to follow.

Development of English Government In 1066, **William the Conqueror** successfully invaded England from France. By 1086, he had completed a census and property survey called the Domesday Book. It helped establish an effective taxation system and treasury.

In 1154, Henry II ascended the English throne. He expanded the justice system. Royal court decisions became the foundation of English **common law,** a system based on custom and prior rulings. Henry II also set up a jury system that was the forerunner of today's grand jury.

Henry's son, King John, abused his power and was forced to sign the **Magna Carta,** or Great Charter. It required the king to obey the laws. It also established two important principles: **due process of law,** or protection from arrest without proper legal procedures, and **habeas corpus,** or protection from imprisonment without being charged with a crime.

John also agreed not to raise taxes before consulting his Great Council of lords and clergy. Under later rulers, this council evolved into **Parliament,** England's legislature. Parliament eventually controlled the "power of the purse," meaning it would not approve new taxes unless the monarch met certain demands.

Growth of the French Monarchy Unlike the English, early French monarchs did not rule a united kingdom. Then in 987, Hugh Capet became king and began expanding royal power. The Capetians stabilized the kingdom over the next 300 years. In 1179, Philip II took the throne. He gained control of English lands in Normandy and expanded territories in southern France, adding vast areas to his domain, and becoming Europe's most powerful ruler.

Louis IX came to power in 1226. Although he persecuted heretics and Jews and led crusades against Muslims, he also outlawed private wars, ended serfdom, and expanded royal courts. By the time of his death in 1270, France was a centralized monarchy ruling over a unified state. In 1302, the Estates General was set up, but this council of clergy, nobility, and townspeople never gained the "power of the purse" over French royalty.

Conflicts Between Popes and Emperors During the Middle Ages, both popes and European rulers grew more powerful. This increase in power often resulted in conflict.

Rulers of the Holy Roman Empire, which extended from Germany to Italy, confronted the pope over the appointment of Church officials. Pope **Gregory VII** banned **lay investiture,** in which the emperor rather than the pope named and installed bishops. However, Holy Roman Emperor **Henry IV** said that bishops held royal lands under his control, so he had the right to appoint them. In 1076, the pope excommunicated Henry and threatened to crown a new emperor. Henry was forced to humble himself to the pope as a sinner, and Gregory forgave him.

>> Under Pope Innocent III, the Church reached a level of power it would never again attain. Innocent saw himself as second only to God, but above all other men.

>> This Italian illustration from about the 1300s shows a lawyer lecturing his students in a medieval school.

Later, Henry led an army to Rome, sending Gregory into exile. Fifty years later, the Concordat of Worms was accepted, giving popes sole power to invest bishops with religious authority and emperors the right to invest them with lands.

Power struggles over land also occurred during the 1100s and 1200s. Holy Roman Emperor Frederick I, called Frederick Barbarossa or "Red Beard," fought but failed to capture wealthy northern Italian cities. Instead, he arranged for his son to marry the heiress to Sicily and southern Italy, expanding his control there. His grandson, Frederick II, also sought but failed to control northern Italy. Ultimately, the Holy Roman Empire broke up into separate feudal states, while southern Italy went through centuries of chaos.

The Height of Papal Power By the 1200s, the Church reached its peak of power. In 1198, Pope **Innocent III** took office and claimed supremacy over all other rulers. He excommunicated the English and French kings and placed their kingdoms under interdict, barring people from religious sacraments. He also launched a holy war against heretics in southern France, killing tens of thousands.

After Innocent's death, popes continued to claim supremacy, but they were challenged by the monarchs' growing power. In the late 1200s, France's Philip IV successfully challenged the pope on the issue of taxing the clergy. Philip then went on to engineer the election of a French pope.

DESCRIBE What was the political, legal, and economic impact of the ideas contained in the Magna Carta?

Learning, Literature, and Arts of the Middle Ages

Europe in the High Middle Ages experienced a blossoming of education, literature, and the arts. This was influenced by increased prosperity, contact with other cultures, and the rediscovery of ancient learning.

Learning and Science in the Middle Ages By the 1100s, schools sprang up near cathedrals, some evolving into the first universities. Muslim scholars had translated the works of Aristotle and other Greeks into Arabic. In Muslim Spain, they were translated into Latin, the language of European scholars.

In the 1100s, the new translations initiated a revolution in learning. Greek philosophers such as Aristotle had used reason to discover truth. Medieval Christians believed that the Church was the final authority. To resolve this conflict, they asked Christian scholars to use reason to support Christian beliefs. This method is known as **scholasticism.**

The most famous scholastic was **Thomas Aquinas.** He wrote *Summa theologica* to prove that faith and reason could exist in harmony. He also believed in the concept of universal natural laws that supersede government laws, which included giving people the right to challenge unjust rulers.

Scientific learning also reached Europe, including translations of Hippocrates on medicine and Euclid on geometry. Europeans adopted the more streamlined Hindu-Arabic numerals over cumbersome Roman numerals, allowing later scientists and mathematicians to make great strides.

Medieval Literature Latin remained the language of Europe's scholars and churchmen. However, new literature emerged in the **vernacular,** or everyday language of ordinary people. This change brought a flowering of literary works, including *The Divine Comedy,* an Italian classic poem of heaven, hell, and purgatory by **Dante Alighieri,** and a portrait of English medieval life by **Geoffrey Chaucer.**

Arts and Architecture Architecture and the arts also flourished. Fortress-like Romanesque churches gave way to the **Gothic style.** Its key feature was flying buttresses—exterior stone supports that permitted thinner, higher walls and massive windows, bringing light and height to cathedrals.

Other arts during the period include stained glass, religious paintings, and woven wall hangings. A famous example is the Bayeux Tapestry, an embroidered illustration of the Norman Conquest of England. The Gothic style was also applied to the decoration of books, known as illumination.

The Byzantine Heritage Much of the literature, learning, and arts of Europe from this period was influenced by the Byzantines. Byzantine civilization combined Christian beliefs with Greek science, philosophy, and arts. Byzantine artists created unique religious icons and mosaics. Byzantine scholars preserved Greek literature and produced their own great books, especially in the field of history.

DESCRIBE What were some elements of the new learning of medieval Europe?

>> Graceful and beautiful, Notre Dame Cathedral in Paris is one of the most famous examples of Gothic architecture.

Bounce to Activate Gallery

The Late Middle Ages: A Time of Upheaval

Europe faced a series of devastating crises that began in the 1300s. First, widespread crop failures brought famine and starvation. Then plague and war ravaged populations. Europe eventually recovered from these disasters. Still, the upheavals marked the end of the Middle Ages and the beginning of the early modern age.

The Black Death In the mid-1300s a deadly disease called bubonic plague, or the **Black Death,** reached Europe by way of trading ships from the east. It was spread by fleas carried by rats. Eventually, the epidemic killed one-third of all Europeans.

Normal life broke down. People fled cities or hid in their homes. Without workers, production declined. Survivors demanded higher wages, leading to inflation, or rising prices. Landlords tried to limit wages and forced villagers off the land. Some terrified Christians unjustly scapegoated Jews for the plague. In the resulting hysteria, thousands of Jews were murdered.

The plague not only spread death but also social unrest, as bitter, angry peasants revolted. Rulers were able to put down peasant revolts. In the long run, however, the shortage of labor gave peasants the bargaining power to demand higher wages. At the same time, landowning nobles suffered a loss of economic and political power. Thus, the Black Death contributed to the breakdown of feudalism. As Europe recovered, trade again began to expand.

Crisis in the Church By the late Middle Ages, the Church, too, was in crisis. Many monks and priests had died during the plague. Survivors asked tough spiritual questions. The Church could not provide the strong leadership that was needed.

In 1309, Pope Clement V had moved the papal court to Avignon outside the border of southern France. For 70 years, popes at Avignon reigned over a luxurious court. Reformers arose within the Church, calling for change. In 1378, they elected their own pope in Rome. French cardinals elected a rival pope.

This Church schism finally ended in 1417 when a Church council removed authority from all three popes and elected a compromise candidate.

Reformers challenged the power of the Church. In England, John Wycliffe attacked corruption and insisted that the Bible, not the Church, was the source of all Christian truth. The Church responded by persecuting Wycliffe and his followers.

The Hundred Years' War Between 1337 and 1453, England and France fought a series of conflicts known as the Hundred Years' War. English rulers had battled for centuries to hold on to the French lands of their Norman ancestors. But French kings were intent on extending their own power in France. When Edward III of England claimed the French crown in 1337, war erupted anew between these rival powers.

England won early victories with new technology, the longbow. It could discharge three arrows in the time a French crossbowman fired just one. Its arrows pierced all but the heaviest armor.

However, led by 17-year-old Joan of Arc, France began to win battles. In 1429, Joan told the uncrowned king that God sent her to save France. He authorized her to lead an army against the English. In one year, her troops won several victories, but she was captured, tried, and burned at the stake. Her death rallied French forces. With their powerful new weapon, the cannon, they drove the English out of most of France.

Ultimately, the war helped French kings expand their power and led to an increase in French national pride. In England, the war strengthened Parliament as kings turned to Parliament for funds. The longbow and

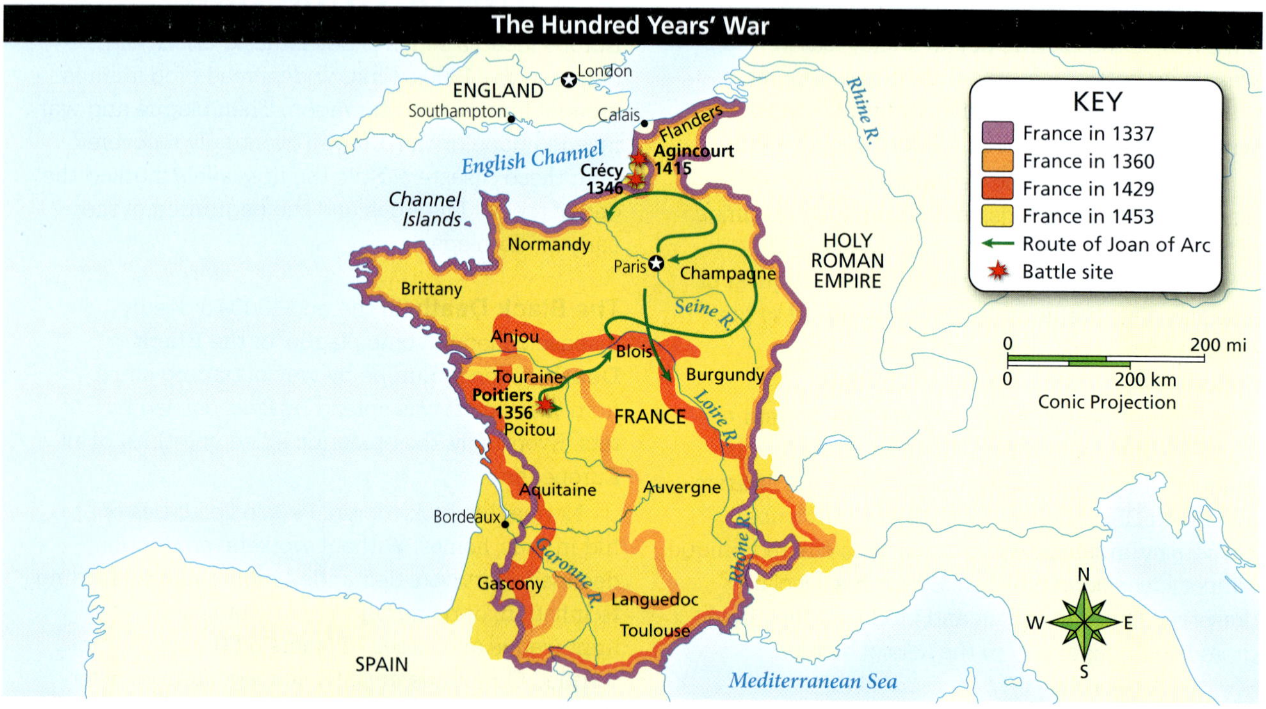

>> The English and French battled for control of France. **Analyze Maps** What regions of France did England gain between 1337 and 1429?

cannon undermined the value of armored knights on horseback. This contributed to the end of feudalism.

CHECK UNDERSTANDING How did the Black Death affect Europe?

Russia and Eastern Europe

Russia has three main geographic regions that shaped early life. The northern forests have poor soil and a cold climate. A band of fertile land farther south attracted farmers. The southern **steppe**—an open, treeless grassland—provided pasture for herds. It allowed nomads to migrate easily from Asia into Europe.

Early History of Russia

Since ancient times, Slavic peoples had lived in areas that later became part of Russia. Vikings came from Scandinavia. The Vikings traveled south along Russia's rivers, trading with the Slavs and with Constantinople. The city of Kiev was at the center of this trade.

Russians date the origins of their country to 862, when a Viking tribe called the Rus began ruling from Novgorod in the north. Rus lands expanded to include Kiev, which became their capital.

Byzantine and Mongol Influence

In the 800s, Constantinople sent missionaries to Russia. Two Orthodox monks, Cyril and Methodius, developed the Cyrillic alphabet, which is still used in Russia. During the reign of the Rus king Vladimir, Orthodox Christianity became the religion of the Rus and they aligned themselves with the Byzantines.

Between 1236 and 1241, Mongols advanced into Russia. They burned Kiev and ruled Russia for the next 240 years. However, as long as they received tribute, the Mongols let Russian princes rule and they tolerated the Russian Orthodox Church. Although trade increased under the Mongols, Mongol rule cut Russia off from Western Europe at a time when Europeans were making great advances.

Rise of the Tsars

The princes of Moscow gained power under the Mongols, and Moscow became Russia's political and spiritual center. In 1380, these princes led other Russians in defeating the Golden Horde at the battle of Kulikovo.

A driving force behind Moscow's successes was Ivan III, or **Ivan the Great.** Between 1462 and 1505, he brought much of northern Russia under his rule. Ivan built the framework for absolute rule. He tried

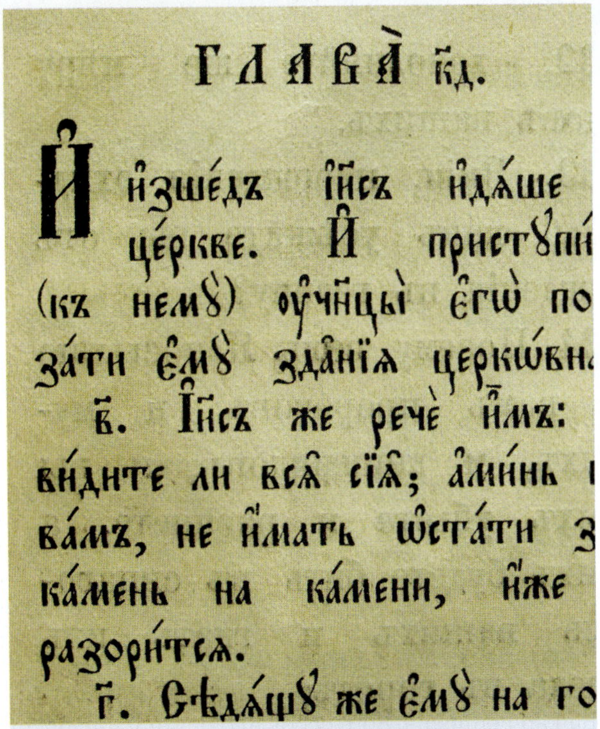
Глава кд.
И изшедъ Іисъ идаше
церкве. И приступи
(къ нему) ученицы его по
зати ему зданія церковн
в. Іисъ же рече имъ:
видите ли вся сія; аминь
вамъ, не имать ѡстати
камень на камени, иже
разорится.
г. Сѣдящу же ему на го

>> Letters were added to the medieval Greek alphabet, with some based on Hebrew, to reflect the rich sounds of the Slavic language.

>> Russian art, such as this religious icon, was heavily influenced by the Byzantine style with its rich, deep colors.

to limit the power of the boyars, or great landowning nobles, and adopted Byzantine court rituals. He sometimes referred to himself as tsar, the Russian word for Caesar.

His grandson, Ivan IV, became the first Russian ruler officially crowned tsar. He further centralized royal power by limiting the privileges of the boyars and granting land to nobles in exchange for military or other service. As the manor system was fading in Western Europe, Ivan IV introduced laws that tied Russian serfs to the land.

However, Ivan IV became unstable and violent. The ways in which he used his power earned him the title **Ivan the Terrible.** By the time he died in 1584, he had introduced Russia to a tradition of extreme absolute power that would shape Russia into modern times.

Eastern Europe: A Diverse Region Eastern Europe lies between Central Europe to the west and Russia to the east. Included in this region is the Balkan Peninsula. Both goods and cultural influences traveled along its rivers.

Many ethnic groups settled in Eastern Europe. An **ethnic group** is a large group of people who share the same language and culture. The West Slavs settled in Poland and other parts of Eastern Europe, while the South Slavs occupied the Balkans. Asian peoples, like the Magyars, as well as Vikings and other Germanic peoples also migrated to Eastern Europe. At times, some groups tried to dominate the region.

Many cultural and religious influences spread to Eastern Europe. Byzantine missionaries brought Eastern Orthodox Christianity and Byzantine culture to the Balkans. German knights and missionaries brought Roman Catholic Christianity to Poland and other areas.

In the 1300s, the Ottomans invaded the Balkans and introduced Islam. Jews who were persecuted in Western Europe fled to Eastern Europe, especially to Poland, where their liberties were protected.

Kingdoms of Eastern Europe During the Middle Ages, Eastern Europe included many kingdoms and small states. The marriage in 1386 of Queen Jadwiga of Poland to Duke Wladyslaw Jagiello of Lithuania made Poland-Lithuania the largest state in Europe. However, power gradually shifted from the monarch to the nobles. The nobles met in an assembly, where a single noble could block passage of a law. Without a strong central government, Poland-Lithuania declined.

The Magyars settled in Hungary and became Roman Catholics. The Hungarian king was forced to sign the Golden Bull of 1222, which strictly limited royal power. The Mongols overran Hungary in

BALKANS DIFFERENT LANGUAGES, RELIGIONS, AND CULTURES

CULTURE	RELIGION	WRITTEN LANGUAGE
Western European Germanic Latin	Roman Catholic	Latin

CULTURE	RELIGION	WRITTEN LANGUAGE
North Africa Arabia	Islam	Arabic Persian

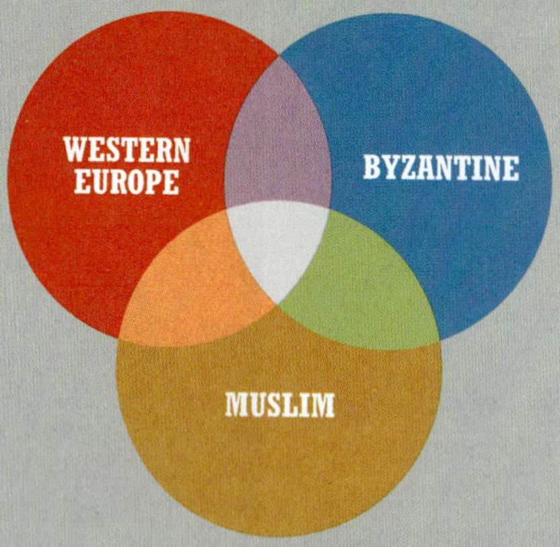

CULTURE	RELIGION	WRITTEN LANGUAGE
Eastern/ Asian	Eastern Orthodox Christian	Cyrrilic

THE AREAS WHERE **CULTURE OVERLAPPED** PRESENTED THE POTENTIAL FOR **CONFLICT**

>> **Analyze Charts** Which cultural influences are present in the Balkans?

1241, killing half of its people. Although they soon withdrew, the Ottoman Turks ended Hungarian independence in 1526.

Some of the South Slavs who settled in the Balkans became the ancestors of the Serbs. Most Serbs became Orthodox Christians and set up a state based on a Byzantine model. Serbia reached its height in the 1300s but could not withstand the advance of the Ottoman Turks. At the battle of Kosovo in 1389, Serbs fought to the death, a memory still honored by their descendants. During almost 500 years of Ottoman rule, Serbs preserved a sense of their own identity.

>> Stefan Dusan was called the Emperor of the Serbs, Greeks, and Albanians. He is considered the greatest ruler of medieval Serbia.

DESCRIBE How did Ivan III and Ivan IV establish authoritarian power in Russia?

ASSESSMENT

1. **Analyze Information** How did the economic system of manorialism work, and how did it affect peasants and nobles?
2. **Synthesize** What were some of the effects of the Great Schism?
3. **Determine Relevance** How did the Crusades accelerate change in Europe?
4. **Analyze Information** How did new knowledge, based on Aristotle and other Greek thinkers, pose a challenge to Christian scholars?
5. **Compare** Compare the effects of the Hundred Years' War on France and England.

>> The oasis of Mecca was an important religious site with a major temple dedicated to pagan gods and goddesses. Its religious significance helped make it a thriving merchant center.

0.8 The religion of Islam, whose followers are called Muslims, emerged in the Arabian Peninsula. There, in A.D. 570, Muhammad was born in Mecca—a trading and religious center. Muhammad worked among nomadic herders called Bedouins. Later, he became a successful merchant and decided to marry at 25. He was known for his honesty in business and devotion to his family.

The Muslim World and Africa

>> Objectives

Describe the central ideas of Islam, and summarize its origin and spread.

Describe Muslim art, architecture, and literature, and summarize the major ideas in mathematics, science, and technology that occurred in Muslim civilization.

Analyze how the gold and salt trade in Africa facilitated the spread of ideas and trade.

>> Key Terms

Muhammad
Mecca
hijra
Kaaba
Quran
hajj
Sharia
Sunni
Shiite
Umayyad
Abbasid
Firdawsi
Omar Khayyám
Ibn Rushd
Ibn Khaldun
al-Khwarizmi
Muhammad al-Razi
Ibn Sina
Ottomans
Safavids
Istanbul
Suleiman
Shah Abbas the Great
Sahara
desertification
Bantu
Nubia
Ghana
Sundiata
Mali
Mansa Musa
Songhai
Axum
Ethiopia
Lalibela
Swahili
Great Zimbabwe
patrilineal
matrilineal
lineage

The Origins of Islam

Muhammad the Messenger Muhammad often meditated on the moral ills of Meccan society, including greed. According to Muslim belief, Muhammad became a prophet at 40 when he was asked by an angel to become God's messenger. When he began teaching, a few listened, but others opposed him with threats. In 622, he and his followers fled Mecca for Yathrib, on a journey called the **hijra**. Later Yathrib was called Medina.

In Medina, thousands adopted Islam and formed strong, peaceful communities. When Meccan leaders grew hostile, Muslims defeated them in battle. Muhammad returned to Mecca in 630, where the **Kaaba**, which Muhammad dedicated to God (Allah), became the holiest Islamic site. Muhammad died in 632.

Teachings of Islam The sacred text of Islam is the **Quran**. To Muslims, the Quran contains the sacred word of God as revealed to Muhammad. It is the final authority on all matters discussed in the text. The Quran teaches about what Muslims believe to be God's will and provides a guide to life. Its ethical standards emphasize honesty, generosity, and social justice.

Muslims believe that priests are not necessary to mediate between people and God. Muslims gather in mosques to pray. All observant Muslims perform five basic duties, known as the Five Pillars of Islam: declaring faith, praying five times daily, giving charity to the poor, fasting during their holy month, and making the **hajj**, or pilgrimage to Mecca, if a person is able.

Because Jews and Christians worship the same God and study what are considered God's earlier revelations, Muslims call them "People of the Book." Although Jews and Christians did not have the same rights as Muslims in early Muslim societies and often faced burdensome taxes and restrictions, they were to a limited degree able to practice their religions.

Islam as a Way of Life The **Sharia** is a body of laws that interprets the Quran and applies religious principles to legal situations. According to the Quran, women are spiritually equal to men but have different roles. In different places, Muslims interpret women's roles and rights differently. In some cases, Muslims adopted practices of conquered peoples, such as requiring upper-class women to wear veils.

INFER Why do Muslims follow the Five Pillars of Islam?

A Muslim Empire

In 632, Abu Bakr became the first caliph, or successor to Muhammad. He converted all Arab tribes to Islam and united them under his leadership. Once united, the Arabs defeated the Persian empire and parts of the Byzantine empire. However, a schism between **Sunni** and **Shiite** Muslims occurred after Muhammad's death and still exists today.

Sunni and Shiite Beliefs Members of both branches of Islam believe in the same God, look to the Quran for guidance, and follow the Five Pillars of Islam. However, Sunnis and Shiites differ in such areas as religious practice, law, and daily life. Shiites believe that Muhammad's successors must be descendants of his son-in-law, Ali. They also should be religious leaders and interpret the Quran. Sunnis believe that any pious male Muslim from Muhammad's tribe can lead without performing religious functions. Today, about 90 percent of Muslims are Sunni. Sufis, who may be Sunni or Shiite, meditate and fast to gain communion with God.

Umayyad Caliphs Create an Arab Empire In the 700s, a powerful Meccan clan set up the Sunni **Umayyad** caliphate. They directed conquests that extended Muslim rule from Spain to the Indus River Valley. Their empire lasted until 750. The Muslims brought many people under their rule. Muslim

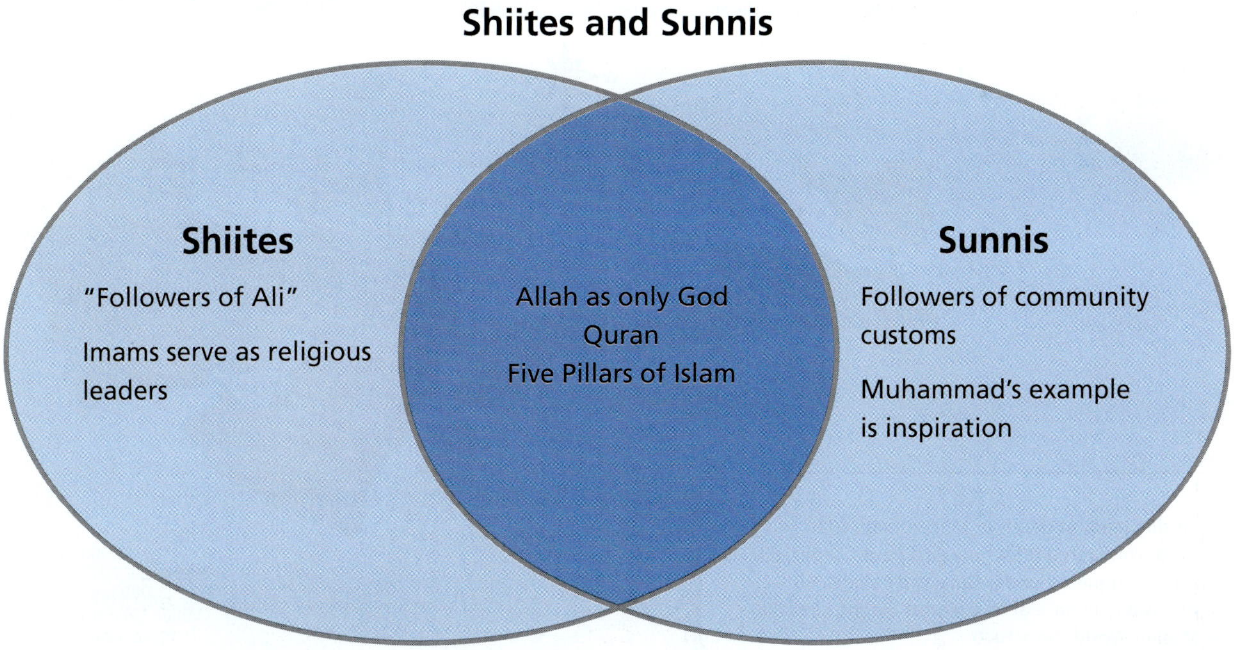

>> **Analyze Charts** This diagram shows the common beliefs held by Sunnis and Shiites, as well as their differences. What is a belief they share?

leaders imposed a special tax on non-Muslims, but Jews, Christians, and Zoroastrians could worship and some held important positions. Many people converted to Islam.

Changes Under the Abbasids However, the Umayyads later faced economic tensions and opposition from those who did not have the same privileges as Muslims. After capturing Damascus in 750, with strong support from Shiites and non-Arabs, Abu al-Abbas founded the **Abbasid** dynasty. The Abbasids ended conquests and supported education and learning. They enjoyed a golden age, with a more efficient government and a beautiful new capital, Baghdad, in the former Persian empire. They allowed Persian officials to hold important government offices, and Persian traditions to influence the caliphate. Mosques with minarets, or slender towers, graced the cities, and markets sold goods from far-off lands.

In Spain, one of the Umayyads established a separate state. Muslims ruled parts of Spain until 1492. They were tolerant of other religions, supported scholars, and constructed grand buildings.

As the empire declined, independent dynasties took power. Seljuk Turks gained power and their sultan, or ruler, controlled Baghdad by 1055, keeping the Abbasid caliph as a figurehead. Beginning in 1216, the Mongols attacked across southwest Asia. In 1258, they burned and looted Baghdad, ending the Abbasid dynasty.

INFER Why did the Abbasids make changes to the Arab Muslim empire?

The Achievements of Muslim Civilization

Muslim civilization enjoyed a golden age under the Abbasids. Their empire stretched into Asia, the Middle East, Africa, and Europe. Merchants crossed the Sahara, traveled the Silk Road to China, and sailed to India and Asia. New products and ideas were exchanged, and the religion of Islam was introduced to many regions. All this fueled the Muslim economy, leading to the development of partnerships, the use of credit, and a banking system. Artisans created manufactured goods for trade, and the government helped improve farming through large irrigation systems.

Muslim society allowed some social mobility, the ability to move up in social class through religious, scholarly, or military achievements. Most slaves were household servants and some were able to purchase their freedom. The children of some slaves could become free under another system.

Spread of Islam, 632–1000

>> **Analyze Maps** Islam spread across northern Africa and into the Mediterranean. Near what important city was the further spread of Islam into Europe stopped?

Bounce to Activate Timeline

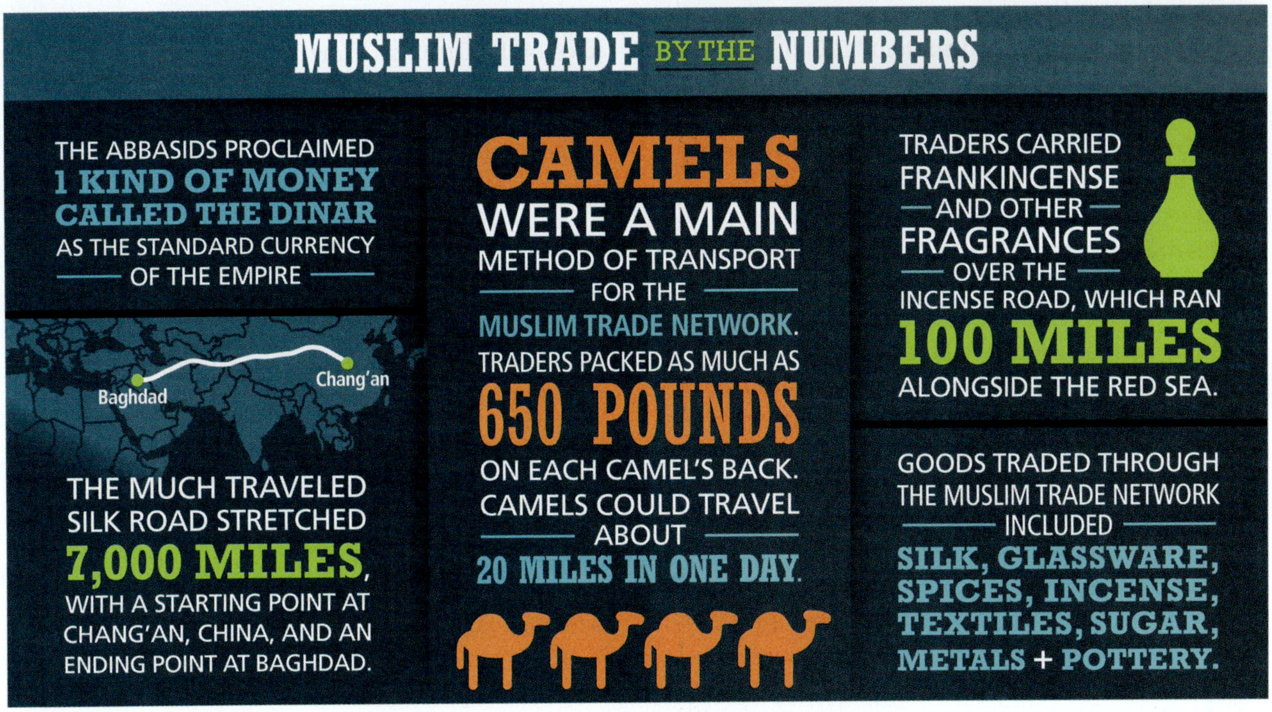

>> **Analyze Data** Trade across the desert brought great wealth to Muslim merchants. How do you think having a standard currency in the Abbasid caliph affected trade?

Diversity in Art, Literature, and Architecture

The diverse cultures in the empire, as well as Islam, influenced art and literature. Early oral poetry told tales of nomadic life, while later poets developed elaborate rules for poems. Great Muslim poets include **Firdawsi**, who told the history of Persia, and **Omar Khayyám**, who wrote about fate and life in The Rubáiyát. Storytellers often used short anecdotes to entertain people. In architecture, buildings reflected Byzantine influences, and mosques included domes and minarets. Muslim artists also used calligraphy, the art of beautiful handwriting, for decoration on buildings and in books.

An Emphasis on Knowledge Muslims made great strides in education. Both boys and girls were educated so they could study the Quran. Several cities supported learning centers with vast libraries. There, scholars translated Greek, Hindu, and Buddhist texts. Known in Europe as Averröes, the philosopher **Ibn Rushd** believed that knowledge should meet the standards of reason. Another Muslim thinker, **Ibn Khaldun**, studied history scientifically and advised others in avoiding errors.

In mathematics, **al-Khwarizmi** pioneered the study of algebra. **Muhammad al-Razi**, chief physician in the hospital at Baghdad, wrote books on diseases and medical practices. **Ibn Sina**, a famous Persian physician, compiled an encyclopedia of medical knowledge. Both doctors' works guided medical study in Europe for 500 years. Other physicians improved ways to save eyesight and mix medicines.

DESCRIBE What new business practices did merchants introduce in Muslim lands?

The Ottoman and Safavid Empires

Centuries after the Abbasids lost control of the Muslim empire two new Muslim dynasties—the **Ottomans** and **Safavids**—dominated the Middle East and parts of Eastern Europe. New military technology allowed these two groups to develop strong central governments. Cannons and muskets gave greater firepower to foot soldiers. The period from 1450 to 1650 is sometimes called the "age of gunpowder empires."

Growth of the Ottoman Empire The Ottomans were Turkish-speaking nomads who had expanded into Asia Minor and the Balkan Peninsula by the 1300s. They were successful in capturing Constantinople in 1453. The city was renamed **Istanbul** and became the capital of the Ottoman empire.

The Ottoman empire enjoyed a golden age under **Suleiman**, who ruled from 1520 to 1566. He expanded the empire into Asia, Africa, and Europe. Although he was defeated at Vienna in 1529, the empire remained the largest and most powerful in Europe and the Middle East for centuries.

Ottomans Control Trade The Ottoman empire controlled major trade routes between Europe, Asia and Africa and Istanbul became one of the great trading capitals of the world. The Ottoman Navy dominated all trade in the eastern Mediterranean. Eventually the Portuguese and other European navies commanded new trade routes around South Africa and ended Ottoman control of both land and sea routes.

Ottoman Society The top two social classes in Ottoman society—military men and intellectuals, such as scientists and lawyers—were nearly all Muslims. Below them were men involved in trade and production, and then farmers. All people belonged to religious communities, which provided for education and legal matters. The Jewish community, which had been expelled from Spain, possessed international banking connections that benefited the Ottomans.

Ottomans converted some young Christian boys to Islam and trained them for government service. Some were chosen for the janizaries, an elite force of the Ottoman army. The brightest became government officials.

Ottoman culture included great poets, painters, and architects. However, after Suleiman's death, the empire declined. By the 1700s, it had lost control of areas in Europe and Africa.

The Rise of the Safavids By the early 1500s, the Safavids united an empire in Persia (modern Iran). They were Shiite Muslims who fought with Sunni Ottomans to the west and the Mughals in India to the east. Their greatest king, or shah, was **Shah Abbas the Great** who ruled from 1588 to 1629. He centralized the government, created a strong military, and developed alliances with Europeans. Abbas lowered taxes and encouraged industry. He tolerated other religions and built a capital at Isfahan, which became a center for silk trading.

After Abbas' death, the empire suffered from religious disputes until its end in 1722. In the late 1700s, a new dynasty, the Qajars, won control of Iran, made Tehran the capital, and ruled until 1925.

DRAW CONCLUSIONS What was the effect of Shah Abbas centralizing the government and the economy, creating a powerful military, and tolerating non-Muslims?

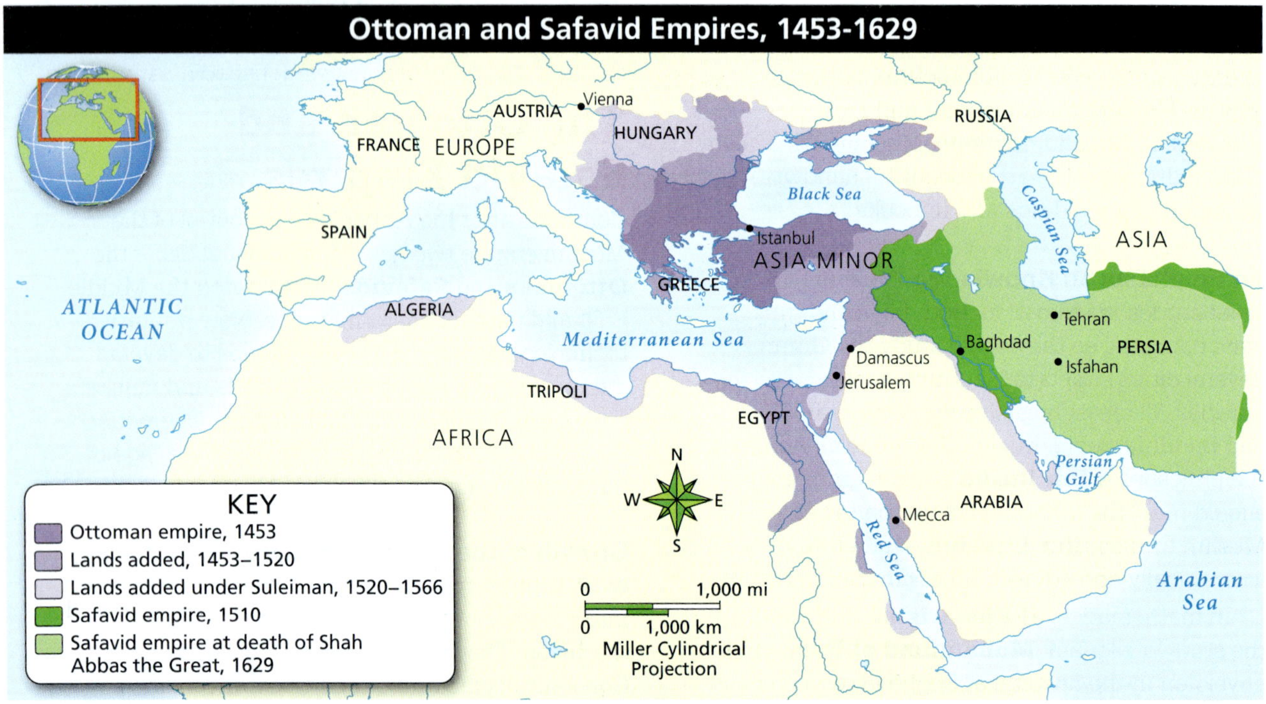

>> **Analyze Maps** At its greatest extent, the Ottoman empire stretched across three continents, while the Safavid empire controlled most of what is today Iran. Into what regions did the Ottoman empire expand under Suleiman?

Africa's Vegetation Regions

>> **Analyze Maps** Africa consists of four major vegetation regions, each of which impacted people living in those areas. Why might people have migrated from the desert into the savannah?

Early Civilizations of Africa

Africa includes tropical rain forests, grassy plains called savannas, and deserts such as the vast **Sahara**. Deserts, rain forests, the interior plateau, and rivers with cataracts, or waterfalls, limited travel and trade. On the other hand, an interior valley and the Mediterranean and Red seas provided overseas trade routes to Asia and Europe. By A.D. 200, camel caravans helped transport goods across the Sahara. Valuable minerals also encouraged trade.

Before 2500 B.C., there were grasslands and savanna in the Sahara. Due to climate change, however, the area slowly dried up and became desert—a process called **desertification**. As a result, people migrated to find new farmland. Between 1000 B.C. and A.D. 1000, people from West Africa moved south and east. They spoke **Bantu** languages. These Bantu peoples merged with existing peoples and brought skills in farming and ironworking, as well as their language and beliefs.

Nubia and Egypt Flourish About 2700 B.C., the civilization of **Nubia**, or Kush, developed on the upper Nile. Egypt controlled Nubia for about 500 years beginning in 1500 B.C. Early Nubian culture was influenced by Egyptian architecture and religion.

Forced to move by Assyrian invaders, the Nubians established a new capital in Meroë about 500 B.C. Meroë developed into a successful trade center. Nearby areas were rich in iron ore and timber. Using wood to fuel smelting furnaces, the Nubians made iron tools and weapons, improving their defense. The Nubians also established a new religion and a system of writing.

North Africa in the Ancient World In A.D. 350, Nubia was conquered by an invader from the south, King Ezana of Axum. While Nubia was thriving along the Nile, Carthage emerged along the Mediterranean in North Africa. Founded by Phoenician traders, Carthage forged a huge empire from 800 B.C. to 146 B.C. At the end of the Third Punic War, however, Rome destroyed Carthage. The Romans then utilized North Africa's farmlands to provide grain for their armies. They also built roads and cities, and later brought Christianity to the area. Muslim Arabs took control of North Africa in the 690s. Islam replaced Christianity, and traders later carried the religion to West Africa. Arabic replaced Latin as North Africa's main language.

ANALYZE INFORMATION What was the effect of the Bantu migrations on the development of African culture?

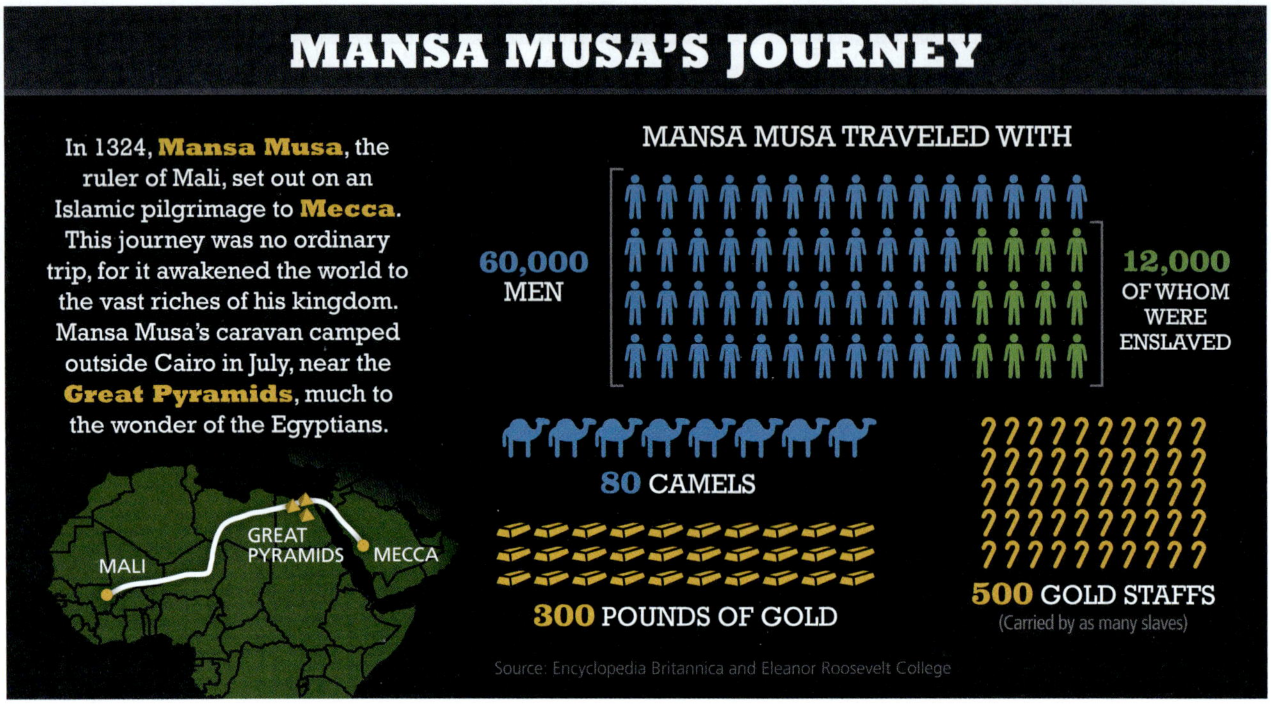

>> **Analyze Data** Mansa Musa's pilgrimage to Mecca in 1324 was a sight to behold as he traveled in grand style. Based on the numbers, what percentage of those who traveled with him were enslaved?

Kingdoms of West Africa

After early farmers moved from the Sahara to more fertile lands to the south, they began to produce more food than they needed, or a surplus. They were then able to trade surplus food for goods from other villages. A trade network developed that eventually connected Africa with Asia and Europe. Cities developed along the trade routes.

Much of the trade exchanged gold for salt, each a valuable product, or commodity. Gold was common in West Africa, while salt was plentiful in the Sahara. However, people needed salt to stay healthy and preserve food. In fact, traders might exchange one pound of salt for one pound of gold.

Ghana About A.D. 800, the ancient West African kingdom of **Ghana** became a center of trade. From there, the king controlled the salt and gold trade. In addition, the king administered justice and other government activities and kept the peace. Ghana was very prosperous and attracted Muslim merchants and traders from the north. They brought new ideas about military technology, business, and government. Later, Ghana was swallowed up by a new power, the rising kingdom of Mali.

Mali About 1235, **Sundiata** established the empire of **Mali**. He gained control of trade routes, the gold mining regions, and the salt supplies. **Mansa Musa**, Mali's greatest ruler, came to power about 1312. He fostered justice and religious freedom. His pilgrimage to Mecca created ties to Muslim states and brought Islamic scholars to Mali to provide religious instruction.

Songhai After Mali weakened, another kingdom, **Songhai**, developed in West Africa. After 1492, Songhai's emperor Askia Muhammad established a Muslim dynasty, expanded the territory, and improved the government. He strengthened ties to other Muslim states and built mosques and schools. However, internal conflicts weakened the empire, which was conquered by the sultan of Morocco around 1591.

Smaller Societies and Kingdoms Smaller societies, such as Benin, also flourished in the region from A.D. 500 to 1500. In the rain forests of the Guinea coast in the 1300s, the people of Benin built farming villages. They also traded pepper, ivory, and slaves to neighbors. At the same time, the Hausa built clay-walled cities. These cities grew into commercial centers, where artisans produced goods, and merchants traded with Arabs. Many Hausa rulers were women.

DESCRIBE What impact did trade have on the West African kingdom of Ghana?

Trading States of East Africa

After 100 B.C., the kingdom of **Axum** spread from the Ethiopian highlands to the Red Sea coast. Axum included the upland capital city of Axum and the port of Adulis on the Red Sea. The peoples of Axum were descended from African farmers and people from the Middle East. By about A.D. 400, Axum controlled a rich trade network connecting Africa, India, and the Mediterranean. Traders exchanged many cultural influences in their travels.

Axum became a Christian kingdom in the 300s. At first, this helped strengthen trade ties with other Christian countries. When Islam began spreading across North Africa in the 600s, however, Axum became isolated and lost power. Civil war and economic decline combined to weaken Axum.

Ethiopia Axum's legacy, however, survived for centuries in a portion of present-day **Ethiopia**. There, Christianity was a unifying influence that helped give Ethiopia a unique identity among Muslim neighbors. A distinct culture developed in Ethiopia. In the 1200s, under King **Lalibela**, Christian churches were carved below ground into mountain rocks. Ethiopian Christianity absorbed local customs.

City-States of East Africa After Axum declined, Arab and Persian traders established Muslim communities along the East African coast. By the 600s, ships regularly took advantage of monsoon winds to sail to India and back, and the cities in East Africa grew wealthy by trading goods with Africa, Southeast Asia, and China.

The cities were independent, and although they competed for power, relations among them were generally peaceful. By the 1000s, the mixture of cultures created unique architecture, as well as a new language and culture, both called **Swahili**. The language was Bantu-based, using some Arabic words and written in Arabic.

Great Zimbabwe, the capital of a great inland Zimbabwe empire, was built by a succession of

African Kingdoms and Trading States, 1000 B.C.–A.D. 1600

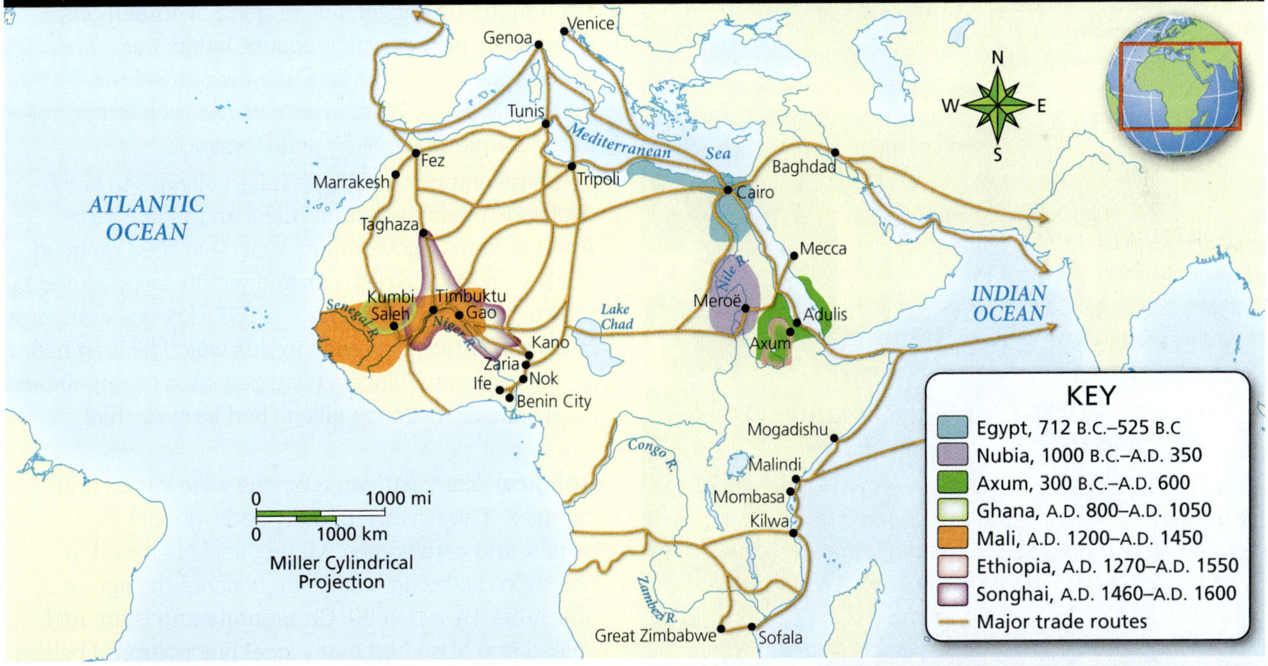

>> **Analyze Maps** The people of early Africa developed a system of trade routes that connected much of the continent. Why do you think most of these trade routes bordered oceans and rivers?

Bounce to Activate Map

>> This wooden figure of a mother and child shows the value one sub-Sahara African society placed on women.

Bantu-speaking peoples between 900 and 1500. It reached its height around 1300. The city included great stone buildings, and its people mined gold and traded goods across the Indian Ocean. By the 1500s, the empire of Zimbabwe was in decline. Later, Portuguese traders tried, but failed, to find the region's source of gold.

IDENTIFY CENTRAL IDEAS What was the impact of trade on the city-states of East Africa?

Diverse Peoples and Traditions in Africa

In small societies in medieval Africa, the nuclear family, or one set of parents and their children, lived and worked together. In other societies, the family included several generations. **Patrilineal** families passed inheritances through the father's side of the family, while **matrilineal** families passed property down through the mother's side. Each family belonged to a **lineage**, a group of households with a common ancestor, and a clan included several lineages descended from a common ancestor.

Government and Power Political patterns depended on the size and culture of a community. In small societies, political power was often shared among a number of people. Village decisions were often made by consensus, or general agreement, after open discussions. Because elders had experience, their opinions usually carried the greatest weight. Women sometimes took strong roles in the marketplace or as peacemakers.

Large empires usually required villages to obey decisions made by distant rulers and their courts. Another form of government that developed grouped many villages into districts and provinces governed by the king's officials. Around A.D. 1500, Kongo, a kingdom in central Africa, governed in this way. The king had limited powers. Villagers were governed by appointed royal officials, but each village had its own chief.

>> King Alvaro II, ruler of Kongo, made alliances and trade agreements with Europeans, such as the Dutch depicted in this illustration.

Religion Early African religions were varied and complex. They involved many gods, goddesses, rituals, and ceremonies. Many people believed in one supreme being, and some honored the spirits of ancestors. By A.D. 1000, Christianity and Islam had spread and absorbed many local practices and beliefs.

Art and Literature The tradition of African arts includes the Egyptian pyramids, built 4,000 years ago. Much art served decorative, religious, or ceremonial purposes, such as cloths, pottery, and jewelry. Objects often had symbolic meanings, such as the bright blue-and-gold kente cloth of West Africa, which was reserved for the wealthy and powerful.

Medieval written histories from Africa provide records of laws, religion, and society. Arabic provided a common written language in Muslim areas, and Muslim scholars gathered in important cities. In West Africa, griots, or professional storytellers, recited ancient stories. Griots preserved both histories and traditional folk tales in the same way that the epics of Homer or Aryan India were passed orally from generation to generation. Folktales and other stories encouraged a sense of community and common values.

IDENTIFY CENTRAL IDEAS How did literature help to reinforce social ties?

>> A kente cloth was often woven from bright colors of silk and cotton.

ASSESSMENT

1. **Infer** How do the Quran and Sharia guide Muslims?
2. **Compare and Contrast** In what ways are Sunni and Shiite beliefs alike and different?
3. **Cite Evidence** What evidence supports the fact that learning was important in the Arab Muslim empire?
4. **Draw Conclusions** How did Africa's geographic features influence migration, cultural development, and trade?
5. **Determine Relevance** What was the importance of art in medieval African cultures?

>> Akbar's tolerance of different Indian cultures and his willingness to include them in government was one of his strengths as a ruler.

Bounce to Activate Flipped Video

0.9 After 550, rival princes fought for control of India. Around 1000, Muslim armies moved in. Muslim attacks included onslaughts that killed many Hindus and destroyed Buddhist temples. Muslims triumphed due to military superiority, rivalries among Hindu princes, and the many Hindus who converted to Islam. By the 1100s, a sultan controlled northern India. From the capital in Delhi, the Delhi sultanate ruled from 1206 to 1526.

>> Objectives

Explain how Muslim and Hindu civilizations interacted in India and describe the historical origins and central ideas of Sikhism.

Describe China during the Tang and Song dynasties, summarize how the Mongols took control of China, and explain how the Ming restored Chinese rule.

Describe the Silla, Korya, and Choson dynasties of Korea.

Summarize the development of government and culture in feudal Japan.

Describe the many cultures of Southeast Asia

>> Key Terms

Sikhism
Guru Nanak
"Five Ks"
Babur
Akbar
Nur Jahan
Shah Jahan
Tang dynasty
Tang Taizong
Song dynasty
Genghis Khan
Kublai Khan
Marco Polo
Ming
Zheng He
Silla
Koryo
Choson
hangul
Shinto
samurai
bushido
Zen
stupa
paddy

Civilizations of Asia

The Delhi Sultanate and Mughal India

Muslim rulers reorganized Indian government and increased trade. During the Mongol raids of the 1200s, scholars fled from Baghdad to India, bringing Persian and Greek learning with them. These newcomers helped turn Delhi into a place where art and architecture flourished. However, in 1389, Mongols attacked Delhi, destroying much of its culture.

The Meeting of Islam and Hinduism The Muslim advance brought two utterly different religions and cultures face to face. Hinduism was an ancient religion that had evolved over thousands of years. Hindus recognized many sacred texts and prayed before statues representing many gods and goddesses. They believed these statues represented various forms of the Absolute, or God. Islam, by contrast, was a newer faith with a single sacred text. Muslims were devout monotheists. Hindus accepted differences in caste status, while Muslims taught the equality of all believers before God.

Eventually, the Delhi sultans grew more tolerant of their Hindu subjects. Hindus were allowed to practice their religion as long as they paid a poll tax, and some rajahs, or local Hindu rulers, continued governing. Many Hindus converted to Islam, and Muslims followed some Hindu customs and ideas. A new language, Urdu, blended Arabic, Persian, and the Indian language spoken in Delhi.

Sikhism Emerges In the late 1400s, a young man named Nanak founded the religion of **Sikhism** (SIK iz um) in the Punjab region of South Asia. **Guru Nanak** preached a faith recognizing one God for all humanity.

In addition to the belief in one God for all humanity, the basic Sikh beliefs include the equality of all people in the eyes of God, regardless of their race, gender, social class, or religion. This belief in equality and tolerance was a radical concept during the 1500s and 1600s, when Sikhism was developing and beginning to spread.

Many Sikhs wear distinctive clothing that includes the five Sikh articles of faith, called the **"Five Ks"** among English-speaking Sikhs because they each begin with the English letter *k*. As articles of faith, each object holds a deep personal and religious meaning for the Sikh wearing it.

Mughal India In 1526, **Babur** led Turkish and Mongol armies into northern India to establish the Mughal dynasty, which would last until 1857. Babur's grandson, **Akbar**, known as Akbar the Great, ruled from 1556 to 1605. He established a strong central government that had paid officials; he also modernized the army and encouraged international trade. He allowed Hindus to work in government and promoted peace through religious tolerance.

After Akbar's death, his son's wife, **Nur Jahan**, managed the government skillfully. She was the most powerful woman in Indian history until the twentieth century. Akbar's grandson, **Shah Jahan**, ruled when Mughal literature, art, and architecture were at their height. He built the Taj Mahal, a tomb for his wife. It is a spectacular building and a great monument of the Mughal empire.

EXPLAIN How did Muslim and Hindu cultures interact?

Golden Ages in China: Tang and Song Dynasties

After the Han dynasty collapsed, China broke apart. During the Sui dynasty (589–618), the emperor Sui Wendi reunited north and south. In 618, the general Li Yuan and his son Li Shimin led a revolt and established the **Tang dynasty**. Eight years later, Li Shimin compelled his aging father to step down. Li Shimin then took the throne under the name

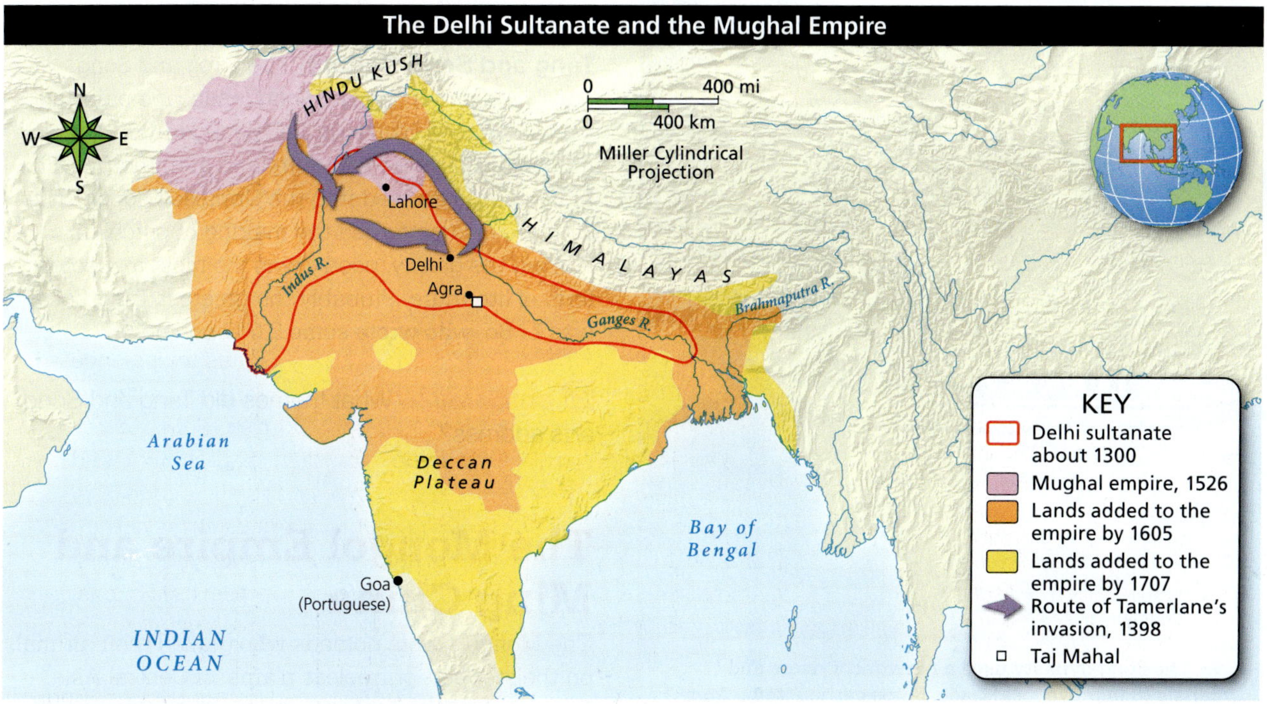

>> Two Muslim dynasties ruled much of the Indian subcontinent. The Delhi sultanate lasted more than 300 years before the Mughal dynasty replaced it. **Analyze Maps** Describe Tamerlane's route into India.

>> Wu Zhao rose from a lowly position at court to a position of influence over the Tang emperor. Upon his death, she became the first woman to claim the throne.

Tang Taizong. Later Tang rulers conquered many territories and forced Vietnam, Tibet, and Korea to become tributary states, or self-governing states that sent tribute. Other Tang rulers, such as Empress Wu Zhao, restored the Han system of uniform government. Tang emperors also undertook land reform in which they redistributed land to peasants. However, the Tang dynasty eventually weakened. In 907, the last Tang emperor was overthrown.

The Song Dynasty In 960, Zhao Kuangyin founded the **Song dynasty**. The Song ruled for 319 years. They faced the constant threat of invaders from the north. Nonetheless, the Song period was a time of great achievement. A new type of faster-growing rice was imported from Southeast Asia. The rise in productivity created food surpluses, freeing more people to pursue commerce, learning, or the arts.

An Ordered Society Under the Tang and Song, China was a well-ordered society. At its head was the emperor. Scholar-officials had the highest social status. Most of them came from the gentry, or wealthy, landowning class. The vast majority of Chinese were poor peasant farmers. Merchants had the lowest status because their riches came from the labor of others. Women had higher status during this period than they did later. However, when a woman married, she could not keep her dowry, the payment that a woman brings to a marriage. She could also never remarry.

>> The Song dynasty used a network of rivers and canals to improve local trade. Ships carried items from different parts of China to trading ports.

Bounce to Activate Gallery

Tang and Song Culture The Tang and Song developed a rich culture. Song landscape painting was influenced by Daoist beliefs. Buddhist themes influenced Chinese sculpture and architecture. The Indian stupa evolved into the Chinese pagoda. The Chinese also perfected the making of porcelain. Among the gentry, poetry was the most respected form of literature. Probably the greatest Tang poet was Li Bo, who wrote some 2,000 poems.

SUMMARIZE What themes did Tang and Song arts address?

The Mongol Empire and Ming China

The Mongols were nomads who grazed their animals on the steppes, or treeless plains, of Central Asia. Mongol clans spent much of their time warring with one another. In the early 1200s, however, a

The Mongol Empire

>> Analyze Maps At its height, the Mongol empire was the world's largest up to that time. Describe the growth of the empire between 1227 and 1294. Did Genghis Khan or his successors conquer the most land?

Mongol chieftain united these clans. He took the name **Genghis Khan**, meaning "Universal Ruler." Under his leadership, Mongol forces conquered a vast empire. After his death, his heirs continued to expand the Mongol empire. For the next 150 years, they dominated much of Asia. The Mongols established peace and order within their domains. They controlled and protected the Silk Road, and trade flourished.

Mongols Rule China Genghis Khan's grandson, **Kublai Khan**, toppled the last Song emperor in China in 1279. He named his dynasty the Yuan. Only Mongols could serve in his military and in the highest government jobs, but he allowed Chinese officials to continue to rule in the provinces. He welcomed many foreigners to his court, including Ibn Battuta and **Marco Polo**. Polo's writings about the wealth and splendor of China sparked European interest in Asia. Chinese products, including gunpowder and porcelain, made their way to Europe.

Chinese Rule Restored by the Ming The Yuan dynasty declined after Kublai Khan's death in 1294. Finally, Zhu Yuanzhang formed a rebel army that toppled the Mongols. In 1368, he founded the **Ming**, or "brilliant," dynasty.

Ming China was immensely productive. Better methods of fertilizing improved farming. The Ming repaired the canal system, which made trade easier and allowed cities to grow.

Flourishing Trade and Culture The Ming carefully limited trade with Europeans. By accepting only silver or gold in exchange for goods in high demand in Europe, such as silk, tea, and porcelain, the Ming caused a massive flow of precious metals into China.

The arts and literature also flourished in Ming China. Ming artists developed their own styles of painting and created beautiful blue-and-white porcelain. Ming writers composed novels and the world's first detective stories.

Ming Math, Science, and Technology Mathematicians during the Ming period turned to popular and practical application. Making calculations with an **abacus**, a much earlier invention, now spread swiftly within and beyond China.

Many Ming scholars sought to integrate their own traditions with the Western science and technology they were learning from Jesuit missionaries. In 1629, Xu Guangqi led an imperial research program to reform the inaccurate Chinese calendar. Assisted by Jesuits, Chinese scholars used Western ideas and technology, including telescopes, to make observations of the heavenly bodies.

Chinese Fleets Explore the Seas Early Ming rulers sent Chinese fleets into distant waters to show the glory of their empire. The most famous voyages were those of **Zheng He**. Between 1405 and 1433, he commanded seven expeditions that explored the coasts of Southeast Asia, India, the Persian Gulf, and East Africa. However, after Zheng He died in 1435, the Ming emperor banned the building of seagoing ships, and overseas expeditions came to a halt. Historians are not sure why.

DESCRIBE How did Kublai Khan organize Mongol rule in China?

Korea and Its Traditions

Korea is located on a peninsula that juts south from the Chinese mainland. Because of its location, Korea has been strongly influenced by China. The earliest Koreans probably migrated from Siberia and northern Manchuria. They evolved their own ways of life before they were influenced by China. In 108 B.C., the Han emperor, Wudi, invaded Korea. The invasion brought with it Confucian traditions and Chinese ideas.

Early Kingdoms Between A.D. 100 and 668, local rulers forged three kingdoms in Korea: Koguryo, Paekche, and Silla. The three kingdoms often warred with one another or with China. Still, Chinese ideas continued to spread there. Missionaries brought Buddhism to Korea. Korean monks then traveled to China and brought home Chinese arts and learning. In 668, the **Silla** kingdom united the Korean peninsula. Under the Silla dynasty, Korea became a tributary state of China. As Chinese influence increased, Confucian views took root. However, Koreans adapted Confucian ideas to fit their own traditions.

The Koryo Dynasty The **Koryo** dynasty replaced the Silla in 935. Confucianism and Buddhism were both influential during this time. Koreans used woodblock printing from China to produce Buddhist texts. They learned to make Chinese porcelain. They then perfected the technique for making celadon, a porcelain with an unusual blue-green glaze.

The Choson Dynasty The Mongols first invaded Korea in 1231 and occupied the country until the 1350s. When their rule collapsed, the Koryo returned

Korea's Three Kingdoms, A.D. 300–A.D. 600

>> The three early kingdoms of Korea shared an ethnic background, culture, and language, although they were frequently at war with each other. **Analyze Maps** Which of these kingdoms was probably most influenced by Chinese civilization? Why?

to power. However, in the late 1300s the Korean general Yi Song-gye overthrew them and set up the **Choson** dynasty. This was the longest-lasting, but final, Korean dynasty.

In 1443, King Sejong decided to replace complex Chinese writing. Sejong had experts develop **hangul**, the Korean phonetic alphabet. Hangul spread quickly because it was easier to use than written Chinese. Its use led to an extremely high literacy rate.

In the 1590s, the Japanese armies invaded Korea. To stop the invaders at sea, Korean Admiral Yi Sun-shin sailed armored ships into the Japanese fleet. Eventually, the Japanese armies withdrew from Korea. As they left, they carried off many Korean artisans in order to introduce their skills to Japan.

SUMMARIZE Summarize two technological achievements of the Koryo dynasty and explain how they showed Korea's cultural influences.

>> Celadon is created with a slip, or wash of liquid clay, that contains iron and is applied before glazing. When the pottery is fired at a high temperature, the iron colors the surface.

The Island Kingdom of Japan

Japan sits on an archipelago, or chain of islands. In early times, surrounding seas both protected and isolated Japan. This region has many volcanoes, earthquakes, and tidal waves called tsunamis.

Early Japan Early Japanese society was divided into clans. The clans honored kami, or powers that were natural or divine. The worship of these forces of nature became known as **Shinto**. Missionaries from Korea introduced Buddhism to Japan in the 500s. They also brought knowledge of Chinese culture. In the 600s, Prince Shotoku sent nobles to study in China. The visitors brought back Chinese technology and arts. In 710, the Japanese emperor built a new capital at Nara, modeled after the Chinese capital.

The Japanese kept some Chinese ways but discarded others. This process is known as selective borrowing. The Japanese revised the Chinese writing system and added kana, symbols representing syllables. From 794 to 1185, Heian was the Japanese capital. Heian women, such as Murasaki Shikibu, produced some of the most important works of Japanese literature.

>> Prince Shotoku was an advisor to Empress Suiko. He revolutionized Japan by creating a government based on Chinese practices and Buddhist teachings.

Japan's Feudal Age Japan evolved into a feudal society. Theoretically, the emperor was the head of this society, but really he was powerless. The shogun, or supreme military commander, had the real power. Minamoto Yoritomo was appointed shogun in 1192. He set up the Kamakura shogunate. The shogun distributed land to lords, called daimyo, who agreed to support him with their armies. They, in turn, granted land to lesser warriors called **samurai**. Samurai developed a code of values, known as **bushido**. The code emphasized honor, bravery, and loyalty to one's lord.

>> After the Battle of Sekigahara in 1600, Tokugawa Ieyasau seized control of central Japan. He used strict administrative regulations to control anyone who challenged his power.

Bounce to Activate Chart

A United Japan Kublai Khan tried to invade Japan in 1274 and 1281, but typhoons wrecked the Mongol ships during both invasions. However, after the attempted invasions, the Kamakura shogunate crumbled. By 1590, Toyotomi Hideyoshi had brought most of Japan under his control. In 1600, Tokugawa Ieyasu defeated his rivals to become master of Japan. The Tokugawa shoguns created an orderly society. With peace restored to the countryside, agriculture improved and trade flourished.

During Japan's feudal age, a Buddhist sect known as **Zen** won widespread acceptance. Zen monks were great scholars, yet they stressed the importance of reaching a moment of "non-knowing."

APPLY CONCEPTS How did honor, bravery, and absolute loyalty to one's lord affect Japanese feudal society?

The Many Cultures of Southeast Asia

Southeast Asia is made up of two regions: mainland Southeast Asia, which includes present-day Myanmar, Thailand, Cambodia, Laos, Vietnam, and Malaysia; and island Southeast Asia, which consists of more than 20,000 islands. These islands include the present-day nations of Indonesia, Singapore, Brunei, and the Philippines. Historically, sea trade between China and India had to pass through the Malacca or Sunda straits, so the islands that controlled these straits were strategically important. Women took part in the spice trade and had greater equality there than they did elsewhere in Asia. Matrilineal descent, or inheritance through the mother, was an accepted custom in this region.

>> Indian styles are evident in this Buddhist monument, the Borodudur temple in Central Java, which was long overgrown and covered in volcanic ash before its intricate carvings were discovered.

Indian Culture Spreads In the early centuries A.D., Indian merchants and Hindu priests slowly spread their culture through Southeast Asia. Later, monks introduced Theravada Buddhism. Indian traders eventually carried Islam to Indonesia, and as far east as the Philippines. Trade with India brought prosperity. Merchants exchanged cotton cloth, jewels, and perfume for timber, spices, and gold.

Empires and Kingdoms of Southeast Asia

>> **Analyze Maps** From which direction did the Mongol invasion take place?

Kingdoms and Empires A series of kingdoms and empires developed in Southeast Asia. The kingdom of Pagan arose in present-day Myanmar. In 1044, King Anawrahta united the region and brought Buddhism to his people. He filled his capital city with magnificent **stupas**, or dome-shaped shrines.

Indian influences also shaped the Khmer empire, which reached its peak between 800 and 1350. Its greatest rulers controlled much of present-day Cambodia, Thailand, and Malaysia. Khmer rulers became Hindus, but most people were Buddhists. In Indonesia, the trading empire of Srivijaya flourished from the 600s to the 1200s. Both Hinduism and Buddhism reached Srivijaya.

The heart of northern Vietnam was the Red River delta. There, the river irrigated fertile rice **paddies**. In 111 B.C., Han armies conquered the region, and China remained in control for the next 1,000 years. During that time, the Vietnamese absorbed Confucian ideas. Unlike the rest of Southeast Asia, where Theravada Buddhism had the strongest impact, Vietnam adopted Mahayana Buddhism from China. In A.D. 39, two noble sisters, Trung Trac and Trung Nhi, led an uprising that briefly drove out the Chinese. Finally, in 939, Vietnam was able to break free from China.

GENERATE EXPLANATIONS How did Hinduism, Buddhism, and Islam become established in Southeast Asia?

ASSESSMENT

1. **Analyze Information** How did the relationship between Muslims and Hindus in India change over time?
2. **Draw Conclusions** In what ways did the rise of the Tang dynasty unify and benefit China?
3. **Identify Cause and Effect** How did Ming China impact global trade?
4. **Synthesize** How are Korea's history and culture linked to those of China and Japan?
5. **Check Understanding** How did the Tokugawas unite Japan, and what was the effect of unification?

>> The growth of urban areas helped spur and encourage a renewal of culture known as the Renaissance. This 19th century reconstruction of a 15th century painting shows Florence, Italy, in 1490.

0.10 From the 1300s to the 1600s, Europe experienced a time of great creativity and social change. It started with the Renaissance in Italy, a golden age in the arts. Later, northern Europe, too, enjoyed a creative upsurge. The Renaissance spirit of inquiry led to a revolution in science. Meanwhile, Christians launched their own revolution aimed at reforming the Church's practices. This Protestant Reformation had profound effects on European society.

>> Objectives

Describe the origins, characteristics, and impact of the Renaissance.

Explain why the Protestant Reformation started, identify its leaders, and describe how it affected Europe.

Analyze the development and importance of the Scientific Revolution.

>> Key Terms

humanism
vernacular
perspective
Leonardo da Vinci
Michelangelo
William Shakespeare
Johannes Gutenberg
Martin Luther
theocracy
Henry VIII
Galileo Galilei
scientific method
Isaac Newton

The Renaissance and Reformation

The Italian Renaissance

The Renaissance marked the transition between medieval and early modern times. During the Renaissance, Western Europe witnessed the growth of cities and trade, which greatly extended people's horizons.

A New Worldview Most important, the Renaissance changed the way people saw themselves and their world. Spurred by a reawakened interest in the learning of ancient Greece and Rome, creative Renaissance minds set out to transform their own age. Their era, they felt, was a time of rebirth after the disorder and disunity of the medieval world.

Renaissance Europe did not really break with its medieval past. Much of the classical heritage had survived, including the Latin language and knowledge of ancient thinkers such as Euclid and Aristotle. Yet the Renaissance did produce new attitudes toward culture and learning. Unlike medieval scholars, who debated the nature of life after death, Renaissance thinkers were eager to explore the richness and variety of human experience in the here and now.

Renaissance Humanism At the heart of the Italian Renaissance was an intellectual movement known as **humanism**. Humanist scholars studied classical Greek and Roman cultures, hoping to use the wisdom of the ancients to increase their understanding of their own times. Though most humanists were pious Christians, they focused on worldly, or secular, subjects rather than on the religious issues that had occupied medieval thinkers.

Francesco Petrarch (PEE trahrk), who lived in Florence, a city in northern Italy in the 1300s, was an early Renaissance humanist. Petrarch assembled a library of Greek and Roman manuscripts. An influential poet, Petrarch wrote in Latin and also in the **vernacular**, or everyday language of ordinary people.

The Renaissance Begins in Italy The Renaissance began in Italy in the mid-1300s and later spread north to the rest of Europe. It reached its height in the 1500s. The Renaissance emerged in Italy for several reasons.

The Renaissance was marked by a reawakened interest in the culture of ancient Rome. Since Italy was the center of ancient Roman civilization, it was only natural for this reawakening to begin there. Architectural remains, antique statues, coins, and inscriptions were all daily reminders of the glory of ancient Rome.

Italy's location also helps explain why the Renaissance began there. During the Middle Ages, the city-states of Florence, Milan, Venice, and Genoa had grown into prosperous centers of trade. At these and other Italian ports, ships brought goods, people, and ideas from the Muslim world, which had preserved much learning from ancient Greece and Rome—learning that had been lost in Europe.

The Arts Flourish A class of wealthy and powerful merchants emerged in Italy's city-states. They stressed individual achievement and spent lavishly to support the arts. The Renaissance gained its most glorious expression in its paintings, sculpture, and architecture.

Painters produced portraits of well-known figures of the day, reflecting the humanist interest in individual achievement. They also painted scenes from Greek and Roman history and mythology. In the process, they developed new techniques for representing humans and landscapes in a realistic way. Painters used shadings of light and dark to make objects look round and real, resulting in more dramatic scenes. They also discovered and applied the rules of **perspective**. By making distant objects smaller than those close to the viewer, they gave the impression of space and depth on a flat surface, adding to the realism of scenes.

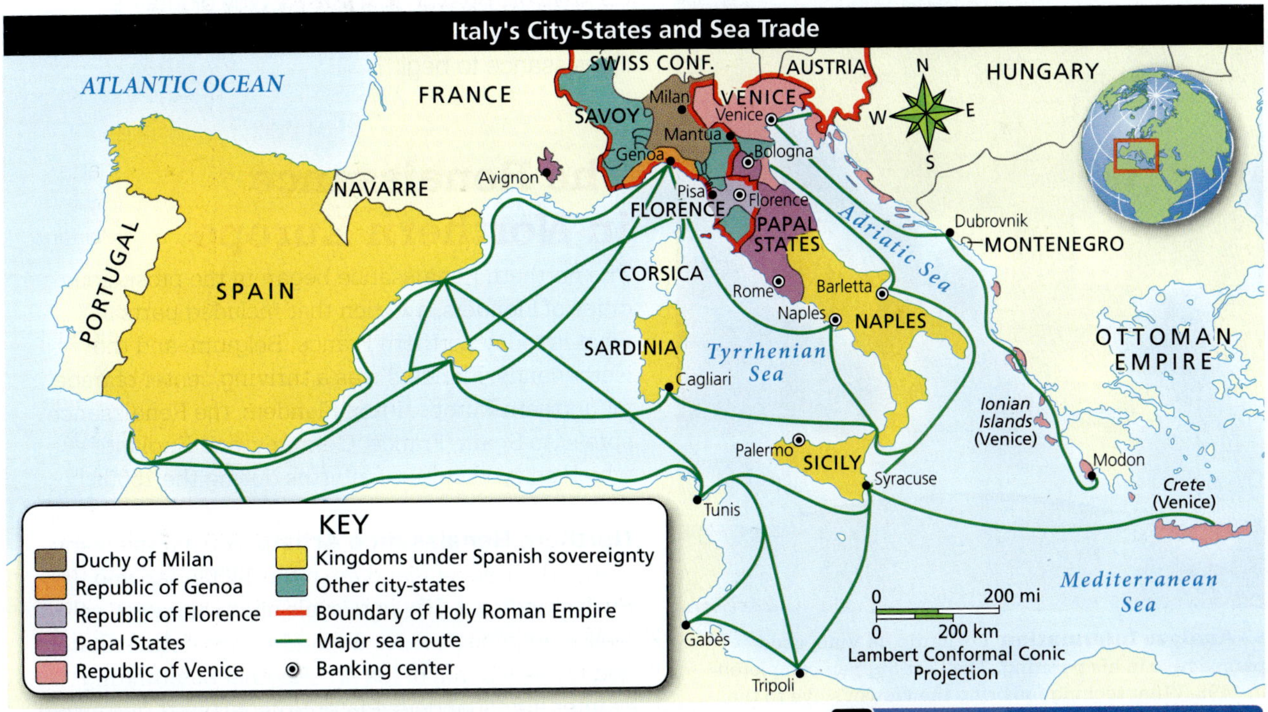

>> **Analyze Maps** The states and kingdoms of Italy lay at the center of Europe's sea trade. Why were so many banking centers located in Italy?

Bounce to Activate Map

Like the painters of the time, Renaissance sculptors and architects studied ancient Greek and Roman works and revived many classical forms. The sculptor Donatello, for example, created a life-size statue of a soldier on horseback. It was the first such figure done since ancient times. Architects adopted the columns, arches, and domes used by the Greeks and Romans.

Artists of Florence Florence, perhaps more than any other city, came to symbolize the Italian Renaissance. Many outstanding Renaissance artists called the city their home. Among the most brilliant were Leonardo da Vinci, Michelangelo, and Raphael.

Leonardo da Vinci, born in 1452, is admired today for the freshness and realism of his paintings. One of his masterpieces, the *Mona Lisa*, is a portrait of a woman whose mysterious smile has intrigued viewers for centuries. Another, *The Last Supper*, which shows Jesus and his disciples, is an excellent example of the use of perspective. Although Leonardo thought of himself as an artist, his interests extended to botany, anatomy, optics, music, architecture, and engineering.

Like Leonardo, **Michelangelo**, born in 1475, had many talents. He excelled as a sculptor, painter, architect, poet, and engineer. Michelangelo's marble sculpture *David*, a statue of the biblical shepherd who killed the giant Goliath, recalls the harmony and grace of ancient Greek sculptures. His murals on the vast curved ceiling of the Sistine Chapel in Rome include dramatic scenes from the biblical book of *Genesis*. As an architect, Michelangelo drew the design for the enormous dome of St. Peter's Cathedral in Rome.

>> Analyze Information Leonardo da Vinci used perspective in his painting, *The Last Supper*, completed in 1498. What techniques bring the viewer's eye to the central figure of Jesus?

A few years younger than Leonardo and Michelangelo, Raphael (rah fa EL) studied the works of those great masters. His paintings blend Christian and classical styles. Among his best-known works is *School of Athens*, which pictures an imaginary gathering of great thinkers and scientists, including Plato, Aristotle, Socrates, and the Arab philosopher Averroës.

Books Guide Courtiers and Rulers Poets, artists, and scholars mingled with politicians at the courts of Renaissance rulers. A literature of "how to" books sprang up to help ambitious men and women who wanted to rise in the Renaissance world.

In *The Book of the Courtier*, Baldassare Castiglione (kahs teel YOH nay) described the manners, skills, learning, and virtues that a member of the court should have. Niccolò Machiavelli (mahk ee uh VEL ee) wrote a different kind of handbook. In *The Prince*, published in 1513, he stressed that the end justifies the means. He urged rulers to use whatever methods necessary to achieve their goals.

CHECK UNDERSTANDING Why did Italy's history and geography make it an ideal place for the Renaissance to begin?

The Renaissance in Northern Europe

The northern Renaissance began in the prosperous cities of Flanders, a region that included parts of what is today northern France, Belgium, and the Netherlands. Flanders was a thriving center of trade for northern Europe. From Flanders, the Renaissance spread to Spain, France, Germany, and England, which enjoyed cultural rebirths during the 1500s.

Northern Renaissance Artists Among the many talented artists of Flanders in the 1400s, Jan van Eyck stands out. His portrayals of townspeople as well as religious scenes abound in rich details that add to the realism of his art. Another outstanding painter from Flanders, Pieter Bruegel (BROY gul), used vibrant colors to portray animated scenes of peasant life. Bruegel influenced later Flemish artists, who painted scenes of ordinary people in their daily lives.

Van Eyck, Bruegel, and other Flemish artists developed and applied new techniques for using oil paint. Thus they were able to produce strong colors and a hard-surfaced paint that could survive for centuries.

Another influential artist of the northern Renaissance was the German painter and printmaker Albrecht Dürer (DYOOR ur). In 1494, he made the first of several trips to Italy to study the works and techniques of Italian masters. At home, he employed the new methods in his own paintings, engravings, and prints. Dürer had a keen, inquiring mind. Because of his wide-ranging interests, which extended far beyond art, he is sometimes called the "German Leonardo."

>> William Shakespeare (1564–1616), English author, playwright, and poet.

Bounce to Activate Gallery

Northern Renaissance Humanists and Writers

Like the Italian humanists, northern European humanist scholars stressed classical learning. They believed that the revival of ancient learning should be used to bring about religious and moral reform.

The great Dutch humanist and writer Desiderius Erasmus (ih RAZ mus), became a priest in 1492. He used his knowledge of classical languages to produce a new Greek edition of the New Testament and a Latin translation of the Bible. At the same time, Erasmus called for a translation of the Bible into the vernacular. "I disagree very much with those who are unwilling that Holy Scripture, translated into the vernacular, be read by the uneducated." Erasmus sought other reforms as well. He challenged the worldliness of the Church and urged a return to early Christian traditions.

Erasmus's friend, the English humanist Sir Thomas More, pressed for social and economic reforms. In *Utopia*, he describes an ideal society, where private property does not exist, the people live in peace, no one is poor, and all are educated.

The French humanist François Rabelais (rab uh LAY) had a varied career as a monk, a physician, a Greek scholar, and an author. Rabelais wrote in the French vernacular. Although his *Gargantua and Pantagruel* is a comic tale, his characters offer opinions on religion, education, and other serious subjects.

The towering figure of Renaissance literature was the English poet and playwright **William Shakespeare**. Between 1590 and 1613, he wrote 37 plays that are still performed around the world. They include comedies such as *A Midsummer Night's Dream*, histories such as *Richard III*, and tragedies such as *Romeo and Juliet, Hamlet,* and *Macbeth*. Shakespeare's genius was his ability to express universal themes in everyday realistic settings. His work explores Renaissance ideals such as the complexity of the individual and the importance of the classics. At the same time, his characters speak in language that the common people can understand.

The Printing Revolution In Germany in 1456, **Johannes Gutenberg** (GOOT un burg) printed a complete edition of the Christian Bible using a printing press with movable metal type. With the Gutenberg Bible, the European age of printing had begun.

The development of the printing press set off revolutionary changes that would transform Europe. No longer would books have to be slowly copied out by hand. Because they were so much easier to produce, they became more affordable. More people learned to read and write, gaining access to new ideas that greatly expanded their horizons.

Printing influenced both religious and secular, or nonreligious, thought. "The preaching of sermons is speaking to a few of mankind," noted an English author, "but printing books is talking to the whole world."

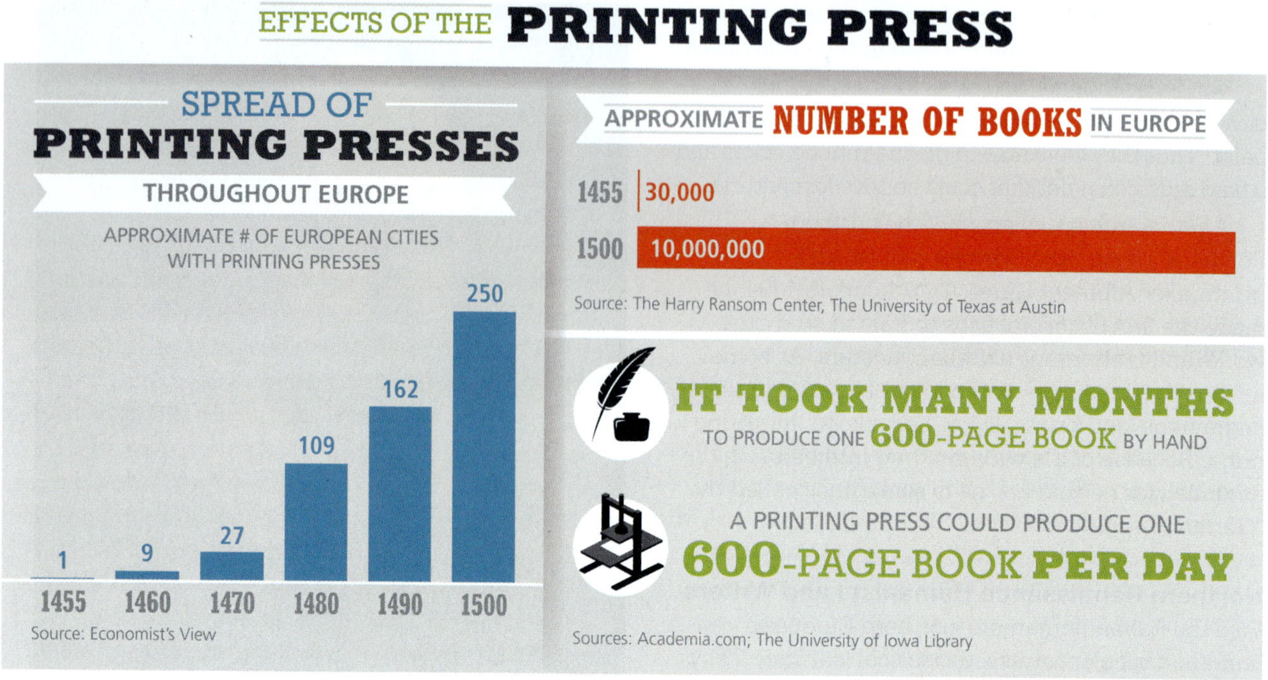

>> **Analyze Charts** The chart shows the effects of the printing press in Europe. Is it likely or unlikely that in 1500 only the largest European capital cities had printing presses?

The new printing presses contributed to the religious turmoil that engulfed Europe in the 1500s. By then, many Christians could read the Bible for themselves. As a result, the ideas of religious reformers spread faster and to a larger audience than ever before.

CHECK UNDERSTANDING What Renaissance themes did artists, humanists, and writers of northern Europe express?

The Protestant Reformation

During the Renaissance, Christians from all levels of society grew impatient with the worldliness of the Roman Catholic Church and the corruption of the clergy. In the 1500s, the movement for reform unleashed forces that would shatter Christian unity in Europe. This reform movement is known as the Protestant Reformation.

Causes of the Reformation Starting in the late Middle Ages, the Church had become increasingly caught up in worldly affairs. Popes competed with Italian princes for political power. They fought long wars to protect their territories in Italy against invasions by secular rulers.

Like secular princes, popes led lavish lives. They hired painters and sculptors to beautify churches and spent vast sums to rebuild the Cathedral of St. Peter in Rome. To finance such projects, the Church increased fees for services such as marriages and baptisms. By the late 1400s, some clergy had also begun promoting the sale of indulgences.

An indulgence was a type of pardon that lessened the time of punishment a soul faced for sins committed during a person's lifetime. Indulgences could be bought with money or a gift to the Church. Many Christians, especially in northern Europe, protested such practices.

Martin Luther Challenges the Church Protests against Church practices continued to grow. In the early 1500s, these protests erupted into a full-scale revolt. The person who triggered the revolt was a German monk and professor of theology named **Martin Luther**. Luther had grown increasingly disillusioned with what he saw as the corruption and worldliness of the Church. An incident in his native town of Wittenberg, Germany, prompted him to act.

In 1517, a German priest, Johann Tetzel, set up a pulpit on the outskirts of the town. With the approval of the pope, he sold indulgences to any Christian who contributed money for the rebuilding of the Cathedral of St. Peter in Rome. Tetzel claimed that purchase of these indulgences would assure entry into heaven not only for the buyers but for their dead relatives as well.

To a pious man like Luther, Tetzel's actions were an outrage. In response, Luther drew up a list of 95 Theses, or arguments, against indulgences. He posted the list on the door of a church in Wittenberg. In the 95 Theses, he argued that indulgences had no basis in the Bible, that the pope had no authority to release souls from purgatory (where sinners atoned for their sins), and that Christians could be saved only through faith.

The Church called on Luther to recant, or give up his views. Instead, he developed even more radical doctrines that went way beyond a condemnation of indulgences. Before long, Luther was urging Christians to reject the tyranny of Rome. Many Germans backed him, accepting his teachings and renouncing the authority of the pope.

Luther's teachings rested on several key beliefs. First, he argued that salvation could be achieved through faith alone, rejecting the Church doctrine that a person could be saved only by performing good deeds. Second, he declared that the sole source of religious truth was the Bible, denying the traditional authority of Church councils and the pope. Third, he rejected the idea that priests and the Church hierarchy had special powers. All Christians, he said, had equal access to God through faith and the Bible.

Luther called for other changes in Church practices, including a simplified mass that focused more on the sermon rather than ritual. The Lutheran Churches set up by his followers adopted these and other changes.

Luther's Reforms Gain Further Support In 1521, Pope Leo X excommunicated Luther, and the new Holy Roman Emperor, Charles V, declared him an outlaw. But he continued to write, and support for his reforms grew. The printing press spread Luther's writings throughout Germany and Scandinavia. Fiery preachers denounced Church abuses. By 1530, the Lutherans were using a new name, *Protestant*, for those who "protested" papal authority.

Many clergy viewed Luther's reforms as the answer to corruption in the Roman Catholic Church. German princes embraced Lutheran beliefs for more selfish reasons. Some saw Lutheranism as a way to throw off the rule of both the Church and the Holy Roman Emperor. Others welcomed a chance to seize valuable Church property in their territories.

Many peasants also took up Luther's demand for reform. They hoped to gain support for social and economic change. In 1524, a Peasants' Revolt erupted across Germany. The rebels called for an end to serfdom and for changes to ease their harsh lives. Luther, however, strongly favored social order and respect for political authority. As the Peasants' Revolt grew more violent, Luther denounced it. The nobles brutally suppressed the rebellion.

John Calvin Takes Reform in a New Direction

In the wake of Luther's revolt against the Church, other reformers challenged Church authority. The most important of them was John Calvin, who set forth his religious beliefs in his *Institutes of Christian Religion*, published in 1536. Like Luther, Calvin believed that salvation was gained through faith alone and that the Bible was the only source of religious truth. But Calvin put forth a number of ideas of his own.

Calvin taught that God alone had long ago determined who would achieve eternal life and who would not. This idea, known as predestination, led Calvinists to reason that the world was divided into two types of people—saints and sinners. Calvinists tried to live like saints, believing that only those who were saved could live truly Christian lives.

In 1541, Protestants in the city-state of Geneva, in present-day Switzerland, asked Calvin to lead their

>> Martin Luther nails his 95 Theses to the church door in Wittenberg. The theses also contained an invitation to church leaders to debate Luther on the issues raised by his theses. The invitation was ignored.

community. In keeping with his teachings, Calvin set up a **theocracy**, or government run by church leaders. Citizens faced fines or harsher punishments for offenses such as fighting, swearing, laughing in church, or dancing.

By the late 1500s, Calvinism had taken root in Germany, France, the Netherlands, England, and Scotland. This new challenge to the Roman Catholic Church embroiled Europe in religious turmoil.

Reformation Ideas Spread In England, turmoil arose not from religious reformers but from the king, **Henry VIII**. In 1527, Henry asked the pope to annul, or cancel, his marriage to Catherine of Aragon. The pope refused. Henry reacted by taking over the English Church, which became known as the Anglican Church. Henry had little interest in adhering to Protestant doctrines. His Anglican Church retained most Catholic forms of worship.

When Henry died in 1547, his nine-year-old son inherited the throne as Edward VI. After Edward died in his teens, his half-sister Mary Tudor, a pious Catholic, came to the throne. She tried and failed to make England Catholic again, but not before hundreds of English Protestants had been burned at the stake for heresy. On Mary's death, the throne passed to her Protestant half-sister, Elizabeth, who adopted a policy of religious compromise. The monarch remained head of the Anglican Church, and England remained firmly Protestant, but Elizabeth preserved many traditional Catholic ideas.

Meanwhile, a vigorous reform movement took place within the Catholic Church itself. This Catholic Reformation (also known as the Counter-Reformation) sought to revive the moral authority of the Church. In 1545, Pope Paul III called Catholic religious leaders together at the Council of Trent. The council took steps to end abuses in the Church, providing stiff penalties for worldliness and corruption. The reforms succeeded in bringing many Protestants back into the Church. By 1600, the majority of Europeans remained Catholic.

DRAW CONCLUSIONS What effects did Martin Luther's teachings have on northern Europe?

The Scientific Revolution

The Renaissance and Reformation both looked to the past for models. The Renaissance spirit of inquiry led scientists to explore beyond the knowledge of

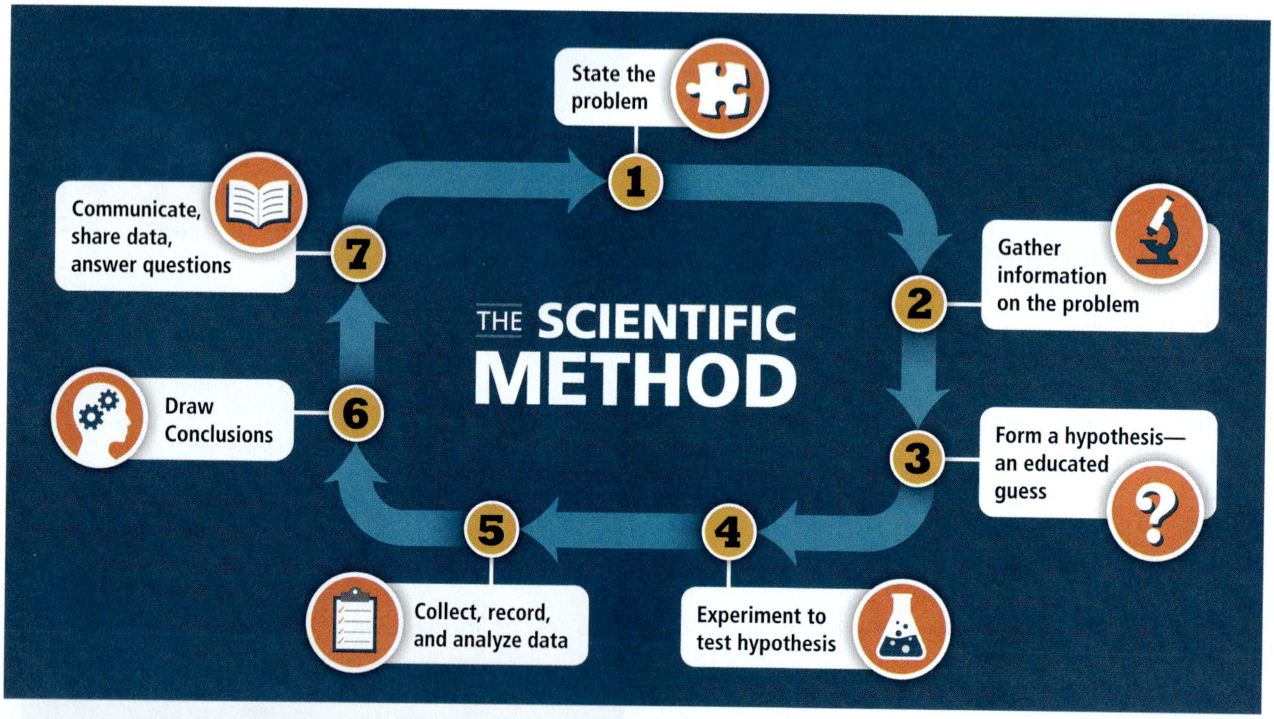

>> **Analyze Information** The scientific method, still used today, is based on careful observation and measurement of data. Why do you think it's critical to follow each step in sequence and to follow the same procedure for each step?

the ancients. In the 1500s, there arose a new way of thinking about the physical universe. It marked the start of what is now called the Scientific Revolution.

Changing Views of the Universe The Greek astronomer Ptolemy had taught that Earth was the center of the universe. European scholars—and the Church—accepted this view. In 1543, Polish scholar Nicolaus Copernicus (koh PUR nih kus) proposed a sun-centered model of the universe. Most experts rejected this theory, but others built on it.

One of them, **Galileo Galilei**, assembled a telescope and made observations of the planets that supported Copernicus's theory. The Church condemned Galileo, because his ideas challenged the Christian teaching that the heavens were fixed, unmoving, and perfect. In 1633, Galileo was put on trial for his views. He spent the rest of his life under house arrest.

A New Scientific Method By this time, a new approach to science had emerged. Based on observation, experimentation, and complex mathematics, this approach became known as the **scientific method**. Over time, the scientific method evolved into a step-by-step process to collect, measure, and explain data.

The new scientific method was really a revolution in thought. Two giants of this revolution, the Englishman Francis Bacon and the Frenchman René Descartes, devoted themselves to understanding how truth is determined. They argued that truth can be known only after a long process of investigation.

Scientific Breakthroughs The 1500s and 1600s saw dramatic changes in the sciences, especially medicine and chemistry. In 1543, Belgian scientist Andreas Vesalius (vuh SAY lee us) published the first accurate and detailed study of human anatomy. In the early 1600s, English scholar William Harvey described, for the first time, how blood circulates through the body.

During this time, scientists began relying on new technology to learn more about how the body works. Dutch inventor Anton van Leeuwenhoek (LAY wun hohk) perfected the single-lens microscope, which he used to see cells and microorganisms such as bacteria. English chemist Robert Boyle explained that all matter was composed of tiny particles that behaved in knowable ways.

In the late 1600s, using complex mathematics, **Isaac Newton** showed that a single force keeps the planets in their orbits around the sun. He called this force gravity. Newton argued that nature follows uniform laws and that all motion in the universe can be measured and describe mathematically. His transformative ideas make him one of the most influential scientists of all time.

>> Isaac Newton performs an experiment to analyze how light is made up of a spectrum of different colors.

EXPLAIN What was the purpose of the scientific method?

ASSESSMENT

1. **Analyze Information** What were some of the characteristics of the Italian Renaissance?
2. **Identify Cause and Effect** How did the invention of the printing press affect European society?
3. **Analyze Information** How did Luther's ideas spark the Protestant Reformation?
4. **Recognize Ideologies** How did the theories of Copernicus and Galileo change the way people understood the universe?

>> On their way to the Indies, Vasco da Gama's ships rounded the southern tip of Africa, shown here in the distance.

0.11 Beginning in the late 1400s, European nations sent explorers across the oceans in search of riches. Desire for wealth led European nations to establish colonies in the Americas. Eventually, European exploration and increased trade stimulated a global exchange, a commercial revolution, and changes in European society. Exploration and trade also changed the lives of people in Asia, Africa, and the Americas.

>> Objectives

Understand the major causes of European exploration.

Analyze the results of the first encounters between the Spanish and Native Americans.

Explain how triangular trade worked.

Explain how European exploration led to the Columbian Exchange.

>> Key Terms

Moluccas
cartographer
Prince Henry
Vasco da Gama
Christopher Columbus
circumnavigate
Taíno
conquistadors
immunity
Hernán Cortés
New France
Pilgrims
French and Indian War
plantations
triangular trade
Middle Passage
Asante kingdom
Oyo empire
Columbian Exchange
Commercial Revolution
capitalism
free enterprise system
entrepreneur
mercantilism

New Global Connections

Europeans Explore Overseas

European Trade with Asia Europeans had traded with Asia long before the Renaissance. The Crusades introduced Europeans to many luxury goods from Asia. Asian goods flowed to Europe along complex overland trade routes. The most valued trade items were spices, such as cloves, cinnamon, and pepper, to flavor food, make medicines and perfumes. The chief source of spices was the **Moluccas**, an island chain in present-day Indonesia.

The Drive to Explore In the 1400s, Arab and Italian merchants controlled most trade between Asia and Europe. Muslim traders brought spices and other goods to Mediterranean ports. From there, Italian traders carried them to European markets.

Europeans wanted to cut out the Muslim and Italian middlemen and gain direct access to the riches of Asia. The Atlantic powers sought a new route to Asia.

Many explorers hoped to get rich by entering the spice trade or conquering other lands. Some missionaries and soldiers ventured

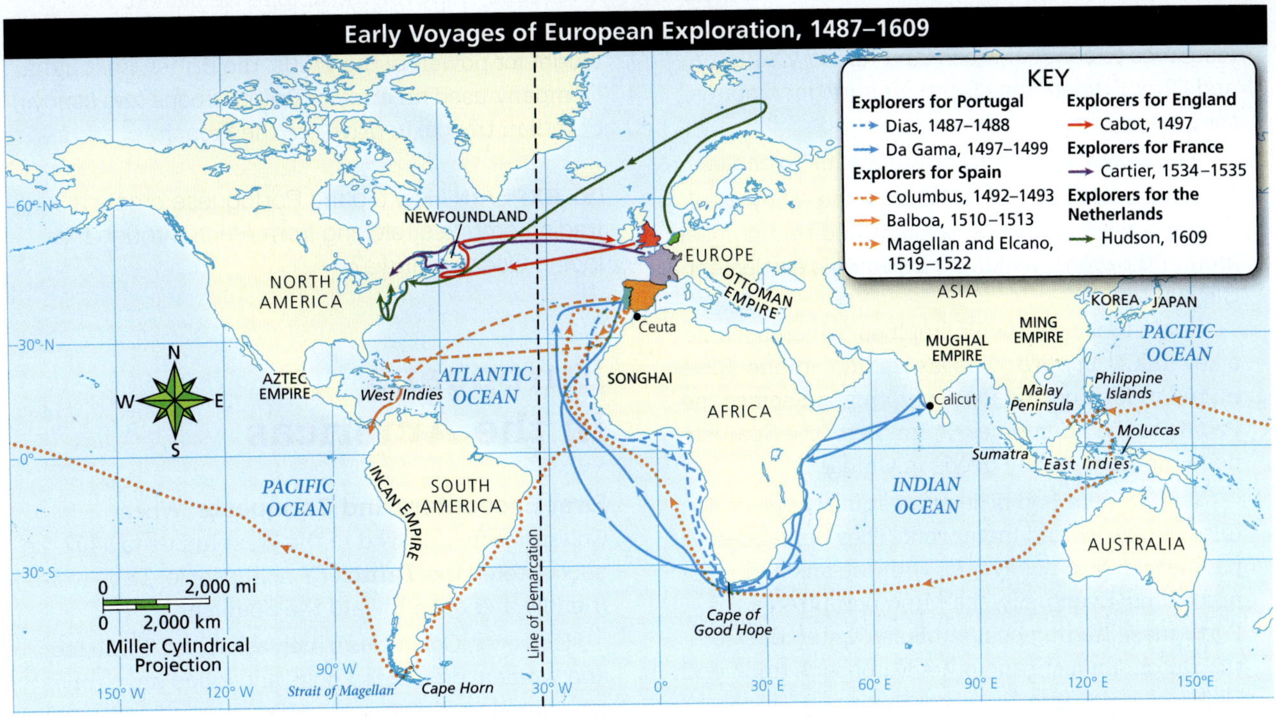

>> **Analyze Maps** Portugal led the way in exploring the world by ship. Spain and other countries soon followed. How did Magellan's route to Asia differ from the routes of other explorers?.

overseas to win new converts to Christianity. The Renaissance spirit of curiosity also fed a desire to learn more about lands beyond Europe.

Improved Technology Improvements in technology helped Europeans cross vast oceans. **Cartographers** created more accurate maps. European sailors learned how to use the astrolabe to determine latitude at sea. Europeans also designed larger and better ships.

Portugal Explores Africa and Beyond

Portugal led the way in exploration. **Prince Henry** saw that the Portuguese could convert Africans to Christianity. He also believed that in Africa he would find the sources of the gold Muslim traders controlled.

In West Africa, the Portuguese established trading posts to trade muskets, tools, and cloth for gold, ivory, hides, and slaves. These were not colonies peopled by settlers. Instead, the Portuguese left just enough men and firepower to defend their forts.

The Portuguese attacked East African coastal cities, expelling the Arabs who controlled the East African trade network and taking over this thriving commerce. In 1497, Portuguese navigator **Vasco da Gama** led four ships around the Cape of Good Hope and reached the great spice port of Calicut on the west coast of India. He returned with a very profitable spice cargo. Other fleets and merchants followed, building a vast Portuguese trading empire.

The Search for Routes to Asia and the Pacific Inspired by successful Portuguese voyages, **Christopher Columbus** wanted to reach the East Indies by sailing west across the Atlantic but reached the previously unknown continents of North and South America.

Once Europeans realized that the Americas blocked a sea passage to India, they hunted for a route around or through the Americas. In 1513, the Spanish adventurer Vasco Núñez de Balboa made his way through Panama's tropical forests and gazed at the Pacific Ocean.

In September 1519, Ferdinand Magellan set out from Spain with five ships to find a way to the Pacific. After great difficulties, he reached the Pacific and then sailed westward. The voyage's survivors became the first people to **circumnavigate,** or sail around, the world.

Europeans Trade with Asia In 1510, the Portuguese seized the island of Goa off the coast of

India, making it their major military and commercial base. However, they had neither the strength nor the resources to conquer much land territory. In India and China, where they faced far stronger empires, they merely sought permission to trade.

The Dutch were the first Europeans to challenge Portuguese domination of Asian trade. They used their sea power to set up colonies and trading posts around the world, including a strategic settlement at Cape Town.

Spain took over the Philippines, which became a key link in Spain's overseas trading empire. Silver mined in Mexico and Peru was shipped across the Pacific to the Philippines. From there, the Spanish used the silver to buy goods in China.

The Chinese had little interest in Europe or its inferior textiles and metalwork. They demanded payment in gold or silver for Chinese silk and porcelains. Eventually, the Ming permitted a Portuguese trading post at Macao. Later, they let the Dutch, English, and other Europeans trade with Chinese merchants.

The Mughal empire was larger, richer, and more powerful than any European kingdom, and the Mughal emperors granted Europeans trading rights.

>> *First Tribute to Columbus* (1892) by Spanish artist José Garnelo y Alda represents the first meeting with the Taíno. **Hypothesize** Do you think the encounter actually appeared like this? Why or why not?

Over time, however, the empire weakened. As Mughal power faltered, French and English traders fought for power. In the 1700s, the British East India Company used an army of British troops and sepoys, or Indian troops, to drive out the French.

EXPLAIN How did the Portuguese create a trading empire stretching from Africa through the Indian Ocean to India?

Europeans in the Americas

First Encounters and Conquests When Columbus first arrived in the West Indies in 1492, he encountered the **Taíno** (TY noh) people. They were friendly and open toward the Spanish.

However, Columbus's men assaulted Taíno men and women, demanded gold, and killed any Taínos who dared to resist.

A wave of Spanish **conquistadors** (kahn KEES tuh dawrz), or conquerors, soon arrived in the Americas and repeated Columbus's encounter. The conquistadors seized the Native Americans' gold and made them pan for more. The Spanish also forced the Native Americans to convert to Christianity.

From the Caribbean, explorers probed the coasts of the Americas. Spanish guns and cannons were superior to the Native Americans' arrows and spears, and European metal armor provided them with better protection. They also had horses.

Europeans unknowingly carried diseases, such as smallpox, measles, and influenza, to which Native Americans had no **immunity**, or natural protection. These diseases spread rapidly and wiped out entire villages.

The Spanish conquistadors **Hernán Cortés** and Francisco Pizarro formed alliances with Native American groups and took advantage of civil war to conquer the Aztecs in Mexico and the Incas in Peru. The Tupian Indians in Brazil were largely wiped out by disease. In the 1530s, Portugal began to issue grants of land to Portuguese nobles, who agreed to develop the land and share profits with the crown.

The Spanish Colonial Empire Spanish settlers and missionaries followed the conquistadors to the Americas. In time, the huge Spanish empire stretched from California in the north to Argentina in the south. Spain divided these lands into four provinces, including New Spain (Mexico) and Peru.

European Colonization of North America, about 1700

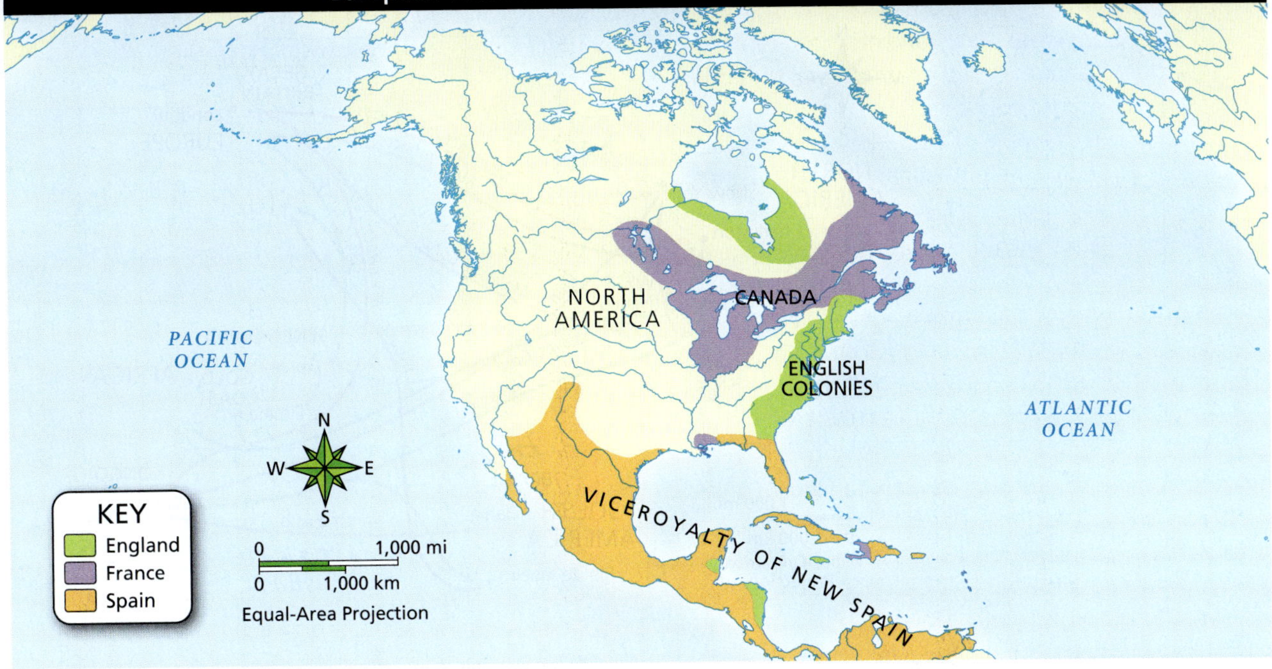

>> England, France, and Spain controlled large parts of North America. Their colonies differed from each other in a number of ways.

Bounce to Activate Map

Spain imposed its culture, language, religion, and way of life on millions of new subjects in its empire. The Spanish built new Spanish-style cities on top of the ruins of Native American cities. The Catholic Church worked with the government to convert Native Americans to Christianity.

Although Spanish culture was dominant in the cities, the blending of diverse traditions changed people's lives throughout the Americas. Settlers learned Native American styles of building, ate foods native to the Americas, and traveled in Indian-style canoes. Indian artistic styles influenced the newcomers. At the same time, Europeans taught their religion to Native Americans. They also introduced animals, especially the horse, thereby transforming the lives of many Native Americans.

Africans contributed to this cultural mix with their farming methods, cooking styles, and crops. African drama, dance, and song heightened Christian services. In Cuba, Haiti, and elsewhere, Africans forged new religions that blended African and Christian beliefs.

DESCRIBE How did the Spanish conquistadors treat the Taínos?

European Colonies in North America During the 1600s, France, the Netherlands, England, and Sweden joined Spain in settling North America.

At first, Europeans were disappointed that North America did not yield gold treasure or offer a water passage to Asia, as they had hoped. Before long, though, the English and French were turning profits by growing tobacco in Virginia, fishing off the North Atlantic coast, and trading furs from New England and Canada with Europe.

French claims in Canada—which the French called **New France**—quietly grew while French rulers were distracted by wars at home in Europe. French explorers and fur traders gradually traveled inland with the help of Native American allies, who sought support against rival Native American groups.

Jesuits and other missionaries soon followed the explorers. The population of New France grew slowly. Settlers faced the long winters of the harsh Canadian climate. By the early 1700s, French forts, missions, and trading posts stretched from Quebec to Louisiana, and the population was growing.

The English built their first permanent colony at Jamestown, Virginia, in 1607. Its early years were filled with disaster. In 1620, another group of English settlers landed at Plymouth, Massachusetts. They were **Pilgrims**—English Protestants who rejected the Church of England. They sought religious freedom.

At first, settlers in the English colonies just struggled to survive. Early on, they abandoned dreams of finding riches like the Spanish had.

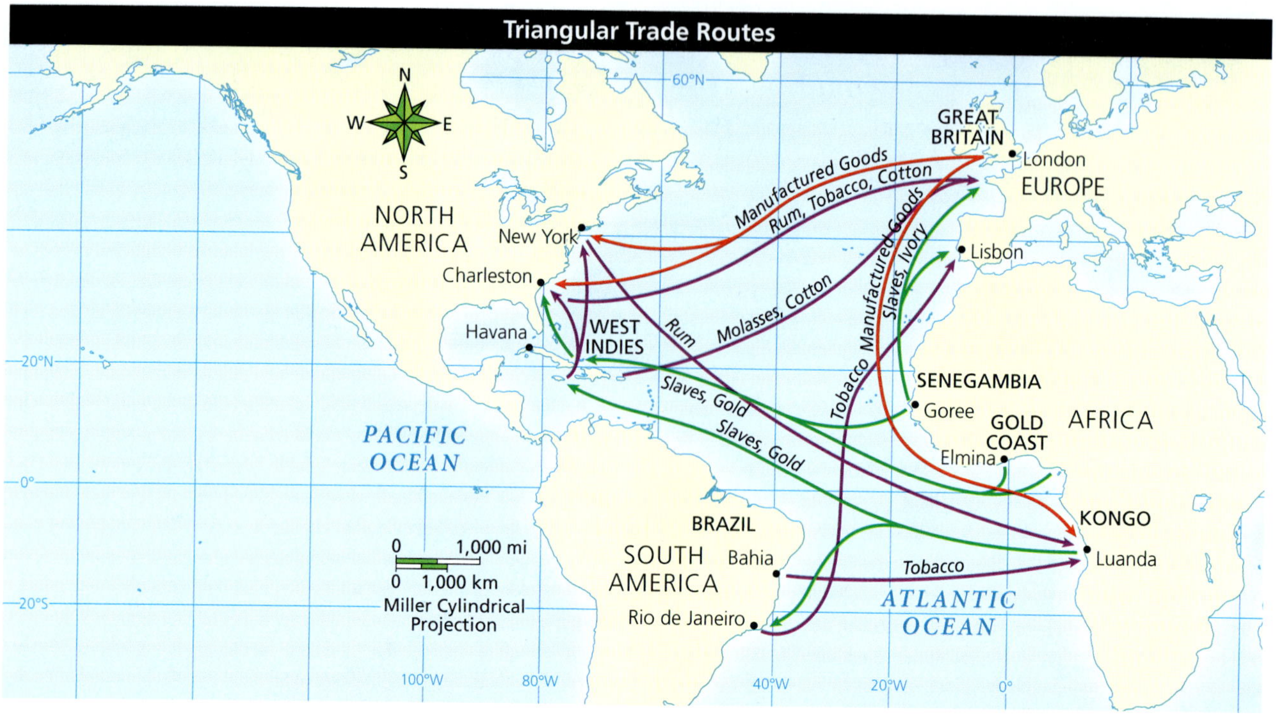

>> **Analyze Maps** This map shows triangular trade routes that started in the 1500s. What trade goods were slaves exchanged for in North America?

Bounce to Activate Map

Instead, they learned to create wealth by using the resources native to their surroundings.

A Power Struggle Begins By the 1600s, Spain, France, England, and the Netherlands all had colonies in North America. This included fierce competition in the Caribbean, as European nations battled to acquire the profitable sugar-producing colonies. Europeans began to fight—both in the colonies and around the world—to protect and expand their interests.

By the 1700s, Britain and France emerged as bitter rivals for power. Their clashes in Europe often ignited conflicts in the Caribbean, North America, India, and Africa.

In 1754, fighting broke out between the French and British in North America. In the British colonies, it marked the beginning of the **French and Indian War**. By 1756, that regional conflict was linked to the Seven Years' War in Europe. The war soon spread to India and other parts of the globe.

During the war, British soldiers and colonial troops launched a series of campaigns against the French in Canada and on the Ohio frontier. In 1759, the British captured Quebec, capital of New France, and then Montreal. The 1763 Treaty of Paris officially ended the worldwide war and ensured British dominance in North America.

The Slave Trade and Its Impact on Africa

The African Slave Trade Expands In the 1400s and 1500s, as you have read, Europeans set up small forts on the coast of West Africa in order to resupply their ships and profit from local trade, especially in gold. As Europeans built colonies in the Americas, they needed large numbers of laborers to make their colonies profitable. By the 1600s, they increasingly turned to Africa to provide that labor.

At first, the Portuguese and other Europeans brought a few Africans back to Europe as slaves. There, Africans were seen as exotic servants of the rich. As European colonies in the Americas grew, however, Europeans turned to slave laborers to clear **plantations,** or the large estates run by an owner or an owner's overseer.

Europeans lacked the resources to travel inland to seize slaves. Instead, they relied on local African rulers and traders to bring captives—usually from other African nations—to coastal trading posts. There, the traders exchanged captured Africans for weapons, gunpowder, textiles, iron, and other goods.

Over the next 300 years, however, it grew into a huge, profitable business. By the 1700s and 1800s, traders had shipped tens of thousands of enslaved

Africans across the Atlantic to work on tobacco and sugar plantations in the Americas. These slaves were property.

As the slave trade grew, some African leaders tried to slow it down or even stop it altogether. But in the end, the system that supported the trade was too strong for them to resist.

IDENTIFY CAUSE AND EFFECT Why did the African slave trade expand?

The Atlantic Slave Trade The Atlantic slave trade formed one part of a three-legged international trade network known as **triangular trade**. This was a triangle-shaped series of Atlantic trade routes linking Europe, Africa, and the Americas.

Triangular trade worked in the following way. On the first leg, merchant ships brought European goods—including guns, cloth, and cash—to Africa. In Africa, the merchants traded these goods for slaves. On the second leg, known as the **Middle Passage,** the slaves were transported to the Americas. There, the enslaved Africans were exchanged for sugar, molasses, and other products manufactured at plantations owned by Europeans.

On the final leg, merchants carried sugar, molasses, cotton, and other American goods such as furs, salt fish, and rum made from molasses. These goods were shipped to Europe, where they were traded at a profit for the European commodities that merchants needed to return to Africa.

To merchants, the Middle Passage was just one leg of triangular trade. For enslaved Africans, the Middle Passage was a horror.

Most Africans were taken from inland villages. After they were enslaved, they were forced to march to coastal ports. Many captives died along the way. Others tried to escape, and were often quickly recaptured and brutally punished. Once purchased by European traders, Africans were packed below the decks of slave ships, usually in chains. Hundreds of men, women, and children were crammed into a single vessel for voyages that lasted from three weeks to three months.

Disease was the biggest threat to the lives of the captives and the profit of the merchants. Of the slaves who died, most died of dysentery. Many died of smallpox. Slave ships became "floating coffins" on which up to half the Africans on board died from disease or brutal mistreatment.

Impact of the Slave Trade Historians continue to debate how many Africans were carried to the Americas during the Atlantic slave trade. Some historians estimate that about 2,000 Africans were sent to the Americas each year during the 1500s.

>> **Analyze Charts** Based on this information, what percentage of slaves died during passage to the Americas? Where in the Americas did most slaves end up?

Bounce to Activate Chart

In the 1780s, when the slave trade reached its peak, that number approached 80,000 a year. By the mid-1800s, when the overseas slave trade was finally ended, an estimated 11 million enslaved Africans had been forcibly carried to the Americas. Another 2 million probably died under the brutal conditions of the Middle Passage.

The slave trade brought great profits to many and provided the labor needed by colonial economies. Yet the slave trade had a devastating impact on African societies. Millions of people in Africa were brutalized by the slave trade and slavery itself. Many others died during the horrific Middle Passage.

In some parts of Africa, the slave trade had little or no impact. In other areas, it disrupted whole societies. The slave trade triggered wars, increased tensions among neighboring peoples, and led to the rise of strong new states. The rulers of these states battled rivals for control of the slave trade.

The **Asante kingdom** (uh SAHN teh) emerged in the area occupied by present-day Ghana. In the late 1600s, an able military leader, Osei Tutu, unified his people to defeat the neighboring Denkyera. Efficient government officials, chosen by merit, managed the royal monopolies on gold mining and the slave trade.

The Asante traded with Europeans on the coast, exchanging gold and slaves for firearms. They also played rival Europeans against one another to protect themselves. In this way, they built a wealthy, powerful state.

The **Oyo empire** arose from successive waves of settlement by the Yoruba people of present-day Nigeria. It began as a relatively small forest kingdom. Beginning in the late 1600s, however, its leaders used wealth from the slave trade to build up an impressive army that conquered the neighboring kingdom of Dahomey. The Oyu also continued to gain wealth by trading with European merchants at the port city of Porto-Novo.

The Atlantic slave trade brought people from different societies in Africa to the Americas. Although most came from West Africa, that region was home to diverse communities from small chiefdoms to larger states and kingdoms. A rich variety of African traditions, languages, beliefs, stories, music, and other cultural elements were added to the emerging new cultures of the Americas.

>> The African slave trade expanded in response to Europeans' increasing use of enslaved workers on plantations in the Americas.

Effects of Global Contact

The Columbian Exchange The European voyages of exploration in the 1500s and 1600s set off a chain of events that brought major changes to the world. Over the next centuries, European exploration and expansion overseas affected people from Asia, Africa, and the Americas to Europe itself.

When Columbus returned to Spain in March 1493, he brought with him plants and animals that he had found in the Americas. Later that year, Columbus returned to the Americas with some 1,200 settlers and a collection of European animals and plants. In this way, Columbus began a vast global exchange that would profoundly affect the world. Because this exchange began with Columbus, we call it the **Columbian Exchange**.

In the Americas, Europeans found a variety of foods that were new to them, including tomatoes, peppers, corn, and potatoes. They eagerly transported these to Europe. Europeans also carried a wide variety of plants and animals to the Americas, including wheat and grapes from Europe and bananas and sugar cane from Africa and Asia. Cattle, pigs, goats, and chickens, unknown before the European encounter, joined the Native American diet. Horses and donkeys transported people and goods quickly.

The Columbian Exchange

TRANSFERRED FROM THE WESTERN HEMISPHERE		TRANSFERRED FROM THE EASTERN HEMISPHERE	
Corn	Turkeys	Wheat	Coffee
Potatoes	Pineapples	Sugar	Horses
Sweet Potatoes	Tomatoes	Bananas	Pigs
Beans	Cocoa	Rice	Cows, oxen
Peanuts	Cassava/manioc	Oats	Goats
Squash	Silver	Barley	Chickens
Pumpkins	Quinine	Rye	Smallpox
Chili peppers	Sunflowers	Grapes	Typhus

>> **Analyze Charts** The Columbian Exchange affected people around the world. What livestock were introduced to the Americas by the Columbian Exchange?

The Columbian Exchange resulted in the migration of millions of people. Shiploads of Europeans sailed to the Americas in search of new opportunities. The Atlantic slave trade forcibly brought millions of Africans to the Americas. Native American populations, however, declined drastically.

The vast movement of people led to the diffusion, or transfer, of ideas and technologies. Europeans and Africans brought their beliefs and customs to the Americas. In Europe and elsewhere, people adapted ideas and inventions from distant lands.

IDENTIFY CAUSE AND EFFECT How did the Columbian Exchange affect global population?

A Commercial Revolution The opening of direct links with Asia, Africa, and the Americas had far-reaching economic consequences for Europeans and their colonies. Europe underwent a period of economic growth and change known as the **Commercial Revolution,** which spurred the growth of modern capitalism, banking, and investing. By the 1500s, prices began to rise in many parts of Europe. At the same time, there was much more money in circulation. Earnings were often retained in banks or reinvested in the economy.

A rise in prices that is linked to a sharp increase in the amount of money available is called inflation. The period in European history when inflation rose rapidly is known as the price revolution. Inflation was fueled by the enormous amount of silver and gold flowing into Europe from the Americas by the mid-1500s. When prices began to rise, output also increased.

Expanded trade and the push for overseas empires spurred the growth of European **capitalism,** or the investment of money to make a profit. In a capitalist economy, also called a **free enterprise system,** most businesses are privately owned and economic decisions are made between buyers and sellers based on supply and demand. Other key elements of capitalism include the accumulation and investment of capital (money) and competition within a free market.

During the Commercial Revolution, **entrepreneurs,** or enterprising business people, organized, managed, and took on the risks of doing business. Entrepreneurs provided jobs for workers and paid for raw materials, transport, and other costs of production.

As trade increased, entrepreneurs sought to expand into overseas ventures. Distant markets could be risky since governments were often small or weak in those places, but capitalists, because of their resources, were more willing to take risks.

Mercantilism European monarchs enjoyed the benefits of the Commercial Revolution. In the fierce competition for trade and empire, they adopted a new economic policy, known as **mercantilism,**

>> As European rulers embraced mercantilism and expanded trade, their ports became thriving centers of commerce. This painting depicts the crowded port of Toulon, France, in the mid-1700s.

which was aimed at strengthening their national economies. Mercantilists believed that a nation's real wealth was measured in its gold and silver treasure. To build its supply of gold and silver, they said, a nation must export more goods than it imported.

To mercantilists, overseas colonies existed for the benefit of the parent country. They provided resources and raw materials not available in Europe. In turn, they enriched a parent country by serving as a market for its manufactured goods.

To achieve these goals, European powers passed strict laws regulating trade with their colonies. Colonists could not set up their own industries to manufacture goods. They were also forbidden from buying goods from a foreign country. In addition, only ships from the parent country or the colonies themselves could be used to send goods into or out of the colonies.

ASSESSMENT

1. **Identify Cause and Effect** Why did Europeans explore Africa, Asia, and the Americas beginning in the 1400s?
2. **Draw Conclusions** How did the decline of Mughal India aid European traders in the region?
3. **Draw Conclusions** Why were Native Americans unable to defeat the Spanish conquistadors?
4. **Identify Steps in a Process** How did the three steps of the triangular trade network function?
5. **Analyze Information** How was the impact of the Columbian Exchange positive in some ways but negative in other ways?

PEARSON realize
PearsonSchool.com/CASS

Go online to PearsonSchool.com/CASS and use the texts, quizzes, interactivities, Interactive Reading Notepads, Flipped Videos, and other resources from this Topic to prepare for the Topic Test.

- Etexts
- Quizzes
- Interactivities
- Interactive Reading Notepads
- Flipped Videos

While online you can also check the progress you've made learning the topic and course content by viewing your grades, test scores, and assignment status.

California Topic 0 Quick Study Guide

LESSON SUMMARIES

Use these Lesson Summaries, and the longer versions available online, to review the key ideas for each lesson in this Topic.

Lesson R.1: Origins of Civilization

The change from nomadic to farming life during the Neolithic Agricultural Revolution led to the emergence of civilizations.

Lesson R.2: The Ancient Middle East and Egypt

The earliest civilizations developed in the river valleys of Africa and Asia. The fertile land between the Tigris and Euphrates rivers laid the foundation for the development of Sumer, the world's first civilization. The Nile River shaped the civilization of Egypt.

Lesson R.3: Ancient India and China

As civilizations developed in the Nile Valley and the Fertile Crescent, people in India and China carved out their own civilizations.

Lesson R.4: The Americas

Three advanced civilizations—those of the Mayas, the Aztecs, and the Incas—developed in Middle and South America. In North America diverse culture groups emerged.

Lesson R.5: Ancient Greece

The Minoans and the Mycenaeans shaped the first Greek civilizations. As Greek city states grew, they developed different types of government, including an early form of democracy.

Lesson R.6: Ancient Rome and the Origins of Christianity

Rome expanded across the Mediterranean to build a huge, diverse empire. Christianity, which emerged in Roman-held lands in the Middle East, spread quickly throughout the Roman Empire.

Lesson R.7: Medieval Christian Europe

In time, the Roman Empire broke apart, with the eastern half flourishing as the Byzantine Empire and the western half dividing into small kingdoms. In the West, a new social system called feudalism developed. At the same time, the Christian Church grew in strength.

Lesson R.8: The Muslim World and Africa

Muhammad introduced the religion of Islam to the Arabian Peninsula. Islam spread throughout the Middle East and northern Africa. Kingdoms in Africa rose and developed during this period.

Lesson R.9: Civilizations of Asia

India experienced tremendous changes while China experienced long periods of peace, order, and advancement. Mongol warriors swept through much of Asia, claiming a mighty empire.

Lesson R.10: The Italian Renaissance

New ways of thinking in Western Europe brought about many achievements in the arts as well as changes to the Church and scientific advancements.

Lesson R.11: New Global Connections

In the 1400s, Europeans began an age of exploration, which led to growing influence on other people around the world.

VISUAL REVIEW

Use these graphics to review some of the key terms, people, and ideas from this Topic.

Key Stages of Human Development

OLD STONE AGE

- creation of tools and weapons
- use of fire
- spoken language
- belief in a spiritual world
- creation of cave paintings
- burial of the dead

NEW STONE AGE

- farming and domestication of plants and animals
- settling of permanent villages
- appearance of differences in wealth
- creation of first calendars
- more elaborate tools and new technologies

RISE OF CIVILIZATIONS

- production of surpluses of food
- expansion of population
- development of cities and governments
- government oversight of large-scale projects
- belief in polytheistic religions
- job specialization
- development of social classes
- development of arts and architecture

Early Empires

Date	Empire	Leader
2300 B.C.	Akkadian Empire	*Sargon*
1500s B.C.	Egyptian Empire	*Thutmose I*
321 B.C.	Maurya Empire	*Chandragupta*
300s B.C.	Alexander's Empire	*Alexander*
221 B.C.	Qin Empire	*Shi Huangdi*
27 B.C.	Roman Empire	*Augustus*
A.D. 500s	Byzantine Empire	*Justinian*
A.D. 632	Muslim Empire	*Abu Bakr*
A.D. 1200s	Mongol Empire	*Genghis Khan*
A.D.1235	Mali Empire	*Sundiata*

Religions of the World

JUDAISM	HINDUISM	BUDDHISM	CHRISTIANITY	ISLAM
• Initiated by Abraham's dedication to one God	• Originated with the Aryans	• Founded by Siddhartha Gautama, the Buddha	• Based on the teaching of Jesus	• Introduced by Muhammad
• Began in Canaan in Southwest Asia	• Began in India	• Began in India and adopted in China	• Began in Roman Empire (Southwest Asia)	• Began on Arabian Peninsula
• Follow the laws expressed in the Torah, which also tells the history of the ancient Israelites	• Achieve moksha, or union with Brahman, by following laws of karma and dharma through various cycles of life	• Achieve nirvana, or union with the universe, by following the Four Noble Truths and the Eightfold Path	• Emphasize God's love, justice, morality, forgiveness, and service to others as expressed in Christian Bible	• Follow the teachings of the Quran, which provides a guide to life for Muslims

California Topic 0 Assessment

KEY TERMS, PEOPLE, AND IDEAS

1. Why is the **Neolithic Revolution** considered a turning point in history?
2. How did the **Fertile Crescent** affect the development of early civilizations?
3. How did the beliefs of the ancient Israelites differ from those of neighboring people?
4. What influence did the ideas of **Confucius** have on Chinese civilization?
5. What elements of Olmec culture were used by the Maya and Incas?
6. How was a Greek city-state or polis different from a modern city?
7. Why was the establishment of **due process of law** important to the people of the Middle Ages?
8. What role did **cartographers** play in European exploration?
9. Why is **Johannes Gutenberg** remembered in history?

CRITICAL THINKING

10. **Identify Cause and Effect** Which feature(s) of civilization do you think most allowed empires to develop?
11. **Use Evidence** What evidence supports the idea that laws were central to early Judaism?
12. **Compare and Contrast** What similarities and differences exist between Hindu and Buddhist teachings about the way a person should live?
13. **Draw Inferences** What goals did Shi Huangdi proclaim for China?
14. **Compare and Contrast** How were the farming methods developed by the Aztec and the Inca different? How were they similar?
15. **Draw Conclusions** What basic ideas of the Greeks were instrumental in the design of the Parthenon?
16. **Compare and Contrast** How was Roman law similar to and different from Jewish law?
17. **Identify Main Ideas** Describe the central ideas and major religious influences of Christianity. What beliefs was Christianity based on? How were Christian beliefs different from those of Judaism? How was Christianity tolerated and what was its influence?
18. **Identify Cause and Effect** Describe the impact of important concepts contained in the Magna Carta. Consider the rights for nobles and rules affecting the monarchs, due process of law, and habeas corpus. How was taxation affected under King John's rule at the time?
19. **Summarize** How did Islam develop and spread to other lands?
20. **Identify Cause and Effect** How did the development of trading centers in the African gold-salt trade influence the spread of ideas and trade?
21. **Draw Conclusions** Why do you think some Europeans were willing to give up their old life to become colonists in the Americas?
22. **Draw Conclusions** King Asoka had stone pillars set up across India announcing laws or edicts. The following are excerpts from several of the pillars. (a) How did Asoka feel about other religions? (b) How does Asoka's laws teach values?

> "Whoever honors his own [religion] and disparages another man's, whether from blind loyalty or with the intention of showing his own [religion] in a favorable light, does his own [religion] the greatest possible harm. . . .
>
> All the good deeds that I have done have been accepted and followed by the people. And so obedience to mother and father, obedience to teachers, respect for the aged, kindliness . . . to the poor and weak, and to slaves and servants have increased and will continue to increase. . . . And this progress of Righteousness . . . has taken place in two manners, by enforcing conformity to Righteousness and by exhortation. . . ."

23. **Writing Activity** In the excerpt below a student from ancient Sumeria describes his day at school. Use the excerpt and what you have read to describe the role scribes had in Sumerian society and to explain why strict discipline was required.

> "I recited my tablet, ate my lunch, prepared my new tablet, wrote it, finished it. Then they assigned me my oral work, and in the afternoon they assigned me my written work. When school was dismissed, I went home, entered the house, and found my father sitting there. I told my father of my written work, then recited my tablet to him, and my father was delighted. . . . When I awoke early in the morning, I faced my mother and said to her: 'Give me my lunch, I want to go to school.' My mother gave me two rolls and I set out. In school, the monitor in charge of punctuality said to me 'Why are you late?' Afraid and with pounding heart, I entered before my teacher and made a respectful curtsey."
>
> — Samuel Noah Kramer, *History Begins at Sumer*

DOCUMENT-BASED QUESTIONS

When anthropologists make new finds, they are not always sure exactly what they have discovered. Read the documents below describing the finds of researchers, and then answer the questions that follow.

DOCUMENT A

"Scientists have discovered a new species of ancient human that lived 18,000 years ago on an island east of the Java Sea—a prehistoric hunter. . . . These "little people" stood about three feet tall and had heads the size of a grapefruit. . . . The research team . . . described the remains—a fairly complete skull, the jawbone and much of the skeleton—as those of a 30-year-old woman. . . . The team also found . . . the remains of between five and seven people in all."

—*Guy Gugliotta, washingtonpost.com, October 28, 2004*

DOCUMENT B

"So what was this strange creature, and what was it doing on [the island of] Flores? The [researchers] have had to make difficult choices in deciding how to classify the creature, although it is clear that this person was definitely not a modern human. The small brain size and the hip-bone shape might favor classification as an australopithecine, whereas the size and shape of the skull might suggest a primitive form of *H. erectus*. Given the unique combination of features, the [researchers] have decided to give the specimen a new name: *Homo floresiensis*."

—*Chris Stringer, news@nature.com, October 27, 2004*

DOCUMENT C

"The researchers estimate that the tiny people lived on [the island of] Flores from about 95,000 years ago until at least 13,000 years ago. The scientists base their theory on charred bones and stone tools found on the island. The [tools] were apparently used to hunt big game. . . . The Flores people used fire in hearths for cooking and hunted stegodon, a primitive dwarf elephant found on the Island. . . . Almost all of the stegodon bones, associated with the human artifacts are of juveniles [youths], suggesting the tiny humans selectively hunted the smallest stegodons."

—*Hillary Mayell, nationalgeographic.com, October 27, 2004*

DOCUMENT D

An adult *Homo floresiensis* skull (left) beside an adult modern human skull

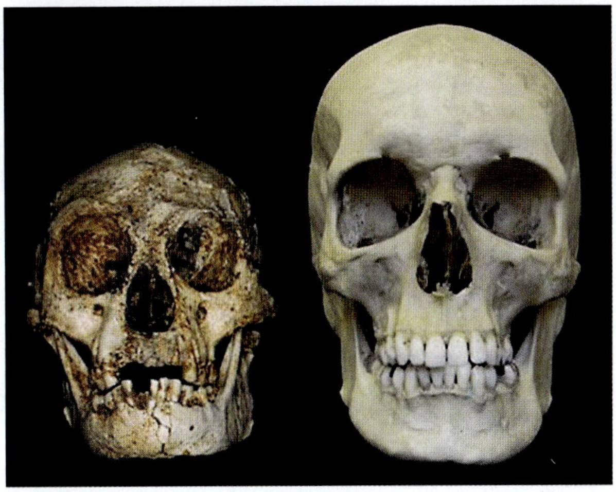

24. Documents B and C describe the discovery of
- **A.** modern human remains
- **B.** australopithecine remains
- **C.** *Homo erectus* remains
- **D.** *Homo floresiensis* remains

25. Which is NOT a theory that researchers have expressed about the tiny hominids whose remains were found in Flores?
- **A.** The tiny hominids lived at least 13,000 years ago.
- **B.** The tiny hominids were juveniles.
- **C.** The tiny hominids had small heads and brains.
- **D.** The tiny hominids hunted dwarf elephants.

26. Which is the most accurate conclusion that can be drawn from Document D about the relative sizes of *Homo floresiensis* and modern human adults?
- **A.** Modern human adults have larger bodies than *Homo floresiensis* adults.
- **B.** Modern human adults have larger skulls than *Homo floresiensis* adults.
- **C.** The modern human skull pictured is larger than the *Homo floresiensis* skull pictured.
- **D.** The *Homo floresiensis* skull pictured is older than the modern human skull pictured.

27. Writing Tasks Which information given in Documents A, B, C, and D seems the most reliable to you? Use your knowledge and specific information from these documents to support your opinion.

End-of-Topic Practice

1. Study the chart that explains the process archaeologists follow when excavating for evidence of how early hominids lived. Which of the following is the missing step?

   A Geologists examine seeds and animal bones at the site

   B Archaeologists record the description and location of each artifact

   C Botanists analyze blood stains found on artifacts

   D Zoologists determine the age of the rocks surrounding the dig

---

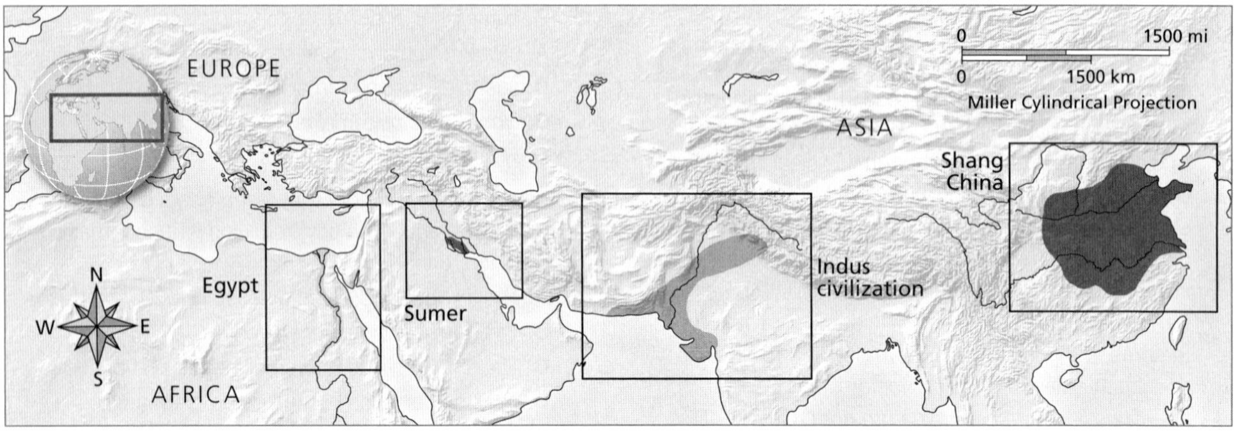

2. Which of the following generalizations is true for all of the places indicated on the map?

   F They developed complex economies by trading wheat and corn with other societies.

   G They were home to all of the people in the regions at the time.

   H They developed cities with complex social classes.

   J They invented terraced farming to grow enough food for their populations.

3 How might the lives of Athenian and Spartan citizens?

A Athenian citizens farmed, male citizens voted, physical activity was important; Spartan citizens voted and farmed

B Athenian citizens pursued interests in art and architecture, eventually developed a strong navy, were citizens of a democracy; Spartan citizens were strong soldiers, were citizens of a monarchy

C Spartan citizens farmed, built strong navies, and were noted architects; Athenian citizens lived under a monarchy, were strong soldiers

D Spartans were famous soldiers, citizens of a democracy, and noted intellectuals; Athenian citizens voted in citizen assemblies, concentrated on land warfare

---

4 Which statement is true about the Middle Ages in Europe?

F The many manors in a region of Europe were interdependent.

G Vassals held the highest place in feudal society.

H Only lords and their family were allowed on manors.

J War was a way of life for members of the noble class.

If you have trouble with. . .				
Question	1	2	3	4
See Lesson	R.1	R.2, R.3	R.5	R.7

[**ESSENTIAL QUESTION**] How much power should the government have?

1 Absolutism and Revolution (1550–1850)

>> The execution of Queen Marie Antoinette during the French Revolution

Enduring Understandings

- Absolute monarchs such as Louis XIV of France exerted complete authority over their kingdoms.
- England developed a limited monarchy with a written constitution.
- Enlightenment philosophers applied reason to political, social, and economic problems.
- Ideas such as natural rights shaped the American Revolution and the U.S. Constitution.
- An unequal social system sparked the French Revolution, in which the monarchy was replaced by a republic.
- As emperor of France, Napoleon Bonaparte began a series of wars that had lasting effects on Europe and the Americas.

NBC LEARN

Learn about King Louis XIV of France, the greatest of the absolute monarchs.

Bounce to Activate My Story Video

California Topic 1 Overview

In this Topic, you will learn about the events of the age of Absolutism and Revolution. Look at the lesson outline and explore the timeline. As you study this Topic, you will complete the Quest team project.

LESSON OUTLINE

1.1 Absolute Monarchy in Spain and France
Analysis CST.1, CST.2, HRE.4, HI.1

1.2 Rise of Austria, Prussia, and Russia
HSS 10.1.1; Analysis CST.1, HRE.4, HI.1

1.3 Triumph of Parliament in England
HSS 10.2, HSS 10.2.2; Analysis CST.1, CST.3, HRE.4, HI.1

1.4 The Enlightenment
HSS 10.2.1; Analysis CST.1, CST.2, HRE.4, HI.1

1.5 The American Revolution
HSS 10.1.3, HSS 10.2, HSS 10.2.1, HSS 10.2.2, HSS 10.2.3; Analysis CST.1, CST.2, HRE.4, HI.1

1.6 The French Revolution Begins
HSS 10.2, HSS 10.2.2, HSS 10.2.4; Analysis CST.1, CST.2, CST.3, HRE.4, HI.1

1.7 A Radical Phase
HSS 10.2, HSS 10.2.4; Analysis CST.1, CST.2, CST.3, HRE.4, HI.1

1.8 The Age of Napoleon
HSS 10.2.4, HSS 10.2.5; Analysis CST.1, CST.2, HRE.4, HI.1

Key Events of the Age of Absolutism and Revolution

1500 Crown of Louis XV of France

1556 Philip II becomes King of Spain.

1642 English Civil War begins.

1688 Glorious Revolution in England.

1789 Bastille stormed in Paris, starting the French Revolution.

1804 Napoleon crowns himself emperor of France.

1814 Congress of Vienna meets.

1815 Napoleon is defeated at Waterloo.

1500 | 1600 | 1700 | 1800 | 1900

QUEST! TEAM PROJECT

Becoming a Human Rights Advocate

What rights should everyone have? In this Quest, you will examine different ideas about what rights people are entitled to. Then your team will draft a human rights bill with the group's conclusion about the rights everyone should have.

STEP 1
Watch the video of President Obama discussing human rights at a press conference with President Hu. What did you learn?

STEP 2
Examine the documents discussing human rights. What general conclusions can you make? What viewpoints are presented?

STEP 3
Draw up a list of human rights that you feel should be universal. Then write a letter to your senator stating why this human rights bill is needed.

STEP 4
Edit, then revise your bill and your letter. Reflect on how human rights have changed through the years.

PEARSON realize™ PearsonSchool.com/CASS

Go ONLINE for complete Quest materials

VIDEO ETEXT WRITING RUBRIC PDF ASSESSMENT

>> This photo shows a jeweled crown worn by King Louis XV of France. Crowns were a symbol of the wealth, power, and prestige of the monarch.

1.1 During the Renaissance and Reformation, European rulers continued to centralize power at the expense of their nobles and the clergy. As wars of religion raged in many European lands, monarchs battled to impose royal law and restore order in their kingdoms.

Bounce to Activate Flipped Video

>> Objectives

Identify the characteristics of absolute monarchy, including the concept of divine right.

Explain how Spanish power grew under Charles V and Philip II.

Understand how France built a centralized monarchy after the wars of religion.

Evaluate Louis XIV as an absolute monarch.

Describe how the arts flourished in Spain and France.

>> Key Terms

Hapsburg empire
Charles V
Philip II
absolute monarchy
armada
El Greco
Miguel de Cervantes
Huguenots
Henry IV
Edict of Nantes
Cardinal Richelieu
Louis XIV
intendant
Jean-Baptiste Colbert
Versailles
levée
balance of power
divine right

Absolute Monarchy in Spain and France

Ruling with Absolute Power

Between about 1500 and 1800, the old feudal order gave way to individual nation-states with strong central governments. Monarchs presided over government bureaucracies that enforced the law and collected taxes. They used income not only to support lavish Renaissance courts but also to strengthen their military power.

Powerful States and Rulers The emergence of strong unified nation-states occurred at different times in different parts of Europe.

The rulers of some countries, such as Spain and France, set up **absolute monarchies.** The chief characteristic of this political system is that a ruler has complete authority over the government and the lives of the people.

During the Age of Absolutism, as this period is called, powerful new dynasties emerged. The Hapsburgs in Spain and the Bourbons in France passed power from generation to generation within the family while they added lands to their kingdoms through skillfully arranged marriages.

Absolute monarchs often had parliaments or other bodies, but these bodies had no real power. The ruler could dissolve them at will. In theory, absolute monarchs had total power, but in practice, to preserve power, they had to balance the interests of different groups from nobles and clergy to the middle class and peasants.

Divine Right to Rule During the Age of Absolutism, European monarchs embraced the idea of **divine right,** meaning that their authority to rule came directly from God. They used divine right theory to justify their power. As God's representative on Earth, monarchs could command absolute obedience from their subjects. In the 1600s, a French bishop and court preacher, Jacques Bossuet (bah soo WAY) defended the theory of divine right and royal absolutism, saying that absolute power was necessary to protect the people.

> "The royal power is absolute. . . Without this absolute authority the king could neither do good nor repress evil. It is necessary that his power be such that no one can escape him."
>
> —Jacques Bossuet, "Politics Drawn from the Very Words of Scripture," 1679

Still, absolute monarchs who claimed to rule by divine right were expected to act for the good of their people.

By 1700, absolute monarchs reigned over most of the great powers in Europe, except England. In time, however, thinkers and others challenged divine right theory along with the entire system of absolute monarchy. They called, instead, for limits on government power and for governments to be responsible to the people.

☑ **IDENTIFY** What are the characteristics of an absolute monarchy?

Spain and the Hapsburg Empire

By the 1500s, Spain had emerged as the first modern European power. Through their marriage, Queen Isabella and King Ferdinand had unified the country. They pursued a policy of imposing religious unity and financed Columbus's voyage, which would lead to the Spanish conquest of the Americas. Wealth from the Americas would help Spain to become the most powerful nation in Europe.

Charles V Wears Two Crowns In 1516, Ferdinand and Isabella's grandson, Charles I, became king of Spain, and thereby ruler of the Spanish colonies in the Americas as well. When his other grandfather died in 1519, Charles I also became heir to the sprawling **Hapsburg empire,** which included the German states of the Holy Roman Empire and the Dutch Netherlands. As ruler of the Hapsburg empire, Charles took the name **Charles V,** the title by which historians now usually refer to him.

Ruling two empires involved Charles in constant warfare. He continued a long Hapsburg struggle with France over rival claims in Italy.

As a devout Catholic, he fought to suppress Protestantism in the German states. After years of religious conflict, however, Charles was forced to allow the German princes to choose their own religion.

His greatest foe was the Ottoman empire, which at the time controlled the Balkans in southeastern Europe. Under Suleiman, Ottoman forces advanced across central Europe to the walls surrounding Vienna, Austria. Although Austria held firm during the siege, the Ottomans occupied much of Hungary following their crushing victory at the Battle of Mohács. Ottoman naval forces also continued to challenge Spanish power in the Mediterranean.

>> In the early 1500s, Charles V became ruler over both the Spanish and the Hapsburg empires. He faced constant warfare, particularly against the Ottomans.

>> This painting shows the abdication of Charles V 1555. He divided the Hapsburg empire between his son, Philip II of Spain, and his brother, Holy Roman Emperor Ferdinand I. **Infer** What types of problems could have contributed to Charles V's decision to resign?

>> The Spanish fleet was victorious over the Ottomans at the Battle of Lepanto in 1571.

The Empire Is Divided The **Hapsburg empire** proved to be too scattered and cumbersome for any one person to rule. Exhausted, Charles gave up his titles in 1556 and entered a monastery. He divided his empire, leaving the Hapsburg lands in central Europe to his brother Ferdinand, who became Holy Roman emperor. He gave Spain, the Netherlands, some southern Italian states, and Spain's overseas empire to his son Philip, who became Philip II.

SUMMARIZE Why did Charles V divide the Hapsburg Empire?

Philip II Becomes an Absolute Monarch

During his 42-year reign, **Philip II** expanded Spanish influence, strengthened the Catholic Church, and made his own power absolute. Thanks in part to silver from Spanish colonies in the Americas, he made Spain the foremost power in Europe.

A Dedicated Ruler Philip surpassed Ferdinand and Isabella in making every part of the government responsible to him. He reigned as an absolute monarch, claiming divine right. Like his father, he was hard working, devout, and ambitious. Unlike many other monarchs, Philip devoted most of his time to government work. He seldom hunted, never jousted, and lived as simply as a monk. The king's isolated, somber palace outside Madrid, known as the Escorial (es kohr YAHL), reflected his character. It served as a church, a residence, and a tomb for the royal family.

Philip saw himself as the guardian of the Roman Catholic Church. The great undertaking of his life was to defend the Catholic Reformation and turn back the rising Protestant tide in Europe. Within his empire, Philip enforced religious unity, turning the Inquisition against Protestants and other people thought to be heretics.

The Wars of Philip II Philip fought many wars to advance Spanish Catholic power. In the Mediterranean, Spain and its Italian allies soundly defeated an Ottoman fleet at the Battle of Lepanto in 1571. Although Christians hailed this as a great victory, the Ottoman Empire would remain a major power in the Mediterranean region for three more centuries.

During the last half of his reign, Philip battled Protestants and other rebels in the Netherlands. At

>> **Integrate Information** Which country divided Philip's empire? Based on the map, why was England in a position to disrupt Spanish shipping?

the time, the region included 17 provinces that are today Belgium, the Netherlands, and Luxembourg. It was the richest part of Philip's empire.

Protestants in the region resisted Philip's efforts to crush their faith. Protestants and Catholics alike opposed high taxes and autocratic Spanish rule, which threatened local traditions of self-government.

In the 1560s, riots against the Inquisition sparked a general uprising in the Netherlands. Savage fighting raged for decades. In 1581, the northern, largely Protestant provinces declared their independence from Spain and became known as the Dutch Netherlands. They did not gain official recognition, however, until 1648. The southern, mostly Catholic provinces of the Netherlands remained part of the Spanish Empire.

The Spanish Armada By the 1580s, Philip saw England's Queen Elizabeth I as his chief Protestant enemy. First secretly, then openly, Elizabeth had supported the Dutch against Spain. She encouraged English captains, known as sea dogs, to plunder Spanish treasure ships and loot Spanish cities in the Americas. To Philip's dismay, Elizabeth made Francis Drake, the most daring sea dog, a knight instead of punishing him as a pirate.

To end English attacks and subdue the Dutch, Philip prepared a huge **armada,** or fleet, to carry a Spanish invasion force to England. In 1588, the Spanish Armada sailed with more than 130 ships, 20,000 men, and 2,400 pieces of artillery. The Spanish were confident of victory. "When we meet the English," predicted one Spanish commander, "God will surely arrange matters so that we can grapple and board them, either by sending some strange freak of weather or, more likely, just by depriving the English of their wits."

This prediction did not come to pass. In the English Channel, lumbering Spanish ships were outmaneuvered by the lighter, faster English ships. Strong winds favored the English, scattering the Armada. After further disasters at sea, the tattered remnants limped home in defeat.

Decline of the Spanish Empire While the defeat of the Spanish Armada ended Philip's plan to invade England, it had little short-term effect on his power. In the long-term, however, Spanish power slowly faded. The decline was due in part to Philip's successors, who were less able rulers than he.

Economic problems were also to blame. Costly overseas wars drained wealth out of Spain almost as fast as it came in. Treasure from the Americas led Spain to neglect farming and commerce. The government heavily taxed the small middle class, weakening a group that in other European nations supported royal power. The expulsion of Muslims and Jews from Spain deprived the economy of many skilled artisans and merchants. Finally, the influx of American gold and silver led to soaring inflation. As Spain's power dwindled in the 1600s and 1700s, Dutch, English, and French fleets challenged—and eventually surpassed—Spanish power both in Europe and around the world.

SUMMARIZE What were Philip II's motivations for waging war?

Arts and Literature of Spain's Golden Century

The century from 1550 to 1650 is often referred to as Spain's *siglo de oro* (SEEG loh day OHR oh), or "golden century," for the brilliance of its arts and literature. Philip II was an enthusiastic patron of the arts and also founded academies of science and mathematics.

Painting Among the famous painters of this period was a man known as **El Greco,** meaning "the Greek." Though not Spanish by birth, El Greco became a master of Spanish painting. Born on the Greek island of Crete, El Greco had studied in Italy before settling in Spain. He produced haunting religious pictures and striking portraits of Spanish nobles, done in a dramatically elongated style.

El Greco's use of vibrant colors influenced the work of Diego Velázquez (vuh LAHS kes), court painter to King Philip IV. Velázquez is perhaps best known for his vivid portraits of Spanish royalty.

Literature Spain's golden century produced several outstanding writers. Lope de Vega (LOH pay duh VAY guh), a peasant by birth, wrote more than 1,500 plays, including witty comedies and action-packed romances.

During Spain's golden age, **Miguel de Cervantes** (sur VAN teez) wrote Europe's first modern novel. *Don Quixote* pokes fun at medieval tales of chivalry. The elderly Don Quixote has read too many tales of days when fictional knights were bold. Imagining himself a medieval knight, he sets out across the Spanish countryside dressed in rusty armor. By his side is his practical servant, Sancho Panza.

Don Quixote mocks the traditions of Spain's feudal past. At the same time, Cervantes depicts with affection both the earthy realism of Sancho and the foolish but heroic idealism of Don Quixote.

DESCRIBE What was the *siglo de oro*?

>> The Spanish painter El Greco was born Domenikos Theotokopoulos in Greece. The *View of Toledo,* shown here, was one of the very few landscapes done by El Greco. It shows his elongated, dramatic style.

Bounce to Activate Gallery

Royal Power Expands in France

Like Philip II in Spain, French rulers were determined to expand royal power. France was torn apart by wars of religion in the late 1500s. Then a new dynasty, the Bourbons, rose to power and built the foundations for an absolute monarchy in France.

Wars of Religion After the Hundred Years' War, French kings slowly consolidated power over their lands. In the 1500s, rivalry with Spain and the Protestant Reformation posed new challenges for France. Religious wars between the Catholic majority and French Protestants, called **Huguenots** (HYOO guh nahts), tore France apart. Leaders on both sides used the strife to further their own ambitions.

Each side committed terrible acts of violence. The worst began on St. Bartholomew's Day (a Catholic holiday), August 24, 1572.

While Huguenot and Catholic nobles were gathered for a royal wedding, a Catholic plot led to the massacre of 3,000 Huguenots. In the next few days, thousands more were slaughtered. For many, the St. Bartholomew's Day Massacre symbolized the complete breakdown of order in France.

Henry IV Restores Order In 1589, a Huguenot prince inherited the French throne as **Henry IV.** Henry was the first ruler in the Bourbon dynasty. As a Huguenot, Henry had battled Catholic forces. Once on the throne, he realized he would face severe problems ruling a largely Catholic country, so he converted to Catholicism. "Paris is well worth a Mass," he is supposed to have said. To protect Protestants, however, he issued the **Edict of Nantes** in 1598. It granted the Huguenots religious toleration and other freedoms.

Henry IV then set out to restore royal power and rebuild a land shattered by war. His goal, he said, was not the victory of one sect over another, but "a chicken in every pot"—a good Sunday dinner for every peasant. Under Henry, the government reached into every area of French life.

Royal officials administered justice, improved roads, built bridges, and revived agriculture. By building the royal bureaucracy and reducing the influence of nobles, Henry IV laid the foundations for royal absolutism.

>> The St. Bartholomew's Day Massacre began at a royal wedding in Paris in 1572. Thousands of French Huguenots were massacred.

Richelieu Strengthens Royal Authority When Henry IV was killed by an assassin in 1610, his nine-year-old son, Louis XIII, inherited the throne. For a time, nobles reasserted their power. Then, in 1624, Louis appointed **Cardinal Richelieu** (ree shul YOO) as his chief minister. This cunning, capable leader devoted the next 18 years to strengthening the central government.

Richelieu was determined to destroy the power of two groups that defied royal authority—nobles and Huguenots. He defeated the private armies of the nobles and destroyed their fortified castles. While reducing their independence, Richelieu tied the nobles to the king by giving them high posts at court or in the royal army. At the same time, he smashed the walled cities of the Huguenots and outlawed their armies. Yet he allowed them to continue to practice their religion.

Richelieu handpicked his able successor, Cardinal Mazarin (ma za RAN). When five-year-old **Louis XIV** inherited the throne in 1643, the year after Richelieu's death, Mazarin was in place to serve as chief minister. Like Richelieu, Mazarin worked tirelessly to extend royal power.

>> Cardinal Richelieu, one of the architects of French absolutism, was principle advisor to Louis XIII. The Siege of La Rochelle, shown here, was a battle in Richelieu's campaign to bring the Huguenots under royal authority.

IDENTIFY SUPPORTING DETAILS How did the Edict of Nantes affect Huguenots?

Louis XIV, an Absolute Monarch

Soon after Louis XIV became king, disorder again swept France. In an uprising called the *Fronde*, nobles, merchants, peasants, and the urban poor each rebelled in order to protest royal power or preserve their own. On one occasion, rioters drove the boy king from his palace. It was an experience Louis would never forget.

When Mazarin died in 1661, the 23-year-old Louis resolved to take complete control over the government himself. "I have been pleased to entrust the government of my affairs to the late Cardinal," he declared. "It is now time that I govern them myself."

"I Am the State" Like his great-grandfather Philip II of Spain, Louis XIV firmly believed in his divine right to rule. He took the sun as the symbol of his absolute power.

Just as the sun stands at the center of the solar system, he argued, so the Sun King stands at the center of the nation. Louis is often quoted as saying, "*L'état, c'est moi*" (lay TAH seh MWAH), which in English translates as "I am the state."

During his reign, Louis did not once call a meeting of the Estates General, the medieval assembly made up of representatives of all French social classes. In fact, the Estates General did not meet between 1614 and 1789. Thus, the Estates General played no role in checking royal power.

Louis Centralizes Power Louis spent many hours each day attending to government affairs. To strengthen the state, he followed the policies of Richelieu. He expanded the bureaucracy and appointed **intendants,** royal officials who collected taxes, recruited soldiers, and carried out his policies in the provinces.

The king often appointed wealthy middle-class men to government jobs. In this way, Louis cemented ties with the middle class and limited the influence of nobles.

Under Louis XIV, the French army became the strongest in Europe. The state paid, fed, trained, and supplied up to 300,000 soldiers. Louis used this highly disciplined army to enforce his policies at home and abroad.

Colbert Strengthens the Economy The French economy grew under the king's brilliant finance minister, **Jean-Baptiste Colbert** (kohl behr). Colbert had new lands cleared for farming, encouraged mining and other basic industries, and built up luxury trades such as lacemaking. To protect French manufacturers, Colbert put high tariffs on imported goods.

>> **Make Generalizations** What do all Louis XIV's efforts to strengthen absolutism have in common?

Colbert also fostered overseas colonies, such as New France in North America and several colonies in India. Imposing mercantilist policies, he regulated trade with the colonies to enrich the royal treasury.

Colbert's policies helped make France the wealthiest state in Europe. Yet not even his financial genius could produce enough income to support the huge costs of Louis's court and his many foreign wars.

RECALL Why did Louis XIV choose the sun as his symbol?

The Royal Palace at Versailles

In the countryside near Paris, Louis XIV turned a royal hunting lodge into the immense palace of **Versailles** (ver SY). There, he presided over both his court and the government. Versailles became the perfect symbol of the power of the Sun King.

Louis spared no expense in making Versailles the most magnificent building in Europe. Its halls and salons displayed the finest paintings and statues. Some depicted the king as Apollo, the ancient Greek god of the sun. Chandeliers and mirrors glittered with gold. In the royal gardens, millions of flowers, trees, and fountains were set out in precise geometric patterns, reflecting royal power over nature.

>> Louis XIV, who came to the throne at a young age, ruled France for more than 72 years. He believed in the divine right of kings and was a powerful absolute monarch.

Elaborate Court Ceremonies Louis XIV perfected elaborate ceremonies that emphasized his own importance. Each day began in the king's bedroom with a ritual known as the **levée** (luh VAY), or rising. High-ranking nobles competed for the honor of holding the royal washbasin or handing the king his diamond-buckled shoes. At night, the ceremony was repeated in reverse. Wives of nobles vied to serve women of the royal family.

Rituals such as the levée served a serious purpose. French nobles were descendants of the feudal lords who had held power in medieval times. At liberty on their estates, these nobles were a threat to the power of the monarchy. By luring nobles to Versailles, Louis turned them into courtiers angling for privileges rather than rival warriors battling for power. His tactic worked because he carefully protected their prestige and continued their privilege of not paying taxes.

>> The Hall of Mirrors is one of the most famous rooms at the Versailles Palace. This elaborate palace was the principal residence of Louis XIV and a monument to his power.

Bounce to Activate Gallery

A Flowering of French Culture The king and his court supported a "splendid century" of the arts.

>> English troops fight the French in this 1704 battle in the War of the Spanish Succession, one of the many foreign wars of Louis XIV.

The king sponsored musical entertainments and commissioned plays by the best writers. The age of Louis XIV came to be known as the classical age of French drama.

In painting, music, architecture, and decorative arts, French styles became the model for all Europe. A new form of dance drama, ballet, gained its first great popularity at the French court. As a leading patron of culture, Louis sponsored the French Academies, which set high standards for both the arts and the sciences.

SUMMARIZE How did Louis XIV secure support from the nobility?

The Legacy of Louis XIV

Louis XIV ruled France for 72 years—far longer than any other monarch. During that time, French culture, manners, and customs set the standard for European tastes. The Sun King made France the strongest state in Europe. In both foreign and domestic affairs, however, many of Louis's policies were costly failures.

Costly Wars Louis XIV poured vast resources into wars meant to expand French borders. However, rival rulers joined forces to check these ambitions. Led by the Dutch or the English, these alliances fought to maintain the **balance of power.** The goal was to maintain a distribution of military and economic power to prevent any one country from dominating Europe.

In 1700, Louis's grandson Philip V inherited the throne of Spain. To maintain the balance of power, neighboring nations led by England fought to prevent the union of France and Spain.

The War of the Spanish Succession dragged on until 1713, when an exhausted France signed the Treaty of Utrecht (YOOtrekt). Philip remained on the Spanish throne, but France agreed never to unite the two crowns.

Huguenots Face Persecution Perhaps Louis's most costly mistake was his treatment of the Huguenots. Louis saw the Protestant minority as a threat to religious and political unity. In 1685, he revoked, or withdrew, the Edict of Nantes.

Facing renewed persecution, more than 100,000 Huguenots fled France. They settled mainly in England, the Netherlands, Germany, Poland, and the Americas. The Huguenots had been among the hardest working and most prosperous of Louis's subjects. Their loss was a serious blow to the French economy, just as the expulsion of Spanish Muslims and Jews had hurt Spain.

IDENTIFY CAUSE AND EFFECT How did Louis's actions weaken the French economy?

ASSESSMENT

1. **Identify** What factors led to the rise of absolute monarchies?
2. **Summarize** How did Spanish power grow under Charles V? under Philip II?
3. **Identify Supporting Details** How did France build a centralized monarchy after the wars of religion?
4. **Support a Point of View with Evidence** Would you consider Louis XIV a successful absolute monarch? Give examples from the text to support your answer.
5. **Connect** What impact did Spanish king Philip II and French king Louis XIV have on the arts?

1.2 During the Reformation, the many German-speaking states within the Holy Roman Empire were plunged into religious wars. Some princes remained loyal to the Roman Catholic Church. Others accepted the teachings of Protestant reformers like Martin Luther or John Calvin. By the early 1600s, war raged across much of the Holy Roman Empire.

>> At the Battle of White Mountain in 1620, forces led by the Holy Roman emperor destroyed the Bohemian army.

Bounce to Activate Flipped Video

Rise of Austria, Prussia, and Russia

The Thirty Years' War

A Fragmented "Empire" By early modern times, as the French philosopher Voltaire later observed, the Holy Roman Empire was neither holy, nor Roman, nor an empire. Instead, by the seventeenth century it had become a patchwork of several hundred small, separate states.

In theory, these states were ruled by the Holy Roman emperor, who was chosen by seven leading German princes called **electors.** In practice, the emperor had little power over the many rival princes. This power vacuum contributed to the outbreak of the Thirty Years' War.

Religion further divided the German states. The north had become largely Protestant, while the south remained Catholic.

Conflict Erupts The Thirty Years' War was actually a series of wars. It began in Bohemia, the present-day Czech Republic. Ferdinand, the Catholic Hapsburg king of Bohemia, sought to suppress Protestants and to assert royal power over nobles.

>> Objectives

Outline the causes and results of the Thirty Years' War.

Understand how Austria and Prussia emerged as great powers.

Explain the steps Peter the Great took to modernize Russia.

Describe how Russia grew under Peter the Great and Catherine the Great.

Describe how European nations tried to maintain a balance of power.

>> Key Terms

elector
mercenary
depopulation
Peace of Westphalia
Maria Theresa
War of the Austrian Succession
Prussia
Frederick William I
Frederick II
Peter the Great
westernization
boyar
autocratic
warm-water port
St. Petersburg
Catherine the Great
partition

In May 1618, a few rebellious Protestant nobles tossed two royal officials out of a castle window in Prague. This act, known as the Defenestration of Prague, sparked a general revolt, which Ferdinand moved to suppress. As both sides sought allies, what began as a local conflict widened into a general European war.

The following year, Ferdinand was elected Holy Roman Emperor. With the support of Spain, Poland, and other Catholic states, he tried to roll back the Reformation by force. Early on, he defeated rebellious Bohemians and their Protestant allies. Alarmed, Protestant powers like the Netherlands and Sweden sent troops into Germany.

Political motives quickly outweighed religious issues. Catholic and Protestant rulers shifted alliances to suit their own interests. At one point, Catholic France joined Lutheran Sweden against the Catholic Hapsburgs.

A Time of Chaos The fighting took a terrible toll. Roving armies of **mercenaries,** or soldiers for hire, burned villages, destroyed crops, and killed without mercy. Murder and torture were followed by famine and disease. Wolves, not seen in settled areas since the Middle Ages, stalked the deserted streets of once-bustling villages.

The war led to a severe **depopulation,** or reduction in population. Exact statistics do not exist, but historians estimate that as many as one third of the people in the German states may have died as a result of the war.

Peace Is Restored Finally, in 1648, the exhausted combatants accepted a series of treaties, known as the **Peace of Westphalia.** Because so many powers had been involved in the conflict, the treaties ended with a general European peace and settled other international problems.

Among the combatants, France emerged a clear winner, gaining territory on both its Spanish and German frontiers. The Hapsburgs were not so fortunate. They had to accept the almost total independence of all the princes of the Holy Roman Empire. In addition, the Netherlands and the Swiss Federation (present-day Switzerland) won recognition as independent states.

The Thirty Years' War left German lands divided into more than 360 separate states—"one for every day of the year." These states still acknowledged the rule of the Holy Roman emperor. Yet each state had its own government, currency, church, armed forces, and foreign policy.

The German-speaking states, if united, had the potential to become the most powerful nation in

Europe After the Thirty Years' War (1648)

>> **Analyze Maps** After the Thirty Years' War, the Peace of Westphalia redrew the map of Europe. Who controlled Bohemia after 1648?

Bounce to Activate Map

Europe. They remained fragmented, however, and would not be joined into a single nation for another 223 years.

IDENTIFY CAUSE AND EFFECT What were some effects of the Peace of Westphalia?

Hapsburg Austria Expands

The Thirty Years' War took a terrible toll on the people of the German states. Out of the ashes, however, rose two great German-speaking powers: Austria and Prussia. Like Louis XIV in France, their rulers tried to centralize power and rule as absolute monarchs.

A Diverse Empire Though weakened by war, the Hapsburgs still wanted to create a strong united state. They kept the title "Holy Roman emperor" but focused their attention on expanding their own lands. To Austria, their base of power, they added Bohemia, Hungary, and, later, parts of Poland and some Italian states.

Uniting these lands proved difficult. Not only were they divided by geography, they included a number of diverse peoples and cultures as well. By the 1700s, the Hapsburg Empire included Germans, Magyars, Slavs, and others. In many parts of the empire, people had their own languages, laws, political assemblies, and customs.

The Hapsburgs did exert some control over these diverse peoples. They sent German-speaking officials to Bohemia and Hungary and settled Austrians on lands they had seized in these provinces. They also put down revolts in Bohemia and Hungary. Still, the Hapsburgs never developed a fully centralized governmental system like that of France.

Empress Maria Theresa In the early 1700s, a new challenge threatened Hapsburg Austria. Emperor Charles VI had no male heir. His daughter, **Maria Theresa,** was intelligent and capable, but no woman had yet ruled Hapsburg lands in her own name. Charles persuaded other European rulers to recognize his daughter's right to succeed him. When he died, however, many ignored their pledge.

Shortly after Charles's death in 1740, Frederick II of Prussia seized the rich Hapsburg province of Silesia. This action sparked the eight-year **War of the Austrian Succession.**

>> The War of the Austrian Succession challenged Maria Theresa's right to rule the Holy Roman Empire. In 1745, French forces defeated British and Austrian troops at the Battle of Fontenoy, shown here.

Maria Theresa set off for Hungary to appeal for military help from her Hungarian subjects. The Hungarians were ordinarily unfriendly to the Hapsburgs. But she made a dramatic plea before an assembly of Hungarian nobles. According to one account, the nobles rose to their feet and shouted, "Our lives and blood for your Majesty!" She eventually got further help from Britain and Russia.

Reforms of an Absolute Monarch Maria Theresa never succeeded in forcing Frederick out of Silesia. Still, she did preserve her empire and win the support of most of her people. Equally important, she strengthened Hapsburg power by reorganizing the bureaucracy and improving tax collection. She forced nobles and clergy to pay taxes and tried to ease the burden of taxes and labor services on peasants.

Maria Theresa was an absolute monarch who believed that her decisions were for the good of her subjects. Like other rulers at the time, she strengthened royal authority by limiting the power of nobles and the Church.

IDENTIFY CAUSE AND EFFECT What caused the War of the Austrian Succession?

Prussia Emerges

While Austria was molding a strong Catholic state, **Prussia** emerged as a new Protestant German-speaking power in the north. In the 1600s, the Hohenzollern (HOH un tsahl urn) family ruled scattered lands across north Germany. After the Peace of Westphalia, ambitious Hohenzollern rulers united their holdings by taking over states between them. Like absolute rulers elsewhere, they imposed royal power on all their subjects and reduced the independence of their nobles, called Junkers (YOON kerz).

Creating an Efficient Bureaucracy To achieve their goals, Hohenzollern rulers set up an efficient central bureaucracy and forged one of the best-trained armies in Europe. One Prussian military leader boasted, "Prussia is not a state which possesses an army, but an army which possesses a state."

Emperor **Frederick William I,** who came to power in 1713, gained the loyalty of the Junkers by giving them positions in the army and government. His tactic reduced the nobles' independence and increased his own control. By 1740, Prussia was strong enough to challenge its rival Austria.

>> Hohenzollern rulers united their lands to create a Prussian empire. This 18th-century print shows a Prussian army camp in Pomerania, territory that lay between East Prussia and West Prussia.

Frederick the Great That year, young **Frederick II** inherited the throne. From an early age, Frederick was trained in the art of war, as his father insisted.

> His tutor must take the greatest pains to imbue my son with a sincere love for the soldier's profession and to impress upon him that nothing else in the world can confer upon a prince such fame and honor as the sword.
>
> —Frederick William I

However, Frederick preferred playing the flute and writing poetry. His father despised these pursuits and treated the young prince so badly that he tried to flee the country. Discovering these plans, Frederick William put his son in solitary confinement. Then he forced the 18-year-old prince to watch as the friend who had helped him was beheaded.

Frederick's harsh military training had an effect. After becoming king in 1740, Frederick II lost no time in using his army. He boldly seized Silesia from Austria, sparking the War of the Austrian Succession.

In several later wars, Frederick continued to brilliantly use his disciplined army, forcing all to recognize Prussia as a great power. His exploits and his power as an absolute monarch earned him the name Frederick the Great.

SUMMARIZE How did Frederick William increase his power?

Peter the Great Modernizes Russia

From 1604 to 1613, Russia was in a period of disorder, plagued by foreign invasions and internal rebellion. The rise of the first Romanov tsar restored a measure of order. Still, Russia remained a medieval state, untouched by the Renaissance or Reformation and largely isolated from Western Europe.

At the end of the century, a tsar emerged who was strong enough to regain the absolute power of earlier tsars. Just 10 years old when he took the throne in 1682, Peter I took control of the government seven years later. **Peter the Great,** as he came to be called, used his power to put Russia on the road to becoming a great modern power.

Peter Visits the West The young tsar was a striking figure, nearly seven feet tall, with a booming laugh and a furious temper. Although he was not well educated, he was immensely curious. He spent hours in the Moscow neighborhood where many Dutch,

Scottish, English, and other foreigners lived. There, he heard of the new technology that was helping Western European monarchs forge powerful empires.

In 1697, Peter set out to learn about Western technology and ways for himself. He spent hours walking the streets of European cities, noting the manners and homes of the people. He visited factories and art galleries, learned anatomy from a doctor, and even had a dentist teach him how to pull teeth.

In England, Peter was impressed by Parliament. "It is good," he said, "to hear subjects speaking truthfully and openly to their king."

The Westernization of Russia Returning to Russia, Peter brought a group of technical experts, teachers, and soldiers he had recruited in Europe. He then embarked on a policy of **westernization,** the adoption of Western ideas, technology, and culture.

Some changes had a symbolic meaning. He forced the **boyars,** or landowning nobles, to shave their traditional beards and wear Western-style clothes. To end the practice of secluding upper-class women in separate quarters, he held grand parties at which women and men were expected to dance together. Russian nobles opposed this radical mixing of the sexes in public, but they had to comply.

To impose his will, Peter became the most **autocratic** of Europe's absolute monarchs, meaning that he ruled with unlimited authority. Determined to centralize royal power, he brought the Russian Orthodox Church under his control. He forced the haughty boyars to serve the state in civilian or military jobs.

Extending Serfdom Peter knew that nobles would serve the state only if their own interests were protected. Therefore, he passed laws ensuring that nobles retained control over their lands. This included the serfs who were tied to those lands.

Under Peter's rule, serfdom spread in Russia at a time when it was dying out in Western Europe. Further, he forced some serfs to become soldiers or to work as laborers on roads, canals, and other government projects.

A Harsh, Effective Ruler Peter showed no mercy to any who resisted his new order. When elite palace guards revolted, he had more than 1,000 of the rebels tortured and executed. Then, as an example of his power, he left their rotting corpses outside the palace walls for months.

Peter was known not only for cruelty but also for remaking Russia. He imported Western technology,

>> In this image, Peter the Great is studying the building plans for St. Petersburg. The establishment of the city was one of his most important and long-lasting achievements.

Bounce to Activate Gallery

>> While visiting the Netherlands, Peter the Great disguised himself as a ship carpenter's apprentice to study shipbuilding. **Draw Conclusions** Why might Peter disguise himself like this?

simplified the Russian alphabet, and set up academies for the study of mathematics, science, and engineering. To pay for his reforms, Peter adopted mercantilist policies, such as encouraging exports. He improved waterways and canals, developed mining and textile manufacturing, and backed new trading companies. Peter succeeded in refashioning Russia from a medieval backwater into a rising European—and Asian—power.

CATEGORIZE What policies did Peter use to solidify his control over the nobles?

>> Peter wanted to gain access to a warm-water port and the open sea. His first step toward this goal was to capture Azov, a town in what is now southwestern Russia, from the Turks. This painting shows the successful capture of Azov in 1696.

Expanding Russia's Borders

From his earliest days as tsar, Peter worked to build Russia's military power. He created the largest standing army in Europe, built a world-class navy from scratch, and set out to extend Russian borders to the west and south. To achieve these goals meant fighting Russia's neighbors.

Seeking a Warm-Water Seaport Peter's chief goal was to win a **warm-water port,** a port that was not frozen in winter. Russian seaports, located along the Arctic Ocean, were covered in ice most of the year. A warm-water port would increase Russia's ability to trade with the West.

The nearest warm-water coast was located along the Black Sea. To gain control of this territory, Peter had to push through the powerful Ottoman Empire. In the end, Peter was unable to defeat the Ottomans and gain his warm-water port. The drive to achieve this goal motivated future Russian tsars, and by the late 1700s, Catherine the Great would succeed.

>> **Analyze Maps** This historical map shows the city of St. Petersburg, built by Peter the Great. What are the benefits of St. Petersburg's location? What are the challenges?

The Great Northern War In 1700, Peter began a long war against the kingdom of Sweden, which at the time dominated the Baltic region. Early on, Russia suffered humiliating defeats. A Swedish force of only 8,000 men defeated a Russian army five times its size. Undaunted, Peter rebuilt his army, modeling it after European armies.

Finally, in 1709, he defeated the Swedes and won territory along the Baltic Sea. On this land, Peter would build a magnificent new capital city, **St. Petersburg.**

A "Window on the West" St. Petersburg became the great symbol of Peter's desire to forge a modern, Western-oriented Russia nation. Seeking to open a "window on the West," he located the city along the swampy shores of the Neva River, near the Baltic coast. He forced tens of thousands of serfs to drain the swamps. Many thousands died, but Peter's plan for the city succeeded.

On his journey to the West, Peter had visited Louis XIV's splendid new palace of Versailles. Like the Sun King, Peter invited the best European architects and artisans to design and build the palaces for his new city. Peter even planned the city's parks and boulevards himself, modeling them on those he had seen at Versailles.

Expanding to the East Peter also expanded the Russian empire eastward toward the Pacific. Russian traders and raiders also crossed the plains and rivers of Siberia. Under Peter, Russia signed a treaty with China that recognized Russia's claim to lands north of China and defined the common border of the two empires.

In the early 1700s, Peter hired the Danish navigator Vitus Bering to explore what became known as the Bering Strait between Siberia and Alaska. After Peter's death, Russian traders built outposts in Alaska and northern California. Few Russians moved east of the Ural Mountains at this time, but the expansion made Russia the largest country in the world. It still is today, nearly 300 years later.

A Mixed Legacy When Peter died in 1725, he left a mixed legacy. He had expanded Russian territory, gained ports on the Baltic Sea, and created a mighty army. He had also ended Russia's long period of isolation. From the 1700s on, Russia would be increasingly involved in the affairs of Western Europe. Yet many of Peter's ambitious reforms died with him. Nobles, for example, soon ignored his policy of service to the state.

Like earlier tsars, Peter the Great had used terror to enforce his absolute power. His policies contributed to the growth of serfdom, which served only to widen the gap between Russia and the West that Peter had sought to narrow.

IDENTIFY CAUSE AND EFFECT What impact did Peter's defeat of Sweden have on Russia's expansion?

Catherine the Great

Peter's successors in the Romanov dynasty were ineffective rulers. Russian nobles quickly reasserted their independence. Then a new monarch took the

>> The Bering expedition brought the Russians to the west coast of North America.

>> Catherine the Great, shown here in a 1794 portrait, took over the rule of Russia after the assassination of her husband, Tsar Peter III.

reins of power firmly in hand. She became known to history as **Catherine the Great.**

A German Princess Becomes Tsar A German princess by birth, Catherine came to Russia at the age of 15 to wed the heir to the Russian throne. She learned Russian, embraced the Russian Orthodox faith, and won the loyalty of the people.

In 1762, a group of Russian army officers loyal to her deposed and murdered her mentally unstable husband, Tsar Peter III. Whether or not Catherine was involved in the assassination is uncertain. In any case, with the support of the military, she ascended the Russian throne.

Catherine Embraces Reform Catherine proved to be an efficient, energetic empress. She reorganized the provincial government, codified laws, and began state-sponsored education for both boys and girls.

Like Peter the Great, Catherine embraced Western ideas and worked to bring Russia fully into European cultural and political life. At court, she encouraged French language and customs, wrote histories and plays, and organized performances. She was also a serious student of the French thinkers who led the intellectual movement known as the Enlightenment.

An Absolute Monarch Like rulers in France and Spain, Catherine was an absolute monarch. Like them, she could be ruthless. She granted a charter to the boyars outlining important rights, such as exemption from taxes. She also allowed them to increase their stranglehold on the peasants. When peasants rebelled against the harsh burdens of serfdom, Catherine harshly suppressed the uprisings. Under Catherine, conditions grew even worse for Russian peasants and serfdom continued to spread.

Like Peter the Great, Catherine was determined to expand Russia's borders. After a war against the Ottoman Empire, she achieved the Russian dream of a warm-water port on the Black Sea. She also took steps to seize territory from neighboring Poland.

The Partitions of Poland Poland-Lithuania had once been a great European power. However, its rulers were unable to centralize their power or diminish the influence of the Polish nobility. In the 1770s, three powerful neighboring monarchs—Catherine of Russia, Frederick II of Prussia, and Joseph II of Austria—hungrily eyed Poland.

To avoid fighting one another, the three monarchs agreed in 1772 to **partition,** or divide up, Poland. Poland was partitioned three times between the 1770s and 1790s. Russia took the eastern part, where many Russians and Ukrainians lived. Austria and

>> Analyze Maps Russia expanded its borders from 1689 to 1796. Which five cities could probably serve as warm-water ports?

Prussia divided up the rest. By 1795, the independent kingdom of Poland had vanished from the map. Not until 1919 would a free Polish state reappear.

COMPARE How were Catherine's goals similar to those of Peter?

Five Great European Powers

By 1750, five European powers had come to dominate European affairs. They were Austria, Prussia, France, Britain, and Russia. All five had strong centralized governments. Although Spain and the Ottoman Empire ruled parts of Europe, these once powerful empires were in decline.

Struggles for Power As these five nation-states competed with one another, they formed various alliances to maintain the balance of power. Though nations sometimes switched partners, two basic rivalries persisted. Prussia battled Austria for control of the German-speaking states. At the same time, Britain and France competed for power and influence both in Europe and in their growing overseas empires.

On occasion, these rivalries resulted in worldwide conflict. The Seven Years' War, which lasted from 1756 until 1763, was fought on four continents.

In Europe, Prussia and Britain battled Austria, France, Russia, and Sweden. Britain and France also battled for power in India, Africa, and North America, where the conflict became known as the French and Indian War.

Absolutism at Its Peak Absolutism reached its peak in the mid-1700s. Four of the five great European powers were ruled by absolute monarchs. Britain, with its strong Parliament, was the only exception.

At the same time, new ideas were circulating about natural rights and the role of government. In time, demands for change and reform would topple French absolutism, revolutionize European societies, and transform the balance of power in Europe.

DESCRIBE How did European nations maintain a balance of power?

>> The Seven Years' War in Europe pitted Europe, Prussia, and Britain against Austria, France, Russia, and Sweden. This painting shows a December 1757 battle in which the Prussians defeated the Austrians.

ASSESSMENT

1. **Identify Cause and Effect** What were the causes and results of the Thirty Years' War?
2. **Identify** How were the goals of Austria and Prussia similar?
3. **Describe** How did European nations try to maintain a balance of power?
4. **List** What steps did Peter the Great take to modernize Russia?
5. **Describe** How did Russia grow under Peter the Great and Catherine the Great?

>> Henry VIII consulted with Parliament frequently. Here, he presides as chairman over the House of Lords.

Bounce to Activate Flipped Video

1.3 During the age of absolutism, English monarchs, like rulers on the continent, tried to increase royal power and claim the divine right to rule. Their efforts, however, ran into the obstacle of Parliament, which during the Middle Ages had acquired the power of the purse. Only Parliament could grant monarchs the funds they needed to pursue their ambitions. And Parliament at times stood firm against royal absolutism.

>> Objectives

Describe the relationship between Parliament and the monarchy under the Tudors and Stuarts.

Explain how English government developed after the English Civil War.

Identify the causes of the Glorious Revolution and the ideas contained in the English Bill of Rights.

Identify the characteristics of limited monarchy and constitutional government in England.

>> Key Terms

James I
dissenter
Puritan
Charles I
Oliver Cromwell
English Bill of Rights
limited monarchy
constitutional government
cabinet
prime minister
oligarchy

Triumph of Parliament in England

Tudor Monarchs Work with Parliament

Henry VIII From 1485 to 1603, England was ruled by Tudor monarchs. Although the Tudors believed in divine right, they shrewdly recognized the value of good relations with Parliament. When Henry VIII broke with the Roman Catholic Church, he turned to Parliament to legalize his actions. Parliament approved the Act of Supremacy, making the monarch head of the Church of England.

A constant need for money led Henry to consult Parliament frequently. Although he had inherited a bulging treasury, he quickly used up his funds fighting overseas wars. To levy new taxes, the king had to seek the approval of Parliament. Members of Parliament tended to vote as Henry's agents instructed. Still, they became accustomed to being consulted on important matters.

Elizabeth I When Henry's daughter Elizabeth I gained the throne, she too both consulted and controlled Parliament. In theory, the monarch called Parliament for advice. In practice, Elizabeth rarely asked for its view. During her 45-year reign, she summoned Parliament only 13 times. All but one time, she asked for money.

When Parliament met, the queen's advisers conveyed her wishes. Certain subjects, such as foreign policy or the queen's marriage, were forbidden. Her skill in handling Parliament helped make "Good Queen Bess" a popular and successful ruler.

CHECK UNDERSTANDING Why did Henry VIII work with Parliament?

Stuart Monarchs Clash with Parliament

Elizabeth died childless in 1603. The throne passed to her relatives the Stuarts, the ruling family of Scotland. The Stuarts were neither as popular as the Tudors nor as skillful in dealing with Parliament. They also inherited problems that Henry and Elizabeth had long suppressed. The result was a "century of revolution" that pitted the Stuart monarchs against Parliament.

James I Asserts Divine Right When the first Stuart monarch, **James I,** took the throne, he agreed to rule according to English laws and customs. Soon, however, he was lecturing Parliament about divine right. In 1610, the king made a speech in Parliament.

> The state of Monarchy is the supremest thing upon earth; for kings are not only God's lieutenants upon earth and sit upon God's throne, but even by God himself they are called gods. . . . Kings are justly called gods for that they exercise a manner or resemblance of Divine power on earth . . . And to the King is due both the affection of the soul and the service of the body of his subjects....
>
> —King James I

Parliament was not impressed with the king's claim to rule by divine right. Instead, James faced

>> James I, the first Stuart king of England, ruled England from 1603 to 1625.

>> King James gave Greek and Hebrew scholars specific instructions for translating the Christian Bible into English. The King James Bible is considered a literary masterpiece.

repeated clashes with Parliament, mostly over money and foreign policy that involved the king's wars in Europe. James lived extravagantly and had to ask Parliament for funds to finance his lavish court.

More than once, when members wanted to discuss foreign policy before voting funds, James dissolved Parliament and raised money without their consent. These actions poisoned relations between the king and Parliament.

James also found himself embroiled in religious disputes. He clashed with **dissenters,** Protestants who differed with the Church of England. One group were called **Puritans** because they sought to "purify" the English church of Catholic practices. Puritans called for simpler services and a more democratic church without bishops. James rejected their demands, vowing to "harry them out of this land or else do worse."

Charles I Clashes with Parliament In 1625, **Charles I** inherited the throne. Like his father, Charles behaved like an absolute monarch. He imprisoned his foes without trial and squeezed the nation for money. By 1628, however, his need to raise taxes forced Charles to summon Parliament. Before voting any funds, Parliament insisted that Charles sign the Petition of Right.

>> Charles I and his troops stormed into the House of Commons to arrest radicals.

Bounce to Activate Timeline

This document prohibited the king from raising taxes without Parliament's consent or from jailing anyone without legal justification.

Charles did sign the Petition, but he then dissolved Parliament in 1629. For 11 years, he ignored the Petition and ruled without Parliament. During that time, he created bitter enemies, especially among Puritans. His Archbishop of Canterbury, William Laud, tried to force all clergy to follow strict Anglican rules, dismissing or imprisoning dissenters. Many people felt that the archbishop was trying to revive Catholic practices.

In 1637, Charles and Laud tried to impose the Anglican prayer book on Scotland. The Calvinist Scots revolted. To get funds to suppress the Scottish rebellion, Charles once again had to summon Parliament in 1640. When it met, however, Parliament launched its own revolt.

The Long Parliament Begins The 1640 Parliament became known as the Long Parliament because it lasted on and off until 1653.

Its actions triggered the greatest political revolution in English history. In a mounting struggle with Charles I, Parliament tried and executed his chief ministers, including Archbishop Laud. It called for the abolition of bishops and declared that the Parliament could not be dissolved without its own consent.

Charles lashed back. In 1642, he led troops into the House of Commons to arrest its most radical leaders. They escaped through a back door and soon raised their own army. The clash now moved to the battlefield.

DESCRIBE What was the Petition of Right?

The English Civil War

The civil war that followed lasted from 1642 to 1651. Like the Fronde that occurred about the same time in France, the English Civil War posed a major challenge to absolutism. But while the forces of royal power won in France, in England the forces of revolution triumphed.

Cavaliers and Roundheads At first, the odds seemed to favor the supporters of Charles I, called Cavaliers. Many Cavaliers were wealthy nobles, proud of their plumed hats and fashionably long hair. Well trained in dueling and warfare, the Cavaliers expected a quick victory. But their foes proved to be tough fighters with the courage of their convictions.

The forces of Parliament were composed of country gentry, town-dwelling manufacturers, and Puritan clergy. They were called Roundheads because their hair was cut close around their heads. The Roundheads found a leader of genius in **Oliver Cromwell.** A Puritan member of the lesser gentry, Cromwell proved himself to be a skilled general.

He organized the "New Model Army" for Parliament into a disciplined fighting force. Cromwell's army defeated the Cavaliers in a series of decisive battles. By 1647, the king was in the hands of parliamentary forces.

Execution of the King Eventually, Parliament set up a court to put the king on trial. It condemned him to death as "a tyrant, traitor, murderer, and public enemy." On a cold January day in 1649, Charles I stood on a scaffold surrounded by his foes. "I am a martyr of the people," he declared. Showing no fear, the king told the executioner that he himself would give the sign for him to strike. After a brief prayer, Charles knelt and placed his neck on the block. On the agreed signal, the executioner severed the king's neck with a single stroke.

The execution sent shock waves throughout Europe. In the past, a king had occasionally been assassinated or killed in battle. But for the first time, a ruling monarch had been tried and executed by his own people. The parliamentary forces had sent a clear message that, in England, no ruler could claim absolute power and ignore the rule of law.

IDENTIFY CAUSE AND EFFECT What was the result of the English Civil War?

>> Oliver Cromwell led parliamentary forces in the English Civil War.

>> Charles I was beheaded in January 1649. It was the first time a ruling monarch had been tried and executed by his own people.

Cromwell and the Commonwealth

After the execution of Charles I, the House of Commons abolished the monarchy and the House of Lords, and established the Church of England. It declared England a republic, known as the Commonwealth, under the leadership of Oliver Cromwell.

Challenges to the Commonwealth The new government faced many threats. Supporters of Charles II, the uncrowned heir to the throne, attacked England by way of Ireland and Scotland. Cromwell led forces into Ireland and brutally crushed the uprising. He then took harsh measures against the Irish Catholic majority that are still vividly remembered in that nation today. In 1652, Parliament passed a law exiling most Catholics to barren land in the west of Ireland. Any Catholic found disobeying this order could be killed on sight.

Squabbles also splintered forces within the Commonwealth. One group, called Levellers, thought that poor men should have as much say in government as the gentry, lawyers, and other leading citizens. "The poorest he that is in England hath a life to live as the greatest he," wrote one Leveller. In addition, woman Levellers asserted their right to petition Parliament. These ideas horrified the gentry, who dominated Parliament.

Cromwell suppressed the Levellers, as well as more radical groups who threatened ownership of private property. In 1653, as the challenges to order grew, Cromwell took the title Lord Protector. From then on, he ruled as a virtual dictator, using the army to back up his orders.

England Under the Puritans Under the Commonwealth, Puritan preachers tried to root out godlessness and impose a "rule of saints." The English Civil War thus ushered in a social revolution as well as a political one.

Parliament enacted a series of laws designed to make sure that Sunday was set aside for religious observance.

Anyone over the age of 14 who was caught "profaning the Lord's Day" could be fined. To the Puritans, theaters were frivolous. So, like John Calvin in Geneva, Cromwell closed all theaters. Puritans also frowned on taverns, gambling, and dancing.

Puritans felt that every Christian, rich and poor, must be able to read the Bible. To spread religious knowledge, they encouraged education for all people. By mid-century, families from all classes were sending their children to school, girls as well as boys.

Puritans pushed for changes in marriage to ensure fidelity. In addition to marriages based on business interests, they encouraged marriages based on love. Still, as in the past, women were seen mainly as subordinate to men.

Although Cromwell did not tolerate open worship by Roman Catholics, he believed in religious freedom for other Protestant groups. He even welcomed Jews back to England after more than 350 years of exile.

Puritan Rule Ends Oliver Cromwell died in 1658. Soon after, the Puritans lost their grip on England. Many people were tired of military rule and strict Puritan ways. In 1660, a newly elected Parliament invited Charles II to return to England from exile.

England's "kingless decade" ended with the Restoration, or return of the monarchy. Yet Puritan ideas about morality, equality, government, and

>> Analyze Information The Puritans sought societal and moral reforms. How did Puritans feel about education?

education endured. These ideas were already shaping England's colonies in North America, where many Puritans had settled.

DESCRIBE What was the Commonwealth?

From Restoration to Glorious Revolution

In late May 1660, cheering crowds welcomed Charles II back to London. An observer described the celebration as a triumph.

> This day came in his Majesties Charles the Second to London after a sad, and long Exile . . . with a Triumph of above 20,000 horse and [soldiers], brandishing their swords, and shouting with inexpressible joy; the [ways strewn] with flowers, the bells ringing, the streets hung with [tapestry].
>
> —John Evelyn, Diary

>> Crowds welcomed Charles II back after the monarchy was restored.

A Popular King With his charm and flashing wit, young Charles II was a popular ruler. He reopened theaters and taverns and presided over a lively court in the manner of Louis XIV.

Charles restored the official Church of England but encouraged toleration of other Protestants such as Presbyterians, Quakers, and Baptists. Although Charles accepted the Petition of Right, he shared his father's belief in absolute monarchy and secretly had Catholic sympathies. Still, he shrewdly avoided his father's mistakes in dealing with Parliament.

Charles was a strong supporter of science and the arts. He helped found the Royal Society, a group formed to advance scientific knowledge. Its early members, such as Isaac Newton, Robert Hooke, and Robert Boyle, advanced the study of mathematics, biology, physics, and chemistry. Charles was equally supportive of the arts, especially architecture. After the Great Fire of 1666 destroyed much of London, Charles appointed the great architect, Sir Christopher Wren, to rebuild the city.

The Glorious Revolution Charles's brother, James II, inherited the throne in 1685. Unlike Charles, James practiced his Catholic faith openly. He angered his subjects by suspending laws on a whim and appointing Catholics to high office. Many English Protestants feared that James would restore the Roman Catholic Church.

In 1688, alarmed parliamentary leaders invited James's Protestant daughter, Mary, and her Dutch Protestant husband, William III of Orange, to become rulers of England. When William and Mary landed with their army, James II fled to France. This bloodless overthrow of the king became known as the Glorious Revolution.

The English Bill of Rights Before they could be crowned, William and Mary had to accept several acts passed by Parliament in 1689 that became known as the **English Bill of Rights.** The Bill of Rights ensured the superiority of Parliament over the monarchy. It required the monarch to summon Parliament regularly and ensured that the House of Commons kept control over spending. A king or queen could no longer interfere in parliamentary debates or suspend laws. The Bill of Rights also barred any Roman Catholic from sitting on the throne.

The Bill of Rights also restated the traditional legal rights of English citizens, such as trial by jury. It abolished excessive fines and cruel or unjust punishment. It affirmed the principle of habeas corpus. That is, no person could be held in prison without first being charged with a specific crime. The legal ideas contained in the English Bill of

Rights would later have a strong influence on the United States.

Soon after, the separate Toleration Act of 1689 granted limited religious freedom to Puritans, Quakers, and other Protestant dissenters. Still, only members of the Church of England could hold public office. And Catholics were allowed no religious freedom.

A Limited Monarchy The Glorious Revolution turned England into a **limited monarchy,** a type of government in which a constitution or legislative body limits the monarch's powers. English rulers still had much power, but they had to obey the law and govern in partnership with Parliament. In an age of absolute monarchy elsewhere in Europe, the limited monarchy in England was quite radical.

Among the people who lived at the time of the Glorious Revolution was the political thinker, John Locke. Events in England helped shape his philosophy. Much later, Locke's ideas about government and natural rights would influence the Americans who drew up the Declaration of Independence and the United States Constitution.

DEFINE What was the Glorious Revolution?

England's Constitutional Government Evolves

In the century following the Glorious Revolution, three new political institutions arose in Britain: political parties, the cabinet, and the office of prime minister. The appearance of these institutions was part of the evolution of Britain's **constitutional government**—that is, a government whose power is defined and limited by law.

Political Parties In the late 1600s, political parties emerged in England as a powerful force in politics. At first, there were just two political parties—Tories and Whigs.

Tories were generally aristocrats who sought to preserve older traditions. They supported broad royal powers and a dominant Anglican Church.

Whigs backed the ideas embodied in the Glorious Revolution. They were more likely to reflect urban business interests, support religious toleration, and favor Parliament over the crown. For much of the 1700s Whigs dominated Parliament.

The Cabinet System The cabinet, another new feature of government, evolved in the 1700s after the British throne passed to a German prince. George I spoke no English and relied on the leaders

Influence of the Glorious Revolution

	English Bill of Rights	Writings of John Locke	Constitutional Government
OUTCOME IN ENGLAND	• People elect representatives to Parliament, which is supreme over the monarch. • All citizens have natural rights.	• People have natural rights such as life, liberty, and property. • There is a social contract between people and government.	• Government is limited and defined by law. • Political parties, the cabinet, and the office of prime minister arise.
	↓	↓	↓
IMPACT ON THE UNITED STATES	• Colonists believed that they too had rights, including the right to elect people to represent them.	• Locke's ideas shaped the American Revolution and the writing of the Declaration of Independence and the Constitution.	• Government is limited and defined by law. • The new nation formed a constitutional government with two parties and even stronger provisions for the separation of powers.

>> **Analyze Charts** A common protest during the American Revolution was "no taxation without representation." Which outcome in England influenced that idea?

Bounce to Activate Gallery

in Parliament to help him rule. Under George I and his German-born son George II, a handful of parliamentary advisors set policy. They came to be referred to as the **cabinet** because of the small room, or "cabinet," where they met.

In time, the cabinet gained official status. It was made up of leaders of the majority party in the House of Commons. The cabinet remained in power so long as it enjoyed the support of the Commons.

If the Commons voted against a cabinet decision, the cabinet resigned. The cabinet system (also called a parliamentary system) was later adopted by other countries in Europe and elsewhere around the globe.

The Prime Minister Over time, the head of the cabinet came to be known as the **prime minister.** This person was always the leader of the majority party in the House of Commons.

Eventually, the prime minister became the chief official of the British government and the prime minister's power would exceed that of the monarch. From 1721 to 1742, the able Whig leader Robert Walpole molded the cabinet into a unified body by requiring all members to agree on major issues. Although the title was not yet in use, Walpole is often called Britain's first prime minister.

>> The marketplace brought different classes of people together, but the classes differed widely in terms of political power. **Interpret** In this painting, how can you tell the different classes apart?

Rule by an Oligarchy Even as Parliament and the cabinet assumed new powers, British government was far from democratic. Rather, it was an **oligarchy**—a government in which the ruling power belongs to a few people.

Landowning aristocrats were believed to be the "natural" ruling class. The highest nobles held seats in the House of Lords. Other wealthy landowners and rich business leaders in the cities controlled elections to the House of Commons. The right to vote was limited to a relatively few male property owners, whose votes were often openly bought.

The lives of most people contrasted sharply with those of the ruling elite. The majority made a meager living from the land.

In the 1700s, even that poor existence was threatened. Wealthy landowners, attempting to increase agricultural production, bought up farms and took over common lands, evicting tenant farmers and small landowners. Because they controlled Parliament, they easily passed laws ensuring that their actions were legal. A small but growing middle class included successful merchants and manufacturers. These prosperous and often wealthy people controlled affairs in the towns and cities. Some improved their social standing by marrying into the landed gentry. The middle class also produced talented inventors and entrepreneurs who would soon help usher in the Industrial Revolution.

CHECK UNDERSTANDING What were the new political institutions that developed as a result of Britain's constitutional government?

ASSESSMENT

1. **Check Understanding** Why was James I resistant to working with Parliament?
2. **Define** What was the Long Parliament?
3. **Recall** Who was Oliver Cromwell?
4. **Describe** What did the English Bill of Rights mean to Parliament?
5. **Identify Central Ideas** What is the main feature of a constitutional government?

Primary Sources

English Bill of Rights

Introduction

When the Catholic king, James II, was forced from the English throne in 1688, Parliament offered the crown to his Protestant daughter Mary and her husband, William of Orange. Parliament, however, insisted that William and Mary submit to a bill of rights. This document sums up the powers that Parliament had been seeking since the Petition of Right in 1628.

The second primary source is from The Petition of Right, which Parliament wrote in 1628 to protest the overreach of authority by King Charles I.

>> William and Mary accept the crown.

Primary Source

Whereas, the late King James II . . . did endeavor to subvert and extirpate [eliminate] the Protestant religion and the laws and liberties of this kingdom . . . and whereas the said late king James II having abdicated the government, and the throne being vacant. . . . The said Lords [Parliament] . . . being now assembled in a full and free representative [body] of this nation . . . do in the first place . . . declare.

- That the pretended [untruthfully claimed] power of suspending the laws or the execution of laws by regal authority without consent of Parliament is illegal;
- That the pretended power of dispensing with laws or the execution of laws by regal authority, as it hath been assumed and exercised of late, is illegal; . . .
- That levying [collecting] money for or to the use of the Crown by pretence of prerogative [a right exclusive to a king or queen], without grant of Parliament, for longer time, or in other manner than the same is or shall be granted, is illegal;
- That it is the right of the subjects to petition [make a request of] the king, and all commitments and prosecutions for such petitioning are illegal;

CITE EVIDENCE On what grounds did Parliament draw up the English Bill of Rights?

- That the raising or keeping a standing army within the kingdom in time of peace, unless it be with consent of Parliament, is against law;
- That the subjects which are Protestants may have arms for their defence suitable to their conditions and as allowed by law;
- That election of members of Parliament ought to be free;
- That the freedom of speech and debates or proceedings in Parliament ought not to be impeached [discredited] or questioned in any court or place out of Parliament;
- That excessive bail ought not to be required, nor excessive fines imposed, nor cruel and unusual punishments inflicted;
- That jurors ought to be duly [done at a proper time] impaneled [registered on a panel of jurors] and returned [released from service], and jurors which pass upon men in trials for high treason ought to be freeholders [property owners with unconditional rights];
- That all grants and promises of fines and forfeitures of particular persons before conviction are illegal and void;

- And that for redress [correction] of all grievances, and for the amending, strengthening and preserving of the laws, Parliaments ought to be held frequently.

DRAW CONCLUSIONS Why might Parliament have included the point that its members should be elected freely? What larger concept is supported by this point?

Primary Source

III. And whereas also by the statute called 'The Great Charter of the Liberties of England,' it is declared and enacted, that no freeman may be taken or imprisoned or be disseized [deprived] of his freehold or liberties [or his free customs, or be outlawed or exiled, or in any manner destroyed] but by the lawful judgment of his peers, or by the law of the land.

VI. And whereas of late great companies of soldiers and mariners have been dispersed into divers counties of the realm, and the inhabitants against their wills have been compelled to receive them into their houses, and there to suffer them to sojourn against the laws and customs of this realm, and to the great grievance and vexation of the people.

X. They do therefore humbly pray your most excellent Majesty, that no man hereafter be compelled to make or yield any gift, loan, benevolence, tax, or such like charge, without common consent by act of parliament; and that none be called to make answer, or take such oath, or to give attendance, or be confined, or otherwise molested or disquieted concerning the same or for refusal thereof; and that no freeman, in any such manner as is before mentioned, be imprisoned or detained; and that your Majesty would be pleased to remove the said soldiers and mariners, and that your people may not be so burdened in time to come.

CITE EVIDENCE How did the Petition of Right protect a person who is arrested?

ASSESSMENT

1. **Analyze Interactions** Review the American Declaration of Independence. What similarities do you notice between the two documents?
2. **Determine Central Ideas** Which ideas in the English Bill of Rights and the Petition of Right influenced the formation of the United States government?
3. **Cite Evidence** How did the English Bill of Rights expand the rights of common Englishmen? Cite specific examples from the text to support your answer.
4. **Determine Central Ideas** How did the English Bill of Rights make Parliament more powerful? Provide specific examples from the text in your response.

>> Sir Isaac Newton was a key figure in the Scientific Revolution. Among his many discoveries was gravity.

Bounce to Activate Flipped Video

1.4 During the Scientific Revolution of the 1500s and 1600s, European scholars made advances in physics, chemistry, biology, and medicine. Like ancient scholars, the thinkers of the Scientific Revolution relied on reason, but they also developed a new "scientific method" to test their theories and observations. Using mathematics and the scientific method, they discovered a series of laws that governed the physical universe.

>> Objectives

Describe how science led to the Enlightenment.

Explain the political philosophies of Hobbes, Locke, Voltaire, Montesquieu, and Rousseau.

Summarize the economic ideas of the physiocrats and Adam Smith.

Describe how Enlightenment ideas spread and influenced the arts.

Understand the role of enlightened despots.

>> Key Terms

natural law
Thomas Hobbes
John Locke
social contract
natural rights
philosophe
Montesquieu
Voltaire
Jean-Jacques Rousseau
laissez faire
Adam Smith
free market
free enterprise system
censorship
salon
baroque
rococo
enlightened despot
Joseph II

The Enlightenment

Scientific Revolution Leads to the Enlightenment

The Scientific Revolution, in turn, helped spark the Enlightenment in which thinkers emphasized the use of reason to uncover "natural" laws that governed human life. During the Enlightenment of the 1600s and 1700s, thinkers developed new ideas about government and basic human rights.

While scientists and mathematicians developed laws about natural phenomena like the law of gravity, European thinkers searched for similar laws that governed human life. Like scientists, they emphasized the power of reason, rather than religious beliefs. During the 1600s and 1700s, these thinkers developed new ideas about **natural laws**—unchanging principles, discovered through reason, that govern all human conduct.

Using the methods of the Scientific Revolution, European thinkers and reformers set out to study human behavior and solve the problems of society. The German philosopher Immanuel Kant used the word *enlightenment* to describe this new approach. During the Enlightenment, also called the Age of Reason, philosophers emphasized the power of human reason to uncover general laws of nature that shape all of human experience.

The Enlightenment continued a trend that began during the Renaissance. During the Middle Ages, Europe had been dominated by the Church. Feudal monarchs, like later absolute rulers, looked to the Church to justify their royal authority. The Renaissance placed a new emphasis on secularism and individual achievement.

The Scientific Revolution and Enlightenment also stressed science and natural law rather than religious authority. Enlightenment thinkers turned away from absolutism and divine right toward democracy and individual rights. Their ideas would encourage revolutionary leaders in Europe and the Americas. Though Christianity would remain a strong force in western culture, most governments became increasingly secular. The French Revolution in particular would see a radical decline in Church influence on government.

EXPLAIN How was the Scientific Revolution directly related to the development of the concept of natural law?

Hobbes and Locke on the Role of Government

During the 1600s, two English thinkers, **Thomas Hobbes** and **John Locke,** set forth ideas that were to become key to the Enlightenment. Both men lived through the upheavals of the English Civil War. Yet they reached different conclusions about human nature and the purpose and proper role of government.

Hobbes Argues for Powerful Government In 1651, Thomas Hobbes outlined his ideas in a work titled *Leviathan*. In it, he argued that people were naturally cruel, greedy, and selfish. If not strictly controlled, they would fight, rob, and oppress one another. Life in the "state of nature"—without laws or other control—would be "solitary, poor, nasty, brutish, and short."

To escape that "brutish" life, said Hobbes, people entered into a **social contract,** an agreement by which they gave up their freedom for an organized society. Hobbes believed that only a powerful government could ensure an orderly society. For him, such a government was an absolute monarchy, which could impose order and compel obedience. Not surprisingly, Hobbes had supported the Stuart kings in their struggle against Parliament.

Locke Focuses on Natural Rights John Locke had a more optimistic view of human nature. He thought people were basically reasonable and moral.

Further, they had certain **natural rights,** or rights that belonged to all humans from birth. These included the right to life, liberty, and property.

In *Two Treatises of Government,* Locke argued that people formed governments to protect their natural rights. The best kind of government, he said, had limited power and was accepted by all citizens. Thus, unlike Hobbes, Locke rejected absolute monarchy.

Locke proposed a radical idea about this time. A government, he said, has an obligation to the people it governs. If a government fails its obligations or violates people's natural rights, the people have the right to overthrow that government. Given these ideas, Locke supported the overthrow of James II in the Glorious Revolution of 1688. In Locke's view, the king deserved to lose his throne because he had violated the rights of the English people.

Locke's idea would one day influence leaders of the American Revolution, such as Benjamin Franklin, Thomas Jefferson, and James Madison. Locke's idea of the right of revolution would also echo across Europe and Latin America in the centuries that followed.

>> This illustration from Thomas Hobbes's book *Leviathan* reflects his belief in a powerful ruler. The monarch rises above all society, just as the mythological Leviathan, or sea monster, rises above all the seas.

Bounce to Activate Chart

CONTRAST How did Hobbes and Locke differ in their views on the role of government?

The *Philosophes*

In the 1700s, France saw a flowering of Enlightenment thought. French ***philosophes*** (fee loh ZOHFS), or philosophers, felt that nothing was beyond the reach of human reason. As they examined ideas about government, law and society, they called for reforms to protect people's natural rights. Their ideas, like those of Locke, would shift political thought and strongly influence the development of democratic-republican government.

Montesquieu Calls for Separation of Powers

An early and influential *philosophe* was Baron de **Montesquieu** (MAHN tus kyoo). Montesquieu studied the governments of Europe, from Italy to England. He read about ancient and medieval Europe, and learned about Chinese and Native American cultures. He sharply criticized absolute monarchy.

In 1748, Montesquieu published *The Spirit of the Laws,* in which he discussed governments throughout history. Montesquieu felt that the best way to protect liberty was to divide the various functions and powers of government among three branches: the legislative, executive, and judicial.

He also felt that each branch of government should be able to serve as a check on the other two, an idea that we call checks and balances. Montesquieu's beliefs would influence the Framers of the United States Constitution.

Voltaire Supports Freedom of Thought

Probably the most famous of the *philosophes* was François-Marie Arouet, who took the name **Voltaire.** "My trade," said Voltaire, "is to say what I think." He used biting wit as a weapon to expose the abuses of his day. He targeted corrupt officials and idle aristocrats. With his pen, he battled inequality, injustice, and superstition. He detested the slave trade and deplored religious prejudice.

Voltaire's outspoken attacks offended both the French government and the Catholic Church. He was imprisoned and forced into exile. Even as he saw his books outlawed and sometimes even burned, he continued to defend the principle of freedom of speech.

Diderot Edits the *Encyclopedia*

Denis Diderot (DEE duh roh) worked for years to produce a 28-volume set of books called the *Encyclopedia.* As the editor, Diderot did more than just compile articles. His purpose was "to change the general way

Montesquieu: Separation of Powers

	FUNCTION	EXAMPLES IN U.S. GOVERNMENT	EXAMPLES IN BRITISH GOVERNMENT
LEGISLATIVE	Creates law	Congress	Parliament
EXECUTIVE	Enforces law	President	Prime minister
JUDICIAL	Applies law	Supreme Court	U.K. Supreme Court

>> **Analyze Charts** Montesquieu believed in the separation of the powers of government into branches. Who currently heads the executive branch of government in the United States?

of thinking" by explaining ideas on topics such as government, philosophy, and religion.

Diderot's *Encyclopedia* included articles by leading thinkers of the day, including Montesquieu and Voltaire. In these articles, the *philosophes* denounced slavery, praised freedom of expression, and urged education for all. They attacked divine-right theory and traditional religions.

The French government viewed the *Encyclopedia* as an attack on public morals, and the pope threatened to excommunicate Roman Catholics who bought or read the volumes. Despite these and other efforts to ban the *Encyclopedia*, more than 4,000 copies were printed between 1751 and 1789.

Rousseau Promotes the Social Contract The most controversial *philosophe* was **Jean-Jacques Rousseau** (roo SOH). Rousseau believed that people in their natural state were basically good. This natural innocence, he felt, was corrupted by the evils of society, especially the unequal distribution of property.

In 1762, Rousseau set forth his ideas about government and society in *The Social Contract*. Rousseau felt that society placed too many limitations on people's behavior. He believed that some controls were necessary, but that they should be minimal. Additionally, only governments that had been freely elected should impose these controls. Rousseau put his faith in the "general will," or the best conscience of the people. The good of the community as a whole, he said, should be placed above individual interests. Woven through Rousseau's work is a hatred of all forms of political and economic oppression.

Women and the Enlightenment The Enlightenment slogan "free and equal" did not apply to women. Though the *philosophes* said women had natural rights, their rights were limited to the areas of home and family.

By the late 1700s, a small but growing number of women protested this view. Germaine de Staël in France and Mary Wollstonecraft in Britain argued that women were being excluded from the social contract itself. Their arguments, however, were ridiculed and often sharply condemned.

Wollstonecraft was a British writer and thinker. She accepted that a woman's first duty was to be a good mother but felt that a woman should be able to decide what was in her own interest without depending on her husband. In her book *A Vindication of the Rights of Woman*, Wollstonecraft called for equal education for girls and boys. Only education, she argued, could give women the tools they needed to participate equally with men in public life. Her ideas would influence the women's rights movement that emerged in the next century.

>> Writer Mary Wollstonecraft was a passionate advocate for social and educational equality for women.

Enlightenment Thinkers and Slavery While Enlightenment philosophy declared that equality and the protection of natural rights belonged to all, this was not meant for everyone. These rights were often expressly applied to white males. Most Enlightenment thinkers saw no contradiction in this. Montesquieu, for example, did not support slavery, claiming it was "against nature's wishes." But he argued that enslavement of Africans was acceptable. In similar fashion, Immanuel Kant adhered to the same views. Diderot, however, felt slavery was morally wrong. "Slavery," he wrote, "violates religion, morality, natural laws, and all the rights of human nature."

IDENTIFY SUPPORTING DETAILS What political philosophies did Jean-Jacques Rousseau set forth in *The Social Contract*?

New Economic Ideas

French thinkers known as physiocrats focused on economic reforms. Like the *philosophes*, physiocrats based their thinking on natural laws. The physiocrats claimed that their rational economic system was based on the natural laws of economics.

Laissez-Faire Economics

Physiocrats rejected mercantilism, which required government regulation of the economy to achieve a favorable balance of trade. Instead, they urged a policy of **laissez faire** (les ay FEHR), allowing business to operate with little or no government interference. Physiocrats supported free trade and opposed tariffs.

Adam Smith and *The Wealth of Nations*

Scottish economist **Adam Smith** greatly admired the physiocrats. In his influential work *The Wealth of Nations*, he argued that the **free market,** the natural forces of supply and demand, should be allowed to operate and regulate business. Smith favored a **free enterprise system** in which commerce and business compete for profit with little or no government interference.

Smith tried to show how manufacturing, trade, wages, profits, and economic growth were all linked to the market forces of supply and demand. Wherever there was a demand for goods or services, he said, suppliers would seek to meet that demand in order to gain profits.

Smith was a strong supporter of laissez faire. However, he felt that government had a duty to protect society, administer justice, and provide public works. Adam Smith's ideas about free enterprise would help to shape productive economies in the 1800s and 1900s.

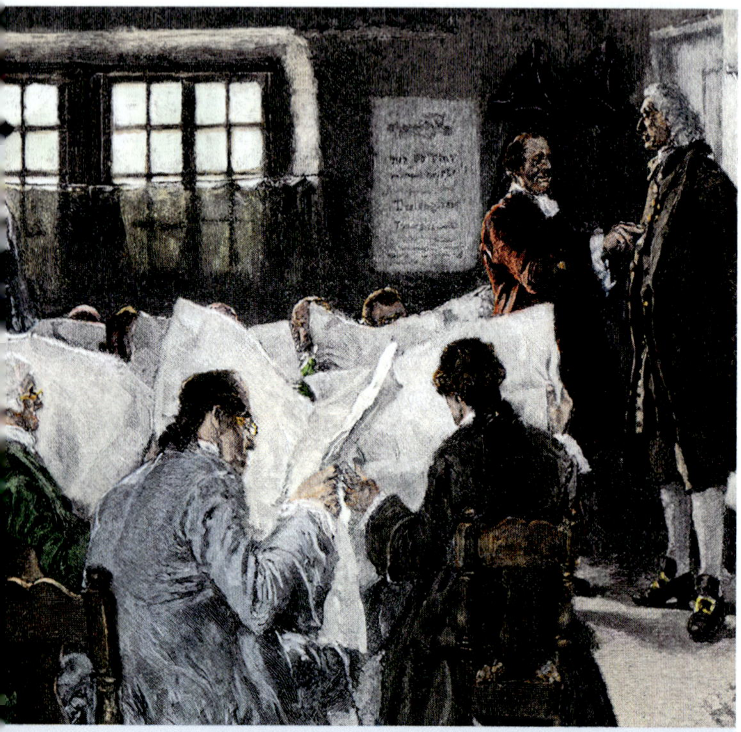

>> Enlightenment ideas spread through the printing of pamphlets and newspapers available to citizens.

COMPARE AND CONTRAST How is laissez-faire policy different from mercantilism?

Spread of Enlightenment Ideas

From France, Enlightenment ideas flowed across Europe and beyond. Everywhere, thinkers examined traditional beliefs and customs in the light of reason and found them flawed. Literate people eagerly read Diderot's *Encyclopedia* as well as small pamphlets turned out by printers that discussed a broad range of issues. More and more people came to believe that reform was necessary in order to achieve a just society.

During the Middle Ages, most Europeans had accepted without question a society based on divine-right rule, a strict class system, and a belief in heavenly reward for earthly suffering. In the Age of Reason, such ideas seemed unscientific and irrational. A just society, Enlightenment thinkers taught, should ensure social justice and happiness in this world. While many people embraced these new ideas, other groups rejected calls for change.

Writers Confront Censorship

Most, but not all, government and church authorities felt they had a sacred duty to defend the old order. They believed that God had set up the old order.

To protect against the attacks of the Enlightenment, they waged a war of **censorship,** or restricting access to ideas and information. They banned and burned books and imprisoned writers.

To avoid censorship, writers like Montesquieu and Voltaire sometimes disguised their ideas in works of fiction. In the *Persian Letters*, Montesquieu used two fictional Persian travelers, named Usbek and Rica, to mock French society. The hero of Voltaire's satirical novel *Candide*, published in 1759, travels across Europe and even to the Americas and the Middle East in search of "the best of all possible worlds." Voltaire slyly uses the tale to expose the corruption and hypocrisy of European society.

In England, Jonathan Swift published *Gulliver's Travels* in 1726. The story uses fantasy to satirize, or make fun of, English political life.

In a famous scene, Gulliver is bound by the Lilliputians, tiny six-inch-tall characters, and is unable to move. The harder Gulliver tries to break free, the more the Lilliputians attack him. Swift uses the story to comment on the pettiness of nations and their rulers.

Salons Spread Ideas New literature, the arts, science, and philosophy were regular topics of discussion in **salons,** or informal social gatherings at which writers, artists, *philosophes*, and others exchanged ideas. The salon originated in the 1600s, when a group of noblewomen in Paris began inviting a few friends to their homes for poetry readings. By the 1700s, some middle-class women began holding salons. There, middle-class citizens met with nobles on an equal basis to discuss Enlightenment ideas.

Through the salons, Enlightenment ideas spread among the educated people of Europe. Madame Geoffrin (zhoh FRAN) ran one of the most respected salons. In her home on the Rue St. Honoré (roo sant ahn ur AY), she brought together the brightest and most talented people of her day.

The young musical genius Wolfgang Amadeus Mozart played for her guests, and Diderot was a regular at her weekly dinners for philosophers and poets.

Slow Change for the Majority At first, most Europeans were untouched by the spread of Enlightenment ideas. They remained what they had always been—peasants living in small rural villages. Echoes of serfdom still remained throughout Europe despite advances in Western Europe. Centuries-old traditions continued to shape European society, which only very slowly began to change.

By the late 1700s, ideas about equality and social justice had finally seeped into peasant villages across Europe. Some peasants welcomed ideas about equality and an end to the old order. Others did not. Upheavals in France and elsewhere quickened the pace of change. By the early 1800s, war and changing economic conditions began to transform life for people across Europe.

IDENTIFY CENTRAL IDEAS How did those opposed to Enlightenment ideas try to stop the spread of information?

>> During the Enlightenment, Madame Geoffrin's salons were popular gatherings for intellectual discussions.

Arts and Literature of the Enlightenment

In the 1600s and 1700s, the arts evolved to meet changing tastes. As in earlier periods, artists and composers had to please their patrons, the men and women who commissioned works from them or gave them jobs.

Changing Styles in Art and Architecture In the age of Louis XIV, courtly art and architecture were either in the Greek and Roman tradition or in a grand, ornate style known as **baroque.** Baroque paintings were huge, colorful, and full of excitement. They glorified historic battles or the lives of saints. Such works matched the grandeur of European courts at that time.

By the mid-1700s, architects and designers developed a new style that reflected changing tastes. Unlike the heavy splendor of the baroque, **rococo** art was lighter, more personal, elegant and charming. Rococo furniture and tapestries featured delicate shells and flowers, and more pastel colors were used. Portrait painters showed noble subjects in charming rural settings, surrounded by happy servants and pets. Although this style was criticized by the *philosophes* for its superficiality, it was popular with the upper and middle classes.

New Trends in Music During the Enlightenment, composers and musicians developed new forms of music. Their music followed ordered structured forms well suited to the Age of Reason. At the same time, their work transcended, or rose above, the culture of the Enlightenment and remains popular all over the world today.

Ballets and opera—plays set to music—were performed at royal courts, and opera houses sprang up from Italy to England. In the past, only the highest people in society could afford to commission new works of music. By the mid-1700s, wealthy middle class people commissioned works and hired musicians to perform them. Among the towering musical figures of the era was Johann Sebastian Bach.

A devout German Lutheran, Bach wrote beautiful religious works for organ and choirs. His skills playing the organ and harpsichord were recognized during his lifetime, but he is now generally regarded as one of the greatest composers in history. Bach was a master of counterpoint, a technique that weaves two or more independent melodies together to create a new harmony.

Another German-born composer, George Frideric Handel, spent much of his life in England, where his music was extremely popular with the general public. There, he wrote *Water Music* and other pieces for King George I, as well as more than 30 operas. His most celebrated choral work, the *Messiah*, is often performed at Christmas and Easter. The stirring "Hallelujah Chorus" from the *Messiah* conveys universal themes of joy and celebration.

In 1761, a six-year-old prodigy, Wolfgang Amadeus Mozart, burst onto the European scene. He gained instant celebrity as a composer and performer.

During his brief life, the young man from Salzburg in Austria composed an amazing variety of music with remarkable speed. His operas reflected Enlightenment criticism of a class-ridden world full of hypocrisy and lies. At age 35, Mozart died in poverty, leaving a musical legacy that thrives today.

>> Johann Sebastian Bach plays the piano with his family in a 1870 painting. Many of Bach's children became important musicians.

Bounce to Activate Gallery

The Novel Takes Shape By the 1700s, literature developed new forms and a wider audience. Middle-class readers, for example, liked stories about their own times told in straightforward prose. One result was an outpouring of novels, or long works of prose fiction.

English novelists wrote many popular stories. Daniel Defoe wrote *Robinson Crusoe*, an exciting tale about a sailor shipwrecked on a tropical island. In a novel called *Pamela*, Samuel Richardson used a series of letters to tell a story about a servant girl. This technique was adopted by other authors of the period.

DRAW CONCLUSIONS How did literature change as Enlightenment ideas spread?

The Enlightened Despots

Discussions of Enlightenment theories enlivened the courts of Europe. *Philosophes* hoped to convince European rulers to adopt their ideas and introduce reforms. Some monarchs did accept Enlightenment ideas. They became **enlightened despots,** or absolute rulers who used their power to bring about political and social change.

Frederick the Great As king of Prussia from 1740 to 1786, Frederick II exerted extremely tight control over his subjects. Still, he saw himself as the "first servant of the state," with a duty to work for the common good.

Frederick openly praised Voltaire's work and invited him to Berlin. He asked French scientists to help him set up a Prussian academy of science. As king, he tried to reduce the use of torture and allowed a free press. He also tolerated religious differences, welcoming victims of religious persecution. "In my kingdom," he said, "everyone can go to heaven in his own fashion."

Most of Frederick's reforms were directed at making the Prussian government more efficient. To do this, he reorganized the government's civil service and simplified laws. Although Frederick did believe in enlightened reform, his efforts to improve government meant more power for himself.

Catherine the Great Catherine II, empress of Russia, read the works of the *philosophes* and exchanged letters with Voltaire and Diderot. She praised Voltaire as someone who had "fought the united enemies of humankind: superstition, fanaticism, ignorance, trickery." Catherine admired the Enlightenment ideas of equality and liberty.

Catherine experimented with implementing Enlightenment ideas. Early in her reign, she made some limited reforms in law and government. Catherine abolished torture and granted some religious tolerance for Christians and Muslims in her lands. However, she increased restrictions and taxes on Jews. She granted nobles a charter of rights and spoke out against serfdom. Still, like Frederick in Prussia, Catherine did not intend to give up power. Her main political contribution to Russia was an expanded empire.

Joseph II The most radical of the enlightened despots was **Joseph II** of Austria, the son and successor of Maria Theresa. Joseph was an eager student of the Enlightenment, and he traveled in disguise among his subjects to learn of their problems.

Like his mother, Joseph worked to modernize Austria's government. He chose talented middle-class officials rather than nobles to head departments and imposed a range of political and legal reforms. Despite opposition, Joseph granted more rights to and eased some restrictions on Protestants and Jews in his Catholic empire. He ended censorship by allowing a free press and attempted to bring the Catholic Church under royal control. He sold the property of many monasteries that were not involved in education or care of the sick and used the proceeds to build hospitals. Joseph even abolished serfdom. Like many of his other reforms, however, this measure was canceled after his death.

ANALYZE INFORMATION What did Frederick the Great mean by, "In my kingdom, everyone can go to heaven in his own fashion"?

>> Catherine the Great expressed an interest in many Enlightenment ideas. She often met with scholars to learn more. **Interpret** What type of scholar do you think she is meeting in this painting? Explain.

ASSESSMENT

1. **Explain** Explain the influence of scientific ideas on the progression of thought from the Scientific Revolution to the Enlightenment.
2. **Identify Central Ideas** What are some ways in which Enlightenment ideas spread?
3. **Identify Central Ideas** Explain the components of the free-enterprise system.
4. **Draw Conclusions** Why might some absolute monarchs have been willing to consider Enlightenment ideas, while others were not?
5. **Identify Central Ideas** In what way were the ideas of John Locke and Jean-Jacques Rousseau similar?

Primary Sources

The *Encyclopedia*, "Slave Trade": Louis de Jaucourt

Introduction

The *Encyclopedia*, edited by French philosopher and writer Denis Diderot, was published between 1751 and 1772. This *Encyclopedia* article presents Louis de Jaucourt's viewpoint on the slave trade. Jaucourt (1704–1799) created about a quarter of the entire *Encyclopedia*—more than 17,000 informative articles on biology, history, society, and many other subjects.

The second excerpt, from *Observations on the Feeling of the Beautiful and the Sublime*, was written by Immanuel Kant (1724–1804), a German Enlightenment philosopher. It states his views about Africans. Kant deeply influenced modern thinkers in many fields.

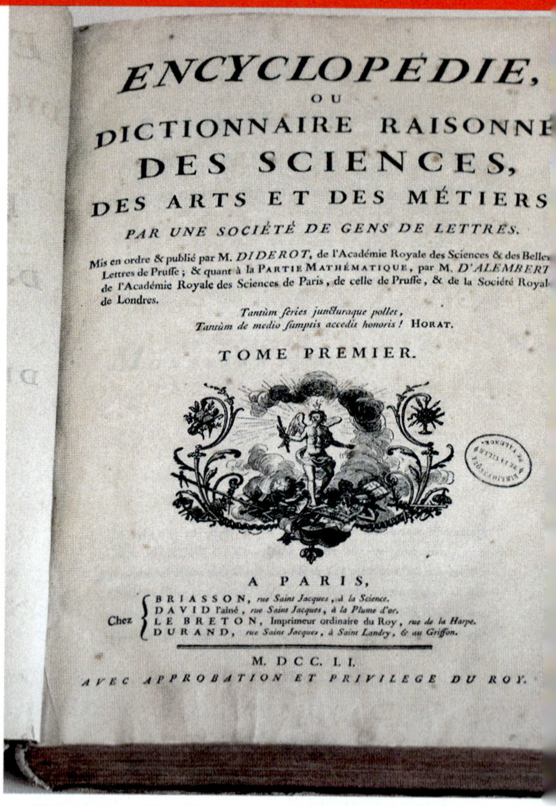

>> *Encyclopedia* title page, first edition 1751

Primary Source

The Slave Trade (Commerce of Africa) is the buying of unfortunate Negroes by Europeans on the coast of Africa to use as slaves in their colonies. This buying of Negroes, to reduce them to slavery, is one business that violates religion, morality, natural laws, and all the rights of human nature.

Negroes, says a modern Englishman full of enlightenment and humanity, have not become slaves by the right of war; neither do they deliver themselves voluntarily into bondage, and consequently their children are not born slaves. Nobody is unaware that they are bought from their own princes, who claim to have the right to dispose of their liberty, and that traders have them transported in the same way as their other goods, either in their colonies or in America, where they are displayed for sale.

If commerce of this kind can be justified by a moral principle, there is no crime, however atrocious it may be, that cannot be made legitimate. Kings princes, and magistrates are not the proprietors of their subjects: they do not, therefore, have the right to dispose of their liberty and to sell them as slaves.

DETERMINE AUTHOR'S POINT OF VIEW According to Jaucourt, is it acceptable for Europeans to buy Africans to use as slaves? Explain why or why not.

On the other hand, no man has the right to buy them or to make himself their master. Men and their liberty are not objects of commerce; they can be neither sold nor bought nor paid for at any price. We must conclude from this that a man whose slave has run away should only blame himself, since he had acquired for money illicit goods whose acquisition is prohibited by all the laws of humanity and equality.

There is not, therefore, a single one of these unfortunate people regarded only as slaves who does not have the right to be declared free, since he has never lost his freedom. Consequently the sale that has been completed is invalid in itself. This Negro does not divest himself and can never divest himself of his natural right; he carries it everywhere with him, and he can demand everywhere that he be allowed to enjoy it.

EXPLAIN AN ARGUMENT What does Jaucourt say about the right of traders to buy and sell slaves? How does he argue that all slaves have the right to be declared free?

Primary Source

The Negroes of Africa have by nature no feeling that rises above the trifling. Mr. Hume [a Scottish philosopher] challenges anyone to cite a single example in which a Negro has shown talents, and asserts that among the hundreds of thousands of blacks who are transported elsewhere from their countries, although many of them have even been set free, still not a single one was ever found who presented anything great in art or science or any other praiseworthy quality, even though among the whites some continually rise aloft from the lowest rabble, and through superior gifts earn respect in the world.

CITE EVIDENCE What evidence does Kant provide to show the inferiority of "the Negroes of Africa"?

So fundamental is the difference between these two races of man, and it appears to be as great in regard to mental capacities as in color. The religion of fetishes so widespread among them is perhaps a sort of idolatry that sinks as deeply into the trifling as appears to be possible to human nature. A bird's feather, a cow's horn, a conch shell, or any other common object, as soon as it becomes consecrated by a few words, is an object of veneration and of invocation in swearing oaths. The blacks are very vain but in the Negro's way, and so talkative that they must be driven apart from each other with thrashings.

DRAW INFERENCES How does Kant view the religion of African cultures?

>> Immanuel Kant

ASSESSMENT

1. **Identify** According to Jaucourt, do Europeans know how Africans become slaves? Identify the stages of the enslavement process.
2. **Determine Author's Purpose** Why do you think Louis de Jaucourt wrote his article about slave trading?
3. **Summarize** How does Kant characterize "the Negroes of Africa"?
4. **Predict** How do you think other Enlightenment thinkers might have responded to Kant's characterization of "the Negroes of Africa"?

>> England had a vast trading network that included its thirteen North American colonies. This image shows the busy port of Charleston, South Carolina.

Bounce to Activate Flipped Video

1.5 **By the 1770s, Britain was a major power in Europe with territories around the globe. Although upheavals in the 1600s had created a limited monarchy, a new king was eager to recover powers the crown had lost.**

>> Objectives

Describe how Britain became a global power.

Understand the events and ideas leading up to the American Revolution, including the impact of the Enlightenment.

Summarize key events of the American Revolution.

Identify the political and legal ideas in the Declaration of Independence and the United States Constitution.

>> Key Terms

George III
Stamp Act
George Washington
Benjamin Franklin
Thomas Jefferson
popular sovereignty
Yorktown, Virginia
Treaty of Paris
James Madison
federal republic
checks and balances

The American Revolution

Britain Becomes a Global Power

Trade and Commerce Britain's rise to global prominence had multiple causes. England's location and long seagoing tradition placed it in a position to build a vast trading network. By the 1600s, England had trading outposts and colonies in the West Indies, North America, and India. A new merchant class expanded trade and competed vigorously with Spanish, Portuguese, and Dutch traders.

During the 1700s, thousands of settlers sailed to North America to build colonies. At the same time, British merchants expanded into the profitable slave trade, carrying enslaved people from West Africa to the Americas.

Britain's economic policies added to its prosperity. England offered a climate favorable to business and commerce. It put fewer restrictions on trade than some of its neighbors, such as France.

Territorial Expansion In the 1700s, Britain was generally on the winning side in European conflicts. In the Treaty of Utrecht, which ended the War of the Spanish Succession, France gave

Nova Scotia and Newfoundland to Britain. As a result of the French and Indian War, Britain gained all of French Canada, as well as rich islands in the Caribbean in 1763.

At home, England grew by merging with neighboring Scotland. In 1701, the Act of Union united the two countries in the United Kingdom of Great Britain. The union brought economic advantages.

Free trade between both lands created a larger market for farmers and manufacturers. The United Kingdom also included Wales, and in 1801 Ireland would be added to Great Britain.

George III Takes Power In 1760, **George III** began a 60-year reign. Unlike his German father and grandfather, the new king was born in England. He spoke English and loved Britain. But George was eager to recover the powers the crown had lost since the Glorious Revolution. Following his mother's advice, "George, be a king!" he set out to reassert royal power. He wanted to end Whig domination, choose his own ministers, dissolve the cabinet system, and make Parliament follow his will.

Gradually, George found seats in Parliament for "the king's friends." With their help, he began to assert his leadership. Many of his policies, however, would prove disastrous. He angered colonists in North America, leading 13 English colonies to declare independence.

Britain's loss of its American colonies discredited the king. Increasingly, too, he suffered from bouts of mental illness. By 1788, cabinet rule was restored in Britain.

ANALYZE INFORMATION What were some of the elements that led to Britain's rise to global prominence in the 1700s?

The British Colonies in America

By 1750, a string of prosperous colonies stretched along the eastern coast of North America. They were part of Britain's growing empire. Colonial cities such as Boston, New York, and Philadelphia were busy commercial centers that linked North America to the West Indies, Africa, and Europe. Colonial shipyards produced many vessels for this trade.

Britain applied mercantilist policies to its colonies in an attempt to strengthen its own economy by exporting more than it imported. To this end, in the 1600s, Parliament had passed the Navigation Acts to regulate colonial trade and manufacturing. For the most part, however, these acts were not rigorously enforced. Therefore, activities like smuggling were common and not considered crimes by the colonists.

By the mid-1700s, the colonies were home to diverse religious and ethnic groups. Social

British Territory in North America (1763)

>> **Analyze Maps** What do all of the colonies on this map have in common?

distinctions were more blurred than in Europe, although wealthy landowners and merchants dominated government and society. In politics, as in much else, there was a good deal of free discussion.

Colonists felt entitled to the rights of English citizens, and their colonial assemblies exercised much control over local affairs. Many also had an increasing sense of their own destiny separate from Britain.

DESCRIBE Why did Americans believe they had the same rights as English citizens?

Discontent in the Colonies

The French and Indian War had drained the British treasury. George III and his advisors insisted that colonists pay the costs of their own defense, including troops still stationed in frontier posts.

Growing Tensions Parliament passed new taxes on the colonies. The Sugar Act of 1764 taxed imports, while the **Stamp Act** of 1765 taxed items such as newspapers and pamphlets. Although the new taxes were not burdensome, colonists bitterly resented them as an attack on their rights. "No taxation without representation," they protested. Since they had no representatives in Parliament, they believed that Parliament had no right to tax them. Parliament repealed the Stamp Act, but asserted its right to tax the colonists.

>> Benjamin Franklin, Thomas Jefferson, John Adams, Robert R. Livingston, and Roger Sherman served as the committee to draft the Declaration of Independence.

Bounce to Activate Illustration

A series of violent clashes intensified the colonists' anger. In March 1770, British soldiers in Boston opened fire on a crowd that was pelting them with stones and snowballs. Colonists called the death of five protesters the Boston Massacre.

Then, in December 1773, a handful of colonists hurled a cargo of recently arrived British tea into the harbor to protest a tax on tea. The incident became known as the Boston Tea Party. When Parliament passed harsh laws to punish Massachusetts, other colonies rallied to help Massachusetts.

As tensions rose, representatives from 12 colonies gathered in Philadelphia in 1774. At the First Continental Congress, representatives discussed how to respond to Britain's harsh moves against Massachusetts.

Among the participants were the radical but fair-minded John Adams, the Virginia planter and soldier **George Washington,** and **Benjamin Franklin,** a leading figure of the American Enlightenment.

Declaring Independence In April 1775, the crisis between the colonists and the British exploded into war. At the battles of Lexington and Concord in Massachusetts, colonists clashed with British troops—the opening shots of the American Revolution. Soon after, the Second Continental Congress met and set up a Continental Army with George Washington in command.

In 1776, Congress took a momentous step, voting to declare independence from Britain. Young **Thomas Jefferson** of Virginia was the principal author of the Declaration of Independence. Jefferson's political philosophy was heavily influenced by Enlightenment thinkers, especially John Locke. The document clearly reflects Locke's political and legal ideas, including the idea of natural law. It announced that people have "certain inalienable rights, that among them are life, liberty, and the pursuit of happiness."

In the Declaration, Jefferson further stated that people had the right "to alter or to abolish" unjust governments, echoing Locke's ideas about the right to revolt. He then carefully detailed the colonists' grievances against Britain, such as imposing taxes without consent, dissolving colonial legislatures at will, and depriving many colonists of their legal right to trial by jury. Because Parliament had trampled colonists' natural rights, he argued, the colonists had the right to rebel and set up a new government to protect them.

The document spelled out the political principle of **popular sovereignty,** the idea that all government power comes from the people. Aware of the risks involved, on July 4, 1776, American leaders signed the Declaration, pledging "our lives, our fortunes, and our sacred honor" to the cause of the United States of America.

DRAW CONCLUSIONS Why did the colonists object so strongly to the idea of taxation without representation?

The American Revolution

At first, the American cause looked bleak. The colonists themselves were divided. About one third of the American colonists were Loyalists, or those who supported Britain. Many others refused to fight for either side.

Military Strengths and Weaknesses The colonists faced severe military disadvantages as well. The British had a large number of trained soldiers, a huge fleet, and plentiful money. They occupied most major American cities. The Americans lacked military resources, had little money to pay soldiers, and did not have a strategic plan.

Still, the colonists had some advantages. They were battling for their own independence on their own familiar home ground. Although the British held New York and Philadelphia, colonists controlled the countryside. And they had a strong, inspiring military leader in George Washington.

As the war unfolded, the British relied on Loyalists as well as Native American groups, some of whom sided with them. The British also sought support among African Americans held in slavery. They offered freedom to any who would join their side.

Alliance with France The first turning point in the war came in 1777, when the Americans triumphed over the British at the Battle of Saratoga. This victory persuaded France to join the Americans against its old rival, Britain. The alliance brought the Americans desperately needed supplies, trained soldiers, and French warships. Spurred by the French example, the Netherlands and Spain added their support.

>> George Washington encouraged his men to fight on despite heavy odds.

Hard times continued, however. In the brutal winter of 1777–1778, Continental troops at Valley Forge suffered from cold, hunger, and disease. Throughout this crisis and others, Washington was patient, courageous, and determined. He held the ragged army together.

Victory for the Americans Finally, in 1781, with the help of a French fleet, Washington forced the surrender of a British army at **Yorktown, Virginia.** With that defeat, the British war effort crumbled.

Two years later, American, British, and French diplomats signed the **Treaty of Paris,** ending the war. Britain formally recognized the independence of the United States of America. Britain also accepted the new nation's western frontier as the Mississippi River.

GENERATE EXPLANATIONS Why was the selection of George Washington as head of the American army essential to the ultimate success of the American Revolution?

>> James Madison is known as the father of the U.S. Constitution because he was instrumental in drafting the document.

>> The U.S. Constitution, shown here, set up a series of checks and balances in which each branch of government can limit the powers of the other branches.

Bounce to Activate Chart

The United States Constitution

The Articles of Confederation was the new nation's first constitution. It proved to be too weak to rule effectively. To address this problem, the nation's leaders gathered once more. Among them were George Washington, **James Madison,** and Benjamin Franklin. During the hot summer of 1787, they hammered out the Constitution of the United States. This framework for a strong, flexible government has remained in place for more than 200 years.

The Impact of the Enlightenment The Framers of the Constitution had absorbed the ideas of Locke, Montesquieu, and Rousseau. Like Rousseau, the framers saw government in terms of a social contract among members of the community. A central feature of the new federal government—the separation of powers among the legislative, executive, and judicial branches—was borrowed directly from Montesquieu.

The framers were also influenced by the ideas of an English legal scholar of the 1700s, William Blackstone, who shared many of Locke's ideas. Blackstone's writings greatly informed the legal ideas contained in the Constitution and a good portion of American law to the present day. For example, his famous statement that "the law holds it better that ten guilty persons escape, than that one innocent party suffer" is reflected in the Constitutional rights given to people accused of crimes.

A Framework of Government The Constitution created a **federal republic,** with power divided between the federal, or national, government and the states. It provided for both an elected legislature and an elected president.

To prevent any branch of government from becoming too powerful, the Constitution set up a series of **checks and balances.** Under this system, each branch of the government has the right to monitor and limit each of the other branches.

The Bill of Rights, or the first ten amendments to the Constitution, recognized the idea that citizens have basic rights that the government must protect. These included freedom of religion, speech, and the press.

It also affirmed legal ideas, such as the right to trial by jury and the principle that no one may be forced to testify against him- or herself. The Bill of Rights, like the Constitution, put Enlightenment ideas into practice.

Symbol of Freedom From the start, the new republic was a symbol of freedom for many. The Declaration of Independence, along with the Bill of Rights, put forth the idea that there are certain rights that belong to everyone. The American Revolution became the example to follow. Nationalists in other countries demanded freedom. Today, it is still a prototype for wars of independence.

In 1789, most countries in Europe were ruled by hereditary absolute monarchs. The United States stood out as a beacon to Europeans who took up the cry for liberty and freedom.

Demands for written constitutions and a limit to royal power would bring great changes to Europe by the decades ahead. Revolutionaries in Latin America were also inspired by the example of the United States.

Under the Constitution, citizens enjoy many rights, but they also have many responsibilities. They are expected to vote, sit on juries, and keep informed on topics of local and national interest. Noncitizens who reside in the United States also enjoy its constitutional rights and protections and have responsibilities such as paying taxes and abiding by local, state, and federal laws.

ANALYZE CONTEXT How did the ideas of the Enlightenment influence the United States Constitution and the Bill of Rights?

ASSESSMENT

1. **Identify Main Ideas** How did trade play a role in Britain's becoming a global power?
2. **Identify Cause and Effect** Why did North America's geography make it difficult for the British to win the war?
3. **Check Understanding** Why did colonists wait to declare independence from Britain?
4. **Hypothesize** Why do you think many countries over time have emulated the principles outlined in the Declaration of Independence and the U.S. Constitution?
5. **Describe** In what way does the Bill of Rights put the ideas of the Enlightenment into practice?

Primary Sources

Declaration of Independence

Introduction

By signing the Declaration of Independence, members of the Continental Congress sent a clear message to Britain that the American colonies were free and independent states. Starting with its preamble, the document spells out all the reasons the people of the United States have the right to break away from Britain.

>> Presenting the Declaration of Independence.

Primary Source

When in the Course of human events, it becomes necessary for one people to dissolve the political bands which have connected them with another, and to assume among the powers of the earth, the separate and equal station to which the Laws of Nature and of Nature's God entitle them, a decent respect to the opinions of mankind requires that they should declare the causes which impel [force] them to the separation.

We hold these truths to be self-evident, that all men are created equal, that they are endowed [gifted] by their Creator with certain unalienable [cannot be taken away] Rights, that among these are Life, Liberty and the pursuit of Happiness. That to secure these rights, Governments are instituted among Men, deriving their just powers from the consent of the governed. That whenever any Form of Government becomes destructive of these ends, it is the Right of the People to alter or to abolish it, and to institute new Government, laying its foundation on such principles and organizing its powers in such form, as to them shall seem most likely to effect their Safety and Happiness. Prudence [cautiousness], indeed, will dictate that Governments long established should not be changed for light and transient causes; and accordingly all experience hath shown that mankind are more disposed to suffer, while evils are sufferable, than to right themselves by abolishing the forms to which they are accustomed. But when a long train of abuses and usurpations [unjust uses of power], pursuing invariably the same Object evinces a design to reduce them under absolute Despotism [rule of absolute power], it is their right, it is their duty, to throw off such Government, and to provide new Guards for their future security. Such has been the patient sufferance of these Colonies; and such is now the necessity which constrains them to alter their former Systems of Government. The history of the present King of Great Britain is a history of repeated injuries and usurpations, all having in direct object the establishment of an absolute Tyranny over these States. To prove this, let Facts be submitted to a candid world.

He has refused his Assent to Laws, the most wholesome and necessary for the public good. He has forbidden his Governors to pass Laws of immediate and pressing importance, unless suspended in their operation till his Assent should be obtained; and when so suspended, he has utterly neglected to attend to them. He has refused to pass other Laws for the accommodation of large districts of people, unless those people would relinquish [give up] the right of Representation in the Legislature, a right inestimable [priceless] to them and formidable to tyrants only. He has called together legislative bodies at places unusual, uncomfortable, and distant from the depository of their public Records, for the sole purpose of fatiguing them into compliance with his measures. He has dissolved Representative Houses repeatedly, for opposing with manly firmness his invasions on the rights of the people. He has refused for a long time, after such dissolutions [closing down], to cause others to be elected; whereby the Legislative powers, incapable of Annihilation, have returned to the People at large for their exercise; the State remaining in the mean time exposed to all the dangers of invasion from without, and convulsions [riots] within.

He has kept among us, in times of peace, Standing Armies without the Consent of our legislatures. He has affected to render the Military independent of and superior to the Civil power. He has combined with others to subject us to a jurisdiction foreign to our constitution, and unacknowledged by our laws; giving his Assent to their Acts of pretended Legislation: For quartering [lodging] large bodies of armed troops among us: For protecting them, by a mock Trial, from punishment for any Murders which they should commit on the Inhabitants of these States: For cutting off our Trade with all parts of the world: For imposing Taxes on us without our Consent: For depriving us in many cases, of the benefits of Trial by Jury: For transporting us beyond Seas to be tried for pretended offences: For abolishing the free System of English Laws in a neighbouring Province, establishing therein an Arbitrary government, and enlarging its Boundaries so as to render it at once an example and fit instrument for introducing the same absolute rule into these Colonies:

. . . He has kept among us, etc. He has abdicated Government here, by declaring us out of his Protection and waging War against us. He has plundered our seas, ravaged our Coasts, burnt our towns, and destroyed the lives of our people. . .

In every stage of these Oppressions We have Petitioned for Redress [correction of wrongs] in the most humble terms: Our repeated Petitions have been answered only by repeated injury. A Prince, whose character is thus marked by every act which may define a Tyrant, is unfit to be the ruler of a free people.

Nor have We been wanting in attentions to our British brethren. We have warned them from time to time of attempts by their legislature to extend an unwarrantable jurisdiction over us. We have reminded them of the circumstances of our emigration and settlement here. We have appealed to their native justice and magnanimity [generosity], and we have conjured [begged] them by the ties of our common kindred, to disavow these usurpations, which would inevitably interrupt our connections and correspondence. They too have been deaf to the voice of justice and of consanguinity [relation by blood]. We must, therefore, acquiesce in the necessity, which denounces our Separation, and hold them, as we hold the rest of mankind, Enemies in War, in Peace Friends.

We, therefore, the Representatives of the United States of America, in General Congress, Assembled, appealing to the Supreme Judge of the world for the rectitude [justness] of our intentions, do, in the Name, and by Authority of the good People of these Colonies, solemnly publish and declare, That these United Colonies are, and of Right ought to be Free and Independent States; that they are Absolved from all Allegiance to the British Crown, and that all political connection between them and the State of Great Britain, is and ought to be totally dissolved; and that as Free and Independent States, they have full Power to levy War, conclude Peace, contract Alliances, establish Commerce, and to do all other Acts and Things which Independent States may of right do. And for the support of this Declaration, with a firm reliance on the protection of Divine Providence, we mutually pledge to each other our Lives, our Fortunes and our sacred Honor.

ASSESSMENT

1. **Identify Cause and Effect** How might the ideas about equality expressed in the Declaration of Independence have influenced later historical movements, such as the abolitionist movement and the women's suffrage movement?

2. **Identify Key Steps in a Process** Why was the Declaration of Independence a necessary document for the founding of the new nation?

3. **Draw Inferences** English philosopher John Locke wrote that government should protect "life, liberty, and estate." How do you think Locke's writing influenced ideas about government put forth in the Declaration of Independence?

4. **Analyze Structure** How does the declaration organize its key points from beginning to end?

>> Delegates of the Third Estate took the Tennis Court Oath in June 1789 and vowed to create a new constitution.

Bounce to Activate Flipped Video

1.6 On April 28, 1789, unrest exploded at a Paris wallpaper factory. A rumor had spread that the factory owner was planning to cut wages even though bread prices were soaring. Enraged workers vandalized the owner's home and then rioted through the streets.

>> Objectives

Describe the social divisions of France's old order.

Trace the causes of the French Revolution.

Identify the reforms enacted by the National Assembly, including the Declaration of the Rights of Man and the Citizen.

>> Key Terms

ancien régime
estates
bourgeoisie
deficit spending
Louis XVI
Jacques Necker
Estates-General
cahiers
Tennis Court Oath
Bastille
faction
Marquis de Lafayette
Olympe de Gouges
Marie Antoinette

The French Revolution Begins

The Old Regime in France

The rioting reflected growing unrest in Paris and throughout France. In 1789, France faced not only an economic crisis but also widespread demands for far-reaching changes. By July, the hungry, unemployed, poorly paid people of Paris were taking up arms against the government, a move that would trigger the French Revolution.

In 1789, France, like the rest of Europe, still clung to an outdated social system that had emerged in the Middle Ages. Under this **ancien régime,** or old order, everyone in France belonged to one of three social classes, or **estates.** The First Estate was made up of the clergy; the Second Estate was made up of the nobility; and the Third Estate comprised the vast majority of the population.

First Estate: the Clergy During the Middle Ages, the Church had exerted great influence throughout Christian Europe. In 1789, the French clergy still enjoyed enormous wealth and privilege. The Church owned about 10 percent of the land, collected tithes, and paid no direct taxes to the state. High Church leaders such as bishops and abbots were usually nobles who lived very well. Parish priests, however, often came from humble origins and might be as poor as their peasant congregations.

The First Estate did provide some social services. Nuns, monks, and priests ran schools, hospitals, and orphanages. But during the Enlightenment, *philosophes* targeted the Church for reform.

They criticized the idleness of some clergy, the Church's interference in politics, and its intolerance of dissent. In response, many clergy condemned the Enlightenment for undermining religion and moral order.

Second Estate: the Nobility The Second Estate was the titled nobility of French society. In the Middle Ages, noble knights had defended the land. In the 1600s, Richelieu and Louis XIV had crushed the nobles' military power but had given them other rights—under strict royal control. Those rights included top jobs in government, the army, the courts, and the Church.

At Versailles, ambitious nobles competed for royal appointments while idle courtiers enjoyed endless entertainments. Many nobles, however, lived far from the center of power. Though they owned land, they received little financial income. As a result, they felt the pinch of trying to maintain their status in a period of rising prices.

Many ambitious nobles came to hate absolutism and resented the royal bureaucracy that employed middle-class men in positions that once had been reserved for them. They feared losing their traditional privileges, especially their freedom from paying taxes.

Third Estate: From Middle Class to Peasantry

The Third Estate was the most diverse social class. At the top sat the **bourgeoisie** (boor zhwah ZEE), or middle class. The bourgeoisie included prosperous bankers, merchants, and manufacturers, as well as lawyers, doctors, journalists, and professors.

The bulk of the Third Estate, however, consisted of rural peasants. Some were prosperous landowners who hired laborers to work for them. Others were tenant farmers or day laborers.

Among the poorest members of the Third Estate were urban workers. They included apprentices, journeymen, and others who worked in industries such as printing or cloth making.

Many women and men earned a meager living as servants, construction workers, or street sellers of everything from food to pots and pans. A large

>> **Analyze Political Cartoons** What does this cartoon say about the relationship between the three social classes in France?

Bounce to Activate Cartoon

>> Merchants were among the bourgeoisie, France's middle class.

number of the urban poor were unemployed. To survive, some turned to begging or crime.

Widespread Discontent From rich to poor, members of the Third Estate resented the privileges enjoyed by their social "betters." Wealthy bourgeois families in the Third Estate could buy political office and even titles, but the best jobs were still reserved for nobles. Urban workers earned miserable wages. Even the smallest rise in the price of bread, their main food, brought the threat of greater hunger or even starvation. In 1775, before the French Revolution, peasants rioted over the high price of bread in an event called the "Flour War."

Because of traditional privileges, the First and Second Estates paid almost no taxes. Peasants were burdened by taxes on everything from land to soap to salt. Though they were technically free, many owed fees and services that dated back to medieval times, such as the corvée (kawr VAY), which was unpaid labor to repair roads and bridges.

Peasants were also incensed when nobles, hurt by rising prices, tried to reimpose old manor dues. In towns and cities, Enlightenment ideas about equality led people to question the inequalities of the old regime. Why, people demanded, should the first two estates have such great privileges at the expense of the majority? Throughout France, the Third Estate called for the privileged classes to pay their share.

CONTRAST How did the lives of the Third Estate differ from the lives of clergy and nobles?

France's Economic Crisis

Along with social unrest, France faced economic woes, especially a mushrooming financial crisis. The crisis was caused in part by years of **deficit spending.** This occurs when a government spends more money than it takes in.

A Nation in Debt Louis XIV had left France deeply in debt. The Seven Years' War and the American Revolution strained the treasury even further. Costs generally had risen in the 1700s, and the lavish court soaked up millions. To bridge the gap between income and expenses, the government borrowed more and more money. By 1789, half of the government's income from taxes went to paying the interest on this enormous debt.

To solve the financial crisis, the government would have to increase taxes, reduce expenses, or both. However, the nobles and clergy fiercely resisted any attempt to end their exemption from taxes.

FRANCE IN ECONOMIC CRISIS

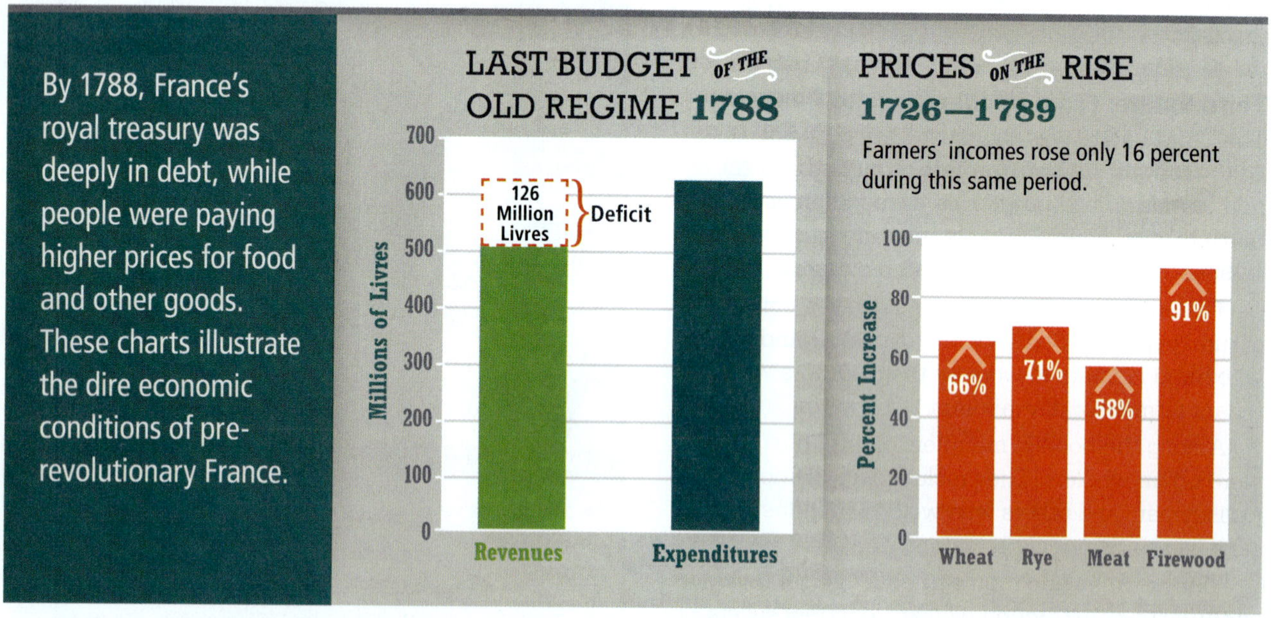

>> **Analyze Charts** As France's deficit grew, so did the suffering of the poor. How much did the price of firewood rise between 1726 and 1789?

A Crumbling Economy Other economic woes added to the crisis. A general economic decline began in the 1770s. Then in the late 1780s, bad harvests set food prices soaring and brought hunger to poorer peasants and city dwellers.

Hard times and lack of food inflamed these people. In towns, people rioted, demanding bread. In the countryside, peasants began to attack the manor houses of nobles.

Failure of Reform The heirs of Louis XIV were not the right men to solve the economic crisis that afflicted France. Louis XV, who ruled from 1715 to 1774, pursued pleasure before serious business and ran up more debts.

The next king, **Louis XVI**, was well-meaning but weak and indecisive. He did wisely choose **Jacques Necker,** a financial expert, as an advisor. Necker urged the king to reduce extravagant court spending, reform government, and abolish burdensome tariffs on internal trade. When Necker proposed taxing the First and Second Estates, however, the nobles and high clergy forced the king to dismiss him.

As the crisis deepened, the pressure for reform mounted. The wealthy and powerful classes demanded, however, that the king summon the **Estates-General,** the legislative body consisting of representatives of the three estates, before making any changes. No French king had called the Estates-General for 175 years. They feared that nobles would try to recover the feudal powers they had lost under absolute rule.

To reform-minded nobles, the Estates-General seemed to offer a chance of carrying out changes like the ones the English had achieved through the Glorious Revolution. They hoped to bring the absolute monarch under the control of nobles and guarantee their own privileges.

DESCRIBE What were some of the main reasons France was in serious economic trouble in the late 1700s?

>> The poor made up the majority of the Third Estate. Here, they are shown rioting during the "Flour War," a brief 1775 uprising brought on by higher bread prices.

Louis XVI Calls the Estates-General

As 1788 came to a close, France tottered on the verge of bankruptcy. Bread riots were spreading, and nobles, fearful of taxes, were denouncing royal tyranny. A baffled Louis XVI finally summoned the Estates-General to meet at Versailles the following year.

The Cahiers In preparation, Louis had all three estates prepare **cahiers** (kah YAYZ), or notebooks, listing their grievances. Many cahiers called for reforms such as fairer taxes, freedom of the press, or regular meetings of the Estates-General. In one town, shoemakers denounced regulations that made leather so expensive they could not afford to make shoes. Servant girls in the city of Toulouse demanded the right to leave service when they wanted and insisted that "after a girl has served her master for many years, she receive some reward for her service."

The cahiers testified to boiling class resentments. One called tax collectors "bloodsuckers of the nation who drink the tears of the unfortunate from goblets of gold." Another one of the cahiers condemned the courts of nobles as "vampires pumping the last drop of blood" from the people. Yet another complained that "20 million must live on half the wealth of France while the clergy . . . devour the other half."

The Tennis Court Oath Delegates to the Estates-General from the Third Estate were elected, though only propertied men could vote. Thus, the delegates were mostly lawyers, middle-class officials, and writers. They were familiar with the writings of

Voltaire, Rousseau, and other *philosophes*, as well as with the complaints in the cahiers. They went to Versailles not only to solve the financial crisis but also to insist on reform.

The Estates-General convened in May 1789. From the start, the delegates were deadlocked over the issue of voting. Traditionally, each estate had met and voted separately. Each group had one vote.

Under this system, the First and Second Estates always outvoted the Third Estate two to one. This time, the Third Estate wanted all three estates to meet in a single body, with votes counted "by head." After weeks of stalemate, delegates of the Third Estate took a daring step. In June 1789, claiming to represent the people of France, they declared themselves to be the National Assembly. A few days later, the National Assembly found its meeting hall locked and guarded. Fearing that the king planned to dismiss them, the delegates moved to a nearby indoor tennis court.

As curious spectators looked on, the delegates took their famous **Tennis Court Oath.** They swore "never to separate and to meet wherever the circumstances might require until we have established a sound and just constitution." When reform-minded clergy and nobles joined the Assembly, Louis XVI grudgingly accepted it.

>> The storming of the Bastille on July 14, 1789, was the opening event of the French Revolution.

At the same time, though, royal troops gathered around Paris. Rumors spread that the king planned to dissolve the Assembly.

DESCRIBE Why did the Third Estate want the Estates-General to meet as a single body?

Storming the Bastille

On July 14, 1789, the city of Paris seized the spotlight from the National Assembly meeting in Versailles. The streets buzzed with rumors that royal troops were going to occupy the capital. More than 800 Parisians assembled outside the **Bastille,** a grim medieval fortress used as a prison for political and other prisoners. The crowd demanded weapons and gunpowder believed to be stored there.

The commander of the Bastille refused to open the gates and opened fire on the crowd. In the battle that followed, many people were killed. Finally, the enraged mob broke through the defenses. Thomas Jefferson was at the time American minister to France and described the scene as one of chaos and violence.

> The people rushed against the place, and almost in an instant were in possession of a fortification, defended by 100 men, of infinite strength, which in other times had stood several regular sieges and had never been taken. . . . They took all the arms, discharged the prisoners and such of the garrison as were not killed in the first moment of fury, carried the Governor and Lieutenant governor to the Greve (the place of public execution), cut off their heads, and set them through the city in triumph to the Palais royal.
>
> —Thomas Jefferson, letter to John Jay, July 14, 1789

The mob killed the commander and five guards and released the handful of prisoners who were being held there. However, they found no weapons.

For the French, the Bastille was a powerful symbol of the tyranny, inequalities, and injustices of the old order. The storming of the Bastille signaled the end of the absolute monarchy and a step toward freedom. It also marked the beginning of the French

Revolution. Today, July 14 is a national holiday when the French celebrate the birth of modern France.

IDENTIFY CENTRAL IDEAS What was the main motivation behind the Parisians' attack on the Bastille?

Revolts in Paris and the Provinces

The political crisis of 1789 coincided with the worst famine in memory. Starving peasants roamed the countryside or flocked to towns, where they swelled the ranks of the unemployed. As grain prices soared, even people with jobs had to spend as much as 80 percent of their income on bread.

The "Great Fear" In such desperate times, rumors ran wild and set off what was later called the "Great Fear." Tales of attacks on villages and towns spread panic. Other rumors asserted that government troops were seizing peasant crops.

Inflamed by famine and fear, peasants unleashed their fury on nobles who were trying to reimpose medieval dues. Defiant peasants set fire to old manor records and stole grain from storehouses. The attacks eventually died down, but they clearly showed peasant anger with the injustice of the old order.

Paris in Arms Paris, too, was in turmoil. As the capital and chief city of France, it was the revolutionary center. A variety of factions competed to gain power. A **faction** is a group or clique within a larger group that has different ideas and opinions than the rest of the group.

Moderates looked to the **Marquis de Lafayette,** the aristocratic "hero of two worlds" who had fought alongside George Washington in the American Revolution. Lafayette headed the National Guard, a largely middle-class militia organized in response to the arrival of royal troops in Paris. The Guard was the first group to don the tricolor—a red, white, and blue badge that was eventually adopted as the national flag of France.

A more radical group, the Paris Commune, replaced the royalist government of the city. It could mobilize whole neighborhoods for protests or violent action to further the revolution. Newspapers and political clubs—many even more radical than the Commune—blossomed everywhere.

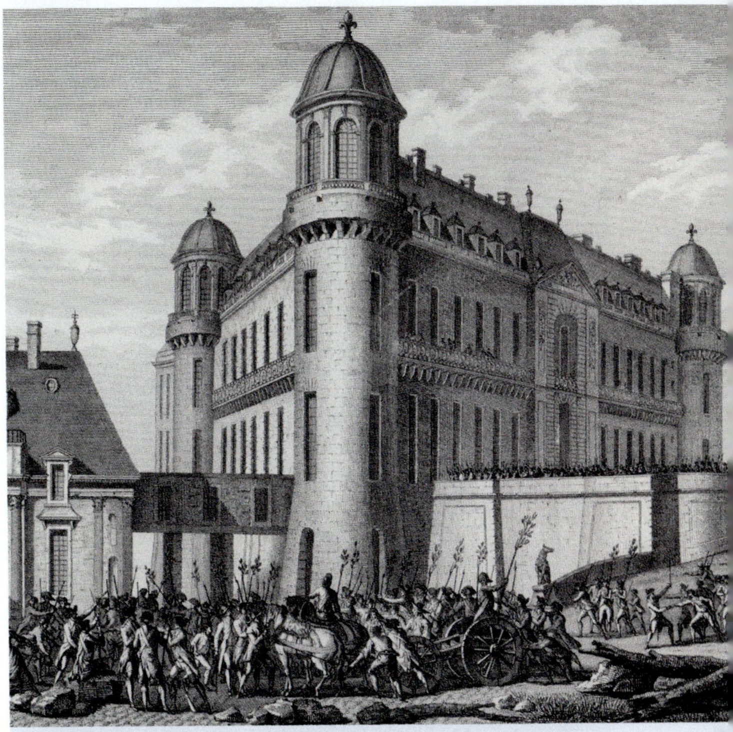

>> Peasant rebellions during the Great Fear began amid rumors that the king and other aristocrats wanted to overthrow the Third Estate.

Some demanded an end to the monarchy and spread scandalous stories about the royal family and members of the court.

IDENTIFY MAIN IDEAS What stoked the "Great Fear"?

The National Assembly

Peasant uprisings and the storming of the Bastille stampeded the National Assembly into action. On August 4, in a combative all-night meeting, nobles in the National Assembly voted to end their own privileges. They agreed to give up their old manorial dues, exclusive hunting rights, special legal status, and exemption from taxes.

An End to Special Privilege "Feudalism is abolished," announced the proud and weary delegates at 2 A.M. As the president of the Assembly later observed, "We may view this moment as the dawn of a new revolution, when all the burdens weighing on the people were abolished, and France was truly reborn."

Were nobles sacrificing much with their votes on the night of August 4? Both contemporary observers

>> The ideals of the Enlightenment inspired the Declaration of the Rights of Man and the Citizen.

Bounce to Activate Illustration

>> On October 5, 1789, thousands of women marched on the royal palace at Versailles hoping to draw attention to their poor living conditions.

and modern historians note that the nobles gave up nothing that they had not already lost. In the months ahead, the National Assembly turned the reforms of August 4 into law, meeting a key Enlightenment goal—the equality of all male citizens before the law.

Declaration of the Rights of Man In late August, as a first step toward writing a constitution, the Assembly issued the Declaration of the Rights of Man and the Citizen. The document was modeled in part on the American Declaration of Independence, written 13 years earlier. All men, the French declaration announced, were "born and remain free and equal in rights." They enjoyed natural rights to "liberty, property, security, and resistance to oppression." Like the writings of Locke and the *philosophes*, the declaration insisted that governments exist to protect the natural rights of citizens.

The declaration further proclaimed that all male citizens were equal before the law. Every French man had an equal right to hold public office "with no distinction other than that of their virtues and talents."

It affirmed the legal idea that no person could be arrested, tried or imprisoned except according to the law. In addition, the declaration asserted freedom of religion and called for taxes to be levied according to ability to pay. Its principles were captured in the enduring slogan of the French Revolution, "Liberty, Equality, Fraternity."

Some women were disappointed that the Declaration of the Rights of Man did not grant equal citizenship to them. In 1791, **Olympe de Gouges** (oh LAMP duh GOOZH) demanded equal rights in her Declaration of the Rights of Woman and the Female Citizen. "Woman is born free," she proclaimed, "and her rights are the same as those of man." She called for all citizens, men or women, to be equally eligible for all public offices. De Gouges and other women who pushed the cause of women's rights were often ridiculed or sometimes imprisoned and executed.

Women March on Versailles Louis XVI did not want to accept the reforms of the National Assembly. Nobles continued to enjoy gala banquets while people were starving.

By autumn, anger again turned to action. On October 5, about six thousand women marched 13 miles in the pouring rain from Paris to Versailles. "Bread!" they shouted. They demanded to see the king.

Much of the crowd's anger was directed at the queen, **Marie Antoinette.** She was the daughter

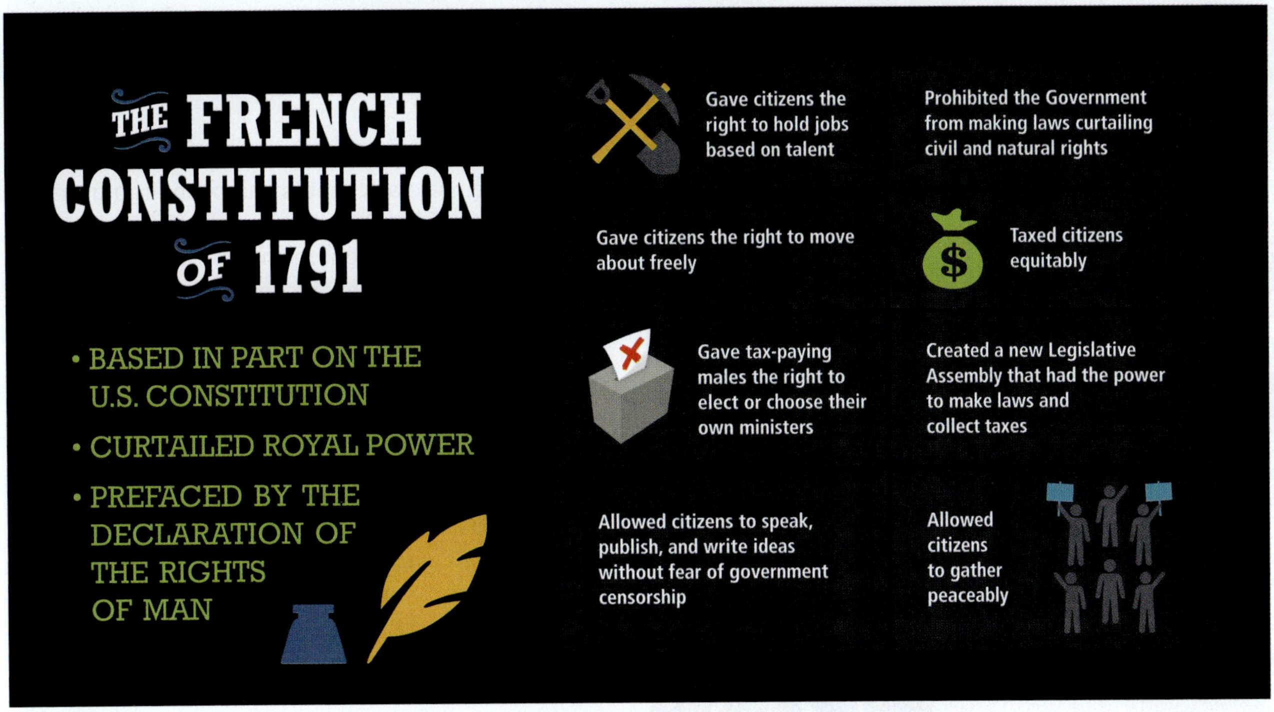

>> **Analyze Charts** The Constitution of 1791 turned France upside down by destroying the old order. What powers did the Legislative Assembly now have?

of Maria Theresa of Austria. Ever since she had married Louis, she had come under attack for being frivolous and extravagant. She eventually grew more serious and even advised the king to compromise with moderate reformers. Still she remained a source of scandal. "Death to the Austrian!" the women who marched on Versailles shouted.

Lafayette and the National Guard eventually calmed the crowd. Still the women refused to leave Versailles until the king met their most important demand—to return to Paris. Not too happily, the king agreed. The next morning, the crowd, with the king and his family in tow, set out for the city. At the head of the procession rode women perched on the barrels of seized cannons. Crowds along the way cheered the king, who now wore the tricolor.

In Paris, the royal family moved into the Tuileries (TWEE luh reez) palace. For the next three years, Louis was a virtual prisoner.

DESCRIBE Why did the women who marched on Versailles want King Louis XVI to return to Paris?

Reforms of the National Assembly

The National Assembly soon followed the king to Paris. Its largely bourgeois members worked to draft a constitution and to solve the continuing financial crisis.

Controlling the Church To pay off the huge government debt—much of it owed to the bourgeoisie—the Assembly voted to take over and sell Church lands. In an even more radical move, the National Assembly put the French Catholic Church under state control. Under the Civil Constitution of the Clergy, issued in 1790, bishops and priests became elected, salaried officials. The Civil Constitution ended papal authority over the French Church and dissolved convents and monasteries.

Reaction to the Civil Constitution was swift and angry. Many bishops and priests refused to accept the document while the pope condemned it.

Large numbers of French peasants, who were conservative concerning religion, also rejected the changes. When the government punished clergy who refused to support the Civil Constitution, a huge gulf opened between revolutionaries in Paris and the peasantry in the provinces.

>> Revolutionaries captured King Louis XVI as he tried to escape.

The Constitution of 1791 The National Assembly completed its main task by producing a constitution. The Constitution of 1791 set up a limited monarchy in place of the absolute monarchy that had ruled France for centuries. A new Legislative Assembly had the power to make laws, collect taxes, and decide on issues of war and peace. Lawmakers would be elected by tax-paying male citizens over age 25.

To make government more efficient, the constitution replaced the old provinces with 83 departments of roughly equal size. It abolished the old provincial courts, and it reformed laws.

To moderate reformers, the Constitution of 1791 seemed to complete the revolution. Reflecting Enlightenment goals, it ensured equality before the law for all male citizens and ended Church interference in government. At the same time, it put power in the hands of men with the means and leisure to serve in government.

The Royal Family Tries to Escape Meanwhile, Marie Antoinette and others had been urging the king to escape their humiliating situation. Louis finally gave in. One night in June 1791, a coach rolled north from Paris toward the border. Inside sat the king disguised as a servant, the queen dressed as a governess, and the royal children.

The attempted escape failed. In a town along the way, Louis's disguise was uncovered by someone who held up a piece of currency with the king's face on it. A company of soldiers escorted the royal family back to Paris, as onlooking crowds hurled insults at the king. In place of the old shouts of "Long Live the King!" people cried, "Long Live the Nation." To many, Louis's dash to the border showed that he was a traitor to the revolution. As new crises arose, the French Revolution entered a new, more radical phase.

DESCRIBE How did the National Assembly try to reform the French Catholic Church?

ASSESSMENT

1. **Apply Concepts** How did France's social divisions in the late 1700s contribute to the revolution?
2. **Draw Conclusions** Why was the conflict between the clergy and the Third Estate the most divisive in the course of the revolution?
3. **Compare** How might the complaints of a peasant and a merchant compare during the revolution?
4. **Identify Cause and Effect** What characteristics of the Third Estate helped fuel the Revolution?
5. **Connect** What did the Tennis Court Oath foretell about the coming events of the French Revolution?

Declaration of the Rights of Man and the Citizen

Introduction

The National Assembly issued this document in 1789 after having overthrown the established government in the early stages of the French Revolution. The document was modeled in part on the English Bill of Rights and on the American Declaration of Independence. The basic principles of the French declaration were those that inspired the revolution, such as the freedom and equality of all male citizens before the law. The Articles below identify additional principles.

In 1791, Olympe de Gouge presented the Declaration of the Rights of Woman and the Female Citizen to challenge the Declaration of the Rights of Man and the Citizen. The second primary source lists some of the ideas in the document.

>> The Declaration of the Rights of Man

Primary Source

If you need extra support, click on the icon between the text. Therefore the National Assembly recognizes and proclaims, in the presence and under the auspices [approval and support] of the Supreme Being, the following rights of man and of the citizen:

1. Men are born and remain free and equal in rights. Social distinctions may be founded only upon the general good.
2. The aim of all political association is the preservation of the natural and imprescriptible [that which cannot be rightfully taken away] rights of man. These rights are liberty, property, security, and resistance to oppression. . . .
4. Liberty consists in the freedom to do everything which injures no one else. . . .
5. Law can only prohibit such actions as are hurtful to society. . . .
6. Law is the expression of the general will. Every citizen has a right to participate personally, or through his representative, in its formation. It must be the same for all, whether it protects or punishes. All citizens, being equal in the eyes of the law, are equally eligible to all dignities and to all public positions and occupations, according to their abilities, and without distinction except that of their virtues and talents.
7. No person shall be accused, arrested, or imprisoned except in the cases and according to the forms prescribed by law. . . .
11. The free communication of ideas and opinions is one of the most precious of the rights of man. Every citizen may, accordingly, speak, write, and print with freedom. . . .
13. A common contribution is essential for the maintenance of the public [military] forces and for the cost of administration. This should be equitably distributed among all the citizens in proportion to their means.

Primary Source

1. Woman is born free and remains equal to man in rights. Social distinctions may be based only on common utility.

2. The purpose of all political association is the preservation of the natural rights of woman and man. These rights are liberty, property, security, and especially resistance to oppression.
3. The principle of all sovereignty rests essentially in the nation, which is but the reuniting of woman and man. No body and no individual may exercise authority which does not emanate expressly from the nation.
6. The law should be the expression of the general will. All citizenesses and citizens should take part. . . .All citizenesses and citizens being equal in its eyes, should be equally admissible to all public dignities, offices and employments, according to their ability, and with no other distinction than that of their virtues and talents.
13. For maintenance of public authority and for expenses of administration, taxation of women and men is equal; she takes part in all forced labor service, in all painful tasks; she must therefore have the same proportion in the distribution of places, employments, offices, dignities and in industry.
17. Property belongs to both sexes whether united or separated; it is for each of them an inviolable and sacred right, and no one may be deprived of it . . .

ANALYZE ARGUMENTS In what ways does de Gouge demand that women be regarded as equal citizens?

ASSESSMENT

1. **Draw Conclusions** Many of the Declaration's principles are broad and idealistic. Choose one to analyze, addressing the potential problems that could arise when it becomes implemented as a law.
2. **Paraphrase** Tell in your own words what the Declaration says about law and fairness. Pay particular attention to Article 6 as you formulate your answer.
3. **Summarize** Explain how the Declaration protects individual liberties. Cite details in the text to support your response.
4. **Draw Conclusions** How did de Gouges hope to show the failings of the French Revolution in terms of rendering equality for men and women?

1.7 The outbreak of the French Revolution stirred debate all over Europe and the United States. Supporters of the Enlightenment, such as Thomas Jefferson, saw the French experiment as the dawn of a new age for justice and equality. European rulers and nobles, however, denounced the French Revolution.

>> The September massacres lasted six days and resulted in more than 1,368 deaths.

Bounce to Activate Flipped Video

A Radical Phase

>> **Objectives**

Explain why the French Revolution entered a more radical phase.

Understand how radicals abolished the French monarchy.

Analyze the causes and course of the Reign of Terror.

Describe France under the Directory.

Identify how the French Revolution changed life in France.

>> **Key Terms**

émigré
sans-culottes
Jacobin
suffrage
Maximilien Robespierre
Reign of Terror
guillotine
Napoleon Bonaparte
Nationalism
Marseilles

Radicals Gain Strength

Fear of the "French Plague" European rulers were horrified by the French Revolution, which threatened absolute monarchy. They increased border patrols to stop the spread of the "French plague." Fueling those fears were the horror stories that were told by **émigrés** (EM ih grayz)—nobles, clergy, and others who had fled France. Émigrés reported attacks on their privileges, their property, their religion, and even their lives. Even "enlightened" rulers turned against France. Catherine the Great of Russia burned Voltaire's letters and locked up critics.

Edmund Burke, a British statesman who earlier had defended the American Revolution, bitterly condemned revolutionaries in Paris. He predicted all too accurately that the revolution would become more violent. "When ancient opinions and rules of life are taken away," he warned, "we have no compass to govern us."

Threats from Abroad The failed escape of Louis XVI brought further hostile rumblings from abroad. In August 1791, the king of Prussia and the emperor of Austria—who was Marie Antoinette's brother—issued the Declaration of Pilnitz. In this document, the two monarchs threatened to protect the French monarchy.

The declaration may have been mostly a bluff, but revolutionaries in France took the threat seriously and prepared for war. The revolution was about to enter a new, more radical phase.

Radicals Seek Power In October 1791, the newly elected Legislative Assembly took office. Faced with crises at home and abroad, it survived for less than a year. Economic problems fed renewed turmoil.

Assignats (AS ig nats), the revolutionary currency, dropped in value, causing prices to rise rapidly. Uncertainty about prices led to hoarding and caused additional food shortages.

In Paris and other cities, working-class men and women, called **sans-culottes** (sanz koo LAHTS), pushed the revolution into more radical action. Sans-culottes means "without breeches." Men wore long trousers instead of the fancy knee breeches that men of the upper class wore. By 1791, many sans-culottes demanded an end to the monarchy and the creation of a republic. They also wanted the government to guarantee them a living wage.

Within the Legislative Assembly, several hostile factions competed for power. The sans-culottes found support among radicals, especially the Jacobins. A revolutionary political club, the **Jacobins** were mostly middle-class lawyers or intellectuals. They used pamphleteers and sympathetic newspaper editors to advance the republican cause.

Opposing the radicals were moderate reformers and officials who wanted no more reforms at all. The radicals soon held the upper hand in the Legislative Assembly.

War Breaks Out In April 1792, the war of words between French revolutionaries and European monarchs moved onto the battlefield. Eager to spread the revolution and destroy tyranny abroad, the Legislative Assembly declared war first on Austria and then on Prussia, Britain, and other states. The great powers expected to win an easy victory against France, a land divided by revolution. In fact, the fighting that began in 1792 lasted on and off until 1815.

The war abroad heightened tensions in Paris. Well-trained Prussian forces were cutting down raw French recruits. In addition, royalist officers were deserting the French army, joining émigrés and others hoping to restore the king's power.

CITE EVIDENCE How did the monarchs of Europe react to the French Revolution?

Political Map of Europe, 1792

>> Europe in the 1790s was dominated by monarchies. **Analyze Maps** Why do you suppose France's neighbors were afraid of the French Revolution?

The Monarchy Is Abolished

In 1793, the Revolution entered a radical phase. For a year, France experienced one of the bloodiest regimes in its long history as determined leaders sought to extend and preserve the Revolution.

New Outbreaks of Violence Battle disasters overseas quickly inflamed revolutionaries in Paris. They thought the king was in league with the enemies. On August 10, 1792, a crowd of Parisians stormed the royal palace of the Tuileries and slaughtered the king's guards. The royal family fled to the Legislative Assembly.

A month later, citizens attacked prisons that held nobles and priests accused of political offenses. More than 1,000 prisoners were killed, including many ordinary criminals.

Historians disagree about the people who carried out these "September massacres." Some call them bloodthirsty mobs. Others describe them as patriots defending France. In fact, most were ordinary citizens fired to fury by real and imagined grievances.

>> Marie Antoinette's lavish lifestyle and disregard for the masses contributed to her unpopularity and later execution.

The National Convention Backed by Paris crowds, radicals then took control of the Assembly. Radicals called for the election of a new legislative body called the National Convention. **Suffrage**, the right to vote, was to be extended to all male citizens, not just to property owners.

The Convention that met in September 1792 was a more radical body than earlier Assemblies. It voted to abolish the monarchy and establish a republic. Deputies then drew up a new constitution. The Jacobins, who controlled the Convention, set out to erase all traces of the old order. They seized lands of nobles and abolished titles of nobility. All men and women were called "Citizen." Louis XVI became Citizen Capet, from the dynasty that ruled France during the Middle Ages.

Execution of a King and Queen During the early months of the Republic, the Convention also put Louis XVI on trial as a traitor to France. The king was convicted by a single vote and sentenced to death.

On a foggy morning in January 1793, Louis mounted a scaffold in a public square in Paris. He started to speak, "Frenchmen, I die innocent. I pardon the authors of my death. I pray God that the blood about to be spilt will never fall upon the head of France. . . ." Then a roll of drums drowned out his words. Moments later, the king was beheaded. The executioner lifted the king's head by its hair and held it before the crowd.

In October, Marie Antoinette was also executed. The popular press celebrated her death. The queen, however, showed great dignity as she went to her death. Her son, who might once have become Louis XVII, died of unknown causes in the dungeons of the Revolution.

☑ **CONTRAST** What was the main difference between earlier Assemblies and the National Convention, which met in September 1792?

The Reign of Terror

By early 1793, danger threatened France on all sides. The country was at war with much of Europe, including Britain, the Netherlands, Spain, and Prussia. In the Vendée (vahn DAY) region of France, royalists and priests led peasants in rebellion against the government.

In Paris, the sans-culottes demanded relief from food shortages and inflation. The Convention itself was bitterly divided between Jacobins and a rival group, the Girondins.

Committee of Public Safety To deal with the threats to France, the Convention created the Committee of Public Safety. The 12-member committee had almost absolute power. Preparing France for all-out war, it ordered all citizens to contribute to the war effort. They urged young men to go into battle, women to make tents or serve in hospitals, and children to turn old lint into linen.

Spurred by revolutionary fervor, recruits marched off to defend the republic. Young officers developed effective tactics to win battles with masses of ill-trained but patriotic forces. Soon, French armies overran the Netherlands. They later invaded Italy. At home, they crushed peasant revolts. European monarchs shuddered as the revolutionaries carried "freedom fever" into conquered lands.

Robespierre, the Incorruptible At home, the government battled counterrevolutionaries under the guiding hand of **Maximilien Robespierre** (ROHBZ pyehr). Robespierre, a shrewd lawyer and politician, quickly rose to the leadership of the Committee of Public Safety. Among Jacobins, his selfless dedication to the revolution earned him the nickname "the incorruptible." His enemies called him a tyrant.

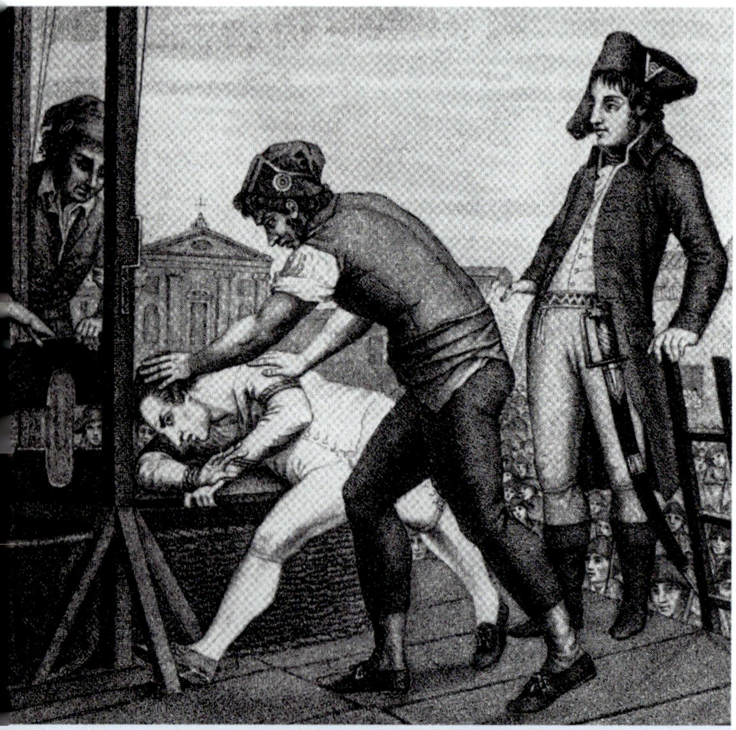

>> Robespierre was beheaded on July 287, 1794, a victim of the Terror he helped create.

Bounce to Activate Gallery

"Death to the Traitors" Robespierre was one of the chief architects of the **Reign of Terror**, which lasted from September 1793 to July 1794. Revolutionary courts conducted hasty trials. Spectators greeted death sentences with cries of "Hail the Republic!" or "Death to the traitors!" In a speech given on February 5, 1794, Robespierre explained that the terror was necessary to protect the Revolution and achieve its goals.

During the Reign of Terror, about 300,000 citizens were arrested. About 17,000 were executed. They included nobles and clergy, peasants, and sans-culottes, along with middle-class citizens who had once supported the Revolution.

> It is necessary to stifle the domestic and foreign enemies of the Republic or perish with them. . . . The first maxim of our politics ought to be to lead the people by means of reason and the enemies of the people by terror.
>
> —Maximilien Robespierre

Many were victims of mistaken identity or were falsely accused by their neighbors. Many more were packed into hideous prisons, where deaths from disease were common.

The engine of the Terror was the **guillotine** (GIL uh teen). Its fast-falling blade extinguished life instantly. A member of the legislature, Dr. Joseph Guillotin (gee oh TAN), had introduced it as a more humane method of beheading than the uncertain ax. Still, the guillotine quickly became a symbol of horror.

Within a year, the Terror consumed those who initiated it. Weary of bloodshed and fearing for their own lives, members of the Convention turned on the Committee of Public Safety. On the night of July 27, 1794, Robespierre was arrested. The next day he was executed. After the heads of Robespierre and other radicals fell, executions slowed dramatically.

DRAW CONCLUSIONS How did radicals such as Robespierre justify the use of terror?

Reaction and the Directory

In reaction to the Terror, the Revolution entered a third stage. Middle class and professional people dominated this stage of the Revolution.

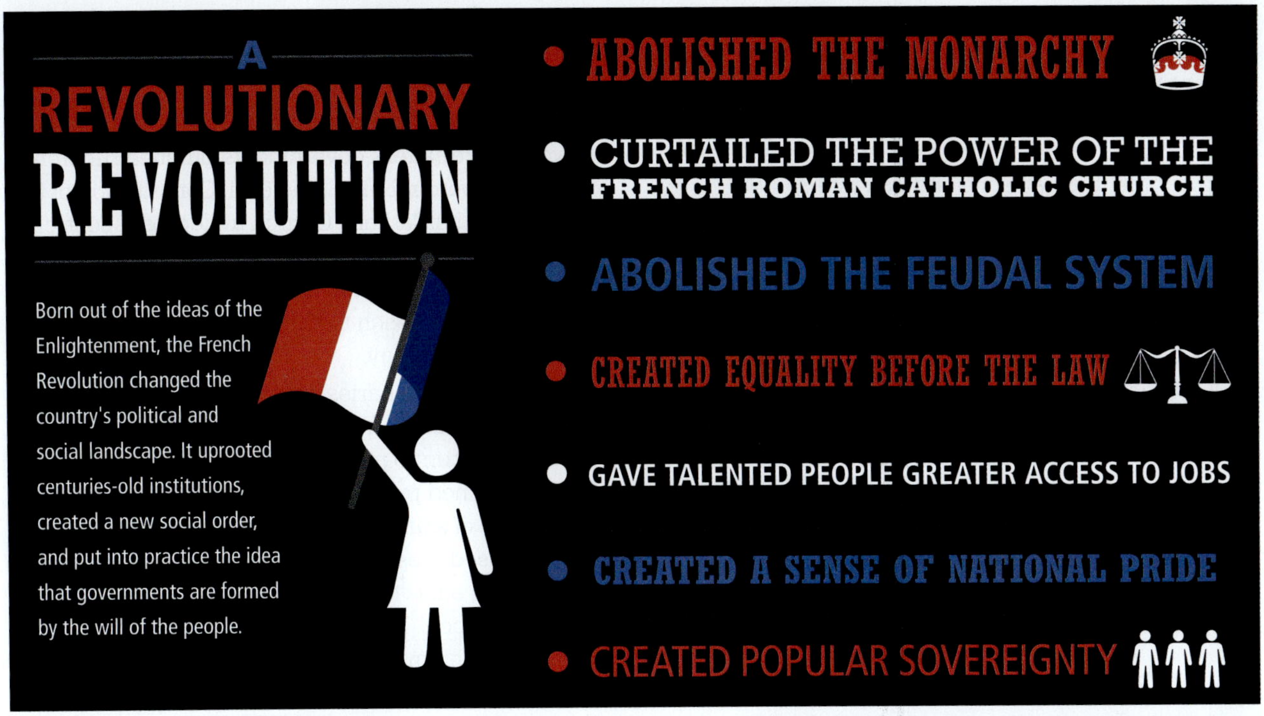

>> **Analyze Charts** The French Revolution changed the country's political and social landscape. How did the Revolution change the social order?

Bounce to Activate Timeline

Moving away from the excesses of the Convention, moderates produced another constitution, the third since 1789. The Constitution of 1795 set up a five-man Directory and a two-house legislature elected by male citizens of property. The Directory held power from 1795 to 1799.

Weak, but willing to use force against its enemies, the Directory faced many challenges. Although France made peace with Prussia and Spain, the war continued with Austria and Great Britain. Corrupt leaders lined their own pockets but failed to solve pressing problems. When rising bread prices stirred hungry sans-culottes to riot, the Directory quickly suppressed them.

Another threat to the Directory was the revival of royalist feeling. Many émigrés were returning to France, and devout Catholics, who resented measures that had been taken against the Church, were welcoming them. In the election of 1797, supporters of a constitutional monarchy won the majority of seats in the legislature.

Despite its failings, the Directory consolidated many reforms of the National Convention. It set up a system of elite schools and helped the French economy to recover from the upheavals of the Terror. During the Directory, France had strengthened its armies and won several important battles.

As chaos threatened, politicians turned to **Napoleon Bonaparte,** a popular military hero who had won a series of brilliant victories against the Austrians in Italy. The politicians planned to use him to advance their own goals. To their dismay, however, before long Napoleon would outwit them all to become ruler of France.

IDENTIFY CAUSE AND EFFECT Why did Catholics welcome the return of the émigrés?

The Revolution Transforms France

By 1799, the 10-year-old French Revolution had dramatically changed France. It had dislodged the old social order, overthrown the monarchy, and brought the Church under state control.

New symbols such as the red "liberty caps" and the tricolor confirmed the liberty and equality of all male citizens. The new title "citizen" applied to people of all social classes. Elaborate fashions and powdered wigs gave way to the practical clothes and simple haircuts of the sans-culottes.

Nationalism Spreads Revolution and war gave the French people a strong sense of national identity. In earlier times, people had felt loyalty to local authorities. As monarchs centralized power, loyalty shifted to the king or queen. Instead, the government rallied sons and daughters of the Revolution to defend the nation itself.

Nationalism, a strong feeling of pride in and devotion to one's country, spread throughout France. The French people attended civic festivals that celebrated the nation and the Revolution. A variety of dances and songs on themes of the Revolution became immensely popular.

By 1793, France was a nation in arms. From the port city of **Marseilles** (mahr say), troops marched to a rousing new song. It urged the "children of the fatherland" to march against the "bloody banner of tyranny." This song, "La Marseillaise" (mahr say ez), would later become the French national anthem.

Social Reform Revolutionaries pushed for social reform and religious toleration. They set up state schools to replace religious ones and organized systems to help the poor, old soldiers, and war widows. With a major slave revolt raging in the colony of St. Domingue (Haiti), the government also abolished slavery in France's Caribbean colonies.

>> During the radical phase of the French Revolution, many Christian churches were renamed Temples of Reason. Religious symbols were covered. On some churches, the revolutionary motto "Liberté, egalité, fraternité" was inscribed on the stone facade.

Religion and the Revolution During the Revolution, different governments pursued different policies toward religion. The Civil Constitution of the Clergy put the Catholic Church under state control. Unlike the United States whose Constitution forbade the establishment of any official state church, France supported the French Catholic Church by paying the salaries of the clergy.

Many revolutionaries embraced the ideas of religious toleration. Yet this Enlightenment ideal often fell victim to politics. During the radical phase, leaders banned public religious worship and removed the names of saints from streets and buildings. Any who opposed these moves faced persecution or death. This effort to de-Christianize France had little popular support. In the end, the Catholic Church was restored with limited rights.

Comparison with the American Revolution The French Revolution came on the heels of the American Revolution. The two revolutions had both similarities and differences.

Both grew out of Enlightenment ideals such as liberty, freedom, and the rights of citizens. Both began with calls for reform, but ended up with a complete change of government. In the colonies and in France, people rose up against oppressive monarchies and high taxes. Each revolution broke out after years of increasing discontent with powerful rulers who imposed their will on the people.

Historians have compared the causes of the American and French Revolutions, and emphasized the role of the ideas behind the Glorious Revolution in helping to inspire both later events. Although the political traditions and social climate of France and the colonies differed, both the French and American colonists wanted a government that was responsible to its people. The colonists saw themselves as citizens of Britain, entitled to the same rights. The British people had won these rights by limiting the power of their monarch through the Magna Carta in 1215 and the Glorious Revolution of 1688. The violation of these rights by Parliament, over 70 years later, was one cause of the American Revolution.

France was an absolute monarchy, but here too the ideas behind the Glorious Revolution played a role. The Glorious Revolution had confirmed the supremacy of Parliament over the monarch in Britain. French revolutionary leaders were influenced by this political development, as well as by the ideals behind the American Revolution and the U.S. Constitution.

In both countries, the people set up a republican form of government. In France, the first republic did not last, but in the United States, it has lasted until the present.

The short-lived republic of France had a government organized with separation of powers. The National Assembly became the legislative branch, and the king would represent the executive branch. Citizen rights were protected, but equal rights were not fully extended to women.

In both England and pre-revolutionary France, the state supported an official church. In America, although many of the leaders of the Revolution were deeply religious, the First Amendment to the Constitution forbade the establishment of any state-supported church. In France, a state-supported Catholic Church remained a powerful force for more than a century.

ANALYZE INFORMATION Describe several ways the Revolution changed French society.

ASSESSMENT

1. **Compare and Contrast** Compare and contrast the views of France's radical revolutionaries to the views of its moderates.
2. **Check Understanding** Why was the Committee of Public Safety allowed to terrorize France during the Reign of Terror?
3. **Describe** How did the Directory's actions ultimately lead to the rise of Napoleon?
4. **Describe** What actions did the French take after the Revolution to show their patriotism?
5. **Identify Cause and Effect** What was it about the nature of the French Revolution that led to political and social reform?

>> Napoleon was a military genius who dominated Europe for more than a decade.

Bounce to Activate Flipped Video

1.8 From 1799 to 1815, Napoleon Bonaparte dominated France and Europe. A hero to some, an evil force to others, he gave his name to the final phase of the French Revolution—the Age of Napoleon.

>> Objectives

Describe how Napoleon Bonaparte rose to power.

Explain the impact of Napoleon and the Napoleonic Wars.

Identify the reasons for Napoleon's fall from power.

Understand how the Congress of Vienna tried to restore order to Europe.

>> Key Terms

plebiscite
Napoleonic Code
Napoleonic Wars
annex
Continental System
guerrilla warfare
abdicate
Congress of Vienna
legitimacy
Concert of Europe

The Age of Napoleon

Napoleon on the Rise

Early Years Napoleon was born in Corsica, a French-ruled island in the Mediterranean. At age nine, he was sent to France to be trained for a military career. When the revolution broke out, he was an ambitious 20-year-old lieutenant, eager to make a name for himself.

Napoleon favored the Jacobins and republican rule. However, he found the conflicting ideas and personalities of the French Revolution confusing. He wrote to his brother in 1793: "Since one must take sides, one might as well choose the side that is victorious, the side which devastates, loots, and burns. Considering the alternative, it is better to eat than be eaten."

Military Success During the turmoil of the Revolution, Napoleon rose quickly in the army. In December 1793, he drove British forces out of the French port of Toulon (too LOHN).

He then went on to win several dazzling victories against the Austrians, capturing most of northern Italy and forcing the Hapsburg emperor to make peace. Hoping to disrupt British trade with India, he led an expedition to Egypt in 1798. The Egyptian campaign proved to be a disaster, but Napoleon managed to hide stories of the worst losses from his admirers in France.

Success fueled Napoleon's ambition. By 1799, he moved from victorious general to political leader. That year, he helped overthrow the weak Directory and set up a three-man governing board known as the Consulate. Another constitution was drawn up, but Napoleon soon took the title First Consul. In 1800, he forced Spain to return Louisiana Territory to France. In 1802, Napoleon had himself named consul for life.

Napoleon Crowns Himself Emperor Two years later, Napoleon had acquired enough power to assume the title Emperor of the French. He invited the pope to preside over his coronation in Paris. During the ceremony, however, Napoleon took the crown from the pope's hands and placed it on his own head. By this action, Napoleon meant to show that he owed his throne to no one but himself.

At each step on his rise to power, Napoleon had held a **plebiscite** (PLEB uh syt), or popular vote by ballot. Each time, the French strongly supported him, even after he had assumed absolute power as emperor. To understand why, we must look at his policies.

CITE EVIDENCE How did Napoleon rise to power so quickly in France?

Napoleon Reforms France

Napoleon consolidated his power by strengthening the central government. Order, security, and efficiency replaced liberty, equality, and fraternity as the slogans of the new regime.

Social and Economic Reforms To restore economic prosperity, Napoleon controlled prices, encouraged new industry, and built roads and canals. He set up a system of public schools under strict government control to ensure well-trained officials and military officers.

At the same time, Napoleon backed off from some of the Revolution's social reforms. He made peace with the Catholic Church in the Concordat of 1801. The Concordat kept the Church under state control but recognized religious freedom for Catholics. Revolutionaries who opposed the Church denounced the agreement, but Catholics welcomed it.

Napoleon won support across class lines. He encouraged émigrés to return, provided they take an oath of loyalty. Peasants were relieved when he recognized their right to lands they had bought from the Church and nobles during the Revolution.

The middle class, who had benefited most from the Revolution, approved of Napoleon's economic reforms and the restoration of order after years of chaos. Napoleon also opened jobs to all, based on talent, a popular policy among those who remembered the old aristocratic monopoly of power.

The Napoleonic Code Among Napoleon's most lasting reforms was a new code of laws, popularly called the **Napoleonic Code**. It embodied Enlightenment principles such as the equality of all citizens before the law, religious toleration, and the abolition of feudalism.

At the same time, the Napoleonic Code undid some reforms of the French Revolution. Women, for example, lost most of their newly gained rights and could not exercise the rights of citizenship. Male heads of households regained complete authority over their wives and children. Again, Napoleon valued order and authority over individual rights.

DESCRIBE What were some of the reforms Napoleon introduced?

>> At Napoleon's coronation, he placed the crown on his own head to show that he was the source of his own power, not the pope.

The Napoleonic Wars

From 1804 to 1812, Napoleon furthered his reputation on the battlefield. In a series of conflicts known as the **Napoleonic Wars,** he battled the combined forces of the greatest European powers. He took great risks and even suffered huge losses. "I grew up on the field of battle," he once said, "and a man such as I am cares little for the life of a million men." By 1812, his Grand Empire reached its greatest extent.

As a military leader, Napoleon valued rapid movements and made effective use of his large armies. He developed a new plan for each battle so opposing generals could never anticipate what he would do next. His enemies paid tribute to his leadership. Napoleon's presence on the battlefield, said one, was "worth 40,000 troops."

Redrawing the Map of Europe As Napoleon created a vast French empire, he redrew the map of Europe. He **annexed**, or incorporated, into his empire the Netherlands, Belgium, and parts of Italy and Germany.

He also abolished the tottering Holy Roman Empire and created a 38 member Confederation of the Rhine under French protection. He cut Prussian territory in half, turning part of old Poland into the Grand Duchy of Warsaw.

Napoleon controlled much of Europe through forceful diplomacy. One tactic was placing friends and relatives on the thrones of Europe. For example, after unseating the king of Spain, he placed his own brother, Joseph Bonaparte, on the throne. He also forced alliances on European powers from Madrid to Moscow. At various times, the rulers of Austria, Prussia, and Russia reluctantly signed treaties with the "Corsican ogre," as defeated monarchs called him.

In France, Napoleon's successes boosted the spirit of nationalism. Great victory parades filled the streets of Paris with cheering crowds. The people celebrated the glory and grandeur that Napoleon had gained for France.

The Continental System Of all the major European powers, Britain alone remained outside Napoleon's European empire. With only a small army, Britain relied on its sea power to stop Napoleon's drive to rule the continent. In 1805, Napoleon prepared to invade England. But at the Battle of Trafalgar, fought off the southwest coast of Spain, British Admiral Horatio Nelson smashed the French fleet.

Napoleon's Europe (1804-1815)

>> Analyze Maps Napoleon reshaped the map of Europe with his military and political conquests. Who were Napoleon's allies?

Bounce to Activate Map

With an invasion ruled out, Napoleon struck at Britain's lifeblood, its commerce. He waged economic warfare through the **Continental System**, which closed European ports to British goods. Britain responded with its own blockade of European ports. A blockade involves shutting off ports to keep people or supplies from moving in or out.

During their long struggle, both Britain and France seized neutral ships suspected of trading with the other side. British attacks on American ships sparked anger in the United States and eventually triggered the War of 1812.

In the end, Napoleon's Continental System failed to bring Britain to its knees. Although British exports declined, Britain's powerful navy kept vital trade routes open to the Americas and India. Meanwhile, trade restrictions created a scarcity of goods in Europe, sent prices soaring, and intensified resentment against French power.

Impact of Napoleon's Conquests French armies under Napoleon spread ideas of the revolution across Europe. They backed liberal reforms in the lands they conquered. In some places, they helped install revolutionary governments that abolished titles of nobility, ended Church privileges, opened careers to men of talent, and ended serfdom and manorial dues. The Napoleonic Code, too, influenced countries in continental Europe and Latin America.

IDENTIFY CAUSE AND EFFECT How did Napoleon come to dominate most of Europe by 1812?

Challenges to the French Empire

In 1812, Napoleon continued his pursuit of European domination and invaded Russia. This campaign began a chain of events that eventually led to his downfall. Napoleon's final defeat brought an end to the era of the French Revolution.

Seeds of Defeat Napoleon's successes contained seeds of defeat. Although nationalism spurred French armies to success, it worked against them, too. Many Europeans who had welcomed the ideas of the French Revolution nevertheless saw Napoleon and his armies as foreign oppressors. They resented the Continental System and Napoleon's effort to impose French culture on them.

From Rome to Madrid to the Netherlands, nationalism unleashed revolts against France. In the

>> This painting depicts the Battle of Trafalgar, in which the British navy defeated the French on October 21, 1805.

>> Napoleon, shown here crossing the Alps on horseback, attempted to spread French culture across Europe.

Bounce to Activate Timeline

German states, leaders encouraged national loyalty among German-speaking people to counter French influence.

>> Spanish patriots bravely resisted French invaders. In his famous painting *Third of May 1808*, Spanish artist Francisco Goya shows the execution of Spanish resistance leaders by French troops.

Resistance in Spain Resistance to foreign rule bled French-occupying forces dry in Spain. Napoleon introduced reforms that sought to undermine the Spanish Catholic Church. But many Spaniards remained loyal to their former king and devoted to the Church. When the Spanish resisted the invaders, well-armed French forces responded with brutal repression. Far from crushing resistance, however, the French response further inflamed Spanish nationalism. Efforts to drive out the French intensified.

Spanish patriots conducted a campaign of **guerrilla warfare**, or hit-and-run raids, against the French. (In Spanish, guerrilla means "little war.") Small bands of guerrillas ambushed French supply trains or troops before retreating into the countryside. These attacks kept large numbers of French soldiers tied down in Spain when Napoleon needed them elsewhere.

Austria Seeks Revenge Spanish resistance encouraged Austria to resume hostilities against the French. In 1805, at the Battle of Austerlitz, Napoleon had won a crushing victory against an Austro-Russian army of superior numbers. Now, in 1809, the Austrians sought revenge. But once again, Napoleon triumphed—this time at the Battle of Wagram. By the peace agreement that followed, Austria surrendered lands populated by more than three million subjects.

>> The French invasion of Russia became a disaster when the lack of food and supplies combined with a hard winter to nearly destroy Napoleon's army.

Napoleon Invades Russia Tsar Alexander I of Russia was once an ally of Napoleon. The tsar and Napoleon planned to divide Europe if Alexander helped Napoleon in his Continental System. Many countries objected to this system, and Russia became unhappy with the economic effects of the system as well. Yet another cause for concern was that Napoleon had enlarged the Grand Duchy of Warsaw that bordered Russia on the west.

These and other issues led the tsar to withdraw his support from the Continental System. Napoleon responded to the tsar's action by assembling an army with soldiers from 20 nations, known as the Grand Army.

In 1812, with about 600,000 soldiers and 50,000 horses, Napoleon invaded Russia. To avoid battles with Napoleon, the Russians retreated eastward, burning crops and villages as they went. This scorched-earth policy left the French hungry and cold as winter came.

Napoleon entered Moscow in September. His triumph, however, was short-lived.

The Retreat from Moscow Even as French troops entered Moscow, Napoleon realized that he would not be able to feed and supply his army through the long Russian winter. In October, he turned homeward.

The 1,000-mile retreat from Moscow turned into a desperate battle for survival. Russian attacks and the brutal Russian winter took a terrible toll. Fewer than 20,000 soldiers of the once-proud Grand Army survived. Many died. Others deserted. French general Michel Ney sadly concluded, "General Famine and General Winter, rather than Russian bullets, have conquered the Grand Army."

Napoleon rushed to Paris to raise a new force to defend France. His reputation for success had been shattered.

ANALYZE INFORMATION What led to Napoleon's disaster in Russia?

>> Once the scourge of Europe, Napoleon eventually fell from power. This painting shows Napoleon in exile.

Napoleon Falls from Power

The disaster in Russia changed the course of the Napoleonic Wars. Russia, Britain, Austria, and Prussia formed a new alliance against a weakened France. In 1813, they defeated Napoleon in the Battle of the Nations at Leipzig.

Napoleon Abdicates Briefly The next year, Napoleon **abdicated**, or stepped down from power. The victors exiled him to Elba, an island in the Mediterranean. They then recognized Louis XVIII, brother of Louis XVI, as king of France.

The restoration of Louis XVIII did not go smoothly. He agreed to accept the Napoleonic Code and honor the land settlements made during the Revolution. However, many émigrés rushed back to France bent on revenge. An economic depression and the fear of a return to the old regime helped rekindle loyalty to Napoleon.

As the victorious allies gathered in Vienna for a general peace conference, Napoleon escaped his island exile and returned to France. Soldiers flocked to his banner. As citizens cheered Napoleon's advance, Louis XVIII fled. In March 1815, Napoleon entered Paris in triumph.

Napoleon Is Defeated at Waterloo Napoleon's triumph was short-lived. His star soared for only 100 days, while the allies reassembled their forces. On June 18, 1815, the opposing armies met near the town of Waterloo in Belgium. British forces under the Duke of Wellington and a Prussian army commanded by General Blücher crushed the French in an agonizing day-long battle. Once again, Napoleon was forced to abdicate and to go into exile on St. Helena, a lonely island in the South Atlantic. This time, he would not return.

Napoleon's Legacy Napoleon died in 1821, but his legend lived on in France and around the world. His contemporaries as well as historians today have long debated his legacy. Was he "the Revolution on horseback," as he claimed? Or was he a traitor to the Revolution?

No one, however, questions Napoleon's impact on France and on Europe. The Napoleonic Code consolidated many changes of the Revolution. The France of Napoleon was a centralized state with a constitution. Elections were held with expanded, though limited, suffrage. Many more citizens had rights to property and access to education than under the old regime. Still, French citizens lost many rights promised so fervently by republicans during the Convention.

On the world stage, the Napoleonic Wars spread the ideas of the French Revolution. He failed to make Europe into a French empire. Instead, he sparked nationalist feelings across Europe. The abolition of the Holy Roman Empire would eventually help in creating a new Germany.

Napoleon's impact also reached across the Atlantic. In 1803, his decision to sell France's vast Louisiana Territory to the American government doubled the size of the United States and ushered in an age of American expansion.

ANALYZE INFORMATION Why were the French so eager for Napoleon to return to France after his escape from Elba?

The Congress of Vienna

After Waterloo, diplomats and heads of state again sat down at the **Congress of Vienna**. They faced the monumental task of restoring stability and order in Europe after years of war.

The Congress met for 10 months, from September 1814 to June 1815. It was a brilliant gathering of European leaders. Diplomats and royalty dined and danced, attended concerts and ballets, and enjoyed parties arranged by their host, Emperor Francis I of Austria. The work fell to Prince Clemens von Metternich of Austria, Tsar Alexander I of Russia, and Lord Robert Castlereagh of Britain. Defeated France was represented by Prince Charles Maurice de Talleyrand.

Goals of the Congress The chief goal of the Vienna decision makers was to create a lasting peace by establishing a balance of power and protecting the system of monarchy. Each of the leaders also pursued his own goals. Metternich, the dominant figure at the Congress, wanted to restore things to the way they were in 1792. Alexander I urged a "holy alliance" of Christian monarchs to suppress future revolutions.

Lord Castlereagh was determined to prevent a revival of French military power. The aged diplomat Talleyrand shrewdly played the other leaders against one another so France would be accepted as an equal partner.

Restoring Peace and Order The peacemakers redrew the map of Europe. To contain French ambitions, they ringed France with strong countries. In the north, they added Belgium and Luxembourg to Holland to create the kingdom of the Netherlands.

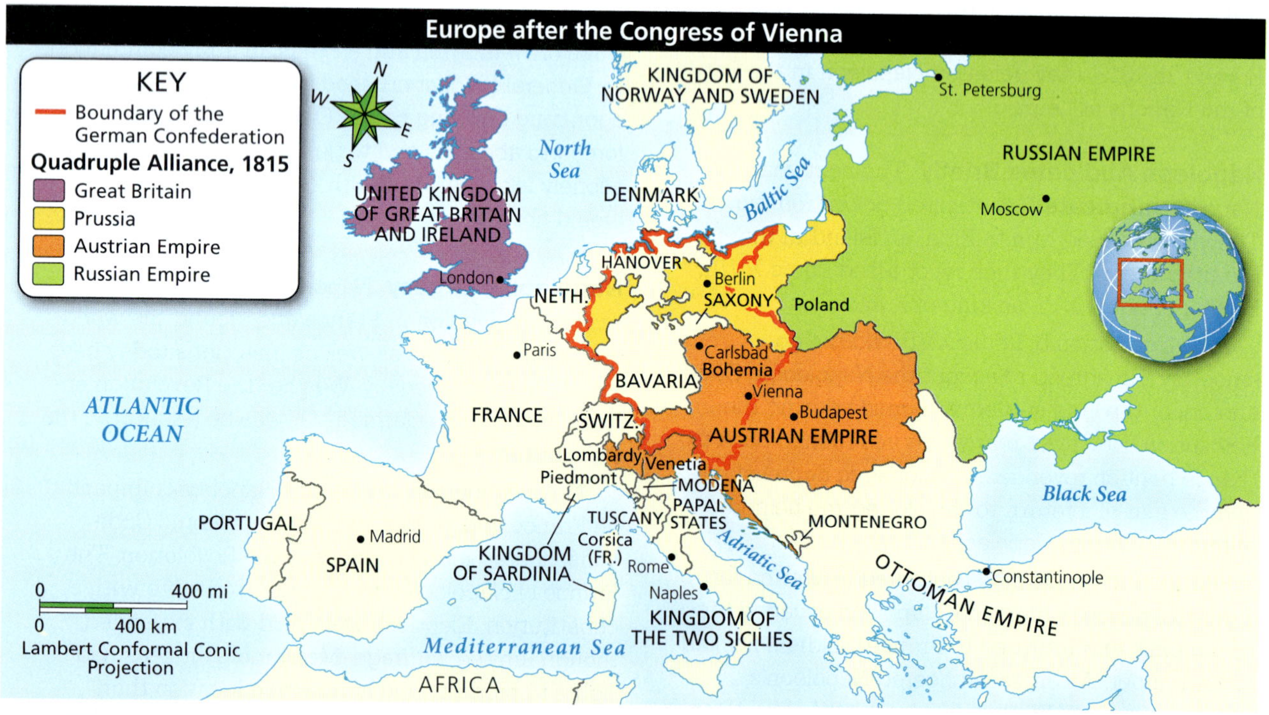

>> Analyze Maps Why did the Congress of Vienna enlarge some of the countries around France?

To prevent French expansion eastward, they gave Prussia lands along the Rhine River. They also allowed Austria to reassert control over northern Italy.

To turn back the clock to 1792, the architects of the peace promoted the principle of **legitimacy**, restoring hereditary monarchies that the French Revolution or Napoleon had unseated. Even before the Congress began, they had put Louis XVIII on the French throne. Later, they restored "legitimate" monarchs in Portugal, Spain, and the Italian states.

Successes and Failures To protect the new order, Austria, Russia, Prussia, and Great Britain extended their wartime alliance. In the Quadruple Alliance, the four nations pledged to act together to balance power and suppress uprisings. They then set up the **Concert of Europe**, a loose organization whose goal was to preserve the agreements set up by the Congress of Vienna. The four great powers—and later France—worked to suppress any uprising inspired by the French Revolution. The Concert of Europe was the first modern international peace keeping organization.

The Vienna statesmen achieved their immediate goals in creating a lasting peace. Peace lasted in Europe for the next 100 years. Although smaller wars broke out, Europe would not see war on a Napoleonic scale until 1914. They failed, however, to foresee how powerful new forces such as nationalism would shake the foundations of Europe and Latin America in the future.

ANALYZE INFORMATION What was the chief goal of the Congress of Vienna?

ASSESSMENT

1. **Identify** What political views did Napoleon spread in Europe that angered monarchs?
2. **Describe** In what way was the Continental System an act of economic warfare? Why did it fail?
3. **Describe** In what way did Napoleon's actions doom his dream of creating a French empire in Europe?
4. **Compare and Contrast** Compare and contrast the goals of Prince Clemens von Metternich of Austria and Britain's Lord Castlereagh during the Congress of Vienna.
5. **Draw Conclusions** Why might some of the French have resisted a return to a monarchy?

California Topic 1 Quick Study Guide

LESSON SUMMARIES

Use these Lesson Summaries, and the longer versions available online, to review the key ideas for each lesson in this Topic.

Lesson 1: Absolute Monarchy in Spain and France

Both King Philip of Spain and Louis XIV ruled as absolute monarchs. Claiming rule by divine right, both rulers unified their nations and centralized power.

Lesson 2: Rise of Austria, Prussia, and Russia

After the brutal Thirty Years' War, Austria and Prussia emerged as great powers. In Russia, Peter the Great centralized royal power, sought to expand Russia, and started a program to modernize the nation.

Lesson 3: Triumph of Parliament in England

English monarchs attempted to expand royal power, but the British Parliament asserted its rights against royal claims to absolute power. The monarchy was abolished and then restored.

Lesson 4: The Enlightenment

The Scientific Revolution of the 1500s and 1600s changed the way people in Europe viewed the world. Enlightenment thinkers believed that social, political, and economic problems could be solved through the use of reason.

Lesson 5: The American Revolution

By 1750, thirteen prosperous colonies in North America were part of Britain's growing empire. As relations became strained with Britain, colonists bitterly resented what they saw as restrictions on their rights. The opposition would lead to revolution, independence, and the founding of the United States of America.

Lesson 6: The French Revolution Begins

Enlightenment ideas led people to question the social, economic, and political inequalities of the old regime. As social unrest increased, citizens stormed the Bastille, a prison for political prisoners. The revolution had begun.

Lesson 7: A Radical Phase

The moderate, first phase of the revolution which attempted to limit the power of the monarchy and guarantee basic rights gave way to the radical phase during which the monarchy was abolished, the king and queen were executed, and a Reign of Terror began.

Lesson 8: The Age of Napoleon

From 1799 to 1815, Napoleon Bonaparte gained power and built an empire that included much of Europe.

VISUAL REVIEW

Use these graphics to review some of the key terms, people, and ideas from this Topic.

Key Rulers

- **Spain:** Charles V (Charles I of Spain); Philip II
- **France:** Henry IV; Louis XIV
- **Britain:** Henry VIII; Elizabeth I; James I; Charles I; Oliver Cromwell; Charles II; James II; William and Mary
- **Austria:** Ferdinand; Charles VI; Maria Theresa
- **Prussia:** Frederick William; Frederick the Great
- **Russia:** Peter the Great; Catherine the Great

American Declaration of Independence

Main Ideas

- All men are created equal and have natural rights to life, liberty, and the pursuit of happiness.
- It is the government's obligation to protect these rights.
- If a government fails to protect these rights, the people can revolt and set up a new government.

Enlightenment Ideas Influence Democracy

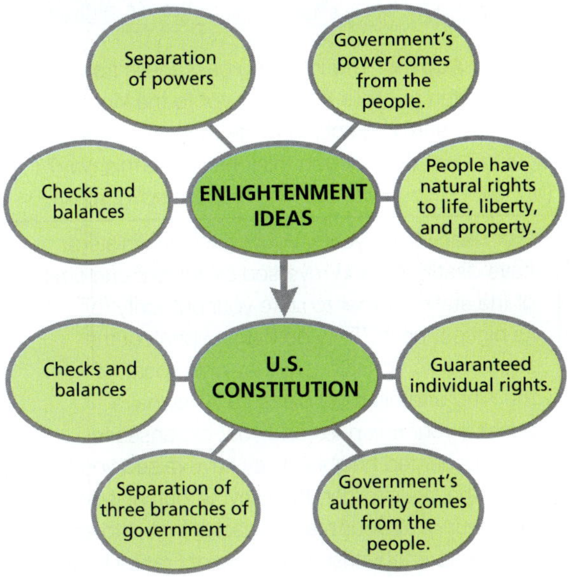

Causes and Effects of the French Revolution

CAUSE AND EFFECT

LONG-TERM CAUSES

- Corrupt and inconsistent leadership
- Prosperous members of the Third Estate resent privileges of the First and Second Estates
- Spread of Enlightenment ideas

IMMEDIATE CAUSES

- Huge government debt
- Poor harvests and rising price of bread
- Failure of Louis XVI to accept financial reforms
- Formation of National Assembly
- Storming of Bastille

↓

THE FRENCH REVOLUTION

↓

IMMEDIATE EFFECTS

- Declaration of the Rights of Man and the Citizen adopted.
- France adopts its first written constitution.
- Revolutionary France fights coalition of European powers.
- Monarchy abolished; execution of king and queen.
- Reign of Terror

LONG-TERM EFFECTS

- Napoleon gains power.
- Napoleonic Code established.
- French public schools set up.
- French conquests spread nationalism.
- Congress of Vienna convenes to restore stability to Europe.
- Revolutions occur elsewhere in Europe and in Latin America.

California Topic 1 Assessment

KEY TERMS, PEOPLE, AND IDEAS

1. How did monarchs use the concept of **divine right** to support absolute rule?
2. How did **Peter the Great** envision Russia's future?
3. What is the connection between the policy of **laissez faire** and natural economic laws?
4. According to John Locke what is the purpose of government?
5. Compare the development of constitutional monarchy in England with that of France.
6. How did the Declaration of Independence influence the writing of the Declaration of the Rights of Man and the Citizen?
7. What role did **Robespierre** assume in the French Revolution?
8. After the fall of Napoleon, how did the Congress of Vienna affect nationalism in Europe?
9. How did the Glorious Revolution change English government?

CRITICAL THINKING

10. **Summarize** Why was the government of Britain an oligarchy rather than a democracy?
11. **Compare** How did Thomas Hobbes's view of government differ from John Locke's? Did the ideas of either influence the new government of the United States? Explain.
12. **Explain** Trace the shift in ideas that moved the French Revolution from constitutional monarchy to democratic despotism.
13. **Draw Conclusions** How did the ideas of a "just society" change during the Age of Reason?
14. **Synthesize Information** How did the Enlightenment impact both the American and French revolutions?
15. **Analyze Information** How did the American Revolution impact the way rebellions were fought and the expectations?
16. **Analyze Cartoons** Look at the cartoon below. The figure on the left represents the British; the other figure represents Napoleon. What are both men carving? Explain.

17. **Writing Activity** The following passage is from a letter written to Louis XIV by a tutor to the king's children, Fenelon. Fenelon wrote the letter without signing it. (a) Why do you think he sent it this way? (b) How do you think the king responded? Explain.

> "For nearly thirty years, your principal Ministers have destroyed and reversed all ancient customs of the state in order to raise your authority to its highest pitch. They no longer speak of the state and its constitution; they only speak of the King and his royal pleasure. They have pushed your revenues and your expenses to unprecedented heights. They have raised you up to the sky in order, they say, to outshine the grandeur of all your predecessors; that is to say, in order to impoverish the whole of France for the introduction of monstrous luxuries of court. . . . Meanwhile, your people die of hunger. The cultivation of the soil is almost stagnant, and no longer offers employment to working men. All commerce is destroyed."
>
> —Archbishop Francois de Fenelon, *Letters*

DOCUMENT-BASED QUESTIONS

The struggle between English monarchs and Parliament raged through the seventeenth century, and was fought on battlefields and legal fronts. Read the documents below, then answer the questions that follow.

DOCUMENT A

"THE KINGS THEREAFTER in Scotland were before any estates or ranks of men within the same, before any Parliaments were holden or laws made; and by them was the land distributed (which at first was wholly theirs), states erected and decerned, and forms of government devised and established. And it follows of necessity that the Kings were the authors and makers of the laws and not the laws of the Kings."

—*True Law of Free Monarchies, 1598*

DOCUMENT B

"The Petition exhibited to his Majesty by the lords Spiritual and Temporal, and Commons, in this present Parliament assembled, concerning divers Rights and Liberties of the Subjects, with the King's Majesty's royal answer thereunto in full Parliament. . . . Your subjects have inherited this freedom, that they should not be compelled to contribute to any tax, tallage, aid, or other like charge not set by common consent, in parliament. . . . No man, of what estate or condition that he be, should be put out of his land or tenements, nor taken, nor imprisoned, nor disinherited nor put to death without being brought to answer by due process of law."

—*The Petition of Right, 1628*

DOCUMENT C

"Men, being, as has been said, by nature all free, equal, and independent, no one can be . . . subjected to the political power of another without his own consent. The only way whereby anyone divests himself of his natural liberty, and puts on the bonds of civil society is by agreeing with other men to join and unite into a community. . . .

It is evident, that *absolute monarchy*, which by some men is counted the only government in the world, is indeed *inconsistent with civil society*."

—*Two Treatises on Government* by John Locke, 1690

DOCUMENT D

A mid-1600s engraving depicts Charles I as a political and religious martyr.

18. What is the main point of Document A?

A. Kings are subject only to laws of parliament.
B. Kings make laws but are not subject to them.
C. Kings no longer have the power of life and death over subjects.
D. Parliament now has the power of life and death over subjects.

19. Document B is a declaration of whose rights?

A. the kings rights
B. Parliament's rights
C. subjects' rights
D. the landed aristocracy's rights

20. Document C

A. supports Document A.
B. supports Document B.
C. supports both Document A and Document B.
D. supports Documents A and D.

21. **Writing Tasks** Would you describe the rise of Parliament in England as an evolution or a revolution? Use the documents along with information from this Topic in your response.

End-of-Topic Practice

1 Why did Thomas Hobbes support absolutism?

A He believed kings ruled by divine right and knew best how to govern citizens who would otherwise be constantly at war.

B He claimed that men naturally are cruel and greedy. They need a strong common power to keep an organized society.

C He saw society as a group of individuals who willingly entered into a contract that would ensure liberty and protection under the banner of one strong ruler in a democratic state.

D He believed that effective government rose from absolute authority and this, along with the assistance of Parliament, would create the best society.

> *"That whenever any Form of Government becomes destructive of these ends, it is the Right of the People to alter or to abolish it . . ."*

2 This excerpt from the Declaration of Independence shows that events during the American Revolution and the French Revolution were partly based on which Enlightenment ideas?

F The evils of divine-right theory listed in Diderot's encyclopedia articles

G Western opinions about religious prejudice and the slave trade

H A social contract giving up organized society for individual freedoms

J Locke's theory about the right to overthrow a government if it fails its duties

3 How did the English Bill of Rights change the relationship between Parliament and the monarchy?

A It established a constitutional monarchy which limited the power of the monarchy.

B It allowed the monarchy to equally share power with Parliament.

C It established political parties which held elections annually.

D The monarchy was given absolute power.

---

4 Which Enlightenment philosopher would Napoleon have agreed with?

F Adam Smith since Napoleon allowed laissez-faire policies in the republic.

G Thomas Hobbes because Napoleon agreed with his views of absolute sovereignty.

H Rousseau since Napoleon created the Napoleonic Code to include Rousseau's views on religious tolerance and universal suffrage.

J John Locke because Napoleon endorsed his democratic principles of government.

If you have trouble with. . .				
Question	1	2	3	4
See Lesson	1.4	1.5, 1.6	1.3	1.4, 1.8

PEARSON realize
PearsonSchool.com/CASS

Go **ONLINE** for digital resources

VIDEO AUDIO ETEXT ACTIVITY WRITING GAMES PDF ASSESSMENT

[ESSENTIAL QUESTION] How do science and technology affect society?

2 The Industrial Revolution (1750–1914)

>> A furnace for manufacturing iron in England

Enduring Understandings

- Agricultural changes, the factory system, and steam power sparked the Industrial Revolution.
- Effects of industrialization included rapid urbanization and the rise of a new middle class.
- Early working conditions in factories and mines were harsh, but later improved.
- Laissez-faire economists like Adam Smith favored free enterprise and limited government control, while Karl Marx called for workers to control means of production.
- In the second Industrial Revolution, technology revolutionized production, transportation, and communication.
- Differing responses to industrial society led to new artistic movements

NBC LEARN

Share the experiences of a worker in an early 19th century textile mill.

Bounce to Activate My Story Video

California Topic 2 Overview

In this Topic, you will learn about the events of The Industrial Revolution. Look at the lesson outline and explore the timeline. As you study this Topic, you will complete the Quest team project.

LESSON OUTLINE

Key Events of the Industrial Revolution

1760s
Watt improves the steam engine.

1807
Robert Fulton develops the first successful steamboat.

1848
Marx and Engels publish *The Communist Manifesto*.

1859
Charles Darwin publishes *On the Origin of Species*.

1750 — 1800s — 1850 — 1900

QUEST! TEAM PROJECT

Making Policy Decisions

Your team is part of a government think tank on economics. You will do important research that will be used to make important decisions. Your current study is about economic policies that will help improve the nation's living standards. There are many questions. In this Quest you will explore one: Who Should Control Economic Decisions?

STEP 1
Gather the documents. Analyze the content of each. List the conclusions. Then have a discussion about the different systems.

STEP 2
Choose the documents with a viewpoint the team will consider and evaluate. Outline your report. Then, still using evidence, consider arguments that could be used to oppose the team's decision.

STEP 3
Review, edit, and revise the report. Remember to support your decision with evidence. Then consider why the team's choice might be opposed.

STEP 4
Present your final report to the class. Reflect on what you have researched. How is the current economic system affecting the nation's families? Should changes be made?

PEARSON realize
PearsonSchool.com/CASS

Go ONLINE for complete Quest materials

VIDEO ETEXT WRITING RUBRIC PDF ASSESSMENT

>> Industrial cities and towns grew up around factories like this one. Factories provided resources, goods, and jobs. **Understand Cause and Effect** Based on this image, how do you think life changed because of industrialization?

Bounce to Activate Flipped Video

2.1 For thousands of years following the rise of civilization, most people lived and worked in small farming villages. Then a chain of events set in motion in the mid-1700s changed that way of life. Today, we call this period of economic change the Industrial Revolution. Production shifted from simple hand tools to complex machines, and sources of energy shifted from human and animal power to steam and, later, electricity.

>> Objectives

Describe how changes in agriculture helped spark the Industrial Revolution.

Analyze why the Industrial Revolution began in Britain.

Explain the role of steam technology and textile manufacturing in the Industrial Revolution.

Describe how the factory system and transportation revolution advanced industry.

Trace how the Industrial Revolution spread.

>> Key Terms

Industrial Revolution
anesthetic
enclosure
James Watt
smelt
capital
enterprise
entrepreneur
putting-out system
Eli Whitney
turnpike
Liverpool
Manchester

The Industrial Revolution Begins

New Ways of Working Change Life

Like the Enlightenment, which occurred around the same time, the Industrial Revolution was partly an outgrowth of the Scientific Revolution of the 1600s and 1700s. The Scientific Revolution focused attention on the physical world, and thinkers used the scientific method to conduct controlled experiments. This scientific approach helped inventors to devise new technologies to improve life. These technologies would change the way work was done.

In contrast with most political revolutions, the Industrial Revolution was neither sudden nor swift. It was a long, slow, uneven process. Yet it affected people's lives as much as previous political changes and revolutions had. From its beginnings in Britain, it spread to the rest of Europe, to North America, and around the globe.

A Rural Way of Life In 1750, most people worked the land, using handmade tools. They lived in simple cottages lit by firelight and candles. They made their own clothing and grew their own food.

In nearby towns, they might exchange goods at a weekly outdoor market.

Like their ancestors, these people knew little of the world that existed beyond their village. The few who left home traveled only as far as their feet or a horse-drawn cart could take them. Those bold adventurers who dared to cross the seas were at the mercy of the winds and tides.

Growing Cities With the onset of the Industrial Revolution, the rural way of life began to disappear. By the 1850s, many country villages had grown into industrial towns and cities. Those who lived there were able to buy clothing and food that someone else produced.

Industrialization Brings Great Change Unlike earlier times, industrial-age travelers were able to move rapidly between countries and continents by train or steamship. Urgent messages flew along telegraph wires. New inventions and scientific "firsts" poured forth each year.

Between 1830 and 1855, for example, an American dentist first used an **anesthetic,** or drug that prevents pain during surgery; an American inventor patented the first sewing machine; a French physicist measured the speed of light; and a Hungarian doctor introduced antiseptic methods to reduce the risk of women's dying in childbirth. By the early 1900s, our familiar world of skyscraper cities and carefully planned suburbs had begun to emerge.

How and why did these great changes occur? Historians point to a series of interrelated causes that helped trigger the industrialization of the West. The "West" referred originally to the industrialized countries of western Europe and North America, but today includes many more.

IDENTIFY MAIN IDEAS How did the Industrial Revolution lead to social and economic changes in Europe?

A New Agricultural Revolution

Oddly enough, the Industrial Revolution was made possible in part by a change in the farming fields of western Europe. The first agricultural revolution took place some 11,000 years ago, when people learned to farm and domesticate animals. Then, about 300 years ago, a second agricultural revolution took place that greatly improved the quality and quantity of farm products.

Farmers Reclaim Land and Renew Soil The Dutch led the way in this new agricultural revolution. They built earthen walls known as dikes to reclaim land from the sea. They also combined smaller fields into larger ones to make better use of the land, and they used fertilizer from livestock to renew the soil.

In the 1700s, British farmers expanded on Dutch agricultural experiments.Educated farmers exchanged news of experiments through farm journals. Some farmers mixed different kinds of soils to get higher crop yields. Others tried out new methods of crop rotation.

Lord Charles Townshend urged farmers to grow turnips, which restored exhausted soil. Jethro Tull invented a new mechanical device, the seed drill, to aid farmers. It deposited seeds in rows to maximize land use rather than scattering them over land, a practice that wasted seeds by spacing plants irregularly.

Wealthy Landowners Enclose Lands Meanwhile, wealthy landowners pushed ahead with a practice called **enclosure.** Enclosure is the process of taking over and consolidating, or combining, lands formerly shared by peasant farmers. In the 1500s, landowners had enclosed land to gain more pastures for sheep in order to increase wool output. By the

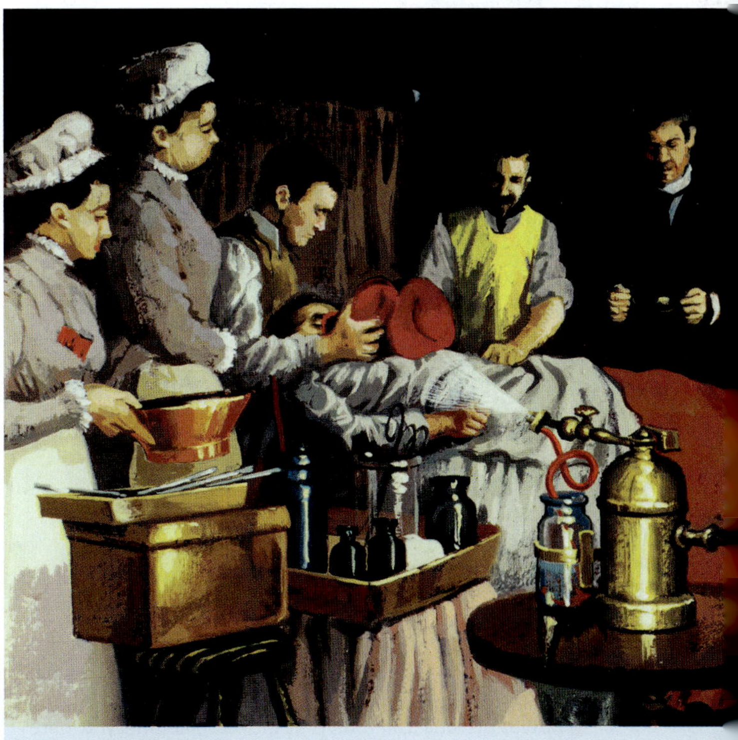

>> An American dentist demonstrates the use of ether as a surgical anesthetic in 1846.

1700s, they wanted to create larger fields that could be cultivated more efficiently. The British Parliament passed laws that made it easier for landowners to enclose lands.

As millions of acres were enclosed, farm output rose. Profits also rose because consolidated fields needed fewer workers. However, such progress had a human cost. Many farm laborers were thrown out of work, and small farmers were forced off their land because they could not compete with large landholders. Villages shrank when people left in search of work.

This shift in the labor force became a key factor in industrialization. Jobless farm workers migrated to towns and cities. Many found work in the new factories, tending to the machines of the Industrial Revolution.

Population Grows Because of Better Farming

Not only did people move to towns and cities, but an overall boom in population also occurred. The improved farming practices of the agricultural revolution contributed to this rapid population growth. Precise population statistics for the 1700s are rare, but those that do exist are striking. Britain's population, for example, soared from about 5 million in 1700 to almost 9 million in 1800.

The population of Europe as a whole shot up from roughly 120 million to about 180 million during the same period. Such growth had never before been seen.

Why did this population increase occur? The population boom was due more to declining death rates than to rising birth rates. The agricultural revolution reduced the risk of famine. Since people ate better, they were healthier. Also, by the late 1800s, better hygiene and sanitation, along with improved medical care, further slowed deaths from disease. During the Industrial Revolution, this growing population tended the machines and bought the goods produced by factories.

CHECK UNDERSTANDING How did an agricultural revolution contribute to population growth?

WATT'S STEAM-ENGINE

>> Watt's engine used steam and atmospheric pressure to power pistons and rods that moved machinery. It had a separate condenser to keep the water hot, conserving energy.

Coal, Steam, and the Energy Revolution

Another major factor that contributed to the Industrial Revolution was an "energy revolution." In the past, the energy for work came mostly from the muscles of humans and animals. In the 1700s, inventive minds found ways to use water power more efficiently and harnessed new sources of energy. Among the most important energy sources was coal, which was used to develop the steam engine.

James Watt and the Steam Engine

In 1712, inventor Thomas Newcomen developed a steam engine powered by coal to pump water out of mines. Later, in 1764, Scottish engineer **James Watt** looked at Newcomen's invention and set out to make improvements on the engine in order to make it more efficient. Watt's engine would become a vital power source of the Industrial Revolution.

The steam engine was first used to power machines, but later was adapted to power locomotives and steamships.

Producing Better Iron

Coal was also a vital source of fuel in the production of iron, a material needed for the construction of machines and steam engines. The Darby family of Coalbrookdale, England, pioneered new methods of producing iron. In 1709, Abraham Darby used coal instead of charcoal to **smelt** iron, or separate iron from its ore.

Resources and Industry in England, 1750

>> **Analyze Maps** Notice where various resources and industries were located in 1750. Why is the location of navigable rivers important to resources and industry?

Darby's experiments led him to produce less expensive and better-quality iron, which was used to produce parts for the steam engines. Both his son and grandson continued to improve on his methods. In fact, Abraham Darby III built the world's first iron bridge. In the decades that followed, high-quality iron was used more and more widely, especially after the world turned to building railroads.

IDENTIFY SUPPORTING DETAILS What did the Darby family contribute to the Industrial Revolution?

Why Did the Industrial Revolution Start in Britain?

Historians have fiercely debated why the Industrial Revolution began in Britain in the 1700s. They have identified a number of advantages Britain had. No single one was unique to Britain, but taken together they helped Britain take an early lead. This complex combination included natural resources, labor, capital, and entrepreneurship. Economists call these the four factors of production; that is, the elements necessary to produce goods. In addition to these factors, growing demand for goods and new technology provided the essential building blocks for Britain's leap forward.

Natural Resources and Geography During the 1700s, Britain began to take greater advantage of its abundant natural resources. Although Britain was a relatively small nation, it had large supplies of coal to power steam engines. Britain also had plentiful iron, which was used to build machines.

Britain's geography also provided an advantage. As an island nation with many ports, Britain had long benefited from trade. Its ships brought raw materials from its overseas empire and exported finished goods. Britain also had streams and rivers that could be harnessed to provide water power. Many rivers were later developed with canals and then used to transport goods to internal markets.

Labor and Capital A large number of workers were needed to mine the coal and iron, build the factories, and run the machines. The agricultural revolution of the 1600s and 1700s freed many men and women from farm labor. The population boom that resulted from changes in agriculture further swelled the available work force. The growing population also increased the demand for goods, which industry supplied.

To develop mining and other industries, capital was needed. **Capital** is money used to invest in enterprises. An **enterprise** is a business organization in an area such as shipping, mining, railroads, or factories. Many businesspeople were ready to risk their profits in new ventures. The capital that helped Britain industrialize came from landowners, banks, and merchants who profited from overseas trade, including the slave trade.

Entrepreneurs and Inventors Britain also had plenty of skilled mechanics. They developed practical new inventions and partnered with entrepreneurs to profit from them. An **entrepreneur** is someone who manages and assumes the financial risks of starting new businesses.

Technology was important to the Industrial Revolution, but did not cause it. Only when other necessary conditions existed, including demand and capital, did technology pave the way for industrialization.

A Favorable Climate for Business In addition to the advantages already cited, Britain had a stable government that supported economic growth. Other countries in Europe imposed heavy river tolls and other barriers to growth. Britain had far fewer blocks to the movement of goods. The government built a strong navy that protected its empire, including shipping and overseas trade.

Raw Cotton, Great Britain 1710–1849 in millions of pounds

ANNUAL AVERAGE CONSUMPTION		ANNUAL AVERAGE CONSUMPTION	
1710–19	1.3	1780–89	15.5
1720–29	1.5	1790–99	28.6
1730–39	1.7	1800–09	59.6
1740–49	2.1	1810–19	93.4
1750–59	2.8	1820–29	166.5
1760–69	3.5	1830–39	320.7
1770–79	4.8	1840–49	526.3

SOURCE: 1697–1780: Wadsworth and Mann [1931], 1780–1810: Baines [1835] 1810–1849: Ellison [1886]

>> **Analyze Charts** This chart shows the gradual increase in cotton use in Britain during the Industrial Revolution. What factors changed the British cotton industry and helped to make it the "workshop of the world"?

Social attitudes adjusted to changing economic conditions. Although members of the upper class looked down on business and business people, they did not reject the great wealth produced by the new entrepreneurs. Religious groups encouraged thrift and hard work. These goals led inventors, bankers, and other risk-takers to devote their energies to new enterprises.

CHECK UNDERSTANDING What conditions in Britain paved the way for the Industrial Revolution?

Textile Industry Initiates Industrialization

The Industrial Revolution first took hold in Britain's largest industry—textiles. In the 1600s, cotton cloth imported from India had become popular. British merchants tried to organize a cotton cloth industry at home. They developed the **putting-out system,** also known as the cottage industry, in which raw cotton was distributed to peasant families who spun it into thread and then wove the thread into cloth in their own homes. Skilled artisans in the towns then finished and dyed the cloth.

Technology Speeds Production Under the putting-out system, production was slow. The process of using manually operated machines for spinning and weaving took time. As the demand for cloth grew, inventors came up with a series of remarkable devices that revolutionized the British textile industry. For example, John Kay's flying shuttle enabled weavers to work so fast that they soon outpaced spinners. James Hargreaves solved that problem by producing the spinning jenny in 1764, which spun many threads at the same time. Five years later, Richard Arkwright patented the water frame, a spinning machine that could be powered by water.

Meanwhile, in America, these faster spinning and weaving machines presented a challenge—how to produce enough cotton to keep up with England. Raw cotton grown in the South had to be cleaned of dirt and seeds by hand, which is a time-consuming task. To solve this, **Eli Whitney** invented a machine called the cotton gin that separated the seeds from the raw cotton at a fast rate. He finished the cotton gin in 1793, and cotton production increased at a rapid rate.

The First Factories The new machines doomed the putting-out system. They were too large and expensive to be operated at home. Instead, manufacturers built long sheds to house the machines. At first, they located the sheds near rapidly moving streams, harnessing the water power to run the machines. Later, machines were powered by steam engines.

Spinners and weavers now came each day to work in these first factories, which brought together workers and machines to produce large quantities of goods. Early observers were awed at the size and output of these establishments. One onlooker noted: "The same [amount] of labor is now performed in one of these structures which formerly occupied the industry of an entire district."

IDENTIFY CAUSE AND EFFECT What technology brought about advances in the British textile industry?

>> Workers and machines filled the early factories of the Industrial Revolution. Machines dramatically increased the quantity of goods that could be produced.

Bounce to Activate Gallery

A Revolution in Transportation

As production increased, entrepreneurs needed faster and cheaper methods of moving goods from place to place. Some capitalists invested in **turnpikes,** private roads built by entrepreneurs who charged travelers a toll, or fee, to use them. Goods traveled faster as a result, and turnpikes soon linked every part of Britain. Other entrepreneurs had canals dug to connect rivers together or to connect inland towns with coastal ports. Engineers also built stronger bridges and upgraded harbors to help the expanding overseas trade.

Canals Improve Transportation During the late 1700s and early 1800s, British factories needed an efficient, inexpensive way to receive coal and raw materials and then to ship finished goods to market. In 1763, when the Bridgewater Canal opened, it not only made a profit from tolls, but it shortened the trip enough to cut in half the price of coal in Manchester.

The success of this canal set off a canal-building frenzy. Entrepreneurs formed companies to construct canals for profit. Not all the canals that were built had enough traffic to support them, however, and bankruptcy often resulted. Then, beginning in the 1830s, canals lost their importance as steam locomotives made railroads the new preferred form of transportation.

>> Steam locomotives made travel faster than ever before. The locomotives burned coal to produce steam and traveled overland routes on iron rails.

Bounce to Activate Map

The Steam Locomotive Drives Railroads It was the invention of the steam locomotive that made the growth of railroads possible. In the early 1800s, pioneers like George Stephenson developed steam-powered locomotives to pull carriages along iron rails. The railroad did not have to follow the course of a river. This meant that tracks could go places where rivers did not, allowing factory owners and merchants to ship goods swiftly and cheaply over land. The world's first major rail line, from **Liverpool** to **Manchester,** opened in England in 1830.

In the following decades, railroad travel became faster and railroad building boomed. By 1870, rail lines crisscrossed Britain, Europe, and North America.

Cheaper Goods Lead to More Demand As the Industrial Revolution got under way, it triggered a chain reaction. Once inventors developed machines that could produce large quantities of goods more efficiently, prices fell. Lower prices made goods more affordable and thus attracted more consumers. Additional consumers then further fed the demand for goods. This new cycle caused a wave of economic and social changes that dramatically affected the way people lived.

DRAW CONCLUSIONS How did the development of railroads advance the Industrial Revolution?

Industrialization Spreads

The start of industrialization had largely been forged from iron, powered by steam engines, and driven by the British textile industry. By the mid-1800s, the Industrial Revolution entered a second phase. By then, it had spread outside Britain. New industrial powers emerged. Factories powered by electricity used innovative processes to turn out new products. Changes in business organization contributed to the rise of giant companies. As the twentieth century dawned, this second Industrial Revolution transformed the economies of the Western world.

Other Nations Industrialize During the early Industrial Revolution, Britain stood alone as the world's industrial giant. To protect its head start, Britain tried to enforce strict rules against exporting inventions.

For a while, the rules worked. Then, in 1807, British mechanic William Cockerill opened factories in Belgium to manufacture spinning and weaving machines. Belgium became the first European nation after Britain to industrialize. By the mid-1800s, other nations had joined the race, and several newcomers were challenging Britain's industrial supremacy.

How were other nations able to catch up with Britain so quickly? First, nations such as Germany,

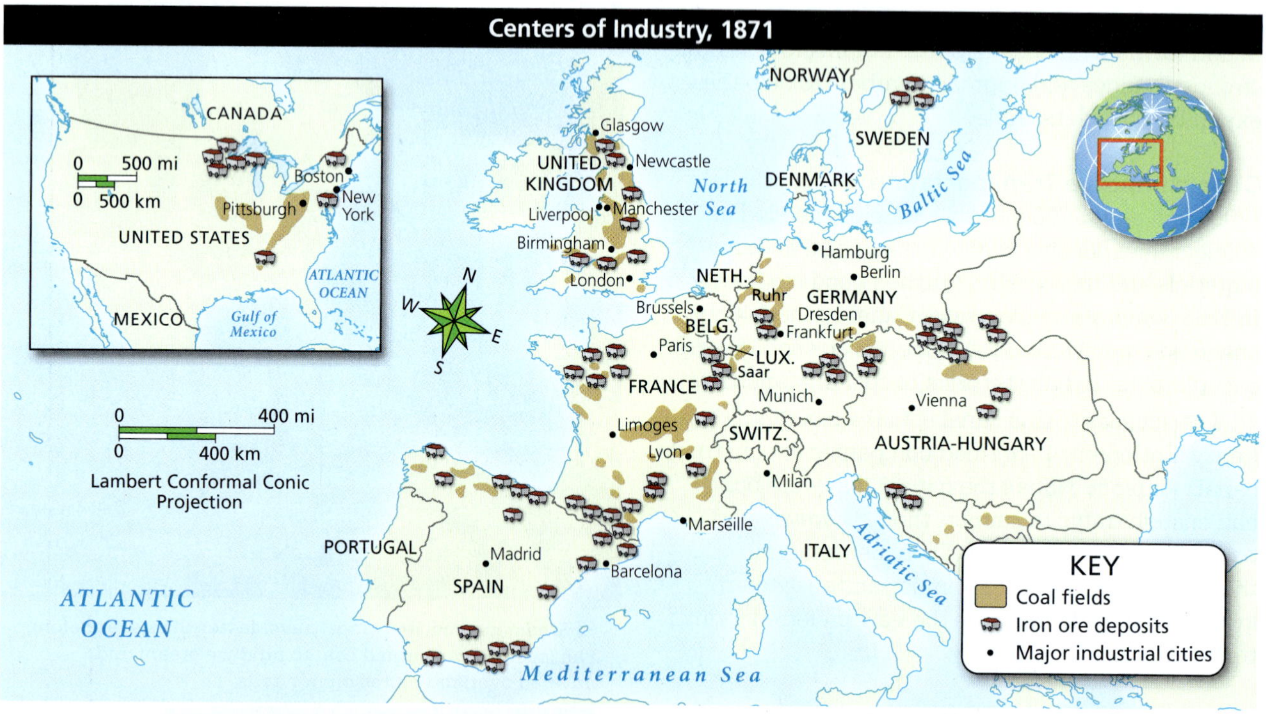

>> **Analyze Maps** By 1871, industrialization had spread through Europe and across the Atlantic to America. Which major industrial cities were probably shipping centers as well? Identify two nations that were at a disadvantage for industrialization.

France, and the United States had more abundant supplies of coal, iron, and other resources than Britain did. Also, they had the advantage of being able to follow Britain's lead. Like Belgium, latecomers often borrowed British experts or technology. The first American textile factory was built in Pawtucket, Rhode Island, with plans smuggled out of Britain. American inventor Robert Fulton powered his steamboat with one of James Watt's steam engines.

Two countries in particular—Germany and the United States—thrust their way to industrial leadership. Germany united into a powerful nation in 1871. Within a few decades, it became Europe's leading industrial power. Across the Atlantic, the United States advanced even more rapidly, especially after the Civil War.

With a large labor force, plenty of resources, and entrepreneurs who had capital, by 1900 the United States was manufacturing about 30 percent of the world's industrial goods. It had surpassed Britain as the leading industrial nation.

>> A street scene in Chicago, Illinois, from the early 1900s shows how the urban landscape was altered by industrialization. **Compare and Contrast** How is the scene similar to and different from a typical city street today?

Industry Spreads Unevenly Other nations industrialized more slowly, particularly those in eastern and southern Europe. These nations often lacked natural resources or the capital to invest in industry. Although Russia did have resources, social and political conditions slowed its economic development. Only in the late 1800s, more than 100 years after Britain, did Russia move toward industrialization.

In East Asia, however, Japan offered a remarkable success story. Although Japan lacked many basic resources, it industrialized rapidly after 1868 because of a political revolution that made modernization a priority. Canada, Australia, and New Zealand also built thriving industries during this time.

Social, Economic, and Political Changes Like Britain, the new industrial nations underwent social changes, such as rapid urbanization. Early in the history of industrialization, men, women, and children worked long hours in difficult and dangerous conditions. By 1900, however, these conditions had begun to improve in many industrialized nations.

The factory system produced huge quantities of new goods at lower prices than ever before. In time, ordinary workers were buying goods that in earlier days only the wealthy could afford. The demand for goods created jobs, as did the building of cities, railroads, and factories. Politics changed, too, as leaders had to meet the demands of an industrial society.

Globally, industrial nations competed fiercely, altering patterns of world trade. Because of their technological and economic advantage, the Western powers came to dominate the world more than ever before.

ANALYZE INFORMATION What factors allowed other nations to industrialize after Britain?

ASSESSMENT

1. **Identify Patterns** What would you identify as the important changes in human life caused by the Industrial Revolution?
2. **Identify Cause and Effect** How did technological advances in agriculture affect the Industrial Revolution?
3. **Generate Explanations** Why was a supply of coal crucial to the Industrial Revolution?
4. **Synthesize** How did the four factors of production determine which nations were able to industrialize after Britain? Cite specific examples from the text.
5. **Cite Evidence** How did industrialization enable Western powers to dominate world affairs?

>> Men, women, and children worked side by side in many factories. Conditions in cotton mills could be cramped, as this photograph inside a mill in Lancashire shows.

2.2 **The Industrial Revolution brought great riches to most of the entrepreneurs who helped set it in motion. It also provided employment for farmers and farmhands displaced by the changes in agriculture. But these jobs came with a heavy price. Millions of workers who crowded into the new factory towns endured dangerous working conditions, unsanitary and overcrowded housing, and unrelenting poverty.**

Bounce to Activate Flipped Video

>> Objectives

Outline the growth of industrial cities and the emergence of new social classes.

Describe the working conditions in factories and mines.

Analyze the benefits and challenges of industrialism.

Describe the ideas of Adam Smith and other thinkers regarding free enterprise.

Identify the origins and characteristics of socialism and communism.

>> Key Terms

urbanization
tenement
labor union
standard of living
social mobility
free market
Thomas Malthus
Jeremy Bentham
utilitarianism
socialism
means of production
Robert Owen
Karl Marx
communism
proletariat
social democracy

Social Impact of Industrialism

Industry Causes Urban Growth

In time, reforms would curb many of the worst abuses of the early Industrial Age in Europe and the Americas. As standards of living increased, people at all levels of society would benefit from industrialization.

The Industrial Revolution brought rapid **urbanization,** or the movement of people to cities. Changes in farming, soaring population growth, and an ever-increasing demand for workers led masses of people to migrate from farms to cities. Almost overnight, small towns around coal or iron mines mushroomed into cities. Other cities grew up around the factories that entrepreneurs built in once-quiet market towns.

The British market town of Manchester numbered 17,000 people in the 1750s. Within a few years, it exploded into a center of the textile industry. Its population soared to 40,000 by 1780 and 70,000 by 1801. Visitors described the "cloud of coal vapor" that polluted the air, the pounding noise of steam engines, and the filthy stench of its river. This growth of industry and rapid population growth dramatically changed the location and distribution of two resources—labor and people.

IDENTIFY SUPPORTING DETAILS What led to the massive migration of people from farms to cities?

The Rise of New Social Classes

The Industrial Revolution helped create both a new middle class and a new urban working class. The middle class included entrepreneurs and others who profited from the growth of industry and the rise of cities. The middle class enjoyed a comfortable lifestyle.

When farm laborers and others moved to the new industrial cities, they took jobs in factories or mines. In rural villages, they had strong ties to a community, where their families had lived for generations. In the cities, they felt lost and bewildered. In time, though, factory and mine workers developed their own sense of community.

The Lives of the New Middle Class Those who benefited most from the Industrial Revolution were the entrepreneurs who set it in motion. The Industrial Revolution created this new middle class, or bourgeoisie (boor zhwah ZEE), whose members came from a variety of backgrounds. Some were merchants who invested their profits in factories. Others were inventors or skilled artisans who developed

new technologies. Some rose from "rags to riches," a pattern that the age greatly admired. Middle-class families lived in well-built, well-furnished homes. In time, middle-class neighborhoods had paved streets and a steady water supply. These families dressed and ate well. The new middle class took pride in their hard work and their determination to "get ahead." Only a few had sympathy for the poor.

As a sign of their new and improved status, middle-class women sought to imitate the wealthy women of the upper classes. They did not do physical labor or work outside the home. They hired maidservants to care for their homes and look after their children.

The Lives of the Working Class While the wealthy and the middle class lived in pleasant neighborhoods, vast numbers of poor struggled to survive in foul-smelling slums. They packed into tiny rooms in **tenements,** or multistory buildings divided into apartments. These tenements had no running water, only community pumps. Early

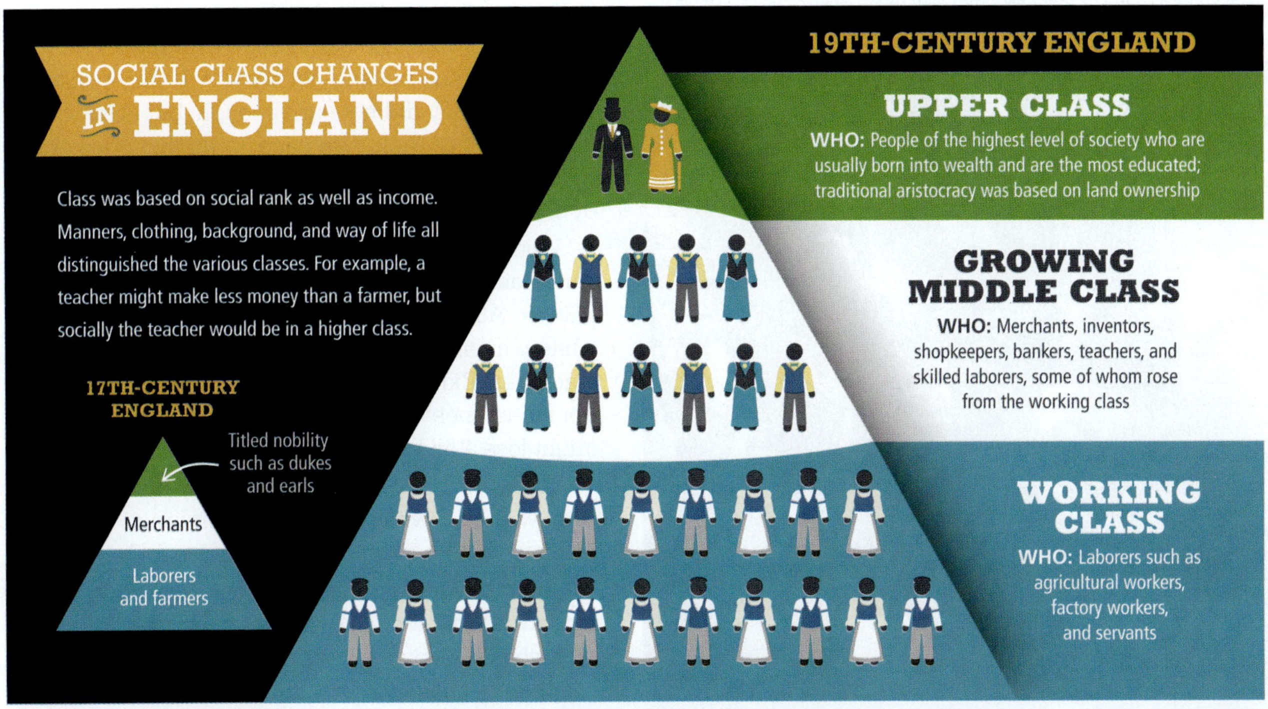

>> The expanding middle class included working-class people who found new opportunities because of industrialization. **Analyze Charts** Which class changed the least due to industrialization?

industrial cities had no sewage or sanitation systems, so waste and garbage rotted in the streets.

Sewage was also dumped into rivers, which created an overwhelming stench and contaminated drinking water. This led to the spread of diseases such as cholera.

Workers' Protests During the early Industrial Revolution, there were no **labor unions,** organizations of workers who bargained for better pay and working conditions. As the Industrial Revolution began, weavers and other skilled artisans resisted the new "labor-saving" machines that were replacing their jobs.

From 1811 to 1813, protesting workers, called Luddites (LUD yts), smashed machines and burned factories. The Luddites were harshly crushed. Although frustrated workers continued to protest, they were forbidden to form worker associations and strikes were outlawed.

Methodists Help the Poor Many working-class people found comfort in a religious movement called Methodism. John Wesley had founded the Methodist movement in the mid-1700s. Wesley stressed the need for a personal sense of faith. He encouraged his followers to improve themselves by adopting sober, moral ways.

Methodist meetings featured hymns and sermons promising forgiveness of sin and a better life to come. Methodist preachers took this message of salvation into the slums. There, they tried to rekindle hope among the working poor. They set up Sunday schools where followers not only studied the Bible but also learned to read and write. Methodists helped channel workers' anger away from revolution and toward reform.

>> John Wesley, founder of Methodism, is shown preaching at his father's grave in a churchyard in Epworth, Lincolnshire, where he was born and raised.

MAKE GENERALIZATIONS How did members of the working class react to their new experiences in industrial cities?

Harsh Conditions in Factories and Mines

The heart of the new industrial city was the factory. There, the technology of the machine age imposed a harsh and dangerous way of life on workers. The miners who supplied the coal and iron for the Industrial Age faced equally unsafe working conditions.

Hazards of the Factory System Working in a factory system differed greatly from working on a farm. In rural villages, people worked long hours for low wages, but their work varied according to the season. Life was also hard for poor rural workers who were part of the putting-out system. If they worked too slowly, they did not earn enough, but at least they worked at their own pace. In the factories of industrial towns, workers faced a rigid schedule set by the factory whistle.

Working hours in early factories were long, with shifts lasting from 12 to 16 hours, six or seven days a week. A factory whistle announced time to eat a hasty meal, then quickly sent them back to the machines. Exhausted workers suffered accidents from machines that had no safety devices. They might lose a finger, a limb, or even their lives.

In textile mills, workers constantly breathed air filled with lint, which damaged their lungs. Those workers who became sick or injured lost their jobs.

At first, women made up much of the new industrial work force. Employers often preferred to hire women workers. They thought women could adapt more easily to machines and were easier to manage than men. More important, they were able to pay women less than men, even for the same work.

Factory work created a double burden for women. Their new jobs took them out of their homes for 12 hours or more a day. They then returned to their tenements, which might consist of one damp room with a single bed. They had to feed and clothe their families, clean, and cope with such problems as sickness and injury.

Dangers in the Mines As the demand for coal and iron grew, more mines were opened. Although miners were paid more than factory workers, conditions in the mines were even harsher than in the factories. Miners worked in darkness, and the coal dust destroyed their lungs. There were always the dangers of explosions, flooding, and collapsing tunnels.

Women and children worked in mines, carting heavy loads of coal. Children were frequently hired to work in mines because they could climb through narrow shafts. Many spent their days on all fours or carried heavy baskets of coal up flimsy ladders.

Children Perform Risky Work Children had always worked on rural farms or as servants and apprentices. However, child labor took on new dimensions during the Industrial Revolution. Since children had helped with farm work, parents accepted the idea of child labor. The wages children earned were needed to keep their families from starving.

Factories and mines hired many boys and girls. These children often started working at age seven or eight, a few as young as five. Nimble-fingered and quick-moving, they changed spools in the hot and humid textile mills where sometimes they could not see because of all the dust. They also crawled under machinery to repair broken threads in the mills.

Conditions were even worse for children who worked in the mines. Some sat all day in the dark, opening and closing air vents. Others hauled coal carts in the extreme heat.

In the early 1800s, Parliament passed a series of laws, called "factory acts," to reform child labor practices. These early efforts were largely ignored. Then, in 1833, Michael Sadler headed up a committee to look into the conditions of child workers in the textile industry. The Sadler Report contained firsthand accounts of child labor practices and helped bring the harsh labor conditions to light. As a result, Parliament passed new regulations to ease working conditions for children.

An 1833 law forbade the hiring of children under the age of nine and limited the working hours of older children in the textile industry. Over time,

>> Before child labor laws, working-class children like these boys in Pennsylvania worked long hours on hazardous jobs. Many of these mineworkers were aged 10 or even younger. **Hypothesize** Why did mine owners hire children for certain jobs?

Bounce to Activate Gallery

Parliament passed other laws to improve working conditions in both factories and mines and to limit the work day of both adults and children to 10 hours. It also enacted laws to require the education of children and to stop the hiring of children and women in mines.

DRAW CONCLUSIONS How did the Industrial Revolution change the lives of men, women, and children?

Benefits of the Industrial Revolution

Since the 1800s, people have debated whether the Industrial Revolution was a blessing or a curse. The early Industrial Age brought great hardships and much misery. Although the first factories did provide jobs and wages to displaced farm workers, the conditions under which they labored were generally terrible. In time, however, reformers, along with labor unions, pushed for laws to improve working conditions in factories, mines, and other industries. Despite the negative aspects of industrialization, the new industrial world eventually brought many advantages.

Better Standards of Living The factory system produced huge quantities of new goods at lower prices than ever before. In time, as wages and working conditions improved, ordinary workers were able to buy goods that in earlier days only the wealthy had been able to afford. Slowly, too, the **standard of living** rose for workers. The standard of living refers to the level of material goods and services available to people in a society. Families ate more varied diets, lived in better homes, and dressed in inexpensive, mass-produced clothing. Advances in medicine ensured healthier lives.

New job opportunities opened up for skilled and unskilled workers. The building of cities, railroads, and factories provided jobs. The demand for goods and the growth of new industries, such as railroads and eventually automobiles, created more job opportunities.

New Worlds for Entrepreneurs The new industrial world was more open to change and innovation than the old rural world. Enterprising people opened new businesses and invented new products. The British potter Josiah Wedgwood, for example, was an entrepreneur who combined science and new industrial methods of production. Wedgwood experimented with new materials to improve the quality of his pottery. He set up a factory that gave each different job to a specially skilled worker. Wedgwood also used his pottery to spread ideas about social justice, especially the abolition of the slave trade. His factory cast antislavery medallions, worn by many, that carried the image of a slave in chains with the words "Am I not a man and a brother?"

>> In *The Wealth of Nations,* Adam Smith proposed ideas about free market competition that are still applied today.

Social and Political Impact The Industrial Revolution opened new opportunities for success and increased **social mobility,** or the ability of individuals or groups to move up the social scale. In the past, birth determined a person's rank in society. Although birth still gave nobles their status, some families were able to move up the social ladder through successful enterprise. By the late 1800s, many people embraced the "rags to riches" idea, whereby a person could achieve great wealth and status through hard work and thrift.

With social mobility came greater political rights. As the middle class expanded, its members pushed for political influence. Gradually throughout the 1800s, working-class men gained the right to vote. From 1831 to 1885, the number of voters in England and Wales increased from 366,000 to almost 8 million. The growing number of voters gave the working class more power as politicians began to have to appeal to their concerns. Later, women also earned the right to vote. Labor unions won the right to bargain with employers for better wages, hours, and working conditions.

CHECK UNDERSTANDING Why was the Industrial Revolution seen as both a blessing and a curse?

Laissez-Faire Economics

Many thinkers and economists tried to understand the staggering changes taking place in the early Industrial Age. As heirs to the Enlightenment, these thinkers looked for natural laws to explain the world of business and economics. Their ideas would influence governments down to the present. Among the most influential schools of thought were laissez-faire economics, utilitarianism, and socialism.

Adam Smith and Laissez-Faire Economics During the Enlightenment, thinkers looked for natural laws that governed the world of business and economics. Physiocrats argued that natural laws should be allowed to operate without interference. As part of this philosophy, they believed that government should not interfere in the free operation of the economy. In the early 1800s, middle-class business leaders embraced this laissez-faire, or "hands-off," approach.

The main proponent of laissez-faire economics was Adam Smith, author of the bestseller *The Wealth of Nations*. Smith asserted that a **free market,** or unregulated exchange of goods and services, would come to help everyone, not just the rich. The free market, Smith said, would produce more goods at lower prices, making them affordable to everyone. A growing economy would also encourage capitalists to reinvest profits in new ventures.

As the Industrial Revolution spread, later supporters of this free-enterprise capitalism pointed to the successes of the early Industrial Revolution, in which government had played a limited role. Governments had taken steps to create a favorable atmosphere for business, such as Britain's laws to outlaw the export of inventions or the tariffs passed by the United States in 1789 to protect American industry, but played little role in the day-to-day operation of industry.

>> Laissez-faire thinker Thomas Malthus believed that the increasing population put too great a strain on the food supply. He suggested smaller family sizes as a solution to ending poverty.

Malthus on Population Growth Like Smith, **Thomas Malthus** was a laissez-faire thinker whose writings influenced economic ideas for generations. In his 1798 book *An Essay on the Principle of Population*, he grimly predicted that poverty was unavoidable because the population was increasing faster than the food supply.

Malthus wrote: "The power of population is [far] greater than the power of the Earth to produce subsistence for man." He thought that the only checks on population growth were nature's "natural" methods of war, disease, and famine. As long as population kept increasing, he went on, the poor would suffer. He thus urged families to have fewer children and discouraged charitable handouts and vaccinations.

During the early 1800s, with industrial workers living and working in harsh conditions, many people accepted Malthus's bleak view. His view was proved wrong, however. Although the population boom did continue, the food supply grew even faster.

As the century progressed, living conditions in the Western world slowly improved, and people eventually did begin to have fewer children. By the 1900s, population growth was no longer a problem in the West, but it did continue to afflict many nations elsewhere.

Ricardo and the "Iron Law of Wages" Another influential British laissez-faire economist, David Ricardo, dedicated himself to economic studies after reading Smith's *The Wealth of Nations*. Like Malthus, Ricardo claimed that the poor had too many children and had little chance to escape poverty. In his "Iron Law of Wages," Ricardo noted that when wages were high, families had more children. But more children increased the supply of labor, which led to lower wages and higher unemployment. Because of such gloomy predictions, economics became known as the "dismal science."

Neither Malthus nor Ricardo was a cruel man. Still, both opposed any government help for the poor. In their view, the best cure for poverty was not government relief but the unrestricted "laws of the free market." They felt that individuals should be left to improve their lot through thrift, hard work, and limiting the size of their families.

IDENTIFY CAUSE AND EFFECT How did the ideas that Adam Smith discussed in *The Wealth of Nations* support the free enterprise system?

>> Philosopher and economist John Stuart Mill supported extending suffrage. Mill believed that political power through voting could lead to necessary reforms.

>> Widespread poverty, as shown here, motivated socialists to seek a more equitable economic system.

Utilitarians Support Limited Government

Other thinkers sought to modify laissez-faire doctrines to justify some government intervention. By 1800, British philosopher and economist **Jeremy Bentham** was advocating **utilitarianism,** or the idea that the goal of society should be "the greatest happiness for the greatest number" of its citizens. To Bentham, all laws or actions should be judged by their "utility." In other words, did they provide more pleasure or happiness than pain? Bentham strongly supported individual freedom, which he believed guaranteed happiness. Still, he saw the need for government to become involved under certain circumstances.

Bentham's ideas influenced the British philosopher and economist John Stuart Mill. Although he believed strongly in individual freedom, Mill wanted the government to step in to improve the hard lives of the working class.

"The only purpose for which power can be rightfully exercised over any member of a civilized community, against his will," Mill wrote, "is to prevent harm to others." Therefore, while middle-class business and factory owners were entitled to increase their own happiness, the government should prevent them from doing so in a manner that would harm workers.

Mill further called for giving the vote to workers and women. These groups could then use their political power to win reforms. Most middle-class people rejected Mill's ideas. Only in the later 1800s were his views slowly accepted. Today's democratic governments, however, have absorbed many ideas from Mill and the other utilitarians.

CHECK UNDERSTANDING What did John Stuart Mill see as the proper role of government?

Socialist Thought Emerges

While the champions of laissez-faire economics favored the free market and individual rights, other thinkers focused on social inequality and what they claimed were the evils of industrial capitalism. They argued that industrialization had created an unjust gulf between rich and poor.

The Socialist Point of View To end poverty and injustice, some thinkers offered a radical solution—socialism. Under **socialism,** the people as a whole rather than private individuals would own and operate the **means of production**—the farms, factories, railways, and other large businesses that produced and distributed goods. In practice, when socialist governments gained power in the 1900s, they tended to regulate the production and distribution of goods, which often proved inefficient.

Socialism grew out of the Enlightenment faith in progress and human nature and its concern for social justice. Socialist thinkers developed a number of different ideas about how to achieve their goals. The early experiments in socialism differed greatly from what later socialist governments would do.

Owen and Utopian Socialism A number of early socialists established communities in which all work was shared and all property was owned in common. When there was no difference between rich and poor, they said, fighting between people would disappear. These early socialists were called Utopians. To critics, the name implied that they were impractical dreamers.

One of these social reformers was **Robert Owen.** Owen himself was an industrial success story. He started life as a poor Welsh boy and became a successful mill owner. Unlike most industrialists at the time, Owen refused to use child labor. He campaigned vigorously for laws that limited child labor and encouraged the organization of labor unions.

Like other Utopians, Owen believed there was a way he could change society for the better. To prove his point, he set up a model community around a mill in New Lanark, Scotland, to put his own ideas into practice. At his factory in New Lanark, he built homes for workers, opened a school for children, and generally treated employees well. He wanted to show that an employer could offer decent living and working conditions and still run a profitable business.

IDENTIFY What were the characteristic beliefs of early socialists?

Marx and the Origins of Communism

In the 1840s, **Karl Marx,** a German philosopher, condemned the ideas of the Utopians as unrealistic idealism. He formulated a new theory, "scientific socialism," which he claimed was based on a scientific study of history. He teamed up with another German socialist, Friedrich Engels, whose father owned a textile factory in England.

Marxist Theory Marx and Engels wrote a pamphlet, *The Communist Manifesto,* which they

>> This well-known Marxist poster proclaims in German, "Workers of all countries, unite!" **Determine Point of View** Why should workers unite, according to Marx?

Bounce to Activate Chart

published in 1848. "A spectre [ghost] is haunting Europe," it began, "the spectre of communism." According to Marx, **communism** would bring a classless society in which the means of production would be owned in common for the good of all.

In fact, wherever communism came to be practiced in the 1900s, it brought a system of government in which the state led by a small elite controlled all economic and political life and exercised authoritarian control over the people.

In *The Communist Manifesto*, Marx theorized that economics was the driving force in history. He argued that there was "the history of class struggles" between the "haves" and the "have-nots." The "haves" had always owned the means of production and thus controlled society and all its wealth. In industrialized Europe, Marx said, the "haves" were the bourgeoisie. The "have-nots" were the **proletariat,** or working class.

According to Marx, the modern class struggle pitted the bourgeoisie against the proletariat. In the end, he predicted, the proletariat would be triumphant. Workers would then take control of the means of production and set up a classless, communist society. In such a society, the struggles of the past would end because wealth and power would be shared equally.

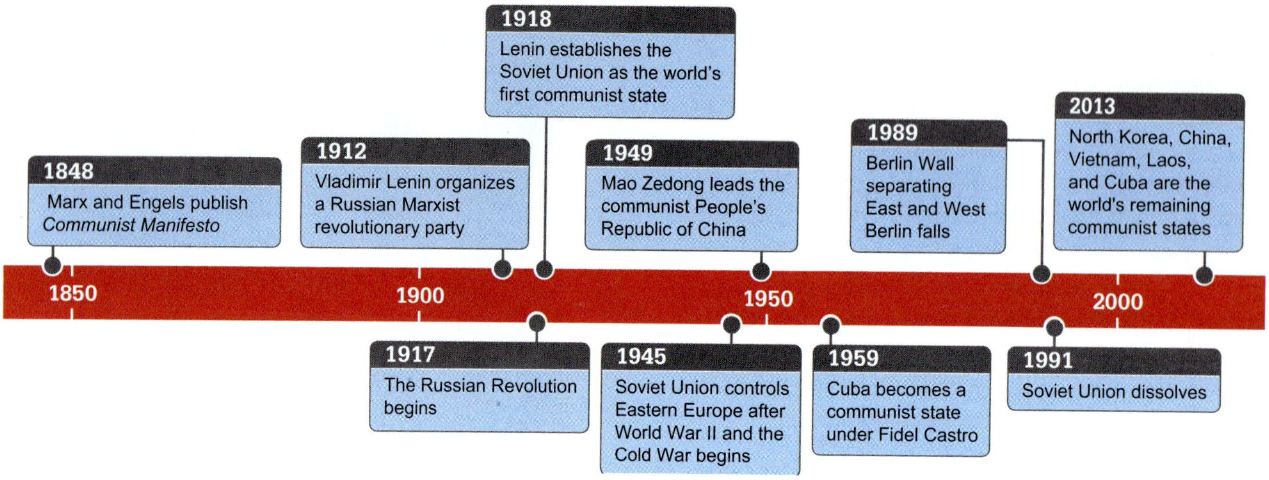

>> Since Marx's lifetime, communism has spread globally and then declined. **Analyze Charts** How much time elapsed between the Soviet Union's gaining control of Eastern Europe and the end of the Soviet Union?

Marx despised capitalism. He believed it created prosperity for only a few and poverty for many. He called for an international struggle to bring about its downfall. "Workers of all countries," he urged, "unite!"

Marxism Finds Support At first, Marxist ideas had little impact. In time, however, they would gain supporters around the world. In western Europe, communist political parties emerged and promoted the goals of violent revolution to achieve a classless society. Marx's ideas would never be practiced exactly as he imagined. Even so, Karl Marx remains a key historic figure, not only in his lifetime but in the century to come.

In the 1860s, German socialists adapted Marx's beliefs to form **social democracy,** a political ideology in which there is a gradual transition from capitalism to socialism instead of a sudden violent overthrow of the system. By the late 1800s, a rift formed between strict Marxists, who believed in revolution to end capitalism, and social democrats, who believed in the possibility of peaceful reform.

In the late 1800s, Russian socialists embraced Marxism and formed a communist party to bring about revolution. In 1917, the Russian Revolution set up a communist government there that lasted until 1991. During the 1900s, revolutionaries in countries from China to Cuba adapted Marxist ideas to their own situations and needs. Independence leaders in Asia, Latin America, and Africa often experimented with Marxist ideas.

Marxism Loses Its Appeal Marx claimed that his ideas were based on scientific laws. However, many of his ideas turned out to be wrong. He predicted that the misery of the proletariat would touch off a world revolution. Instead, by 1900, the standard of living of the working class improved in industrially developed countries. He also predicted that workers would unite across national borders to wage class warfare.

Instead, people continued to feel stronger ties to their own countries than to any international workers' movement. Finally, by the late 1900s, the few nations that had experimented with communism were moving away from government control of the economy and were adding elements of free-market capitalism.

CHECK UNDERSTANDING What did Marx predict was the future of the proletariat?

ASSESSMENT

1. **Summarize** How did the middle class live during the Industrial Revolution?
2. **Describe** What was life like for working-class women during the Industrial Revolution?
3. **Cite Evidence** What key social and economic changes did industrialization bring about, both for the better and for the worse? Explain your answer with evidence from the text.
4. **Identify Main Ideas** What were the historical origins and characteristics of the free enterprise system?
5. **Identify Patterns** How did the Industrial Revolution impact the development of modern economic systems? In your answer, identify the economic systems that arose during that period.

2.3 The first phase of industrialization was forged from iron, powered by steam engines, and driven by the British textile industry. By the mid-1800s, the Industrial Revolution was entering a new phase in which new factories powered by new sources of energy used new processes to turn out new products. At the same time, new forms of business organization led to the rise of giant new companies.

>> Henry Ford introduced the moving assembly line in 1913. These men are assembling the flywheel magneto—the first part of the Model T to be manufactured on a moving assembly line.

Bounce to Activate Flipped Video

The Second Industrial Revolution

>> **Objectives**

Describe the impact of new technology on industry, transportation, and communication.

Understand how big business emerged.

Summarize the impact of medical advances in the later 1800s.

Describe how cities changed and grew.

Explain how conditions for workers gradually improved.

>> **Key Terms**

Henry Bessemer
Alfred Nobel
Michael Faraday
dynamo
Thomas Edison
interchangeable parts
assembly line
Orville and Wilbur Wright
Guglielmo Marconi
stock
corporation
cartel
germ theory
Louis Pasteur
Robert Koch
Florence Nightingale
Joseph Lister
urban renewal
mutual-aid society

Science and Technology Change Industry

During the early Industrial Revolution, inventions such as the steam engine were generally the work of gifted tinkerers. They experimented with simple machines to make them better.

During the second Industrial Revolution, the pace of change quickened as companies hired professional chemists and engineers to create new products and machinery. The union of science, technology, and industry spurred economic growth.

The Bessemer Process Transforms Steel British engineer **Henry Bessemer** and American inventor William Kelly independently developed a new process for making steel from iron. In 1856, Bessemer patented this process. Steel was lighter, harder, and more durable than iron, so it could be produced very cheaply. Steel quickly became the major material used in tools, bridges, and railroads. As steel production soared, industrialized countries measured their success in steel output. In 1880, for example, the average German steel mill produced less than 5 million metric tons of steel a year. By 1910, that figure had reached nearly 15 million metric tons.

Innovations in Chemistry During the same period, chemists created hundreds of new products, from medicines such as aspirin to perfumes and soaps. Newly developed chemical fertilizers played a key role in increasing food production.

In 1866, the Swedish chemist **Alfred Nobel** invented dynamite, an explosive much safer than others used at the time. It was widely used in construction and, to Nobel's dismay, in warfare. Dynamite earned Nobel a huge fortune, which he willed to fund the famous Nobel prizes that are still awarded today.

Electricity Replaces Steam Power In the late 1800s, a new power source—electricity—replaced steam as the dominant source of industrial power. Scientists like Benjamin Franklin had tinkered with electricity a century earlier. The Italian scientist Alessandro Volta developed the first battery around 1800. Later, the English chemist **Michael Faraday** created the first simple electric motor and the first **dynamo,** a machine that generates electricity. Today, all electrical generators and transformers work on the principle of Faraday's dynamo.

>> After inventing the light bulb, Thomas Edison supervised the building of the first electric power system in New York City.

In the 1870s, the American inventor **Thomas Edison** made the first electric light bulb. Soon, Edison's "incandescent lamps" illuminated whole cities. The pace of city life quickened, and factories could continue to operate after dark. By the 1890s, cables carried electrical power from dynamos to factories.

Improved Methods of Production The basic features of the factory system remained the same during the 1800s. Factories still used large numbers of workers and power-driven machines to mass-produce goods. To improve efficiency, however, manufacturers designed products with **interchangeable parts,** identical components that could be used in place of one another. Interchangeable parts simplified both the assembly and repair of products. By the early 1900s, manufacturers had introduced another new method of production, the **assembly line.**

Workers on an assembly line add parts to a product that moves along a belt from one work station to the next. A different person performs each task along the assembly line. While not all factories used assembly lines, the factory system always relied on the division of labor. Each worker was assigned one task, such as putting the sole on a shoe or sewing a collar on a shirt. Once that task was done, the worker handed the product to the next person, who then performed his or her task. Interchangeable parts, the division of labor, and the assembly line all made production more efficient. They also lowered the price of factory goods, making them affordable to more people.

IDENTIFY CAUSE AND EFFECT How did the assembly line and division of labor affect manufacturing?

Advances in Transportation and Communication

During the second Industrial Revolution, transportation and communications were transformed by technology. Steamships replaced sailing ships, and railroad building took off. In Europe and North America, rail lines connected inland cities and seaports, mining regions, and industrial centers. In the United States, a transcontinental railroad provided rail service from the Atlantic to the Pacific. In the same way, Russians built the Trans-Siberian Railroad, linking Moscow in European Russia to Vladivostok on the Pacific. Railroad tunnels and bridges crossed the Alps in Europe and the Andes in South America.

Passengers and goods rode on rails in India, China, Egypt, and South Africa.

The Age of the Automobile The transportation revolution took a new turn when a German engineer, Nikolaus Otto, invented a gasoline-powered internal combustion engine. In 1886, Karl Benz received a patent for the first automobile, which had three wheels. A year later, Gottlieb Daimler (DYM lur) introduced the first four-wheeled automobile. People laughed at the "horseless carriages," but they quickly changed the way people traveled.

The French nosed out the Germans as early automakers. Then the American Henry Ford started making models that reached the breathtaking speed of 25 miles per hour. In the early 1900s, Ford began using the assembly line to mass-produce cars, making the United States a leader in the automobile industry.

The First Airplane The invention of the internal combustion engine changed life and industry in other ways. Motorized threshers and reapers boosted farm production. Even more dramatically, the internal combustion engine made possible sustained, pilot-controlled flight. In 1903, American bicycle makers **Orville and Wilbur Wright** designed and flew a flimsy airplane at Kitty Hawk, North Carolina. Although their flying machine stayed aloft for only a few seconds, it ushered in the air age.

Soon, daredevil pilots were flying airplanes across the English Channel and over the Alps. Commercial passenger travel, however, would not begin until the 1920s.

A Communications Revolution A revolution in communications also made the world smaller. An American inventor, Samuel F. B. Morse, developed the telegraph, which could send coded messages over wires by means of electricity. His first telegraph line went into service between Washington, D.C., and Baltimore in 1844. By the 1860s, an undersea cable was relaying messages between Europe and North America. This trans-Atlantic cable was an amazing engineering accomplishment for its day.

Communication soon became even faster. In 1876, the Scottish-born American inventor Alexander Graham Bell patented the telephone. By the 1890s, the Italian pioneer **Guglielmo Marconi** had invented the radio, which allowed wireless communication over long distances. In 1901, Marconi received a radio message, using Morse code, sent from Britain to Canada. As Marconi had predicted, radio soon became a key part of a global communications network that linked every corner of the world.

>> In 1903, Orville and Wilbur Wright tested their flying machine at Kitty Hawk, North Carolina. By 1905, they had built an airplane that could stay in the air for 39 minutes.

Bounce to Activate Timeline

IDENTIFY CAUSE AND EFFECT How did Nikolaus Otto's invention of the internal combustion engine affect the Industrial Revolution? What can you infer about its impact on Western nations?

The Rise of Big Business

By the late 1800s, what we call "big business" came to dominate industry. Big business refers to an establishment that is run by entrepreneurs who finance, manufacture, and distribute goods or services on a large scale. As time passed, some big businesses came to control entire industries.

Investors Form Corporations The latest technologies required the investment of large amounts of money, or capital. To get the needed capital, owners sold **stock,** or shares in their companies, to investors. Each stockholder became owner of a tiny part of a company. Large-scale companies, such as steel foundries, needed so much capital that they sold hundreds of thousands of shares. These businesses formed giant **corporations,** businesses that are owned by many investors who buy shares of stock. With large amounts of capital, corporations could expand into many areas.

Monopolies Dominate Industry Some powerful business leaders created monopolies and trusts, huge corporate structures that controlled entire industries or areas of the economy. In Germany, Alfred Krupp inherited a steelmaking business from his father. He bought up coal and iron mines along with the supply lines that carried raw materials to feed the steel business. Later, he and his son acquired plants that made tools, railroad cars, and weapons.

In the United States, John D. Rockefeller dominated the petroleum industry by gaining control of oil wells, oil refineries, and oil pipelines. Andrew Carnegie, who started out as a poor immigrant from Scotland, worked his way up to build an American steel empire. He later used his wealth to fund libraries, universities, and other charities.

Sometimes, a group of corporations would join forces and form a **cartel,** an association to fix prices, set production quotas, or control markets. In Germany, a single cartel fixed prices for 170 coal mines.

Opposing Views of Big Business The rise of big business sparked a stormy debate. Admirers saw the Krupps, Rockefellers, and Carnegies as "captains of industry" and praised their vision and skills. They pointed out that capitalists invested their wealth in worldwide ventures, such as railroad building, that employed thousands of workers and added to the general prosperity. They also claimed that monopolies increased efficiency by driving out less efficient corporations.

To critics, the aggressive magnates were "robber barons" who ruthlessly destroyed competing companies in pursuit of profit. With the competition gone, they were free to raise prices. Destroying competition, critics argued, damaged the free-enterprise system. Reformers called for laws to prevent monopolies and regulate large corporations. By the early 1900s, some governments did move against monopolies. However, the political and economic power of business leaders often hindered efforts at regulation.

>> This 1899 American political cartoon shows a monopoly as an octopus-like monster covering a city. **Analyze Political Cartoons** Which side of the debate about the effects of monopolies does this cartoon support? Explain.

DRAW CONCLUSIONS Why was there a move toward developing monopolies?

Better Medicine, Nutrition, and Health

The population explosion that had begun during the 1700s continued through the 1800s. Between 1800 and 1900, the population of Europe more than doubled. This rapid growth was not due to larger families. In fact, families in most industrializing countries had fewer children. Instead, populations soared because the death rate fell. Nutrition improved, thanks in part to improved methods of farming, food storage, and distribution. Medical advances and improvements in public sanitation also slowed death rates.

Combating Disease Since the 1600s, scientists had known of microscopic organisms, or microbes. Some scientists speculated that certain microbes might cause specific infectious diseases. Yet most doctors scoffed at this **germ theory.** Not until 1870 did French chemist **Louis Pasteur** (pas TUR) clearly show the link between microbes and disease. Pasteur went on to make other major contributions to medicine, including the development of vaccines against rabies and anthrax. He also discovered a process called pasteurization that killed disease-carrying microbes in milk.

In the 1880s, the German doctor **Robert Koch** identified the bacterium that caused tuberculosis, a respiratory disease that claimed about 30 million human lives in the 1800s. The search for a tuberculosis cure, however, took half a century. By 1914, yellow fever and malaria had been traced to microbes carried by mosquitoes.

Population Growth of Major Cities During the Industrial Revolution

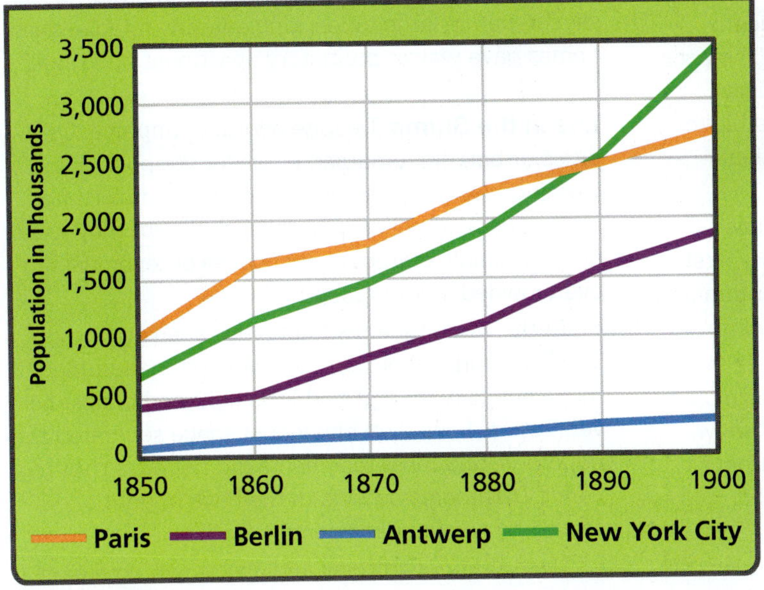

Life Expectancy During the Industrial Revolution

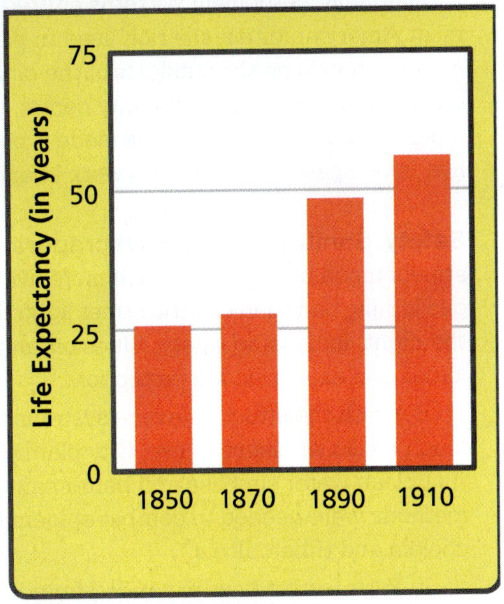

>> Longer life expectancies contributed to population booms in major cities. **Analyze Graphs** Which city's population grew the most? How did life expectancy change between 1850 and 1910?

Bounce to Activate Gallery

As people understood how germs caused disease, they bathed and changed their clothes more often. In European cities, better hygiene helped decrease the rate of disease.

Improving Hospital Care By the 1840s, anesthesia was being widely used to relieve pain during surgery. The use of anesthetic gas allowed doctors to experiment with operations that had never before been possible.

Yet, throughout the century, hospitals could be dangerous places. Surgery was performed with dirty instruments in dank rooms. Often, a patient would survive an operation, only to die days later of infection. For the poor, being admitted to a hospital was often a death sentence. Wealthy or middle-class patients insisted on treatment in their own homes.

"The very first requirement in a hospital," said British nurse **Florence Nightingale,** "is that it should do the sick no harm." As an army nurse during the Crimean War, Nightingale insisted on better hygiene in field hospitals. After the war, she worked to introduce sanitary measures in British hospitals. She also founded the world's first school of nursing.

The English surgeon **Joseph Lister** discovered how antiseptics prevented infection. He insisted that surgeons sterilize their instruments and wash their hands before operating. Eventually, the use of antiseptics drastically reduced deaths from infection.

DRAW CONCLUSIONS Why was the improvement in hospital care especially important to the poor?

City Life Changes

As industrialization progressed, cities came to dominate the West. Cities grew as rural people streamed into urban areas for work. By the end of the 1800s, European and American cities had begun to take on many of the features of cities today.

New Cityscapes Growing wealth and industrialization altered the basic layout of European cities. City planners created spacious new squares and boulevards. They lined these avenues with government buildings, offices, department stores, and theaters.

The most extensive **urban renewal,** or rebuilding of the poor areas of a city, took place in Paris in the 1850s. Georges Haussmann, chief planner for Napoleon III, destroyed many tangled medieval streets full of tenement housing. In their place, he built wide boulevards and splendid public buildings.

The project was designed after Paris had experienced frequent uprisings, where poor city dwellers and their leaders set up barricades across narrow streets to battle the authorities. Haussmann's plan provided jobs, and the wide new boulevards made it harder for rebels to block streets and easier for troops to move around the city.

Gradually, settlement patterns shifted. In most American cities, the rich lived in pleasant neighborhoods on the outskirts of the city. The poor crowded into slums near the city center, within reach of factories. Trolley lines made it possible to live in one part of the city and work in another.

Safety, Sanitation, and Skyscrapers Paved streets made urban areas much more livable. First gas lamps, and then electric street lights illuminated the night, increasing safety. Cities organized police forces and expanded fire protection.

Beneath the streets, sewage systems made cities much healthier places to live. City planners knew that clean water supplies and better sanitation methods were needed to combat epidemics of cholera and tuberculosis.

In Paris, sewer lines expanded from 87 miles (139 kilometers) in 1852 to more than 750 miles (1200 kilometers) by 1911. The massive new sewer systems of London and Paris were costly, but they cut death rates dramatically.

By 1900, architects were using steel to construct soaring buildings. The Eiffel Tower became the symbol of Paris and the heights to which modern structures could reach. American architects like Louis Sullivan pioneered a new structure, the skyscraper. In large cities, single-family middle-class homes gave way to multistory apartment buildings.

>> It was not uncommon for more than one family to share a tiny apartment in tenement buildings. **Analyze Images** What evidence does this photograph provide about the lives of the urban poor?

Life in the Slums Despite efforts to improve cities, urban life remained harsh for the poor. Some working-class families could afford better clothing, newspapers, or tickets to a music hall. But they went home to small, cramped row houses or tenements in overcrowded neighborhoods.

In the worst tenements in cities such as London and New York, whole families were often crammed into a single room that had little light and almost no ventilation. Less than one foot of space separated the buildings, and most tenements did not have running water. Bathrooms outside in the back might be shared by as many as twenty people.

Unsanitary conditions and overcrowding meant diseases spread quickly. Unemployment or illness meant lost wages that could ruin a family, leaving it homeless. High rates of crime and alcoholism were a constant curse. Conditions had improved somewhat from the early Industrial Revolution, but slums remained a fact of city life.

The Lure of City Life Despite their drawbacks, cities attracted millions. New residents were drawn as much by the excitement as by the promise of work. For tourists, too, cities were centers of action.

Music halls, opera houses, and theaters provided entertainment for every taste. Museums and libraries offered educational opportunities. Sports, from tennis to bare-knuckle boxing, drew citizens of all classes. Tree-lined parks offered a chance for fresh air, walks, and picnics, while reminding people of life in the country.

DRAW CONCLUSIONS How did industrialization change the face of cities?

The Working Class Wins New Rights

Workers tried to improve the harsh conditions of industrial life. They protested low wages, long hours, unsafe conditions, and the constant threat of unemployment. At first, business owners and governments tried to silence protesters. By mid-century, however, workers began to make progress.

The Growth of Labor Unions Workers formed **mutual-aid societies,** self-help groups to aid sick or injured workers. Men and women joined socialist parties or organized unions. In 1830 and 1848, revolutions had broken out across Europe, sparked by political and social unrest. The revolts left vivid images of widespread worker discontent that governments could no longer ignore.

By the late 1800s, most Western countries had granted all men the vote. Workers also won the right to organize unions to bargain on their behalf. Germany legalized labor unions in 1869. Britain, Austria, and France followed. By 1900, Britain had about three million union members, and Germany had about two million.

The main tactic of unions was the strike, or work stoppage. Workers used strikes to demand better working conditions, wage increases, or other benefits from their employers. Violence was often a result of strikes, particularly if employers called in the police or hired nonunion workers to keep their operations going.

Pressured by unions, reformers, and working-class voters, governments passed laws to regulate working conditions. Early laws forbade employers to hire very young children. Later laws outlawed child labor entirely and banned the employment of women in mines. Other laws limited work hours and improved safety. By 1909, British coal miners had won an eight-hour day, setting a standard for workers in other countries.

In Germany, and then elsewhere, Western governments established old-age pensions, as well as disability insurance for workers who were hurt or became ill. These programs protected workers from dying in poverty once they were no longer able to work.

>> Miners and steelworkers go on strike in Belgium. **Draw Conclusions** Who do you think the men on horseback are? Why are they there? Explain.

An Improved Standard of Living Wages varied throughout the industrialized world, with unskilled laborers earning less than skilled workers. Women received less than half the pay of men doing the same work. Farm laborers barely scraped by during the economic slump of the late 1800s. Periods of unemployment brought desperate hardships to industrial workers and helped boost union membership.

Overall, though, standards of living for workers did rise. Working-class people began to benefit from higher wages and better working conditions. They, too, were able to afford a larger variety of goods and services. Many benefited from the growing movement to provide public education. Some were able to get access to health care. Efforts to curb diseases led to vaccination programs that reached into poor communities. Some workers were able to move out of overcrowded slums into the outer ring of cities and travel to work on subways and trolleys. Despite improvements in the standard of living, however, a large gap divided workers from the middle class.

DRAW CONCLUSIONS What were some ways that life improved for workers?

ASSESSMENT

1. **Identify Main Ideas** Identify the major effects of new technology and transportation on industry during the Industrial Revolution.
2. **Draw Conclusions** Why did big business emerge during the Industrial Revolution, and how did it affect free enterprise?
3. **Identify Central Issues** How did the Industrial Revolution bring about important changes to human life in cities? Identify changes for the better and for the worse.
4. **Apply Concepts** How did the working class begin to improve its conditions during the late 1800s?
5. **Identify** Describe the contributions of Louis Pasteur and how they impacted society during the Industrial Revolution.

Primary Sources

How the Other Half Lives: Jacob Riis

Introduction

Jacob Riis immigrated to the United States from Denmark in 1870. After living for several years in extreme poverty, he found a job as a police reporter for the *New York Tribune*. He became one of the leading muckrakers of the Progressive Era. Riis's writing and photographs helped expose the harsh living conditions in the crowded tenements of New York City. This excerpt is from Riis's 1890 book, *How the Other Half Lives*.

Annie Daniel, a physician and public health reformer in New York, worked to both educate the public about and improve living conditions in tenements. The second primary source is from her speech "The Wreck of the Home: How Wearing Apparel is Fashioned in the Tenements".

>> A city tenement

Primary Source

The problem of the children becomes, in these swarms, to the last degree perplexing. Their very number make one stand aghast [horrified]. I have already given instances of the packing of the child population in East Side tenements. They might be continued indefinitely until the array [orderly arrangement] would be enough to startle any community. For, be it remembered, these children with the training they receive—or do not receive—with the instincts they inherit and absorb in their growing up, are to be our future rulers, if our theory of government is worth anything. More than a working majority of our voters now register from the tenements.

DETERMINE CENTRAL IDEAS According to Riis, why should all Americans be concerned about tenement children?

I counted the other day the little ones, up to ten years or so, in a Bayard Street tenement that for a yard has a triangular space in the center with sides fourteen or fifteen feet long, just room enough for a row of ill-smelling closets [toilets] at the base of the triangle and a hydrant at the apex [highest point]. There was about as much light in this "yard" as in the average cellar. I gave up my self-imposed task in despair when I had counted one hundred and twenty-eight in forty families. . . .

SUMMARIZE What is the tenement like on Bayard Street that Riis describes?

Bodies of drowned children turn up in the rivers right along since summer whom no one seems to know anything about. When last spring some workmen, while moving a pile of lumber on a North River pier, found under the last plank the body of a little lad crushed to death, no one had missed a boy, though his parents afterward turned up. The truant [a pupil who misses school without permission] officer assuredly does not know, though he spends his life trying to find out, somewhat illogically, perhaps, since the department that employs him admits that thousands of poor children are crowded out of the schools year by year for want of room.

SUMMARIZE What is Riis's complaint about the education received by tenement children?

Primary Source

". . . The new law relating to manufacturing in tenement-houses, provides that thirty- three distinct industries may be carried on in the living rooms of the workers–manufacturing all of which requires hand work or simple machinery. Every garment worn by a woman is found being manufactured in tenement rooms. The coarsest home-wrappers to the daintiest lace gown for a fine evening function are manufactured in these rooms. Corsets and shoes are the most uncommon. The adornments of woman's dress, the flowers and feathers for her hats, the hats themselves–these I have seen being made in the presence of small-pox, on the lounge with the patient. In this case the hats belonged to a Broadway firm. All clothing worn by infants and young children–dainty little dresses–I have seen on the same bed with children sick of contagious diseases and into these little garments is sewed some of the contagion. . . ."

DRAW CONCLUSIONS What conditions detailed in this excerpt might have resulted in laws to protect the consumer and the worker?

ASSESSMENT

1. **Identify Supporting Details** What details in this excerpt may have shocked readers of the time period? Why do you think muckrakers sought to shock their audience?
2. **Determine Meaning** To whom does the "Other Half" in the title refer? Why do you think Riis uses this phrase?
3. **Identify Cause and Effect** How do you think Riis's account might have contributed to social reforms for tenement housing?
4. **Explain** What advantage might the "putting out system" described by Daniels provide the manufacturer? Why does Daniel see the worker as abused?

>> Until the late 1800s, the only education available for British students was at either religious schools or "ragged schools," which were schools for poor children. The Education Act of 1902 established a system of public grammar schools.

Bounce to Activate Flipped Video

2.4 The Industrial Revolution slowly changed the old social order in the Western world. For centuries, the two main classes were nobles and peasants. While middle-class merchants, artisans, and lawyers played important roles, they still had a secondary position in society. With the spread of industry, a more complex social structure emerged.

>> Objectives

Identify what values shaped the new social order.

Describe how the role of women changed in the Industrial Revolution.

Explain the impact of education, new scientific ideas, and religion.

Analyze how romanticism, realism, and impressionism reflected the culture of the Industrial Age.

>> Key Terms

cult of domesticity
temperance movement
Elizabeth Cady Stanton
women's suffrage
Sojourner Truth
John Dalton
Charles Darwin
racism
social gospel
William Wordsworth
romanticism
Lord Byron
Victor Hugo
Ludwig van Beethoven
realism
Charles Dickens
Gustave Courbet
Louis Daguerre
impressionism
Claude Monet
Vincent van Gogh

Changing Ways of Life and Thought

The New Social Order

The New Class Structure By the late 1800s, a new upper class emerged in western Europe. It came to include not only the old nobility but also wealthy families who had acquired their riches from business and industry. Rich entrepreneurs married into aristocratic families, gaining the status of noble titles. Nobles needed the money brought by the industrial rich to support their lands and lifestyle. By tradition, the upper class held the top jobs in government and the military.

Below this tiny elite, a growing middle class was pushing its way up the social ladder. At its highest rungs were the upper middle class, made up of mid-level business people and professionals such as doctors and scientists. With comfortable incomes, they enjoyed a wide range of material goods. Next came the lower middle class, which included teachers, office workers, shop owners, and clerks. On much smaller incomes, they struggled to keep up with their "betters."

Industrial workers and rural peasants were at the base of the social ladder. The size of this working class varied across Europe. In highly industrialized Britain, workers made up more than 30 percent of the population in 1900. In western Europe and the United States, the number of farmworkers dropped, but many families still worked the land. The rural population was higher in eastern and southern Europe, where industrialization was more limited.

Middle Class Values By midcentury, the growing middle class had developed its own way of life. A strict code of etiquette governed social behavior.

Rules dictated how to dress for every occasion, how to give a dinner party, how to pay a social call, when to write letters, and how long to mourn for relatives who had died.

Parents strictly supervised their children, who were expected to be "seen but not heard." A child who misbehaved was considered to reflect badly on the entire family. Servants, too, were seen as a reflection of their employers. Even a small middle-class household was expected to have at least a cook and a housemaid.

The Ideal Home and Family Middle-class families tended to include just the nuclear family, parents and children, rather than the larger extended families of the past. They lived in a large house, or perhaps one of the new apartment houses. Rooms were crammed with large, overstuffed furniture. Clothing reflected middle-class tastes for luxury and respectability.

Within the family, the division of labor between wife and husband changed. Earlier, middle-class women had helped run family businesses out of the home.

By the later 1800s, most middle-class husbands went to work in an office or shop. A successful husband was one who earned enough to keep his wife at home. Women spent their time raising children, directing servants, and doing religious or charitable service.

Books, magazines, and popular songs supported a **cult of domesticity** that idealized women and the home. Women and girls stitched sayings like "home, sweet home" into needlework that was hung on parlor walls. The ideal woman was seen as a tender, self-sacrificing caregiver who provided a nest for her children and a peaceful refuge for her husband to escape from the hardships of the working world.

This ideal rarely applied to the bottom rungs of the social ladder. Lower-middle-class women might work alongside their husbands in stores. Working-class women labored for low pay in garment factories or worked as domestic servants. Young women might leave domestic service after they married, but often had to seek other employment. Despite long days working for wages, they were still expected to take full responsibility for child care and homemaking.

IDENTIFY MAIN IDEAS How did the roles of men and women in middle-class households change as a result of the Industrial Revolution?

The Struggle for Women's Rights

Some individual women and women's groups protested restrictions on women's lives. They sought a broad range of rights. Across Europe and the United States, politically active women campaigned for fairness in marriage, divorce, and property laws. Women's groups also supported the **temperance movement,** a campaign to limit or ban the use of alcoholic beverages. Temperance leaders pointed out that drinking threatened family life. They also argued that banning alcohol would create a more productive and efficient workforce.

These reformers faced many obstacles. In Europe and the United States, women could not vote. They were barred from most schools and had little, if any,

>> In industrialized cities, many members of the working class lived in tenement buildings like this. **Infer** What can you infer about working-class life from the way these people are dressed indoors?

protection under the law. A woman's husband or father controlled all of her property.

The Campaign Begins In the late 1700s, women such as Olympe de Gouges in France and Mary Wollstonecraft in England had begun to call for women's rights. Later, their successors—mostly from the middle class—took up the struggle. In the United States, Lucretia Mott, **Elizabeth Cady Stanton,** and Susan B. Anthony campaigned for the abolition of slavery. In the process, they realized the severe restrictions on their own lives. They became the founders of the American women's rights movement.

Over time, women began to break the barriers that kept them out of universities and professions. By the late 1800s, a few women trained as doctors or lawyers. Others became explorers, researchers, or inventors, often without recognition. For example, Julia Brainerd Hall worked with her brother to develop an aluminum-producing process. Their company became hugely successful, but Charles Hall received almost all of the credit.

The Suffrage Movement By the late 1800s, married women in some countries had won the right to control their own property. The struggle for political rights proved far more difficult. In the United States, the Seneca Falls Convention of 1848 demanded that women be granted the right to vote. In Europe, groups dedicated to **women's suffrage,** or women's right to vote, emerged in the later 1800s.

Among men, some liberals and socialists supported women's suffrage. In general, though, suffragists faced intense opposition. Some critics claimed that women were too emotional to be allowed to vote. Others argued that women needed to be "protected" from grubby politics or that a woman's place was in the home, not in government.

To such claims, **Sojourner Truth,** an African American suffragist, is credited with replying, "Nobody ever helps me into carriages, or over mud puddles, or gives me any best place! And ain't I a woman?"

On the edges of the Western world, women made faster strides. In New Zealand, Australia, and some western territories of the United States, women won the vote by the early 1900s. There, women who had "tamed the frontier" alongside men were not dismissed as weak and helpless. In the United States, Wyoming became the first state to grant women the right to vote. In much of the Western world, however, the women's suffrage struggle took much longer. By 1920, women in Britain and the United States had finally won the vote.

>> In Britain, the first petition for women's suffrage was presented to Parliament in 1867. The suffragist movement continued until Parliament finally granted women over 30 the right to vote in 1918. Women gained the same voting rights as men in 1928.

Bounce to Activate Gallery

IDENTIFY MAIN IDEAS What were the arguments against women's suffrage?

The Rise of Public Education

By the late 1800s, reformers persuaded many governments to set up public schools and require basic education for all children. Teaching "the three Rs"—reading, writing, and 'rithmetic—was thought to produce better citizens. In addition, industrialized societies recognized the need for a literate workforce. Schools taught punctuality, obedience to authority, disciplined work habits, and patriotism. In European schools, children also received basic religious education.

Improving Public Schools At first, elementary schools were primitive. Many teachers had little schooling themselves. In rural areas, students attended class only during the times when they were not needed on the farm or in their parents' shops.

By the late 1800s, a growing number of children were in school, and the quality of elementary education improved. Teachers received training at normal schools, where the latest "norms and standards" of educational practices were taught. By the late 1800s, more schools were being set up in western Europe and elsewhere to train teachers.

In England, schooling girls and boys between the ages of five and ten became compulsory after 1881. At the same time, governments began to expand secondary schools, known as high schools in the United States. In secondary schools, students learned the "classical languages," Latin and Greek, along with history and mathematics.

In general, only middle-class families could afford to have their sons attend these schools, which trained students for more serious study or for government jobs. Middle-class girls were sent to school primarily in the hope that they might marry well and become better wives and mothers. Generally, girls' schools did not teach much science or mathematics, which were considered unnecessary and inappropriate for young women.

Higher Education Grows Colleges and universities expanded in this period, too. Most university students were the sons of middle or upper-class families. The university curriculum emphasized ancient history and languages, philosophy, religion, and law. By the late 1800s, universities added courses in the sciences, especially in chemistry and physics. At the same time, engineering schools trained students who would have the knowledge and skills to build the new industrial society.

Some women sought greater educational opportunities. By the 1840s, a few small colleges for women opened, including Bedford College in England and Mount Holyoke in the United States. In 1863, the British reformer Emily Davies campaigned for female students to be allowed to take the entrance examinations for Cambridge University. She succeeded, but as late as 1897, male Cambridge students rioted against granting degrees to women.

DRAW CONCLUSIONS Why did more children attend school in the late 1800s than before?

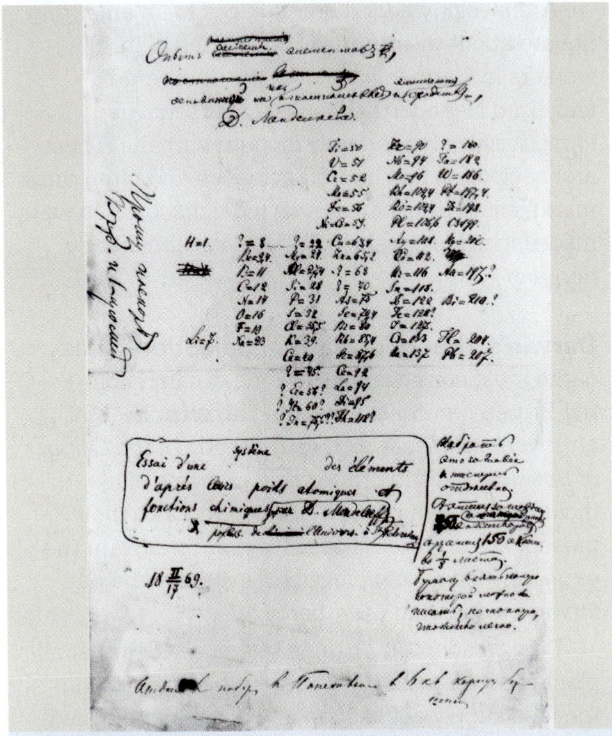

>> This image shows Dmitri Mendeleyev's 1869 manuscript of the periodic table. In 1871, he created a version with gaps where he believed elements that had not yet been discovered would fit.

New Directions in Science

Science in the service of industry brought great changes in the later 1800s. At the same time, researchers advanced startling theories about the natural world. Their new ideas challenged long-held beliefs.

Modern Atomic Theory A crucial breakthrough in chemistry came in the early 1800s when the English Quaker schoolteacher **John Dalton** developed modern atomic theory. The ancient Greeks had speculated that all matter was made of tiny particles called atoms. Dalton showed that each element has its own kind of atoms. Earlier theories put forth the idea that all atoms were basically alike. Dalton also showed how different kinds of atoms combine to make all chemical substances. In 1869, the Russian chemist Dmitri Mendeleyev (men duh LAY ef) drew up a table that grouped elements according to their atomic weights. His table became the basis for the periodic table of elements used today.

The Question of Earth's Age The new science of geology opened avenues of debate. In *Principles of Geology,* Charles Lyell offered evidence to show that Earth had formed over millions of years. His successors concluded that Earth was at least two billion years old and that life had not appeared until long after Earth was formed. These ideas did not seem to agree with biblical accounts of creation.

Archaeology added other pieces to an emerging debate about the origins of life on Earth. In 1856, workers in Germany accidentally uncovered fossilized Neanderthal bones. Later scholars found fossils of other early modern humans. These archaeologists had limited evidence and often drew mistaken conclusions. But as more discoveries were made, scholars developed new ideas about early humans.

Darwin's Theory of Natural Selection Some of the most controversial new ideas came from the British naturalist **Charles Darwin.** In 1859, after years of research, he published *On the Origin of Species.* Darwin argued that all forms of life, including human beings, had evolved into their present state over millions of years. To explain the extremely long, slow process of evolution, he put forward a startling new theory.

Darwin adopted Thomas Malthus's idea that all plants and animals produced more offspring than the food supply could support. As a result, he said, members of each species constantly competed to survive. Natural forces "selected" those with physical traits best adapted to their environment to survive and to pass the trait on to their offspring. Darwin called this process natural selection. Later, some people called it "survival of the fittest."

>> Darwin's theories about evolution sparked much debate. **Analyze Political Cartoons** How does the portrayal of Darwin as a monkey relate to his theories? Do you think the cartoonist accepts the theories?

The Uproar Over Darwin Like the ideas of Nicolaus Copernicus and Isaac Newton in earlier times, Darwin's theory ignited a furious debate between scientists and theologians. To many Christians, the Bible contained the only true account of creation. It told that God created the world and all forms of life within seven days. Darwin's theory, they argued, reduced people to the level of animals and undermined belief in God and the soul. While some Christians eventually came to accept the idea of evolution, others did not. Controversy over Darwin's theories has continued to the present day.

Social Darwinism Although Darwin himself never promoted any social ideas, some thinkers used his theories to support their own beliefs about society. The idea that natural selection applied to human society, especially to warfare and economic competition, became known as Social Darwinism. It was British philosopher Herbert Spencer who coined the phrase "survival of the fittest."

Social Darwinists argued that industrial tycoons earned their success because they were more "fit" than those they put out of business. War brought progress by weeding out weak nations. Victory was seen as proof of superiority.

Social Darwinism encouraged **racism,** the unscientific belief that one racial group is superior to another, and had horrific consequences for people throughout the world. For example, Social Darwinism was used to justify harsh treatment of the mentally ill and countless acts of violence toward people of "different" religions, races, and ethnicities. By the late 1800s, many Europeans and Americans claimed that the success of Western civilization was due to the supremacy of the white race. Such powerful ideas would have a long-lasting impact on world history.

IDENTIFY CENTRAL IDEAS How did science begin to challenge existing beliefs in the late 1800s?

The Role of Religion

Despite the challenge of new scientific ideas, religion continued to be a major force in Western society. Christian churches and Jewish synagogues remained at the center of communities. Religious leaders influenced political, social, and educational developments.

The grim realities of industrial life stimulated feelings of compassion and charity. Christian and Jewish labor unions and political parties pushed for reforms. Individuals, church groups, and Jewish organizations all tried to help the working poor. Catholic priests and nuns set up schools and hospitals in urban slums. Many Protestant churches backed the **social gospel,** a movement that urged Christians to social service. They campaigned for reforms in housing, healthcare, and education.

Motivated by their religious values, Christians and Jews founded many organizations to help those in need. In Paris, Frédéric Ozanum established the St. Vincent de Paul Society in 1833. By 1878, William and Catherine Booth had set up the Salvation Army in London.

It both spread Christian teachings and provided social services. Their daughter, Evangeline Booth, later helped bring the Salvation Army to North America. In 1881, the Jewish community in New York founded the Hebrew Immigrant Aid Society, which provided shelter, food, employment, and education to many new immigrants.

IDENTIFY SUPPORTING DETAILS What social services did religious organizations provide?

>> The hardships of industrial life led to the creation of numerous charitable organizations, including the Salvation Army, which provided many services to the needy.

The Romantics Turn from Reason

The Industrial Age shaped the arts as well as society and science. Many writers turned away from the harsh realities of industrial life to celebrate the peace and beauty of nature. These writers were part of a cultural movement called romanticism. **Romanticism** emphasized imagination, freedom, and emotion. (Romance, in the sense of romantic love, was not the focus of the movement.) From the late 1700s to 1850, romanticism shaped much of Western literature and arts.

Romantic Poetry Romantic writers, artists, and composers rebelled against the Enlightenment emphasis on reason, order, and emotional restraint. Instead, romantic writers focused on simple, direct language that conveyed intense feelings and glorified nature.

English poet **William Wordsworth** helped launch this cultural movement with the publication of *Lyrical Ballads* in 1789. Wordsworth rejected formal styles and conventions, and instead experimented with poetic forms and focused on

>> Romantic paintings often focused on nature and emotion. Note the romantic features of this portrait of William Wordsworth. His arms are crossed, and his head is down as though he is brooding about something. A dramatic landscape looms behind him.

common people and subjects, like the peace and beauty of the sunset.

> It is a beauteous evening, calm and free,
>
> The holy time is quiet as a Nun
>
> Breathless with adoration; the broad sun
>
> Is sinking down in its tranquility
>
> —William Wordsworth, *Complete Poetical Works*

Poets such as William Blake, Samuel Taylor Coleridge, John Keats, and Percy Bysshe Shelley were also leading lights of the romantic movement.

Mysterious Heroes Romantic writers created a new kind of hero—a mysterious, melancholy figure who felt out of step with society. "My joys, my grief, my passions, and my powers, / Made me a stranger," wrote Britain's George Gordon, **Lord Byron.** He himself was a larger-than-life figure equal to those he created.

After a rebellious, wandering life, he joined Greek forces battling for independence from Turkish rule. When he died of a fever there, his legend bloomed. Moody, isolated romantic heroes came to be described as "Byronic."

The romantic hero often hid a guilty secret and faced a grim destiny. German writer Johann Wolfgang von Goethe (GUR tuh) wrote the dramatic poem *Faust.* The aging scholar Faust makes a pact with the devil, exchanging his soul for youth. After much agony, Faust wins salvation by accepting his duty to help others. In *Jane Eyre*, British novelist Charlotte Brontë weaves a tale about a quiet governess and her brooding, Byronic employer, whose large mansion conceals a terrifying secret.

>> In many of his paintings, romantic artist J.M.W. Turner focused on the effects of light and color. **Analyze Images** How does *A View on the Rhine* exemplify the characteristics of romantic art?

Glorifying the Past Romantic writers combined history, legend, and folklore. Sir Walter Scott's novels and ballads evoked the turbulent history of Scottish clans or medieval knights. Alexandre Dumas (doo MAH) and **Victor Hugo** re-created France's past in novels like *The Three Musketeers* and *The Hunchback of Notre Dame.*

Architects, too, were inspired by old styles and forms. Churches and other buildings, including the British Parliament, were modeled on medieval Gothic styles. To people living in the 1800s, medieval towers and lacy stonework conjured up images of a glorious past.

Romanticism in Music The orchestra, as we know it today, took shape in the early 1800s. The first composer to take full advantage of the broad range of instruments was the German composer **Ludwig van Beethoven.** Beethoven's stirring music transcended his own time and culture by conveying universal emotions such as love, loss, death, joy, and fear. For example, the famous opening of his Fifth Symphony conveys the sense of fate knocking on one's door.

His Sixth Symphony captures a joyful day in the countryside, interrupted by a violent thunderstorm. In all, Beethoven produced nine symphonies, five piano concertos, a violin concerto, an opera, two masses, and dozens of shorter pieces that are still popular today.

Romantic composers also tried to stir deep emotions. The piano music and passionate playing of the Hungarian composer Franz Liszt moved audiences to laugh or weep. Other composers wove traditional folk music into their works to glorify their nations' past. In his piano works, Frederic Chopin (shoh PAN) used Polish peasant dances to convey the sorrows and joys of people living under foreign occupation.

Romanticism in Art Painters, too, broke free from the discipline and strict rules of the Enlightenment. Landscape painters like J.M.W. Turner sought to capture the beauty and power of nature. Using bold brush strokes and colors, Turner often showed tiny human figures struggling against sea and storm.

Romantics painted many subjects, from simple peasant life to medieval knights to current events. Bright colors conveyed violent energy and emotion. The French painter Eugène Delacroix (deh luh KRWAH) filled his canvases with dramatic action. In *Liberty Leading the People,* the Goddess of Liberty carries the revolutionary tricolor as French citizens rally to the cause.

IDENTIFY CAUSE AND EFFECT How was romanticism a reaction to the Enlightenment and the Industrial Revolution?

>> Romantic painter Eugene Delacroix turned to foreign lands and ancient times to portray the exotic or simpler ways of life. Although the painting focuses on peasant musicians rather than nature, it still seems idealized rather than harshly realistic.

Artists Represent Real Life

By the mid-1800s, a new artistic movement, **realism,** took hold in the West. Realism was an attempt to represent the world as it was, without the heightened sentiment and idealized emotions of the romantics. Realists often stressed the harsh side of life in urban slums or peasant villages. Many writers and artists were committed to improving the lot of the unfortunates whose lives they depicted.

>> This poster shows characters from a play based on Victor Hugo's novel *Les Misérables*. In the center is Jean Valjean, who was arrested for stealing a loaf of bread to keep his sister's child from starving.

Novelists Expose Social Wrongs The English novelist **Charles Dickens** vividly portrayed the lives of slum dwellers and factory workers, including children. In *Oliver Twist,* Dickens tells the story of a nine-year-old orphan raised in a grim poorhouse. When a desperately hungry Oliver asks for more food, he is smacked in the head by his well-fed master and sent off to work. Later, he runs away to London. There he is taken in by Fagin, a villain who trains homeless children to become pickpockets.

The book shocked many middle-class readers with its picture of poverty, mistreatment of children, and urban crime. Yet Dickens's humor and colorful characters made him one of the most popular novelists in the world.

French novelists also portrayed the ills of their time. With *Les Misérables* (lay miz ehr AHB), Victor Hugo moved from romanticism to realism. The novel showed how hunger drove a good man to crime and how the law hounded him ever after. The novels of Émile Zola painted an even grimmer picture. In *Germinal,* Zola exposed class warfare in the French mining industry. To Zola's characters, neither the Enlightenment faith in reason nor the romantic emphasis on feelings mattered at all.

Realism on Stage Norwegian dramatist Henrik Ibsen brought realism to the stage. His plays attacked the hypocrisy he observed around him. *A Doll's House* shows a woman caught in a straitjacket of social rules. In *An Enemy of the People,* a doctor discovers that the water in a local spa is polluted. Because the town's economy depends on its spa, the citizens denounce the doctor and suppress the truth. Ibsen's realistic dramas had a wide influence in Europe and the United States.

Realism in Art Realist painters also rejected the romantic emphasis on imagination. Instead, they focused on ordinary subjects, especially working-class men and women. "I cannot paint an angel," said the French realist **Gustave Courbet** (koor BAY), "because I have never seen one." Instead, he painted works such as *The Stone Breakers,* which shows two rough laborers on a country road. Later in the century, *The Gross Clinic,* by American painter Thomas Eakins, shocked viewers with its realistic depiction of an autopsy conducted in a medical classroom.

>> In 1839, Louis Daguerre perfected an effective method of photography. His camera changed both art and society.

>> Realist painters focused on everyday subjects. *The Gross Clinic,* shown here, shows medical students dissecting a body. It is considered Eakins's masterpiece. **Analyze Images** Why were viewers so shocked by this painting? Why might Eakins have chosen this subject?

CONTRAST How did realism differ from romanticism?

New Directions in the Visual Arts

By the 1840s, a new art form, photography, was emerging. **Louis Daguerre** (dah GEHR) in France and William Fox Talbot in England had improved on earlier technologies to produce successful photographs. At first, many photos were stiff, posed portraits of middle-class families or prominent people. Other photographs reflected the romantics' fascination with faraway places.

In time, photographers used the camera to present the grim realities of life. During the American Civil War, Mathew B. Brady preserved a vivid, realistic record of the corpse-strewn battlefields. Other photographers showed the harsh conditions in industrial factories or slums.

The Impressionists Photography posed a challenge to painters. Why try for realism, some artists asked, when a camera could do the same thing better?

By the 1870s, a group of painters took art in a new direction, seeking to capture the first fleeting impression made by a scene or object on the viewer's eye. The new movement, known as **impressionism,** took root in Paris, capital of the Western art world.

Since the Renaissance, painters had carefully finished their paintings so that no brush strokes showed. But impressionists like **Claude Monet** (moh NAY) and Edgar Degas (day GAH) brushed strokes of color side by side without any blending. According to new scientific studies of optics, the human eye would mix these patches of color.

By concentrating on visual impressions rather than realism, artists achieved a fresh view of familiar subjects. Monet, for example, painted the cathedral of Rouen (roo AHN), France, dozens of times from the same angle, capturing how it looked in different lights at different times of day.

The Postimpressionists Later painters, called postimpressionists, developed a variety of styles. Georges Seurat (suh RAH) arranged small dots of color to define the shapes of objects.

Vincent van Gogh experimented with sharp brush lines and bright colors. His unique brushwork lent a dreamlike quality to everyday subjects. Desperately poor, he sold few paintings in his short, unhappy life. Today, Van Gogh's masterpieces sell for millions of dollars each.

Paul Gauguin (goh GAN) also developed a bold, personal style. He rejected the materialism of Western life and went to live on the island of Tahiti in the South Pacific. His most famous works depict the people of Tahiti. In his paintings, people look flat, as in "primitive" folk art. But his brooding colors and black outlining of shapes convey intense feelings and images.

CONNECT How did photography influence the development of painting?

>> After being rejected by France's most prestigious art exhibition, a group of painters held their own exhibition in 1874. One of the paintings, Claude Monet's *Impression: Sunrise,* gave the impressionist movement its name.

Bounce to Activate Gallery

ASSESSMENT

1. **Identify Cause and Effect** In what ways were the new artistic styles of the 1800s a reaction to changes in society?
2. **Draw Conclusions** Why did the movement to change women's roles in society face strong opposition?
3. **Infer** Why did reformers think free public education would lead to social change?
4. **Identify Supporting Details** How did the Industrial Revolution change the old social order and long-held traditions in the Western world?
5. **Infer** Referring to *Oliver Twist*, Charles Dickens wrote that "to show [criminals] as they really are, for ever skulking uneasily through the dirtiest paths of life . . . would be a service to society." How does his claim reflect the goals of realism?

LESSON SUMMARIES

Use these Lesson Summaries, and the longer versions available online, to review the key ideas for each lesson in this Topic.

Lesson 1: The Industrial Revolution Begins

Life in farming villages that sustained most people for centuries underwent changes in the mid-1700s. This time of change is called the Industrial Revolution. It would have an impact on every aspect of life in Western Europe and the United States.

Lesson 2: Social Impact of Industrialism

With changes in farming, many people moved to the city. This movement or urbanization had benefits and problems. In addition, workers had to adjust to the difficulties of a factory system.

Lesson 3: The Second Industrial Revolution

Advances in science—the Bessemer Process, the use of electricity, along with numerous inventions to improve factory production—advances in transportation and communication, changed the way people worked and lived.

Lesson 4: Changing Ways of Life and Thought

The Industrial Revolution challenged long-held values and traditions. The rise of the middle class brought new social values and a strict etiquette code. Women campaigned for voting rights and reformers worked to make education accessible to all children. New cultural ideas embraced romanticism, then realism, in the arts.

VISUAL REVIEW

Use these graphics to review some of the key terms, people, and ideas from this Topic.

Key People

INVENTORS/DEVELOPERS
Henry Bessemer—steel processing
Michael Faraday—dynamo
Thomas Edison—electric light bulb
Gottlieb Daimler—automobile
Samuel F.B. Morse—telegraph
Alexander Graham Bell—telephone
Guglielmo Marconi—radio

SCIENTISTS
Louis Pasteur—vaccinations, pasteurization
Joseph Lister—antiseptics
John Dalton—modern atomic theory
Charles Darwin—theory of natural selection

REFORMERS
Florence Nightingale—sanitary measures in hospitals
Elizabeth Cady Stanton—women's rights
Susan B. Anthony—women's rights
William and Catherine Booth—Salvation Army

ARTISTS, WRITERS, AND COMPOSERS
William Wordsworth—romantic writer
Lord Byron—romantic writer
Ludwig van Beethoven—romantic composer
Charles Dickens—realist writer
Émile Zola—realist writer
Gustave Courbet—realist painter
Claude Monet—impressionist painter
Edgar Degas—impressionist painter
Vincent van Gogh—postimpressionist painter

Impact of the Industrial Revolution

KEY EFFECTS OF THE INDUSTRIAL REVOLUTION

INDUSTRIALIZATION	URBANIZATION	SOCIAL STRUCTURE
• Germany, France, and the U.S. join Great Britain as Industrial powers. • Rise of Factories; new production methods • Advances in transportation and communication • Rise of big business • Growth of labor unions	• Advances in medicine and science • Population growth due to falling death rates • Higher standard of living	• Three social classes emerge • Middle class expands • Rise of urban working class • Reform movements grow • Public education expands

California Topic 2 Assessment

KEY TERMS, PEOPLE, AND IDEAS

1. What is the practice of **enclosure**? How were small farmers affected?
2. How did **James Watt's** invention contribute to the technology of the Industrial Revolution?
3. How did the division of labor affect manufacturing?
4. How did natural resources in Britain contribute to the rise of the Industrial Revolution?
5. How did the Industrial Revolution affect the **standard of living**?
6. What policy did **Thomas Malthus** advocate for ending poverty?
7. According to Adam Smith, what were the benefits of a **free market**?
8. How did **Romanticism** reflect a new way of thinking?
9. What were the goals of social reformers in the United States?

CRITICAL THINKING

10. **Describe** How did industrialization gradually spread to other nations? What were the effects?
11. **Summarize** How did Robert Owen seek to improve social conditions?
12. **Synthesize Information** How did the rise of cities challenge the economic and social order of the time?
13. **Summarize Information** What laws helped workers in the late 1800s?
14. **Draw Conclusions** During the early years of the Industrial Revolution, the government exercised a policy of laissez faire economics. What were the effects on business? Were there benefits to this policy?
15. **Recognize Cause and Effect** Why did life expectancy rise steadily between 1850 and 1900?
16. **Use Primary Sources** Read the excerpt below from Karl Marx and Friedrich Engels. It gives their view on workers in the Industrial Revolution. Discuss how Marx feels a worker might regard his or her job. What made the job this way for the worker?

> "Owing to the extensive use of machinery and to division of labor, the work of the proletarians has lost all individual character, and consequently, all charm for the workman. He becomes [a limb] of the machine, and it is only the most simple, most monotonous, and most easily acquired knack that is required of him. Hence, the cost of production of a workman is restricted entirely to the means of [survival] that he requires for his maintenance. . . . . ."
>
> *—Karl Marx and Friedrich Engels, The Communist Manifesto*

17. **Writing Activity** After James Watt decided to produce and market an improved steam engine, he needed money to carry out his dream. He found a partner—Matthew Boulton. Extremely pleased Boulton declared :

> "I have at my disposal what the whole world demands, something which will uplift civilization more than ever by relieving man of all undignified drudgery. I have *steam power*."

Discuss the significance of this technology in starting the Industrial Revolution. How did it impact the spread of the industrial revolution? Use your knowledge of the Topic to explain the significance of steam power.

DOCUMENT-BASED QUESTIONS

The birth of the modern city helped to define the Industrial Age. Read the documents below, then answer the questions that follow.

DOCUMENT A

"The first shock of a great earthquake had, just at that period, rent the whole neighborhood to its center. Traces of its course were visible on every side. Houses were knocked down; streets broken through and stopped; deep pits and trenches dug in the ground; enormous heaps of earth and clay thrown up; buildings that were undermined and shaking, propped by great beams of wood. . . . In short, the yet unfinished and unopened Railroad was in progress; and, from the very core of all this dire disorder, trailed smoothly away, upon its mighty course of civilization and improvement."

—*from Dombey and Son by Charles Dickens*

DOCUMENT B

SELECTED INVENTIONS, 1824–1911	
Cement	1824
Locomotive	1830
Dynamite	1866
Telephone	1876
Cash register	1879
Electric trolley car	1884–1887
Steel alloy	1891
Self-starting auto	1911

SOURCE: *The World Almanac*, 2004

DOCUMENT C

POPULATION OF MAJOR CITIES

CITY	1850	1900
Berlin, Germany	419,000	1,889,000
London, England	2,685,000	6,586,000
Moscow, Russia	365,000	989,000
New York, United States	696,000	3,437,000
Paris, France	1,053,000	2,714,000

SOURCE: *International Historical Statistics*

DOCUMENT D

Brooklyn Bridge, 1883

18. The cause of the earthquake described in Document A was

A. an underground fault in London.
B. poorly constructed tall buildings.
C. construction of a railroad.
D. deep pits and trenches in the ground.

19. Which inventions from Document B had the most impact on New York City at the time Document D was created?

A. trolley cars, steel alloy, cash registers
B. dynamite, telephones, cash registers
C. cement, locomotives, telephones
D. cement, locomotives, dynamite

20. Which trend does Document C illustrate?

A. the shift in population from Europe to the United States
B. the shift in population from East Coast to West Coast
C. the increase in population of cities
D. the decease in rural population

21. **Writing Tasks** What were the most significant features of the modern city? Why? Use the information from Documents A through D as well as what you have learned in this Topic to support your opinion.

End-of-Topic Practice

1 How did the Industrial Revolution change the economy?

A There was an increase in subsistence farming, or farming to maintain a family, and fewer consumer goods on the market.

B There was an increase in domestic production and subsistence farming.

C Subsistence farming decreased and more consumer goods arrived on the market.

D With improved agricultural methods, subsistence farming increased along with factory production.

---

2 Why was it important for workers to gain voting rights during the Industrial Revolution?

F Voting created pressure for governments to regulate working conditions.

G Voting enabled people to start strikes or revolts without interference.

H Voting minimized the government's feeling of worker discontent.

J Voting allowed workers to form societies such as the mutual-aid society.

> *"Betty Harris, age 37: I was married at 23, and went into a colliery when I was married. I used to weave when about 12 years old; can neither read nor write. I work for Andrew Knowles, of Little Bolton (Lancs), and make sometimes 7s a week, sometimes not so much. I am a drawer, and work from 6 in the morning to 6 at night. Stop about an hour at noon to eat my dinner; have bread and butter for dinner; I get no drink. I have two children, but they are too young to work. I worked at drawing when I was in the family way. I know a woman who has gone home and washed herself, taken to her bed, delivered of a child, and gone to work again under the week."*

3 Read the excerpt. Which of these helped to change the roles of working-class women during the Industrial Age?

A Efforts of political activists successfully changed work conditions.

B Changes in laws guaranteed income for women with children.

C Women's suffrage in the late 1800s empowered women.

D Women had a large voice in the labor union movements.

---

4 How did factory systems enhance industrialization efforts?

F Expensive interchangeable parts improved parts repair.

G New inventions were tested by the government before use.

H Assembly line methods were efficient with division of labor.

J Division of labor excluded women and children from risky jobs.

If you have trouble with. . .				
Question	1	2	3	4
See Lesson	2.1	2.2	2.2, 2.4	2.2

[ESSENTIAL QUESTION] What are the Challenges of Diversity?

3 Nationalism and the Spread of Democracy (1790–1914)

>> A statue of Simón Bolívar

Enduring Understandings

- After Napoleon's defeat, conservatives tried to restore monarchies while liberals called for constitutional governments.
- Nationalism and liberalism led to a series of revolutions in Europe.
- Influenced by the American and French revolutions, Latin American colonies won independence.
- Nationalism led to the unification of Germany and Italy but threatened the Austrian and Ottoman empires.
- In Britain and the United States, democracy expanded as more people won the right to vote.
- After France's defeat by Prussia, the Third Republic was established.
- In Russia, the cycle of reform and repression led to instability.

NBC LEARN

Learn more about The Liberator, Simón Bolívar.

Bounce to Activate My Story Video

California Topic 3 Overview

In this Topic, you will learn more about the events which occurred during the era of Nationalism and the Spread of Democracy. As you study this Topic, you will complete the Quest team project.

LESSON OUTLINE

3.1 Revolutions Sweep Europe
Analysis CST.1, CST.2, HRE.4, HI.1

3.2 Latin American Nations Win Independence
Analysis CST.1, CST.2, CST.3, HRE.4, HI.1

3.3 The Unification of Germany
Analysis CST.1, CST.2, HRE.4, HI.1

3.4 The Unification of Italy
Analysis CST.1, CST.2, HRE.4, HI.1

3.5 Democratic Reforms in Britain
HSS 10.3.4; Analysis CST.1, CST.2, HRE.4, HI.1

3.6 Divisions and Democracy in France
Analysis CST.1, CST.2, HRE.4, HI.1

3.7 Growth of the United States
Analysis CST.1, CST.2, HRE.4, HI.1

3.8 Nationalism in Eastern Europe and Russia
Analysis CST.1, CST.2, HRE.4, HI.1

Key Events of Nationalism and the Spread of Democracy

1800 | 1850 | 1900 | 1950

1800
Nationalism rises in Germany.

1804
Haiti declares independence from France.

1819
Simón Bolívar seizes Bogata from Spain.

1830s
Mazzini founds Young Italy to encourage unification.

1848
Revolutions break out across much of Europe.

1861
Alexander II frees the serfs.

1870
Bismarck unifies the German empire.

1905
Revolution breaks out in St. Petersburg.

QUEST! TEAM PROJECT

Preparing for a debate

What caused the Irish Potato famine is a question that has and still sparks controversy. Who or what is to blame for the famine that took the lives of over one million people? In this Quest, you will read different viewpoints. Then you will take a stand and defend your position.

STEP 1
Review what you know about the political and economic situation in Britain and Ireland during the nineteenth century.

STEP 2
Turn to the different sources and consider the varying viewpoints and the supporting evidence. Evaluate the sources.

STEP 3
Team members will choose YES or NO positions. Write your position outlines. Use strong supporting evidence. Review, edit, and revise your position paper.

STEP 4
In 1997, British prime minister Tony Blair apologized for Britain's role in the famine. Was the apology needed? Reflect on what you have learned as the discussion begins.

PEARSON realize™
PearsonSchool.com/CASS
Go ONLINE for complete Quest materials
VIDEO ETEXT WRITING RUBRIC PDF ASSESSMENT

>> Prince Metternich served as the foreign minister of Austria from 1809 to 1848. To suppress revolutionary ideas, he urged conservatives to censor the press and crush protests in their countries.

3.1 At the Congress of Vienna in 1815, the powerful rulers of Europe sought to suppress revolutionary ideas, preserve their own power, and set up a lasting peace. Prince Clemens von Metternich, a commanding force at the congress, warned of the dangers of the "revolutionary seed" spread by the French Revolution and Napoleon. Revolutionary ideas, he warned, not only threatened Europe's monarchs, but also undermined the values of the old social order.

Bounce to Activate Flipped Video

>> Objectives

Compare the goals of conservatives and liberals in 19th century Europe.

Identify the influence of liberty, equality, and nationalism on political revolutions.

Describe the causes and results of the revolutions of 1830 and 1848.

>> Key Terms

ideology
universal manhood suffrage
autonomy
radical
Louis Philippe
recession
Napoleon III
Louis Kossuth
absolutism

Revolutions Sweep Europe

A Clash of Ideologies

> Passions are let loose. . . to overthrow everything that society respects as the basis of its existence: religion, public morality, laws, customs, rights, and duties, all are attacked, confounded [defeated], overthrown, or called in question.
>
> —Prince Clemens von Metternich

Unlike the monarchs attending the Congress of Vienna, other voices loudly opposed Metternich's views. In the decades after 1815, people with opposing **ideologies,** or systems of thought and belief, plunged Europe into turmoil.

Conservatives Favor Old Order The Congress of Vienna was a victory for the conservative forces, which included monarchs and their officials, noble landowners, and church leaders. To preserve the old political and social order, European monarchs worked together to ensure stability and prevent revolution. This arrangement is sometimes called the Concert of Europe. In addition to the conservative ruling class of Europe, conservative ideas appealed to peasants, who wanted to preserve traditional ways.

Conservatives of the early 1800s wanted to return to the way things had been before 1789. They had benefited under the old order. They wanted to restore royal families to the thrones they had lost when Napoleon swept across Europe. They supported a social hierarchy in which lower classes respected and obeyed their social superiors.

Conservatives also backed an established church—Catholic in Austria and southern Europe, Protestant in northern Europe, and Eastern Orthodox in eastern Europe.

Conservatives believed that talk about natural rights and constitutional government could lead only to chaos, as in France in 1789. If change had to come, they argued, it must come slowly. Conservatives felt that their own interest in peace and stability benefited everyone. Conservative leaders like Metternich opposed freedom of the press, which could spread revolutionary ideas. Metternich urged monarchs to crush protests in their own lands and help others to douse the flames of rebellion wherever they erupted.

>> **Analyze Political Cartoons** A determined Prince Metternich stands firm, with an angry crowd behind him. Who does the crowd represent, and what do they want?

Bounce to Activate Cartoon

IDENTIFY MAIN IDEAS What was the primary goal of conservatives in the Concert of Europe?

Liberalism and Nationalism Spur Revolts

Challenging the conservatives at every turn were the liberals. Liberals embraced the ideas of the Enlightenment and the French Revolution. Their goals, and the rising tide of nationalism, ignited revolts across Europe.

Liberals Defend Natural Rights Because liberals spoke mostly for the bourgeoisie, or middle class, their ideas are sometimes called "bourgeois liberalism." Liberals included business owners, bankers, and lawyers, as well as politicians, newspaper editors, writers, and others who helped to shape public opinion.

Liberals wanted governments to be based on written constitutions and separation of powers. They opposed the old notion of the divine right of monarchs and the tradition of a ruling aristocracy. Liberals called for rulers elected by the people and responsible to them. Thus, most liberals favored a republican form of government over a monarchy,

>> **Compare** After the Congress of Vienna, liberals repeatedly protested and rebelled against the conservative order. How do the liberal protesters in this image differ in appearance from the image of the conservative leader Metternich in the previous text?

or at least wanted the monarch to be limited by a constitution.

Liberals defended natural rights such as liberty and equality. They stood for property rights and freedom of religion. Liberals of the early 1800s saw the role of government as limited to protecting these basic rights. In their view, only male property owners or others with a financial stake in society should have the right to vote. Not until later in the 1800s did liberals support the principle of **universal manhood suffrage,** giving all adult men the right to vote.

Liberals also strongly supported the laissez-faire economics of Adam Smith and David Ricardo. They saw the free market as an opportunity for capitalist entrepreneurs to succeed. As capitalists, and often employers, liberals had different goals from those of workers laboring in factories, mines, and other enterprises of the early Industrial Revolution.

Nationalism Grows Another challenge to Metternich's conservative order came from the rise of nationalist feelings. Like liberalism, nationalism was an outgrowth of the Enlightenment and the French Revolution. Nationalism, like liberalism, would feed the flames of revolt against the established order.

For centuries, European rulers had gained or lost lands through wars, marriages, and treaties. They exchanged territories and the people in them like pieces in a game. As a result, by 1815 Europe had several empires that included many nationalities. The Austrian, Russian, and Ottoman empires, for example, each included diverse peoples.

During the 1800s, national groups who shared a common heritage demanded their own states. Each group had its own leaders who inspired and organized the struggle. Although nationalism gave people a sense of identity and the goal of achieving an independent homeland, it also had negative effects. It often bred intolerance and led to persecution of other ethnic or national groups.

HYPOTHESIZE Why would nationalism lead to intolerance and persecution of other ethnic or national groups?

Rebellions Erupt in Eastern Europe

Spurred by the ideas of liberalism and nationalism, revolutionaries fought against the old order. Although these ideas stirred unrest in Western Europe, the first successful nationalist revolts occurred in Eastern Europe. Eastern Europe was home to a mix of peoples and religions. In the early 1800s, several Balkan peoples in southeastern Europe rebelled against the Ottomans, who had ruled them for more than 300 years.

Goals of Liberals and Conservatives

LIBERALS	CONSERVATIVES
Ideas appealed to middle class of educated business people and professionals.	Ideas appealed to royalty, nobility, church leaders, and uneducated peasants.
GOALS: Governments based on written constitutions Separation of powers Natural rights of individuals (liberty, equality, and property) Republican form of government Laissezfaire economics Revolution, if necessary, to achieve goals	**GOALS:** Royal families on their thrones Traditional social hierarchy Authority of established churches Respect and obedience to authority Stability and order Suppression of revolutions

>> **Analyze Charts** Conservatives and liberals had very different ideas about the role of government. How did their different ideologies affect European politics in the early-to-mid-1800s?

Serbia Gains Independence The first Balkan people to revolt were the Serbs. From 1804 to 1817, the Serbian independence leaders Karageorge (ka rah JAWR juh) and Milos Obrenovic (oh BRAY noh vich) battled Ottoman forces in two major uprisings.

Although Serbs had support from Russia, which shared its Slavic heritage and Eastern Orthodox Christianity, the Serbs faced a terrible struggle. The fighting took a huge toll. During this period, Serbian literature and culture flourished, further strengthening Serbian nationalism.

Gradually, Serbia gained a degree of **autonomy,** or self-rule, within the Ottoman empire. An 1830 agreement gave Serbs complete control over their own internal affairs, although European countries did not recognize Serbia's independence until 1878. Serbia continued its close ties with Russia, which it saw as a protector of its hard-won freedom.

Greeks Revolt Against Ottoman Rule In 1821, the Greeks revolted, seeking to end centuries of Ottoman rule. At first, the Greeks were badly divided. But years of suffering in long, bloody wars of independence helped shape a national identity. Leaders of the rebellion justified their struggle as "a national war, a holy war, a war the object of which is to reconquer the rights of individual liberty." The Greeks had the support of romantic writers such as English poet Lord Byron, who went to Greece to aid the fight for independence.

The Greek rebels won the sympathy of even the conservative powers of Europe. In the late 1820s, Britain, France, and Russia forced the Ottomans to grant independence to some Greek provinces. By 1830, Greece was independent. The European powers, however, pressured the Greeks to accept Otto von Wittelsbach, a German prince, as their king. This move was meant to show that the European powers did not support nationalist revolutions.

Other Challenges to the Old Order During the 1820s, other revolts erupted along the fringe of Europe. In Spain, Portugal, and several Italian states, rebels demanded constitutional governments. The unrest posed a challenge to the conservative rulers of Europe. Spurred on by Metternich, a French army marched over the Pyrenees to suppress a revolt in Spain. Austrian forces crossed the Alps to smash Italian rebels.

Troops dampened the fires of liberalism and nationalism, but could not smother them. In the next decades, sparks would flare anew. Added to liberal and nationalist demands were the goals of the new industrial working class. By the mid-1800s, social reformers and agitators were urging workers to support socialism or other ways of reorganizing property ownership, further contributing to the unrest of this period.

>> Uprisings flared up repeatedly across Europe, especially in Paris.

HYPOTHESIZE Why would a monarch order his army to suppress an uprising in another country?

Revolutions of 1830 and 1848

In the 1820s, conservative forces quickly suppressed the liberal uprisings in Spain, Portugal, and the Italian states. They could not, however, end Europe's age of revolutions. Liberal French leader Alexis de Tocqueville warned that the revolutions of the 1820s were not over.

> We are sleeping on a volcano. . . Do you not see that the Earth trembles anew? A wind of revolution blows, the storm is on the horizon.
>
> —Alexis de Tocqueville

Conservatives and Liberals in France The Congress of Vienna had restored Louis XVIII to the French throne. The new ruler wisely issued a constitution, the Charter of French Liberties. It created a two-house legislature and allowed limited freedom of the press. Still, the king retained much power.

Louis's efforts at compromise satisfied few people. Ultra royalists despised constitutional government and wanted to restore the old regime. These "ultras" included many high clergy and émigré nobles who had returned to France after the revolution.

Opposing the ultras were the liberals. They wanted to extend suffrage and win a share of power for middle-class citizens like themselves. Another group, the **radicals,** or people who favor extreme change, called for a republic like France had in the 1790s. The working class still wanted what it had hoped to win in 1789: decent pay and bread the people could afford.

Citizens Lead the July Revolution When Louis XVIII died in 1824, his younger brother, Charles X, inherited the throne. Charles, a strong believer in **absolutism,** rejected the very idea of the charter. In July 1830, he suspended the legislature, limited the right to vote, and restricted the press.

In Paris, angry citizens threw up barricades across the narrow streets. From behind the barricades, people fired on the soldiers and pelted them with stones and roof tiles. Within days, rebels controlled Paris. The revolutionary tricolor flew from the towers of Notre Dame cathedral. A frightened Charles X abdicated and fled to England.

>> French rebels erected barricades in the streets using household items and whatever else they could find that might offer protection during battles with government soldiers.

Louis Philippe, the "Citizen King" Radicals and liberals who had united against Charles X disagreed over a new government. Radicals wanted to set up a republic. Liberals, however, insisted on a constitutional monarchy and chose **Louis Philippe** as king. Louis Philippe was a cousin of Charles X and in his youth had supported the revolution of 1789.

The French called Louis Philippe the "citizen king" because he owed his throne to the people. Louis got along well with the liberal bourgeoisie. He dressed like them in a frock coat and top hat. Sometimes he strolled the streets, shaking hands with well-wishers. Liberal politicians filled his government.

Under Louis Philippe, the upper bourgeoisie prospered. Louis extended suffrage, but only to France's wealthier citizens. The vast majority of the people still could not vote. The king's other policies also favored the middle class at the expense of the workers.

RECALL What actions did Charles X take in 1830, and how did French rebels respond?

Demands for Reform Spread

The July Revolution in Paris inspired uprisings elsewhere in Europe. Metternich later said, "When France sneezes, Europe catches cold." Most of the uprisings were suppressed. But here and there, rebels did force changes on conservative governments. Even when they failed, revolutions frightened rulers badly enough to encourage reforms later in the century.

Belgium Wins Independence The one notable success in 1830 took place in Belgium. In 1815, the Congress of Vienna had united the Austrian Netherlands (present-day Belgium) and the Kingdom of Holland under the Dutch king. The Congress had

Revolutions of 1830

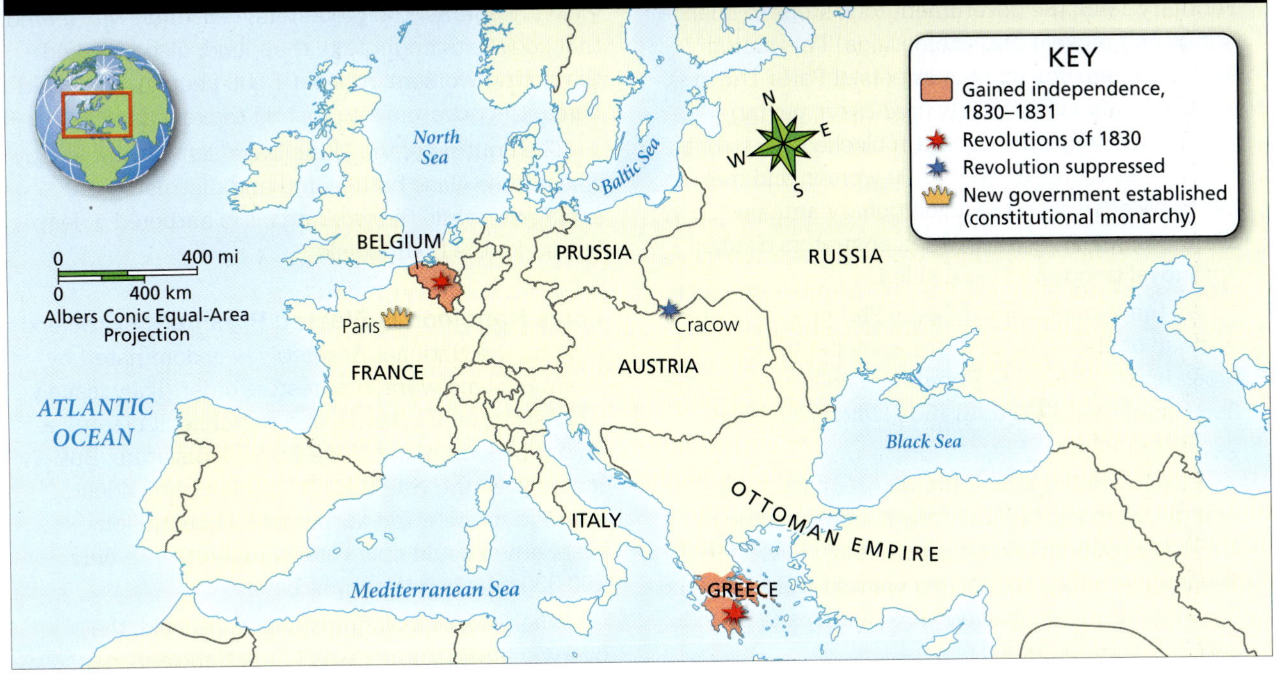

>> **Analyze Maps** What were the results of the revolutions of 1830?

wanted to create a strong barrier to help prevent French expansion in the future.

The Belgians resented the new arrangement. The Belgians and Dutch had different languages, religions, and economic interests. The Belgians were Catholic, while the Dutch were largely Protestant. The Belgian economy was based on manufacturing, while the Dutch relied on trade.

News of the 1830 Paris uprising ignited a revolutionary spark in Belgium. Students and workers, along with other citizens, threw up barricades in Brussels, the capital. The Dutch king hoped for help from Britain and France. These two countries backed Belgian demands for independence, expecting to benefit from the separation of Belgium and Holland. As a result, in 1831, Belgium became an independent state with a liberal constitution. Soon after, the major European powers signed a treaty recognizing Belgium as a "perpetually neutral state."

Polish Nationalists Defeated Nationalists in Poland also staged an uprising in 1830. But, unlike the Belgians, the Poles failed to win independence for their country.

In the late 1700s, Russia, Austria, and Prussia had divided up Poland. Poles had hoped that the Congress of Vienna would restore their homeland in 1815. Instead, the great powers handed most of Poland to Russia.

In 1830, Polish students, army officers, and landowners rose in revolt. The rebels failed to gain widespread support, however, and were brutally crushed by Russian forces. Some survivors fled to Western Europe and the United States, where they kept alive the dream of freedom.

COMPARE AND CONTRAST How were the Belgian and Polish revolutions of 1830 different?

The Revolution of 1848 in France

By the 1840s, discontent in France was again reaching a boiling point. The Industrial Revolution was changing life in France, especially in the cities. Politically, France remained divided. Radicals still wanted a republic. Utopian socialists called for an end to private ownership of property. Even liberals denounced Louis Philippe's government for corruption.

Discontent grew when a **recession,** or period of reduced economic activity, hit France. Factories closed and workers lost their jobs. Poor harvests led to rising food prices. In Paris, conditions were ripe for revolution.

Violence Erupts During "February Days" In February 1848, the government took steps to silence critics and prevent public meetings. This action sent angry crowds into the streets of Paris. During the "February Days," overturned carts, paving stones, and toppled trees again blocked the streets. Church bells rang alarms, while women and men on the barricades sang the revolutionary anthem "La Marseillaise." A number of demonstrators clashed with royal troops and were killed.

As the turmoil spread, Louis Philippe abdicated. A group of liberal, radical, and socialist leaders proclaimed the Second Republic. The First Republic had lasted from 1792 until 1804, when Napoleon became emperor.

From the start, deep differences divided the new government. Middle-class liberals wanted moderate political reforms. Socialists wanted far-reaching social and economic change and forced the government to set up national workshops to provide jobs for the unemployed.

Workers Lose Out During "June Days" By June, however, upper- and middle-class interests had won control of the government. They saw the national workshops as a waste of money and shut them down. Furious, workers again took to the streets of Paris. This time, however, bourgeois liberals turned violently against the protesters. Peasants, who feared that socialists might take their land, also attacked the rioting workers. At least 1,500 people were killed before the government crushed the rebellion.

The fighting of the "June Days" left a bitter legacy. The middle class both feared and distrusted the socialists, while the working class harbored a deep hatred for the bourgeoisie.

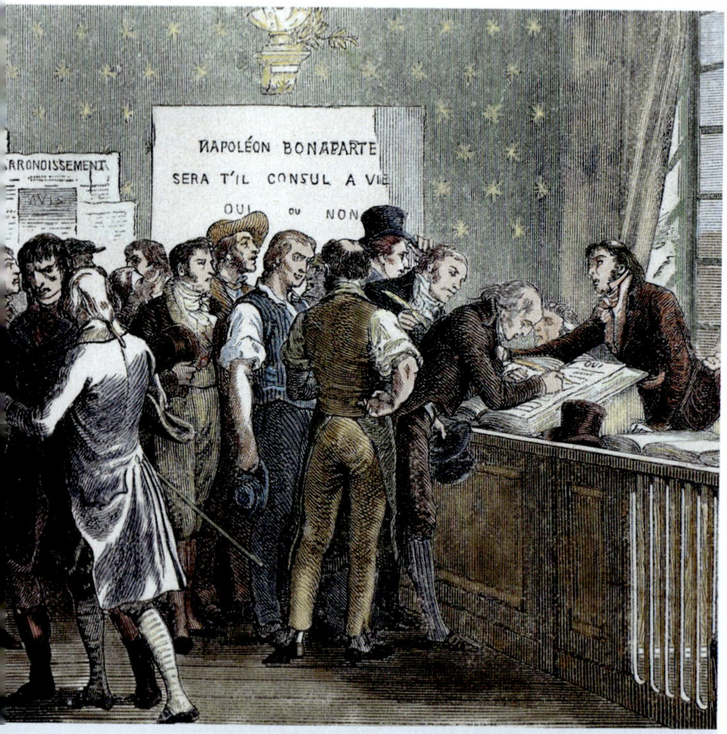

>> During the Second Republic, the National Assembly issued a constitution that gave the vote to all adult men.

Louis Napoleon is Elected President By the end of 1848, the National Assembly was dominated by members who wanted to restore order. They issued a constitution for the Second Republic. It created a strong president and a one-house legislature. But it also gave the vote to all adult men, the widest suffrage in the world at the time. Nine million Frenchmen could now vote, compared with only 200,000 who had that right before.

When elections for president were held, the overwhelming winner was Louis Napoleon, nephew of Napoleon Bonaparte. The "new" Napoleon attracted the working classes by presenting himself as a man who cared about social issues such as poverty. At the same time, his famous name, linked with order and past French glory, helped him with conservatives.

Napoleon III Establishes the Second Empire Once in office, Louis Napoleon used his position as a stepping-stone to greater power. By 1852, he had proclaimed himself emperor, taking the title **Napoleon III.** Thus ended the short-lived Second Republic.

Like his celebrated uncle, Napoleon III used a plebiscite, or ballot in which voters have a direct say on an issue, to win public approval for his seizure of power. A stunning 90 percent of voters supported his move to set up the Second Empire. Many thought that a monarchy was more stable than a republic or hoped that Napoleon III would restore the glory days of Napoleon Bonaparte.

Napoleon III, like Louis Philippe, ruled at a time of rapid economic growth. For the bourgeoisie, the early days of the Second Empire brought prosperity and contentment. In time, however, Napoleon III would embark on foreign adventures that would bring down his empire and end French leadership in Europe.

CONTRAST How did the French governments created after the Revolutions of 1830 and 1848 differ?

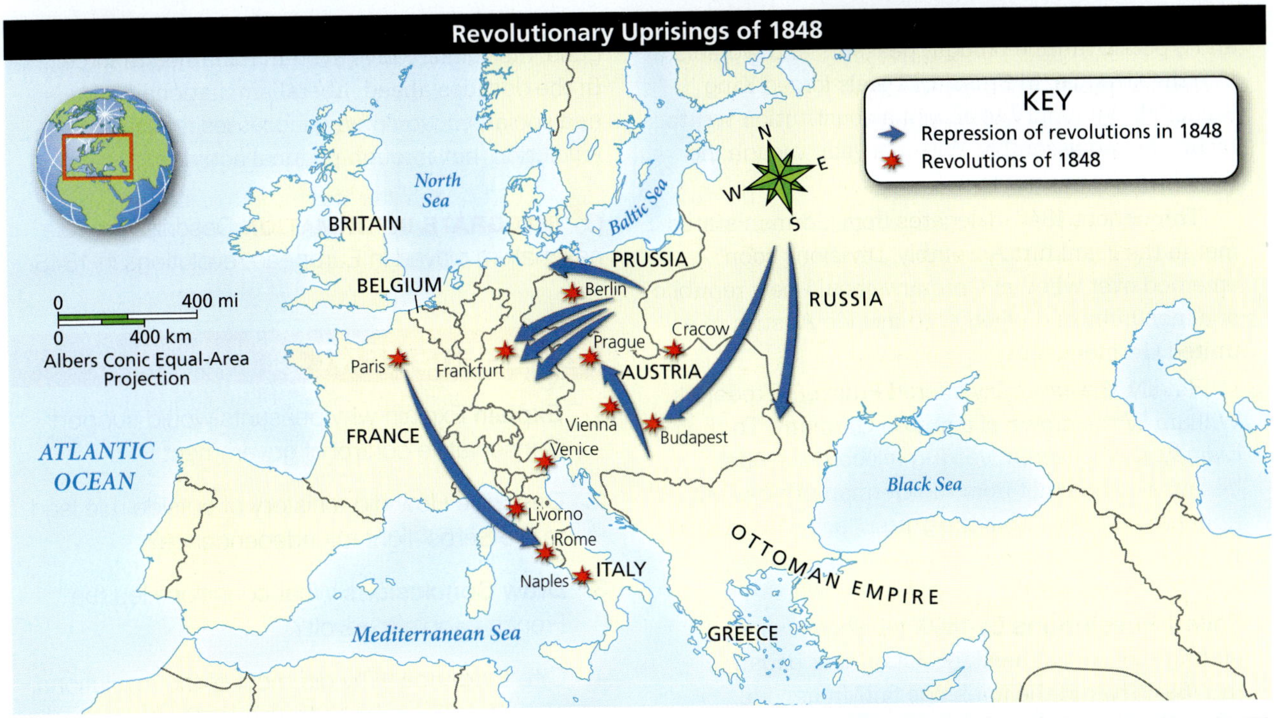

>> **Analyze Maps** France's successful 1848 uprising sparked revolutions throughout Europe. How does the map show the difficulties conservatives had in stopping the spread of revolutionary ideas?

Bounce to Activate Map

Revolution Spreads Across Europe

The Revolution of 1848 in France triggered a wave of revolutions across Europe, just as it had in 1830. For opponents of the old order, it was a time of such hope that they called it the "springtime of the peoples." Although events in France touched off the revolts, grievances had been piling up for years.

European middle-class liberals wanted a greater share of political power, as well as protections for the basic rights of all male citizens. Workers demanded relief from the miseries of the Industrial Revolution. And nationalists of all classes ached to throw off foreign rule.

Revolts Shake the Austrian Empire In the Austrian empire, revolts broke out in the major cities, starting in Vienna. Metternich, who had long dominated Austrian politics, tried to suppress the revolts. Even though he censored the press, books were smuggled to universities throughout the empire. Students demanded change. When workers joined the students on the streets of Vienna, Metternich resigned and fled in disguise.

Revolution quickly spread to other parts of the Austrian empire. In Budapest, Hungarian nationalists led by journalist **Louis Kossuth** demanded an independent government, an end to serfdom, and a written constitution. In Prague, the Czechs made similar demands. Overwhelmed by events, the Austrian government agreed to the reforms. The gains were temporary, however. Austrian troops soon regained control of Vienna and Prague and smashed the rebels in Budapest.

Revolts in Italy Uprisings also erupted in the Italian states. Nationalists wanted to end Hapsburg domination. As elsewhere, nationalist goals were linked to demands for liberal reforms such as constitutional government. Workers suffering economic hardships demanded even more radical changes.

From Venice in the north to Naples in the south, Italians set up independent republics. Revolutionaries expelled the pope from Rome. Before long, the forces of reaction returned, backed by military force. Austrian troops ousted the new governments in northern Italy. A French army restored the pope to power. Elsewhere, liberal reforms were canceled.

Rebellion in the German States In the German states, university students demanded national unity and liberal reforms. Economic hard times and a potato famine brought peasants and workers into the struggle. In Prussia, liberals forced King Frederick William IV to accept a constitution written by an elected assembly. Within a year, though, he dissolved the assembly.

Throughout 1848, delegates from German states met in the Frankfurt Assembly. Divisions soon emerged over whether Germany should be a republic or a monarchy and whether to include Austria in a united German state.

Finally, the assembly offered Prussia's Frederick William IV the crown of a united Germany. To their dismay, the conservative king rejected the offer because it came not from the German princes but from the people—"from the gutter," as he described it.

Failed Revolutions By 1850, rebellions faded, ending the age of liberal revolution that began in 1789. Why did the uprisings fail? In general, revolutionaries did not have mass support. Also, opposing goals divided liberals,who wanted moderate political reforms, and workers, who sought radical economic changes. And rulers did not hesitate to use force to crush the uprisings.

At mid century, although Metternich was gone, his conservative system remained in force. In the decades ahead, liberalism, nationalism, and socialism would win successes not through revolution, but through political activity.

INTEGRATE INFORMATION Describe the role nationalism played in European revolutions in 1848.

ASSESSMENT

1. **Explain** Explain why peasants would support Conservative control of government.
2. **Describe** How did a history of outside rule lead to the Serbs' fight for independence?
3. **Draw Conclusions** What conditions led the French people to revolt?
4. **Cite Evidence** Why did most of the revolutions of 1848 fail to achieve their goals?
5. **Identify Main Ideas** Explain the main ideologies that led to the uprisings throughout Europe.

3.2 By the late 1700s, the revolutionary fever that gripped Western Europe had spread to Latin America. There, discontent was rooted in the social, racial, and political system that had emerged during 300 years of Spanish rule. By 1825, most of Latin America was freed from colonial rule.

>> Simón Bolívar was a Venezuelan-born military and political leader. Inspired by Enlightenment ideals, he led revolutions to end Spanish rule in Latin America.

Bounce to Activate Flipped Video

Latin American Nations Win Independence

Latin America Ripe for Revolution

A Complex Social Structure Spanish-born **peninsulares,** members of the highest social class, dominated Latin American political and social life. Only they could hold top jobs in government and the Church. Many **creoles**—the European-descended Latin Americans who owned the haciendas, ranches, and mines—bitterly resented their second-class status. Merchants fretted under mercantilist policies that tied the colonies to Spain.

Meanwhile, a growing population of **mestizos,** people of Native American and European descent, and **mulattoes,** people of African and European descent, were angry at being denied the status, wealth, and power that were available to whites. Native Americans suffered economic misery under the Spanish, who had conquered the lands of their ancestors. In the Caribbean region and parts of South America, masses of enslaved Africans who worked on plantations longed for freedom.

>> Objectives

List the causes of growing discontent in Latin America, including the influence of the Enlightenment.

Trace the influence of the American and French Revolutions on Latin America.

Describe the revolutions in Haiti, Mexico, and Central America.

Explain how South American nations won independence, including the role of Simón Bolívar.

>> Key Terms

peninsular
creole
mestizo
mulatto
Simón Bolívar
Toussaint L'Ouverture
Father Miguel Hidalgo
Father José Morelos
José de San Martín
Dom Pedro

Enlightenment Ideas Reach Latin America

In the 1700s, educated creoles read the works of Enlightenment thinkers. They watched colonists in North America throw off British rule and were inspired by their success. Translations of the Declaration of Independence and the Constitution of the United States circulated among the creole elite.

During the French Revolution, young creoles like **Simón Bolívar** (boh LEE vahr) traveled in Europe and were inspired by the ideals of "liberty, equality, and fraternity." Yet, despite their admiration for Enlightenment ideas and revolutions in other lands, most creoles were reluctant to act.

The Uprisings Begin The spark that finally ignited widespread rebellion in Latin America was Napoleon's invasion of Spain in 1808. Napoleon ousted the Spanish king and placed his brother Joseph on the Spanish throne. In Latin America, leaders saw Spain's weakness as an opportunity to reject foreign domination and demand independence from colonial rule.

CHECK UNDERSTANDING In what ways did the American and French Revolutions influence Latin Americans?

Haiti Fights for Freedom

Even before Spanish colonists hoisted the flag of freedom, revolution had erupted in a French-ruled colony on the island of Hispaniola. In Haiti, as the western part of the island is now called, French planters owned very profitable sugar plantations worked by nearly a half million enslaved Africans. Sugar plantations were labor-intensive. The slaves were overworked and underfed.

Toussaint L'Ouverture Leads a Slave Revolt

Embittered by suffering and inspired by the talk of liberty and equality, the island's slaves rose up in revolt in 1791. The rebels were fortunate to find an intelligent and skillful leader in **Toussaint L'Ouverture** (too SAN loo vehr TOOR), a self-educated former slave. Although untrained, Toussaint was a brilliant general and inspiring commander.

Toussaint's army of former slaves faced many enemies. Some mulattoes joined French planters against the rebels. France, Spain, and Britain all sent armies against them.

The fighting took more lives than any other revolution in the Americas. But by 1798, the rebels had achieved their goal: Slavery was abolished, and Toussaint's forces controlled most of the island.

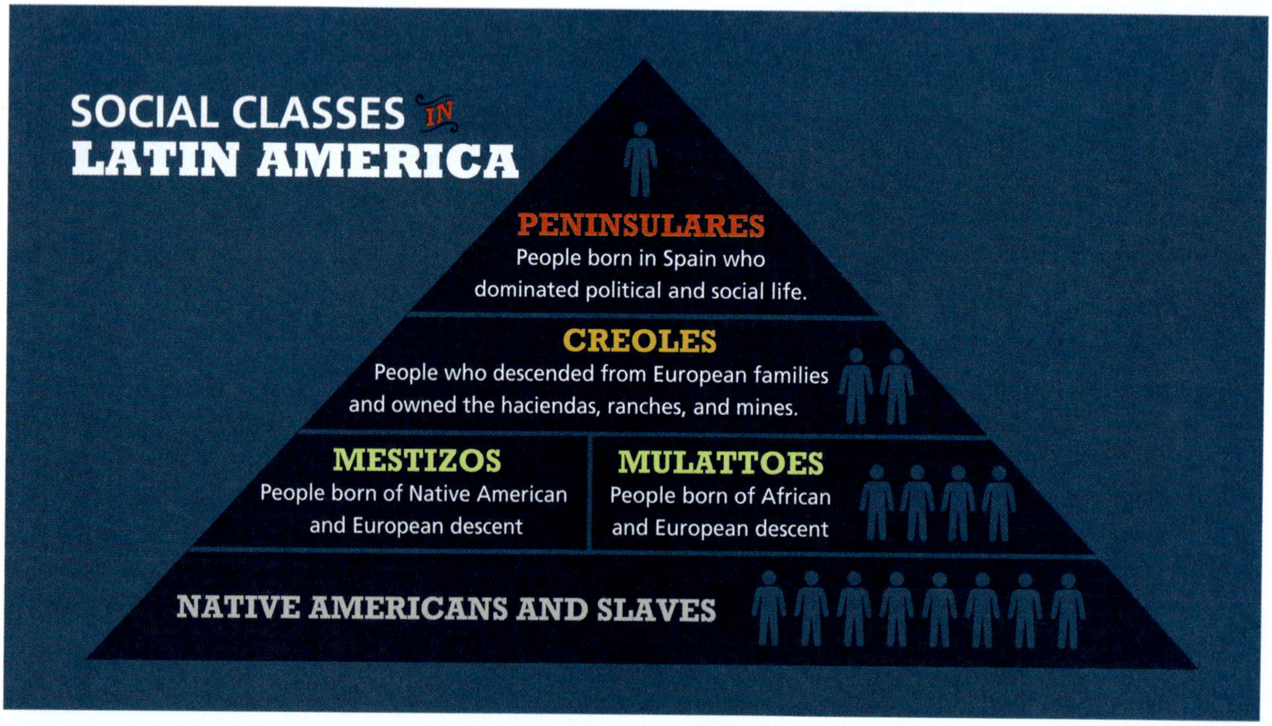

>> **Analyze Charts** In Spain's Latin American colonies, the social structure reflected inequality among the classes. Why would creoles be likely to support and lead revolutions in Latin America?

Haitian Independence In 1802, Napoleon Bonaparte sent a large army to reconquer the former colony. Toussaint urged his countrymen to take up arms once again to resist the invaders. In April 1802 the French agreed to a truce, but then they captured Toussaint and carried him in chains to France. He died there in a cold mountain prison a year later.

The struggle for freedom continued, however, and late in 1803, with yellow fever destroying their army, the French surrendered. In January 1804, the island declared itself an independent country under the name of Haiti. In the following years, rival Haitian leaders fought for power. Finally, in 1820, Haiti became a republic.

CHECK UNDERSTANDING What conditions led to the Haitian fight for independence?

>> **Draw Conclusions** Toussaint's army defeated British, Spanish, and French armies to end slavery in Haiti and win independence from France. Why would the British and Spanish join the fight against the rebels?

Revolts in Mexico and Central America

The slave revolt in Haiti frightened creoles in Spanish America. Although they wanted power themselves, most had no desire for economic or social changes that might threaten their way of life. In 1810, however, a creole priest in Mexico, **Father Miguel Hidalgo** (hee DAL goh), raised his voice for freedom.

Mexico's Battle for Independence Begins Father Hidalgo presided over the poor rural parish of Dolores. On September 15, 1810, he rang the church bells summoning the people to prayer. When they gathered, he startled them with an urgent appeal, "My children, will you be free?" Father Hidalgo's speech became known as "el Grito de Dolores"—the cry of Dolores. It called Mexicans to fight for independence.

A ragged army of poor mestizos and Native Americans rallied to Father Hidalgo and marched to the outskirts of Mexico City. At first, some creoles supported the revolt. However, they soon rejected Hidalgo's call for an end to slavery and his plea for reforms to improve conditions for Native Americans. They felt that these policies would cost them power.

After some early successes, the rebels faced growing opposition. Less than a year after he issued the "Grito," Hidalgo was captured and executed, and his followers scattered.

>> Father Hidalgo led the Mexican independence movement, battling Spanish forces for almost a year before his capture and execution.

José Morelos Continues the Fight Another priest picked up the banner of revolution. **Father José Morelos** was a mestizo who called for wide-ranging social and political reform. He wanted to improve conditions for the majority of Mexicans, abolish slavery, and give the vote to all men. For four years,

Morelos led rebel forces before he, too, was captured and shot in 1815.

Spanish forces, backed by conservative creoles, hunted down the surviving guerrillas. They had almost succeeded in ending the rebel movement when events in Spain had unexpected effects.

Mexico Wins Independence In Spain in 1820, liberals forced the king to issue a constitution. This move alarmed Agustín de Iturbide (ee toor BEE day), a conservative creole in Mexico. He feared that the new Spanish government might impose liberal reforms on the colonies as well.

Iturbide had spent years fighting Mexican revolutionaries. Suddenly, in 1821, he reached out to them. Backed by creoles, mestizos, and Native Americans, he overthrew the Spanish viceroy. Mexico was independent at last. Iturbide took the title Emperor Agustín I. Soon, however, liberal Mexicans toppled the would-be monarch and set up the Republic of Mexico.

New Republics in Central America Spanish-ruled lands in Central America declared independence in the early 1820s. Iturbide tried to add these areas to his Mexican empire. After his overthrow, local leaders set up a republic called the United Provinces of Central America. The union soon fragmented into the separate republics of Guatemala, Nicaragua, Honduras, El Salvador, and Costa Rica.

>> Bolívar leads his army against Spanish troops in the struggle to free South America from Spanish control.

Bounce to Activate Gallery

HYPOTHESIZE Why do you think Mexico's first two independence leaders were priests?

Discontent Sparks Revolts in South America

In South America, Native Americans had rebelled against Spanish rule as early as the 1700s, though with limited results. It was not until the 1800s that discontent among the creoles sparked a widespread drive for independence.

Bolívar Fights for Independence In the early 1800s, discontent spread across South America. As you read earlier, educated creoles like Simón Bolívar admired the French and American revolutions. They dreamed of winning their own independence from Spain.

In 1808, when Napoleon Bonaparte occupied Spain, Bolívar and his friends saw the occupation as a signal to act. In 1810, Bolívar led an uprising that established a republic in his native Venezuela. Bolívar's new republic was quickly toppled by conservative forces, however. For years, civil war raged in Venezuela. The revolutionaries suffered many setbacks. Twice Bolívar was forced into exile on the island of Haiti.

Then, Bolívar conceived a daring plan. He would march his army across the Andes and attack the Spanish at Bogotá, the capital of the viceroyalty of New Granada (present-day Colombia). First, he cemented an alliance with the hard-riding llañeros, or Venezuelan cowboys. Then, in a grueling campaign, he led an army through swampy lowlands and over the snowcapped Andes. Finally, in August 1819, he swooped down to take Bogotá from the surprised Spanish.

Other victories followed. By 1821, Bolívar had succeeded in freeing Caracas, Venezuela. "The Liberator," as he was now called, then moved south into Ecuador, Peru, and Bolivia. There, he joined forces with another great leader, **José de San Martín.**

San Martín Joins the Fight Like Bolívar, San Martín was a creole. He was born in Argentina but went to Europe for military training. In 1816, this gifted general helped Argentina win freedom from Spain. He then joined the independence struggle in other areas.

>> **Analyze Maps** What was Gran Colombia? Why is it not on maps of present-day South America?

Bounce to Activate Map

He, too, led an army across the Andes, from Argentina into Chile. He defeated the Spanish in Chile before moving into Peru to strike further blows against colonial rule. San Martín turned his command over to Bolívar in 1822, allowing Bolívar's forces to win the final victories against Spain.

Civil Wars Break Out The wars of independence ended by 1824. Bolívar then worked tirelessly to unite the lands he had liberated into a single nation, called Gran Colombia. Bitter rivalries, however, made that dream impossible. Before long, Gran Colombia split into four independent countries: Colombia, Panama, Venezuela, and Ecuador.

Bolívar faced another disappointment as power struggles among rival leaders triggered destructive civil wars. Before his death in 1830, a discouraged Bolívar wrote, "We have achieved our independence at the expense of everything else." Contrary to his dreams, South America's common people had simply exchanged one set of masters for another.

Brazil Gains Independence When Napoleon's armies conquered Portugal, the Portuguese royal family fled to Brazil. When the king returned to Portugal, he left his son **Dom Pedro** to rule Brazil. "If Brazil demands independence," the king advised Pedro, "proclaim it yourself and put the crown on your own head."

In 1822, Pedro followed his father's advice. A revolution had brought new leaders to Portugal who planned to abolish reforms and demanded that Dom Pedro return. Dom Pedro refused to leave Brazil. Instead, he became emperor of an independent Brazil. He accepted a constitution that provided for freedom of the press, freedom of religion, and an elected legislature. Brazil remained a monarchy until 1889, when social and political turmoil led it to become a republic.

COMPARE AND CONTRAST How did the goals of the Latin American revolutions differ from their results?

ASSESSMENT

1. **Draw Conclusions** How did the social structure contribute to discontent in Latin America?
2. **Identify Central Issues** Explain why creoles did not support Hidalgo or Morelos and how this affected the fight for independence.
3. **Draw Conclusions** What advantages did the Haitian slaves have over the French soldiers?
4. **Identify Main Ideas** Describe the challenges Simón Bolívar faced while liberating South America.
5. **Check Understanding** How do we know that Bolívar's political goals for South America were not achieved?

>> Napoleon rides triumphantly into Berlin. French rule inspired German nationalism and demands for a unified German state.

3.3 In the early 1800s, German-speaking people lived in a number of small and medium-sized states, as well as in Prussia and the Austrian Hapsburg empire. Napoleon's invasions unleashed new forces in these lands, especially a sense of German nationalism. Early efforts to unify Germany failed, but by 1862 a strong-willed Prussian official, Otto von Bismarck, set out to build a strong, unified German state.

Bounce to Activate Flipped Video

>> Objectives

Identify the factors that promoted German nationalism.

Analyze how Bismarck achieved German unification.

Describe the German empire under Bismarck.

Explain the policies of Kaiser William II.

>> Key Terms

Otto von Bismarck
chancellor
Realpolitik
annex
kaiser
Reich
Kulturkampf
William II
social welfare

The Unification of Germany

Moving Toward a Unified Germany

Impact of Napoleonic Invasions Between 1806 and 1812, Napoleon made important territorial changes in German-speaking lands. He annexed lands along the Rhine River for France. He dissolved the Holy Roman Empire by forcing the emperor of Austria to agree to the lesser title of king. He also organized a number of German states into the Rhine Confederation.

At first, some Germans welcomed the French emperor as a hero with enlightened, modern policies. He encouraged freeing the serfs, made trade easier, and abolished laws against Jews. However, not all Germans appreciated Napoleon and his changes. As people fought to free their lands from French rule, a sense of German nationalism emerged. They began to demand a unified German state.

Napoleon's defeat did not resolve the issue. At the Congress of Vienna, Metternich opposed nationalist demands. A united Germany, he argued, would require dismantling the governments of the many German states. Instead, conservative peacemakers created the German Confederation, a weak alliance headed by Austria.

New Efforts to Bring Unity In the 1830s, Prussia created an economic union called the Zollverein (TSAWL fur yn). It dismantled tariff barriers between many German states. Still, Germany remained politically fragmented.

In 1848, liberals meeting in the Frankfurt Assembly again demanded German political unity. They offered the throne of a united German state to Frederick William IV of Prussia. The Prussian ruler, however, rejected the notion of a throne offered by "the people."

☑ **DESCRIBE** What impact did the Napoleonic Wars have on Germany?

Bismarck Becomes the Architect of German Unity

Where others had failed in uniting Germany, **Otto von Bismarck** succeeded. Bismarck came from Prussia's Junker (YOONG kur) class, made up of conservative landowning nobles. Bismarck first served Prussia as a diplomat in Russia and France, and then as prime minister to King William I. In 1871, he became **chancellor,** or the highest official, of a united Germany.

Blood and Iron In his "blood and iron" speech delivered in 1862, Otto von Bismarck set the tone for his future policies. He wanted Prussian legislators to vote for more money to build up the army. Liberal members opposed the move. Bismarck rose and dismissed their concerns with a speech that has become known as the "blood and iron" speech.

> Germany does not look to Prussia's liberalism, but to her power. . . .The great questions of the day are not to be decided by speeches and majority resolutions—that was the mistake of 1848 and 1849—but by blood and iron!
>
> —Otto von Bismarck, 1862

Master of Realpolitik Bismarck's success was due in part to his strong will. He was a master of **Realpolitik** (ray AHL poh lee teek), or realistic politics based on the needs of the state. In the case

Bismarck Unites Germany, 1865–1871

>> **Analyze Maps** By 1871, Germany had been unified. In what year was the North German Confederation formed?

Bounce to Activate Timeline

of Realpolitik, power was more important than principles.

Although Bismarck was the architect of German unity, he was not really a German nationalist. His main goal was to increase Prussia's power, not to fulfill German nationalist aims. Bismarck's primary loyalty was to the Hohenzollerns (hoh un TSAWL urnz), the ruling dynasty of Prussia. Through unification, he hoped to bring more power to the Hohenzollerns.

A Powerful Military As Prussia's prime minister, Bismarck first moved to build up the Prussian army. Despite Bismarck's "blood and iron" speech, the liberal legislature refused to vote for funds for the military. In response, Bismarck strengthened the army with money that had been collected for other purposes. With a powerful, well-equipped military, he was then ready to pursue an aggressive foreign policy. Over the next decade, Bismarck led Prussia into three wars. Each war increased Prussian prestige and power and paved the way for German unity.

War with Denmark and Austria Bismarck's first maneuver was to form an alliance in 1864 with Austria. Prussia and Austria then seized the provinces of Schleswig and Holstein from Denmark. After a brief war, Prussia and Austria "liberated" the two provinces and divided up the spoils. Austria was to administer Holstein and Prussia was to administer Schleswig.

In 1866, Bismarck invented an excuse to attack Austria. The Austro-Prussian War lasted just seven weeks and ended in a decisive Prussian victory. Prussia then **annexed,** or took control of, several other north German states.

Bismarck dissolved the Austrian-led German Confederation and created a new confederation dominated by Prussia. Austria and four other southern German states remained independent. Bismarck's motives, as always, were strictly practical. Attempting to conquer Austria might have meant a long and risky war for Prussia.

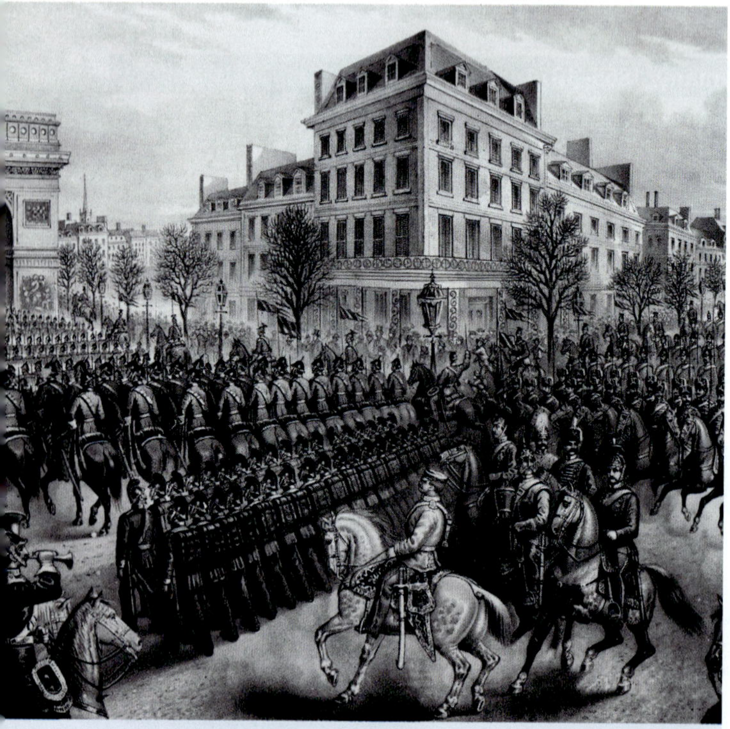

>> Bismarck used war with France as a way to unite the German states. Here, a triumphant Prussian army enters Paris.

The Franco-Prussian War In France, the Prussian victory over Austria angered Napoleon III. A growing rivalry between the two nations led to the Franco-Prussian War of 1870.

Germans recalled only too well the invasions of Napoleon I some 60 years earlier. Bismarck played up the image of the French menace to spur German nationalism. For his part, Napoleon III did little to avoid war, hoping to mask problems at home with military glory.

Bismarck furthered the crisis by rewriting and then releasing to the press a telegram that reported on a meeting between King William I and the French ambassador. Bismarck's editing of the "Ems dispatch" made it seem that William I had insulted the Frenchman. Furious, Napoleon III declared war on Prussia, as Bismarck had hoped.

A superior Prussian force, supported by troops from other German states, smashed the badly organized and poorly supplied French soldiers. Napoleon III, old and ill, surrendered within a few weeks. France had to accept a humiliating peace. The Franco-Prussian War left a bitter legacy for the French and a strong desire for revenge against Germany.

The German Empire Is Created Delighted by the victory over France, princes from the southern German states and the North German Confederation persuaded William I of Prussia to take the title **kaiser** (KY zur), or emperor. In January 1871, German nationalists celebrated the birth of the Second **Reich,** or empire. They called it that because they considered it heir to the Holy Roman Empire, set up in the 900s and abolished by Napoleon I in 1806.

A constitution drafted by Bismarck set up a two-house legislature. The Bundesrat (BOON dus raht), or upper house, was appointed by the rulers of the German states. The Reichstag (RYKS tahg), or lower house, was elected by universal male suffrage. Still, the new German nation was far from democratic. Because the Bundesrat could veto any decisions of the Reichstag, real power remained in the hands of the emperor and his chancellor.

EXPLAIN How did Bismarck unify the German states?

Germany Becomes an Industrial Giant

In January 1871, German princes gathered in the glittering Hall of Mirrors at the French palace of Versailles. They had just defeated Napoleon III in the Franco-Prussian War. Once home to French kings, the palace seemed the perfect place to proclaim the new German empire. To the winners as well as to the losers, the symbolism was clear: French domination of Europe had ended. Germany was now the dominant power in Europe.

In the aftermath of unification, the German empire emerged as the industrial giant of the European continent. By the late 1800s, German chemical and electrical industries were setting the standard worldwide. Among the European powers, German shipping was second only to Britain's.

>> Germany became a leader in various industries, including the production of chemicals, electronics, steel, weapons, and optical equipment.

Economic Progress Germany, like Great Britain, had several factors that helped it industrialize. Germany's spectacular growth was due in part to ample iron and coal resources, the basic ingredients for industrial development. A disciplined and educated workforce also helped the economy. The German middle class and educated professionals helped to create a productive and efficient society that prided itself on its sense of responsibility and deference to authority. Germany's rapidly growing population—from 41 million in 1871 to 67 million by 1914—also provided a huge home market along with a larger supply of industrial workers.

The new nation also benefited from earlier progress. During the 1850s and 1860s, German entrepreneurs had founded large companies and built many railroads. The house of Krupp (kroop) boomed after 1871, becoming an enormous industrial complex that produced steel and weapons for a world market.

Between 1871 and 1914, the business tycoon August Thyssen (TEES un) built a small steel factory of 70 workers into a giant empire with 50,000 employees. Optics was another important industry. German industrialist and inventor Carl Zeiss built a company that became known for its telescopes, microscopes, and other optical equipment.

Promoting Economic Growth German industrialists were the first to see the value of applied science in developing new products such as synthetic chemicals and dyes. Industrialists, as well as the government, supported research and development in the universities and hired trained scientists to solve technological problems in their factories.

The German government promoted economic development. After 1871, it issued a single currency for Germany, reorganized the banking system, and coordinated railroads built by the various German states. When a worldwide depression hit in the late 1800s, Germany raised tariffs to protect home industries from foreign competition. The leaders of the new German empire were determined to

>> Bismarck was a leader in international affairs, using a mix of force and diplomacy to further German interests. Bismarck (center) at the 1878 Congress of Berlin.

maintain economic strength as well as military power.

DESCRIBE What factors did Germany possess that made industrialization possible?

The Iron Chancellor

As chancellor of the new German empire, Bismarck pursued several foreign-policy goals. He wanted to keep France weak and isolated while building strong links with Austria and Russia. He respected British naval power but did not seek to compete in that arena. "Water rats," he said, "do not fight with land rats." Later, however, he would take a more aggressive stand against Britain as the two nations competed for overseas colonies.

On the domestic front, Bismarck applied the same ruthless methods he had used to achieve unification. The Iron Chancellor, as he was called, sought to erase local loyalties and crush all opposition to the imperial state. He targeted two groups—the Catholic Church and the Socialists. In his view, both posed a threat to the new German state.

Bismarck Challenges the Catholic Church After unification, Catholics made up about a third of the German population. Bismarck, who was Lutheran, distrusted Catholics—especially the clergy— whose first loyalty, he believed, was to the pope instead of to Germany.

In response to what he saw as the Catholic threat, Bismarck launched the ***Kulturkampf*** (kool TOOR kahmpf), or "battle for civilization," which lasted from 1871 to 1878. His goal was to make Catholics put loyalty to the state above allegiance to the Church. The chancellor had laws passed that gave the state the right to supervise Catholic education and approve the appointment of priests. Other laws closed some religious orders, expelled the Jesuits from Prussia, and made it compulsory for couples to be married by civil authority.

Bismarck's moves against the Catholic Church backfired. The faithful rallied behind the Church, and the Catholic Center party gained strength in the Reichstag. A realist, Bismarck saw his mistake and worked to make peace with the Church.

>> **Analyze Political Cartoons** In this political game of chess, Bismarck and Pope Pius IX try to checkmate each other. How does this image reflect the relationship between Bismarck and the Pope? How would each player define victory?

Bounce to Activate Cartoon

Bismarck Attacks the Socialists Bismarck also saw a threat to the new German empire in the growing power of socialism. Under socialism, the people are supposed to own and operate the means of production. Socialism had support among some Germans. By the late 1870s, German Marxists had organized the Social Democratic party, which called for parliamentary democracy and laws to improve conditions for the working class. Bismarck feared that socialists would undermine the loyalty of German workers and turn them toward revolution. Bismarck had laws passed that dissolved socialist groups, shut down their newspapers, and banned their meetings. Once again, repression backfired. It served to unite workers to support the socialist cause.

Bismarck Changes Course Bismarck then changed course. He set out to woo workers away from socialism by sponsoring laws to protect them. By the 1890s, Germans had health and accident insurance as well as old-age insurance to provide retirement benefits. Thus, under Bismarck, Germany was a pioneer in social reform. Its system of economic safeguards became the model for other European nations.

Although workers benefited from Bismarck's plan, they did not abandon socialism. In fact, the Social Democratic party continued to grow. By 1912, it held more seats in the Reichstag than any other party. Yet Bismarck's program showed that conditions for workers could be improved without a revolution. Later, Germany and other European nations would build on Bismarck's social policies, greatly increasing government's role in providing for the needs of its citizens.

CHECK UNDERSTANDING Why did Bismarck try to dissolve socialist groups?

>> **Analyze Political Cartoons** Bismarck tries to push the scary looking "Socialist Jack" back into the box. What did Bismarck do after his anti-socialist laws strengthened the socialist cause?

Kaiser William II

In 1888, **William II** succeeded his grandfather as kaiser. The new emperor, supremely confident, wished to put his own stamp on Germany. In 1890, he shocked Europe by asking the dominating Bismarck to resign. "There is only one master in the Reich," he said, "and that is I." William II seriously believed that his right to rule came from God.

> My grandfather considered that the office of king was a task that God had assigned to him. . . . That which he thought I also think. . . . Those who wish to aid me in that task . . . I welcome with all my heart; those who oppose me in this work I shall crush.
>
> —William II

>> Otto von Bismarck leaves his Berlin office in 1890 after Kaiser William II forced him to resign as chancellor.

>> Kaiser William II wanted a German navy strong enough to build an overseas empire. His decision to expand German military and naval power contributed to international tensions.

Social Welfare Not surprisingly, William resisted efforts to introduce democratic political reforms. At the same time, however, his government continued the idea of **social welfare,** or programs provided by the state for the benefit of its citizens. These programs, designed to combat support for socialists, helped improve conditions not only for workers and the elderly, but also German society in general.

His government also provided services such as cheap transportation and electricity. An excellent system of public schools, which had flourished under Bismarck, taught students obedience to the emperor along with reading, writing, and mathematics.

Strengthening the Military Like his grandfather, William II lavished funds on the German military machine, already the most powerful in Europe. He also launched an ambitious campaign to expand the German navy and win an overseas empire to rival those of Britain and France. William's nationalism and aggressive military stance helped increase tensions on the eve of World War I.

RECALL Why did William II ask Bismarck to resign?

ASSESSMENT

1. **Recall** Describe Germany's economic changes after unifying in 1871.
2. **Describe** Why did Germany pioneer social reform under Bismarck?
3. **Connect** Why did the German government issue a single currency for all of Germany?
4. **Compare** How did Kaiser William II continue Bismarck's policies?
5. **Identify Main Ideas** Why do you think the German empire was committed to maintaining its economic strength?

3.4 **Although the peoples of the Italian peninsula spoke the same language, they had not been politically united since Roman times. Over the centuries, ambitious foreign conquerors had turned Italy into a battleground, occupying parts or all of the peninsula. By the early 1800s, nationalism inspired Italian patriots to dream of ousting foreign rulers and reuniting Italy.**

>> Giuseppe Garibaldi leads his Red Shirts against troops of the Kingdom of the Two Sicilies.

Bounce to Activate Flipped Video

The Unification of Italy

>> **Objectives**

List the key obstacles to Italian unity.

Evaluate the roles played by Cavour and Garibaldi in Italian unification.

Describe the challenges that faced the new nation of Italy.

>> **Key Terms**

Camillo Cavour
Giuseppe Garibaldi
anarchist
emigration

First Steps to Italian Unity

Obstacles to Unity Frequent warfare and foreign rule had led people to identify with local regions. The people of Florence considered themselves Tuscans, those of Venice Venetians, those of Naples Neapolitans, and so on. But as in Germany, the invasions of Napoleon had sparked dreams of national unity.

The Congress of Vienna, however, ignored the nationalists who hoped to end centuries of foreign rule and achieve unity. To Prince Metternich of Austria, Italy was merely a "geographical expression," not a nation. Moreover, a divided Italy suited Austrian interests. At Vienna, Austria took control of much of northern Italy, while Hapsburg monarchs ruled various other Italian states. In the south, a French Bourbon ruler was put in charge of Naples and Sicily.

In response, nationalists organized secret patriotic societies and focused their efforts on expelling Austrian forces from northern Italy. Between 1820 and 1848, nationalist revolts exploded across the region. Each time, Austria sent in troops to crush the rebels.

>> Giuseppe Mazzini, the founder of Young Italy, dreamed of a unified Italian republic. Due to his failed attempts at revolution, he spent many years in exile but continued to inspire Italian nationalism.

Bounce to Activate Map

Mazzini's Young Italy In the 1830s, the nationalist leader Giuseppe Mazzini founded Young Italy. The goal of this secret society was "to constitute Italy, one, free, independent, republican nation." In 1849, Mazzini helped set up a revolutionary republic in Rome, but French forces soon toppled it. Like many other nationalists, Mazzini spent much of his life in exile, plotting and dreaming of a united Italy.

Nationalism Spreads "Ideas grow quickly," Mazzini once said, "when watered by the blood of martyrs." Although revolution had failed, nationalist agitation had planted seeds for future harvests.

To nationalists like Mazzini, a united Italy made sense not only because of geography, but also because of a common language and shared traditions. Nationalists reminded Italians of the glories of ancient Rome and the medieval papacy. To others, unity made practical economic sense. It would end trade barriers among the Italian states and stimulate industry.

CHECK UNDERSTANDING What forces hindered Italian unity?

>> Prime Minister Cavour (middle) served Sardinia's King Victor Emmanuel II (right) with great success. Cavour improved the economy and brought other Italian states under Sardinian rule.

Bounce to Activate Gallery

The Struggle for Italy

After 1848, leadership of the Risorgimento (ree sawr jee MEN toh), or Italian nationalist movement, passed to the kingdom of Sardinia, which included Piedmont, Nice, and Savoy as well as the island of Sardinia. Its constitutional monarch, Victor Emmanuel II, hoped to join other states to his own, thereby increasing his power.

Cavour, a Crafty Politician In 1852, Victor Emmanuel made Count **Camillo Cavour** (kah VOOR) his prime minister. Cavour came from a noble family but favored liberal goals. He was a flexible, practical, crafty politician, willing to use almost any means to achieve his goals. Like Bismarck in Prussia, Cavour was a monarchist who believed in Realpolitik.

Once in office, Cavour moved first to reform Sardinia's economy. He improved agriculture, had railroads built, and encouraged commerce by supporting free trade. Cavour's long-term goal, however, was to end Austrian power in Italy and annex the provinces of Lombardy and Venetia.

Cavour Plots with France In 1855, Sardinia, led by Cavour, joined Britain and France against Russia in the Crimean War. Sardinia did not win territory, but it did have a voice at the peace conference. Sardinia also gained the attention of Napoleon III.

In 1858, Cavour negotiated a secret deal with Napoleon, who promised to aid Sardinia in case it faced a war with Austria. A year later, the shrewd Cavour provoked that war. With help from France, Sardinia defeated Austria and annexed Lombardy. Meanwhile, nationalist groups overthrew Austrian-backed rulers in several other northern Italian states. These states then joined with Sardinia.

Garibaldi's "Red Shirts" Next, attention shifted to the Kingdom of the Two Sicilies in southern Italy. There, **Giuseppe Garibaldi** (gah ree BAHL dee), a longtime nationalist and an ally of Mazzini, was ready for action.

Like Mazzini, Garibaldi wanted to create an Italian republic. He did not hesitate, however, to accept aid from the monarchist Cavour. By 1860, Garibaldi had recruited a force of 1,000 red-shirted volunteers. Cavour provided weapons and allowed two ships to take Garibaldi and his "Red Shirts" south to Sicily. With surprising speed, Garibaldi's forces won control of Sicily, crossed to the mainland, and marched triumphantly north to Naples.

>> **Analyze Political Cartoons** Garibaldi suggests that Pope Pius IX trade his papal cap for the cap of "liberty" that he offers. What does Garibaldi want? How do you think the Pope feels about the offer?

Unity Achieved Garibaldi's success alarmed Cavour, who feared that the nationalist hero would set up his own republic in the south. To prevent this, Cavour urged Victor Emmanuel to send Sardinian troops to deal with Garibaldi. Instead, the Sardinians overran the Papal States and linked up with Garibaldi and his forces in Naples.

In a patriotic move, Garibaldi turned over Naples and Sicily to Victor Emmanuel. Shortly afterward, southern Italy voted to approve the move, and in 1861, Victor Emmanuel II was crowned king of Italy.

Two areas remained outside the new Italian nation: Rome and Venetia. Cavour died in 1861, but his successors completed his dream. Italy formed an alliance with Prussia in the Austro-Prussian War and won the province of Venetia. Then, during the Franco-Prussian War in 1870, France was forced to withdraw its troops from Rome. For the first time since the fall of the Roman empire, Italy was a united land.

DESCRIBE What steps did Cavour take to promote Italian unity?

Italy Faces New Challenges

The new Italian nation faced a host of problems. Like the German empire that Bismarck cemented together out of many states, Italy had no tradition of political unity. Few Italians felt ties to the new nation. Strong regional rivalries left Italy unable to solve critical national issues.

Regional Differences The greatest regional differences were between the north and the south. The north was richer and had more cities than the south. For centuries, northern Italian cities had flourished as centers of business and culture. The south, on the other hand, was rural and poor. Its population was booming, but illiterate peasants could extract only a meager existence from the exhausted farmland.

Conflict with the Papal States Hostility between Italy and the Roman Catholic Church further divided the nation. Popes bitterly resented the seizure of the Papal States and of Rome. The government granted the papacy limited rights and control over church properties. Popes, however, saw themselves as "prisoners" and urged Italian Catholics—almost all Italians—not to cooperate with their new government.

Political and Social Turmoil Under Victor Emmanuel, Italy was a constitutional monarchy

>> Italian emigrant families with their baggage and belongings wait to board a ship at this crowded port. **Draw Conclusions** Why did many Italians emigrate to other countries in the early 1900s?

with a two-house legislature. The king appointed members to the upper house, which could veto bills passed by the lower house. Although the lower house consisted of elected representatives, only a small number of men had the right to vote.

In the late 1800s, unrest increased as radicals on the left struggled against a conservative government. Socialists organized strikes while **anarchists,** people who want to abolish all government, turned to sabotage and violence.

Slowly, the government extended suffrage to more men and passed laws to improve social conditions. Still, the turmoil continued. To distract attention from troubles at home, the government set out to win an overseas empire in Ethiopia.

Economic Progress Despite its problems, Italy did develop economically, especially after 1900. Although the nation lacked important natural resources such as coal, industries did sprout up in northern regions. Industrialization, of course, brought urbanization as peasants flocked to the cities to find jobs in factories. As in other countries, reformers campaigned to improve education and working conditions.

The population explosion of this period created tensions, but an important safety valve was **emigration,** or movement away from their homeland. Many Italians left for the United States, Canada, and Latin American nations.

By 1914, the country was significantly better off than it had been in 1861. But it was hardly prepared for the great war that broke out in that year.

DESCRIBE What problems did Italians face after unification?

ASSESSMENT

1. **Analyze Context** Why would Prince Metternich of Austria oppose the idea of Italian unification?
2. **Describe** How did Cavour's appointment as prime minister of the kingdom of Sardinia help the cause of Italian unification?
3. **Analyze Information** Garibaldi could easily have kept the Kingdom of the Two Sicilies with himself as king. Why do you think he turned over control to Victor Emmanuel II instead?
4. **Cite Evidence** Why did conflict in Italy continue even after unification?
5. **Explain** Why do you think Rome and Venetia initially remained separate after unification?

3.5 In his 1845 novel, *Sybil, or The Two Nations*, Benjamin Disraeli describes the tremendous gap between the living conditions of the rich and the poor. In one scene, a man boasts to a stranger that Queen Victoria "reigns over the greatest nation that ever existed."

>> **Draw Conclusions** Poor living conditions, such as in this London slum, were a common sight in British industrial cities in the early 1800s. How do you think scenes like this affected British government leaders?

Bounce to Activate Flipped Video

Democratic Reforms in Britain

"Two Nations": The Rich and the Poor

> Which nation? asks one of the strangers, "for she reigns over two... Two nations; between whom there is no [communication] and no sympathy; who are as ignorant of each other's habits, thoughts, and feelings, as if they were ... inhabitants of different planets.
>
> What are these "two nations," Egremont asks. "The Rich and the Poor," the stranger replies.
>
> —Benjamin Disraeli, *Sybil*

Benjamin Disraeli and other British leaders worked to bridge the gap between the "two nations" by expanding democratic rights and introducing social reforms to end deeply rooted inequalities.

>> Objectives

Understand how political reforms in Britain affected suffrage and the nature of Parliament.

Identify the influence of Queen Victoria and the values she represented.

Describe social and economic reforms enacted by Parliament in the 1800s.

Describe the efforts by British women to win the vote.

Explain the struggle for Irish home rule and the impact of famine on Ireland.

>> Key Terms

rotten borough
electorate
secret ballot
Queen Victoria
Benjamin Disraeli
William Gladstone
parliamentary democracy
free trade
repeal
abolition
capital offense
penal colony
absentee landlord
home rule

Unlike some of its neighbors in Europe, Britain generally achieved change through reform rather than revolution.

Parliament In Need of Reform In 1815, Britain was a constitutional monarchy with a parliament and two political parties. Still, it was far from democratic. Parliament was made up of the House of Lords and the House of Commons. The House of Lords were hereditary nobles and high-ranking clergy in the Church of England. They had the right to veto any bill passed by the House of Commons.

Members of the Commons were elected, but less than five percent of the people could vote. Wealthy country squires, or landowners, along with nobles, dominated politics and heavily influenced voters. In addition, old laws banned Catholics and non-Anglican Protestants from voting or serving in Parliament. In the 1820s, after fierce debates, Parliament finally ended these religious restrictions.

Pressure for Reform Builds An even greater battle soon erupted over making Parliament more representative. During the Industrial Revolution, centers of population shifted. Some rural towns lost so many people that they had few or no voters. Yet local landowners in these **rotten boroughs** still sent members to Parliament.

At the same time, populous new industrial cities like Manchester and Birmingham had no seats in Parliament because they had not existed as population centers in earlier times.

>> During the early 1800s, the British Parliament was not very democratic. The House of Lords, shown here around 1830, could veto any bill passed by the House of Commons.

Reform Act of 1832 In the 1830s, as revolts flared in France and elsewhere, Whigs and Tories were battling over a bill to reform Parliament.

The Whig Party largely represented middle-class and business interests. The Tory Party spoke for nobles, landowners, and others whose interests and income were rooted in agriculture. In the streets, supporters of reform chanted, "The Bill, the whole Bill, and nothing but the Bill!" Their shouts seemed to echo the cries of revolutionaries on the continent.

Parliament finally passed the Great Reform Act in 1832. It redistributed seats in the House of Commons, giving representation to large towns and cities and eliminating rotten boroughs. It also enlarged the **electorate,** the body of people allowed to vote, by granting suffrage to more men. The act did, however, keep a property requirement for voting.

The Reform Act of 1832 did not bring full democracy, but it did give a greater political voice to middle-class men. Land-owning nobles, however, remained a powerful force in the government and in the economy.

The Chartist Movement The reform bill did not satisfy the demands of more radical reformers like the Chartists, who stood for working class interests. In the 1830s, they drew up the People's Charter, a petition setting out their goals. They demanded universal male suffrage, annual parliamentary elections, and salaries for members of Parliament. Another key demand was for a **secret ballot,** which would allow people to cast their votes without announcing them publicly.

Twice the Chartists presented petitions with over a million signatures to Parliament. Both petitions were ignored. In 1848, as revolutions swept Europe, the Chartists prepared a third petition and organized a march on Parliament. Fearing violence, the government banned the march.

Soon after, the unsuccessful Chartist movement declined. In time, however, Parliament would pass most of the major reforms proposed by the Chartists.

ANALYZE INFORMATION How did reformers' efforts make the British parliament more democratic?

The Victorian Age

From 1837 to 1901, the great symbol in British life was **Queen Victoria.** Her reign was the longest in British history. Although she exercised little real political power, she set the tone for what is now called the Victorian age.

Victorian Ideals As queen, Victoria came to embody the values of her age. These Victorian ideals included duty, thrift, honesty, hard work, and above all respectability. Victoria herself embraced a strict code of morals and manners. As a young woman, she married a German prince, Albert, and they raised a large family.

Although she outranked Albert, she treated him with the devotion a dutiful wife was expected to have for her husband. When he died in 1861, Victoria went into deep mourning and dressed in black for the rest of her long reign. She was fond of her 36 grandchildren, some of whom later became ruling monarchs.

>> Queen Victoria in 1887. Her reign began in 1837 and lasted till her death at age 81 in 1901.

Growing British Confidence Under Victoria, the British middle class—and growing numbers of the working class—felt great confidence in the future. That confidence grew as Britain expanded its already huge empire. Victoria, the empress of India and ruler of some 300 million subjects around the world, became a revered symbol of British might.

During her reign, Victoria witnessed growing agitation for social reform. The queen herself commented that the lower classes "earn their bread and riches so deservedly that they cannot and ought not to be kept back." As the Victorian era went on, reformers continued the push toward greater social and economic justice.

DRAW CONCLUSIONS When Queen Victoria stated that the lower classes "earn their bread and riches so deservedly that they cannot and ought not to be kept back," what did she mean?

>> **Hypothesize** In the 1800s and early 1900s, Parliament passed laws to extend and protect suffrage for men. Why were private booths and a police officer needed in this English polling station?

Bounce to Activate Timeline

Reforms Increase Parliamentary Democracy

In the 1860s, a new era dawned in British politics. The old political parties regrouped under new leadership. Benjamin Disraeli forged the Tories into the modern Conservative Party. The Whigs, led by **William Gladstone,** evolved into the Liberal Party. Between 1868 and 1880, as the majority in Parliament swung between the two parties,

Gladstone and Disraeli alternated as prime minister. Both fought for important reforms.

Expanding Male Suffrage Disraeli and the Conservative Party pushed through the Reform Bill of 1867. By giving the vote to many working-class men, the new law almost doubled the size of the electorate.

In the 1880s, it was the turn of Gladstone and the Liberal Party to extend suffrage. Their reforms gave the vote to farmworkers and most other men.

By century's end, almost-universal male suffrage, the secret ballot, and other Chartist ambitions had been achieved. Britain had truly transformed itself from a constitutional monarchy to a **parliamentary democracy,** a form of government in which the executive leaders (usually a prime minister and cabinet) are chosen by and responsible to the legislature (parliament), and are also members of it.

Victory for Democracy In the early 1900s, many bills passed by the House of Commons met defeat in the House of Lords. In 1911, a Liberal government passed measures to restrict the power of the Lords, including their power to veto tax bills. The Lords resisted. Finally, the government threatened to create enough new lords to approve the law, and the Lords backed down.

People hailed the change as a victory for democracy. In time, the House of Lords would become a largely ceremonial body with little power. The elected House of Commons would reign supreme.

COMPARE AND CONTRAST What were the origins of the Liberal and Conservative parties? Which groups did they represent?

>> London dock workers unload tea from cargo ships. British customs officials monitored such activities and collected tariffs on foreign imports. **Summarize** Who opposed tariffs, and why?

Economic and Social Reforms

During the early and mid-1800s, Parliament passed a series of social and economic reforms. Many laws were designed to help working class families whose labor supported the new industrial society. Among the most controversial reforms was the issue of **free trade,** or trade between countries without quotas, tariffs, or other restrictions. It pitted landowners and farmers against the middle and working classes.

Abolishing the Corn Laws Britain, like other European nations, taxed foreign imports in order to protect local economies. By the early 1800s however, supporters of free trade, usually middle-class business leaders, wanted to end these protective tariffs. Like Adam Smith, they argued that a laissez-faire policy would increase prosperity for all. Without tariffs they said, merchants would have larger markets in which to sell their goods, and consumers would benefit from open competition.

Some British tariffs were repealed in the 1820s. However, fierce debate erupted over the Corn Laws, which imposed high tariffs on imported grain. (In Britain, "corn" refers to all cereal grains, such as wheat, barley, and oats.) Farmers and wealthy landowners supported the Corn Laws because they kept the price of British grain high. Free traders, however, wanted Parliament to **repeal,** or cancel, the Corn Laws. They argued that repeal of these laws would lower the price of grain, make bread cheaper for workers, and open up trade in general.

Parliament finally repealed the Corn Laws in 1846, after widespread crop failures swept many parts of Europe. Liberals hailed the repeal as a victory for free trade and laissez-faire capitalism. However, in the late 1800s, economic hard times led Britain and other European countries to impose protective tariffs on many goods again.

Abolition of Slavery During the 1700s, Enlightenment thinkers had turned the spotlight on the evils of the slave trade. At the time, British ships were carrying more Africans to the Americas than any other European country. Middle-class reformers in Britain increased pressure for **abolition,** calling for an end to slavery and the slave trade.

In Parliament, William Wilberforce led the movement to end the slave trade. A dedicated social reformer, Wilberforce also held strong religious convictions. Wilberforce helped shift political thought by persistently introducing anti-slavery motions for decades in Parliament. Finally, in 1807, Britain became the first European power to abolish the slave trade.

Banning the slave trade did not end slavery. Although the Congress of Vienna condemned slavery, it had taken no action. In Britain, liberals preached the immorality of slavery. Finally, in 1833, Parliament passed a law banning slavery in all British colonies.

Crime and Punishment Other reforms were aimed at the criminal justice system. In the early 1800s, more than 200 crimes were punishable by death. Such **capital offenses** included not only murder but also shoplifting, sheep stealing, and impersonating an army veteran.

In practice, some juries refused to convict people charged with crimes, because the punishments were so harsh. Executions were public occasions, and the hanging of a well-known murderer might attract thousands of curious spectators. By 1868 however, Parliament banned public hangings, and executions then took place behind prison walls. Afterward, instead of receiving a proper burial, the criminal's body might be given to a medical college for dissection.

Reformers began to reduce the number of capital offenses. By 1850, the death penalty was reserved for murder, piracy, treason, and arson. Many petty criminals were instead transported to **penal colonies,** or settlements for convicts, in the new British territory of Australia. Additional reforms improved prison conditions and outlawed imprisonment due to debt.

☑ **DRAW CONCLUSIONS** How did the Corn Laws affect the lower classes?

>> **Analyze Political Cartoons** In this cartoon, the British prime minister opens a particular gate. What change in policy does the cartoon depict? Explain.

>> Harsh working conditions and deadly accidents were common in British coal mines. With the Mines Act of 1842, Parliament prohibited all females and boys under age 10 from working in underground mines.

Victories for the Working Class

"Four [ghosts] haunt the Poor: Old Age, Accident, Sickness and Unemployment," declared Liberal politician David Lloyd George in 1905. "We are going to [expel] them."

As early as the 1840s, Parliament passed some laws aimed at improving conditions for workers. Later in the 1800s and early 1900s, Parliament passed additional reforms, designed to help the working class whose labor supported the new industrial society.

Working Conditions Improve As you have read, working conditions in the early industrial age were grim and often dangerous. Gradually, Parliament passed laws to regulate conditions in factories and mines. In 1842, for example, mine owners were forbidden to employ women or children under age 10. An 1847 law limited women and children to a 10-hour day. Later in the 1800s, the government regulated many safety conditions in factories and mines—and sent inspectors to see that the laws were enforced. Other laws set minimum wages and maximum hours of work.

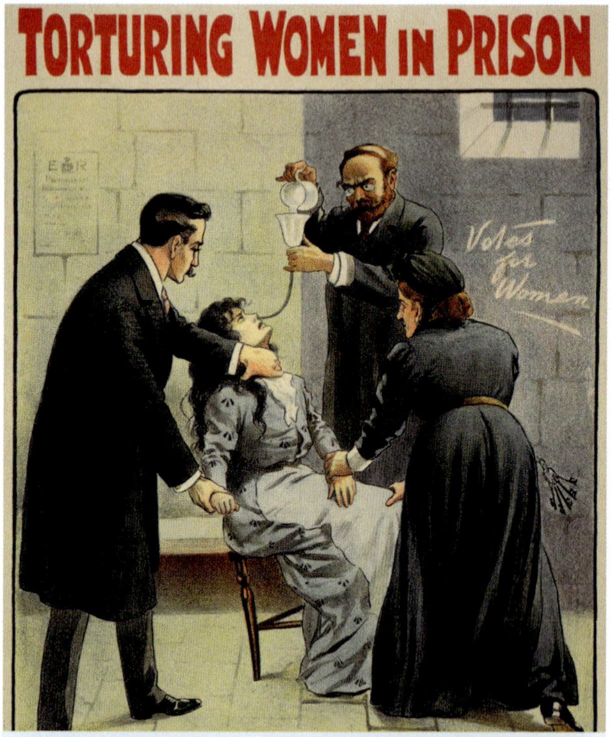

>> When some jailed English suffragists went on hunger strikes, prison officials force-fed them to keep them alive. The suffragists used posters like this to gain popular support for their cause.

Labor Unions Expand Early in the Industrial Revolution, labor unions were outlawed. Under pressure, government and business leaders slowly accepted worker organizations. Trade unions were made legal in 1825 but it remained illegal to go on strike until later in the century.

Despite restrictions, unions spread, and gradually they won additional rights. Between 1890 and 1914, union membership soared. Besides winning higher wages and shorter hours for workers, unions pressed for other laws to improve the lives of the working class.

Other Social Reforms During the late 1800s and early 1900s, both political parties enacted social reforms to benefit Britain's citizens. Disraeli sponsored laws to improve public health and housing for workers in cities. Under Gladstone, an education act called for free elementary education for all children. Gladstone also pushed to open up government jobs based on merit rather than on birth or wealth.

Another force for reform was the Fabian Society, a socialist organization founded in 1883. The Fabians promoted gradual change through legal means rather than by violence. Though small in number, the Fabians had a strong influence on British politics.

The Labour Party Emerges In 1900, socialists and union members backed the formation of a new political party, which became the Labour Party. (*Labour* is the British spelling of *labor.*) The Labour Party would quickly grow in power and membership until, by the 1920s, it surpassed the Liberal Party and became one of Britain's two major parties.

In the early 1900s, Britain began to pass social welfare laws modeled on those Bismarck had introduced in Germany. They protected workers with accident, health, and unemployment insurance as well as old-age pensions. One result of such reforms was that the Marxist idea of a communist revolution gained only limited support among the British working class. The middle class hailed reforms as proof that democracy was working.

IDENTIFY CENTRAL IDEAS What reforms improved the lives of children in Britain?

Women Struggle for the Vote

In Britain, as elsewhere, women struggled against strong opposition for the right to vote. Women themselves were divided on the issue. Some women opposed suffrage altogether. Queen Victoria, for example, called the women's suffrage struggle "mad, wicked folly." Even women in favor of suffrage disagreed about how best to achieve it.

Radicals Take Action By the early 1900s, Emmeline Pankhurst, a leading suffragist, had become convinced that even more aggressive tactics were necessary to bring victory. Pankhurst and other radical suffragists interrupted speakers in Parliament, shouting, "Votes for women!" until they were carried away. They collected petitions and organized huge public demonstrations.

When mass meetings and other peaceful efforts brought no results, some women turned to more drastic, violent protests. They smashed windows or even burned buildings. Pankhurst justified such tactics as necessary to achieve victory. "There is something that governments care for far more than human life," she declared, "and that is the security of property, so it is through property that we shall strike the enemy." Many suffragists went on hunger strikes, risking their lives to achieve their goals.

Some titled women, like Lady Constance Lytton, joined the protests. Imprisoned after a demonstration, Lytton gave a false name and vowed to stay on a hunger strike until women won the vote. A doctor, unaware of her identity, force-fed Lytton through a tube. The painful ordeal failed to weaken Lytton's resolve. "No surrender," she whispered. "No surrender."

The Tide Turns Even middle-class women who disapproved of such radical and violent actions increasingly demanded votes for women. Still, Parliament refused to grant women's suffrage. Not until 1918 did Parliament finally grant suffrage to women over age 30. Younger women did not win the right to vote for another decade.

DRAW CONCLUSIONS Why might some women have disagreed with the idea of giving women the vote?

The Irish Question

Throughout the 1800s, Britain faced the ever-present "Irish question." The English had begun conquering Ireland in the 1100s. In the 1600s, English and Scottish settlers colonized Ireland, taking possession of much of the best farmland.

>> The Irish potato blight caused great hardship, famine, and death. Without potatoes to sell, thousands of tenants could not pay rent and were evicted.

Bounce to Activate Gallery

The Irish never accepted English rule. They bitterly resented settlers, especially **absentee landlords** who owned large estates but did not live on them. Many Irish peasants lived in desperate poverty, while paying high rents to landlords living in England. In addition, the Irish, most of whom were Catholic, had to pay tithes to support the Church of England. Under these conditions, resistance and rebellion were common.

Irish Nationalism Grows Like the national minorities in the Austrian empire, Irish nationalists campaigned vigorously for freedom and justice in the 1800s. Nationalist leader Daniel O'Connell, nicknamed "the Liberator," organized an Irish Catholic League and held mass meetings to demand repeal of unfair laws. "My first object," declared O'Connell, "is to get Ireland for the Irish."

Under pressure from O'Connell and other Irish nationalists, Britain slowly moved to improve conditions in Ireland. In 1829, Parliament passed the Catholic Emancipation Act, which allowed Irish Catholics to vote and hold political office. Yet many injustices remained. Absentee landlords could evict tenants almost at will. Other British laws forbade the teaching and speaking of the Irish language.

Irish Home Rule The famine in Ireland caused by the potato blight left the Irish with a legacy of bitterness and distrust toward Britain. The Great Hunger fueled movements in Ireland that pitted radicals, such as the Fenians, who wanted an independent Ireland, against moderates who called for **home rule,** or local self-government.

In the 1870s, moderates found a rousing leader in the Irish nationalist, Charles Stewart Parnell. He rallied Irish members of Parliament to work for home rule. The "Irish question" disrupted British politics for decades. At times, political parties were so deeply split over the Irish question that they could not take care of other business.

As prime minister, Gladstone pushed for reforms in Ireland. He ended the use of Irish tithe money to support the Anglican church and tried to ease the hardships of Irish tenant farmers. New laws prevented landlords from charging unfair rents and protected the rights of tenants to the land they worked.

Finally, in 1914, Parliament passed a home rule bill. But it delayed putting the new law into effect when World War I broke out that year. As you will read, the dream of the Fenians was partly achieved in 1921, when the southern counties of Ireland finally became an independent nation.

MAKE GENERALIZATIONS How did absentee landlords feed the growth of Irish nationalism?

ASSESSMENT

1. **Identify Central Issues** Which groups would benefit from repealing the high tariffs known as the Corn Laws? Why?
2. **Draw Conclusions** How did the political, social, and economic reforms of the early 1800s in Britain reflect the growing power of the middle class?
3. **Support Ideas with Examples** Why did many people view the criminal justice system in Britain during the 1800s as unjust? Provide specific examples.
4. **Draw Conclusions** How did the Fabian Society reflect Victorian ideals?
5. **Identify Central Issues** What were two of the reforms that improved conditions in Ireland?

3.6 After the revolution of 1848, Napoleon III, nephew of Napoleon Bonaparte, rose to power and set up the Second Empire. His appeal cut across lines of class and ideology. The bourgeoisie saw him as a strong leader who would restore order. His promise to end poverty gave hope to the lower classes. People of all classes were attracted by his name, a reminder of the days when France had towered over Europe. Unlike his famous uncle, however, Napoleon III would bring France neither glory nor an empire.

>> Napoleon III hoped to restore glory to France. Here he commands victorious French troops at the Battle of Solferino during the second Italian War of Independence in 1859.

Bounce to Activate Flipped Video

Divisions and Democracy in France

>> **Objectives**

List the domestic and foreign policies of Napoleon III.

Describe the challenges and political reforms of the Third Republic.

Explain how the Dreyfus Affair divided France and contributed to the growth of the Zionist movement.

>> **Key Terms**

Napoleon III
Suez Canal
premier
coalition
Dreyfus Affair
libel
Zionism

Napoleon III and the Second Empire

Napoleon III Limits Liberties On the surface, the Second Empire looked like a constitutional monarchy. In fact, Napoleon III ruled almost as a dictator, with the power to appoint his cabinet, the upper house of the legislature, and many officials. Although the assembly was elected by universal male suffrage, appointed officials "managed" elections so that supporters of the emperor would win. Debate was limited, and newspapers faced strict censorship.

In the 1860s, Napoleon III began to ease controls. He lifted some censorship and gave the legislature more power. He even issued a new constitution that extended democratic rights.

Economic Growth Like much of Europe, France prospered at mid-century. Napoleon III promoted investment in industry and large-scale ventures such as railroad building and the urban renewal of Paris. During this period, a French entrepreneur, Ferdinand de Lesseps (LAY seps), organized the building of the **Suez Canal** in Egypt to link the Mediterranean with the Red Sea and the Indian Ocean.

Workers enjoyed some benefits of economic growth. Napoleon legalized labor unions, extended public education to girls, and created a small public health program. Still, in France, as in other industrial nations, many people lived in great poverty.

Foreign Affairs Napoleon's worst failures were in warfare and foreign affairs. In the 1860s, he tried to place Maximilian, an Austrian Hapsburg prince, on the throne of Mexico. Through Maximilian, Napoleon hoped to turn Mexico into a French satellite. But after a large commitment of troops and money, the venture failed. Mexican patriots resisted fiercely, and the United States protested. After four years, France withdrew its troops. Maximilian was overthrown and shot by Mexican patriots.

Napoleon's successes were almost as costly as his failures. He helped Italian nationalists defeat Austria, and in return, the regions of Nice (nees) and Savoy were ceded to France. But this victory soon backfired when a united Italy emerged as a rival on France's border. And, though France and Britain won the Crimean War, France had little to show for its terrible losses except a small foothold in the Middle East.

>> During the Prussian siege of Paris, the French government established municipal canteens to provide low-cost food for the starving people of the city.

Bounce to Activate Gallery

Defeat in the Franco-Prussian War At this same time, France was growing increasingly concerned about the rise of a great European rival, Prussia. The Prussian leader Otto von Bismarck shrewdly manipulated the French and lured Napoleon into war in July 1870.

The Franco-Prussian War was a disaster for France. Napoleon III was forced to surrender to the Germans, ending the Second Empire. A brutal four-month siege of Paris by Prussian forces reduced residents to near starvation. People ate rats and killed circus animals for food. During the siege, Parisians used carrier pigeons and balloons to communicate with the outside world.

In 1871, a newly elected French Assembly accepted a harsh peace with Germany. France had to surrender the provinces of Alsace and Lorraine and pay a huge sum to Germany. The sting of defeat left the French burning to avenge their loss.

The Franco-Prussian War ended a long period of French domination of Europe that had begun under Louis XIV. Yet a Third Republic rose from the ashes of the Second Empire of Napoleon III. Economic growth, democratic reforms, and fierce nationalism all played a part in shaping modern France.

DESCRIBE the government of France during the Second Empire.

The Third Republic Faces New Struggles

At the end of the Franco-Prussian War, a new government, known as the Third Republic, was set up in France. Even as a new National Assembly took power and made peace with Germany, France was plunged into a new crisis. Once again, the crisis was centered in Paris.

The Paris Commune In early 1871, an uprising broke out in Paris. Rebels set up the Paris Commune. Like the radical government during the French Revolution, its goal was to save the Republic from royalists. Communards, as the rebels were called, included workers and socialists as well as bourgeois republicans. As patriots, they rejected the harsh peace that the National Assembly had signed with

Germany. Radicals dreamed of creating a new socialist order.

The National Assembly ordered the Paris Commune to disband. When the Communards refused, the government sent troops to retake Paris. For weeks, civil war raged. As government troops advanced, the rebels set fire to several government buildings, toppled Paris monuments, and slaughtered a number of hostages. Finally, government forces butchered some 30,000 Communards. The suppression of the Paris Commune left bitter memories that deepened social divisions within France.

>> The Paris Commune, determined to save the Republic from royalists, rebelled against the new National Assembly. The Communards erected barricades throughout Paris.

Coalition Governments Despite its shaky beginnings, the Third Republic remained in place for 70 years. The new republic had a two-house legislature. The powerful lower house, or Chamber of Deputies, was elected by universal male suffrage. Together with the Senate, it elected the president of the republic. However, the president had little power and served mostly as a figurehead. Real power was in the hands of the **premier** (prih MIR), or prime minister.

Unlike Britain, with its two-party system, France had many parties, reflecting the wide splits within the country. Among them were royalists, constitutional monarchists, moderate republicans, and radicals. With so many parties, no single party could win a majority in the legislature. In order to govern, politicians had to form **coalitions,** or alliances of various parties. Once a coalition controlled enough votes, it could then name a premier and form a cabinet.

Multiparty systems and coalition governments are common in Europe. Such alliances allow citizens to vote for a party that most nearly matches their own beliefs. Coalition governments, however, are often unstable. If one party deserts a coalition, the government might lose its majority in the legislature. The government then falls, and new elections must be held. In the first 10 years of the Third Republic, 50 different coalition governments were formed and fell.

>> **Analyze Political Cartoons** The Boulanger scandal rocked France. Boulanger leads as his supporters follow. What does the image of the man with the large banner suggest about Boulanger's goals?

Bounce to Activate Cartoon

Scandals Rock the Third Republic Despite frequent changes of governments, France made economic progress. It paid Germany the huge sum required by the peace treaty and expanded its overseas empire. By the beginning of the twentieth century, France was the largest democratic country in Europe, with a constitution that protected basic rights. Its overseas empire was second only to that of Britain. But in the 1880s and 1890s, a series of political scandals shook public trust in the government.

One crisis involved the minister of war, General Georges Boulanger (boo lahn zhay), who rallied royalists, workers, the military, and ultranationalists eager for revenge on Germany. Accused of plotting to overthrow the republic, Boulanger fled to Belgium. In another scandal, a nephew of the president was caught selling nominations for the Legion of Honor, France's highest award. The president was forced to resign.

Even more disturbing was a crisis that began in 1894. Known as the Dreyfus Affair, it scarred French politics and society for decades.

DESCRIBE a coalition government.

The Dreyfus Affair

The most serious and divisive scandal began in 1894. The scandal involved a French army officer, Captain Alfred Dreyfus, who was charged with treason. His trial and conviction ignited a decades-long controversy known as the **Dreyfus Affair.**

>> Analyze Political Cartoons This 1899 caricature, *The Traitor,* shows Dreyfus as a lindworm, a mythical dragon or serpent with a poisonous bite. Why was this figure used to represent Dreyfus?

Dreyfus on Trial Alfred Dreyfus was accused of spying for Germany. After a military trial, Dreyfus was convicted of treason. The military claimed to have plenty of written evidence against Dreyfus. Yet neither Dreyfus nor his lawyer was allowed to see it. The army claimed secrecy was needed to protect France.

The injustice was rooted in anti-Semitism. The military elite detested Dreyfus, the first Jewish person to reach such a high position in the army. Although Dreyfus proclaimed his innocence, he was convicted and condemned to life imprisonment on Devil's Island, a desolate penal colony off the coast of South America.

A Long Struggle for Justice The Dreyfus Affair scarred French politics and society for decades. Royalists, ultranationalists, and Church officials charged Dreyfus supporters, or "Dreyfusards," with undermining France. Paris echoed with cries of "Long live the army!" and "Death to traitors!" Dreyfusards, mostly liberals and republicans, upheld ideals of justice and equality in the face of massive public anger.

By 1896, new evidence pointed to another officer, Ferdinand Esterhazy, as the spy. Still, the army refused to grant Dreyfus a new trial.

In 1898, French novelist Émile Zola joined the battle. In an article headlined *J'Accuse!* (I Accuse!), he charged the army and government with suppressing the truth. As a result, Zola was convicted of **libel,** or the knowing publication of false and damaging statements. He fled into exile.

Eventually, the Dreyfusards made progress, and the army had to release its evidence against Dreyfus. Much of it turned out to be forged. In 1906, a French court cleared Dreyfus of all charges and reinstated him in the army. Even though justice had triumphed, the Dreyfus Affair left lasting scars.

Growing Anti-Semitism The Dreyfus case reflected the rise of anti-Semitism in Europe. The Enlightenment and the French Revolution had spread ideas about religious toleration. In Western Europe, some Jews had gained jobs in government, universities, and other areas of life. Others had achieved success in banking and business, but most struggled to survive in the ghettos of Eastern Europe or the slums of Western Europe.

By the late 1800s, however, anti-Semitism was again on the rise. Anti-Semites were often members of the lower middle class who felt insecure in their social and economic position. Steeped in the new nationalist fervor, they adopted an aggressive intolerance for outsiders and a violent hatred of Jews.

The Rise of Zionism The Dreyfus case and pogroms in Russia stirred Theodor Herzl (HURT sul), a Hungarian Jewish journalist living in France. In the face of growing anti-Semitism, Herzl called for Jews to set up their own nation state. He helped spur the growth of **Zionism,** a nationalist movement devoted to rebuilding a Jewish state in the Jews' ancient homeland. Many Jews had kept this dream alive since the destruction of the temple in Jerusalem by the Romans. In 1897, Herzl organized the First Zionist Congress in Basel, Switzerland.

DRAW CONCLUSIONS What solution did Zionists propose to address widespread anti-Semitism?

Reforms in France

Although shaken by the Dreyfus affair, France achieved serious reforms in the early 1900s. Like Britain, France passed laws regulating wages, hours, and safety conditions for workers. It set up a system of free public elementary schools. Creating public schools was also part of a campaign to reduce the control of the Roman Catholic Church over education in France.

Separation of Church and State Like Bismarck in Germany, French reformers tried to limit or even end Church involvement in government. Republicans viewed the Church as a conservative force that opposed progressive policies. In the Dreyfus Affair, it had backed the army and ultranationalists.

From 1899 to 1905, the government enacted a series of reforms. It closed Church schools, along with many convents and monasteries. In 1905, it passed a law to separate church and state and stopped paying the salaries of the clergy. Catholics, Protestants, and Jews all enjoyed freedom of worship, but the new laws ensured that none had any special treatment from the government.

Rights for Women Under the Napoleonic Code, French women had few rights. By the 1890s, a growing women's rights movement in France sought legal reforms. It made some gains, such as an 1896 law giving married women the right to their own earnings.

In 1909, Jeanne-Elizabeth Schmahl founded the French Union for Women's Suffrage. Schmahl and other women sought to win the vote through legal means. Yet even liberal men were reluctant to grant women suffrage. They feared that women would vote for Church and conservative causes. In the end, French women did not win the vote until 1946.

>> One of the many reforms in early 1900s France was the establishment of free public elementary schools.

DESCRIBE How did French women try to change their role in French society in the late 1800s?

ASSESSMENT

1. **Identify Main Ideas** What political changes did the end of the Franco-Prussian War bring to France?
2. **Draw Conclusions** Explain the effect of Napoleon III's foreign policy failures.
3. **Explain** How did coalition governments affect France?
4. **Draw Conclusions** Why was the Dreyfus Affair an important event in French history?
5. **Analyze Information** Why did French women not get the vote until 1946?

>> Most people migrating west traveled in wagons, like the settlers moving through this mountain pass.

3.7 In the 1800s, the United States was a beacon of hope for many people. The American economy was growing rapidly, offering jobs to newcomers. The Constitution and the Bill of Rights held out the hope of political and religious freedom. Not everyone shared in the prosperity or the ideals of democracy. Still, by the early 1900s, the United States had undertaken reforms to ensure equality for all its citizens.

Bounce to Activate Flipped Video

>> Objectives

Describe the territorial expansion of the United States.

Summarize the causes and effects of the Civil War.

Explain how American democracy grew in the 1800s.

Analyze the impact of economic growth and social reform on the United States.

>> Key Terms

expansionism
Louisiana Purchase
Manifest Destiny
secede
segregation

Growth of the United States

The United States Expands

Territorial Gains From the earliest years of its history, the United States had followed a policy of **expansionism,** or extending the nation's boundaries. At first, the United States stretched only from the Atlantic coast to the Mississippi River. In 1803, President Thomas Jefferson bought the Louisiana territory from France. In one stroke, the **Louisiana Purchase** virtually doubled the size of the nation.

By 1846, the United States had expanded to include Florida, Oregon, and the Republic of Texas. The Mexican War (1846–1848) added California and the Southwest.

Manifest Destiny With growing pride and confidence, Americans claimed that their nation was destined to spread across the entire continent, from sea to sea. This idea became known as **Manifest Destiny.** Some expansionists even hoped to absorb Canada and Mexico. In fact, the United States did go far afield. In 1867, it bought Alaska from Russia and in 1898, annexed the Hawaiian Islands.

DESCRIBE Describe the United States' territorial gains during the 1800s.

Expanding Democracy

In 1800, the United States had the most liberal suffrage in the world, but still only white men who owned property could vote. States slowly chipped away at requirements. By the 1830s, most white men had the right to vote. Democracy was still far from complete, however.

By mid-century, reformers were campaigning for many changes. Some demanded a ban on the sale of alcoholic beverages. Others called for better treatment of the mentally ill or pushed for free elementary schools. But two campaigns stood out above all others because they highlighted the limits of American democracy—the abolition movement and the women's rights movement.

The Abolition Movement In the early 1800s, a few Americans began to call for an immediate and complete end to slavery. One of these abolitionists was William Lloyd Garrison, who pressed the antislavery cause through his newspaper, the *Liberator*. Another was Frederick Douglass. He had been born into slavery and escaped, and he spoke eloquently in the North about the evils of the system.

By the 1850s, the battle over slavery had intensified. As each new state entered the union, proslavery and antislavery forces met in violent confrontations to decide whether slavery would be legal in the new state. Harriet Beecher Stowe's novel *Uncle Tom's Cabin* helped convince many northerners that slavery was a great social evil.

Women Seek Equality Women worked hard in the antislavery movement. Lucretia Mott and Elizabeth Cady Stanton traveled to London for the World Antislavery Convention—only to find they were forbidden to speak because they were women. Gradually, American women began to protest the laws and customs that limited their lives. In 1848, Mott and Stanton organized the Seneca Falls Convention, the first women's rights convention, to address the problems faced by women.

The convention passed a resolution, based on the Declaration of Independence. It began, "We hold these truths to be self evident: that all men and women are created equal."

Expansion of the United States, 1783–1898

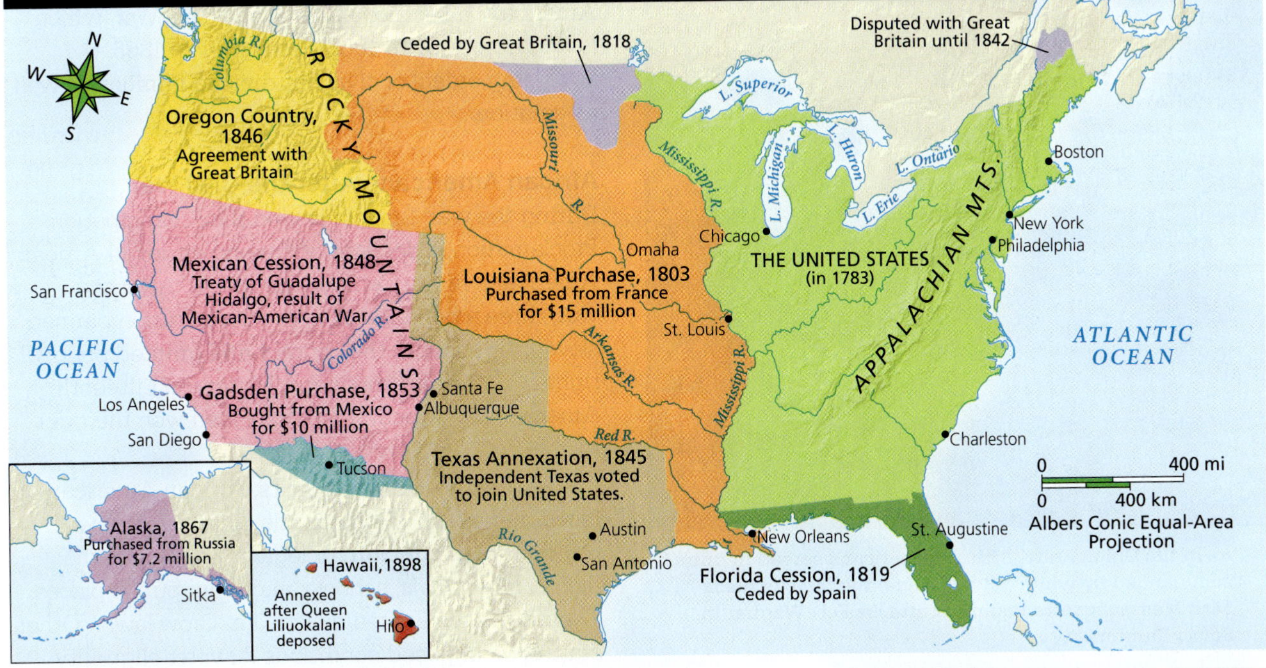

>> **Analyze Maps** Over the course of two centuries, the United States expanded its territory from east of the Mississippi River to the Pacific Ocean and beyond. How did the United States acquire territory on the Pacific coast?

Bounce to Activate Map

>> Lucretia Mott organized the Seneca Falls Convention with Elizabeth Cady Stanton in 1848.

Bounce to Activate Timeline

>> In the Union army, African Americans served in units commanded by white officers. Here, the famous black 54th Massachusetts Regiment attacks Fort Wagner in South Carolina.

The women's rights movement set as its goals equality before the law, in the workplace, and in education. Some women also demanded the right to vote. The idea of women's suffrage sparked controversy. Many Americans, both women and men, thought it was ridiculous. Support for this idea, however, slowly grew.

DRAW CONCLUSIONS How did the abolitionist and women's rights movements highlight the limits of American democracy?

The Civil War

By the mid-1800s, the South and the North were developing along different paths. While the South remained largely rural and agricultural, the North was industrializing and had rapidly growing cities. Along with economic differences, the issue of slavery was increasingly driving a wedge between North and South.

The division reached a crisis in 1860 when Abraham Lincoln was elected president. Lincoln opposed extending slavery into new territories. Southerners feared that he would eventually abolish slavery altogether and that the federal government would infringe on their states' rights.

A Costly Civil War Soon after Lincoln's election, most southern states **seceded,** or withdrew, from the Union and formed the Confederate States of America. This action sparked the Civil War, which lasted from 1861 to 1865. From 1861 to 1865, the agonizing ordeal of civil war divided families as well as a nation.

African Americans After the Civil War

During the war, Lincoln issued the Emancipation Proclamation, a declaration freeing enslaved African Americans in the Confederate states. After the war, three amendments to the Constitution banned slavery throughout the country and granted political rights to African Americans. Under the Fifteenth Amendment, African American men won the right to vote.

Despite these amendments, African Americans faced many restrictions. In the South, state laws imposed **segregation,** or legal separation of the races, in hospitals, schools, and other public places. These laws were often called "Jim Crow laws." Other state laws imposed conditions for voter eligibility that, despite the Fifteenth Amendment, prevented African Americans from voting.

POST–CIVIL WAR AMENDMENTS

After the Civil War, three amendments were added to the Constitution that addressed slavery and the status of former slaves.

	13TH AMENDMENT	14TH AMENDMENT	15TH AMENDMENT
RATIFIED	December 6, 1865	July 9, 1868	February 3, 1870
SECTION 1	Neither slavery nor involuntary servitude, except as a punishment for crime whereof the party shall have been duly convicted, shall exist within the United States, or any place subject to their jurisdiction.	All persons born or naturalized in the United States ... are citizens of the United States and of the State wherein they reside. No State shall make or enforce any law which shall abridge the privileges or immunities of citizens of the United States; nor shall any State deprive any person of life, liberty, or property, without due process of law.	The right of citizens of the United States to vote shall not be denied or abridged by the United States or by any State on account of race, color, or previous condition of servitude...
SUMMARY	Slavery is outlawed.	Gives former slaves citizenship in the United States and the individual states where they live.	Provides African American men the right to vote.

>> After the Civil War, three amendments to the Constitution changed America. **Analyze Charts** What was the purpose of these amendments, and why were they necessary?

African Americans also faced economic hardships. Newly freed African Americans had no land, and many ended up working as tenant farmers. Some headed west to work as cowhands or buy farmland. Others migrated to northern cities to find jobs in factories.

The South had fewer resources, fewer people, and less industry than the North. Still, Southerners fought fiercely to defend their cause. At first, the South won victories. At one point, Confederate armies under General Robert E. Lee drove northward as far as Gettysburg, Pennsylvania, before being driven back. In the last years of the war, Lincoln's most successful general, Ulysses S. Grant, used the massive resources of the North in a full-scale offensive against the South.

After devastating losses, the Confederacy finally surrendered in 1865. The struggle cost more than 600,000 lives—the largest casualty figures of any American war. Although the war left a bitter legacy, it did guarantee that the nation would remain undivided.

SYNTHESIZE How did the 15th Amendment expand democracy in the United States?

Economic Growth and Reform

As in Western Europe, the Industrial Revolution was transforming the United States at mid-century. By 1900, it led the world in industrial and agricultural output, thanks to many factors. It had vast natural resources, a stable government, and a growing population—supplied mostly by immigrants.

The free enterprise system and the protection of property rights allowed entrepreneurs to invest in expanding businesses. The building of railroads and new technologies that improved communication further helped farming and industry.

Business and Labor By 1900, giant monopolies controlled whole industries. Scottish-born Andrew Carnegie built the nation's largest steel company, while John D. Rockefeller's Standard Oil Company dominated the world's petroleum industry. Big business enjoyed tremendous profits. The growing prosperity was not shared by all. In factories, wages were low and conditions were often brutal. To defend their interests, American workers organized labor unions such as the American Federation of Labor. Unions sought better wages, hours, and working conditions. Struggles with management sometimes erupted into violent confrontations. Slowly, however, workers made gains.

The Push for Reform When economic hard times hit in the late 1800s, the farmers also organized to defend their interests. In the 1890s, they joined city workers to support the new Populist party. The Populists never became a major party, but their platform of reforms, such as an eight-hour workday, eventually became law.

By 1900, reformers known as Progressives pressed for change. They sought laws to ban child labor, limit working hours, regulate monopolies, and give voters more power. In addition Progressives backed women's suffrage. After a long struggle, American suffragists finally won the vote in 1920, when the Nineteenth Amendment went into effect.

DRAW CONCLUSIONS How did immigration help economic growth after the Civil War?

ASSESSMENT

1. **Describe** What was Manifest Destiny and how did it affect the United States?
2. **Describe** How did a free enterprise system aid the growth of the United States?
3. **Connect** How did the expansion of the United States set the stage for the Civil War?
4. **Analyze Information** What was the impact of economic growth on the United States?
5. **Synthesize** What problems did workers face during the late 1800s and early 1900s and how did they try to enact change?

Primary Sources

Democracy in America: Alexis de Tocqueville

Introduction

Alexis de Tocqueville, a young French writer, visited the United States in 1831. During his travels, he observed firsthand the impact of Jacksonian democracy. After returning to France, Tocqueville began writing *Democracy in America,* a detailed look at American politics, society, economics, religion, and law. The first volume was published in 1835. The book is still studied and quoted by historians and politicians today. In these excerpts from *Democracy in America,* Tocqueville discusses the role of the American people in their government and gives his view of the American character.

Another observer of American institutions, Thomas Jefferson, describes his vision for the new nation in "Notes on the State of Virginia" written in 1785.

>> Settlers traveling west

Primary Source

The general principles which are the groundwork of modern constitutions–principles which were imperfectly known in Europe, and not completely triumphant even in Great Britain, in the seventeenth century–were all recognized and determined by the laws of New England: the intervention of the people in public affairs, the free voting of taxes, the responsibility of authorities, personal liberty, and trial by jury, were all positively established without discussion. From these fruitful principles consequences have been derived and applications have been made such as no nation in Europe has yet ventured to attempt.

DRAW CONCLUSIONS In Tocqueville's view, how did America differ from countries in Europe and Great Britain? Based on this, what can you conclude about Tocqueville's own frame of reference?

. . . it is at least true that in the United States the county and the township are always based upon the same principle, namely, that everyone is the best judge of what concerns himself alone, and the most proper person to supply his private wants.

DETERMINE CENTRAL IDEAS Recall that laissez-faire is the economic principle that says business should be free from government interference. In what way could the idea of laissez-faire be applied to this section of Tocqueville's text?

In America the people name those who make the law and those who execute it; they themselves form the jury that punishes infractions [violations] of the law. Not only are the institutions democratic in their principle, but also in all their developments; thus the people name their representatives directly and generally choose them every year in order to keep them more completely under their dependence. It is therefore really the people who direct. . . . This majority is composed principally of peaceful citizens who, either by taste or by interest, sincerely desire the good of the country. Around them parties constantly agitate. . . .

EXPLAIN AN ARGUMENT What does Tocqueville mean when he says that American institutions are "democratic" both in their "principle" and their "developments"?

The American taken randomly [chosen without a plan] will therefore be a man ardent [intense] in his desires, enterprising [full of energy; willing to take on new projects], adventurous—above all, an innovator [a person who creates a new way of doing something]. This spirit is in fact found in all his works; he introduces it into his political laws, his religious doctrines, his theories of social economy, his private industry; he brings it with him everywhere, into the depths of the woods as into the heart of towns.

DRAW CONCLUSIONS Choose two of the "works" mentioned in this section and describe how a "random" American, according to Tocqueville, might pursue them with a spirit of innovation.

To evade the bondage of system and habit, of family maxims, class-opinions, and in some degree, of national prejudices; to accept tradition only as a means of information, and existing facts only as a lesson used in doing otherwise and doing better; to seek the reason of things for oneself, and in oneself alone; to tend to results without being bound to means, and to aim at the substance through the form;—such are the principle characteristics of what I shall call the philosophical method of the Americans. But if I go further, and if I seek among those characteristics the principle one which includes almost all the rest, I discover that, in most operations of the mind, each American appeals only to the individual effort of his own understanding.

EXPLAIN AN ARGUMENT Explain why Tocqueville regards the principle of individualism as such a crucial social value.

Primary Source

We never had an interior trade of any importance. Our exterior commerce has suffered very much from the beginning of the present contest. During this time we have manufactured within our families the most necessary articles of clothing. Those of cotton will bear some comparison with the same kinds of manufacture in Europe; but those of wool, flax and hemp are very coarse, unsightly, and unpleasant: and such is our attachment to agriculture, and such our preference for foreign manufactures, that be it wise or unwise, our people will certainly return as soon as they can, to raising raw materials, and exchanging them for finer manufactures than they are able to execute themselves.

ASSESSMENT

1. **Determine Central Ideas** In what way do the people "direct" the American democracy, according to Tocqueville?
2. **Summarize** What impressed Tocqueville during his time in America? Cite examples to support your answer.
3. **Draw Conclusions** In what way could Tocqueville's book be relevant today?
4. **Summarize** How does Jefferson encourage the industry of farming?

3.8 In Eastern and Central Europe, the Austrian Hapsburgs and the Ottoman Turks ruled lands that included diverse ethnic groups. During the 1800s, nationalist feelings spread among these subjected people, which contributed to tensions in Europe. Nationalism, which had brought unity to countries like Germany and Italy, would undermine multi-ethnic empires like that of the Austrian Hapsburgs and the Ottoman Turks. Why did nationalism bring new strength to some countries and weaken others?

>> Nationalist revolts broke out in 1848 across the multinational Austrian Hapsburg empire. Vienna burns during the fighting in October of that year.

Bounce to Activate Flipped Video

Nationalism in Eastern Europe and Russia

Nationalism Endangers Old Empires

The Lands of the Hapsburg Empire The Hapsburgs were the oldest ruling house in Europe. In addition to their homeland of Austria, over the centuries they had acquired the territories of Bohemia and Hungary, as well as parts of Romania, Poland, Ukraine, and northern Italy. By the 1800s, ruling such a vast empire made up of many nationalities posed a challenge for the Hapsburg monarchs, especially as the tide of nationalism rose.

Austrian Hapsburgs Face Challenges Since the Congress of Vienna, the Austrian emperor Francis I and his foreign minister Metternich had upheld conservative goals against liberal forces. "Rule and change nothing," the emperor told his son. Under Francis and Metternich, newspapers could not even use the word constitution, much less discuss this key demand of liberals.

>> Objectives

Explain how nationalism challenged Austria and the Ottoman Empire.

Summarize major obstacles to progress in Russia.

Describe the cycle of absolutism, reform, and reaction followed by the tsars.

Explain how industrialization contributed to the outbreak of revolution in 1905.

>> Key Terms

Francis Joseph
Ferenc Deák
Dual Monarchy
colossus
Alexander II
Crimean War
emancipation
zemstvo
pogrom
refugee
Duma
Peter Stolypin

The government also tried to limit industrial development, which would threaten traditional ways of life.

The Hapsburgs, however, could not hold back the changes that were engulfing Europe. By the 1840s, factories were springing up. Soon, the Hapsburgs found themselves facing the problems of industrial life that had long been familiar in Britain—the growth of cities, worker discontent, and the stirrings of socialism.

Nationalist Demands Equally disturbing to the old order were the urgent demands of nationalists. The Hapsburgs presided over a multinational empire. Of its 50 million people at mid-century, fewer than a quarter were German-speaking Austrians. Almost half belonged to different Slavic groups, including Czechs, Slovaks, Poles, Ukrainians, Serbs, Croats, and Slovenes. Often, rival groups shared the same region. The empire also included large numbers of Hungarians and Italians. The Hapsburgs ignored nationalist demands as long as they could. When nationalist revolts broke out in 1848, the government crushed them.

>> Francis Joseph inherited the Hapsburg throne while still a teenager. He made some limited reforms, but not enough to save his empire.

Reforms of Francis Joseph Amid the turmoil, 18-year-old **Francis Joseph** inherited the Hapsburg throne. He would rule until 1916, presiding over the empire during its fading days.

An early challenge came when Austria suffered its humiliating defeat at the hands of France and Sardinia in 1859. Francis Joseph realized he needed to strengthen the empire at home. Accordingly, he made some limited reforms. He granted a new constitution that set up a legislature. This body, however, was dominated by German-speaking Austrians.

The reforms thus satisfied none of the other national groups that populated the empire. The Hungarians, especially, were determined to settle for nothing less than self-government.

HYPOTHESIZE What alternatives might Francis Joseph have had in responding to nationalist demands?

The Dual Monarchy

Austria's disastrous defeat in the 1866 war with Prussia brought renewed pressure for change from Hungarians within the empire. One year later, **Ferenc Deák** (DEH ahk), a moderate Hungarian leader, helped work out a compromise that created a new political power known as the **Dual Monarchy** of Austria-Hungary.

The Creation of Austria-Hungary Under the agreement, Austria and Hungary were separate states. Each had its own constitution and parliament. Francis Joseph ruled both, as emperor of Austria and king of Hungary. The two states also shared ministries of finance, defense, and foreign affairs, but were independent of each other in all other areas.

Nationalist Unrest Increases Although Hungarians welcomed the compromise, other subject peoples resented it. Restlessness increased among various Slavic groups, especially the Czechs in Bohemia.

Some nationalist leaders called on Slavs to unite, insisting that "only through liberty, equality, and fraternal solidarity" could Slavic peoples fulfill their "great mission in the history of mankind." By the early 1900s, nationalist unrest often left

>> **Analyze Maps** By 1914, there were several new, independent countries in the Balkans, such as Serbia, Bulgaria, and Romania. Based on the map, do you think the people of these new countries felt that their independence was secure? Explain.

Bounce to Activate Map

the government paralyzed in the face of pressing political and social problems.

DRAW CONCLUSIONS Why did the Dual Monarchy fail to end nationalist demands?

The Ottoman Empire Declines

Like the Hapsburgs, the Ottomans ruled a multinational empire. It stretched from Eastern Europe and the Balkans to North Africa and the Middle East. There, as in Austria, nationalist demands tore at the fabric of the empire.

Nationalism in the Balkans In the Balkans, Serbia won autonomy in 1830, and southern Greece won independence during the 1830s. But many Serbs and Greeks still lived in the Balkans under Ottoman rule. The Ottoman empire was also home to other national groups, such as Bulgarians and Romanians. During the 1800s, various subject peoples staged revolts against the Ottomans, hoping to set up their own independent states.

Dividing Ottoman Lands Such nationalist stirrings became mixed up with the ambitions of the great European powers. In the mid-1800s, Europeans came to see the Ottoman empire as "the sick man of Europe." Eagerly, they scrambled to divide up Ottoman lands. Russia pushed south toward the Black Sea and Istanbul, which Russians still called Constantinople.

Austria-Hungary took Bosnia and Herzegovina, angering Serbs. They had ambitions to expand their influence in the area. Meanwhile, Britain and France set their sights on other Ottoman lands in the Middle East and North Africa.

Balkan Wars In the end, a complex web of competing interests contributed to a series of crises and wars in the Balkans. Russia fought several wars against the Ottomans. France and Britain sometimes joined the Russians and sometimes the Ottomans.

Germany supported Austrian authority over the discontented national groups. But Germany also encouraged the Ottomans because of their strategic location in the eastern Mediterranean. In between, the subject peoples revolted and then fought among themselves. By the early 1900s, observers were referring to the region as the "Balkan powder keg."

The explosion that came in 1914 helped set off World War I.

DRAW CONCLUSIONS How did Balkan nationalism contribute to the decline of the Ottoman Empire?

Russia Tries Reform

During the 1800s, Russia expanded its empire eastward into Asia but faced rising demands for reform at home. Reformers hoped to bring Enlightenment ideals such as constitutional government and social justice. They called for an end to autocratic rule and urged the tsar to modernize Russia. Under pressure, tsars introduced some reforms, but soon reverted to repression when ongoing unrest threatened their throne.

Russia Expands By 1815, Russia was not only the largest, most populous nation in Europe but also a great world power. Since the 1600s, explorers, soldiers, and traders seeking furs had expanded Russia's empire eastward across Siberia to the Pacific.

>> Russian nobles celebrate the coronation of Tsar Nicholas II in 1896. Russian royalty and nobility lived lives of wealth and luxury.

In their efforts to gain warm water ports, Peter the Great and Catherine II added lands on the Baltic and Black seas. During the 1800s, as tsars sought to contain the Ottoman and British empires, they expanded into the Caucasus region and Central Asia. In the process, Russia acquired a vast multinational empire over parts of Europe and Asia.

Other European powers, including Britain and France, watched the Russian **colossus,** or giant, anxiously. Russia had immense natural resources. Its vast size gave it global influence. But Western Europeans disliked its autocratic government and feared its expansionist aims. At the same time, Russia remained economically undeveloped.

Obstacles to Progress By the 1800s, tsars saw the need to modernize but resisted reforms that would undermine their absolute rule. While they wavered, Russia fell further behind the West in economic and social developments.

A great obstacle to progress was the rigid social structure. Landowning nobles dominated society and rejected any change that would threaten their privileges. The middle class was small and weak.

Most Russians were serfs, or laborers bound to the land and to the landowners who controlled them. While serfdom had almost disappeared in Western Europe by the 1700s, it had survived and even spread in Russia.

Russian Serfdom Most serfs were peasants. Others were servants, artisans, or soldiers forced into the tsar's army. As industry expanded, some masters sent serfs to work in factories but took much of their pay.

Enlightened Russians knew that serfdom was inefficient. As long as most people had to serve the whim of their masters, Russia's economy would remain backward. Landowning nobles had no reason to improve agriculture and took little interest in industry.

The Tsars Have Absolute Power For centuries, tsars had ruled with absolute power, imposing their will on their subjects. On occasion, the tsars made limited attempts at liberal reform, such as easing censorship or making legal and economic reforms to improve the lives of serfs. However, in each instance the tsars drew back from their reforms when they began to fear losing the support of nobles.

In short, the liberal and nationalist changes brought about by the Enlightenment and the French Revolution had almost no effect on Russian autocracy.

The tsarist motto was the "three pillars of absolutism." They were: orthodoxy, or strong ties between the Russian Orthodox Church and the government; autocracy, or absolute government; and nationality, or Russian nationalism, which called for respect for Russian traditions and suppression of non-Russian groups within the empire.

IDENTIFY CENTRAL ISSUES Why did industrialization and reform come more slowly to Russia than to Western Europe?

Emancipation and Stirrings of Revolution

During much of the 1800s, tsars moved back and forth between reform and repression. In mid-century, the tsar **Alexander II** moved toward reform, but his death at the hands of an assassin led to a return to repression.

The Crimean War Alexander II came to the throne during the **Crimean War.** The war had broken out after Russia tried to seize Ottoman lands along the Danube River. Britain, France, and Sardinia stepped in to help the Ottomans by sending armies into the Russian Crimea, a peninsula that juts into the Black Sea.

The war, which ended in a Russian defeat, revealed the country's backwardness. Russia had only a few miles of railroads, and the military bureaucracy was hopelessly inefficient.

Emancipation of the Serfs Russia's defeat in the Crimean War triggered widespread calls for change. Russian liberals demanded changes, and students demonstrated, seeking reform. Pressed from all sides, Alexander II finally agreed to reforms. In 1861, he issued a royal decree that required **emancipation,** or freeing, of the serfs.

Freedom brought problems. Former serfs had to buy the land they had worked, but many were too poor to do so. Also, the lands allotted to peasants were often too small to farm efficiently or to support a family. Peasants remained poor, and discontent festered.

Still, emancipation was a turning point. Many peasants moved to the cities, taking jobs in factories and building Russian industries. Equally important, freeing the serfs boosted the drive for further reform.

Limited Reforms Along with emancipation, Alexander II set up a system of local government.

>> The 1881 assassination of Alexander II prompted further repression by his son and successor, Alexander III.

Bounce to Activate Gallery

Elected assemblies, called **zemstvos,** were made responsible for matters such as road repair, schools, and agriculture. Through this system, Russians gained some experience of self-government at the local level.

The tsar also introduced legal reforms such as trial by jury. He eased censorship and tried to reform the military. A soldier's term of service was reduced from 25 years to 15, and brutal discipline was limited. Alexander also encouraged the growth of industry in Russia.

Dissent Continues Alexander's reforms failed to satisfy many Russians. Peasants had freedom but not land. Liberals wanted a constitution and an elected legislature. Radicals, who had adopted socialist ideas from the West, demanded even more revolutionary changes. The tsar, meanwhile, moved away from reform and toward repression.

In the 1870s, some socialists went to live and work among peasants, preaching reform and revolution. They had little success. The peasants scarcely understood them and sometimes turned them over to the police.

The failure of this movement, combined with renewed government repression, sparked anger among radicals, leading some to embrace violence.

>> Jewish men view the damage done to their sacred Torah scrolls during an 1881 pogrom. Pogroms targeted Jewish communities in Russia.

>> An iron foundry in Lysva, Russia, in 1900. **Draw Conclusions** How did industrialization affect demands for reform in Russia?

On March 13, 1881, terrorists assassinated Alexander II.

Return to Repression Alexander III responded to his father's assassination by returning to repression. To wipe out liberals and revolutionaries, he increased the power of the secret police, restored strict censorship, and exiled critics to Siberia.

The tsar also launched a program of Russification aimed at suppressing the cultures of non-Russian peoples within the empire. Alexander insisted on one language, Russian, and one church, the Russian Orthodox Church. Poles, Ukrainians, Finns, Armenians, Muslims, Jews, and many others suffered persecution.

Persecution and Pogroms Russia had acquired a large Jewish population when it carved up Poland and expanded into Ukraine. Under Alexander III, the persecution of Russia's Jewish population increased.

The tsar limited the number of Jews allowed to study in universities or practice certain professions. He revived old laws that forced Jews to live in restricted areas.

Official persecution encouraged **pogroms,** or violent mob attacks on Jewish people. Gangs beat and killed Jewish people and looted and burned their homes and stores. Faced with savage persecution, many left Russia. They became **refugees,** or people who flee their homeland to seek safety elsewhere. Large numbers of Russian Jews went to the United States.

IDENTIFY CAUSE AND EFFECT Why did emancipation fail to meet the needs of the serfs and lead to continued discontent?

The Beginnings of Industrialization

By the late 1800s, Russia had finally entered the industrial age under Alexander III and his son Nicholas II. Russia had several factors of production needed to industrialize. It had vast natural resources, including land and minerals. Its large population included peasants and the beginnings of an urban working class. Over time, a new industrial class emerged with the capital and drive to invest in economic development.

In the 1890s, the government focused on economic development. It encouraged the building of railroads to connect iron and coal mines with factories and to transport goods across Russia.

It secured foreign capital to invest in transportation and industry. Loans from France helped Russia build the Trans-Siberian Railway, which stretched 5,000 miles from European Russia to the Pacific Ocean.

Political Turmoil Grows Industrialization increased social and political problems. Government officials and business leaders applauded economic growth. Nobles opposed it, fearing the changes it brought.

Industrialization also created new social ills as peasants flocked to cities to work in factories. Instead of a better life, they found long hours and low pay in dangerous conditions. In the slums around the factories, poverty, disease, and discontent multiplied. These conditions provided fertile ground for radicals, who sought supporters among the new industrial workers. At factory gates, Socialists often handed out pamphlets that preached the revolutionary ideas of Karl Marx, who won support among the new industrial workers.

HYPOTHESIZE Why did industrialization increase radicalism among Russian peasants?

>> Russian soldiers fire on peaceful protesters in front of the Winter Palace in St. Petersburg in January 1905. This event came to be known as Bloody Sunday.

The Road to Revolution

When war broke out between Russia and Japan in 1904, Nicholas II called on his people to fight for "the Faith, the Tsar, and the Fatherland." Despite patriotic slogans and great sacrifices, the Russians suffered one humiliating defeat after another.

Bloody Sunday News of the military disasters unleashed pent-up discontent created by years of oppression. Protesters poured into the streets. Workers went on strike, demanding shorter hours and better wages. Liberals called for a constitution and reforms to overhaul the government.

As the crisis deepened, a young Orthodox priest, Father George Gapon, organized a peaceful march for Sunday, January 22, 1905. He felt certain that the tsar would help his people if only he understood their sufferings. Marchers flowed through the streets of St. Petersburg toward the tsar's Winter Palace. Chanting prayers and singing hymns, workers carried holy icons and pictures of the tsar. They also brought a petition for justice and freedom.

Fearing the marchers, the tsar had fled the palace and called in soldiers. As the people approached, they saw troops lined up across the square. Suddenly, gunfire rang out. Hundreds of men and women fell dead or wounded in the snow. One

>> Protesters march in St. Petersburg in 1905. Bloody Sunday led to uprisings against the tsar throughout Russia.

>> The first session of the Duma meets in St. Petersburg in 1906. Its liberal members wanted political and social reforms, prompting the tsar to dismiss it after only a few months.

woman stumbling away from the scene moaned: "The tsar has deserted us! They shot away the orthodox faith." Indeed, the slaughter marked a turning point for Russians. "Bloody Sunday" killed the people's faith and trust in the tsar.

Unrest Explodes into Revolution In the months that followed Bloody Sunday, discontent exploded across Russia. Strikes multiplied. In some cities, workers took over local government. In the countryside, peasants revolted and demanded land. Minority nationalities called for autonomy. Terrorists targeted officials, and some assassins were cheered as heroes by discontented Russians.

At last, the clamor grew so great that Nicholas was forced to announce sweeping reforms. In the October Manifesto, he promised "freedom of person, conscience, speech, assembly, and union." He agreed to summon a **Duma,** or elected national legislature. No law, he declared, would go into effect without approval by the Duma.

Post-Revolution Reforms The manifesto won over moderates, leaving Socialists isolated. These divisions helped the tsar, who had no intention of letting strikers, revolutionaries, and rebellious peasants challenge him.

In 1906, the first Duma met, but the tsar quickly dissolved it when leaders criticized the government. Nicholas then appointed **Peter Stolypin** (stuh LIP yin) a conservative, as his prime minister. Arrests, pogroms, and executions followed as the conservative Stolypin sought to restore order.

Stolypin realized that Russia needed reform, not just repression. To regain peasant support, he introduced moderate land reforms. He strengthened the zemstvos and improved education before he was assassinated in 1911.

Several more Dumas met during this period, but new voting laws made sure they were conservative. By 1914, Russia was still an autocracy, but one simmering with unrest.

DRAW CONCLUSIONS What does Bloody Sunday suggest about the relationship between the tsar and the Russian people?

ASSESSMENT

1. **Identify Cause and Effect** What effect did nationalism have on the Hapsburg and Ottoman empires?
2. **Synthesize** How did the concept of liberty influence nationalism and revolution in Eastern Europe?
3. **Integrate Information** How did the struggle for basic human rights such as life, liberty, and freedom of expression influence the Revolution of 1905?
4. **Analyze Information** Tsar Alexander II declared that it is "better to abolish serfdom from above than to wait until it will be abolished by a movement from below." Explain his statement.
5. **Hypothesize** Why would a policy such as "Russification" lead to increased nationalism?

PEARSON realize™
PearsonSchool.com/CASS

Go online to PearsonSchool.com/CASS and use the texts, quizzes, interactivities, Interactive Reading Notepads, Flipped Videos, and other resources from this Topic to prepare for the Topic Test.

- Etexts
- Quizzes
- Interactivities
- Interactive Reading Notepads
- Flipped Videos

While online you can also check the progress you've made learning the topic and course content by viewing your grades, test scores, and assignment status.

California Topic 3 Quick Study Guide

LESSON SUMMARIES

Use these Lesson Summaries, and the longer versions available online, to review the key ideas for each lesson in this Topic.

Lesson 1: Revolutions Sweep Europe

After 1815, opposing ideologies between conservatives, liberals and nationalists thrust Europe into turmoil for more than thirty years. Conservatives strongly denounced ideas on natural rights and constitutional government. Liberals favored constitution-based governments, and Nationalists hoped to regain lost territories and establish new homelands.

Lesson 2: Latin American Nations Win Independence

By the late 1700s, the revolutionary fervor that gripped Western Europe spread to Latin America. There, nations that had endured years of social, racial, and political injustice revolted.

Lesson 3: The Unification of Germany

Otto von Bismarck, the chancellor of Prussia, was determined to build a strong, unified German state. In 1871, he became chancellor of the German empire.

Lesson 4: The Unification of Italy

At the Congress of Vienna, Italian nationalists hoped to end centuries of foreign rule and achieve unity. By 1871, Italy was a united nation with its capital in Rome. Long-time nationalist Giuseppe Garibaldi and his Red Shirts played an important role in achieving this goal.

Lesson 5: Democratic Reforms in Britain

In 1815, Britain was a constitutional monarchy with a parliament and two political parties. With the support of Queen Victoria, Parliament passed a wide variety of social reform measures that included the abolition of the slave trade and laws to benefit the working class. However, the women's suffrage remained an issue.

Lesson 6: Divisions and Democracy in France

The Franco-Prussian War ended a long reign of French domination in Europe. Under Napoleon III, democratic reform, economic growth, and nationalism shaped modern France.

Lesson 7: Growth of the United States

In the 1800s, the United States represented hope for many people. In the 1800s, the nation was expanding, developing industry, and gradually extending its democratic principles to all citizens.

Lesson 8: Nationalism in Eastern Europe and Russia

In Eastern Europe, the Austrian Hapsburgs and the Ottoman Turks ruled lands that included diverse ethnic groups. Strong nationalist feelings among these subject people contributed to tensions building across Europe. In Russia, reformers hoped to free Russia from autocratic rule and social injustice.

VISUAL REVIEW

Use these graphics to review some of the key terms, people, and ideas from this Topic.

Effects of Nationalism

NATIONALISM BY REGION				
GERMANY	**ITALY**	**AUSTRIA**	**BALKANS**	**RUSSIA**
• German states unite under William I. • Empire takes leading role in Europe. • Bismarck becomes known as the Iron Chancellor.	• Mazzini founds Young Italy. • Garibaldi leads Red Shirts. • Victor Emmanuel II makes Cavour prime minister of Sardinia. • Italian states become unified by 1871.	• Francis I and Metternich uphold conservative goals. • Dual Monarchy with Hungary is set up. • Nationalist groups grow restless. • Empire becomes weakened.	• Serbians achieve autonomy in 1830. • Greeks achieve independence in the 1830s. • European nations divide up Ottoman lands. • "Balkan powder keg" helps set off World War I.	• Serfs are freed in 1861. • Alexander III encourages persecution and pogroms. • Russia enters the industrial age late. • Bloody Sunday leads to revolution in 1905. • Duma has limited power.

Independence Movements in Latin America

CAUSE AND EFFECT	
LONG-TERM CAUSES	**IMMEDIATE CAUSES**
• European domination • Spread of Enlightenment ideas • American and French Revolutions • Growth of nationalism	• Social injustices • Revolutionary leaders emerge • Napoleon invades Spain.

↓

INDEPENDENCE MOVEMENTS

↓

IMMEDIATE EFFECTS	LONG-TERM EFFECTS
• Toussaint L'Ouverture leads slave revolt in Haiti. • Bolivar, San Martin, and others lead successful revolts. • Colonial rule ends in much of Latin America.	• Numerous independent nations in Latin America • Continuing efforts to achieve stable democratic governments and to gain economic independence

Key Events in the United States 1800s–Early 1900s

1803	Louisiana Purchase
1846–1848	Mexican War
1849	California Gold Rush
1861–1865	Civil War
1867	Purchase of Alaska
1869	Completion of Transcontinental Railroad
1882	Formation of Standard Oil Trust
1898	Spanish-American War; Hawaiian islands annexed
1908	Development of Henry Ford's Model T

California Topic 3 Assessment

KEY TERMS, PEOPLE, AND IDEAS

1. How did reforms affect the social and political status of Britain?
2. What was the first step on Haiti's road to independence?
3. Is the term Iron Chancellor an appropriate title for **Otto von Bismarck**? Explain.
4. How did regional differences in Italy initially prevent unity in the new nation?
5. How did the Great Reform Act of 1832 affect the **electorate**?
6. What effect did the **Dreyfus Affair** have on France?
7. Was **Manifest Destiny** in the United States accepted by everyone? Explain.
8. What was the **dual monarchy**?
9. Discuss the causes of the Latin American independence movement.

CRITICAL THINKING

10. **Synthesize Information** How did ideas from the Enlightenment and the Napoleonic Code influence nationalist movements in Europe during the 1840s?
11. **Summarize** How did Britain and France slowly extend democratic rights during the 1800s and early 1900s?
12. **Comparing** (a) How does the French system of political parties differ from the American system? (b) How do these differences affect the stability of governments under each system?
13. **Summarize** What sparked the Irish nationalist movement?
14. **Draw Conclusions** What social changes in the United States after the Civil War prompted political reform?
15. **Find the Main Idea** What territorial and economic changes promoted German unity?
16. **Analyze Cartoons** Look at the cartoon below. (a) What event is represented? (b) How does the cartoon reflect the goals of nationalists?

17. **Writing Activity** In 1814, after a defeat in Caracas, Venezuela, Simón Bolívar fled to the British colony of Jamaica. There he wrote the following letter. Describe the purpose of the letter. Why do you think he called Spain an "unnatural stepmother"? What do you think were the effects of the publication of this letter? Explain.

> "There is nothing we have not suffered at the hands of that unnatural stepmother—Spain. . . . Americans, under the existing Spanish system, occupy a position in society no better than that of serfs suitable for labor. . . And even this status is surrounded with galling restrictions, such as the prohibition against the cultivation of European crops. . . To this add the exclusive trading privileges. . . in short do you wish to know what our future was?—simply the cultivation of the fields of indigo, grain, coffee, sugar cane, cacao, and cotton. . . . digging in the earth to mine gold for the insatiable greed of Spain."
>
> —Simón Bolívar, "Letter From Jamaica"

DOCUMENT-BASED QUESTIONS

The Dreyfus Affair divided and scarred French society and politics. Read the documents below, then answer the questions that follow.

DOCUMENT A

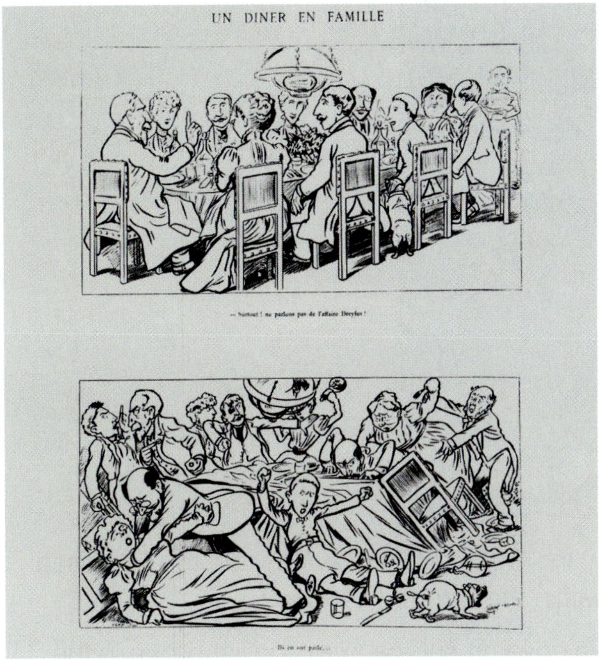

"Un Diner En Famille"

Translation: "It is agreed that there should be no talk of the affair! But they did talk about it . . ."

—*From Le Figaro by Caran d'Ache, February, 1898*

DOCUMENT B

". . . if my voice ceased to be heard, it would mean that it had been extinguished forever, for if I have survived, it has been in order to insist on my honor—my property and the patrimony of our children—and in order to do my duty, as I have done it everywhere and always, and as it must always be done, when right and justice are on one's side, without ever fearing anything or anyone."

—*From a letter to his wife Lucie, by Alfred Dreyfus, September 1898, published in Cinq Années*

DOCUMENT C

"I accuse the offices of War of having conducted in the press, particularly in L'Eclair and in L'Echo de Paris, an abominable campaign designed to mislead public opinion and to conceal their wrongdoing."

"Finally, I accuse the first Court Martial of having violated the law in convicting a defendant on the basis of a document kept secret, and I accuse the second Court Martial of having covered up . . . [and] knowingly acquitting a guilty man."

—*From "J'Accuse" a letter to the President of the Republic by Émile Zola*

18. Document A illustrates

A. why many French families believed Dreyfus was guilty.

B. why Dreyfus was unfairly convicted of treason.

C. how the Dreyfus case divided France.

D. how anti-Semitism was a factor in the Dreyfus case.

19. In Document B, Dreyfus suggests that his wish to prove his innocence helped to

A. keep him close to his family.

B. keep him alive.

C. make the Army take illegal actions.

D. make anti-Semitic groups angry.

20. Which statement best summarizes Zola's letter in Document C?

A. Although the French military convicted the wrong man, they attempted to carry out a fair trial.

B. The French military was fooled by handwriting experts, who tried to convict the wrong man.

C. The French military knowingly and illegally convicted an innocent man.

D. The French military showed that the army was anti-Semitic at the highest levels.

21. Writing Tasks On July 21, 1906, a French general knighted Alfred Dreyfus a member of the Legion of Honor. Well wishers attended the ceremony in the courtyard of the Ecole Militaire. Suppose you are reporting on the event for an American newspaper. Write a news story, using the documents on this page along with information from the Topic.

End-of-Topic Practice

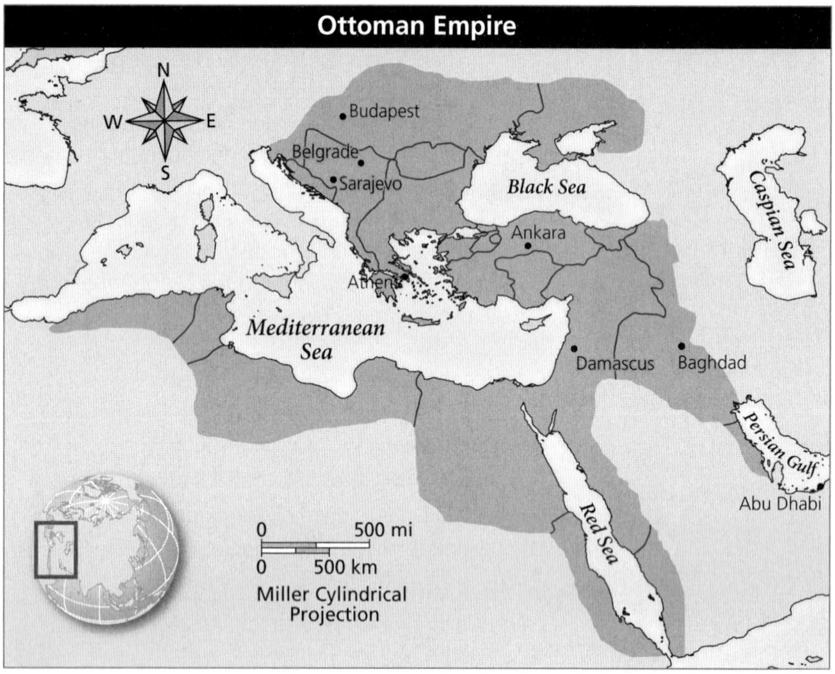

1. Look at the map of the states that were ruled by the Ottoman Empire. Why did the European idea of nationalism lead to political revolutions within the Ottoman Empire?

   A It led the rulers of the empire to reorganize the government, causing conflict between the different Ottoman states.

   B It led the different peoples in the empire to desire the ability to govern themselves, causing conflict with the imperial rulers.

   C It led the citizens of the empire to want to imitate Western democratic institutions, causing conflict with the conservative Ottoman bureaucracy.

   D It led the rulers of the various Ottoman states to push the central government for reforms, causing conflict between religious sects inside the empire.

---

2. How did Napoleon Bonaparte's ouster of the Spanish king in 1808 influence Latin American independence movements?

   F Latin American independence movements feared French involvement.

   G Latin American leaders wanted to copy Napoleon's military strategy.

   H Latin American leaders feared delays in their own independence.

   J Spain's weakness showed that Latin America could also overthrow foreign rule.

3 What military and diplomatic strategy did Bismarck use to create a viable German Empire?

A With his skillful understanding of realpolitik, he arranged numerous diplomatic missions to Austria and small provinces.

B He provoked conflicts with Austria and France that resulted in war and the annexation of land.

C His blood and iron speech rallied German nationalists who then supported his desire to go to war against Austria.

D His goal was to form a confederation that united the smaller principalities.

". . .in an age when the mass of the working classes were without either organization or political experience, they were not easily pursued together. The struggles between the conflicting interest of economic reform and political democracy, corresponding as it did to a difference in outlook between north and south, and to the rival policies of revolution and persuasion, ultimately broke up the [Chartist] movement."

—R.H. Tawney, Introduction to William Lovett's autobiography

4 The factors which led to the decline of the Chartist movement are described above. How did some of the ideas of the Chartist movement eventually affect British government?

F It convinced Parliament that universal civil rights should be granted to all citizens.

G It destroyed the push for a secret ballot, but later the secret ballot became part of the Reform Act of 1832.

H It convinced Parliament that universal suffrage is best restricted to the wealthy and educated.

J It expanded social freedoms for the poor and working class.

If you have trouble with. . .				
Question	1	2	3	4
See Lesson	3.1	3.2	3.3	3.5

PEARSON realize
PearsonSchool.com/CASS

Go ONLINE for digital resources

VIDEO AUDIO ETEXT ACTIVITY WRITING GAMES PDF ASSESSMENT

[ESSENTIAL QUESTION] Why Do People Move?

4 The Age of Imperialism (1800–1914)

>> Hafiz Abdul Karim attends to Queen Victoria, 1893

Enduring Understandings

- Motives for imperialism included the need for natural resources and new markets, racism, and the desire to spread Christianity.
- Using superior military technology, European powers divided up most of Africa and Southeast Asia, while India became a British colony.
- Many people resisted European rule, but Ethiopia and Siam avoided colonization.
- As Chinese power declined, western nations established spheres of influence in China.
- Japan responded to outside influences by rapidly modernizing and becoming an imperialist power.
- Latin American nations faced economic imperialism and the influence of the United States.

NBC LEARN

Learn how Menelik II helped Ethiopia resist colonization during the Age of Imperialism.

Bounce to Activate My Story Video

California Topic 4 Overview

In this Topic, you will learn about the events of the Age of Imperialism. Look at the lesson outline and explore the timeline. As you study this Topic, you will complete the Quest team project.

LESSON OUTLINE

4.1 The New Imperialism
HSS 10.4.1, HSS 10.4.2; Analysis CST.1, CST.2, HRE.4, HI.1

4.2 European Colonies in Africa
HSS 10.4.2, HSS 10.4.4; Analysis CST.1, CST.2, HRE.4, HI.1

4.3 Europe and the Muslim World
HSS 10.4, HSS 10.4.2, HSS 10.4.3, HSS 10.4.4; Analysis CST.1, CST.2, HRE.4, HI.1

4.4 India Becomes a British Colony
HSS 10.4, HSS 10.4.2, HSS 10.4.3, HSS 10.4.4; Analysis CST.1, CST.2, CST.3, HRE.4, HI.1

4.5 China and the West
HSS 10.4, HSS 10.4.2, HSS 10.4.3, HSS 10.4.4; Analysis CST.1, CST.2, HRE.4, HI.1

4.6 The Modernization of Japan
HSS 10.4, HSS 10.4.2; Analysis CST.1, CST.2, HRE.4, HI.1

4.7 Southeast Asia and the Pacific
HSS 10.4, HSS 10.4.2, HSS 10.4.3, HSS 10.4.4; Analysis CST.1, CST.2, HRE.4, HI.1

4.8 The Americas in the Age of Imperialism
HSS 10.4, HSS 10.4.2, HSS 10.4.3, HSS 10.4.4; Analysis CST.1, CST.2, CST.3, HRE.4, HI.1

Key Events of the Age of Imperialism

1800 | 1825 | 1850 | 1875 | 1900 | 1925

1830 France begins efforts to conquer Algeria in North Africa.

1853 American ships commanded by Commodore Perry arrive in Japan.

1857 The Sepoy rebellion breaks out in India.

1868 Meiji restoration begins in Japan.

1886 Britain annexes Burma.

1899 The Boer War starts in South Africa.

1910 Japan annexes Korea.

1911 Sun Yixian becomes president of Chinese republic.

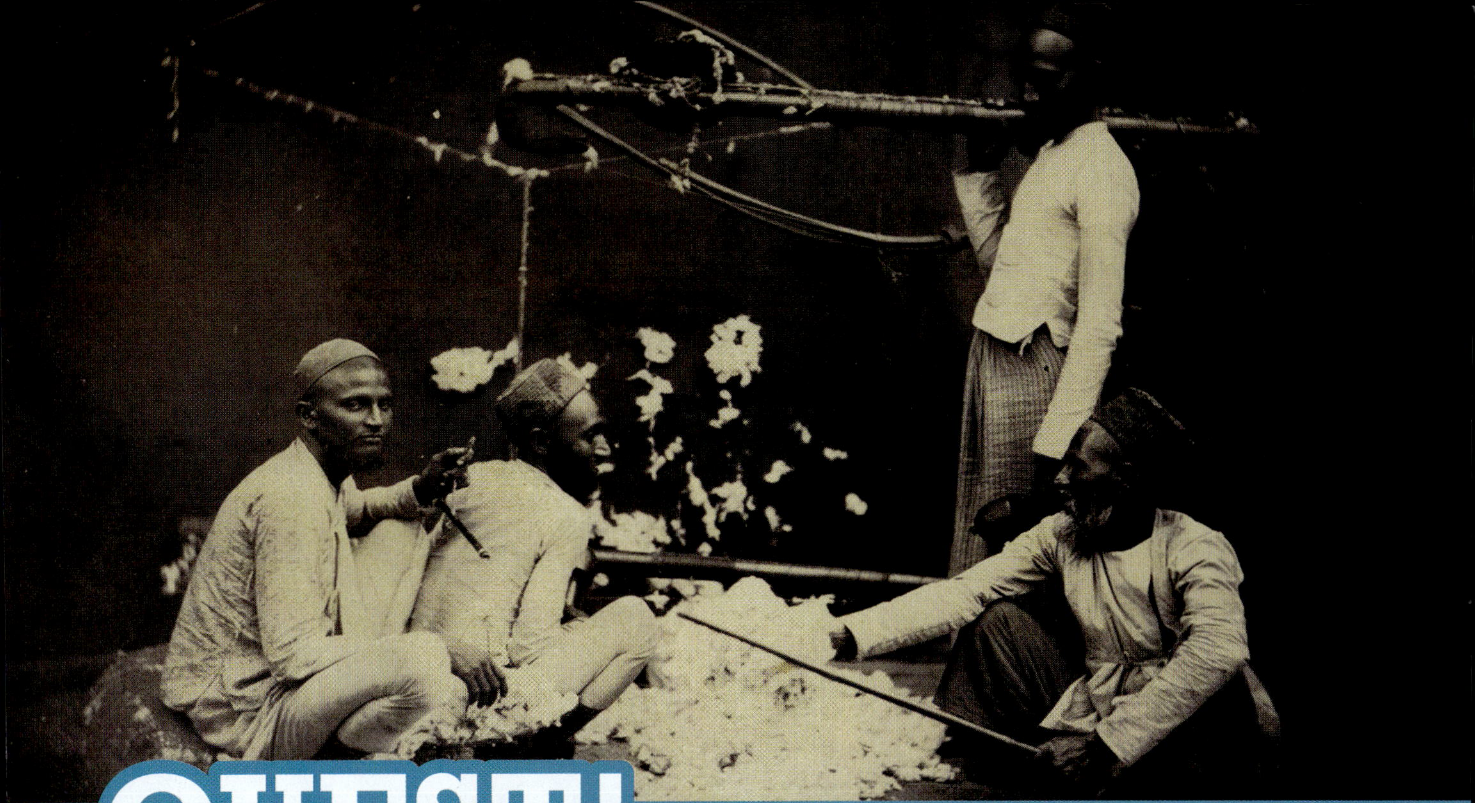

QUEST! TEAM PROJECT

Create a Power Point Presentation

How did imperialism affect India? In this Quest, you will work with your team to prepare a power point presentation that addresses the effects.

STEP 1

Examine the photo of the polo team in India in 1880. What does it tell you about British rule in India? What does it tell you about Indian traditions?

STEP 2

Study the documents on imperialism. Prepare a team chart listing what you have learned. Ask questions, evaluate the sources. Draft an outline for your presentation. Have team members choose a YES or NO side.

STEP 3

Begin preparing boards for your presentation. Try to use graphics to enhance your presentation. Refer to websites that may help you set up your power point presentation.

STEP 4

Share your presentation with your classmates. Reflect on the impact of British imperialism in India. Are there still effects of imperialism on India and other countries today?

PEARSON realize™ PearsonSchool.com/CASS

Go ONLINE for complete Quest materials

VIDEO ETEXT WRITING RUBRIC PDF ASSESSMENT

>> The Netherlands played a leading role in the first phase of imperialism, from 1500 to 1800. The Dutch East India Company protected Dutch trade in the Indian Ocean and even had the right to make treaties and maintain its own armed forces.

4.1 During the Industrial Revolution, the Western world was transformed. Advances in science and technology, industry, transportation, and communication strengthened the West, making it more powerful than any society in history.

Bounce to Activate Flipped Video

>> Objectives

Explain the political, economic, and social causes of European imperialism.

Understand how technology and other factors contributed to the spread of imperialism.

Describe the characteristics of imperial rule.

Summarize the cultural, political, and social effects of imperialism.

>> Key Terms

imperialism
protectorate
sphere of influence

The New Imperialism

Motivations for the New Imperialism

Armed with new economic and political power, Western nations set out to expand their overseas empires. Between 1870 and 1914, European nations brought much of the world and its people under their control.

European Expansion During the Age of Discovery European imperialism did not begin in the 1800s. **Imperialism** is the policy of one country's political, economic, or cultural domination over other lands and territories. During the Age of Discovery from the 1400s to the 1600s, Spain, Portugal, Britain, and France set up colonies in the Americas. Spain also seized control of the Philippine Islands.

Elsewhere, European nations gained only small outposts overseas. Portugal, Spain, and the Netherlands won footholds in Southeast Asia. The British and French were fierce rivals for trading rights in India. Europeans built trading forts on the coasts of Africa and negotiated limited trade with China and Japan.

Between 1500 and 1800, Europe had relatively little influence on the lives of the peoples in China, India, or Africa. Europeans traded with merchants in these lands but did not control any large territory, except in the Americas.

Expansion Turns into Empire Building By the 1800s, European nations with strong central governments had become more powerful. As the Industrial Revolution took off, some European nations grew rich. Spurred on by their new economic and military strength, these nations embarked on a path of aggressive expansion that modern historians call the "new imperialism." The new imperialism was a period in which industrial nations scrambled for territories that would provide them with raw materials and serve as markets for their manufactured goods.

In just a few decades, beginning in the 1870s, Europeans brought much of the world under their control. The new imperialism exploded out of a combination of causes. The main causes can be categorized as: economic, political, military, humanitarian, and religious.

Need for Resources Drives Further Expansion The Industrial Revolution created needs and desires that spurred overseas expansion. Manufacturers wanted access to natural resources such as rubber, petroleum, manganese for steel, and palm oil for machinery. They also wanted to expand their global markets by increasing the number of consumers to whom they could sell their manufactured goods.

Bankers, too, backed overseas expansion, which would provide new opportunities for investments. For some countries, colonies offered a valuable outlet for rapidly growing populations.

Political and Military Motives Political and military issues were closely linked to economic motives. Steam-powered merchant ships and naval vessels needed bases around the world to take on coal and supplies. Industrial powers seized islands or harbors to satisfy these needs.

Nationalism, a driving force in Europe throughout the 1800s, played a major role too. As Europeans started seizing territories overseas, it set off a race among rival nations. When France moved into West Africa, rival nations like Britain and Germany seized nearby African lands to halt further French expansion.

Western leaders claimed that colonies were needed to protect their national security interests. Sometimes, Western nations acquired colonies for the prestige of ruling a global empire.

Humanitarian and Religious Goals Many Westerners felt a genuine concern for their "little brothers" beyond the seas. Missionaries, doctors, and colonial officials believed they had a duty to spread what they saw as the blessings of Western civilization, including its medicine, law, and the Christian religion.

Influence of Social Darwinism Behind the idea that the West had a civilizing mission was a growing sense of racial superiority in the West. Many Westerners had embraced the ideas of Social Darwinism. They applied Darwin's ideas about natural selection and survival of the fittest to human societies. European races, they argued, were superior to all others, and imperial conquest of weaker races was simply nature's way of improving the human species.

Although this reasoning was never part of Darwin's ideas, it became popular among many people in the West. As a result, the cultural heritage of millions of non-Westerners was destroyed because their societies were deemed inferior.

SUMMARIZE What main factors contributed to European imperialism in the 1800s?

>> The growth of European industrial economies required raw materials to fuel its factories. New colonies provided both natural resources and new markets for European manufactured goods.

Bounce to Activate Map

Western Imperialism Spreads Rapidly

Starting in the late 1800s, the great powers of Europe divided up almost all of Africa along with large chunks of Asia. The European powers included Britain, France, Germany, Austria-Hungary, Russia, and Italy. The United States acquired the Philippines and gained influence in parts of Latin America.

Every corner of the globe was claimed by a Western power. Leading the way were explorers, missionaries, merchants, soldiers, and settlers. The reasons for the success of Western imperialism in the late 1800s and early 1900s varied and so did the kinds of governments imposed by Western powers on their newly acquired territories.

Vulnerable Non-Western States While European nations had grown stronger in the 1800s, several older civilizations were in decline. In the Middle East, the once powerful Ottomans faced many challenges from within their diverse empire. Weak rulers in Mughal (MOO gul) India triggered internal unrest with less tolerant policies toward Hindus. In China, Qing (ching) rulers resisted calls for modernization with disastrous consequences.

>> American author Mark Twain was an outspoken critic of both imperialism and the brutal Belgian rule in the Congo. In 1905, he published *King Leopold's Soliloquy*, which brought international attention to the situation.

Bounce to Activate Gallery

In West Africa, wars among African peoples and the damaging effects of the slave trade had undermined long-established kingdoms and city-states. Newer African states were not strong enough to resist the Western onslaught. Many Africans lived in small communities with no strong, centralized kingdom to protect them.

Western Advantages European powers had the advantages of strong economies, well-organized governments, and powerful armies and navies. Superior technology, including riverboats and the telegraph, as well as improved medical knowledge also played a role. The discovery of quinine in 1817 and other new medicines helped Europeans survive deadly tropical diseases such as malaria that had prevented them from exploring tropical regions in Africa.

Equally important, new weaponry gave Westerners a huge advantage. Advances such as Maxim guns—the earliest machine guns—along with repeating rifles and steam-driven warships were very strong arguments in persuading Africans and Asians to accept Western control.

Finally, Europeans often played rival groups within a region against one another. In India, the British successfully used rivalries between Hindu and Muslim princes to their advantage. In Africa, Europeans encouraged divisions among local rulers to keep them from joining forces against the newcomers.

Some Resist Imperialism People in Africa and Asia strongly resisted Western expansion. Many people fought the invaders, even though they had no weapons to equal the Maxim gun. Rulers in some areas tried to strengthen their societies against outsiders by reforming their own Muslim, Hindu, or Confucian traditions.

Although European powers defeated almost all the armed resistance, the struggle against imperialism continued. European rule turned many native peoples into forced laborers with no freedom of movement. By the early 1900s, nationalist movements were emerging. Western-educated Africans and Asians used Enlightenment ideas about freedom and liberty to call for an end to colonial rule. Tens of thousands in colonies around the world joined national liberation movements.

Critics at Home In the West, a small group of anti-imperialists emerged. Some argued that colonialism was a tool of the rich. Others opposed imperialist expansion because they wanted to focus on improving conditions for people in the West rather than imposing change on other cultures. Still others called imperialism immoral. Westerners, they pointed out, were moving toward greater democracy at home but were imposing undemocratic rule on other peoples.

EXPLAIN How did Western imperialism spread through Africa and Asia so quickly?

Types of Imperial Rule

The new imperialism took several forms. In many areas, imperial powers established colonies. They sent governors, officials, and soldiers to control the people and set up a colonial bureaucracy. France and Britain, the leading imperial powers, developed different kinds of colonial rule.

Direct and Indirect Rule The French practiced direct rule, sending officials and soldiers from France to administer their colonies. Their goal was to impose French culture on their colonies and turn them into French provinces. Direct rule reflected the European belief that colonial people were incapable of ruling themselves.

The British, by contrast, used indirect rule. Under the system of indirect rule, a British governor and council of advisers made laws for each colony. Local rulers loyal to the governor retained some authority and served as agents for the British. The British encouraged the children of the local ruling class to get an education in Britain. In that way, a new generation was groomed to become agents of indirect rule—and of Western civilization.

Indirect rule differed from direct rule because it did not replace traditional rulers with European officials. Yet local rulers had only limited power and did not influence government decisions. Under both direct and indirect rule, the result was the same. Traditional rulers no longer had power or influence.

Other Types of Imperial Rule In some places, Western powers established a protectorate. In a **protectorate,** local rulers were left in place but were expected to follow the advice of European advisers on issues such as trade or missionary activity. A protectorate had certain advantages over a colony. It cost less to run than a colony and usually did not require a large commitment of military forces unless a crisis occurred.

A third form of Western control was the **sphere of influence,** an area in which an outside power claimed exclusive investment or trading privileges.

>> The French practiced direct rule in their colonies. Here, French soldiers speak with an Algerian man. **Infer** What were the costs and benefits of direct rule?

Europeans carved out spheres of influence in China and elsewhere to prevent conflicts among themselves. The United States claimed parts of Latin America as its sphere of influence, holding off European powers that might compete with its interest.

COMPARE AND CONTRAST Compare and contrast how Britain and France ruled their colonies.

The Effects of Imperialism

The new imperialism profoundly affected the political, economic, and social life of societies around the world. Colonial rule disrupted old civilizations and ways of life. European powers imposed alien cultures on people who had different values and religious beliefs.

Another effect of imperialism was the continuous spread of early globalization. The term "globalization" may be recent but the changes represented by the term are historical and occurred long before the twentieth century. The Industrial Revolution and Imperialism were developments that had worldwide consequences. New inventions replaced the old models of transportation and communication which not only changed life during the industrial revolution but affected colonization and imperialism. With powerful weapons and sea vessels, Western countries were able to conquer areas in other parts of the world. These events changed trade, political systems, cultures, economies, and populations. Global migration and economic exchange had begun.

Political Changes In conquered territories, European nations set up governments that reflected their own traditions. They introduced European legal systems that relied on abstract principles of right and wrong. By contrast, traditional African forms of justice had emphasized consensus, or general agreement. Many African societies saw these foreign principles as unjust, especially when Europeans used these laws to take land from local people.

As Europeans carved up the world, they drew borders around the territories they claimed. Often, these artificially-drawn borders split ethnic or cultural groups. Or they lumped people who shared no common heritage together into one colony.

>> Missionaries brought not only religion, but cultural change. Girls at this French missionary school in China learn Christmas carols. **Analyze Context** What evidence can you find in the photo that this is a missionary school?

Economic Changes European powers expected their colonies to be profitable. Colonial rulers therefore tapped local mineral and agricultural resources. Where mineral resources were lacking, colonial powers developed cash crops, such as rubber, cotton, palm oil, and peanuts. A cash crop is raised to be sold for money on the world market. The rise or fall of prices for cash crops affected standards of living in the colonies.

During the Age of Imperialism, a new global economic pattern emerged. Colonies provided raw materials for the factories of the industrial powers. European colonial powers then sold their manufactured goods to their colonies. The export of cash crops and natural resources in exchange for manufactured goods left colonies dependent on markets in the industrial world. Imports of machine-made goods destroyed indigenous cottage industries.

Growth of a Money Economy The costs of governing colonies were huge, from salaries for officials and the military, to the costs of building roads, railroads, and schools. To pay for these costs, colonial governments required local people to pay taxes in cash.

The only way people could earn cash was to sell their labor, working on large plantations or in factories and mines owned by Europeans. Some became indentured servants or forced laborers who were shipped to other parts of the world to work on plantations or building projects.

Social and Cultural Changes The rise of the money economy contributed to the breakdown of traditional cultures. Until Europeans arrived, most people lived in close-knit villages that had subsistence economies. People produced the goods they needed or traded for goods they could not produce. As the money economy grew, people needed to have cash.

To earn money, men often took jobs in distant mines or plantations. Their long absences undermined family life. Some families moved to colonial cities, hoping to improve their positions. As a result, the close-knit village life declined.

Christian missionaries worked hard to win converts, urging newcomers to the faith to reject traditional beliefs and customs. Missionaries set up schools that emphasized the superiority of Western civilization. Impressed by European wealth, power, and teachings, many colonial people embraced Christianity, rejected their traditional cultures, and accepted the idea of European superiority.

Improvements Bring Benefits and Disadvantages Although the new imperialism broke down traditional patterns of life, some people argue that colonial rule brought important benefits. Europeans developed their colonies economically, building roads and railroads and setting up telegraph systems.

Improvements in transportation and communication had advantages and disadvantages. They made travel easier and faster. Economic development created jobs that enabled colonial people to acquire new skills, although most were forced to work for very low wages.

Roads and railroads were built to benefit colonial rulers, not the people they controlled. Railroads linked plantations and mines to ports, where cash crops and raw materials were shipped overseas. New transportation systems allowed colonial governments to extend their control and encouraged the migration of workers.

Colonial governments and missionaries introduced improved medical care and better methods of sanitation. Missionaries set up hospitals and clinics and dedicated their lives to improving healthcare. New crops, tools, and farming methods increased food production. In many places, colonial rule secured peace by ending local warfare.

CATEGORIZE How is migrating to find work a cultural as well as an economic effect of imperialism?

>> Coffee and tea were grown on plantations for the export market. Land used for these and other cash crops was not used to grow food. **Summarize** How did growing cash crops like coffee change colonized people's lives?

ASSESSMENT

1. **Identify Cause and Effect** How did the Industrial Revolution lead to the new imperialism?
2. **Cite Evidence** How did Western nations come to dominate much of the world in the late 1800s?
3. **Distinguish** Why was Social Darwinism important to the new imperialism?
4. **Summarize** What were the long-term effects of imperialism on the colonized peoples?
5. **Predict Consequences** How might grouping several rival ethnic groups into one political unit cause friction once that region gains independence?

>> Europeans began trading along the African coast in the 1500s. Centuries later, they began moving into the continent's interior.

4.2 Between 1870 and 1914, Britain, France, Germany, and other European powers scrambled to carve up the African continent. They set up dozens of colonies and ruled over the lives of millions of people. Although people in Africa resisted, they could not hold back the tide of European conquest.

Bounce to Activate Flipped Video

>> Objectives

Describe the forces that shaped Africa in the early 1800s.

Explain why European contact with Africa increased.

Analyze how European nations carved up Africa.

Describe African resistance to imperialism.

>> Key Terms

Usman dan Fodio
Shaka
paternalistic
David Livingstone
Henry Stanley
Leopold II
Boer War
Samori Touré
Yaa Asantewaa
Nehanda
Menelik II
elite

European Colonies in Africa

Africa Before Imperialism

Africa is a huge continent, nearly three times the size of Europe, with diverse regions and cultures. Before the scramble for Africa, people living on the continent spoke hundreds of languages and had developed varied governments. Some people lived in large centralized states, while others lived in village communities. Many still lived in nomadic societies.

North Africa North Africa includes the fertile land along the Mediterranean and the enormous Sahara. For centuries before 1800, the region had been part of the Muslim world. In the early 1800s, much of North Africa, including Egypt, was still ruled by the weakening Ottoman empire.

Islamic Conquest in West Africa In the great savanna region of West Africa, an Islamic reform movement brought change. It began among the Fulani people in what is today northern Nigeria. There, the scholar and preacher **Usman dan Fodio** (oo SMAHN dahn foh DEE oh) denounced the corruption of the local Hausa rulers. He called for social and religious reforms to purify and revive Islam. Under Usman and other leaders, several new Muslim states arose, built on trade, farming, and herding.

Usman dan Fodio ruled the Sokoto Caliphate, the largest empire in Africa since the fall of Songhai. At its height in the mid-1800s, it stretched for 1,500 miles and included 30 emirates, or smaller states. During this time, literacy increased, local wars were quieted, and trade improved. Their success inspired other Muslim reform movements in West Africa. Between about 1780 and 1880, other Islamic leaders replaced old rulers or set up new states in West Africa.

In the forest regions, strong states like the Asante (uh SAHN teh) kingdom had emerged. The Asante traded with both Europeans and Muslims. Asante power was limited, however. They controlled several smaller states that felt no loyalty to the central government. These tributary states were ready to turn to other protectors who might help them defeat their Asante rulers. European powers would exploit this lack of unity.

>> When Europeans arrived in Tanzania, they encountered small village communities like this Utiri village.

Bounce to Activate Map

East Africa Islam had long influenced coastal regions of East Africa, from the Red Sea south to port cities like Mombasa (mahm BAH suh) and Kilwa (KEEL wah). These cities had suffered setbacks when the Portuguese arrived in the early 1500s.

Yet East African cities still sent trading ships to the Red Sea or Persian Gulf. The cargoes were human captives, who had been seized in the interior and marched to the coast. From there, they were shipped as slaves to the Middle East. Ivory and copper from Central Africa were also exchanged for goods such as cloth and firearms.

>> East African port cities often served as centers for the slave trade. This slave market was on the island of Zanzibar.

Southern Africa In the early 1800s, southern Africa was in turmoil as a result of the Zulu wars. The Zulu people had migrated into southern Africa in the 1500s. By the 1800s, they had emerged as a major force in southern Africa under a ruthless and brilliant leader, **Shaka.**

Shaka's war disrupted life across southern Africa. Groups driven from their homelands by the Zulus then adopted Shaka's tactics.

They migrated north, conquering still other peoples and creating their own powerful states. By the 1830s, the Zulus faced a new threat, the arrival of well-armed, mounted Boers, descendants of Dutch farmers who were migrating north from the Cape Colony.

In 1806, the Cape Colony had passed from the Dutch to the British. Many Boers resented British laws that abolished slavery and otherwise interfered with their way of life. To escape British rule, they loaded their goods into covered wagons and started north. Several thousand Boer families joined this "Great Trek."

As the migrating Boers came into contact with Zulus, fighting quickly broke out. At first, Zulu regiments held their own. But in the end, Zulu spears could not defeat Boer guns. The struggle for control of the land would rage until the end of the century.

Impact of the Slave Trade For centuries, Europeans had taken Africans as slaves to work the plantations and mines of the Americas. Arabs and Africans had also traded in slaves. Beginning in the early 1800s, European nations slowly outlawed the slave trade, though it took years to end.

In Britain and the United States, abolitionists promoted the idea of returning freed slaves to Africa. In 1787, the British organized Sierra Leone in West Africa as a colony for former slaves. Later, some free blacks from the United States settled in nearby Liberia. By 1847, Liberia had become an independent state.

Slavery still existed, however. Arab and African slave traders continued to seize people from Central and East Africa to work as slaves in the Middle East and Asia well into the 1800s. Thus the demand for slaves remained and the slave trade continued in Africa. As reports of this slave trade spread, abolitionists and European explorers demanded action to end it.

>> Freetown, Sierra Leone, was settled by freed slaves from all over the world. Many had their origins in regions of Africa. Sierra Leone became a center of education for Africans.

SUMMARIZE What factors shaped each of the main regions of Africa during the early 1800s?

European Contact Increases

From the 1400s through the 1700s, Europeans traded along the African coast, but they knew very little about the continent. They relied on Africans to bring slaves and trade goods, such as ivory and gold, from the interior to their trading posts on the coast.

European interest in Africa increased during the Age of Imperialism. Spurred on by trading companies and a desire for adventure, Europeans explored the rivers of Africa. In the past, difficult geography, resistance by Africans, and diseases had all kept Europeans from moving into the interior of Africa. In the 1880s, medical advances and river steamships helped Europeans move inland.

Explorers Push into Africa's Interior In the early 1800s, European explorers began pushing into the interior of Africa. Daring adventurers like Mungo Park and Richard Burton set out to map the course and sources of the great African rivers such as the Niger, the Nile, and the Congo.

Some explorers were self-promoters who wrote glowing accounts of their bold deeds. While they were fascinated by African geography, they had little understanding of the peoples they met. All, however, endured great hardships while exploring Africa.

Missionaries Follow Explorers Catholic and Protestant missionaries followed the explorers. All across Africa, they sought to win people to Christianity. The missionaries were sincere in their desire to help Africans. They built schools and medical clinics alongside churches. They also focused attention on the evils of the slave trade.

Still, missionaries, like most Westerners, took a **paternalistic** view of Africans, meaning they saw them as children in need of guidance. To them, African cultures and religions were "degraded." They urged Africans to reject their own traditions in favor of Western civilization.

Africa in 1914

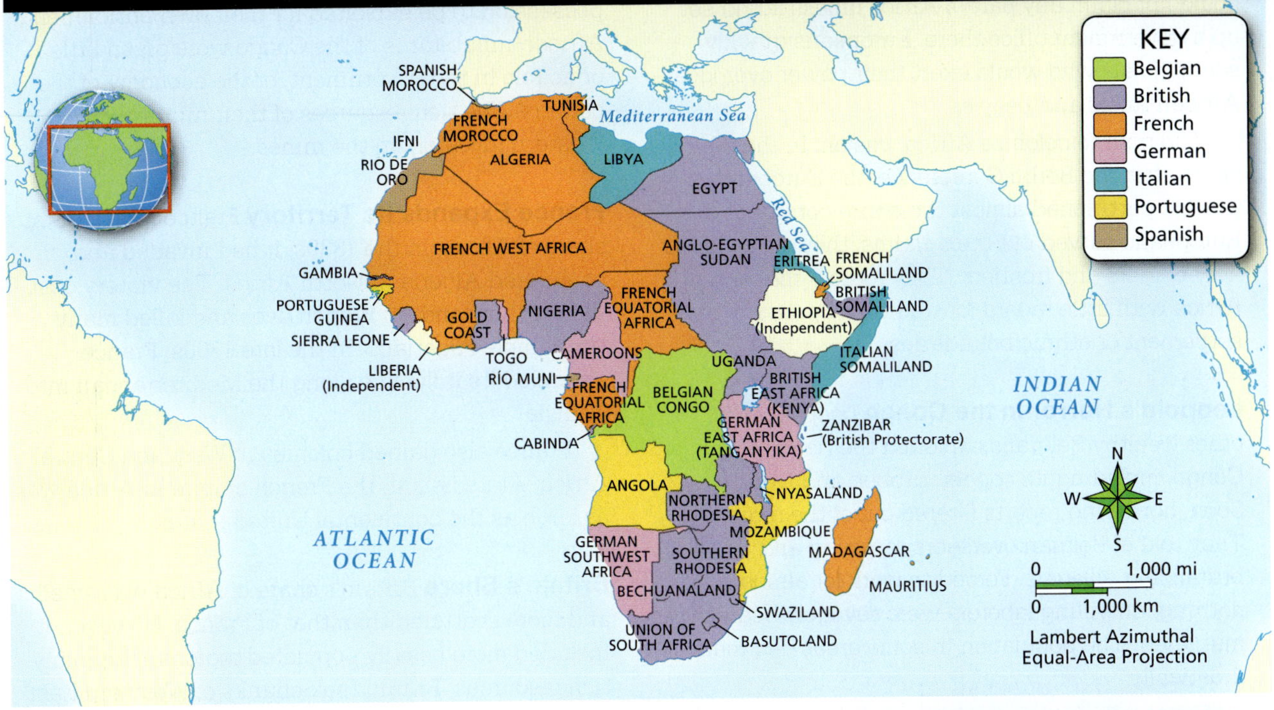

>> **Analyze Maps** One goal of British imperialists in Africa was to gain control "from Cairo to the Cape" (South Africa). Which colony stood in the way of that plan? Which European country controlled that colony?

Bounce to Activate Map

Livingstone's Explorations More than anyone else, **David Livingstone,** a British doctor and missionary, captured the imaginations of Westerners. For 30 years, he crisscrossed Africa. He wrote about the many peoples he met with more sympathy and less bias than did most Europeans.

He relentlessly opposed the slave trade, which remained a profitable business for some. The only way to end this cruel traffic, he believed, was to open up the interior of Africa to Christianity and trade.

Europeans credited Livingstone with "discovering" the huge waterfalls on the Zambezi River. He named them Victoria Falls, after Britain's Queen Victoria. The Africans who lived nearby, however, had long known the falls as Mosi oa Tunya, "the smoke that thunders."

Livingstone blazed a trail that others soon followed. In 1869, the journalist **Henry Stanley** trekked into Central Africa to find Livingstone, who had not been heard from for years. He finally tracked him down in 1871 in what is today Tanzania, greeting him with the now-legendary question "Dr. Livingstone, I presume?"

RECALL Why did European contact with Africa increase in the late 1800s?

European Nations Scramble for Colonies

Shortly after Stanley met up with Livingstone, King **Leopold II** of Belgium hired Stanley to explore the Congo River basin and arrange trade treaties with African leaders. Publicly, Leopold spoke of a civilizing mission to carry the light "that for millions of men still plunged in barbarism will be the dawn of a better era." Privately, he dreamed of conquest and profit.

Leopold's activities in the Congo set off a scramble by other nations. Before long, Britain, France, and Germany were pressing rival claims to the region. The scramble for Africa had begun. It would end with the partition of virtually the entire continent among the great powers of Europe.

The Berlin Conference To avoid bloodshed, European powers met at an international conference in 1884. It took place not in Africa but in Berlin, Germany. No Africans were invited to the conference.

At the Berlin Conference, European powers recognized Leopold's private claims to the Congo Free State but called for free trade on the Congo and Niger rivers.

They further agreed that a European power could not claim any part of Africa unless it had set up a government office there. Europeans quickly sent officials who would exert their power over local African rulers and peoples.

The rush to colonize Africa was on. In the 20 years after the Berlin Conference, the European powers partitioned almost the entire continent. As Europeans carved out their claims, they established new borders and frontiers. They redrew the map of Africa with little regard for traditional patterns of settlement or ethnic boundaries.

Leopold's Horror in the Congo Leopold and other wealthy Belgians exploited the riches of the Congo, including its copper, rubber, and ivory. Soon, horrifying reports filtered out of the region. They told of Belgian overseers torturing and brutalizing villagers. Forced to work for almost nothing, unwilling laborers were savagely beaten or mutilated. The population in some areas declined drastically.

Eventually, international outrage forced Leopold to turn over his personal colony to the Belgian government. It became the Belgian Congo in 1908. Under Belgian rule, the worst abuses were ended.

>> A major resource that the Belgians wanted from the Congo was rubber. **Cite Evidence** What evidence in the photo indicates that these rubber workers were slaves?

Still, the Belgians regarded the Congo as a possession to be exploited for their own enrichment. African inhabitants of the Congo were given little or no role in the government, or the economy of the country. The rich resources of their mines went to Western investors in the mines.

France Expands Its Territory France took a giant share of Africa. In the 1830s, it had invaded and conquered Algeria in North Africa. The victory cost tens of thousands of French lives and killed many times more Algerians. In the late 1800s, France extended its influence along the Mediterranean into Tunisia.

France also gained colonies in West and Central Africa. At its height, the French empire in Africa was as large as the continental United States.

Britain's Share Britain's share of Africa was smaller and more scattered than that of France. However, it included more heavily populated regions with many rich resources. Britain took chunks of West and East Africa. It gained control of Egypt, pushed south into the Sudan, and ruled much of southern Africa.

The British industrialist Cecil Rhodes was a passionate imperialist who had made a fortune in mining in southern Africa. Rhodes dreamed of building a "Cape to Cairo" railway to link British possessions from Cape Town, South Africa, to Cairo, Egypt.

I care nothing about money for its own sake," he once wrote, "but it is a power—and I do like power." Rhodes helped Britain extend its African empire by one million square miles. The British colony of Rhodesia (now Zimbabwe), was named after him.

The Boer War In southern Africa, Britain clashed with the Boers, who were descendants of Dutch settlers. Britain had acquired the Cape Colony from the Dutch in 1806. The Boers—Dutch farmers—resented British rule and many had migrated north to set up their own republics.

In the late 1800s, however, the discovery of gold and diamonds in the Boer republics led to conflict with Britain. The **Boer War,** which lasted from 1899 to 1902, involved bitter guerrilla fighting. The British won, but at great cost.

In 1910, the British united the Cape Colony and the former Boer republics into the Union of South Africa. The new constitution set up a government run by whites and laid the foundation for a system of complete racial segregation that would remain in force until 1993.

Others Nations Join the Scramble Other European powers joined the scramble for African colonies. They wanted to bolster their national image and further their economic growth and influence. The Portuguese carved out colonies in Angola and Mozambique. Italy reached across the Mediterranean to occupy Libya and then pushed into the "horn" of Africa, at the southern end of the Red Sea.

Germany was newly united in 1871 under the expert leadership of Bismarck. At first, Bismarck had little interest in overseas expansion, but eventually realized the importance of colonies. In the 1880s, Germany took lands in Southwest Africa (now Namibia) and East Africa (now part of Tanzania) as well as what are today Cameroon and Togo. A German politician, trying to ease the worries of European rivals, explained, "We do not want to put anyone in the shade, but we also demand our place in the sun."

IDENTIFY CAUSE AND EFFECT How did King Leopold II set off a scramble for colonies in Africa?

>> French troops capture the city of Mascara in December 1835, during the French–Algerian War. **Infer** What advantages do the Algerian troops have? What advantages do the French troops have?

African Resistance

Europeans met armed resistance across the continent. In North Africa, the Algerians fought French expansion for years. In West Africa, **Samori Touré** (sah MAWR ee too RAY) fought French forces. Elsewhere in West Africa, the Ibo and Fulani struggled for years against the British advance. In southern Africa, the Zulus resisted British domination, handing them several grave defeats before the British finally succeeded.

Women Leaders of the Resistance In West Africa, the British faced the powerful Asante kingdom in a series of wars. When their king was exiled, the Asante people put themselves under the command of their queen, **Yaa Asantewaa** (YA uh ah sahn TAY wuh). She led the fight against the British in the last Asante war.

Another woman, **Nehanda** (neh HAHN duh), was a spiritual leader of the Shona people in what is today Zimbabwe. Nehanda inspired the Shona to resist British rule. In the 1890s, she and her husband were captured and executed by the British. Her courage, however, inspired later generations to fight for freedom.

Ethiopia Remains Independent In East Africa, the ancient Christian kingdom of Ethiopia successfully resisted European colonization and remained independent. Like feudal Europe, Ethiopia had been divided up among a number of rival princes who ruled their own domains.

In the late 1800s, however, a reforming ruler, **Menelik II,** began to modernize his country. He hired European experts to plan modern roads and bridges and set up a Western school system. He imported the latest weapons and European officers to help train his army. Thus, when Italy invaded Ethiopia in 1896,Menelik was prepared. At the battle of Adowa (AH duh wuh), the Ethiopians smashed the Italian invaders. Ethiopia, along with Liberia, were the only African nations to preserve independence.

Resistance Against Germany In East Africa, the Germans fought wide-ranging wars against groups resisting foreign rule. During the 1890s, the Uhehe harried German forces. The Germans gained control by using terror. Any groups linked to the resistance were killed or driven off the land. Some were turned into forced laborers for settlers. In 1905, another rebellion, the Maji Maji War, erupted. In that conflict too, the Germans triumphed only after burning acres and acres of farmland, leaving thousands of local people to die of starvation.

Two factors limited African resistance in East Africa. First, the slave trading states in East Africa

>> During the Age of Imperialism, some Africans adopted Western dress. The man wearing a Western jacket behind the Asante king was an Asante official.

had disrupted many small societies and made some Africans more sympathetic to European expansion. Second, the outbreak of rinderpest, a cattle disease, caused a disastrous famine. The epidemic, which killed 95 percent of all cattle in some areas, led to malnutrition and other diseases that affected people's ability to fight the invaders.

A New African Elite During the Age of Imperialism, a Western-educated African **elite,** emerged in both Africa and other parts of the world. Some middle-class people in Africa admired Western ways and rejected their own culture. Others valued their ancient traditions and condemned Western societies that upheld liberty and equality for white Western people only. By the early 1900s, African leaders were forging nationalist movements to pursue self-determination and independence.

DESCRIBE How did Ethiopians resist imperialism?

ASSESSMENT

1. **Describe** Name one development in each region of Africa in the early 1800s.
2. **Identify Cause and Effect** How did imperialist European powers claim control over most of Africa by the end of the 1800s?
3. **Analyze Information** What impact did explorers and missionaries have on Africa?
4. **Infer** Why do you think the Europeans did not invite Africans to the Berlin Conference?
5. **Summarize** How did Africans resist European imperialism?

4.3 In 1800, the Muslim world extended from North Africa to Southeast Asia. Much of this world was ruled by three giant Muslim empires—the Ottomans in the Middle East, the Mughals in India, and the Safavids (sah FAH vidz) in Persia. By this time, however, all three empires were in decline.

>> During the Battle of the Pyramids in 1798, Napoleon and his army captured the Egyptian city of Cairo.

Bounce to Activate Flipped Video

Europe and the Muslim World

>> **Objectives**

Explain how internal and external pressures shaped the Muslim world.

Identify the challenges facing the Ottoman empire and Persia.

Describe the ways Egypt tried to modernize, including the opening of the Suez Canal.

>> **Key Terms**

Muhammad Ahmad
Mahdi
pasha
sultan
genocide
Muhammad Ali
concession

Unrest in Muslim Regions

Napoleon Bonaparte's 1798 invasion of Egypt opened a new era in European contact with the Muslim world. It focused attention on the fading power of the Ottoman empire. By the early 1800s, European countries were nibbling at the fringes of the Muslim world. Before long, they would strike at its heartland.

Declining Empires The decay of these once-mighty empires had many causes. Central governments had lost control over powerful groups such as landowning nobles, military elites, and urban craft guilds. Corruption was widespread. In some places, Muslim scholars and religious leaders were allied with the state. In other areas, they helped to stir discontent against governments.

Muslim Reform Efforts In the 1700s and 1800s, reform movements sprang up across the Muslim world. Reformers in parts of Africa and Asia generally stressed religious piety and strict rules of behavior. Efforts to reform the practice of Islam touched off revolts and demands for political change.

Islamic revivals arose in Africa. Usman dan Fodio struggled to reform Muslim practices in northern Nigeria. In the Sudan, south of Egypt, **Muhammad Ahmad** (AHK mud) announced that he was the **Mahdi** (mahk DEE), the long-awaited savior of the faith. In the 1880s, the Mahdi and his followers fiercely resisted British expansion into the region. In modern Sudan, followers of the Mahdi still have much influence.

Another Islamic reform movement, the Wahhabi (wah HAHB ee) movement in Arabia, rejected the schools of theology and law that had emerged in the Ottoman empire. In their place, they wanted to recapture the purity and simplicity of Muhammad's original teachings.

In a true Islamic society, they declared, the government furthered the goals of Islam. An Arab prince led a Wahhabi revolt against Ottoman rule. Although the revolt was put down, the Wahhabi movement survived. Its teachings remain influential in the kingdom of Saudi Arabia today.

European Imperialism In addition to internal decay and stresses, the old Muslim empires faced the threat of Western imperialism. Through a mix of diplomacy and military threats, European powers won treaties giving them favorable trading terms. They then demanded special rights for Europeans residing in Muslim lands. They used excuses such as the need to protect their citizens' rights to intervene in local affairs. At times, they took over an entire region.

EXPLAIN How did Western powers gain the upper hand in Muslim regions of the world?

The Ottoman Empire Declines

At its height, the Ottoman empire extended across the Middle East, North Africa, and parts of Eastern Europe. By 1800, however, it faced serious challenges. Ambitious **pashas,** or provincial rulers, had increased their power. Economic problems and corruption added to Ottoman decay.

Nationalist Revolts As ideas of nationalism spread from Western Europe, internal revolts weakened the multi-ethnic Ottoman empire. Subject peoples in Eastern Europe, North Africa, and the Middle East threatened to break away.

In the Balkans, Greeks, Serbs, Bulgarians, and Romanians gained their independence. Revolts against Ottoman rule also erupted in Arabia, Lebanon, and Armenia. The Ottomans suppressed these uprisings, but another valuable territory, Egypt, slipped out of their control.

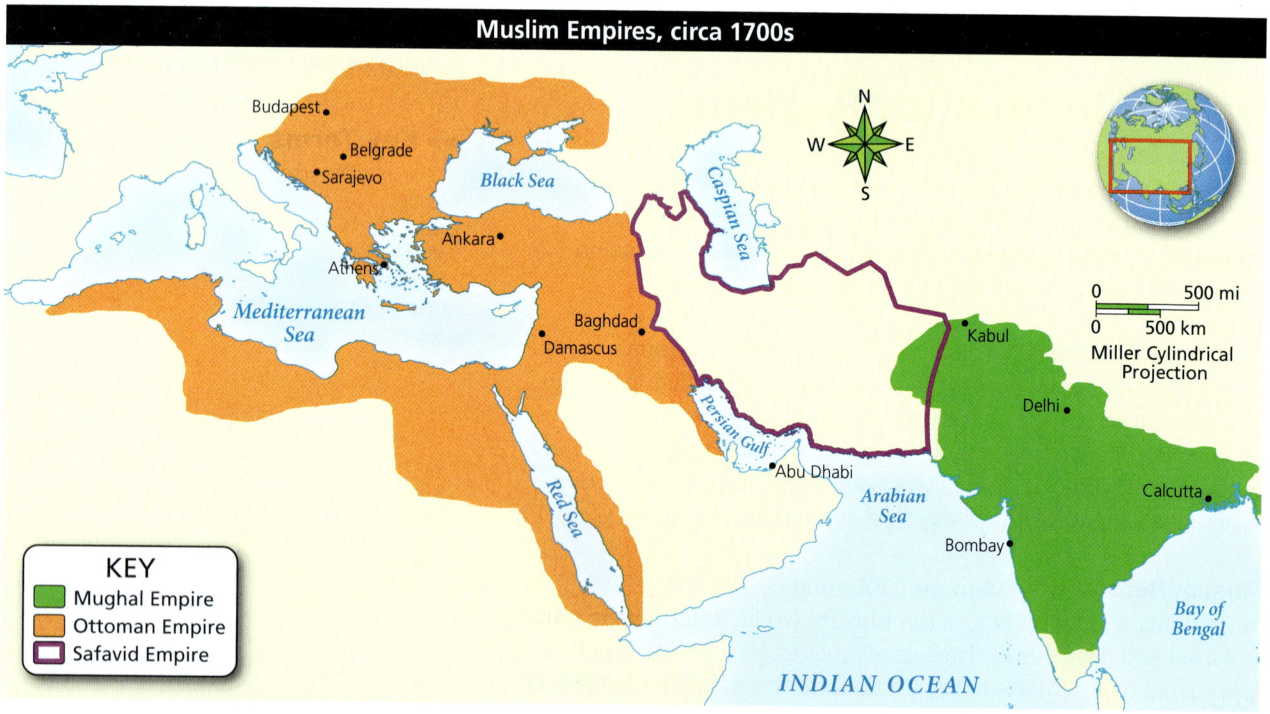

>> **Analyze Maps** Western imperialism gained steam at a time when the three major Muslim empires were in decline. In which empire might ethnic diversity have created internal challenges? Why?

Increasing European Pressure Britain, France, and Russia each sought to benefit from the slow crumbling of the Ottoman empire. After seizing Algeria in the 1830s, France cast its attention on other Ottoman-ruled lands. Russia schemed to gain control of the Turkish straits—the Bosporus (BAHS puh rus) and the Dardanelles. Control of these straits would give the Russians access to the Mediterranean Sea.

Britain tried to thwart Russia's ambitions, which it saw as a threat to its own power in the Mediterranean and beyond to India. During the Crimean War in the 1850s, Britain and France joined forces to help the Ottoman empire resist Russian expansion. By the late 1880s, however, France and Britain had extended their own influence over Ottoman lands. Finally, in 1898, the newly united German empire hoped to increase its influence in the region by building a Berlin-to-Baghdad railway.

Thanksgiving on the other side—No. 1 Thanksgiving on the other side—No. 2

THE POWERS WAITING TO DIVIDE THE TURKEY WHICH RUSSIA IS STILL PURSUING

>> **Analyze Political Cartoons** The European powers hoped to carve up the crumbling Ottoman empire for themselves. How do you know which figure in the cartoon represents the Ottoman empire?

Bounce to Activate Cartoon

Efforts to Westernize Since the late 1700s, several Ottoman rulers had seen the need for reform and looked to the West for ideas. They reorganized the bureaucracy and system of tax collection. They built railroads, improved education, and hired Europeans to train a modern military. Young men were sent to the West to study science and technology. Many returned with Western political ideas about democracy and equality.

The reforms also brought improved medical care and revitalized farming. These improvements, however, were a mixed blessing. Better health care resulted in a population explosion. The growing population increased competition for the best land, which led to unrest.

The adoption of Western ideas about government increased tension. Many officials objected to changes that were inspired by a foreign culture. For their part, repressive **sultans,** rulers of the Ottoman Turkish empire, rejected reform and tried to rebuild the autocratic power enjoyed by earlier rulers.

The Young Turks In the 1890s, a group of liberals formed a movement called the Young Turks. They insisted that reform was the only way to save the Ottoman empire. In 1908, the Young Turks overthrew the sultan. Before they could achieve their planned reforms, however, the Ottoman empire was plunged into the world war that erupted in 1914.

Armenian Genocide By the late 1800s, Turkish nationalism had grown stronger. In the 1890s, it took an ugly, intolerant course.

Traditionally, the Ottomans allowed its diverse religious and ethnic groups to live in their own communities and practice their own religions. By the 1890s, however, nationalism was igniting new tensions between Ottoman rulers and minority peoples. Spurred by Turkish nationalism, Ottoman rulers feared a further breakup of the empire. These tensions led to increasing persecution and eventually a brutal genocide of the Armenians, a Christian people concentrated in the eastern mountains of the empire. **Genocide** is a deliberate and systematic killing of people who belong to a particular racial, ethnic, or cultural group.

The Muslim Turks accused Christian Armenians of supporting Russian plans against the Ottoman empire. Using this as a pretext, they installed repressive policies against the Armenians in the 1890s. When Armenians protested, the sultan had tens of thousands of them slaughtered. Survivors fled, many of them to the United States. Still, over the next 25 years, another million or more Armenians were killed by the Turks or died from disease and starvation. The Armenian genocide would reach new heights during World War I.

DESCRIBE How were efforts to Westernize problematic for the Ottoman empire?

Modernization in Egypt

Egypt in 1800 was a semi-independent province of the Ottoman empire. In the early 1800s, it made great strides toward reform. Its success was due to **Muhammad Ali,** an Albanian Muslim soldier who was appointed governor of Egypt in 1805. Ali had helped to oust the French from Egypt. They were remnants of Napoleon's forces that had occupied the land for several years. The French occupation had disrupted Egypt's traditional government, which gave Muhammad Ali an opportunity to remake Egypt.

Reform Efforts Muhammad Ali is sometimes called the "founder of modern Egypt." He introduced a number of political and economic reforms. First, he ended the power of the old ruling oligarchy and seized huge farms from the old landowning class. He reduced the power of religious leaders and crushed any protest against his rule. He then set out to rebuild Egypt along modern lines. He improved tax collection and backed large irrigation projects to increase farm output.

Muhammad Ali ordered Egyptian farmers to plant a new kind of cotton, to be sold as a cash crop. By expanding cotton production and encouraging the development of many local industries, Ali brought Egypt into the growing network of world trade.

Muhammad Ali also brought Western military experts to Egypt to help him build a well-trained, modern army. He promoted education and the study of medicine. Before he died in 1849, he had set Egypt on the road to becoming a major Middle Eastern power.

The Suez Canal Muhammad Ali's successors lacked his skills, and Egypt came increasingly under foreign control. In 1858, a French entrepreneur, Ferdinand de Lesseps (LAY seps), organized a company to build the Suez Canal, a waterway connecting the Mediterranean and Red seas. Europe hailed its opening in 1869 because it greatly reduced the travel time between Europe and Asia. To Britain, especially, the canal was a "lifeline" to India, where its influence was increasing.

In 1875, the ruler of Egypt was unable to repay loans he had contracted for the canal and other modernization projects. To pay his debts, he sold his shares in the canal. The British prime minister Disraeli quickly bought them, giving Britain a controlling interest in the canal.

>> The British used their military strength to protect their interest in the Suez Canal. These troops were sent to Egypt during the 1882 Anglo-Egyptian War. **Identify Cause and Effect** Why would the British want to protect their control of the Suez Canal?

Bounce to Activate Gallery

Becoming a British Protectorate Britain soon expanded its influence in Egypt. When a nationalist revolt erupted in 1882, Britain made Egypt a protectorate. In theory, the governor of Egypt was still an official of the Ottoman government. In fact, he followed policies dictated by Britain.

Under British influence, Egypt continued to modernize. At the same time, nationalist discontent simmered and flared into protests and riots well into the next century.

GENERATE EXPLANATIONS How did Egypt fall under British control?

European Imperialism in Persia

Like the Ottoman empire, Persia faced major challenges in the 1800s. At first, the Qajar (kah JAHR) shahs, who ruled Persia from 1794 to 1925, exercised absolute power like the Safavids before them. Still, they did take steps to introduce reforms. The government improved finances and sponsored the building of railroads and telegraph lines. By the early 1900s, it was even experimenting with liberal reforms.

The Great Game Reform, however, did not save Persia from Western imperialism. Both Russia and Britain battled for influence in the area. Russia wanted to protect its southern frontier and expand into Central Asia. Britain wanted to protect its interests in India.

Throughout the 1800s, Britain was determined to stop Russia's southward expansion,fearing that Russia might win control of northern India. Cartoons of the time showed the British lion pitted against the Russian bear. The competition between Russia and Britain in the region became known as the "Great Game." During this time, the two European powers sought to increase their influence in the Ottoman empire, Persia, Afghanistan, and Tibet. Persia was a particular focus of their rivalry.

For a time, each nation set up its own sphere of influence in Persia. Russia operated in the north and Britain in the south. The discovery of oil in the early 1900s upset the balance and generally heightened foreign interest in the region. Both Russia and Britain plotted to win control of the Persian oil fields and gain other rights.

Tensions Within Persia During the Age of Imperialism, Persia experienced changes similar to those of other regions subject to European expansion. It became a supplier of raw materials for industrial Europe and a market for its manufactured goods. Local Persian industries declined, unable to compete with factory-made goods. Much land was converted into producing cash crops, reducing local food production.

To raise money, the Persian government granted **concessions,** or special rights given to foreign companies or individuals. The money was supposed to be used to modernize the country but was often wasted on the extravagant Persian court. Persian nationalists and reformers protested the concessions, even more so after Russia sent troops to protect its concessions.

Persian nationalists included two very different groups. Some Persians, especially from the growing urban middle classes, wanted to move swiftly to adopt Western ways. Others, led by Muslim religious leaders, condemned the Persian government and Western influences. The religious leaders often spoke for the masses of the people who lived in rural poverty and resented government interference in their traditional way of life.

>> The discovery of oil in Persia led to a greater British and Russian presence in the country, which sparked a nationalist backlash.

ANALYZE INFORMATION For what reason did Persia attract foreign interest in the early 1900s?

ASSESSMENT

1. **Make Generalizations** What was the goal of the Wahhabi reform movement?
2. **Identify Cause and Effect** What effect did nationalism have on the Ottoman empire during the 1800s?
3. **Express Ideas Clearly** Who was Muhammad Ali, and why was he a significant figure?
4. **Summarize** How did Britain gain control of the Suez Canal?
5. **Generate Explanations** Why did foreign interest in Persia increase in the early 1900s?

>> **Draw Conclusions** An official of the British East India Company rides in an Indian procession in the early 1800s. How does the painting convey the power of the British?

Bounce to Activate Flipped Video

4.4 **During the 1500s and 1600s, the Mughals presided over a powerful empire in India. By the mid-1700s, however, the Mughal empire was in decline. When Mughal rulers were strong, the British East India Company gained only limited trading rights on the fringe of the empire.**

>> Objectives

Understand the causes and effects of the Sepoy Rebellion.

Explain the impact of British rule on India.

Describe how the British and Indians viewed one another.

Trace the origins of Indian nationalism.

>> Key Terms

sati
sepoy
viceroy
deforestation
Ram Mohun Roy
purdah

India Becomes a British Colony

The British East India Company

As Mughal power declined, the company's influence grew and it drove its rival France out of India. By the mid-1800s, the British East India Company controlled three fifths of India. In the 1800s, Britain turned its commercial interests in India into political ones.

Exploitation of Indian Diversity Even when Mughal power was at its height, India was home to many people and cultures. As Mughal power crumbled, India became fragmented. Indians speaking dozens of different languages and with different traditions were not able to unite against the newcomers.

The British took advantage of Indian divisions by playing rival princes against each other. When local disputes led to conflict, the British stepped in. Where diplomacy or intrigue did not work, the British used their superior weapons to overpower local rulers.

Implementation of British Policies The East India Company's main goal in India was to make money, and leading officials often grew rich. At the same time, the company did work to improve roads, preserve peace, and reduce banditry.

By the early 1800s, British officials introduced Western education and legal procedures. Missionaries converted Indians to Christianity, which they felt was superior to Indian religions. The British also pressed for social change. They worked to end forms of indentured servitude in India and to improve the position of women within the family. One law banned **sati** (SUH tee), a custom practiced mainly by the upper classes. It called for a widow to join her husband in death by throwing herself on his funeral pyre.

However, the British used caste differences to their advantage. Caste was used to determine how the native population could best serve British rule. The census the British implemented made caste distinctions more rigid and permanent.

Increasing Discontent In the 1850s, the British East India Company took several unpopular steps that deepened anger with the British. The company had relied on Indian soldiers, called **sepoys,** (SEE poyz), that it had recruited for service. Sepoys had helped the company expand its control of India. As its empire grew, the British required sepoys to serve anywhere, either in India or overseas. For some orthodox Hindus, however, overseas travel was an offense against their religion. The East India Company, prompted by Indian reformers, also passed a law that allowed widows to remarry.

The final insult came in 1857 when the British issued new rifles to the sepoys. Troops had to bite off the tips of cartridges before loading them into the rifles. The cartridges, however, were greased with animal fat—either from cows, which Hindus considered sacred, or from pigs, which were forbidden to Muslims. When troops refused the order to "load rifles," they were dismissed without pay or imprisoned.

The Sepoy Rebellion Angry sepoys rose up against their British officers. The Sepoy Rebellion swept across northern and central India. Several sepoy regiments marched off to Delhi, the old Mughal capital. There, they hailed the last Mughal ruler as their leader. Other sepoys called on both Hindus and Muslims to support the uprising.

In some places, the sepoys brutally massacred British men, women, and children. The British soon rallied and crushed the revolt. They then took terrible revenge for their earlier losses, torching villages and slaughtering thousands of unarmed Indians.

Impact of the Rebellion The Sepoy Rebellion left a bitter legacy of fear, hatred, and mistrust on both sides. It also brought major changes in British policy.

>> **Infer** Indian sepoys were soldiers employed by the British East India Company in the mid-1800s. What item or items in the image reflect India's culture, and which show a British influence?

Bounce to Activate Gallery

>> During the Sepoy Rebellion, the British battled Indian forces around Delhi, a city that was alternately controlled by both the British and the sepoys.

In 1858, Parliament ended the rule of the East India Company and put India directly under the British crown. It sent more troops to India, taxing Indians to pay the cost of these occupying forces.

The rebellion slowed the "reforms" that had angered Hindus and Muslims. In India, discontent continued to feed a growing nationalist movement. Indian nationalists later called the 1857 uprising India's First War of Independence.

IDENTIFY CAUSE AND EFFECT What was the primary cause of the Sepoy Rebellion?

India Under British Rule

After 1858, Parliament set up a system of colonial rule in India which became known as the British Raj. A British **viceroy** in India governed in the name of the queen, and British officials held the top positions in the civil service and army. Indians filled most other jobs. With their cooperation, the British made India the "brightest jewel" in the crown of their empire.

British policies were designed to fit India into the overall British economy. At the same time, British officials felt they were helping India to modernize. In their terms, modernizing meant adopting not only Western technology but also Western culture.

>> This railway station was built in India in 1878 during the British Raj. British architects incorporated traditional Indian architectural features into the design.

Bounce to Activate Illustration

An Unequal Partnership Britain saw India both as a market and as a source of raw materials. To this end, the British built roads and an impressive railroad network. Improved transportation let the British sell their factory-made goods across the subcontinent and carry Indian cotton, jute, and coal to coastal ports for transport to factories in England.

New methods of communication, such as the telegraph, also gave Britain better control of India. After the Suez Canal opened in 1869, British trade with India soared. But it remained an unequal partnership, favoring the British. The British flooded India with inexpensive, machine-made textiles, ruining India's once-prosperous hand-weaving industry.

Britain also transformed Indian agriculture. It encouraged nomadic herders to settle into farming and pushed farmers to grow cash crops, such as cotton, that could be sold on the world market. However, British land policies resulted in peasants losing property, leading to a steady decline in the standard of living for most Indians. Clearing new farmlands led to massive **deforestation,** or cutting of trees, and other environmental destruction.

The Strain of Population Growth The British introduced medical improvements as new farming methods increased food production. The result was rapid population growth.

The rising numbers put a strain on the food supply, especially as farmland was turned over to growing cash crops instead of food. In the late 1800s, terrible famines swept India.

Benefits of British Colonial Rule On the positive side, British rule brought some degree of peace and order to the countryside. Railroads helped Indians move around the country, while the telegraph and postal system improved communication. Greater contact helped bridge regional differences and develop a sense of national unity.

The upper classes, especially, benefited from some British policies. They sent their sons to British schools, where they were trained for posts in the civil service and military. Indian landowners and princes, who still ruled their own territories, grew rich from exporting cash crops.

IDENTIFY CAUSE AND EFFECT What were some impacts of British colonial rule on agriculture in India?

SOME EFFECTS OF THE BRITISH RAJ

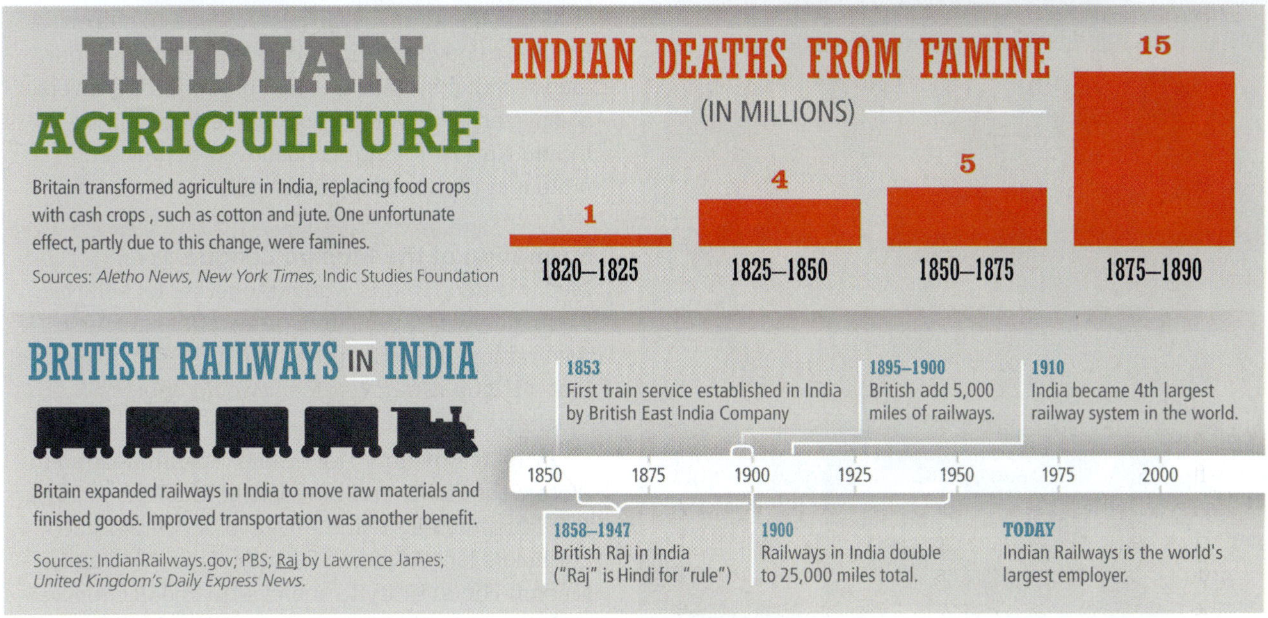

>> **Support a Point of View with Evidence** The graph and timeline show some effects of the British Raj. All things considered, was British rule a positive or a negative for India? Why?

Diverse Views on Culture

Some educated Indians, impressed by British power and technology, urged India to follow a Western model of progress. These mostly upper-class Indians had learned English and adopted many Western ways. Other Indians felt that the path to freedom lay within their own Hindu or Muslim cultures.

Indian Attitudes In the early 1800s, **Ram Mohun Roy** combined both views. A great scholar, he knew Sanskrit, Persian, and Arabic classics, as well as English, Greek, and Latin works. Roy felt that India could learn from the West. At the same time, he wanted to revitalize and reform traditional Indian culture.

Roy condemned some traditions, such as rigid caste distinctions, child marriage, sati, and **purdah** (PUR duh), the isolation of women in separate quarters. But he also set up educational societies that helped revive pride in Indian culture. Because of his influence on later leaders, he is often hailed today as the founder of Indian nationalism.

Westerner Attitudes The British disagreed among themselves about India. A few admired Indian theology and philosophy. As Western scholars translated Indian classics, they acquired respect for India's ancient heritage. Western writers and philosophers borrowed ideas from Hinduism and Buddhism.

On the other hand, few British people knew about Indian achievements and dismissed Indian culture with contempt. In an essay on whether Indians should be taught in English or their own languages, British historian Thomas Macaulay arrogantly wrote that "a single shelf of a good European library is worth the whole native literature of India and Arabia." This view of Indian civilization was commonly accepted in Britain and elsewhere in Europe.

☑ **COMPARE AND CONTRAST** What were some differing views among British people about the culture of India?

The Growth of Indian Nationalism

Under British rule, a class of Western-educated Indians emerged. The British expected this elite class to support British rule. As it turned out, exposure to European ideas had another effect. By the late 1800s, Western-educated Indians were

>> AC Mazumdar served as president of the Indian National Congress, which pushed for self-rule for India.

spearheading a nationalist movement. Schooled in Western ideals such as democracy and equality, they were determined to end foreign rule.

Indian National Congress By the late 1800s, Indians, especially from the educated class, were discussing how to change British rule. In 1885, nationalist leaders organized the Indian National Congress, which became known as the Congress party.

At first, members of the Indian National Congress called for reforms in British rule. Over time, they called for greater democracy, which they felt should allow a class of educated Indians like themselves to help rule the country. The Indian National Congress looked forward to eventual self-rule but supported Western-style modernization.

Some members of the party began to call on Indians to boycott British goods in favor of Indian-made products. They reached out to India's diverse social classes. Overall, though, members of the Indian National Congress believed in peaceful protest to gain their objectives.

Formation of the Muslim League At first, Muslims and Hindus worked together for self-rule. In time, however, Muslims grew to resent Hindu domination of the Congress party. They also worried that a Hindu-run government would oppress Muslims.

In 1906, Muslims formed the Muslim League to protect the rights and interests of Muslims in India. The Muslim League initially favored British rule, but before long, it called for self-rule, as well as for Muslim-Hindu unity to achieve this goal. Eventually, by 1930, members of the league began talking of a separate Muslim country.

IDENTIFY CAUSE AND EFFECT What was one cause of the Indian nationalist movement?

ASSESSMENT

1. **Analyze Information** Why did the Sepoy Rebellion leave "a bitter legacy of fear, hatred, and mistrust on both sides"?
2. **Analyze Information** What was one specific rule put in place by the East India Company that angered and offended sepoys?
3. **Analyze Information** What were the positive and negative effects of British rule on Indians?
4. **Infer** How did Ram Mohun Roy view the British?
5. **Analyze Information** How did British rule contribute to the development of Indian nationalism?

4.5 For centuries, Chinese regulations had strictly controlled foreign trade, ensuring that China had a favorable balance of trade with other nations. Balance of trade refers to the difference in value between how much a country imports and how much it exports. By the 1800s, however, Western nations were using their growing power to weave a web of influence over East Asia, which tilted the balance of trade in their favor.

>> The antiquated Chinese fleet was outmatched by larger, more technologically advanced British warships during the Opium War.

Bounce to Activate Flipped Video

China and the West

>> **Objectives**

Describe how Westerners tried to gain trade rights in China.

Explain how reformers tried to strengthen China.

Understand why the Qing dynasty fell.

>> **Key Terms**

balance of trade
trade surplus
trade deficit
indemnity
extraterritoriality
Taiping Rebellion
Sino-Japanese War
Open Door Policy
Guang Xu
Boxer Uprising
Sun Yixian
Opium War

Economic Interest in China

Chinese rulers had limited the activities of foreign traders. European merchants were restricted to a small area in southern China. China sold them silk, porcelain, and tea in exchange for gold and silver. Under this arrangement, China enjoyed a **trade surplus,** exporting more than it imported. Westerners, on the other hand, had a **trade deficit** with China, buying more from the Chinese than they sold to them. In 1796, the British requested more trading rights. The emperor Qianlong refused, saying that there was nothing in the West that China needed.

By the late 1700s, two developments were underway that transformed China's relations with the Western world. First, China entered a period of decline.

Second, the Industrial Revolution created a need for expanded markets for European goods. At the same time, it gave the West superior military power.

The Opium War During the late 1700s, British merchants discovered they could make huge profits by trading opium grown in India for Chinese tea. Soon, many Chinese had become addicted to the drug. Silver flowed out of China in payment for the drug, disrupting the economy.

The Chinese government outlawed opium and executed Chinese drug dealers. They called on Britain to stop the trade. The British refused, insisting on the right of free trade. In 1839, Chinese warships clashed with British merchants, triggering the **Opium War.** British gunboats, equipped with the latest in firepower, bombarded Chinese coastal and river ports. With outdated weapons and fighting methods, the Chinese were easily defeated.

Unequal Treaties In 1842, Britain made China accept the Treaty of Nanjing (NAHN jing). It was the first of a series of "unequal treaties" that forced China to give up rights to Western powers. Under the Treaty of Nanjing, Britain received a huge **indemnity,** or payment for losses in the war. The British also gained the island of Hong Kong. China had to open five ports to foreign trade and grant British citizens in China **extraterritoriality,** the right to live under their own laws and be tried in their own courts.

Finally, the treaty included a "most favored nation" clause. It said that if the Chinese granted rights to another nation, Britain would automatically receive the same rights.

The Opium War was the first of a series of trading wars that set a pattern for later encounters between China and the West. France and the United States soon forced China to sign treaties, giving them rights similar to those the British had won. Western powers then continued to squeeze China to win additional rights, such as opening more ports to trade and letting Christian missionaries preach in China.

>> Troops from the Qing dynasty clash with peasant rebels during the Taiping Rebellion.

DESCRIBE Describe how British trade with China triggered the Opium War.

The Taiping Rebellion and a Weakened China

By the 1800s, the Qing dynasty was in decline. Irrigation systems and canals were poorly maintained, leading to massive flooding of the Yellow River valley. The population explosion that had begun a century earlier created great hardships for China's peasants as they tried to feed more and more people.

An extravagant imperial court, tax evasion by the rich, and widespread official corruption added to the peasants' burden. Even the honored civil service was rocked by bribery and cheating scandals. As poverty and misery increased, peasants rebelled.

The Taiping Rebellion Throughout its long history, China was plagued by peasant uprisings, but the frequency and extent of revolts grew in the 1800s. The most shattering was the **Taiping Rebellion** (TY ping), which lasted from 1850 to 1864.

Its leader, Hong Xiuquan (shyoo CHWAHN), was a village teacher who had failed the civil service exams several times. Inspired by religious visions, he set himself up as a revolutionary prophet.

He wanted to topple the hated Qing dynasty and set up a "Heavenly Kingdom of Great Peace"—the Taiping. Hong, influenced by both Confucian and Christian teachings, called for radical change. He wanted land reform, community ownership of property, equality of women and men, and strict morality.

Hong won followers among the poor and outcast. At first, some Westerners sympathized with the rebels but then realized that if the Qing dynasty fell, their trading rights could be lost. As the powerful Taiping movement spread, rebels won control of large parts of China. It took the government 15 years and vast sums of money to defeat the rebellion.

The Taiping Rebellion almost toppled the Qing dynasty. It is estimated that more than 20 million Chinese died in the fighting. The Qing government survived, but it had to share power with regional commanders who had helped crush the rebellion.

>> **Analyze Maps** Western powers carved out spheres of influence throughout China. What area was occupied by Japan beginning in 1897?

Bounce to Activate Map

During the rebellion, Europeans kept up pressure on China. Russia seized lands in northern China. It then built the port of Vladivostok on the Pacific coast.

EXPLAIN How did the Taiping Rebellion and other internal problems weaken the Qing dynasty?

Reform Efforts in China

By the mid-1800s, educated Chinese were divided over the need to reform China by adopting Western ways. Most saw no reason to build new industries because China's wealth came from land. Although Chinese merchants were allowed to do business, they were not seen as a source of economic prosperity for the country.

Scholar-officials also disapproved of the ideas of Western missionaries, whose emphasis on individual choice challenged the Confucian order. They saw Western technology as dangerous, too, because it threatened Confucian ways that had served China successfully for so long.

The imperial court was a center of conservative opposition. By the late 1800s, the empress Ci Xi (tsih shih) had gained power. A strong-willed ruler, she surrounded herself with advisers who were deeply committed to Confucian traditions.

Self-Strengthening Movement Some Chinese, however, wanted to adapt Western ideas. In the 1860s, reformers launched the "self-strengthening movement." They imported Western technology, setting up factories to make modern weapons.

They developed shipyards, railroads, mining, and light industry. The Chinese translated Western works on science, government, and the economy.

The movement made limited progress though, because the government did not rally behind it. Also, while China was undertaking a few selected reforms, the Western powers—and Japan—were moving ahead rapidly.

The Sino-Japanese War The island nation of Japan modernized rapidly after 1868. It then joined the Western imperialists in the competition for a global empire.

In 1894, Japanese pressure on China led to the **Sino-Japanese War.** It ended in disaster for China, with Japan gaining Korea and the island of Taiwan. When the two powers met at the peace table, there was a telling difference in outlook. Japanese officials dressed in Western-style clothing while the Chinese wore traditional robes.

Spheres of Influence The crushing defeat revealed China's weakness. Western powers moved swiftly

>> **Analyze Political Cartoons** The dogs represent the United States, Japan, and Britain. They guard an open door that says "China Trade." Which country opened the door?

>> Chinese rebels nicknamed Boxers wanted to drive out foreigners from their country. **Identify Cause and Effect** Why were the Boxers angry about the foreign presence in China?

Bounce to Activate Gallery

to carve out spheres of influence along the Chinese coast. The British took the Chang River valley.

The French acquired the territory near their colony of Indochina. Germany and Russia gained territory in northern China.

The United States, a longtime trader with the Chinese, did not take part in the carving up of China. It feared that European powers might shut out American merchants. In 1899, it called for a policy to keep Chinese trade open to everyone on an equal basis. The imperial powers more or less accepted the idea of an **Open Door Policy,** as it came to be called. No one, however, consulted the Chinese about the policy.

Hundred Days of Reform Defeated by Japan and humiliated by Westerners, Chinese reformers looked for a scapegoat. Reformers blamed conservative officials for not modernizing China. They argued that Confucius himself had been a reformer and that China could not look to a golden age in the past but must modernize as Japan had.

In 1898, a young emperor, **Guang Xu** (gwahng shoo), launched the Hundred Days of Reform. New laws set out to modernize the civil service exams, streamline government, and encourage new industries. Reforms affected schools, the military, and the bureaucracy.

Conservatives soon rallied against the reform effort. The emperor was imprisoned, and the aging empress Ci Xi reasserted control. Reformers fled for their lives.

IDENTIFY Identify reformers' solutions for China's problems.

The Fall of the Qing Dynasty

By 1900, China was in turmoil. Anger against foreigners was growing. While the Chinese welcomed some Western ideas, they resented Christian missionaries who showed little respect for Chinese traditions and Confucian ideas. The presence of foreign troops was another source of discontent.

Protected by extraterritoriality, foreigners ignored Chinese laws and lived in their own communities. In Western neighborhoods, signs announced: "Dogs and Chinese Not Allowed."

The Boxer Uprising Anti-foreign feeling finally exploded in the **Boxer Uprising.** In 1899, groups of

Chinese peasants had formed a secret society, the Righteous Harmonious Fists. Westerners watching them train in the martial arts dubbed them Boxers. Their goal was to drive out the "foreign devils" who were polluting the land with their non-Chinese ways, strange buildings, machines, and telegraph lines.

In late 1899 and throughout 1900, the Boxers attacked and killed foreigners across China. In response, the Western powers and Japan organized a multinational force.

After taking some losses, this force crushed the Boxers and rescued foreigners besieged in Beijing. The empress Ci Xi had at first supported the Boxers but reversed her policy as they retreated.

Consequences of the Uprising In the aftermath of the Boxer Uprising, foreign powers forced China to make still more concessions. The defeat, however, forced even Chinese conservatives to support Westernization. In a rush of reforms, China admitted women to schools and stressed science and mathematics in place of Confucian thought. More students were sent abroad to study.

During the early 1900s, China expanded economically. Mining, shipping, railroads, banking, and exports of cash crops grew. Small-scale Chinese industry developed with the help of foreign capital. A Chinese business class emerged, and a new urban working class began to press for rights in the same way Western workers had done.

Growth of Chinese Nationalism Although the Boxer Uprising failed, the flames of Chinese nationalism spread. Reformers who wanted to strengthen China's government introduced a constitutional monarchy. Some reformers called for a republic.

A passionate spokesman for a Chinese republic was **Sun Yixian** (soon yee SHYAHN), also known as Sun Yat-sen. In the early 1900s, he organized the Revolutionary Alliance to rebuild China on "Three Principles of the People." The first principle was nationalism, or freeing China from foreign domination. The second was democracy, or representative government. The third was livelihood, or economic security for all Chinese.

A Republic Is Born When Ci Xi died in 1908, a two-year-old boy inherited the throne. China slipped into chaos. In 1911, uprisings swiftly spread. Peasants, students, warlords, and even court politicians helped topple the Qing dynasty, ending China's 2000-year old monarchy.

>> Known as the Father of Modern China, Sun Yixian founded the Chinese Nationalist Party and became the first president of China after the fall of the Qing dynasty.

Sun Yixian hurried home from a trip to the United States. In early 1912, he was sworn in as president of the new Chinese republic. The republic faced overwhelming problems and was almost constantly at war with itself or foreign invaders.

IDENTIFY CAUSE AND EFFECT What caused the Qing dynasty to fall?

ASSESSMENT

1. **Sequence Events** Describe the sequence of conflicts and their consequences that weakened Qing China.
2. **Generate Explanations** How did Western powers gain greater trading rights in China?
3. **Summarize** What internal problems threatened the Qing dynasty?
4. **Summarize** What were the goals of Chinese reformers?
5. **Synthesize** Describe how a republic replaced the Qing dynasty.

>> **Generate Explanations** Emperor Mutsuhito took the name "Meiji," or "enlightened rule," when he came to power. What made his rule "enlightened"?

4.6 **In 1853, United States warships arrived off the coast of Japan demanding Japan open its ports to trade. Japanese leaders debated how to respond. Some resisted giving up their longstanding policy of seclusion. Others felt that the wiser course was to learn from the foreigners.**

Bounce to Activate Flipped Video

The Modernization of Japan

>> Objectives

Identify the problems faced by Tokugawa Japan.

Explain how the United States opened Japan to the outside world.

Analyze the causes and effects of the Meiji Restoration.

Describe how Japan began to build an empire.

>> Key Terms

Matthew Perry
Mutsuhito
Tokyo
Meiji Restoration
Diet
zaibatsu
homogeneous society
First Sino-Japanese War
Russo-Japanese War

Unrest in Tokugawa Japan

In the end, Japan abandoned its isolation. As a defense against Western imperialism, Japan decided to learn from the West. It swiftly transformed itself into a modern industrial power and then set out on its own imperialist path.

The Tokugawa Shoguns By 1603, Tokugawa Ieyasu had gained the office of shogun, the top military commander in Japan. This ended a long period of lawlessness and chaos in Japan. Although the emperor still lived in his capital of Kyoto, the shogun held the real power in Edo. The Tokugawa shoguns reimposed centralized feudalism on Japan, bringing the daimyo under their control and presiding over a long period of peace.

In 1637, the Tokugawas closed Japan to foreigners, and barred Japanese from traveling overseas. Their only window on the world was through Nagasaki, where the Dutch were allowed very limited trade.

For almost 250 years, Japan developed in isolation. During that time, the economy expanded, especially internal commerce. Farm output grew, and bustling cities sprang up.

Hardships Grow Economic growth, however, brought changes that put strains on the country. Daimyo suffered financial hardship because their wealth was in land. In a commercial economy, money was needed. Daimyo had the heavy expense of maintaining households in both Edo and their own domains.

Lesser samurai were unhappy, too, because they were no longer fighters. Many were government bureaucrats. Even though they were noble, they lacked the money to live as well as urban merchants. Merchants in turn resented their place at the bottom of the social ladder. No matter how rich they were, they had no political power. Peasants, meanwhile, suffered under heavy taxes.

The government responded by trying to revive old ways, emphasizing farming over commerce and praising traditional values. Efforts at reform failed. By the 1800s, many groups were discontent and had little loyalty to the old system.

IDENTIFY CAUSE AND EFFECT By the mid-1800s, why did so many groups of people in Japan feel discontented?

The Opening of Japan

While the shogun faced troubles at home, disturbing news reached him from abroad. With alarm, he heard of how the British had defeated China in the Opium War and how imperialists had forced China to sign unequal treaties. Japanese officials realized it would not be long before Western powers sought trading rights in Japan.

External Pressure Leads to Internal Revolt

In July 1853, a fleet of well-armed American ships commanded by Commodore **Matthew Perry** sailed into Tokyo Bay. Perry carried a letter from the president of the United States. It demanded that Japan open its ports to trade.

The shogun's advisers debated what to do. Japan did not have the ability to defend itself against the powerful United States Navy. In the Treaty of Kanagawa in 1854, the shogun Iesada agreed to open three Japanese ports to American ships, where they could take on supplies.

The United States soon won trading and other rights, including extraterritoriality. Britain, France, and Russia demanded and won similar rights. Like the Chinese, the Japanese deeply resented the humiliating terms of these unequal treaties. Some bitterly criticized the shogun for not taking a strong stand against the foreigners.

Foreign pressure deepened the social and economic unrest. As the crisis worsened, many young, reform-minded samurai rallied around the emperor, long regarded as a figurehead.

In 1867, discontented daimyo and samurai led a revolt that unseated the shogun and "restored" the emperor, **Mutsuhito** to power. He moved from Kyoto, the old imperial capital, to the shogun's palace in Edo, which was renamed **Tokyo,** or "eastern capital." The emperor took the name Meiji (MAY jee), which means "enlightened rule."

The Meiji Restoration The young emperor, just 15 years old, began a long reign known as the **Meiji Restoration.** This period, which lasted from 1868 to 1912, was a major turning point in Japanese history.

The Meiji reformers, who ruled in the emperor's name, were determined to strengthen Japan against the West. Their goal was summarized in their motto, "A rich country, a strong military."

The new leaders set out to study Western ways, adapt them to Japanese needs, and eventually protect Japan from having to give in to Western demands. In 1871, members of the government

>> In this Japanese woodblock print, Japanese boats go out to meet one of Commodore Matthew Perry's ships in Tokyo Bay.

Bounce to Activate Illustration

traveled abroad to learn about Western governments, economies, technology, and customs. The government brought experts from Western countries to Japan and sent young samurai to study in Europe and the United States.

SUMMARIZE How did Japan react when it was forced to accept unequal treaties?

Transformation during the Meiji Period

The Meiji reformers faced an enormous task. They were committed to replacing the rigid feudal order with a completely new political and social system and to building a modern industrial economy. Change did not come easily. However, Japan adapted foreign ideas with great speed and success.

Reforming Government The reformers wanted to create a strong central government, equal to those of Western powers. After studying the governments of various European countries, they adapted the German model. In 1889, the emperor issued the Meiji constitution. It set forth the principle that all citizens were equal before the law. Like the German system, however, it gave the emperor autocratic, or unlimited, power. A legislature, or **Diet,** was formed, made up of one elected house and one house appointed by the emperor. Suffrage, or the right to vote, was also limited.

Japan then set up a Western-style bureaucracy with separate departments to supervise finance, the army, the navy, and education. To strengthen the military, it turned to Western technology and ended the special privileges of samurai. In the past, samurai alone were warriors. In modern Japan, as in the modern West, all men were subject to military service.

>> This woodblock print shows the announcement of the new Meiji constitution in 1889, which created a European-style government in Japan. **Analyze Images** What other European influences do you see in the print?

Bounce to Activate Gallery

Rapid Industrialization Meiji leaders made the economy a major priority. They encouraged Japan's business class to adopt Western methods. The government set up a modern banking system, built railroads, improved ports, and organized a telegraph and postal system.

To get industries started, the government typically built factories and then sold them to wealthy business families who developed them further. With such support, business dynasties like the Mitsubishi and Kawasaki families soon ruled over industrial empires that rivaled the Rockefellers in the United States or the Krupps in Germany. These powerful banking and industrial families were known as **zaibatsu** (zy baht soo).

By the 1890s, industry was booming. With modern machines, silk manufacturing soared. Shipyards, copper and coal mining, and steel making also helped make Japan an industrial powerhouse. As in other industrial countries, the population grew rapidly, and many peasants flocked to the growing cities for work.

Social Changes The constitution ended legal distinctions between classes, thus freeing more people to build the nation. The government set up schools and a university. It hired Westerners to teach modern technology to the new generation.

Despite the reforms, class distinctions survived in Japan as they did in the West. Also, although literacy increased and some women gained an education, women in general were still assigned a secondary role in society.

The reform of the Japanese family system, and women's position in it, became the topic of major debates in the 1870s. Reformers wanted women to become full partners in the process of nation building and to learn skills that would allow them to live on their own.

Investment in Meiji Japan

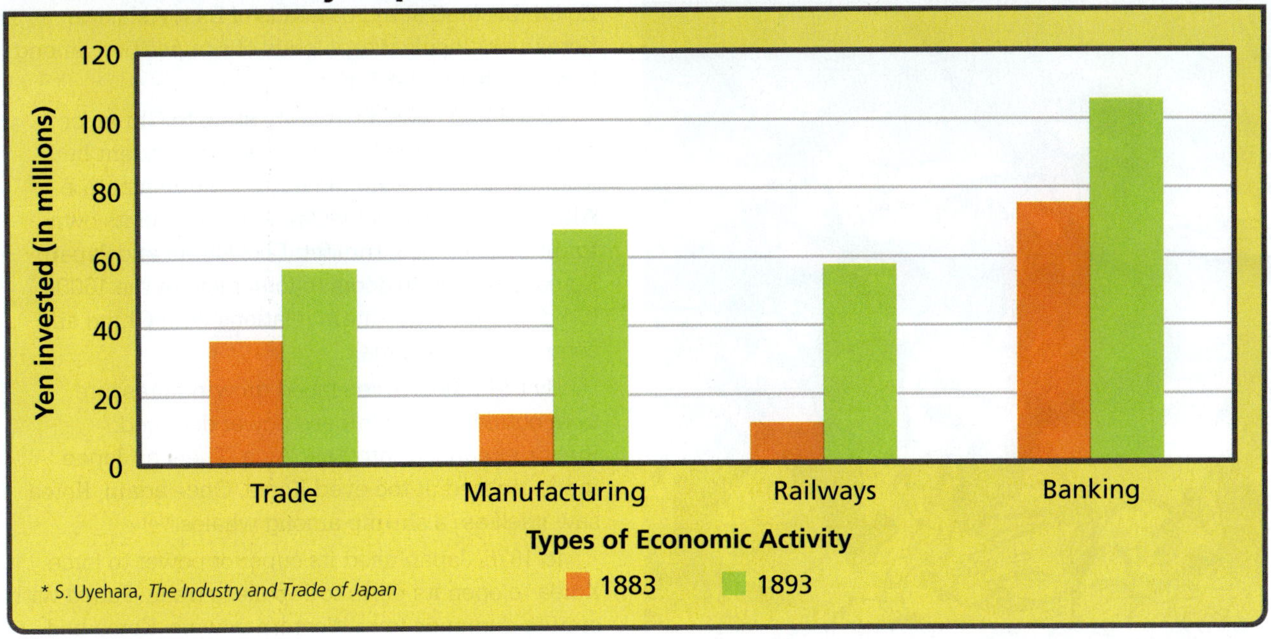

>> **Analyze Charts** Meiji reformers worked to industrialize Japan. How does the chart reflect this goal?

While the government agreed to some increases in education for women, it dealt harshly with other attempts at change. It took away earlier political and legal rights that women had won. After 1898, Japanese women were forbidden any political participation and legally were lumped together with minors.

An Amazing Success Japan modernized with amazing speed during the Meiji period. Its success was due to a number of causes. It was a **homogeneous society**—that is, its people shared a common culture and language. Economic growth during Tokugawa times had set Japan on the road to development. Japan also had experience in learning and adapting ideas from foreign nations, such as China.

Like other people faced with Western imperialism, the Japanese were determined to resist foreign rule. By the 1890s, Japan was strong enough to force Western powers to revise the unequal treaties. By then, it was already competing with the West and acquiring its own overseas empire.

SUMMARIZE What changes did the reforms of the Meiji Restoration bring about in Japan?

Japan Builds an Empire

As in Western industrial nations, Japan's economic needs fed its imperialist desires. As a small island nation, Japan lacked many basic resources, including coal, that were essential for industrial growth. Spurred by nationalism and a strong ambition to equal the West, Japan sought to build an empire. With its modern army and navy, it maneuvered for power in East Asia.

Japan Expands In 1894, competition between Japan and China for power in Korea led to the **First Sino-Japanese War.** ("Sino" means "Chinese.") Although China had far greater resources, Japan had benefited from modernization. To the surprise of China and the West, Japan won easily. It used its victory to gain treaty ports in China and control over the island of Taiwan. The war showed that Japan had joined the Western powers in the race for empire.

Ten years later, Japan successfully challenged Russia, its other rival for power in Korea and Manchuria. During the **Russo-Japanese War,** Japan's armies defeated Russian troops in Manchuria, and its navy destroyed almost an entire Russian fleet. For the first time in modern history, an Asian power humbled a European nation.

In the 1905 Treaty of Portsmouth, Japan gained control of Korea as well as rights in parts of Manchuria. This foothold on the mainland would fuel its ambitions in East Asia.

>> **Analyze Political Cartoons** Japan began its imperialist agenda in Korea. Based on the cartoon, who else had imperialist ambitions in Korea?

>> Japan's victory in the Russo-Japanese War forced Russia to abandon its imperialist policies in East Asia.

Korea Imperialist rivalries put the spotlight on Korea. Located at a crossroads of East Asia, the Korean peninsula was a focus of competition among Russia, China, and Japan.

Korea had been a tributary state to China for many years. A tributary state is independent but acknowledges the supremacy of a stronger state. Although influenced by China, Korea had its own traditions and government. Like China and Japan, Korea had shut its doors to foreigners in the 1600s. It did, however, maintain relations with China and sometimes with Japan.

By the 1800s, Korea faced growing pressure from outsiders. As Chinese power declined, Russia expanded into East Asia. Then, as Japan industrialized, it too eyed Korea. Once again, Korea saw itself as "a shrimp among whales."

In 1876, Japan used its superior power to force Korea to open its ports to Japanese trade. Faced with similar demands from Western powers, Korea had to accept unequal treaties. After defeating China and then Russia, Japan made Korea a protectorate. In 1910, it annexed Korea outright, absorbing the kingdom into the Japanese empire.

Japanese Rule in Korea Japan ruled Korea for 35 years. Like Western imperialists, the Japanese set out to modernize their newly acquired territory. They built factories, railroads, and communications systems. Development, however, generally benefited the colonial power. Under Japanese rule, Koreans produced more rice than ever before, but most of it went to feed the Japanese.

The Japanese were as unpopular in Korea as Western imperialists were elsewhere. They imposed harsh rule on their colony and deliberately set out to erase the Korean language and identity. Repression bred resentment. And resentment, in turn, nourished a Korean nationalist movement.

Nine years after annexation, a nonviolent protest against the Japanese began on March 1, 1919, and soon spread throughout Korea. The Japanese crushed the uprising and massacred many Koreans. The violence did not discourage people who worked to end Japanese rule. Instead, the March First Movement became a rallying symbol for Korean nationalists.

The Koreans would have to wait many years to regain their freedom. By the early 1900s, Japan was the strongest power in Asia. In competition with Western nations, Japan continued to expand in East Asia. In time, Japanese ambitions to control a sphere of influence in the Pacific would put it on a collision course with several Western powers, especially Britain and the United States.

GENERATE EXPLANATIONS How did industrialization help start Japan on an imperialist course?

ASSESSMENT

1. **Cite Evidence** What was one cause of discontent in Tokugawa, Japan?
2. **Identify Main Ideas** What demand did the United States make on Japan in 1853?
3. **Make Generalizations** What was the goal of the Meiji reformers?
4. **Identify Cause and Effect** What was the main reason Japan become an imperialist power?
5. **Summarize** Why was the Russo-Japanese War significant?

>> This sculpture in Tapgol Park in Seoul, South Korea, honors the fight for Korean independence from Japanese rule.

>> The headquarters of the Dutch East India Company was called Batavia Castle. It was located in present-day Jakarta. The East India Company built trading and military bases throughout the Spice Islands.

Bounce to Activate Flipped Video

4.7 By the mid-1800s, leaders throughout Southeast Asia faced the growing threat of Western imperialism. Before long, Western industrial powers divided up the region in their race for raw materials, new markets, and Christian converts.

>> Objectives

Describe how Europe and the United States built colonies in Southeast Asia.

Explain how imperialism spread to the islands of the Pacific.

Analyze how Australia and New Zealand achieved self-rule.

>> Key Terms

French Indochina
Mongkut
Spanish-American War
Liliuokalani
indigenous
penal colony
Maori

Southeast Asia and the Pacific

European Imperialism in Southeast Asia

Southeast Asia commands the sea lanes between India and China. The region had long been influenced by both civilizations. In the 1500s and 1600s, European merchants gained footholds in Southeast Asia, but most of the peoples of the region remained independent.

When the Industrial Revolution set off the Age of Imperialism, the situation changed. Western powers, especially the Dutch, British, and French, used modern armies and technology to colonize much of Southeast Asia.

The Dutch East Indies In the 1600s, the Dutch East India Company gained control of the fabled riches of the Moluccas, or Spice Islands. The Dutch then reached out to dominate the rest of the East Indies—what is now Indonesia. The region included larger islands, such as Java, Sumatra, and Borneo, as well as many smaller islands.

By 1800, the Dutch government had taken over these areas from the Dutch East India Company. During the next century, the

Dutch faced uprisings, but they gradually extended their control. Like other imperialist powers, the Dutch expected their Southeast Asia colonies to produce profitable crops of coffee, indigo, and spices. Under colonial rule, local people were forced to work as slave labor on plantations, raising anger and criticism.

The British in Burma and Malaya In the early 1800s, the rulers of Burma (present-day Myanmar) clashed with the British, who were expanding eastward from India. The Burmese misjudged British strength and suffered disastrous defeats in several wars. By 1886, Britain had annexed Burma. The Burmese, however, constantly resisted British rule.

At the same time, the British pushed south through the Malay Peninsula. The bustling port of Singapore grew up at the southern tip of the peninsula. Singapore stood on the sea route between the Indian Ocean and the China Sea. Soon, rubber and tin from Malaya, along with profits from Asian trade were flowing through Singapore to enrich Britain.

The French in Indochina The French, meanwhile, were building an empire on the Southeast Asian mainland. Like other imperialist powers, they wanted political influence, raw materials, and markets in the region.

In the early 1800s, French missionaries began winning converts in what is today Vietnam. In response to growing Western influence, Vietnamese officials tried to suppress Christianity by killing converts and priests. The French used the murders as a reason to invade.

Like the Burmese, the Vietnamese misjudged European power. Starting in 1858, the French attacked and took over parts of Vietnam. The Vietnamese fought fiercely but could not withstand superior European firepower. The French eventually seized all of Vietnam, Laos, and Cambodia. The West referred to these holdings as **French Indochina.**

Siam Stays Independent The kingdom of Siam (present-day Thailand) lay between British-ruled Burma and French Indochina. Siam escaped becoming a European colony partly because its rulers did not underestimate Western power and avoided incidents that might provoke invasion.

Although the king of Siam, **Mongkut** (mahng KOOT), had to accept some unequal treaties, he set Siam on the road to modernization. He and his son, Chulalongkorn, who ruled from 1868 to 1910, reformed the government, modernized the army,

>> **Analyze Maps** Europeans sought to exploit the vast natural resources of Southeast Asia. According to the map, to which resources did the Dutch have exclusive access?

and hired Western experts to train Thais in the new technology.

They abolished slavery and gave women some choice in marriage. Thai students traveled abroad and spread Western ways when they returned home. As Siam modernized, Chulalongkorn bargained to remove the unequal treaties.

In the end, both Britain and France saw the advantage of making Siam a buffer, or neutral zone, between them. In the early 1900s, they guaranteed its independence. But to prevent other imperialist powers from pushing into Siam, each set up its own sphere of influence there.

Characteristics of Colonial Southeast Asia By the 1890s, Europeans controlled most of Southeast Asia. They introduced modern technology and expanded commerce and industry. Europeans directed the mining of tin, the harvesting of rubber, and the building of harbors and railroads. But these changes benefited the European colonizers far more than they did the Southeast Asians.

DESCRIBE How did the Burmese and the Vietnamese respond to colonization attempts?

>> During the Spanish-American War, the U.S. Navy destroyed Spanish ships in the Battle of Manila Bay in the Philippines.

Bounce to Activate Map

Military Might and the Philippines

In the 1500s, Spain had seized the Philippines and extended its rule over the islands. Catholic missionaries spread Christianity among the Filipinos and the Catholic Church gained enormous power and wealth. Many Filipinos accused the Church of abusing its position. By the late 1800s, their anger fueled strong resistance to Spanish rule.

Leaders like José Rizal, a doctor who had studied abroad, called on Filipinos to use nonviolent means to win reforms. Although captured and executed by the Spanish, Rizal continued to inspire Filipinos eager to free their country from foreign rule.

Battles in the Philippines The United States became involved in the Philippines almost by accident. In 1898, war broke out between Spain and the United States over Cuba's effort to win independence from Spain. During the **Spanish-American War,** American battleships destroyed the Spanish fleet, which was stationed in the Philippines.

Seizing the moment, Filipino leaders declared independence from Spain. Rebel soldiers threw their support into the fight against Spanish troops. In return for their help, the Filipino rebels expected the United States to recognize their independence. Instead, the peace settlement with Spain placed the Philippines under American control.

Bitterly disappointed, Filipino nationalists renewed their struggle. From 1899 to 1901, Filipinos led by Emilio Aguinaldo (ah gee NAHL doh) battled American forces. Thousands of Americans and hundreds of thousands of Filipinos died. In the end, the Americans crushed the rebellion. The United States set out to modernize the Philippines, promising Filipinos self-rule some time in the future.

IDENTIFY MAIN IDEAS How did the United States gain control of the Philippines?

Strategic Holdings in the Pacific Islands

In the 1800s, the industrialized powers began to take an interest in the islands of the Pacific. The thousands of islands splashed across the Pacific include the three regions of Melanesia, Micronesia, and Polynesia.

At first, American, French, and British whaling and sealing ships looked for bases to take on supplies while they were operating in the Pacific. Missionaries, too, moved into the region and opened the way for political involvement. For much of the 1800s, whalers, merchants, and missionaries were the only visitors to the Pacific Islands.

From Ports of Call to Colonies By the late 1800s, nationalist rivalries led European powers to claim Pacific islands as colonies. France set up a protectorate over Tahiti, but soon made it a colony. The race was on for control of the Pacific Islands.

In 1878, the United States secured an unequal treaty from Samoa, a group of islands in the South Pacific. The United States gained rights such as extraterritoriality and a naval station.

Other nations gained similar agreements. As their rivalry increased, the United States, Germany, and Britain agreed to a triple protectorate over Samoa.

Beginning in the mid-1800s, American sugar growers pressed for power in the Hawaiian Islands. When the Hawaiian queen **Liliuokalani** (lih lee uh oh kuh LAH nee) tried to reduce foreign influence, American planters overthrew her in 1893. They then asked the United States to annex Hawaii, which it did in 1898. Supporters of annexation argued that if the United States did not take Hawaii, Britain or Japan might do so.

>> Queen Liliuokalani reduced benefits to American businesses operating in Hawaii, generating opposition from businessmen like Sanford Dole of the pineapple industry.

Imperialist Rivalry By 1900, the United States, Britain, France, and Germany had claimed nearly every island in the Pacific. Japan, too, wanted a share of the region. Eventually, it would gain German possessions in the Pacific, setting the stage for a growing rivalry with the United States.

Although small in size, the Pacific Islands offered economic benefits to colonial powers. In Hawaii, sugarcane plantations were profitable. Elsewhere, imperial powers tapped into local resources such as nickel, or even guano, bird droppings used to make fertilizer. For imperialist powers locked in a global race for colonies, the Pacific Islands provided useful ports for their merchant ships and warships.

RECALL Why did some Americans think the United States should control Hawaii?

Europeans in Australia

The Dutch in the 1600s were the first Europeans to reach Australia—the world's largest island and smallest continent. In 1770, Captain James Cook claimed Australia for Britain. For a time, however, Australia remained too distant to attract European settlers.

Australia's Indigenous People Like most regions claimed by imperialist powers, Australia had long been inhabited by other people. The first settlers had reached Australia about 40,000 years ago, probably from Southeast Asia. These **indigenous,** or original, inhabitants were called Aborigines, a European word for earliest people to live in a place. Today, many Australian Aborigines call themselves Kooris.

Isolated from the larger world, the Aborigines lived in small hunting and food-gathering bands, much as their Stone Age ancestors had. Aboriginal groups spoke as many as 250 distinct languages. When white settlers arrived in Australia, the indigenous population suffered disastrously just as it had in the Americas after the arrival of Columbus.

A Penal Colony Events in North America and Britain ended Australia's isolation. During the 1700s, Britain had sent convicts to its North American colonies, especially to Georgia. The American Revolution closed that outlet just as the Industrial Revolution was disrupting British society. British prisons were filled with poor people arrested for minor crimes such as stealing food, or serious crimes, such as murder.

To fill the need for prisons, Britain made Australia into a **penal colony,** a place to send people convicted of crimes. The first British ships, carrying about 700 convicts, arrived in Botany Bay, Australia, in 1788. The men, women, and children who survived the grueling eight-month voyage faced more hardships on shore. Many were city dwellers with no farming skills. Under the brutal discipline of soldiers, work gangs cleared land for settlement.

Emigration to Australia In the early 1800s, Britain encouraged free citizens to emigrate to Australia by offering them land and tools. As the newcomers occupied coastal lands, they thrust aside or killed the Aborigines.

In time, a prosperous wool industry grew up as settlers found that the land and climate suited sheepherding. In 1851, a gold rush in eastern Australia set off a population boom as gold hunters from around the world headed to the island continent. Many gold hunters stayed on to become ranchers and farmers.

They pushed into the rugged interior known as the Outback and displaced the Aborigines as they carved out huge sheep ranches and wheat farms. By the late 1800s, Australia had won a place in the growing world economy.

Self-Rule in Australia Australia was made up of separate colonies scattered around the continent. Britain worried about interference from other imperialist European powers. To counter this threat and to boost development, it responded to Australian demands for self-rule. In 1901, Britain helped the colonies unite into the independent Commonwealth of Australia. The new country kept its ties to Britain by recognizing the British monarch as its head of state.

The Australian constitution set up a federal system that limited the power of the central government. Its Parliament has a Senate and House of Representative, but its executive is a prime minister chosen by the majority party in Parliament.

Unlike Britain and the United States, Australia quickly granted women the right to vote. In 1856, some Australian states introduced the secret ballot, which became known as the Australian ballot. Later, other countries adopted this practice.

IDENTIFY CAUSE AND EFFECT What effects did colonization have on Australia's indigenous population?

>> Fireworks blaze over Perth, Australia, on Australia Day, which commemorates Australia's first European settlers. **Infer** How might Australia's aboriginal population feel about the celebration of Australia Day?

Bounce to Activate Chart

New Zealand's Story

About 1,000 miles southeast of Australia lies New Zealand. It consists of several islands. New Zealand was the last landmass in the world to be settled. Like Australia, New Zealand had its own indigenous people, the **Maori** (MAH oh ree).

Arrival of the Maori The ancestors of the Maori had reached New Zealand from Polynesia in the 1200s. These seafaring people were skilled navigators who relied on the winds, stars, and ocean currents to reach land.

In New Zealand, the Maori lived in small hunting bands and raised sweet potatoes and yams brought with them on their voyages. They had an extensive oral history, in which they recorded long genealogies, or family trees. They engaged in warfare but also traded with one another.

Arrival of Europeans In 1642, a Dutch explorer was the first European to reach New Zealand. Captain James Cook claimed the islands for Britain in 1769. The first Europeans arrived in New Zealand in the late 1700s.

Early settlements were outposts for whalers, seal hunters, and lumbering operations. In 1814, missionaries arrived to convert the Maori to Christianity.

White settlers were attracted to New Zealand by its mild climate and good soil. They introduced sheep and cattle and were soon exporting wool, mutton, and beef. Maori and Europeans traded in basic goods, exchanging potatoes and pork for European firearms.

Maori Struggles In 1840, Britain annexed New Zealand in part to keep the French from claiming any of it. Unlike Australia, where the Aborigines were spread thinly across a large continent, the Maori were concentrated in a smaller area. About 100,000 Maoris lived in New Zealand before the arrival of Europeans.

As colonists poured in, they took over more land. Disputes over land led to a series of fierce wars with the Maori. Even though Europeans offered to buy land,the Maori were unwilling to give up land they had farmed collectively for generations.

Many Maori died in clashes with settlers. Still more perished from disease brought by Europeans. By 1872, the Maori resistance had crumbled. The Maori population had fallen drastically, to less than 45,000. Only recently has the Maori population started to grow again.

The Nation of New Zealand Like settlers in Australia, white New Zealanders achieved self-rule. In 1893, New Zealand became the first modern country to give women the right to vote. In 1907, New Zealand became a dominion within the British empire with its own parliament, prime minister, and elected legislature.

Like Australia, New Zealand won independence faster than other territories claimed by the British. One reason was that both had large populations of white settlers. Imperialist nations like Britain felt that whites could govern themselves. Nonwhites in places like India were thought to be incapable of shouldering such responsibility.

COMPARE AND CONTRAST Compare and contrast the European settlement of Australia and New Zealand.

>> Traditional Maori tattooing, which often covers the face, reveals important information about the wearer's family and identity, such as tribal affiliations and social status.

ASSESSMENT

1. **Identify Supporting Details** How did industrialized powers divide up the various lands of Southeast Asia and the Pacific?
2. **Contrast** How was Siam different from the other nations of Southeast Asia?
3. **Draw Conclusions** Why were Filipino rebels disappointed when the United States took control of the Philippines?
4. **Synthesize** Describe how Hawaii became part of the United States.
5. **Identify Cause and Effect** Why did Britain grant self-rule to Australia and New Zealand?

>> **Check Understanding** The United States helped Cuba fight Spain in the Spanish-American War. The U.S. Navy destroyed a Spanish fleet off Santiago de Cuba in 1898. What did the United States gain after the war?

Bounce to Activate Flipped Video

4.8 **After the wars of independence in the early 1800s, Latin American nations hoped to build democratic governments. That dream soon faded as power struggles erupted across the region. During the Age of Imperialism, Latin American economies became increasingly dependent upon those of more developed countries. Britain, and later the United States, invested heavily in Latin America.**

>> Objectives

Identify the political problems faced by new Latin American nations.

Describe Mexico's struggle to achieve stability.

Explain why Latin America entered a cycle of economic dependence.

Analyze the influence of the United States on Latin America, including the opening of the Panama Canal.

Analyze how Canada achieved self-rule.

>> Key Terms

regionalism
caudillo
Benito Juárez
La Reforma
peonage
Monroe Doctrine
Panama Canal
confederation
dominion
métis

The Americas in the Age of Imperialism

Political Problems Linger

Simón Bolívar had hoped to create a single Latin American nation. After all, the people shared a common language, religion, and cultural heritage. But feuds among leaders, geographic barriers, and local nationalism shattered that dream of unity. In the end, 20 separate nations emerged.

These new nations wrote constitutions modeled on that of the United States. They set up republics with elected legislatures. During the 1800s, however, most Latin American nations were plagued by revolts, civil war, and dictatorships.

The Legacy of Colonialism Many problems facing the new nations had their origins in colonial rule. Spain and Portugal had kept tight control on their colonies, giving them little experience with self-government. The wars of independence barely changed the colonial social and political hierarchy. Creoles simply replaced *peninsulares* as the ruling class. The Roman Catholic Church kept its privileged position and still controlled huge amounts of land.

For most people—mestizos, mulattoes, blacks, and Indians—life did not improve after independence. The new constitutions guaranteed equality before the law, but deep-rooted inequalities remained. Voting rights were limited. Racial prejudice was widespread, and land remained in the hands of a few. Owners of haciendas ruled their great estates, and the peasants who worked them, like medieval European lords.

The Rise of Dictators With few roads and no tradition of unity, the new nations were weakened by **regionalism,** or loyalty to a local area. Local strongmen, called ***caudillos*** (kow THEE yohs), assembled private armies to resist the central government.

At times, popular caudillos, sometimes former military leaders, gained national power. They looted treasuries and ignored constitutions. Supported by the military, they ruled as dictators.

Power struggles among competing strongmen led to frequent revolts that changed little except the name of the leader. In the long run, power remained in the hands of a privileged few who had no desire to share it.

Conservatives and Liberals As in Europe, the ruling elite in Latin America were divided between conservatives and liberals. Conservatives defended the traditional social order, favored press censorship, and strongly supported the Catholic Church. They wanted to maintain the current social order, fearing that change would bring chaos and disorder.

Liberals backed Enlightenment ideas of liberty, equality, and popular sovereignty. They supported laissez-faire economics, religious toleration, and freedom of the press. They wanted to weaken the power of the Catholic Church by breaking up its vast landholdings and ending its monopoly on education. Liberals saw themselves as enlightened supporters of progress but often showed little concern for the needs of the majority of the people.

IDENTIFY CAUSE AND EFFECT What political obstacles to democracy were caused by lingering effects of colonial rule in Latin America?

Mexico's Search for Stability

During the 1800s, each Latin American nation followed its own course. Mexico provides an example of the challenges facing many Latin American nations.

In the years after independence, large landowners, army leaders, and the Catholic Church dominated Mexican politics. Deep social divisions separated wealthy creoles from mestizos and Indians who lived in desperate poverty. Bitter battles between conservatives and liberals led to revolts and the rise of dictators.

Santa Anna and War With the United States

Between 1833 and 1855, an ambitious and cunning *caudillo*, Antonio López de Santa Anna, gained and lost power many times. Allied with Spain during Mexico's war of independence, Santa Anna switched sides when he saw that Spain was losing. Following a similar pattern as president, he first posed as a liberal reformer. Then, after critics opposed his reforms, he reversed his stand. When in power, Santa Anna ruled as a dictator.

Settlers in Mexico's northern territory of Texas took advantage of the chaos in Mexico to seek independence in 1835. Many settlers had moved to Texas from the United States and wanted to ensure a stable government. Santa Anna marched north to crush the rebels. Although he overwhelmed Texas forces at the Alamo, he was soon defeated and captured. In 1836, he was forced to recognize the independent Republic of Texas.

>> Life did not improve for many Latin Americans after they gained independence. Here, peasant women process crops grown on a hacienda in Mexico in the 1800s.

Santa Anna returned to Mexico in disgrace, but reemerged as a hero in a brief conflict with France. In 1846, after the United States annexed Texas, war broke out between Mexico and the United States. Santa Anna took command of Mexican forces, but was again defeated.

In the Treaty of Guadalupe-Hidalgo, which ended the war in 1848, Mexico lost almost half its territory to the United States. The humiliating defeat forced Santa Anna into exile and triggered new violence between conservatives and liberals in Mexico.

La Reforma Brings Changes to Mexico In 1855, **Benito Juárez** (WAHR ez) and other liberals gained power and opened an era of reform known as **La Reforma.**

Juárez, of Zapotec Indian heritage, offered hope to the oppressed people of Mexico. He and his fellow reformers revised the Mexican constitution to strip the military of power and end the special privileges of the Church. They ordered the Church to sell unused lands to peasants.

Conservatives resisted La Reforma, unleashing a disastrous civil war. Juárez was elected president in 1861 and expanded his reforms. Conservative opponents turned to Europe for help. Mexico owed large debts to several European countries, including France. In 1863, Napoleon III sent troops to Mexico and set up Austrian archduke Maximilian as emperor.

For four years, Juárez's forces battled against Mexican conservatives and French forces. When France withdrew its troops, Maximilian was captured and shot. In 1867, Juárez returned to power and tried to renew reform, but opponents resisted. Juárez died in office in 1872 never achieving all the reforms he envisioned. He did, however, bring mestizos into politics, separate church and state, and help to unite Mexico.

>> Benito Juárez, a Mexican lawyer and politician, brought reforms to Mexico and served several terms as president. His reforms helped unite Mexico and bring mestizos into politics.

A Dictator's Order, Progress, and Oppression After Juárez died, General Porfirio Díaz, a hero of the war against the French, used the military to seize power. From 1876 to 1880 and 1884 to 1911, he ruled as a dictator. In the name of "Order and Progress," he strengthened the army, local police, and central government. Any opposition was brutally crushed.

Under his harsh rule, Mexico made impressive economic advances. It build railroads, increased foreign trade, developed some industry, and expanded mining. Growth, however, had a high cost. Capital for development came from foreign investors, to whom Díaz granted special rights. He also let wealthy landowners buy up Indian lands.

The rich prospered, but most Mexicans remained poor. Many Indians and mestizos fell into **peonage** to their employers. In the peonage system, hacienda owners would give workers advances on their wages and require them to stay on the hacienda until they had paid back what they owed. Wages remained low, and workers were rarely able to repay the hacienda owner.

Most Mexicans lived in desperate poverty even as they worked on haciendas or in the new factories. Many children died in infancy. Other children worked 12-hour days and never learned to read or write.

SUMMARIZE What reforms did Juárez achieve to help Mexico attempt a more stable government and society?

The Economics of Latin America's Dependence

Under colonial rule, mercantilist policies made Latin America economically dependent on Spain and Portugal. Colonies sent raw materials such as cash

>> Analyze Maps The map shows European and U.S. possessions in Latin America in the early 1900s. Imperialists often acted to protect business interests. What explains the strong U.S. interest in Latin America?

crops or precious metals to the parent country and had to buy manufactured goods from them.

Strict laws kept colonists from trading with other countries. Other laws prohibited the building of local industries that would have competed with the parent country. Overall, these policies kept the colonies from developing their own economies.

The Cycle of Economic Dependence After independence, this pattern changed very little. The new Latin American republics did adopt free trade, welcoming all comers. Britain and the United States rushed into the new markets, replacing Spain as Latin America's chief trading partners. But the region remained as economically dependent as before.

Economic dependence occurs when less developed nations export raw materials and commodities to industrial nations and import manufactured goods, capital, and technological know-how. The relationship is unequal because the more developed nations control the prices and terms of trade.

Foreign Investment and Influence In the 1800s, foreign goods flooded Latin America,creating large profits for foreigners and for a handful of local business people. Foreign investment, which could yield enormous profits, was often accompanied by local interference. Investors from Britain, the United States, and other nations pressured their governments to take action if political events or reform movements in a Latin American country seemed to threaten their interests.

Limited Economic Growth After 1850, some Latin American economies did grow. Industrial countries needed increasing quantities of raw materials and other products from Latin America. With foreign capital, Latin American countries were able to develop mining and agriculture. Chile exported copper and nitrates. Argentina expanded its livestock and wheat production. Brazil added coffee and rubber to its traditional cash crop of sugar. By the early 1900s, both Venezuela and Mexico were developing profitable oil industries.

Throughout the region, foreigners invested in modern ports and railroads to carry goods from the interior to coastal cities. As in the United States at the time, European immigrants poured into Latin America. The newcomers helped to promote economic activity, and a small middle class emerged.

Thanks to trade, investment, technology, and migration, Latin American nations moved into the world economy. Yet internal development was limited. Local industries grew slowly, in part because of the social structure.

The tiny elite at the top benefited from the economic upturn. Their wealth grew, but very little trickled down to the masses of people at the bottom. The poor earned too little to buy consumer goods. Without a strong demand, many industries failed to develop.

IDENTIFY CAUSE AND EFFECT What were some negative effects of foreign investment in Latin America?

The United States Wields Power and Influence

As Latin American nations tried to build stable governments and develop their economies, the United States expanded across North America. At first, the young republics in the Western Hemisphere looked favorably on each other. Simón Bolívar praised the United States as a "model of political virtues and moral enlightenment." In time however, Latin American nations began to feel threatened by the "Colossus of the North," the giant power that cast its shadow over the entire hemisphere.

COASTING.
The old horse was too slow for Uncle Sam.

>> **Analyze Political Cartoons** This cartoon portrays the early 1900s entry of the United States into competition with European powers for territory in the Eastern Hemisphere. Why are the Europeans shouting at Uncle Sam?

Bounce to Activate Cartoon

The Monroe Doctrine of 1823 In the 1820s, Spain plotted to recover its American colonies. Britain opposed any move that might close the door to trade with Latin America. Britain asked the United States to join it in a statement opposing any new colonization of the Americas.

American President James Monroe, however, wanted to avoid any "entangling alliance" with Britain. Acting alone, he issued the **Monroe Doctrine** in 1823. "The American continents," it declared, "are henceforth not to be considered as subjects for future colonization by any European powers."

The United States lacked the military power to enforce the Monroe Doctrine. But with the support of Britain's strong navy, the doctrine discouraged European interference. For more than a century, the Monroe Doctrine would be the key to United States policy in the Americas.

The United States Expands As a result of the Mexican American War, the United States acquired the thinly populated regions of northern Mexico, gaining all or part of the present-day states of California, Arizona, New Mexico, Nevada, Utah, and Colorado. The victory fed dreams of future expansion. Before the century had ended, the United States controlled much of North America and was becoming involved in overseas conflicts.

Cuba and the Spanish American War For decades, Cuban patriots had battled to free their island from Spanish rule. As they began to make headway, the United States joined their cause, declaring war on Spain in 1898. The brief Spanish-American War ended in a crushing defeat for Spain.

In the peace treaty ending the war, the United States acquired Puerto Rico in the Caribbean and the Philippines and Guam in the Pacific. Cuba was granted independence, but in 1901, the United States forced Cubans to add the Platt Amendment to their constitution. The amendment gave the United States naval bases in Cuba and the right to intervene in Cuban affairs.

U.S. Intervention in Latin America American investments in Latin America soared in the early 1900s. Citing the need to protect those investments, in 1904 the United States issued the Roosevelt Corollary to the Monroe Doctrine. Under this policy, the United States claimed "international police power" in the Western Hemisphere. When the Dominican Republic failed to pay its foreign debts, the United States sent in troops. Americans collected customs duties, paid off the debts, and remained for years.

In the next decades, the United States sent troops to Cuba, Haiti, Mexico, Honduras, Nicaragua, and other countries in Central America and the Caribbean. Like European powers in Africa and Asia, the United States intervened in Latin America to protect American lives and investments. Still, its actions triggered outrage and resentment across Latin America.

The Panama Canal From the late 1800s, the United States had wanted to build a canal across Panama in Central America. A canal would let American warships move between the Atlantic and Pacific coasts and protect its coastlines on either side of the continent. Shorter shipping times would also greatly reduce the cost of trade.

Panama, however, belonged to Colombia, which refused to sell the United States land for the canal. In 1903, the United States backed a revolt by Panamanians against Colombia. The Panamanians quickly won independence and gave the United States control of the land to build the canal.

Construction began in 1904. Engineers solved many difficult problems in the course of building the canal, including cutting through mountains and excavating about 232 million cubic yards of dirt, rocks, and debris.

The **Panama Canal** opened in 1914. It was an engineering marvel that boosted American trade and shipping worldwide. The canal cut the distance of a sea journey between cities such as New York and San Francisco by thousands of miles.

To people in Latin America, however, the canal was another example of "Yankee imperialism." During the 1900s, nationalist feeling in the hemisphere was often expressed as anti-Americanism. In 2000, Panama finally gained complete control over the canal, which now forms a vital part of the Panamanian economy.

IDENTIFY CAUSE AND EFFECT How did the United States influence the direction of Cuban history?

>> **Analyze Information** Two men stand inside one of the Panama Canal lock's enormous gates. The gates allow water to flow in and out, raising or lowering ships to different levels. What does the perspective of the photo indicate about the scale of the project?

Bounce to Activate Gallery

>> By the late 1700s, there were still parts of Canada that had not yet been reached by European settlers. By the mid-1800s, the country had begun to grow, and settlements spread to new areas.

Canada Achieves Self-Rule

In North America, Canada developed slowly in the shadow of its powerful neighbor to the south. Canada's first European rulers were the French. When France lost Canada to Britain in 1763, thousands of French-speaking Catholic settlers remained there.

After the American Revolution, about 30,000 British loyalists fled from the United States to Canada. Unlike the earlier French settlers,they were English-speaking and Protestant. Rivalries between these two groups have been an ongoing issue in Canada ever since.

Native Americans formed another strand of the Canadian heritage. In the 1790s, various groups of Native American people lived in eastern Canada. Others, in the west and the north, remained largely undisturbed by white settlers. Canadians today refer to all these Native American groups as First Nations.

Unrest in the Two Canadas To ease ethnic tensions between European settlers, Britain passed the Constitutional Act of 1791. The act created two provinces: English-speaking Upper Canada (now Ontario) and French-speaking Lower Canada (now Quebec). Each had its own laws, legislature, and royal governor. French traditions and the Catholic Church were protected in Lower Canada while English traditions and laws guided Upper Canada.

During the early 1800s, unrest grew in both colonies. The people of Upper Canada resented the power held by a small British elite who controlled the government. In Lower Canada, people felt that British officials ignored their needs.

In 1837, discontent flared into rebellion in both Upper and Lower Canada. William Lyon Mackenzie led the revolt in Upper Canada, crying, "Put down the villains who oppress and enslave our country!" Louis Joseph Papineau, the head of the French Canadian Reform party, led the rebellion in Lower Canada.

Britain's Response The British had learned a lesson from the American Revolution. While they hurried to put down the disorder, they sent an able politician, Lord Durham, to compile a report on the causes of the unrest. In 1839, the Durham Report called for the two Canadas to be united and given control over their own affairs.

In 1840, Parliament passed the Act of Union, a major step toward self-government. It joined the two Canadas and gave Canada an elected legislature to determine domestic policies. Britain kept control of foreign policy and trade.

>> Analyze Maps Canada grew throughout the late 1800s. This map shows Canadian provinces from 1867 to 1914 and their natural resources. List the natural resources of Manitoba and Nova Scotia.

The Dominion of Canada Like the United States, Canada expanded westward in the 1800s and new settlements were built. As the country grew, two Canadians, John Macdonald and George-Etienne Cartier, urged **confederation,** or unification, of British settlements in North America. They included Nova Scotia, New Brunswick, Prince Edward Island, and British Columbia, as well as the united Upper and Lower Canadas.

Like many Canadians at the time, the two leaders feared that the United States might try to dominate Canada. Confederation, they thought, would strengthen the new nation against American ambitions and help it develop economically.

Britain finally agreed to the plan. In 1867, it passed the British North America Act, which created the Dominion of Canada. A **dominion** is a self-governing nation. As a dominion, Canada had its own parliament, modeled on that of Britain. By 1900, Canada also controlled its own foreign policy. Still, Canada maintained close ties with Britain.

Like Australia and New Zealand, Canada won independence and self-rule faster and easier than British colonies in Africa or Asia. Many Canadians shared the same language and cultural heritage as Britain. Racial attitudes also played a part, as Britain considered white Canadians better able to govern themselves than the non-white populations elsewhere in their empire.

Canada Expands John MacDonald, Canada's first prime minister, encouraged expansion. To unite the far-flung regions of Canada, he called for a transcontinental railroad. In 1885, the Canadian Pacific Railway opened,linking eastern and western Canada. Wherever the railroad went, settlers followed. It moved people and products, such as timber, grain, minerals, and manufactured goods across the country.

As in the United States, westward expansion destroyed the way of life of Native American people. Most were forced to sign treaties giving up their lands. Some resisted. Louis Riel led a revolt of the **métis,** people of mixed Native American and French Canadian descent. These French-speaking Catholics accused the government of stealing their land and trying to destroy their language and religion. Government troops put down the uprising and executed Riel.

In the late 1800s and early 1900s, more immigrants flooded into Canada from Germany, Italy, Poland, Russia, Ukraine, China, and Japan. They joined the English, Scottish, and Irish settlers who had arrived earlier. These groups enriched Canada economically and culturally.

By 1914, Canada was a flourishing independent nation. Still, two issues plagued Canada. First, French-speaking Canadians were determined to preserve their separate heritage, making it hard for Canadians to create a single national identity. Second, the United States exerted a powerful economic and cultural influence that threatened to dominate Canada. Both issues have continued to affect Canada to the present day.

ANALYZE INFORMATION What were some reasons that Canada achieved self-rule faster and easier than other British colonies?

ASSESSMENT

1. **Connect** How was Latin America's ruling elite similar to Europe's ruling class, and why was that a political problem?
2. **Identify Cause and Effect** How did dictator General Porfirio Díaz contribute to economic and political instability in Mexico?
3. **Identify Cause and Effect** How did colonial rule contribute to Latin America's continuing economic dependence after colonialism?
4. **Identify Cause and Effect** What effects did the Monroe Doctrine and Roosevelt Corollary have on Latin America?
5. **Summarize** How did the British respond to the Canadians' desire for self-rule?

California Topic 4 Quick Study Guide

LESSON SUMMARIES

Use these Lesson Summaries, and the longer versions available online, to review the key ideas for each lesson in this Topic.

Lesson 1: The New Imperialism

During the 1800s, some European nations set up colonies in Africa and Asia to acquire the natural resources needed to meet manufacturing demands. Claiming cultural superiority, Europeans felt Western culture should be spread, but colonial resistance to Western domination rose.

Lesson 2: European Colonies in Africa

In the late 1800s, Britain, France, and other European nations began a scramble for African territories. Within twenty years, Europeans had carved up the continent and dominated millions of Africans.

Lesson 3: Europe and the Muslim World

Napoleon's Egyptian campaign highlighted the decline of the Ottoman empire and opened a new era of European contact with the Muslim regions. European nations soon moved in to benefit from the crumbling empire.

Lesson 4: India Becomes a British Colony

In the early 1600s, the British East India Company won trading rights on the fringe of the Mughal empire. As Mughal power declined, the company's influence grew. After the Sepoy Rebellion, Parliament ended the rule of the British East India Company and after 1858, set up colonial rule in India.

Lesson 5: China and the West

After defeat in the Opium Wars with Britain, China was forced to accept terms of an unequal treaty which resulted in concessions to Western powers. Qing China declined as Western powers used diplomacy and war to gain power in East Asia.

Lesson 6: The Modernization of Japan

When Japan chose to abandon its centuries of isolation, the country, pressured by the United States, opened its markets to the West. During the Meiji Restoration, Japan rapidly modernized. By the early 1900s, Japan was the strongest empire in Asia.

Lesson 7: Southeast Asia and the Pacific

As they had in Africa, Western industrial powers pushed into Southeast Asia in their need to acquire raw materials, new markets, and to spread Christianity.

Lesson 8: The Americas in the Age of Imperialism

The economy of Latin America became dependent on industrialized nations for investment, technology, and manufactured goods.

VISUAL REVIEW

Use these graphics to review some of the key terms, people, and ideas from this Topic.

Western Imperialism

AFRICA

- Berlin Conference
- Raw materials exploited
- Boer War
- Racial segregation in South Africa
- Western-educated African elite
- Nationalism grows

MUSLIM REGIONS

- Islamic reform movements
- Internal revolts
- Armenian genocide
- Egypt modernizes

INDIA

- British East India Company
- Changes to legal and caste systems
- Sepoy Rebellion
- Indians forced to raise cash crops
- Population growth and famine
- Indian National Congress
- Muslim League

CHINA

- Opium War
- Unequal trade treaties
- Self-strengthening movement
- Sino-Japanese War
- Boxer Uprising

New Imperialism

CAUSES

- Industrial Revolution strengthens the West
- Newly industrialized nations seek new markets
- European nations compete for power

EFFECTS

- Europeans claim and conquer large empires in Africa and Asia
- Western powers spread their ideas and adopt elements of nonwestern cultures
- Local people resist European domination
- Some nonwestern leaders attempt reforms in an effort to modernize

California Topic 4 Assessment

KEY TERMS, PEOPLE, AND IDEAS

1. Why did Europeans seek to expand their overseas empires in the 1800s? What two European nations would colonize most of Africa?
2. What role did the **Boer War** play in Britain's bid for colonial power in Africa?
3. How did Social Darwinism become a factor in the New Imperialism?
4. What events sparked the **Boxer uprising** in China?
5. Why do people in India refer to the Sepoy Rebellion as the First War of Independence?
6. What problems faced new nations in Latin America as a result of colonial rule?
7. What role did **Commodore Matthew Perry** assume in establishing relations with Japan?
8. How did the **Monroe Doctrine** affect Latin America?
9. Why did the United States want to build the **Panama Canal**?

CRITICAL THINKING

10. **Synthesize Information** How did the Industrial Revolution contribute to the new imperialism?
11. **Analyze Information** Describe the ideology of Sun Yixian in his quest for a new China.
12. **Draw Conclusions** How did European imperialism cause political conflict among peoples in different colonies?
13. **Create a Timeline** Use the information you have learned to create a timeline of events during the age of imperialism. The timeline should have the following: You will create a timeline for Africa, Japan, China, and the Americas. Label events between 1800 and 1925. Choose events which were significant in the development of or impact of imperialism in a particular region.
14. **Analyze Information** How did the Monroe Doctrine establish new goals for U.S. foreign policy?
15. **Evaluate Information** How did British rule lead to growing Indian nationalism?
16. **Use Primary Sources** The excerpt below gives one perspective of citizens who endured colonial rule. Some Chinese citizens wanted to adopt Western ideas. In 1896, Liang Ch'i-ch'ao, an influential Chinese thinker, was unhappy with conditions in China. (a) Why do you think Ch'i-ch'ao was a major supporter of reform in China? (b) What kind of "move" do you think "secret societies" were waiting to make?

> "Whenever there is a flood or drought, communications are severed, there is no way to transport famine relief, the dead are abandoned to fill the ditches or are disregarded, and nine out of ten houses are emptied. . . . The members of secret societies are scattered over the whole country, waiting for the chance to move. Industry is not developed, commerce is not discussed, the native goods daily become less salable. . . ."
> —*Liang Ch'i-ch'ao, On the Harm of Not Reforming*

17. **Writing Activity** Read the following passage on European Fashions. A Brazilian writer describes how the richer class dresses. Use your knowledge of what you have learned about imperialism and the excerpt below to discuss why the elite in Pernambuco dressed so impractically. What did it say about the values of the elite?

> "At that time . . . Brazil did not manufacture a yard of silk, a shoe, a spool of thread; everything was imported. . . . Men's clothing for a tropical climate was made of English wool suitable for life in the unheated homes of an English winter. I asked myself: how did they stand the heat? The ladies when they took off their shoes at home used slippers of heavy wool, as if they were in Siberia. . . . Except for the poor, I never saw in the Pernambuco [the writer's hometown] of my time anyone dressed in light clothing.
> —*Gilbert Amado, Historia da Minha Infancia*

DOCUMENT-BASED QUESTIONS

The Armenian massacre has been called the "forgotten genocide." It refers to the destruction, between 1895 and 1923, of the Christian Armenians of Turkey under the Muslim Ottoman government. Read the documents below, then answer the questions that follow.

DOCUMENT A

"As it got worse, all of us, and all the people, began gathering in our school. The word came around that the Turks were going on the streets and killing all the Armenians and leaving them on the streets. I, myself, was in school already, so I simply stayed there. Then orders came from the school that we, too, should run away. But where? All the buildings were on fire! The Turks were burning everything. There was a whole group of us running away from the school."

—Annalin, a survivor from Smyrna on events of 1922

DOCUMENT B

"The massacre of Armenian subjects in the Ottoman Empire in 1896 . . . was amateur and ineffective compared with the largely successful attempt to exterminate [them] during the First World War in 1915. . . . [This] genocide was carried out under the cloak of legality by cold-blooded governmental action. These were not mass-murders committed spontaneously by mobs of private people. . . ."

—Arnold Toynbee, British historian, cited in Experiences

DOCUMENT C

"The 1,000 Armenian houses are being emptied of furniture by the police one after the other. The furniture, bedding and everything of value is being stored in large buildings about the city. . . . The goods are piled in without any attempt at labeling or systematic storage. A crowd of Turkish women and children follow the police about like a lot of vultures and seize anything they can lay their hands on and when the more valuable things are carried out of the house by the police they rush in and take the balance. . . . I suppose it will take several weeks to empty all the houses and then the Armenian shops and stores will be cleared out."

—From a report to the American embassy by Oscar S. Heizer, American consul in Tebizond, July 1915

DOCUMENT D

"The proportion of Armenians killed by the Turks in World War I out of the general number of Armenians in the Ottoman Empire was no less than that of the Jewish victims [during the Holocaust] out of the total Jewish population in Europe. Nor are the methods of killing unique. . . . The type of murder committed by the Germans in the USSR—mass machine-gunning—was the traditional method of mass murder in our century, and the death marches of Jews in the closing stages of the war had their precedent in the Armenian case as well. Nor is the fact that in the case of the Holocaust it was a state machine and a bureaucracy that was responsible for the murder unique, because there, too, the Young Turks had preceded the German Nazis in planning the execution of a population with such means as were modern at the time."

—From Remembrance and Denial by Richard G. Hovannisian

18. According to Document B, the 1915 massacre of Armenians

A. went unpunished.

B. was ineffective and unsuccessful.

C. was not as well documented as the 1896 massacre.

D. was committed with the knowledge of the Turkish government.

19. Document C shows that the Turkish police

A. tried to protect the property of Armenian citizens despite their government's orders.

B. tried to help Armenian citizens as best they could.

C. took part in stealing the property of Armenian citizens.

D. protested to the American embassy to try to help their friends.

20. According to Document D, the Armenian Massacre and the Holocaust

A. were committed by the same people.

B. were carried out in a similar way.

C. had very few similarities, except for the large number of murders.

D. both took place in Germany.

21. **Writing Tasks** Ismayale Kemal Pasha, a governor in Marash, tried to save Armenian citizens, despite orders from his superiors to carry out the genocide without remorse. Suppose Ismayale Kemal Pasha explained his decision to help in a memoir. Write a brief explanation from his point of view. Use these documents along with information from the Topic in your writing.

End-of-Topic Practice

1 Which scenario best illustrates a major political motivation that influenced European imperialism?

A The breakup of the Ottoman Empire started a scramble among European nations for colonies.

B Britain and Germany seized territory in West Africa to prevent France from claiming more land.

C Belgium seized territory in Africa in order to dominate the international rubber and copper trade.

D The Dutch East India Company patrolled the waters of the Indian Ocean with its own fleet to protect its trading vessels.

---

2 How did Ethiopia resist colonizing by Italy?

F Always interested in new technologies, Menelik studied war strategies of Britain and France.

G Menelik entered into unequal trade agreements with several European nations with the understanding that Ethiopia would be a protectorate.

H Menelik reached out to neighboring leaders to plan a defense strategy that proved successful.

J While negotiating treaties with Italy, Menelik started importing weapons from France and Russia and enlisted training advice for his army from European officers.

"In April 1884 the Viceroy, Lord Ripon, wrote to Lord Kimberley, the Secretary of State for India, on a question of government policy which was becoming daily more pressing: 'You may rely upon it that there are few Indian questions of greater importance in the present day than those which relate to the mode in which we are to deal with the growing body of natives educated by ourselves in Western learning and Western ideas.'"

3 Which statement best explains the concern expressed by Lord Ripon?

A Many Western-educated Indians felt that the ideas of democracy and human rights could best be realized by remaining under British rule.

B Many Western-educated Indians were afraid that the ideas of democracy and human rights would let Muslims dominate an independent India.

C Many Western-educated Indians disagreed with the ideas of democracy and human rights and yearned to reestablish traditional rule in India.

D Many Western-educated Indians were impressed with the ideas of democracy and human rights and wanted to end imperial rule and establish self-rule.

---

4 How did Latin American countries receive the Monroe Doctrine?

F It represented solidarity with the United States and recognition of newly independent republics.

G It represented intention by the United States to monopolize Latin American trade and their internal affairs.

H It thrust Latin American countries into political turmoil—they preferred to manage contact with European powers as they wished.

J It protected Latin America against British invasion.

If you have trouble with. . .				
Question	1	2	3	4
See Lesson	4.1	4.2	4.4	4.8

PEARSON realize™
PearsonSchool.com/CASS

Go ONLINE for digital resources

VIDEO AUDIO ETEXT ACTIVITY WRITING GAMES PDF ASSESSMENT

[ESSENTIAL QUESTION] When is war justified?

5 World War I and the Russian Revolution (1914–1924)

>> American soldiers in World War I

Enduring Understandings

- Imperial rivalries, militarism, extreme nationalism, and a system of competing alliances contributed to the outbreak of World War I.
- Trench warfare and modern military technology led to a long stalemate and high casualty rates.
- U.S. entry into the war led to an Allied victory.
- Woodrow Wilson tried to build a lasting peace based on his Fourteen Points, but the Treaty of Versailles punished Germany harshly.
- In Russia, wartime hardships sparked the March Revolution, forcing the tsar to abdicate.
- Lenin and the Bolsheviks seized power in the November Revolution and began to build a communist state in Russia.

NBC LEARN

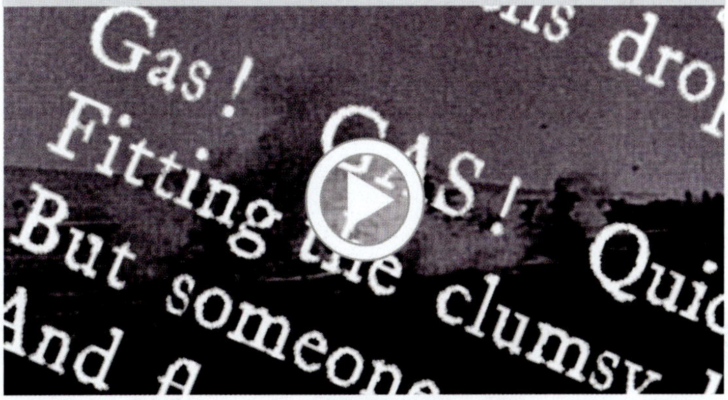

See World War I through the eyes of an English soldier and poet.

Bounce to Activate My Story Video

California Topic 5 Overview

In this Topic, you will learn about the events of World War I. Look at the lesson outline and explore the timeline. As you study this Topic, you will complete the Quest team project.

LESSON OUTLINE

5.1 World War I Begins
HSS 10.5, HSS 10.5.1; Analysis CST.1, CST.2, HRE.4, HI.1

5.2 Fighting the Great War
HSS 10.5, HSS 10.5.2, HSS 10.5.4, HSS 10.5.5; Analysis CST.1, CST.2, HRE.4, HI.1

5.3 World War I Ends
HSS 10.5, HSS 10.5.3, HSS 10.5.4, HSS 10.6, HSS 10.6.1, HSS 10.6.2; Analysis CST.1, CST.2, HRE.4, HI.1

5.4 Revolution in Russia
HSS 10.5.3, HSS 10.7.1, HSS 10.8.1; Analysis CST.1, CST.2, HRE.4, HI.1

Key Events of World War I

1914
Archduke Ferdinand and his wife are assassinated in Sarajevo.

1917
The United States joins the Allies. March and October revolutions erupt in Russia.

1919
Delegates to the Paris Peace Conference draft the Treaty of Versailles.

1910 — 1915 — 1920 — 1925

1916
More than two million soldiers are killed in the battle of Verdun and the battles of the Somme.

1918
Armistice with Germany ends the war.

1920
Communist government wins civil war in Russia.

QUEST! TEAM PROJECT

Create a Video Docudrama about World War I

How did the war change the lives of civilians, soldiers, and leaders? In this Quest, you will read about the changes, then create a docudrama of people's experiences during that time.

STEP 1
As you begin the project, review what you know about World War I. Assign topics to be researched. List questions. Prepare story outlines.

STEP 2
Become familiar with the requirements of making a docudrama. There are websites you can use.

STEP 3
After information is gathered and evaluated, start writing the first narrative draft. Review, edit, and revise your presentation.

STEP 4
Present your completed video to your classmates, and your family and friends. Use this opportunity to reflect on the impact of war as it affected people then and now.

PEARSON realize™
PearsonSchool.com/CASS
Go ONLINE for complete Quest materials
VIDEO ETEXT WRITING RUBRIC PDF ASSESSMENT

>> Archduke Francis Ferdinand and his wife, Sophie, were assassinated on June 28, 1914, just one hour after this photograph was taken.

5.1 By 1914, Europe had enjoyed a century of relative peace. Idealists hoped for a permanent end to the scourge of war. International events, such as the first modern Olympic games in 1896 and the First Universal Peace Conference in 1899, were steps toward keeping the peace. "The future belongs to peace," said French economist Frédéric Passy (pa SEE).

Bounce to Activate Flipped Video

>> Objectives

Describe how imperialism, nationalism, and militarism pushed Europe closer to war.

Identify the key event that sparked World War I.

Trace how the alliance system drew nations into the war.

>> Key Terms

entente
militarism
Alsace and Lorraine
ultimatum
mobilize
neutrality

World War I Begins

European Powers Form Alliances

Not everyone was so hopeful. "I shall not live to see the Great War," warned German Chancellor Otto von Bismarck, "but you will see it, and it will start in the east." It was Bismarck's prediction, rather than Passy's, that came true.

Nations Form Alliances Despite efforts to ensure peace, the late 1800s saw growing rivalries among the great powers of Europe, including Britain, France, Germany, Austria-Hungary, Italy, and Russia. In an atmosphere of fear and distrust, the great powers set out to protect themselves by forming alliances. Nations signed treaties pledging to defend each other. These alliances were intended to create powerful combinations that no one would dare attack. Gradually, two rival alliances evolved.

The Triple Alliance The first major alliance had its origins in Bismarck's day. He knew that France longed to avenge its defeat in the Franco-Prussian War. Sure that France would not attack Germany without help, Bismarck signed treaties with other powers. By 1882, Germany had formed the Triple Alliance with Italy and Austria-Hungary. Although Bismarck had previously signed an alliance with Russia, Kaiser William II did not preserve that alliance, leaving Russia free to seek other allies.

In 1914, when war did erupt, Germany and Austria-Hungary fought on the same side. They became known as the Central Powers.

The Triple Entente A rival bloc took shape in 1893, when France and Russia signed a secret treaty. France was eager to end its isolation and balance the growing power of Germany. In 1904, France and Britain signed an **entente** (ahn TAHNT), a nonbinding agreement to follow common policies. Though not as formal as a treaty, the entente led to close military and diplomatic ties. Britain later signed a similar agreement with Russia, creating the Triple Entente. When war began, these powers became known as the Allies.

Britain and France had been rivals for hundreds of years, and France had invaded Russia during the Napoleonic Wars. Still, these three powers joined together in the Triple Entente because they feared Germany wanted to dominate Europe.

Other Alliances Other states were drawn into alliances. Germany signed a treaty with the Ottoman empire. As early as 1867, Britain had signed a treaty to protect Belgium's right to remain neutral in any European conflict. Italy had a secret treaty with France not to attack it. And Russia had agreed to protect Serbia. Britain forged ties with Japan.

Rather than easing tensions, the growth of rival alliance systems made governments increasingly nervous. A local conflict could mushroom into a general war. In 1914, that threat became a reality.

ANALYZE INFORMATION Why did the European nations form opposing alliances?

Major Causes of World War I

During the late 1800s and early 1900s, tensions were increasing among the great powers of Europe. Aggressive nationalism, economic competition, imperialism, militarism, and an arms race all helped fuel an atmosphere of suspicion and distrust.

Economic and Imperial Rivalry Economic rivalries helped sour the international atmosphere. Germany, the newest of the great powers, was growing into an economic and military powerhouse. Britain felt threatened by Germany's rapid growth. Germany, in turn, thought the other great powers

>> Germany, led by Kaiser William II (left), and Austria-Hungary, led by Emperor Francis Joseph (right), became close allies in the years before World War I.

>> A Parisian newspaper presented this view of imperialism. The caption says "France freely gives Morocco civilization, peace, and wealth." **Hypothesize** Who might have opposed this viewpoint? Why?

did not give it enough respect. It also worried about future economic competition from Russia, which had a huge population and vast natural resources.

Imperialism also divided European nations. In 1905 and again in 1911, competition for colonies brought France and Germany to the brink of war in Morocco, then under France's influence. Although diplomats kept the peace, Germany did gain some territory in central Africa. As a result of the two Moroccan crises, Britain and France strengthened their ties against Germany.

Militarism and the Arms Race The late 1800s saw a rise in **militarism,** or the glorification of the military. Under militarism, the armed forces and readiness for war came to dominate national policy. Militarists painted war in romantic colors. Young men dreamed of blaring trumpets and dashing cavalry charges—not at all the sort of conflict they would soon face.

With international tensions on the rise, the great powers began to build up their armies and navies. The fiercest competition was the naval rivalry between Britain and Germany. To protect its vast overseas empire, Britain had built the world's most respected navy. As Germany began acquiring overseas colonies, it began to build up its own navy. Suspicious of Germany's motives, Britain in turn increased naval spending. Newspapers dramatized the arms race and stirred national public opinion against rival countries.

The arms race helped military leaders gain influence. On matters of peace and war, civilian governments turned to military leaders for advice. Germany generals and British admirals enjoyed great respect and got more funds to build up their forces. As militarism and the arms race fed each other, tensions grew.

Nationalism Aggressive nationalism also caused tension. Nationalism was strong in both Germany and France. Germans were proud of their new empire's military power and industrial leadership. The French were bitter about their 1871 defeat in the Franco-Prussian War and yearned to recover the parts of the border provinces of **Alsace and Lorraine** that had been taken in the war.

In Eastern Europe, Russia sponsored a powerful form of nationalism called Pan-Slavism. It held that all Slavic peoples shared a common nationality. As the largest Slavic country, Russia felt that it had a duty to lead and defend all Slavs. By 1914, it stood ready to support Serbia, a proud young Slavic nation, against any threat.

Two old multinational empires particularly feared rising nationalism. Austria-Hungary worried that nationalism might foster rebellion among the many minority populations within its empire. Ottoman

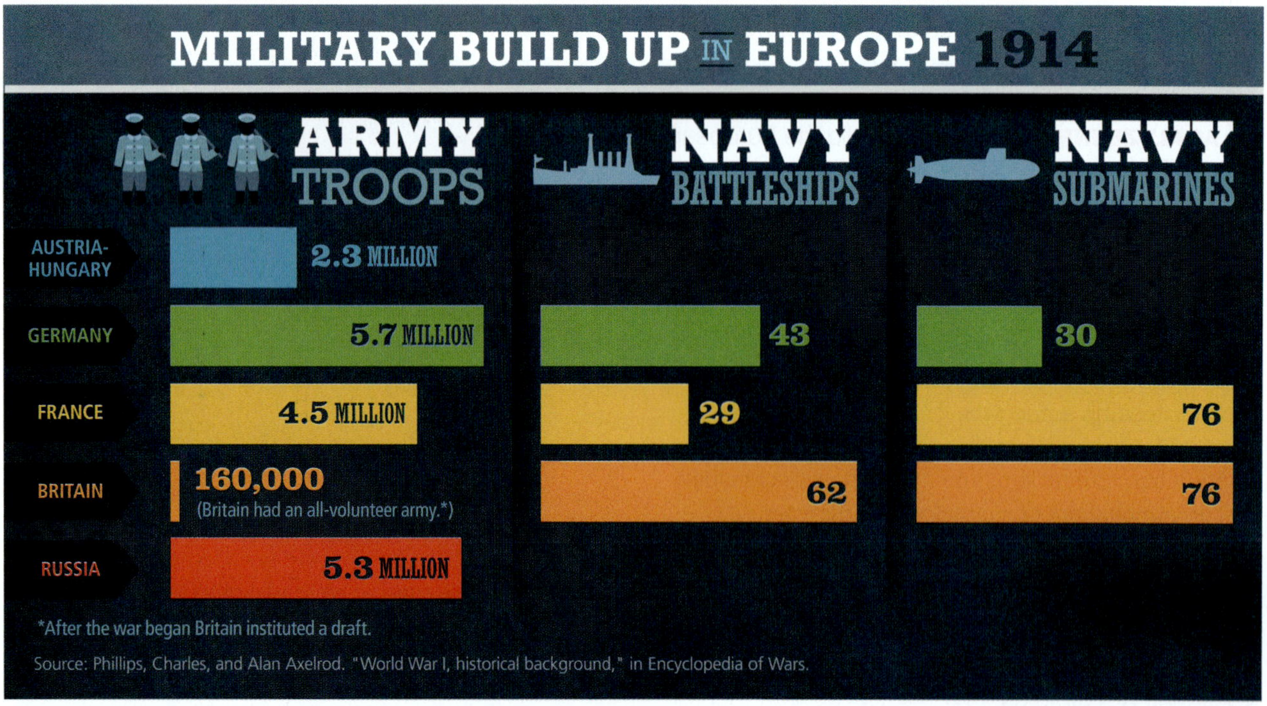

>> **Analyze Data** According to this infographic, which country had the most soldiers? Which country had the largest navy?

Turkey felt threatened by nearby new nations, such as Serbia. If realized, Serbia's dream of a South Slav state could take territory away from both Austria-Hungary and Turkey.

In 1912, several Balkan states—Serbia, Greece, Bulgaria and Montenegro—attacked Turkey and succeeded in taking a large area of land away from Turkish control. The next year, they fought among themselves over the spoils of war. These brief but bloody Balkan wars raised tensions to a fever pitch. By 1914, the Balkans were called the "powder keg of Europe"—a barrel of gunpowder that a tiny spark might cause to explode.

IDENTIFY CAUSE AND EFFECT How did imperialism heighten tensions in Europe?

The Balkan Powder Keg Explodes

As Bismarck had predicted, the Great War began in Eastern Europe. A regional conflict between tiny Serbia and the huge empire of Austria-Hungary grew rapidly into a general war that would mark one of history's significant turning points.

Archduke Francis Ferdinand Is Assassinated

The crisis began when Archduke Francis Ferdinand of Austria-Hungary announced that he would visit Sarajevo (sa ruh YAY voh), the capital of Bosnia. Francis Ferdinand was the nephew and heir of the aging Austrian emperor, Francis Joseph. At the time of his visit, Bosnia was under the rule of Austria-Hungary. But it was also the home of many Serbs and other Slavs.

News of the royal visit angered many Serbian nationalists. They viewed the Austrians as foreign oppressors. Some members of Unity or Death, a Serbian terrorist group commonly known as the Black Hand, vowed to take action.

The archduke ignored warnings of anti-Austrian unrest in Sarajevo. On June 28, 1914, he and his wife, Sophie, rode through Sarajevo in an open car. As the car passed by, a conspirator named Gavrilo Princip (GAV ree loh PREEN tseep) seized his chance and fired twice into the car. Moments later, the archduke and his wife were dead.

Austria Declares War on Serbia When news of the assassination of Francis Ferdinand reached Vienna, the government of Emperor Francis Joseph blamed Serbia. Austria-Hungary believed that Serbia would stop at nothing to achieve its goal of a South Slav empire. Austria decided its only course was to punish Serbia.

>> This political cartoon was published in 1912 in the British magazine *Punch*. **Analyze Political Cartoons** What view of the Balkans does this cartoon present?

Bounce to Activate Cartoon

In Berlin, Kaiser William II was horrified at the assassination. He wrote to Francis Joseph, advising him to take a firm stand toward Serbia. Instead of urging restraint, Germany gave Austria a "blank check," or permission to undertake whatever action it chose.

For weeks, diplomats shuttled notes among the great powers, trying to head off a conflict. Backed by Germany, however, Austria-Hungary sent Serbia a harsh **ultimatum,** or final set of demands. To avoid war, said the ultimatum, Serbia must end all anti-Austrian agitation and punish any Serbian official involved in the murder plot. It must even let Austria join in the investigation. Austria-Hungary gave Serbia 48 hours to reply.

Serbia agreed to most, but not all, of the terms of Austria's ultimatum. This partial refusal gave Austria the opportunity it was seeking. On July 28, 1914, Austria declared war on Serbia.

INTEGRATE INFORMATION How did Austria's alliance system influence Austria's decision to send Serbia an ultimatum?

>> To aid its ally Serbia, Russia mobilized its army, including these Cossacks. As World War I began, European armies still sent cavalry units into battle.

>> In August 1914, Germany invaded neutral Belgium to reach France. Here, the German infantry advances across a Belgian field filled with flowers.

The Alliance System Leads to War

The war between Austria and Serbia might have been another "summer war," like most European wars of the previous century. However, the carefully planned alliances soon drew the great powers into the conflict.

Russia and France Support Serbia After receiving Austria's ultimatum, Serbia turned to its ally, Russia. From St. Petersburg, Nicholas II telegraphed William II. The tsar asked the kaiser to urge Austria to soften its demands. When this plea failed, Russia began to **mobilize,** or prepare its military forces for war. On August 1, Germany responded by declaring war on Russia.

Russia, in turn, appealed to its ally France. In Paris, nationalists saw a chance to avenge France's defeat in the Franco-Prussian War. Though French leaders had some doubts, they gave Russia the same kind of backing Germany offered to Austria. When Germany demanded that France keep out of the conflict, France refused. Germany then declared war on France.

Germany Marches Through Belgium By early August, the battle lines were hardening. Italy and Britain still remained uncommitted. Italy chose to stay neutral for the time being. **Neutrality** is a policy of supporting neither side in a war. Britain had to decide quickly whether or not to support its ally France. Then, Germany's war plans suddenly made the decision for Britain.

Germany's worst fear was a war on two fronts, with France attacking from the west and Russia from the east. Years earlier, General Alfred Schlieffen (SHLEE fun) had developed a strategy to avoid a two-front war. Schlieffen reasoned that Russia's lumbering military would be slow to mobilize. Under the Schlieffen Plan, Germany first had to defeat France quickly. Then it would concentrate its forces against Russia.

To ensure a swift victory in the west, the Schlieffen Plan required German armies to march through neutral Belgium and then swing south behind French lines. The goal was to encircle and crush France's army. The Germans embarked on the plan by invading Belgium on August 3.

However, Germany had signed a treaty with Britain and France guaranteeing Belgian neutrality. Outraged by the invasion of Belgium, Britain declared war on Germany on August 4.

Once the machinery of war was set in motion, it seemed impossible to stop. Military leaders insisted that they must mobilize their forces immediately

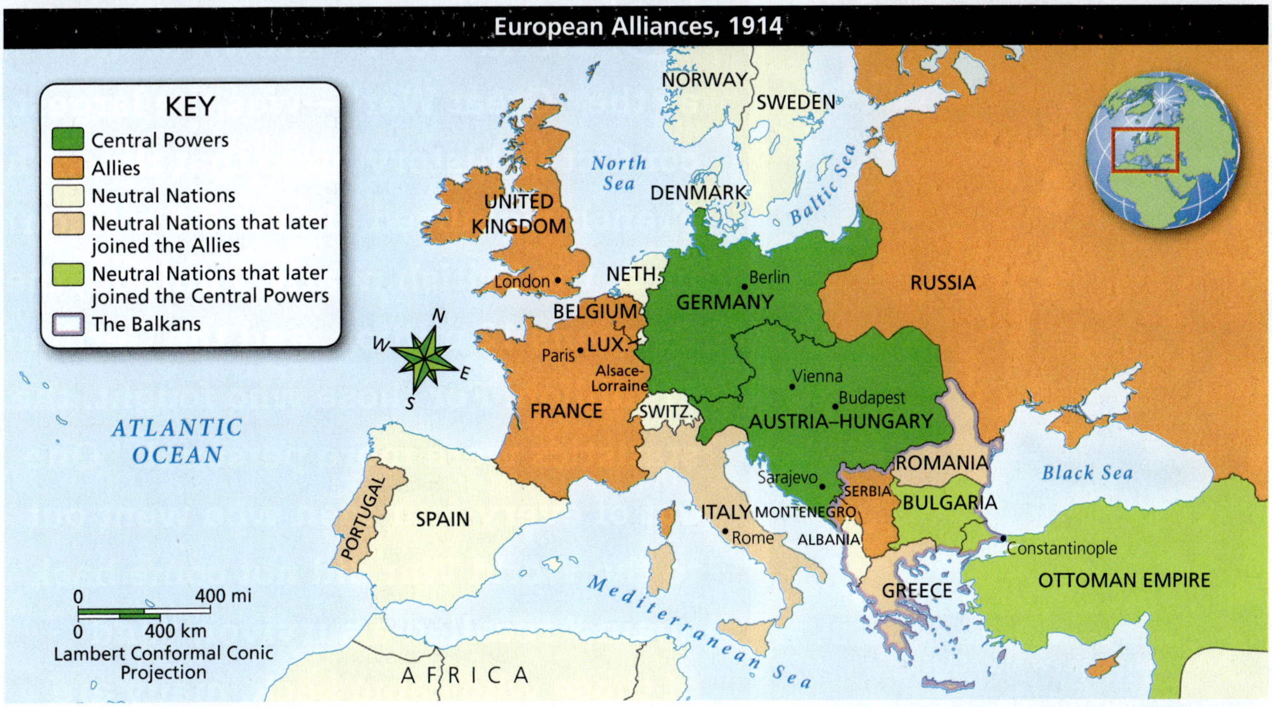

>> **Analyze Maps** How does this map help explain the expansion of World War I from a localized to a global war?

Bounce to Activate Chart

to accomplish their military goals. These military timetables made it impossible for political leaders to negotiate instead of fight.

Whose Fault? How did an assassination lead to all-out war in just a few weeks? During the war, each side blamed the other. Afterward, the victorious Allies blamed Germany. Today, most historians agree that all parties must share blame for a catastrophe nobody wanted.

Each great power believed its cause was just. Austria wanted to punish Serbia for encouraging terrorism. Germany felt that it must stand by its one dependable ally, Austria. Russia saw the Austrian ultimatum to Serbia as an effort to oppress Slavic peoples.

France feared that if it did not support Russia, it would have to face Germany alone later. Britain felt committed to protect Belgium, but also feared the growing power of Germany.

Once the machinery of war was set in motion with the Austrian ultimatum and mobilization of troops, political leaders could no longer save the peace. Although government leaders made the decisions, most people on both sides were committed to military action. Young men rushed to enlist, cheered on by women and their elders. Now that war had come at last, it seemed an exciting adventure.

British diplomat Edward Grey was less optimistic. As armies began to move, he predicted, "The lamps are going out all over Europe. We shall not see them lit again in our lifetime."

IDENTIFY CENTRAL ISSUES How did Germany's invasion of Belgium bring Britain into the war ?

ASSESSMENT

1. **Generate Explanations** How were economic competition and imperialism causes of World War I?
2. **Identify Cause and Effect** Was nationalism a cause of World War I? Why or why not? Give examples.
3. **Identify Central Issues** What is militarism, and how did it influence the nations of Europe prior to World War I?
4. **Integrate Information** How did a single event start a chain reaction that sparked World War I ?
5. **Draw Conclusions** How did the alliance system spread the original conflict between Austria-Hungary and Serbia into a general war involving many countries?

>> Austrian soldiers advance into Russian Poland during the winter of 1915.

5.2 World War I—known at the time as the "Great War"—was the largest conflict in history up to that time. The French mobilized almost 8.5 million men, the British nearly 9 million, the Russians 12 million, and the Germans 11 million. For those who fought, the statistics were more personal. "One out of every four men who went out to the World War did not come back again," recalled a survivor, "and of those who came back, many are maimed and blind and some are mad."

Bounce to Activate Flipped Video

>> Objectives

Understand how trench warfare led to a stalemate on the Western Front.

Identify and describe the impact of modern military technology on the fighting.

Outline the course of the war on multiple European fronts.

Explain how World War I was a global conflict.

>> Key Terms

stalemate
zeppelin
U-boat
convoy
Dardanelles
T. E. Lawrence

Fighting the Great War

A New Kind of War

The early enthusiasm for the war soon faded. There were no stirring cavalry charges, no quick and glorious victories. This was a new kind of war, far deadlier than any before.

Stalemate on the Western Front As the war began, German forces fought their way through Belgium toward Paris, following the Schlieffen Plan. The Belgians resisted more than German generals had expected, but the German forces prevailed. However, Germany's plans for a quick defeat of France soon faltered.

The Schlieffen Plan failed for several reasons. First, Russia mobilized more quickly than expected. After Russian forces won a few small victories in eastern Prussia, German generals hastily shifted some troops to the east. This move weakened their forces in the west. Then, in September 1914, British and French troops pushed back the German drive along the Marne River. The first battle of the Marne ended Germany's hopes for a quick victory on the Western Front.

Both sides then began to dig deep trenches to protect their armies from fierce enemy fire. They did not know that the conflict would turn into a long, deadly **stalemate,** a deadlock in which neither side is able to defeat the other. Battle lines in France would remain almost unchanged for four years.

Trench Warfare On the Western Front, the warring armies burrowed into a vast system of trenches, stretching from the Swiss frontier to the English Channel. An underground network linked bunkers, communications trenches, and gun emplacements.

There, millions of soldiers roasted under the broiling summer sun or froze through long bitter winters. They shared their food with rats and their beds with lice.

Between the opposing trench lines lay "no man's land," an empty tract, pocketed with shell holes. Through coils of barbed wire, soldiers peered over the edge of their trenches, watching for the next enemy attack. They themselves would have to charge into this man-made desert when officers gave the order.

Sooner or later, soldiers obeyed the order to go "over the top." With no protection but their rifles and helmets, they charged across no man's land toward the enemy lines. With luck, they might overrun a few trenches. In time, the enemy would launch a counterattack, with similar results. Each side then rushed in reinforcements to replace the dead and wounded. The struggle continued, back and forth, over a few hundred yards of territory.

High Casualty Rates To break the stalemate on the Western Front, both the Allies and the Central Powers launched massive offensives in 1916. German forces tried to overwhelm the French at Verdun (vur DUN). The French defenders held firm, sending up the battle cry "They shall not pass." The 11-month struggle cost more than a half a million casualties, or soldiers killed, wounded, or missing, on both sides.

An Allied offensive at the Somme River (sum) was even more costly. In a single grisly day, nearly 60,000 British soldiers were killed or wounded. In the five-month battle, more than one million soldiers were killed, without either side winning an advantage.

Some soldiers wrote about their experiences on the front lines:

> The blue French cloth mingled with the German grey upon the ground, and in some places the bodies were piled so high that one could take cover from shell-fire behind them. The noise was so terrific that orders had to be shouted by each man into the ear of the next. And whenever there was a momentary lull in the tumult of battle and the groans of the wounded,

Europe in World War I, 1914

>> **Analyze Maps** Who do you think was in a better strategic position at the start of the war, the Allies or the Central Powers? Why?

Bounce to Activate Map

>> This German soldier was one of the many casualties of the fighting during World War I. Massive offenses and new military technology combined to produce extremely high casualty rates.

Bounce to Activate 3D Model

>> Poison gas and machine guns are two examples of the military technology that killed and wounded so many. These British machine gunners wear gas masks during the Battle of the Somme, in July 1916.

Bounce to Activate Gallery

one heard, high up in the blue sky, the joyful song of birds! Birds singing just as they do at home in spring-time! It was enough to tear the heart out of one's body!

—German soldier Richard Schmieder, writing from the trenches in France

IDENTIFY CAUSE AND EFFECT How did the failure of Germany's Schlieffen Plan to quickly defeat France affect the future course of the war?

Modern Military Technology

The enormous casualties suffered on the Western Front were due in part to the destructive power of modern weapons. Two significant weapons were the rapid-fire machine gun and the long-range artillery gun. Machine guns mowed down waves of soldiers. Artillery allowed troops to shell the enemy from more than 10 miles away. The shrapnel, or flying debris from artillery shells, killed or wounded even more soldiers than the guns.

Poison Gas Efforts to overcome the stalemate of trench warfare led to the use of poison gas. Early on, the French used tear gas grenades, but by 1915, the Germans began employing poison gas on a large scale. Even though the Allies condemned the use of poison gas, both sides developed and used different kinds of poison gases. Poison gas blinded or choked its victims or caused agonizing burns and blisters. It could be fatal. Though soldiers were eventually given gas masks, poison gas remained one of the most dreaded hazards of the war.

One British soldier recalled the effects of being gassed:

> I suppose I resembled a kind of fish with my mouth open gasping for air. It seemed as if my lungs were gradually shutting down and my heart pounded away in my ears like the beat of a drum. . . . To get air into my lungs was real agony.
>
> —William Pressey, quoted in *People at War 1914–1918*

Poison gas was an uncertain weapon. Shifting winds could blow the gas back on the soldiers who launched it. As both sides invented masks to protect against gas attacks, it became less useful. After the war, disgust and horror with the use of poison gas led to its ban in 1925, which is still in effect today.

Tanks, Airplanes, and Submarines During World War I, advances in technology, such as the gasoline-powered engine, led the opposing forces to use tanks, airplanes, and submarines against each other. In 1916, Britain introduced the first armored tank. Mounted with machine guns, the tanks were designed to move across no man's land. Still, the first tanks broke down often. They failed to break the stalemate.

Both sides also used aircraft. At first, planes were utilized simply to observe enemy troop movements. In 1915, Germany used **zeppelins** (ZEP uh linz), large gas-filled balloons, to bomb the English coast. Later, both sides equipped airplanes with machine guns. Pilots known as "flying aces" confronted each other in the skies. These "dogfights" were spectacular, but had little effect on the course of the war on the ground.

Submarines proved much more important. German **U-boats,** nicknamed from the German word for submarine, *Unterseeboot,*did tremendous damage to the Allied side, sinking merchant ships carrying vital supplies to Britain. To defend against the submarines, the Allies organized **convoys,** or groups of merchant ships protected by warships.

☑ **INFER** How did U-boat attacks affect the fighting on land?

>> On the Italian front, soldiers trekked through the Alps using snowshoes and skis. At times, they even engaged in battle while wearing their skis. **Analyze Visuals** Based on this image, what else besides deadly weapons caused high casualty rates?

Other European Fronts

From the outset of World War I, Germany and Austria-Hungary battled Russia on the Eastern Front. There, battle lines shifted back and forth, sometimes over large areas. Even though the armies were not mired in trench warfare, casualties rose even higher than on the Western Front. The results were just as indecisive.

Mounting Russian Losses in the East In August 1914, Russian armies pushed into eastern Germany. Then, the Russians suffered a disastrous defeat at Tannenberg. Reeling from the disaster, the Russians retreated. After Tannenberg, the warring armies in the east fought on Russian soil.

As the least industrialized of the great powers, Russia was poorly equipped to fight a modern war. Although Russian factories geared up to produce rifles and other machinery for war, Russia lacked the roads and railroads to carry goods to the front. As the war raged on, some troops even lacked rifles. Still, Russian commanders continued to send masses of peasant soldiers into combat.

War in Southern Europe Southeastern Europe was another battleground. In 1915, Bulgaria joined the Central Powers and helped defeat its old rival Serbia. Romania, hoping to gain some land in Hungary, joined the Allies in 1916, only to be crushed by the Central Powers.

Also in 1915, Italy declared war on Austria-Hungary and later on Germany. The Allies had agreed in a secret treaty to give Italy some Austrian-ruled lands on its northern border. Over the next two years,the Italians and Austrians fought numerous battles, with few major breakthroughs. In October 1917, Italy suffered a major setback during the battle of Caporetto, but French and British forces stepped in to stop the Central Powers from advancing into Italy. Still, Caporetto proved as disastrous for Italy as Tannenberg had been for Russia.

CONTRAST How was the Eastern Front different from the Western Front?

A Global Conflict

Though most of the fighting took place in Europe, World War I was a global conflict. In 1914, Japan joined the Allies by declaring war on Germany. Japan used the war as an excuse to seize German outposts in China and islands in the Pacific. Japan's advances in East Asia and the Pacific would have far-reaching consequences in the years ahead as ambitious Japanese leaders set out to expand their footholds in China.

The Ottoman Empire Joins the War Because of its strategic location, the Ottoman empire was a desirable ally. If the Ottoman Turks had joined the Allies, the Central Powers would have been almost completely encircled. However, the Turks joined the Central Powers in late October 1914. The Turks then cut off crucial Allied supply lines to Russia through the **Dardanelles,** a vital strait connecting the Black Sea and the Mediterranean.

In 1915, the Allies sent a massive force of British, Indian, Australian, and New Zealander troops to attempt to open up the strait. At the battle of Gallipoli (guh LIP uh lee), Ottoman troops trapped the Allies on the beaches of the Gallipoli peninsula. In January 1916, after 10 months and more than 200,000 casualties, the Allies finally withdrew from the Dardanelles.

Despite their victory at Gallipoli, the war did not go well for the Ottomans on a second front, the Middle East. The Ottoman empire included vast areas of Arab land. In 1916, Arab nationalists led by Husayn ibn Ali declared a revolt against Ottoman rule. The British government sent Colonel **T. E. Lawrence**—later known as Lawrence of Arabia—to support the Arab revolt. Lawrence led guerrilla raids against the Ottomans, dynamiting bridges and supply trains. Eventually, the Ottoman empire lost a great deal of territory to the Arabs, including the key city of Baghdad.

Deportation and Mass Murder of Armenians Meanwhile, the Ottoman empire was fighting Russia on a third front in the Caucasus Mountains. This region was home to ethnic Armenians, some of whom lived under Ottoman rule and some of whom lived under Russian rule. As Christians, the Armenians were a minority in the Ottoman empire and did not have the same rights as Muslims. Still, they prospered—much to the resentment of their neighbors.

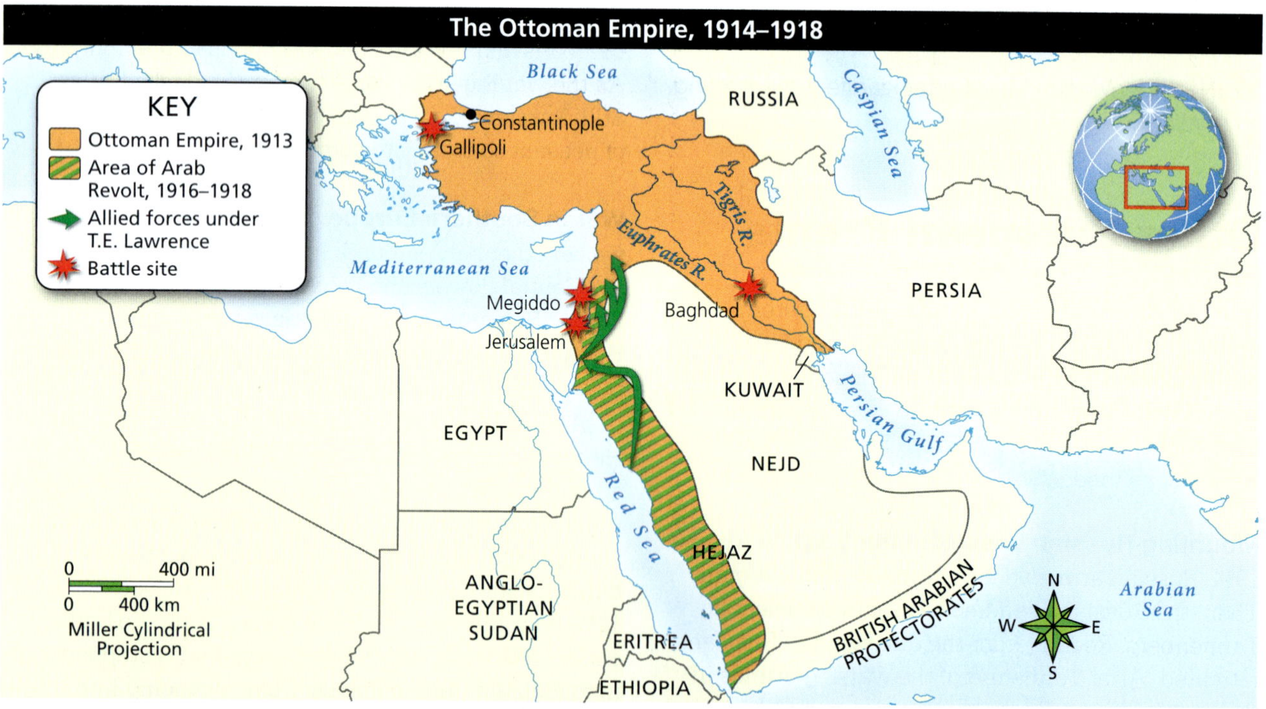

>> **Analyze Maps** How did the Arab revolt against the Ottoman empire affect the Allied cause?

Starting in 1915, the Ottoman government embarked on a brutal campaign against the Armenians, some of whom had joined the Russian forces. Claiming Armenians were traitors, the government ordered the deportation of the entire Armenian population from the war zone. But Henry Morgenthau, the U.S. ambassador to the Ottoman Empire, disputed Ottoman claims that the deportations were a wartime necessity:

> ". . . When the Turkish authorities gave the orders for these deportations, they were merely giving the death warrant to a whole race . . . in their conversations with me, they made no particular attempt to conceal the fact."
>
> —Henry Morgenthau, *Ambassador Morgenthau's Story*

During barbarous forced marches, between 600,000 and 1.5 million Armenians were killed or died from hunger or thirst. A later wave of atrocities forced most of the remaining Armenians from Turkey. Many Armenians fled to other countries, including the United States.

Survivors of the genocide were not able to return to their homeland. Their property was seized by the new Turkish government. Today nearly ten million Armenians are part of the Armenian diaspora. At Morgenthau's urging, the United States government organized the Near East Relief Agency to aid genocide victims.

European Colonies and the War European colonies were also drawn into the struggle. The Allies overran scattered German colonies in Africa and Asia. They also turned to their own colonies and dominions for troops, laborers, and supplies. Colonial recruits from British India and French West Africa fought on European battlefields. Canada, Australia, and New Zealand sent troops to Britain's aid.

People in the colonies had mixed feelings about serving. Some were reluctant to serve rulers who did not treat them fairly. Other colonial troops volunteered eagerly. They expected that their service would be a step toward citizenship or independence. Such hopes would be dashed after the war.

SUMMARIZE What were the major features and immediate effects of the war in the Middle East?

>> Troops from Europe's colonies fought in World War I. These soldiers in a dugout near Verdun in 1915 are from French Africa.

ASSESSMENT

1. **Identify Central Issues** What is a stalemate, and why did one develop on the Western Front?
2. **Identify Cause and Effect** What were the effects of major new military technologies on World War I?
3. **Draw Conclusions** How did the Ottoman empire's entry into the war on the side of the Central Powers have a negative impact on Russia?
4. **Support Ideas with Evidence** How did the war contribute to the mass murder of the Armenian people? Include details from the text.
5. **Synthesize** How did imperialism influence the war?

>> Delegates gathered in Paris in 1919 to discuss peace terms. The treaty between the Allies and Germany was signed in June in the Hall of Mirrors, shown here, at the palace of Versailles.

5.3 By 1917, European societies were cracking under the strain of war. Casualties on the fronts and shortages at home sapped morale. The stalemate dragged on, seemingly without end. Soon, however, the departure of one country from the war and the entry of another would tip the balance and end the stalemate.

Bounce to Activate Flipped Video

>> Objectives

Describe how World War I became a total war.

Explain how U.S. entry into the war led to an Allied victory.

List the effects of World War I in terms of financial costs, high casualty rates, and political impact.

Describe the issues at the Paris Peace Conference and the impact of Woodrow Wilson's Fourteen Points.

Summarize the terms and impact of the Treaty of Versailles.

>> Key Terms

total war
conscription
contraband
Lusitania
propaganda
atrocity
Fourteen Points
self-determination
armistice
pandemic
reparation
radical
collective security
mandate

World War I Ends

Governments Direct Total War

As the struggle wore on, nations realized that a modern, mechanized war required the channeling of a nation's entire resources into the war effort, or **total war.** To achieve total war, governments began to take a stronger role in directing the economic and cultural lives of their people.

Recruiting and Supplying Huge Armies Early on, both sides set up systems to recruit, arm, transport, and supply armies that numbered in the millions. All of the warring nations except Britain immediately imposed universal military **conscription,** or "the draft," which required all young men to be ready for military or other service. Britain, too, instituted conscription in 1916. Germany set up a system of forced civilian labor as well.

Governments raised taxes and borrowed huge amounts of money to pay the costs of war. They rationed food and other products, from boots to gasoline. In addition, they introduced other economic controls, such as setting prices and forbidding strikes.

Blockades and Submarines Impact Economies At the start of the war, Britain's navy formed a blockade in the North Sea to keep ships from carrying supplies into and out of Germany.

International law allowed wartime blockades to confiscate **contraband,** or military supplies and raw materials needed to make military supplies. Items such as food and clothing were exempt. Still, the British blockade stopped both types of goods from reaching Germany. As the war progressed, it became harder and harder to feed the German and Austrian people. In Germany, the winter of 1916 and 1917 was remembered as "the turnip winter," because the potato crop failed and people ate turnips instead.

To retaliate, Germany used U-boats to create its own blockade. In 1915, Germany declared that it would sink all ships carrying goods to Britain. In May 1915, a German submarine torpedoed the British liner ***Lusitania*** off the coast of Ireland. Almost 1,200 passengers were killed, including 128 Americans. Germany justified the attack, arguing that the *Lusitania*was carrying weapons.

When American President Woodrow Wilson threatened to cut off diplomatic relations with Germany, Germany agreed to restrict its submarine campaign. Before attacking any ship, U-boats would surface and give warning, allowing neutral passengers to escape to lifeboats. Unrestricted submarine warfare stopped—for the moment.

>> This painting portrays the sinking of the *Lusitania* by a German submarine. Unrestricted submarine warfare worsened American public opinion of Germany.

The Propaganda War Total war also meant controlling public opinion. Even in democratic countries, special boards censored the press. Their aim was to keep complete casualty figures and other discouraging news from reaching the public. Government censors also restricted popular literature, historical writings, motion pictures, and the arts.

Both sides waged a propaganda war. **Propaganda** is the spreading of ideas to promote a cause or to damage an opposing cause. Allied propaganda played up the brutality of Germany's invasion of Belgium.

The British and French press circulated tales of **atrocities,** horrible acts committed against innocent people. Although some atrocities did occur, often the stories were distorted by exaggerations or completely made up.

Governments also used propaganda to motivate military mobilization, especially in Britain before conscription started in 1916. In France and Germany, propaganda urged civilians to loan money to the government.

>> Posters such as this British one helped to stoke patriotic emotions. **Determine Author's Purpose** What did the creators of this poster hope that men would do after viewing this image?

Bounce to Activate Gallery

Women Contribute to the War Effort Women played a critical role in total war. As millions of men left to fight, women took over their jobs and kept national economies going. Many women worked in war industries, manufacturing weapons and supplies. Others joined women's branches of the armed forces. When food shortages threatened Britain, volunteers in the Women's Land Army went to the fields to grow their nation's food.

Nurses shared the dangers of the men whose wounds they tended. At aid stations close to the front lines, nurses often worked around the clock, especially after a big "push" brought a flood of casualties. In her diary, English nurse Vera Brittain describes sweating through 90-degree days in France, "stopping hemorrhages, replacing intestines, and draining and reinserting innumerable rubber tubes" with "gruesome human remnants heaped on the floor."

War work gave women a new sense of pride and confidence. After the war, most women had to give up their jobs to men returning home. Still, they had challenged the idea that women could not handle demanding and dangerous jobs. In many countries, including Britain, Germany, and the United States, women's support for the war effort helped them finally win the right to vote, after decades of struggle.

DRAW CONCLUSIONS How can total war increase the power of government and have a lasting political impact?

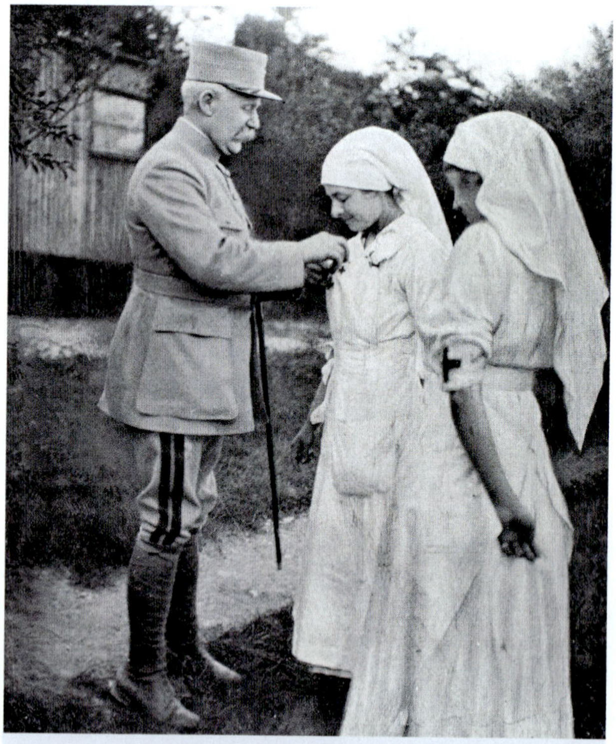

>> Women worked as nurses at the front in difficult and dangerous conditions. Here, a French general honors a nurse who took part in the battle of Verdun in 1916.

Morale Breaks Down

Despite inspiring propaganda, by 1917 the morale of troops and civilians had plunged. Germany was sending 15-year-old recruits to the front, and Britain was on the brink of bankruptcy.

War-Weary Civilians and Soldiers Long casualty lists, food shortages, and the failure of generals to win promised victories led to calls for peace. Instead of praising the glorious deeds of heroes, war poets like British soldier Siegfried Sassoon began denouncing the leaders whose errors wasted so many lives.

> You smug-faced crowds with kindling eye
>
> Who cheer when soldier lads march by,
>
> Sneak home and pray you'll never know
>
> The hell where youth and laughter go.
>
> —Siegfried Sassoon, "Suicide in the Trenches"

As morale collapsed, troops in some French units mutinied. In Italy, many soldiers deserted during the retreat at Caporetto. In Russia, soldiers left the front to join in a full-scale revolution back home.

Revolution in Russia Three years of war had hit Russia especially hard. Stories of incompetent generals and corruption eroded public confidence. In March 1917, bread riots in St. Petersburg erupted into a revolution that brought down the Russian monarchy. (You'll learn more about the causes and effects of the Russian Revolution in another lesson.) The new Russian government continued the war effort.

At first, the Allies welcomed the overthrow of the tsar. They hoped Russia would institute a democratic government and become a stronger ally. But in October of that year, a second revolution brought V. I. Lenin to power. Lenin had promised to pull Russian troops out of the war. Early in 1918, Lenin signed the Treaty of Brest-Litovsk (brest lih TAWFSK) with Germany. The treaty ended Russian participation in World War I.

Russia's withdrawal had an immediate impact on the war. With Russia out of the struggle, Germany could concentrate its forces on the Western Front. In the spring of 1918, the Central Powers stood ready to achieve the great breakthrough they had sought for so long. But by then, Germany faced a new opponent. The United States had been dragged into the war.

CITE EVIDENCE What evidence shows that soldiers' morale declined and negatively affected the war effort?

The United States Enters the War

Soon after the Russian Revolution began, another event altered the balance of forces. The United States declared war on Germany. Many factors contributed to the decision of the United States to exchange neutrality for war in 1917.

Unrestricted Submarine Warfare A major reason for the U.S. entry into the war was German submarine attacks. After the sinking of the Lusitania and under pressure from President Wilson, Germany had agreed to restrict its submarine campaign. By early 1917, however, Germany was desperate to break the stalemate in the war. On February 1, the German government announced that it would resume unrestricted submarine warfare. Wilson angrily denounced Germany.

Anti-German Sentiment Grows Many Americans supported the Allies because of cultural ties. The United States shared a cultural history and language with Britain and sympathized with France as another democracy. On the other hand, some German Americans favored the Central Powers. So did many Irish Americans, who resented British rule of Ireland, and Russian Jewish immigrants, who did not want to be allied with the tsar. The resumption of unrestricted submarine warfare, however, increased anger toward Germany and spurred support for the Allies.

Another German move also angered Americans. In early 1917, the British intercepted a message from the German foreign minister, Arthur Zimmermann, to his ambassador in Mexico. In the note, Zimmerman wrote that if Mexico joined Germany in the event of war with the United States, Germany would help Mexico "to reconquer the lost territory in New Mexico, Texas, and Arizona." Britain revealed the Zimmermann note to the American government. When the note became public, anti-German feeling intensified in the United States.

>> Soldiers ate, slept, fought and died in the trenches. As the war dragged on and casualties mounted, morale was severely tested.

>> Germany resumed unrestricted submarine warfare in 1917. Here, President Wilson reads a German message and ponders what to do. **Analyze Political Cartoons** What does the overflowing waste basket suggest?

Wilson Asks for a "War to End War" In April 1917, Wilson asked Congress to declare war on Germany. "We have no selfish ends to serve," he stated. Instead, he painted the conflict idealistically as a war "to make the world safe for democracy" and later as a "war to end war."

The United States needed months to recruit, train, supply, and transport a modern army across the Atlantic. But by 1918, about two million American soldiers had joined the war-weary Allied troops fighting on the Western Front. Although relatively few American troops engaged in combat, their arrival gave Allied troops a much-needed morale boost. Just as important to the debt-ridden Allies was American financial aid.

Wilson's Fourteen Points Though he had failed to maintain American neutrality, Wilson still hoped to be a peacemaker. In January 1918, he issued the **Fourteen Points,** a list of his terms for resolving both this war and future wars. He called for freedom of the seas, free trade, large-scale reductions of arms, and an end to secret treaties. For Eastern Europe, Wilson favored **self-determination,** the right of people to choose their own form of government. Finally, Wilson urged the creation of a "general association of nations" to keep the peace in the future.

INFER Why did President Woodrow Wilson think that World War I was "the war to end wars"?

The Great War Ends

A final showdown on the Western Front began in early 1918. The Germans badly wanted to achieve a major victory before eager American troops arrived in Europe.

Final Offensives In March 1918, the Germans launched a huge offensive on the Western Front with troops newly freed from fighting in Russia. By July, the spring offensive had driven the Allies back 40 miles, the biggest German breakthrough in three years. The rapid push exhausted the German forces and cost heavy casualties.

By then, fresh American troops were pouring into the Western Front. The Allies launched a counter-offensive, slowly driving German forces back through France and Belgium. In September, German generals told the Kaiser that the war could not be won.

Germany Asks for Peace Uprisings exploded among hungry city dwellers across Germany. German commanders advised the kaiser to step down. William II did so in early November, fleeing into exile in the Netherlands.

WOODROW WILSON'S FOURTEEN POINTS	
1. No secret treaties	10. Peoples of Austria-Hungary should have freest opportunity for autonomous development.
2. Freedom of the seas	
3. Free trade	
4. Large-scale reduction of arms	11. Occupation forces to be evacuated from Romania, Serbia and Montenegro; Serbia should have free and secure access to the sea
5. Impartial adjustment of colonial claims based on interests of governments and native populations.	
6. Evacuation of all Russian territory; providing Russia the best opportunity for self-determination	12. Autonomous development for the non-Turkish peoples of the Ottoman Empire; free passage for all ships through the Dardanelles
7. Evacuation and restoration of Belgium as a sovereign nation	13. Independence for Poland, with free and secure access to the sea
8. Liberation of France; return of the region of Alsace-Lorraine to France	14. Formation of a general association of nations to guarantee to its members political independence and territorial integrity (the League of Nations)
9. Readjustment of Italy's frontiers based on recognizable lines of nationality	

>> **Analyze Information** Which of Wilson's Fourteen Points deal with countries having free access to international commerce? Why did Wilson consider this so important?

The Costs of World War I

COUNTRY	ALLIES				CENTRAL POWERS	
	RUSSIA	BRITISH EMPIRE	FRANCE	UNITED STATES	GERMANY	AUSTRIA-HUNGARY
MOBILIZED FORCES	12,000,000	8,904,467	8,410,000	4,355,000	11,000,000	7,800,000
KILLED	1,700,000	908,371	1,357,800	116,516	1,773,700	1,200,000
WOUNDED	4,950,000	2,090,212	4,266,000	204,002	4,216,058	3,620,000
PRISONERS AND MISSING	2,500,000	191,652	537,000	4,500	1,152,800	2,200,000
TOTAL CASUALTIES	9,150,000	3,190,235	6,160,800	323,018	7,142,558	7,020,000
CASUALTY RATE	76%	36%	73%	7%	65%	90%
FINANCIAL COSTS	$25 billion	$55 billion	$48 billion	$32 billion	$60 billion	$22 billion

SOURCE: *The Harper Encyclopedia of Military,* History, R. Ernest Dupuy and Trevor N. Dupuy; *The Great War,* www.pbs.org.

>> World War I ended in 1918, but its human and economic costs would be felt for decades. Many nations had thrown all their resources into the fight, and their losses were staggering.

By autumn, Austria-Hungary was also reeling toward collapse. As the government in Vienna tottered, the subject nationalities revolted, splintering the empire of the Hapsburgs. Bulgaria and the Ottoman empire also asked for peace.

The new German government sought an **armistice,** or agreement to end fighting, with the Allies. At 11 A.M. on November 11, 1918, the Great War at last came to an end.

The Human Toll The human and material costs of the war were staggering. More than 8.5 million men had died in battle. More than twice that number had been wounded, many of them disabled for life. Historians estimate that at least 6 million civilians also lost their lives as a result of the war.

The devastation was made even worse in 1918 by a deadly **pandemic** of influenza. A pandemic is the spread of a disease across a large area—in this case, the whole world. In just a few months, the flu killed more than 20 million people worldwide.

The Economic Toll In battle zones from France to Russia, homes, farms, factories, roads, and churches had been shelled into rubble. People had fled these areas as refugees. Now they had to return and start to rebuild. The costs of reconstruction and paying off huge war debts would burden an already battered world.

Shaken and disillusioned, people everywhere felt bitter about the war. The Allies blamed the conflict on their defeated foes and insisted that the losers make **reparations,** or payments for war damage. The stunned Central Powers, who had viewed the armistice as a cease-fire rather than a surrender, looked for scapegoats on whom they could blame their defeat.

The Political Toll Under the stress of war, governments had collapsed in Russia, Germany, Austria-Hungary, and the Ottoman empire. Political **radicals,** or people who wanted to make extreme changes, dreamed of building a new social order from the chaos. Conservatives warned against the spread of Bolshevism, or communism, as it was soon called.

Unrest also swept through Europe's colonial empires. African and Asian soldiers had discovered that the imperial powers were not as invincible as they seemed. Colonial troops returned home with a more cynical view of Europeans and renewed hopes for independence.

GENERATE EXPLANATIONS Why might the war cause an economic recession or depression in Europe?

Making the Peace

Just weeks after the war ended, President Wilson boarded a steamship bound for France. He had decided to go in person to Paris, where Allied leaders would make the peace. Wilson was certain that he could bring a "just peace" to the world. "Tell me what is right," Wilson urged his advisors, "and I'll fight for it."

To a weary, angry world, Wilson seemed a symbol of hope. His talk of democracy and self-determination raised expectations for a just and lasting peace—even in defeated Germany. Sadly, it would not be that easy. Europe was a shattered continent. Its problems, and those of the world, would not be solved for many years afterward.

Allies Have Conflicting Goals The victorious Allies met at the Paris Peace Conference to discuss the fate of Europe, the former Ottoman empire, and various colonies around the world. The Central Powers and Russia, under its new communist government, were not allowed to take part in the negotiations.

Wilson was one of three strong leaders who dominated the Paris Peace Conference. He was a dedicated reformer and at times was so stubbornly convinced that he was right that he could be hard to work with. Wilson urged for "peace without victory" based on the Fourteen Points.

Two other Allied leaders at the peace conference had different aims. British Prime Minister David Lloyd George had promised to build a postwar Britain "fit for heroes"—a goal that would cost money. The chief goal of the French leader, Georges Clemenceau (KLEM un soh), was to weaken Germany so that it could never again threaten France. "Mr. Wilson bores me with his Fourteen Points," complained Clemenceau. "Why, God Almighty has only ten!"

>> In this cartoon, President Wilson says to the dove, "Here's your olive branch. Now get busy." **Analyze Political Cartoons** Does the cartoonist think Wilson's solution will work?

Obstacles to Settlement Crowds of other representatives circled around the "Big Three" with their own demands. Among the most difficult issues were the secret agreements made by the Allies during the war. Italy had signed one such treaty. The Italian prime minister, Vittorio Orlando (awr LAN doh), insisted that the Allies honor their secret treaty to give former Austro-Hungarian lands to Italy. Such agreements often violated the idea of self-determination.

Self-determination posed other problems. Many people who had been ruled by Russia, Austria-Hungary, or the Ottoman empire now demanded national states of their own. The territories claimed by these peoples often overlapped, so it was impossible to satisfy them all. Some ethnic groups became unwanted minorities in newly created states.

Wilson had to compromise on his Fourteen Points. However, he stood firm on his goal of creating an international League of Nations. The League would be based on the idea of **collective security,** a system in which a group of nations acts as one to preserve the peace of all. Wilson felt sure that the League could correct any mistakes made in Paris.

The Treaty of Versailles In June 1919, the Allies ordered representatives of the new German Republic to sign the treaty they had drawn up at the palace of Versailles (vur SY) outside Paris. The German delegates were horrified. The Treaty of Versailles forced Germany to assume full blame for causing the war.

It also imposed huge reparations that would burden an already damaged German economy. The reparations covered not only the destruction caused by the war, but also pensions for millions of Allied soldiers or their widows and families. The total cost of German reparations would come to over $400 billion in today's money.

Europe, 1920

>> **Analyze Maps** Based on this map and the text, why were many Germans unhappy with the territorial changes that occurred after World War I?

Bounce to Activate Map

Other parts of the treaty were aimed at weakening Germany. The treaty severely limited the size of the once-feared German military. It returned Alsace and Lorraine to France, removed hundreds of square miles of territory from western and eastern Germany, and stripped Germany of its overseas colonies. The treaty compelled many Germans to leave the homes they had made in Russia, Poland, Alsace-Lorraine, and the German colonies to return to Germany or Austria.

The Germans signed because they had no choice. However, German resentment of the Treaty of Versailles would poison the international climate for 20 years. It would help spark an even deadlier world war in the years to come.

COMPARE POINTS OF VIEW How did the goals of the Big Three Leaders—Wilson, Lloyd George, and Clemenceau—conflict?

Effects of the Peace Settlements

The Allies drew up separate treaties with the other Central Powers. These treaties redrew the map of Eastern Europe and affected colonial peoples around the globe. Like the Treaty of Versailles, these treaties left widespread dissatisfaction.

New Nations in Europe A key principle of Wilson's Fourteen Points was self-determination. This goal helped a band of new nations emerge in Eastern Europe where the German, Austrian, and Russian empires had once ruled.

Poland became an independent nation after more than 100 years of foreign rule. The Baltic states of Latvia, Lithuania, and Estonia fought for and achieved independence. Three new republics—Czechoslovakia, Austria, and Hungary—rose in the old Hapsburg heartland. In the Balkans, the peacemakers created a new South Slav state, Yugoslavia, dominated by Serbia.

Despite the settlement, Eastern Europe remained a center of political conflict and unrest. The new nations were also relatively poor, with agricultural economies and little capital for industry.

The Mandate System European colonies in Africa, Asia, and the Pacific had looked to the Paris Peace Conference with high hopes. Nationalist leaders in these regions expected that the peace would bring new respect and an end to imperial rule. They took up Wilson's call for self-determination.

However, the leaders at Paris applied self-determination only to parts of Europe. Outside Europe, the victorious Allies added to their overseas empires.

>> Delegates attend the first meeting of the League of Nations on December 4, 1920, in the Hall of Reformation in Geneva, Switzerland.

The treaties created a system of **mandates,** territories administered by Western powers. Britain and France gained mandates over German colonies in Africa. Japan and Australia were given mandates over some Pacific islands. The treaties handled lands that used to be part of the Ottoman empire as if they were colonies, too.

In theory, mandates were to be held until they were able to stand alone. In practice, they became colonies, remaining under the political and economic control of the Allied powers. From Africa to the Middle East and across Asia, people living in the mandates felt betrayed by the peacemakers.

Widespread Discontent Germans and colonial peoples were not the only groups dissatisfied by the peace. Italy was angry because it did not get all the lands promised in its secret treaty with the Allies. Japan protested the refusal of the Western powers to recognize its claims in China. At the same time, China was forced to accept Japanese control over some former German holdings. Russia, excluded from the peace talks, resented the reestablishment of a Polish nation and three independent Baltic states on lands that had been part of the Russian empire.

All of these discontented nations bided their time. They waited for a chance to revise the peace settlements in their favor.

The League of Nations The Paris Peace Conference did offer one beacon of hope with the establishment of the League of Nations. More than 40 nations joined the League. They agreed to negotiate disputes rather than resort to war and to take common action against any aggressor state.

Wilson's dream had become a reality, or so he thought. On his return from Paris, Wilson faced resistance from his own Senate.

Some Republican senators, led by Henry Cabot Lodge, wanted to restrict the treaty so that the United States would not be obligated to fight in future wars. Lodge's reservations echoed the feelings of many war-weary Americans. Wilson would not accept Lodge's compromises. In the end, the Senate refused to ratify the treaty, and the United States never joined the League.

The loss of the United States weakened the League's power. In addition, the League had no power outside of its member states. As time soon revealed, the League could not prevent war. Still, it was a first step toward something genuinely new—an international organization dedicated to maintaining peace and advancing the interests of all peoples.

DRAW CONCLUSIONS How did the refusal of the United States to join the League of Nations weaken the League's power?

ASSESSMENT

1. **Identify Cause and Effect** How did World War I affect the role of women in society?
2. **Analyze Context** Why did it take so long for the United States to enter World War I?
3. **Make Generalizations** How does a long war with a high number of casualties generally affect civilians' and soldiers' opinions of their government?
4. **Compare and Contrast** After World War I, why were conditions ripe for social and political change in Russia, but not in the United States?
5. **Predict Consequences** How might the harsh provisions of the Treaty of Versailles affect conditions in Germany?

The Fourteen Points: Woodrow Wilson

Introduction

In a speech to Congress on January 8, 1918, President Wilson laid out America's war aims and his vision for peace after the war. His speech included fourteen key points upon which he believed the peace following the war must be based. However, not all of Wilson's ideas were adopted at the Paris Peace Conference.

Following the Fourteen Points is an excerpt from the opening speech of Premier Georges Clemenceau of France at the Versailles conference in 1919. It is his response to the Fourteen Points.

>> Woodrow Wilson

Primary Source

. . . What we demand in this war, therefore, is nothing peculiar [unique] to ourselves. It is that the world be made fit and safe to live in; and particularly that it be made safe for every peace-loving nation which, like our own, wishes to live its own life, [and] determine its own institutions [choose its own government]. . . . The program of the world's peace, therefore, is our only program; and that program, the only possible program as we see it, is this:

DISTINGUISH AMONG FACT, OPINION, AND REASONED JUDGMENT When Wilson says, "The program of the world's peace, therefore, is our only program, the only possible program as we see it, is this," is this a fact, an opinion, or a reasoned judgment? Explain your answer.

1. Open covenants [formal agreements] of peace, openly arrived at, after which there shall be no private international understandings of any kind but [instead] diplomacy shall proceed always frankly [openly and honestly] and in the public view.

EXPLAIN AN ARGUMENT Why might Wilson think that prohibiting secret agreements between nations is necessary in order to avoid war?

2. Absolute freedom of navigation upon the seas, outside territorial waters, alike in peace and in war, except as the seas may be closed in whole or in part by international action for the enforcement of international covenants.

PARAPHRASE Restate Point 2 in your own words.

3. The removal, so far as possible, of all economic barriers and the establishment of an equality of trade conditions among all the nations consenting to the peace and associating themselves for its maintenance.

4. Adequate guarantees given and taken that national armaments will be reduced to the lowest point consistent with domestic safety.

ANALYZE WORD CHOICES What two things does Wilson leave unspecified in Point 4?

5. A free, open-minded, and absolutely impartial adjustment of all colonial claims, based upon a strict observance of the principle that in determining all such questions of sovereignty the interests of the populations concerned must have equal weight with the equitable claims of the government whose title is to be determined. . . .

14. A general association [organization] of nations must be formed under specific covenants for the purpose of affording mutual guarantees of political independence and territorial integrity to great and small states alike.

INTEGRATE INFORMATION FROM DIVERSE SOURCES Does such an association of nations exist today? If so, what is it?

Primary Source

I come now to the order of the day. The first question is as follows: "The responsibility of the authors of the war." The second is thus expressed: "Penalties for crimes committed during the war." . . . [The task at hand] is a very vast field. But we beg of you to begin by examining the question as to the responsibility of the authors of the war. I do not need to set forth our reasons for this. If we wish to establish justice in the world we can do so now, for we have won victory and can impose the penalties demanded by justice. We shall insist on the imposition of penalties on the authors of the abominable crimes committed during the war. Has anyone any question to ask in regard to this? If not, I would again remind you that every delegation should devote itself to the study of this first question, which has been made the subject of reports by eminent jurists, and of a report which will be sent to you entitled, "An Inquiry into the Criminal Responsibility of the Emperor William II."

ASSESSMENT

1. **Compare and Contrast** Points 6–13 deal with specific territorial issues, such as breaking up the Ottoman and Austro-Hungarian Empires and restoring sovereignty to Belgium and Poland. To an American in 1918, how would those points be different from the ones excerpted here?
2. **Draw Conclusions** Preventing war seems like an admirable goal. Why might a country reject some or all of Wilson's points?
3. **Integrate Information From Diverse Sources** Why might isolationists oppose some or all of Wilson's Fourteen Points?
4. **Draw Inferences** What political impact do you think Wilson's Fourteen Points had?
5. **Explain** What demands, if met, would have convinced France to embrace the Fourteen Points?

5.4 The year 1913 marked the 300th anniversary of the Romanov dynasty. Everywhere, Russians honored the tsar and his family. Tsarina Alexandra felt confident that the people loved Nicholas too much to ever threaten him. "They are constantly frightening the emperor with threats of revolution," she told a friend, "and here,—you see it yourself—we need merely to show ourselves and at once their hearts are ours."

>> Vladimir Ilyich Lenin took his revolutionary ideas directly to the people, addressing crowds in the streets.

Bounce to Activate Flipped Video

Revolution in Russia

Causes of the February Revolution

Appearances were deceiving. In March 1917, the first of two revolutions would topple the Romanov dynasty and pave the way for even more radical changes. These revolutions are known to Russians as the February and October Revolutions, and to many westerners as the March and November Revolutions.

In 1917, Russia still used an old calendar, which was 13 days behind the one used in Western Europe. Russia did not adopt the Western calendar until 1918.

Roots of Discontent In 1914, the huge Russian empire stretched from Eastern Europe east to the Pacific Ocean. Unlike Western Europe, Russia was slow to industrialize despite its huge potential. Landowning nobles, priests, and an autocratic tsar controlled the government and economy. Much of the majority peasant population endured stark poverty. As Russia began to industrialize, a small middle class and an urban working class emerged.

>> Objectives

Explain the causes of the February (March) Revolution.

Describe the goals of Lenin and the Bolsheviks in the October Revolution.

Summarize the outcome of the civil war in Russia.

Analyze how Lenin built a Communist state in the Soviet Union.

>> Key Terms

proletariat
soviet
Cheka
commissar
V. I. Lenin

After the Revolution of 1905, Nicholas had failed to solve Russia's basic political, economic, and social problems. The elected Duma set up after the revolution had no real power. Moderates pressed for a constitution and social change. But Nicholas II, a weak and ineffective leader, blocked attempts to limit his authority. Like past tsars, he relied on his secret police and other enforcers to impose his will. A corrupt bureaucracy and an overburdened court system added to the government's problems.

Revolutionaries hatched radical plots. Some hoped to lead discontented peasants to overthrow the tsarist regime. Marxists tried to ignite revolution among the **proletariat**—the growing class of factory and railroad workers, miners, and urban wage earners. A revolution, they believed, would occur when the time was ripe.

World War I Intensifies Discontent The outbreak of war in 1914 fueled national pride and united Russians. Armies dashed to battle with enthusiasm. But like the Crimean and Russo-Japanese wars, World War I quickly strained Russian resources. Factories could not turn out enough supplies. The transportation system broke down, delivering only a trickle of crucial materials to the front. By 1915, many soldiers had no rifles and no ammunition. Badly equipped and poorly led, they died in staggering numbers. In 1915 alone, Russian casualties reached two million.

>> Gregory Rasputin's followers, including the tsarina Alexandra, considered him a mystic and a faith healer. His opponents called him the "mad monk."

In a patriotic gesture, Nicholas II went to the front to take personal charge. The decision proved a disastrous blunder. The tsar was no more competent than many of his generals. Worse, he left domestic affairs to the tsarina, Alexandra.

In Nicholas's absence, Alexandra relied on the advice of Gregory Rasputin, an illiterate peasant and self-proclaimed "holy man." The tsarina came to believe that Rasputin had miraculous powers after he helped her son, who suffered from hemophilia, a disorder in which any injury can result in uncontrollable bleeding.

By 1916, Rasputin's influence over Alexandra had reached new heights and weakened confidence in the government. Fearing for the monarchy, a group of Russian nobles killed Rasputin on December 29, 1916.

Tsar Nicholas II Steps Down By March 1917, disasters on the battlefield, combined with food and fuel shortages on the home front, brought the monarchy to collapse. In St. Petersburg (renamed Petrograd during the war), workers were going on strike. Marchers, mostly women, surged through the streets, shouting, "Bread! Bread!" Troops refused to fire on the demonstrators, leaving the government helpless. Finally, on the advice of military and political leaders, the tsar abdicated.

Duma politicians then set up a provisional, or temporary, government. Middle-class liberals in the government began preparing a constitution for a new Russian republic. At the same time, they continued the war against Germany.

IDENTIFY CAUSE AND EFFECT What were the causes of the Russian Revolution of March 1917?

Lenin Leads the Bolsheviks

Outside the provisional government, revolutionary socialists plotted their own course. In Petrograd and other cities, they set up **soviets,** or councils of workers and soldiers. At first, the soviets worked democratically within the government. Before long, though, the Bolsheviks, a radical socialist group, took charge. The leader of the Bolsheviks was a determined revolutionary, V. I. Lenin.

The Making of a Revolutionary **V. I. Lenin** was born Vladimir Ilyich Ulyanov(ool YAHN uf) in 1870 to a middle-class family. He adopted the name Lenin when he became a revolutionary.

When he was 17, his older brother was arrested and hanged for plotting to kill the tsar. The execution branded his family as a threat to the state and made the young Vladimir hate the tsarist government. As a young man, Lenin read the works of Karl Marx and participated in student demonstrations. He spread Marxist ideas among factory workers along with other socialists, including Nadezhda Krupskaya (nah DYEZ duh kroop SKY uh), the daughter of a poor noble family.

In 1895, Lenin and Krupskaya were arrested and sent to Siberia. During their imprisonment, they were married. After their release, they went into exile in Switzerland. There, they worked tirelessly to spread revolutionary ideas that would eventually succeed in shifting political thought in Russia and other nations.

Lenin Adapts Marxism Lenin adapted Marxist ideas to fit Russian conditions. Marx had predicted that the industrial working class would rise spontaneously to overthrow capitalism. But Russia did not have a large urban proletariat. Instead, Lenin called for an elite group to lead the revolution and set up a "dictatorship of the proletariat." Though this elite revolutionary party represented a small percentage of socialists, Lenin gave them the name Bolsheviks, meaning "majority."

In Western Europe, many leading socialists had come to think that socialism could be achieved through gradual and moderate reforms such as higher wages, increased suffrage, and social welfare programs.

A group of socialists in Russia, the Mensheviks, favored this approach. The Bolsheviks rejected it. To Lenin, reforms of this nature were merely capitalist tricks to repress the masses. Only revolution, he said, could bring about needed changes.

In March 1917, Lenin was still in exile. As Russia stumbled into revolution, Germany saw a chance to weaken its enemy by helping Lenin return home. Lenin rushed across Germany to the Russian frontier in a special train. He greeted a crowd of fellow exiles and activists with this cry: "Long live the worldwide Socialist revolution!"

EXPLAIN Explain how Lenin adapted Marxist ideas to Russian society and government.

>> In this 1920 painting, "Bolshevik," by Boris Kustodiev, a giant carries a red banner through a Russian city. **Analyze Art** Who or what does the giant symbolize?

Bounce to Activate Chart

The October Revolution Brings the Bolsheviks to Power

Lenin threw himself into the work of furthering the revolution. Another dynamic Marxist revolutionary, Leon Trotsky, helped lead the fight. To the hungry, war-weary Russian people, Lenin and the Bolsheviks promised "Peace, Land, and Bread."

Causes of the October Revolution Meanwhile, the provisional government, led by Alexander Kerensky, continued the war effort and failed to deal with land reform. Those decisions proved fatal. Most Russians were tired of war. Troops at the front were deserting in droves. Peasants wanted land, while city workers demanded an end to the desperate shortages.

In July 1917, the government launched the disastrous Kerensky Offensive against Germany. By November, according to one official report, the army was "a huge crowd of tired, poorly clad, poorly fed, embittered men." Growing numbers of troops mutinied. Peasants seized land and drove off fearful landlords.

The Bolsheviks Seize Power Conditions were ripe for the Bolsheviks to make their move. In November 1917, squads of Red Guards—armed factory workers—joined mutinous sailors from the Russian fleet in attacking the provisional government. In just a matter of days, Lenin's forces overthrew the provisional government.

The Bolsheviks quickly seized power in other cities. In Moscow, it took a week of fighting to blast the local government out of the walled Kremlin, the former tsarist center of government. Moscow became the Bolsheviks' capital, and the Kremlin their headquarters.

"We shall now occupy ourselves in Russia in building up a proletarian socialist state," declared Lenin.

The Bolsheviks ended private ownership of land and distributed land to peasants. Workers were given control of the factories and mines. A new red flag with an entwined hammer and sickle symbolized union between workers and peasants. Throughout the land, millions thought they had at last gained control over their own lives. In fact, the Bolsheviks—renamed Communists—would soon become their new masters.

>> A crusading white knight slays the red dragon in this Russian civil war propaganda poster. Its title is "For a United Russia." **Draw Conclusions** Which side in the Russian civil war made this poster? Why?

DESCRIBE Describe the reasons for the fall of Kerensky's government.

Civil War Erupts in Russia

After the Bolshevik Revolution, Lenin quickly sought peace with Germany. Russia signed the Treaty of Brest-Litovsk in March 1918, giving up a huge chunk of its territory and its population. The cost of peace was extremely high, but the Communist leaders knew that they needed all their energy to defeat a collection of enemies at home. Russia's withdrawal affected the hopes of both the Allies and the Central Powers.

The Opposing Forces For three years, civil war raged between the "Reds," as the Communists were known, and the counterrevolutionary "Whites." The "White" armies were made up of tsarist imperial officers, Mensheviks, democrats, and others, all of whom were united only by their desire to defeat the Bolsheviks. Nationalist groups from many of the former empire's non-Russian regions joined them in their fight. Poland, Estonia, Latvia, and Lithuania broke free, but nationalists in Ukraine, the Caucasus, and central Asia were eventually subdued.

The Allies intervened in the civil war. They hoped that the Whites might overthrow the Communists and support the fight against Germany. Britain, France, and the United States sent forces to help the Whites. Japan seized land in East Asia that tsarist Russia had once claimed. The Allied presence, however, did little to help the Whites. The Reds appealed to nationalism and urged Russians to drive out the foreigners. In the long run, the Allied invasion fed Communist distrust of the West.

Brutality was common in the civil war. Counterrevolutionary forces slaughtered Communist prisoners and tried to assassinate Lenin. The Communists shot the former tsar and tsarina and their five children in July 1918 to keep them from becoming a rallying symbol for counterrevolutionary forces.

Terror and War Communism The Communists used terror not only against the Whites, but also to control their own people. They organized the **Cheka,** a secret police force much like the tsar's. The Cheka executed ordinary citizens, even if they were only suspected of taking action against the revolution. The Communists also set up a network of forced labor camps in 1919—which grew under Stalin into the dreaded Gulag.

The Union of Soviet Socialist Republics, 1923

>> **Analyze Maps** Russia was by far the largest of the various republics that made up the Soviet Union. How do you think nationalism affected the Soviet Union?

Bounce to Activate Map

The Communists adopted a policy known as "war communism." They took over banks, mines, factories, and railroads. Peasants in the countryside were forced to deliver almost all of their crops to feed the army and hungry people in the cities. Peasant laborers were drafted into the military or forced to work in factories.

Meanwhile, Trotsky turned the Red Army into an effective fighting force. He used former tsarist officers under the close watch of **commissars,** Communist party officials assigned to the army to teach party principles and ensure party loyalty. Trotsky's passionate speeches roused soldiers to fight. So did the order to shoot every tenth man if a unit performed poorly.

The Reds' position in the center of Russia gave them a strategic advantage. The White armies were forced to attack separately from all sides. They were never able to cooperate effectively with one another. By 1921, the Communists had managed to defeat their scattered foes.

INTEGRATE INFORMATION How did Lenin and Trotsky use brutality and terror to win the Russian Civil War?

The Communist Soviet Union Emerges

Russia was in chaos. Millions of people had died since the beginning of World War I. Millions more perished from famine and disease. Lenin faced the enormous problem of rebuilding a shattered state and economy.

New Government, Old Problems In 1922, Lenin's Communist government united much of the old Russian empire into the Union of Soviet Socialist Republics (USSR), or Soviet Union. The Communists produced a constitution that seemed both democratic and socialist. It set up an elected legislature, later called the Supreme Soviet, and gave all citizens over 18 the right to vote. All political power, resources, and means of production would belong to workers and peasants. The Soviet Union was a multinational state made up of European and Asian peoples. In theory, all the member republics shared certain equal rights.

Reality, however, differed greatly from theory. The Communist party, not the people, reigned supreme. Just as the Russian tsars had, the party used the army and secret police to enforce its will. Russia, which was the largest republic, dominated the other republics.

>> Lenin (left) and Stalin (right) appear together here. But British art historian David King claims that Stalin's image was airbrushed into the photo. **Hypothesize** Why would Stalin want photos of him appearing with Lenin?

Lenin Abandons War Communism On the economic front, Lenin retreated from his policy of "war communism," which had brought the economy to near collapse. Under party control, factory and mine output had fallen. Peasants stopped producing grain, knowing the government would only seize it.

In 1921, Lenin adopted the New Economic Policy, or NEP. It allowed some capitalist ventures. Although the state kept control of banks, foreign trade, and large industries, small businesses were allowed to reopen for private profit. The government also stopped squeezing peasants for grain. Under the NEP, peasants held on to small plots of land and freely sold their surplus crops.

Lenin's compromise with capitalism helped the Soviet economy recover and ended armed resistance to the new government. By 1928, food and industrial production climbed back to prewar levels. The standard of living improved, too. But Lenin always saw the NEP as just a temporary retreat from communism. His successor would soon return the Soviet Union to "pure" communism.

Stalin Comes to Power Lenin died in 1924 at the age of 54. His death set off a power struggle among Communist leaders. The chief contenders were Trotsky and Joseph Stalin. Trotsky was a brilliant Marxist thinker, a skillful speaker, and an architect of the Bolshevik Revolution. Stalin, by contrast, was neither a scholar nor an orator. He was, however, a shrewd political operator and behind-the-scenes organizer. Trotsky and Stalin differed on the future of communism. Trotsky urged support for a worldwide revolution against capitalism. Stalin, who was more cautious, wanted to concentrate on building socialism at home first.

Eventually, Stalin isolated Trotsky within the party and stripped him of party membership. Trotsky fled the country in 1929, but continued to criticize Stalin. In 1940, a Stalinist agent murdered Trotsky in Mexico.

In 1922, Lenin had expressed grave doubts about Stalin's ambitious nature: "Comrade Stalin . . . has concentrated an enormous power in his hands; and I am not sure that he always knows how to use that power with sufficient caution." Just as Lenin had warned, in the years that followed, Stalin used ruthless measures to win dictatorial power.

DESCRIBE What capitalist measures did Lenin incorporate into his New Economic Policy?

ASSESSMENT

1. **Identify Cause and Effect** How did the actions of Tsar Nicholas II and his wife lead to revolution in Russia?
2. **Draw Conclusions** How did World War I help to pave the way for the Russian Revolution?
3. **Compare and Contrast** Compare and contrast Lenin's idealistic vision of a socialist state with the reality of communism in the new Soviet Union.
4. **Distinguish** Differentiate between the February Revolution and the October Revolution. What were the outcomes of each?
5. **Hypothesize** If World War I had not taken place, do you think the Russian Revolution would have happened? Support your argument with facts.

PEARSON realize™
PearsonSchool.com/CASS

Go online to PearsonSchool.com/CASS and use the texts, quizzes, interactivities, Interactive Reading Notepads, Flipped Videos, and other resources from this Topic to prepare for the Topic Test.

- Etexts
- Quizzes
- Interactivities
- Interactive Reading Notepads
- Flipped Videos

While online you can also check the progress you've made learning the topic and course content by viewing your grades, test scores, and assignment status.

California Topic 5 Quick Study Guide

LESSON SUMMARIES

Use these Lesson Summaries, and the longer versions available online, to review the key ideas for each lesson in this Topic.

Lesson 1: World War I Begins

By the early 1900s, many efforts had been made to promote peace. But, more powerful forces were pushing Europe to the brink of war. Aggressive nationalism, economic competition, militarism, and alliances were among the factors that could increase tension and start a war.

Lesson 2: Fighting the Great War

On June 28, 1914, Archduke Francis Ferdinand of Austria-Hungary and his wife Sophie were riding in an open car, through the streets of Sarajevo, the capital of Bosnia. News of the visit angered many Serbian nationalists who viewed Austria-Hungary as oppressors. As the car traveled, the couple was assassinated by a Serbian nationalist. This was the spark that ignited the war.

Lesson 3: World War I Ends

The "Great War" was the largest conflict in history up to that time. The early enthusiasm for the war soon disappeared. Modern weapons resulted in huge numbers of casualties and prevented either side from gaining an advantage.

Lesson 4: Revolution in Russia

After the Revolution of 1905, Czar Nicholas II failed to solve Russia's basic political, economic, and social problems. Discontent sparked new eruptions. In March 1917, the first of two revolutions would destroy the Romanov dynasty and pave the way for even more radical changes.

VISUAL REVIEW

Use these graphics to review some of the key terms, people, and ideas from this Topic.

Causes and Effects of World War I

CAUSE AND EFFECT

LONG-TERM CAUSES	IMMEDIATE CAUSES
• Rivalries among European powers • European alliance system • Militarism and arms race • Nationalist tensions in the Balkans	• Austria-Hungary's annexation of Bosnia and Herzegovina • Fighting in the Balkans • Assassination of Archduke Francis Ferdinand • Russian mobilization • German invasion of Belgium

↓

WORLD WAR I

↓

IMMEDIATE EFFECTS	LONG-TERM EFFECTS
• Enormous cost in lives and property • Revolution in Russia • Creation of new nations in Eastern Europe • German reparations • German loss of overseas colonies • Balfour Declaration • League of Nations	• Economic impact of war debts on Europe • Stronger central governments • Emergence of United States and Japan as important powers • Growth of nationalism in colonies • Rise of fascism • Increased anti-Semitism in Germany • World War II

Key Events in the Russian Revolution

- **1914–1917** World War I pressures Russia.
- **March 1917** March Revolution causes tsar to abdicate; the provisional government takes power.
- **November 1917** Bolsheviks under Lenin topple provisional government (November Revolution).

Financial Costs of World War I

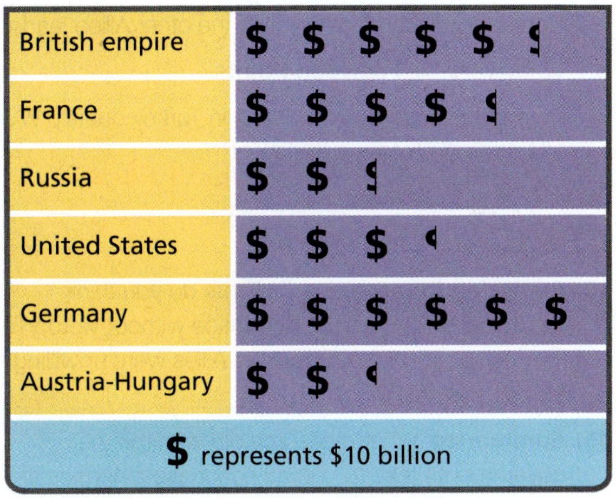

SOURCE: *The Harper Encyclopedia of Military History*, R.Ernest Dupuy and Trevor N. Dupuy

California Topic 5 Assessment

KEY TERMS, PEOPLE, AND IDEAS

1. Why did the United States enter WWI? How did this affect the outcome of the war?
2. How did the **Lusitania** incident affect relations between the United States and Germany?
3. What factors contributed to the **stalemate** on the Western Front?
4. Why do some historians label the strategy used in WWI as a **"total war"** effort?
5. How did imperialism affect WWI?
6. Why might some colonial troops have been willing to fight in the War?
7. How did Woodrow Wilson's goals at the Paris Peace Conference differ from those of the other Allied leaders?
8. What were the **Fourteen Points**?
9. How did the rise of nationalism in Turkey during WWI affect the Armenian population?

CRITICAL THINKING

10. **Analyzing Information** (a) What do you think Woodrow Wilson meant by "peace without victory"? (b) Why do you think European Allies were unwilling to accept this idea?
11. **Summarize** What measures did wartime governments take to control national economies and public opinion?
12. **Summarize** How did the Versailles Treaty shift geographic borders in Europe and the Middle East after WWI?
13. **Recognize Causes and Effects** What were the causes and effects of the civil war in Russia?
14. **Predict Consequences** One member of the Paris Peace Conference said of the negotiations "This is not a peace; it is an armistice for twenty years." Do you agree or disagree? Explain
15. **Analyze Information** How did the loss of the United States as a member nation affect the League of Nations?
16. **Analyze Images** Look at the image below of a trench used during WW I. (a) How do you think soldiers were affected with this kind of warfare? (b) Why might some historians feel this was the best way to fight the war?

17. **Writing Activity** Aggressive nationalism was among the causes of World War I. Helmuth von Moltke, a military leader described the strategy Germany should use at the beginning of World War I.

> "The German people must be made to see that we have to attack because of our enemy's provocation. Things must be so built up that war will seem as a deliverance from the great armaments, the financial burdens, the political tensions. . . Germany must regain what she formerly lost."

Some historians are of the opinion that the major cause of World War I was Germany's desire to be a world power. Is there evidence to support this view? Use your knowledge of the Topic and the quote to write a response.

DOCUMENT-BASED QUESTIONS

The entry of the United States into the war in April 1917 was a turning point in World War I. Read the documents below, then answer the questions that follow.

DOCUMENT A

American Soldiers Arrive in Europe, 1918

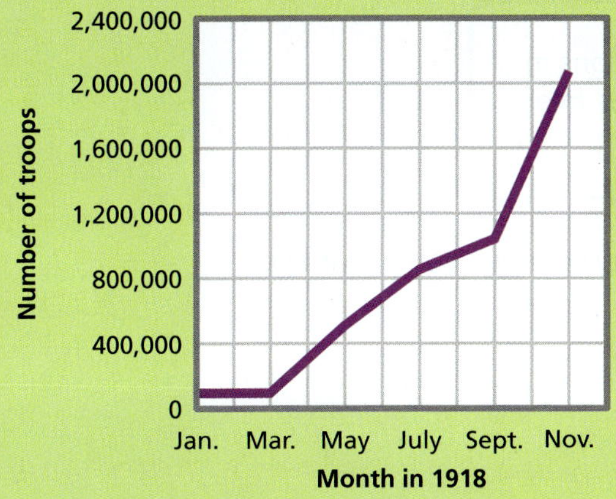

SOURCE: *The First World War: An Eyewitness History*, Joe H. Kirchberger

DOCUMENT B

"British shipping losses, especially since the declaration of unrestricted submarine warfare, had risen dangerously. . . . But the entry of the United States into the war made the German submarine warfare an evident failure, because thereafter the number of ships convoyed and the number of ships protecting the convoys was increased steadily. Convoys of ships transporting food, war materials, and troops arrived safely in Britain, and the rate of shipping construction soon exceeded the rate of loss."

—The End of the European Era. 1890 to the Present. by Felix Gilbert and David Clay Large

DOCUMENT C

Winston Churchill, who served in Britain's navy and army during World War I, wrote about the effect American troops had on their tired Allies.

"The impression made upon the hard-pressed French by this seemingly inexhaustible flood of gleaming youth in its first maturity of health and vigour was prodigious [amazing]. None were under twenty, and few were over thirty . . . the French Headquarters were thrilled with the impulse of new life. . . . Half trained, half organized, with only their courage, their numbers and their magnificent youth behind their weapons, they were to buy their experience at a bitter price. But this they were quite ready to do."

DOCUMENT D

Loans from the United States to Allies

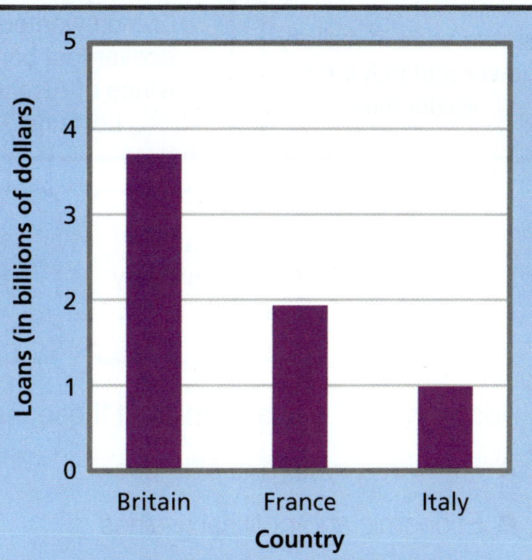

SOURCE: *The End of the European Era. 1890 to the Present.* Felix Gilbert and David Clay Large

18. How would you describe the arrival of American troops in Europe in 1918?

A. slow at first, but rapid after March

B. steady throughout the year

C. rapid at first, but slow after March

D. No American troops arrived in Europe in 1918.

19. How did the United States navy help break Germany's submarine blockade of Britain?

A. by completely destroying the German submarine fleet

B. by finding new routes around the German submarine fleet

C. by strengthening the convoys

D. by sending supplies to France rather than Britain

20. Based on Document C, how did Churchill feel about American soldiers?

A. They were experienced but had a poor attitude toward the war.

B. They were energetic and willing to fight, although not experienced.

C. They were well-trained and energetic.

D. They were neither energetic nor experienced.

21. **Writing Tasks** How did the United States help bring about the Allied victory in 1918? Use your knowledge of World War I and specific evidence from the documents to support your points.

End-of-Topic Practice

German pride in military power and industrial leadership	French wanted to recover lost border province of Alsace and Lorraine	Russian defense and aid to Pan-Slavism
Minority populations within Austria-Hungary empire	Military tensions in Balkan states over territory	

1 According to the chart, which of these reasons helped cause World War I?

A Forming a system of alliances

B Economic and political rivalries

C Build-up of military forces

D Extreme nationalism

---

2 How did imperialism help cause World War I?

F As the Ottoman empire declined, imperialist rivalry led to the first anti-France alliances in Europe.

G The new imperialism encouraged competition and a breakdown of diplomatic relations in Europe.

H Compromises among European nations were attempted but failed as France and Germany continued aggressive colonizing in Africa and the Ottoman Empire.

J Colonial disputes continued, ultimately leading to the August Crisis in 1914.

> *"Once war was declared, the army attempted to mobilize the troops very quickly. The fatigued British and French troops, who had been fighting since August 1914, sorely needed the relief offered by the American forces."*

3 Based on an analysis of the excerpt, why was there a need for American forces?

A American forces contradicted propaganda that the Allies were weaker than others.

B American forces helped break the stalemate that had resulted in prolonged trench warfare.

C American forces showed support for the nations that were bombed most heavily.

D American forces allayed concerns that food rationing was occurring on the front lines.

---

4 What advantages helped the Bolsheviks to rise to power in 1917?

F Members of the provisional government gradually joined the Bolshevik party.

G As Bolsheviks gained power, their message gradually spread to German and French workers who soon supported their cause.

H The Bolsheviks, who appealed to peasants and workers, were well organized and led by a determined leader, Lenin.

J The Bolshevik party was largely populated by former Red Guards, workers, and peasants, who cheered the goals of Trotsky and Lenin.

If you have trouble with. . .				
Question	1	2	3	4
See Lesson	5.1	5.1	5.3	5.4

PEARSON realize
PearsonSchool.com/CASS

Go ONLINE for digital resources

VIDEO AUDIO ETEXT ACTIVITY WRITING GAMES PDF ASSESSMENT

[ESSENTIAL QUESTION] What should governments do?

6 The World Between the Wars (1910–1939)

>> Wealthy women attend the opera in Paris the 1920s

Enduring Understandings

- Economic and political inequalities led to the Mexican Revolution.
- Examples of resistance to imperialism included Pan-Africanism, Pan-Arabism, and Gandhi's civil disobedience campaign in India.
- In China, the nationalists under Jiang Jieshi and the communists under Mao Zedong competed for power.
- Postwar disillusion and new mass media reshaped western culture.
- A global economic depression caused widespread misery and threatened the stability of democratic governments.
- Authoritarian and totalitarian states such as Japan, the Soviet Union, Italy, and Germany placed loyalty to the state above individual rights.

NBC LEARN

Explore the efforts of Mohandas Gandhi to win independence for India.

Bounce to Activate My Story Video

California Topic 6 Overview

In this Topic, you will learn about the events that occurred between the world wars from 1910–1939. Look at the lesson outline and explore the timeline. As you study this Topic, you will complete the Quest team project.

LESSON OUTLINE

6.1 Revolution and Nationalism in Latin America
Analysis CST.1, CST.2, HRE.4, HI.1

6.2 Nationalist Movements in Africa and the Middle East
Analysis CST.1, CST.2, CST.3, HRE.4, HI.1

6.3 India Seeks Self Rule
Analysis CST.1, CST.2, HRE.4, HI.1

6.4 New Forces in China and Japan
Analysis CST.1, CST.2, HRE.4, HI.1

6.5 The West After World War I
HSS 10.6.4, HSS 10.8.2; Analysis CST.1, CST.2, CST.3, HRE.4, HI.1

6.6 Fascism Emerges in Italy
HSS 10.6.3, HSS 10.7, HSS 10.7.3; Analysis CST.1, CST.2, HRE.4, HI.1

6.7 The Soviet Union Under Stalin
HSS 10.6.3, HSS 10.7, HSS 10.7.2, HSS 10.7.3; Analysis CST.1, CST.2, HRE.4, HI.1

6.8 The Rise of Nazi Germany
HSS 10.6.3, HSS 10.7, HSS 10.7.3; Analysis CST.1, CST.2, HRE.4, HI.1

Key Events of the World Between WWI and WWII

1910 Mexican Revolution begins.

1912 Black South Africans form the African National Congress party.

1920 The Weimar Republic is established in Germany.

1922 Mussolini comes to power.

1928 Stalin launches his Five Year Plans.

1932 Stalin's failed plans thrust the Soviet Union into mass starvation.

1933 Adolf Hitler becomes chancellor of Germany.

1935 The Nazi Party passes the Nuremberg Laws that limit the rights of Jews.

1910 1915 1920 1925 1930 1935 1940

QUEST! TEAM PROJECT

Civic Discussion: Lenin and Stalin

After the death of Bolshevik leader Lenin, Stalin gained control of the Communist party. In this quest, you will prepare a discussion to address whether Lenin sowed the seeds for Stalin's brutal dictatorship.

STEP 1
Begin the discussion about the question. Review what you know about the topic. List major points that can be used in answering the question.

STEP 2
Review the documents. Evaluate the evidence. Discuss the conclusions. Then have team members take sides. Outline discussion points.

STEP 3
Work with your group to determine the strongest arguments. Prepare your discussion. Review, edit, and revise.

STEP 4
Present your discussion. Reflect on the importance of understanding issues from multiple perspectives.

PEARSON realize™
PearsonSchool.com/CASS
Go ONLINE for complete Quest materials
VIDEO ETEXT WRITING RUBRIC PDF ASSESSMENT

>> Peasants joined the Mexican revolution in the hopes of improving their lives. Most were untrained and had few supplies, but they continued to fight for social, political, and economic change.

Bounce to Activate Flipped Video

6.1 By 1910, the dictator Porfirio Díaz had ruled Mexico for almost 35 years, winning re-election as president again and again. On the surface, Mexico enjoyed peace and economic growth. Díaz welcomed foreign investors who developed mines, built railroads, and drilled for oil.

>> Objectives

Identify causes and effects of the Mexican Revolution.

Analyze the effects of economic and political nationalism on Latin America.

Trace the changing relationship between Latin America and the United States.

>> Key Terms

Porfirio Díaz
hacienda
Emiliano Zapata
Venustiano Carranza
nationalization
Lázaro Cárdenas
economic nationalism
cultural nationalism
Good Neighbor Policy

Revolution and Nationalism in Latin America

The Mexican Revolution

Seeds of Discontent However, underneath the surface, discontent rippled through Mexico. The country's prosperity benefited only a small group. The majority of Mexicans were mestizos or Indian peasants who lived in desperate poverty. Most of these peasants worked on **haciendas,** or large plantations, controlled by the landowning elite.

Some peasants moved to cities, where they found jobs in factories, or worked in mines. Everywhere, they earned meager wages. In Mexican cities, middle-class liberals, who embraced the ideals of democracy, opposed the Díaz dictatorship.

The unrest boiled over in 1910 when Francisco Madero, a liberal reformer from an elite family, demanded free elections. After being imprisoned by Diaz, he hoisted the flag of revolution. Soon, revolutionaries all across Mexico joined Madero's cause. Faced with rebellion in several parts of the country, Díaz resigned in 1911.

A Complex Struggle Madero became president of Mexico, but he turned out to be too liberal for conservatives and not radical enough for the revolutionaries. In 1913, he was murdered by one of his generals, Victoriano Huerta. Huerta ruled as a military dictator, but was quickly faced with rebellion.

During a long, complex power struggle, several radical leaders emerged. They sometimes joined forces but then fought each other. In southern Mexico, **Emiliano Zapata** led a peasant revolt. Zapata, an Indian peasant farmer, understood the misery of peasant villagers. The battle cry of the Zapatistas, as these rebels were called, was "Tierra y libertad!" which means "land and freedom."

Francisco "Pancho" Villa, a hard-riding rebel from the north, fought mostly for personal power but won the intense loyalty of his peasant followers. Villa and Zapata formed an uneasy coaltion with **Venustiano Carranza,** a rich landowner who wanted political reform but opposed social change.

Fighting flared across Mexico for a decade, killing as many as a million Mexicans. Peasants, small farmers, ranchers, and urban workers were drawn into the violent struggle. Soldaderas, women soldiers, cooked, tended the wounded, and even fought alongside men.

During the revolution, President Woodrow Wilson of the United States twice sent troops to Mexico. In 1914, U.S. forces helped depose, or remove, Huerta. In 1916, they tried to hunt down Pancho Villa, whose raid into New Mexico had killed 16 Americans. After the overthrow of Huerta, Carranza turned on Villa and Zapata and defeated them. In 1917, Carranza was elected president of Mexico. That year, he reluctantly signed a new constitution.

SEQUENCE EVENTS Explain the events of the Mexican Revolution in order.

>> Francisco Madero served as president for less than two years before he was overthrown. Though he accomplished little, he remained an inspiration to revolutionaries.

Bounce to Activate Gallery

>> During the Constitutional Convention in Querétaro, Venustiano Carranza chaired the committee that drafted the Constitution of 1917. The Congress approved it on February 5, 1917.

Economic and Social Reforms

Venustiano Carranza had called for a new constitution during the Mexican Revolution. But he did not like the one he had reluctantly signed in 1917 and did not institute its reforms. In 1920, rival revolutionaries arranged for his assassination. The constitution, however, survived. With some revisions, it is still in effect today.

The Constitution of 1917 The Constitution of 1917 addressed three major issues: land, religion, and labor. The constitution strengthened government control over the economy. It permitted the breakup of large estates, placed restrictions on foreigners owning land, and allowed **nationalization,** or government takeover, of natural resources. Church land was made "the property of the nation." The constitution set a minimum wage and protected the workers' right to strike.

Although the constitution gave suffrage only to men, it did give women some rights. Women doing the same job as men were entitled to the same pay. In response to women activists' efforts to change the Mexican government, Carranza also passed laws allowing married women to draw up contracts, take part in legal suits, and have equal authority with men in spending family funds.

The PRI Takes Control In 1929, the government organized what later became the Institutional Revolutionary Party (PRI). The PRI made political choices to accommodate many groups in Mexican society, including business and military leaders, peasants, and workers. Its leaders backed social reform, even while it kept power in its own hands and suppressed political opposition. It also boosted Mexican industry. Over time, the PRI brought stability to Mexico and carried out many desired reforms. The PRI dominated Mexican politics until 2000.

Social and Economic Reforms At first, the Constitution of 1917 was just a set of goals to be achieved in the future. But in the 1920s and 1930s, as the government finally restored order, it began to carry out reforms.

In the 1920s, the government helped some Indian communities regain lands that had been taken from them. In the 1930s, President **Lázaro Cárdenas** made the decision to redistribute millions of acres of land to peasants under a communal land program. The government supported labor unions and launched a massive effort to combat illiteracy. Schools and libraries were set up. For the first time, Mexicans in rural areas who grew up speaking various Indian languages learned Spanish.

Dedicated teachers, often young women, worked for low pay. While they taught basic skills, they also spread ideas of nationalism that began to bridge the gulf between the regions and the central government. As the revolutionary era ended, Mexico became the first Latin American nation to pursue real social and economic reforms for the majority of its people.

Under the PRI, the government also took a strong role in directing the economy. In 1938, labor disputes broke out between Mexican workers and the management of some foreign-owned petroleum companies. In response, President Cárdenas nationalized Mexico's oil resources. American and

Land Distributed in Mexico by President, 1915–1940

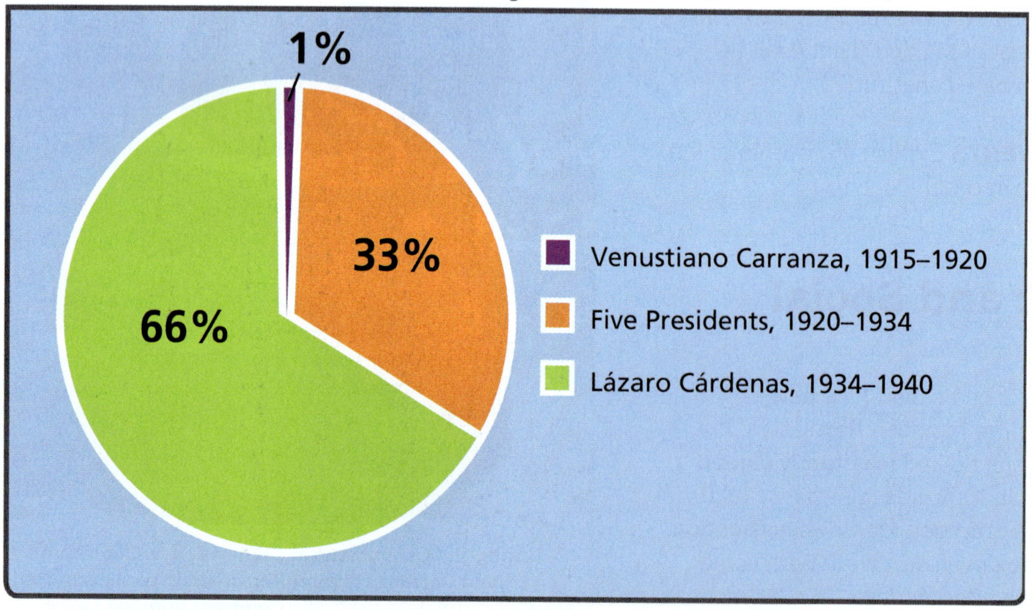

>> **Analyze Graphs** Between 1915 and 1940, nearly 75 million acres of land were distributed to Mexico's people, fulfilling one goal of the constitution. Which president redistributed the most land?

British oil companies resisted Cárdenas's decision, but eventually accepted compensation for their losses. Mexicans felt that they were at last gaining economic independence from foreign influence.

IDENTIFY CENTRAL IDEAS How did the PRI accommodate many groups in Mexican society while keeping power for itself?

>> The Institutional Revolutionary Party (PRI) created a more stable government in Mexico and increased the representation of peasants and urban laborers.

Nationalism Spreads in Latin America

The issues facing Mexico were echoed in other Latin American nations. In the early 1900s, Latin America's economy was booming because of exports. Latin Americans sold their plentiful natural resources and cash crops to industrialized countries. In return, they bought products made in those countries.

Stable governments helped to keep the region's economy on good footing. Some Latin American nations, such as Argentina and Uruguay, had democratic constitutions. However, military dictators or small groups of wealthy landowners held the real power. The tiny ruling class kept the economic benefits of the booming economy for themselves. The growing middle class and the lower classes—workers and peasants—had no say in their own governments.

Economic Nationalism

During the 1920s and 1930s, world events affected Latin American economies. After World War I, trade with Europe fell off. The Great Depression that struck the United States in 1929 spread around the world in the 1930s. Prices for Latin American exports plunged as demand dried up. At the same time, the cost of imported consumer goods rose. Latin American economies, dependent on export trade, declined rapidly.

A tide of **economic nationalism,** or emphasis on home control of the economy, swept Latin American countries. It was directed largely at ending economic dependence on the industrial powers, especially the United States and Britain. Since consumers could no longer afford costly imports, local entrepreneurs set up factories to produce goods at home. They urged their governments to raise tariffs, or taxes on imports, to protect these new industries. Following Mexico's lead, some nations nationalized resources or took over foreign-owned industries.

>> Students rally to support President Lázaro Cárdenas's nationalization of the foreign-owned oil industry. One of the signs reads: "We will collaborate enthusiastically in the betterment of Mexico."

The drive to create domestic industries had limited success. In Mexico, Argentina, Brazil, and a few other countries, some areas of manufacturing grew. Mexico and Venezuela also benefited from a growing demand for their oil. But most Latin American nations lacked the resources to build large industries. As in the past, the unequal distribution of wealth hurt efforts at economic development. Only a few in the wealthy ruling class benefited from economic growth.

Political Nationalism The Great Depression also triggered political changes in Latin America. The economic crisis caused people to lose faith in the ruling oligarchies and the ideas of liberal government. Liberalism, a belief in the individual and in limited government, was a European theory. People began to feel that it did not work in Latin America.

In the midst of economic crisis, authoritarian governments with strong nationalist goals gained power in many countries. Authoritarian rulers imposed stability and supported economic nationalism, but suppressed opposition political parties and silenced critics.

Cultural Nationalism By the 1920s, an upsurge of national feeling led Latin American writers, artists, and thinkers to reject European influences. Instead, they took pride in their own culture, with its blend of Western and Native American traditions.

In Mexico, **cultural nationalism,** or pride in one's own national culture, was reflected in the revival of mural painting, a major art form of the Aztecs and Maya. Diego Rivera, José Clemente Orozco (oh ROHS koh), and other muralists created magnificent works that reflected Mexican culture and history. On the walls of public buildings, they portrayed the struggles of the Mexican people for liberty. The murals have been a great source of national pride ever since.

Relations with the United States Nationalism affected how Latin American nations saw the United States. During and after World War I, investments by the United States in Latin America soared, while British influence declined. The United States continued to play the role of international policeman, intervening to restore order when it felt its interests were threatened.

During the Mexican Revolution, the United States stepped in with military force to support the leaders who favored American interests. This interference stirred up anti-American feelings, which increased throughout Latin America during the 1920s. For example, in Nicaragua, Augusto César Sandino led a guerrilla movement against United States forces occupying his country.

U.S. Intervention in Latin America, 1920–1930

COUNTRY	YEAR(S)	TYPE/REASON
Nicaragua	1912–1934	20-year occupation to fight guerrillas; from 1926–1933, sought to capture nationalistic forces led by Augusto César Sandino
Haiti	1914–1934	19-year occupation after revolutions
Dominican Republic	1916–1924	8-year Marine occupation
Cuba	1917–1933	Military occupation and establishment of economic protectorate under Platt Amendment
Panama	1918–1920	Police duty after elections; protection of United Fruit plantations
Guatemala	1920–1921	Two-week intervention against unionists; support of a coup
Costa Rica / Panama	1921	Troop intervention in border dispute
Mexico	1923	Air Force defense of Calles from rebellion
Honduras	1924–1925	Two landings during election unrest
Panama	1925	Marine suppression of general strike
El Salvador	1932	Warship support of ruling general during revolt

>> **Analyze Charts** During the early 1900s, the United States regularly intervened in Latin American conflicts. What was the most common form of intervention?

The Good Neighbor Policy In the 1930s, President Franklin Roosevelt took a new approach to Latin America. He pledged to follow "the policy of the good neighbor."

Under the **Good Neighbor Policy,** the United States agreed to stop interfering in the affairs of Latin American nations. The United States withdrew troops stationed in Haiti and Nicaragua and lifted the Platt Amendment, which had limited Cuban independence.

When Mexico nationalized its oil industry in 1938, Roosevelt resisted demands by some Americans to intervene. The Good Neighbor policy survived until 1945 when global tensions led the United States to intervene once again in the region.

SYNTHESIZE How did political and cultural nationalism grow in Latin America?

>> Artist Diego Rivera portrayed the history of Mexico in this mural. The bottom represents Aztec civilization. The top half focuses on the Mexican Revolution and the future of Mexico.

Bounce to Activate Gallery

ASSESSMENT

1. **Identify Central Ideas** How did Mexican artists express cultural nationalism?
2. **Identify Cause and Effect** What caused many Mexicans to struggle for change in the early 1900s?
3. **Identify Central Issues** How did nationalism affect Latin America?
4. **Assess Credibility** How did the PRI fulfill some goals of the Mexican Revolution but not others?
5. **Cite Evidence** What role did the United States play after World War I and during the Mexican Revolution? Cite evidence to support your response.

>> Throughout Africa, Europeans operated mines and paid Africans low wages to work in them. Here, South Africans are working in a diamond mine owned by a Dutch company.

6.2 During the early 1900s, more and more Africans felt the impact of colonial rule. European nations exploited, or took advantage, of their colonies to produce profits for the parent country. Although the peoples of Africa had long tried to resist foreign imperialism, calls for change spread, fueling new nationalist movements.

Bounce to Activate Flipped Video

>> Objectives

Explain how Africans resisted colonial rule.

Describe the rise of nationalism in Africa.

Describe how Turkey and Persia modernized.

Understand how the mandate system contributed to Arab nationalism and to conflict between Jews and Arabs.

>> Key Terms

apartheid
Pan-Africanism
Marcus Garvey
négritude movement
Asia Minor
Atatürk
Reza Khan
Pan-Arabism
Balfour Declaration

Nationalist Movements in Africa and the Middle East

Africans Protest Colonial Rule

Exploitation of African Colonies European governments expected their colonies to be profitable. To do so, they exploited the mineral resources of Africa, sending raw materials to feed European factories. In Kenya and Rhodesia, white settlers forced Africans off the best land. Also in Kenya, the British made all Africans carry identification cards, pay a tax, and live or travel only in certain areas.

Everywhere, farmers were forced to work on European-run plantations or in mines to earn money to pay taxes. Those farmers who kept their own land had to grow cash crops, like cotton, for the benefit of the colonizers instead of food. This led to famines in some regions. Increasingly, African people lost their self-sufficiency and became dependent on European goods.

Protesting Imperialism During World War I, more than one million Africans had fought on behalf of their colonial rulers. Many had hoped that their service would lead to more rights and opportunities. Instead, the situation after World War I remained mostly the same or even worsened.

Many Western-educated Africans criticized the injustice of imperial rule. Although they had trained for professional careers, the best jobs went to Europeans.

Inspired by President Woodrow Wilson's call for self-determination, Africans condemned the colonial system that excluded them from controlling their own lands. During the 1920s and 1930s, a new generation of leaders proud of their unique heritage struggled to restore Africa for Africans. Protests and opposition to imperialism multiplied. Some of this new generation turned to socialism or the writings of Marx and Lenin.

While large-scale revolts were rare, protests were common. In Kenya, the Kikuyu people protested the loss of their land to white settlers and denounced forced labor and heavy taxes. In the 1920s, Ibo women in Niberia revolted against British policies that threatened their rights. The British eventually ended the "Women's War" with gunfire.

A Policy of Segregation in South Africa

Between 1910 and 1940, whites strengthened their grip on South Africa. They imposed a system of racial segregation to ensure white economic, political, and social supremacy. New laws, for example, restricted better-paying jobs in mines to whites only.

Blacks were pushed into low-paid, less-skilled work. South African blacks had to carry passes at all times. They were evicted from the best land and forced to live on crowded "reserves," which were located in dry, infertile areas.

Other laws chipped away at the rights of blacks. In one South African province, educated blacks who owned property had been allowed to vote in local elections. In 1936, the government abolished that right. The system of segregation would become even stricter after 1948, when **apartheid**(uh PAHR tayt), a policy of rigid racial segregation, became law.

Yet South Africa was also home to a vital nationalist movement. African Christian churches and African-run newspapers demanded rights for black South Africans. In 1912, they formed a political party, later called the African National Congress (ANC), to protest unfair laws and demand a change to South Africa's white government. Their efforts had no immediate effect, but the ANC did build a framework for political action in later years.

IDENTIFY CAUSE AND EFFECT How did Africans think that fighting on behalf of their colonial rulers during World War I would impact their lives?

A Rising Tide of African Nationalism

In the 1920s, a movement known as Pan-Africanism began to nourish the nationalist spirit and strengthen resistance. **Pan-Africanism** emphasized the unity of Africans and the people of African descent worldwide. Among its most inspiring leaders was Jamaica-born **Marcus Garvey.** He preached a forceful, appealing message of "Africa for Africans" and demanded an end to colonial rule. Garvey's ideas influenced a new generation of African and African American leaders.

The Pan-African Congress African American scholar and activist W.E.B. DuBois (doo BOYS) organized the first Pan-African Congress in 1919. It met in Paris, where the Allies were holding their peace conference.

>> Opposition to imperialism grew among Africans in the 1920s and 1930s. In 1929, Ibo market women in Nigeria demanded a voice in decisions that affected their markets. The "Women's War" soon became a full-fledged revolt.

Bounce to Activate Map

Delegates from African colonies, the West Indies, and the United States called on the Paris peacemakers to approve a charter of rights for Africans and an end to colonialism. Although the Western powers ignored their demands, the Pan-African Congress established cooperation among African and African American leaders.

Writers Celebrate African Culture A literary movement further awakened nationalism and self-confidence among Africans. French-speaking writers from West Africa and the Caribbean who were living in Paris founded the **négritude movement.** Writers of the négritude movement expressed pride in their African roots and culture and protested colonial rule. Their work often transcended their time and place to convey universal themes, such as the human desire for freedom and dignity.

The best known writer of the négritude movement was the Senegalese poet Léopold Senghor. Senghor celebrated Africa's rich cultural heritage. He fostered African pride by rejecting the negative views of Africa spread by colonial rulers. Later, Senghor would take an active role in Senegal's drive to independence, and he would serve as its first president in 1960.

>> Léopold Senghor inspired many writers of the négritude movement, including Birago Diop and Mongo Beti. He was admired throughout the world as a writer and statesman.

Bounce to Activate Gallery

Independence for Egypt African nationalism brought little political change, except to Egypt. During World War I, Egyptians had been forced to provided food and workers to help Britain. Simmering resistance to British rule flared as the war ended. Western-educated officials, peasants, landowners, Christians, and Muslims united behind the Wafd (WAHFT) party, which launched strikes and protests.

In 1922 Britain finally agreed to Egyptian independence. In fact, British troops stayed in Egypt to guard the Suez Canal and to back up the Egyptian monarch, King Faud. Displeased with this state of affairs, during the 1930s many young Egyptians joined an organization called the Muslim Brotherhood. This group fostered a broad Islamic nationalism that rejected Western culture and denounced corruption in the Egyptian government.

>> Atatürk (center) sought to modernize, Westernize, and secularize Turkey. He is still honored throughout the nation. His portrait appears on postage stamps and all currency.

SYNTHESIZE How did the négritude movement reflect the history of African culture, and how did this affect Africans?

Modernization of Turkey and Persia

Nationalist movements greatly affected the Middle East in the aftermath of World War I. The defeated Ottoman empire was near collapse in 1918. Its Arab lands were divided between Britain and France. However, in **Asia Minor,** a peninsula in western Asia between the Black Sea and the Mediterranean Sea, ethnic Turks resisted Western control and fought to build a modern nation.

Atatürk Takes Power In 1920, the Ottoman sultan reluctantly signed the Treaty of Sèvres, in which the empire lost its Arab and North African lands. The sultan also had to give up some land in Asia Minor to a number of Allied countries, including Greece. A Greek force landed in the city of Smyrna (now Izmir) to assert Greece's claims.

Turkish nationalists, led by the determined and energetic Mustafa Kemal, overthrew the sultan, defeated the Greeks, and declared Turkey a republic. Kemal later took the name **Atatürk** (ah tah TURK), meaning "father of the Turks." He negotiated a new treaty. Among other provisions, the treaty called for about 1.3 million Greeks to leave Turkey, while some 400,000 Turks left Greece.

Westernization of Turkey Between 1923 and his death in 1938, Atatürk forced through an ambitious program of radical reforms. His goals were to modernize Turkey along Western lines and to separate religion from government.

To achieve these goals, Atatürk mandated that Islamic traditions in several fields be replaced with Western alternatives. For example, he replaced Islamic law with laws based on a European model, replaced the Arabic alphabet with the Latin alphabet, and forced people to wear Western-style clothing. Under Atatürk, state schools replaced religious schools.

Atatürk's government encouraged industrial expansion. The government built railroads, set up factories, and hired westerners to advise on how to make Turkey economically independent.

To achieve his reforms, Atatürk ruled with an iron hand. To many Turks, he was a hero who was transforming Turkey into a strong, modern power. Some Turkish Muslims, however, rejected Atatürk's dictatorial powers and his formation of a secular government. To them, the Quran and Islamic customs provided all the guidance needed.

>> Atatürk stands before a crowd, pointing to letters of the Roman alphabet. He introduced the western alphabet to Turkey as one of his many modernizing reforms.

>> Reza Khan, seated here on the throne of the shahs, overthrew the reigning shah in 1925. On December 16, 1926, the Grand Council of Persia appointed Reza Khan king.

Persian Nationalism and Reform The success of Atatürk's reforms inspired nationalists in neighboring Persia (present-day Iran). Persian nationalists greatly resented the British and Russians, who had won spheres of influence over Persia in 1907. In 1925, an ambitious army officer, **Reza Khan,** overthrew the shah. He set up his own dynasty, with himself as shah.

Like Atatürk, Reza Khan rushed to modernize Persia and make it fully independent. He built factories, roads, and railroads and strengthened the army. He forced Persians to wear Western clothing and set up modern, secular schools. In addition, he moved to replace Islamic law with secular law and encouraged women to take part in public life. The shah had the support of wealthy urban Persians. However, Muslim religious leaders fiercely condemned his efforts to introduce Western ways.

Reza Khan also persuaded the British company that controlled Persia's oil industry to give Persia a larger share of the profits and insisted that Persian workers be hired at all levels of the company. In the decades ahead, oil would become a major factor in Persia's economy and foreign policy.

INFER Why did Muslim religious leaders disapprove of Reza Khan's reforms?

Nationalism and Conflict in the Middle East

After World War I, the vast Ottoman empire was partitioned into Turkey and several new nations that would make up the modern Arab world. Several Arab lands sat above large oil reserves, giving them global importance in a world that was increasingly dependent on gasoline-powered engines. Instead of granting independence to the Arab states carved out of the Ottoman empire, European powers turned them into mandates under their control.

The Rise of Pan-Arabism Partly in response to foreign influence, Arab nationalism grew after World War I. One form of Arab nationalism was **Pan-Arabism.** This nationalist movement was built on the shared heritage of Arabs who lived in lands from the Arabian Peninsula to North Africa.

Today, this area includes Syria, Jordan, Iraq, Egypt, Algeria, and Morocco. Pan-Arabism emphasized the common history and language of Arabs and recalled the golden age of Arab civilization. The movement sought to free Arabs from foreign domination and unite them in their own state.

>> **Analyze Maps** Population movement, the Treaty of Versailles, and foreign influences changed the Middle East after World War I. How did foreign influences affect the Middle East?

The Pan-Arab movement however, faced obstacles. Arabs generally were not united. They tended to identify with their particular tribe, sect, religion, or region rather than with a single, unified nation-state.

European-Controlled Mandates During World War I, some Arab leaders had helped the Allies against the Ottoman empire. These leaders expected to create their own kingdoms after the war. Even before the revolt, however, France and Britain had secretly agreed that they would take over the Arab lands within the Ottoman empire.

The Treaty of Versailles gave control of German and Ottoman colonies to various Allied nations in the form of mandates.The mandates were authorized by the League of Nations.

The former Ottoman territories in the Middle East were put under the control of two Allies. France was given mandates in Syria and Lebanon, and Britain received mandates in Palestine and Iraq. Later, Britain gave a large part of the Palestinian Mandate, TransJordan, to an Arab ally, King Abdullah.

Arabs felt betrayed by the West—a feeling that has endured to this day. During the 1920s and 1930s, their anger erupted in frequent protests and revolts against Western imperialism. A major center of turmoil was the British Mandate of Palestine. There, Arab nationalists increasingly clashed with Jewish nationalists, known as Zionists.

Conflicting Promises About Palestine Since Roman times, Jews in the diaspora had dreamed of returning to their ancient homeland of Israel. In 1897, Theodor Herzl (HURT sul) responded to growing anti-Semitism, or prejudice against Jewish people, in Europe by founding the modern Zionist political movement. His goal was to reestablish a Jewish homeland in the region called Palestine.

In tsarist Russia, brutal pogroms prompted thousands of Jews to migrate to Palestine. They joined the small Jewish community that had lived there since biblical times.

During World War I, the Allies made two vague and conflicting sets of promises that greatly impacted Arab and Jewish nationalists. First, in an effort to gain Arab support for the British war effort, Britain promised Arabs their own kingdoms in former Ottoman lands.

Then, in 1917, the British attempted to win Jewish support by issuing the **Balfour Declaration.** The declaration affirmed Britain's support for the idea of establishing "a national home for Jewish people" in the Palestine Mandate.

>> In the early 1920s, the first oil wells were drilled in Persia (now Iran). This photograph shows an oil strike at the oil fields in Masjed Soleyman.

Many Jews took this to mean that Britain was announcing its intention to establish a Jewish homeland, but the Balfour Declaration stopped short of making this promise.

The declaration noted that "nothing shall be done which may prejudice the civil and religious rights of existing non-Jewish communities in Palestine, or the rights and political status enjoyed by Jews in any other country." The conflicting promises made to Arab and Jewish settlers set the stage for conflict between Arab and Jewish nationalists.

A Bitter Struggle Begins From 1919 to 1940, tens of thousands of Arabs and Jews immigrated to the Palestine Mandate. Both the Zionist movement and the effects of anti-Semitism in Europe encouraged Jewish immigration. Despite great hardships, Jewish immigrants set up factories, built new towns, and established farming communities. At the same time, the Arab population almost doubled. Some were immigrants from nearby lands. As a result, the population of the Palestine Mandate included a changing mix of settlers. The Jewish population, which was less than 60,000 in 1919, grew to about 400,000 in 1936, while the Muslim population increased from about 568,000 in 1919 to about 1 million in 1940.

At first, some Arabs welcomed the money and modern technical skills that the newcomers brought with them. But as more Jews moved to Palestine Mandate, tensions between the two groups developed.

Jewish organizations tried to purchase as much land as they could, while many Arabs sought to slow down or stop Jewish immigration. Arabs attacked Jewish communities, hoping to discourage Jewish immigration. To protect themselves, the Jewish settlers established their own military defense force. Competing claims to the land continue to lie at the heart of the Arab-Israeli conflict

IDENTIFY CAUSE AND EFFECT Why did the Palestine Mandate become a center of conflict after World War I?

ASSESSMENT

1. **Synthesize** What significance does the phrase "Africa for Africans" have?
2. **Draw Conclusions** How did nationalism contribute to changes in Africa and the Middle East following World War I?
3. **Identify Central Ideas** How did Africans resist colonial rule?
4. **Compare and Contrast** What are the similarities in the way Atatürk and Reza Khan modernized Turkey and Persia and changed their governments?
5. **Identify Cause and Effect** How did the mandate system affect the Middle East?

6.3 Indians had long struggled to end British control. Since 1885, the Indian National Congress party, called the Congress party, had pressed for self-rule within the British empire but had not yet called for full independence.

>> The Salt March, shown here, began at Gandhi's ashram in Sabermati. When Gandhi reached the shore, he picked up a handful of salt and claimed he was shaking the British empire's foundation.

Bounce to Activate Flipped Video

India Seeks Self-Rule

India's Struggle for Independence Begins

During World War I, more than a million Indians had served overseas. Under pressure from Indian nationalists, the British promised Indians greater self-government in return for their service.

However, when the fighting ended, Britain proposed only a few minor reforms. The reforms did little to change the system of bureaucratic rule. The British continued to have little regard for Indian beliefs and customs. Indian frustrations continued to mount, and many began calling for independence from British rule.

A New Leader Emerges Congress party members were mostly middle-class, Western-educated elite who had little in common with the masses of Indian peasants. Then a new leader named **Mohandas Gandhi** emerged and was able to unite Indians across class lines. Admiring Indians came to call him Mahatma, or "Great Soul."

>> Objectives

Explain the impact of World War I and the Amritsar massacre on Indian nationalism.

Evaluate the ideas of Mohandas Gandhi.

Analyze how Gandhi led resistance to political oppression in India.

>> Key Terms

Mohandas Gandhi
Amritsar massacre
ahimsa
civil disobedience
untouchable
boycott
Muhammad Ali Jinnah

>> **Analyze Images** Because the Jallian wala Bagh in Amritsar had only one entrance, demonstrators could not escape the gunfire. How does this painting help you understand the public's reaction to the massacre?

Bounce to Activate Chart

>> In 1913, Muhammad Ali Jinnah joined the Muslim League. Although he and Gandhi disagreed on many things, both believed that a political union between Muslims and Hindus was necessary for Indian independence.

Gandhi came from a middle-class Hindu family. At age 19, he went to England to study law. Then, like many Indians, Gandhi went to South Africa. For 20 years, Gandhi fought laws that discriminated against Indians in South Africa. In his struggle against injustice, he began to develop a tactic of nonviolent, or passive, resistance. He called it satyagraha, or "soul force."

In 1915, Gandhi returned to India and was hailed as a national hero for his work in Africa. Gandhi joined the Congress party, and began to campaign for the rights of Indian workers. He was not, however, calling for Indian independence. His views changed thanks to a tragic event in 1919.

The Muslim League Other leaders also worked for Indian independence. **Muhammad Ali Jinnah** was one of the most influential leaders of India's large Muslim population. He was a leader of the Muslim League, which was founded in 1906 to protect Muslim interests. Jinnah and others feared that the Congress Party was only looking out for Hindu interests. The Indian Congress Party, while made up primarily of Hindus, also had Muslim members.

In the early decades of the century, the Congress party and the Muslim League cooperated in working to achieve an independent India. As time passed, however, the two organizations began to diverge.

The Amritsar Massacre In 1919, the British passed the Rowlatt Acts, which allowed British officials to arrest and imprison any Indian citizen suspected of sedition, or urging people to disobey the government. These political prisoners could then be tried without a jury.

Gandhi opposed the act, which also threatened freedom of the press, and helped organize protests. When violence threatened, he called for an end to the protest campaign.

On April 13, 1919, a large but peaceful crowd of protesters, most of them Sikhs, jammed into an enclosed field in Amritsar, a city in northern India. The protest took place during Vaisakhi, the most prominent holiday in the Sikh tradition. The British commander, General Reginald Dyer, had banned public meetings, but many in the crowd were unaware of the order. As Indian leaders spoke, Dyer ordered his troops to open fire on the unarmed crowd, killing nearly 400 people and wounding more than 1,100.

The **Amritsar massacre** was a turning point for many Indians, including Gandhi. Up to that point, Gandhi had hoped to win partial self-rule for India.

After Amritsar, he was convinced that India must seek full independence.

IDENTIFY CAUSE AND EFFECT What motivated the Indian independence movement after World War I?

Gandhi's Philosophy of Civil Disobedience

In 1921, Gandhi was elected president of the Congress party. He remained the dominant figure in Indian politics for more than twenty years. His words, actions, and ideas inspired Indians of all religious and ethnic backgrounds.

Nonviolent Protest Gandhi was horrified by the violence at Amritsar, but he also condemned Indian acts of violence in response to the massacre. Instead, he preached a philosophy of nonviolent protest that he had first begun to develop during his years in South Africa. His philosophy was based on the ancient Hindu and Jain doctrine of **ahimsa** (uh HIM sah), or nonviolence and reverence for all life. By using the power of love, Gandhi believed, people could convert even the worst wrongdoer to the right course of action. To fight against injustice, he advocated the use of nonviolent resistance. Hindu tradition also informed Gandhi's belief that all Indians regardless of religion had a common spiritual character and common interests.

Gandhi's philosophy reflected Western as well as Indian influences. He admired Christian teachings about love. He believed in the American philosopher Henry David Thoreau's ideas about **civil disobedience,** the refusal to obey unjust laws. Gandhi also embraced Western ideas of democracy and nationalism.

Inspired by both Indian and Western ideas, Gandhi rejected the inequalities of the Indian caste system and fought hard to end the harsh treatment of **untouchables,** the lowest caste of Indian society. He called these outcasts Harijans, or "children of God." Gandhi also urged equal rights for all Indians, women as well as men.

Restoring National Pride Over the next two decades, Gandhi initiated a series of nonviolent actions against British rule. He called for Indians to **boycott,** or refuse to buy, British goods, especially cotton textiles. The move was designed to boost local Indian industries and help restore Indian pride. For centuries, India had produced fine textiles, which

>> Gandhi taught his ways to people throughout India. Here, he speaks to harijan workers at his ashram, or spiritual retreat, in the village of Sevagram.

Bounce to Activate Gallery

had declined under British rule. Gandhi wanted to rebuild such traditional industries.

He made the spinning wheel the symbol of the nationalist movement. In a symbolic move, he abandoned Western-style clothing for the *dhota,* the simple white garments traditionally worn by village Indians.

Through his own example, Gandhi inspired Indians to "get rid of our helplessness." When protests led to violent riots, Gandhi would fast, pray, and call on patriotic Indians to practice self control. His campaigns of civil disobedience attracted wide support, and his nonviolent protests caught the attention of the British government and the world.

IDENTIFY CENTRAL IDEAS What force did Gandhi propose using to free India from British colonial rule, and what was the basis for his ideas?

Gandhi Takes a Stand

To mobilize mass support, Gandhi decided to take a stand against the British salt monopoly, which he saw as a symbol of British oppression. Natural salt was available along the shore, and people had traditionally gotten their salt supplies by boiling seawater. But under colonial rule, the British claimed the sole right to produce and sell salt. By taxing those sales, they collected money to maintain their government in India.

The Salt March Early in 1930, Gandhi wrote to the British viceroy in India. He stated his intention to break the hated salt laws and condemned British rule as "a curse."

On March 12, 1930, Gandhi set out with 78 followers on a 240-mile march to the sea. As the tiny band passed through villages, crowds responded to Gandhi's message. By the time they reached the sea, the marchers numbered in the thousands.

On April 6, Gandhi waded into the surf and picked up a lump of sea salt by the edge of the water. He was soon arrested and jailed.

Still, Indians followed his lead. Coastal villagers started collecting salt and evaporating seawater to make it. Indians sold salt on city streets—and went to jail. As Gandhi's campaign gained force, tens of thousands of Indians were imprisoned.

World Opinion Shifts All around the world, newspapers criticized Britain's harsh reaction to the protests. Stories revealed how police brutally clubbed peaceful marchers who tried to occupy a government saltworks. "Not one of the marchers even raised an arm to fend off the blows," wrote an outraged American newspaper.

The Salt March embarrassed Britain, which prided itself on its democratic traditiions. Slowly, Gandhi's campaign forced Britain to hand over some power to Indians. Britain also agreed to meet other demands of the Congress party.

The Future of India In 1939, a new world war exploded. Britain outraged Indian leaders by postponing independence and bringing Indians into the war without consulting them. Angry nationalists launched a campaign of noncooperation and were jailed. Millions of Indians, however, did help Britain during World War II.

When the war ended in 1945, India's independence could no longer be delayed. As it neared, Muslim fears of the Hindu majority increased. Conflict between Hindus and Muslims would trouble the new nation in the years to come.

ANALYZE INFORMATION How did the Salt March force Britain to respond to Indian demands?

ASSESSMENT

1. **Identify Cause and Effect** What impact did the Amritsar massacre have on the Indian independence movement?
2. **Draw Conclusions** Why was Gandhi able to unite Indians and shift political thought when earlier attempts had not succeeded?
3. **Identify Cause and Effect** How did Gandhi and the National Congress party work for independence in India?
4. **Analyze Information** What were Gandhi's key ideas? How did Gandhi implement these ideas in his fight against political oppression?
5. **Infer** How might fighting discrimination in South Africa have influenced Gandhi when he returned to India?

Primary Sources

Hind Swaraj: Mohandas Gandhi

Introduction

Mohandas Gandhi led a successful, peaceful revolution in India against British rule. In the following excerpt from his book *Hind Swaraj (Indian Home Rule),* Gandhi explains the ideas behind his nonviolent method of passive resistance in the form of an imaginary conversation between an editor and a reader. *Hind Swaraj* was first published in 1909 in South Africa, but was banned in India.

Both Gandhi and Martin Luther King, Jr. were influenced by Henry Thoreau's ideas on civil disobedience. In the second primary source, King, who was influenced by Gandhi's stance on passive resistance, refers to Thoreau in his book *The Autobiography of Martin Luther King, Jr.*

>> Mohandas Gandhi

Primary Source

Editor: Passive [accepting or allowing] resistance is a method of securing rights by personal suffering; it is the reverse of resistance by arms. When I refuse to do a thing that is repugnant [offensive] to my conscience, I use soul-force. For instance, the government of the day has passed a law which is applicable to me. I do not like it. If by using violence, I force the government to repeal the law, I am employing what may be termed body-force. If I do not obey the law, and accept the penalty for its breach [act of breaking a law], I use soul-force. It involves sacrifice of self.

COMPARE AND CONTRAST How are "soul-force" and "body-force" related?

Everybody admits that sacrifice of self is infinitely superior to sacrifice of others. Moreover, if this kind of force is used in a cause that is unjust, only the person using it suffers. He does not make others suffer for his mistakes. Men have before now done many things which were subsequently found to have been wrong. No man can claim that he is absolutely in the right, or that a particular thing is wrong, because he thinks so, but it is wrong for him so long as that is his deliberate judgment. It is therefore meet [proper] that he should not do that which he knows to be wrong, and suffer the consequence whatever it may be. This is the key to the use of soul-force.

DISTINGUISH AMONG FACT, OPINION, AND REASONED JUDGMENT Why does Gandhi say that right and wrong are judgments, not facts?

Reader: You would then disregard laws—this is rank [complete and utter] disloyalty. We have always been considered a law-abiding nation. You seem to be going even beyond the extremists. They say that we must obey the laws that have been passed, but that, if the laws be bad, we must drive out the lawgivers even by force.

Editor: Whether I go beyond them or whether I do not is a matter of no consequence to either of us. We simply want to find out what is right, and to act accordingly. The real meaning of the statement that we are a law-abiding nation is that we are passive resisters. When we do not like certain laws, we do not break the heads of law-givers, but we suffer and do not submit to the laws.

IDENTIFY CENTRAL IDEAS According to Gandhi, why is it acceptable to disregard laws?

Primary Source

In King's discussion of civil disobedience he says, "an individual who breaks a law that conscience tells him is unjust, and who willingly accepts the penalty of imprisonment in order to arouse the conscience of the community over its injustice, is in reality expressing the highest respect for law."

Similarly, King says, "In no sense do I advocate evading or defying the law, as would the rabid segregationist. That would lead to anarchy. One who breaks an unjust law must do so openly, lovingly, and with a willingness to accept the penalty."

During my student days I read Henry David Thoreau's essay *On Civil Disobedience* for the first time. Here, in this courageous New Englander's refusal to pay his taxes and his choice of jail rather than support a war that would spread slavery's territory into Mexico, I made my first contact with the theory of nonviolent resistance. Fascinated by the idea of refusing to cooperate with an evil system, I was so deeply moved that I reread the work several times. I became convinced that noncooperation with evil is as much a moral obligation as is cooperation with good. No other person has been more eloquent and passionate in getting this idea across than Henry David Thoreau. As a result of his writings and personal witness, we are the heirs of a legacy of creative protest. The teachings of Thoreau came alive in our civil rights movement; indeed, they are more alive than ever before. Whether expressed in a sit-in at lunch counters, a freedom ride into Mississippi, a peaceful protest in Albany, Georgia, a bus boycott in Montgomery, Alabama, these are outgrowths of Thoreau's insistence that evil must be resisted and that no moral man can patiently adjust to injustice.

DRAW CONCLUSIONS What does King mean when he says "we are the heirs of a legacy of creative protest"?

ASSESSMENT

1. **Draw Inferences** Why does Gandhi advocate suffering and self-sacrifice?
2. **Analyze Style and Rhetoric** Why do you think Gandhi chooses to structure his book as a conversation between an editor and a reader? How does this help him to get his point across?
3. **Draw Conclusions** Gandhi helped bring about Indian independence from British rule. Why do you think his approach was effective in enacting social and political change?
4. **Explain** How did King and Gandhi unite their roles as religious leaders with their roles as social activists?

6.4 A new Chinese republic took shape after the fall of the Qing dynasty in 1911. Nationalists like Sun Yixian set the goal of "catching up and surpassing the powers, east and west." But that goal would remain a distant dream as China suffered the turmoil of civil war and foreign invasion.

>> Mao was introduced to communist ideas while he was working at Peking University as a librarian's assistant. He later became the leader of the Chinese Communist Party.

Bounce to Activate Flipped Video

New Forces in China and Japan

>> **Objectives**

Explain the key challenges faced by the Chinese republic in the early 1900s.

Analyze the struggle between nationalists and Communists in China.

Summarize the effects of liberal changes in Japan in the 1920s.

Describe the rise of extreme nationalism and militarism in Japan.

Describe the impact of the Japanese invasion of China.

>> **Key Terms**

Twenty-One Demands
May Fourth Movement
vanguard
Guomindang
Jiang Jieshi
Mao Zedong
Long March
ultranationalist
Manchuria
Hirohito

Trouble in the Chinese Republic

Struggles for Power Sun Yixian, the "father of modern China," hoped to rebuild China on the Three Principles of the People—nationalism, democracy, and economic security for everyone. But he made little progress. One problem, he noted, was that the Chinese people felt more loyalty to families and clans than to the nation.

> Therefore, even though we have four hundred million people gathered together in one China, in reality they are just a heap of loose sand. Today we are the poorest and weakest nation in the world and occupy the lowest position in international affairs. Other men are the carving knife and serving dish, we are the fish and the meat.
>
> —Sun Yixian

In 1912, Sun Yixian stepped down as president in favor of Yuan Shikai (yoo AHN shih KY), a powerful general. Sun hoped that Yuan would create a strong central government. Instead, the ambitious general tried to set up a new dynasty. The military, however, did not support Yuan, and opposition divided the nation. When Yuan died in 1916, China plunged into still greater disorder.

In the provinces, local warlords seized power. As rival armies battled for control, the economy collapsed and millions of peasants suffered terrible hardships. Famine and attacks by bandits added to their misery.

Foreign Imperialism During this period of upheaval, foreign powers increased their influence over Chinese affairs. They dominated Chinese port cities and extended their influence inland. During World War I, Japanese officials presented Yuan Shikai with the **Twenty-One Demands,** a list of demands that sought to make China a Japanese protectorate.

With China too weak to resist, Yuan gave in to some of the demands. Then, at the Paris Peace Conference in 1919, the Allies gave Japan control over some former German possessions in China. That news infuriated Chinese Nationalists.

>> Jiang Jieshi led the Guomindang after Sun's death in 1925. He headed the Guomindang government in China from 1928 to 1949.

The May Fourth Movement Seeks Reform In response, student protests erupted in Beijing on May 4, 1919, and later spread to cities across China. "China's territory may be conquered," they declared, "but it cannot be given away!" The students organized boycotts of Japanese goods and businesses.

The protests set off a cultural and intellectual ferment known as the **May Fourth Movement.** Western-educated leaders blamed the imperialists' success on China's own weakness. As in Meiji Japan, Chinese reformers wanted to learn from the West and use that knowledge to end foreign domination. Most reformers rejected Confucian traditions in favor of Western science and ideas such as democracy and nationalism.

Women played a key role in the May Fourth Movement. They campaigned to end traditional practices, such as footbinding and the seclusion of women within the home. Their work helped open doors for women in education and the economy.

Chinese Communism Is Born Some Chinese turned to the revolutionary ideas of Marx and Lenin. The Russian Revolution seemed to offer a model of how a strong, well-organized party could transform a nation.

The Soviet Union trained Chinese students and military officers to become the **vanguard,** or elite leaders, of a communist revolution. By the 1920s, a small group of Chinese Communists had formed their own political party.

IDENTIFY CAUSE AND EFFECT How did warlord uprisings and foreign imperialism lead to the May Fourth movement?

Nationalists and Communists

In 1921, Sun Yixian and his **Guomindang** (gwoh meen DAWNG) or Nationalist party, established a government in south China. Sun planned to raise an army to defeat the warlords and unite China. When Western democracies refused to help, Sun accepted aid from the Soviet Union and joined forces with the small group of Chinese Communists to defeat the warlords. However, he still believed that China's future should be based on his Three Principles of the People.

The Nationalists and Jiang Jieshi After Sun's death in 1925, an energetic young army officer, **Jiang Jieshi** (jahng jeh shur), took over the Guomindang. Jiang Jieshi was determined to

Civil War in China, 1927–1936

>> **Analyze Maps** The Guomindang and the Communists waged a long and bitter war for control of China. What natural features made the Long March difficult?

Bounce to Activate Chart

smash the power of the warlords and reunite China, but he had little interest in either democracy or communism.

In 1926, Jiang Jieshi began the Northern Expedition in order to crush or win over local warlords as he advanced on Beijing. In mid-campaign, Jiang turned on his sometime ally the Chinese Communists, who he saw as a threat to his power. The Communists were winning converts among the small working class in cities like Shanghai.

Early in 1927, on orders from Jiang, Guomindang troops slaughtered Communist Party members and the workers who supported them. In Shanghai and elsewhere, thousands of people were killed. This massacre marked the beginning of a bitter civil war between the Communists and the Guomindang that lasted for 22 years.

Communism and Mao Zedong Among the Communists who escaped Jiang's attack was a young revolutionary of peasant origins, **Mao Zedong** (mow dzuh doong). Unlike earlier Chinese Communists, Mao believed that the Communists should seek support not among the small urban working class but among the large peasant masses.

Although the Communists were pursued at every turn by Guomindang forces, Mao was optimistic about eventual success. In southeastern China, Mao and the Communists redistributed land to peasants and offered them schooling and health care.

The Long March Jiang Jieshi, however, was determined to destroy the "Red bandits," as he called the Communists. He led the Guomindang in a series of "extermination campaigns" against them. Mao and about 100,000 of his followers fled the Guomindang in an epic retreat known as the **Long March.** From 1934 to 1935, they trekked more than 6,000 miles, facing daily attacks as they crossed rugged mountains and raging rivers. Mao's forces used guerrilla, or irregular hit-and-run, tactics to fight back. Only about 20,000 of the marchers survived the ordeal.

During the march, the Communists enforced strict discipline. Soldiers were told to treat peasants politely, pay for goods they wanted, and avoid damaging crops. Such behavior made Mao's forces welcome among peasants, many of whom had suffered greatly at the hands of the Guomindang.

For decades, the Long March stood as a symbol of communist heroism and inspired new recruits to follow Mao. At the end of the Long March, the Communists set up a new base in a remote region of northern China. There, Mao rebuilt his forces and plotted new strategies for fighting the Guomindang.

IDENTIFY SUPPORTING DETAILS How did the communists manage to survive Jiang's "extermination campaigns"?

China Faces Japanese Imperialism

While Jiang was pursuing the Communists across China, the country faced another danger. In 1931, Japan invaded Manchuria in northeastern China, adding it to the growing Japanese empire. As Japanese aggression increased, some of Jiang's generals pushed him to form a united front with the Communists against Japan.

In 1937, the Japanese struck again, starting what became the Second Sino-Japanese War. Airplanes bombed Chinese cities, and Japanese troops overran eastern China, including Beijing and Guangzhou. Jiang Jieshi and his government retreated to the interior and set up a new capital at Chongqing (chawng CHING).

After a lengthy siege, Japanese troops marched into the city of Nanjing (nahn jing) on December 13. Nanjing was an important cultural center and had been the Guomindang capital before Chongqing.

>> During the Russo-Japanese War in 1904–1905, Japan used Korea as a base for its military operations against Russia. Japanese leaders later annexed Korea.

After the city's surrender, the Japanese killed hundreds of thousands of soldiers and civilians and brutalized still more. The cruelty and destruction became known as the "Rape of Nanjing."

The invasion suspended China's civil war as the Guomindang and Communists formed a temporary, uneasy alliance. Jiang's army battled Japanese troops, while Communists engaged in guerrilla attacks against the invaders. The Soviet Union sent advisors and equipment to help. Great Britain, France, and the United States gave economic aid.

EXPLAIN Why did the Japanese invasion help unify the Chinese temporarily?

Conflicting Forces in Japan

The Japanese invasions of China were part of a rising tide of Japanese imperialism. Like China, Japan sought to become a major world power, equal to Western nations. However, Japan lacked the resources needed to fuel its industrial achievements. The small nation looked to the West as an example, attempting to conquer lands to form a huge empire. As you will see, the invasion of China takes on new meaning when viewed from the Japanese perspective.

Unlike China in the 1920s, which was shaken by conflict and economic turmoil, Japan was a powerful, united country with a growing industrial economy. Beneath the surface, however, conflicts brewed that would undermine its moves toward democratic reforms.

Expansion and Economic Growth During World War I, the Japanese economy enjoyed remarkable growth. Its exports to Allied nations soared. Heavy industrial production grew, making Japan a true industrial power. At the same time, it sought to win international recognition as equal to the Western powers.

While Western powers battled in Europe, Japan expanded its influence throughout East Asia. Japan had already annexed Korea as a colony in 1910. During the war, Japan also sought further rights in China with the Twenty-One Demands. After the war, Japan was given some former German possessions in East Asia, including the Shandong province in China.

Liberal Reforms of the 1920s During the 1920s, Japan moved toward more widespread democracy.

Political parties grew stronger. Elected members of the Diet—the Japanese parliament—exercised their power. In 1925, all adult men, regardless of class, won the right to vote. Western ideas about women's rights brought some changes.

Overall, however, the status of Japanese women remained below that of men. They would not win suffrage until 1945.

Despite greater democracy, powerful business leaders, called the zaibatsu (zy baht soo), strongly influenced the government through donations to political parties. They pushed for policies that favored international trade and their own interests.

Japan's aggressive expansion threatened its economic relationship with the Western powers. To improve relations, moderate Japanese politicians decided to slow down foreign expansion. In 1922, Japan signed an agreement with the United States, Britain, Italy, and France to limit the size of its navy. It also agreed to leave Shandong. The government reduced military spending.

>> Members of the Japanese Woman Suffrage League approach the government with 20,000 signed petitions demanding the right to vote.

Lurking Problems Behind its seeming well-being, Japan faced some grave problems. The economy grew more slowly in the 1920s than at any time since the country had modernized. Rural peasants did not share in the nation's prosperity. In the cities, factory workers earning low wages were attracted to the ideas of Marx and Lenin.

In the cities, members of the younger generation were also in revolt against tradition. They adopted Western fads and fashions. Also, they rejected family authority for the Western ideal of individual freedom, shocking their elders.

During the 1920s, tensions between the government and the military simmered not far below the surface. Conservatives, especially military officers, blasted government corruption, including payoffs by powerful zaibatsu. They also condemned Western influences for undermining basic Japanese values of obedience and respect for authority.

A devastating earthquake, one of the most destructive quakes in history, struck the Tokyo area in 1923. The earthquake and the widespread fires it caused resulted in the deaths of over 100,000 people and damaged more than 650,000 buildings. Almost half of surviving workers lost their jobs because so many businesses were destroyed. With help from the government, the Tokyo area gradually recovered—just as Japan faced a worldwide economic crisis.

>> In 1923, Tokyo suffered from one of the most destructive earthquakes in history, the Great Kanto Earthquake. The quake caused fires and tidal waves and killed more than 100,000 people.

SUMMARIZE How did democratic participation in Japan both grow in the 1920s? How was it limited?

The Ultranationalist Reaction

In 1929, the Great Depression rippled across the Pacific, striking Japan with devastating force. Trade suffered as foreign buyers could no longer afford to purchase Japanese silks and other exports. Unemployment in the cities soared, while rural peasants were only a mouthful from starvation.

Increasing Unrest Economic disaster fed the discontent of the leading military officials and extreme nationalists, or **ultranationalists.** They condemned politicians for agreeing to Western demands to stop overseas expansion. Western industrial powers, they pointed out, had long ago grabbed huge empires. By comparison, Japan's empire was tiny.

Japanese nationalists were further outraged by racial policies in the United States, Canada, and Australia that shut out Japanese immigrants. The Japanese took great pride in their industrial achievements. They bitterly resented being treated as second-class citizens in other parts of the world.

As the economic crisis worsened, nationalists demanded renewed expansion. An empire in Asia, they argued, would provide much-needed raw materials as well as an outlet for Japan's rapidly growing population. They set their sights on the northern Chinese province of **Manchuria.** This region was rich in natural resources, and Japanese businesses had already invested heavily there.

The Manchurian Incident In 1931, a group of Japanese army officers provoked an incident that provided an excuse to seize Manchuria. They set explosives and blew up tracks on a Japanese-owned railroad line. Then they claimed that the Chinese had committed the act. Claiming self-defense, the army attacked Chinese forces.

Without consulting their own government, the Japanese military forces conquered all of Manchuria and set up a puppet state there that they called Manzhouguo (man choo KWOO). They brought in Puyi, the last Chinese emperor, to head the puppet state.

Politicians in Tokyo objected to the army's highhanded actions, but public opinion sided with the military. When the League of Nations condemned Japanese aggression against China, Japan simply withdrew from the League. The League's member states failed to take military action against Japanese aggression. Japan also nullified its naval disarmament agreements with the Western powers.

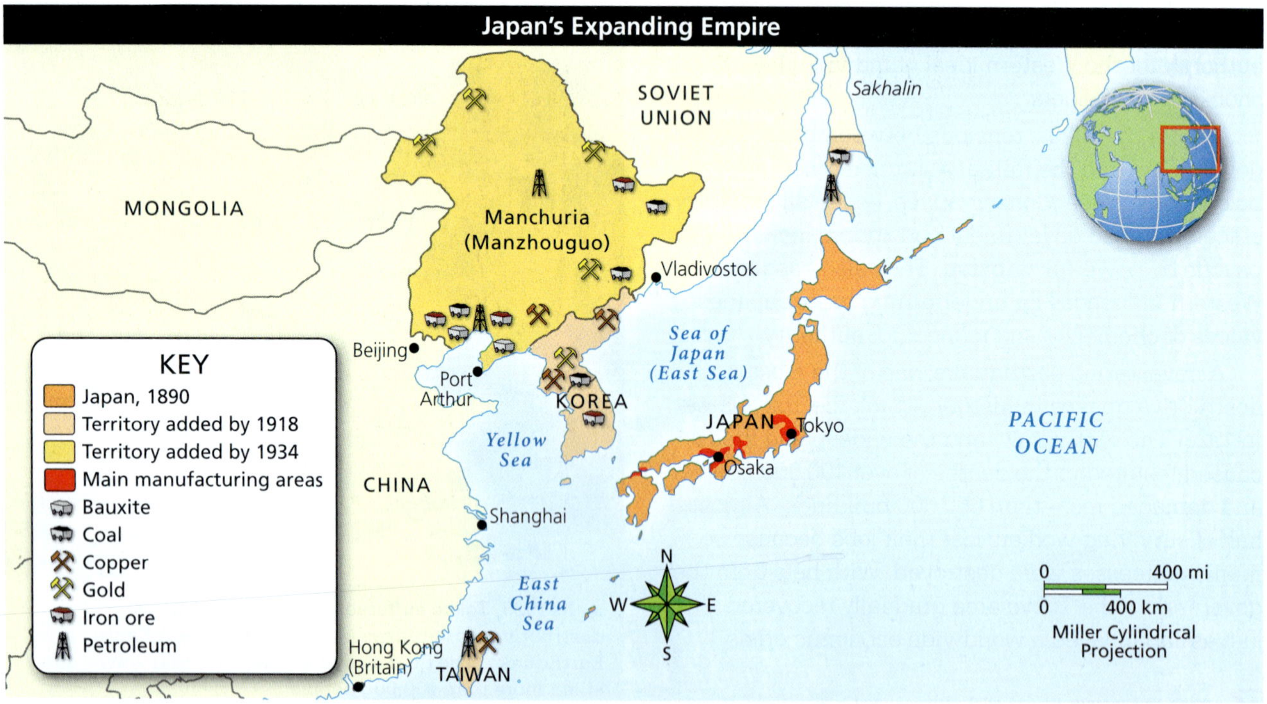

>> **Analyze Maps** Japan expanded its territory in Asia between 1918 and 1934. From the conquered lands, the Japanese acquired natural resources to fuel industry. Where were Japan's main manufacturing areas located?

IDENTIFY CAUSE AND EFFECT How did the Great Depression lead to calls for renewed expansion?

Militarists Gain Power

In the early 1930s, ultranationalists were winning support from the people for renewing foreign conquests and taking a tough stand against the Western powers. Members of extreme nationalist societies assassinated a number of politicians and business leaders who opposed expansion. Military leaders plotted to overthrow the government and, in 1936, briefly occupied the center of Tokyo.

Revival of Traditional Values Civilian government survived, but by 1937, the unrest forced the government to accept military domination. To please the ultranationalists, the government cracked down on socialists and suppressed most democratic freedoms. It revived ancient warrior values and built a cult around Emperor **Hirohito,** who had ascended to the throne in 1926. According to Japanese tradition, the emperor was descended from the sun goddess and was himself a living god.

In theory, Hirohito was the nation's supreme authority. In practice, however, he merely approved the policies that his ministries formulated. To spread its nationalist message, the government used schools to teach students absolute obedience to the emperor and service to the state.

Expansion into China Japan took advantage of China's civil war to increase its influence there. By 1937, as you have read, its armies had invaded the Chinese mainland and overran eastern China.

Japan expected to complete its conquest of China within a few years. But in 1939, while the two nations were locked in deadly combat, World War II broke out in Europe. That conflict swiftly spread to Asia, where France and Britain had large empires.

In 1936, Japan had allied with two aggressive European powers, Germany and Italy. These three powers signed the Tripartite Pact in September 1940, cementing the alliance known as the Axis Powers. That alliance, combined with renewed Japanese conquests, would turn World War II into a brutal, wide-ranging conflict waged not only across the continent of Europe but across Asia and the islands of the Pacific as well.

>> Japanese soldiers occupied Beijing in 1937. Japan took control of large parts of China during the Second Sino-Japanese War, from 1937 to 1945.

Bounce to Activate Gallery

IDENTIFY CAUSE AND EFFECT How did Japanese militarists rise to power in the 1930s?

ASSESSMENT

1. **Summarize** What political and economic changes occurred in Japan during the 1920s?
2. **Identify Cause and Effect** Why did the new republic of China fall into chaos after 1912?
3. **Integrate Information** Why did the Communists and the Guomindang cooperate during the Northern Expedition in 1926? How did the expedition affect their long-term relationship?
4. **Infer** Judging from the example of Japan, why might a nation turn to military leaders and extreme nationalists during a crisis? Cite details from the text.
5. **Identify Central Ideas** How did the Japanese invasion affect the civil war in China?

>> Duke Ellington was a composer, pianist, and bandleader. He referred to his music as "American Music" rather than "jazz." His career spanned the 1920s to the 1970s.

6.5 The catastrophe of World War I shattered the sense of optimism that had grown in the West since the Enlightenment. Despair gripped survivors on both sides as they added up the staggering costs of the war. Europeans mourned a generation of young men who had been lost on the battlefields.

Bounce to Activate Flipped Video

The West After World War I

>> Objectives

Analyze how Western society and culture changed after World War I.

Identify the contributions of modern scientists such as Marie Curie and Albert Einstein.

Summarize the domestic and foreign policy issues that the Western democracies faced after World War I.

Describe how the global depression began and spread.

Explain the responses of Britain, France, and the United States to the Great Depression.

>> Key Terms

flapper
Miriam Ferguson
Prohibition
Marie Curie
Albert Einstein
psychoanalysis
Harlem Renaissance
abstract art
dada
surrealism
Maginot Line
Kellogg-Briand Pact
disarmament
general strike
overproduction
finance
Federal Reserve
Great Depression
Franklin D. Roosevelt
New Deal

Social Change After World War I

Many people talked about a "return to normalcy," to life as it had been before 1914. But rebellious young people rejected the moral values and rules of the Victorian Age and chased after excitement. Gertrude Stein, an American writer living in Paris, called them the "lost generation." Others saw them as immoral pleasure-seekers.

The Roaring Twenties During the 1920s, new technologies helped create a mass culture shared by millions in the world's developed countries. Affordable cars, improved telephones, and new forms of media such as motion pictures and radio brought people around the world closer together than ever before.

In the 1920s, many radios tuned into the new sounds of jazz. In fact, the decade in the West is often called the Jazz Age. African American musicians combined Western harmonies with African rhythms to create jazz. Jazz musicians, like trumpeter Louis Armstrong and pianist Duke Ellington, took simple melodies and improvised endless subtle variations in rhythm and beat.

Throughout the 1920s, the popularity of jazz moved from the United States to Europe. Europeans embraced American popular culture, with its greater freedom and willingness to experiment. The nightclub and jazz were symbols of that freedom. Jazz came to embody the universal themes of creativity and self-expression.

Much of today's popular music has been influenced by jazz. It has transcended the "Roaring Twenties" American culture to become an international musical language.

After the war, rebellious young people, disillusioned by the war, rejected the moral values and rules of the Victorian Age and chased after excitement. During the Jazz Age, this rebellion was exemplified by a new type of liberated young woman called the **flapper.** The first flappers were American, but their European sisters soon adopted the fashion. Flappers rejected old ways in favor of new, exciting freedoms.

> The Flapper awoke from her lethargy (tiredness) ... bobbed her hair, put on her choicest pair of earrings and a great deal of audacity (boldness) and rouge and went into battle. She flirted because it was fun to flirt and ... refused to be bored chiefly because she wasn't boring ... Mothers disapproved of their sons taking the Flapper to dances, to teas, to swim, and most of all to heart.
>
> —Zelda Fitzgerald, flapper and wife of author F. Scott Fitzgerald

Women's Progress Flappers were highly visible, but they were a small minority. Most women saw mixed progress in the postwar period. During the war, women had held a wide range of jobs. Although most women left those jobs when the war ended, their war work helped them win the vote in many Western countries, such as Britain, Germany, the Netherlands, and the United States. A few women were elected to public office, such as Texas governor **Miriam Ferguson** or Lady Nancy Astor, the first woman to serve in the British Parliament.

By the 1920s, labor-saving devices had become common in middle class homes. Washing machines, vacuum cleaners, and canned foods lightened the burden of household chores. Some women then sought work outside the home or did volunteer work to help the less fortunate.

In the new atmosphere of emancipation, women sought higher education and pursued careers in many areas—from sports to the arts. Women golfers, tennis players, swimmers, and pilots set new records.

Women worked as newspaper reporters, published bestselling novels, and won recognition as artists. Most professions, though, were still dominated by men. Women doing the same work as men earned much less.

Diverse Reactions to the Jazz Age Not everyone approved of the freewheeling lifestyle of the Jazz Age. In 1920, the Eighteenth Amendment to the Constitution of the United States ushered in **Prohibition,** which banned the manufacture and sale of alcoholic beverages. Temperance reformers had long sought the amendment to stop alcohol abuse. It was later repealed in part because it had spurred the growth of organized crime, which supplied illegal alcohol to speakeasies, or illegal bars.

In the United States in the early 1900s, a Christian fundamentalist movement swept rural areas. Fundamentalists support traditional Christian beliefs. Popular fundamentalist preachers traveled around the country holding inspirational revival meetings. Some used the new technology of radio to spread their message.

SOLVE PROBLEMS What problem was Prohibition intended to solve? How well did it succeed?

>> Amelia Earhart was an American aviation pioneer and author. She was the first woman to fly solo across the Atlantic Ocean. She was also an avid supporter of women's rights.

Scientific Discoveries

Even before World War I, new ideas and scientific discoveries were challenging long-held ideas about the nature of the world and even of people. Like the war, science helped feed a sense of uncertainty that flowed through Western culture.

Curie Experiments with Radioactivity The ancient Greeks were the first to propose that all matter is composed of tiny, indivisible atoms. Over the centuries, most scientists came to accept this idea. But discoveries made in the early 1900s showed that the atom was more complex than anyone suspected.

The Polish-born French scientist **Marie Curie** and others experimented with an atomic process called radioactivity. They found that the atoms of certain elements, such as radium and uranium, spontaneously release charged particles. As scientists studied radioactivity further, they discovered that it can change atoms of one element into atoms of another. Such findings proved that atoms are not solid and indivisible.

>> Albert Einstein received the 1921 Nobel Prize in Physics and is well known for his mass-energy formula. Einstein fled Germany and became an American citizen in 1940.

Einstein Proposes the Theory of Relativity In 1905 and 1916, the German-born physicist **Albert Einstein** introduced his theories of relativity. Einstein argued that measurements of space and time are not absolute but are determined by many factors, including the relative position of the observer. Einstein's ideas raised questions about Newtonian science, which compared the universe to a machine operating according to absolute laws.

In the postwar years, many scientists came to accept the theories of relativity. To the general public, however, Einstein's ideas were difficult to understand. They seemed to further reinforce the unsettling sense of a universe whirling beyond the understanding of human reason.

In 1934, building on Curie's and Einstein's theories, Italian physicist Enrico Fermi and other scientists around the world discovered atomic fission, or the splitting of the nuclei of atoms in two. This splitting produces a huge burst of energy. In the 1940s, Fermi (now an American), along with fellow American physicists J. Robert Oppenheimer and Edward Teller, would use this discovery to create the devastating atomic bomb.

Fleming Discovers Penicillin In 1928, the Scottish scientist Alexander Fleming made a different type of scientific discovery. One day, he picked up a discarded laboratory dish that he had used to grow bacteria. The dish had grown some mold, which had killed the bacteria. Fleming called this nontoxic mold "penicillin." Fleming's penicillin was the first antibiotic, or medicine used to kill micro-organisms such as bacteria. Later scientists developed a wide range of antibiotics.

Freud Analyzes the Mind The Austrian physician Sigmund Freud (froyd) also challenged faith in reason. He suggested that the subconscious mind drives much of human behavior. Freud said that learned social values such as morality and reason help people to repress, or check, powerful urges. But an individual feels constant tension between repressed drives and social training. This tension, argued Freud, may cause psychological or physical illness.

Freud pioneered **psychoanalysis,** a method of studying how the mind works and treating mental disorders. Although many of his theories have been discredited, Freud's ideas have had an extraordinary impact far beyond medicine. They strongly influenced the art and literature of the postwar West.

IDENTIFY PATTERNS How did scientific discoveries in the 1920s change people's views of the world?

Literature Reflects New Perspectives

In the 1920s, war novels, poetry, plays, and memoirs flowed off the presses. Novels such as *All Quiet on the Western Front* by German author Erich Remarque exposed the grim horrors faced by soldiers in World War I. Other writers heaped scorn on the leaders who took them into war. Their realistic works stripped away any romantic notions about the glories of warfare and reflected a powerful disgust with war that influenced an entire generation.

The Lost Generation To many postwar writers, the war symbolized the moral breakdown of Western civilization. In 1922, the English poet T. S. Eliot published *The Waste Land.* This long poem portrays the modern world as spiritually empty and barren.

In *The Sun Also Rises,* the American novelist Ernest Hemingway shows the rootless wanderings of young people who lack deep convictions. "I did not care what it was all about," says the narrator. "All I wanted to know was how to live in it." In *The Great Gatsby,* American novelist F. Scott Fitzgerald exposed the emptiness of the 1920s world of flappers and parties.

American poet Gertrude Stein considered herself, her writer friends, and young people part of a "lost generation." They had become adults during or right after World War I and were disillusioned by the upheaval of the war and its aftermath.

Literature Explores the Inner Mind As Freud's ideas became popular, many writers began to explore the inner workings of the mind. Some experimented with stream of consciousness. In this technique, a writer appears to present a character's random thoughts and feelings without imposing any logic or order. In the novel *Mrs. Dalloway,* British novelist Virginia Woolf used stream of consciousness to explore the thoughts of people going through the ordinary actions of their everyday lives. In *Finnegans Wake,* the Irish novelist James Joyce explored the inner mind of a hero who remains sound asleep throughout the novel.

>> Austrian neurologist Sigmund Freud founded the field of psychoanalysis. In his later years, Freud used psychoanalysis to interpret religion and culture.

>> F. Scott Fitzerald's 1925 novel *The Great Gatsby* is a portrait of the Jazz Age and Roaring Twenties. It emphasizes the glittering but empty life of parties and excess.

The Harlem Renaissance A more optimistic literary movement arose in the United States during the 1920s. The **Harlem Renaissance** was an African American cultural awakening. It began in Harlem, a neighborhood in New York City that was home to many African Americans. African American writers and artists expressed their pride in their unique culture.

Among its best known figures was the poet and playwright Langston Hughes. In his poem, "The Negro Speaks of Rivers," Hughes reflects on the rivers associated with the African and African-American experience from the Euphrates, Congo, and Nile to the Mississippi. Novelist and anthropologist Zora Neale Hurston studied African American folklore and traditions.

COMPARE POINTS OF VIEW How did postwar authors show disillusionment with prewar institutions?

Modern Art and Architecture

In the early 1900s, many Western artists rejected traditional styles. Instead of trying to reproduce the real world, they explored other dimensions of color, line, and shape. Painters like Henri Matisse (ma TEES) utilized bold, wild strokes of color and odd distortions to produce works of strong emotion. He and fellow artists outraged the public and were dubbed *fauves*(fohv), or wild beasts, by critics.

>> Pablo Picasso, one of the most important artists of the 20th century, co-developed the movement known as Cubism. He painted *Woman Sitting in an Armchair* in 1920.

Bounce to Activate Gallery

Painters Embrace Revolutionary Trends Before World War I, the Spanish artist Pablo Picasso and the French artist Georges Braque (brak) created a revolutionary new style called cubism. Cubists painted three-dimensional objects as complex patterns of angles and planes. By redefining objects into separate shapes, they offered a new view of reality.

Later, the Russian Vasily Kandinsky and the Swiss Paul Klee moved even further away from representing reality. They created a new style of **abstract art,** composed only of lines, colors, and shapes, sometimes with no recognizable subject matter at all.

During and after the war, the dada movement burst onto the Paris art world. **Dada** was a European art movement that rejected traditional artistic values by producing works that seemed like absurd nonsense. Dada was a revolt against civilization. Paintings and sculptures by Jean Arp and Max Ernst were intended to shock and disturb viewers. Some Dadaists created works made of objects they found abandoned or thrown away.

Cubism and dada both helped to inspire **surrealism,** a movement that attempted to portray the workings of the unconscious mind. Surrealism rejected rational thought, which had produced the horrors of World War I, in favor of irrational or unconscious ideas. The Spanish surrealist Salvador Dali used images of melting clocks and burning giraffes to suggest the chaotic dream state described by Freud.

Architecture Reflects a New World Architects, too, rejected classical traditions and developed new styles to match a new urban, industrialized world. The famous Bauhaus school in Germany influenced architecture by blending science and technology with design. Bauhaus buildings used glass, steel, and concrete but very little ornamentation.

The American architect Frank Lloyd Wright reflected the Bauhaus belief that the function of a building should determine its form. He used materials and forms that fit a building's environment. He believed that "a building should grace its environment rather than disgrace it." One of Wright's most famous designs is Fallingwater, a house in Pennsylvania built on a waterfall. The structure works in harmony with the surrounding environment, as Wright intended.

IDENTIFY CAUSE AND EFFECT What effect did World War I have on artistic movements in the 1920s?

Postwar Politics in the West

As nations recovered from the war, people began to feel hope rising out of their disillusionment. But soon, the "lost generation" would face a new crisis that would revive many old problems and spark new conflicts.

In 1919, the three Western democracies—Britain, France, and the United States—appeared powerful. They had ruled the Paris Peace Conference and boosted hopes for democracy among the new nations of Eastern Europe. Beneath the surface, however, postwar Europe faced grave problems. To make matters worse, many members of the younger generation who might have become the next great leaders had been killed in the war.

At first, the most pressing issues were finding jobs for returning veterans and rebuilding war-ravaged lands like France and Belgium. Economic problems fed social unrest and made radical ideas more popular. The Russian Revolution unleashed fears of the spread of communism. Some people saw socialism as the answer to economic hardships. Others embraced nationalist political movements.

Political Parties Clash in Britain In Britain during the 1920s, the Labour party surpassed the Liberal party in strength. The Labour party gained support among workers by promoting a gradual move toward socialism. The Liberal party passed some social legislation, but it traditionally represented middle-class business interests. As the Liberal party faltered, the middle class began to back the Conservative party, joining the upper class, professionals, and farmers. With this support, the Conservative party held power during much of 1920s. After a massive strike of over three million workers in 1926, Conservatives passed legislation limiting the power of workers to strike.

Irish Independence at Last Britain still faced the "Irish question." In 1914, Parliament passed a home-rule bill that was shelved when the war began. Militant Irish nationalists, however, were unwilling to wait any longer. On Easter 1916, a small group launched a revolt against British rule. Although the Easter Rising was quickly suppressed, it stirred wider support for the Irish cause.

>> Fallingwater, a Pennsylvania home designed by architect Frank Lloyd Wright, incorporates nature into its design. It appears to hover over a tranquil waterfall.

>> The major outcomes of the Paris Peace Conference were five peace treaties ending World War I, including the Treaty of Versailles with Germany, and the creation of the League of Nations.

When Parliament again failed to grant home rule in 1919, members of the Irish Republican Army (IRA) began a guerrilla war against British forces and their supporters. In 1922, moderates in Ireland and Britain reached an agreement. Most of Ireland became the independent Irish Free State. The largely Protestant northern counties remained under British rule. The settlement ended the worst violence, but the IRA and others never accepted the division of Ireland. In years to come, Catholics in the north faced discrimination, creating new tensions and conflict.

Peacetime Troubles in France Like Britain, France emerged from World War I both a victor and a loser. Fighting on the Western front had destroyed much of northern France. The French had suffered huge casualties. Survivors felt battered and insecure.

After the war, political divisions and financial scandals continued to plague the Third Republic. Several parties—from conservatives to communists—competed for power. During the postwar years, France was again ruled by a series of coalition governments that created temporary alliances among rival political parties.

Postwar Fears in the United States In contrast, the United States emerged from World War I in good shape. A late entrant into the war, it had suffered relatively few casualties and little loss of property. However, the United States did experience some domestic unrest. Fear of radicals and the Bolshevik Revolution in Russia set off a "Red Scare" in 1919 and 1920. Police rounded up suspected foreign-born radicals, and a number were expelled from the United States.

The "Red Scare" fed growing demands to limit immigration. Millions of immigrants from southern and eastern Europe had poured into the United States between 1890 and 1914. Some native-born Americans sought to exclude these newcomers, whose cultures differed from those of earlier settlers from northern Europe. In response, Congress passed laws limiting immigration from Europe. Earlier laws had already excluded or limited Chinese and Japanese immigration.

>> Analyze Political Cartoons This political cartoon's original caption was "Communism. A Destructive Worm." What message is the cartoonist conveying in this cartoon?

IDENTIFY CENTRAL ISSUES What political issues did France face after World War I?

International Relations

In addition to problems at home, the three democracies faced a difficult international situation. The peace settlements that ended World War I caused friction, especially in Germany and among some ethnic groups in Eastern Europe.

Allies Disagree Over Direction France's chief concern after the war was securing its borders against Germany. The French remembered the German invasions of 1870 and 1914. To prevent a third invasion, France built massive fortifications called the **Maginot Line**(ma zhee NOH) along its border with Germany. The Maginot Line offered a sense of security—a false one. The line would be of little use when Germany invaded again in 1940.

In its quest for security, France also strengthened its military and sought alliances with other countries, including the Soviet Union. It insisted on strict enforcement of the Versailles treaty and complete payment of reparations. France's goal was to keep the German economy weak.

Britain was more interested in protecting its overseas empire and rebuilding trade than in punishing Germany. British leaders strongly supported the limits on German naval power. Still, during the postwar period, many British leaders began to think that the Treaty of Versailles had been too harsh on Germany, and they called for easing its terms. They feared that if Germany became too weak, the Soviet Union and France would become too powerful.

Searching for Peace During the 1920s and 1930s, many people worked for peace. Hopes soared in 1925 when representatives from seven European nations signed a series of treaties at Locarno, Switzerland. These treaties settled Germany's disputed borders with France, Belgium, Czechoslovakia, and Poland.

The Locarno treaties became the symbol of a new era of peace. "France and Germany Ban War Forever," trumpeted a *New York Times* headline.

The hopeful "spirit of Locarno" was echoed in **Kellogg-Briand Pact,** signed in 1928. Almost every independent nation signed this agreement, promising to "renounce war as an instrument of national policy." Although the Kellogg-Briand Pact outlawed war, it provided no way of enforcing the ban.

In the same optimistic spirit, the great powers also pursued **disarmament,** the reduction of armed forces and weapons. The United States, Britain, France, Japan, and other nations signed treaties to reduce the size of their navies. However, they failed to agree on limiting the size of their armies.

>> Analyze Political Cartoons This political cartoon, called "The Doormat," makes a statement about the world's reaction to Japan's rising militarism. Who is the doormat in the cartoon, and why might this be the case?

Bounce to Activate Cartoon

The League of Nations Despite grumblings about the Versailles treaty, people around the world put their hope in the League of Nations. From its headquarters in Geneva, Switzerland, the League encouraged cooperation and tried to get members to make a commitment to stop aggression. At first, the League did have some successes. Although the United States never joined, the League grew in the 1920s. In 1926, after signing the Locarno agreements, Germany joined the League. Later, the Soviet Union was also admitted.

Despite its lofty aims, the League of Nations was powerless to stop aggression. In 1931, the League vigorously condemned Japan's invasion of Manchuria, but it had no military means to stop it. Ambitious dictators in Europe noted the League's weakness. They began to rearm and pursue aggressive foreign policies.

☑ **COMPARE POINTS OF VIEW** Why did Britain and France disagree over how to enforce the Treaty of Versailles?

Economics in the Postwar Era

The war affected economies all over the world, hurting some and helping others. Britain and France both owed huge war debts to the United States. Both relied on reparation payments from Germany to pay back their loans. Meanwhile, the crushing reparations and other conditions hurt Germany's economy.

Britain and France Recover Britain faced serious economic problems in the 1920s. It was deeply in debt, and its factories were out of date. Unemployment was severe. Wages remained low, leading to worker unrest and frequent strikes. In 1926, a **general strike,** or strike by workers in many different industries at the same time, lasted nine days and involved some three million workers.

In comparison, the French economy recovered fairly rapidly. Financial reparations and territories gained from Germany helped. Still, economic swings did occur, adding to an unstable political scene.

Despite these problems, Europe made a shaky recovery during the 1920s. Economies returned to peacetime manufacturing and trade. Veterans gradually found jobs, although unemployment never ceased to be a problem. Middle-class families enjoyed a rising standard of living.

The American Economy Booms In contrast, the United States emerged from the war as the world's leading economic power. In the affluent 1920s, middle-class Americans enjoyed the benefits of capitalism. American loans and investments backed the recovery in Europe. As long as the American economy prospered, the global economy remained stable.

IDENTIFY CAUSE AND EFFECT How did World War I and its peace treaties affect the international economy?

The Great Depression

During the 1920s, European nations made a shaky recovery from World War I, helped in part by American loans and investments. As long as the American economy was healthy, the global economy remained relatively prosperous. Then, at the end of the decade, an economic crisis began in the United States and spread to the rest of the world. This global economic slump, called the **Great Depression,** was the longest, most severe economic downturn to strike the industrialized Western world.

Overproduction and a Drop in Demand Both the American and the world economy had weak points. In the industrial world, a major problem was **overproduction,** meaning that factories and farms produced more goods than were being sold. In other words, supply outpaced demand.

By the 1920s, improved technology and farming methods had led to higher output. When demand for goods slowed, prices fell. Consumers benefited from the lower prices, but farmers, miners, and other suppliers of raw materials did not. Overproduction created a backlog of unsold goods, leading businesses to cut back on output and lay off workers. Unemployed workers had no money to spend on buying goods, which slowed demand further and brought more layoffs. This cycle then had a ripple effect throughout the economy.

Crash Leads to Collapse Meanwhile, a crisis in **finance**—the management of money matters, including the circulation of money, loans, investments, and banking—was brewing. Few saw the danger. Prices on the New York Stock Exchange were at an all-time high. Eager investors acquired stocks through risky methods. To slow the run on the stock market, the **Federal Reserve,** the central banking system of the United States, raised interest rates in 1928 and again in 1929.

In the autumn of 1929, jitters about the economy caused brokers to call in the loans made to investors. When investors were unable to repay, financial panic set in. Stock prices crashed in October, wiping out the fortunes of many investors. The stock market

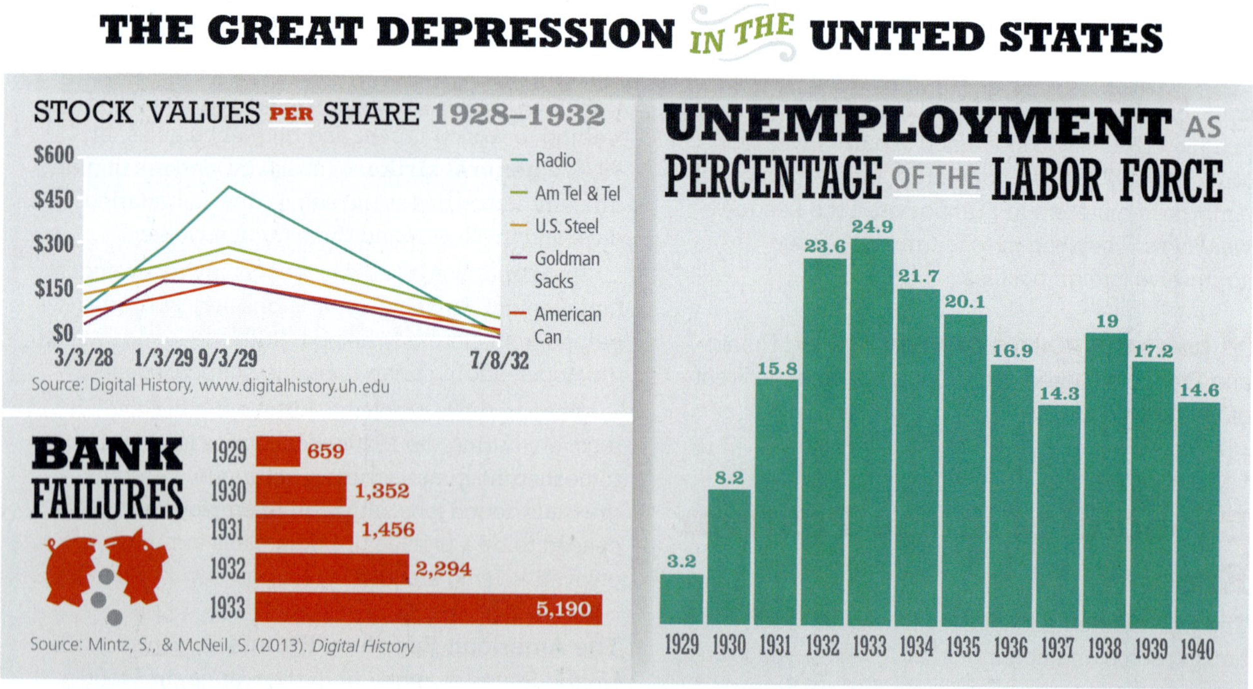

>> **Analyze Information** In what year did unemployment and bank failures peak in the United States?

crash worsened the economic decline. The Great Depression had begun.

Over the next few years, consumer spending and investment fell, causing still more businesses and factories to close. Millions of people lost their jobs. The cycle spiraled steadily downward. By 1933, between 13 to 15 million Americans were jobless and almost half the banks had closed. The jobless could not afford to buy goods, so more factories had to close, which in turn increased unemployment. People slept on park benches and lined up to eat in soup kitchens.

The Depression Spreads Around the World

The economic problems quickly spread around the world. American banks stopped investing or making loans abroad and demanded repayment of foreign loans. Without new investments, European prosperity slowed. Hardest hit were countries, like Britain and Germany, that owed the most to the United States.

In Germany, unemployment rose steeply, leaving one in four workers jobless. Britain was less badly hurt, but its industries and trade were depressed.

Desperate governments tried to protect their economies from foreign competition. The United States imposed the highest tariffs in its history. The policy backfired when other nations retaliated by raising their tariffs. In the end, all countries lost access to the global markets as world trade continued to shrink. The collapse of world trade spread the misery of the Great Depression beyond the industrial world to Latin America, Africa, and Asia.

GENERATE EXPLANATIONS What were three root causes of the Great Depression?

Western Democracies React to the Depression

The Great Depression led to changes in government economic policies. For more than a century, Western governments had backed laissez-faire capitalism, the policy that calls for little or no government interference in the economy. During the 1930s, governments in Britain, France, the United States, and elsewhere stepped in to ease the impact of the Great Depression. None of their methods provided a quick fix, but they did alleviate some of the suffering.

International Industrial Production, 1926–1938

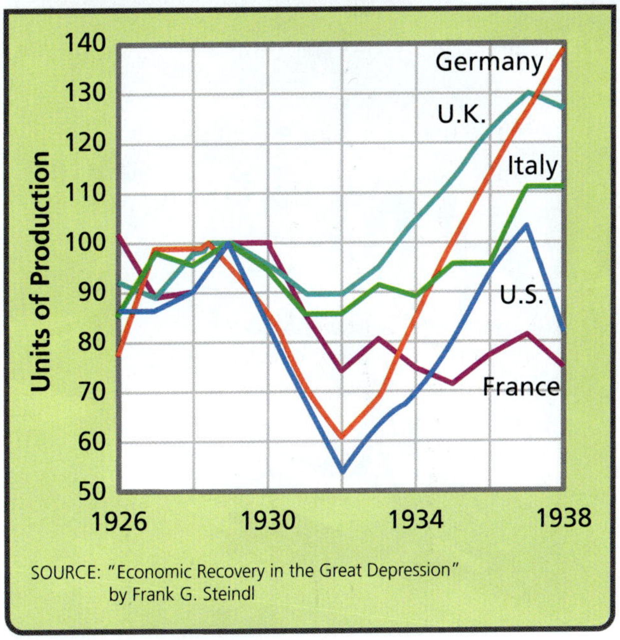

>> **Analyze Information** In which two countries did industrial production decline the most?

Britain and France Search for Solutions

In response to the Depression, Britain set up a coalition government made up of leaders from all three of its major political parties. The government provided some unemployment benefits. It kept tariffs low throughout the British Empire to boost trade but raised tariffs against the United States and other countries. By the mid-1930s, Britain was slowly recovering from the worst of the Great Depression. Still, unemployment remained high, and the recovery was uneven.

The Great Depression took longer to hurt France than some other countries. However, by the mid-1930s, France was feeling the pinch of decreased production and unemployment. In response, several leftist parties united behind the socialist leader Leon Blum. His Popular Front government tried to solve labor problems and passed some social legislation. But it could not satisfy more radical leftists. Strikes soon brought down Blum's government. Democracy survived, but the country lacked strong leadership able to respond to the clamor for change.

Roosevelt's New Deal

Meanwhile, in the United States, President Herbert Hoover firmly believed that the government should not intervene in private business matters. Even so, he did try a variety of limited measures to solve the crisis. Nothing worked.

>> Striking workers walk down a boulevard in Paris in June 1936.

In 1932, Americans elected a new President, **Franklin D. Roosevelt,** or FDR. Roosevelt argued that the government had to take an active role in combating the Great Depression. He introduced the **New Deal,** a massive package of economic and social programs.

Under the New Deal, the federal government took a more active role in managing the economy than ever before. New laws regulated the stock market and protected bank deposits. Government programs created jobs and gave aid to farmers. A new Social Security system provided pensions for the elderly and other benefits.

As the New Deal programs were being put into effect, a natural disaster in 1934 hit several central states. After years of drought and overfarming, huge winds blew across the plains. The winds picked up and carried away the topsoil exposed by erosion, creating the Dust Bowl. The storms destroyed crops, land, and equipment. Thousands of farmers lost their land. Many migrated to the cities of the West Coast in search of work and a new life.

The New Deal failed to end the Great Depression, although it did ease the suffering for many. Still, some critics fiercely condemned FDR's expansion of the role of government. The debate about the size and role of the U.S. federal government continues to this day.

Loss of Faith in Democracy As the Depression dragged on, many people lost faith in the ability of democratic governments to solve the problems of the modern world. Misery and hopelessness created fertile ground for extremists who promised radical solutions. Communists gloated over what they called the failure of capitalism. Right-wing extremists played on themes of intense nationalism, the failure of democracy, the virtues of authoritarian rule, and the need to rearm. By the late 1930s, aggressive rulers once again threatened the peace.

EXPLAIN How did the U.S. government react to the Great Depression?

ASSESSMENT

1. **Identify Central Ideas** What cultural changes did Western society experience after World War I?
2. **Make Generalizations** How did the ideas of Einstein and Curie contribute to a sense of uncertainty?
3. **Synthesize** How did Britain and France emerge from World War I as both victors and losers?
4. **Summarize** What were three causes of the Great Depression?
5. **Identify Cause and Effect** How did the Great Depression change government in the United States?

6.6 "I hated politics and politicians," said Italo Balbo. Like many Italian veterans of World War I, he had come home to a land of economic chaos and political corruption. Italy's constitutional government, he felt, "had betrayed the hopes of soldiers, reducing Italy to a shameful peace." Disgusted and angry, Balbo rallied behind a fiercely nationalist leader, Benito Mussolini. Mussolini's rise to power in the 1920s served as a model for ambitious strongmen elsewhere in Europe.

>> Mussolini and the National Fascist Party led the March on Rome in October 1922. Fewer than 30,000 men participated in the march, but the king feared a civil war and asked Mussolini to form a cabinet.

Bounce to Activate Flipped Video

Fascism Emerges in Italy

>> **Objectives**

Describe the rise of Mussolini.

Summarize Mussolini's policies as leader of Italy.

Identify the characteristics of totalitarianism and fascism.

>> **Key Terms**

Benito Mussolini
Black Shirt
March on Rome
totalitarian state
fascism

The Rise of Mussolini

Postwar Discontent When Italy agreed to join the Allies in 1915, France and Britain secretly promised to give Italy certain Austro-Hungarian territories that had large Italian populations. When the Allies won, Italy received some of the promised territories, but others became part of the new Yugoslavia. The broken promises outraged Italian nationalists.

In the postwar years, disorders within Italy multiplied. Inspired in part by the Russian Revolution, peasants seized land, and workers went on strike or seized factories. Their actions frightened landowners and industrialists who had traditionally held power.

Amid the chaos, returning veterans faced unemployment. Trade declined and taxes rose. The government, split into feuding factions, seemed powerless to end the crisis.

Mussolini and the Fascist Party Into this turmoil stepped Benito Mussolini. The son of a socialist blacksmith and a teacher, Mussolini had been a socialist in his youth. During the war, however, he rejected socialism for intense nationalism. In 1919, he organized veterans and other discontented Italians into the

Fascist party. They took the name from the Latin *fasces*, a bundle of sticks wrapped around an ax. In ancient Rome, the fasces symbolized unity and authority.

Mussolini was a fiery and charismatic speaker. He promised to end corruption and replace turmoil with order. He also spoke of reviving Roman greatness, pledging to turn the Mediterranean into a "Roman lake" once again. He held a great deal of power over crowds when he gave his rousing speeches.

> [Only joy at finding such a leader] can explain the enthusiasm [Mussolini] evoked at gathering after gathering, where his mere presence drew the people from all sides to greet him with frenzied acclamations. Even the men who first came out of mere curiosity and with indifference or even hostile feelings gradually felt themselves fired by his personal magnetic influence. . .
>
> —Margherita G. Sarfhatti, ***The Life of Benito Mussolini*** (tr. Frederic Whyte)

Control by Terror Mussolini organized his supporters into "combat squads." The squads wore black shirts to emulate an earlier nationalist revolt. These **Black Shirts,** or party militants, rejected the democratic process in favor of violent action. They broke up socialist rallies, smashed leftist presses, and attacked farmers' cooperatives. Fascist gangs used intimidation and terror to oust elected officials in northern Italy. Hundreds were killed as new gangs of Black Shirts sprang up all over Italy. Many Italians accepted these actions because they, too, had lost faith in constitutional government.

>> The fasces, a bundle of sticks wrapped around an ax, was an ancient Roman symbol of unity and authority. Fascists adopted the name and symbol for their party.

In 1922, the Fascists made a bid for power. At a rally in Naples, they announced their intention to go to Rome to demand that the government make changes. In the **March on Rome,** tens of thousands of Fascists swarmed toward the capital. Fearing civil war, King Victor Emmanuel III asked Mussolini to form a government as prime minister. Mussolini entered the city triumphantly on October 30, 1922. Without firing a shot, Mussolini thus obtained a legal appointment from the king to lead Italy.

DRAW CONCLUSIONS How did postwar disillusionment contribute to Mussolini's rise?

Mussolini's Totalitarian Rule

At first, Fascists held only a few cabinet posts in the new government. By 1925, though, Mussolini had assumed more power and taken the title Il Duce (eel DOO chay), "The Leader." He suppressed rival parties, muzzled the press, rigged elections, and replaced elected officials with Fascist supporters. In 1929, Mussolini received recognition from Pope Pius XI in return for recognizing Vatican City as an independent state, although the pope continued to disagree with some of Mussolini's goals.

In theory, Italy remained a parliamentary monarchy. In fact, it was a dictatorship upheld by terror. Critics were thrown into prison, forced into exile, or murdered. Secret police and propaganda bolstered the regime.

The State Controls the Economy To spur economic growth and end conflicts between owners and workers, Mussolini brought the economy under state control. However, he preserved capitalism.

Under Mussolini's corporate state, representatives of business, labor, government, and the Fascist party controlled industry, agriculture, and trade. This policy did help business, and production increased. This success came at the expense of workers. They were forbidden to strike, and their wages were kept low.

Loyalty to the State To the Fascists, the individual was unimportant except as a member of the state. Men, women, and children were bombarded with slogans glorifying the state and Mussolini. "Believe! Obey! Fight!" loudspeakers blared and posters proclaimed. Men were urged to be ruthless, selfless warriors fighting for the glory of Italy. Women were pushed out of paying jobs. Instead, Mussolini called on women to "win the battle of motherhood." Those who bore more than 14 children were given a medal by Il Duce himself.

Shaping the young was a major Fascist goal. Fascist youth groups toughened children and taught them to obey strict military discipline. Boys and girls learned about the glories of ancient Rome.

Young Fascists marched in torchlight parades, singing patriotic hymns and chanting, "Mussolini is always right." By the 1930s, a generation of young soldiers stood ready to back Il Duce's drive to expand Italian power.

Building a Totalitarian State Mussolini and the Fascist Party built the first modern **totalitarian state.** In this form of government, a one-party dictatorship regulates every aspect of the lives of its citizens. Fascist Italy served as a model for fascist rule in other European nations. Still, Fascist rule in Italy was never as absolute as those imposed by the communists in the Soviet Union or the Nazis in Germany.

Mussolini's rule was fascist in nature, as was Hitler's. However, totalitarian governments rise under other kinds of ideology as well, such as communism in Stalin's Soviet Union.

All of these totalitarian governments shared common features. They were single-party dictatorships in which the state controlled the economy. The party was led by a dictator, who used police spies and terrorism to control the people and demanded unquestioning obedience. The government controlled the media and enforced strict censorship. It used every means possible to indoctrinate, or mold, its citizens' ideas and thoughts.

IDENTIFY MAIN IDEAS How did the Fascist party transform Italy's government and economy?

Characteristics of Fascism

Historians still debate the real nature of Mussolini's fascist ideology. Mussolini coined the term, but fascists had no unifying theory as Marxists did.

>> Mussolini viewed children as the Fascists of the future and took great interest in education and the youth program. Boys were taught to be strong soldiers and girls were taught to be strong, nurturing mothers.

Bounce to Activate Gallery

Today, we generally use the term **fascism** to describe any centralized, authoritarian government that is not communist whose policies glorify the state over the individual and are destructive to basic human rights. In the 1920s and 1930s, though, fascism meant different things in different countries.

Features of Fascism All forms of fascism, however, shared some basic features. They were rooted in extreme nationalism. Fascists glorified action, violence, discipline, and, above all, blind loyalty to the state.

Fascists also pursued aggressive foreign expansion. Echoing the idea of "survival of the fittest," Fascist leaders glorified warfare as a noble struggle for survival. "War alone," declared Mussolini, "brings to its highest tension all human energy and puts the stamp of nobility upon peoples who have the courage to face it."

Fascists were also antidemocratic. They rejected the Enlightenment emphasis on reason and the concepts of equality and liberty. To them, democracy led to corruption and weakness. They claimed democracy put individual or class interests above national goals and destroyed feelings of community.

>> This poster depicts Mussolini working alongside Italian builders. Like much Fascist propaganda, it was designed to convey a sense of purpose and strength.

Bounce to Activate Chart

Instead, fascists emphasized emotion and the need for individuals to serve the state.

The Appeal of Fascism Given its restrictions on individual freedom, why did fascism appeal to many Italians? First, it promised a strong, stable government and an end to the political feuding that had paralyzed democracy in Italy. Mussolini projected a sense of power and confidence at a time of disorder and despair. His intense nationalism also revived national pride, which helped further the shift of political thought throughout Italy.

At first, Il Duce received good press outside Italy. Newspapers in Britain, France, and North America applauded the discipline and order of Mussolini's government. "He got the trains running on time," admirers said. Only later, when Mussolini embarked on a course of foreign conquest, did Western democracies protest.

Fascism and Communism Compared Three systems of government competed for influence in postwar Europe. Democracy endured in Britain and France but faced an uphill struggle in hard times. In Italy, fascism offered a different option. As the Great Depression spread, other nations—most notably Germany—looked to fascist leaders. Communism emerged in Russia and won support elsewhere.

Fascists were the sworn enemies of socialists and communists. While communists called for a worldwide revolution of the working class, fascists pursued nationalist goals. Fascists supported a society with defined classes. They found allies among business leaders, wealthy landowners, and the lower middle class. Communists touted a classless society. They won support among both urban and agricultural workers.

Despite basic differences, in practice these two ideologies had much in common. Both flourished during economic hard times by promoting extreme programs of social change. In both communist Russia and fascist Italy, dictators imposed totalitarian governments in order to bring about their revolutions. Both encouraged blind devotion to the state or a charismatic leader. Both used terror to guard their power. In both, a party elite claimed to rule in the name of the national interest.

COMPARE POINTS OF VIEW Describe the similarities between fascism and communism.

ASSESSMENT

1. **Identify Cause and Effect** What problems did Italy face after World War I, and how did these problems help Mussolini win power?
2. **Summarize** Describe one of Mussolini's economic or social goals, and explain the actions he took to achieve it.
3. **Compare and Contrast** List two similarities and two differences between fascism and communism.
4. **Explain** Why is control of the media important in a totalitarian state?
5. **Contrast** How did fascist values differ from democratic principles and goals?

6.7 By 1921, Lenin and the Communists had won the civil war that followed the Russian Revolution. They were then faced with the enormous task of rebuilding Russian society. Millions of Russians had died since the outbreak of World War I, from fighting and from famine, and Russia was in a state of chaos. Lenin's policy of "war communism" outraged the people and brought the Russian economy to the brink of collapse.

>> One million Russians attended Lenin's funeral march in Red Square. His death set off a power struggle within the Soviet Union.

Bounce to Activate Flipped Video

The Soviet Union Under Stalin

Stalin Builds a Command Economy

That year, Lenin introduced his New Economic Policy, which allowed limited capitalism. This brief compromise with capitalism helped the Soviet economy recover and ended the armed resistance to Lenin's government.

Stalin Takes Charge Lenin died in January 1924. Tens of thousands of people lined up in Moscow's historic Red Square to view his body. Lenin's widow, Nadezhda Krupskaya, had wanted to bury him simply next to his mother. But Joseph Stalin wanted to preserve Lenin's body and put it on permanent display. In the end, Lenin's body was displayed in Red Square for more than 65 years. By preserving Lenin's body, Stalin wanted to show that he would carry on the goals of the revolution.

In fact, Stalin moved the Soviet Union in directions Karl Marx had never foreseen. Marx had predicted that under communism the state would eventually wither away. Instead, Stalin turned the Soviet Union into a totalitarian state controlled by a powerful and complex bureaucracy. For almost 30 years, Stalin held more power than any other leader in history.

>> Objectives

Explain how Stalin built a command economy in the Soviet Union.

Describe how Stalin used terror to build a totalitarian state.

Analyze Stalin's use of propaganda to control thought and the arts.

Summarize the characteristics of Soviet society under Stalin.

Understand the goals of Soviet foreign policy.

>> Key Terms

command economy
collective
kulak
Gulag
socialist realism
Osip Mandelstam
Boris Pasternak
russification
atheism
Comintern

Stalin's Five-Year Plans Once in power, Stalin set out to make the Soviet Union a modern industrial power. In the past, said Stalin, Russia had suffered because of its economic backwardness. In 1928, he proposed the first of several "five-year plans" aimed at building heavy industry, improving transportation, and increasing farm output.

To achieve his goals, Stalin brought all economic activity under government control. The government owned all businesses and distributed all resources. The Soviet Union developed a **command economy,** in which government officials made all basic economic decisions. By contrast, in a capitalist system, the free market determines most economic decisions. Privately owned businesses compete to win the consumer's choice. This competition regulates the price and quality of goods.

Stalin's five-year plans set high production goals, especially for heavy industry and transportation. The government pushed workers and managers to meet these goals by giving bonuses to those who succeeded—and by punishing those who did not. Between 1928 and 1939, large factories, hydroelectric power stations, and huge industrial complexes rose across the Soviet Union. Oil, coal, and steel production grew. Mining expanded, and new railroads were built.

Industrial Policy Yields Mixed Results During this time, the West was in the grip of the Great Depression. The Soviet Union had little international trade, so it was insulated from many of the harshest effects of the global economic crisis. Some people in Europe and North American pointed to the industrial growth of the Soviet Union as proof that Stalin's economic policies were successful—ignoring the fact that this success came at a staggering human cost.

Despite impressive progress in some areas, Soviet workers had little to show for their efforts. Some former peasants did become skilled factory workers or managers. Overall, though, the standard of living remained low. Wages were low, workers were forbidden to strike, and consumer goods were scarce. Central planning was often inefficient, causing shortages of some goods and surpluses of others. Many managers, concerned only with meeting production quotas, turned out large quantities of low-quality goods.

During and after the Stalin era, the Soviet Union continued to produce well in heavy industry, such as the manufacture of farm machinery. But its planned economy failed to match the capitalist world in making consumer goods, such as clothing and cars.

Forced Collectivization in Agriculture Causes Misery Stalin also brought agriculture under government control, but at a horrendous cost. The

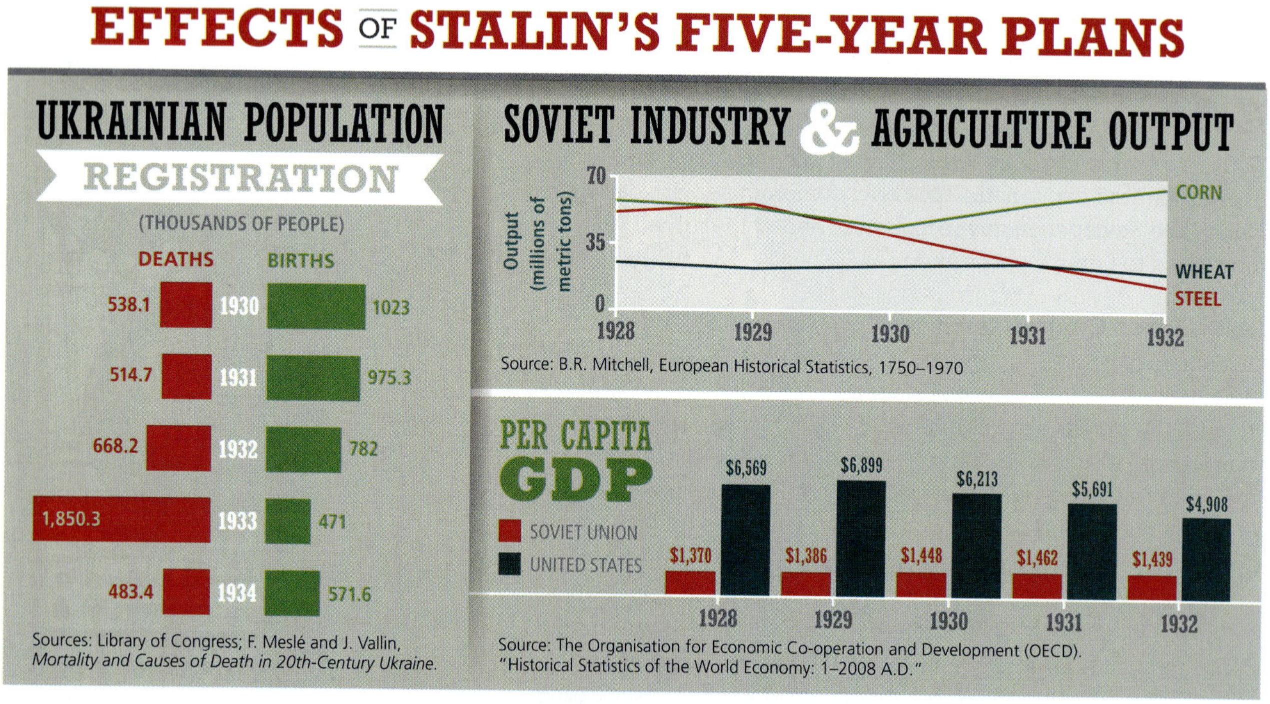

>> Analyze Information Describe the effect of the Five-Year Plans on steel and corn production.

government wanted farmers to produce more grain to feed workers in the cities. It also hoped to sell grain abroad to earn money.

Under Lenin's New Economic Plan (NEP), peasants had held on to small plots of land. Many had prospered. Stalin saw that system as being inefficient and a threat to state power. Stalin wanted all peasants to farm on either state-owned farms or **collectives,** large farms owned and operated by peasants as a group.

On collectives, the government provided tractors, fertilizers, and better seed, and peasants learned modern farm methods. Peasants were permitted to keep their houses and personal belongings, but all farm animals and implements had to be turned over to the collective. The state set all prices and controlled access to farm supplies.

Many peasants resisted collectivization by killing farm animals, destroying tools, and burning crops. The government responded with brutal force. Stalin targeted **kulaks,** or wealthy farmers.

In 1929, Stalin declared his intention to "liquidate the kulaks as a class." To this end, the government confiscated kulaks' land and sent them to slave labor camps, where thousands were executed or died from overwork.

Despite the repression, angry peasants continued to resist by growing just enough to feed themselves. In response, the government seized all of their grain for the cities, purposely leaving the peasants to starve. In 1932, this ruthless policy, combined with poor harvests, led to a terrible famine. Later called the Terror Famine, it caused between five and eight million people to die of starvation in the Ukraine alone. Millions more died in other parts of the Soviet Union.

Although collectivization increased Stalin's control of the peasantry, it did not improve farm output. During the 1930s, grain production inched upward, but meat, vegetables, and fruits remained in short supply. Feeding the population would remain a major problem in the Soviet Union.

☑ **EXPLAIN** How did Stalin take control of the Soviet Union's economic life?

Control Through Terror

In addition to tactics like the Terror Famine, Stalin's totalitarian state used secret police, torture, and violent purges to ensure obedience. Stalin tightened his grasp on every aspect of Soviet life, stamping out any signs of dissent even within the Communist elite.

>> This propaganda poster supports one element of Stalin's Five-Year Plan for industry: the creation of an industrial area in Siberia that took advantage of the region's vast coal reserves.

>> The Gulag was the system of Soviet forced-labor camps. It housed political prisoners as well as actual criminals and became a symbol of political repression in the Soviet Union.

Terror as a Weapon Stalin ruthlessly used terror as a weapon against his own people. He perpetrated crimes against humanity, carried out politically motivated mass murders, and systematically violated his people's individual rights. Police spies did not hesitate to open private letters or plant listening devices. A vast network of internal spies reported on groups or individuals. Nothing appeared in print without official approval. There was no free press, and no safe method of voicing protest. Grumblers or critics were rounded up and sent to the **Gulag,** a system of brutal labor camps, where many died.

Stalin's Great Purge Even though Stalin's power was absolute, he had obsessive fears that rival party leaders were plotting against him. In 1934, he launched the Great Purge. During this reign of terror, Stalin and his secret police cracked down especially on Old Bolsheviks, or party activists from the early days of the revolution. His net soon widened to target army heroes, industrial managers, writers, and ordinary citizens. They were charged with a wide range of crimes, from counter-revolutionary plots to failure to meet production quotas.

Between 1936 and 1938, Stalin staged a series of spectacular public "show trials" in Moscow. Former Communist leaders confessed to all kinds of crimes after officials tortured them or threatened their families or friends.

Many of the purged party members were never tried but were sent straight to the Gulag. Secret police files reveal that at least four million people were purged during the Stalin years. Some historians estimate the toll to be much greater.

Impact of the Great Purge The purges increased Stalin's power. The purges destroyed the older generation of revolutionaries, replacing them with younger party members who owed absolute loyalty to Stalin. The program of terror increased Stalin's power by impressing on the Soviet people the dangers of disloyalty.

However, the Soviet Union paid a heavy price. Among the victims of the purges were experts in industry, economics, and engineering, and many of the Soviet Union's most talented writers and thinkers. The purged also included most of the nation's military leaders and about half of its military officers. The loss of so many military leaders would come back to haunt Stalin in 1941, when Germany invaded the Soviet Union.

IDENTIFY CAUSE AND EFFECT In what ways did Stalin's terror tactics harm the Soviet Union?

>> Stalin used propaganda to win the hearts and minds of Soviet citizens. This poster reads, "Thanks to dear Stalin for a happy childhood."

Bounce to Activate Gallery

Stalin Builds a Totalitarian State

The use of terror and intimidation was one of the major characteristics of Stalin's totalitarian stage. Like other totalitarian rulers, Stalin sought to control the hearts and minds of Soviet citizens. He tried to do this by tirelessly distributing propaganda, censoring opposing ideas, imposing Russian culture on minorities, and replacing religion with communist ideology.

Propaganda and the "Cult of Personality" Stalin tried to boost morale and faith in the communist system by making himself a godlike figure. He used propaganda as a tool to build up a "cult of personality" around himself.

Using modern technology, the party bombarded the public with relentless propaganda. Radios and loudspeakers blared into factories and villages. In movies, theaters, and schools, citizens heard about communist successes and the evils of capitalism.

Billboards and posters urged workers to meet or exceed production quotas. Headlines in the

The Soviet Union, 1928–1941

>> **Analyze Maps** Stalin used terror and labor camps to control the huge, multinational Soviet Union. In which part of the Soviet Union was the heaviest concentration of Gulag labor camps?

Communist party newspaper *Pravda,*or "Truth," linked enemies at home to foreign agents seeking to overthrow the Communist regime.

Censoring the Arts At first, the Bolshevik Revolution had meant greater freedom for Soviet artists and writers. Under Stalin, however, the heavy hand of state control also gripped the arts. The government controlled what books were published, what music was heard, and which works of art were displayed. Stalin required artists and writers to follow a style called **socialist realism.** Its goal was to show Soviet life in a positive light. Artists and writers could criticize the bourgeois past, but their overall message had to promote hope in the socialist future. Popular themes for socialist realist artists were peasants, workers, and heroes of the revolution—and, of course, Stalin.

Artists who ignored socialist realism guidelines could not get materials, work space, or jobs. Writers, artists, and composers also faced government persecution. The Jewish poet **Osip Mandelstam,** for example, was imprisoned, tortured, and exiled for composing a satirical verse about Stalin. Out of fear for his wife's safety, Mandelstam finally submitted to threats and wrote an "Ode to Stalin." **Boris Pasternak,** who would later win fame for his novel *Doctor Zhivago,* was afraid to publish anything at all during the Stalin years. Rather than write in the favored style of socialist realism, he translated foreign literary works instead.

Despite restrictions, some Soviet writers produced magnificent works whose themes reflected the history and culture of Stalinist Russia. Yevgeny Zamyatin's classic anti-Utopian novel *We* became well known outside of the Soviet Union, but was not published in his home country until 1989. The novel depicts a nightmare future in which people go by numbers, not names, and the "One State" controls people's thoughts.

And Quiet Flows the Don, by Mikhail Sholokhov, passed the censor. The novel tells the story of a man who spends years fighting in World War I, the Russian Revolution, and the civil war. Sholokhov later won the Nobel Prize for literature.

Russification of the Republics Yet another way Stalin controlled the cultural life of the Soviet Union was by promoting a policy of **russification,** or imposing Russian culture on the diverse Soviet empire. During the Soviet era, the U.S.S.R. came to include 15 separate republics. Russia, or the Russian Soviet Federated Socialist Republic, was the largest and dominant republic. The others, such as Uzbek and the Ukraine, had their own languages, historical traditions, and cultures.

At first, Stalin encouraged the autonomy, or independence, of these cultures. However, in the late 1920s, Stalin turned this policy on its head and systematically tried to promote Russian culture. He appointed Russians to high-ranking positions in non-Russian SSRs and required the Russian language to be used in schools and businesses. Many Russian citizens were sent to settle in the other republics, furthering the spread of Russian customs and culture.

Communists Wage War on Religion In accordance with the ideas of Marx, **atheism,** or the belief that there is no god, became the official Soviet state policy. Early on, the Communists targeted the Russian Orthodox Church, which had strongly supported the tsars. The party seized most religious property, converting many churches into offices and museums. Many priests and other religious leaders were killed in the purges or sent to die in prison camps.

Other religions were persecuted as well. At one show trial, 15 Roman Catholic priests were charged with teaching religion to the young, a counter-revolutionary activity. The state seized Jewish synagogues and banned the use of Hebrew. Islam was also officially discouraged.

The Communists tried to replace religion with their own ideology. Like a religion, communist ideology had its own "sacred" texts—the writings of Marx and Lenin—and its own shrines, such as the tomb of Lenin. Portraits of Stalin replaced religious icons in Russian homes. However, millions of Soviets continued to worship, in private and sometimes in public, in defiance of government prohibitions.

>> To weaken the power of the Russian Orthodox Church, the party seized church property and converted churches into offices and museums. Here, Red Army soldiers carry off religious relics from a church.

Bounce to Activate Chart

IDENTIFY CENTRAL IDEAS How did Stalin use censorship and propaganda to support his rule?

Soviet Society Under Stalin

The terror and cultural coercion of Stalin's rule made a mockery of the original theories and promises of communism. The lives of most Russians did change. But, while the changes had some benefits, they were often outweighed by continuous shortages and restricted freedoms.

The Soviet Elite Takes Control The Communists destroyed the old social order of landowning nobles at the top and peasants at the bottom. But instead of creating the classless society that Marx had predicted, they created a society where a few elite groups emerged as a new ruling class. At the top of society were members of the Communist party. Only a small fraction of Soviet citizens could join the party. Many who did so were motivated by a desire to get ahead, rather than a belief in communism. The Soviet elite also included industrial managers, military leaders, scientists, and some artists and writers.

The elite enjoyed benefits denied to most people. They lived in the best apartments in the cities and rested at the best vacation homes in the country. They could shop at special stores for scarce consumer goods. On the other hand, Stalin's purges often targeted the elite.

Limited Benefits Although excluded from party membership, most people did enjoy several new benefits. The party required all children to attend free Communist-built schools. The state supported technical schools and universities as well.

Schools served many important goals. Educated workers were needed to build a modern industrial state. The Communist party also set up programs for students outside school. These programs included sports, cultural activities, and political classes to train teenagers for party membership. However, in addition to important basic skills, schools also taught communist values, such as atheism, the glory of collective farming, and love of Stalin.

The state also provided free medical care, day care for children, inexpensive housing, and public recreation. While these benefits were real, many people still lacked vital necessities. Although the state built massive apartment complexes, housing was scarce. Entire families might be packed into a single room. Bread was plentiful, but meat, fresh fruit, and other foods remained in short supply.

Women Win Greater Equality Long before 1917, women such as Lenin's wife, Nadezhda Krupskaya, worked for the revolution, spreading radical ideas among peasants and workers. In 1905, Alexandra Kollontai noted "how little our party concerned itself with the fate of working class women." After becoming the only high-ranking woman in Lenin's government, she continued her campaign for women's rights.

Under the Communists, women won equality under the law. They gained access to education and a wide range of jobs.

By the 1930s, many Soviet women were working in medicine, engineering, or the sciences. By their labor, women contributed to Soviet economic growth. They worked in factories, in construction, and on collectives. Within the family, their wages were needed because men and women earned the same low salaries.

>> Soviet ideology stressed gender equality in labor and education. Many Soviet women held jobs and earned advanced degrees.

GENERATE EXPLANATIONS How did Communist schools benefit the state and Communist party?

Soviet Foreign Policy

Between 1917 and 1939, the Soviet Union pursued two very different goals in foreign policy. As communists, both Lenin and Stalin wanted to bring about the worldwide revolution that Marx had predicted. But as Soviets, they wanted to guarantee their nation's security by winning the support of other countries. The result was a contradictory and generally unsuccessful foreign policy.

Promoting Communist Revolution In 1919, Lenin formed the Communist International, or **Comintern.** Its purpose was to encourage worldwide revolution. To this end, it aided revolutionary groups around the world and urged colonial peoples to rise up against imperialist powers.

The Comintern's support of revolutionary groups outside the Soviet Union and its loud propaganda against capitalism made Western powers suspicious of the Soviet Union.

In the United States, fear of Bolshevik plots led to the "Red Scare" in the early 1920s. Britain temporarily broke off relations with the Soviet Union when evidence revealed Soviet schemes to turn the 1926 general strike into a revolution.

Seeking Recognition Even while the Comintern supported the global communist struggle, the Soviet Union sought international recognition and trade with capitalist countries, especially the United States and Britain. In 1933, the United States and Soviet Union finally set up diplomatic relations, and the following year, the Soviets joined the League of Nations. However, mistrust still poisoned relations, especially after the Great Purge.

In the early years of Stalin's rule, the Soviet Union remained, for the most part, isolated from the West. By the late 1930s, however, Stalin feared a growing threat from Nazi Germany. In April 1939, he suggested that Russia, France, and Britain form an alliance against Germany. Western suspicions of Soviet intentions made an agreement impossible. Within months, Stalin made an about-face and signed an alliance with Nazi Germany.

ANALYZE INFORMATION How did the Soviet Union's foreign policy goals contradict one another?

ASSESSMENT

1. **Identify Cause and Effect** What were the goals and results of Stalin's five-year plans?
2. **Contrast** For those not in the elite party, how did life change under Soviet rule?
3. **Explain** How did Stalin attempt to control thought in the Soviet Union?
4. **Summarize** What methods did Stalin use to create a totalitarian state?
5. **Compare** What foreign policy goals did both Lenin and Stalin pursue?

6.8 As World War I drew to a close, Germany tottered on the brink of chaos. Under the threat of a socialist revolution, Kaiser William II abdicated. Moderate leaders signed the armistice and later, under protest, the Treaty of Versailles.

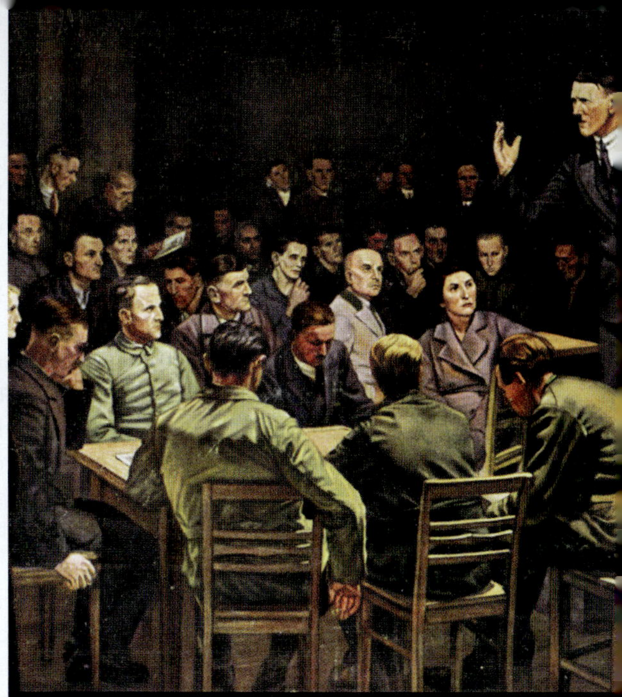

>> The Nazi Party was active between 1920 and 1945. Hitler served as the party's leader starting in 1921. Initially, the Nazis focused on anti-big business and anti-capitalist rhetoric.

Bounce to Activate Flipped Video

The Rise of Nazi Germany

>> **Objectives**

Summarize the political and economic problems faced by the Weimar Republic.

Analyze Hitler's rise to power.

Describe the political, social, economic, and cultural policies of Nazi Germany.

Explain why Eastern Europe turned to authoritarian rule.

>> **Key Terms**

chancellor
Ruhr Valley
hyperinflation
Adolf Hitler
Third Reich
Gestapo
Nuremberg Laws

The Weimar Republic

In 1919, German leaders drafted a constitution in the city of Weimar (VY mahr). It created a democratic government known as the Weimar Republic. The constitution set up a parliamentary system led by a **chancellor,** or prime minister. It gave women the right to vote and included a bill of rights. However, the Weimar Republic faced numerous problems, including political extremists, extreme inflation, and the Great Depression, all of which led to the Republic's eventual fall.

Political Turmoil The republic faced severe problems from the start. Politically, it was weak because Germany, like France, had many small parties. The chancellor had to form coalitions that easily fell apart.

The government, led by moderates, came under constant fire from both the left and right. Communists demanded radical changes like those Lenin had brought to Russia. Conservatives—including the old Junker nobility, military officers, and wealthy bourgeoisie—attacked the government as too liberal and weak. They longed for another strong leader like Bismarck.

Germans of all classes blamed the Weimar Republic for the hated Versailles treaty, with its war guilt clause and heavy reparations. Bitter, they looked for scapegoats. Many scapegoated Marxists or German Jews for Germany's economic and political problems.

Economic Hardship Economic disaster fed unrest. In 1923, when Germany fell behind in reparations payments, France occupied the coal-rich **Ruhr Valley,** (roor) taking over its iron, coal, and steel industries. German workers in the Ruhr protested using passive resistance and refused to work. To pay the workers, the German government printed huge quantities of paper money.

Inflation soon spiraled out of control, spreading misery and despair. The German mark became almost worthless. An item that cost 100 marks in July 1922 might have cost 944,000 marks by August 1923. Such an extremely rapid and sharp increase in prices is known as **hyperinflation.** Salaries rose by billions of marks, but they still could not keep up with skyrocketing prices. Many middle-class families saw their savings wiped out.

>> **Analyze Political Cartoons** The terms of the Treaty of Versailles resulted in Germany losing large amounts of territory as well as its overseas colonies. What do you think the turkey in this cartoon represents?

Bounce to Activate Timeline

Recovery and Depression With help from the Western powers, the government did bring inflation under control. In 1924, the United States gained British and French approval for a plan to reduce German reparations payments. Under the Dawes Plan, France withdrew its forces from the Ruhr, and American loans helped the German economy recover.

Germany began to prosper. Then the Great Depression hit, reviving memories of the miseries of 1923. Germans turned to an energetic leader, Adolf Hitler, who promised to solve the economic crisis and restore Germany's former greatness.

Culture in the Weimar Republic Despite political and economic turmoil, culture flourished in the Weimar Republic. The tumultuous times helped to stimulate new cultural movements, such as dadaist art and Bauhaus architecture. Berlin attracted writers and artists from around the world, just as Paris did. The German playwright Bertolt Brecht sharply criticized middle-class values with *The Three-Penny Opera.* The artist George Grosz, through scathing drawings and paintings, blasted the failings of the Weimar Republic.

Most of the art and music produced during the Weimar Republic reflected the culture of that time. However, many believed that this modern culture and the Weimar Republic itself were not in keeping with Germany's illustrious past. They condemned the new culture as immoral and rejected American influences, such as jazz.

SUPPORT IDEAS WITH EXAMPLES Describe the problems of the Weimar Republic.

Hitler Leads the Nazi Party

The Great Depression sent the German economy into a downward spiral. As discontent rose, Germans began to listen to the ideas of **Adolf Hitler**, who had operated on the fringe of German politics for a decade.

Early Years Hitler was born in Austria in 1889. When he was 18, he went to Vienna, then the capital of the multinational Hapsburg empire. German Austrians made up just one of many ethnic groups in Vienna. Yet they felt superior to Jews, Serbs, Poles, and other groups. While living in Vienna, Hitler developed the fanatical anti-Semitism, or prejudice against Jewish people, that would later play a major role in his rise to power.

Hitler went to Germany and fought in the German army during World War I. In 1919, he joined a small group of right-wing extremists. Like many ex-soldiers, he despised the Weimar government, which he saw as weak. Within a year, he was the unquestioned leader of the National Socialist German Workers, or Nazi, party. Like Mussolini, Hitler organized his supporters into fighting squads. Nazi "storm troopers" fought in the streets against their political enemies.

Hitler's Ideological Manifesto In November 1923, Hitler tried to follow Mussolini's example by staging a small-scale coup known as the Beer Hall Putsch in Munich. The coup failed, and Hitler was soon behind bars. While in prison, Hitler wrote *Mein Kampf ("My Struggle").*It would later become the basic book of Nazi goals and ideology.

Mein Kampf reflected Hitler's obsessions—extreme nationalism, racism, and anti-Semitism. Germans, he said, belonged to a superior "master race" of Aryans, or light-skinned Europeans, whose greatest enemies were the Jews.

Hitler's ideas were rooted in a long tradition of European anti-Semitism, dating back to the persecutions of the Middle Ages. The rise of nationalism in the 1800s caused people to identify Jews as ethnic outsiders. Hitler viewed Jews not as members of a religion but as a separate race. (He defined a Jew as anyone with one Jewish grandparent.) Echoing a familiar right-wing theme, he blamed Germany's defeat in World War I on a conspiracy of Marxists, Jews, corrupt politicians, and business leaders.

In his recipe for revival, Hitler urged Germans everywhere to unite into one great nation. Germany must expand, he said, to gain *Lebensraum* (LAY buns rowm), or living space, for its people. Slavs and other inferior races must bow to Aryan needs. To achieve its greatness, Germany needed a strong leader, or Führer (FYOO rur). Hitler was determined to become that leader.

Hitler Comes to Power After less than a year, Hitler was released from prison. He soon renewed his table-thumping speeches. The Great Depression played into Hitler's hands. As unemployment rose, Nazi membership grew to almost a million. Hitler's program appealed to veterans, workers, the lower middle classes, small-town Germans, and business people alike. He promised to end reparations, create jobs, and defy the Versailles treaty by rearming Germany.

>> A Nazi propaganda poster from 1934 urges the German people to support their country by purchasing German produce.

With the government paralyzed by divisions, both Nazis and Communists won more seats in the Reichstag, or lower house of the legislature. Fearing the growth of communist political power, conservative politicians turned to Hitler. Although they despised him, they believed they could control him. Thus, with conservative support, Hitler was appointed chancellor in 1933 through legal means under the Weimar constitution.

Within a year, Hitler was dictator of Germany. He and his supporters suspended civil rights, destroyed the Communists, and disbanded other political parties. Germany became a one-party, totalitarian state. Like Stalin in Russia, Hitler purged his own party, brutally executing Nazis he felt were disloyal. Nazis learned that Hitler demanded unquestioning obedience.

Hitler's rise to power raises disturbing questions that we still debate today. Why did Germany turn from democracy to totalitarianism? How could a ruthless, hate-filled dictator gain the enthusiastic support of many Germans?

CHECK UNDERSTANDING Describe the ideology of Hitler and the Nazi Party.

The Third Reich

Once in power, Hitler and the Nazis moved to build a new Germany. Like Mussolini, Hitler appealed to nationalism by recalling past glories. Germany's First Reich, or empire, was the medieval Holy Roman Empire, which had lasted more than 800 years. The Second Reich was the empire forged by Bismarck in 1871. Under Hitler's new **Third Reich,** he boasted, the German master race would dominate Europe for a thousand years. His aggressive goals would eventually lead Germany—and the world—into another war.

To combat the Great Depression, Hitler launched large public works programs (as did Britain and the United States). Tens of thousands of people were put to work building highways and housing or replanting forests. Hitler also repudiated, or rejected, the Versailles treaty. He launched a crash program to rearm Germany and schemed to unite Germany and Austria.

Like Mussolini, Hitler preserved capitalism but brought big business and labor under government control. Few objected to this loss of freedom because their standard of living rose. Nazi propaganda highlighted the improvements.

>> The Gestapo was the official secret police agency of Nazi Germany. It was formed in 1933 and was under the administration of Heinrich Himmler by April 1934.

A Totalitarian State Emerges To achieve his goals, Hitler organized an efficient but brutal system of terror, repression, and totalitarian rule. Nazis controlled all areas of German life—from government to religion to education. Elite, black-uniformed troops, called the SS, enforced the Führer's will. His secret police, the **Gestapo** (guh STAH poh), rooted out opposition.

At first, many Germans welcomed Hitler, who took forceful action to ease the effects of the Great Depression and promised to revive German greatness. Any people who criticized Hitler became victims of terror or were cowed into silence in fear for their own safety.

Anti-Semitism Campaign Begins In his fanatical anti-Semitism, Hitler set out to drive Jews from Germany. In 1935, the Nazis passed the **Nuremberg Laws,** which deprived Jews of German citizenship and placed severe restrictions on them. They were prohibited from marrying non-Jews, attending or teaching at German schools or universities, holding government jobs, practicing law or medicine, or publishing books. Nazis beat and robbed Jews and roused mobs to do the same. Many German Jews fled, seeking refuge in other countries, but these countries often closed their doors and limited Jewish immigration.

On November 7, 1938, a young German Jew whose parents had been deported to their native Poland shot and wounded a German diplomat in Paris. Hitler used the incident as an excuse to stage an attack on all Jews. The incident became known as *Kristallnacht* (krih STAHL nahkt), or the "Night of Broken Glass." On the night of November 9 and into the following day, Nazi mobs in Germany, Austria, and Czechoslovakia smashed the windows of Jewish homes and businesses. The experience was terrifying for Jews.

> They broke our windowpanes, and the house became very cold.". . . We were standing there, outside in the cold, still in our night clothes, with only a coat thrown over... Then they made everyone lie face down on the ground. . .'Now, they will shoot us,' we thought. We were very afraid."
>
> —Sophie Nussbaum, quoted in ***48 Hours of Kristallnacht***

Over 1,000 synagogues were burned and more than 7,000 Jewish businesses destroyed. Many Jewish schools, hospitals and homes were damaged, and many Jews were injured and killed. The Nazis arrested 30,000 Jews and forced them into concentration camps.

Kristallnacht reflected so badly on Germany that it was not repeated. Yet Hitler made the Jewish victims of the attacks pay for the damage. Before long, Hitler and his henchmen were making even more sinister plans for what they called the "Final Solution"—the extermination of all Jews.

Nazi Social Policies Like Italian Fascists and Soviet Communists, the Nazis indoctrinated young people with their ideology. In passionate speeches, the Führer spewed his message of racism.

He urged young Germans to destroy their so-called enemies without mercy. On hikes and in camps, the "Hitler Youth" pledged absolute loyalty to Germany and undertook physical fitness programs to prepare for war. School courses and textbooks were rewritten to reflect Nazi racial views.

Like Mussolini's Fascists, Nazis sought to limit women's roles. Women were dismissed from upper-level jobs and turned away from universities. To raise the birthrate, Nazis offered "pure-blooded Aryan" women rewards for having more children.

Still, Hitler's goal to keep women in the home and out of the workforce applied mainly to the privileged. As German industry expanded, women factory workers were needed.

Purifying German Culture The Nazis used education and the arts as propaganda tools to purge, or purify, German culture. At huge public bonfires, Nazis burned books of which they disapproved. They denounced modern art, saying that it was corrupted by Jewish influences. They condemned jazz because of its African roots. Instead, the Nazis glorified old German myths such as those re-created in the operas of Richard Wagner (VAHG nur).

Hitler despised Christianity as "weak" and "flabby." He sought to replace religion with his racial creed. To control the churches, the Nazis combined all Protestant sects into a single state church. They closed Catholic schools and muzzled the Catholic clergy. Although many clergy either supported the new regime or remained silent, some courageously spoke out against Hitler.

DESCRIBE How did the Nazi Party maintain its control of Germany?

Authoritarian Rule in Eastern Europe

Like Germany, most new nations in Eastern Europe slid from democratic to authoritarian rule in the postwar era. In 1919, a dozen countries were carved out of the old Russian, Austro-Hungarian, Ottoman, and German empires. Although they differed from one another in important ways, they faced some common problems. They were small countries whose rural agricultural economies lacked capital to develop industry. Social and economic inequalities separated poor peasants from wealthy landlords. None had much experience with the democratic process.

Further complicating the situation, rivalries left over from World War I hindered economic cooperation between countries. Each country in the region tried to be independent of its neighbors, which hurt all of them. The region was hit hard by the Great Depression.

Ethnic Rivalries Old rivalries between ethnic and religious groups created severe tensions. In Czechoslovakia, Czechs and Slovaks were unwilling partners. More than three million Germans lived in northern Czechoslovakia, and some of them wanted to join Hitler's Nazi Germany.

Serbs dominated the new state of Yugoslavia, but restless Slovenes and Croats living there pressed for independence. In Poland, Hungary, and Romania, conflict flared among various ethnic minorities.

Dictators Replace Democracy Economic problems and ethnic tensions contributed to

>> The Hitler Youth program emphasized activism, physical training, and Nazi ideology, as well as absolute obedience to Hitler and the Nazi Party.

Bounce to Activate Gallery

instability, which in turn helped fascist rulers gain power. In Hungary, military strongman Nicholas Horthy (HAWR tay) overthrew a Communist-led government in 1919. By 1926, the military hero Joseph Pilsudski (peel SOOT skee) had taken control of Poland. Eventually, right-wing dictators emerged in every Eastern European country except Czechoslovakia and Finland.

Like Hitler, these dictators promised order and won the support of the military and wealthy. They also turned to anti-Semitism, using Jewish people as scapegoats for many national problems. Meanwhile, strong, aggressive neighbors eyed these small, weak states of Eastern Europe as tempting targets. Before long, Eastern Europe would fall into the orbit of Hitler's Germany and then of Stalin's Soviet Union.

IDENTIFY CENTRAL ISSUES How did World War I impact the growth of authoritarian states in Eastern Europe?

ASSESSMENT

1. **Describe** Describe the weaknesses of the Weimar Republic.
2. **Support Ideas with Examples** How was Hitler able to shift political thought in Germany in order to establish and maintain a totalitarian state?
3. **Identify Cause and Effect** Describe the effects of Eastern Europe's economic problems and ethnic and religious tensions.
4. **Describe** Describe Hitler's fanatical anti-Semitism and how he tried to drive Jewish people from Germany.
5. **Summarize** Why did the Nazi Party glorify old German myths and denounce modern art?

PEARSON realize™
PearsonSchool.com/CASS

Go online to PearsonSchool.com/CASS and use the texts, quizzes, interactivities, Interactive Reading Notepads, Flipped Videos, and other resources from this Topic to prepare for the Topic Test.

- Etexts
- Quizzes
- Interactivities
- Interactive Reading Notepads
- Flipped Videos

While online you can also check the progress you've made learning the topic and course content by viewing your grades, test scores, and assignment status.

California Topic 6 Quick Study Guide

LESSON SUMMARIES

Use these Lesson Summaries, and the longer versions available online, to review the key ideas for each lesson in this Topic.

Lesson 1: Revolution and Nationalism in Latin America

Revolution swept through Mexico between 1910 and 1920. As the revolution spread, Indian peasants battled to end centuries of oppression and to win land. It was a long and difficult struggle.

Lesson 2: Nationalist Movements in Africa and the Middle East

After World War I, nationalist sentiment contributed to many changes in Africa and the Middle East.

Lesson 3: India Seeks Self Rule

During WWI, as thousands of Indian troops died on distant battlefields, Indian nationalists grew angry that they had no freedom at home. In the 1920s a leader emerged—Mohandas Gandhi. In his struggle against injustice, he adopted the weapon of nonviolent resistance. Eventually, his ideas would inspire many others.

Lesson 4: New Forces in China and Japan

Civil war and foreign invasions plagued the new Chinese republic. Japan, in the 1930s, had a military dominated government that emphasized service to the nation and a policy of imperialistic expansion.

Lesson 5: The West After World War I

In 1919, three western democracies – Great Britain, France, and the United States—appeared powerful. They had ruled the Paris Peace Conference and boosted hopes for democracy among the new nations of Eastern Europe. But postwar all faced difficult political and economic crises. The Great Depression of the 1930s marked a period of global economic collapse.

Lesson 6: Fascism Emerges in Italy

In 1919, Italian nationalists were outraged by the Paris peace treaties. Disorder grew in the country with economic and political upsets. Mussolini rose in the midst of this turmoil. Supporters rallied to his claims to end corruption and restore Italy to its former glory. But his government would become a dictatorship upheld by terror—critics were harshly suppressed.

Lesson 7: The Soviet Union Under Stalin

Stalin turned the Soviet Union into a totalitarian state that regulated every aspect of the lives of its citizens.

Lesson 8: The Rise of Nazi Germany

In 1919, the German republic was entangled in economic and political difficulties. These hardships helped Adolf Hitler rise to power. But under Hitler, the Nazi government would use terror, repression, and one-party rule to establish a totalitarian state.

VISUAL REVIEW

Use these graphics to review some of the key terms, people, and ideas from this Topic.

Nationalism Around the World 1910–1939

LOCATION	GOALS	EXPRESSION
Mexico	To reject foreign influence	Nationalizing foreign companies; emphasizing Latin American culture
Africa	To fight for rights under colonial system	Organizing resistance, including protests, boycotts, strikes squatting; founding of associations and political parties
Turkey and Persia	To strengthen countries by modernizing and westernizing	Secularizing daily life; adopting Western ways; building industry
The Middle East	To create a Pan-Arab state	Resisting mandate system; ongoing friction between Jewish settlers and Palestinians
India	To gain independence from British	Protesting British rule using nonviolent methods, under Gandhi's leadership
China	To lessen foreign domination of China	Resisting Japanese encroachment; attempting to strengthen China
Japan	To build an empire	Issuing the Twenty-One demands; invading China multiple times

Effects of World War I on World Events

EFFECTS OF WORLD WAR I

- Trade fell off in Latin America after war.
- Resistance to colonial rule grew when war service failed to improve treatment of African and Indian colonies.
- Atatürk united Turkey and fought to renegotiate the Treat of Sévres.
- The Allies broke promises in the Middle East, fostering bitterness.
- Japan expanded its influence in China.

Three Totalitarian States: Italy, the Soviet Union, and Germany

COUNTRY	DICTATOR IN POWER	IDEOLOGY	EXAMPLE OF TERROR TACTICS
Italy	Benito Mussolini in power in 1922	Fascist; Fanatic nationalism	Black Shirts suppressed dissent.
Soviet Union	Joseph Stalin in power 1924	Communist	Stalin sends millions to Gulag labor camps.
Germany	Adolf Hitler in power in 1933	Fascist; Racial policies of hatred, aimed particularly at Jews	Nazis began to restrict and terrorize German Jews.

California Topic 6 Assessment

KEY TERMS, PEOPLE, AND IDEAS

1. What prompted the push for **economic nationalism** in Latin America after WWI?
2. What postwar issues did most European nations face after WWI?
3. What philosophy did **Gandhi** follow? How did he use this philosophy in his move for an independent India?
4. Once in power, how did Stalin attempt to improve the economy of Russia? What were the results?
5. How did geography determine Japan's goal toward expanding its empire?
6. What change in social attitude did the **flapper** represent in 1920s America?
7. How did postwar disillusionment pave the way for the rise of totalitarian governments?
8. How did **overproduction** become one cause of the **Great Depression**?
9. Why did Hitler pass the **Nuremberg Laws**?

CRITICAL THINKING

10. **Drawing Conclusions** Why did Palestine become a center of conflict after World War I?
11. **Synthesize Information** Two literary movements arose in the United States during the 1920s—works by writers who were part of the Lost Generation and works by writers who represented the Harlem Renaissance. What factors after the war shaped these movements?
12. **Explain** What similarities exist in the governing of totalitarian regimes?
13. **Draw Conclusions** How did postwar disillusionment pave the way for the rise of totalitarian governments?
14. **Analyze Information** How did Britain, France, and the United States respond to the Great Depression?
15. **Evaluate Information** How did the Treaty of Versailles lay the seeds for the rise of Hitler in Germany?
16. **Analyze Image** Look at the image below. This is a propaganda poster to support Stalin's Five Year economic plan. How does the poster show a bright outlook for the economy?

17. **Writing Activity** The following excerpt is from the Manifesto of the Second Pan-African Congress. The members wrote it to detail their beliefs. (a) What does it say about the spread of democracy? (b) How would it encourage African pride and nationalism? Use your knowledge of the Topic and information in the excerpt to write your paragraph.

> "The absolute equality of races—physical, political, and social—is the founding stone of world peace and human advancement...
>
> That is the vast range of time, one group should in its industrial technique, or social organization, or spiritual vision, lag a few hundred years behind another, or forge fitfully ahead, ... is proof of the essential richness and variety of human nature... The doctrine of racial equality does not interfere with individual liberty, rather it fulfills it...
>
> The habit of democracy must be made to encircle the earth. Despite the attempt to prove that its practice is the secret and divine gift of the few, no habit is more natural or more widely spread...
>
> —*Manifesto of the Second Pan-African Congress*

DOCUMENT-BASED QUESTIONS

In 1930, Mohandas Gandhi organized the Salt March to protest the British salt monopoly. Read the documents below, then answer the questions that follow.

DOCUMENT A

"Wherever possible, civil disobedience of the salt laws should be started. These laws can be violated in three ways. It is an offense to manufacture salt wherever there are facilities for doing so. The possession and sale of contraband salt, which includes natural salt or salt earth, [is] also an offense. The purchasers of such salt will be equally guilty. To carry away the natural salt deposits on the seashore is likewise violation of the law. So is the hawking of such salt. In short, you may choose any one or all of these devices to break the salt monopoly."

—*Gandhi on the Salt March*

DOCUMENT B

"The Salt Satyagraha started with a dramatic long march by Gandhi and a group of picked companions from Sabarmati to the coast at Dandi, 240 miles away, where he proceeded to make salt illegally by boiling sea water. The march was a publicity enterprise of great power as the press followed the party's progress . . . As he journeyed . . ., deliberately challenging established authority, village headmen began to resign in large numbers . . . in April, [India's Viceroy, Lord] Irwin reported to London that in Gujarat 'the personal influence of Gandhi threatens to create a position of real embarrassment to the administration . . . as in some areas he has already achieved a considerable measure of success in undermining the authority of Government.'"

—*Modern India: The Origins of Asian Democracy by Judith M. Brown*

DOCUMENT C

"Suddenly, at a word of command, scores of native policemen rushed upon the advancing marchers and rained blows on their heads with their steel-shod *lathis*. Not one of the marchers even raised an arm to fend off the blows. They went down like tenpins. . . . The survivors, without breaking ranks, silently and doggedly marched on until struck down."

—*Webb Miller, a British journalist reporting on a march to the salt deposits at Dharsana*

DOCUMENT D

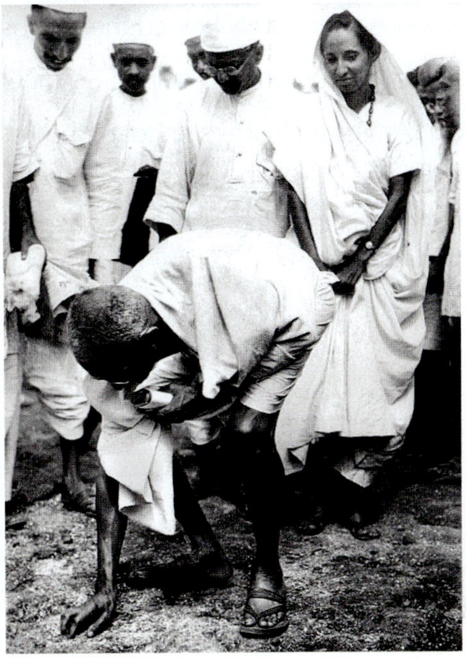

Gandhi picking up salt at the coastal village of Dandi in India, April 6, 1930

18. In Document A, Gandhi was mainly addressing
- **A.** British authorities.
- **B.** journalists around the world.
- **C.** the British people.
- **D.** the Indian people.

19. In Document B, the historian describes the effect of the Salt March on
- **A.** the supply of salt.
- **B.** the authority of the British government.
- **C.** protesters in other countries.
- **D.** Gandhi's health.

20. Which words from Document C reflect the attitude of the reporter toward the marchers?
- **A.** suddenly, command
- **B.** steel-shod, lathis, ten-pins
- **C.** fend, blows
- **D.** silently, doggedly

21. **Writing Tasks** How was the Salt March a turning point in India's struggle for independence? Use what you have learned from these documents and the Topic in your response.

PEARSON realize™ PearsonSchool.com/CASS

Go ONLINE to practice
ASSESSMENT

End-of-Topic Practice

1 Which of these effectively helped the independence movement in Africa in the 1900s?

A The Muslim Brotherhood helped Egyptians gain independence from Britain.

B African American leaders encouraged revolutionary changes through the négritude movement.

C The Pan-African Congress held in Paris at the time of the peace conference put an end to colonialism.

D Pan-Africanism movements emphasized the unity of Africans for eventual self-rule.

Britain	• Most of Ireland breaks away to be self-govening • Fears that Soviet Union and France would become too powerful if Germany was weakened
France	• Insistence that Germany pay war reparations • Security is key goal; strengthened military and alliances
United States	• Political efforts to restrict growing immigration from Europe • Signed disarmament treaty but did not join League of Nations

2 Look at the chart. How did World War I impact the political, economic, and social systems in the three countries?

F Britain and France both wanted to strengthen its borders from future attacks.

G The United States wanted to restrict immigration by declining to join the League of Nations.

H All three nations wanted peace but were fearful of future war influences.

J The French disagreed with British and U.S. disarmament policies.

> *"More than 57 years after the death of Soviet dictator Joseph Stalin, scholars continue to uncover long-hidden truths about his rise to absolute power and the reign of 'Great Terror' that took more than a million lives and exiled many millions more."*

3 According to the excerpt, what is the legacy of Joseph Stalin?

A His five-year plans for agricultural projects were brilliant but were defeated by wealthy farmers.

B He effectively built an economic giant but, because of poor product quality, failed to compete globally.

C He built the Soviet Union into a powerful totalitarian state using the secret police, Gulag, torture, and death.

D His autocratic rule failed in every political, economic, and social aspect of life for the Soviets.

---

4 Hitler's economic recovery plan

F increased his popularity because it employed millions of German citizens when the rest of the world was in the midst of the Great Depression.

G caused a drop in German manufacturing and led to unemployment of many factory workers.

H increased his popularity because it led to a renewal of trade and the gradual buildup of the military in spite of the demands of the Paris Treaty.

J caused inflation and overproduction but after adjustments, employment increased.

If you have trouble with. . .				
Question	1	2	3	4
See Lesson	6.2	6.5	6.7	6.8

[ESSENTIAL QUESTION] When is war justified?

7 World War II (1930–1945)

>> Allied troops landing at the beach at Normandy, France

Enduring Understandings

- Western democracies responded to Axis aggression with appeasement until the Nazi invasion of Poland.
- Early in World War II, Axis forces overran most of Europe and the Pacific, then the tide began to turn in favor of the Allies.
- Neutral at first, the United States joined the Allies after the Japanese bombing of Pearl Harbor.
- The Nazis carried out a plan to exterminate European Jews, now known as the Holocaust.
- After the failed Nazi siege of Stalingrad and the D-Day landings at Normandy, Allied troops closed in on Germany.
- The dropping of atomic bombs on Japan ended the war, but the decision was controversial.

NBC LEARN

Witness an interview with a survivor of the bombing of Britain.

Bounce to Activate My Story Video

California Topic 7 Overview

In this Topic, you will learn about the events of World War II. Look at the lesson outline and explore the timeline. As you study this Topic, you will complete the Quest team project.

LESSON OUTLINE

7.1 Aggression, Appeasement, and War
HSS 10.8, HSS 10.8.1, HSS 10.8.2; Analysis CST.1, CST.2, HRE.4, HI.1

7.2 Axis Powers Advance
HSS 10.8, HSS 10.8.3, HSS 10.8.4; Analysis CST.1, CST.2, HRE.4, HI.1

7.3 The Holocaust
HSS 10.8, HSS 10.8.5; Analysis CST.1, CST.2, CST.3, HRE.4, HI.1

7.4 The Allies Turn the Tide
HSS 10.8, HSS 10.8.3, HSS 10.8.4; Analysis CST.1, CST.2, HRE.4, HI.1

7.5 Victory for the Allies
HSS 10.8, HSS 10.8.3, HSS 10.8.4, HSS 10.8.6, HSS 10.9.8; Analysis CST.1, CST.2, HRE.4, HI.1

Key Events of World War II

1939
Germany invades Poland. France and Britain declare war on Germany.

1940
France falls to Germany. Roosevelt wins a third term.

1941
Germany invades the Soviet Union. Japan attacks Pearl Harbor.

1942
Allies win the Battle of Midway. Nazi leaders plan "Final Solution" for Europe's Jews.

1944
Allied troops land in Normandy on D-Day

1945
Germany surrenders. U.S. drops atomic bombs on Japan. Japan surrenders.

1939 1940 1941 1942 1943 1944 1945

QUEST! TEAM PROJECT

Create a World War II Tribute

The arrival of war always changes the usual pace of life. Much is sacrificed and rearranged for the national good. In this Quest, you will explore life during World War II and commemorate a special tribute to a person or an event.

STEP 1
Decide what is needed in a good tribute. Choose the kind of tribute you will create. Brainstorm ideas.

STEP 2
Choose an event, person, or experience to honor. Outline a draft of the presentation. Consider researching multimedia elements, books, or picture collections.

STEP 3
Complete the first generation of your tribute. Review, edit, and revise.

STEP 4
Share your presentation with classmates, family, and community. Reflect on what you learned about World War II. When is war justified? Discuss current issues and wars facing the United States.

PEARSON realize™ PearsonSchool.com/CASS

Go ONLINE for complete Quest materials

VIDEO ETEXT WRITING RUBRIC PDF ASSESSMENT

>> Germany rebuilt its military during the 1930s in defiance of the Treaty of Versailles. Here, troops stand at attention during a Nazi rally in Nuremberg, Germany.

7.1 **Throughout the 1930s, the rulers of Germany, Italy, and Japan were preparing to build new empires. After the horrors of World War I, the leaders of Britain, France, and the United States tried to avoid conflict through diplomacy. During the 1930s, the two sides tested each other's commitment and will.**

Bounce to Activate Flipped Video

>> Objectives

Describe how the Western democracies responded to aggression.

Explain the significance of the Spanish Civil War.

Understand how German aggression led Europe into World War II.

>> Key Terms

appeasement
pacifism
Neutrality Acts
Axis powers
Francisco Franco
Anschluss
Sudetenland
Nazi-Soviet Pact

Aggression, Appeasement, and War

A Pattern of Aggression

Challenges to peace followed a pattern. Dictators took aggressive action but met only verbal protests and pleas for peace from the democracies. Mussolini, Hitler, and Japanese militarists viewed that desire for peace as weakness and responded with new acts of aggression. With hindsight, we can see the shortcomings of the policies followed by the democracies. These policies, however, were the product of long and careful deliberation. At the time, many people believed they would prevent war.

Japanese Imperialism Grows One of the earliest tests had been posed by Japan. Japanese military leaders and ultranationalists thought that Japan should have an empire equal to those of the Western powers. In pursuit of this goal, Japan seized the Chinese province of Manchuria in 1931. When the League of Nations condemned the aggression, Japan simply withdrew from the organization.

Japan's easy success strengthened the militarist faction in Japan. In 1937, Japanese armies overran much of eastern China, starting the Second Sino-Japanese War. Once again, Western protests did not stop Japan's acts of imperialism.

Italy Invades Ethiopia In Italy, Mussolini decided to act on his own imperialist ambitions. Italy's defeat by the Ethiopians at the battle of Adowa in 1896 still rankled after almost 40 years. In 1935, Italy invaded Ethiopia, located in northeastern Africa. Although the Ethiopians resisted bravely, their outdated weapons were no match for Mussolini's tanks, machine guns, poison gas, and airplanes.

The Ethiopian king Haile Selassie (HY luh suh lah SEE) appealed to the League of Nations for help. The League voted sanctions against Italy for violating international law. League members agreed to stop selling weapons or other war materials to Italy. But the sanctions did not extend to petroleum, which fueled modern warfare. In addition, the League had no power to enforce the sanctions. By early 1936, Italy had conquered Ethiopia.

Hitler Violates the Treaty of Versailles Hitler had also tested the will of the Western democracies, as well as of the League of Nations, and found it weak. First, he built up the German military in defiance of the Treaty of Versailles. Then, in 1936, he sent troops into the "demilitarized" Rhineland bordering France—another treaty violation. Germans hated the Versailles treaty, and Hitler's successful challenge made him more popular at home.

The Western democracies denounced his moves but took no real action. Instead, they adopted a policy of **appeasement,** or giving in to the demands of an aggressor in order to keep the peace.

Reasons for Appeasement The Western policy of appeasement developed for a number of reasons. France was demoralized, suffering from political divisions at home. It could not take on Hitler without British support. The British, however, had no desire to confront the German dictator. Some even thought that Hitler's actions constituted a justifiable response to the terms of the Treaty of Versailles, which they believed had been too harsh on Germany.

In both Britain and France, many saw Hitler and fascism as a defense against a worse evil—the spread of Soviet communism. Additionally, the Great Depression sapped the energies of the Western democracies. Finally, widespread **pacifism,** or opposition to all war, and disgust with the destruction from the previous war pushed many governments to seek peace at any price.

>> **Analyze Political Cartoons** British cartoonist David Low was known for speaking out against the policy of appeasement. How does this cartoon reflect his message?

Bounce to Activate Cartoon

>> Here, Japanese cavalry have successfully occupied the northern section of Manchuria. The freezing weather did not stop Japanese imperalism.

The United States Remains Neutral As war clouds gathered in Europe in the mid-1930s, the United States Congress passed a series of **Neutrality Acts.** One law forbade the sale of arms to any nation at war. Others outlawed loans to warring nations and prohibited Americans from traveling on ships of warring powers. The fundamental goal of American policy, however, was to avoid involvement in a European war, not to prevent such a conflict.

Formation of the Axis Powers Germany, Italy, and Japan were encouraged by the apparent weakness of the western democracies. The three aggressor nations formed what became known as the **Axis powers,** or the Rome-Berlin-Tokyo Axis. The Axis powers agreed to fight Soviet communism. They also agreed not to interfere with one another's plans for territorial expansion. The agreement cleared the way for these anti-democratic, aggressor powers to take even bolder steps.

RECALL Describe the early acts of aggression of Germany, Italy, and Japan.

The Spanish Civil War

In 1936, Spain was plunged into civil war. Although the Spanish civil war was a local struggle, it soon drew other European powers into the fighting.

From Monarchy to Republic In the early 1900s, Spain was a monarchy dominated by a landowning upper class. Most Spaniards were poor peasants or urban workers. In 1931, popular unrest against the old order forced the king to leave Spain. A republic was set up with a new, more liberal constitution.

The republican government passed a series of controversial reforms. It took over some Church lands, redistributed some land to peasants, and ended some privileges of the old ruling class. These moves split the country. Communists and others on the left demanded more radical reforms. Conservatives and the military rejected the changes.

In 1936, a conservative general named **Francisco Franco** led a revolt that touched off a bloody civil war. Franco's forces, called Nationalists, rallied conservatives to their side. Supporters of the republic, known as Loyalists, included communists, socialists, and supporters of democracy.

Other Countries Get Involved People from other nations soon jumped in to support both sides. Hitler and Mussolini sent arms and forces to help Franco. The Soviet Union sent soldiers to fight against fascism alongside the Spanish Loyalists. Although the governments of Britain, France, and the United States remained neutral, individuals from those countries, as well as other countries, also fought with the Loyalists. Anti-Nazi Germans and anti-Fascist Italians joined the Loyalist cause as well.

A Bloody War Both sides committed horrible atrocities. The ruinous struggle took more than 500,000 lives.

Acts of Aggression

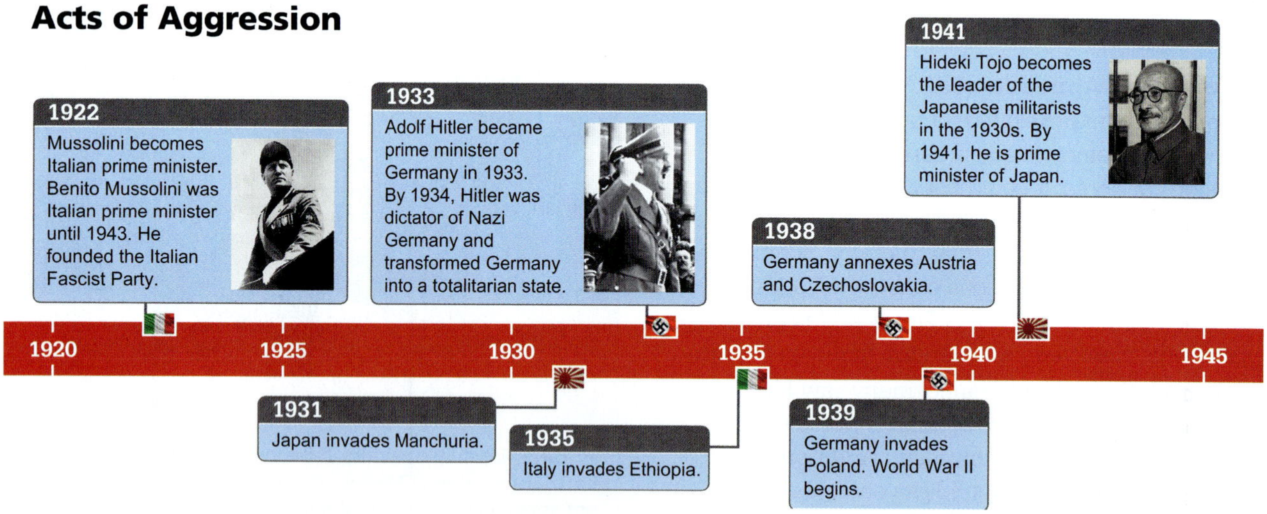

>> Italy, Germany, and Japan formed an alliance and continued their aggressive actions. **Analyze Information** Why was it important for these three nations to form an alliance?

One of the worst horrors was a German air raid on Guernica, a small Spanish market town, in April 1937. Germans timed their attack for an afternoon on a market day with thousands of people in town. German planes dropped their load of bombs, and then swooped low to machine-gun anyone who had survived the bombs. Nearly 1,000 innocent civilians were killed.

To Nazi leaders, the attack on Guernica was an experiment to identify what their new planes could do. To the rest of the world, it was a grim warning of the destructive power of modern warfare. Later, commentators viewed the Spanish Civil War as a "dress rehearsal" for World War II because it had allowed new tactics and weapons to be tested, which would soon be used in a new global war.

By 1939, Franco had triumphed. Once in power, he created a fascist dictatorship similar to the dictatorships of Hitler and Mussolini. He rolled back earlier reforms, killed or jailed enemies, and used terror to promote order.

RECALL Explain how other countries got involved in the Spanish Civil War.

>> Robert Capa's famous photograph, *The Fallen Soldier*, shows the death of a Loyalist militiaman during the Spanish Civil War. The Loyalists were supported by most urban workers and peasants, along with much of the educated middle class, which preferred a liberal democracy.

German Aggression Continues

In the meantime, Hitler pursued his goal of bringing all German-speaking people into the Third Reich. He also took steps to gain "living space" for Germans in Eastern Europe. Hitler, who believed in the superiority of the German people, thought that Germany had a right to conquer the Slavs to the east. Hitler claimed, "I have the right to remove millions of an inferior race that breeds like vermin."

Hitler also had economic and military reasons for expanding eastward. He wanted access to the natural resources of Eastern Europe, which would help boost production of military equipment. New lands would also provide additional markets for German products.

Germany Annexes Austria From the outset, Nazi propaganda had found fertile ground in Austria. By March, 1938, Hitler was ready to engineer the **Anschluss**(AHN shloos), or union of Austria and Germany.

When Austria's chancellor refused to agree to Hitler's demands, Hitler sent in the German army to "preserve order." To indicate his new role as ruler of Austria, Hitler made a speech from the Hofburg Palace, the former residence of the Hapsburg emperors.

>> On March 15, 1938, Hitler gave a speech at the Hofburg Palace in Vienna announcing annexation of Austria by Nazi Germany.

>> British prime minister Neville Chamberlain believed he had delivered peace to Europeans. After the Munich Pact, he assured a jubilant crowd in London that they could sleep soundly, as he returned from Germany bringing peace with honor.

>> German troops ride in a convoy through the streets of Prague during the occupation of Czechoslovakia in March 1939. Czech citizens lined the streets and watched silently in the rain and sleet.

Bounce to Activate Timeline

The Anschluss violated the Versailles treaty and created a brief war scare. Hitler quickly silenced any Austrians who opposed annexation. And since the Western democracies took no action, Hitler easily had his way.

The Czech Crisis Germany turned next to Czechoslovakia. At first, Hitler insisted that the three million Germans in the **Sudetenland** (soo DAY tun land)—a region of western Czechoslovakia—be given autonomy. Czechoslovakia was one of only two remaining democracies in Eastern Europe. (Finland was the other.) Still, Britain and France were not willing to go to war to save it. As British and French leaders searched for a peaceful solution, Hitler increased his demands. The Sudetenland, he said, must be annexed to Germany.

At the Munich Conference in September 1938, British and French leaders again chose appeasement. They caved in to Hitler's demands and then persuaded the Czechs to surrender the Sudetenland without a fight. In exchange, Hitler assured Britain and France that he had no further plans to expand his territory.

The Munich Pact Returning from Munich, British Prime Minister Neville Chamberlain told cheering crowds that he had achieved "peace for our time." He told Parliament that the Munich Pact had "saved Czechoslovakia from destruction and Europe from Armageddon." French leader Edouard Daladier (dah lahd yay) reacted differently to the joyous crowds that greeted him in Paris. "The fools, why are they cheering?" he asked.

British politician Winston Churchill, who had long warned of the Nazi threat, judged the diplomats harshly: "They had to choose between war and dishonor. They chose dishonor; they will have war." Churchill vocalized his strong opposition to appeasement and the Munich Pact in a speech he gave in the House of Commons. He warned:

> "And do not suppose that this is the end. This is only the beginning of the reckoning. This is only the first sip, the first foretaste of a bitter cup which will be proffered to us year by year unless by a supreme recovery of moral health and martial vigour, we arise again and take our stand for freedom as in the olden time."
>
> —Winston Churchill, October 5, 1938

Churchill's warning was largely ignored amid the celebration of the Munich Pact. However, he would very soon play a dominant role in the war he had predicted.

CHECK UNDERSTANDING How did Hitler justify taking over Austria and the Sudetenland?

World War II Begins

Just as Churchill predicted, Europe plunged rapidly toward war. In March 1939, Hitler broke his promises and gobbled up the rest of Czechoslovakia. The democracies finally accepted the fact that appeasement had failed. At last, thoroughly alarmed, they promised to protect Poland, most likely the next target of Hitler's expansion.

Nazi-Soviet Pact In August 1939, Hitler stunned the world by announcing a nonaggression pact with his great enemy—Joseph Stalin, the Soviet dictator. Publicly, the **Nazi-Soviet Pact** bound Hitler and Stalin to peaceful relations. Secretly, the two agreed not to fight if the other went to war and to divide up Poland and other parts of Eastern Europe between them.

The pact was based not on friendship or respect but on mutual need. Hitler feared communism as Stalin feared fascism.

But Hitler wanted a free hand in Poland. Also, he did not want to fight a war with the Western democracies and the Soviet Union at the same time. For his part, Stalin had sought allies among the Western democracies against the Nazi menace. Mutual suspicions, however, kept them apart. By joining with Hitler, Stalin tried to protect the Soviet Union from the threat of war with Germany and grabbed a chance to gain land in Eastern Europe.

Germany Invades Poland On September 1, 1939, a week after the Nazi-Soviet Pact, German forces invaded Poland. Two days later, Britain and France declared war on Germany. World War II had begun. History had again arrived at one of its great turning points.

The devastation of World War I and the awareness of the destructive power of modern technology made the idea of more fighting unbearable. Unfortunately, the war proved to be even more horrendous than anyone had imagined.

>> The cartoon portrays the two long-time enemies, Hitler and Stalin, uniting in marriage, representing the nonaggression pact they signed. **Analyze Political Cartoons** Why would the cartoonist caption this cartoon "Wonder how long the honeymoon will last?"

IDENTIFY CENTRAL IDEAS Why did Britain and France end their policy of appeasement?

ASSESSMENT

1. **Identify Central Issues** Why did the western powers follow a policy of appeasement even though it seemed to encourage more aggression?
2. **Synthesize** Why did Germany and Italy become involved in the Spanish Civil War?
3. **Infer** Why did Churchill believe the Munich Pact was the "beginning of the reckoning"?
4. **Describe** How did the Nazi-Soviet Pact contribute to the start of World War II?
5. **Identify Central Ideas** What reaction did Britain have to Germany's invasion of Poland in 1939?

>> On June 22, 1941, under the code name Operation Barbarossa, Germany invaded the Soviet Union. It was the largest German military operation of World War II. German authorities planned to annihilate the Communist nation.

Bounce to Activate Flipped Video

7.2 World War II lasted from 1939 to 1945. It pitted the Axis powers against the Allies, which eventually included Britain, France, the Soviet Union, China, the United States, and 43 other nations. Unlike World War I, with its defensive trenches, the new global conflict was a war of aggressive movement. In the early years, things went badly for the Allies as Axis forces swept across Europe, North Africa, and Asia.

>> Objectives

Trace the course of German aggression and British resistance in Europe.

Describe the Nazi invasion of the Soviet Union.

Explain how Japanese imperialism and the attack on Pearl Harbor brought the United States into the war.

>> Key Terms

blitzkrieg
Luftwaffe
Dunkirk
Vichy
Erwin Rommel
Lend-Lease Act
Atlantic Charter
Hideki Tojo

Axis Powers Advance

Axis Domination of Europe

Germany's "Lightning War" The Nazi invasion of Poland revealed the power of Hitler's **blitzkrieg,** or "lightning war." The blitzkrieg used tank and air power technology to strike a devastating blow against the enemy.

First, the **Luftwaffe,** or German air force, bombed airfields, factories, towns, and cities. Screaming dive bombers attacked troops and civilians. Then fast-moving tanks and troop transports pushed their way into the defending Polish army, encircling whole divisions and forcing them to surrender.

As Germany attacked from the west, Stalin's forces invaded from the east, grabbing lands promised to them under the Nazi-Soviet Pact. Within a month, Poland ceased to exist as an independent nation. Because of Poland's location and the speed of the attacks, Britain and France could do nothing beyond declaring war on Germany.

Hitler passed the winter without much further action. Stalin's armies, however, forced the Baltic states of Estonia, Latvia, and Lithuania to host bases for the Soviet military. Soviet forces also seized part of Finland, which put up stiff but unsuccessful resistance.

In April 1940, Hitler launched a blitzkrieg against Norway and Denmark, both of which soon fell. Next, his forces slammed into the Netherlands and Belgium.

The Rescue at Dunkirk During that first winter, the French hunkered down behind the Maginot Line, a border created by the French in the 1930s to protect from German invasion. Britain sent troops to wait with them. Some reporters referred to this quiet time as the "phony war."

In May 1940, German forces surprised the French and British by attacking through the Ardennes Forest in Belgium, an area that was considered invasion proof. Bypassing the Maginot Line, German troops poured into France. Retreating British forces were soon trapped between the Nazi army and the English Channel.

In a desperate gamble, the British sent all available naval vessels, merchant ships, and even fishing and pleasure boats across the channel to pluck stranded troops off the beach of **Dunkirk.** Despite German air attacks, the improvised armada ferried more than 300,000 troops to safety in Britain. This heroic rescue raised British morale.

France Surrenders Meanwhile, German forces were heading south toward Paris. In June, Mussolini had declared war on France and Britain. He sent Italian troops to attack France from the south.

Overrun and demoralized, France surrendered. On June 22, 1940, Hitler forced the French to sign the surrender documents in the same railroad car in which Germany had signed the armistice ending World War I. Following the surrender, Germany occupied northern France. In the south, the Germans set up a "puppet state," with its capital at **Vichy** (VEE shee).

Some French officers escaped to England and set up a government-in-exile. Led by Charles de Gaulle, these "free French" worked to liberate their homeland. Within France, resistance fighters used guerrilla tactics against German forces.

Operation Sea Lion With the fall of France, Britain stood alone in Western Europe. Hitler was sure that the British would sue for peace. But Winston Churchill, who had replaced Neville Chamberlain as prime minister, had other plans. Churchill's defiance gave voice to the determination of the British.

> "We shall defend our island, whatever the cost may be, we shall fight on the beaches, we shall fight on the landing grounds, we shall fight in the fields and in the streets, we

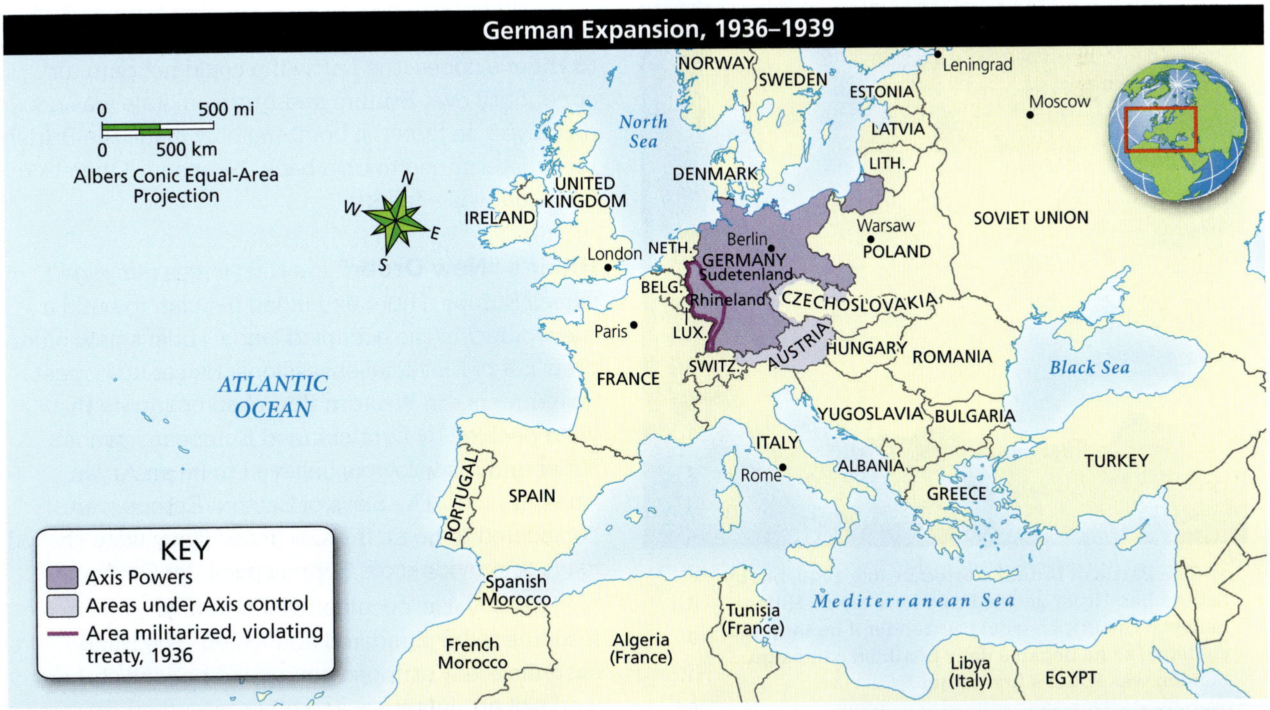

>> Germany advanced aggressively from 1936 to 1939, until its invasion of Poland sparked another world war. **Analyze Maps** How did Germany violate the Treaty of Versailles?

Bounce to Activate Map

shall fight in the hills; we shall never surrender."

Winston Churchill, June 4, 1940

>> In his first speech in Parliament, Prime Minister Winston Churchill vowed, "I have nothing to offer but blood, toil, tears and sweat." He ended with the words, "Come then, let us go forward together with our united strength."

Faced with this defiance, Hitler made plans for Operation Sea Lion—the invasion of Britain. In preparation for the invasion, he launched massive air strikes against the island nation.

Beginning in August 1940, German bombers began a daily bombardment of England's southern coast. For a month, Britain's Royal Air Force valiantly battled the Luftwaffe. Then the Germans changed their tactics. Instead of bombing military targets in the south, they began to bomb London and other cities.

England Survives the Blitz German bombers first appeared over London late on September 7, 1940. All through the night, relays of aircraft showered high explosives and firebombs on the sprawling capital. The bombing continued for 57 nights in a row and then sporadically until the next May. These bombing attacks are known as "the Blitz." Much of London was destroyed, and thousands of people lost their lives.

London did not break under the Blitz. Defiantly, Parliament continued to meet. Citizens carried on their daily lives, seeking protection in shelters and then emerging to resume their routines when the all-clear sounded. Even Churchill and the British king and queen chose to support Londoners by joining them in bomb shelters rather than fleeing to the countryside.

German planes continued to bomb London and other cities off and on until May 1941. But contrary to Hitler's hopes, the Luftwaffe could not gain air superiority over Britain, and British morale was not destroyed. In fact, the bombing only made the British more determined to turn back the enemy. Operation Sea Lion was a failure.

>> The Battle of Britain started in July 1940, but by September, Hitler decided on a new tactic. Hitler believed the British would surrender if he targeted civilians, so he began a daily bombing campaign. London was Hitler's first target.

Bounce to Activate Gallery

Hitler's "New Order" As Nazi forces rampaged across Europe, Hitler expanded his plan to build a "new order" in the occupied lands. Hitler's new order grew out of his racial obsessions. He set up puppet governments in Western European countries that were peopled by light-skinned Europeans, whom Hitler and his followers believed to be an Aryan "master race." The Slavs of Eastern Europe were considered to be an inferior "race." They were shoved aside to provide more "living space" for Germans.

To the Nazis, occupied lands were an economic resource to be plundered and looted. The Nazis systematically stripped conquered nations of their works of art, factories, and other resources. To counter resistance movements that emerged in occupied countries, the Nazis took savage revenge, shooting hostages and torturing prisoners.

War in North Africa and the Balkans Axis armies also pushed into North Africa and the Balkans. In September 1940, Mussolini ordered forces from Italy's North African colony of Libya into Egypt. When the British army repulsed these invaders, Hitler sent one of his most brilliant commanders, General **Erwin Rommel,** to North Africa. The "Desert Fox," as he was called, chalked up a string of successes in 1941 and 1942. He pushed the British back across the desert toward Cairo, Egypt.

In October 1940, Italian forces invaded Greece. They encountered stiff resistance, and in 1941 German troops once again provided reinforcements. Both Greece and Yugoslavia were added to the growing Axis empire. Even after the Axis triumph, however, Greek and Yugoslav guerrillas plagued the occupying forces. Meanwhile, both Bulgaria and Hungary had joined the Axis alliance. By 1941, the Axis powers or their allies controlled most of Europe.

DESCRIBE Describe how the Axis powers gained control of most of Europe in 1941.

>> Erwin Rommel led the military operation in Libya. Rommel was sent to North Africa to help the Italian forces fight the British. Rommel was an expert at tank warfare.

Nazis Attack the Soviet Union

After the failure in Britain, Hitler turned his military might to a new target—the Soviet Union. The decision to invade the Soviet Union took pressure off Britain. It also proved to be one of Hitler's costliest mistakes.

In June 1941, Hitler broke the Nazi-Soviet Pact by invading the Soviet Union in Operation Barbarossa, a plan which took its name from the medieval Germanic leader, Frederick Barbarossa. Hitler made his motives clear. He wanted to gain "living space" for Germans and to win control of regions rich in resources."If I had the Ural Mountains with their incalculable store of treasures in raw materials," he declared, "Siberia with its vast forests, and the Ukraine with its tremendous wheat fields, Germany under National Socialist leadership would swim in plenty." He also wanted to crush communism in Europe and defeat his powerful rival, Stalin.

A Rapid Advance Hitler unleashed a new blitzkrieg in the Soviet Union. About three million German soldiers invaded. The Germans caught Stalin unprepared. His army was still suffering from the purges that had wiped out many of its top officers.

The Soviets lost two and a half million soldiers trying to fend off the invaders. As they were forced back, Soviet troops destroyed factories and farm equipment and burned crops to keep them out of enemy hands. But they could not stop the German war machine. By autumn, the Nazis had smashed deep into the Soviet Union and were poised to take Moscow and Leningrad (present-day St. Petersburg).

Winter Halts the Blitzkrieg There, however, the German advance stalled. Like Napoleon's Grand Army in 1812, Hitler's forces were not prepared for the fury of "General Winter." By early December, temperatures plunged to 0°F (-18°C).

Cold was a killer. German troops had set out in summer and had no warm winter uniforms. Fuel froze in tanks, and much of the Germans' mechanized equipment was useless. Thousands of German soldiers starved or froze to death.

Siege of Leningrad The Soviets, meanwhile, suffered appalling hardships. In September 1941, the two-and-a-half-year siege of Leningrad began. Food was rationed to two pieces of bread a day. Desperate Leningraders ate almost anything. For example, they boiled wallpaper scraped off walls because its paste was said to contain potato flour.

Although more than a million Leningraders died during the siege, the city did not fall to the Germans. Hoping to gain some relief for his exhausted people, Stalin urged Britain to open a second front in Western Europe. Although Churchill could not offer much real help, the two powers did agree to work together.

IDENTIFY SUPPORTING DETAILS Why did Hitler nullify the Nazi-Soviet Pact by invading the Soviet Union?

U.S. Involvement in the War

When the war began in 1939, the United States declared its neutrality. Although isolationist feeling remained strong, many Americans, including President Franklin Delano Roosevelt, sympathized with those who battled the Axis powers. In time, Roosevelt found ways around the Neutrality Acts to provide aid, including for Britain, as it stood alone against Hitler.

Roosevelt Supports the Allies In March 1941, FDR persuaded Congress to pass the **Lend-Lease Act.** It allowed him to sell or lend war materials to "any country whose defense the President deems vital to the defense of the United States." The United States, said Roosevelt, would not be drawn into the war, but it would become "the arsenal of democracy," supplying arms to those who were fighting for freedom.

To show further support, Roosevelt met secretly with Churchill on a warship in the Atlantic in August 1941. The two leaders issued the **Atlantic Charter,** which set goals for the war—"the final destruction of the Nazi tyranny"—and for the postwar world. They pledged to support "the right of all peoples to choose the form of government under which they will live" and called for a "permanent system of general security."

Growing Tensions with Japan Although Roosevelt viewed Hitler as the greatest menace to world peace, it was tensions with Japan that finally brought the United States into the war. The United States held several possessions in the Pacific, including the Philippines and Hawaii.

When war broke out in Europe in 1939, the Japanese saw a chance to grab European possessions in Southeast Asia. Japanese forces took control across Asia and the Pacific. Japan claimed that its mission was to help Asians escape Western colonial rule. In fact, the real goal was a Japanese

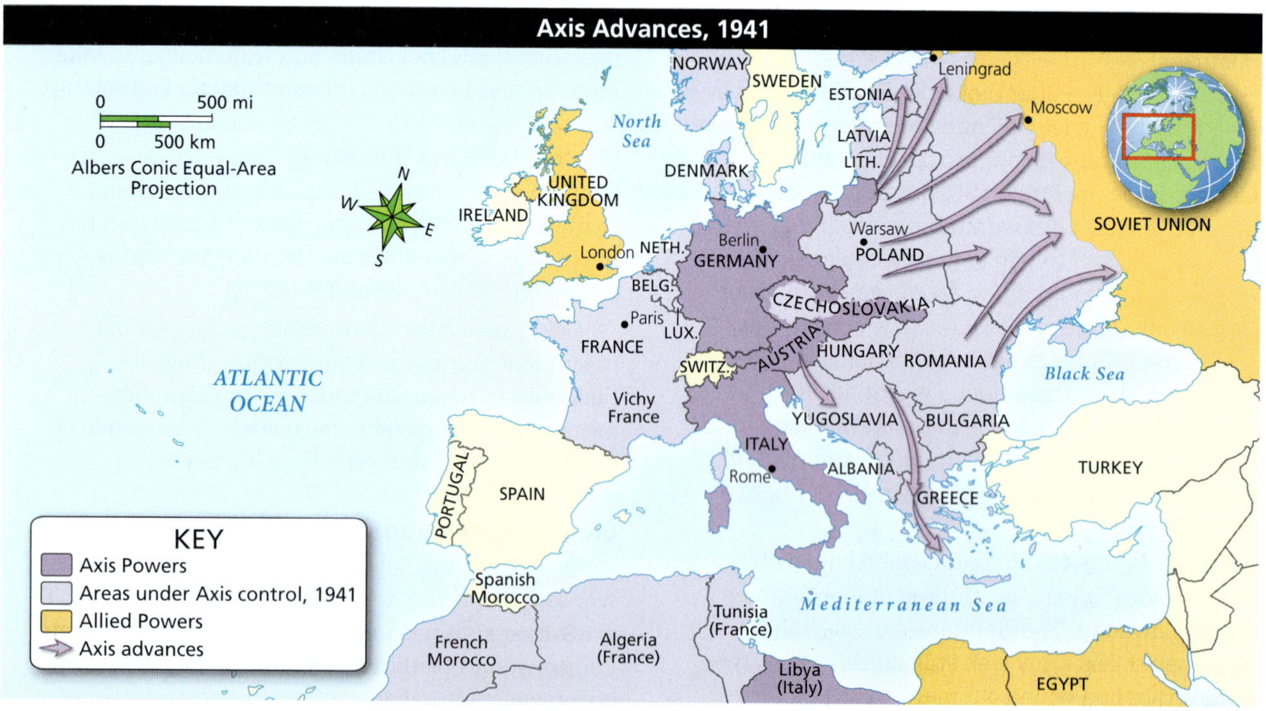

>> The Soviet Union joined the Allies after Germany's invasion. **Analyze Maps** How might this new enemy affect Germany's war effort in geographic terms?

empire in Asia. The rich resources of the region, including oil, rubber, and tin, would be of immense value in fighting Japan's war against the Chinese.

In 1940, with Europeans distracted by war, Japan advanced into French Indochina and the Dutch East Indies. In response, the United States banned the sale of war materials, such as iron, steel, and oil, to Japan. Japanese leaders saw this move as a threat to Japan's economy and its Asian sphere of influence.

Japan and the United States held talks to ease the growing tension. But extreme militarists were gaining power in Japan, including General **Hideki Tojo** who became prime minister in 1941. Prior to the war, Tojo had strongly supported the invasion of China and the formation of the alliance with Germany and Italy. Tojo and other militarists hoped to seize more lands in Asia and the Pacific and believed the United States was interfering with their plans.

The Attack on Pearl Harbor With talks at a standstill, General Tojo ordered a surprise attack. Early on December 7, 1941, Japanese airplanes bombed the American fleet at Pearl Harbor in Hawaii. The attack took the lives of about 2,400 people and destroyed battleships and aircraft.

The next day, a grim-faced President Roosevelt told the nation that December 7 was "a date which will live in infamy." He asked Congress to declare war on Japan. On December 11, Germany and Italy, as Japan's allies, declared war on the United States.

Japanese Victories in the Pacific In the long run, the Japanese attack on Pearl Harbor would be as serious a mistake as Hitler's invasion of the Soviet Union. But in the months immediately after Pearl Harbor, European and American possessions in the Pacific fell one by one to the Japanese.

The Japanese captured the Philippines and other islands held by the United States. They overran the British colonies of Hong Kong, Burma, and Malaya, advanced deeper into the Dutch East Indies, and completed the takeover of French Indochina. By 1942, the Japanese empire stretched from Southeast Asia to the western Pacific Ocean.

The Japanese invaders treated the Chinese, Filipinos, Malaysians, and other conquered people with great brutality. In China, the Philippines, Malaysia, and elsewhere, they killed and tortured civilians. They seized food crops, destroyed cities and towns, and made local people into slave laborers. Whatever welcome the Japanese had first met as "liberators" soon turned to hatred. In the Philippines, Indochina, and elsewhere, resistance forces organized to wage guerrilla warfare against the Japanese invaders.

>> On Sunday morning, December 7, 1941, the U.S. naval base at Pearl Harbor, Hawaii, was jolted awake by a surprise air attack. Japanese planes dropped bombs and torpedoes, stunning Americans.

IDENTIFY CENTRAL ISSUES Why did Japanese leaders view the United States as an enemy?

ASSESSMENT

1. **Integrate Information** How were people of occupied territories treated by the Axis powers?
2. **Describe** Explain why Hitler's blitzkrieg tactics were successful at the beginning of the war.
3. **Synthesize** What was the role of Winston Churchill during World War II?
4. **Describe** Explain the purpose of Hitler's "new order."
5. **Synthesize** What role did Japanese imperialism play in igniting World War II?

>> The Warsaw Uprising ended on October 2, 1944. The entire civilian population of the Warsaw ghetto was expelled; most were sent to labor and death camps.

Bounce to Activate Flipped Video

7.3 Hitler came to power in the midst of the Great Depression, promising to end reparations, create jobs, and defy the hated Versailles treaty by rearming Germany. Hitler also played on anti-Semitism, which had existed for centuries in Europe. Hitler saw Jews as a separate, inferior race whom he blamed for Germany's defeat in World War I. He launched a campaign against the Jews, which began with persecution and escalated to mass murder.

>> Objectives

Identify the roots of Nazi persecution of the Jews.

Describe how the Nazis carried out a program of genocide.

Describe the various acts of Jewish resistance.

Summarize the response of the Allies to the Holocaust.

>> Key Terms

concentration camp
crematorium
Holocaust
Auschwitz

The Holocaust

The Nazi Campaign Against the Jews

Early Persecution The Nuremberg Laws of 1935 put Nazi racist ideology into practice. They removed citizenship from German Jews and banned marriage between Jews and non-Jews. Before long, the Nazis imposed other restrictions that forced Jews from their jobs and homes and embarked on escalating violence and terror against Jews. Schools and the Hitler Youth Movement taught children that Jews were "polluting" German society and culture.

Anti-Semitic propaganda triggered one of the most violent early attacks on Jews. In November 1938, Nazi-led mobs smashed windows, looted, and destroyed Jewish homes, businesses, and places of worship. This wave of violence in Germany and Austria became known as Kristallnacht, or Night of Broken Glass.

Nazi Concentration Camps After gaining power in 1933, the Nazis began rounding up political opponents and placing them in **concentration camps,** detention centers for civilians who were considered enemies of the state. Before long, they were sending Jews, communists, and others they despised to these camps.

By 1934, Hitler had given Heinrich Himmler the power to take full control of the concentration camps throughout Germany.

After World War II began, the Nazis built many more camps for Jews from Poland and other parts of Eastern Europe as well as resistance fighters, Roma (Gypsies), Slavs, and other "racially undesirable elements." The physically and mentally disabled, homosexuals, and ordinary criminals were also sent to the camps. So, too, were political and religious leaders who spoke out against the Nazis.

During the war, Nazis used people in the camps as forced laborers, who. had to produce weapons and other goods for the German war effort. They faced brutal mistreatment, hunger, disease, and execution. Hundreds of thousands of people were murdered.

> "I was 9 weeks in Majdanek, 9 weeks, you see, 9 weeks! And I never washed my face the whole 9 weeks because then in the barracks there was no water. We had to go out, you know, in a shed, washing the face, or needing to go to the toilet."
>
> —Solomon Radasky, a Holocaust Survivor

Brutal Medical Experiments In some camps, Nazi doctors conducted painful and deadly medical experiments on prisoners. They tested dangerous new drugs on prisoners and tried out treatments designed to help Axis forces survive injuries. They also ran experiments to try to prove Nazi racial ideas.

Josef Mengele, a physician at the notorious Auschwitz concentration camp, conducted experiments to see how different ethnic groups responded to contagious diseases such as malaria or yellow fever. Still other experiments were linked to the Nazi goal of sterilizing people they claimed were "inferior races."

Hitler's "Final Solution" As Nazi troops advanced into Eastern Europe, they forced Jews in Poland and elsewhere to live in ghettos, or restricted areas where they were sealed off from the surrounding city. By 1941, however, Hitler and other Nazi had devised what they called the "Final Solution to the Jewish question." Their goal was the extermination of all European Jews. This campaign of genocide eventually became known as the **Holocaust.**

Hitler took steps to carry out his Final Solution. After the Nazi invasion of the Soviet Union in 1941, mobile killing units followed the German army and murdered over a million Jewish men, women, and children in Eastern Europe.

Nazi Concentration Camps, 1933–1945

>> **Analyze Maps** Where were the death camps located? How did this location reflect the goals of the "Final Solution"?

Bounce to Activate Map

Hitler then had six "death camps" built in Poland. There, the Nazis shipped Jews and others marked for extermination from all over occupied Europe. Nazi engineers designed efficient means of killing millions of men, women, and children.

As the prisoners reached the camps, they were stripped of their clothes and valuables. Their heads were shaved. Guards separated men from women, and children from their parents. The young, elderly, and sick were murdered immediately. Falsely told they were to be disinfected, they were herded into fake "shower rooms" and gassed. Then their bodies were burned in specially designed **crematoriums.** The Nazis worked younger, healthier prisoners to death or used them for their inhumane "medical" experiments.

By June 1945, the Nazis had massacred more than six million Jews. Almost as many other "undesirable" people were killed as well.

SYNTHESIZE Describe the escalation of Hitler's campaign against the Jews.

>> Anne Frank was one of over a million Jewish children who was murdered by the Nazis or died of disease in the horrifying conditions of the concentration camps. She and her family lived in hiding in Amsterdam for over two years until they were found and sent to concentration camps. Anne's diary remains a key document of the Holocaust.

Jewish Resistance

Jewish people resisted the Nazis even though they knew their efforts could not succeed. In the early 1940s, Jews in the ghettos of Eastern Europe at times took up arms. The largest uprising occurred in the Warsaw ghetto in occupied Poland.

The Warsaw Ghetto Uprising In July 1942, the Nazis began sending Polish Jews from the Warsaw ghetto to the Treblinka death camp and to slave labor camps. As the mass deportations continued, Jewish groups organized an underground resistance movement.

By the spring of 1943, the German plan to liquidate the Warsaw ghetto was clear, and resistance groups planned a full-scale revolt. Armed with smuggled weapons and homemade bombs, the Jews took over the ghetto and prepared to fight to the end.

After holding out for a month, the resistance forces were crushed. The ghetto was in ruins, and thousands were killed in the fighting. Any survivors were sent to death camps or forced labor camps. Although the uprising was doomed, the courage of the resistance inspired uprisings elsewhere

Continuing Resistance A few Jews escaped the Warsaw ghetto and from ghettos elsewhere in Eastern Europe. About 25,000 Jews, many of them teenagers, joined resistance groups waging guerrilla warfare against the Nazis. These fighters were called partisans. Some joined Soviet units or formed their own Jewish units. In Western Europe, Jews were active in the French and Belgian resistance movements.

Jewish resistance took different forms. In addition to armed uprisings and fighting with guerrilla forces, a few Jews challenged Nazi death camps. Uprisings occurred at Treblinka and Sobibor. In October 1944, a group of Jews in **Auschwitz,** the largest Nazi death camp, destroyed one of the gas chambers.

Jews also resisted by hiding or sending their children into hiding. And despite Nazi persecution, they preserved their culture and traditions as best they could.

Hiding Jews In some parts of Europe, friends, neighbors, or even strangers protected Jews. When Mussolini undertook a vicious campaign against Italian Jews, peasants hid Jews in their villages. Denmark and Bulgaria saved almost all their Jewish populations. The Danish resistance movement, assisted by many common citizens, coordinated the flight of over 7,000 Jews to safety in nearby Sweden.

Many individuals who were not Jewish took great risks to save Jewish lives. One of the best-known stories of the Holocaust is about Anne Frank and her tale of silent resistance. Anne and her family hid for just over two years in her father's Amsterdam office building, while eight people from the office worked together to secretly feed and care for the family in hiding. There are many similar stories of courageous citizens who helped to hide and protect Jewish friends, neighbors, and strangers.

Most people, however, closed their eyes to what was happening. Many people collaborated, or cooperated, with the Nazis, actively taking part in killing Jews or informing on Jews in hiding. In France, the Vichy government helped ship thousands of Jews to their deaths. Strict immigration policies in many Western countries as well as conscious efforts to block Jewish immigration prevented many Jews from gaining refuge elsewhere.

INFER Explain why the Jews in the Warsaw Ghetto decided to fight back.

>> Passengers on the refugee ship *St. Louis* were turned away from Cuba and the U.S. In June 1939, the ship was forced to return to Europe and an uncertain fate.

The Allies Respond to the Holocaust

Even before the war started, some people outside Germany expressed concern about the Nazi persecution of the Jews. Still, the response was limited. The United States and other countries could have accepted many more Jewish refugees from Germany and Austria.

The Question of Jewish Refugees In the summer of 1938, delegates from 32 countries met in France to discuss the "refugee problem." During the nine-day meeting, delegates expressed sympathy for the refugees, but most countries, including the United States and Britain, offered excuses for not accepting more refugees. In the midst of the Great Depression, many Americans worried that refugees would take jobs away from them and overburden social welfare programs. Widespread racial prejudices among the Allies, including anti-Semitic attitudes, also played a role in the failure to admit more Jewish refugees.

In 1939, the United States refused asylum to Jewish refugees on board the ship the *St. Louis*. The passengers were forced to return to Germany.

On the eve of World War II, Britain briefly lifted some restrictions and accepted almost 10,000 mostly Jewish children from Nazi Europe. Their parents were not allowed to accompany the children, and many children never saw their parents again.

The Allies Take Limited Action After the war began, the Allies were mostly concerned with military strategy. Throughout 1940 and 1941, Britain was fighting the war against the Nazis alone. Even when reliable reports concerning the murder of the Jews started to surface, the Allies were slow to respond. Despite urgent calls from resistance groups in occupied Europe, the Allies did not undertake any military operations.

By 1942, the Allies knew that Jews were being taken to death camps in Poland, but often kept this information classified. They refused to release early photographs taken of the camps. Over the next two years, both Britain and the United States considered the idea of bombing Auschwitz, but neither country took action, focusing instead on their ultimate war aim to defeat the Nazis. The only way to rescue Jews, argued some U.S. officials, was to win the war as fast as possible.

President Roosevelt began to respond to reports of Jewish genocide in 1944. He established the War Refugee Board, a government agency that worked with the Red Cross to save thousands of Eastern

European Jews. Its greatest success was due to the brave actions of Raoul Wallenberg, a Swedish diplomat, in Hungary. Wallenberg issued thousands of Swedish passports to Hungarian Jews, which saved them from being deported to Auschwitz. Overall, the War Refugee Board is credited with saving as many as 200,000 Jews.

The Liberation of the Concentration Camps

The Allies only became fully aware of the enormity of the Nazi genocide program toward the end of the war, as Soviet and American troops began liberating the camps. These liberators, hardened by war, were not prepared to see the piles of dead bodies, the warehouses full of human hair and jewelry, the ashes from the crematoriums, or the half-dead, emaciated survivors.

Soviet forces were the first to liberate a major Nazi camp in Majdanek, Poland. The Nazis had been surprised by the rapid Soviet advance and attempted to destroy the evidence of mass murders by demolishing the camp. In the summer of 1944, the Soviets also liberated the Belzec, Sobibor, and Treblinka killing centers. By January 1945, the Soviets had liberated Auschwitz.

American and British forces also liberated many camps in Germany. On April 11, 1945, U.S. forces freed more than 20,000 prisoners at Buchenwald. British forces liberated concentration camps in northern Germany, and in mid-April 1945 freed more than 60,000 prisoners from the Bergen-Belsen concentration camp.

Most of the prisoners they released were in critical condition because of a typhus epidemic. More than 10,000 prisoners died within a few weeks of liberation from the effects of malnutrition.

Impact of the Holocaust By 1945, the Nazis had massacred some six million Jews in the Holocaust, two-thirds of European Jews. Nearly five million other people were killed as well. The scale and savagery of the Holocaust are unequaled in history. The Nazis deliberately set out to destroy the Jews for no reason other than their religious and ethnic heritage. Today, the record of that slaughter is a vivid reminder of the monstrous results of racism and intolerance.

Survivors of the Holocaust often had nowhere to go in Europe. Their homes, villages, and communities had been destroyed. Many ended up in refugee camps in Allied-occupied Germany, waiting to find new homes in other countries. They still faced discrimination, however, and many countries refused to accept them.

As the horrors of the Holocaust were revealed, worldwide support for an independent Jewish

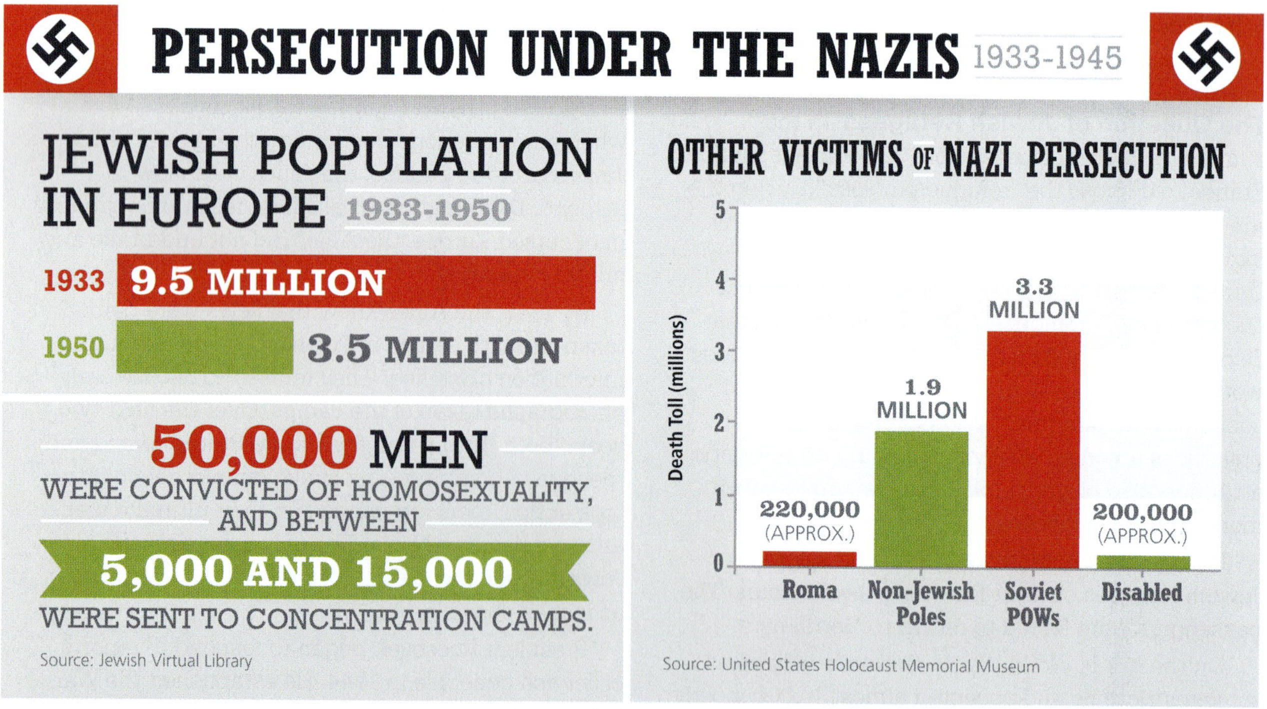

>> **Analyze Information** Besides the Jewish population, what was the next-largest group of victims of Nazi persecution? Why do you think that group was targeted?

homeland increased. On May 14, 1948, Jewish leader David Ben-Gurion proclaimed the establishment of the State of Israel in the former British Palestine Mandate, site of the ancient Jewish kingdom of Israel. Many displaced Holocaust survivors immigrated to Israel to make a new start.

The Holocaust had a significant impact on international law. The term "genocide" for an attempt to deliberately destroy a race was created in 1944 to describe the Nazi Final Solution. Four years later, nations signed the Convention on the Prevention and Punishment of the Crime of Genocide which established genocide as a crime that could be prosecuted in international courts.

Today, people in the United States and around the world are working to make sure the Holocaust is not forgotten. Holocaust museums can be found in many states and countries. Some of the concentration camps, such as Auschwitz, have been preserved and stand as authentic memorials to honor those who died and those who survived.

DRAW CONCLUSIONS Why were Soviet and American forces finally able to liberate many concentration camp victims?

>> Holocaust museums around the world attract millions of visitors each year. Their goal is to remind the world of the horrors of genocide.

Bounce to Activate Gallery

ASSESSMENT

1. **Synthesize** In what was Hitler's campaign against German Jews rooted?
2. **Compare and Contrast** Describe the difference between Hitler's "Final Solution" and the Nazis' earlier persecution of the Jews.
3. **Recall** In what ways did Jews resist Nazi persecution?
4. **Infer** Why did the Allied Powers refuse admittance to Jewish refugees before Hitler's launch of the "Final Solution"?
5. **Synthesize** Why are people from around the world making sure the Holocaust is not forgotten?

Primary Sources

The Diary of a Young Girl: Anne Frank

Introduction

In 1933, Adolf Hitler was elected Chancellor of Germany. During World War II, his Nazi Party rounded up European Jews, many of whom were transported to death camps. Anne Frank was a young Jewish girl who hid with her family in small concealed rooms in her father's office. Frank kept a diary from June 12, 1942 to August 1, 1944, when her family's hiding place was discovered. She died in a concentration camp in 1945. Frank's father survived and published her diary to share Anne's story with the world.

>> Anne Frank

Primary Source

Saturday, June 20, 1942

My father was thirty-six when he married my mother, who was then twenty-five. My sister Margot was born in 1926 in Frankfort-on-Main. I followed on June 12, 1929, and, as we are Jewish, we emigrated to Holland in 1933, where my father was appointed Managing Director of Travies N.V. This firm is in close relationship with the firm of Kolen & Co. in the same building, of which my father is a partner.

The rest of our family, however, felt the full impact of Hitler's anti-Jewish laws, so life was filled with anxiety. In 1938 after the pogroms [organized killing and other persecution of Jews], my two uncles (my mother's brothers) escaped to the U.S.A. My old grandmother came to us, she was then seventy-three. After May 1940 good times rapidly fled: first the war, then the capitulation [surrender], followed by the arrival of the Germans, which is when the sufferings of us Jews really began.

ANALYZE SEQUENCE List the chronology of events that Anne Frank describes in this passage from June 20. What does this sequence of events suggest about life for European Jews during the 1930s and early 1940s?

Anti-Jewish decrees followed each other in quick succession. Jews must wear a yellow star. Jews must hand in their bicycles. Jews are banned from trains and are forbidden to drive. Jews are only allowed to do their shopping between three and five o'clock and then only in shops which bear the placard [sign] "Jewish shop." Jews must be indoors by eight o'clock and cannot even sit in their own gardens after that hour. Jews are forbidden to visit theaters, cinemas, and other places of entertainment. Jews may not take part in public sports. Swimming baths, tennis courts, hockey fields, and other sports grounds are all prohibited to them. Jews may not visit Christians. Jews must go to Jewish schools, and many more restrictions of a similar kind.

So we could not do this and were forbidden to do that. But life went on in spite of it all. Jopie [Jacqueline van Mearsen, Anne's best friend] used to say to me, "You're scared to do anything, because it may be forbidden." Our freedom was strictly limited. Yet things were still bearable.

DRAW CONCLUSIONS Choose a decree described in this passage, and explain how it limited Jews' rights and freedoms.

Thursday, November 19, 1942

Countless friends and acquaintances have gone to a terrible fate. Evening after evening the green and gray army lorries [trucks] trundle [roll] past. The Germans ring at every front door to inquire if there are any Jews living in the house. If there are, then the whole family has to go at once. If they don't find any, they go on to the next house. No one has a chance of evading [avoiding] them unless one goes into hiding. Often they go around us with lists, and only ring when they know they can get a good haul. Sometimes they let them off for cash—so much per head, it seems like the slave hunts of olden times. But it's certainly no joke; it's much too tragic for that. In the evenings when it's dark, I often see rows of good, innocent people accompanied by crying children, walking on and on, in charge of a couple of these chaps, bullied and knocked about until they almost drop. No one is spared—old people, babies, expectant mothers, the sick—each and all join in the march of death.

How fortunate we are here, so well cared for and undisturbed. We wouldn't have to worry about all this misery were it not that we are so anxious about all those dear to us whom we can no longer help.

I feel wicked sleeping in a warm bed, while my dearest friends have been knocked down or have fallen into a gutter somewhere out in the cold night. I get frightened when I think of close friends who have now been delivered into the hands of the cruelest brutes that walk the earth. And all because they are Jews!

SUMMARIZE As Frank describes in her diary, how has life changed for Jews from June to November 1942?

Wednesday, May 3, 1944

Why all this destruction? The question is very understandable, but no one has found a satisfactory answer to it so far. Yes, why do they make still more gigantic planes, still heavier bombs and, at the same time, prefabricated [mass-produced] houses for reconstruction? Why should millions be spent daily on the war and yet there's not a penny available for medical services, artists, or for poor people?

Why do some people have to starve, while there are surpluses [extra amounts] rotting in other parts of the world? Oh, why are people so crazy?

Saturday, July 15, 1944

In spite of everything I still believe that people are really good at heart. I simply can't build up my hopes on a foundation consisting of confusion, misery, and death. I see the world gradually being turned into a wilderness, I hear the ever approaching thunder, which will destroy us too, I can feel the sufferings of millions and yet, if I look up into the heavens, I think that it will all come right, that this cruelty too will end, and that peace and tranquility [calm] will return again.

EXPLAIN AN ARGUMENT Why does Frank describe people as "crazy"? What problems does she observe?

ASSESSMENT

1. **Draw Inferences** What was the purpose of the restrictions the Nazis imposed on Jews? What were the effects of these laws?
2. **Analyze Style and Rhetoric** How would you describe the tone of Frank's diary? How does she relate to her subject matter?
3. **Determine Central Ideas** How does reading Frank's diary differ from reading a secondary source about the Holocaust? What might her diary teach readers today that other sources cannot?

>> Women learned new skills in order to participate in the war effort. In some countries, they served in combat and worked in manufacturing. Women also offered day care for children of those who worked or served.

Bounce to Activate Flipped Video

7.4 As 1942 began, the Allies were in trouble. German bombers flew unrelenting raids over Britain, and the German army advanced deep into the Soviet Union. In the Pacific, the Japanese onslaught seemed unstoppable. But helped by extraordinary efforts on the home front and a series of military victories, the tide was about to turn.

>> Objectives

Understand how nations committed all of their resources to fighting World War II.

Explain how the Allies began to push back the Axis powers in Europe and the Pacific.

Describe the Normandy landings and the Allied advance toward Germany.

>> Key Terms

Franklin Delano Roosevelt
Winston Churchill
Joseph Stalin
internment
Rosie the Riveter
aircraft carrier
Dwight Eisenhower
Stalingrad
D-Day
Yalta Conference
Dwight Eisenhower

The Allies Turn the Tide

A Commitment to Total War

Like the Axis powers they were fighting, the Allies committed themselves to total war. In total war, nations devote all of their resources to the war effort.

Governments Redirect Resources To achieve maximum war production, democratic governments in the United States and Great Britain increased their economic and political power. They directed economic resources into the war effort, ordering factories to stop making cars or refrigerators and to turn out airplanes or tanks instead.

They raised money by holding war bond drives. By buying bonds, citizens lent their government certain sums of money that would be returned with interest later.

Wartime economic policies placed limits on individual economic freedoms. Governments implemented programs to ration, or control, the amount of certain vital goods consumers could buy. Rationed items included rubber, tin, gasoline, and certain food items. Prices and wages were also regulated. In the United States, the war stimulated the economy by creating millions of new jobs. Unemployment, which had remained high during the Great Depression, was almost wiped out.

Limits on Individual Rights Under the pressures of war, even democratic governments limited the rights of citizens. They censored the press and used propaganda to win public support for the war. In the United States and Canada, racial prejudice and concerns about security led to the **internment,** or confinement during wartime, of citizens of Japanese descent. Japanese Americans on the West Coast and Japanese Canadians were forced to move to camps inland, where conditions were very poor.

In Britain, Germans, Austrians, and Italians were subjected to internment, although some of them, including Jewish refugees from Nazi Germany, were released. Some 40 years later, both the United States and Canada provided former internees with reparations, or payment for damages. For most, the compensation came too late.

Women Help Win the War As men joined the military, millions of women around the world replaced them in essential war industry jobs. Women, symbolized by the character **"Rosie the Riveter"** in the United States, built ships and planes and produced munitions.

British and American women served in the armed forces in many auxiliary roles—driving ambulances, delivering airplanes, and decoding messages. In occupied Europe, women fought in the resistance. Marie Fourcade, a French woman, helped downed Allied pilots escape to safety. Soviet women served in combat roles. Soviet pilot Lily Litvak, for example, shot down 12 German planes before she herself was killed.

IDENTIFY CENTRAL ISSUES What changes did the Allies make at home to ensure that they had sufficient resources for fighting World War II?

Progress on Three Fronts

During 1942 and 1943, the Allies won several victories that would turn the tide of battle. They fought on three main fronts— in North Africa and Italy, in the Soviet Union, and in the Pacific.

Japan Suffers Setbacks In the Pacific, the Japanese suffered their first serious setback at the Battle of the Coral Sea. The battle lasted for five days in May 1942. For the first time in naval history,

WWII GDP COMPARED TO AIRCRAFT AND TANK PRODUCTION 1939–1945

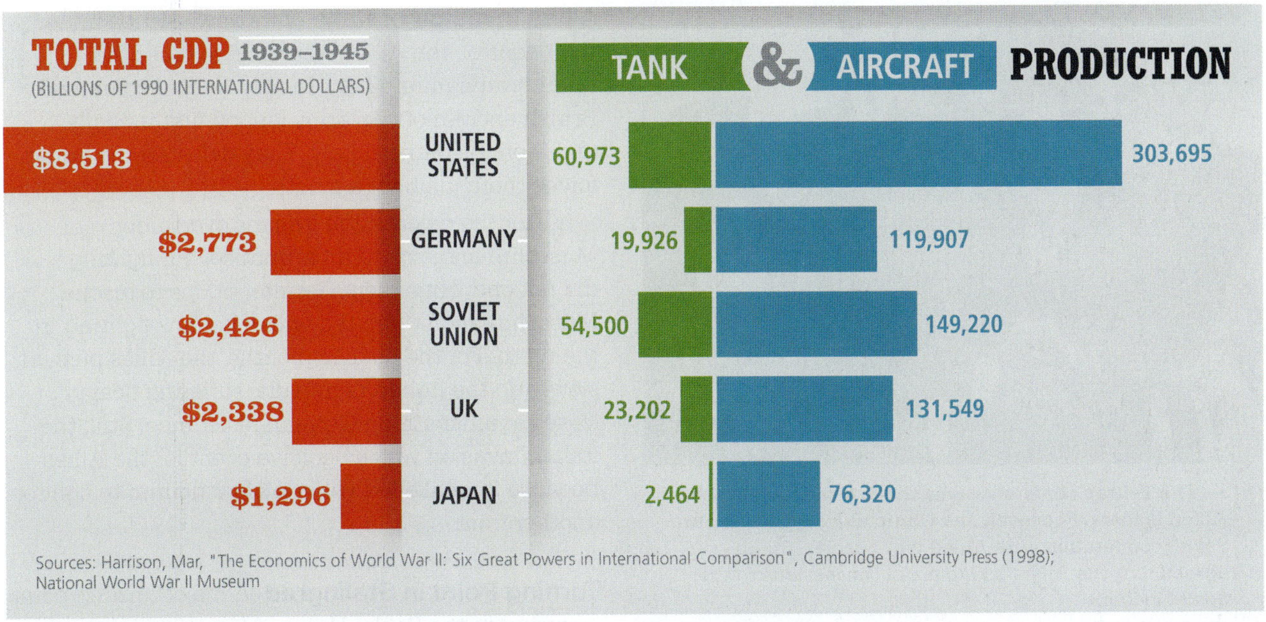

>> The Allies' commitment to all-out war meant a shift in manufacturing from commercial to military goods and equipment. Producing for the war effort also helped keep Americans employed. **Analyze Charts** What generalization can you make about GDP and war production based on the data in the chart?

ships engaged in a battle in which they never even saw each other. Attacks were carried out by planes launched from **aircraft carriers,** or ships that transport aircraft and accommodate the take-off and landing of airplanes. The Allies prevented Japan from seizing several important islands. More importantly, the Americans sank one Japanese aircraft carrier and several cruisers and destroyers.

This Allied victory was followed by an even more impressive win at the Battle of Midway in June 1942, which was also fought entirely from the air. The Americans destroyed four Japanese carriers and more than 250 planes. The battle was a devastating blow to the Japanese. After Midway, Japan was unable to launch any more offensive operations.

The loss was a setback to Japanese prime minister Hideki Tojo. Tojo, who also served as war minister, had been popular during Japan's string of victories. After Midway, he faced increasing opposition at home.

"Big Three" Strategize After the United States entered the war, the Allied leaders met periodically to hammer out their strategy. In 1942, the "Big Three"—**Franklin Delano Roosevelt, Winston Churchill,** and **Joseph Stalin**—agreed to focus on finishing the war in Europe before trying to end the war in Asia.

>> The Tehran conference was the first meeting of the Allied leaders. Roosevelt and Churchill sought to ensure Soviet cooperation with Allied war policies. Stalin agreed, but the Allies had to make concessions to the Soviet leader.

From the outset, the Allies distrusted one another. Churchill and Roosevelt feared that Stalin wanted to dominate Europe. Stalin believed the West wanted to destroy communism. None of the new Allies wanted to risk a breakdown in their alliance, however. At a conference in Tehran, Iran, in late 1943, Churchill and Roosevelt yielded to Stalin by agreeing to let the borders outlined in the Nazi-Soviet Pact stand, against the wishes of Poland's government-in-exile.

Stalin also wanted Roosevelt and Churchill to open a second front against Germany in Western Europe to relieve the pressure on the Soviet Union. Roosevelt and Churchill replied that they did not yet have the resources. Stalin saw the delay as a deliberate policy to weaken the Soviet Union.

Victory in North Africa In North Africa, British forces led by General Bernard Montgomery fought Rommel. After the fierce Battle of El Alamein in November 1942, the Allies finally halted the Desert Fox's advance. Allied tanks drove the Axis back across Libya into Tunisia.

Later in 1942, American General **Dwight Eisenhower** took command of a joint British and American force in Morocco and Algeria. Advancing on Tunisia from the west, the Allies trapped Rommel's army, which surrendered in May 1943.

Allied Invasion of Italy With North Africa under their control, the Allies were able to cross the Mediterranean into Italy. In July 1943, a combined British and American army landed first in Sicily and then in southern Italy. They defeated the Italian forces there in about a month.

After the defeats, the Italians overthrew Mussolini and signed an armistice, but fighting did not end. Hitler sent German troops to rescue Mussolini and stiffen the will of Italians fighting in the north. For the next 18 months, the Allies pushed slowly up the Italian peninsula, suffering heavy losses against strong German resistance. Still, the Italian invasion was a decisive event for the Allies because it weakened Hitler by forcing him to fight on another front.

Turning Point in Stalingrad A major turning point occurred in the Soviet Union. After their lightning advance in 1941, the Germans were stalled outside Moscow and Leningrad. In 1942, Hitler launched a

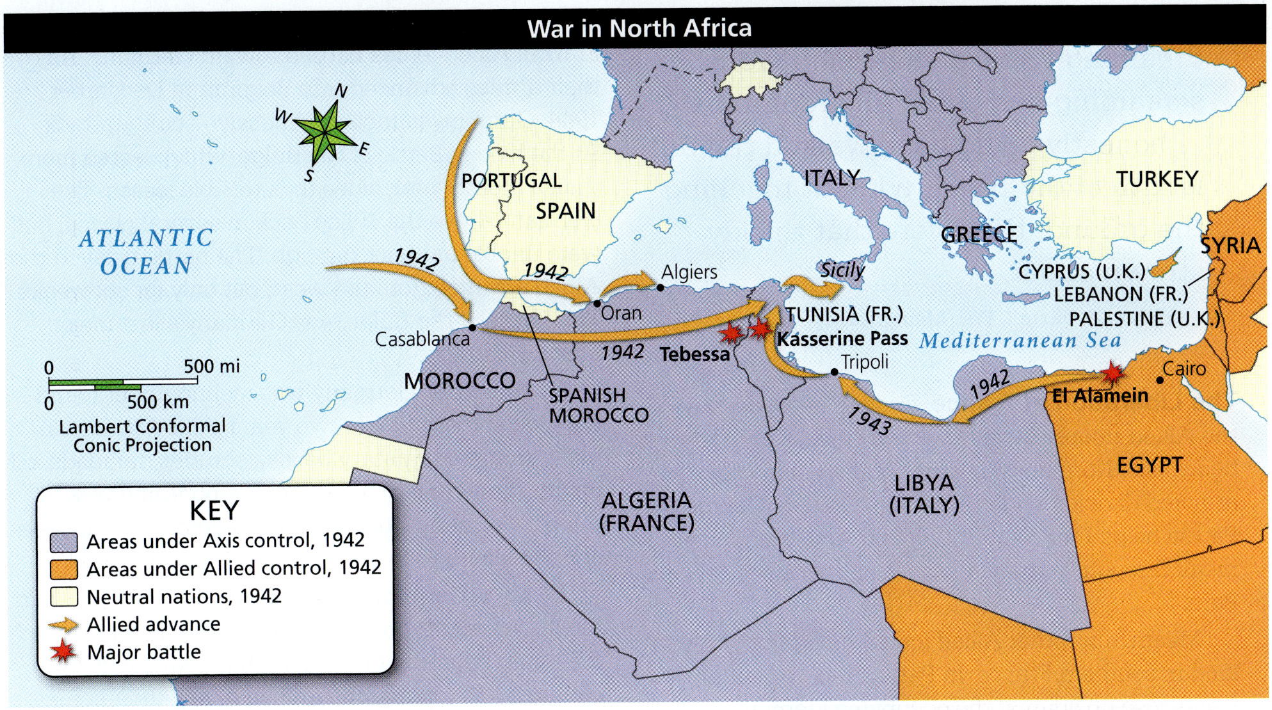

>> The Allies had tremendous challenges to overcome in order to regain control of western Europe and Africa from the Axis. **Analyze Maps** By what two routes did the Allies meet in Tunisia? What do you think was their reason for meeting at this location?

Bounce to Activate 3D Model

new offensive. This time, he aimed for the rich oil fields of the south.

His troops, however, got only as far as **Stalingrad.** The Battle of Stalingrad was one of the costliest of the war. Hitler was determined to capture Stalin's namesake city, and Stalin was equally determined to defend it. The battle began when the Germans surrounded the city.

As winter closed in, a bitter street-by-street, house-by-house struggle raged. A German officer wrote that soldiers fought for two weeks for a single building. Corpses "are strewn in the cellars, on the landings and the staircases," he said. In November, the Soviets encircled their attackers. Trapped, without food or ammunition and with no hope of rescue, the German commander finally surrendered in January 1943.

After the Battle of Stalingrad, the Red Army took the offensive and drove the invaders out of the Soviet Union entirely. Hitler's forces suffered irreplaceable losses of both troops and equipment. By early 1944, Soviet troops were advancing into Eastern Europe.

DRAW CONCLUSIONS What was the impact of the Battles of Coral Sea and Midway?

A Second Front in Europe

By 1944, the Western Allies were at last ready to open a second front in Europe by invading France. General Dwight Eisenhower was made the supreme Allied commander. He and other Allied leaders faced the enormous task of planning the operation and assembling troops and supplies.

To prepare the way for the invasion, Allied bombers flew constant missions over Germany. They targeted factories and destroyed aircraft that might be used against the invasion force. They also destroyed many German cities and bombed railroads and bridges in France that could carry German troops and supplies to the front.

The Normandy Landings The Allies chose June 6, 1944—known as **D-Day**—for the invasion of France. Just before midnight on June 5, Allied planes dropped paratroopers behind enemy lines. Then, at dawn, thousands of ships ferried 156,000 Allied troops across the English Channel. The troops fought their way to shore amid underwater mines and raking machine-gun fire, and the casualties mounted as they reached the shore.

> It all seemed unreal, a sort of dreaming while awake, men were screaming and dying all around me. . . I honestly could have walked the full length of the beach without touching the ground, they were that thickly strewn about.
>
> —Melvin B. Farrell, *War Memories*

The Liberation of France Despite heavy losses, the Allied troops clawed their way inland from the beaches of Normandy. In early August, a massive armored division under American General George S. Patton helped the joint British and American forces break through German defenses and advance toward Paris.

Meanwhile, other Allied forces sailed from Italy to land in southern France. In Paris, French resistance forces rose up against the occupying Germans. Under pressure from all sides, the Germans retreated. On August 25, the Allies entered Paris. Within a month, all of France was free.

Advancing Toward Germany After freeing France, Allied forces battled toward Germany. As their armies advanced into Belgium in December 1944, Germany launched a massive counterattack. At the bloody Battle of the Bulge, which lasted more than a month, both sides took terrible losses. The Germans drove the Allies back in several places, but were unable to break through. The battle delayed the Allied advance from the west, but only for six weeks. The Battle of the Bulge was Germany's last major offensive attack.

By this time, Germany was reeling under round-the-clock bombing. For two years, Allied bombers had hammered military bases, factories, railroads, oil depots, and cities. The goal of the bombing was to cripple Germany's industries and destroy the morale of its civilians.

By 1945, Germany could no longer defend itself in the air. In one 10-day period, bombing almost erased the huge industrial city of Hamburg, killing 40,000 civilians and forcing one million to flee their homes. In February 1945, Allied raids on Dresden killed as many as 135,000 people. The attack on Dresden later stirred controversy because the city was not an industrial center and had long been seen as one of Europe's most beautiful cities.

>> After the Allies had encircled Germany, they continued to bomb German industrial and military centers. German defenses were eliminated, and the European war came to an end. **Analyze Maps** From which direction did the Allies come when they launched the D-Day invasion?

Bounce to Activate Map

Meanwhile, the Soviet army battled through Germany and advanced on Berlin from the east. Hitler's support within Germany was declining, and he had already survived one assassination attempt by senior officers in the German military. By early 1945, the defeat of Germany seemed inevitable.

The Yalta Conference As the Allies advanced on Germany, the Big Three met in the Soviet city of Yalta. At the **Yalta Conference** in February 1945, Roosevelt, Churchill, and Stalin planned for the final stages of the war and for post-war Europe. The meeting took place in an atmosphere of distrust. Stalin insisted that the Soviet Union needed to maintain control of Eastern Europe to be able to protect itself from future aggression. Churchill and Roosevelt favored self-determination for Eastern Europe, which would give people the right to choose their own form of government. Although Stalin agreed to hold free elections in the newly liberated nations of Eastern Europe, he soon showed he had no intention of upholding that promise.

The three leaders also outlined a plan for postwar Germany. It would be temporarily divided into four zones, to be governed by American, French, British, and Soviet forces.

Although the war in Europe was almost over, the Allies were less certain of the outcome in the Pacific. Roosevelt and Churchill were eager to get the Russians to declare war on Japan. Stalin agreed that the Soviet Union would enter the war against Japan within three months of Germany's surrender. In return, Churchill and Roosevelt promised Stalin that the Soviets would take possession of southern Sakhalin Island, the Kuril Islands, and an occupation zone in Korea.

EXPLAIN How did the Allied advance toward Germany limit that country's ability to wage war?

>> The Allies launched a massive invasion on the fortified beaches of Normandy, France. By the end of D-Day, they had a foothold in Nazi-occupied France and had taken a major step toward its liberation.

Bounce to Activate Chart

ASSESSMENT

1. **Draw Conclusions** What actions did democratic governments take during the war that many citizens would probably reject in peace time?
2. **Summarize** Describe the strategy involved in the invasion of Normandy on D-Day.
3. **Identify Cause and Effect** How did the total war effort in the United States affect the nation's economy?
4. **Identify Main Ideas** What was the significance of Hitler's offensive in the southern Soviet Union?
5. **Interpret** How did Allied nations limit the individual rights of certain people during World War II? Why did this happen?

>> The Allied strategy in Europe was to encircle Germany, advancing from the south, west, and east. Here, Soviet and American soldiers meet at the Elbe River in eastern Germany.

Bounce to Activate Flipped Video

7.5 By early spring 1945, the war in Europe was nearing its end. That April, the Allies lost a key leader, Franklin Roosevelt. Though he did not live to see the final victory, he knew the defeat of the Nazis was inevitable.

>> Objectives

Understand the reasons for the final defeat of the Nazis.

Describe how the Allies began to push back the Japanese in the Pacific.

Explain how the dropping of the atomic bombs ended the war.

Describe the aftermath of World War II and the founding of the United Nations.

>> Key Terms

Douglas MacArthur
kamikaze
Hiroshima
Nagasaki
Nuremberg Trials
United Nations (UN)
Bataan Death March
"island-hopping"
Manhattan Project
Harry Truman
V-E Day

Victory for the Allies

End of the War in Europe

Germany Is Defeated By March 1945, the Allies had crossed the Rhine into western Germany. From the east, Soviet troops closed in on Berlin. In late April, American and Soviet soldiers met and shook hands at the Elbe River. All over Europe, Axis armies began to surrender.

In Italy, guerrillas captured and executed Mussolini. As Soviet troops fought their way into Berlin, Hitler committed suicide in his underground bunker. After just 12 years, Hitler's "thousand-year Reich" was bomb-ravaged and in ruins. On May 7, Germany surrendered.

Officially, the war in Europe ended the next day, May 8, 1945, which was proclaimed **V-E Day** (Victory in Europe).

Reasons for Victory in Europe The Allies were able to defeat the Axis powers in Europe for a number of reasons. By 1942, Germany and its allies had to fight on several fronts simultaneously. Hitler insisted on making major military decisions himself and some proved disastrous, especially the invasion of the Soviet Union. He underestimated the ability of the Soviet Union to fight in defense of their land.

The enormous productive capacity of the United States was another factor. By 1944, the United States was producing twice as much as all of the Axis powers combined. Meanwhile, Allied bombing hindered German production. Oil became so scarce because of bombing that the Luftwaffe was almost grounded by the time of the D-Day invasion.

With victory in Europe achieved, the Allies could focus all their attention on defeating Japan in the Pacific. There, they still faced stiff opposition.

INFER Why were the Allies able to defeat the Axis in Europe?

Battles in the Pacific

During the war in the Pacific, the Japanese at first won a string of victories. They also controlled much of China and Southeast Asia. Despite the early Japanese advances, the Allies slowly turned the tide.

Bataan Death March Just hours after Pearl Harbor, the Japanese bombed the Philippines, which the United States had controlled since 1898. By May 1942, the Japanese had gained control of the islands. After the U.S. and Filipino defenders of Bataan surrendered, the Japanese forced their prisoners to march more than 60 miles in incredible heat with almost no water or food. The cruel **Bataan Death March** resulted in the death of as many as 10,000 prisoners.

One survivor described the ordeal as "a macabre litany of heat, dust, starvation, thirst, flies, filth, stench, murder, torture, corpses, and wholesale brutality that numbs the memory." Many Filipino civilians risked—and sometimes lost—their lives to give food and water to captives on the march.

Americans Take the Offensive After the battle of Midway, the United States took the offensive. That summer, United States Marines landed at Guadalcanal in the Solomon Islands. Victory at Guadalcanal marked the beginning of an **"island-hopping"** campaign. The goal of the campaign was to recapture some Japanese-held islands while bypassing others. Each captured island served as a stepping stone to the next objective. As a result, American forces, led by General **Douglas MacArthur,** gradually moved north towards Japan.

On the captured islands, the Americans built air bases to enable them to carry the war closer to Japan. By 1944, the United States Navy, commanded by Admiral Chester Nimitz, was blockading Japan, and American bombers pounded Japanese cities

World War II in the Pacific, 1941–1945

>> After winning the war in Europe, the Allies poured all their resources into victory in the Pacific theater. **Analyze Maps** Based on the map, how would you describe the Allied strategy to defeat Japan?

Bounce to Activate Map

>> Kamikaze attacks were a desperate attempt to ward off American advances. Japanese pilots crashed into Allied aircraft carriers and other ships, killing American sailors along with themselves.

>> President Harry S. Truman and U.S. Secretary of State James Byrne examine a map of Europe aboard the U.S.S. *Augusta* on their way to the "big three" conference in Potsdam in the summer of 1945.

and industries. In October 1944, MacArthur began the fight to retake the Philippines. The British, meanwhile, were pushing Japanese forces back into the jungles of Burma and Malaya. Despite such setbacks, the militarists who dominated the Japanese government rejected any suggestions of surrender.

INFER Why might a naval blockade prove to be an effective war strategy?

End of the War in the Pacific

With war won in Europe, the Allies poured their resources into defeating Japan. By mid-1945, most of the Japanese navy and air force had been destroyed. Yet the Japanese still had an army of two million men. The road to victory, it appeared, would be long and costly.

Japanese Resistance As American forces closed in on Japan, the Japanese put up fierce resistance. By 1944, young Japanese **kamikaze** (kah muh KAH zee) pilots were undertaking suicide missions, crashing their explosive-laden airplanes into American warships.

The next year, in bloody battles on the islands of Iwo Jima from February to March 1945 and Okinawa from April to July 1945, Japanese forces showed that they would fight to the death rather than surrender. Some American officials estimated that an invasion of Japan would cost a million or more casualties.

A Powerful New Weapon While Allied military leaders planned for invasion, scientists offered another way to end the war. Since the early 1900s, scientists had understood that matter, made up of atoms, could be converted into pure energy. In military terms, this meant that by splitting the atom, scientists could create an explosion far more powerful than any yet known.

During the war, Allied scientists—some of them German and Italian refugees—raced to harness the atom before the Germans could. In July 1945, the top secret **Manhattan Project,** successfully tested the first atomic bomb at Alamogordo, New Mexico.

News of this test was brought to the new American president, **Harry Truman.** He realized that the atomic bomb was a terrible new force for destruction. Still, after consulting with his advisors, he decided to use the new weapon against Japan. Truman believed that dropping the atomic bomb would bring the war to a faster end and save American lives.

At the time, Truman was meeting with other Allied leaders in the city of Potsdam, Germany. They issued a warning to Japan to surrender or face "complete destruction" and "utter devastation." When the Japanese ignored the warning, the United States took action.

Dropping of the Atomic Bombs On August 6, 1945, an American plane dropped an atomic bomb over the city of **Hiroshima.** The bomb flattened four square miles and instantly killed more than 70,000 people. In the months that followed, many more would die from radiation sickness, a deadly aftereffect of exposure to radioactive materials.

Truman warned the Japanese that if they did not surrender, they could expect "a rain of ruin from the air, the like of which has never been seen on this Earth." And on August 8, the Soviet Union declared war on Japan and invaded Manchuria. Again, Japanese leaders did not respond. The next day, the United States dropped a second atomic bomb, this time on the city of **Nagasaki.** More than 40,000 people were killed in this second explosion.

Some members of the Japanese cabinet wanted to fight on. Other leaders disagreed. Finally, on August 10, Emperor Hirohito intervened, an action unheard of for a Japanese emperor. He forced his government to surrender. On September 2, 1945, the formal peace treaty was signed on board the American battleship *Missouri,* anchored in Tokyo Bay. After more than five years of fighting, World War II was over.

An Ongoing Controversy Using the atomic bomb against Japan brought a quick end to World War II. It also unleashed terrifying destruction. Ever since, people have debated whether or not the United States should have used the bomb.

For President Truman, using the bomb was a difficult decision. He later explained that he made his decision based only on military considerations. He was concerned that Japan would not surrender without an invasion, and that would cost an enormous loss of lives. After all, the Japanese still had a home army of 2 million.

Critics of Truman's decision argued that Japan was almost defeated at that point and the bomb was not needed. They also claim that by using the atomic bomb, the United States unleashed a dangerous arms race that grew over the next decades.

Growing differences between the United States and the Soviet Union may also have influenced Truman's decision. Truman may have hoped the bomb would impress the Soviets with American power. The debate over Truman's decision has continued to the present.

>> After Japan failed to accept Allied surrender terms, Truman ordered the atomic bombings of Hiroshima and Nagasaki. The destruction was unlike anything the world had seen.

Bounce to Activate Timeline

INTERPRET What was the purpose of the declaration issued by the Allies at Potsdam?

Aftermath of the War

Even as the Allies celebrated victory, the appalling costs of the war began to emerge. The war had killed as many as 50 million people around the world. In Europe alone, over 30 million people had lost their lives, more than half of them civilians. The Soviet Union suffered the worst casualties, with over 20 million dead.

Europe in Ruins "Give me ten years and you will not be able to recognize Germany," Hitler had predicted in 1933. Indeed, Germany in 1945 was an unrecognizable ruin. Parts of Poland, the Soviet Union, Japan, China, and other countries also lay in ruins. Total war had gutted cities, factories, harbors, bridges, railroads, farms, and homes.

>> Representatives of the four major Allies sat in judgment of Nazi war criminals. It was the first time that war criminals were punished for "crimes against humanity" during war.

>> Prime Minister Tojo did not have the same totalitarian powers as Hitler and Mussolini. Still, he was tried and executed for war crimes committed by Japan during the war.

Over 20 million refugees wandered Europe. Amid the devastation, hunger, disease, and mental illness took their toll for years after the fighting ended. As they had after World War I, the Allies faced difficult decisions about the future.

The Holocaust Is Revealed Numbers alone did not tell the story of the Nazi nightmare in Europe or the Japanese brutality in Asia. During the war, the Allies were aware of the existence of Nazi concentration camps and death camps. But only at war's end did they learn the full extent of the inhumanity of the Holocaust. American General Dwight Eisenhower, who visited the camps, was stunned to come "face to face with indisputable evidence of Nazi brutality and ruthless disregard of every sense of decency."

War Crimes Trials At wartime meetings, the Allies had agreed that Axis leaders should be tried for "crimes against humanity." In Germany, the Allies held the **Nuremberg Trials** in the city where Hitler had staged mass rallies in the 1930s. Nearly 200 Germans and Austrians were tried for war crimes. Most were found guilty. A handful of top Nazis received death sentences. Others were imprisoned.

Similar war crimes trials were held in Italy and Japan. Among those found guilty and executed was Japanese prime minister Tojo. Many of those accused of war crimes were never captured or brought to trial. However, the trials showed that political and military leaders could be held accountable for actions in wartime.

The war crimes trials served another purpose. By exposing the savagery of the Axis regimes, they further discredited the totalitarian and militarist ideologies that had led to the war. Yet disturbing questions remained. Why had ordinary people in Germany, Poland, France, and elsewhere accepted—and even collaborated in—Hitler's "Final Solution"? How could the world prevent dictators from again terrorizing Europe or Asia?

The Allies tried to address those issues when they occupied Germany and Japan. The United States felt that strengthening democracy would ensure tolerance and peace. The Western Allies built new governments in occupied Germany and Japan with democratic constitutions to protect the rights of all citizens. In German schools, for example, Nazi textbooks and courses were replaced with a new curriculum that taught democratic principles. In Japan, the occupying forces under General MacArthur helped Japanese politicians to create a new constitution that gave power to the Japanese people, rather than the emperor and military elite.

UNITED NATIONS STRUCTURE

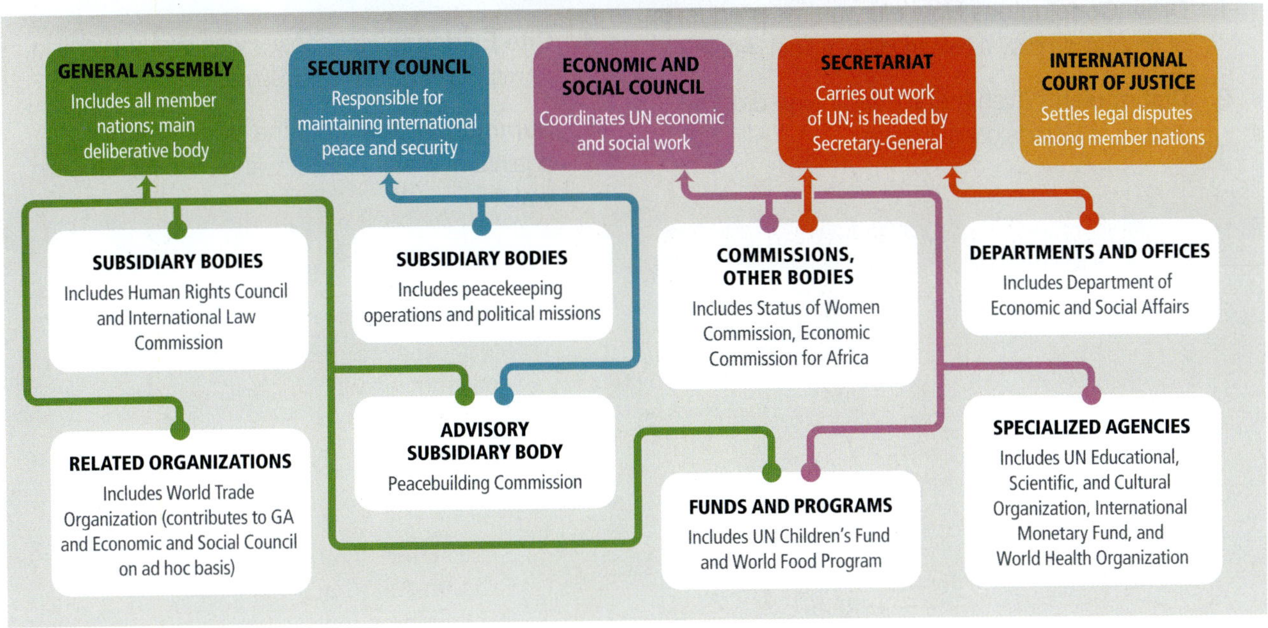

>> The United Nations' originating mission included maintaining international peace and security and solving economic, social, cultural, and humanitarian problems. **Analyze Charts** Under which of the five departments is the World Health Organization?

ANALYZE INFORMATION What were the main goals of the Allies' post-war policies toward the defeated Axis countries?

The United Nations Is Formed

In April 1945, delegates from 50 nations convened in San Francisco to draft a charter for the **United Nations (UN).** They hoped that, unlike the ineffective League of Nations, the UN would be able to keep peace among nations by providing a forum where differences could be resolved peacefully. In the years to follow, the UN would play a greater role in world affairs than its predecessor did.

Structure of the United Nations Under the UN Charter, each of the member nations has one vote in the General Assembly. A much smaller body called the Security Council has greater power. Each of its five permanent members—the United States, the Soviet Union (today Russia), Britain, France, and China—has the right to veto any council decision. The goal was to give these great powers the authority to ensure the peace.

The Security Council has the power to apply economic sanctions or send a peace-keeping military force to try to resolve disputes. Still, differences between the United States and Russia have continued to hamper Security Council decisions. Since the fall of the Soviet Union in 1991, more peacekeeping delegations have been approved.

UN Activities Over time, the work of the UN would go far beyond peacekeeping. It has taken on many issues from human rights and economic development to health and education. UN agencies have worked to end diseases such as smallpox and set up vaccination programs around the world. It has set up refugee camps and organized resettlement programs for refugees from war zones. It has worked with national governments to reduce poverty and protect the environment.

From the first, the UN has faced critics. Some have argued that the UN is ineffective in preventing or resolving conflicts. Others claim that UN resolutions interfere with national governments or are biased. Differences have also risen between rich industrial nations and the poorer nations of the world. And some smaller nations have criticized the veto power of the five permanent members of the Security Council.

CONTRAST What is the difference between the United Nations General Assembly and the Security Council?

ASSESSMENT

1. **Draw Conclusions** How did wartime production of resources play a role in Hitler's final defeat?
2. **Distinguish** Which military campaign did the victory at Guadalcanal initiate?
3. **Infer** Why did Japanese emperor Hirohito call for Japan to surrender?
4. **Cite Evidence** How costly was World War II in terms of European and Soviet casualties?
5. **Summarize** How were the Nazis' "crimes against humanity" dealt with at the Nuremberg trials?

Primary Sources

Charter of the United Nations

Introduction

After World War I, more than 50 countries joined together to form the League of Nations. The League was supposed to prevent future wars by providing a forum for the peaceful settlement of international disputes. The United States never joined the League.

The idea of an international peacekeeping organization was revisited after World War II. In 1944, representatives from the United States, the Soviet Union, China, and the United Kingdom met for several months to work out the framework for the United Nations.

In 1945, representatives of 50 countries met in San Francisco to sign the United Nations charter, bringing the organization into being.

Here are the preamble and first two articles of that charter.

>> The United Nations

Primary Source

WE THE PEOPLES OF THE UNITED NATIONS DETERMINED

- to save succeeding [later] generations from the scourge of war, which twice in our lifetime has brought untold sorrow to mankind, and
- to reaffirm faith in fundamental human rights, in the dignity and worth of the human person, in the equal rights of men and women and of nations large and small, and
- to establish conditions under which justice and respect for the obligations arising from treaties and other sources of international law can be maintained, and
- to promote social progress and better standards of life in larger freedom,

AND FOR THESE ENDS

- to practice tolerance and live together in peace with one another as good neighbours, and
- to unite our strength to maintain international peace and security, and
- to ensure, by the acceptance of principles and the institution of methods, that armed force shall not be used, save in the common interest, and
- to employ international machinery for the promotion of the economic and social advancement of all peoples,

HAVE RESOLVED TO COMBINE OUR EFFORTS TO ACCOMPLISH THESE AIMS

Accordingly, our respective Governments, through representatives assembled in the city of San Francisco, who have exhibited their full powers found to be in good and due form, have agreed to the present Charter of the United Nations and do hereby establish an international organization to be known as the United Nations.

CHAPTER I: PURPOSES AND PRINCIPLES

Article 1

The Purposes of the United Nations are:

1. To maintain international peace and security, and to that end: to take effective collective measures for the prevention and removal of threats to the peace, and for the suppression of acts of aggression or other breaches of the peace, and to bring about by peaceful means, and in conformity with the principles of justice and international law, adjustment or settlement of

international disputes or situations which might lead to a breach of the peace;

2. To develop friendly relations among nations based on respect for the principle of equal rights and self-determination of peoples, and to take other appropriate measures to strengthen universal peace;
3. To achieve international co-operation in solving international problems of an economic, social, cultural, or humanitarian character, and in promoting and encouraging respect for human rights and for fundamental freedoms for all without distinction as to race, sex, language, or religion; and
4. To be a centre for harmonizing the actions of nations in the attainment of these common ends.

Article 2

The Organization and its Members, in pursuit of the Purposes stated in Article 1, shall act in accordance with the following Principles.

1. The Organization is based on the principle of the sovereign equality of all its Members.
2. All Members, in order to ensure to all of them the rights and benefits resulting from membership, shall fulfill in good faith the obligations assumed by them in accordance with the present Charter.
3. All Members shall settle their international disputes by peaceful means in such a manner that international peace and security, and justice, are not endangered.
4. All Members shall refrain in their international relations from the threat or use of force against the territorial integrity or political independence of any state, or in any other manner inconsistent with the Purposes of the United Nations.
5. All Members shall give the United Nations every assistance in any action it takes in accordance with the present Charter, and shall refrain from giving assistance to any state against which the United Nations is taking preventive or enforcement action.
6. The Organization shall ensure that states which are not Members of the United Nations act in accordance with these Principles so far as may be necessary for the maintenance of international peace and security.
7. Nothing contained in the present Charter shall authorize the United Nations to intervene in matters which are essentially within the domestic jurisdiction of any state or shall require the Members to submit such matters to settlement under the present Charter; but this principle shall not prejudice the application of enforcement measures under Chapter VII.

PARAPHRASE Paraphrase Article 1, Purpose 1.

ASSESSMENT

1. **Cite Evidence** The government of a country is inflicting terrible human rights abuses on members of the opposition party. Based on the excerpt, can the United Nations intervene? Cite the part(s) of the charter that support your opinion.
2. **Explain an Argument** Several years of drought in western Asia have led to widespread famine. The UN arranges to bring convoys of food to starving people. One country, a member of the UN, does not want to let relief workers come inside its borders. Does any part of the charter cited here support or rebut the country's position? Explain your answer.
3. **Draw Conclusions** Has the United Nations been successful in its mission "to save succeeding generations from the scourge of war"? Explain your answer.

PEARSON realize™
PearsonSchool.com/CASS

Go online to PearsonSchool.com/CASS and use the texts, quizzes, interactivities, Interactive Reading Notepads, Flipped Videos, and other resources from this Topic to prepare for the Topic Test.

- Etexts
- Quizzes
- Interactivities
- Interactive Reading Notepads
- Flipped Videos

While online you can also check the progress you've made learning the topic and course content by viewing your grades, test scores, and assignment status.

California Topic 7 Quick Study Guide

LESSON SUMMARIES

Use these Lesson Summaries, and the longer versions available online, to review the key ideas for each lesson in this Topic.

Lesson 1: Aggression, Appeasement, and War

Dictators in Germany and Italy, along with militarists in Japan, pursued ambitious goals for empire. Dictators took aggressive actin but met only verbal protests and please for peace from the democracies.

Lesson 2: Axis Powers Advance

The early years of World War II were marked by Axis victories. Germany invaded Poland and soon country after country gave way to Axis powers. With the fall of France in 1940, Britain stood alone in Western Europe.

Lesson 3: The Holocaust

Before the war, Hitler started his policy of killing all people he considered "racially inferior" particularly Jews. Millions were sent to death camps and killed in what became known as the Holocaust. Almost as many other "undesirable" people were killed as well.

Lesson 4: The Allies Turn the Tide

In 1942 and 1943, the tide of the war began to turn as Allied forces won key victories. By 1944, the Allies were ready to open a second front in Europe—with the planned D-Day invasion of France. With France free, focus turned on conquering Germany and defeating Japan.

Lesson 5: Victory for the Allies

After freeing France, Allies closed in on France. Germany surrendered. On August 6, 1945, an American plane dropped an atomic bomb on Hiroshima. Japan surrendered.

VISUAL REVIEW

Use these graphics to review some of the key terms, people, and ideas from this Topic.

Key Causes of World War II

- Failure of Word War I peace settlement, Treaty of Versailles
- Global economic depression
- Fascism, militarism, and imperialism in Germany, Italy, and Japan
- Weakness of the League of Nations
- British and French appeasement

Reasons for Allied Victory

Location of Germany—surrounded by enemies
Location of Japan—dependent on imported goods
Poor military decisions by Axis leaders
Huge productive capability of the United States
Better technology developed and used by Allies

Key Political Leaders

Allies

- Franklin Delano Roosevelt, *U.S. president*
- Harry S Truman, *U.S. president*
- Neville Chamberlain, *British prime minister*
- Winston Churchill, *British prime minister*
- Joseph Stalin, *Soviet dictator*
- Charles de Gaulle, *leader of Free French*

Axis Powers

- Adolf Hitler, *German dictator*
- Benito Mussolini, *Italian dictator*
- Hirohito, *Japanese emperor*
- Tojo Hideki, *Japanese prime minister*

Acts of Aggression

1931	Japan invades Manchuria
1935	Italy invades Ethiopia
1938	Germany annexes Austria and Czechoslovakia
1939	Germany invades Poland. World War II begins

California Topic 7 Assessment

KEY TERMS, PEOPLE, AND IDEAS

1. Why did France, Great Britain, and the United States adopt a policy of **appeasement** in response to Axis aggression?
2. Why did President Truman finally decide to drop the atomic bomb on Japan?
3. Did the **Lend Lease Act** violate America's stand of neutrality during the beginning of WWII? Explain.
4. Why were Hitler's **blitzkrieg** tactics successful at the beginning of the war?
5. What were the expectations of Stalin, Roosevelt, and Churchill at their 1943 strategy meeting in Tehran?
6. What role did **Rosie the Riveter** play in gathering cooperation at home for the war effort?
7. Why did Allied nations limit individual rights during the war? How were rights limited?
8. Why did Hitler begin a campaign against the Jews? How did it become the Final Solution?
9. How did the **Nuremberg Trials** change the way the global community felt about human rights?

CRITICAL THINKING

10. **Analyze Information** How did the rise of the totalitarian state after WWI emphasize extreme nationalism and loyalty?
11. **Summarize** Prepare a chart that lists the causes of WWII. Then consider the statement made by some historians that WWII was the continuation of WWI. Do you agree or disagree? Explain your position.
12. **Draw Conclusions** What post-war plans did the Allies have? What decisions were made at the Yalta Conference?
13. **Compare and Contrast** Why was the United Nations more likely to succeed as an international peace organization than the League of Nations?
14. **Summarize** What was the Bataan Death March?
15. **Analyze Information** Discuss the German, Italian, and Japanese drives for power in the 1930s. Create a graphic organizer that lists the locations and dates of Axis aggression, the motivating factors, and the results of the campaigns. Include the significance of the events to the start of WWII.
16. **Analyze Maps** Look at the map below. What does it show? Why did the Allies choose to invade Normandy? What challenges did the Allies face in the D-Day invasion of Normandy?
17. **Writing Activity** The excerpt below is from a speech Winston Churchill gave in the House of Commons. He voices his opinion of the Munich Pact as a way to approach Axis aggression. Discuss his opinion of the agreement. How effective does he think it will be? What solution does he suggest? Why? Use your knowledge of the Topic and the excerpt to write your answer.

> "And do not suppose that this is the end. This is only the beginning of the reckoning. This is only the first sip, the first foretaste of a bitter cup which will be pre-offered to us year by year unless by a supreme recovery of moral health and martial vigour, we arise again and take our stand for freedom as in the olden time."
>
> —*Winston Churchill, October 5, 1938*

World War II in Europe, 1942–1945

DOCUMENT-BASED QUESTIONS

Perhaps no decision in American history has been more hotly debated than Harry S Truman's decision to drop atomic bombs on Hiroshima and Nagasaki, Japan, in August 1945. Read the documents below, then answer the questions that follow.

DOCUMENT A

"It was believed with deep apprehension that many thousands, probably tens of thousands, of lives of Allied combatants would have been spent in the continuation of our air and sea bombardment and blockade. . . . But the people who would have suffered most, had the war gone on much longer and their country invaded, were the Japanese. One American incendiary air raid on the Tokyo area in March 1945 did more damage and killed and injured more Japanese than the bomb on Hiroshima."

—The Atomic Bomb and the End of World War II by Herbert Feis

DOCUMENT B

"Even without the use of the atomic bombs, the war would probably have ended before an American invasion of Kyushu [one of the four main islands of Japan] became necessary. Conditions in Japan were steadily deteriorating . . . The destruction of cities from B-29 raids, diminishing food supplies, [and] decreased public morale fostered enough discontent to worry the emperor and his advisors. . . . Even without the atomic attacks, it seems likely that the emperor at some point would have acted in the same way that he did in the aftermath of Hiroshima to end the war."

—Prompt and Utter Destruction: Truman and the Use of Atomic Bombs Against Japan by J. Samuel Walker

DOCUMENT C

In the spring of 1945, the Allies' island-hopping campaign in the Pacific brought them closer to the heart of Japan. When American troops invaded first the island of Iwo Jima, then the island of Okinawa, the Japanese fought fiercely, but unsuccessfully, to keep them from gaining control. They knew that the Allies planned to use the islands as a base for an invasion of Japan itself.

Troops Killed at Iwo Jima and Okinawa, 1945

BATTLE	JAPANESE TROOPS KILLED	AMERICAN TROOPS KILLED
Iwo Jima	21,000	6,800
Okinawa	100,000	12,000

SOURCE: Encyclopedia Britannica

DOCUMENT D

18. Which of the following cities experienced the most damage from the American bombing raids?

A. Tokyo
B. Yokohama
C. Hiroshima
D. Osaka

19. Which of the following statement BEST summarizes Herbert Feis's explanation for Truman's use of the atomic bomb?

A. Use of the atomic bombs would cause more destruction.
B. Use of the atomic bombs would save lives.
C. Use of the atomic bombs would ensure surrender.
D. Use of the atomic bombs would make it more difficult for Japan to rebuild its military.

20. J. Samuel Walker's main argument against the use of atomic bombs is that

A. atomic bombs were more destructive than conventional bombs.
B. an American invasion would not have been as destructive as the bombs.
C. the war would have ended anyway.
D. the Japanese emperor opposed the use of atomic bombs.

21. **Writing Tasks** Which of the historians quoted in Documents A and B do you agree with most strongly? Why? Use your knowledge of World War II and specific evidence from the documents to support your opinion.

End-of-Topic Practice

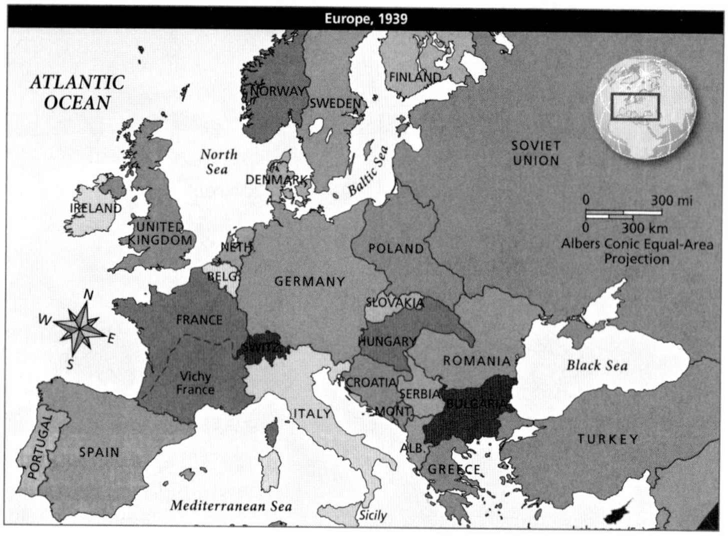

1 Which location on the map was the site of a major historical turning point in 1939?

A Poland, because the USSR invaded it to attack Nazi Germany

B Poland, because Germany invaded it to take the Polish Corridor

C France, because the USSR invaded it to defeat German troops stationed in Paris

D France, because Germany invaded it to knock the French out of the war before attacking Poland

---

2 How is the role of German leader Adolf Hitler during World War II best explained?

F He was responsible for sending German troops to fight against the Italians in 1941.

G He was responsible for the surrender of Britain in 1940 when he sent German planes to bomb London, destroying the city.

H He was responsible for the involvement of the United States in the war by attacking their naval base in Pearl Harbor in 1941.

J He was responsible for the outbreak of the war in 1939 when Germany successfully invaded Poland in a "blitzkrieg" operation.

3 In what ways did people resist Nazi persecution of Jews?

A They joined resistance movements which bombed Nazi military sites.

B They worked to smuggle Jewish children out of Germany and Denmark.

C At the death camps some prisoners fought back by destroying death chambers.

D Many were received by families in the United States who wanted to help them escape persecution.

---

4 When discussing President Roosevelt's Executive Order 9066, Anselm Adams states " I have not said the evacuation was JUST, but that it was justified." How was the order justified at the time it was ordered?

F After Pearl Harbor, the Supreme Court upheld the denial of rights to Japanese and German citizens.

G After Pearl Harbor, the U.S. government felt it necessary to evacuate Japanese citizens to relocation centers.

H During the war, the United States could not accommodate large number of Jewish refugees, so they were ordered to return to Europe.

J During the war, citizens of German and Italian birth were forced to leave the United States.

If you have trouble with. . .				
Question	1	2	3	4
See Lesson	7.1, 7.2	7.1, 7.2	7.3	7.4

[ESSENTIAL QUESTION] How Should We Handle Conflict?

8 The Cold War Era (1945–1991)

>> Protesters on the Berlin Wall, 1989

Enduring Understandings

- Conflicts over Eastern Europe and Germany quickly eroded the wartime alliance between the United States and the Soviet Union.
- In the Cold War, the two superpowers did not confront one another directly, but competed for influence around the world.
- Communism spread to China and Cuba, while Japan became a prosperous democracy.
- The nuclear arms race and the wars in Korea and Vietnam increased Cold War tensions.
- Political oppression and the failures of the command economy led to growing discontent in the Soviet Union and Eastern Europe.
- The Cold War ended with the breakup of the Soviet Union.

NBC LEARN

Hear a former resident of East Germany describe life behind the iron curtain during the Cold War.

Bounce to Activate My Story Video

California Topic 8 Overview

In this Topic, you will learn about the events of the Cold War era. Look at the lesson outline and explore the timeline. As you study this Topic, you will complete the Quest team project.

LESSON OUTLINE

8.1 A New Global Conflict
HSS 10.9, HSS 10.9.1, HSS 10.9.2, HSS 10.9.3, HSS 10.9.8; Analysis CST.1, CST.2, HRE.4, HI.1

8.2 The Western Democracies and Japan
HSS 10.9, HSS 10.9.1; Analysis CST.1, CST.2, HRE.4, HI.1

8.3 Communism in East Asia
HSS 10.9, HSS 10.9.3, HSS 10.9.4; Analysis CST.1, CST.2, HRE.4, HI.1

8.4 War in Southeast Asia
HSS 10.9, HSS 10.9.2, HSS 10.9.3; Analysis CST.1, CST.2, HRE.4, HI.1

8.5 The Cold War Ends
HSS 10.9.5, HSS 10.9.7; Analysis CST.1, CST.2, HRE.4, HI.1

Key Events of the Cold War

1945 World War II ends.

1949 Germany is divided.

1950–1953 Korean War.

1959 Fidel Castro leads communist revolution in Cuba.

1961 Berlin Wall is built.

1964 U.S. enters Vietnam War.

1975 Vietnam War ends.

1989 Eastern Europeans overthrow communist rulers.

1991 Soviet Union breaks up and the Cold War ends.

1945 1955 1965 1975 1985 1995

QUEST! TEAM PROJECT

Launching a Seminar

Did the end of the Cold War make the world safer? You are part of an international affairs seminar for a Cold War Studies institute. In this Quest, you will prepare a presentation that addresses that question.

STEP 1
Review what you already know about the rivalry between the U.S. and the Soviet Union after WWII. Read and evaluate the primary sources. Ask questions.

STEP 2
In addition to the primary sources, interview one or two people who lived through that era. Gather all your information. Divide the groups into YES or NO groups. Create a preliminary outline of your presentation.

STEP 3
As you prepare your presentations, use charts, timelines, and maps to support your viewpoint. Review, edit, and revise.

STEP 4
Consider opposing arguments. Then have the "institute" members vote on a decision. What did you learn from the opposing group? Reflect on the effect of the Cold War on present international affairs.

PEARSON realize PearsonSchool.com/CASS
Go ONLINE for complete Quest materials
VIDEO ETEXT WRITING RUBRIC PDF ASSESSMENT

>> Churchill, Truman, and Stalin shake hands at the Potsdam Conference, held in Germany in July, 1945. Still at war with Japan, the leaders of the wartime alliance hid the growing tensions among them.

Bounce to Activate Flipped Video

8.1 Amid the rubble of war, a new power structure emerged. In Europe, Germany was defeated. France and Britain were exhausted. Two other powers, the United States and the Soviet Union, emerged as superpowers, nations with the economic resources and military might to dominate the globe. The United States abandoned its traditional policy of isolationism to counter what President Truman saw as the communist threat.

>> Objectives

Summarize how the outcome of World War II contributed to the development of the Cold War.

Identify continuing Cold War conflicts in Germany and Eastern Europe.

Explain the growth of the nuclear arms race.

Analyze how the Cold War became a global conflict.

Compare the United States and the Soviet Union in the Cold War.

>> Key Terms

superpower
Cold War
Truman Doctrine
containment
Marshall Plan
North Atlantic Treaty Organization (NATO)
Warsaw Pact
détente
Fidel Castro
John F. Kennedy
ideology
Nikita Khrushchev
Leonid Brezhnev

A New Global Conflict

Wartime Alliance Breaks Apart

Tensions Grow Among the Allies During the war, the Soviet Union and the nations of the West had cooperated to defeat Nazi Germany. However, differences between the two nations were long apparent before the end of WWII. The relationship had long been a tense one. The United States did not trust Soviet Russia and remained concerned about Joseph Stalin's tyrannical rule of his country. An embargo that the United States imposed against Germany was extended to include Russia.

In turn, the Russians resented the refusal of the United States, during the 1920s, to recognize their government and to accept them as a legitimate part of the international community. They also blamed the late entry of the United States into WWII for the deaths of millions of Russians. By 1945, the wartime alliance was crumbling. Conflicting ideologies and mutual distrust soon led to the conflict known as the Cold War.

The **Cold War** was a state of tension and hostility between nations aligned with the United States on one side, and the Soviet

Union on the other side. There was no armed conflict between the United States and the Soviet Union, the major rivals during the Cold War.

At wartime conferences and postwar discussions, the Allies had forged a united front. At the Yalta Conference, Churchill and Roosevelt accepted some of Stalin's demands regarding Eastern Europe. They also agreed to the Allied occupation of Germany and the principle of reparations. Despite these agreements, tensions among the Allies deepened once the war ended, helping to create a divided world during the Cold War.

The Cold War Begins At first, the focus of the Cold War was Eastern Europe. Stalin had two main goals in Eastern Europe. First, he wanted to spread communism into the area. Second, he wanted to create a buffer zone of friendly governments as a defense against Germany, which had invaded Russia during World War I and again in 1941.

As the Red Army pushed German forces out of Eastern Europe, it left behind occupying forces. The Soviet dictator pointed out that the United States was not consulting the Soviet Union about peace terms for Italy or Japan, both of which were defeated and occupied by American and British troops. In the same way, the Soviet Union would determine the fate of the Eastern European lands that it occupied.

Roosevelt and Churchill rejected Stalin's view, making him promise "free elections" in Eastern Europe. Stalin ignored that pledge. Most Eastern European countries had existing Communist parties, many of which had actively resisted the Nazis during the war. Backed by the Red Army, these local Communists in Poland, Czechoslovakia, and elsewhere destroyed rival political parties and even assassinated democratic leaders. By 1948, pro-Soviet communist governments were in place throughout Eastern Europe.

GENERATE EXPLANATIONS What postwar issues caused the Western Allies and the Soviet Union to disagree?

Soviet Aggression Grows

Stalin soon showed his aggressive intentions outside of Eastern Europe. In Greece, Stalin backed communist rebels who were fighting to overturn a right-wing monarchy supported by Britain. By 1947, however, Britain could no longer afford to defend Greece. Stalin was also menacing Turkey and the vital shipping lane through the Dardanelles.

The Iron Curtain In 1946, Winston Churchill, former prime minister of Britain, spoke of how the Soviet Union was sealing off the countries in Eastern Europe that its armies had occupied at the end of World War II. He said an "iron curtain" has descended across the Continent."

In the West, the "iron curtain" became a symbol of the Cold War fear of communism. It described the division of Europe into an "eastern" and a "western" bloc. In the East were the Soviet-dominated, communist countries of Eastern Europe. In the West were the Western democracies led by the United States.

The Truman Doctrine President Truman saw communism as an evil force threatening countries around the world. To deal with the growing communist threat in Greece and Turkey, he took action. On March 12, 1947, Truman outlined a new policy to Congress. The policy, known as the **Truman Doctrine,** was rooted in the idea of **containment,** limiting communism to the areas already under Soviet control. Stalin, however, saw containment as "encirclement" by the capitalist world that wanted to isolate the Soviet Union.

>> The Red Army entered Berlin in April 1945. The Soviets installed communist governments in East Germany and throughout Eastern Europe in the postwar years.

The Truman Doctrine would guide the United States for decades. It made clear that Americans would resist Soviet expansion in Europe or elsewhere in the world. Truman soon sent military and economic aid and advisers to Greece and Turkey so that they could withstand the communist threat.

Marshall Plan Aids Europe Postwar hunger and poverty made Western European lands fertile ground for communist ideas. To strengthen democratic governments, the United States offered a massive aid package called the **Marshall Plan.** Under it, the United States funneled food and economic assistance to Europe to help countries rebuild. Billions of dollars in American aid helped war-shattered Europe recover rapidly and reduced communist influence there.

President Truman also offered aid to the Soviet Union and its satellites, or dependent states, in Eastern Europe. However, Stalin declined and forbade Eastern European countries to accept American aid. Instead, he promised help from the Soviet Union in its place.

A Divided Germany Defeated Germany became another focus of the growing tensions between the Soviet Union and the United States. The Soviets took reparations for their massive war losses by dismantling and moving factories and other resources from its occupation zone to help rebuild the Soviet Union. Above all, the Soviets feared the danger of a restored Germany.

The Western powers also took some reparations, but they wanted to create a stable, democratic Germany. Therefore, they united their zones of occupation and encouraged Germans to rebuild industries with Marshall Plan aid. The Soviets were furious at this move and strengthened their hold on Eastern Germany.

Germany became a divided nation. In West Germany, the Western democracies let the people write a constitution and regain self-government. In East Germany, the Soviets installed a socialist dictatorship tied to Moscow.

>> An airplane brings food and other supplies to Berlin as part of the Berlin Airlift. **Cite Evidence** Based on this image, how much progress has been made in the rebuilding of Berlin? Provide evidence.

The Berlin Airlift Stalin's resentment at Western moves to rebuild Germany triggered a crisis over Berlin. Even though it lay deep within the Soviet zone, the former German capital was occupied by all four victorious Allies. In June 1948, Stalin tried to force the Western Allies out of Berlin by sealing off every railroad and highway into the Western sectors of the city. The Western powers responded to the blockade by mounting a round-the-clock airlift. For more than a year, cargo planes supplied West Berliners with food and fuel. Their success forced the Soviets to end the blockade. Although the West had won a victory in the Cold War, the crisis deepened the hostility between the two camps.

New Alliances Tensions continued to grow. In 1949, the United States, Canada, and ten other countries formed a new military alliance called the **North Atlantic Treaty Organization (NATO).** Members pledged to help one another if any one of them were attacked.

In 1955, the Soviet Union responded by forming its own military alliance, the **Warsaw Pact.** It included the Soviet Union and seven satellites in Eastern Europe. Unlike NATO, however, the Warsaw Pact was often invoked by the Soviets to keep its satellites in order.

The Propaganda War Both sides participated in a propaganda war. The United States spoke of defending capitalism and democracy against communism and totalitarianism. The Soviet Union claimed the moral high ground in the struggle

NATO and Warsaw Pact, 1977

>> Though some countries remained neutral, in general, Western European nations were part of NATO, while Eastern European nations joined the Warsaw Pact. **Analyze Maps** Which Warsaw Pact countries bordered NATO nations?

against Western imperialism. Yet, linked to those stands, both sides sought world power.

IDENTIFY MAIN IDEAS Why did the United States establish the NATO alliance? What was the Soviet Union's response?

Two Opposing Sides in Europe

As the Cold War deepened, the superpowers—the United States and the Soviet Union—faced off against each other in Europe and around the world. For more than 40 years, the Cold War loomed over Europe. In general, the superpowers avoided direct confrontation. Yet several incidents brought Europe to the brink of war.

The Berlin Wall Berlin was a key focus of Cold War tensions. The city was divided into democratic West Berlin and communist East Berlin. In the 1950s, West Berlin became a showcase for West German prosperity. Unhappy with communism, many low-paid East Germans fled into West Berlin.

To stop the flight, the East German government built a wall in 1961 that separated the two sectors of the city. When completed, the Berlin Wall was a massive concrete barrier, topped with barbed wire and patrolled by guards. The wall showed that workers, far from enjoying a communist paradise, had to be forcibly kept from fleeing.

Revolts in Eastern Europe During the Cold War, the Soviet Union had more than 30 divisions of troops stationed across the region. Yet, in East Germany, Poland, Hungary, and elsewhere, unrest simmered. In 1953, about 50,000 workers confronted the Soviet army in the streets of the German capital. The uprising spread to other East German cities, but the protesters could not withstand Soviet tanks.

In 1956, economic woes in Poland touched off riots and strikes. To end the turmoil, the Polish government made some reforms, but dissatisfaction with communism remained. That year, Imre Nagy (nahj), a communist reformer and strong nationalist, gained power in Hungary. He ended one-party rule, ejected Soviet troops, and withdrew from the Warsaw Pact. In response, the Soviet Union invaded Hungary and ended the reforms. Nagy was later executed.

In early 1968, Czechoslovakian leader Alexander Dubcek introduced greater freedom of expression and limited democracy. This movement of freedom became known as the "Prague Spring." Soviet leaders feared that democracy would threaten communist power and Soviet domination. Once again, the Soviets responded with force, sending Warsaw Pact troops to oust Dubcek and end the reforms.

IDENTIFY CAUSE AND EFFECT How was Europe divided following the end of World War II?

The Nuclear Arms Race

One of the most frightening aspects of the Cold War was the arms race. Each side wanted to be able to withstand an attack by the other. At first, the United States, which had the atomic bomb, was the only nuclear power. By 1949, however, the Soviet Union had also developed an atomic bomb. By 1953, both sides in the Cold War had developed the far more destructive military technology—the hydrogen bomb.

The Balance of Terror The United States and the Soviet Union spent vast sums to develop new, more deadly nuclear and conventional weapons. They invested still more to improve "delivery systems"—the bombers, missiles, and submarines to launch these terrifying weapons of mass destruction.

Critics of the arms race argued that a nuclear war would destroy both sides. Yet each superpower wanted to be able to deter the other from launching its nuclear weapons.

By the 1960s, the terrifying possibility of nuclear war led to the idea of mutually assured destruction (MAD), which meant that if one side launched a nuclear attack, the other side would retaliate in kind, and both sides would be destroyed. Even though MAD might discourage nuclear war, the fear of such a conflict haunted the world. In the words of Winston Churchill, the balance of power had become a "balance of terror."

Disarmament Talks To reduce the threat of nuclear war, the two sides met at disarmament talks. Although mutual distrust slowed progress, the rival powers did reach some agreements. In 1963, they agreed to the Nuclear Test Ban Treaty, which prohibited the testing of nuclear weapons in the atmosphere.

In 1969, the United States and the Soviet Union began the Strategic Arms Limitation Talks (SALT) to limit the number of nuclear weapons held by each

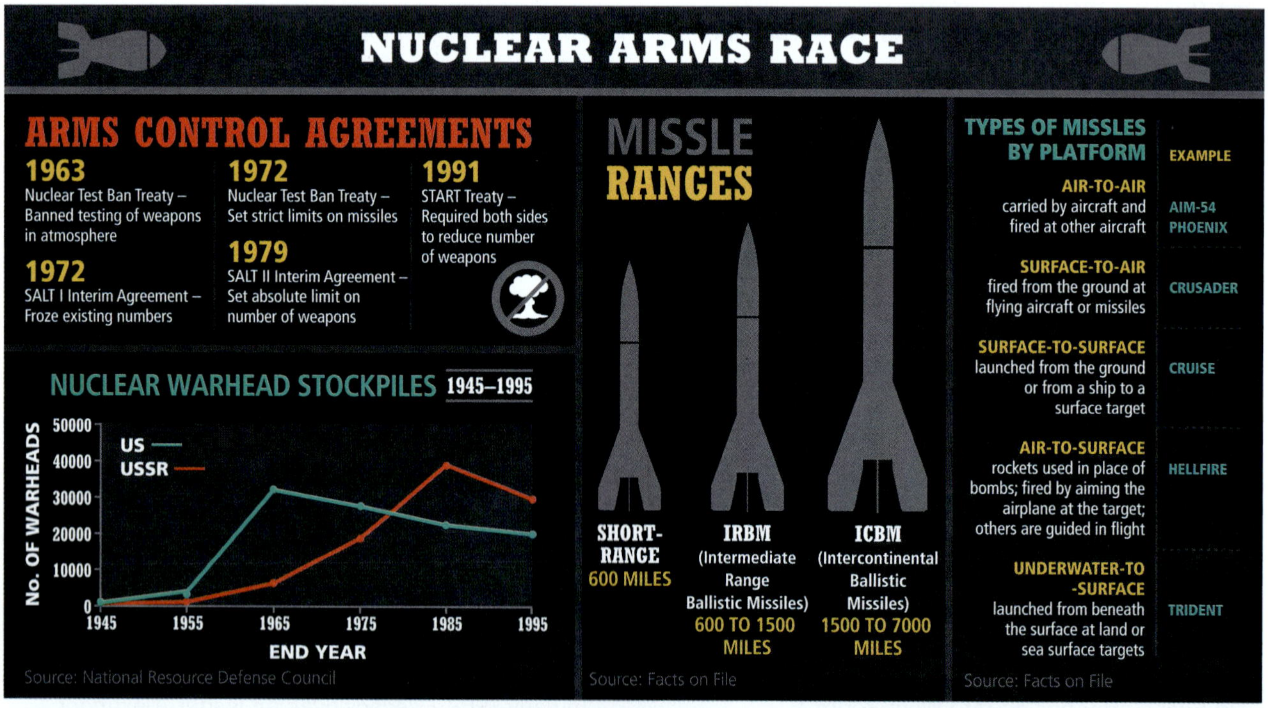

>> **Analyze Charts** Compare the Nuclear Test Ban Treaty of 1963, the SALT II Treaty of 1972, and the START Treaty of 1991. How did each of the later treaties advance beyond the treaty that came before it?

Bounce to Activate Gallery

side. In 1972 and 1979, both sides signed agreements setting these limits.

In 1991, the United States and Russia negotiated a Strategic Arms Reduction Treaty (START), which has been renewed in recent years. These START agreements led to the removal of a large number of nuclear weapons.

An Era of Détente During the 1970s, American and Soviet leaders promoted an era of **détente** (day TAHNT), or relaxation of tensions. Détente brought new agreements to reduce nuclear stockpiles as both sides turned to diplomacy to resolve issues. The era of détente ended in 1979, when the Soviet Union invaded Afghanistan.

Limiting the Spread of Nuclear Weapons By the late 1960s, Britain, France, and China had developed their own nuclear weapons. By then, many world leaders were eager to stop the spread of nuclear weapons. In 1968, dozens of nations signed the Nuclear Non-Proliferation Treaty (NPT). They agreed not to develop nuclear weapons and cooperate in the peaceful use of nuclear energy.

INTEGRATE INFORMATION What factors discouraged the use of nuclear weapons in the Cold War?

>> The United States had many military bases overseas, and its navy played a vital role in maintaining the U.S. presence around the world.

The Cold War Around the World

The superpowers waged the Cold War not only in Europe, but also around the world. By the end of World War II, the Soviets were helping communist forces in China, Korea, and elsewhere. The United States took action to respond to the global threat of communism.

Establishing Alliances and Bases To stop the spread of communism, the United States sought regional alliances with friendly powers. In Europe, it backed NATO. In Asia, the United States promoted another regional alliance, the Southeast-Asia Treaty Organization (SEATO). It included the United States, Britain, France, Australia, Pakistan, Thailand, New Zealand, and the Philippines.

The United States also formed military alliances with individual nations, such as Japan and South Korea. Often, these agreements included the right to set up American military bases. As a result, American bases circled the globe from North America to Europe, Asia, and the islands of the Pacific.

Meanwhile, the Soviet Union formed its own alliances. In addition to the Warsaw Pact in Europe, the Soviet Union formed alliances with newly independent nations in Africa and Asia. However, the Soviet Union had few bases overseas.

Where the Cold War Got Hot Because both superpowers had a global reach, local conflicts in many places played into the Cold War. Often, the United States and its allies supported one side, and the Soviet bloc supported the other. Through such struggles, the superpowers could confront each other indirectly, rather than head to head.

Political shifts around the world added to Cold War tensions. When communist forces won control of mainland China in 1949, the United States feared that a tide of communism would sweep around the world. During this period, European colonies in Africa and Asia battled for independence. Liberation leaders and guerrillas frequently sought help from one or the other Cold War power.

On occasion, the Cold War erupted into "shooting wars," especially in Asia. Both Korea and Vietnam were torn by brutal conflicts in which the United States, the Soviet Union, and China played crucial roles. More commonly, however, the superpowers provided weapons, training, or other aid to opposing forces in Asia, Africa, or Latin America.

The United States and Latin America The United States was especially concerned about the threat of communism in the Western Hemisphere. Seeing reform movements in Latin American countries as communist threats, it backed right-wing, anti-communist dictators and helped topple elected socialist leaders. In 1962, Cuba, a small island nation just 90 miles from Florida, became the chief focus of United States concern.

The Communist Revolution in Cuba In the 1950s, a young lawyer, **Fidel Castro,** organized an armed rebellion against the corrupt dictator who then ruled Cuba. By 1959, Castro had led his tiny guerrilla army to victory and set about transforming the country into a communist state.

During the Cuban Revolution, Castro nationalized, or took over, foreign-owned businesses. He put most land under government control and distributed the rest to peasant farmers. While Castro imposed harsh authoritarian rule, he did at first improve conditions for the poor. But Castro's revolution angered many Cubans, especially from the middle class. Critics were jailed or silenced. Hundreds of thousands of Cubans fled to the United States.

>> The Soviet Union celebrated the anniversary of the Bolshevik Revolution with this military parade in Moscow in 1969.

The United States, alarmed as Castro turned to the Soviet Union for support, attempted to bring down the communist regime next door. In 1961, President **John F. Kennedy** backed a plan by anti-Castro exiles to invade Cuba and lead an uprising against Castro.

The poorly planned plot was a disaster. An invasion force landed at the Bay of Pigs in Cuba, but was quickly crushed. News of the plot helped Castro rally Cuban popular opinion against foreign interference, and the bungled invasion hurt the reputation of the United States.

The Cuban Missile Crisis In 1962, the United States imposed a trade embargo on Cuba. Castro, seeking closer ties with the Soviet Union, let the Soviets build nuclear missile bases in Cuba. The threat of Soviet nuclear bases in its backyard outraged the United States and touched off a dangerous crisis.

In October 1962, President Kennedy imposed a naval blockade on Cuba. Kennedy demanded that the Soviet Union remove its nuclear missiles from Cuba, and for a few tense days, the world faced the risk of nuclear war. Finally, however, Soviet Premier Nikita Khrushchev backed down. He agreed to remove the Soviet missiles, but won a secret pledge from Kennedy to not invade Cuba.

MAKE GENERALIZATIONS How did the United States and the Soviet Union confront each other around the world during the Cold War?

The Soviet Union During the Cold War

Victory in World War II brought few rewards to the Soviet people. Stalin continued his ruthless policies. He filled labor camps with "enemies of the state" and seemed ready to launch new purges when he died in 1953.

Soviet Communism In the Soviet Union, the government controlled most aspects of public life. Communists valued obedience, discipline, and economic security. They sought to spread their communist **ideology,** or value systems and beliefs, around the globe.

The Soviet Union also aimed to spread its command economy to other countries. In a command economy, the government makes most economic decisions. A huge bureaucracy, rather than supply and demand, decided what to produce, how much, and for whom. Government planners in Moscow often had little knowledge of local conditions. The government owned most of the property.

Collectivized agriculture remained so unproductive that the Soviet Union often had to import grain to feed its people. Nor could Russia's command economy match the free-market economies of the West in producing consumer goods. Since workers had lifetime job security, they had little incentive, or reason, to produce better-quality goods.

Stalin's Successors After Stalin's death in 1953, **Nikita Khrushchev** (KROOSH chawf) emerged as the new Soviet leader. In 1956, he shocked top Communist Party members when he publicly denounced Stalin's abuse of power. Khrushchev maintained the Communist Party's tight political control, but he closed prison camps and eased censorship. He called for a "peaceful coexistence" with the West.

Khrushchev's successor, **Leonid Brezhnev** (BREZH nef), held power from the mid-1960s until he died in 1982. Under Brezhnev, dissidents, or people who criticized the government, faced arrest and imprisonment.

>> Americans who feared nuclear war built bomb shelters in their backyards and stocked them with canned goods and other supplies.

Dissidents Resist Despite the risk of harsh punishment, some courageous people dared to criticize the government. Andrei Sakharov (SAH kuh rawf), a brilliant physicist, spoke out against human rights abuses. He was exiled to a remote Soviet city.

Another critic, Aleksandr Solzhenitsyn (sohl zhuh NEET sin), wrote a letter to a friend criticizing Stalin. He was sent to a prison camp. Under Khrushchev, he was released and wrote fictional works that drew on his experiences in Soviet prison camps. His writings were banned in the Soviet Union, and in 1974, he was deported to West Germany. Despite the government's actions, Sakharov and Solzhenitsyn inspired others to resist communist repression and demand greater freedom.

☑ **CHECK UNDERSTANDING** How did the Soviet Union handle critics of its policies?

The United States in the Cold War

The Cold War was not just a military rivalry. It was also a competition between two contrasting economic and political value systems. Unlike the communist countries, the democratic, capitalist countries, led by the United States, gave citizens the freedom to make economic and political choices. These nations valued freedom and prosperity. They held that economic freedom and free market principles helped improve the human condition—especially compared to the command economies of the communist world.

Free Markets While communist countries had command economies, capitalist countries had market economies. In market economies, producers and consumers make economic decisions. Prices are based on supply and demand in a free market. Property is privately owned. Producers compete to offer the best products for the lowest prices. By deciding what to buy, consumers ultimately decide which products are produced. In a free enterprise system, producers who win consumers' business make profits and grow.

The United States economy is basically a market economy. However, the United States and Western Europe have what can be called mixed economies, because their governments have an economic role.

The Cold War at Home Early in the Cold War, fierce anti-communists in the United States warned that Soviet agents were operating everywhere within the country. The House Un-American Activities Committee (HUAC) led a campaign to identify supposed communist sympathizers. In the early 1950s, Senator Joseph McCarthy charged many innocent citizens with harboring communist sympathies. Government probes produced little evidence of subversion. Eventually, the Senate condemned McCarthy's reckless behavior, but not before his charges and the investigations of the HUAC had ruined the careers of thousands of Americans.

The fear of a nuclear war also affected Americans. Some families built fallout shelters, where they could hide in the event of a nuclear bomb. Schools conducted air-raid drills in which children were taught to duck under their desks. Although these measures would not have protected children in a nuclear attack, the drills reflected the widespread fear of nuclear war.

DISTINGUISH How did the United States respond to the threat of communism at home and around the world?

ASSESSMENT

1. **Identify Central Ideas** What foreign policy did the United States establish with the Truman Doctrine?
2. **Make Generalizations** What kinds of conflicts resulted from the global confrontation between the two superpowers?
3. **Infer** How did the buildup of nuclear weapons discourage their actual use?
4. **Cite Evidence** List three occasions when the Soviet Union put down revolts in Eastern Europe during the Cold War.
5. **Compare and Contrast** How were the United States and the Soviet Union alike during the Cold War? How were they different?

8.2 Despite the tensions of the Cold War, the United States enjoyed a period of great prosperity and growth in the postwar decades. Its booming economy became a symbol of the power of capitalism and democratic freedoms in the ongoing propaganda war against communism.

>> New York City was chosen as the headquarters of the new United Nations.

The Western Democracies and Japan

>> Objectives

Analyze the postwar American economy.

Identify developments in American society and government.

Explain how Western Europe rebuilt and moved toward greater unity.

Describe how Japan changed after World War II.

>> Key Terms

suburbanization
interdependence
recession
segregation
discrimination
Dr. Martin Luther King, Jr.
Konrad Adenauer
welfare state
Margaret Thatcher
European Union
gross domestic product (GDP)

Postwar Prosperity in the United States

In the postwar decades, the American economic system flourished. American businesses expanded into markets around the globe. The dollar was the world's strongest currency. Foreigners flocked to invest in American industry and to buy U.S. government bonds. America's wealth was a model for other democracies and a challenge to the stagnant economies of the communist world.

America in a Central Role During the Cold War, the United States was a global political leader. The headquarters of the League of Nations had been symbolically located in neutral Switzerland. The headquarters of the newly formed United Nations was built in New York City.

The United States also played a leading economic role. America had emerged untouched from the horrendous destruction of the Second World War. Other nations needed American goods and services, and foreign trade helped the United States achieve a long postwar boom. The long postwar peace among democratic nations helped to spread this boom worldwide.

An Economic Boom In 1945, the United States produced 50 percent of the world's manufactured goods. Factories soon shifted from making tanks and bombers to peacetime production. With the Cold War looming, government military spending increased, creating many jobs in defense industries.

During the 1950s and 1960s, the American economy was booming. At home, a growing population demanded homes, cars, refrigerators, and thousands of other products. Overseas, American businesses were investing in Europe's recovery and expanding into new markets. American cultural influences spread, and people around the globe enjoyed American movies, television programs, and music—especially jazz and rock and roll.

America's postwar economic strength impacted social systems in the United States. Although segments of the population were left behind, many Americans grew more affluent and moved from the cities to the suburbs. The movement to communities outside an urban core is known as **suburbanization.** Suburbanites typically lived in single-family houses with lawns and access to good schools. Suburban highways allowed residents to commute to work by car.

During the postwar decades, many Americans also moved to the Sunbelt, or the states in the South and Southwest of the United States. Jobs in these states were becoming more plentiful than in the industrialized North. The warmer climate was an added bonus. The availability of air conditioning and water for irrigation helped make the movement to the Sunbelt possible.

>> In the postwar boom, Americans moved out of the cities and into the suburbs, where they could own a home with a yard. **Connect** What role did the car play in the suburbanization of America?

Bounce to Activate Gallery

A Wider Role for Government In the postwar decades, the government's role in the economy grew. Under President Truman, Congress created generous benefits that helped veterans attend college or buy homes. Other Truman programs expanded FDR's New Deal, providing greater security for the elderly and poor.

Truman's successor, Dwight Eisenhower, tried to reduce the government's role in the economy. At the same time, he approved government funding to build a vast interstate highway system. This program spurred the growth of the auto, trucking, and related industries. Highways and home building changed the face of the nation. Suburbanization led to the decay of many inner-city neighborhoods.

The United States and the Global Economy In the postwar decades, the United States profited from the growing global economy. But **interdependence**—mutual dependence of countries on goods, resources, and knowledge from other parts of the world—brought problems, too. In the 1970s, a political crisis in the Middle East led to a global oil shortage and soaring oil prices. In the United States, people waited in long lines for costly gasoline, which made Americans aware of how much they relied on imported oil.

The oil crisis and other economic issues brought periods of **recession,** or economic downturn. For the most part, recessions were fairly mild.

Other economic issues, however, such as competition from nations in Asia and elsewhere posed challenges for the United States. During the 1980s, the United States lost manufacturing jobs to Asia and Latin America. Some American corporations even moved their operations overseas to take advantage of lower wages.

Still, the United States remained a rich nation and a magnet for immigrants. These newcomers came largely from Latin America and Asia. By the 1980s, some Americans were calling for stricter laws to halt illegal immigration.

IDENTIFY MAIN IDEAS How was the U.S. economy linked to the broader global economy during the Cold War?

The United States Responds to New Challenges

The 1950s seemed a peaceful time within the United States. Yet changes were underway that would reshape American society. Among the most far-reaching was the Civil Rights Movement, which sought to ensure the promise of equal opportunity for all Americans.

>> Segregated drinking fountains were a common sight in the southern states.

The Civil Rights Movement Although African Americans had won freedom nearly a century before, many states, especially in the South, denied them equality. **Segregation,** or forced separation, was legal in education and housing. African Americans also faced **discrimination,** or unequal treatment and barriers, in jobs and voting. The Civil Rights Movement of the 1950s and 1960s renewed earlier efforts to end racial injustice.

In 1954, the Supreme Court issued a landmark ruling in *Brown* v. *Board of Education of Topeka.* It declared that segregated schools were unconstitutional. President Eisenhower and his successors used federal power to uphold the order to desegregate public schools.

Martin Luther King, Jr. By 1956, a gifted preacher, **Dr. Martin Luther King, Jr.,** had emerged as a leader of the Civil Rights Movement. Inspired by Gandhi's campaign of civil disobedience in India, King organized boycotts and led peaceful marches to end segregation in the United States. Many Americans of all races joined the Civil Rights Movement. Their courage in the face of sometimes brutal attacks stirred the nation's conscience.

In 1963, at a huge civil rights rally, King made a stirring speech. "I have a dream," he proclaimed, "that one day this nation will rise up and live out the true meaning of its creed: 'We hold these truths to be self-evident, that all men are created equal.'"

>> People from all over the country came to the March on Washington, held on August 28, 1963. Martin Luther King Jr. was a keynote speaker. **Analyze Information** How do the demands on the signs represent the civil rights movement?

Progress and Problems In time, Congress responded. It outlawed segregation in public accommodations, protected the rights of black voters, and required equal access to housing and jobs. Despite these victories, racial prejudice survived, and African Americans faced many economic obstacles. Poverty and unemployment plagued African American communities in urban areas.

Still, the Civil Rights Movement provided wider opportunities. Many African Americans won elected offices or gained top jobs in business and the military.

Other Groups Demand Equality The Civil Rights Movement inspired other groups, such as Native Americans and Latinos, to campaign for equality. Women, too, renewed their efforts to gain equal rights. New civil rights laws banned discrimination based on gender as well as race in hiring and promotion. More women won political office, and some made progress into high positions in business.

The Great Society During the 1960s, the government further expanded social programs to help the poor and disadvantaged. President Lyndon Johnson created a program that he called the Great Society. It funded Medicare, which ensured health care for the elderly, job training and low-cost housing for the poor, and support for education. Many Americans came to rely on these programs in the next decades.

The Conservative Response In the 1980s, conservatives challenged costly social programs and the growth of government. President Ronald Reagan called for cutbacks in government spending on social programs. Congress ended some welfare programs, reduced government regulation of the economy, and cut taxes. At the same time, military spending increased.

Government spending and tax cuts greatly increased the national deficit, the gap between what a government spends and what it takes in through taxes and other sources. As the deficit grew, conservatives crusaded for deeper cuts in social and economic programs. Debate raged about how far to cut spending on programs ranging from education and welfare to environmental protection.

☑ **CITE EXAMPLES** Over time, how did the U.S. government expand opportunities for individuals? Give examples.

Rebuilding Western Europe

The impact of—and recovery from—World War II on the political and economic systems of Europe was profound. With Marshall Plan aid from the United States, Western European countries recovered from

U.S. Military Spending, 1960-1980

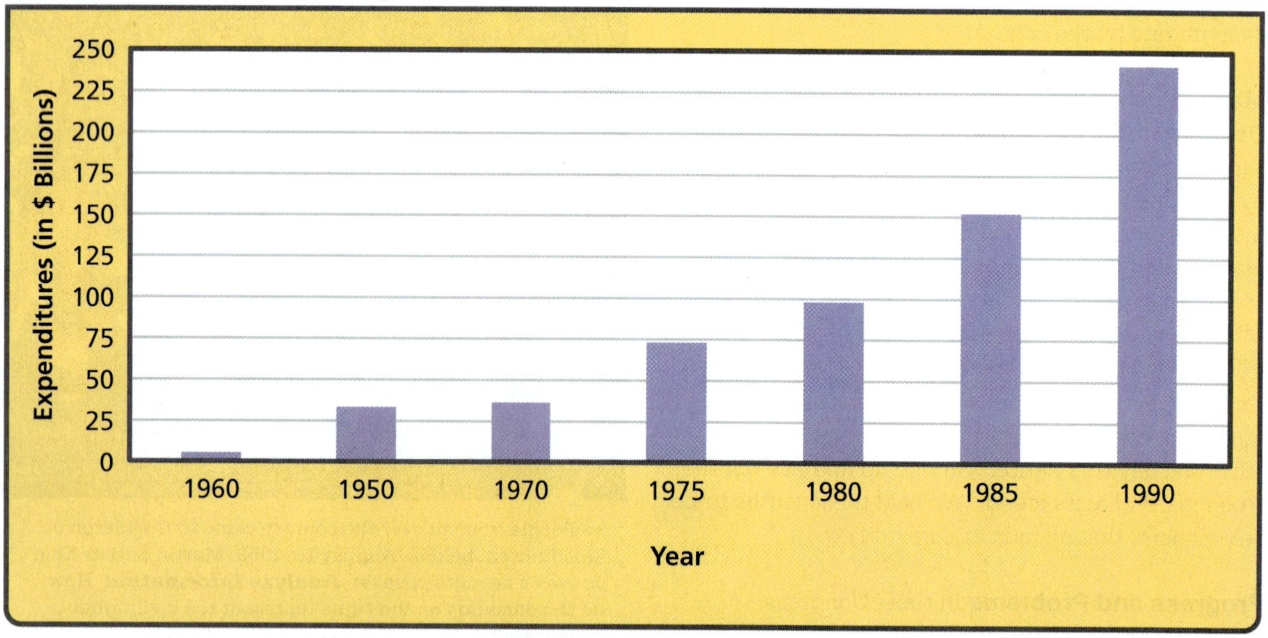

>> **Analyze Charts** U.S. military spending increased dramatically during the Cold War years. In which five-year period did military spending increase the most?

EAST AND WEST GERMANY IN 1968 AN ECONOMIC COMPARISON

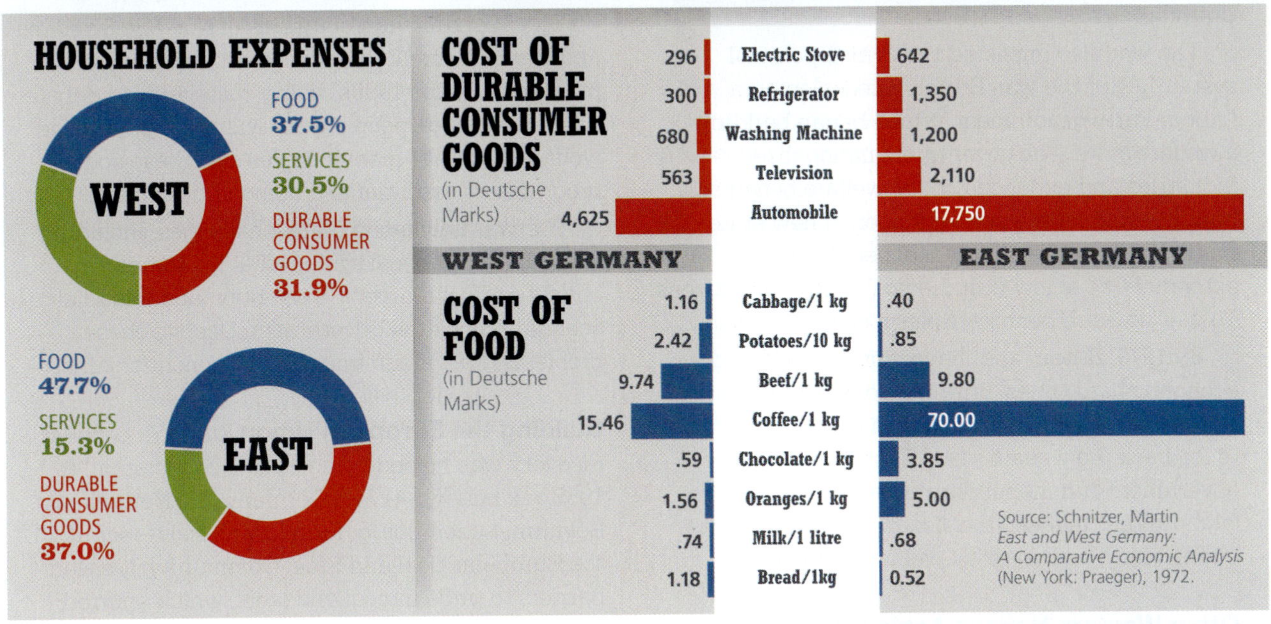

>> **Analyze Charts** What types of goods were expensive in East Germany in 1968? What types of goods were inexpensive?

Bounce to Activate Chart

World War II. They rebuilt industries, farms, and transportation networks destroyed during the war. In the 1950s, economies in Western Europe boomed. Standards of living rose dramatically, and people began to enjoy comforts unheard of in earlier times.

West Germany's Economic Miracle The early postwar years were a desperate time for Germany. People were starving amid a landscape of destruction. The Cold War left Germany divided. West Germany was a member of the Western alliance. East Germany lay in the Soviet orbit. Over the next decades, differences between the two Germanys widened.

Early on, the United States rushed aid to West Germany in order to strengthen it against the communist tide sweeping Eastern Europe. From 1949 to 1963, a strong-minded chancellor, **Konrad Adenauer** (AD eh now er), led West Germans as they rebuilt cities, factories, and trade.

Despite high taxes to pay for the recovery, West Germany created a booming industrial economy. This "economic miracle" raised European fears of a German revival. But West German leaders worked closely with France and the United States in NATO and other international organizations.

While West Germany remained a capitalist country, some later chancellors belonged to the Socialist party. They expanded the **welfare state.** Under this political system, a government keeps most features of a capitalist economy but takes much responsibility for the social and economic needs of its people. In the welfare state, a government provides national health care, unemployment insurance, old-age pensions, and support for qualified students to attend college.

Germany Reunites The postwar decades brought no economic miracle to East Germany. Under communist rule, its economy stagnated. The Soviet Union exploited East German workers and industry for its own benefit. Still, unemployment was low, and East German workers had some basic benefits such as health care and free education.

By 1989, communism was declining in the Soviet Union. Without Soviet power to back them, East Germany's communist leaders were forced out of office. The Berlin Wall was torn down, and in 1990, Germany was reunited.

While Germans welcomed unity, the change brought new challenges. Prosperous West Germans had to pay higher taxes to finance the rebuilding of the east. At the same time, East Germans faced a difficult transition to a market economy.

Britain Recovers World War II left Britain physically battered and economically drained. After the war, Britain could no longer afford its overseas colonies, which demanded independence. Britain gave up global leadership to its close ally, the United States.

The war also impacted the British political system. After the war, British voters elected a Labour Party government, which began building a welfare state. The government nationalized industries and expanded social welfare benefits. It built housing for the poor and opened new state-funded universities. A national health service extended free or low-cost medical care to all citizens. To pay for these benefits, taxes rose tremendously.

By 1979, Britain and the rest of Europe faced economic hard times. Britain's Conservative party, led by **Margaret Thatcher,** won power and set out to roll back the welfare state. Thatcher privatized government-run industries, curbed the power of labor unions, reduced the size of the government bureaucracy, and cut back welfare services.

Other Western Nations Achieve Prosperity

Other nations in Western Europe, including France, the Netherlands, and Belgium, rebuilt after the war, helped by Marshall Plan aid. Like Britain, these Europeans powers had to give up their overseas colonial empires. France faced bloody conflicts in Vietnam and Algeria, which it tried to hold on to in the face of nationalist demands for independence.

The Scandinavian countries of Norway, Sweden, and Denmark created extensive socialist welfare programs. By the 1990s, rising costs revived debate about how much people were willing to pay for the welfare state. Yet many peoples saw these social programs as essential to a democratic society.

Postwar Italy faced many challenges, including a multiparty political system that led to frequent changes of government. Corruption and financial scandals shook the government. Despite these problems, Italy made impressive economic gains.

>> British miners protest the closure of a government-operated coal mine. Many British industries were once again privatized under Prime Minister Margaret Thatcher.

Building the European Union Europe's postwar recovery was helped by economic cooperation. In 1952, six nations—West Germany, the Netherlands, Belgium, Luxembourg, France, and Italy—set up the European Coal and Steel Community. It eased barriers to trade in coal and steel, which spurred economic growth. Later, these nations formed the European Community to expand free trade. Over time, it ended tariffs, or taxes on imports, and allowed workers and capital to move freely across national borders.

In 1993, the European Community was renamed the **European Union** (EU). Since then, it has expanded to include 28 nations, including Britain, Ireland, Denmark, and other European countries. The EU set up a common currency, the euro, which is used by 17 European nations. The EU became a powerful economic force and promoted regional trade and peace by replacing destructive competition with an amazing degree of cooperation.

COMPARE What are some advantages and disadvantages of the welfare state in Europe?

Japan Is Transformed

In 1945, Japan, like Germany, lay in ruins. It had suffered perhaps the most devastating damage of any nation involved in World War II. Tens of thousands of Japanese were homeless and hungry.

Occupation Bring Changes The war had a deep impact on the political system of Japan. Under General Douglas MacArthur, the American military government set two main goals for the occupation of Japan: to destroy militarism and to ensure democratic government. Japan's armed forces were disbanded. War crime trials were held to punish those responsible for wartime atrocities.

In 1946, Japan adopted a new constitution, which set up a parliamentary democracy. Although the Japanese emperor lost all political power, he remained the symbolic head of the nation. Japan renounced war and banned any military forces, except for its own defense.

To build Japanese democracy, American occupying forces backed changes to the economic and social systems. They opened the education system to all people and emphasized legal equality for women. A land-reform program bought out large landowners and gave land to tenant farmers, erasing lingering traces of feudalism in Japan. Other reforms protected the rights of workers.

>> The American occupation of Japan lasted about seven years and resulted in a firm friendship between the former enemies.

Japan and the Cold War By 1950, Japan was on the road to recovery. At the same time, the Cold War was making the United States eager to end the occupation. As the Cold War erupted into armed conflict in nearby Korea, the United States and Japan signed a peace treaty, and in 1952, the occupation ended.

Japan and the United States had close ties during the Cold War. The American military operated out of bases that they had set up in Japan, while Japan enjoyed the protection of the American "nuclear umbrella." The two nations were trading partners, and in time, competitors for global markets.

The Japanese Economic Miracle Between 1950 and 1975, Japan produced its own economic miracle, even more spectacular than Germany's. It chalked up huge jumps in **gross domestic product (GDP).** GDP is the total value of all goods and services produced by a nation in a particular year.

>> Japan became an export powerhouse by building cars, electronics, and other products.

Japan's success was built on producing goods for export. At first, it manufactured textiles. Later, it shifted to selling steel and machinery. By the 1970s, Japanese cars, cameras, and televisions found eager buyers on the world market. Soon, a wide range of Japanese electronic goods were competing with Western, and especially American, products.

Japan's economic miracle was due in part to its new modern factories built after the war. Because Japan spent little on its military, it could invest more in its economy. It benefited from an educated and skilled workforce and imposed tariffs and regulations that limited imports and helped Japanese manufacturers at home.

By the 1980s, Japan was seen as an economic superpower. Its vast trade network reached around the world and resulted in a trade surplus for Japan. By the 1980s, United States manufacturers were angered by what they saw as unfair competition, and the United States pushed Japan to open its economy to more imports. Japan's stunning economic growth ended in the 1990s. However, it continued as a major world economic power.

IDENTIFY What factors explain Japan's economic success in the decades after World War II?

ASSESSMENT

1. **Compare Points of View** How did Democrats and Republicans differ on the best ways to improve opportunity for Americans?
2. **Identify Cause and Effect** What challenges did American democracy face during the 1950s and 1960s? How did Americans respond to these challenges?
3. **Compare** During the Cold War, how was economic development in Western Europe similar to, or different from, that of Japan?
4. **Infer** How would Europe benefit economically from greater unity?
5. **Make Generalizations** How was trade important to the economic development of Western Europe, the United States, and Japan during the postwar decades?

8.3 Civil war raged across China during the late 1940s as Mao Zedong (mow dzuh doong) and his Communist forces fought to overthrow Jiang Jieshi's Nationalists. In 1949, Mao's forces triumphed. The defeated Jiang and his supporters fled to the island of Taiwan. After decades of struggle, China was finally united, with the Chinese Communists in control. They renamed the country the People's Republic of China.

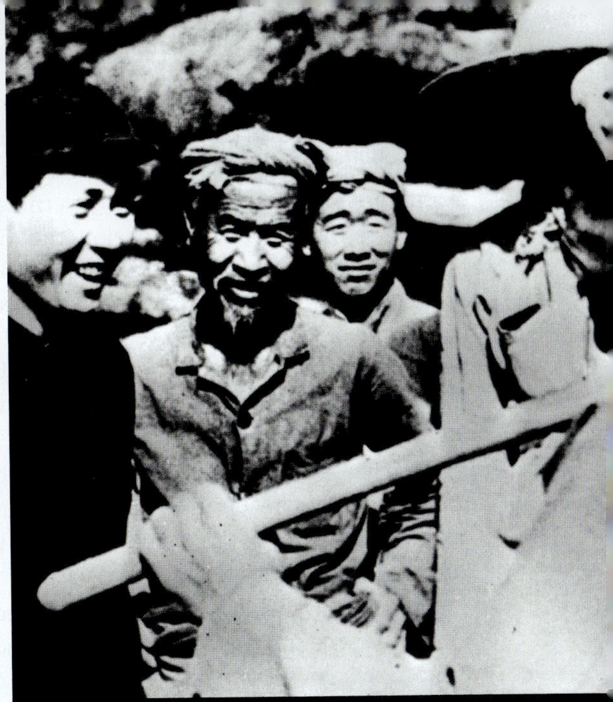

>> The support of Chinese peasants helped Mao Zedong (left) and the communists achieve victory in China's civil war.

Bounce to Activate Flipped Video

Communism in East Asia

>> **Objectives**

Analyze how Mao Zedong turned China into a communist state.

Describe China's role in the Cold War.

Explain the causes and impact of the Korean War.

>> **Key Terms**

Mao Zedong
collectivization
Great Leap Forward
Cultural Revolution
38th parallel
Kim Il Sung
Syngman Rhee
Pusan Perimeter
demilitarized zone

The Chinese Communist Victory

Soon afterward, the Communists conquered Tibet, claiming it was part of China. In 1959, as the Chinese cracked down, Tibet's revered religious leader, the Dalai Lama, was forced to flee to India.

How the Communists Won Mao's victory in China was due to several causes. Mao had won the support of China's huge peasant population. Peasants had long suffered from brutal landlords and crushing taxes. The Communists promised to redistribute land to peasants and end oppression by landlords. Many women backed the Communists, who rejected the old inequalities of Chinese society. Finally, Mao's army outfought Jiang's armies with guerrilla tactics they had perfected fighting the Japanese.

Jiang and the Nationalists who ruled China had failed to end widespread economic hardship. Many Chinese resented corruption in Jiang's government and his reliance on support from Western powers that had long dominated China. Many educated Chinese were drawn to the Communists' vision of a new China free from foreign domination.

Remaking Chinese Life Once in power, the Communists set out to turn China from a backward peasant society into a modern industrial nation. Communist ideology guided the government's efforts to reshape the economy and society that China had inherited from the dynastic period. To build socialism, China nationalized all businesses and tried to increase coal and steel output and develop heavy industry. With help from the Soviet Union, the Chinese built hydroelectric plants, dams, and railroads.

To boost agriculture, Mao at first distributed land to peasants. Before long, the government imposed **collectivization,** or the forced pooling of peasant land and labor to increase productivity.

To increase literacy, reformers simplified Chinese characters, making it easier to learn to read and write. Schools were opened for young and old. The Communists sent health-care workers to remote rural areas. Although many had little training, they did help reduce disease and teach better hygiene.

Under China's new constitution, women won equality under the law. Although Chinese woman made real progress, they did not enjoy full equality. Often paid less than men for the same work, women toiled in fields and factories while still maintaining the home.

>> The government forced collectivization on Chinese farmers in order to increase productivity. During the Great Leap Forward, tractors arrive at a farmer's cooperative.

Communism Takes a Huge Toll Like Lenin in the Soviet Union, Mao Zedong built a one-party, Communist totalitarian state. Communist ideology replaced Confucian beliefs and traditional religions. Buddhists, Christians, and others faced persecution and death. The government attacked crime and corruption. It did away with the old landlord and business classes. In their place, peasant and workers were honored as the builders of the new China.

These revolutionary changes came at an enormous human cost. Communist leaders committed politically motivated mass murder, as hundreds of thousands of landlords, middle class property owners, and others suffered persecution, torture, and death. Many more were sent to forced labor camps, where they died under brutal conditions.

Great Leap Forward Fails From 1958 to 1960, Mao pursued a policy known as the **Great Leap Forward,** which was designed to increase farm and industrial output. To make agriculture more efficient, he created communes. The communes were composed of several villages, thousands of acres of land, and up to 25,000 people.

Rural communes set up "backyard" industries to produce steel and other products. The Great Leap Forward was a disastrous failure. Backyard industries turned out useless goods. The commune system slowed food output. Bad weather added to the problems and led to a terrible famine. Between 1959 and 1961, as many as 55 million Chinese are thought to have starved to death.

The Cultural Revolution In 1966, Mao launched a new program known as the **Cultural Revolution.** Its goal was to purge China of "bourgeois" (non revolutionary) tendencies. He urged young Chinese to experience revolution firsthand, as his generation had.

During the Cultural Revolution, bands of teenaged Red Guards, waving copies of the "Little Red Book," *Quotations From Chairman Mao Tse-tung,* attacked people they considered bourgeois. The accused were publicly humiliated, beaten, and sometimes murdered. Skilled workers and managers were forced out of their jobs and sent to work on rural farms or put into forced labor camps. Schools and factories closed. As the economy stalled and unrest rose, Mao finally had the army restore order.

COMPARE What were the main successes and failures of the Chinese Communist Revolution?

China and the Cold War

The Communist victory in China dominated the Cold War in the years after 1949. The United States had supported Jiang Jieshi in the civil war. After Jiang fled to Taiwan, the United States continued to support the Nationalist government there, providing military and economic aid as it faced shelling from the mainland. For decades, the United States refused to recognize the People's Republic of China, or, as many Americans called it, "Red China."

An Uneasy Alliance with the Soviet Union

Despite a treaty of friendship between China and the Soviet Union, the two communist giants were uneasy allies. In fact, Chinese communism differed from Soviet communism. In the 1950s, Stalin sent economic and technical experts to help China modernize. But he and Mao disagreed on many issues, especially on Marxist ideology. A key difference was the role of the peasantry. Mao believed that peasants were the major force behind communist revolution, while Soviets trusted in a "revolutionary elite" of urban intellectuals and workers.

By 1959, border clashes and disputes over ideology led the Soviets to withdraw all aid and advisors from China and end their alliance. Western powers welcomed the split, which eased fears of the global threat posed by communism.

China and the United States The rift between the United States and China deepened when they supported opposing sides in the Korean War. For years, the United States tried to isolate China, which it saw as an aggressive communist power seeking to expand across Asia.

As the Cold War dragged on, however, the United States reassessed its policy towards China. There were strategic advantages to improving relations with China after its split with the Soviet Union. By "playing the China card," the United States might isolate the Soviets between NATO in the west and a hostile China in the east.

In 1971, China won admission to the United Nations. A year later, American President Richard Nixon visited Mao in Beijing, opening the door to improved relations. Formal diplomatic relations finally came in 1979.

The Nationalists in Taiwan During the Cold War, Jiang Jieshi (Chiang Kai-shek) exercised authoritarian rule over Taiwan, hoping one day to regain control of China. By the early 1990s, however,

>> Mao Zedong's "Little Red Book" of quotations became required reading for all Chinese. Here, peasants take a break from their work in the fields to read it. **Infer** Why do you think the picture of Mao is displayed?

Bounce to Activate Gallery

>> **Analyze Political Cartoons** The Soviet Union and China, both communist, had a tense relationship. In 1978, China rejected a Soviet proposal to improve relations. Who does the bear represent? Who has the upper hand in this cartoon?

Taiwan had made the transition to democratic government.

On the mainland, Mao and his successors saw Taiwan as a breakaway province and insisted that it must someday be reunited with China. Tensions between Taiwan and the mainland continued throughout the Cold War, but in recent years, trade and other links between the two have grown. Although few countries recognized Taiwan, it became an economic powerhouse in Asia and a center of computer technology.

SUMMARIZE How did China's relationships with the Soviet Union and the United States change during the Cold War?

The Two Koreas

In 1950, the Cold War erupted into a "shooting war" in Korea, a peninsula on the northeastern edge of Asia. The Korean War pitted UN forces, largely from the Western democracies, against communist North Korea, which was supported by the Soviet Union and China. It was a key event of the Cold War.

A Nation Divided Korea was an independent kingdom until Japan annexed the country in 1910 and imposed a harsh regime. After Japan's defeat in World War II, Soviet and American forces agreed to divide Korea temporarily along the **38th parallel** of latitude. American forces occupied the south, while the Soviets held the north.

During the Cold War, Korea's division—like Germany's—seemed to become permanent. North Korea, ruled by the dictator **Kim Il Sung,** became a communist ally of the Soviet Union.

In South Korea, the United States backed an authoritarian—but noncommunist—leader, **Syngman Rhee.** Each leader wanted to reunite the country—under his own rule.

The Korean War Begins In June 1950, North Korean forces invaded South Korea and soon overran most of the peninsula. Backed by the UN, which condemned the invasion, the United States organized an international force to help South Korea.

UN forces, mostly Americans and South Koreans under the command of General Douglas MacArthur, fell back in the face of the North Korean advance. They took up a defensive line known as the **Pusan Perimeter,** holding their ground against repeated North Korean attacks. MacArthur then landed troops at Inch'on, behind enemy lines, and drove the invaders back across the 38th parallel. He continued to push northward toward the Yalu River on the border of China.

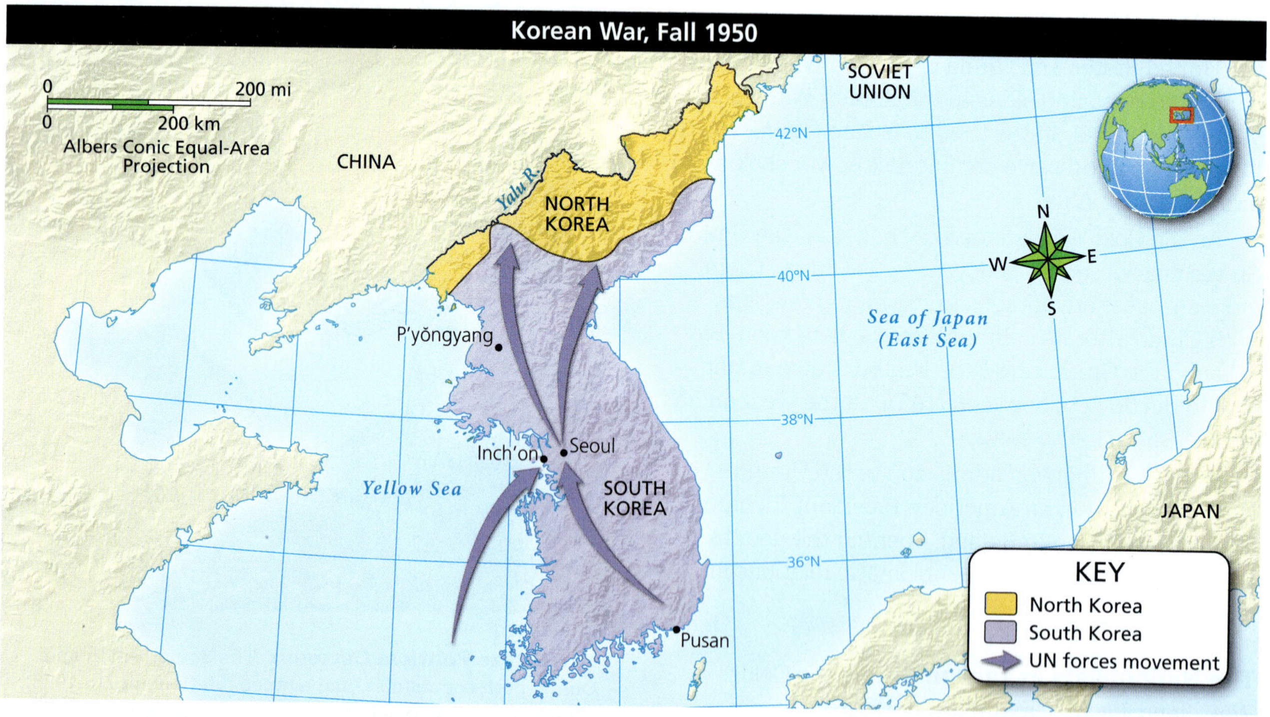

>> Analyze Maps War broke out in Korea in 1950. Communist North Korea invaded South Korea in an effort to reunite Korea. In the fall of 1950, who controlled most of the Korean Peninsula?

Bounce to Activate Map

China Responds MacArthur's success alarmed China, which feared an American invasion. Mao Zedong sent Chinese troops to help the North Koreans. In tough winter fighting, the Chinese and North Koreans pushed the UN forces back across the 38th parallel. The Korean War then turned into a long, deadly stalemate.

Korea Remains Divided Fighting continued until 1953, when both sides signed an armistice to end the fighting. Almost two million North Korean and South Korean troops dug in on either side of the **demilitarized zone (DMZ),** an area with no military forces, near the 38th parallel. American forces, too, remained in South Korea to guarantee the peace. The ceasefire has held for more than 60 years, but no peace treaty has ever been negotiated.

After the war, the two Koreas slowly rebuilt their economies which were destroyed by the fighting and by the Japanese occupation. Korea itself remained a focus of Cold War rivalry. The United States funneled aid to South Korea, while the Soviets helped communist North Korea.

South Korea Prospers For decades, a dictatorial government backed by the military ruled South Korea. By 1987, however, growing prosperity and fierce student protests forced the government to ease controls and hold direct elections. The country also faced new social pressures as more people moved to the cities, undermining traditional rural ways of life.

North Korea Isolates Itself Under Kim Il Sung, North Korea recovered from the war, but by the late 1960s, growth stalled. Kim emphasized self-reliance and kept North Korea isolated from much of the world. When its old partners, the Soviet Union and China, tried out economic reforms in the 1980s, North Korea clung to hardline communism and its command economy in which the government controlled economic decisions.

In North Korea, a barrage of propaganda glorified Kim as the "Great Leader." Kim's successors, his son and grandson, continued to isolate the country and impose ruthless totalitarian control over all aspects of life.

For years, North Koreans lived on the edge of starvation as the country suffered from food shortages, natural disasters, and economic mismanagement. North Korea, meanwhile, poured resources into developing nuclear weapons in spite of international condemnation.

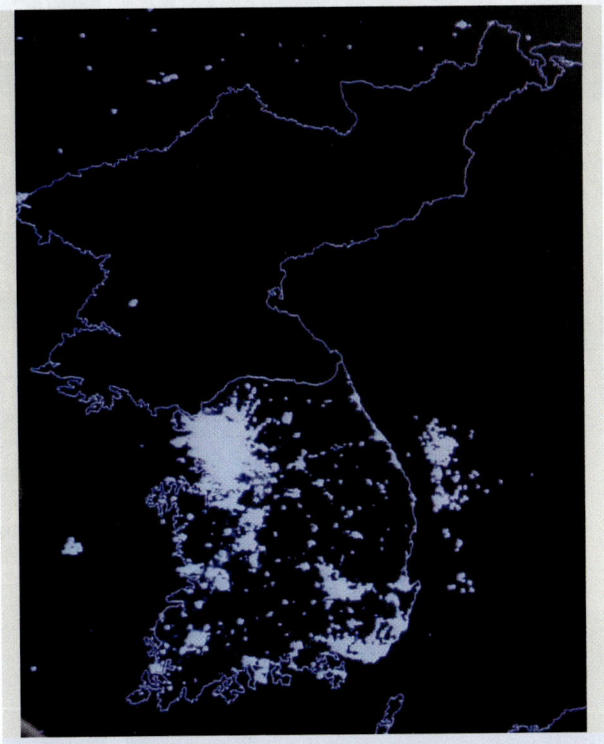

>> South Korea has a modern economy and infrastructure, while North Korea's infrastructure is limited. This 2006 nighttime satellite image shows an eerily dark North Korea and a brightly lit South Korea.

EXPLAIN Explain why China became involved in the Korean War.

ASSESSMENT

1. **Contrast** How did Chinese communism differ from Soviet communism?
2. **Infer** How did the United States use the changing relationship between China and the Soviet Union to its own advantage?
3. **Predict** How might Korea be different if UN forces had not stepped in to oppose the North Korean invasion in 1950?
4. **Summarize** Why was the Great Leap Forward a failure?
5. **Recall** How did North Korea's economic performance compare with South Korea's?

>> Vietnam became the focus of Cold War tensions when communist guerrillas fighters fought against French rule. Here, Viet Minh troops enter Hanoi on October 14, 1954.

Bounce to Activate Flipped Video

8.4 During World War II, Japan seized much of Southeast Asia from the European colonial powers that ruled the region. After Japan's defeat, local nationalists rejected European efforts to reclaim their colonial empires. Some Southeast Asian nations won freedom without much violence. Others, like Vietnam, faced long wars of liberation.

>> Objectives

Describe events in Indochina after World War II.

Explain how the United States became involved in the Vietnam War.

Explore the end of the Vietnam War.

Summarize the impact of the war on Vietnam and Cambodia.

>> Key Terms

guerrilla
Ho Chi Minh
Dien Bien Phu
domino theory
Viet Cong
Tet Offensive
Khmer Rouge
Pol Pot

War in Southeast Asia

The Road to War in Southeast Asia

Cold War tensions complicated the drive for freedom. The United States supported independence for colonial people in principle. But the West was anxious to stop the spread of communism. As a result, the United States helped anti-communist leaders win power, even if they had little popular support.

The Long War Begins In mainland Southeast Asia, an agonizing liberation struggle tore apart the region once known as French Indochina. It affected the emerging nations of Vietnam, Cambodia, and Laos. The 30-year conflict was a key event of the Cold War and had two major phases: the battle against the French from 1946 to 1954, and the Cold War conflict that involved the United States and lasted from 1955 to 1975.

In 1946, the French set out to reestablish their authority over Indochina. In Vietnam, the French faced opposition forces led by **Ho Chi Minh** (hoh chee min). Ho, a nationalist and a communist, had waged warfare against Japanese occupying forces using

guerrillas, or small groups of loosely organized soldiers making surprise raids.

In 1954, Ho Chi Minh's guerilla forces decisively defeated French troops at the battle of **Dien Bien Phu** (dyen byen foo). The defeat forced France to end its efforts to reclaim Indochina. Cambodia, and Laos meanwhile, had won independence separately.

Vietnam Is Divided By 1954, the struggle in Vietnam had become part of the Cold War. At an international conference that year, Western and communist powers agreed to a temporary division of Vietnam.

Ho and the communists ruled North Vietnam. A fierce anti-communist government, led by Ngo Dinh Diem (ngoh Dinh dee EM) and supported by the United States, ruled South Vietnam.

The agreement called for elections to be held to reunite Vietnam within a year. The elections never took place, however, largely because the Americans and Diem feared the communists might win.

Although prodded by the United States, Diem refused to undertake needed reforms, and his increasingly dictatorial rule and corrupt government alienated many South Vietnamese. By 1959, South Vietnam was facing a growing challenge from both communist guerrillas and rising discontent with Diem.

IDENTIFY CENTRAL IDEAS Why did Vietnamese guerrillas fight the French in Indochina?

The United States Enters the War

American officials believed in the **domino theory,** which held that a communist victory in South Vietnam would cause noncommunist governments across Southeast Asia to fall to communism—like a row of dominoes. To prevent such a disaster, the United States stepped in to shore up the Diem government.

However, there were limits to what American power could achieve in Vietnam. President John F. Kennedy realized that the United States alone could not prop up the unpopular Diem government in South Vietnam. In an interview, he noted:

> I don't think that unless a greater effort is made by the Government to win popular support that the war can be won out there. . . . We can help them, we can give them equipment, we can send our men out there as advisors, but they have to win it, the people of Vietnam, against the Communists.
>
> —President John F. Kennedy

Diem was overthrown and killed in early November 1963 by South Vietnamese military leaders. After Diem's death, the United States became more deeply involved in Vietnam, working with the ruling generals against the growing threat from communist rebels.

American Involvement In North Vietnam, Ho Chi Minh was determined to reunite the country under communist rule. He helped the **Viet Cong,** the communist rebels trying to defeat South Vietnam's government. At first, the United States sent only supplies and military advisers to South Vietnam. But as the Viet Cong won control of more areas, the United States was dragged into the fighting, turning a local struggle into a major Cold War conflict.

In August 1964, the *Maddox,* an American warship in the Gulf of Tonkin, reported attacks by North Vietnamese torpedo boats in retaliation for

>> U.S. soldiers search for Viet Cong hideouts in the jungle northeast of Saigon.

Bounce to Activate Gallery

South Vietnamese commando raids nearby. Without mentioning the commando raids, President Lyndon Johnson used the attacks to win congressional approval for the Gulf of Tonkin Resolution. It authorized the president to take all necessary measures to prevent further aggression.

The United States soon began bombing targets in North Vietnam, although no war was ever declared. When air strikes failed to force Ho to abandon the war, the United States committed more and more troops to the conflict. By 1969, more than 500,000 American troops were serving in Vietnam. Meantime, the Soviet Union and China sent aid—but no troops—to help North Vietnam.

Guerrilla Warfare Like the French before them, American forces faced a guerrilla war. Many rebels in South Vietnam were local peasants who knew the countryside. They often found safe haven among villagers who resented the foreign troops and bombings that destroyed their homes and crops. American forces were hard put to tell whether villagers were rebels or innocent civilians.

Supplies for the guerrillas came from North Vietnam, along a series of trails, known as the Ho Chi Minh Trail. These trails wound through the rainforests of neighboring Laos and Cambodia. In an effort to stop the flow of supplies, the United States sent bombers and ground troops across the border into these nations, widening the war in Southeast Asia.

The Tet Offensive Even with massive American help, South Vietnam could not defeat the Viet Cong and their North Vietnamese allies. In January 1968, communist forces launched the **Tet Offensive,** a series of attacks by the Viet Cong on cities across the south. North Vietnamese forces assaulted an American marine base. The attacks were unexpected because they took place during Tet, the Vietnamese New Year.

During bloody fighting, the communists lost many troops and were unable to hold any cities against the American counterattacks. Still, the Tet Offensive marked a turning point in American public opinion. Up to then, Americans believed that the war was winnable. Tet shook public confidence in the war and its leaders.

APPLY CONCEPTS How did the domino theory lead the United States to send troops to Vietnam?

>> **Analyze Maps** The Tet Offensive was a series of attacks by communist guerrillas on South Vietnamese cities. Through which countries did the Ho Chi Minh Trail pass on the way to South Vietnam?

Bounce to Activate Timeline

The Vietnam War Ends

In the United States, the bombing of North Vietnam and increasing American casualties helped inflame anti-war opinion. Growing numbers of American troops were prisoners of war (POWs) or missing in action (MIAs). Many opponents called the Vietnam War a quagmire, or swamp, in which the United States was trapped without the possibility of victory.

American Opposition to the War Grows As the United States committed more troops and poured vast sums into the war, the nation grew increasingly divided. At first, the majority of Americans backed the war effort to stop the spread of communism. By the mid-1960s, a growing number of Americans were calling for an end to the war. They questioned why the United States was sending its troops to fight in a local conflict in Southeast Asia.

By 1967, the anti-war movement was spreading. Television news programs relayed vivid pictures of American casualties and the burning ruins of Vietnamese villages. On college campuses, students rallied against the war, especially as more young men faced the draft, or compulsory military service.

Prominent leaders from all walks of life joined the protests in cities across the nation. Many Americans had mixed feelings. "I want to get out," said one woman, "but I don't want to give up."

A Negotiated Peace Faced with mounting protests at home, President Johnson, who had greatly widened the war, decided not to run for a second term in 1968. His successor, President Richard Nixon, eventually arranged a cease-fire agreement in 1973. Under the agreement, the United States began to withdraw troops from South Vietnam. North Vietnam agreed it would not send any more troops to the south. The accord left South Vietnam to determine its own future.

Vietnam Is Reunited Two years after American troops withdrew, the North Vietnamese captured Saigon, capital of South Vietnam. In 1976, they renamed the city Ho Chi Minh City, in honor of their liberation leader. Hanoi, the capital of North Vietnam, became the capital of the reunited nation.

The communist victors imposed harsh rule on the south. Tens of thousands of Vietnamese fled in small boats. Many of these "boat people" drowned. Survivors ended up in refugee camps in nearby countries. Eventually, some were accepted into the United States or other countries.

Vietnam had to rebuild a land mangled by decades of war. Recovery was slow due partly to

>> People gathered on the Mall in Washington, D.C., on November 15, 1969, to protest the Vietnam War. The Peace Moratorium was estimated to be the largest demonstration in U.S. history.

>> Between the 1973 ceasefire and the final American pullout in 1975, refugees flooded seaports in Vietnam to escape. This Vietnamese navy ship carried more than 7,000 refugees.

>> The Khmer Rouge used children as soldiers in its five-year-long civil war to establish a communist government in Cambodia.

government inefficiency and partly to an American-led boycott of Vietnam. For years, the country was mired in poverty. By the 1990s, however, a new generation of Vietnamese leaders opened the door to investors by introducing free-market reforms. After the Cold War ended, the United States and Vietnam edged toward better relations.

Politically Motivated Mass Murder in Cambodia During the Vietnam War, fighting spilled over into neighboring Cambodia. The North Vietnamese sent supplies through Cambodia to guerrilla forces in South Vietnam. In 1969, the United States bombed those routes and then briefly invaded Cambodia.

After the Americans left, Cambodian communist guerrillas, the **Khmer Rouge** (kuh MEHR roozh), gained ground and overthrew the government in 1975. Led by the brutal dictator **Pol Pot,** the Khmer Rouge unleashed a reign of terror. To destroy all Western influences, they drove people from the cities and forced them to work in the fields. They slaughtered, starved, or worked to death more than one million Cambodians, about a third of the population. The international community failed to readily respond to the genocide.

In 1979, Vietnam invaded and occupied Cambodia, ending the genocide. From 1979 until 1994, no international legal action was taken against Khmer Rouge for his crimes. Pol Pot and his forces retreated to remote areas. In 1993, UN peacekeepers supervised elections. Despite guerrillas who still terrorized parts of the country, a new government began to rebuild Cambodia. In 1997 at Cambodia's request, the United Nations set up a committee to investigate the crimes. The recommendation was an international tribunal to try Khmer Rouge and other Cambodian leaders for war crimes and crimes against humanity.

SUMMARIZE Why did the United States withdraw its troops from Vietnam?

ASSESSMENT

1. **Draw Conclusions** Why did the French withdraw from Indochina in the 1950s?
2. **Apply Concepts** How was American involvement in Vietnam an extension of the Truman Doctrine?
3. **Compare Points of View** What different opinions did Americans have about U.S. involvement in the Vietnam War?
4. **Synthesize** When the text states that "dominoes fell" after the Vietnam War, what does this mean?
5. **Summarize** How did the local struggle in Vietnam reflect the larger Cold War conflict?

8.5 During the Cold War, relations between the Soviet Union and the United States swung back and forth between confrontation and détente. The superpowers confronted each other over issues such as the Berlin Wall, Soviet intervention in Eastern Europe, and Cuba. However, in the 1970s, Soviet leader Leonid Brezhnev pursued détente and disarmament with the United States.

>> Missiles are paraded in Red Square in Moscow. The heavy military commitments of the Soviet Union was one of the factors that led to its decline.

Bounce to Activate Flipped Video

The Cold War Ends

The Soviet Union Declines

Détente came to an abrupt end in 1979, after the Soviet Union invaded Afghanistan to ensure its influence in that neighboring nation. Like the Vietnam War in the United States, the Afghan War drained the Soviet economy and provoked a crisis at home.

The Soviets in Afghanistan The Soviet Union invaded Afghanistan in late 1979 to support an Afghan communist government that had seized power a year earlier. The new government's efforts to introduce social reforms and redistribute land roused bitter resentment among the anti-communist, devoutly Muslim Afghan people. As insurgencies, or uprisings, threatened the government, the Soviet Union stepped in.

For ten years, Soviet forces battled widely scattered groups of **mujahedin** (moo jah heh DEEN), or Muslim guerrilla fighters. Despite 100,000 troops, the Soviets controlled only the cities, not the countryside. When the Soviets turned to bombing rural areas, millions of Afghan refugees fled into neighboring Pakistan. The United States funneled weapons and other military supplies to help the insurgents battle Soviet troops.

By the late 1980s, the Afghan War had become a quagmire for the Soviet Union. It was draining badly needed resources

>> Objectives

Understand why the Soviet Union declined.

Identify the reforms introduced by Mikhail Gorbachev.

Describe the collapse of communism in Eastern Europe and the Soviet Union.

Evaluate how the end of the Cold War affected the remaining communist nations and the United States.

>> Key Terms

mujahedin
Mikhail Gorbachev
glasnost
perestroika
Lech Walesa
Solidarity
Václav Havel
Nicolae Ceausescu

and costing many casualties. In 1989, the Soviets withdrew from Afghanistan to focus on troubling issues at home.

The Command Economy Stagnates The Soviet economy faced severe problems. Unlike the economies of Western Europe and the United States, which experienced booms during the Cold War, the communist economies of Eastern Europe and the Soviet Union stagnated. Central economic planning led to inefficiency and waste. In competition with free market economies of the West, the Soviet command economy began to collapse. It could not match the West in production of quality consumer goods. People saw little improvement in their lives and envied their western neighbors.

The arms race put an additional strain on the Soviet economy. By the 1980s, both superpowers were spending massive sums on costly weapons systems. U.S. President Ronald Reagan began a massive military buildup, partly because he believed that the Soviet Union could not afford to spend as much on defense as the United States. When Reagan launched a new round of missile development, it was clear that the Soviet economy could not afford to match it.

>> Gorbachev struggled at home, but the United States welcomed Soviet reforms. President Ronald Reagan and Mikhail Gorbachev shake hands before a summit near Geneva in 1985. In a 1987 speech near the Berlin Wall, Reagan urged Gorbachev to "tear down this wall!"

Gorbachev Tries Reform In 1985, an energetic new leader, **Mikhail Gorbachev** (GAWR buh chawf), came to power in the Soviet Union. In foreign policy, Gorbachev sought to end Cold War tensions. To ease tensions, Gorbachev renounced the Brezhnev Doctrine, which had asserted the Soviet Union had a right to intervene militarily in any Warsaw Pact nation.

He signed arms control treaties with the United States and eventually pulled Soviet troops out of Afghanistan.

At home, Gorbachev launched a two-pronged effort at reform. First, he called for **glasnost,** or openness. He ended censorship and encouraged people to talk openly about the country's problems.

Second, he urged **perestroika** (pehr uh STROY kuh), or the restructuring of government and the economy. Gorbachev's reforms also included a lessening of restraints on emigration. Natan Sharansky, a Soviet scientist and human rights activist, had been imprisoned for ten years for treason. Long denied permission to emigrate, he was released in exchange for a Soviet spy in 1986 and settled in Israel.

Streamlining government and reducing the size of the bureaucracy, he hoped, would boost efficiency and output. He backed some free-market ideas, including limited private enterprise. But he still wanted to keep the essence of communism.

Corrupt or inefficient officials were dismissed. To produce more and higher-quality goods, factory managers, instead of central planners, were made responsible for decisions. To increase food supplies, farmers were allowed more land on which to grow food to sell on the free market.

IDENTIFY SUPPORTING DETAILS What economic problems did the Soviets face in the 1970s and 1980s?

The Soviet Union Collapses

Gorbachev faced a host of problems. His policies brought rapid change that led to economic turmoil. Shortages grew worse, and prices soared. Factories that could not survive without government help closed, throwing thousands out of work. Old-line Communists and bureaucrats whose careers were at stake denounced the reforms. At the same time, other critics demanded even more changes.

Former Soviet Union, 1992

>> **Analyze Maps** The Soviet Union officially dissolved in 1991, and many former republics gained independence. Which of the former Soviet republics is the largest?

Bounce to Activate Map

The Soviet Empire Crumbles Glasnost encouraged unrest in the multinational Soviet empire. The Baltic republics of Estonia, Latvia, and Lithuania, which had been seized by the Soviet Union in 1940, broke away in 1990, declaring independence soon after. In Eastern Europe, countries from Poland to Bulgaria broke out of the Soviet orbit, beginning in 1989. Russia's postwar empire seemed to be collapsing.

In mid-1991, Soviet hardliners tried to overthrow Gorbachev and restore the old order. Their attempted coup failed, but it further weakened Gorbachev. By year's end, as other Soviet republics declared independence, Gorbachev resigned.

End of the Soviet Union In December 1991, the Union of Soviet Socialist Republics was officially dissolved after almost 70 years. Its 15 republics became separate independent nations. Russia, the largest republic, had dominated the Soviet Union.

After the breakup, Russia and its new president, Boris Yeltsin, faced a difficult future. They struggled to build a market economy and prevent violent conflict between pro-democracy and pro-communist groups. Like Russia, the other former Soviet republics like Ukraine and Kazakhstan faced hard times. They wanted to build stable governments and improve their standards of living. But ethnic violence and economic troubles proved obstacles. Some republics had stores of nuclear weapons, which they agreed to give up in exchange for aid and investment from the West.

SUMMARIZE How did Gorbachev's reforms lead to a new map of Europe and Asia?

Eastern Europe Transformed

During the Cold War, Eastern Europe lay in the Soviet orbit. Efforts to resist Soviet domination were met with harsh repression. Despite the Soviet threat, some nations in Eastern Europe slowly made reforms. After Mikhail Gorbachev announced that the Soviet Union would no longer intervene in Eastern Europe, a "democracy movement" swept the region, and the nations of Eastern Europe were remarkably transformed.

Poland Struggles Toward Democracy Poland was the Soviet Union's most troublesome satellite. In 1956, protests had led to some reforms, but dissatisfaction with communism remained strong. The Roman Catholic Church, which often faced persecution, became a rallying symbol for Poles who opposed the communist regime.

>> Lech Walesa traveled to Italy in 1981 to meet Pope John Paul II, the first Polish pope. The pope was a great supporter of the Solidarity movement.

Bounce to Activate Timeline

>> Residents of East and West Berlin walk atop the Berlin Wall in front of the Brandenburg Gate on November 11, 1989. The wall was torn down shortly after.

In 1980, economic hardships ignited strikes of shipyard workers. Led by **Lech Walesa** (lek vah WEN suh), they organized an independent labor union, called **Solidarity.** It soon claimed millions of members, who pressed for political change.

Under pressure from the Soviet Union, the Polish government outlawed Solidarity and arrested its leaders, including Walesa. Still, unrest simmered. Walesa became a national hero and the Polish government eventually released him from prison.

Pressure from the world community further strained Poland's communist government and helped hasten its collapse. Pope John Paul II visited Poland, met with Solidarity leaders, and criticized communist policies. The pope was the former Karol Wojtyla, archbishop of the Polish city of Cracow.

In the late 1980s, Poland—like the Soviet Union—began to introduce radical economic reforms. It legalized Solidarity and in 1989 sponsored the first free elections in 50 years. Lech Walesa was soon elected president of Poland. The new government began a difficult but peaceful transition from socialism to a market economy. It helped mark the start of the collapse of Soviet domination and communism in Eastern Europe.

Revolution and Freedom By 1989, the "democracy movement" in Eastern Europe was sweeping out old governments and ushering in new ones. People took to the streets, demanding reform.

In the 1970s and 1980s, Hungary had quietly introduced some modest economic reforms. Later, in the spirit of glasnost, Hungarians began to criticize their government more openly. Under growing pressure, the communist government allowed other political parties and opened its border with Austria.

That move allowed thousands of East Germans to escape into Hungary, and from there, to the West. Within a few months, Germans tore down the Berlin Wall, a move that would soon lead to the reunification of Germany.

One by one, communist governments fell across Eastern Europe. In Czechoslovakia, **Václav Havel** (VAHTS lahv HAH vul), a dissident writer and human rights activist, was elected president. Most changes came peacefully, but when **Nicolae Ceausescu** (chow SHES koo), Romania's long time dictator, refused to step down, he was overthrown and executed.

For the first time since 1945, Eastern European countries were free to settle their own affairs. They withdrew from the Warsaw Pact and requested that Soviet troops leave. By then, Soviet power itself was crumbling.

Ethnic Tensions in Eastern Europe Centuries of migrations and conquest left most Eastern European nations with ethnically diverse populations. Most countries had a majority population with one or more ethnic minorities that asserted their own identities. Nationalism helped unite some countries such as Poland and Hungary, but it was also a divisive force.

Faced with ethnic tensions, Czechoslovakia peacefully split into two countries, the Czech Republic and Slovakia. In 1991, however, ethnic conflict tore apart the Balkan nation of Yugoslavia.

The Breakup of Yugoslavia During World War II, a skilled guerrilla leader, Josip Tito, had battled Germany occupying forces. Later, Tito set up a communist government in Yugoslavia, but he pursued a path independent of Moscow. He refused to join the Warsaw Pact and claimed to be neutral in the Cold War.

After Tito's death and the fall of communism, a wave of nationalism tore Yugoslavia apart. The country consisted of six republics, including Bosnia-Herzegovina, Croatia, Macedonia, Montenegro, Serbia, and Slovenia. In 1992, Slovenia and Croatia broke away after a bitter conflict with Serbia. That year, another conflict erupted in Bosnia, which declared independence.

Most Bosnians were Muslims, but many Serbs and Croats lived there. Bosnian Serbs rejected independence, and with money and arms from Serbia, they seized much of Bosnia. In a brutal war, Serbs practiced "ethnic cleansing," forcibly removing other ethnic groups from the areas they controlled. Hundreds of thousands of Bosnians became refugees. Others were tortured or killed. Sarajevo, the capital of Bosnia, came under a deadly siege by Bosnian Serb forces.

Restoring Peace Bosnia became a test case for the role of the United States and the Western powers in the post Cold-War world. For three years, the UN tried unsuccessfully to bring about peace. In 1994, as Bosnian Serbs advanced, the United States and its NATO allies began air strikes against Serbian targets in Bosnia.

In 1995, the United States helped broker a peace agreement, known as the Dayton Accords, which ended the war in Bosnia. NATO peacekeepers enforced the agreements in the troubled Balkan region, and the various new nations set out to recover from the brutal ethnic conflict.

IDENTIFY CAUSE AND EFFECT How did glasnost in the Soviet Union contribute to the end of communist rule in Eastern Europe?

>> At a 1992 peace demonstration in Sarajevo, the capital of Bosnia, protesters crouch to avoid fire from Serbian snipers on a hotel roof. The Bosnian special forces soldier returns fire.

Communism Declines Around the World

The collapse of communism in the Soviet Union and Eastern Europe affected other communist nations. Cuba, which had long depended on Soviet aid and support, faced severe difficulties. Its economy suffered, too, from sanctions imposed by the United States decades earlier.

In 2006, Raul Castro, brother of the ailing leader, Fidel Castro, took over the Cuban government. He allowed some market reforms and sought investment from countries in Europe, Asia, and Latin America. Despite some economic easing, Castro kept tight political control over the island nation.

Other Communist Nations Adopt Market Reforms China began to introduce limited market reforms, such as allowing some private enterprise and foreign investment, in the early 1980s. The reforms brought increased prosperity for some Chinese. By the early 2000s, China's economy was booming, and its many new factories were turning out manufactured goods for a growing global market.

In China, as in Cuba, economic change did not bring political reform. The Chinese Communist party

>> The role of the United States as the sole remaining superpower means that the U.S. military often responds to problems and conflicts all over the world.

kept its monopoly on power, and the government cracked down on any signs of discontent.

China's government undertook no major political reforms. However, as the global economic crisis that began in 2008 led to factory closings, protests by unemployed workers increased. China's government responded with a $600 billion stimulus package to retrain workers and improve productivity.

Different Paths for Vietnam and North Korea

Two other communist nations in Asia, Vietnam and North Korea, took different paths. Vietnam allowed some market reforms and won increased foreign investment. North Korea, however, clung to its old ideology, continuing its strict isolation from the world.

COMPARE How did other communist countries react to the collapse of the Soviet bloc?

The Post-Cold War World

When the Cold War ended in the early 1990s, Americans hoped for a more peaceful world. But as the sole superpower, the United States played a leading role in trying to resolve world conflicts. The United States led coalition forces in several missions around the world.

The United States and its European allies were also eager to help the new nations of Eastern Europe to make the difficult transition to democracy and capitalism. They provided advice and loans, but also required far-reaching economic reforms.

The Move Toward Market Economies In the aftermath of the Cold War, the nations of Eastern Europe—as well as Russia and the former Soviet republics—set out to build stable democratic governments and replace their old command economies with free-market economies. Although the experiences of each nation differed, all faced similar challenges.

To attract badly needed foreign investment, governments had to push radical economic reforms. They privatized industries and stopped keeping prices for basic goods and services low. They ended many benefits from the old days such as free tuition at universities. At first, the changes brought hardships such as high unemployment, soaring prices, and crime. Consumer goods were more plentiful, but few people could afford them.

A further stumbling block to progress was the global economic recession that started in 2008. Economic hard times brought a rise of anti-foreign sentiment along with anti-Semitic and anti-Roma (Gypsy) hate speech from extremist groups. Despite these challenges, the governments of Eastern Europe remained democratic.

SUMMARIZE What steps did former Communist nations have to take to transition to market economies?

ASSESSMENT

1. **Draw Conclusions** Why was the Soviet Union unable to keep up with the market economies of the West?
2. **Summarize** How did Gorbachev's reforms lead to the breakup of the Soviet empire?
3. **Identify Cause and Effect** Why were Eastern Europeans able to break free of communist governments and Soviet domination in the late 1980s?
4. **Infer** How did the collapse of the Soviet Union affect the United States?
5. **Infer** Why might some communist nations have adopted market principles after the fall of the Soviet Union?

"Tear Down This Wall": Ronald Reagan

Introduction

On June 12, 1987, President Reagan spoke in West Berlin, near the Berlin Wall, not far from where the Brandenburg Gate stood in the eastern sector. His speech acknowledged the new Soviet leader Mikhail Gorbachev's efforts at reform in the Soviet Union. However, Reagan was not satisfied with Gorbachev's limited measures. He challenged the Soviet leader to show a real commitment to reform by tearing down the Berlin Wall that had stood between East and West Berlin since 1961. This wall symbolized the division between communism and democracy.

Twenty eight years later in 1989 the wall came down. The second primary source is an excerpt from an article, written twenty years later, from *Time* magazine. It revisits Reagan's decisions about the speech before it was given.

>> Ronald Reagan and Mikhail Gorbachev

Primary Source

In the 1950s, Khrushchev predicted: "We will bury you." But in the West today, we see a free world that has achieved a level of prosperity and well-being unprecedented [never having happened or existed before] in all human history. In the Communist world, we see failure, technological backwardness, declining standards of health, even want of the most basic kind—too little food. Even today, the Soviet Union still cannot feed itself. After these four decades, then, there stands before the entire world one great and inescapable conclusion: Freedom leads to prosperity. Freedom replaces the ancient hatreds among the nations with comity [courtesy] and peace. Freedom is the victor [winner].

ANALYZE WORD CHOICES Reagan characterizes Khrushchev's statement "We [Communism] will bury you" as a prediction and not as a threat. If that is true, what did Khrushchev mean when he said "We will *bury you*"?

And now the Soviets themselves may, in a limited way, be coming to understand the importance of freedom. We hear much from Moscow about a new policy of reform and openness. Some political prisoners have been released. Certain foreign news broadcasts are no longer being jammed. Some economic enterprises have been permitted to operate with greater freedom from state control.

DETERMINE MEANING What does it mean to "jam" a radio or television broadcast?

Are these the beginnings of profound changes in the Soviet state? Or are they token gestures, intended to raise false hopes in the West, or to strengthen the Soviet system without changing it? We welcome change and openness; for we believe that freedom and security go together, that the advance of human liberty can only strengthen the cause of world peace. There is one sign the Soviets can make that would be unmistakable, that would advance dramatically the cause of freedom and peace.

General Secretary Gorbachev, if you seek peace, if you seek prosperity for the Soviet Union and Eastern Europe, if you seek liberalization: Come here to this gate! Mr. Gorbachev, open this gate! Mr. Gorbachev, tear down this wall!

Primary Source

Twenty years ago, on the morning of June 12, 1987, Reagan arrived in Berlin, on the occasion of the city's 750th birthday. He was scheduled to speak on the Western side of the Brandenburg Gate, for years the city's symbolic dividing line. His speechwriters had drafted an address intended as much for Soviet leader Mikhail Gorbachev, with whom Reagan was forging a close relationship, as for the 20,000 people who gathered to hear him speak. In the speech, Reagan would call on Gorbachev to tear down the Berlin Wall, but that language was opposed strongly by Reagan's National Security Council and the State Department, who feared it would be used by hard-liners in the Kremlin to discredit Gorbachev. When the President's entourage arrived in Berlin, Reagan's team was still arguing over the final wording. State and NSC submitted yet another draft of the speech. But in the limousine ride to the Wall, Reagan told his deputy chief of staff, Kenneth Duberstein, that he intended to issue the fateful challenge to Gorbachev. "It's the right thing to do," he said.

Two decades later, what can we learn from the epochal events that followed–the fall of the Berlin Wall, the reunification of Germany and the collapse of the Soviet Union? "People were afraid of the consequences of what Reagan would say," George Shultz, Reagan's long-serving Secretary of State, told me over lunch in Berlin last week. "But it turns out he [Reagan] was right. Saying something like, 'Mr. Gorbachev, tear down this wall'–that could be perceived as provocative. Things were breaking and were in a lot of flux. But knowing Ronald Reagan as I did, I would have said don't bother. He was going to express his feelings.

ASSESSMENT

1. **Determine Central Ideas** According to the first paragraph of this passage, why should Gorbachev tear down the Berlin Wall?
2. **Determine Author's Purpose** What was the purpose of Reagan's speech?
3. **Distinguish Among Fact, Opinion, and Reasoned Judgment** When Reagan says, "freedom is the victor," is that a fact, an opinion, or a reasoned judgment? Cite evidence from the speech to support your answer.
4. **Draw Conclusions** At the time Reagan spoke, little attention was given to his speech. Why do you think the speech gradually gained significance?

PEARSON realize
PearsonSchool.com/CASS

Go online to PearsonSchool.com/CASS and use the texts, quizzes, interactivities, Interactive Reading Notepads, Flipped Videos, and other resources from this Topic to prepare for the Topic Test.

- Etexts
- Quizzes
- Interactivities
- Interactive Reading Notepads
- Flipped Videos

While online you can also check the progress you've made learning the topic and course content by viewing your grades, test scores, and assignment status.

LESSON SUMMARIES

Use these Lesson Summaries, and the longer versions available online, to review the key ideas for each lesson in this Topic.

Lesson 1: A New Global Conflict

During the war, the Soviet Union and the nations of the West had cooperated to defeat Nazi Germany. By 1945, the wartime alliance was crumbling. The United States and the Soviet Union became superpowers. They also became tense rivals in a conflict known as the Cold War.

Lesson 2: The Western Democracies and Japan

After World War II, western ideas and technology helped Japan rebuild and become an economic superpower.

Lesson 3: Communism in East Asia

Even though communism in the Soviet Union did not develop as promised, many leaders still favored communism. In China, leaders such as Mao Zedong still believed communism could overturn the old order and yield economic and political success.

Lesson 4: War in Southeast Asia

For decades after the end of WWII, Southeast Asia was shaped by the nationalist drive for independence. The struggle for Vietnam became part of the Cold War.

Lesson 5: The Cold War Ends

In the 1980s, the Soviet economy began to crumble. Efforts at reform failed. After years of Communist rule, the Soviet Union collapsed and was replaced by Russia and other independent republics.

Go ONLINE for lesson summaries

AUDIO READING GAMES

VISUAL REVIEW

Use these graphics to review some of the key terms, people, and ideas from this Topic.

Cold War Contrasts

COMMUNIST COUNTRIES	INDUSTRIALIZED DEMOCRACIES
Compete in arms race to maintain "balance of terror."	Compete in arms race to maintain "balance of terror."
Form Warsaw Pact. China follows separate path.	Form NATO and SEATO.
Seek to spread communism.	Seek to contain communism.
Command economies.	Market economies.
Economic stagnation, low standards of living.	Economic "miracles", prosperity with scattered recessions
Repress of dissent, labor camps	Free expression, but fears lead to an episode of McCarthyism
Power is closely held by communist parties.	Democracy is established in Japan, civil rights movement extends democracy in United States.
Lost arms race.	Won arms race.

Cold War Hot Spots

KOREA	VIETNAM
Divided into communist north and noncommunist, U.S.-supported south.	Divided into communist north and noncommunist, U.S.-supported south.
China provided troops to support North Korea.	China and the Soviet Union provided economic and military aid, but not troops, to North Vietnam.
The United States led United Nations troops supporting South Korea.	The United States and some allies provided troops to support South Vietnam.
Warfare mainly involved regular troops.	Viet Cong fighting in the south were mainly guerrillas.
United States troops remained in South Korea after war.	United States troops withdrew before the war ended.
Korean War ended in a stalemate between the two sides and a ceasefire.	Vietnam War ended when North Vietnam defeated South Vietnam and reunited the country.

Steps in the Collapse of the Soviet Empire

- The command economy could not create wealth or raise living standards as quickly as market economies.
- The Soviet Union could not afford the expense of maintaining a "balance of terror" in the arms race.
- East Europeans resisted communism and Soviet control.
- Soviet military failure in Afghanistan led to calls for change.
- Reforms in Russia included glasnost, or freedom of expression, and perestroika, or market reforms.
- East Germans forced their government to open the Berlin Wall.
- Eastern European nations rejected Soviet control and adopted market economies and democracy.
- Glasnost led to drive for independence by Soviet ethnic minorities and the breakup of the Soviet Union.
- Soviet Union was divided into 15 independent nations.
- The Warsaw Pact was dissolved.

California Topic 8 Assessment

KEY TERMS, PEOPLE, AND IDEAS

1. How did the Yalta Conference cause a postwar power shift between the United States, Britain, and the Soviet Union?
2. What was the **iron curtain**? Why did Churchill choose that term?
3. What was the state of the economy in post-war United States?
4. Discuss the establishment of organizations such as NATO and the **Warsaw Pact**. What did each organization represent to western and communist nations?
5. Why did Japan experience an economic upturn decades after WWII?
6. What role did **collectivization** have in the communist economy?
7. What were the goals of Mao's economic plan **"The Great Leap Forward"**? Why did it fail?
8. What are proxy wars? Were the Vietnam War and the Korean war proxy wars? Explain.
9. Why did uprisings in Eastern Europe increase during the early years of the Cold War?

CRITICAL THINKING

10. **Explain** How did perestroika and glasnost contribute to the end of communism?
11. **Analyze Information** How did the Truman Doctrine underscore Truman's belief that the key to preventing the fall of nations to communism was to attack the "conditions of misery and want" that led to totalitarianism?
12. **Summarize** How did postwar production push the United States into an economic boom? Why was the economic performance of Eastern Europe and the Soviet Union different?
13. **Synthesize Information** What was the effect of World War II on the status of women in the United States?
14. **Draw Conclusions** Why did the Korean War end in a stalemate?
15. **Summarize** How did a local struggle in Vietnam become a major Cold War conflict?
16. **Analyze Images** The picture below shows residents of Berlin gathering around and on top of the Berlin Wall. (a) what does the gathering of people indicate about the changed feeling in Berlin? (b) The wall was torn down shortly after. How did the fall of the wall represent a change in history?

17. **Writing Activity** The excerpt below is from Robert Kaiser, a reporter for the *Washington Post* who was stationed in Moscow. He describes what is needed to shop at the stores in Moscow. What does it reveal about the Soviet command system? Could the command system have been another factor in the collapse of communism? Use your knowledge of the Topic and what you have learned about the free market economy when writing your response.

> "A good shopper will jump into a queue [line] wherever he or she finds it, taking a place and then asking what is being offered at the other end,
>
> The queue is everywhere in Soviet life ... the queue to buy a private car may be five years long. ... At the neighborhood bread store, three lines are not uncommon; one to make a selection; another to pay the cashier, a third to exchange the cashier's receipt for the chosen loaf."
>
> *—Robert G. Kaiser, Russia from the Inside*

DOCUMENT-BASED QUESTIONS

The United States and the Soviet Union confronted each other in the Cold War—a global conflict that included a nuclear arms race. Read the documents below, then answer the questions that follow.

DOCUMENT A

"Seeing that their government had reasserted control over its own frontiers, the East Germans were heartened by the solidification and fortification of their state. . . .I know there are people who claim that the East Germans are imprisoned in paradise and that the gates of the Socialist paradise are guarded by armed troops. I'm aware that a defect exists, but I believe it's a necessary and only temporary defect."

—*Khrushchev Remembers by Nikita Khrushchev*

DOCUMENT B

". . . I hope the Prime Minister has understood all the implications of what I said," Nixon went on, with an oblique [indirect] reference to Berlin. "What I mean is that the moment we place either one of these powerful nations, through an ultimatum, in a position where it has no choice but to accept dictation or fight, then you are playing with the most destructive force in the world."

Khrushchev: (flushed, wagging a finger near Nixon's face): We too are giants. If you want to threaten, we will answer threat with threat.

Nixon: We never engage in threats.

Khrushchev: You wanted indirectly to threaten me. But we have means at our disposal that can have very bad consequences.

Nixon: We have too.

—*Time, August 3, 1959*

DOCUMENT C

Fortifications that kept East Germans from crossing into West Germany.

DOCUMENT D

18. The author's purpose in Document A was to

A. explain East German discipline.

B. offer a balanced perspective on the Cold War.

C. argue for a fortified barrier between East and West Germany.

D. explain the role of the Soviet Union in East Germany.

19. The tone of the exchange in Document B is

A. friendly and joking

B. tense and hostile

C. cautious

D. businesslike

20. Document D shows that

A. West Berlin was located inside West Germany.

B. the border between East and West Germany passes through Berlin.

C. East Germany surrounded West Gemany.

D. two East German borders separated West Berlin from West Germany.

21. **Writing Activity** How was the Cold War fought? Use what you have read in the Topic, along with these documents, to write a response.

End-of-Topic Practice

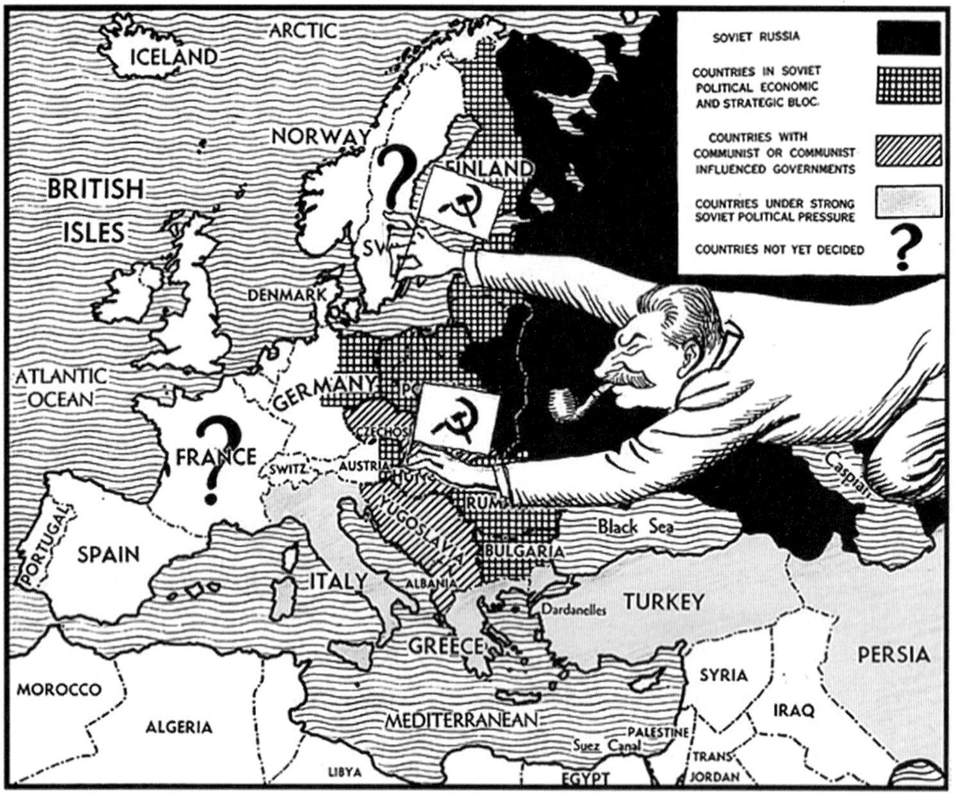

1 Why did relations between the United States and the USSR fall apart after World War II?

A Stalin wanted to continue the war until he dominated Western Europe.

B Stalin wanted to create a buffer zone of satellite states to prevent invasion.

C Stalin demanded to annex all of the land once owned by Germany.

D Stalin wanted to be paid for all of the damage that Germany had committed in the USSR.

---

2 Why did Chinese peasants readily support Mao Zedong and the Communist Party during the Chinese civil war?

F They welcomed the opportunity to exercise decision making privileges in special group communes.

G There was less government corruption and more jobs were available in the cities.

H The Communists redistributed land to peasants and ended both military oppression and oppression by landlords.

J The Communists set up work communes which provided fertile land plots to all peasants.

3 How did the Communist revolution in Vietnam impact the Cold War?

A It weakened relations between the Soviet Union and China as they disagreed about tactics and which side to support.

B The United States and the Soviet Union continued to funnel aid and military supplies to their allied regions, escalating the conflict.

C It caused the Soviet Union to demand a withdrawal of U.S. forces from all of Asia to protect the actions of South Vietnam.

D Ho Chi Minh broke a peace treaty signed by Western and Communist powers that called for the reunification of North and South Vietnam, causing the Vietnam War.

> *"In the mid-1980s, through glasnost—openness and freedom—and perestroika—economic restructuring—Gorbachev had demonstrated willingness to loosen government strangleholds in the Soviet Union and Eastern Europe, including East Germany."*

4 How did Gorbachev's policies described in the excerpt lead to the collapse of communism in the Soviet Union?

F He took advantage of a weakened government to overthrow military hardliners who had ruined the economy.

G He thought that limited capitalism under glasnost would be better than a command economy.

H His open policies and reforms worsened the Soviet economy, which encouraged unrest there and in Eastern Europe.

J His perestroika (restructuring) plans caused ethnic violence directed toward centralized government planning.

If you have trouble with. . .				
Question	1	2	3	4
See Lesson	8.1	8.3	8.4	8.5

[**ESSENTIAL QUESTION**] What should governments do?

9 New Nations Emerge (1945–Present)

>> Women in Kenya celebrating the anniversary of winning independence

Enduring Understandings

- As European imperial powers declined after World War II, colonies in Africa and Asia gained independence.
- South Asia was partitioned into Hindu-dominated India and Muslim-dominated Pakistan, setting the stage for decades of conflict.
- Some African nations achieve independence peacefully, while others had to fight for their freedom.
- In the Middle East, the new Jewish State of Israel faced immediate opposition from its Arab neighbors.
- Factors shaping the modern Middle East include Islam, oil, and religious and ethnic diversity.

NBC LEARN

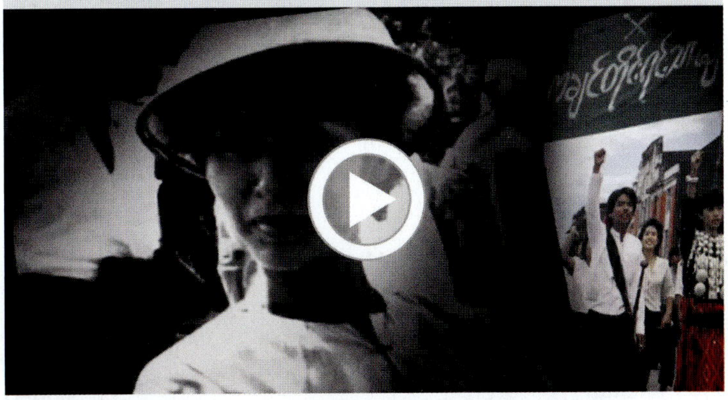

Learn about Aung San Suu Kyi's efforts to bring democracy to Myanmar.

Bounce to Activate My Story Video

California Topic 9 Overview

In this Topic, you will learn about the events that occurred as new nations emerged after World War II. Look at the lesson outline and explore the timeline. As you study this Topic, you will complete the Quest team project.

LESSON OUTLINE

9.1 New Nations in South Asia and Southeast Asia
Analysis CST.1, CST.2, HRE.4, HI.1

9.2 African Nations Win Independence
HSS 10.9.3, HSS 10.10, HSS 10.10.1, HSS 10.10.2; Analysis CST.1, CST.2, HRE.4, HI.1

9.3 The Modern Middle East Takes Shape
HSS 10.9.2, HSS 10.9.6, HSS 10.10, HSS 10.10.1, HSS 10.10.2; Analysis CST.1, CST.2, CST.4, HRE.4, HI.1

9.4 Conflicts in the Middle East
HSS 10.9.6, HSS 10.10.1, HSS 10.10.2; Analysis CST.1, CST.2, HRE.4, HI.1

Key Events as New Nations Emerge

1947 India and Pakistan gain independence after partition.

1948 Israel is founded.

1957 Ghana becomes the first African nation south of the Sahara to win independence.

1979 Iranian revolution.

1990–2002 African nations move toward democracy.

1993 Oslo accords are signed bringing partial peace between Israelis and Palestinians.

1994 Ethnic conflict in Rwanda leads to genocide.

2011 Arab nations erupt in pro-democracy protests during "Arab Spring."

1940 1950 1960 1970 1980 1990 2000 2010 2020

QUEST! TEAM PROJECT

Presenting a position paper

Is genocide a preventable crime? You are part of the global conversation about this topic at the United Nations. Review the outcome of the Genocide Convention at the United Nations in 1948. In this Quest, you will research and explore this issue.

STEP 1

First, research the laws and action plans which are in place to prevent genocide. Are these actions effective? Discuss with your team. Prepare a list of questions you might want to address as you continue.

STEP 2

Review the primary sources. Discuss the various viewpoints. Begin a draft outline of your position paper.

STEP 3

Review, edit, and revise your paper. Your team is ready to address the General Assembly of the United Nations on the issue of genocide. What were the viewpoints of other teams?

STEP 4

Reflect on what you have learned. Consider this quote: The Genocide Convention said "never again" to genocide. But it has become "again" and ''again". Discuss the issue.

PEARSON realize™ PearsonSchool.com/CASS

Go ONLINE for complete Quest materials

VIDEO ETEXT WRITING RUBRIC PDF ASSESSMENT

>> Indians celebrated independence from Britain during this parade in Mumbai on August 15, 1947.

9.1 At the same time that the Cold War was unfolding, a global independence movement was reshaping the world. The European colonial powers, especially Britain and France, had been weakened by World War II. Their military and financial resources were exhausted, and so was their will to hold on to their colonial empires. While nationalists in the colonies were ready to fight for their freedom, many war-weary Europeans had no desire for further conflict.

Bounce to Activate Flipped Video

>> Objectives

Explain how independence led to the partition of India.

Describe the national development of India, Pakistan, and Bangladesh.

Define the role of South Asia in the Cold War.

Explain the impact of independence on nations of Southeast Asia.

>> Key Terms

partition
Sikh
Kashmir
Jawaharlal Nehru
dalits
Indira Gandhi
Punjab
Golden Temple
Bangladesh
nonalignment
autocratic
Aung San Suu Kyi
Sukarno
Suharto
East Timor
Ferdinand Marcos
Benigno Aquino
Corazon Aquino

New Nations in South Asia and Southeast Asia

Independence and Partition in South Asia

Among the first new nations to win independence were the former British colonies of South Asia, or the Indian subcontinent. Nationalists in British-ruled India had demanded self-rule since the late 1800s. As independence neared, however, a long-simmering issue surfaced. What would happen to the Muslim minority in a Hindu-dominated India?

The Formation of India and Pakistan Like Mohandas Gandhi, most of the leaders and members of the Congress Party were Hindus. However, the party wanted a unified India that would include both Muslims and Hindus.

The Muslim League, led by Muhammad Ali Jinnah, had a different view of liberation. Although they had cooperated with the Congress Party in the drive for independence, they feared discrimination against the Muslim minority in a unified

India. Therefore, the Muslim League demanded the creation of a separate nation, called Pakistan, that would include the parts of British India where Muslims formed a majority.

After World War II, the British government decided that it could no longer afford to resist Indian demands for independence. As independence approached, violence between Hindus and Muslims worsened, pushing Britain to accept the idea of **partition,** or dividing the subcontinent into two nations. In 1947, British officials hastily drew borders to create Hindu India, and Pakistan made up of two widely separated areas that had large Muslim populations. In August 1947, the two nations celebrated their independence.

Partition Leads to Violence Drawing fair borders for the two new nations was impossible because Hindus and Muslims lived side by side in many areas. As soon as the new borders became known, a mass migration began. On the Pakistani side of the borders, millions of Hindus and **Sikhs** (SIK khs), members of a South Asian religious minority, packed their belongings and fled to the new India. At the same time, millions of Muslims fled from India into newly created Pakistan. An estimated 10 million people left their homes, most of them on foot.

Muslims fleeing along the crowded roads into Pakistan were slaughtered by Hindus and Sikhs. Muslims massacred Hindu and Sikh neighbors. Around one million people died in these massacres. Others died of starvation and exposure on the road.

Horrified at the partition and the violence, Gandhi turned once more to satyagraha, or nonviolent resistance to evil. On January 30, 1948, he was shot and killed by a Hindu extremist. Jawaharlal Nehru told a stricken nation, "The light has gone out of our lives and there is darkness everywhere." Gandhi's death discredited extremists and helped end the worst violence. Still, Hindu-Muslim tensions remained.

The Battle for Kashmir Since independence, India and Pakistan have fought a series of wars over **Kashmir,** a state in the Himalayas. In 1947, Kashmir's Hindu ruler tried to join India. However, Kashmir's Muslim majority wanted to be part of Pakistan. For decades, Kashmiri separatists, often supported by Pakistani militants, have fought Indian troops. Indian and Pakistani forces have also battled along Kashmir's mountainous border. Today, Kashmir remains a flashpoint in the tense relations between India and Pakistan.

A Nuclear Arms Race In the 1970s, first India and then Pakistan developed nuclear weapons programs. By 1998, both nations had successfully tested nuclear weapons. The emergence of these two nuclear powers alarmed neighbors in South Asia and the world, in part because of the ongoing hostility between India and Pakistan. Another concern was the danger that extremists in either country might get access to nuclear technology or even nuclear weapons.

Ongoing Conflict in Sri Lanka The island of Ceylon won freedom from Britain in 1948. Later, it took the name Sri (sree) Lanka. In the 1970s, ethnic tensions sparked a long, brutal guerrilla war in Sri Lanka.

Most Sri Lankans are Buddhists who speak Sinhalese. A large Tamil-speaking Hindu minority living in the north and east charged the government with discrimination. When efforts to win equality failed, Tamil rebels waged war to set up a separate nation. For three decades, terrorism and brutality fed the deadly conflict between government forces and Tamil rebels. In 2009, the government regained control of Tamil-held towns and started to resettle those displaced by the conflict. Since then, Sri Lanka has tried to rebuild its shattered economy, but tensions remained.

>> Indian refugees crowd onto trains after India and Pakistan are separated into two independent states. Muslims fled to Pakistan and Hindus fled to India in one of the largest transfers of population in history.

Bounce to Activate Gallery

>> Indira Gandhi served as India's prime minister for almost 15 years, though not consecutively. She lost her election in 1977 due to unpopular policies, but won back the seat in 1980.

>> Jawaharlal Nehru meets with Indian citizens of Pashtun ethnicity. Pashtuns are ethnic Afghans and are predominantly Muslim.

IDENTIFY MAIN IDEAS Why is Kashmir a source of conflict between India and Pakistan?

Challenges to Modern India

Upon achieving independence, India built on the legacy of British rule to form a parliamentary democracy. Although India is today the world's largest democracy, it has faced many challenges. Ethnic and religious tensions threatened its unity. Its people speak over 100 languages and many dialects. Hundreds of millions of Indians lived in desperate poverty. Despite unrest and diversity, India has emerged as a major world power.

Strong Prime Ministers Set Goals During its early decades, India benefited from strong leadership. The Congress Party, which had spearheaded the independence movement, worked to turn India into a modern nation. From 1947 to 1964, **Jawaharlal Nehru** (juh WAH huhr lahl NAY roo), leader of the Congress Party, was India's prime minister. He worked to build a modern, secular state dedicated to promoting economic growth and social justice. Under Nehru, food output rose, but so did India's population. The government encouraged family planning to reduce the birthrate, but with limited success.

Although India's 1947 constitution banned discrimination against people in the lowest castes, discrimination based on caste continued. Nehru's government set aside jobs and places in universities for **dalits,** and other lower-caste Indians. Still, higher-caste Hindus generally got better schooling and jobs.

Later, Nehru's daughter, **Indira Gandhi,** served as prime minister for most of the years between 1966 and 1984. She had a global influence and challenged traditional discrimination against women.

Religious Conflicts Persist India was a land of many religions. A majority of Indians were Hindu, but millions were Muslim, Sikh, Christian, or Buddhist. At times, religious divisions led to violence.

Some Sikhs wanted greater autonomy for **Punjab,** a prosperous, largely Sikh state in northern India. Sikh dissidents engaged in protests, most of them nonviolent, against government policies. These protests were organized from the **Golden Temple,** the most prominent Sikh house of worship. Indira Gandhi planned an attack to remove Sikh dissidents hiding in the Golden Temple.

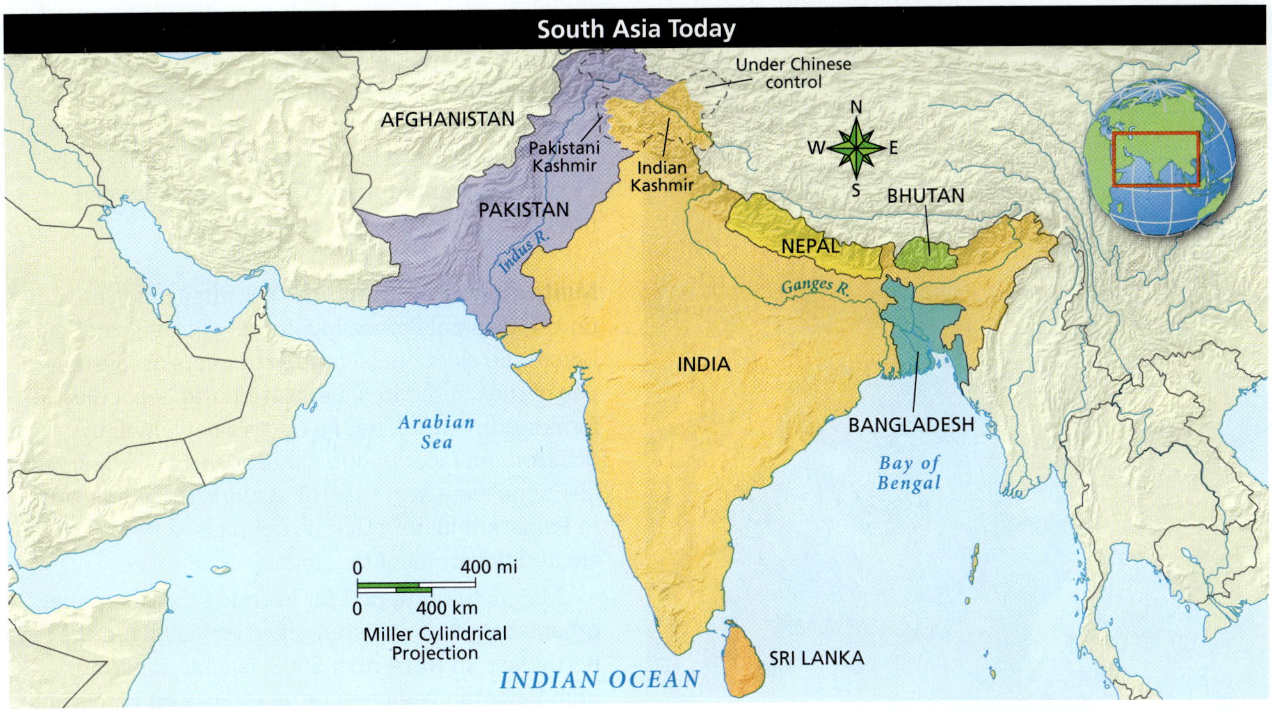

>> **Analyze Maps** This map shows South Asia today. West Pakistan is now called Pakistan. East Pakistan is now called Bangladesh. Ceylon is now called Sri Lanka. What geographic reason made it difficult for Pakistan to retain control of Bangladesh?

Bounce to Activate Map

As news of this planned attack leaked, Sikh activists fortified the Golden Temple with arms and weapons. Indian troops attacked the temple in 1984. Over a thousand Sikhs were killed and many religious artifacts were destroyed. Soon after, Gandhi was assassinated by two of her Sikh bodyguards. In the state-sponsored anti-Sikh riots that followed, thousands more Sikhs were killed.

In the 1980s, the Hindu nationalist party, Bharatiya Janata Party (BJP), began to challenge the secular, or nonreligious, Congress Party. The BJP accused Indira Gandhi of overstepping her authority and favoring minority religions at the expense of Hinduism. They wanted a government based on Hindu traditions. Religious minority groups accused the party of stoking violence.

SUMMARIZE How did the Indian government try to improve conditions for lower castes?

Pakistan and Bangladesh Separate

When Pakistan gained independence in 1947, it was a divided country. West Pakistan and East Pakistan were located on either side of India, separated by a thousand miles. India made trade and travel between the two Pakistans difficult.

Bangladesh Declares Independence Although East and West Pakistanis were Muslim, their languages and cultures differed. Bengalis in the east outnumbered Punjabis in the west, but Punjabis dominated the government. The government concentrated most economic development programs in West Pakistan, while East Pakistan remained deep in poverty. Many Bengalis resented governmental neglect of East Pakistan.

In 1971, Bengalis in East Pakistan declared independence. They named their country **Bangladesh,** or "Bengali nation." Pakistan's military ruler ordered the army to crush the rebellion. Millions of Bengalis fled into India. India responded by attacking and defeating the Pakistani army in Bangladesh. Pakistan was then compelled to recognize the new country.

Pakistan's Unstable Government After independence, Pakistan struggled to build a stable government. Power shifted back and forth between elected civilian leaders and military rulers. Tensions among the country's diverse ethnic groups posed problems. The fiercely independent people in the

>> Afghan children, refugees in Pakistan, are transported by truck. Since the 1970s, millions of Afghan refugees have fled into Pakistan.

northwestern "tribal areas" were left largely on their own and resisted government control.

The activities of Islamic fundamentalists created tension. The fundamentalists wanted a government that followed strict Islamic principles, while other Pakistanis wanted greater separation between religion and state.

Militants in Pakistan In 2008, after nine years in power, General Pervez Musharraf allowed elections. Before the election, Islamic extremists assassinated one of the candidates, Benazir Bhutto, a popular former prime minister. Pakistan's new civilian government faced tough challenges. Still, when new elections were held in 2013, it marked the first time in Pakistani history that power passed from one elected government to another.

Meanwhile, support for Islamic fundamentalist groups based in Pakistan grew, especially in the northwest. In November 2008, Islamic militants from Pakistan launched terror attacks on hotels and tourists in Mumbai, India, fueling tensions between the hostile neighbors.

Islamic traditions were strong in the rugged border area between Pakistan and Afghanistan. When the Soviet Union invaded Afghanistan in 1979, one million Afghan refugees fled into Pakistan. There, many joined Islamic fundamentalist groups to battle the invaders.

After Russia withdrew from Afghanistan, the Taliban, an extreme Islamist group, seized power with the support of Pakistan. The Taliban backed Al Qaeda, which launched terrorist attacks on the United States in 2001. When U.S. forces invaded Afghanistan and overthrew the Taliban, its supporters fled into Pakistan.

By then, Pakistan had withdrawn its support of the Taliban. Still, Taliban fighters and other Islamic extremists set up strongholds in northwestern Pakistan. The Pakistani government waged on and off again war against the militants and reluctantly accepted U.S. aid. Many Pakistanis, however, were outraged by American drone—or pilotless aircraft--attacks on suspected terrorists within its borders. Although the attacks were aimed at militants, they sometimes caused civilian casualties.

>> A woman walks through flooded streets in Dhaka, the capital of Bangladesh.

Bangladesh Struggles Bangladesh ranks among the world's poorest, most crowded countries. Its population, more than half as large as that of the United States, lives in an area the size of Alabama. The large population is crowded on the low-lying Ganges Delta, just a few feet above sea level. Bangladesh has suffered repeatedly from devastating tropical storms and floods. Explosive population growth has strained resources further. More than 50 million people live below the poverty level.

During its early years, Bangladesh was ruled by authoritarian military governments that controlled the economy. In the 1990s, the nation moved from military to democratic rule. The new civilian government encouraged foreign investment. Foreign companies took advantage of cheap labor costs to make clothes in Bangladesh. However, human rights group protested the widespread use of child labor and and dangerous working conditions that have led to the deaths of many workers.

One hopeful program for combating poverty came from the Grameen Bank, founded by Bangladeshi economist Muhammad Yunus. It gave tiny loans, or "microcredit," to poor people so they could open small businesses. Many of the beneficiaries were poor village women who used the funds to buy dairy cows or set up small crafts businesses. Although microcredit helped only a few, it offered a model to poor nations around the world. In 2006, Yunus was awarded the Nobel Peace Prize for his efforts. Since then, many organizations have begun to offer microcredit to millions of the world's poorest families. Such loans helped people create their own jobs, earn enough to educate their children, and gain respect within their communities.

SUMMARIZE How does geography pose challenges for Bangladesh?

South Asia in the Cold War

India and Pakistan were among the first of more than 90 new nations to emerge after World War II. By the 1930s, nationalist movements had taken root in European colonies across Africa, Asia, and the Middle East. After India and Pakistan gained independence, nationalist leaders in other regions demanded the same for their countries.

India, Pakistan, and other new nations condemned colonialism. They also rejected Cold War expansion and the divisions between the West and the Soviet Union. In response, they sought **nonalignment,** or political and diplomatic independence from the Cold War superpowers. In 1955, India and Pakistan helped organize a conference of newly independent nations in Bandung, Indonesia, which marked the birth of the nonaligned movement.

>> In 1983, the Nonaligned Movement held a summit in India. Ugandan president Dr. Apolo Milton Obote and Indian president Zail Singh (front) gathered with other leaders of developing nations.

The nonaligned movement had its first formal meeting in 1961 in Yugoslavia. India was a leader of the nonaligned movement, which came to include more than 100 nations, mainly in Asia, Africa, and Latin America. Because they rejected both the Western allies, or the First World, and the Soviet alliance, or the Second World, the Nonaligned Movement was seen as the voice of a "Third World" of countries.

IDENTIFY MAIN IDEAS What important global role did India and Pakistan play after independence?

Independent Nations in Southeast Asia

Southeast Asia includes part of the Asian mainland and thousands of islands that stretch from the Indian Ocean to the South China Sea. In 1939, most of the region was under colonial rule by European nations or the United States. During World War II, Japan seized the region. After the war, nationalist groups demanded independence and resisted reoccupation by European nations.

Mainland Southeast Asia is a region of contrasts. Thailand and Malaysia have mostly prospered as market economies, although they have been affected by global financial crises. However, nearby Myanmar has suffered under a brutal **autocratic,** or repressive, government with unlimited power.

Malaysia Prospers British colonies on the Malay Peninsula and the island of Borneo gained independence in the 1950s and joined to form the nation of Malaysia. The oil-rich monarchy of Brunei, on Borneo, and the prosperous city-state of Singapore gained independence as separate nations.

Malaysia has a diverse population. Malays make up about 60 percent of the people, but the country is home to many people of Chinese and Indian descent. In general the communities exist in harmony but with little interaction among them.

Ethnic Chinese have long dominated business and grown into a wealthy business class. They helped Malaysia develop profitable industries such as rubber, timber, and electronics. Since the 1970s, the government, however, has taken steps to make sure Malays have access to education and business opportunity. As a result, Malaysia has a more equal distribution of wealth than most countries in the region.

>> Aung San Suu Kyi attends a Burmese cultural event in London. Since her release from house arrest, she has reentered politics and works to improve Myanmar.

Suffering and Oppression in Myanmar Burma won independence from Britain in 1948 and took the name Myanmar in 1989. From 1962 until 2011, a repressive military government held absolute power, suppressed dissent, and isolated the country from the rest of the world. It stood accused of widespread human rights abuses such using forced labor—even child labor—for its own purposes.

Under mounting pressure, the military held elections in 1990. When an opposition party won the election, the military rejected the results. It put the opposition leader, **Aung San Suu Kyi,** (awn sahn soo chee) under house arrest, and jailed, killed, or exiled many opponents. In 1991, Suu Kyi won the Nobel Peace Prize for her "nonviolent struggle for democracy and human rights." The military continued to stifle demands for new elections and crushed peaceful demonstrations by Buddhist monks. It even prevented humanitarian aid from reaching areas of Myanmar that were devastated by a cyclone in 2008.

Since 2011, a civilian government has passed some reforms. Though the new president, Thein Sein, continued the practice of appointing military figures to national office, he worked on substantial reforms, including releasing many political prisoners and enacting laws to protect human rights and freedom of information. Under this government, Aung San Suu Kyi has regained political office as a member of Parliament.

Such political reforms spurred leading countries like the United States to provide develop aid to the impoverished nation. Although it has resources such as lumber and offshore oil deposits, its population lives in poverty.

Ethnic tensions have plagued the country for decades. The Burmese majority has dominated many other ethnic groups. Minority groups faced with persecution under military rule started separatist rebellions. The new government has tried to end long-running conflicts with various ethnic groups, but recently violence has erupted between Buddhists and Muslims.

COMPARE How did Malaysia's approach to ethnic diversity differ from Myanmar's?

Populous Indonesia Faces Challenges

After the Japanese were defeated in World War II, the Netherlands attempted to regain their colony in the Dutch East Indies. Nationalists resisted. In 1949, after an armed struggle, the Dutch East Indies won independence as the nation of Indonesia.

Geography and diversity posed an obstacle to unity in Indonesia and has in some cases led to conflict. Indonesia includes more than 13,000 islands, many very small but some as large as European nations. Javanese make up almost half of the population, but there are hundreds of other ethnic groups. About 90 percent of Indonesians are Muslims, but the population includes substantial Christian, Buddhist, and Hindu minorities.

Search for Stability Upon achieving independence, Indonesia formed a parliamentary government under its first president, **Sukarno.** But Sukarno shifted from democracy to authoritarian rule. In 1967, an army general, **Suharto,** seized power and ruled for the next 31 years.

Under these authoritarian rulers, Indonesia suppressed ethnic and other dissent. In the mid 1960s, the government crushed what it claimed was a communist uprising and massacred thousands of Chinese whose ancestors had settled in Indonesia.

In 1998, riots forced Suharto from power. Since then, elected governments have worked to build democracy, strengthen the economy, and fight corruption. In recent years, it has attracted much foreign investment capital, which has helped it develop an expanding economy.

The Independence Movement in East Timor In 1975, Indonesia seized **East Timor,** which had been a Portuguese colony for centuries. Many of the largely Catholic East Timorese wanted independence. For more than 25 years, they pushed their struggle. The Indonesian government responded by imprisoning leaders, burning towns, and slaughtering civilians.

Helped by UN peacekeepers, East Timor finally won independence in 2002. This very poor new nation struggled to meet its people's need for jobs and decent living standards.

Ethnic Conflicts and Natural Disasters Inspired by East Timor's success in breaking away, several other regions have demanded independence from Indonesia. Rebels in Papua, on the island of New Guinea, sought independence, as did Muslim separatists in Aceh (AH chay) in the northwest.

Islamist extremism has challenged Indonesia's long tradition of religious tolerance. Terrorist groups in Indonesia have targeted foreigners and non-Muslims. In the some parts of the country, fighting between Muslims and Christians has killed thousands.

>> Ferdinand Marcos and his wife, Imelda, meet with the press at their palace. The pair was accused of embezzling government money to fund their lavish lifestyle.

Natural disasters have added to Indonesia's troubles. In 2004, a tsunami (tsoo NAH mee), or giant wave, devastated the coast of Aceh and killed more than 100,000 people. The tsunami also ravaged Thailand, Sri Lanka, and other lands around the Indian Ocean. Following the disaster, rebels in Aceh and the Indonesian government signed a peace accord. Helped by international aid donors, they worked together to rebuild Aceh.

IDENTIFY MAIN IDEAS How has diversity posed challenges to Indonesia?

Struggle for Democracy in the Philippines

Like Indonesia, the Philippines include thousands of islands with diverse ethnic and religious groups. Catholics make up the majority of the population, but many Filipino Muslims live in the south. In 1946, the Philippines gained independence after almost 50 years of American rule. American influence remained strong through military and economic aid.

>> Filipino soldiers perform a counter-terrorism drill in the southern Philippines.

Marcos Becomes a Dictator Although the Filipino constitution set up a democratic government, a wealthy elite controlled politics and the economy. The peasant majority was poor. For years, the government battled Huks (hooks), local communists with strong peasant support. **Ferdinand Marcos,** was elected president in 1965. Marcos had promised reform, but instead became a dictaor. He cracked down on basic freedoms and forced opponents into exile. He even had **Benigno Aquino** (beh NEE nyoh ah KEE noh), a popular rival, murdered.

A Demand for Democracy When Marcos finally held elections in 1986, voters chose **Corazon Aquino** (kawr ah SOHN), the widow of the slain Benigno. Marcos tried to overturn the results, but massive protests forced him to resign in what was called the "people power" revolution. Under Aquino and her successors, this fragile democracy survived, despite many political scandals. Economic growth was limited, and poverty remained widespread. With the highest birth rate in Asia, the population continues to rise rapidly, straining already limited resources.

Clashes with Rebels For decades, various rebel groups have waged guerrilla wars in various parts the Philippines. Some rebels were communists. In a 2012 peace deal, they agreed to work toward peace, despite serious mistrust. Other groups, such as the Moros, wanted a separate Muslim state within the largely Catholic country. After 40 years of fighting, Moro rebels accepted a peace deal, which promised to allow greater Muslim rights in the southern Philippines. Other rebels belonged to a radical Islamist group with links to international terrorist groups such as Al Qaeda. The Filipino government accepted aid from its ally, the United States, to fight terrorists.

IDENTIFY CAUSE AND EFFECT Why has the Philippines had trouble preserving its democracy?

ASSESSMENT

1. **Identify Cause and Effect** Why did the partition of British India cause a refugee crisis?
2. **Summarize** Why did Bangladesh separate from Pakistan?
3. **Draw Conclusions** How did a policy of nonalignment influence the relations of India and Pakistan with the Cold War superpowers?
4. **Compare** Why did policies toward ethnic diversity lead to prosperity in Malaysia but to conflict in other parts of Southeast Asia?
5. **Synthesize** How have religious and ethnic diversity affected the recent history of Indonesia?

Primary Sources

"Freedom from Fear": Aung San Suu Kyi

Introduction

Aung San Suu Kyi, leader of the National League for Democracy in Myanmar (Burma) and winner of the Nobel Peace Prize, has worked courageously for human rights and democracy in her country. Because of her opposition to Myanmar's ruling military junta, she was held under house arrest from 1989 to 1995 and severely restricted until 2010. In this essay, Aung San Suu Kyi describes the need for courage when living under an oppressive government.

The second primary source is from Aung San Suu Kyi's speech after receiving the Nobel Peace Prize, twenty one years after being first named for the honor. At the time, she was still under house arrest and could not leave the country.

>> Aung San Suu Kyi

Primary Source

Fearlessness may be a gift but perhaps more precious is the courage acquired through endeavor, courage that comes from cultivating the habit of refusing to let fear dictate one's actions, courage that could be described as 'grace under pressure'—grace which is renewed repeatedly in the face of harsh, unremitting [not letting up] pressure.

COMPARE AND CONTRAST Why does Suu Kyi compare and contrast fearlessness and courage, saying one is more precious than the other?

Within a system which denies the existence of basic human rights, fear tends to be the order of the day. Fear of imprisonment, fear of torture, fear of death, fear of losing friends, family, property or means of livelihood, fear of poverty, fear of isolation, fear of failure. A most insidious [meant to harm] form of fear is that which masquerades as common sense or even wisdom, condemning as foolish, reckless, insignificant or futile the small, daily acts of courage which help to preserve man's self-respect and inherent [part of one's basic nature] human dignity. It is not easy for a people conditioned by fear under the iron rule of the principle that might is right to free themselves from the enervating [weakening] miasma [harmful atmosphere] of fear. Yet even under the most crushing state machinery courage rises up again and again, for fear is not the natural state of civilized man.

DRAW INFERENCES What do you think might be an example of "the small, daily acts of courage" Suu Kyi references?

The wellspring [source] of courage and endurance in the face of unbridled power is generally a firm belief in the sanctity of ethical principles combined with a historical sense that despite all setbacks the condition of man is set on an ultimate course for both spiritual and material advancement. . . . It is man's vision of a world fit for rational, civilized humanity which leads him to dare and to suffer to build societies free from want and fear. Concepts such as truth, justice and compassion cannot be dismissed as trite [overused and uninteresting] when these are often the only bulwarks [defenses] which stand against ruthless power.

IDENTIFY CAUSE AND EFFECT According to Suu Kyi, from where does courage come? What does it enable individuals to do?

Primary Source

To be forgotten. The French say that to part is to die a little. To be forgotten too is to die a little. It is to lose some of the links that anchor us to the rest of humanity. When I met Burmese migrant workers and refugees during my recent visit to Thailand, many cried out: "Don't forget us!" They meant: "don't forget our plight, don't forget to do what you can to help us, don't forget we also belong to your world." When the Nobel Committee awarded the Peace Prize to me they were recognizing that the oppressed and the isolated in Burma were also a part of the world, they were recognizing the oneness of humanity. So for me receiving the Nobel Peace Prize means personally extending my concerns for democracy and human rights beyond national borders. The Nobel Peace Prize opened up a door in my heart.

ASSESSMENT

1. **Assess an Argument** How is this excerpt from Suu Kyi's essay an example of the courage she advocates?
2. **Draw Conclusions** How do you think essays like "Freedom from Fear" can help bring about political change in places such as Myanmar?
3. **Determine Author's Purpose** President Franklin D. Roosevelt used "freedom from fear" in his 1941 State of the Union, and the phrase is also included in the United Nation's Universal Declaration of Human Rights. Why do you think Suu Kyi chose this phrase for the title of her essay?
4. **Explain** How did the honor of the Nobel peace prize "open a door" for Aung San Suu Kyi?

9.2 In 1945, four European powers—Britain, France, Belgium, and Portugal—controlled almost all of Africa. Only Egypt, Ethiopia, Liberia and white-ruled South Africa were independent nations.

>> Kwame Nkrumah and others wave to a crowd during independence celebrations. **Analyze Visuals** How are the men in this image dressed? What does this reveal about their attitude toward their culture?

Bounce to Activate Flipped Video

African Nations Win Independence

The New Nations of Africa

World War II sparked a rising tide of nationalism in Africa. Japanese victories in Asia shattered the West's reputation as an unbeatable force. Also, African troops who had fought for the Allies were unwilling to accept discrimination when they returned home. Nationalists also won support among workers who had migrated to the cities to work in war industries.

After the war, most European nations lacked the resources and will to fight to hold onto colonies. Faced with nationalist demands, Britain and France introduced political reforms that they thought would gradually lead to independence. But they soon discovered that they could not control the pace of change. Starting in the late 1950s, they gave up direct control of most of their colonies. In countries with large settler populations, however, independence was thwarted for years.

In the new nations, crowds celebrated their freedom, while bands played new national anthems. However, even as independence celebrations took place, African nations faced tough challenges.

>> Objectives

Summarize how African nations won independence.

Analyze the issues facing new African nations and the different paths they took.

Identify examples of and summarize the reasons for ethnic conflict and genocide in African nations.

>> Key Terms

savanna
Kwame Nkrumah
Jomo Kenyatta
coup d'état
Mobutu Sese Seko
Islamist
Katanga
Biafra
Hutus
Tutsis
Darfur

A Geographically Diverse Continent Africa is the world's second-largest continent. It has the world's largest desert—the Sahara—in the north and the smaller Kalahari Desert in the south, as well as fertile coastal strips in North and South Africa. **Savannas,** or grasslands with scattered trees, make up much of the interior. Tropical rain forests cover central Africa's Congo Basin and coastal West Africa.

Africa's population has long been concentrated in the most fertile areas, such as the highlands of East Africa. Like people in other parts of the world, however, millions of Africans are migrating to cities. About 40 percent of Africans live in fast-growing cities.

Africa has rich deposits of minerals such as gold ore, copper ore, and diamonds. However, these resources are distributed unevenly across the continent. Some African nations produce valuable cash crops, including coffee and cacao. Some regions also have large oil reserves. European powers had established colonies in Africa to tap into these natural resources.

Nationalism Leads to Freedom Most nationalist leaders were Western educated. Many were powerful speakers whose words inspired supporters. **Kwame Nkrumah**(KWAH may un KROO muh) in Gold Coast, **Jomo Kenyatta** in Kenya, and Léopold Senghor (sahn GAWR) in Senegal were skilled organizers.

Nationalist leaders organized political parties. In the cities, parties published newspapers, held mass rallies, and mobilized popular support for independence. Colonial powers imprisoned many nationalists, including Nkrumah and Kenyatta. But demonstrations, strikes, and boycotts eventually forced European rulers to negotiate timetables for freedom.

Most African nations won independence through largely peaceful efforts. However, colonies with large numbers of white settlers, such as Algeria and Kenya, were unwilling to grant Africans their freedom. Africans in these colonies were forced to go to war against the colonial powers. Later, you will examine five of these nations in detail.

IDENTIFY CAUSE AND EFFECT How did World War II affect African independence efforts?

>> Some mining operations in Africa employ the most modern technology and machinery, but in poorer nations, older methods are still used. Here, men mine diamonds by hand in Sierra Leone.

A Variety of New Governments

More than 50 new nations were born in Africa during the great liberation. Throughout the continent, Africans had great hopes for the future. After 70 years of colonial rule, Africans were again in control of their destinies. The new nations took different paths to modernization. Some made progress despite huge obstacles. Many others were plunged into crisis by civil war, military rule, or corrupt dictators. In recent decades, a number of African nations have taken steps toward democracy.

Old Boundaries, New Problems In Africa, as in other regions such as Eastern Europe, the question of where to draw national borders created challenges. European colonial powers had drawn boundaries around their colonies without regard to the many rival ethnic groups living there. Most newly independent African nations included a patchwork of peoples with different languages, religions, and traditions.

Within these new nations, people often felt their first loyalty was to their own ethnic group, not to a distant national government. As a result, ongoing conflict between rival ethnic groups has plagued many African nations.

Africa Today

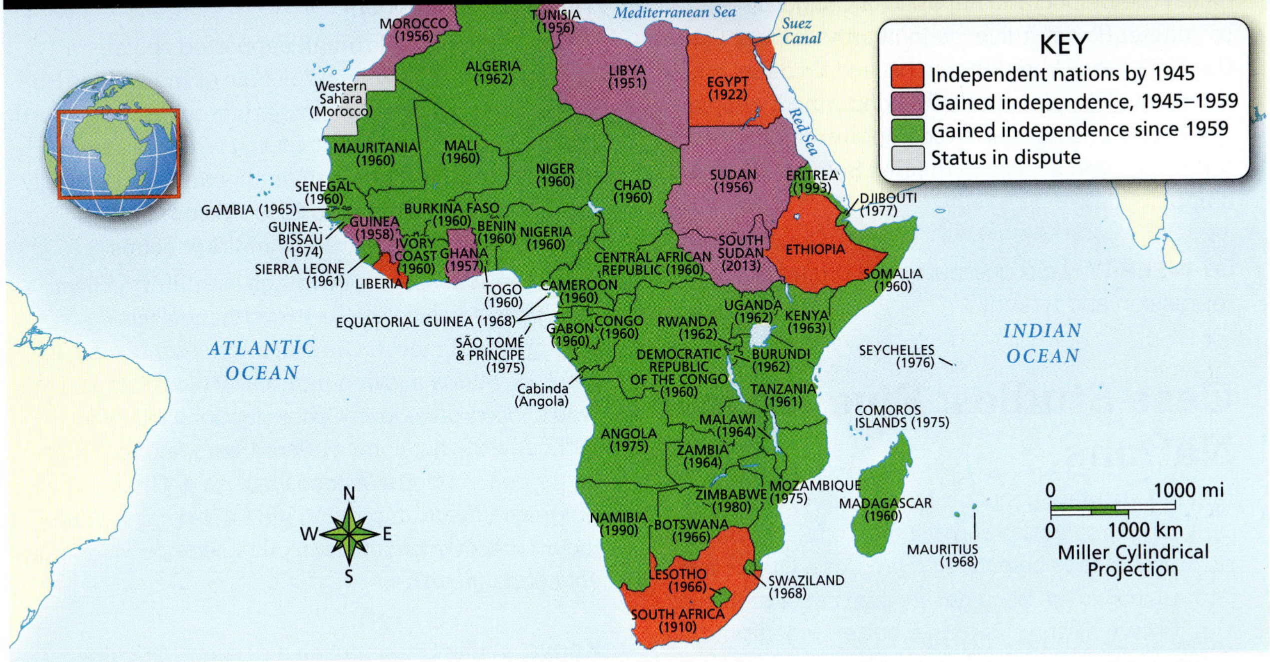

>> Over the course of many years, African nations gained their independence from European powers. **Analyze Maps** What do the dates on this map tell you about when nations gained independence?

Bounce to Activate Map

The Rise of Dictators After independence, the new African nations set up governments modeled on those of the departing colonial rulers. But parliamentary systems did not work in Africa as they had in Europe, where they had evolved over centuries. Creating unified nations with stable governments proved to be a hard goal to reach

Many leaders of the new nations were heroes of the liberation struggle. Some chose to build one-party states. They argued that multiparty systems encouraged disunity, which was often true. Many of these one-party governments became repressive, and some liberation leaders became dictators. Dictators often used their positions to enrich themselves and their supporters at the expense of the nation.

In many nations, unsuccessful policies or corrupt governments led to civil unrest. This in turn, led to military coups (kooz). A coup, or **coup d'état** (koo day TAH), is the forcible overthrow of a government. Some coup leaders became brutal tyrants. Others tried to end corruption and improve conditions. Military leaders usually promised to restore civilian rule. But in many cases, they only surrendered power when they were toppled by another coup.

Democracies Emerge By the 1990s, many African nations were moving away from strongman rule. Africans organized and demanded democratic elections. In some countries, independent newspapers came out, with their editors risking arrest for their publications. Religious leaders spoke out for greater freedom. Outside pressures also played a role. Western governments and lenders, such as the World Bank, demanded political reforms before granting loans needed for economic development.

In response, some governments allowed opposition parties to emerge and lifted censorship. In nations such as Nigeria and Benin, multiparty elections were held, unseating long-ruling leaders.

Outside Influences on African Nations Even after African nations won independence, colonial powers and foreign companies often retained control of businesses and resources in these former colonies. Many new nations remained dependent on their former colonial rulers for aid, trade, and investment.

The new nations were also buffeted by the Cold War. Both the United States and the Soviet Union competed for military and strategic advantage through alliances with several African countries. The United States, for example, backed **Mobutu Sese**

Seko, (seh-say say-koh) the dictator of Zaire (now called the Democratic Republic of Congo). It wanted to counter Soviet influence in nearby Angola. During the 1970s, the United States backed Somalia, while the Soviet Union supported neighboring Ethiopia. Both African countries were important because they controlled access to the Red Sea, a vital world shipping route.

INFER Why did one-party rule often lead to repression and tyranny?

Case Studies: Five African Nations

Making accurate generalizations about Africa is difficult. Every nation is different. Some nations have rich resources to help finance progress. Others are poor in resources. Each has its own set of problems and its own history. To gain a better understanding of the process of nation-building in Africa, we will examine the histories of five important nations.

Ghana In 1957, Ghana was the first African nation south of the Sahara to win independence. Britain had called this colony Gold Coast, for its rich mineral resources. Under independence leader Kwame Nkrumah, it took the name Ghana, after the ancient West African kingdom.

As president, Nkrumah supported socialism and government ownership of major industries. He backed the building of a huge dam to provide electric power, but the project left Ghana with massive debts. Nkrumah's government became increasingly corrupt and dictatorial. In 1966, Nkrumah was toppled by the first of several military coups.

In the 1980s, Jerry Rawlings, a military officer, took power in a coup. He strengthened the economy and moved Ghana toward democracy. In 1992, Rawlings allowed multiparty elections and was chosen president. Other elections followed. Although the economy suffered from falling prices for its main exports of cocoa and gold, Ghana made progress toward improving life for its people. The recent discovery of offshore oil raised hopes for more economic growth.

>> In this image, British troops search a village in Kenya seeking people who participated in the Mau Mau Rebellion.

Kenya While Ghana made a peaceful transition to freedom, Kenya faced an armed struggle. Under colonial rule, white settlers carved out plantations on lands once occupied by the Kikuyu (kee KOO yoo), Kenya's largest ethnic group. White Kenyans then passed laws to ensure their domination over the black majority. Nationalist leader and Kikuyu spokesman Jomo Kenyatta called for nonviolent resistance to end oppressive laws.

In the 1950s, some black Kenyans turned to guerrilla warfare, attacking and killing white settlers. The British called them Mau Mau. Claiming that he was a secret leader of the Mau Mau, the British imprisoned Kenyatta. Both sides committed terrible atrocities during this period, and thousands of Kikuyu were killed. In 1963, the British finally withdrew, and Kenyatta became the first president of an independent Kenya.

Kenyatta and his successor dominated the country for decades. They limited freedom of expression and suppressed other parties. Unrest and international pressure forced Kenya to restore multiparty rule in the 1990s.

Since then, Kenya has faced many challenges from high unemployment to periodic droughts. Corruption and disputed elections have sparked violence and ethnic unrest. With its many national parks and game reserves, tourism is a major industry in Kenya, so any conflict hurts this vital source of income. In 2013 the country held tense but largely peaceful elections.

Algeria Like Kenya, French-ruled Algeria had a large population of European settlers who saw the country as their homeland. France, too, had come to see Algeria as part of their country. From 1954 to 1962, a long, costly war of liberation raged in Algeria.

Algerian nationalists set up the National Liberation Front, which used guerrilla warfare to win freedom. France, which had just lost Vietnam, was unwilling to retreat from Algeria. As the war dragged, both sides suffered huge casualties. Finally, French public opinion turned against the war, and Algeria won independence.

After independence, Algeria suffered periods of military rule and internal conflict. During the 1990s, a civil war erupted between the military and Islamist militants after the government rejected an election won by an Islamist party. **Islamists** are people who want a government based on Islamic law and beliefs. The fighting left an estimated 150,000 people dead. The violence slowed after 1999, but tensions remained. Algeria has also been rocked by suicide bombings by Islamist militants

Algeria's economy has seen some improvements. It first adopted a socialist model of development, but since the 1980s, has moved toward a market economy. Its oil and gas resources have helped the country economically. Still, like many developing countries it faces the problems of high unemployment, widespread poverty, and corruption.

>> Patrice Lumumba was newly independent Congo's first prime minister. Here, Lumumba waves to a crowd after receiving a 41–2 vote of confidence from the Congolese senate in September 1960.

Bounce to Activate Gallery

Democratic Republic of Congo The Democratic Republic of Congo (or Congo), once ruled by Belgium, covers about a million square miles of central Africa. It has rich resources, including vast tropic rainforests, plantations, and great mineral wealth, especially the copper and diamonds.

Belgium was eager to keep control of Congo's resources, such as the copper and diamonds of the **Katanga** province. Fearing a struggle like the French war in Algeria, Belgium suddenly rushed Congo to independence in 1960. But the new nation had no preparation for self-government and no sense of unity. More than 100 political parties sprang up, representing diverse regional and ethnic groups.

Katanga rebelled against Congo shortly after independence. The country's first prime minister, Patrice Lumumba, appealed for Soviet help. This led the United States to back Lumumba's rival, Colonel Joseph Mobutu, later known as Mobutu Sese Seko. Mobutu captured Lumumba, who was soon executed. The United Nations ended the Katanga rebellion in 1963.

For 32 years, Mobutu imposed a harsh, corrupt dictatorship on Congo. Mobutu survived in power in part because his strong anti-communism won favor in the West during the Cold War. Rebels finally forced Mobutu from power in 1997. After his removal, rival leaders again battled to control Congo's government and mineral riches.

Congo's first free elections in 41 years brought Joseph Kabila to power in 2006. Kabila faced immense challenges. He had to ease ethnic tensions, protect Congo's mineral resources, reduce corruption, and heal a country deeply scarred by decades of war.

Nigeria Located in West Africa, Nigeria has the continent's largest population. Its people belong to more than 250 ethnic groups, speak many languages, and practice different religions. The dominant groups are the mainly Christian Ibo (EE boh) and Yoruba (YOH roo buh) in the south, and the Muslim Hausa (HOW suh) in the north.

After gaining independence from Britain in 1960, Nigeria experienced frequent military coups. Military leaders ruled with an iron hand but failed to improve Nigeria's government or its economy. Since 1999, Nigeria has had elected civilian governments.

Ethnic and religious divisions have threatened to tear Nigeria apart. In 1966, the Ibo people in the oil-rich south rebelled and set up the independent Republic of **Biafra.** A brutal civil war led to famine and a huge death toll. After three years, Nigeria crushed the rebels and reunited the country. More recently, Islamists in the north have imposed Sharia law in several areas, causing many Christians to flee. A separatist group, Boko Haram, has launched terrorist attacks throughout the country.

Nigeria has rich oil resources, which has brought benefits as well as disadvantages. When oil prices are high, the country reaps great profits that can be invested in development. But falling oil prices has caused problems and cutbacks in spending. Also oil wealth has contributed to corruption. In the oil-producing Niger Delta region, local people were bitter about the environmental damage caused by oil drilling and the huge profits going to foreign oil companies. Armed groups have attacked pipelines and held foreign oil workers for ransom.

IDENTIFY CENTRAL ISSUES How did the conflicts in Katanga and Biafra reflect the challenges that new African nations faced after independence?

The Wars of Southern Africa

Colonies in southern Africa were among the last to win independence. Unlike the peaceful transition to independence in much of Africa, the road to freedom in southern Africa was marked by long, violent struggles.

>> By the year 2009, when this photo was taken, Robert Mugabe was being forced to share power, but Zimbabwe still faced terrible inflation, food shortages, and disease epidemics.

Zimbabwe During the colonial period, many whites had settled in British-ruled Southern Rhodesia. Whites made up only five percent of Rhodesia's population but owned half the land and controlled the government. White Rhodesians rejected any move to give up power to the black majority. When Britain supported demands for majority rule, whites led by Ian Smith declared independence in 1965.

Guerrilla forces took up arms to win majority rule. They finally succeeded in 1980. Rhodesia became the independent nation of Zimbabwe. Liberation leader Robert Mugabe was elected president.

Although popular at first, Mugabe grew increasingly dictatorial. He cracked down on opponents and ended many basic freedoms. Despite international pressure and an economic crisis, the aging Mugabe held on to power.

Angola and Mozambique Portugal clung fiercely to its profitable colonies of Angola and Mozambique. To achieve independence, nationalist groups had to wage a long guerrilla war. In 1975, Portugal finally agreed to withdraw.

Brutal civil wars, largely supported by foreign powers, soon developed in both countries. White-ruled South Africa feared the rise of strong, black-dominated governments on its borders. As a result, they funded rebel groups in both Mozambique and Angola. The Cold War also fueled tensions. In Angola, the Soviet Union financed Cuban troops who supported the left-wing government, while the United States backed insurgent anti-communist forces.

The fighting continued until 1992 in Mozambique and until 2002 in Angola. Decades of war had ravaged both countries, which slowly began to rebuild.

DRAW CONCLUSIONS Why did fighting continue after Angola achieved independence?

Ethnic Conflict and Genocide

After independence, ethnic conflicts plagued some African nations. The causes were complex. Often one group held political and economic power at the expense of other groups. Weak or unstable governments were unable to build national unity. Regional and cultural differences also fed rivalries that on occasion led to tragic violence. At times, ambitious leaders took advantage of rivalries to increase their own power.

Rwanda and Burundi Power struggles between rival groups led to a deadly genocide in Rwanda, a small central African nation. The country is home to two main groups, the majority **Hutus** and the minority **Tutsis.** Though often considered separate ethnic groups, they speak the same language, share the same culture, follow the same Catholic religion and look alike. In colonial times, the Belgian government had favored Tutsis over the Hutus. After independence, the majority Hutu came into power and violence against Tutsis increased. Over the next 30 years, many Tutsis fled to neighboring countries.

In early 1994, a suspicious plane crash killed the presidents of Rwanda and neighboring Burundi. The crash triggered a coordinated attack on Tutsis. Urged on by extremist Hutu officials, civilians turned on their Tutsi neighbors. At least 800,000 Tutsis and moderate Hutus were brutally slaughtered within a few months. Even as the death toll rose, the world community was slow to act to stop the genocide. By July, a Tutsi-led army had invaded from Burundi, ended the slaughter, and set up a unity government.

Rwandan leaders tried to heal the horrors of the genocide. Almost two million people were tried in traditional community courts where the goal was to achieve truth and reconciliation. The hearings resulted in some convictions, but many of those who took part in the killings remained in their communities. The main leaders of the genocide, however, faced trials in an international court.

Burundi faced similar tensions between Hutus and Tutsis. Violence erupted, but did not lead to genocide as in Rwanda. In 2005, voters approved a new constitution that guaranteed both groups participation in the government and military.

Rebellion and Civil War in Sudan The large, geographically diverse country of Sudan has faced decades of conflict. After independence, the Arab Muslim north dominated the non-Muslim, non-Arab south. A long civil war pitted the north against the south, killing more than a million and a half people.

The Sudanese government and rebels in the south finally agreed to a peace accord. In 2011, the people of South Sudan voted to secede and set up their own independent nation. Relations between the two countries remain strained over disputed borders and the sharing of oil revenues, which both countries desperately need. Within South Sudan itself, tensions threatened civil war as rival groups jockeyed for power.

>> The Kigali Memorial Centre in Kigali, Rwanda, displays photographs of people killed in the genocide. **Analyze Image** How could these photographs affect a person's understanding of the genocide?

>> Children celebrate with a Republic of South Sudan flag cake during Sudanese independence celebrations in 2011.

Another conflict raged in **Darfur,** in the western region of Sudan. There, the rebels were non-Arab Muslims who fought against the Arab-dominated Sudanese government. The government launched a campaign of genocide, encouraging Arab militias to destroy the villages and slaughter the black Sudanese residents. An estimated 300,000 people were killed and more than two million fled their homes.

The United States and other countries sent humanitarian aid to refugees in Darfur. The UN sent peacekeepers to prevent further violence but with little success. The International Criminal Court (ICC) charged Sudan's president, Omar al-Bashir, with crimes against humanity and genocide. However, the ICC is not recognized in Sudan, and no arrest was ever made. In 2010, al-Bashir won reelection, though many believe those elections were not fair or free. The conflict in Darfur has lessened but not ended. The situation is complex with many warring groups and no easy solution.

DESCRIBE Why was there conflict between northern and southern Sudan?

ASSESSMENT

1. **Analyze Information** Where did struggles for independence in Africa turn violent and why?
2. **Compare and Contrast** What were the issues facing the Democratic Republic of Congo and Kenya as they achieved independence and what paths did those countries take?
3. **Synthesize** Why did many new nations in Africa have difficulty building democratic governments?
4. **Summarize** How did the ethnic conflict in Rwanda become a genocide?
5. **Compare** How was the conflict in Darfur similar to the conflict in Rwanda?

Primary Sources

Autobiography: Kwame Nkrumah

Introduction

Kwame Nkrumah led the people of the Gold Coast in their quest for independence from Britain. After succeeding in 1957, Nkrumah became the first prime minister and renamed the country Ghana. In this excerpt from his *Autobiography,* Nkrumah speaks of the need to establish economic independence as a means of maintaining political independence. Nkrumah describes the difficult work of building an independent economy.

Like Ghana, Kenya sought independence from colonial rule. Nationalist leader Jomo Kenyatta became the first prime minister of the Kenyan nation. In the primary source excerpt below, he describes the challenges facing Kenyans.

>> Kwame Nkrumah at an independence celebration.

Primary Source

. . . Independence for the Gold Coast was my aim. It was a colony, and I have always regarded colonialism as the policy by which a foreign power binds territories to herself by political ties with the primary object of promoting her own economic advantage. No one need be surprised if this system has led to disturbances and political tension in many territories. There are few people who would not rid themselves of such domination if they could. . . .

IDENTIFY CAUSE AND EFFECT Why does Nkrumah say it is not surprising that tension and unrest occur in colonies?

I saw that the whole solution to [our] problem lay in political freedom for our people, for it is only when a people are politically free that other races can give them the respect that is due to them. It is impossible to talk of equality of races in any other terms. No people without a government of their own can expect to be treated on the same level as peoples of independent sovereign [self-governing] states. It is far better to be free to govern or misgovern yourself than to be governed by anybody else. . . .

EXPLAIN AN ARGUMENT According to Nkrumah, why are people who live in independent countries better off than people who live in colonies?

Once this freedom is gained, a greater task comes into view. All dependent [subject to the rule of another country] territories are backward in education, in science, in agriculture, and in industry. The economic independence that should follow and maintain political independence demands every effort from the people, a total mobilization of brain and manpower resources. What other countries have taken three hundred years or more to achieve, a once dependent territory must try to accomplish in a generation if it is to survive. . . .

COMPARE AND CONTRAST How does Nkrumah say political dependence is related to economic independence?

Primary Source

True democracy has no colour distinction (difference). It does not choose between black and white. We are here in this tremendous gathering under the Kenya African Union flag to find which road leads us from darkness into democracy. In order to find it we Africans must first achieve the right to elect our own representatives. That is surely the first principle of democracy. We are the only race in Kenya which does not elect its own representatives in the Legislature and we are going to set about to rectify (fix) this situation. We feel we are dominated by a handful of others who refuse to be just.

God said this is our land. . . . We want our cattle to get fat on our land so that our children grow up in prosperity (wealth); we do not want that fat removed to feed others. . . . We want to prosper as a nation, and as a nation we demand equality, that is equal pay for equal work. Whether it is a chief, headman, or laborer he needs increased salary. He needs a salary that compares with a salary of a European who does equal work. We will never get our freedom unless we succeed in this issue. We do not want equal pay for equal work tomorrow—we want it right now. . . . If we work together as one, we must succeed.

IDENTIFY MAIN IDEAS According to Kenyatta, what is the first step toward achieving political independence in Kenya?

ASSESSMENT

1. **Summarize** How does Nkrumah characterize life in a colony?
2. **Summarize** Based on Nkrumah's and Kenyatta's remarks, what challenges did newly emerging nations in Africa face?
3. **Assess an Argument** Do you agree with Nkrumah that it is "far better to be free to govern or misgovern yourself than to be governed by anybody else"? Why or why not?

9.3 The Middle East, as we use the term in this lesson, is the region stretching from Egypt in the west to Iran in the east and from Turkey in the north to the Arabian Peninsula in the south. Although the majority of people in the region today are Muslims, there are also Christian communities and the mostly Jewish nation of Israel.

>> These Iraqi women wear the modified hejab covering their hair. Hejab is required by law in Iran and Saudi Arabia, but it has been freely adopted by many Muslim women worldwide as a sign of their faith.

Bounce to Activate Flipped Video

The Modern Middle East Takes Shape

The Challenges of Diversity

As a world crossroads since ancient times, the Middle East is home to many ethnic groups. Arabs are a majority in some countries, such as Egypt, Saudi Arabia, and Syria. In other countries, the majority populations are non-Arab Muslims, such as the Turks of Turkey and the Persians of Iran.

Mandates Gain Independence At the end of World War I, the Treaty of Versailles and other agreements parceled out many of the lands once dominated by the defeated Central Powers. Britain and France were given mandates over large parts of the Middle East.

Under the mandate system in the Middle East, territories taken from the defeated Ottoman empire were administered, or run, by Europeans. Britain, for example, controlled the Palestine mandate and three provinces of the old Ottoman empire that were joined together into modern-day Iraq. The stated goal of the mandate system was to move the mandates gradually toward independence.

>> Objectives

Analyze the development of modern nations in the Middle East.

Describe the founding of Israel and the impact of the Arab rejection of Israel.

Understand how oil has affected nations of the Middle East.

Examine the impact of Islam on government, law, and the lives of women.

Define the "Arab Spring."

>> Key Terms

kibbutz
Golda Meir
Suez Canal
Gamal Abdel Nasser
Anwar Sadat
Ruhollah Khomeini
theocracy
secular
hejab

From the outset, Arabs resisted the mandates. In British-ruled Palestine, tensions also grew between Arab and Jewish residents. In the Balfour Declaration, Britain had supported a Jewish national home in part of the Palestine mandate, while Arabs in the region demanded self-rule. During the 1930s, independence movements and nationalist calls for an end to European control grew. Following World War II, the former mandates became the independent countries of Iraq, Syria, and Jordan. The Palestine mandate was partitioned into Arab areas and Israel.

Religious and Ethnic Divisions The borders of the new nations were artificially drawn and lumped together diverse ethnic and religious communities. Some ethnic minorities demanded self-rule, or even independence.

Different religious sects, or groups loyal to their own set of beliefs, further divided the new nations. Many countries were home to both Shiite and Sunni Muslims, along with Alawites, Druze, different Christian sects, and Jews. In Iraq and Bahrain, for example, the Shiite majority was ruled by the Sunni minority. Sectarian violence, or conflict based on religious loyalties, posed challenges to unity. Many nations like Syria and Lebanon had diverse groups, including Muslim and Christian Arabs, Assyrians, Greeks, Armenians, and Kurds.

Kurdish Nationalism The Kurds are an ethnic group with their own language and culture. They form important minorities in Turkey, Iran, and Iraq. Kurdish nationalists have long called for an independent homeland. In Turkey, Kurdish rebels resisted government efforts to suppress their culture. In Iraq, a Kurdish uprising in 1991 was brutally suppressed. Today, Kurds in Iraq have much autonomy, but many Kurds still want their own state.

EXPRESS PROBLEMS CLEARLY What is the main cause of ethnic and sectarian violence in the Middle East?

The Founding of Israel

As early as the 1880s, Jews had begun actively organizing and advocating for the re-establishment of a home in their ancient homeland. The horrors of the Holocaust created strong worldwide support for a Jewish state. Many Jews, including Holocaust survivors, migrated to the Palestine Mandate after World War II.

In 1947, the UN drew up a plan to divide, or partition, the Palestine mandate between the Arabs and Jews. The plan called for the division of Palestine into an Arab and a Jewish state. The UN

The Modern Middle East

>> **Analyze Maps** This map shows the countries of the modern Middle East. Saudi Arabia, Kuwait, and Iran are three of the world's largest oil-producing countries. Why might control of the Strait of Hormuz be important?

Bounce to Activate Map

General Assembly voted to adopt the plan. While the Jews accepted partition, Arabs rejected the partition plan. They argued that Palestine was one of the lands that had been promised to them by the British in return for Arab support in World War I.

Arabs and Israelis in Conflict In 1948, when Britain withdrew from the Palestine mandate, Jews proclaimed the independent State of Israel. Neighboring Arab nations launched the first of several wars against Israel, but were defeated.

As a result of these wars, Israel gained control of more territory. After the 1948 war, Jordan took control of the West Bank and East Jerusalem, while Egypt took the Gaza Strip. Today, Palestinian Arabs do not have an independent state, but a series of negotiations over the years has resulted in peace treaties between Israel and Egypt and the creation of an autonomous Palestinian authority within Israeli-controlled territories.

The 1948 Arab-Israeli war created a huge refugee problem. Hundreds of thousands of Palestinian Arabs fled their homes in Israeli territory. The UN housed them in temporary camps in nearby countries, where they remained for decades. At the same time, hundreds of thousands of Jewish refugees expelled from Arab lands fled to Israel.

The Growth of Israel After the 1948 war, Israel developed rapidly. A skilled workforce set up businesses. Kibbutzim produced crops for export. A **kibbutz** (kih BOOTS) is a collective farm.

In 1950, Israel passed a law called the right of return, granting every Jew the right to live in Israel and become an Israeli citizen. This was a response to the Holocaust when countries closed their doors to Jews fleeing the Nazis. This law established Israel as a safe haven for the Jewish people. Jews from around the world migrated to Israel. They joined native Israelis who had struggled to win independence.

An early leader was **Golda Meir,** who had emigrated from Russia to the United States as a child. In the 1920s, she moved to a kibbutz in Palestine and later joined the Jewish independence movement. In 1969, she became Israel's first woman prime minister.

INFER Why did people around the world support a Jewish homeland in Palestine?

>> Israeli flags fly in New York City to celebrate the birth of Israel, which became an independent state on May 14, 1948. **Explain** Why was an Arab state not established as well?

Bounce to Activate Gallery

>> Palestinian women and children flee to Arab-held territories in June 1948. Refugee camps were set up to accept those who could not find shelter. **Recall** How long did some Palestinian refugees live in the refugee camps?

>> This photograph shows members of the royal family of Saudi Arabia, one of the most oil-rich nations on Earth. Most power remains with the king and royal family, but tribal sheikhs also have influence. **Recall** Which other Middle Eastern state has a hereditary monarchy? Which two states have multiparty systems?

>> Gamal Abdel Nasser (left) led Egypt from 1952 until 1970. Here, he and the president of Syria celebrate the union of their countries to form the United Arab Republic in 1958. This Pan-Arab experiment lasted only three years. **Hypothesize** Why is Egypt such an important country in the Middle East?

New Nations in the Middle East

After independence, Middle Eastern nations set out to build strong modern economies. Only a handful of nations in the region had rich oil reserves. Most Middle Eastern nations were poor, and each faced its own set of challenges.

In some countries, nationalist military leaders seized power. They wanted to promote economic growth and end foreign influence, but they were also authoritarian rulers who suppressed critics, often brutally. Some countries, such as Jordan and Saudi Arabia, had hereditary monarchs. Only Israel and Turkey had stable multiparty systems.

Egypt's Leadership in the Arab World Egypt is the most populous nation in the Arab world. Since most of Egypt is desert, its population is crammed into the narrow Nile River valley.

Egypt controls the **Suez Canal,** the vital waterway that provides the shortest sea route between Europe and Asia. Egypt also shares a border with Israel.

In 1952, **Gamal Abdel Nasser** seized power in Egypt. Determined to modernize Egypt and end Western domination, Nasser soon nationalized the Suez Canal, ending British and French control. Nasser's Arab nationalism made him popular in the Arab world. He led two unsuccessful wars against Israel. Egypt relied on Soviet aid during the Cold War.

In 1979, Nasser's successor, **Anwar Sadat,** reduced ties with the Soviet Union and sought aid from the United States. He also became the first Arab leader to make peace with Israel. In exchange for peace, Israel returned the Sinai Peninsula to Egypt. Sadat was assassinated by Islamist extremists in 1981. Hosni Mubarak took over and cracked down hard on extremists, jailing even moderate critics.

The Arab Spring and Its Impact In 2011, popular unrest swept across the Middle East, launching pro-democracy movements, known as the Arab Spring. Frustration with corrupt and dictatorial governments, along with high unemployment, fed demands for change. The Arab Spring, which started in Tunisia, spread to Egypt and other nations. During the Arab Spring, massive street protests forced Egypt's Hosni Mubarak to step down after 30 years in office.

The "Arab Spring" took different paths in different nations. Some governments suppressed the protests. Other countries, such as Egypt, held elections.

Egyptians went to the polls with great hopes in 2012. An Islamist leader, Mohammed Morsi, was elected president. Within a year, however, he was ousted by the Egyptian military after mass protests erupted against his government. New elections are scheduled for 2014.

The results of the Arab Spring also varied from country to country. In Tunisia, Islamist and **secular,** or nonreligious, parties formed a coalition to work together for democratic reform. Hopes for democratic reforms, however, faced an uncertain future in other nations. In Egypt, any new leader will face severe social and economic problems as well the deep divide and ongoing conflict between Islamists and secularists.

Elsewhere, similar political, religious, and other divisions posed challenges. In Syria, pro-democracy protests pitched Syria into a horrendous civil war. Many people grew disillusioned with the "Arab Spring," which had not brought promised changes. Others argued that change would take time.

>> Women played an important role in the Arab Spring movement. This massive demonstration took place in Cairo on July 8, 2011. **Hypothesize** What motivated women to participate in the Arab Spring movement?

An Islamic Revolution in Iran Because of its vast oil fields, Iran was a focus of Cold War rivalries. Its ruler, Shah Mohammad Reza Pahlavi, favored the West but faced nationalist critics at home, led by Mohammad Mosaddeq (MAW sah dek). After Mosaddeq was elected prime minister in 1951, he nationalized the foreign-owned oil industry. The shah, with U.S. help, ousted Mosaddeq and retuned the oil industry to Western control. This move outraged many Iranians.

Although the shah modernized industry, redistributed land to peasants, and gave new rights to women, opposition to his rule grew, especially among the Islamic clergy. In response, the government brutally silenced critics.

The shah's foes rallied behind Ayatollah **Ruhollah Khomeini** (ROO hoh lah koh MAY nee). The Ayatollah, a religious leader, condemned Western influences and accused the shah of violating Islamic law. In 1979, massive protests drove the shah from power. Khomeini and his supporters proclaimed the Islamic Republic of Iran.

>> Ayatollah Khomeini was Iran's ultimate political and religious authority for 10 years after the Iranian Revolution. Khomeini, who died in 1989, is still revered in Iran. This mural is in Tehran.

The new government was a **theocracy,** or government by religious leaders. The Iranian Revolution introduced strict Islamic law. Like the shah, the new leaders silenced critics. In 1979, Islamists seized the American embassy in the capital and held 52 hostages for more than a year.

The new Islamic republic soon faced a long, bloody war with its neighbor Iraq, and tense relations with the West. The United States accused Iran of backing terrorists. Along with its allies, the United

States imposed harsh economic sanctions to keep Iran from developing nuclear weapons. In 2013, Iranians elected a self-proclaimed moderate, Hassan Rouhani, as president.

Hopes rose for an easing of tensions between Iran and the West. At home, however, Rouhani faced an economy hurt by years of economic sanctions and deep political divisions between hardliners and reformists.

Modern Turkey Once the heart of the Ottoman empire, Turkey became a republic in the 1920s under Ataturk. It has the third-largest population in the Middle East after Egypt and Iran. Although it is a Muslim country, most of its people are Turks, not Arabs. Turkey commands a strategic location, straddling Europe and Asia, and has served as a link between Europe and the Middle East. Turkey applied to join the European Union, but some EU members demanded that it make economic and other reforms. Turkey also sought closer ties with its Middle Eastern neighbors.

Although the military intervened in the past, today Turkey is a multiparty democracy with a market economy. Clashes erupted in 2013, however, that pitted the moderate Islamist government against protesters who opposed the growing authoritarianism of the government. The clashes reflected a divide between supporters of the older secularist ideology of Ataturk and those supporting the more Islamist-oriented policies of the government.

CATEGORIZE What types of governments are most common in the Middle East?

The Importance of Oil in the Middle East

Parts of the Middle East have huge oil resources, giving the region global importance. A handful of oil-producing nations prospered. They included Saudi Arabia, Iran, Iraq, Kuwait, and several small states along the Persian Gulf. The oil-producing nations also border vital shipping lanes that carry oil from the region to the world. Even though these oil-rich countries provide aid to their neighbors, most Middle Eastern nations lack oil and have struggled economically.

OPEC In 1960, the oil-producing nations of the Middle East, along with Venezuela, set up the Organization of Petroleum Exporting Countries (OPEC). OPEC wanted to end the power of Western oil companies and set its own oil production quotas and prices.

Oil Reserves in the Middle East

>> **Analyze Maps** This map shows the known oil reserves of Middle Eastern countries. On what body of water do the nations with the largest oil reserves lie?

In 1973, Middle Eastern members of OPEC used oil as a political weapon. They stopped oil shipments to the United States and other countries that had supported Israel in the Yom Kippur War. This oil embargo triggered a global recession and led other countries to try to develop other sources of oil. Since then, OPEC has focused on setting production quotas and has added new members.

Saudi Arabia Saudi Arabia has one of the world's largest oil reserves. It exports vast amounts of oil to the West. In return, it has received military aid from the United States. Its ruling family is committed to Wahhabism, a strict sect within Sunni Islam. Oil wealth allowed Saudi Arabia to modernize its infrastructure, such as transportation and communication systems. At the same time, the government has suppressed opposition.

INFER How can OPEC influence global events?

Islam and the Modern World

After independence, some Middle Eastern countries adopted Western-style secular governments. Leaders in Egypt and Syria, for example, saw secular government as a means to modernization. In time, however, many secular leaders became authoritarian rulers. At the same time, Western cultural influences, introduced during the age of imperialism, spread. In cities, people bought goods imported from the West. They wore Western fashions and watched American television shows and movies.

Islamic Revival Some Muslims claimed that Western culture and capitalism were undermining Islamic society. They called for a return to Sharia, or Islamic law based on the Quran, and to traditional customs and values. These conservative reformers, known as Islamists or Islamic fundamentalists, blamed social and economic ill on the West. Only a renewed commitment to Islam, they declared, could improve conditions for Muslims around the world.

Many Muslims welcomed the Islamic movement as a way to cope with rapid social and economic changes. Moderate Islamists wanted to work toward democratic reforms within Islam. Radical Islamists, or fundamentalist extremists, however, advocated violence to achieve their goal.

Radical Islam Radical Islamic fundamentalist groups in Egypt, Saudi Arabia, and elsewhere sought

>> Men worship at the Sheikh Zayed Mosque in Abu Dhabi, capital of the United Arab Emirates. The mosque is large enough to accommodate more than 40,000 worshipers.

>> Egyptian supporters of the Muslim Brotherhood, an Islamist organization, celebrate the election of Muhammed Morsi. Morsi, who won the first election held in Egypt after the "Arab Spring," was overthrown by the military in 2013.

to overthrow governments that they saw as too closely allied to the West. They also targeted Israel, which had defeated Arabs in several wars, and the United States. Although many governments cracked down on radical Islamic fundamentalists, these groups survived. In 1979, Islamic fundamentalists welcomed Iran's revolution. Iran became the first modern nation to topple a secular government and replace it with a government based on Sharia.

Islam and the Lives of Women Conditions for women vary greatly across the Muslim Middle East. In most countries, women won equality before the law, but women still faced legal and social hurdles, especially to jobs. Over time, however, educated women entered professions such as law and medicine.

In Turkey, Egypt, and Syria, many urban women had given up wearing the **hejab,** or traditional Muslim headscarf, or loose, ankle-length garments meant to conceal. With the Islamic revival, many educated women returned to the hejab as a symbol of their faith. In religiously conservative countries like Saudi Arabia and Iran, women must follow local Islamic traditions, such as wearing the hejab.

Women stood on the front lines of the "Arab Spring" to demand democratic reforms and equal opportunity. "I grew up in a world where we believed we could not do anything," noted a young woman and online activist in Jordan. "Generations believed we could do nothing, and now, in a matter of weeks, we know that we can."

Some women's rights advocates pointed out that their goals were not based on Western values but on the traditions of early Islam that improved the status of women. Women's rights movements faced serious challenges, however. While access to education has improved for women, girls are often less likely to attend school than boys because of the tradition that girls do not need a formal education for their expected roles as wives and mothers. Although governments recognized the productive value of women in the workforce, local cultural restrictions often kept women from holding jobs outside the home.

IDENTIFY CAUSE AND EFFECT Why do Islamists oppose secular government and culture in the Muslim world?

ASSESSMENT

1. **Identify** What are two events that have powerfully influenced the development of the modern nations of the Middle East?
2. **Express Problems Clearly** How do religious and ethnic differences affect the Middle East?
3. **Identify Cause and Effect** What effect did the Arab rejection of the State of Israel have on today's Palestinians?
4. **Describe** What are some ways oil wealth has affected the nations of the Middle East?
5. **Cite Evidence** What influence has Islam had on the government of Iran since the overthrow of the Shah?

9.4 **Modern Israel was established in 1948 under the United Nations Partition Plan. Arab nations rejected the UN plan as illegal, even though it offered Palestinians territory for their own state. Instead, they called for the destruction of Israel.**

>> The Iran-Iraq War lasted eight years and took an enormous toll on both countries. These Iraqi soldiers were photographed near Basra, Iraq, in 1984.

Bounce to Activate Flipped Video

Conflicts in the Middle East

Israel and Palestine

Arab rejection of the State of Israel has led to ongoing conflict. In 1948, five Arab nations invaded the newly independent Israel and were defeated. Israel and its Arab neighbors fought three more wars, in 1956, 1967, and 1973. In these wars, Israel fought for its existence, and in the process of turning back attacking Arab forces gained more land. Between and since these wars, Israel has faced many terrorist attacks within its borders, and ongoing rocket attacks from Gaza and Lebanon. The United States and other nations worked to find a solution to the long-standing conflict.

The West Bank, Gaza, and the Golan Heights In the Six Day War of 1967, in response to ongoing hostility by its Arab neighbors, Israel took control of the West Bank and East Jerusalem from Jordan along with the Gaza Strip and Sinai Peninsula from Egypt. Israel also took the Golan Heights from Syria.

Angered by their loss in the Six Day War, Arab countries held a summit at Khartoum several months later and issued the "Three No's": no recognition of Israel, no negotiations with Israel, and no peace with Israel. In 1973, these Arab nations attacked Israel on

>> Objectives

Explain the ongoing Israeli-Palestinian conflict and the obstacles to peace.

Explain the causes and effects of conflicts in Lebanon and Syria.

Understand why Iraq became a battleground.

>> Key Terms

Yasir Arafat
intifada
Yitzhak Rabin
Jerusalem
militia
Saddam Hussein
no-fly zone
weapon of mass destruction (WMD)
insurgent

Yom Kippur, the holiest day of the Jewish calendar. In the Yom Kippur War, Arabs failed to regain the lands that they had lost to Israel in 1967. Arabs referred to these lands as the "occupied territories." Later, Israel annexed East Jerusalem and the Golan Heights. Israel then allowed Jewish settlers to build homes in some of these territories, which increased bitterness among the Palestinians.

The PLO and Intifada The number of Palestinians in refugee camps grew in the decades after 1948. The majority of these camps were overcrowded, and lacked adequate services such as roads and sewers. Unable to return to Israel, the refugees were also not granted rights in the countries that hosted them. Such conditions fed growing anger. Many Palestinians came to support the Palestinian Liberation Organization (PLO), which led the struggle against Israel.

Led by **Yasir Arafat,** the PLO called for the destruction of Israel and waged guerrilla war against Israelis at home and abroad. The PLO gained world attention with airplane hijackings and the killing of Israeli athletes at the 1972 Olympic Games.

In 1987, Palestinians in the West Bank and Gaza started to resist Israel with **intifadas,** or uprisings. Young Palestinians demanded an end to Israeli control and hurled rocks at or fired on Israeli soldiers. Suicide bombers blew up buses, stores, and clubs in Israel. Israel responded by sealing off and raiding Palestinian towns and targeting terrorist leaders. The violence killed many civilians on both sides.

IDENTIFY CENTRAL IDEAS How did Arab nations respond to the creation of Israel?

The Difficult Road to Peace

During the Cold War, efforts to solve the Arab-Israeli conflict had little success, despite ongoing attempts by the UN, the United States, and other nations . However, as you have read, Egyptian leader Anwar Sadat did take a courageous first step by agreeing to peace talks, the first Arab leader to do so. Israel and Egypt signed a peace accord in 1979 in which Israel returned the Sinai Peninsula to Egypt

The collapse of the Soviet Union led to renewed peace talks. Without Soviet aid, some Arab governments accepted the need to negotiate with Israel. In 1994, Jordan and Israel signed a peace agreement. Talks between Syria and Israel stalled over issues such as the future of the Golan Heights. Israel had taken control of the heights, which Syria had long used to fire on its neighbors.

Israel, 1949

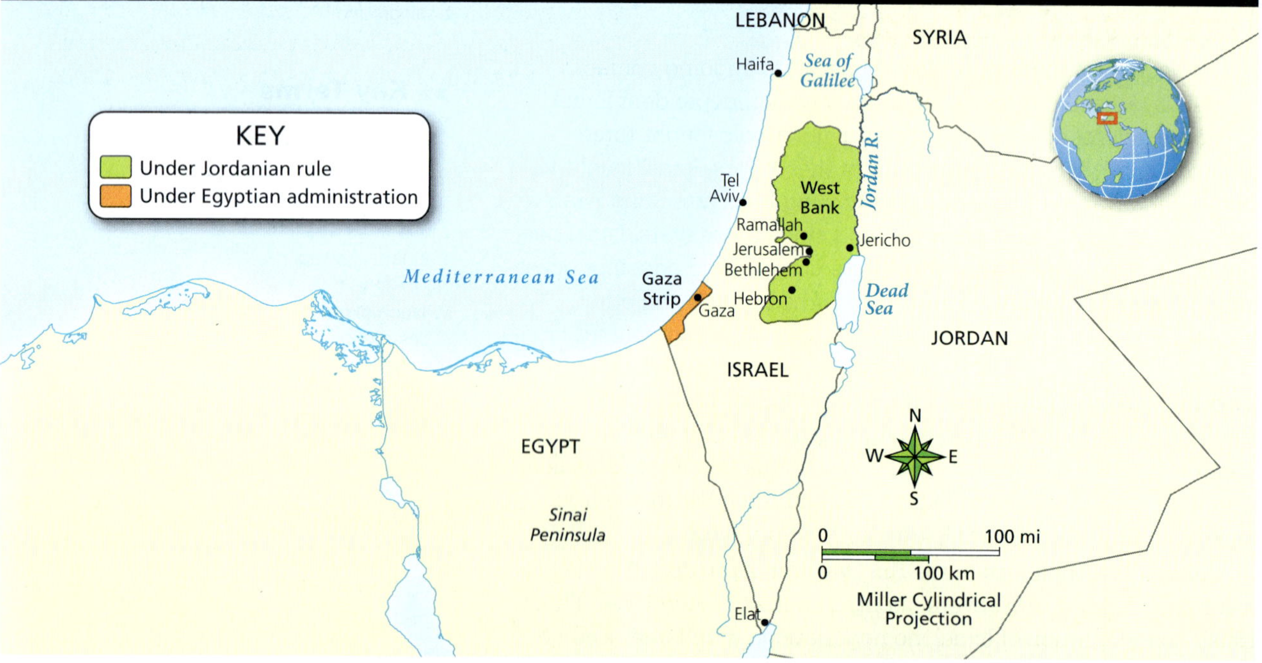

>> **Analyze Maps** This map shows the boundaries of the State of Israel in 1949. How does the map illustrate one challenge to achieving Mideast peace?

Bounce to Activate Map

The Oslo Accords In 1993, Yasir Arafat and Israeli Prime Minister **Yitzhak Rabin**(rah BEEN) signed the Oslo Accords. This plan gave Palestinians in Gaza and the West Bank limited self-rule. They also set up a Palestinian Authority to govern the area. The PLO recognized Israel's right to exist and pledged to stop terrorist attacks on Israel. Arafat led the Palestinian Authority until his death in 2004.

Violence Continues Although Arafat's successor, Mahmoud Abbas (ah BAHS), pledged to stop Palestinian attacks on Israel, violence continued. Fierce divisions split the Palestinian Authority between Fatah, the party of Arafat and his successors, and Hamas, a radical Islamist group. Hamas was funded by Iran and rejected Israel's right to exist. It was ready to use violence to achieve its aims.

In 2007, Hamas seized control of Gaza. Israel then imposed a blockade on Gaza, controlling access to the region in order to stop weapons from reaching Hamas. From Gaza, Hamas launched frequent rocket attacks on Israel. The Israeli military responded with air strikes and several invasions.

During a 50-day war in 2014, Hamas again launched attacks against Israel. In response, Israel targeted Hamas rocket launching sites. The war caused huge damage and many civilian deaths in Gaza. Israel, too, suffered losses. Although a ceasefire was arranged, difficult issues remained. Palestinians demanded an end to the Israeli blockade, which limited their access to food, water, electricity, and other basic necessities. Israelis wanted Hamas to disarm and end its rocket attacks.

Obstacles to Peace Decades of conflict and mistrust have made peace hard to achieve. One obstacle to peace concerns the Palestinian refugees who fled or were forced off their lands in earlier wars. They and their descendants want the "right of return," or the right to resettle on their land in Israel proper. Israelis oppose this demand, which could overwhelm the only Jewish state with large numbers of Palestinians. Israelis view this demand as an attempt to destroy Israel.

A second obstacle is **Jerusalem,** a city sacred to Jews, Christians, and Muslims. Jordan controlled East Jerusalem and the Old City from 1948 to 1967 and did not allow Jewish access to holy sites. Israel gained control in 1967 and later added it to the capital of Israel, reuniting the city of Jerusalem. Muslims and Christians control their holy sites within the city. Palestinians, however, want East Jerusalem to be the capital of a future Palestinian state.

>> In 1977, Egyptian president Anwar Sadat became the first Arab leader to visit and recognize Israel. Here, he exchanges gifts with former Israeli prime minister Golda Meir.

A third stumbling block is the issue of Jewish settlements in East Jerusalem and the West Bank, areas claimed by Palestinians. Israel voluntarily withdrew all of its settlements in the Sinai and in Gaza but has not withdrawn from the West Bank and East Jerusalem. Disagreements about final borders affect negotiations over the future of the West Bank.

Another issue is security. Israel fears that if extremists gained control over a Palestinian state, they could attack Israel as Hamas has done since Israel withdrew from Gaza. Israel therefore wants to limit the military capacity of any Palestinian state and control security in the area. Palestinians argue that security will improve when Palestinians have their own state.

Over time, the Israeli-Palestinian conflict has fueled the anger of fundamentalist, radical Islamist groups such as Hamas in Gaza and Hezbollah in Lebanon. These radical groups reject Israel's right to exist. They condemn its ally, the United States, along with any Arab government involved in the peace process. Ongoing violence and threats from these groups increase Israel's security concerns and impede the peace process.

Another important issue is how to allocate and protect water resources. The distribution of water resources impacts negotiations between Israel and the Palestinians concerning the control of the water supply, water consumption, and the costs of investments in water management. The rights to water resources are also major issues between countries in the region.

A Two-State Solution For years, peace talks have revolved around the idea of a two-state solution, with peaceful coexistence between Israel and a stable, democratic Palestinian state. To achieve this, peacemakers drew up the "road map" to peace, calling for an end to violence and terrorism. Some Israeli and Palestinian leaders accepted the two-state plan. Iran and radical Islamist groups rejected it.

The most recent peace talks opened in the aftermath of the "Arab Spring." The uprisings did little to improve the outlook for peace between Israelis and Palestinians. Islamists won power in some elections, while turmoil engulfed Egypt and Syria.

INTEGRATE INFORMATION Why is Jerusalem so important to both Israelis and Palestinians?

>> A woman is helped by the military after a bombing in Beirut, Lebanon, in 1986. **Analyze Visuals** What does this image tell you about the way that the Lebanese civil war was fought?

Bounce to Activate Timeline

Conflict in Lebanon and Syria

Internal divisions and the ongoing Israeli-Palestinian conflict impacted neighboring Lebanon and Syria. Both nations gained independence in the 1940s. Both are home to diverse religious and ethnic groups.

The Lebanese Civil War Historically, Lebanon was a thriving center of commerce. After gaining independence from France in 1943, its government depended on a delicate balance among diverse Arab Christian sects, such as the Maronites, Sunni and Shiite Muslims, and Druze, people with a religion related to Islam. Palestinian immigration after the 1948 and 1967 wars increased the Muslim population. By the 1970s, Muslims outnumbered Christians. In 1971, PLO fighters were expelled from Jordan after attempting to overthrow its government. The enlarged PLO presence in Lebanon and the intensification of fighting on the Israeli-Lebanese border added to the internal unrest in Lebanon.

Tensions among the diverse groups erupted into civil war that lasted from 1975 to 1990. Christian and Muslim **militias,** or armed groups of citizen soldiers, battled each other. Syria invaded Lebanon and Syrian troops remained for 29 years. Israel briefly invaded Lebanon to stop cross-border attacks first by PLO guerrillas and later by Hezbollah fighters, the militant group backed by Iran and Syria.

Sectarian divisions remained even after a fragile peace was restored. By 2012, the civil war in neighboring Syria threatened renewed violence among rival militias in Lebanon. In addition, a huge number of refugees fled the civil war in Syria, straining Lebanon's resources.

The Syrian Civil War Syria's diverse population includes Armenians, Assyrians, Christians, Druze, Kurds, Alawite Shiites, and Arab Sunnis. For decades, Hafez al-Assad and later his son, Bashir al-Assad, ruled the country and its diverse population with an iron hand. The Assads opposed peace with Israel and supported militant groups such as Hezbollah and Hamas.

During the "Arab Spring," the Syrian government met pro-democracy protests with brutal force, plunging the country into civil war. Rebel groups were deeply divided between moderates and extremist groups. Hezbollah and Iran supported the Assad regime. Western countries, however, hesitated to support the rebels, fearful that weapons could fall into the hands of radical groups. After Assad was accused of using chemical weapons,

The Persian Gulf, 1991

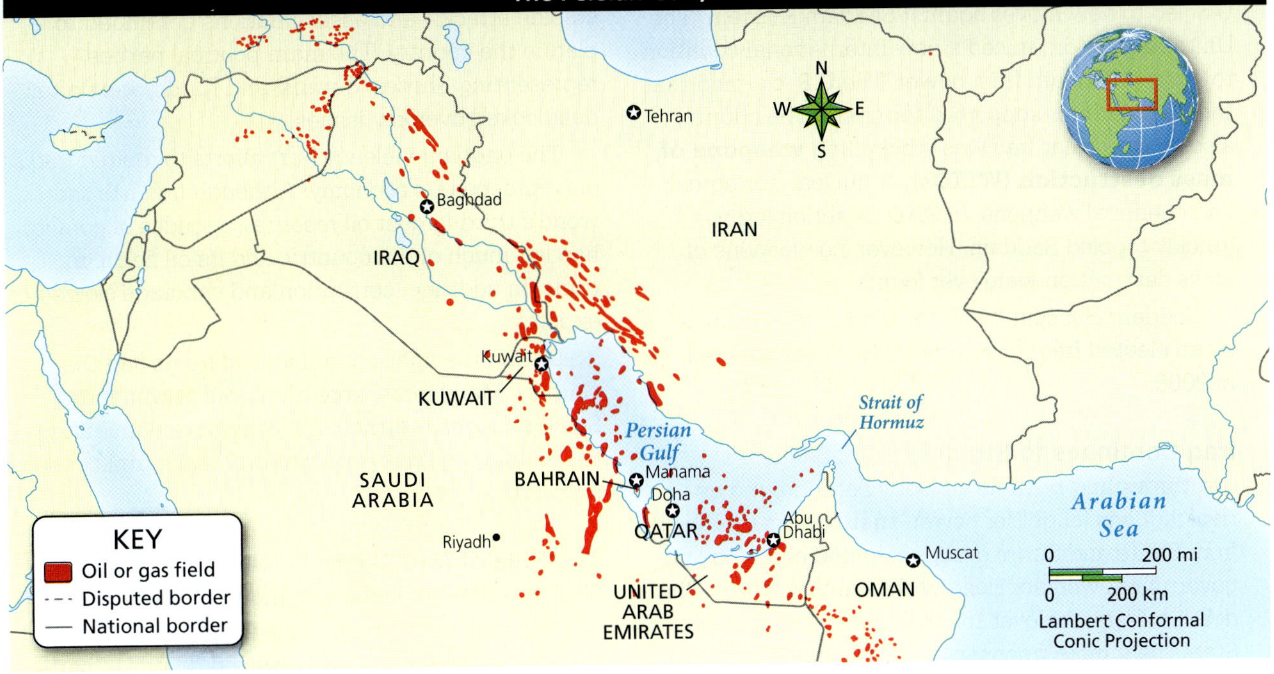

>> **Analyze Maps** The Persian Gulf region has seen numerous wars in recent years. What information on this map suggests one reason why this region is so important to the nations of the industrialized world?

global condemnation forced Syria to agree to give up its chemical arms stockpiles.

As the death toll mounted above 100,000, millions more Syrians were displaced by the fighting. Refugees flooded into nearby countries and raised fears that the Syrian civil war could destabilize the region. International efforts to negotiate peace were complicated by disunity among rebel groups and Assad's continued grip on power.

RECALL What is Hezbollah, and why is it signficant?

Warfare in Iraq

The modern nation of Iraq was carved out of the Ottoman empire after World War I. Its population included Sunni and Shiite Arabs, as well as Kurds who lived in the north. Although Shiites were the majority population, Sunnis controlled the government. Kurds distrusted the government and wanted self-rule.

Divisions among these groups fed tensions in Iraq. During the Cold War, the United States and the Soviet Union competed for influence in Iraq, which had vast oil resources and was strategically located on the Persian Gulf.

The Iran-Iraq War In 1980, Iraq's neighbor Iran was engulfed in its Islamic Revolution. Iraqi dictator, **Saddam Hussein,** took advantage of the turmoil to seize a disputed border region. His action sparked the long, costly Iran-Iraq War. After both sides attacked foreign oil tankers in the Persian Gulf, the United States sent naval forces to protect shipping lanes. The war ended in a stalemate in 1988, but with huge human and economic costs for both Iran and Iraq.

During the war, Saddam Hussein brutally suppressed a Kurdish revolt, using chemical weapons on civilians. His actions sparked international outrage and charges of genocide.

The 1991 Gulf War In 1990, Iraq invaded its oil-rich neighbor, Kuwait. Saddam Hussein wanted Kuwait's vast oil fields and greater access to the Persian Gulf. The United States saw the invasion as a threat to its ally, Saudi Arabia, and to the vital oil resources of the region.

In 1991, a U.S.-led coalition of international forces under the UN banner drove Saddam's forces out of Kuwait. Despite this defeat, Saddam remained in power. He brutally crushed revolts by Shiite Iraqis and Kurds. To protect the Shiites and Kurds, the UN set up **no-fly zones,** or areas where Iraqi aircraft were banned.

The Iraq War The 2001 terrorist attacks on the U.S. led to new moves against Saddam Hussein. The United States organized a new international coalition to remove Saddam from power. The U.S. claimed that the Iraqi dictator supported terrorists. The country also charged that Iraq was stockpiling **weapons of mass destruction (WMDs),** or nuclear, biological, and chemical weapons. In 2003, coalition forces quickly toppled Saddam. However, no weapons of mass destruction were ever found.

Saddam Hussein was later tried for war crimes by an elected Iraqi government. He was executed in 2006.

Iraq Continues to Struggle After Saddam's overthrow, Iraq became a bloody battleground as rival factions fought for power. **Insurgents,** or rebels, from Shiite and Sunni groups targeted civilians and government workers along with coalition forces. The death toll grew to over 162,000 Iraqis. The United States sent more troops in a "surge" to end the fighting.

The United States worked to convince moderate Sunnis, who had prospered under Saddam, to back the newly elected Iraqi government. It also tried to improve Iraqi security forces. In 2011, the last American troops withdrew, leaving a Shiite-led government in control.

Iraq still faced steep hurdles. Car bombings, suicide attacks, and assassinations continued to plague the country. The main political parties, representing Shiites, Sunnis, and Kurds, were often deadlocked over key issues.

The ongoing violence hurt efforts to rebuild Iraq's once-prosperous economy. Although Iraq has the world's third-largest oil reserves, decades of conflict had left much of the country, and its oil fields, in ruins. In addition, corruption and sabotage slowed oil exports.

During the fighting, millions of Iraqis fled the country. Many more were displaced within Iraq. Some refugees returned, but others were unwilling to risk moving back until security and stability were assured.

The Rise of ISIL Tensions between Sunnis and Shiites burst into fierce fighting in 2014. An Al Qaeda breakaway group, known as Islamic State of Iraq and the Levant (ISIL), seized control of parts of northern and eastern Iraq. They won support from some Sunnis who felt oppressed by the Shiite-led government in Baghdad. ISIL militants were also involved in Syria's civil war. They called for an Islamic state to be set up in the region of Syria, Jordan, Iraq, and Lebanon.

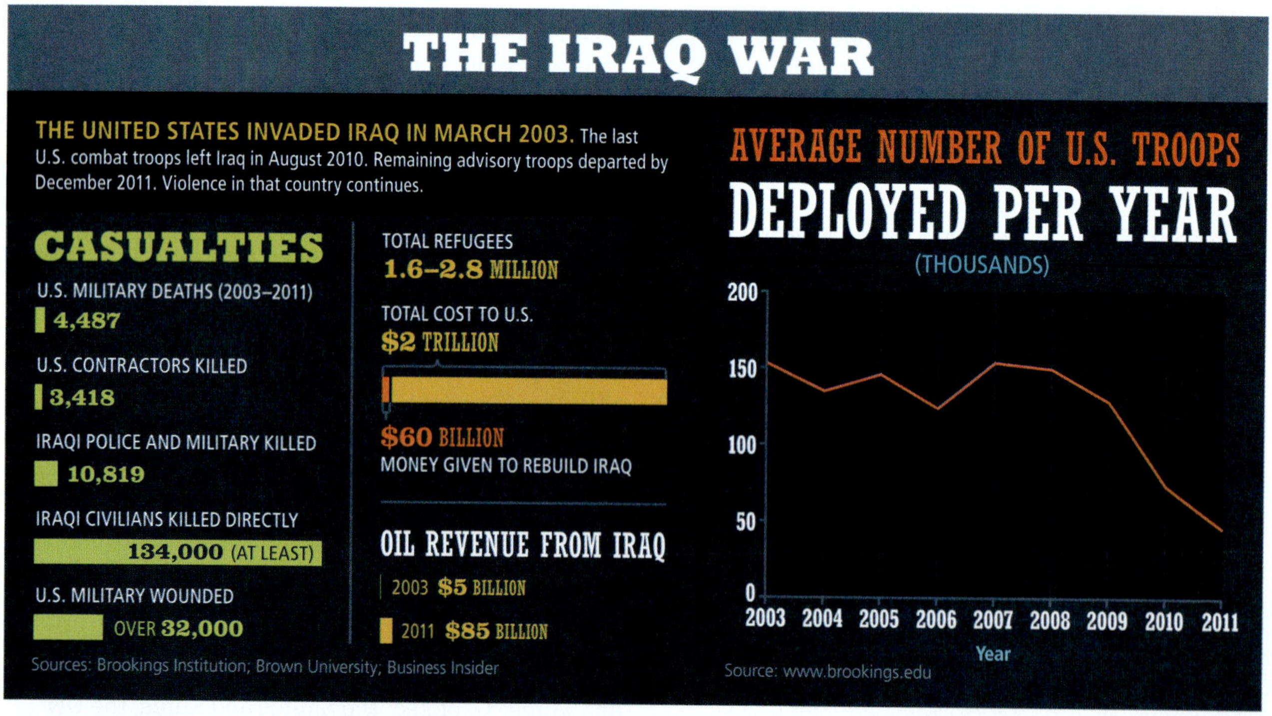

>> Analyze Charts The Iraq War succeeded in its immediate objective, including deposing Saddam Hussein, but the costs were high. How does the information shown here support this generalization?

ISIL militants were known for their brutality in the areas they controlled. They targeted Shiite Muslims, Armenian Christians, and others groups. They also publicly executed several hostages, including American journalists.

The United States launched air strikes to protect various Iraqi minority groups from ISIS atrocities and to destroy weapons and equipment ISIL fighters had seized from the Iraqi army. A new government came to power in Baghdad, hoping to ease tensions with Sunnis and regain control of lost territories.

DRAW CONCLUSIONS Why did Sunni control of government in Iraq create tension in that country?

ASSESSMENT

1. **Identify Central Issues** How did the Israeli-Palestinian conflict begin?
2. **Compare Points of View** Why has peace between Israel and the Palestinians been so difficult to achieve? Include issues from both perspectives.
3. **Identify Cause and Effect** How did the Israeli-Palestinian conflict affect Lebanon and why?
4. **Draw Conclusions** How has the growth of radical Islamic fundamentalism affected conflicts in the Middle East?
5. **Cite Evidence** Why did the removal of Saddam Hussein's regime fail to bring peace to Iraq? Use details from the text in your answer.

California Topic 9 Quick Study Guide

LESSON SUMMARIES

Use these Lesson Summaries, and the longer versions available online, to review the key ideas for each lesson in this Topic.

Lesson 1: New Nations in South Asia and Southeast Asia

After winning independence, Hindu India and Muslim Pakistan pursued separate roads to modernization.

Lesson 2: African Nations Win Independence

During the 1950s and 1960s, dozens of new nations emerged in Africa. As celebration erupted across the continent, people faced many challenges.

Lesson 3: The Modern Middle East Takes Shape

In the Arab world, as in South Asia and in Africa, nationalists sought to free themselves from the legacy of imperialism. Aside from nationalism, the other forces shaping the modern Middle East were diversity, and the availability of resources such as oil and water.

Lesson 4: Conflicts in the Middle East

For new nations in the Middle East, religious, ethnic, and cultural diversity bought concerns and challenges. The major sources of conflict have come from issues between Arab nations and Israel. Major civil wars have engulfed Lebanon, Syria, and Iraq. Revolution has led to conflict in Iran.

VISUAL REVIEW

Use these graphics to review some of the key terms, people, and ideas from this Topic.

Common Themes in New Nations

- Borders drawn by European colonial powers left nations with diverse religion and ethnic groups.
- Ethnic and religious diversity has brought conflict.
- Military coups, one-party systems, and dictatorships kept some countries from achieving democracy.
- Citizens and foreign leaders have forced former dictatorships to hold elections and transition to democracy.
- Natural resources such as oil have been a source of wealth for some nations but have fueled conflicts in others.
- During the Cold War, the United States and Soviet Union competed for influence, particularly in regions with natural resources such as oil, or locations near strategic waterways.

Leaders of New Nations

- Jawaharlal Nehru, *first prime minister of India*
- Indira Gandhi, *first female prime minister of India*
- Aung San Suu Kyi, *leader of Myanmar democracy movement*
- Sukarno, *founder and first president of Indonesia*
- Suharto, *military dictator of Indonesia*
- Corazon Aquino, *democratic president of the Philippines*
- Kwame Nkrumah, *founder and first president of Kenya*
- David Ben-Gurion, *first prime minister of Israel*
- Gamal Abdel Nasser, *an Arab nationalist and first president of Egypt*
- Mohammad Reza Pahlavi, *shah of Iran*
- Ruhollah Khomeini, *leader of the religious government of Iran*

New Nations Emerge

California Topic 9 Assessment

KEY TERMS, PEOPLE, AND IDEAS

1. Why did the **partition** of British India cause a refugee crisis?
2. What goals did **Jawaharlal Nehru** set for modernizing India?
3. Compare the nations of Southeast Asia in the progress they have made toward individual freedom and democracy.
4. What factors led to the support of a Jewish homeland after WWII? How did this initiate the ongoing conflict between the Israelis and the Arabs?
5. What sparked the conflict between the **Hutus** and the **Tutsis**?
6. Why did more nationalist movements rise after World War II?
7. Why did Nasser seize control of the **Suez Canal**? Was the strategy successful? Explain.
8. Describe the roles of **Yasir Arafat** and **Yitzhak Rubin** in the Arab Israeli conflict.
9. Describe one cause of each of the following: (a) the civil war in Lebanon (b) the Iran-Iraq war (c) the Persian Gulf War.

CRITICAL THINKING

10. **Synthesize Information** How has religion influenced the recent history of the Middle East?
11. **Analyze Information** How did the Cold War affect (a) the Middle East (b) Africa?
12. **Summarize** How have the natural resources of the Middle East affected its recent history?
13. **Analyze Information** Discuss the effectiveness of Gamal Abdel Nasser and Indira Gandhi as nationalist leaders.
14. **Compare** How was the conflict in Darfur similar to the one in Rawanda?
15. **Draw Conclusions** Why has the Arab Spring sometimes been referred to as the Arab Awakening? Explain.
16. **Use Primary Sources** In the following passage, Nigerian writer Chinua Achebe describes the changes in traditional Ibo society. Two characters discuss the ways that Europeans have gained power in an African village. Explain what Achebe means by the last sentence in the passage.

> "What has happened to that piece of land in dispute?" asked Okonkwo. "The white man's court has decided that it should belong to Nnama's family, who had given much money to the white man's messengers. . . ." "Does the white man understand our custom about land?" "How can he when he does not even speak our tongue? But he says that our customs are bad; and our own brothers who have take up his religion also say our customs are bad. How do you think we can fight when our own brothers have turned against us? . . . He came quietly with and peacefully with his religion. We . . . allowed him to stay. [Now] He has put a knife on the things that held us together and we have fallen apart."
>
> —*Chinua Achebe, Things Fall Apart*

17. **Writing Activity** The following excerpt is from Prime Minister Nehru's speech before the Indian Assembly when they met to celebrate independence. Describe Nehru's hope for the nation. How does he indicate that this moment has been long fought for? Use your knowlege of the Topic and what you have learned about India's struggle for independence to write your paragraph.

> "Long years ago we made an [appointment] with destiny, and now the time comes when we shall redeem our pledge, not wholly or in full measure, but very substantially. At the stroke of the midnight hour, when the world sleeps, India will awake to life and freedom. A moment comes, which comes but rarely in history, when we step out from the old to the new, when an age ends and when the soul of a nation long suppressed finds utterance."
>
> —*Jawaharlal Nehru, "Tryst With Destiny" speech*

DOCUMENT-BASED QUESTIONS

Kashmir has been claimed by both India and Pakistan and has been a battleground between the two countries. Read the documents below, then answer the questions that follow.

DOCUMENT A

"Mr. Jinnah and his colleagues in the Muslim League, the creators of Pakistan, had always considered that the Vale of Kashmir at least would form part of the new Islamic State . . . When in 1933 Choudhri Rahmat Ali coined the word Pakistan as a suitable name for the State, he intended the letter K in 'Pak' to stand for Kashmir. The geographical and historical links between the Panjab and the Vale of Kashmir were so close that it was inevitable that the two regions should find themselves combined in the thoughts of the protagonists of a separate Islamic State."

—From Crisis in Kashmir, 1947–1966 by Alastair Lamb

DOCUMENT B

DOCUMENT C

Religions of Kashmir, 1941

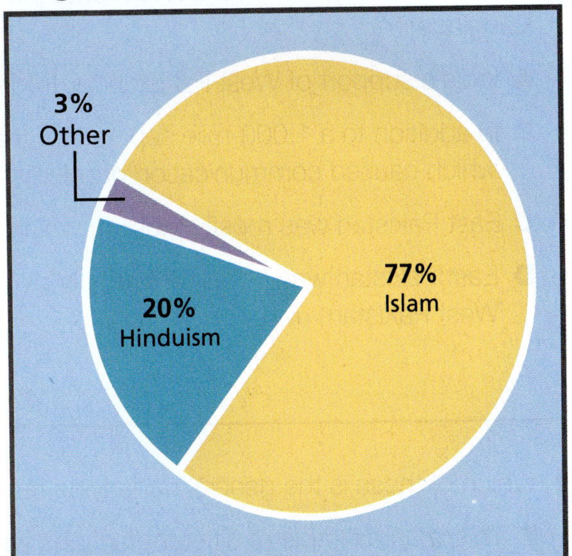

SOURCE: Census of India, 1941

18. According to Document A, Kashmir and Pakistan share

A. the same heroes and poets.
B. a similar history and geography.
C. the same language and literature.
D. similar architecture and art.

19. What argument does the billboard in Document B support?

A. Citizens of Kashmir want to live peacefully.
B. India will never let go of Kashmir.
C. Kashmir is more beautiful than other parts of India.
D. Indians are tired of dealing with Kashmir and its problems.

20. According to Document C, Kashmir's populations

A. is evenly balanced among its different religions.
B. is about one-half Hindu and "Other".
C. only has two religion affiliations.
D. is more than three-quarters Muslim.

21. **Writing Tasks** Why has Kashmir continued to be a volatile spot for so long? What are the main causes of the conflict there? Use information from these documents along with information from the Topic to write your response.

End-of-Topic Practice

1 Why did East Pakistan want to become independent from West Pakistan and become Bangladesh?

A India's support of West Pakistan for trade benefits shrunk East Pakistan's economy.

B In addition to a 1,000-mile separation, the two Pakistans had different majority languages, which caused communication problems.

C East Pakistan was mostly Muslim, which conflicted with the Hinduism of West Pakistan.

D East Pakistan was populated mostly by Bengalis who resented government neglect by West Pakistan rulers.

---

2 Which of these is the general underlying reason for the genocide that occurred in Darfur?

F This is an example of different factions wanting to seize control of oil and gas reserves.

G This is an example of how tensions of ethnic differences over government rule resulted in crimes against humanity.

H This is an example of resentment toward foreign investors who control key economic resources, aided by a minority group.

J This is an example of how Cold War tensions can spill over into civil wars with critical financing.

3 After the failure of the Yom Kippur war, Anwar Sadat

A Changed his strategy and worked to strengthen Egypt's military so that attacks on Israel could continue.

B Changed his strategy to a "Sadat initiative" which meant seeking a diplomatic solution.

C Changed his strategy to call upon neighboring allies to help with his fight against Israel.

D Decided to follow his predecessor Nasser and push aggressive nationalism and militarism.

---

4 The passage below is the text of the Balfour Declaration.

"His Majesty's Government view with favor the establishment in Palestine of a national home for the Jewish people, and will use their best endeavors to facilitate the achievement of this object, it being clearly understood that nothing shall be done which may prejudice the civil and religious rights of existing non-Jewish communities in Palestine, or the rights and political status enjoyed by Jews in any other country."

What impact did the Balfour Declaration have on the Middle East?

F It increased tensions among several ethnic groups in Palestine, resulting in civil wars.

G It allowed the migration of Jews and Palestinians to a former British mandate.

H It healed relations between Zionists and Arab nationalists.

J It fostered an Arab resentment towards the West which still continues.

If you have trouble with. . .				
Question	1	2	3	4
See Lesson	9.1	9.2	9.3	9.4

PEARSON realize™
PearsonSchool.com/CASS

Go **ONLINE** for digital resources

VIDEO AUDIO ETEXT ACTIVITY WRITING GAMES PDF ASSESSMENT

[ESSENTIAL QUESTION] What are the benefits and risks of interdependence?

10 The World Today (1980–Present)

>> An artist's version of our interconnected world

Enduring Understandings

- The industrialized world and the developing world are interdependent economically and politically.
- Developing nations in Africa and Latin America have worked to build stable economies and governments.
- In South Africa, the African majority won a long battle against the apartheid system of white minority rule.
- China and India have developed into economic superpowers.
- Technology, free trade, and international organizations have contributed to globalization.
- Issues of global concern include poverty, human rights, and the environment.
- Terrorism has become a growing concern, especially since September 11, 2001.

NBC LEARN

Learn how young people created a technology-based organization to deal with world issues.

Bounce to Activate My Story Video

California Topic 10 Overview

In this Topic, you will learn about issues and events in The World Today. Look at the lesson outline and explore the timeline. As you study this Topic, you will complete the Quest team project.

LESSON OUTLINE

10.1 Challenges of Development
Analysis CST.1, CST.2, HRE.4, HI.1

10.2 Challenges for African Nations
HSS 10.10.1, HSS 10.10.2; Analysis CST.1, CST.2, CST.4, HRE.4, HI.1, HI.5

10.3 Rapid Development in China and India
HSS 10.9.4, HSS 10.10, HSS 10.10.1, HSS 10.10.2, HSS 10.3; Analysis CST.1, CST.2, CST.4, HRE.4, HI.1

10.4 Latin American Nations Move Toward Democracy
HSS 10.9.2, HSS 10.9.8, HSS 10.10, HSS 10.10.1, HSS 10.10.2; Analysis CST.1, CST.2, HRE.4, HI.1

10.5 The Industrialized World
Analysis CST.1, CST.2, HRE.4, HI.1

10.6 Globalization and Trade
HSS 10.11; Analysis CST.1, CST.2, HRE.4, HI.1

10.7 Social and Environmental Issues
Analysis CST.1, CST.2, CST.4, HRE.4, HI.1, HI.5

10.8 Terrorism and International Security
Analysis CST.1, CST.2, HRE.4, HI.1

10.9 Advances in Science and Technology
HSS 10.11; Analysis CST.1, CST.2, HRE.4, HI.1

Key Events of the World Today

1990(s) Latin American nations move toward democracy.

1994 Open elections bring end of apartheid in South Africa.

2005 China has one of the world's largest economies.

1980 | 1985 | 1990 | 1995 | 2000 | 2005 | 2010 | 2015

1989 Tianamen Square Massacre

2001 Al Qaeda attacks the United States.

2004 Growth of India's economy begins.

2014 China's economy remains strong.

QUEST! TEAM PROJECT

Creating a Case Study Video

What are the differences between developed and developing countries? In this Quest, you will research this question and then create a case study video.

STEP 1
Before starting your research, review what you know about developing and developed countries. Prepare a list of characteristics.

STEP 2
Study the primary sources. Discuss what you have learned. Draw conclusions. Choose one developing country to use as a case study. Choose a characteristic you would like to consider.

STEP 3
Prepare a draft outline. Read, review, and revise. Consider what the team needs to do to create a video or a power point presentation for the case study.

STEP 4
Share your project with your classmates. Reflect on the problems still facing developing countries today. What challenges face developed countries?

PEARSON realize™ PearsonSchool.com/CASS

Go ONLINE for complete Quest materials

VIDEO ETEXT WRITING RUBRIC PDF ASSESSMENT

>> Poverty and rapidly increasing populations often lead to growing slums near urban areas, like these in Brazil. Brazil's slums, or *favelas,* often have serious problems with crime, gangs, and drugs.

Bounce to Activate Flipped Video

10.1 **The new Asian and African nations that won independence after World War II, along with the countries in Latin America, focused on modernization and development. Development is the process of building stable governments, improving agriculture and industry, and raising standards of living. Development involves such goals as building self-sufficient economies and increasing literacy, or the ability to read and write.**

>> Objectives

Understand how nations in the developing world have tried to build strong economies.

Describe obstacles to development in the global South.

Explain how development is changing patterns of life in the developing world.

>> Key Terms

development
literacy
developing world
traditional economy
Green Revolution
fundamentalist
shantytown

Challenges of Development

Working Toward Development

The developing nations emerged during the Cold War, when the world was split between the communist East and the capitalist West. Today, an economic gulf divides the world into two spheres—the relatively rich nations of the global North and the relatively poor nations of the global South.

The Global South The nations working toward development in Africa, Asia, and Latin America are known collectively as the **developing world.** The developing world is sometimes called the global South because most of these nations are located in the zone between the tropics of Cancer and Capricorn. The global South holds 75 percent of the world's people and much of its natural resources.

Some nations have enjoyed strong growth, especially the Asian "tigers"—Taiwan, Hong Kong, Singapore, and South Korea—and the oil-exporting nations of the Middle East. Overall, though, the global South remains generally poor and underdeveloped. Unlike the fully industrialized nations of the global North, newer nations have not had enough time to build up their capital, resources, or industries.

Traditional Economies In the decades since independence, developing nations experienced enormous changes. The changes began during the age of imperialism as a money economy replaced traditional economies. **Traditional economies** rely on custom and tradition, and tend not to change over time. In traditional economies, most people rely on farming, fishing or hunting and use barter to trade for needed goods.

A traditional economy is often called a subsistence economy, where people produce enough for their own need but little surplus. Although vast numbers of people continue to live at subsistence level in rural areas, most developing countries have seen rapid urbanization and have tried to develop agriculture and industry.

Moving Toward Modernization Leaders in the developing world set ambitious economic goals. They wanted to increase food output, develop industry, construct roads, airports, and railroads, and build power plants. To achieve development quickly, some leaders adopted command economies in which the government made most economic decisions and owned most industries.

Developing nations needed vast amounts of capital to finance projects to modernize their economies. After independence, some political leaders tried to speed development by replacing traditional and market economies with government-led command economies. This meant that governments owned most businesses and controlled farming.

Although command economies were meant to promote rapid growth, they often failed. Command economies tended to be inefficient, stifled innovation or change, and restricted freedom. Governments experimented with redistribution of land to give land to peasants, but in many cases, this move did not increase productivity. Since the 1980s, most developing nations have made far-reaching market reforms.

In addition, many developing nations fell into heavy debt. Developing nations needed vast amounts of capital to finance modernization projects. Most borrowed from the industrial world. When prices for their export crops or products were high, they were able to pay interest on their debt. But when prices for their exports fell, they fell heavily into debt.

The 1973 oil crisis followed by a global recession hit developing nations hard. Soaring oil prices and falling exports plunged them into financial disaster. Many nations were unable even to pay interest on their huge debts. To ease the debt crisis, international lenders pushed debtor nations to make

SELECTED DEVELOPED & DEVELOPING NATIONS

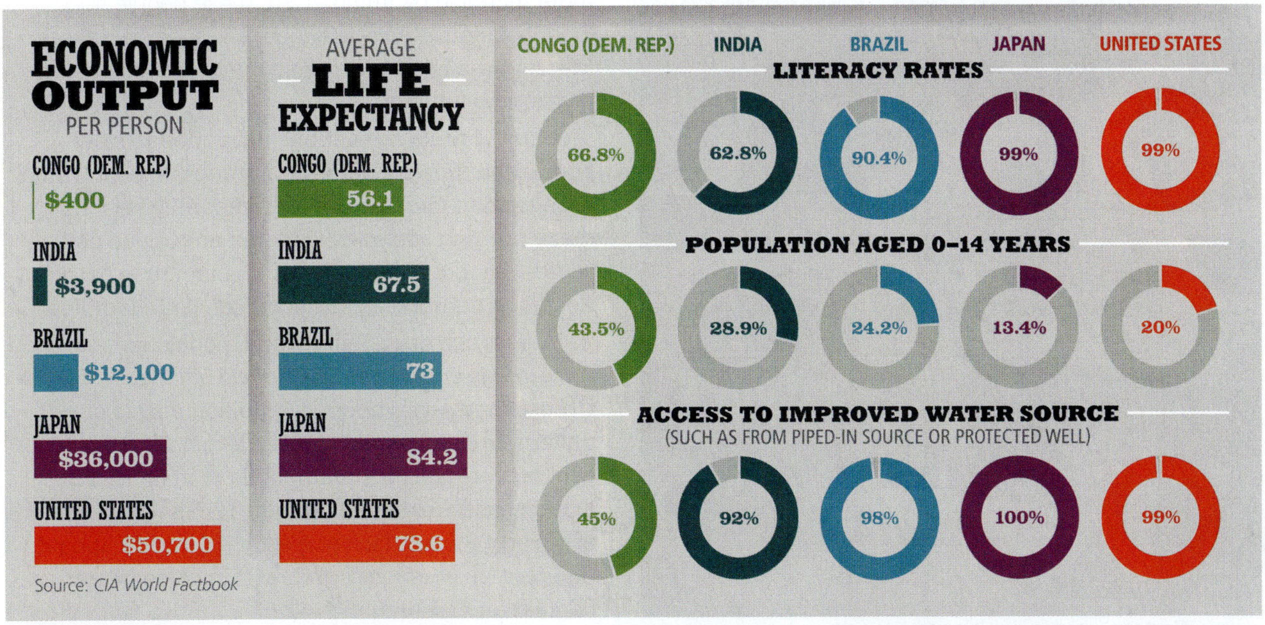

>> This chart compares developed and developing nations on a number of measures. **Analyze Charts** What generalization can you make about the age distribution in developed and developing countries, based on the data in this chart?

Bounce to Activate Map

market reforms. Governments had to privatize, or sell off, industries, ease restrictions on trade, and promote other economic freedoms. They also had to hold free elections. Debtor nations had to undertake these reforms in order to have some of their debt cancelled or to get desperately needed new loans.

Many developing nations have welcomed foreign investment. Investors put money into businesses that produced profits for them and consumer goods for the industrialized world. Some critics have argued that these economic decisions benefited foreign investors more than the developing nation's economy.

As economic opportunities decreased, migration to former imperial powers in Western Europe greatly increased. Workers came looking for jobs and places to live. Europe responded by limiting immigration. Still, the influx continued.

The Green Revolution During the 1950s and 1960s, scientists applied new technology to increasing food production for the world's growing population. They introduced new high-yield seeds that yielded more food per acre than older crops. These new crops, along with new methods of farming, became known as the **Green Revolution.**

>> Western companies that want to reduce labor costs find a large, available workforce in developing nations. In this factory in India, women create computer parts for a rapidly growing electronics industry.

In Mexico, India, Indonesia, and elsewhere, the Green Revolution boosted food output. The Green Revolution had limits, however. It succeeded only in areas with regular moisture. Also, it required chemical fertilizers and pesticides, as well as irrigation systems, which only wealthy farmers with large acreage could afford. Many poor peasants were forced off their small farms, unable to compete with larger, more-efficient enterprises. These landless peasants became farm workers or moved to rapidly growing cities.

DESCRIBE How did leaders of developing nations first try to modernize their economies?

Challenges to Development

While some developing nations have made progress toward modernization, others have not. The reasons varied, but many countries shared similar problems. In parts of Africa, Asia, and Latin America, geography has posed an obstacle to progress. Some newly created African countries are tiny and have few natural resources. Difficult climates, uncertain rainfall, lack of good farmland, and disease have added to the problems of some nations.

Populations Skyrocket Better medical care and greater food supplies have reduced death rates and led to explosive population growth. Each year, the populations of countries like Nigeria, Egypt, and India increase by millions. All these people need food, housing, education, jobs, and medical care. Meeting the needs of so many puts a huge burden on developing nations.

Many developing nations have tried to slow population growth, but few countries, except China, have tried to force people to limit family size. In many farming societies, children are valued as a source of labor and a support for parents in old age. Religious traditions also encourage large families.

Across the developing world, population growth has contributed to a cycle of poverty. The UN estimates that about 870 million people are undernourished, mostly in the developing world. Children are the most vulnerable to malnutrition and diseases related to hunger. The major causes of poverty include lack of resources, hugely unequal distribution of income, and, within some countries, conflict and famine.

Economic Dependence The economic patterns established during the age of imperialism changed little after developing countries won independence.

Most new nations remained economically dependent on their former colonial rulers. They sold agricultural products and raw materials to the industrial world. In turn, they relied on the West for manufactured goods, technology, and investment. In recent years, lower labor costs have led Western companies to relocate their manufacturing operations to the global South.

Some developing nations produce only a single export crop or commodity, such as sugar or cocoa. Their economies depend on global demand for the cash crop or commodity. If demand weakens and prices drop, their economies suffer.

Unstable Governments Civil wars and other conflicts hindered development in some countries. Countries in Central America, the Middle East, Southeast Asia, and Africa have been devastated by civil wars. Military dictators or other authoritarian leaders spent huge sums on weapons and warfare instead of on education, housing, or health care. Corrupt leaders have looted national treasuries and allowed a culture of bribery to thrive.

War has created millions of refugees living in camps both inside and outside their home countries. The loss of their labor has further hurt war-torn countries.

SUMMARIZE How did dependence on colonial rulers affect economic progress in the developing world?

>> In Kolkata, India, a young boy works along with adults in a factory that produces gold jewelry. Many of the hundreds of goldsmiths in Kolkata employ children, who work 14 to 18 hours a day.

Bounce to Activate Gallery

Development Brings Social Change

In recent decades, hundreds of millions of people in the developing world have migrated from rural villages to urban centers. Urbanization has transformed the lives of people in the developing world just as it did in Europe and North America during the Industrial Revolution.

Opportunity Increases for Women Women worked actively in independence movements. After independence, new constitutions granted equality to women, at least on paper. Although women still have less access to education than men, the gap has narrowed. Women are joining the work force in growing numbers and contributing their skills to their nations' wealth. In countries such as India, Argentina, and Liberia, women have served as heads of state. Still, women continued to shoulder a heavy burden of work both inside the home and in the workplace.

Child Labor In traditional economies, children worked alongside parents, farming or herding to meet the family's needs. As modernization and urbanization have changed traditional life, families often move to cities and take whatever jobs they can. Because these jobs pay such low wages, poor families need their children to work in order for the family to survive. Children are sent to work in chemical or textiles factories, mines, workshops.

Worldwide, more than 160 million children between the ages of 5 and 14 work up to 12 hours or more a day. Some young children are chained to looms or other machines. Many children are forced to work full time as farm laborers.

International pressure has led to efforts to reduce child labor. Reformers have called for safer work environments and basic education for child workers. Although many countries have laws about child labor, these laws are often ignored.

Religious Fundamentalism Despite revolutionary changes brought by urbanization, many traditions remain strong. The major world religions and their offshoots still shape modern societies. Since the 1980s, religious revivals have swept many regions. Christian, Muslim, Buddhist, and Hindu reformers have offered their own solutions to the problems of today's world. Some have been called **fundamentalists,** because they stress what they see as the fundamental, or basic, values of their religion. Many seek political power to oppose changes that undermine their valued religious traditions.

Rapid Growth of Cities Across the developing world, people have flooded into cities to find jobs and escape rural poverty. Cities offer not only economic opportunities but also attractions such as entertainment, stores, and sports.

With no money and few jobs, many newcomers cannot afford to ride buses or go to movies. Instead, most settle in **shantytowns,** crowded, dangerous slums on the edges of cities. These slums are as crowded and dangerous as European cities were in the 1800s. They lack basic services such as running water, electricity, or sewer systems. Today, tens of millions of people struggle to survive in these conditions.

In cities, the traditional extended family of rural villages gives way to the nuclear family. As urban children attend school and become literate, they often reject their parents' ways. Without the support of the village and extended family, older beliefs and values are undermined by urban values such as material wealth, education, and job status. People who move from villages to cities frequently suffer a sense of overwhelming stress and isolation.

EXPLAIN In what ways have women's lives changed due to economic development in the developing world?

ASSESSMENT

1. **Express Ideas Clearly** Describe how economic policy in developing nations has changed in the years since independence.
2. **Summarize** What are the main obstacles to economic and political progress in developing nations?
3. **Recall** What are four ways that development has changed life in the developing world?
4. **Contrast** Describe the differences between the global South and the global North.
5. **Explain** What is the Green Revolution, and how did it affect the developing world?

10.2 In the 1950s and 1960s, almost all African nations won independence. In South Africa, the struggle for freedom was different. South Africa had achieved self-rule from Britain in 1910. Self-rule, however, was limited to white settlers. Whites made up less than 15 percent of the population but controlled the government and the economy. The black majority was denied all political and economic rights in their own land. The white-minority government passed racial laws that severely restricted the black majority.

>> Nelson Mandela and F. W. de Klerk won the Nobel Peace Prize in 1994 for their work to end apartheid.

Bounce to Activate Flipped Video

Challenges for African Nations

>> **Objectives**

Summarize the struggle for equality in South Africa and identify how Nelson Mandela led resistance efforts.

Describe how African nations developed their economies.

Understand the challenges African nations face.

>> **Key Terms**

apartheid
African National Congress (ANC)
Sharpeville
Nelson Mandela
Desmond Tutu
F.W. de Klerk
socialism
desertification
urbanization
endangered species
Wangari Maathai
sustainable development

The Struggle for Equality in South Africa

Apartheid Is Established In 1948, the government expanded the existing system of racial segregation, and created the policy known as **apartheid,** or the separation of the races. Under apartheid, all South Africans were registered by race: Black, White, Colored (people of mixed ancestry), Asian. Supporters of apartheid claimed it would allow each race to develop its own culture. In fact, the policy was designed to preserve white control over South Africa.

Under apartheid, blacks were treated like foreigners in their own land. By the early 1900's whites had seized rights to 87% of all land, including all of South Africa's huge mineral wealth. Whites held almost all the decent jobs. Although black workers were needed to work in factories, mines, and other jobs, they were paid less than whites for the same job.

Laws restricted where Black people could live and banned marriages between the races. Among the most hated were the

Pass Laws enacted in 1952, which required all blacks to carry pass books at all times, wherever they went. Blacks schools received less funding than white schools. Low wages and inferior schooling condemned most blacks to poverty.

Resistance Against Apartheid Resistance to white rule began almost as soon as white rule itself was established. The **African National Congress (ANC)** emerged as the main party opposed to apartheid and led the struggle for majority rule. As the government passed ever-harsher laws, the ANC organized larger and larger marches, boycotts, and strikes.

In 1960, police gunned down 69 men, women, and children during a peaceful protest in **Sharpeville,** a black township. The government then outlawed the ANC and cracked down on other groups that opposed apartheid. The Sharpeville massacre was a turning point in the struggle against apartheid, leading some ANC activists to shift from nonviolent protest to armed struggle.

Some leaders, like **Nelson Mandela,** went underground. As an ANC leader, Mandela had first mobilized young South Africans to peacefully resist apartheid laws. As government oppression grew, Mandela joined ANC militants . Mandela was arrested, tried, and, in 1964, condemned to life in prison for treason. He stated at his trial: "I have cherished the ideal of a democratic and free society in which all persons live together in harmony and with equal opportunities. It is an ideal which I hope to live for and to achieve. But if needs be, it is an ideal for which I am prepared to die." Even in prison, he remained a powerful symbol of the struggle for freedom and resistance against political oppression.

In 1976, as a shocked world looked on, government forces killed almost 600 people in protests that began in the township of Soweto. International pressure against the regime began to grow. In the 1980s, demands for an end to apartheid and for Mandela's release began to have an effect. Many countries imposed economic sanctions on South Africa, including the United States, which began to impose sanctions in 1986. In 1984, black South African bishop **Desmond Tutu** won the Nobel Peace Prize for his nonviolent opposition to apartheid.

>> More than 5,000 people attended the funerals of some of the people killed at Sharpeville. **Analyze Visuals** How does this image convey the impact of the Sharpeville massacre?

Bounce to Activate Timeline

Majority Rule Is Established Massive, continuing protests all across South Africa made the country ungovernable. With foreign pressure also mounting, the South African government decided to change. In 1990, South African president **F. W. de Klerk** lifted the ban on the ANC and freed Mandela and other political prisoners. In 1993, Mandela and de Klerk jointly won the Nobel Peace Prize for their efforts in ending apartheid.

Finally in 1994, South Africans of every race were allowed to vote for the first time. Voters chose Nelson Mandela as president in South Africa's first non-racial election. Mandela worked to heal the country's wounds. "Let us build together," he declared. He welcomed old foes into his government, including whites who had supported apartheid. Through his powerful example, he helped shift the political climate in South Africa.

Since 1994, South Africa has faced huge challenges. With majority rule, black South Africans expected a better life. Although South Africa was a rich, industrial country, it had limited resources to spend on housing, education, and other programs. The income and education gap between blacks and whites remained large. Poverty and unemployment were high among blacks. The AIDS epidemic hit South Africa severely.

Although rocked by the 2009 global recession, South Africa recovered and is one of five emerging economic powerhouses, called the BRICS—Brazil, Russia, India, China, and South Africa. These economies, taken together, are seen as a major force in the world today.

SUMMARIZE What factors finally brought about the end of apartheid?

African Nations Face Economic Choices

African economies are diverse. Each country has a different mix of economic resources. A few have rich farmland. Others have cash crops that the world wants, such as cotton, cocoa, tea and coffee. Some countries have great mineral resources, such as diamonds or oil. After achieving independence, each African nation had to make choices as to how to best develop their resources.

Economic Models After independence, many Africans nations were attracted to **socialism,** an economic system in which major economic decisions are made by the government rather than by individuals, companies, and the market. They hoped to industrialize rapidly and looked to the models of the Soviet Union and China, which had made rapid gains in a short period. Some developed their own form of "African socialism," based on traditions of consensus and shared responsibility.

These early models of development did not succeed. By the 1980s, most African nations moved toward market reforms, which international lenders required before making badly needed loans.

Cash Crops or Food Crops? For decades, African governments and multinational corporations worked to boost production of cash crops for export, such as coffee, cocoa, rubber, and cotton. However, the drive to develop cash crops for badly needed income hurt many countries. Land used to grow cash crops could not be used to produce food. Faced with growing populations, some countries had to buy costly imported food. To prevent unrest among the urban poor, many governments then kept food prices artificially low, which was costly.

Today, the demand for both cash crops and food crops remains high. Governments want to produce enough food for their people ,and have encouraged small farmers to adopt new practices to increase food output. At same time, they focus on competing in global markets for cash crops.

Economic Growth in Africa In the past ten years, economic activity across Africa has increased with some nations experiencing strong economic gains. In fact, parts of the continent have posted growth rates equal to, or greater than, parts of Asia.

>> Many industries flourish throughout Africa. In Nigeria, for example, the oil industry is dominant. These men are working on an oil rig in Nigeria's River State.

Progress is due to many causes. Some countries once torn by conflict have restored political stability and made progress, including Rwanda, Ethiopia, Angola, and Mozambique.

Trade has driven much economic growth. African nations have increased trade and other economic ties with industrial giants such as China and India. Some nations have benefited from rising prices for oil, minerals, and other commodities. Many have also reduced foreign debt and brought down high rates of inflation.

As African economies expand, more people prosper, producing a growing middle class. These consumers, in turn, help drive still greater economic growth. South Africa, Botswana, Namibia and all of North Africa are classified as "middle income countries."

Despite improvements, African growth could face setbacks. Global prices for export crops and commodities are subject to swings that can affect growth. Wars, natural disasters, and misguided government policies can also hurt individual countries.

Still, the current growth in Africa has attracted outside investment capital needed to build a strong infrastructure, or underlying transportation and other systems.

Cooperation Furthers Development African nations have benefited from regional and international cooperation. In 1963, African nations set up the Organization of African Unity, which later became the 54-nation African Union (AU). Among its chief goals are encouraging cooperation, promoting economic growth, and seeking peaceful settlements of disputes. Through the African Development Bank, it channels investment capital from foreign sources into development programs.

The UN has also promoted development. It has worked with individual countries and regional organizations like the AU to support democratic government, promote economic growth, and protect the environment. UN programs have introduced drought resistant farming methods to Ethiopia and other regions of limited rainfall. Elsewhere, they have helped poor women open small businesses, which helps families out of poverty.

GENERATE EXPLANATIONS Why did some African governments promote cash crops? What problems did this create?

Continuing Challenges to Development

Effects of Urbanization African nations experienced rapid **urbanization** as millions of people moved from rural areas into cities. Today, some 40 percent of Africans live in cities or towns. As in other developing regions, the newcomers hoped to find a better life. Instead, many faced unemployment and harsh slum conditions.

City life had an impact on families. While respect for elders and for ancestors continue to be major values, modernization has created strains between traditional and modern family values. In cities—and even in some rural areas—Smaller households have replaced the larger extended family. While better health care led to a population boom across Africa, the recent trend has been toward families having fewer children.

Environmental Concerns In Africa, as elsewhere, development and urbanization have contributed to environmental issues. Some nations, especially in the Congo Basin region, have vast forests. But millions of acres of forest are cleared each year. Deforestation, or the clearing of forests for wood and

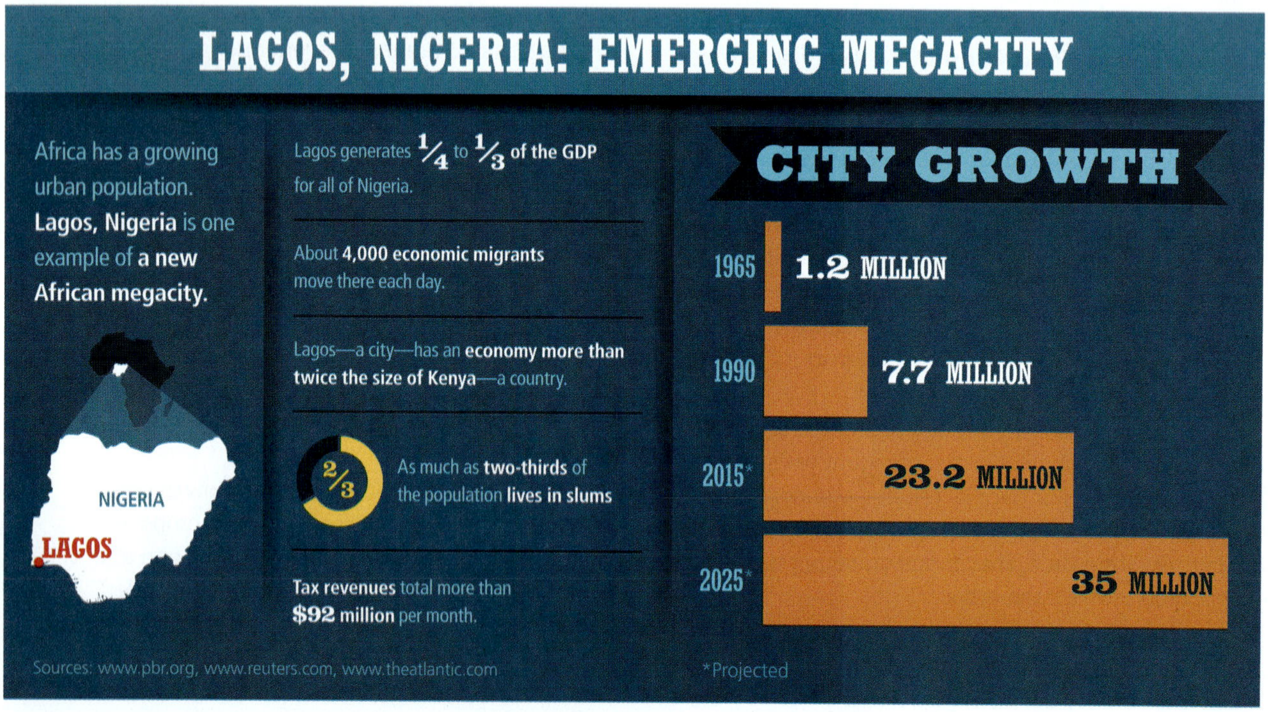

>> Lagos, Nigeria, is growing rapidly and is one of the biggest cities in Africa. **Analyze Data** What does the data shown here tell you about the benefits and drawbacks of rapid urban growth?

farming, has led to soil erosion and other harmful effects.

Deforestation endangers many species of plants and animals. Other animal habitats face destruction through human encroachment and development. The possible loss of these **endangered species** poses a threat to the tourism industries of some countries.

Oil and mining industries create great profits for some countries but also cause widespread pollution. Water pollution is another serious threat, caused by urban and industrial wastes as well as fertilizers, pesticides, and other products used in large scale farming.

Growing awareness of environmental issues has led to national and community efforts to bring change. In Kenya, **Wangari Maathai** challenged government inaction by starting the Green Belt Movement.

Her aim was to restore forest land while opening up opportunities for women in jobs such as planting, marketing, and forestry. Maathai and many other environmentalists want to promote **sustainable development** that meets the needs of the present without compromising the ability of future generations to meet their own needs.

>> Wangari Maathai of Kenya won the Nobel Peace Prize in 2004 for her work in promoting sustainable development.

Drought and Desertification Droughts are common in parts of Africa. The Sahel, a semi-desert region south of the Sahara, has suffered frequent droughts, which has led to **desertification,** or the change of habitable land into desert.

In the Sahel, overgrazing, farming, and deforestation led to destruction of plant life and loss of topsoil. During droughts, herds died off, crops withered, and many people faced famine. International relief efforts eased the famines, but wars that raged in several countries in the Sahel added to the suffering.

Today, an ambitious project called the Great Green Wall is underway to reverse desertification in some 20 African countries by reforesting the Sahel.

A wall of trees is set to reach from Senegal in the west to Dijbouti in the east. Senegal has planted more than 12 million, mostly acacia, trees. The trees can survive in a dry climate and protect the soil from erosion. Acacia trees also produce gum arabic, a substance used in some medicines and other products, which can be exported for profit.

>> Drought is a problem in many areas of Africa. This woman in Kenya digs for water at the bottom of a dry riverbed.

Bounce to Activate Gallery

AIDS and Other Diseases Today, as in the past, malaria remains a major health threat, especially among children. Efforts to combat malaria, such as providing mosquito netting, have slowed death rates.

Still, the World Health Organization estimates that a child in Africa dies of malaria every 30 seconds.

By the 1990s, many African nations were reeling from the deadly effects of AIDS (Acquired Immune Deficiency Syndrome). The disease is caused by HIV, a virus that damages the body's ability to fight infections. In South Africa and Botswana, up to one third of adults were infected with HIV. More than 11 million children in Africa have been orphaned by the AIDS epidemic.

The loss of many skilled and productive workers hurt the economies of some African countries. A global effort to combat AIDS led to the development of drugs to treat people infected with HIV. African nations set up treatment programs and worked hard to stop the spread of AIDS.

IDENTIFY CAUSE AND EFFECT Why has the AIDS epidemic so profoundly affected the economies of Africa?

ASSESSMENT

1. **Summarize** How did Nelson Mandela help shift political thought in South Africa?
2. **Describe** Describe the apartheid regime and the struggle for equality in South Africa.
3. **Infer** Why did some African leaders believe that "African socialism" would work better than a European model? What problems arose?
4. **Identify Central Issues** What do you think is the greatest challenge facing developing African countries today? Give reasons for your answer.
5. **Make Predictions** What effect will urbanization have on Africa? Will it be positive or negative?

Primary Sources

"Glory and Hope": Nelson Mandela

Introduction

Nelson Mandela delivered this speech after having been elected president in South Africa's first multiracial election in 1994. Knowing that the injustices of apartheid would be hard to overcome, Mandela asked the people to work together for peace and justice.

F.W. de Klerk, shown here with Mandela, served as President of South Africa from 1989 to 1994. He worked with Mandela to dismantle the country's system of apartheid. The second primary source is an excerpt from his 1990 speech to Parliament calling for a non-racist South Africa.

>> Nelson Mandela and F.W. de Klerk

Primary Source

Today, all of us do, by our presence here, and by our celebrations . . . confer [give] glory and hope to newborn liberty.

Out of the experience of an extraordinary human disaster that lasted too long must be born a society of which all humanity will be proud.

Our daily deeds as ordinary South Africans must produce an actual South African reality that will reinforce humanity's belief in justice, strengthen its confidence in the nobility of the human soul and sustain all our hopes for a glorious life for all. . . .

DETERMINE MEANING What does Mandela mean by "an actual South African reality"?

The time for the healing of the wounds has come. . . .

The time to build is upon us.

We have, at last, achieved our political emancipation [freedom from bondage or control by others]. We pledge ourselves to liberate all our people from the continuing bondage [slavery] of poverty, deprivation [lack of materials necessary for survival], suffering, gender and other discrimination. . . .

We have triumphed in the effort to implant [insert] hope in the breasts of the millions of our people. We enter into a covenant [binding agreement] that we shall build the society in which all South Africans, both black and white, will be able to walk tall, without any fear in their hearts, assured of their inalienable right to human dignity—a rainbow nation at peace with itself and the world. . . .

SUMMARIZE What freedoms does Mandela call for in this passage?

We understand it still that there is no easy road to freedom.

We know it well that none of us acting alone can achieve success.

We must therefore act together as a united people, for national reconciliation [a settling of differences that results in harmony], for nation building, for the birth of a new world.

Let there be justice for all. Let there be peace for all. Let there be work, bread, water, and salt for all. . . . The sun shall never set on so glorious a human achievement!

PARAPHRASE In one or two sentences, write in your own words how Mandela concludes his speech.

Primary Sources

Primary Source

The Government accepts the principle of the recognition and protection of the fundamental individual rights which form the constitutional basis of most Western democracies. We acknowledge, too, that the most practical way of protecting those rights is vested in a declaration of rights justiciable (subject to a court trial) by an independent judiciary. However, it is clear that a system for the protection of the rights of individuals, minorities and national entities has to form a well-rounded and balanced whole. South Africa has its own national composition and our constitutional dispensation has to take this into account. The formal recognition of individual rights does not mean that the problems of a heterogeneous population will simply disappear. Any new constitution which disregards this reality will be inappropriate and even harmful. Naturally, the protection of collective, minority and national rights may not bring about an imbalance in respect of individual rights. It is neither the Government's policy nor its intention that any group–in whichever way it may be defined–shall be favoured above or in relation to any of the others.

ANALYZE INFORMATION Why does de Klerk warn against an easy compromise of individual rights in South Africa?

ASSESSMENT

1. **Explain an Argument** When apartheid ended, there was a danger of a backlash by blacks against whites who supported apartheid. How does Mandela's speech respond to that danger?
2. **Determine Author's Point of View** How would you describe the tone of Mandela's speech? How does this tone reflect Mandela's view of his country and its future?
3. **Determine Author's Purpose** Why do you think Mandela talks about building a new world, not just a new South Africa?
4. **Describe** The day de Klerk made the speech excerpted here was also the day he announced the release of Mandela from prison after 27 years. Describe what the reaction might have been not only in South Africa but around the world.

10.3 China and India dominate much of Asia. Together, they are home to about two-fifths of the world's population. China is a major industrial nation. Although India's economy is smaller, it has grown rapidly in recent years and is a leading Asian and global power. Both China and India have followed their own paths toward development.

>> Shanghai is China's main industrial center. A population of more than 16 million makes it China's largest city. Increased business has led to growth, but also to problems.

Bounce to Activate Flipped Video

Rapid Development in China and India

Reform and Repression in China

A New Approach to the Chinese Economy Mao Zedong, the architect of China's communist revolution, died in 1976. After his death, more moderate leaders took control of China. By 1981, **Deng Xiaoping** (dung show ping), had adopted a new approach to China's economy. Deng was a practical reformer, more interested in improving economic output than in political purity. "I don't care if a cat is black or white," he declared, "as long as it catches mice."

Deng's program, the Four Modernizations, emphasized agriculture, industry, science, and defense. The plan allowed some features of a market economy, such as some private ownership of property. Communes, or collectively owned farms, were dismantled, and peasant families were allotted plots of land to farm in what was called the "responsibility system." Farmers did not own the land, and the government took a share of their crops. However, farmers could sell any surplus produce and keep the profits.

Entrepreneurs were allowed to set up businesses. Managers of state-run factories were given more freedom, but they had to make their plants more efficient. Deng also welcomed foreign capital

>> Objectives

Describe how China has moved toward a free market economy without allowing democratic reform.

Identify continuing challenges that China faces.

Explain how India has built its economy.

Summarize social reforms in modern India.

>> Key Terms

Deng Xiaoping
Tiananmen Square
one-child policy
Kolkata
Mumbai
Mother Teresa
dalit
Kolkata

and technology. Investors from Japan, Hong Kong, Taiwan, and Western nations invested heavily in China.

Economic reforms brought a surge of growth. In coastal cities, foreign investment created an economic boom. Some Chinese enjoyed a higher standard of living. They bought refrigerators, televisions, and cars. On the other hand, crime and corruption increased and a growing gap developed between poor rural farmers and wealthy city dwellers.

Protest in Tiananmen Square Economic reforms and increased contact with the West led some Chinese to demand greater political freedom. In the late 1980s, students, workers, and others created a democracy movement similar to those sweeping across Eastern Europe. However, Deng and other Chinese Communist leaders were determined to preserve the communist political system.

In 1989, a political crisis erupted as thousands of protesters, many of them students, occupied **Tiananmen (*TYEN* ahn mun) Square,** a huge public plaza in Beijing. Protester waved banners calling for democracy. The government ordered the protesters to disperse. When they refused, the government sent in troops and tanks. Thousands of demonstrators were killed or wounded in the Tiananmen Square Massacre. Many protesters across China were imprisoned and tortured. The crackdown showed that the communist government was determined to keep its monopoly on power.

>> The day after the massacre in Tiananmen Square, a lone protestor stepped in front of a line of tanks. The "Tank Man" became a worldwide symbol of individuals standing against government oppression.

Bounce to Activate Gallery

DRAW CONCLUSIONS What unintended consequences did the Chinese government's reforms during the 1980s have on the Chinese population?

Reforms Bring Growth and Challenges

Economic reforms helped China become an industrial superpower and a rival of the United States. China's achievements were on display to the world when China hosted the 2008 summer Olympic games. Despite its spectacular economic growth, however, China faced serious internal challenges.

Rapid Industrialization In China, as elsewhere, industrialization led to rapid urbanization. Boom times brought millions of rural workers into Chinese cities. They worked for low wages in manufacturing and other jobs. Their needs strained local resources for housing, education, and other services.

Urbanization and industrialization led to widespread air and water pollution. In many cities, air quality is so poor that parents sometimes keep their children indoors. Coal burning and emissions from automobiles are major sources of pollution. Although China has taken steps to fight pollution,economic growth is given priority over the environment. Huge mining operations scar the landscape in some regions, while arid regions face desertification.

The 2009 global financial crisis hurt China, as it hurt other industrialized nation, but its economy was one of the first to recover. By 2011, China had become the world's second-largest economy after the United States. Still, unemployment, which was kept low under Mao, became an issue in China's new economy.

Human Rights Abuses For decades, human rights campaigners both inside China and outside have criticized the government for limiting freedom and jailing critics as well as torturing and executing large numbers of prisoners. Activists protested abuses such as lack of free speech and the use of prison labor to produce goods for export. The

Chinese government has rejected calls from other countries to an end abuses, claiming that outsiders have no right to impose "Western-style" ideas of human rights on China.

China has faced growing unrest from minority groups within its vast country. The Muslim Uighurs as well as Mongols have protested ethnic discrimination and curbs on their religious and cultural freedoms.

A global human rights campaign has focused on Tibet, a region occupied by China in 1950. The government claims that Tibet has been part of China for centuries. China has cracked down hard on Tibetan Buddhists, who have accused China of suppressing their culture and religion. They also resent China's policy of moving Han Chinese into Tibet, which they see as another effort to undermine their traditions.

In November 2013, the Chinese government took more tentative steps toward reform. It announced new policies on some of China's most notorious human rights issues, such as an end to labor camps, which had long been used to punish political dissidents. Other reforms announced by the Chinese government included greater freedoms for farmers to sell land for financial benefit and an improved judicial system. However, many critics still argued that no real political reforms were announced. The government still holds a tight rein on individual rights and freedoms.

China's One-Child Policy With more than 1.3 billion people, China has the world's largest population. To slow population growth, in the 1980s, the government imposed a **one-child policy,** which limited urban families to a single child and allowed rural families two children. The government enforced this harsh policy with steep fines and other penalties. Children born in violation of the policy often could not get an education or other services because they did not have identity cards.

Although the one-child policy was widely condemned, it did slow population growth. Since 2013, the government eased the restriction slightly, allowing couples to have a second child if one of the parents is an only child.

☑ **IDENTIFY CAUSE AND EFFECT** How did the global economic recession affect China?

>> China imposed a strict one-child policy in the 1980s. This mural encourages parents to be satisfied with a single child.

India Builds a Modern Economy

Like China, India is a huge country with a large, diverse population and widespread poverty. After gaining independence in 1947, India set up a democratic government and planned to develop a modern economy.

Developing a Market Economy After independence, India like many developing nations, followed a mixed model of development, using features of both socialism and capitalism. By the late 1980s, however, India had begun to introduce more free market reforms. It privatized some industries and made foreign investment easier. Before long, it emerged as one of the world's fastest-growing economies. Today, India has the third largest economy in Asia, after China and Japan. It is also part of the BRICS—the five fast-emerging economies of Brazil, Russia, India, China, and South Africa.

Indian agriculture benefited from the Green Revolution. High-yield crops, chemical fertilizers, and better irrigation systems increased output.

India, like all nations, has faced economic swings. The 2009 global economic recession hurt growth, but the Indian economy recovered. In recent decades, India has moved into the forefront of information technology, providing computer software and other technological services to the world. Many Western companies have outsourced work to Indian companies, where even skilled workers earned less than their counterparts in the West.

Obstacles to Progress Despite many successes, India faces major economic hurdles. Among them are population and poverty, unemployment, the rural-urban divide, and the need for agricultural development. India, like China, experienced rapid population growth, which hurt efforts to improve standards of living. As food output rose, so did demand. More than one-third of Indians live in poverty, unable to meet basic needs for food, clothing, and shelter. Although India's economy was expanding, it could not provide enough jobs for everyone, leading to high unemployment.

>> As India's economy grows, so does demand for cars. India is now the world's sixth-largest carmaker. Traffic in the narrow streets of crowded cities is a growing problem, as is air pollution.

Bounce to Activate Gallery

As India modernized, tens of millions of people left villages to live in cities, and the gap between rural and urban dwellers grew. Still, an estimated 70 percent of Indians still live in villages. Rural poverty remains high, despite government programs to provide education and jobs. Farming communities still lack roads, electricity and other basic services. Many farm workers still use traditional farming methods and owe much of their output to absentee landowners.

The government has worked to introduce modern farming methods and technology. It has also tried to make Indian farmers less dependent on the seasonal monsoon rainfall. Building modern irrigation systems and repairing old ones is a costly, but ongoing, process.

Impact of Rapid Population Growth With 1.2 billion people, India has the world's second largest population after China. The Indian government supported family planning but did not adopt the harsh policies used in China.

Although India's growth rate has slowed somewhat, it is estimated that India will have the world's larger population by 2030. While middle class families have fewer children than in the past, poor families, especially in rural areas, still see children as an economic resource to work the land and care for parents in old age.

In overcrowded cities like **Kolkata** (or Calcutta) and **Mumbai** (or Bombay), millions lived in poverty without jobs, adequate food, or health care. The government, aid groups, and others tried to help the urban poor. In Kolkata, **Mother Teresa,** a Roman Catholic nun, founded the Missionaries of Charity. This group provided food and medical care to thousands. They treated lepers, AIDS sufferers, and many others. Still, millions more remained in desperate need in both urban and rural areas.

IDENTIFY CAUSE AND EFFECT How did market reforms affect India's economy in the 1990s?

Social Reform in India

Unlike China, which has suppressed social protests, India is a democratic country where activists have pressed social reform. They have addressed many causes, such as protecting women's rights, ending caste discrimination or child labor, and promoting education.

Dalits Education, economic growth, and urbanization continue to undermine Indian's traditional caste system. In India's competitive economy, new classes are emerging based on individual success and wealth. Some older castes are losing their privileged positions while successful entrepreneurs from any caste have gained status. Cities allow for greater social mobility, or the ability of individuals or groups to move up in society.

India's constitution banned discrimination against **dalits,** or people of the lowest caste. To improve conditions, the government set aside jobs and places in universities for members of this group. Overall, conditions for dalits have improved in the past 20 years. However, some discrimination based on caste continued. Higher-caste Hindus generally receive better education and jobs.

Women Work to Improve Their Lives India's constitution granted equal rights to women. In the cities, girls from well-to-do families were educated. Women entered many professions. Some, like Indira Gandhi, won political office. Girls from poor families, however, received little or no education. Some were secluded within the home, and were not allowed to attend school. Although women in rural areas worked the land or contributed to household industries, few received wages. Across India, women organized self-help groups to start small businesses and improve their lives.

Women's rights groups have strongly protested continued inequality and violence against women in India. They have fought for tougher laws for those convicted of crimes against women. Young women and men have demanded an end to discrimination based on gender. They are battling deeply-rooted cultural traditions that gave men authority over women.

The issue of women's rights brings up other human rights concerns in India. Free speech is limited, Christian groups feel they are not adequately protected, and child labor is allowed. Debt bondage—where a person works off his or her debt—still exists. The reports of military abuse are widespread. Soldiers have the power to kill, arrest, search, and detain civilians. The soldiers are not subject to any punishment or prosecution even though the army has the power to try soldiers in military courts. Human rights groups continue to report and fight the abuses. In 2017, the UN Human Rights Council conducted a third review of India's human rights record.

>> This photograph shows Mother Teresa at her mission in Kolkata, surrounded by some of the many poor children she helped in her lifetime.

EXPLAIN How did the Indian government try to improve the status of dalits?

ASSESSMENT

1. **Describe** How did China move toward economic reform without allowing for political reform?
2. **Identify Central Issues** What challenges does the Chinese government continue to face?
3. **Generate Explanations** How has India built a modern economy?
4. **Express Problems Clearly** What social reforms has the Indian government made over the last few decades, and why?
5. **Identify Cause and Effect** How does a rapidly expanding population affect life in India?

>> Flags of the member nations decorate the hall of the Organization of American States headquarters in Washington, D.C. Representatives discuss how to improve the lives of their citizens.

Bounce to Activate Flipped Video

10.4 Latin America comprises Mexico, Central America, the Caribbean, and South America. It includes 33 independent nations, ranging from small islands, such as Grenada, to giant Brazil. It is a diverse region in which each country has its own history and traditions. Despite differences, Latin American nations faced political, economic, and social challenges similar to those of other developing nations—rapid population growth, poverty, illiteracy, political instability, and authoritarian governments.

>> Objectives

Analyze how Latin America has grappled with poverty.

Describe the struggles of Latin American nations to build democratic governments.

Explain the struggle between repression and freedom in Argentina.

>> Key Terms

import substitution
agribusiness
liberation theology
indigenous
Sandinista
contra
Organization of American States (OAS)
Juan Perón
Mothers of the Plaza de Mayo
Oscar Romero

Latin American Nations Move Toward Democracy

Poverty Challenges Latin America

From the 1950s to the 1980s, economic development failed to change deep-rooted inequalities in many Latin American countries. Due to inequality and growing populations, most countries saw little improvement in living standards.

Promoting Industry and Agriculture In Latin America, as in other developing regions, nations often relied heavily on a single cash crop or commodity. If harvests failed or if world demand for that commodity fell, their economies were hard hit.

To reduce dependence on imported goods, many Latin American governments in the 1950s and 1960s adopted a policy of **import substitution,** or manufacturing goods locally to replace expensive imported goods. Results were mixed. Many new industries did not produce efficiently and needed government or foreign capital to survive.

In time, Latin American governments moved from import substitution to promoting exports. They developed a variety of cash crops and encouraged mining and other industries that produced goods for export. Some worked with multinational corporations willing to invest in new projects.

In many Latin American countries, governments backed the growth of **agribusinesses,** giant commercial farms owned by multinational corporations. These agribusinesses produce cash crops that help boost national incomes. In Central America and Brazil, agribusinesses and other developers have cleared tropical rain forests to use as farmland. Deforestation has had both economic benefits and environmental costs. Burning of forest land has destroyed plant and animal habitats, polluted water supplies, and contributed to soil erosion.

The Income Gap One challenge facing Latin American nations is uneven distribution of wealth between rich and poor. This income gap is especially evident in cities, which are divided between comfortable residential neighborhoods and sprawling favelas, or slums. The income gap has long existed in rural areas. In many countries, a tiny elite controls the land, businesses, and factories. These powerful groups oppose changes that might undermine their position. As a result, the gap between the rich and the poor has widened, fueling discontent.

Population Growth Contributes to Poverty

Latin American nations, like the rest of the developing world, experienced a population explosion that contributed to poverty. Although population growth rates slowed somewhat in the 1990s, economies were hard-pressed to keep pace with the needs of their people for housing, education, and other basic services.

In rural areas, population pressures made life more difficult for peasant farmers. Even though a family might own a small plot to grow its own food, most farmers worked on the estates of large landowners for low wages.

Faced with debt and poverty, millions of rural dwellers flocked to cities. Today, more than 75 percent of people in Latin America live in towns and cities. Some newcomers found jobs in factories, offices, and stores. Many more survive by working odd jobs. They fill the shantytowns on the edges of Latin American cities. More than 111 million people in Latin America live in shantytowns.

Economic Activity of Latin America

>> **Analyze Maps** Much of the land in Latin America is devoted to farming. Which type of farming is most widespread?

Bounce to Activate Map

>> Thousands of Catholics crowd into St. Peter's Square in Rome to see and hear Pope Francis on Easter Day 2013. Pope Francis, who is from Argentina, is the first pope from the Americas.

>> This March 1982 photograph shows police detaining people who were protesting the dictatorship in Argentina. Many protesters were jailed, and thousands who disagreed with the government were killed.

The Role of Religion in Latin America The Roman Catholic Church remained a powerful force across Latin America. Although it was often tied to the ruling class, some church leaders spoke up for the poor. During the 1960s and 1970s, many priests, nuns, and church workers crusaded for social justice and an end to poverty. This movement, known as **liberation theology,** urged the church to become a force for reform.

In 2013, people across Latin America celebrated the selection of Argentina's Jorge Bergoglio as pope. He became the first person from the Western Hemisphere to lead the Roman Catholic Church. The new pope took the name Francis, after Francis of Assisi, who had devoted his life to the poor. Pope Francis was well known for his own advocacy for the poor during his life in Argentina and continued to address the issue as pope.

Since the 1980s, evangelical Protestant groups have won many converts in Latin America. Evangelical sects stress the authority of the Bible and belief in salvation through Jesus. Many poor people were attracted to evangelical Christianity. In addition to the Catholic Church and Protestant groups, other world religions had an established place in Latin America.

DRAW CONCLUSIONS What problems did the gap between the rich and the poor cause in Latin America?

Dictatorships and Civil War

Most Latin American countries had constitutions that set up representative governments. Building true democracy, however, was difficult to achieve in nations plagued by poverty and inequality. From the 1950s on, many groups pressed for reforms. They included liberals, socialists, urban workers, peasants, and Catholic priests and nuns. Although they differed over how to achieve their goals, all wanted to improve conditions for the poor.

Conservative forces, however, resisted reforms. Among those who resisted change were the military, the traditional landed elite, and the growing business middle class. Conflict between conservatives and reformers contributed to political instability in many nations.

Military Leaders Seize Power In the 1960s and 1970s, as social unrest increased, military governments in Argentina, Brazil, and Chile seized power. They imposed harsh, autocratic regimes, outlawed political parties, censored the press, and closed universities. They also imprisoned and executed thousands. "Death squads" linked to military rule murdered many more.

Writers, such as Pablo Neruda of Chile and Gabriel García Márquez of Colombia, went into exile after speaking out against repressive governments or social inequality.

Revolutions Break Out In Latin America, as elsewhere, leftists wanted to build socialist societies, which they believed would end inequalities. Some leftists joined guerrilla movements to battle repressive governments. After building a communist state in Cuba, Fidel Castro supported leftist guerrillas in many other parts of Latin America.

Cold War fears about the spread of Marxism complicated efforts for reform. Many conservatives in Latin America saw any call for reform as a communist threat. The United States often supported military governments and conservative groups that were strongly anti-communist.

Civil War in Central America Several Central American nations were torn by civil wars as revolutionaries battled authoritarian governments. In 1954, the United States helped the Guatemalan military overthrow an elected, leftist government. Leftists and others fought the military regime, which responded savagely.

The military targeted Guatemala's **indigenous,** or native, people, slaughtering tens of thousands of Mayans and members of other Indian groups. Fighting ended in 1996, after the government signed a peace accord and held elections.

In El Salvador, too, reformers and leftist revolutionaries challenged the landowning and military elite. During a vicious 12-year civil war, right-wing death squads slaughtered student and labor leaders, church workers, and anyone else thought to sympathize with leftists. One reformer, Archbishop **Oscar Romero,** was assassinated in 1980 while celebrating mass. In 1992, both sides finally agreed to a UN-brokered peace.

In 1979, the **Sandinistas,** socialist rebels in Nicaragua, toppled the Somoza family, which had ruled since 1936. The Sandinistas introduced land reform and other socialist measures. Fearing that Nicaragua could become "another Cuba," U.S. President Ronald Reagan financed the **contras,** guerrillas who fought the Sandinistas. Fighting raged until 1990, when a peace settlement brought multiparty elections.

>> Archbishop Oscar Romero of El Salvador became widely known for defending the poor and oppressed. His sharp criticism of the government gained him a large following, but also many enemies.

Movement Toward Democracy By the 1990s, international pressure and activists within each country pushed military governments to restore civilian rule. Argentina, Brazil, Chile, and other countries held elections. In some countries, such as Brazil, Venezuela, and Bolivia, leftist leaders won office. Since then, many Latin American countries have experienced the peaceful transition of power from one elected government to the another.

Mexico had escaped military rule, but still experienced growing demands for political reform. Between 1930 and 2000, a single political party–the Institutional Revolutionary Party (PRI)–won every election and controlled the government. It claimed to represent all groups in Mexican society from workers and peasants to business and industrial interests as well as the military. Although a few small political parties did exist, PRI bosses moved forcefully against any serious opposition.

Under pressure, the PRI made some reforms in the 1990s. In 2000, Vicente Fox became the first candidate from an opposition party to be elected president.

Fox and later presidents faced tough challenges, ranging from rural poverty to crime, corruption, and violent drug gangs. Despite government pledges for reform, Mexico has remained a disturbing mix of prosperity and poverty. In recent years, some regions of Mexico have suffered from violent crime related to drug trafficking.

IDENTIFY CAUSE AND EFFECT What social and political conditions led to civil wars in many Latin American countries?

U.S.–Latin American Relations

A complex network of ties linked Latin American nations and the United States. Since the late 1800s, the United States has been a looming presence in the Western Hemisphere. It has intervened in local conflicts and taken other steps to ensure its influence in the region.

Today, Latin America and the United States remain closely linked. The **Organization of American States (OAS),** was formed in 1948 to promote democracy, economic cooperation, and peace in the Americas. Although the United States often used its power to dominate the OAS, Latin American members have at times pursued an independent line. The United States is economically linked to Mexico through the North American Free Trade Agreement (NAFTA) and has sought to create a larger free trade area with other Latin American countries

>> American soldiers joined UN forces to keep the peace after the coup in Haiti. Peacekeepers also did practical work, such as building, supplying food, and spreading cement to repair roads.

Despite these links, the United States and Latin American nations view each other very differently. The United States sees itself as the defender of democracy and capitalism in the region. It also provides much-needed aid.

While many Latin Americans admire the wealth of the United States, they often resent what they see as its political, economic, and cultural domination. "North Americans are always among us," said Mexican poet Octavio Paz, "even when they ignore us or turn their back on us. Their shadow covers the whole hemisphere. It is the shadow of a giant."

U.S. Intervention During the Cold War, the United States helped train and equip the military in many Latin American countries and often backed anti-communist dictators. It also returned to a policy of intervention, usually sending its military to stop what it saw as the threat of communism. In 1954, it helped overthrow Guatemala's leftist government. In 1965, the U.S. sent troops to the Dominican Republic when unrest raised fears the island nation could become a "second Cuba." In 1973, the United States secretly backed a military coup in Chile against democratically elected socialist president, Salvador Allende (ah YEN day), putting military dictator Augusto Pinochet (pee noh SHAY) in power.

On other occasions, the United States stepped in for different reasons. In 1989, it sent forces to Panama to bring its drug-smuggling president Manuel Noriega to justice. In 1994, a UN force led by the United States landed in Haiti to restore its elected leader after a military coup. The United States later withdrew its forces from Haiti, leaving UN peacekeepers to protect democracy in the poverty-stricken country. Since then, the United States has provided much aid to Haiti after it was devastated by a strong earthquake and struck by hurricanes.

The War on Drugs As illegal drug use increased in the United States and around the world in the 1970s, criminal gangs in Latin America began producing and smuggling ever-larger quantities of cocaine and other drugs for export. In the 1980s, the U.S. government declared a "war on drugs" and set out to halt the flow of illegal drugs into the country from Colombia, Peru, Bolivia, and elsewhere. It funneled military and financial aid to Latin American governments to destroy drug crops and crush the drug cartels, or criminal gangs that ran the drug trade.

Latin American governments cooperated with U.S. anti-drug efforts. After all, drug lords were bribing government officials and hiring assassins to kill judges, journalists, and others who spoke out against them. But many people argued that the root problem was growing demand for illegal drugs in the United States.

Migration Immigration from Latin America to the United States increased rapidly after the 1970s. Poverty, civil war, and repressive governments led many people to flee their homelands. Many entered the country legally and eventually became citizens. A large number, however, were illegal immigrants. The earnings they sent home helped raise the standard of living for their families in Latin America.

Pressure rose within the United States to halt the flow of illegal immigrants. The United States tightened security along its border with Mexico. Congress debated immigration reform legislation.

Deportation, or the removal of illegal immigrants, gradually eased during the Obama administration. Only undocumented immigrants convicted of serious crimes were deported. However, with the election of President Trump, illegal immigration enforcement increased. All undocumented immigrants were subject to deportation at any time.

At the same time, Latin American countries like Mexico hoped to improve the quality of life and opportunities so fewer citizens left their homelands.

DRAW CONCLUSIONS Why do people in Latin America have mixed opinions of the United States?

The Long Road to Democracy in Argentina

Argentina is among the most prosperous countries in Latin America. During much of the last century, it enjoyed a robust economy based on exports of beef and grain. But it also experienced political and economic upheavals. Since the 1980s, the country has worked to rebuild democracy and recover prosperity.

The Military Takes Control From 1946 to 1955, nationalist president Juan Perón enjoyed great support from workers. He increased the government's economic role, boosted wages, and backed labor unions. Perón was helped greatly by his

>> American soldiers entered Panama to arrest military dictator Manuel Noriega, a major drug dealer. The United States wanted to put an end to the drug trade and to restore freedom to Panama.

>> Juan Perón, shown here with his wife, Eva, made some improvements in Argentina. However, as his government became more repressive and corrupt, he relied increasingly on military force to hold on to power.

>> The Mothers of the Plaza de Mayo gathered weekly in Argentina's capital, carrying photos of their "disappeared" children, who had been kidnapped and probably killed by the government.

Bounce to Activate Gallery

glamorous wife, Eva Perón, who used her influence to help the poor. While Perón wooed the urban poor, his authoritarian government stifled opposition.

When Perón's policies led to an economic crisis, he was ousted in a 1955 military coup. The military was in and out of power for more than two decades. To combat leftist guerrillas, the military waged a "dirty war," torturing and murdering people it claimed were enemies of the state. As many as 20,000 people simply "disappeared." The Dirty War lasted from 1976 to 1983.

In 1977, a group of mothers whose children had disappeared began to meet each week in the Plaza de Mayo in Buenos Aires. They demanded to know what had happened to their missing sons and daughters. The nonviolent protests of the **Mothers of the Plaza de Mayo,** drew worldwide attention.

In 1982, the military hoped to mask economic troubles by seizing the British-ruled Falkland Islands. In the brief but decisive war, the British retook the islands.

Restoration of Democracy Defeat in the Falklands War undermined the military, and it was forced to hold free elections. In 1983, Argentina gained a democratically elected government. Despite economic setbacks and corruption scandals, democracy has survived in Argentina.

Argentina's economy has often experienced cycles of boom-and bust. In 2001, a financial crisis devastated the economy, causing widespread poverty and serious unrest. Eventually, the economy rebounded. Like other nations, Argentina is affected by global economic events as well as by internal crisis.

EXPLAIN Why did the military restore democratic rule in Argentina?

ASSESSMENT

1. **Describe** What changes did Latin American nations make to economic policy to try to cope with poverty and economic hardship?
2. **Identify Cause and Effect** Why did Latin American nations find it difficult to establish democratic governments?
3. **Identify Central Ideas** How have repeated U.S. interventions in Latin America affected Latin American attitudes toward the United States?
4. **Draw Conclusions** Why do you think many of the repressive dictatorships in Latin America were led by the military?
5. **Sequence Events** Describe the changes Argentina's government went through after the 1930s. List significant events in the order in which they occurred.

10.5 The collapse of communism ended decades of division between communist Eastern Europe and democratic Western Europe. Conditions were favorable for the spread of democracy. Trade, business, travel, and communications across the continent became easier. At the same time, many European nations had to deal with issues such as large-scale immigration from the developing world, growing discrimination against foreigners, and rising unemployment.

>> Hong Kong has long been a major trading center of East Asia, thanks to its splendid harbor. Since 1997, when it was returned to China, it has emerged as a prosperous manufacturing and financial center of the new, modernized China.

Bounce to Activate Flipped Video

The Industrialized World

>> **Objectives**

Examine social, political, and economic trends in Europe since the Cold War.

Describe how the breakup of Yugoslavia led to war and genocide.

Analyze the challenges facing Russia since the end of the Soviet Union.

Summarize economic developments in Asia.

>> **Key Terms**

European Union (EU)
euro
default
Vladimir Putin
surplus
deficit
Pacific Rim
Northern Ireland
Good Friday Agreement
Chechnya
multiethnic
Slobodan Milosevic
ethnic cleansing

A New Europe

A Reunited Germany In 1990, after 45 years of division, East Germany and West Germany were reunited. Germans welcomed reunification, even though it brought many challenges. Prosperous West Germans had to pay higher taxes to finance the rebuilding of the east. At the same time, East German faced a difficult transition to a market economy. Still, more than 25 years after reunification, Germany remained an economic giant and a key European leader.

Reunification brought social problems. A few right-wing extremists revived Nazi ideology. Seeing the answer to hard times in racism and hatred, these neo-Nazis viciously attacked foreign workers. Most Germans condemned such actions.

Changes in NATO With the collapse of communism, the Warsaw Pact dissolved. Many democratic nations of Eastern and Central Europe joined NATO, including Poland, Hungary, and the Czech Republic. Today, NATO includes 28 member nations. Russia disliked NATO's expansion, but agreed to a NATO-Russia Council to consult on issues of common interest.

In the post Cold War world, NATO redefined its goals. It helped UN peacekeeping and humanitarian missions. As threats from global terrorism grew, NATO worked to track and uncover terrorist groups and improved preparedness and response to attacks. After the 2001 terrorist attacks on the United States, NATO forces joined the U.S. against the Taliban in Afghanistan. The Taliban had given shelter to the Al Qaeda terrorist who planned the attack.

Growth of the European Union The end of the Cold War also changed trade relations in Europe. In 1993, the European Economic Community became the **European Union (EU),** a bloc of European nations that work together to promote a freer flow of capital, labor, services, and goods. Members also cooperate on security matters. In 2004, the EU added 10 new members mostly from Central and Eastern Europe.

In 2002, the **euro** became the common currency for most of Western Europe. By then, EU passports had replaced national passports. Today, the expanded EU has the world's largest economy and competes with economic superpowers like the United States and Japan. Some European leaders supported even greater economic and political unity for the region. However, many ordinary citizens felt greater loyalty to their own nations than to the EU. Also, the economies of Eastern Europe were weaker than those in the West, causing worries about the EU's overall economic outlook.

Turkey, long a member of NATO, sought to join the EU. But its application faced opposition in part because of human rights issues and the fears of some European nations about admitting a country with a large Muslim population.

The European Debt Crisis The 2009 global economic crisis shook the EU as some member nations came close to bankruptcy. They had borrowed heavily to pay for expensive social and other programs. As the economic crisis worsened, countries such as Spain and Greece were unable to pay their debts. The EU provided financial bailouts, or loans, and required severe cuts in spending. Even as the debt crisis eased, it left a legacy of shaken confidence.

Conflict in Northern Ireland The modern era saw the end of one long-standing conflict. For decades, violence shook Northern Ireland. When Ireland won independence in 1922, Britain kept control of **Northern Ireland,** six counties that had

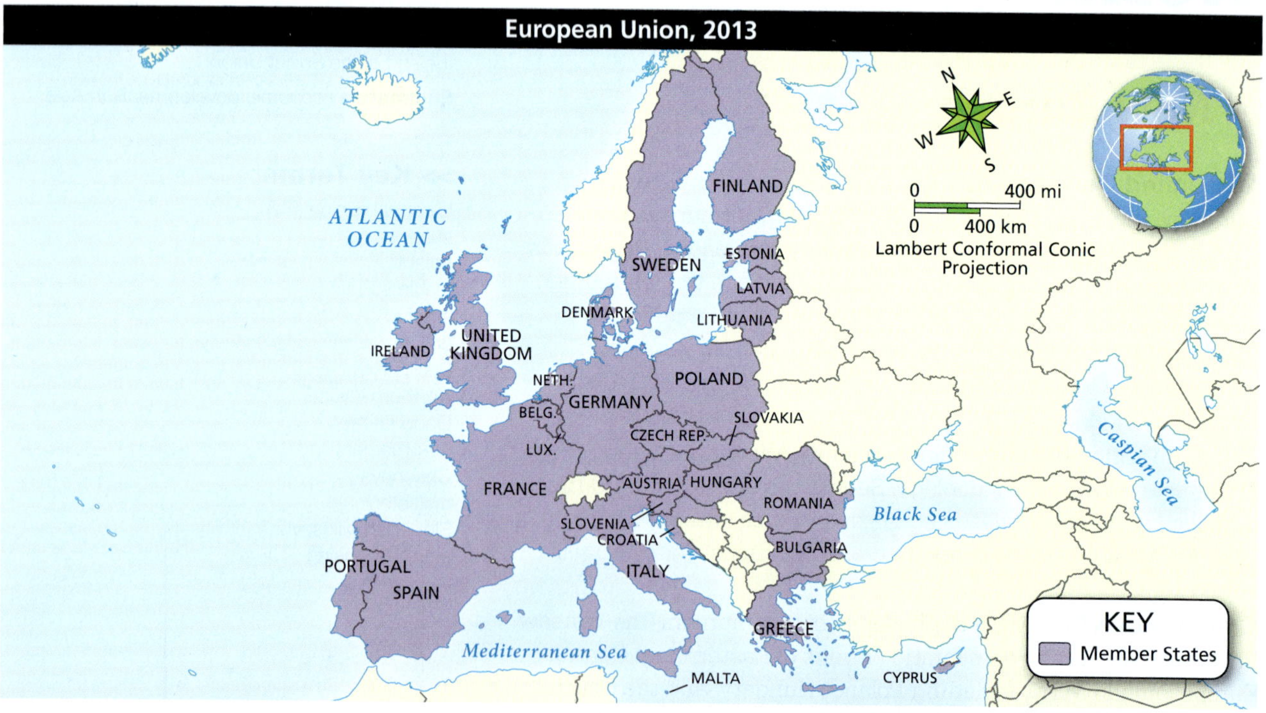

>> This map shows the European Union in 2013. **Analyze Maps** Which EU members border the Black Sea?

Bounce to Activate Map

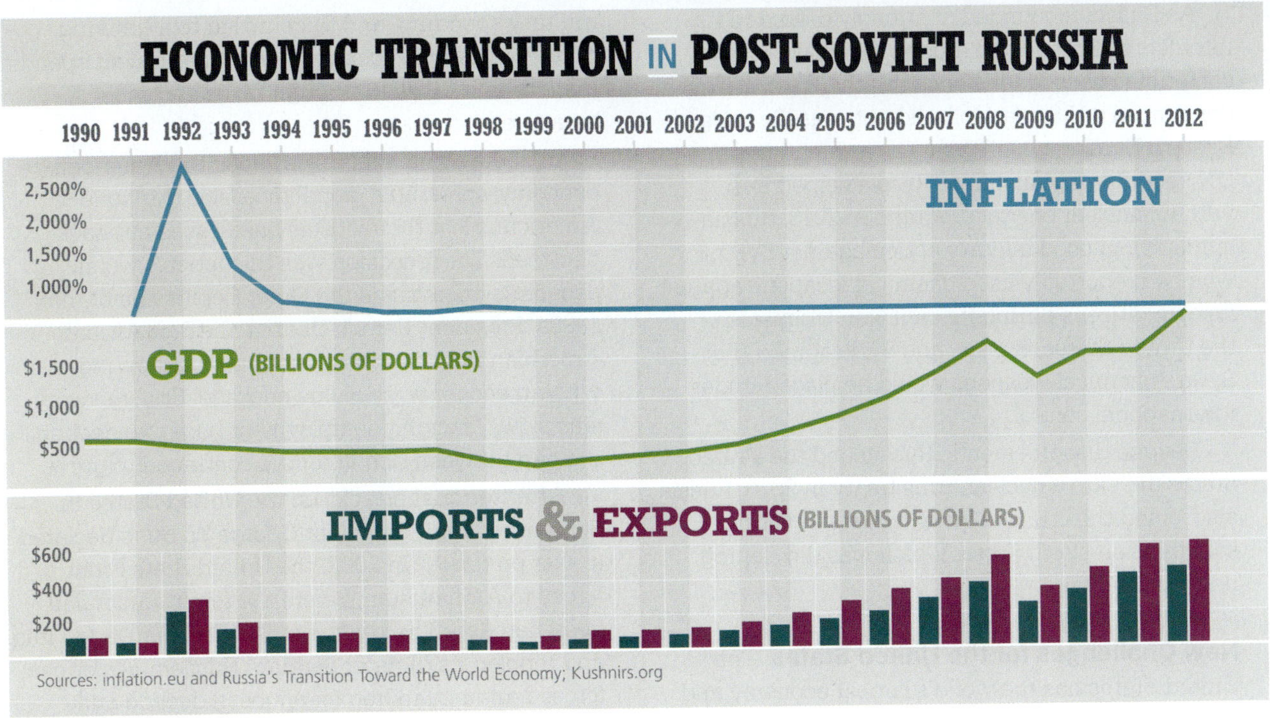

>> **Analyze Graphs** After the fall of the Soviet Union, Russia's economy took time to adapt to a free market economy. In what year did inflation start to drop in Russia?

a Protestant majority. In the face of discrimination, many Catholics demanded civil rights and pressed for unification with Ireland. Protestants wanted Northern Ireland to remain part of Britain.

Violence escalated in the late 1960s as extremists on both sides turned to terrorism. The Irish Republican Army (IRA) attacked Protestants, while armed Protestant groups targeted Catholics. The violence raged for three decades. After Britain sent troops to Northern Ireland, IRA terrorists attacked sites in Britain. Finally, in 1998, both sides signed a peace accord, known as the **Good Friday Agreement.** Protestants and Catholics set up a power-sharing government in 2007. Although isolated acts of violence have occurred, most people expected that peace would be permanent.

CITE EVIDENCE What challenges did Germany face after reunification?

Shifts in Global Power

After the breakup of the Soviet Union, the United States remained the world's sole superpower. Russia struggled economically and was sidelined for a time in foreign affairs. In 2014, Russia hosted the Olympic Games, determined to showcase its return to the world stage as a great power. Despite tensions, the two Cold War rivals cooperated at times while each faced its own issues.

Russia Rebuilds After the breakup of the Soviet Union, Russian president Boris Yeltsin shifted to a market economy. Economic reforms, especially the privatization of many state-run industries and collective farms, brought severe hardships to many Russians as unemployment and prices soared. A financial crisis wiped out the savings of millions. In 1998, Russia barely avoided financial collapse. It **defaulted,** or failed to make payments, on much of its foreign debt. A few Russians, however, grew rich, buying up old Soviet industries at bargain prices. They formed a new wealthy and powerful class.

Since 2000, **Vladimir Putin** has dominated Russian politics. As president, he helped rebuild the economy. Russia benefited from its vast natural resources, especially oil and gas. Rising prices for these exports boosted earnings and gave Putin a powerful tool because Russia was a major supplier of energy to Europe. In 2011, Russia joined the World Trade Organization, the international body that supervises world trade. Even though critics accused Putin's government of corruption and trampling on civil liberties, many Russians supported his policies.

As Russia rebounded, it strongly defended its interests in Europe and around the world, which sometimes caused tensions with the West. It denounced a U.S, plan to build anti-missile sites in Eastern Europe, which it saw as a threat. Despite UN sanctions against Iran, Russia helped Iran with its nuclear energy program. In 2013, Russia similarly opposed military action against Syria, who had reportedly used chemical weapons against its own citizens during its civil war. Ultimately, the United States, Russia, and Syria agreed that Syria's chemical weapons would be placed under international control.

Despite disagreements, Russia and the United States did sign a nuclear arms treaty in 2010. Russia also joined the U.S. and other nations in voting sanctions on North Korea, which was developing nuclear weapons.

New Challenges for the United States The United States has the world's largest economy and strongest military. The country weathered economic ups and downs. The economy boomed in the 1990s, producing a budget **surplus,** or money left over after expenditures. By the early 2000s, slower growth, military spending, and tax cuts led to a growing budget. A **deficit** occurs when a government spends more than it takes in through taxes and other measures.

In 2008, a financial crisis shook the American economy, sparking a global recession. Millions of Americans lost their jobs as businesses cut back or closed. The recession was the nation's worst economic crisis since the Great Depression of the 1930s. President Barack Obama, the first African American President, responded to the growing crisis with an economic stimulus package. Still, recovery was slow. Though unemployment began to decline, the gap between rich and poor continued to grow.

After terrorist attacks on the United States in September 2001, President George W. Bush declared a "war on terror." In 2002, the United States sent forces to Afghanistan, where the terrorist plot had been hatched. The next year, U.S. forces invaded Iraq and toppled its dictator Saddam Hussein. American forces remained in Iraq for almost a decade and continued to provide military support to the Afghan government.

In May 2011, American forces killed Osama bin Laden, the architect of the September 2001 attack. Shortly after, President Obama set a timetable for the withdrawal of troops from Afghanistan. The renewed threat of ISIL extremism in Iraq in 2014 led Obama to call for a renewed commitment to the war on terror.

>> Russian president Vladimir Putin and American president Barack Obama confer at the G20 Summit in Mexico in June 2012. The United States and Russia are powerful forces in the United Nations and other international organizations.

CHECK UNDERSTANDING What troubles did Russia face after the collapse of the Soviet Union?

The Former Soviet Republics

In 1991, the Soviet Union broke up into 15 separate republics. Like Russia, the other former Soviet republics wanted to build stable governments and improve their standard of living. Like Russia, too, they endured hard times as they switched from communism to market economies.

In the Central Asia republics, many skilled Russian workers left, causing a shortage of trained managers and technicians. With help from the UN, the World Bank, and the International Monetary Fund, these nations worked to increase trade and build economic ties with the rest of the world.

Trouble in Chechnya Ethnic divisions caused problems for Russia and other republics. In 1994, Chechen separatists tried to break away from Russian rule. During two wars and ten years of

>> This map shows the Russian Caucasus region, which had been part of the Soviet Union. Three former Soviet republics (Georgia, Armenia, and Azerbaijan) gained independence. There has been ethnic tension in the territories that remain within Russia. **Analyze Maps** Which part of Azerbaijan is separated by Armenia from the main part of the country?

fighting, both sides committed atrocities. Muslim Chechen rebels found support among radical Muslims elsewhere in the Caucasus. Russia finally crushed the Chechen revolt with great brutality.

The war in Chechnya fueled terrorist attacks in Russia. In the early 2000s, Chechen rebels attacked a Moscow theater and killed school children in the city of Beslan. Scattered attacks have continued to the present.

Azerbaijan, Armenia, and Georgia Azerbaijan was plunged into conflict with its neighbor Armenia. Azeris are the majority population in Azerbaijan, except in the region of Nagorno-Karabakh, where ethnic Armenians outnumbered Azeris. When Armenians in this region declared independence, fighting broke out. Backed by troops from Armenia, the Armenians of Karabkh gained control of the territory. More than 800,000 Azeris were forced from their homes.

In Georgia, two provinces tried to break away. Russia backed the separatists, which led to a brief war between Russia and Georgia in 2008. International pressure soon ended the conflict, but tensions remained high.

Troubles in Ukraine Ukraine, Europe's second largest country, was once known as the breadbasket of Europe for its fertile croplands. Recently, it has experienced economic hard times, political unrest, and civil war. Elected governments have tilted back and forth between seeking closer relations with Europe or strengthening ties with Russia. Ukraine depends on Russia for its energy supplies, but many Ukrainians want trade with the EU and even NATO membership.

In 2014, massive street protests led to the collapse of Ukraine's pro-Russian government. Eastern Ukraine, especially Crimea, is home to many ethnic Russians. Backed by Russia, separatists in Crimea broke away, and Russia soon annexed the region despite international condemnation. Elsewhere in eastern Ukraine, separatists armed by Russia battled Ukrainian forces trying to regain control of the region. Separatists even shot down a civilian airplane, killing almost 300 passengers and crew. The ongoing conflict in Ukraine caused severe tensions between Russia and the West.

IDENTIFY CAUSE AND EFFECT What were the causes of the conflicts that erupted in the former Soviet Union?

War in Yugoslavia

The Balkan nation of Yugoslavia was created after World War I out of part of the Austro-Hungarian empire. Yugoslavia was **multiethnic,** or made up of several ethnic groups. The three main groups were Croats, who were Roman Catholic; Serbs, who were Orthodox Christian, and Bosniaks, who were mostly Muslim. In addition, Yugoslavia was home to Montenegrins, Macedonians, Slovenes, and Albanians. Although these groups had distinct customs and religions, most spoke the same language, Serbo-Croatian.

Yugoslavia was divided into six republics: Slovenia, Croatia, Serbia, Bosnia and Herzegovina (often called Bosnia for short), Montenegro, and Macedonia. Each republic had a dominant ethnic group but also was home to other ethnic groups. For decades, the communist leader, Josip Tito kept firm control over these rival groups. People from different groups lived side by side peacefully. Tito died in 1980, and by 1991, as communist rule collapsed, old rivalries fed by ambitious extremists erupted into violence.

Republics Break Away The fall of communism fed nationalist unrest throughout Yugoslavia. The Serbian-dominated government tried to preserve Yugoslavian unity. In 1991, however, Slovenia and Croatia declared independence. This move triggered deadly clashes between Croats and Serbs living Croatia. One by one, other republics declared independence, including Bosnia. Macedonia, and eventually in 2006, tiny Montenegro.

Civil War in Bosnia Some of the worst violence in the Balkans occurred after Bosnia declared independence in 1992. There, civil war erupted among Bosnian Serbs, who wanted to set up their own government, and Bosniaks, who did not want the country divided. The extreme nationalist president of Serbia, **Slobodan Milosevic,** (mih LOH shuh vich), funneled weapons and money to Serbs in Bosnia, which helped fuel the violence.

During the war, all sides committed atrocities. Bosnian Serbs conducted a vicious campaign of **ethnic cleansing,** killing or forcibly removing people from other ethnic groups from areas they wanted to control. Tens of thousands of Muslim Bosniaks were brutalized or killed, sometimes in mass executions. Bosnian fighters took revenge. Croats in Bosnia were also involved in the fighting. For months, the Bosnia capital of Sarajevo was under siege by Bosnian Serbs. Many observers, in the United States and elsewhere, argued that

>> In 1990, Yugoslavia was the dominant country in southeastern Europe. By 2003, it no longer existed, replaced by seven independent nations. **Analyze Maps** Which new nation does not share a border with Serbia?

Bounce to Activate Gallery

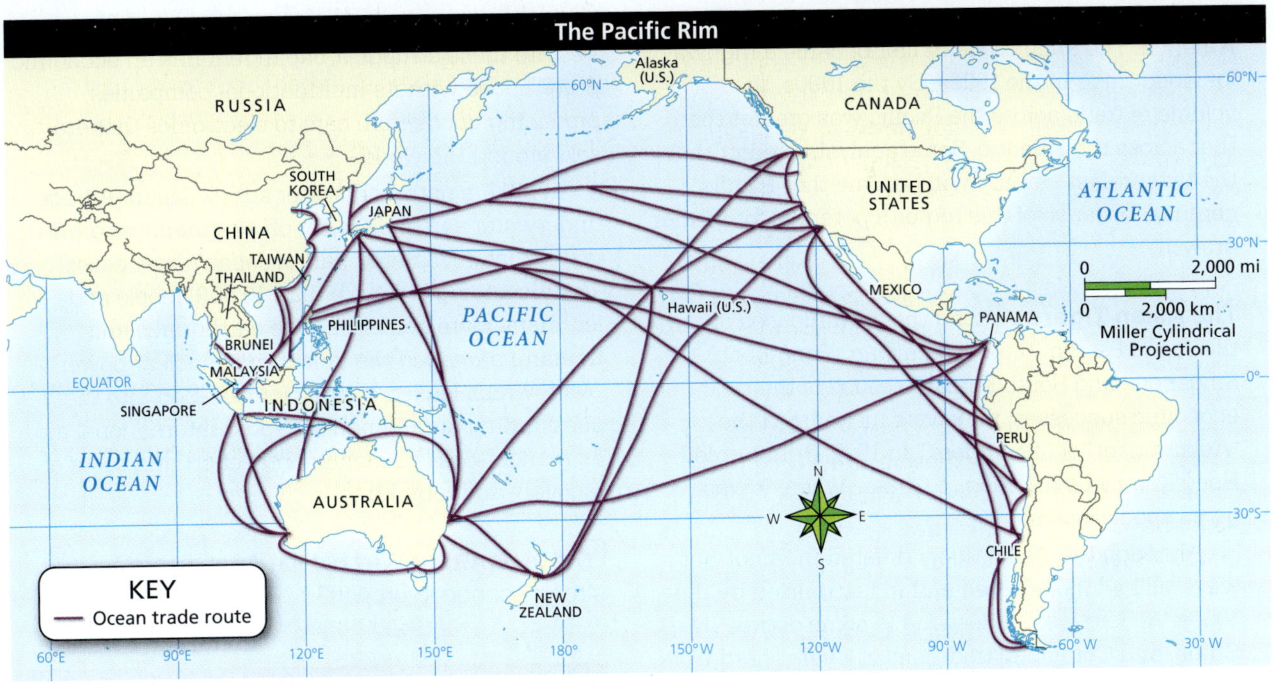

>> The countries of the Pacific Rim have geographic, cultural, and economic ties. The region is a major center of ocean trade routes. **Analyze Maps** According to the map, with which Asian country does the United States trade most?

ethnic cleansing was a form of genocide and that intervention was necessary.

Bosnia became a test case for the Western powers in the post Cold War world. At first, UN forces tried unsuccessfully to keep peace. After much debate, the United States and its NATO allies finally decided to intervene. NATO air strikes against the Bosnian Serb military forced the warring parties to the peace table. In 1995, American negotiators helped the rival groups agree to the Dayton Accords. An international force helped maintain a fragile peace in Bosnia.

War in Kosovo As a tense peace took effect in Bosnia, a crisis broke out in the Serbian province of Kosovo. Most of its people were Muslim Albanians. Serbian president Milosevic responded to separatist moves among Kosovo Albanians with a brutal campaign of ethnic cleansing, NATO launched air attacks against Serbia, forcing Serbia to withdraw its forces from Kosovo.

In 2008, after years of negotiation, Kosovo declared independence. While Kosovo Albanians celebrated, Serbs angrily protested. For them, Kosovo was a historic part of Serbia. A small NATO force remained in Kosovo to keep the peace between the majority Albanians and the minority Serbs.

The wars in the Balkans left bitter memories and tensions. The International Criminal Court held war crimes against various leaders, including Slobodan Milosevic. Despite strained relations, the six nations have moved to restore stability to the region. In 2013, Croatia became the first Balkan nation to join the EU. Albania, Bosnia, and Kosovo have also applied for membership.

IDENTIFY CAUSE AND EFFECT How did the breakup of Yugoslavia lead to ethnic cleansing in Bosnia-Herzegovina?

A New Role for Asia

Much of Asia remains belongs to the developing world. A number of Asian nations, however, are considered newly industrialized countries (NICs). They include the economic giants, China and India, as well as more recent NICs, Thailand, Indonesia, Malaysia, and the Philippines. Like other nations around the world, they have experienced the ups and downs of the global economy.

Strength in the Pacific Rim Most of these newly industrialized Asian countries are part of the global economic force known as the Pacific Rim. The **Pacific Rim,** includes the nations bordering the Pacific Ocean from Asia to North and South America. The Pacific Ocean first became a highway for world trade in the 1500s. By the 1990s, the volume of trade across the Pacific was greater than that across the Atlantic. Some analysts predict that the twenty-first century will become the "Pacific century" because of this region's potential for further growth.

The Asian Tigers Among the powerhouses of the Asian Pacific Rim were Taiwan, Hong Kong, Singapore, and South Korea. Because of their economic successes, they were nicknamed the "Asian tigers" or "four tigers." In 1997, British-ruled Hong Kong was returned to China., where it was given special status.

Although the Asian tigers differed in important ways, all had modernized and industrialized by the 1980s. All four were influenced to some degree by China, and Confucian traditions of loyalty, hard work, and consensus. Each stressed education as a way to increase worker productivity.

The Asian tigers first focused on light industries, such as textiles. As their economies grew, they shifted to higher-priced exports, such as electronics. Their stunning growth was due in part to low wages, long hours, and other worker sacrifices. Like other export-driven economies, the Asian tigers were hurt by the recent global recession, but all have recovered and continue to grow.

Japan Struggles For decades, Japan dominated the Asian Pacific Rim. After Japan suffered a long economic downturn starting in the late 1990s, China's economy boomed. overtaking Japan as the world second largest economy. Like the rest of the world, Japan suffered from the 2009 global recession. Despite these struggles, Japan remains an economic powerhouse with its multinational companies producing goods from cars to electronics that are sold around the world.

In 2011, a natural disaster struck Japan. A huge underwater earthquake set off a tsunami, or giant wave, that devastated part of Japan's east coast. The disaster killed more than 16,000 people and left many more homeless. The earthquake and tsunami damaged the Fukushima nuclear power plant, which leaked dangerous radiation into the surrounding area. Japan accepted international aid as it undertook the monumental effort and costs of recovery and rebuilding.

SUMMARIZE Why did the Asian tigers enjoy strong economic growth?

ASSESSMENT

1. **Summarize** How has Europe changed since the end of the Cold War?
2. **Make Generalizations** What challenges did Russia face after the fall of the Soviet Union?
3. **Identify Cause and Effect** How did nationalism contribute to the violence in the former Yugoslavia?
4. **Summarize** How have developments in Asia changed the global economy?
5. **Compare** What are two similarities between the breakup of the former Yugoslavia and the breakup of the Soviet Union?

10.6 Global trade has existed since ancient times, but it was limited. New technologies and the European age of exploration set off increasing trade and contacts around the world and set the stage for modern globalization. Globalization is the process by which national economies, politics, cultures, and societies become closely linked with those of other nations around the world. Economists use the term to refer to the growth of international investment and financial markets that reduces the control that individual nations have over their own economies. Since the 1980s, the pace and extent of globalization has developed dramatically.

>> This textile plant in India represents one of the many industries that have migrated from European and North American countries to the developing world.

Bounce to Activate Flipped Video

Globalization and Trade

>> **Objectives**

Summarize the impact of globalization on the modern world.

Describe the role of international organizations and treaties in expanding trade.

Analyze the costs and benefits of globalization.

>> **Key Terms**

globalization
interdependence
outsourcing
multinational corporation
World Trade Organization (WTO)
protectionism
bloc
sustainability,

Global Interdependence

Several events in the 1980s and 1990s are closely linked to the rise of globalization. First, economic reforms in China led to increased foreign investment. Second, debt led many Latin American nations to institute reforms that opened the region to trade and investment. Third, the collapse of communism in the Soviet Union and Eastern Europe reconnected these economies to global markets. Finally, new information technologies accelerated the exchange of information and made the world feel more connected.

Working in the Global Economy Rich and poor nations have become increasingly interdependent. **Interdependence** is the dependence of countries on each other for goods, resources, knowledge, and labor from other parts of the world. The nations of the global North control much of the world's capital, trade, and technology. At the same time, they depend on the developing world for many resources.

As the global economy grew, many companies in industrial nations began to outsource jobs to the developing. **Outsourcing** is the practice of sending work to outside enterprises in order to save money or increase efficiency. Many companies in the developed world outsourced technological jobs to India, Russia, China, and the Philippines.

Growth of Multinational Corporations

Over the past 50 years, the world market has become increasingly dominated by multinational corporations. **Multinational corporations** have assets in many countries and sell their goods and services worldwide.

These corporations have invested heavily in the developing world. They brought new technology to industries, built factories, improved transportation networks, and provided much-needed jobs to people in developing nations. Critics, however, have accused multinational corporations of taking large profits out of developing countries, causing environmental damage, and paying low wages.

Global Economic Crises Due to financial interdependence, an economic crisis in one country or region can have a global impact. In 1997, a financial crisis in Thailand spread across Asia. The Asian financial crisis hurt many Asian nations, but did not spread around the world.

More recently, a banking crisis in the United States set off the world's worst economic crisis since the Great Depression. During the 1990s, the United States relaxed regulations on borrowing, allowing banks to make high-risk loans. Many Americans borrowed too much.

By 2008, many homeowners began defaulting on mortgages. Banks became unwilling to loan money to buyers, which contributed to a real estate crash. Nearly every country in the world felt the impact of the U.S. banking crisis, although the severity varied from one country to another. Some European countries, such as Spain, Ireland, and Greece, saw their economies plunge dangerously low and experienced soaring unemployment and social unrest. Developing nations also felt the impact as prices for their goods fell and international aid decreased.

Other nations fared better. Canada's strictly regulated banking system helped to protect the nation better than many others. Wealthy nations, like the United States, shored up their economies and helped banks and other troubled industries survive the crisis. After 2010, a slow but fragile recovery began. Many nations, however, continued to struggle with high unemployment and weak economic growth.

Changing Oil Prices Energy resources play a huge role in the global economy. All nations, for example, need oil for transportation and to manufacture products ranging from plastics to fertilizers. Any

KEY EVENTS OF THE GLOBAL ECONOMIC DOWNTURN 2005–2012

TIMELINE

2007 American homeowners default on mortgages, leading to a banking crisis and a real estate crash.

2008 U.S. banks with too much debt fail. The crisis spreads to other countries.

2009 Economic crises surface in several members of the European Union, threatening the survival of the euro.

2010 Many EU nations are forced to impose austerity measures, cutting spending dramatically.

Sources: www.bloomberg.com, www.britannica.com

GDP OF SELECT NATIONS

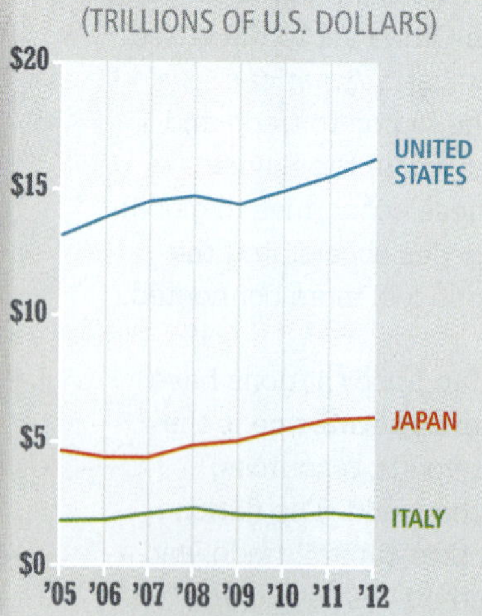

Source: www.data.worldbank.org

THE CRISIS IN PERSPECTIVE

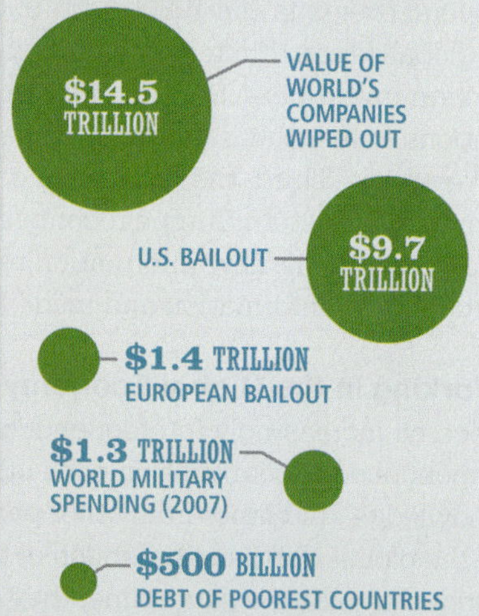

Source: www.globalissues.org; for 2009

>> **Analyze Charts** Which year of the downturn was the low point for the U.S. GDP? For Japan? For Italy? Based on information in the infographic, what is a likely reason why Italy's low point was different from that of the U.S. and Japan?

Bounce to Activate Gallery

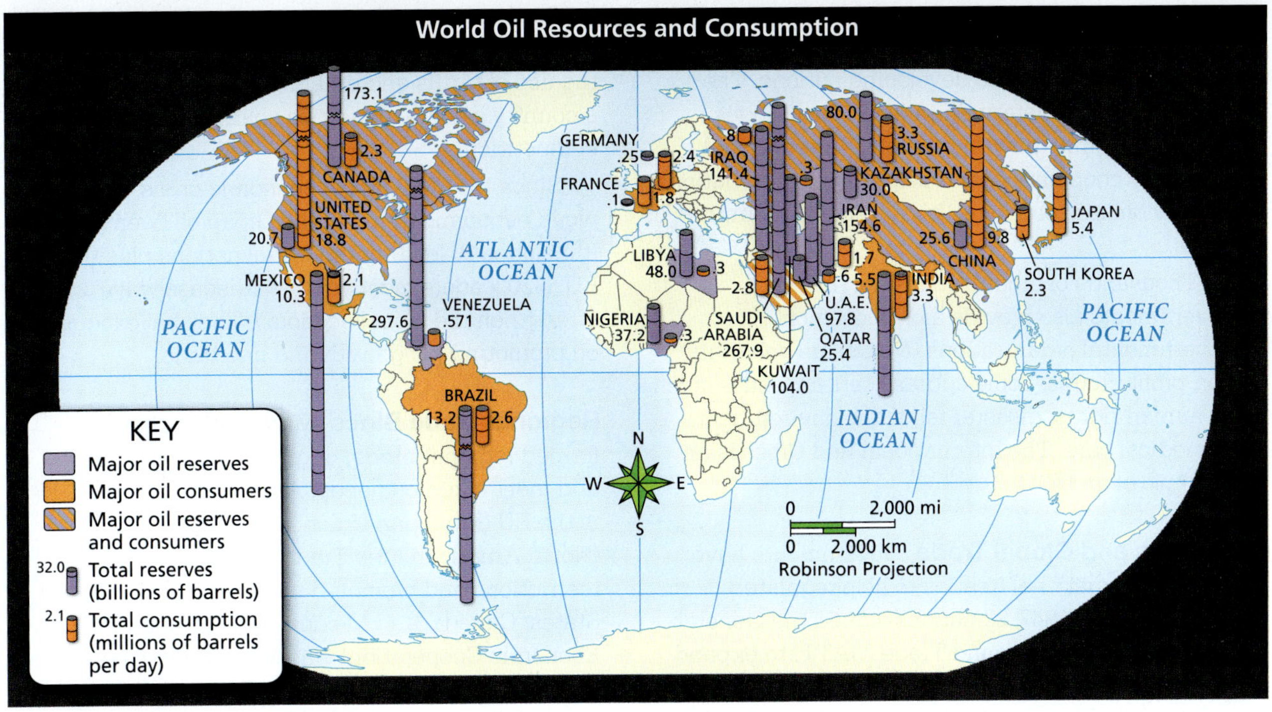

>> This map shows world oil reserves and consumption by country. **Analyze Data** Which nations contain both major oil reserves and are major oil consumers?

change in the global oil supply can have a huge impact worldwide.

In 1973, OPEC limited oil exports and raised prices, creating shortages and setting off a global recession. Since then, whenever oil prices have risen sharply, people have faced economic uncertainties. In 2008, oil prices shot up, partly because the growing economies in China, India, and elsewhere led to increased demand. A year later, as the global economic crisis slowed demand, prices fell. This sudden, rapid change in oil prices has led to renewed calls to develop alternative energy sources. Still, the world has remained largely dependent on oil.

Debt and the Developing World Developing nations borrowed heavily in order to modernize. In the 1980s, bank interest rates rose as the world economy slowed. As demand for their goods fell, poor nations could not repay their debts or even interest on their loans. Their economies stalled as they spent much of their export incomes on payments to foreign creditors.

The debt crisis hurt rich nations, too. Banks were stuck with billions of dollars of bad debts. To ease the crisis, lenders made agreements with debtor nations to lower interest rates or allow more time to repay their loans. Some debts were canceled. In return, debtor nations had to accept market reforms to help improve their economies. Debt has remained a major issue throughout the developing world.

IDENTIFY CAUSE AND EFFECT How do changes in the supply of oil affect economies around the world?

Global Organizations and Trade Agreements

Many international organizations and treaties connect people and nations around the world. These organizations have various goals, such as supporting development, settling economic issues, and promoting free trade.

International Organizations The United Nations is the world's largest international organization. Its membership has grown from 50 nations in 1945 to 193 today. The UN grew rapidly as nations won independence from colonial rule. It expanded again after the former Soviet republics joined.

As the UN expanded, its global role grew. The UN and its many agencies have provided economic and humanitarian aid to developing nations. It has sent peacekeepers to dozens of trouble spots, including Cambodia, Congo, and the Balkans. The UN deals with social development, human rights, and international law.

Various other organizations deal with economic issues. The World Bank, for example, offers loans and technical advice to developing nations. The International Monetary Fund (IMF) encourages global economic growth, promotes international monetary cooperation, and helps developing nations solve economic problems. It also lends to countries in crisis.

Thousands of organizations not linked to governments also provide aid. These non-governmental organizations (NGOs) are voluntary, non-profit groups. Some address certain issues, such as human rights, disaster relief, the environment, or medical care. The International Red Cross is an example of an NGO.

Treaties and Global Trade Governments have signed international treaties to help regulate world trade. In 1947, 23 nations signed the General Agreement on Tariffs and Trade (GATT) to expand world trade and reduce tariffs, or taxes on imported goods. GATT later evolved into the **World Trade Organization (WTO),** which included 159 nations as of 2013.

The WTO seeks to resolve trade disputes among members. Recently, members agreed to offer better access for developing nations to market in rich countries. The WTO opposes **protectionism,** or the use of tariffs and other restrictions that protect a country's home industries against international competition.

Since the 2008 global economic crisis, the major world economic forum is the Group of Twenty (G20). It includes 19 leading industrial nations plus the EU. G20 leaders meet yearly to discuss ways to strengthen the global economy. They have focused on promoting job growth and free trade.

Regional Trade Blocs Many nations have formed regional **blocs,** or groups, to boost trade and meet common needs. Among the largest is the EU (European Union.) In 1994, NAFTA (North American Free Trade Association) eased restrictions and promoted trade among the United States, Canada, and Mexico. APEC (Asian-Pacific Economic Cooperation) was formed to further trade among Pacific Rim nations. OPEC, representing oil-producing countries, regulates the production of oil to stabilize the market.

Regional trade groups perform an important function by lowering trade barriers and encouraging the free exchange of goods and services. Often, regional organizations like the African Union (AU), deal with both economic and political issues.

>> Officials of the African Union meet with European representatives in Addis Ababa, Ethiopia, in 2013. The AU is one of many regional organizations that engages in peacekeeping, emergency relief, and other operations.

SUMMARIZE How do trade blocs benefit nations?

Benefits and Costs of Globalization

Instant communications, modern transportation networks, and increasing economic ties continue to push globalization, which has affected every aspect of life. Even as the world becomes more interdependent, people debate the impact of globalization.

Benefits Competition and the use of low-wage workers in the developing world has allowed multinational corporation to offer goods and services at low prices. People in the industrial world, especially, have benefited from lower prices and a variety of goods. Many developing nations have used increased wealth from global trade to build needed transportation, raise standards of living, and provide better services.

The mass migration of people from rural areas to cities has transformed lives. In cities, people often have better access to education and health care. Urbanization has introduced people to new ideas and technologies. The movement of people, along with modern communication, has furthered the exchange of goods and ideas and contributed to a rich blending of cultures.

Costs Critics argue that the costs of globalization outweigh the benefits. They claim it has offered great profits to companies and nations but few benefits to the poor. Anti-globalizers argue that multinational corporations seek to maximize profits at the expense of worker safety and the environment. They describe globalization as a way for the powerful capitalist economies of the Western world to profit from the weaker nations of the developing world.

Members of the anti-globalization movement reject the emphasis on competition and profit in favor of social responsibility and justice. Many target the World Bank and the IMF because, in exchange for aid, these organizations require developing nations to make tough reforms and cut costly social programs. Such changes result in hardships for a population and few opportunities for economic growth. Others condemn Western cultural dominance.

Environmentalists have also criticized globalization. They claim that industries eager for profits encourage too-rapid development, endangering **sustainability,** or development that balances people's needs today with the need to preserve the environment for future generations.

SUPPORT IDEAS WITH EVIDENCE How has globalization improved the lives of many people around the world?

>> The Pantip Plaza shopping center in Bangkok, Thailand, offers a dizzying array of electronics from around the world. Globalization has greatly enabled the quicker and easier worldwide movement of consumer and other goods.

Bounce to Activate Gallery

>> Some people believe that globalization negatively impacts society. The World Trade Organization has sometimes met with stormy opposition to its role in increasing globalization.

ASSESSMENT

1. **Compare and Contrast** How does globalization affect economies around the world?
2. **Compare** In what ways are developed and developing countries affected differently by economic interdependence? Explain.
3. **Make Generalizations** How do international organizations work to expand trade?
4. **Apply Concepts** Do you think that increased globalization is inevitable? Explain.
5. **Compare Points of View** Describe one of the criticisms against multinational corporations.

>> A homeless child in Katmandu, Nepal, sleeps on the sidewalk. Half of the world's people live in extreme poverty.

Bounce to Activate Flipped Video

10.7 Globalization has spread new technologies, ideas, and greater prosperity to many nations and people. At the same time, the world faces enduring problems, such as poverty, hunger, and disease. Although such problems mainly affect the developing world, they have global dimensions that often require global solutions.

>> Objectives

Explain the impact of poverty, disasters, and disease on nations around the world.

Describe global efforts to protect human rights.

Evaluate the environmental challenges facing the world.

>> Key Terms

tsunami
epidemic
famine
refugee
acid rain
deforestation
erosion
global warming
indigenous peoples

Social and Environmental Issues

Global Challenges

Worldwide Poverty Among the great challenges facing the world is the gap between rich and poor. The gap is huge and growing. It exists in rich nations as well as in poor nations. The gap also exists between rich industrial and poor developing nations.

Half of the world's population, almost 3 billion people, live on less than $2 a day. Almost 1 billion people cannot read or write. Globally, the poor lack access to health care and education. They suffer from hunger and malnutrition and are susceptible to disease. They have little voice in government and face other obstacles that make it hard to escape poverty.

Global poverty is a complex issue with many causes. In the developing world, political upheavals, civil war, corruption, and poor planning hurt efforts to reduce poverty. Rapid population growth has made it harder for countries to provide basic services.

Poverty in the developing world is also due in part to dependence on rich nations, which compete to buy resources and products as inexpensively as possible. Poverty has increased as a result of market reforms required by IMF and World Bank. In order to get new loans, developing nations have had to reduce spending, especially on health, education and development.

The World Bank and other organizations realize that erasing poverty is essential to global security and peace. In this spirit, they call on poor nations to limit population growth. They also encourage rich nations to forgive the debt of poor nations, making more funds available for education, healthcare, and other services.

Although some progress has been made toward reducing poverty, it has been uneven. India, China, and other newly industrialized nations have enjoyed great economic growth, and have fewer people overall living in poverty.

Natural Disasters Natural disasters range from earthquakes, floods, and avalanches to droughts, fires, hurricanes, and volcanic eruptions. They strike all over the world, causing death, destruction, and unsanitary conditions that often lead to disease. Although such events may strike anywhere, they often hit developing nations especially hard due to such factors as heavy population concentrations and inadequate building construction.

In 2004, a huge underwater earthquake in the Indian Ocean triggered a huge **tsunami** (tsoo NAH mee), or massive tidal wave. It swept over islands and along the coasts of 11 countries ringing the Indian Ocean. More than 160,000 people were killed, mainly in Indonesia, Thailand, Sri Lanka, and India. Millions were left homeless or lost their livelihood.

The following year, Hurricane Katrina struck the coastal regions of Louisiana and Mississippi. A 30-foot storm surge and high winds caused a devastating flood in New Orleans and killed more than 1,800 people. The Federal Emergency Management Agency (FEMA) called Katrina "the single most catastrophic natural disaster and costliest hurricane in U.S. history."

A local disaster can disrupt the economy of a country and even have a ripple effect on the global economy. When a typhoon destroyed Myanmar's rice producing region, the country faced a threat of famine One benefit of globalization is that news of natural disasters spreads instantly and triggers a quick aid response.

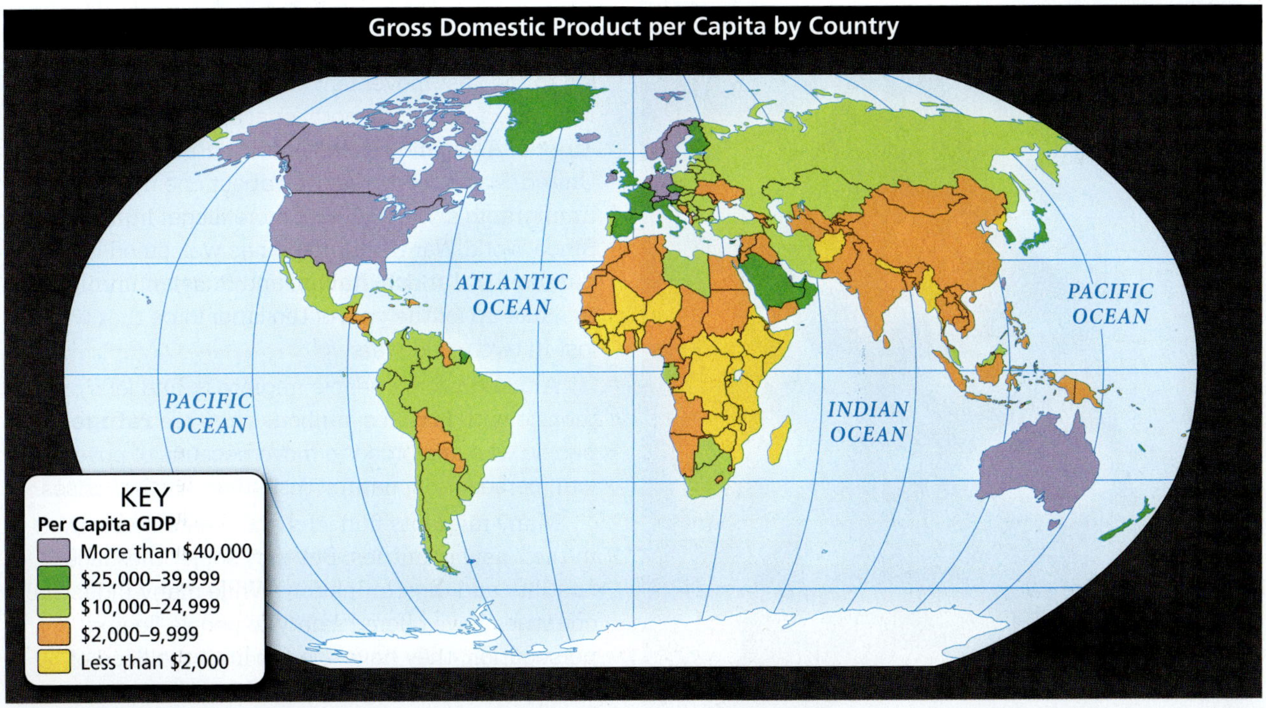

>> **Analyze Maps** This map shows the relative wealth and poverty of nations as determined by the gross domestic product (GDP) per capita. What areas of the world have the highest GDP?

Global Diseases With millions of people on the move daily, diseases spread rapidly. Globalization, however, has allowed health experts around the world to quickly identify and contain outbreaks of disease. In the early 2000s, air travelers spread SARS (severe acute respiratory syndrome), a respiratory disease, from China to more than two dozen countries. Health officials took quick action to stop the SARS outbreak. Following this outbreak, it was clear a better system was needed to detect worldwide health crises. The International Health Regulations, first written in 1969 and revised in 2005, represented an agreement among 196 countries to work together for global health. The regulations require that all countries be able to detect, assess, report, and respond to health crises.

Other diseases, including avian flu (bird flu), mad cow disease, West Nile virus, swine flu (H1N1), and influenza have raised concerns about the global spread of disease. When a disease spreads rapidly across a wide area, it is called an **epidemic**.

The HIV/AIDS epidemic was first reported in 1981 and soon spread around the world. It has taken a staggering human and economic toll, especially in southern Africa and Southeast Asia. The treatment and prevention of AIDS became a global priority.

>> Malaria, transmitted by the mosquito, is common in regions close to the Equator. Netting draped over bedding can help prevent this dangerous disease.

Despite progress, HIV/AIDS continues to spread. Another overlooked problem that is prevalent in both developing and developed countries is obesity. The World Health Organization has worked to develop public awareness campaigns about this ever-growing epidemic. Complications from obesity include strokes, heart disease, and diabetes.

Hunger and Famine For tens of millions of people, hunger is a daily threat. Overall, the world produces enough food to feed the entire population, but food is unevenly distributed. Governments and international organizations have tried to find ways to improve farming and food distribution and to address the underlying causes of poverty and hunger.

In countries racked by conflict or struck by natural disasters, hunger often escalates into famine. A **famine** occurs when large numbers of people in a region or country face death by starvation.

During the 1970s and 1980s, civil wars in Ethiopia and Sudan worsened the effects of drought, leading to widespread famine. Each side in the conflict tried to keep relief supplies from reaching the other. As refugees from the conflicts flooded into camps, international aid groups provided food and water, saving millions of people from starvation.

While famine relief is needed to end a crisis, shipping tons of food to poor nations hurts local farmers. A flood of food forces prices down so that local farmers cannot earn enough to make a living.

People Search for a Better Life Globalization has led to the vast movement of people around the world. Millions of migrants, both legal and illegal, head to Europe, Asia, and North America. Each year, the United States alone receives about one million legal immigrants and 300,000 or more illegal immigrants. Since World War II, Germany has welcomed large numbers of Turkish, Italian, and Russian immigrants to make up for the part of the labor force that was lost in two world wars.

Although some people migrate to find jobs or reunite with families, millions more are **refugees,** people who are forced to move because of poverty, war, persecution, natural disasters, or other crises.

Many migrants find jobs and create better lives in their new countries. But they sometimes face hostility and discrimination. While many industrial countries have offered safety to people fleeing persecution, they have tried to limit the flood of economic migrants, people seeking jobs or better lives. Many people in the developed world resent these economic migrants, claiming they take jobs and services from natural-born citizens.

As migration has grown, so has the smuggling of people across borders. Many illegal immigrants pay smugglers large sums to help them reach their destinations. The UN estimates that human smuggling is a multi-billion dollar global industry.

CONTRAST Explain both the negative and positive effects of globalization on the spread of disease.

Human Rights

In 1948, UN members approved the Universal Declaration of Human Rights. It stated that every person is entitled to basic rights, including "life, liberty and security of person." It called for freedom from slavery, torture, or discrimination along with freedom of thought, conscience and religion." It further recognized the right to work, to receive an education, and to maintain an adequate standard of living.

During the Cold War, 35 nations from the Western world and the Soviet bloc signed the Helsinki Accords that guaranteed such basic rights as freedom of speech, religion, and the press as well as the rights to a fair trial, to earn a living, and to live in safety. Despite such agreements, human rights abuses occur daily around the world. They range from arbitrary arrest to torture and slavery.

World Community Confronts Abuses

Organizations around the world work to protect human rights and end abuses. They include governments and international organizations like the UN. In the 1980s, for example, many nations used economic sanctions to press South Africa to end apartheid.

Citizen groups often take the lead in highlighting abuses. NGOs monitor the actions of governments and pressure them to defend human rights. Human rights groups report on violations covering a range of issues such as attacks on migrant workers or unsafe working conditions in factories. They have reported on attacks against indigenous people by developers who want their lands, Chinese abuses against Tibetan Buddhists, and discrimination against Roma people in some Eastern European countries. North Korea has the world's worst human rights record.

The Struggle for Women's Rights The UN Charter supported "equal rights for men and women." A global women's movement has addressed conditions for women worldwide.

>> In 1946, former First Lady Eleanor Roosevelt became head of the UN Commission on Human Rights, and the only woman to help draft the Universal Declaration of Human Rights.

>> In Saudi Arabia, many women are highly educated but struggle to find jobs. By law, men and women may not work together. Women must have separate offices, entrances, and security guards.

>> Two Hmong women work in a field in Laos. Globally, most women who work outside the home work in agriculture.

Bounce to Activate Gallery

>> Even in wealthy nations, women are more likely to live in poverty than men. This homeless woman in Miami Beach, Florida, pushes her belongings in a shopping cart.

By 1950, women had won the right to vote in most western nations, as well as in Japan, China, Brazil, and other countries. At independence, most African nations guaranteed women the right to vote. Women have headed elected governments in such nations as Argentina, Brazil, Britain, Germany, Israel, India, Liberia, Pakistan, and the Philippines.

Still, a UN report noted that while women represent half of the world's people, "they perform nearly two thirds of all working hours, receive only one tenth of the world's income, and own less than one percent of world property." Women in many countries are subject to violence.

The UN and other groups have condemned violence and discrimination against women. A UN-backed Treaty for the Rights of Women has been ratified by 187 nations. The treaty was designed to ensure gender equality worldwide. The United States has not ratified the treaty. Some groups in the U.S. say the treaty can bring more harm than good to women.

Changing Roles for Women In developed nations, a growing number of women work outside their homes. Some have high-profile jobs as business owners and executives, scientists, and technicians. Yet women often receive less pay than men doing the same work, and many must balance demanding jobs with parenting and housework. Many women work outside the home because families need two incomes to provide the necessities of life.

In the developing world, women often work as subsistence farmers and craftworkers or in domestic service and small-scale manufacturing. In rural areas, especially in Africa, as men migrate to cities to work, women do the farm work in addition to household tasks. In other regions, such as Southeast Asia, young women help support the family or pay for their brothers' education. In some places, cultural traditions confine women to the home or segregate men and women in the workplace. Still, the education gap in the developing world has narrowed. Women from the middle and elite classes have entered the workforce in growing numbers.

The Rights and Protection of Children Human rights groups have drawn attention to the plight of children worldwide. In 1989, UN members approved the Convention on the Rights of the Child, a treaty that outlines basic rights for children, such as the right to life, liberty, education, and healthcare. Providing and protecting these rights has proved difficult. Human rights groups, however, continue to press for change.

Today, almost half the world's children—about 1 billion children—suffer the effects of extreme poverty. Many suffer from HIV/AIDS and have little or no access to treatment. Children have been recruited into armed conflicts, where they are forced to serve as soldiers or even slaves. They are abandoned on the street, sometimes executed for minor offenses, and suffer many other forms of violence. Abuses like these not only damage children but also hurt a country's future development.

In developing countries, tens of millions of children between the ages of 5 and 14 do not attend school. Instead, they work full time. Often, these child laborers work long hours in dangerous, unhealthy conditions for little pay. Many are physically abused by their employers and live in conditions of near slavery. Still, their families need the income the children earn. In some cases, children must work to pay off a family's debt. Human rights groups, the UN, and developed nations have focused a spotlight on child labor in order to end such practices.

>> Decades of armed conflict in Colombia have forced some 41,000 indigenous people from their ancestral lands. Here, displaced families struggle to survive in makeshift huts.

Threats to Indigenous Peoples **Indigenous peoples** are generally those considered to be the descendants of the earliest inhabitants of a region. They include such ethnic and cultural groups as Native Americans, the Aborigines of Australia, and the Maoris of New Zealand. Indigenous peoples in many areas face discrimination and other abuses. Often, their lands have been forcibly taken.

In South America, developers have pushed into once-isolated areas, threatening the ways of life of indigenous peoples. Many Indians have died of diseases carried by the newcomers. During Guatemala's long civil war, the government targeted Mayan villagers, killing tens of thousands. The UN has worked to set standards to protect the rights of indigenous peoples.

CATEGORIZE What common characteristics are found in countries that deny human rights to women?

Development and the Environment

Since earliest times, people have taken what they needed from the environment. In the past, damage was limited because populations were small and technology was simple. Industrialization and the world population explosion have increased threats to the environment.

>> Fire boats battle an explosion on the offshore oil rig Deepwater Horizon in 2010. The disaster in the Gulf of Mexico, off the coast of Louisiana, caused the worst oil spill in U.S. history.

Development improves lives and strengthens economies—but at a price. One of the great challenges for the future is how to achieve necessary development without causing permanent damage to the environment.

Threats to the Environment Since the 1970s, environmentalists have warned about threats to the environment. Strip mining provides ores for industry but destroys land. Chemical pesticides and fertilizers increase food output but harm the soil and water and may cause certain cancers. Oil spills pollute waterways and kill marine life.

Gases from power plants and factories produce **acid rain,** in which toxic chemicals in the air fall back to Earth as rain, snow, or hail. Acid rain has damaged forests, lakes, and farmland, especially in Europe and North America.

Accidents and natural disasters have caused environmental damage. In 1986, a leak from a pesticide plant in India killed 3,600 people and injured 100,000. That same year, an accident at the Chernobyl nuclear power plant in the Soviet Union exposed people, crops, and animals to deadly radiation over a wide area.

In 2011, an earthquake and tsunami damaged Japan's Fukushima nuclear power plant. Radioactive materials leaked into the environment. Such accidents have prompted citizens to call on industries and governments to improve safety measures.

>> A soy plantation in the Amazon rain forest in Brazil shows how acres of forest are cleared for agricultural purposes.

Bounce to Activate Map

Changes to Deserts and Forests As you have read, desertification is a major problem, especially in the Sahel region of Africa. Another threat—especially in Africa, Latin America, and Asia—is **deforestation,** or the cutting of trees without replacing them. In many developing countries, forests are resources that provide needed jobs and increased wealth. People cut trees for firewood or shelter, or to sell in markets abroad. Some burn down forests to make way for farms and cattle ranches, or for industry.

However, once forests are cleared, rains wash nutrients from the soil, destroying its fertility. Deforestation also causes **erosion,** or the wearing away of land, which encourages flooding.

Rain forests like those of the Amazon basin play a key role in absorbing poisonous carbon dioxide from the air and releasing essential oxygen. They are also home to millions of animal and plant species, many of which have become extinct because of deforestation.

Rich nations are the greatest consumers of the world's resources and produce much of the world's pollution. However, they have also led the campaign to protect the environment. They have passed laws to control pollution and ensure conservation in their own countries. In 1992, the UN sponsored the first "earth summit" at which world leaders discussed how to clean up and preserve the planet. Although governments agreed to limit damage, they disagreed over who was responsible and how to pay for any clean up.

The summit raised other hotly debated issues. Should economic development take priority over protecting the environment? Are people, especially in rich nations, willing to do with less in order to preserve the environment? How can emerging nations afford costly safeguards for the environment?

The Debate Over Climate Change Another environmental challenge—one that is hotly debated—is climate change, often referred to as global warming. **Global warming** refers to the increase in Earth's average surface temperature over time. Scientists have recorded the rising temperatures over the past century and a greater rise since 1975. The warming trend is changing precipitation patterns, raising ocean temperatures and sea levels, and causing glaciers to melt.

Most scientists link today's climate change to rising levels of carbon dioxide and other gases released into the atmosphere by human activity such as burning of fossil fuels. "Greenhouse" gases like carbon dioxide trap warmth in Earth's atmosphere.

Some scientists and policymakers, however, disagree with this view. They argue that climate change is due to natural fluctuations in Earth's climate.

The debate over a treaty called the Kyoto Protocol raised a key question: Does economic development have to conflict with protecting the environment? The treaty, signed by 140 countries, with the major exceptions of the United States and Australia, went into effect in 2005. Its purpose is to lower the emissions of carbon dioxide and other "greenhouse" gases. Many developing nations refuse to sign because they say they must exploit their resources in order to develop fully. The United States did not sign because it believes the treaty could strain economic growth. Nations that have signed the treaty, however, argue that developed nations must lead the way in slowing emissions.

IDENTIFY SUPPORTING DETAILS Describe how a regional environmental problem can affect other parts of the world.

ASSESSMENT

1. **Infer** Why might the elimination of poverty be considered essential to global security and peace?
2. **Identify Patterns** What are some of the causes of migration? What characteristics might a migrant look for in a new country?
3. **Identify Central Ideas** How are the human rights of children around the world violated?
4. **Explain** Explain the significance of the United Nations in relation to human rights.
5. **Compare and Contrast** Give three examples of how development can conflict with the preservation of a clean environment.

Universal Declaration of Human Rights

Introduction

The General Assembly of the United Nations adopted this declaration on December 10, 1948. The document sets forth the basic liberties and freedoms to which all people are entitled.

As chairperson of the UN Commission on Human Rights, Eleanor Roosevelt not only helped to draft the document, she also worked to ensure its acceptance. The second primary source is from her speech in Paris on human rights.

>> Eleanor Roosevelt with a copy of the declaration.

Primary Source

Article 1 All human beings are born free and equal in dignity [worthiness] and rights. They are endowed with reason and conscience and should act toward one another in a spirit of brotherhood.

Article 2 Everyone is entitled to all the rights and freedoms set forth in this Declaration, without distinction [difference] of any kind, such as race, colour, sex, language, religion, political or other opinion, national or social origin, property, birth or other status. . . .

Article 3 Everyone has the right to life, liberty and security of person.

Article 4 No one shall be held in slavery or servitude. . . .

Article 5 No one shall be subjected [forced to undergo] to torture or to cruel, inhuman or degrading [humiliating] treatment or punishment.

Article 9 No one shall be subjected to arbitrary arrest, detention or exile.

PARAPHRASE Restate Article 2 in your own words.

Article 13 Everyone has the right to freedom of movement. . . .

Article 18 Everyone has the right to freedom of thought, conscience and religion. . . .

Article 19 Everyone has the right to freedom of opinion and expression. . . .

Article 20 Everyone has the right to freedom of peaceful assembly and association. . . .

Article 23 Everyone has the right to work, to free choice of employment, to just and favourable conditions of work and to protection against unemployment. . . .

Article 25 Everyone has the right to a standard of living adequate [satisfactory] for the health and well-being of himself and of his family, including food, clothing, housing and medical care and necessary social services, and the right to security in the event of unemployment, sickness, disability, widowhood, old age or other lack of livelihood in circumstances beyond his control.

Article 26 Everyone has the right to education. Education shall be free, at least in the elementary and fundamental stages. . . .

DETERMINE MEANING What is meant by the phrase "standard of living" in Article 25? Based on this excerpt, what does it mean for a standard of living to be adequate?

Primary Source

People who continue to be denied the respect to which they are entitled as human beings will not acquiesce forever in such denial.

The Charter of the United Nations is a guiding beacon along the way to the achievement of human rights and fundamental freedoms throughout the world. The immediate test is not only to the extent to which human rights and freedoms have already been achieved, but the direction in which the world is moving. Is there a faithful compliance with the objectives of the Charter if some countries continue to curtail human rights and freedoms instead of to promote the universal respect for an observance of human rights and freedoms for all as called for by the Charter?

The place to discuss the issue of human rights is in the forum of the United Nations. The United Nations has been set up as the common meeting ground for nations, where we can consider together our mutual problems and take advantage of our differences in experience. It is inherent in our firm attachment to democracy and freedom that we stand always ready to use the fundamental democratic procedures of honest discussion and negotiation. It is now as always our hope that despite the wide differences in approach we face in the world today, we can with mutual good faith in the principles of the United Nations Charter, arrive at a common basis of understanding.

EXPLAIN Why does Eleanor Roosevelt feel the United Nations is the best organization to address human rights?

ASSESSMENT

1. **Analyze Interactions** How do you think the U.S. Bill of Rights might have influenced this declaration?
2. **Determine Author's Purpose** Why do you think the members of the United Nations wrote this declaration, and what did they hope it would accomplish?
3. **Determine Central Ideas** Based on this passage, how would you define the term "human rights"?
4. **Draw Conclusions** Why did Eleanor Roosevelt call the Declaration of Human Rights the "international Magna Carta for all mankind"?

>> A soldier takes cover during a 2008 bombing in Mumbai, India. A group of Pakistani terrorists stormed various sites in the city, killing more than 160 people.

Bounce to Activate Flipped Video

10.8 During the Cold War, the United States and the Soviet Union built huge arsenals of nuclear weapons. When the Cold War ended, the question remained about what would happen to these deadly weapons. As the threat of global terrorism increased, keeping nuclear, chemical, and biological weapons out of the hands of dangerous groups has become an important issue.

>> Objectives

Explain how nuclear, biological, and chemical weapons threaten international security.

Analyze the growth of terrorist groups such as al Qaeda.

Explain how the United States and other nations have responded to terrorism from September 11, 2001, to the present.

>> Key Terms

proliferate
terrorism
al Qaeda
Afghanistan
Taliban

Terrorism and International Security

The Threat of New Weapons

The Nuclear Nonproliferation Treaty In 1968, the United States, the Soviet Union, and 60 other nations signed the Nuclear Nonproliferation Treaty (NPT). The purpose of the treaty was to ensure that nuclear weapons did not **proliferate,** or rapidly spread. The treaty was designed to limit nuclear weapons to the five countries that already had them—the United States, the Soviet Union, China, France, and Britain. Since then, the treaty has been renewed, with 190 nations agreeing not to develop or possess nuclear weapons.

Three nations did not sign the NPT: India, Israel, and Pakistan. All three have secretly developed nuclear weapons. North Korea withdrew from the treaty and later tested nuclear weapons.

Western powers accuse Iran of developing nuclear weapons. Iran claims its nuclear program is to produce nuclear power as an energy source only. The UN imposed economic sanctions on Iran to stop its uranium enrichment program, a step toward building nuclear weapons. The sanctions severely hurt the Iranian economy and led Iran to begin talks about its nuclear program. Both sides, however, viewed each other with mistrust.

Nuclear Weapons in Russia The United States and Russia control 95 percent of the world's nuclear weapons. The breakup of the Soviet Union left nuclear weapons sites scattered across Russia and the former Soviet republics. Since the, the United States and Russia have reduced their nuclear arsenals although both still retain thousands of nuclear weapons. With international aid, Russia recovered and then dismantled nuclear weapons from its former territories. In recent years, Russian support for nuclear power programs in Iran have led to renewed tensions between Russia and the United States.

Even while the United States and Russia agreed to further reductions in their nuclear stockpiles, many people worried about nuclear weapons falling into the hands of terrorists. Other nuclear nations, including India or Pakistan, were potential targets for terrorist groups seeking nuclear weapons. Securing all nuclear weapons and materials worldwide remains a top priority

>> Iranian leaders claim that the Iranian nuclear program is for generating power. At an event marking the anniversary of the Islamic revolution, a man carries a sign supporting Iran's nuclear program.

Weapons of Mass Destruction As you have read, weapons of mass destruction (WMDs) include nuclear, biological, and chemical weapons. Nuclear weapons include the atomic bomb. Biological weapons refer mainly to germs that can be released into the air or into water supplies. Chemical weapons are toxins, such as nerve gas and mustard gas.

Recently, the danger from WMDs has grown, as terrorist groups and "rogue states"— nations that ignore international law and threaten other nations— try to acquire them. NATO is working to prevent WMDs from reaching terrorists and has prepared recovery efforts if a WMD attack occurs. The U.S. and other nations also want to make sure that terrorists do not buy knowledge from WMD experts.

COMPARE AND CONTRAST How are rogue nations similar to terrorist organizations? How are they different?

>> Investigators must wear protective gear in order to shield them from possible biological or chemical weapons.

The Growing Threat of Terrorism

Since the 1990s, the world has witnessed a growing threat from terrorism. **Terrorism** is the use of violence, especially against civilians, by groups of extremists to achieve political goals.

Terrorist groups seek to produce widespread fear. They use headline-grabbing tactics to draw attention to their demands. They have attacked hotels and tourists in Mumbai, bombed commuter trains in Madrid, and blown themselves up as "suicide bombers" to kill Israeli or Iraqi civilians. Although terrorists have seldom achieved their larger goals, they have inflicted terrible physical and psychological damage and caused political turmoil. The spread of terrorism has led to greater international cooperation between governments in an effort to prevent further attacks.

Regional Terrorist Groups Terrorist groups operate from a range of motivations. Some want to undermine governments or win freedom for prisoners. Other seek revenge or influence the outcome of a guerrilla war. Terrorist groups have operated around the world for decades. Some have limited local goals.

A Serbian terrorist group played a key role in the outbreak of World War I. In Northern Ireland, the Irish Republican Army (IRA) as well as Protestant paramilitary groups used terrorist tactics, each to achieve its own goals. For more than 40 years, the ETA, a Basque separatist group, used terrorist violence to demand independence for the Basque region in northern Spain. In 2011, the ETA agreed to end its armed activity.

>> Demonstrators in Caracas, Venezuela, protest against the Revolutionary Armed Forces of Colombia, or FARC, in 2008.

Bounce to Activate Map

In South America, leftist groups, such as the Shining Path in Peru and FARC in Colombia, used kidnappings, murder, and bombings to overthrow national governments. They financed their operations with the sale of illegal drugs. In Asia, terrorist groups like Lashkar-e-Omar, were linked to the conflict between India and Pakistan over Kashmir. The Tamil Tigers, a separatist group in Sri Lanka, pioneered the use of suicide bombings as a terrorist weapon and carried out the assassinations of the president of Sri Lanka and Prime Minister Rajiv Gandhi of India. Terrorist groups have operated in the Philippines and in many African countries.

Many countries, including the United States, have experienced "homegrown" terrorism. In 1995, anti-government extremists bombed a federal office building in Oklahoma City, killing 186 people. The 2013 bombings at the Boston Marathon were carried out by extremists linked to international terrorists .

Growth of Terrorism in the Middle East Increasingly, the Middle East has become a training ground and source for terrorism. Much of this activity has stemmed from Arab rejection of the state of Israel and the continuing Israeli-Palestinian conflict. For years, the Palestine Liberation Organization (PLO) used terrorist methods, such as the kidnapping and killing of Israeli athletes at the 1972 Olympic games, to spotlight its goals—the destruction of Israel and the creation of a Palestinian state.

The PLO officially renounced terrorism in 1988. But other terrorist groups have emerged. The Al-Aqsa Martyrs Brigade, Hamas, Hezbollah, and Islamic Jihad are groups that practice terror to achieve their goals. They trained suicide bombers to attack Israeli civilian targets.

These groups found support in poverty-stricken Palestinian refugee camps in Gaza and among Islamic extremists elsewhere in the region. Iran has backed Hamas, Hezbollah, and other groups.

Islamic Fundamentalism By the 1980s, Islamic fundamentalism was on the rise. Fundamentalist movements emerged across the Muslim world from Algeria to Nigeria to Indonesia. Although Saudi Arabia receives military aid from the United States and is a U.S. ally, it supports the strict Wahhabi sect of Islam. Islamist governments gained power in Iran and, for a time, in Afghanistan.

The Islamist movement was partly a response to the rise of secular governments in many Muslim nations and the impact of Western culture. It was also a backlash against foreign support for Israel and the presence of foreign powers in the Middle East. Islamic fundamentalists made Israel or Western nations scapegoats for their nation's problems.

Not all Islamists support terrorism, but in many places, the movement has fed the growth of terrorism. Iran and Saudi Arabia have both provided financial support for terrorist organizations. For some, terrorism is connected to the concept of *jihad,* an Arabic word meaning "struggle." The word is most frequently used to describe an inner struggle in God's service. However, some extremist groups, such as Islamic Jihad, have interpreted the word to mean a violent holy war to defend or spread Islam. Some jihadi extremists seek to become martyrs, or people who die for a cause, by becoming suicide bombers.

Al Qaeda and the September 11 Attacks The best known Islamist terrorist organization is **al Qaeda** (ahl KY duh), which means "the Base" in Arabic. Its founder Osama bin Laden, was a wealthy Saudi businessman who joined Muslim fighters battling Soviet forces in Afghanistan. Later, he called for the overthrow of "un-Islamic" governments and the expulsion of non-Muslims from Muslim countries. Bin Laden fiercely denounced U.S. military presence in Saudi Arabia.

Al Qaeda built a global network to train and finance terrorist activities. In 1998, al Qaeda terrorists bombed U.S. embassies in Kenya and Tanzania. But the major blow came when al Qaeda struck inside the United States.

On September 11, 2001, the Al Qaeda Islamic terrorist group hijacked four commercial passenger airplanes and crashed two of them into the World Trade Center in New York City and one into the Pentagon in northern Virginia. A fourth plane, aimed at the White House, crashed into a Pennsylvania field after passengers rushed the hijackers in the cockpit. Nearly 3,000 people died in the attacks.

President George W. Bush described the events as "evil despicable acts of terror." The swift U.S. response to the terror attacks would have far-reaching consequences in the United States and overseas.

MAKE GENERALIZATIONS What characteristics do global and regional terrorist groups share, regardless of their various goals?

>> The Taliban is an Islamist group that took control of Afghanistan in 1996 and was removed from power in 2001. Here, Taliban members are preparing to surrender their weapons to anti-Taliban forces in Afghanistan.

The U.S. Response to Terrorism

Al Qaeda's attack on the United States shocked the world and led governments around the world to step up efforts to stop terrorism. Since the 9-11 attacks, the United States and other nations have worked together to respond to the global threat of terrorism.

New Security Measures Introduced After the 2001 attacks, the United States made national security a top priority. It strengthened and reorganized its intelligence services and passed new counter terrorism laws. In the United States and elsewhere, rigorous security measures were set up at airports and public buildings. The new security measures were costly, but many felt the expense was justified to ensure safety.

Governments cooperated to track the flow of money to terrorist groups with the goal of cutting off funds and limiting their activities. The United States and the European Union shared bank and credit card data. Other nations coordinated intelligence about terrorist groups, which helped officials identify individuals and targets they planned to attack.

>> Almost 10 years after the September 11 attacks, U.S. forces found and killed Osama bin Laden in Pakistan.

From the start of the "war of terror," critics questioned the impact of the massive security programs. For example, the National Security Agency (NSA) was given broader powers to monitor telephone and Internet communications. Some claimed that governments were using terrorism as an excuse to repress opposition groups or to increase their power. But others felt that the threat was serious enough to justify extreme measures.

The issue exploded publicly after an American computer specialist leaked stolen information about Internet and telephone surveillance. The leaked data showed that the U.S. had not only collected data that violated privacy laws at home but also had spied on its allies overseas. The vast extent of spying raised troubling issues about balancing the right to privacy against the need for security.

War in Afghanistan As part of its "war on terror," the United States made it a priority to find and punish the organizers of the 2001 attacks. Osama bin Laden was based in **Afghanistan.** The government of Afghanistan, an extreme Islamic fundamentalist group called the **Taliban,** refused U.S. demands to surrender the terrorists. The United States then formed a coalition of nations to invade Afghanistan.

In 2002, with the help of Afghan warlords, American and allied forces overthrew the Taliban. Bin Laden and many Taliban leaders escaped capture for many years. Finally, in May 2011, U.S. military and C.I.A. operatives located bin Laden's compound in Pakistan and killed Bin Laden. Al Qaeda survived, but in a more fragmented form.

Coalition forces helped Afghans write a new constitution and hold elections. The new government lifted many harsh Taliban laws, including those against women. From hideouts along the Pakistan border, however, Taliban fighters battled the new Afghan government and its Western allies. Many Pakistanis, including some in official positions, supported and protected these fighters. Since the United States and Pakistan are allies, this caused problems between the two countries.

Even as fighting continued, NATO-led forces ended combat missions in 2014. Some remained to train Afghan troops, but the future of Afghanistan remains uncertain.

War in Iraq In 2003, President Bush urged Congress to agree to an invasion of Iraq, citing intelligence reports that said Iraq was secretly producing WMDs. The Bush administration also suggested that Iraq was involved in the 2001 terrorist attacks against the United States. The war was bitterly debated among Americans and around the world, because no WMDs were found after the U.S. invasion. Many critics also argued that U.S. forces should have remained focused on the war in Afghanistan, which had proven ties to Al Qaeda.

In 2011, President Barack Obama announced the final troop withdrawal from combat mission in Iraq, leaving the Iraqi government and security forces to maintain the peace. However, as the Al Qaeda breakaway group Islamic State of Iraq and the Levant (ISIL) seized parts of Iraq in 2014, Americans began to debate renewed military action.

Iran, Syria, and North Korea Pose Threats

Even as the United States and the world focuses on terrorism, other threats emerged. Developments in Iran, Syria, and North Korea also raised concerns about world security.

When Iran announced a plan to develop nuclear power plants in the early 2000s, the United States and other nations feared that Iran truly intended to develop nuclear weapons. Although Iran insisted its nuclear energy program was for peaceful purposes, the UN Security Council imposed some sanctions on Iran. After years of negotiations with world leaders, Iran agreed in 2013 to some preliminary agreements designed to temporarily suspend its nuclear program while efforts proceed to try to obtain a permanent agreement. World and regional leaders are especially concerned about Iran's nuclear program because Iran already possesses advanced long-range missile technology that may threaten neighboring nations.

Although Syria signed the Nuclear Nonproliferation Treaty (NPT), its nuclear program has been subject to international scrutiny. Its adversarial relationship with Israel raised concerns that Syria might try to develop nuclear weapons. Then, as Syria erupted into civil war, the world's attention turned to Syria's chemical weapons.

In 2013, chemical weapons killed 300 civilians in Damascus. The government and rebels each blamed the other. Although responsibility for the attack remained unclear, President Bashar al-Assad agreed, in a U.S.-Russia brokered deal, to allow international inspectors to dismantle and destroy Syria's chemical weapons cache. In 2017, a far worst chemical attack occurred. Although Assad's government denied responsibility, an outraged international community condemned the attack. The United Nations called for an investigation for possible war crimes. Authorized by President Trump, the United States fired missiles at a Syrian airfield believed to have been the launching site for the gas bombs.

For years, North Korea violated its agreement under the NPT and worked on developing nuclear weapons. Tensions grew as the United States tried to pressure North Korea to stop its nuclear weapons program. In 2003, North Korea withdrew from the NPT. In 2006, it tested a small nuclear bomb, and by 2013 it had conducted three such tests. In 2017, North Korea continued its nuclear development activities with the goal of a successful launch.

Many people feared that if Iran, Syria, or North Korea developed nuclear weapons, nuclear technology could be passed on to terrorist groups. Those nations, if armed with nuclear weapons, might also pose threats to their regions and to world peace.

The New Geopolitics Geopolitics refers to the role of politics on a global scale with an emphasis on how geography is implicated in that politics. With the end of the Cold War, the shift went from the Soviet Union and an emphasis on Europe since Europe and the United States dominated the world, to taking revenge on groups in the Middle East who now used terrorism to threaten world peace.

CONNECT How was the war in Afghanistan related to the terrorist attacks of September 11, 2001?

>> North Korean leader Kim Jong Un uses binoculars to view South Korean territory from a military post near the border. North Korea has been criticized for its nuclear weapons testing.

ASSESSMENT

1. **Check Understanding** How do nuclear, biological, and chemical weapons threaten international security?
2. **Identify Cause and Effect** How has Arab rejection of the state of Israel led to ongoing conflict?
3. **Draw Conclusions** How does Islam influence government and law in fundamentalist Muslim nations?
4. **Generate Explanations** Why did President George W. Bush declare a "war on terror" following September 11, 2001?
5. **Draw Conclusions** What are the reasons for the growth of terrorist groups such as al Qaeda over the past two decades?

>> American astronaut Edwin Aldrin walked on the moon in July 1969. Reflected in his visor are fellow astronaut Neil Armstrong, the first person to step on the moon's surface, and the lunar landing module.

Bounce to Activate Flipped Video

10.9 Since 1945, scientific research and technological development have transformed life for much of the world. Masses of new inventions, the computer revolution, and advances in the medicine and biology have had enormous impact. Among the most dramatic advances was the exploration of space.

>> Objectives

Describe the exploration of space and the innovations that have resulted.

Analyze the development and impact of computer technology and telecommunications.

Summarize key advancements in medicine and biotechnology.

>> Key Terms

artificial satellite
International Space Station (ISS)
Internet
biotechnology
laser
genetics
genetic engineering

Advances in Science and Technology

Space Exploration

By the second half of the twentieth century, there were few places on Earth that people had not begun to explore. Space was seen as the "final frontier"—an unknown world filled with opportunity. Within a few short decades, people had developed the transportation technology to explore space and gained knowledge about this new frontier

The Space Race Rockets are projectiles or vehicles propelled by the ejection of burning gasses from the rear of the rocket. In the early twentieth century, pioneers in rocketry like the American physicist Robert Goddard probed the potential of liquid-fueled rockets.

Goddard believed that a rocket could carry people to the moon. At first people met his ideas with disbelief, but German scientists took an interest in Goddard's work. During World War II German scientists, led by Wernher von Braun, developed Germany's V-2 rockets that flew across the English Channel to rain down on London. Von Braun later became a leader in the U.S. space program.

During the Cold War, the United States and the Soviet Union competed to see which superpower would take the lead in space exploration. This "space race" began in 1957, when Soviet Union launched into orbit *Sputnik*, the first **artificial satellite,**or man-made object that orbits a larger body in space. Four years later, the Soviets sent the first person, Yuri Gargarin, into space.

The United States soon surpassed the Soviets. In 1969, the United States Apollo program landed the first humans on the moon. Both superpowers also explored the military uses of space and sent spy satellites to orbit Earth.

Today, the United States and Russia still have the largest space programs and have even cooperated in joint space ventures. Several other countries have also developed space programs, including China, Pakistan, Japan, France, Britain, and both North Korea and South Korea.

Science in Space In the decades since *Sputnik*and *Apollo*, nations have launched rockets to other planets and beyond. Robotic space vehicles have penetrated the mists of Venus and the rings of Saturn, landed on Mars, and circled the moons of Jupiter. Space missions have pursued a variety of goals. Some take scientific measurements, release permanent satellites or telescopes, or gather information about the composition and formation of the universe itself. On manned space missions, astronauts conduct medical or biological experiments.

Increasingly, nations have worked together to explore space. Russia, the United States, Canada, Japan, and several European countries developed the **International Space Station (ISS).**Construction on the ISS began in 1998 and was completed in 2010.

The ISS has served as a space laboratory, allowing scientists to observe space, conduct research, and develop new space-related technologies. China has its own space station, and plans are underway for other joint stations. Future plans include set up a colony on Mars as well as searching for signs of life in other galaxies.

In the 21st century, space travel and exploration is no longer the business of only governments. Several private companies now launch rockets into space. One California company founded in 2002 has the goal of enabling people to live on other planets.

Space technology has benefited life on earth. Dozens of new products, developed for use in space, are today used on Earth. They include liquid-cooled garments, hang gliders, metalized plastics for use in construction and other areas, foam cushions used in helmets and for medical needs, a blood pump that can be used as a temporary heart, and a lightweight breathing system for firefighters.

Artificial Satellites Thousands of artificial satellites orbit Earth every day. They are used in one of three ways: communications, observation, and navigation. They have both military and non-military uses

Communications satellites, for example, relay information that can be used for television, telephone, and high-speed data transmission. Maintaining stationary orbits over specific points on Earth's surface, communications satellites can transmit phone messages or television pictures anywhere on Earth. Linked to cell phones or computers, they allow people, separated by thousands of miles, to communicate instantly.

Observation satellites provide data to scientists, weather forecasters, and military planners. A satellite can receive transmissions from underwater detectors and track the size and strength of tsunamis. Navigation satellites, or global positioning satellites (GPS), beam precise locations to ships, ground vehicles, airplanes, and even hand-held devices.

INTERPRET What is the International Space Station and what is its significance?

>> An Italian astronaut takes photographs on board the International Space Station in June 2013. Scientists at the station must deal with the long-term effects of weightlessness while they conduct research and develop new technologies.

Bounce to Activate Timeline

The Computer Revolution

The invention of the computer in the twentieth century caused an information revolution. Few aspects of modern life remain untouched by computers. Computers help to run businesses and power plants. They help scientists conduct advanced research. When computers are connected to satellites, they make global communications possible. The development of the computer technology has given rise to the phrase "Information Age."

The Birth of Computers Although most people use computers every day, not everyone can define exactly what a computer is. On the most basic level, a computer is a device for making mathematical calculations and for storing, processing, and rapidly manipulating data. Computers have made it possible to preserve vast amounts of data in a relatively short time. When computers are linked up in a vast network, they allow people to communicate instantaneously over long distances.

Many people contributed to the development of the computer. The first electronic computers were built in the 1940s. They were giant, slow machines, with thousands of vacuum tubes. After the invention of the silicon chip in 1958, the computer was gradually reduced in size. Personal computers became widely available in the 1970s. By installing basic programs, individual users could perform complex and difficult tasks quickly and easily.

Over the next few decades, personal computers replaced typewriters and account books in homes and businesses worldwide. At the same time, computer technology spread into many different fields. Computerized robots operate in factories. Computers remotely control satellites and probes in space, and students use them in school classrooms. Researchers developed computer models to predict disasters or understand environmental changes. Urban planners developed models for future growth of cities. In today's world, computers are everywhere, providing essential information and controlling critical services.

>> Machines like this one, an early "computing machine" for codebreaking used during World War II, marked the start of an information revolution that transformed the world.

The Internet Like the computer, the Internet has no single inventor. In the 1970s, the U.S. government along with several American universities led efforts to link computer systems together via cables and satellites. In 1989, British computer scientist Tim Berners-Lee proposed a system of linked documents that could be reached through a computer network. His proposal quickly developed into the World Wide Web, or Internet. Using the **Internet,** a person can instantly communicate with other users around the world and access vast storehouses of information.

By 2000, the Internet had grown to a gigantic network, linking individuals, governments, and businesses around the world. E-commerce, or buying and selling on the Internet, contributed to economic growth. The Internet affected people in both the industrial and the developing world. It connected people anywhere with access to a computer to a world of ideas and information. Today, it is estimated that about one third of the world's 6.8 billion people use the Internet on a regular basis.

SUMMARIZE What impact have personal computers had on people's lives?

Breakthroughs in Medicine and Biotechnology

Science and technology have revolutionized our understanding of all forms of life and changed the face of our planets. Every year, new developments in medicine improve treatments for diseases . In recent decades, scientists and engineers have made great

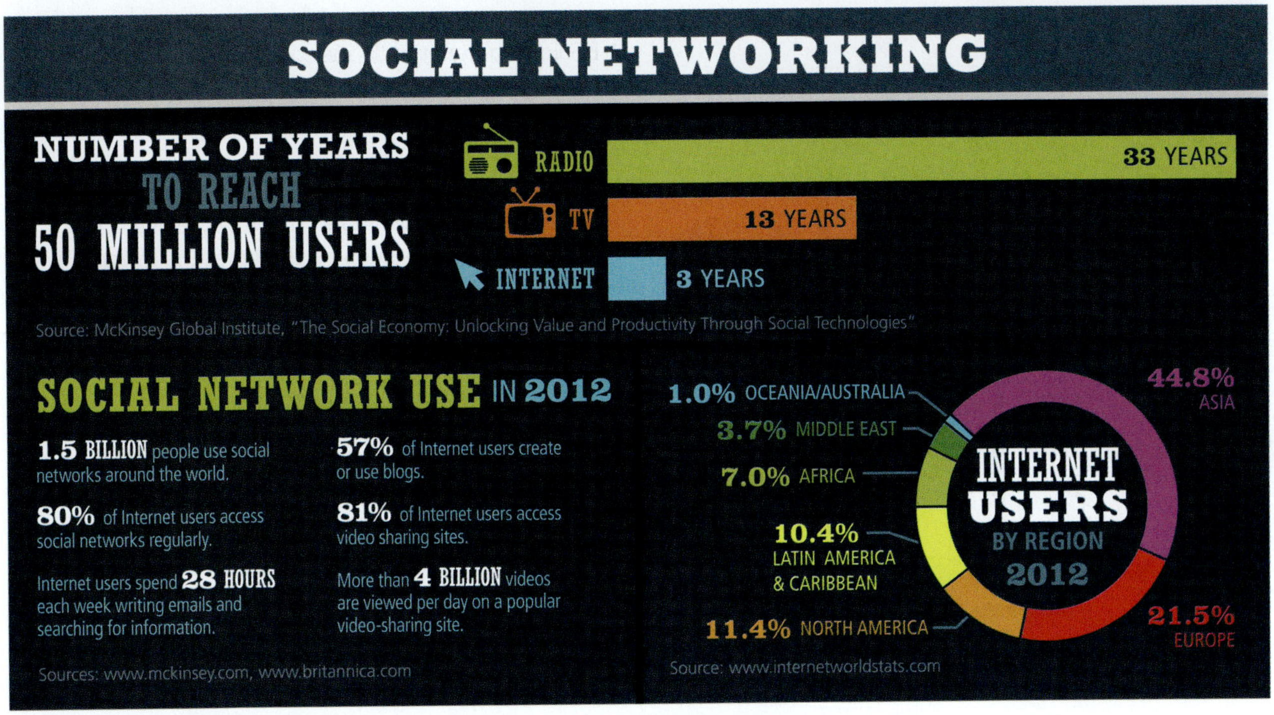

>> **Analyze Graphs** More than 1 billion people around the world use social networking sites. Which region of the world has the highest percentage of Internet users?

advances in **biotechnology,** or the application of biological research to industry, engineering, and technology.

Medical Advances Researchers have found treatments for a number of diseases. In 1952, Jonas Salk developed the first vaccine to prevent polio, a highly infectious disease that causes paralysis. The use of polio vaccines have almost wiped out the disease worldwide. Vaccines have completely eradicated smallpox, once a deadly and much feared disease, Medical researchers continue to work on developing vaccines to protect against many other diseases.

Breakthroughs in surgery also transformed the field of medicine. In the 1970s, surgeons learned to transplant organs, including the human heart, to save lives. Today, lung, kidney, and other transplants are common procedures in the developed world.

New technology such as lasers have made surgery safer and more precise. **Lasers** are high-energy light beams that surgeons use to cut or repair tissues and organs. Scientists have developed a range of treatments for many types of cancers. A growing number of breakthroughs in the diagnosis and treatment of diseases are the result of close partnership between doctors, engineers, and other scientists. The use of computers has also improved both research and communication among researchers around the world.

The Rise of Biotechnology and Genetic Engineering The field of biotechnology has exploded in recent years. Biotechnology is not new. Humans have used biotechnology for thousands of years to produce better plants or breed animals with certain characteristics. Today's biotechnology, however, uses micro-organisms such as bacteria, yeasts, enzymes to carry out certain industrial of manufacturing processes. For example, biotechnology has been used to make synthetic drugs or vaccinations. Scientists have developed ways to use bacteria to treat waste or clean up toxic spills.

Biotechnology is closely linked to **genetics** is the study of genes and heredity. Starting in the 1950s, genetic researchers, spearheaded by John Watson, Francis Crick, and Rosalind Franklin, showed the importance of DNA, the material that carries all the genetic information for living organisms. DNA research has revolutionized medicine, agriculture, forensics—crime-solving—and many other fields. In medicine, it has enabled researchers to identify genes that trigger certain disease and develop drugs to treat some of these diseases.

>> **Analyze Political Cartoons** Below the tomato plant in this cartoon lies a double helix, which is the structural arrangement of DNA. DNA is the genetic information contained in plant or animal cells. What is the cartoonist trying to portray in this cartoon?

Bounce to Activate Timeline

In recent decades, scientists have made great advances in **genetic engineering** or the manipulation of genetic material to produce specific results. Scientists have created new strains of fruits and vegetables that can resist disease or thrive in less favorable conditions such as cold or dry climates. Genetic cloning, or the process of creating identical organisms from the cell of a host organism, has many practical applications in raising livestock and in biological research

Biotechnology and genetic engineering have brought benefits, but also sparked debate. Some people believe that genetically modified foods are unnatural and possibly dangerous. The possibility of cloning genetically identical animals, including humans has raised ethical questions about the role of science in creating and changing life.

Standards of Living Rise Science and technology have changed the way we live. Like older inventions—such as the wheel, printing press, or steam engine—the inventions of the last century have improved lives and helped societies advance. Better diagnoses and treatments of disease have reduced infant mortality and helped people live longer. New genetically modified crops have increased food supplies. Overall, standards of living have risen worldwide.

Technology and information sharing will continue to be tools to solve global problems and build a better future. But to use these tools properly, we must continue to understand and learn from the past.

MAKE GENERALIZATIONS How have scientific advances affected people's standard of living?

ASSESSMENT

1. **Generate Explanations** How have advances in biotechnology and genetic engineering been built on past discoveries?
2. **Synthesize** Why did the United States and the USSR compete against each other to achieve dominance in the space race?
3. **Identify Cause and Effect** What impact has the computer revolution had on globalization?
4. **Summarize** Biotechnology has provided many benefits, but many people worry about its long-term effects. Explain why this is so.
5. **Identify Cause and Effect** What impact do artificial satellites have on modern life?

PEARSON realize
PearsonSchool.com/CASS

Go online to PearsonSchool.com/CASS and use the texts, quizzes, interactivities, Interactive Reading Notepads, Flipped Videos, and other resources from this Topic to prepare for the Topic Test.

- Etexts
- Quizzes
- Interactivities
- Interactive Reading Notepads
- Flipped Videos

While online you can also check the progress you've made learning the topic and course content by viewing your grades, test scores, and assignment status.

California Topic 10 Quick Study Guide

LESSON SUMMARIES

Use these Lesson Summaries, and the longer versions available online, to review the key ideas for each lesson in this Topic.

Lesson 1: Challenges of Development

The Cold War created an ideological split between the communist East and the capitalist West. An economic gulf divides the world into two spheres— the global North which is the industrialized world and the global South which is the developing world.

Lesson 2: Challenges for African Nations

In 1945, four European powers—Britain, France, Belgium, and Portugal – controlled almost all of the African continent. After World War II, a rising tide of nationalism was sweeping over European colonial powers. This spirit would lead many African nations to seek and declare independence. In South Africa, this meant ending the bonds of apartheid.

Lesson 3: Rapid Development in China and India

Both China and India are large countries with diverse populations. By the mid-1990s, China was a major industrial power with a rapidly growing economy. Yet, the nation still faced many challenges. India is the world's largest democratic nation. It too still faces major economic issues.

Lesson 4: Latin American Nations Move Toward Democracy

Latin America's development is influenced by geography, culture, social patterns, and political and economic conditions. Similar to other growing countries, inequality and the growing population continue to contribute poverty.

Lesson 5: The Industrialized World

The end of the Cold War marked the end of communism in many countries. Nations moved to overcome economic problems and to develop new ways of life, trade, and business. Russia and former Soviet Republics work to build stable governments and market -based economies.

Lesson 6: Globalization and Trade

The industrial nations of the global North and the developing nations of the global South have become increasingly interdependent.

Lesson 7: Social and Environmental Issues

Along with globalization come the continuing problems of poverty, hunger, and diseases which usually affect populations in developing countries. Environmental issues confront both developed and developing nations. Modern industry and agriculture have used up natural resources and polluted much of the earth's water, air, and soil.

Lesson 8: Terrorism and International Security

Since the 1960s, incidents of terrorism have increased around the world with the rise of radical Islamic fundamentalism in the 1990s. Terrorist groups deliberately launch attacks against civilians to achieve political goals. Al Qaeda and other terrorist groups launched attacks against targets around the world, including the United States in 2001.

Lesson 9: Advances in Science and Technology

"My village is changing" observed Indian writer Prafulla Mohanti when a road was built there in 1960. Now, villages continue to change with new ways of communication, the computer revolution, and medical and biological advances.

PEARSON realize™
PearsonSchool.com/CASS

Go ONLINE for lesson summaries

AUDIO READING GAMES

VISUAL REVIEW

Use these graphics to review some of the key terms, people, and ideas from this Topic.

Key Components of Globalization

- Interdependence: dependence of countries on goods, resources, knowledge, and labor from other parts of the world
- Advances in communications and transportation
- Rise of huge multinational corporations
- Far-reaching effects of financial crisis, shortages of natural resources, and debt
- Rise of global economy with many global organizations and treaties

Major Challenge to Society Today

- Global poverty, disasters, and disease
- Ensuring human rights for all, including women, children, and indigenous peoples
- Environmental problems including pollution, deforestation, desertification, and climate change
- Threat of misuse of nuclear technology and weapons of mass destruction
- Terrorism

Influential Technology in the Twentieth Century

TECHNOLOGY	DESCRIPTION	USES
Artificial satellite	Man-made object that orbits a larger body	Space exploration, spying and other military purposes; scientific research; navigation; communications
Computer	Device for storing, processing, and rapidly manipulating data	Creating and preserving data; making businesses and homes run more efficiently; controlling satellites and factories
Internet	Network of world computer systems linked by cables and satellites	Instant communication with users around world; instant data retrieval; means of commerce
Biotechnology	Application of biological research to industry	Vaccinations and medicines; industrial

Important Industrialized Regions

REGION	DESCRIPTION	ROLE IN GLOBAL ECONOMY
The United States	World's only superpower	Important world leader, largest trading country in world
The European Union	Union of 25 European nations with distinct governments but common economic, political, and cultural institutions	Currently includes over half of European nations and is growing; world's largest trading region
The Pacific Rim	Geographical Region that includes the countries that border the Pacific Ocean	With many countries and huge populations, potential to be major player in global economy

California Topic 10 Assessment

KEY TERMS, PEOPLE, AND IDEAS

1. How did **Deng Xiaoping** plan to change China's economy?
2. What are the advantages and disadvantages of the **Green Revolution**?
3. How did the **African National Congress** work to help end apartheid in South Africa?
4. What political reforms in China during the 1980s sparked a new political crisis?
5. Similar to China, how has the population boom in India affected the country?
6. What was the goal of **import substitution** in Latin America?
7. What is biotechnology? Why is there a debate about the effects of biotechnology?
8. Discuss the benefits and costs of global interdependence.
9. What are the social and environmental effects of deforestation?

CRITICAL THINKING

10. **Recognize Cause and Effect** What impact has the computer revolution had on globalization?
11. **Summarize** How was the war in Afghanistan related to the 2001 terrorist attacks in the United States?
12. **Analyze Information** Discuss the social and economic consequences of an epidemic in both developing and developed countries.
13. **Analyze information** How has the rise of regional trade blocs such as the European Union affected world economies?
14. **Make Generalizations** Describe the international response to the ethnic cleansing in Bosnia-Herzegovina. How did the response establish further protection for human rights?
15. **Recognize Cause and Effect** Some critics of globalization cite cultural erosion and higher unemployment in the United States as consequences. Discuss why they feel these effects might occur. Those supporting the effects of globalization cite the improvements to the economies of developing nations. Discuss these effects.
16. **Using Primary Sources** Mario Vargas Llosa, a Peruvian writer, described in a 1991 speech what is needed to ensure a successful democracy in Latin America. (a) What does he see as obstacles to this happening? (b) Could his solution be a blueprint for all nations seeking to become more democratic? Explain.

> "The democratization of Latin America . . . is very fragile. To maintain and extend this popular base, governments will have to prove to their citizens that democracy means not only the end of political brutality, but progress . . . benefits in . . . labor, health, and education.
>
> If we want democracy to take hold in our countries, our most urgent task is to broaden it, give it substance, and truth. Democracy is fragile in so many countries because it is superficial, a mere framework within which institutions and political parties go about their business in their traditionally arbitrary, bullying way."
>
> —*Mario Vargas Llosa, Speech, 1991*

17. **Writing Activity** In developing nations, women still shoulder a larger burden of chores. This excerpt is an account of women's lives in the Kenyan countryside. (a) Why are most women the head of household? (b) How are the women working to improve their economic situation? Could this help to ease the poverty? Use your knowledge of the Topic and the excerpt to write your paragraph.

> "One third of all rural households are headed by women, largely because men have migrated to the cities and towns in the hope of finding salaried work. Their wives continue to work the family plots of land and are always busy with some scheme to earn a bit of cash. Everywhere one sees women walking to market with basketloads of vegetables on their heads, infants strapped to their backs. . . . Even while they are walking to market, these women often are waving baskets that they hope to exchange for cash needed for the family's support. . . ."
>
> —*P. Houston, Third World Women Speak Out*

DOCUMENT-BASED QUESTIONS

For many scientists, politicians, and citizens, energy consumption is a troubling issue. Intense debate surrounds the question of which alternate energy sources we should use. Read the documents below, then answer the questions that follow.

DOCUMENT A

United States Energy Consumption by Source, 2014

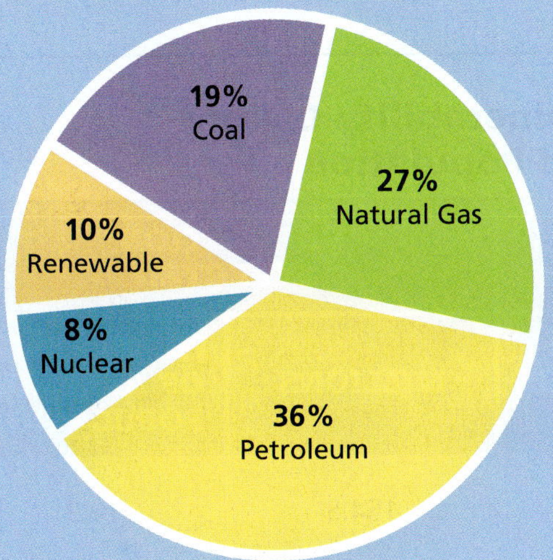

SOURCE: US Energy Information Agency

DOCUMENT B

"As we approach the end of the twentieth century there is no single thing we can do that will have as large an impact on the people of the world during the new century than the development of solar power satellites. They will bring prosperity, an opportunity for the poor nations of the earth to achieve true freedom from want, healing of our environment, and open the vast new frontier of space to all of us.

...With the develoment of solar power satellites we will tap directly into the power of the sun and save the world from impending chaos. There will be hope for the future as we enter the twenty-first century."

—*Sun Power by Ralph Nansen*

DOCUMENT C

"Renewables are nor without their drawbacks. Solar and wind farms cannot generate much electricity on cloudy or still days. As intermittent energy sources, they require vast systems to store the energy they produce, or must rely on the rest of the electrical system for backup. And despite federal subsidies to spur technological innovation, renewable sources have not become economical enough to seriously challenge fossil fuels in an open market."

—*CQ Researcher, November 7, 1997*

18. Which document is supported by the actual U.S. energy consumption data shown in Document A?

A. Document B

B. Document C

C. both Documents B and C

D. neither Document B nor C

19. Which statement best describes the viewpoint of the author of Document B?

A. Biomass generators are a better alternative to fossil fuel than solar powered satellites.

B. Solar powered satellites are the most promising alternative to fossil fuel.

C. Solar powered satellites are not realistic or cost effective as an alternative to fossil fuel.

D. More research must be carried out to determine whether solar powered satellites are a realistic alternative to fossil fuel.

20. According to Document C, all are drawbacks of renewables except which of the following?

A. They are intermittent energy sources.

B. They are not cost-efficient.

C. They rely on traditional electricity sources.

D. They are worse for the environment.

21. **Writing Tasks** What does our energy future look like? Make some predictions for 50 years. Use information from these documents along with information from the Topic to support your predictions.

End-of-Topic Practice

1 How would the rise of trade blocs such as the European Union or NAFTA affect developing countries?

A Trade benefits would include lower import costs and creation of new markets.

B Import costs would rise, reducing the need for new product.

C Standards of living would improve with more products readily available.

D Foreign investments would lessen, drying up job potential and market demand.

Estimates of Land Area Belonging to Vulnerability Classes and Corresponding Number of Impacted Population

VULNERABILITY CLASS	AREA SUBJECT TO DESERTIFICATION		POPULATION AFFECTED	
	SQUARE KILOMETERS	PERCENTAGE	MILLIONS	PERCENTAGE OF AFRICAN POPULATION
Low	4,225,000	14.2	154.5	19.9
Moderate	4,741,000	15.9	196.1	25.3
High	3,213,000	10.8	134.8	17.4
Very High	1,466,000	4.9	22.4	2.9

SOURCE: U.S. Department of Agriculture

2 Using the chart and information from the lessons, which of these represents the problem of desertification in Africa?

F A shortage of basic food supplies is predicted for almost the entire African continent.

G About one fifth of the affected population is in the two worst classes of vulnerability, showing a dangerous level.

H Close to 30 percent of African land is subject to drying out and thus killing livestock and crops.

J People in the lowest vulnerability classes can hardly survive on their own lands without international aid.

3 How have demographic changes in India affected society?

A Slower population growth resulted in less crowded cities and adequate housing for citizens.

B In spite of vigorous reforms, the government could not successfully provide enough food, jobs, and housing for the booming population.

C As in China, India enforced one child per family laws to control population growth and to ease economic hardships.

D India introduced housing reforms, agricultural improvements, and subsidy programs to ease the poverty caused by the population boom.

---

4 How does the U.S. response to terrorism from September 11, 2001, sometimes cause mixed reactions in the United States and other countries?

F Increased efforts to strengthen and coordinate intelligence services to address terrorism may intrude on constitutional rights.

G Security measures at airports mean invasive questions about checked luggage and travel forms

H Public buildings have tighter security that means less accessibility by government workers.

J More scrutiny of personal and business phone calls creates public distrust of government interference.

If you have trouble with. . .				
Question	1	2	3	4
See Lesson	10.1	10.2	10.3	10.8

Stock Connection Blue/Alamy

Constitution Quick Study Guide

Amendments

1st Amendment: Freedom of Religion, Speech, Press, Assembly, and Petition

2nd Amendment: Right to Keep, Bear Arms

3rd Amendment: Lodging Troops in Private Homes

4th Amendment: Search, Seizures, Proper Warrants

5th Amendment: Criminal Proceedings, Due Process, Eminent Domain

6th Amendment: Criminal Proceedings

7th Amendment: Jury Trials in Civil Cases

8th Amendment: Bail; Cruel, Unusual Punishment

9th Amendment: Unenumerated Rights

10th Amendment: Powers Reserved to the States

11th Amendment: Suits Against the States

12th Amendment: Election of President and Vice President

13th Amendment: Slavery and Involuntary Servitude
- Section 1. Slavery and Involuntary Servitude Prohibited
- Section 2. Power of Congress

14th Amendment: Rights of Citizens
- Section 1. Citizenship; Privileges and Immunities; Due Process; Equal Protection
- Section 2. Apportionment of Representation
- Section 3. Disqualification of Officers
- Section 4. Public Debt
- Section 5. Powers of Congress

15th Amendment: Right to Vote—Race, Color, Servitude
- Section 1. Suffrage Not to Be Abridged
- Section 2. Power of Congress

16th Amendment: Income Tax

17th Amendment: Popular Election of Senators
- Section 1. Popular Election of Senators
- Section 2. Senate Vacancies
- Section 3. Inapplicable to Senators Previously Chosen

18th Amendment: Prohibition of Intoxicating Liquors
- Section 1. Intoxicating Liquors Prohibited
- Section 2. Concurrent Power to Enforce
- Section 3. Time Limit on Ratification

19th Amendment: Equal Suffrage—Sex
- Section 1. Suffrage Not to Be Abridged
- Section 2. Power of Congress

20th Amendment: Commencement of Terms; Sessions of Congress; Death or Disqualification of President-Elect
- Section 1. Terms of President, Vice President, members of Congress
- Section 2. Sessions of Congress
- Section 3. Death or Disqualification of President-Elect
- Section 4. Congress to Provide for Certain Successors
- Section 5. Effective Date
- Section 6. Time Limit on Ratification

21st Amendment: Repeal of 18th Amendment
- Section 1. Repeal of Prohibition
- Section 2. Transportation, Importation of Intoxicating Liquors
- Section 3. Time Limit on Ratification

22nd Amendment: Presidential Tenure
- Section 1. Restriction on Number of Terms
- Section 2. Time Limit on Ratification

23rd Amendment: Inclusion of District of Columbia in Presidential Election Systems
- Section 1. Presidential Electors for District
- Section 2. Power of Congress

24th Amendment: Right to Vote in Federal Elections—Tax Payment
- Section 1. Suffrage Not to Be Abridged
- Section 2. Power of Congress

25th Amendment: Presidential Succession; Vice Presidential Vacancy; Presidential Inability
- Section 1. Presidential Succession
- Section 2. Vice Presidential Vacancy
- Section 3. Presidential Inability

26th Amendment: Right to Vote—Age
- Section 1. Suffrage Not to Be Abridged
- Section 2. Power of Congress

27th Amendment: Congressional Pay

The Preamble states the broad purposes the Constitution is intended to serve—to establish a government that provides for greater cooperation among the States, ensures justice and peace, provides for defense against foreign enemies, promotes the general well-being of the people, and secures liberty now and in the future. The phrase We the People emphasizes the twin concepts of popular sovereignty and of representative government.

Legislative Department

Section 1. Legislative power; Congress

Congress, the nation's lawmaking body, is bicameral in form; that is, it is composed of two houses: the Senate and the House of Representatives. The Framers of the Constitution purposely separated the lawmaking power from the power to enforce the laws (Article II, the Executive Branch) and the power to interpret them (Article III, the Judicial Branch). This system of separation of powers is supplemented by a system of checks and balances; that is, in several provisions the Constitution gives to each of the three branches various powers with which it may restrain the actions of the other two branches.

Section 2. House of Representatives

▶ **Clause 1. Election** Electors means voters. Members of the House of Representatives are elected every two years. Each State must permit the same persons to vote for United States representatives as it permits to vote for the members of the larger house of its own legislature. The 17th Amendment (1913) extends this requirement to the qualification of voters for United States senators.

▶ **Clause 2. Qualifications** A member of the House of Representatives must be at least 25 years old, an American citizen for seven years, and a resident of the State he or she represents. In addition, political custom requires that a representative also reside in the district from which he or she is elected.

▶ **Clause 3. Apportionment** The number of representatives each State is entitled to is based on its population, which is counted every 10 years in the census. Congress reapportions the seats among the States after each census. In the Reapportionment Act of 1929, Congress fixed the permanent size of the House at 435 members with each State having at least one representative. Today there is one House seat for approximately every 700,000 persons in the population.

The words "three-fifths of all other persons" referred to slaves and reflected the Three-Fifths Compromise reached by the Framers at Philadelphia in 1787; the phrase was made obsolete, was in effect repealed, by the 13th Amendment in 1865.

---

* The gray words indicate portions of the Constitution altered by subsequent amendments to the document.

▶ **Clause 4. Vacancies** The executive authority refers to the governor of a State. If a member leaves office or dies before the expiration of his or her term, the governor is to call a special election to fill the vacancy.

United States Constitution

PREAMBLE

We the People of the United States, in Order to form a more perfect Union, establish Justice, insure domestic Tranquility, provide for the common defence, promote the general Welfare, and secure the Blessings of Liberty to ourselves and our Posterity, do ordain and establish this Constitution for the United States of America.

Article I.

Section 1.

All legislative Powers herein granted shall be vested in a Congress of the United States, which shall consist of a Senate and House of Representatives.

Section 2.

▶ 1. The House of Representatives shall be composed of Members chosen every second Year by the People of the several States, and the Electors in each State shall have the Qualifications requisite for Electors of the most numerous Branch of the State Legislature.

▶ 2. No Person shall be a Representative who shall not have attained to the age of twenty-five Years, and been seven Years a Citizen of the United States, and who shall not, when elected, be an Inhabitant of that State in which he shall be chosen.

▶ 3. Representatives and direct Taxes* shall be apportioned among the several States which may be included within this Union, according to their respective Numbers, which shall be determined by adding to the whole Number of free Persons, including those bound to Service for a Term of Years and excluding Indians not taxed, three fifths of all other Persons. The actual Enumeration shall be made within three Years after the first Meeting of the Congress of the United States, and within every subsequent term of ten Years, in such Manner as they shall by Law direct. The Number of Representatives shall not exceed one for every thirty Thousand, but each State shall have at Least one Representative; and, until such enumeration shall be made, the State of New Hampshire shall be entitled to choose three, Massachusetts eight, Rhode Island and Providence Plantations one, Connecticut five, New York six, New Jersey four, Pennsylvania eight, Delaware one, Maryland six, Virginia ten, North Carolina five, South Carolina five, and Georgia three.

▶ 4. When vacancies happen in the Representation from any State, the Executive Authority thereof shall issue Writs of Election to fill such Vacancies.

▶5. The House of Representatives shall choose their Speaker and other Officers; and shall have the sole Power of Impeachment.

▶**Clause 5. Officers; impeachment** The House elects a Speaker, customarily chosen from the majority party in the House. Impeachment means accusation. The House has the exclusive power to impeach, or accuse, civil officers; the Senate (Article I, Section 3, Clause 6) has the exclusive power to try those impeached by the House.

Section 3.

▶1. The Senate of the United States shall be composed of two Senators from each State chosen by the Legislature thereof for six Years; and each Senator shall have one Vote.

▶2. Immediately after they shall be assembled in Consequences of the first Election, they shall be divided, as equally as may be, into three Classes. The Seats of the Senators of the first Class shall be vacated at the Expiration of the second Year; of the second Class, at the Expiration of the fourth Year; and of the third Class, at the Expiration of the sixth Year; so that one-third may be chosen every second Year; and if Vacancies happen by Resignation, or otherwise, during the Recess of the Legislature of any State, the Executive thereof may make temporary Appointments until the next Meeting of the Legislature, which shall then fill such Vacancies.

▶3. No Person shall be a Senator who shall not have attained to the Age of thirty Years, and been nine Years a Citizen of the United States, and who shall not, when elected, be an Inhabitant of that State for which he shall be chosen.

▶4. The Vice President of the United States shall be President of the Senate but shall have no Vote, unless they be equally divided.

▶5. The Senate shall choose their other Officers, and also a President pro tempore, in the Absence of the Vice President, or when he shall exercise the Office of President of the United States.

▶6. The Senate shall have the sole Power to try all Impeachments. When sitting for that Purpose, they shall be on Oath or Affirmation. When the President of the United States is tried, the Chief Justice shall preside: And no Person shall be convicted without the Concurrence of two thirds of the Members present.

▶7. Judgment in Cases of Impeachment shall not extend further than to removal from Office, and disqualification to hold and enjoy any Office of honor, Trust, or Profit under the United States: but the Party convicted shall nevertheless be liable and subject to Indictment, Trial, Judgment and Punishment, according to Law.

Section 3. Senate

▶ **Clause 1. Composition, election, term** Each State has two senators. Each serves for six years and has one vote. Originally, senators were not elected directly by the people, but by each State's legislature. The 17th Amendment, added in 1913, provides for the popular election of senators.

▶ **Clause 2. Classification** The senators elected in 1788 were divided into three groups so that the Senate could become a "continuing body." One-third of the Senate's seats are up for election every two years.

The 17th Amendment provides that a Senate vacancy is to be filled at a special election called by the governor; State law may also permit the governor to appoint a successor to serve until that election is held.

▶ **Clause 3. Qualifications** A senator must be at least 30 years old, a citizen for at least nine years, and must live in the State from which elected.

▶ **Clause 4. Presiding officer** The Vice President presides over the Senate, but may vote only to break a tie.

▶ **Clause 5. Other officers** The Senate chooses its own officers, including a president pro tempore to preside when the Vice President is not there.

▶ **Clause 6. Impeachment trials** The Senate conducts the trials of those officials impeached by the House. The Vice President presides unless the President is on trial, in which case the Chief Justice of the United States does so. A conviction requires the votes of two-thirds of the senators present.

No President has ever been convicted. In 1868 the House voted eleven articles of impeachment against President Andrew Johnson, but the Senate fell one vote short of convicting him. In 1974 President Richard M. Nixon resigned the presidency in the face of almost certain impeachment by the House. The House brought two articles of impeachment against President Bill Clinton in late 1998. Neither charge was supported by even a simple majority vote in the Senate, on February 12, 1999.

▶ **Clause 7. Penalty on conviction** The punishment of an official convicted in an impeachment case has always been removal from office. The Senate can also bar a convicted person from ever holding any federal office, but it is not required to do so. A convicted person can also be tried and punished in a regular court for any crime involved in the impeachment case.

Section 4. Elections and Meetings

▶ **Clause 1. Election** In 1842 Congress required that representatives be elected from districts within each State with more than one seat in the House. The districts in each State are drawn by that State's legislature. Seven States now have only one seat in the House: Alaska, Delaware, Montana, North Dakota, South Dakota, Vermont, and Wyoming. The 1842 law also directed that representatives be elected in each State on the same day: the Tuesday after the first Monday in November of every even-numbered year. In 1914 Congress also set that same date for the election of senators.

▶ **Clause 2. Sessions** Congress must meet at least once a year. The 20th Amendment (1933) changed the opening date to January 3.

Section 5. Legislative Proceedings

▶ **Clause 1. Admission of members; quorum** In 1969 the Supreme Court held that the House cannot exclude any member-elect who satisfies the qualifications set out in Article I, Section 2, Clause 2.

A majority in the House (218 members) or Senate (51) constitutes a quorum. In practice, both houses often proceed with less than a quorum present. However, any member may raise a point of order (demand a "quorum call"). If a roll call then reveals less than a majority of the members present, that chamber must either adjourn or the sergeant at arms must be ordered to round up absent members.

▶ **Clause 2. Rules** Each house has adopted detailed rules to guide its proceedings. Each house may discipline members for unacceptable conduct; expulsion requires a two-thirds vote.

▶ **Clause 3. Record** Each house must keep and publish a record of its meetings. The Congressional Record is published for every day that either house of Congress is in session, and provides a written record of all that is said and done on the floor of each house each session.

▶ **Clause 4. Adjournment** Once in session, neither house may suspend (recess) its work for more than three days without the approval of the other house. Both houses must always meet in the same location.

Section 4.

▶1. The Times, Places and Manner of holding Elections for Senators and Representatives, shall be prescribed in each State by the Legislature thereof; but the Congress may at any time by law make or alter such Regulations, except as to the Places of choosing Senators.

▶2. The Congress shall assemble at least once in every Year, and such Meeting shall be on the first Monday in December, unless they shall by Law appoint a different Day.

Section 5.

▶1. Each House shall be the Judge of the Elections, Returns and Qualifications of its own Members, and a Majority of each shall constitute a Quorum to do Business; but a smaller Number may adjourn from day to day, and may be authorized to compel the Attendance of absent Members, in such Manner, and under such Penalties, as each House may provide.

▶2. Each House may determine the Rules of its Proceedings, punish its Members for disorderly Behavior, and, with the Concurrence of two thirds, expel a Member.

▶3. Each House shall keep a Journal of its Proceedings, and from time to time publish the same, excepting such Parts as may in their Judgment require Secrecy; and the Yeas and Nays of the Members of either House on any question shall, at the Desire of one fifth of those Present, be entered on the Journal.

▶4. Neither House, during the Session of Congress, shall, without the Consent of the other, adjourn for more than three days, nor to any other Place than that in which the two Houses shall be sitting.

Section 6.

▶1. The Senators and Representatives shall receive a Compensation for their Services, to be ascertained by Law, and paid out of the Treasury of the United States. They shall in all Cases, except Treason, Felony, and Breach of the Peace, be privileged from Arrest during their Attendance at the Session of their respective Houses, and in going to and returning from the same; and for any Speech or Debate in either House, they shall not be questioned in any other Place.

Section 6. Compensation, Immunities, and Disabilities of Members

▶ **Clause 1. Salaries; immunities** Each house sets its members' salaries, paid by the United States; the 27th Amendment (1992) modified this pay-setting power. This provision establishes "legislative immunity." The purpose of this immunity is to allow members to speak and debate freely in Congress itself. Treason is strictly defined in Article III, Section 3. A felony is any serious crime. A breach of the peace is any indictable offense less than treason or a felony; this exemption from arrest is of little real importance today.

▶2. No Senator or Representative shall, during the Time for which he was elected, be appointed to any civil Office under the Authority of the United States, which shall have been created, or the Emoluments whereof shall have been increased during such time; and no Person holding any Office under the United States, shall be a Member of either House during his Continuance in Office.

▶ **Clause 2. Restrictions on office holding** No sitting member of either house may be appointed to an office in the executive or in the judicial branch if that position was created or its salary was increased during that member's current elected term. The second part of this clause—forbidding any person serving in either the executive or the judicial branch from also serving in Congress—reinforces the principle of separation of powers.

Section 7.

▶1. All Bills for raising Revenue shall originate in the House of Representatives; but the Senate may propose or concur with amendments as on other Bills.

Section 7. Revenue Bills, President's Veto

▶ **Clause 1. Revenue bills** All bills that raise money must originate in the House. However, the Senate has the power to amend any revenue bill sent to it from the lower house.

▶2. Every Bill which shall have passed the House of Representatives and the Senate, shall, before it become a law, be presented to the President of the United States: If he approve, he shall sign it, but if not he shall return it, with his Objections to that House in which it shall have originated, who shall enter the Objections at large on their Journal, and proceed to reconsider it. If after such Reconsideration two thirds of the House shall agree to pass the Bill, it shall be sent, together with the Objections, to the other House, by which it shall likewise be reconsidered, and if approved by two thirds of that House, it shall become a Law. But in all such Cases the Votes of both Houses shall be determined by Yeas and Nays, and the Names of the Persons voting for and against the Bill shall be entered on the Journal of each House respectively. If any Bill shall not be returned by the President within ten Days (Sunday excepted) after it shall have been presented to him, the Same shall be a law, in like Manner as if he had signed it, unless the Congress by their Adjournment, prevent its Return, in which Case it shall not be a Law.

▶ **Clause 2. Enactment of laws; veto** Once both houses have passed a bill, it must be sent to the President. The President may (1) sign the bill, thus making it law; (2) veto the bill, whereupon it must be returned to the house in which it originated; or (3) allow the bill to become law without signature, by not acting upon it within 10 days of its receipt from Congress, not counting Sundays. The President has a fourth option at the end of a congressional session: If he does not act on a measure within 10 days, and Congress adjourns during that period, the bill dies; the "pocket veto" has been applied to it. A presidential veto may be overridden by a two-thirds vote in each house.

▶3. Every Order, Resolution, or Vote to which the Concurrence of the Senate and House of Representatives may be necessary (except on a question of adjournment) shall be presented to the President of the United States; and before the Same shall take Effect, shall be approved by him, or, being disapproved by him, shall be repassed by two thirds of the Senate and House of Representatives, according to the Rules and Limitations prescribed in the Case of a Bill.

▶ **Clause 3. Other measures** This clause refers to joint resolutions, measures Congress often passes to deal with unusual, temporary, or ceremonial matters. A joint resolution passed by Congress and signed by the President has the force of law, just as a bill does. As a matter of custom, a joint resolution proposing an amendment to the Constitution is not submitted to the President for signature or veto. Concurrent and simple resolutions do not have the force of law and, therefore, are not submitted to the President.

Section 8. Powers of Congress

▶ **Clause 1.** The 18 separate clauses in this section set out 27 of the many expressed powers the Constitution grants to Congress. In this clause Congress is given the power to levy and provide for the collection of various kinds of taxes, in order to finance the operations of the government. All federal taxes must be levied at the same rates throughout the country.

▶ **Clause 2.** Congress has power to borrow money to help finance the government. Federal borrowing is most often done through the sale of bonds on which interest is paid. The Constitution does not limit the amount the government may borrow.

▶ **Clause 3.** This clause, the Commerce Clause, gives Congress the power to regulate both foreign and interstate trade. Much of what Congress does, it does on the basis of its commerce power.

▶ **Clause 4.** Congress has the exclusive power to determine how aliens may become citizens of the United States. Congress may also pass laws relating to bankruptcy.

▶ **Clause 5.** has the power to establish and require the use of uniform gauges of time, distance, weight, volume, area, and the like.

▶ **Clause 6.** Congress has the power to make it a federal crime to falsify the coins, paper money, bonds, stamps, and the like of the United States.

▶ **Clause 7.** Congress has the power to provide for and regulate the transportation and delivery of mail; "post offices" are those buildings and other places where mail is deposited for dispatch; "post roads" include all routes over or upon which mail is carried.

▶ **Clause 8.** Congress has the power to provide for copyrights and patents. A copyright gives an author or composer the exclusive right to control the reproduction, publication, and sale of literary, musical, or other creative work. A patent gives a person the exclusive right to control the manufacture or sale of his or her invention.

▶ **Clause 9.** Congress has the power to create the lower federal courts, all of the several federal courts that function beneath the Supreme Court.

▶ **Clause 10.** Congress has the power to prohibit, as a federal crime: (1) certain acts committed outside the territorial jurisdiction of the United States, and (2) the commission within the United States of any wrong against any nation with which we are at peace.

Section 8.

The Congress shall have Power

▶1. To lay and collect Taxes, Duties, Imposts and Excises to pay the Debts and provide for the common Defence and general Welfare of the United States; but all Duties, Imposts and Excises, shall be uniform throughout the United States;

▶2. To borrow Money on the credit of the United States;

▶3. To regulate Commerce with foreign Nations, and among the several States, and with the Indian Tribes;

▶4. To establish an uniform Rule of Naturalization, and uniform Laws on the subject of Bankruptcies throughout the United States;

▶5. To coin Money, regulate the Value thereof, and of foreign Coin, and fix the Standard of Weights and Measures;

▶6. To provide for the Punishment of counterfeiting the Securities and current Coin of the United States;

▶7. To establish Post Offices and post Roads;

▶8. To promote the Progress of Science and useful Arts, by securing, for limited Times to Authors and Inventors the exclusive Right to their respective Writings and Discoveries;

▶9. To constitute Tribunals inferior to the supreme Court;

▶10. To define and punish Piracies and Felonies committed on the high Seas, and Offences against the Law of nations;

11. To declare War, grant Letters of Marque and Reprisal, and make Rules concerning Captures on Land and Water;

Clause 11. Only Congress can declare war. However, the President, as commander in chief of the armed forces (Article II, Section 2, Clause 1), can make war without such a formal declaration. Letters of marque and reprisal are commissions authorizing private persons to outfit vessels (privateers) to capture and destroy enemy ships in time of war; they were forbidden in international law by the Declaration of Paris of 1856, and the United States has honored the ban since the Civil War.

12. To raise and support Armies; but no Appropriation of Money to that Use shall be for a longer Term than two Years;

13. To provide and maintain a Navy;

Clauses 12 and 13. Congress has the power to provide for and maintain the nation's armed forces. It established the air force as an independent element of the armed forces in 1947, an exercise of its inherent powers in foreign relations and national defense. The two-year limit on spending for the army insures civilian control of the military.

14. To make Rules for the Government and Regulation of the land and naval Forces;

Clause 14. Today these rules are set out in three principle statutes: the Uniform Code of Military Justice, passed by Congress in 1950, and the Military Justice Acts of 1958 and 1983.

15. To provide for calling forth the Militia to execute the Laws of the Union, suppress Insurrections and repel Invasions;

16. To provide for organizing, arming, and disciplining the Militia, and for governing such Part of them as may be employed in the Service of the United States, reserving to the States respectively the Appointment of the Officers, and the Authority of training the Militia according to the discipline prescribed by Congress;

Clauses 15 and 16. In the National Defense Act of 1916, Congress made each State's militia (volunteer army) a part of the National Guard. Today, Congress and the States cooperate in its maintenance. Ordinarily, each State's National Guard is under the command of that State's governor; but Congress has given the President the power to call any or all of those units into federal service when necessary.

17. To exercise exclusive Legislation in all Cases whatsoever, over such District (not exceeding ten Miles square) as may, by Cession of Particular States, and the Acceptance of Congress, become the Seat of the Government of the United States, and to exercise like Authority over all Places purchased by the Consent of the Legislature of the State in which the Same shall be, for the Erection of Forts, Magazines, Arsenals, Dockyards and other needful Buildings;—And

Clause 17. In 1791 Congress accepted land grants from Maryland and Virginia and established the District of Columbia for the nation's capital. Assuming Virginia's grant would never be needed, Congress returned it in 1846. Today, the elected government of the District's 69 square miles operates under the authority of Congress. Congress also has the power to acquire other lands from the States for various federal purposes.

18. To make all Laws which shall be necessary and proper for carrying into Execution the foregoing Powers and all other Powers vested by this Constitution in the Government of the United States, or in any Department or Officer thereof.

Clause 18. This is the Necessary and Proper Clause, also often called the Elastic Clause. It is the constitutional basis for the many and far-reaching implied powers of the Federal Government.

Section 9.

1. The Migration or Importation of such Persons as any of the States now existing shall think proper to admit, shall not be prohibited by the Congress prior to the Year one thousand eight hundred and eight, but a Tax or duty may be imposed on such Importation, not exceeding ten dollars for each Person.

Section 9. Powers Denied to Congress

Clause 1. The phrase "such persons" referred to slaves. This provision was part of the Commerce Compromise, one of the bargains struck in the writing of the Constitution. Congress outlawed the slave trade in 1808.

▶ **Clause 2.** A writ of habeas corpus, the "great writ of liberty," is a court order directing a sheriff, warden, or other public officer, or a private person, who is detaining another to "produce the body" of the one being held in order that the legality of the detention may be determined by the court.

▶ **Clause 3.** A bill of attainder is a legislative act that inflicts punishment without a judicial trial. See Article I, Section 10, and Article III, Section 3, Clause 2. An ex post facto law is any criminal law that operates retroactively to the disadvantage of the accused. See Article I, Section 10.

▶ **Clause 4.** A capitation tax is literally a "head tax," a tax levied on each person in the population. A direct tax is one paid directly to the government by the taxpayer—for example, an income or a property tax; an indirect tax is one paid to another private party who then pays it to the government—for example, a sales tax. This provision was modified by the 16th Amendment (1913), giving Congress the power to levy "taxes on incomes, from whatever source derived."

▶ **Clause 5.** This provision was a part of the Commerce Compromise made by the Framers in 1787. Congress has the power to tax imported goods, however.

▶ **Clause 6.** All ports within the United States must be treated alike by Congress as it exercises its taxing and commerce powers. Congress cannot tax goods sent by water from one State to another, nor may it give the ports of one State any legal advantage over those of another.

▶ **Clause 7.** This clause gives Congress its vastly important "power of the purse," a major check on presidential power. Federal money can be spent only in those amounts and for those purposes expressly authorized by an act of Congress. All federal income and spending must be accounted for, regularly and publicly.

▶ **Clause 8.** This provision, preventing the establishment of a nobility, reflects the principle that "all men are created equal." It was also intended to discourage foreign attempts to bribe or otherwise corrupt officers of the government.

Section 10. Powers Denied to the States

▶ **Clause 1.** The States are not sovereign governments and so cannot make agreements or otherwise negotiate with foreign states; the power to conduct foreign relations is an exclusive power of the National Government. The power to coin money is also an exclusive power of the National Government. Several powers forbidden to the National Government are here also forbidden to the States.

▶ **Clause 2.** This provision relates to foreign, not interstate, commerce. Only Congress, not the States, can tax imports; and the States are, like Congress, forbidden the power to tax exports.

▶2. The Privilege of the Writ of Habeas Corpus shall not be suspended, unless when in Cases of Rebellion or Invasion the public safety may require it.

▶3. No Bill of Attainder or ex post facto Law shall be passed.

▶4. No Capitation, or other direct, Tax shall be laid, unless in Proportion to the Census of Enumeration hereinbefore directed to be taken.

▶5. No Tax or Duty shall be laid on Articles exported from any State.

▶6. No Preference shall be given by any Regulation of Commerce or Revenue to the Ports of one State over those of another: nor shall Vessels bound to, or from, one State, be obliged to enter, clear or pay Duties in another.

▶7. No Money shall be drawn from the Treasury, but in Consequence of Appropriations made by Law; and a regular Statement and Account of the Receipts and Expenditures of all public Money shall be published from time to time.

▶8. No Title of Nobility shall be granted by the United States: And no Person holding any Office of Profit or Trust under them, shall, without the Consent of the Congress, accept of any present, Emolument, Office, or Title, of any kind whatever, from any King, Prince, or foreign State.

Section 10.

▶1. No State shall enter into any Treaty, Alliance, or Confederation; grant Letters of Marque and Reprisal; coin Money; emit Bills of Credit; make any Thing but gold and silver Coin a Tender in Payment of Debts; pass any Bill of Attainder, ex post facto Law, or Law impairing the Obligation of Contracts, or grant any Title of Nobility.

▶2. No State shall, without the Consent of the Congress, lay any Imposts or Duties on Imports or Exports, except what may be absolutely necessary for executing its inspection Laws; and the net Produce of all Duties and Imposts, laid by any State on Imports or Exports, shall be for the Use of the Treasury of the United States; and all such Laws shall be subject to the Revision and Control of the Congress.

▶3. No State shall, without the Consent of Congress, lay any Duty of Tonnage, keep Troops, or Ships of War in time of Peace, enter into any Agreement or Compact with another State, or with a foreign Power, or engage in War, unless actually invaded, or in such imminent Danger as will not admit of delay.

▶ **Clause 3.** A duty of tonnage is a tax laid on ships according to their cargo capacity. Each State has a constitutional right to provide for and maintain a militia; but no State may keep a standing army or navy. The several restrictions here prevent the States from assuming powers that the Constitution elsewhere grants to the National Government.

Article II

Section 1.

Executive Department

Section 1. President and Vice President

▶1. The executive Power shall be vested in a President of the United States of America. He shall hold his Office during the Term of four Years, and, together with the Vice President, chosen for the same Term, be elected as follows:

▶ **Clause 1. Executive power, term** This clause gives to the President the very broad "executive power," the power to enforce the laws and otherwise administer the public policies of the United States. It also sets the length of the presidential (and vice-presidential) term of office; see the 22nd Amendment (1951), which places a limit on presidential (but not vice-presidential) tenure.

▶2. Each State shall appoint, in such Manner as the Legislature thereof may direct, a Number of Electors, equal to the whole Number of Senators and Representatives to which the State may be entitled in the Congress: but no Senator or Representative, or Person holding an Office of Trust or Profit, under the United States, shall be appointed an Elector.

▶ **Clause 2. Electoral college** This clause establishes the "electoral college," although the Constitution does not use that term. It is a body of presidential electors chosen in each State, and it selects the President and Vice President every four years. The number of electors chosen in each State equals the number of senators and representatives that State has in Congress.

▶3. The Electors shall meet in their respective States, and vote by Ballot for two Persons, of whom one at least shall not be an Inhabitant of the same State with themselves. And they shall make a List of all the Persons voted for, and of the Number of Votes for each; which List they shall sign and certify, and transmit sealed to the Seat of the Government of the United States, directed to the President of the Senate. The President of the Senate shall, in the Presence of the Senate and House of Representatives, open all the Certificates, and the Votes shall then be counted. The Person having the greatest Number of Votes shall be the President, if such Number be a majority of the whole Number of Electors appointed; and if there be more than one who have such Majority, and have an equal Number of Votes, then, the House of Representatives shall immediately choose by Ballot one of them for President; and if no Person have a Majority, then from the five highest on the List the said House shall in like Manner choose the President. But in choosing the President, the Votes shall be taken by States, the Representatives from each State having one Vote; a quorum for this Purpose shall consist of a Member or Members from two thirds of the States, and a Majority of all the States shall be necessary to a Choice. In every Case, after the Choice of the President, the Person having the greatest Number of Votes of the Electors shall be the Vice President. But if there should remain two or more who have equal Votes, the Senate shall choose from them by Ballot the Vice President.

▶ **Clause 3. Election of President and Vice President** This clause was replaced by the 12th Amendment in 1804.

▶ **Clause 4. Date** Congress has set the date for the choosing of electors as the Tuesday after the first Monday in November every fourth year, and for the casting of electoral votes as the Monday after the second Wednesday in December of that year.

▶ 4. The Congress may determine the Time of choosing the Electors, and the Day on which they shall give their Votes; which Day shall be the same throughout the United States.

▶ **Clause 5. Qualifications** The President must have been born a citizen of the United States, be at least 35 years old, and have been a resident of the United States for at least 14 years.

▶ 5. No Person except a natural born Citizen, or a Citizen of the United States, at the time of the Adoption of this Constitution, shall be eligible to the Office of President; neither shall any person be eligible to that Office who shall not have attained to the Age of thirty-five Years, and been fourteen Years a Resident within the United States.

▶ **Clause 6. Vacancy** This clause was modified by the 25th Amendment (1967), which provides expressly for the succession of the Vice President, for the filling of a vacancy in the Vice Presidency, and for the determination of presidential inability.

▶ 6. In Case of the Removal of the President from Office, or of his Death, Resignation, or Inability to discharge the Powers and Duties of the said Office, the Same shall devolve on the Vice President, and the Congress may by Law provide for the Case of Removal, Death, Resignation or Inability, both of the President and Vice President, declaring what Officer shall then act as President, and such Officer shall act accordingly, until the Disability be removed, or a President shall be elected.

▶ **Clause 7. Compensation** The President now receives a salary of $400,000 and a taxable expense account of $50,000 a year. Those amounts cannot be changed during a presidential term; thus, Congress cannot use the President's compensation as a bargaining tool to influence executive decisions. The phrase "any other emolument" means, in effect, any valuable gift; it does not mean that the President cannot be provided with such benefits of office as the White House, extensive staff assistance, and much else.

▶ 7. The President shall, at stated Times, receive for his Services, a Compensation, which shall neither be increased nor diminished during the Period for which he shall have been elected, and he shall not receive within that Period any other Emolument from the United States, or any of them.

▶ **Clause 8. Oath of office** The Chief Justice of the United States regularly administers this oath or affirmation, but any judicial officer may do so. Thus, Calvin Coolidge was sworn into office in 1923 by his father, a justice of the peace in Vermont.

▶ 8. Before he enter on the Execution of his Office, he shall take the following Oath or Affirmation:
"I do solemnly swear (or affirm) that I will faithfully execute the Office of President of the United States, and will to the best of my Ability, preserve, protect and defend the Constitution of the United States."

Section 2. President's Powers and Duties

▶ **Clause 1. Military, civil powers** The President, a civilian, heads the nation's armed forces, a key element in the Constitution's insistence on civilian control of the military. The President's power to "require the opinion, in writing" provides the constitutional basis for the Cabinet. The President's power to grant reprieves and pardons, the power of clemency, extends only to federal cases.

Section 2.

▶ 1. The President shall be Commander in Chief of the Army and Navy of the United States, and of the Militia of the several States, when called into the actual Service of the United States; he may require the Opinion, in writing, of the principal Officer in each of the executive Departments, upon any Subject relating to the Duties of their respective Offices, and he shall have Power to Grant Reprieves and Pardons for Offences against the United States, except in Cases of Impeachment.

▶ 2. He shall have Power, by and with the Advice and Consent of the Senate, to make Treaties, provided two thirds of the Senators present concur; and he shall nominate, and by and with the Advice and Consent of the Senate, shall appoint Ambassadors, other public Ministers and Consuls, Judges of the supreme Court, and all other Officers of the United States, whose Appointments are not herein otherwise provided for, and which shall be established by Law: but the Congress may by Law vest the Appointment of such inferior Officers, as they think proper, in the President alone, in the Courts of Law, or in the Heads of Departments.

▶ **Clause 2. Treaties, appointments** The President has the sole power to make treaties; to become effective, a treaty must be approved by a two-thirds vote in the Senate. In practice, the President can also make executive agreements with foreign governments; these pacts, which are frequently made and usually deal with routine matters, do not require Senate consent. The President appoints the principal officers of the executive branch and all federal judges; the "inferior officers" are those who hold lesser posts.

▶ 3. The President shall have Power to fill up all Vacancies that may happen during the Recess of the Senate, by granting Commissions which shall expire at the End of their next Session.

▶ **Clause 3. Recess appointments** When the Senate is not in session, appointments that require Senate consent can be made by the President on a temporary basis, as "recess appointments." Recess appointments are valid only to the end of the congressional term in which they are made.

Section 3.

He shall from time to time give to the Congress Information of the State of the Union, and recommend to their Consideration such Measures as he shall judge necessary and expedient; he may, on extraordinary Occasions, convene both Houses, or either of them, and in Case of Disagreement between them, with Respect to the Time of Adjournment, he may adjourn them to such Time as he shall think proper; he shall receive Ambassadors and other public Ministers; he shall take Care that the Laws be faithfully executed, and shall Commission all the Officers of the United States.

Section 3. President's Powers and Duties

The President delivers a State of the Union Message to Congress soon after that body convenes each year. That message is delivered to the nation's lawmakers and, importantly, to the American people, as well. It is shortly followed by the proposed federal budget and an economic report; and the President may send special messages to Congress at any time. In all of these communications, Congress is urged to take those actions the Chief Executive finds to be in the national interest. The President also has the power: to call special sessions of Congress; to adjourn Congress if its two houses cannot agree for that purpose; to receive the diplomatic representatives of other governments; to insure the proper execution of all federal laws; and to empower federal officers to hold their posts and perform their duties.

Section 4.

The President, Vice President and all Civil Officers of the United States, shall be removed from Office on Impeachment for and Conviction of, Treason, Bribery, or other high Crimes and Misdemeanors.

Section 4. Impeachment

The Constitution outlines the impeachment process in Article I, Section 2, Clause 5 and in Section 3, Clauses 6 and 7.

Article III

Section 1.

The judicial Power of the United States, shall be vested in one supreme Court, and in such inferior Courts as the Congress may from time to time ordain and establish. The Judges, both of the supreme and inferior Courts, shall hold their Offices during good Behaviour, and shall, at stated Times, receive for their Services, a Compensation, which shall not be diminished during their Continuance in Office.

Judicial Department

Section 1. Judicial Power, Courts, Terms of Office

The judicial power conferred here is the power of federal courts to hear and decide cases, disputes between the government and individuals and between private persons (parties). The Constitution creates only the Supreme Court of the United States; it gives to Congress the power to establish other, lower federal courts (Article I, Section 8, Clause 9) and to fix the size of the Supreme Court. The words "during good Behaviour" mean, in effect, for life.

Section 2. Jurisdiction

▶ **Clause 1. Cases to be heard** This clause sets out the jurisdiction of the federal courts; that is, it identifies those cases that may be tried in those courts. The federal courts can hear and decide—have jurisdiction over—a case depending on either the subject matter or the parties involved in that case. The jurisdiction of the federal courts in cases involving States was substantially restricted by the 11th Amendment in 1795.

Section 2.

▶1. The judicial Power shall extend to all Cases, in Law and Equity, arising under this Constitution, the Laws of the United States, and Treaties made, or which shall be made, under their Authority;— to all Cases affecting Ambassadors, other public ministers, and Consuls;— to all Cases of Admiralty and maritime Jurisdiction;— to Controversies to which the United States shall be a Party;— to Controversies between two or more States;— between a State and Citizens of another State;— between Citizens of different States;— between Citizens of the same State claiming Lands under Grants of different States, and between a State, or the Citizens thereof, and foreign States, Citizens, or Subjects.

▶ **Clause 2. Supreme Court jurisdiction** Original jurisdiction refers to the power of a court to hear a case in the first instance, not on appeal from a lower court. Appellate jurisdiction refers to a court's power to hear a case on appeal from a lower court, from the court in which the case was originally tried. This clause gives the Supreme Court both original and appellate jurisdiction. However, nearly all of the cases the High Court hears are brought to it on appeal from the lower federal courts and the highest State courts.

▶2. In all Cases affecting Ambassadors, other public Ministers and Consuls, and those in which a State shall be a Party, the supreme Court shall have original Jurisdiction. In all the other Cases before mentioned, the supreme Court shall have appellate Jurisdiction, both as to Law and Fact, with such Exceptions, and under such Regulations as the Congress shall make.

▶ **Clause 3. Jury trial in criminal cases** A person accused of a federal crime is guaranteed the right to trial by jury in a federal court in the State where the crime was committed; see the 5th and 6th amendments. The right to trial by jury in serious criminal cases in the State courts is guaranteed by the 6th and 14th amendments.

▶3. The trial of all Crimes, except in Cases of Impeachment, shall be by Jury; and such Trial shall be held in the State where the said Crimes shall have been committed; but when not committed within any State, the Trial shall be at such Place or Places as the Congress may by Law have directed.

Section 3. Treason

▶ **Clause 1. Definition** Treason is the only crime defined in the Constitution. The Framers intended the very specific definition here to prevent the loose use of the charge of treason—for example, against persons who criticize the government. Treason can be committed only in time of war and only by a citizen or a resident alien.

▶ **Clause 2. Punishment** Congress has provided that the punishment that a federal court may impose on a convicted traitor may range from a minimum of five years in prison and/or a $10,000 fine to a maximum of death; no person convicted of treason has ever been executed by the United States. No legal punishment can be imposed on the family or descendants of a convicted traitor. Congress has also made it a crime for any person (in either peace or wartime) to commit espionage or sabotage, to attempt to overthrow the government by force, or to conspire to do any of these things.

Section 3.

▶1. Treason against the United States shall consist only in levying War against them, or in adhering to their Enemies, giving them Aid and Comfort. No Person shall be convicted of Treason unless on the Testimony of two Witnesses to the same overt Act, or on Confession in open Court.

▶2. The Congress shall have Power to declare the Punishment of Treason, but no Attainder of Treason shall work Corruption of Blood, or Forfeiture except during the Life of the Person attainted.

Article IV

Section 1.

Full Faith and Credit shall be given in each State to the public Acts, Records, and judicial Proceedings of every other State. And the Congress may by general Laws prescribe the Manner in which such Acts, Records and Proceedings shall be proved, and the Effect thereof.

Section 2.

▶1. The Citizens of each State shall be entitled to all Privileges and Immunities of Citizens in the several States.

▶2. A Person charged in any State with Treason, Felony, or other Crime, who shall flee from justice, and be found in another State, shall on Demand of the executive Authority of the State from which he fled, be delivered up, to be removed to the State having Jurisdiction of the Crime.

▶3. No Person held to Service or Labor in one State, under the Laws thereof, escaping into another, shall, in Consequence of any Law or Regulation therein, be discharged from Service or Labor, but shall be delivered up on Claim of the Party to whom such Service or Labor may be due.

Section 3.

▶1. New States may be admitted by the Congress into this Union; but no new State shall be formed or erected within the Jurisdiction of any other State; nor any State be formed by the Junction of two or more States, or Parts of States, without the Consent of the Legislatures of the States concerned as well as of the Congress.

▶2. The Congress shall have Power to dispose of and make all needful Rules and Regulations respecting the Territory or other Property belonging to the United States; and nothing in this Constitution shall be so construed as to Prejudice any Claims of the United States, or of any particular State.

Section 4.

The United States shall guarantee to every State in this Union a Republican Form of Government, and shall protect each of them against Invasion; and on Application of the Legislature, or of the Executive (when the Legislature cannot be convened) against domestic Violence.

Relations Among States

Section 1. Full Faith and Credit

Each State must recognize the validity of the laws, public records, and court decisions of every other State.

Section 2. Privileges and Immunities of Citizens

▶ **Clause 1. Residents of other States** In effect, this clause means that no State may discriminate against the residents of other States; that is, a State's laws cannot draw unreasonable distinctions between its own residents and those of any of the other States. See Section 1 of the 14th Amendment.

▶ **Clause 2. Extradition** The process of returning a fugitive to another State is known as "interstate rendition" or, more commonly, "extradition." Usually, that process works routinely; some extradition requests are contested however—especially in cases with racial or political overtones. A governor may refuse to extradite a fugitive; but the federal courts can compel an unwilling governor to obey this constitutional command.

▶ **Clause 3. Fugitive slaves** This clause was nullified by the 13th Amendment, which abolished slavery in 1865.

Section 3. New States; Territories

▶ **Clause 1. New States** Only Congress can admit new States to the Union. A new State may not be created by taking territory from an existing State without the consent of that State's legislature. Congress has admitted 37 States since the original 13 formed the Union. Five States—Vermont, Kentucky, Tennessee, Maine, and West Virginia—were created from parts of existing States. Texas was an independent republic before admission. California was admitted after being ceded to the United States by Mexico. Each of the other 30 States entered the Union only after a period of time as an organized territory of the United States.

▶ **Clause 2. Territory, property** Congress has the power to make laws concerning the territories, other public lands, and all other property of the United States.

Section 4. Protection Afforded to States by the Nation

The Constitution does not define "a republican form of government," but the phrase is generally understood to mean a representative government. The Federal Government must also defend each State against attacks from outside its border and, at the request of a State's legislature or its governor, aid its efforts to put down internal disorders.

Provisions for Amendment

This section provides for the methods by which formal changes can be made in the Constitution. An amendment may be proposed in one of two ways: by a two-thirds vote in each house of Congress, or by a national convention called by Congress at the request of two-thirds of the State legislatures. A proposed amendment may be ratified in one of two ways: by three-fourths of the State legislatures, or by three-fourths of the States in conventions called for that purpose. Congress has the power to determine the method by which a proposed amendment may be ratified. The amendment process cannot be used to deny any State its equal representation in the United States Senate. To this point, 27 amendments have been adopted. To date, all of the amendments except the 21st Amendment were proposed by Congress and ratified by the State legislatures. Only the 21st Amendment was ratified by the convention method.

Article V

The Congress, whenever two thirds of both Houses shall deem it necessary, shall propose Amendments to this Constitution, or, on the Application of the Legislatures of two thirds of the several States, shall call a Convention for proposing Amendments, which, in either Case, shall be valid to all Intents and Purposes, as Part of this Constitution, when ratified by the Legislatures of three fourths of the several States, or by Conventions in three fourths thereof, as the one or the other Mode of Ratification may be proposed by the Congress; Provided that no Amendment which may be made prior to the Year One thousand eight hundred and eight shall in any Manner affect the first and fourth Clauses in the Ninth section of the first Article; and that no State, without its Consent, shall be deprived of its equal Suffrage in the Senate.

National Debts, Supremacy of National Law, Oath

Section 1. Validity of Debts

Congress had borrowed large sums of money during the Revolution and later during the Critical Period of the 1780s. This provision, a pledge that the new government would honor those debts, did much to create confidence in that government.

Section 2. Supremacy of National Law

This section sets out the Supremacy Clause, a specific declaration of the supremacy of federal law over any and all forms of State law. No State, including its local governments, may make or enforce any law that conflicts with any provision in the Constitution, an act of Congress, a treaty, or an order, rule, or regulation properly issued by the President or his subordinates in the executive branch.

Section 3. Oaths of Office

This provision reinforces the Supremacy Clause; all public officers, at every level in the United States, owe their first allegiance to the Constitution of the United States. No religious qualification can be imposed as a condition for holding any public office.

Article VI

Section 1.

All Debts contracted and Engagements entered into, before the Adoption of this Constitution, shall be as valid against the United States under this Constitution, as under the Confederation.

Section 2.

This Constitution, and the Laws of the United States which shall be made in Pursuance thereof; and all Treaties made, or which shall be made, under the Authority of the United States, shall be the supreme Law of the Land; and the Judges in every State shall be bound thereby, anything in the constitution or Laws of any State to the Contrary notwithstanding.

Section 3.

The Senators and Representatives before mentioned, and the Members of the several State legislatures, and all executive and judicial Officers, both of the United States and of the several States, shall be bound by Oath or Affirmation, to support this Constitution; but no religious Test shall ever be required as a Qualification to any Office or public Trust under the United States.

Ratification of Constitution

The proposed Constitution was signed by George Washington and 37 of his fellow Framers on September 17, 1787. (George Read of Delaware signed for himself and also for his absent colleague, John Dickinson.)

Article VII

The ratification of the Conventions of nine States, shall be sufficient for the Establishment of this Constitution between the States so ratifying the same.

Done in Convention by the Unanimous Consent of the States present the Seventeenth Day of September in the Year of our Lord one thousand seven hundred and Eighty-seven and of the Independence of the United States of America the twelfth. In witness whereof We have hereunto subscribed our Names.

Attest:
William Jackson,
Secretary
George Washington,
President and Deputy from Virginia

New Hampshire
John Langdon
Nicholas Gilman

Massachusetts
Nathaniel Gorham
Rufus King

Connecticut
William Samuel Johnson
Roger Sherman

New York
Alexander Hamilton

New Jersey
William Livingston
David Brearley
William Paterson
Jonathan Dayton

Pennsylvania
Benjamin Franklin
Thomas Mifflin
Robert Morris
George Clymer
Thomas Fitzsimons
Jared Ingersoll
James Wilson
Gouverneur Morris

Delaware
George Read
Gunning Bedford, Jr.
John Dickinson
Richard Bassett
Jacob Broom

Maryland
James McHenry
Daniel of St. Thomas Jenifer
Daniel Carroll

Virginia
John Blair
James Madison, Jr.

North Carolina
William Blount
Richard Dobbs Spaight
Hugh Williamson

South Carolina
John Rutledge
Charles Cotesworth Pinckney
Charles Pinckney
Pierce Butler

Georgia
William Few
Abraham Baldwin

The United States Constitution

Amendments

The first 10 amendments, the Bill of Rights, were each proposed by Congress on September 25, 1789, and ratified by the necessary three-fourths of the States on December 15, 1791. These amendments were originally intended to restrict the National Government—not the States. However, the Supreme Court has several times held that most of their provisions also apply to the States, through the 14th Amendment's Due Process Clause.

1st Amendment. Freedom of Religion, Speech, Press, Assembly, and Petition

The 1st Amendment sets out five basic liberties: The guarantee of freedom of religion is both a protection of religious thought and practice and a command of separation of church and state. The guarantees of freedom of speech and press assure to all persons a right to speak, publish, and otherwise express their views. The guarantees of the rights of assembly and petition protect the right to join with others in public meetings, political parties, interest groups, and other associations to discuss public affairs and influence public policy. None of these rights is guaranteed in absolute terms, however; like all other civil rights guarantees, each of them may be exercised only with regard to the rights of all other persons.

1st Amendment

Congress shall make no law respecting an establishment of religion, or prohibiting the free exercise thereof, or abridging the freedom of speech, or of the press; or the right of the people peaceably to assemble, and to petition the Government for a redress of grievances.

2nd Amendment. Bearing Arms

The right of the people to keep and bear arms was insured by the 2nd Amendment.

2nd Amendment

A well-regulated Militia being necessary to the security of a free State, the right of the people to keep and bear Arms, shall not be infringed.

3rd Amendment. Quartering of Troops

This amendment was intended to prevent what had been common British practice in the colonial period; see the Declaration of Independence. This provision is of virtually no importance today.

3rd Amendment.

No Soldier shall, in time of peace be quartered in any house, without the consent of the Owner, nor, in time of war, but in a manner to be prescribed by law.

4th Amendment. Searches and Seizures

The basic rule laid down by the 4th Amendment is this: Police officers have no general right to search for or seize evidence or seize (arrest) persons. Except in particular circumstances, they must have a proper warrant (a court order) obtained with probable cause (on reasonable grounds). This guarantee is reinforced by the exclusionary rule, developed by the Supreme Court: Evidence gained as the result of an unlawful search or seizure cannot be used at the court trial of the person from whom it was seized.

4th Amendment.

The right of the people to be secure in their persons, houses, papers, and effects, against unreasonable searches and seizures, shall not be violated, and no Warrants shall issue, but upon probable cause, supported by Oath or affirmation, and particularly describing the place to be searched, and the persons or things to be seized.

5th Amendment. Criminal Proceedings; Due Process; Eminent Domain

A person can be tried for a serious federal crime only if he or she has been indicted (charged, accused of that crime) by a grand jury. No one may be subjected to double jeopardy—that is, tried twice for the same crime. All persons are protected against self-incrimination; no person can be legally compelled to answer any question in any governmental proceeding if that answer could lead to that person's prosecution. The 5th Amendment's Due Process Clause prohibits unfair, arbitrary actions by the Federal Government; a like prohibition is set out against the States in the 14th Amendment. Government may take private property for a legitimate public purpose; but when it exercises that power of eminent domain, it must pay a fair price for the property seized.

5th Amendment.

No person shall be held to answer for a capital, or otherwise infamous crime, unless on a presentment or indictment of a Grand Jury, except in cases arising in the land or naval forces, or in the Militia, when in actual service in time of War, or public danger; nor shall any person be subject for the same offence to be twice put in jeopardy of life or limb; nor shall be compelled in any criminal case to be a witness against himself, nor be deprived of life, liberty, or property, without due process of law; nor shall private property be taken for public use, without just compensation.

6th Amendment

In all criminal prosecutions, the accused shall enjoy the right to a speedy and public trial, by an impartial jury of the State and district wherein the crime shall have been committed, which district shall have been previously ascertained by law, and to be informed of the nature and cause of the accusation; to be confronted with the witnesses against him; to have compulsory process for obtaining witnesses in his favor, and to have the Assistance of Counsel for his defence.

6th Amendment. Criminal Proceedings

A person accused of crime has the right to be tried in court without undue delay and by an impartial jury; see Article III, Section 2, Clause 3. The defendant must be informed of the charge upon which he or she is to be tried, has the right to cross-examine hostile witnesses, and has the right to require the testimony of favorable witnesses. The defendant also has the right to be represented by an attorney at every stage in the criminal process.

7th Amendment

In Suits at common law, where the value in controversy shall exceed twenty dollars, the right of trial by jury shall be preserved, and no fact tried by a jury, shall be otherwise re-examined in any Court of the United States, than according to the rules of the common law.

7th Amendment. Civil Trials

This amendment applies only to civil cases heard in federal courts. A civil case does not involve criminal matters; it is a dispute between private parties or between the government and a private party. The right to trial by jury is guaranteed in any civil case in a federal court if the amount of money involved in that case exceeds $20 (most cases today involve a much larger sum); that right may be waived (relinquished, put aside) if both parties agree to a bench trial (a trial by a judge, without a jury).

8th Amendment

Excessive bail shall not be required, nor excessive fines imposed, nor cruel and unusual punishment inflicted.

8th Amendment. Punishment for Crimes

Bail is the sum of money that a person accused of crime may be required to post (deposit with the court) as a guarantee that he or she will appear in court at the proper time. The amount of bail required and/or a fine imposed as punishment must bear a reasonable relationship to the seriousness of the crime involved in the case. The prohibition of cruel and unusual punishment forbids any punishment judged to be too harsh, too severe for the crime for which it is imposed.

9th Amendment

The enumeration in the Constitution, of certain rights, shall not be construed to deny or disparage others retained by the people.

9th Amendment. Unenumerated Rights

The fact that the Constitution sets out many civil rights guarantees, expressly provides for many protections against government, does not mean that there are not other rights also held by the people.

10th Amendment

The powers not delegated to the United States by the Constitution, nor prohibited by it to the States, are reserved to the States respectively, or to the people.

10th Amendment. Powers Reserved to the States

This amendment identifies the area of power that may be exercised by the States. All of those powers the Constitution does not grant to the National Government, and at the same time does not forbid to the States, belong to each of the States, or to the people of each State.

11th Amendment. Suits Against States

Proposed by Congress March 4, 1794; ratified February 7, 1795, but official announcement of the ratification was delayed until January 8, 1798. This amendment repealed part of Article III, Section 2, Clause 1. No State may be sued in a federal court by a resident of another State or of a foreign country; the Supreme Court has long held that this provision also means that a State cannot be sued in a federal court by a foreign country or, more importantly, even by one of its own residents.

11th Amendment

The Judicial power of the United States shall not be construed to extend to any suit in law or equity, commenced or prosecuted against one of the United States by Citizens of another State, or by Citizens or Subjects of any Foreign State.

12th Amendment. Election of President and Vice President

Proposed by Congress December 9, 1803; ratified June 15, 1804. This amendment replaced Article II, Section 1, Clause 3. Originally, each elector cast two ballots, each for a different person for President. The person with the largest number of electoral votes, provided that number was a majority of the electors, was to become President; the person with the second highest number was to become Vice President. This arrangement produced an electoral vote tie between Thomas Jefferson and Aaron Burr in 1800; the House finally chose Jefferson as President in 1801. The 12th Amendment separated the balloting for President and Vice President; each elector now casts one ballot for someone as President and a second ballot for another person as Vice President. Note that the 20th Amendment changed the date set here (March 4) to January 20, and that the 23rd Amendment (1961) provides for electors from the District of Columbia. This amendment also provides that the Vice President must meet the same qualifications as those set out for the President in Article II, Section 1, Clause 5.

12th Amendment

The Electors shall meet in their respective States and vote by ballot for President and Vice President, one of whom, at least, shall not be an inhabitant of the same State with themselves; they shall name in their ballots the person voted for as President, and in distinct ballots the person voted for as Vice President, and they shall make distinct lists of all persons voted for as President, and of all persons voted for as Vice President, and of the number of votes for each, which lists they shall sign and certify, and transmit sealed to the seat of the government of the United States, directed to the President of the Senate;— The President of the Senate shall, in the presence of the Senate and the House of Representatives, open all the certificates and the votes shall then be counted;— the person having the greatest Number of votes for President shall be the President, if such number be a majority of the whole number of Electors appointed; and if no person have such a majority, then, from the persons having the highest numbers not exceeding three on the list of those voted for as President, the House of Representatives shall choose immediately, by ballot, the President. But in choosing the President, the votes shall be taken by States, the representation from each State having one vote; a quorum for this purpose shall consist of a member or members from two thirds of the States, and a majority of all the States shall be necessary to a choice. And if the House of Representatives shall not choose a President whenever the right of choice shall devolve upon them, before the fourth day of March next following, then the Vice President shall act as President, as in case of death or other constitutional disability of the President. The person having the greatest number of votes as Vice President, shall be the Vice President, if such number be a majority of the whole number of Electors appointed, and if no person have a majority, then from the two highest numbers on the list, the Senate shall choose the Vice President; a quorum for the purpose shall consist of two thirds of the whole number of Senators, a majority of the whole number shall be necessary to a choice. But no person constitutionally ineligible to the office of President shall be eligible to that of Vice-President of the United States.

13th Amendment. Slavery and Involuntary Servitude

Proposed by Congress January 31, 1865; ratified December 6, 1865. This amendment forbids slavery in the United States and in any area under its control. It also forbids other forms of forced labor, except punishments for crime; but some forms of compulsory service are not prohibited—for example, service on juries or in the armed forces. Section 2 gives to Congress the power to carry out the provisions of Section 1 of this amendment.

13th Amendment

Section 1. Neither slavery nor involuntary servitude, except as a punishment for crime whereof the party shall have been duly convicted, shall exist within the United States, or any place subject to their jurisdiction.

Section 2. Congress shall have power to enforce this article by appropriate legislation.

14th Amendment

Section 1. All persons born or naturalized in the United States and subject to the jurisdiction thereof, are citizens of the United States and of the State wherein they reside. No State shall make or enforce any law which shall abridge the privileges or immunities of citizens of the United States; nor shall any State deprive any person of life, liberty, or property, without due process of law; nor deny to any person within its jurisdiction the equal protection of the laws.

14th Amendment. Rights of Citizens

Proposed by Congress June 13, 1866; ratified July 9, 1868. Section 1 defines citizenship. It provides for the acquisition of United States citizenship by birth or by naturalization. Citizenship at birth is determined according to the principle of jus soli—"the law of the soil," where born; naturalization is the legal process by which one acquires a new citizenship at some time after birth. Under certain circumstances, citizenship can also be gained at birth abroad, according to the principle of jus sanguinis—"the law of the blood," to whom born. This section also contains two major civil rights provisions: the Due Process Clause forbids a State (and its local governments) to act in any unfair or arbitrary way; the Equal Protection Clause forbids a State (and its local governments) to discriminate against, draw unreasonable distinctions between, persons.

Most of the rights set out against the National Government in the first eight amendments have been extended against the States (and their local governments) through Supreme Court decisions involving the 14th Amendment's Due Process Clause.

Section 2. Representatives shall be apportioned among the several States according to their respective numbers, counting the whole number of persons in each State, excluding Indians not taxed. But when the right to vote at any election for the choice of electors for President and Vice President of the United States, Representatives in Congress, the Executive and Judicial officers of a State, or the members of the Legislature thereof, is denied to any of the male inhabitants of such State, being twenty-one years of age and citizens of the United States, or in any way abridged, except for participation in rebellion, or other crime, the basis of representation therein shall be reduced in the proportion which the number of such male citizens shall bear to the whole number of male citizens twenty-one years of age in such State.

The first sentence here replaced Article I, Section 2, Clause 3, the Three-Fifths Compromise provision. Essentially, all persons in the United States are counted in each decennial census, the basis for the distribution of House seats. The balance of this section has never been enforced and is generally thought to be obsolete.

Section 3. No person shall be a Senator or Representative in Congress, or elector of President and Vice President, or hold any office, civil or military, under the United States, or under any State, who, having previously taken an oath, as a member of Congress, or as an officer of the United States, or as a member of any State legislature, or as an executive or judicial officer of any State, to support the Constitution of the United States, shall have engaged in insurrection or rebellion against the same, or given aid or comfort to the enemies thereof. But Congress may, by a vote of two thirds of each House, remove such disability.

This section limited the President's power to pardon those persons who had led the Confederacy during the Civil War. Congress finally removed this disability in 1898.

Section 4. The validity of the public debt of the United States, authorized by law, including debts incurred for payment of pensions and bounties for services in suppressing insurrection or rebellion, shall not be questioned. But neither the United States nor any State shall assume or pay any debt or obligation incurred in aid of insurrection or rebellion against the United States, or any claim for the loss or emancipation of any slave; but all such debts, obligations and claims shall be held illegal and void.

Section 4 also dealt with matters directly related to the Civil War. It reaffirmed the public debt of the United States; but it invalidated, prohibited payment of, any debt contracted by the Confederate States and also prohibited any compensation of former slave owners.

Section 5. The Congress shall have power to enforce, by appropriate legislation, the provisions of this article.

15th Amendment. Right to Vote—Race, Color, Servitude

Proposed by Congress February 26, 1869; ratified February 3, 1870. The phrase "previous condition of servitude" refers to slavery. Note that this amendment does not guarantee the right to vote to African Americans, or to anyone else. Instead, it forbids the States from discriminating against any person on the grounds of his "race, color, or previous condition of servitude" in the setting of suffrage qualifications.

15th Amendment

Section 1. The right of citizens of the United States to vote shall not be denied or abridged by the United States or by any State on account of race, color, or previous condition of servitude.

Section 2. The Congress shall have power to enforce this article by appropriate legislation.

16th Amendment. Income Tax

Proposed by Congress July 12, 1909; ratified February 3, 1913. This amendment modified two provisions in Article I, Section 2, Clause 3, and Section 9, Clause 4. It gives to Congress the power to levy an income tax, a direct tax, without regard to the populations of any of the States.

16th Amendment

The Congress shall have power to lay and collect taxes on incomes, from whatever source derived, without apportionment among the several States, and without regard to any census or enumeration.

17th Amendment. Popular Election of Senators

Proposed by Congress May 13, 1912; ratified April 8, 1913. This amendment repealed those portions of Article I, Section 3, Clauses 1 and 2 relating to the election of senators. Senators are now elected by the voters in each State. If a vacancy occurs, the governor of the State involved must call an election to fill the seat; the governor may appoint a senator to serve until the next election, if the State's legislature has authorized that step.

17th Amendment

The Senate of the United States shall be composed of two Senators from each State, elected by the people thereof, for six years; and each Senator shall have one vote. The electors in each State shall have the qualifications requisite for electors of the most numerous branch of the State legislatures.

When vacancies happen in the representation of any State in the Senate, the executive authority of such State shall issue writs of election to fill such vacancies: Provided, That the legislature of any State may empower the executive thereof to make temporary appointments until the people fill the vacancies by election as the legislature may direct.

This amendment shall not be so construed as to affect the election or term of any Senator chosen before it becomes valid as part of the Constitution.

18th Amendment. Prohibition of Intoxicating Liquors

Proposed by Congress December 18, 1917; ratified January 16, 1919. This amendment outlawed the making, selling, transporting, importing, or exporting of alcoholic beverages in the United States. It was repealed in its entirety by the 21st Amendment in 1933.

18th Amendment.

Section 1. After one year from the ratification of this article the manufacture, sale, or transportation of intoxicating liquors within, the importation thereof into, or the exportation thereof from the United States and all territory subject to the jurisdiction thereof for beverage purposes is hereby prohibited.

Section 2. The Congress and the several States shall have concurrent power to enforce this article by appropriate legislation.

Section 3. This article shall be inoperative unless it shall have been ratified as an amendment to the Constitution by the legislatures of the several States, as provided in the Constitution, within seven years of the date of the submission hereof to the States by Congress.

19th Amendment. Equal Suffrage—Sex

Proposed by Congress June 4, 1919; ratified August 18, 1920. No person can be denied the right to vote in any election in the United States on account of his or her sex.

19th Amendment

The right of citizens of the United States to vote shall not be denied or abridged by the United States or by any State on account of sex.

Congress shall have power to enforce this article by appropriate legislation.

20th Amendment

Section 1. The terms of the President and Vice President shall end at noon on the 20th day of January, and the terms of Senators and Representatives at noon on the 3d day of January, of the years in which such terms would have ended if this article had not been ratified; and the terms of their successors shall then begin.

Section 2. The Congress shall assemble at least once in every year, and such meeting shall begin at noon on the 3d day of January, unless they shall by law appoint a different day.

Section 3. If, at the time fixed for the beginning of the term of the President, the President elect shall have died, the Vice President elect shall become President. If a President shall not have been chosen before the time fixed for the beginning of his term, or if the President-elect shall have failed to qualify, then the Vice President elect shall act as President until a President shall have qualified; and the Congress may by law provide for the case wherein neither a President elect nor a Vice President elect shall have qualified, declaring who shall then act as President, or the manner in which one who is to act shall be selected, and such person shall act accordingly until a President or Vice President shall have qualified.

Section 4. The Congress may by law provide for the case of the death of any of the persons from whom the House of Representatives may choose a President whenever the right of choice shall have devolved upon them, and for the case of the death of any of the persons from whom the Senate may choose a Vice President whenever the right of choice shall have devolved upon them.

Section 5. Sections 1 and 2 shall take effect on the 15th day of October following the ratification of this article.

Section 6. This article shall be inoperative unless it shall have been ratified as an amendment to the Constitution by the legislatures of three fourths of the several States within seven years from the date of its submission.

20th Amendment. Commencement of Terms; Sessions of Congress; Death or Disqualification of President-Elect

Proposed by Congress March 2, 1932; ratified January 23, 1933. The provisions of Sections 1 and 2 relating to Congress modified Article I, Section 4, Clause 2, and those provisions relating to the President, the 12th Amendment. The date on which the President and Vice President now take office was moved from March 4 to January 20. Similarly, the members of Congress now begin their terms on January 3. The 20th Amendment is sometimes called the "Lame Duck Amendment" because it shortened the period of time a member of Congress who was defeated for reelection (a "lame duck") remains in office.

This section deals with certain possibilities that were not covered by the presidential selection provisions of either Article II or the 12th Amendment. To this point, none of these situations has occurred. Note that there is neither a President-elect nor a Vice President-elect until the electoral votes have been counted by Congress, or, if the electoral college cannot decide the matter, the House has chosen a President or the Senate has chosen a Vice President.

Congress has not in fact ever passed such a law. See Section 2 of the 25th Amendment, regarding a vacancy in the vice presidency; that provision could some day have an impact here.

Section 5 set the date on which this amendment came into force.

Section 6 placed a time limit on the ratification process; note that a similar provision was written into the 18th, 21st, and 22nd amendments.

21st Amendment

Section 1. The eighteenth article of amendment to the Constitution of the United States is hereby repealed.

Section 2. The transportation or importation into any State, Territory, or possession of the United States for delivery or use therein of intoxicating liquors, in violation of the laws thereof, is hereby prohibited.

Section 3. This article shall be inoperative unless it shall have been ratified as an amendment to the Constitution by conventions in the several States, as provided in the Constitution, within seven years from the date of the submission hereof to the States by the Congress.

21st Amendment. Repeal of 18th Amendment

Proposed by Congress February 20, 1933; ratified December 5, 1933. This amendment repealed all of the 18th Amendment. Section 2 modifies the scope of the Federal Government's commerce power set out in Article I, Section 8, Clause 3; it gives to each State the power to regulate the transportation or importation and the distribution or use of intoxicating liquors in ways that would be unconstitutional in the case of any other commodity. The 21st Amendment is the only amendment Congress has thus far submitted to the States for ratification by conventions.

22nd Amendment. Presidential Tenure

Proposed by Congress March 21, 1947; ratified February 27, 1951. This amendment modified Article II, Section I, Clause 1. It stipulates that no President may serve more than two elected terms. But a President who has succeeded to the office beyond the midpoint in a term to which another President was originally elected may serve for more than eight years. In any case, however, a President may not serve more than 10 years. Prior to Franklin Roosevelt, who was elected to four terms, no President had served more than two full terms in office.

22nd Amendment

Section 1. No person shall be elected to the office of the President more than twice, and no person who has held the office of President, or acted as President, for more than two years of a term to which some other person was elected President shall be elected to the office of the President more than once. But this Article shall not apply to any person holding the office of President, when this Article was proposed by the Congress, and shall not prevent any person who may be holding the office of President, or acting as President, during the term within which this Article becomes operative from holding the office of President or acting as President during the remainder of such term.

Section 2. This article shall be inoperative unless it shall have been ratified as an amendment to the Constitution by the legislatures of three fourths of the several states within seven years from the date of its submission to the States by the Congress.

23rd Amendment. Presidential Electors for the District of Columbia

Proposed by Congress June 16, 1960; ratified March 29, 1961. This amendment modified Article II, Section I, Clause 2 and the 12th Amendment. It included the voters of the District of Columbia in the presidential electorate; and provides that the District is to have the same number of electors as the least populous State—three electors—but no more than that number.

23rd Amendment.

Section 1. The District constituting the seat of Government of the United States shall appoint in such manner as the Congress may direct:

A number of electors of President and Vice President equal to the whole number of Senators and Representatives in Congress to which the District would be entitled if it were a State, but in no event more than the least populous State; they shall be in addition to those appointed by the States, they shall be considered, for the purposes of the election of President and Vice President, to be electors appointed by a State; and they shall meet in the District and perform such duties as provided by the twelfth article of amendment.

24th Amendment. Right to Vote in Federal Elections—Tax Payment

Proposed by Congress August 27, 1962; ratified January 23, 1964. This amendment outlawed the payment of any tax as a condition for taking part in the nomination or election of any federal officeholder.

24th Amendment.

Section 1. The right of citizens of the United States to vote in any primary or other election for President or Vice President, for electors for President or Vice President, or for Senator or Representative in Congress, shall not be denied or abridged by the United States or any State by reason of failure to pay any poll tax or other tax.

Section 2. The Congress shall have power to enforce this article by appropriate legislation.

25th Amendment. Presidential Succession, Vice Presidential Vacancy, Presidential Inability

Proposed by Congress July 6, 1965; ratified February 10, 1967. Section 1 revised the imprecise provision on presidential succession in Article II, Section 1, Clause 6. It affirmed the precedent set by Vice President John Tyler, who became President on the death of William Henry Harrison in 1841. Section 2 provides for the filling of a vacancy in the office of Vice President. The office had been vacant on 16 occasions and remained unfilled for the rest of each term involved. When Spiro Agnew resigned the office in 1973, President Nixon selected Gerald Ford per this provision; and, when President Nixon resigned in 1974, Gerald Ford became President and chose Nelson Rockefeller as Vice President.

25th Amendment.

Section 1. In case of the removal of the President from office or of his death or resignation, the Vice President shall become President.

Section 2. Whenever there is a vacancy in the office of the Vice President, the President shall nominate a Vice President who shall take office upon confirmation by a majority vote of both Houses of Congress.

Section 3. Whenever the President transmits to the President pro tempore of the Senate and the Speaker of the House of Representatives his written declaration that he is unable to discharge the powers and duties of his office, and until he transmits to them a written declaration to the contrary, such powers and duties shall be discharged by the Vice President as Acting President.

This section created a procedure for determining if a President is so incapacitated that he cannot perform the powers and duties of his office.

Section 4. Whenever the Vice President and a majority of either the principal officers of the executive departments or of such other body as Congress may by law provide, transmit to the President pro tempore of the Senate and the Speaker of the House of Representatives their written declaration that the President is unable to discharge the powers and duties of his office, the Vice President shall immediately assume the powers and duties of the office as Acting President.

Thereafter, when the President transmits to the President pro tempore of the Senate and the Speaker of the House of Representatives his written declaration that no inability exists, he shall resume the powers and duties of his office unless the Vice President and a majority of either the principal officers of the executive department or of such other body as Congress may by law provide, transmit within four days to the President pro tempore of the Senate and the Speaker of the House of Representatives their written declaration that the President is unable to discharge the powers and duties of his office. Thereupon Congress shall decide the issue, assembling within forty-eight hours for that purpose if not in session. If the Congress, within twenty-one days after receipt of the latter written declaration, or, if Congress is not in session, within twenty-one days after Congress is required to assemble, determines by two-thirds vote of both Houses that the President is unable to discharge the powers and duties of his office, the Vice President shall continue to discharge the same as Acting President; otherwise, the President shall resume the powers and duties of his office.

Section 4 deals with the circumstance in which a President will not be able to determine the fact of incapacity. To this point, Congress has not established the "such other body" referred to here. This section contains the only typographical error in the Constitution; in its second paragraph, the word "department" should in fact read "departments."

26th Amendment.

Section 1. The right of citizens of the United States, who are eighteen years of age or older, to vote shall not be denied or abridged by the United States or by any State on account of age.

Section 2. The Congress shall have the power to enforce this article by appropriate legislation.

26th Amendment. Right to Vote—Age

Proposed by Congress March 23, 1971; ratified July 1, 1971. This amendment provides that the minimum age for voting in any election in the United States cannot be more than 18 years. (A State may set a minimum voting age of less than 18, however.)

27th Amendment.

No law varying the compensation for the services of the Senators and Representatives, shall take effect, until an election of Representatives shall have intervened.

27th Amendment. Congressional Pay

Proposed by Congress September 25, 1789; ratified May 7, 1992. This amendment modified Article I, Section 6, Clause 1. It limits Congress's power to fix the salaries of its members—by delaying the effectiveness of any increase in that pay until after the next regular congressional election.

PEARSON realize
PearsonSchool.com/CASS

Go online to PearsonSchool.com/CASS and use the texts, quizzes, interactivities, Interactive Reading Notepads, Flipped Videos, and other resources from this Topic to prepare for the Topic Test.

- Etexts
- Quizzes
- Interactivities
- Interactive Reading Notepads
- Flipped Videos

While online you can also check the progress you've made learning the topic and course content by viewing your grades, test scores, and assignment status.

Sequence

Sequence means "order," and placing things in the correct order is very important. What would happen if you tried to put toppings on a pizza before you put down the dough for the crust? When studying history, you need to analyze the information by sequencing significant events, individuals, and time periods in order to understand them. Practice this skill by using the reading below. Which words indicate sequence?

> **The Persian Empire** Before modern times, Iran was called Persia. Ancient Persia was influenced by Mesopotamian civilization, in modern-day Iraq. Around 550 B.C., the Persian king Cyrus the Great conquered the Babylonian empire, in Mesopotamia, and many other lands. He created the Persian empire.
>
> Cyrus and the rulers who followed him spread Persian control from modern Pakistan and Afghanistan in the east to modern Turkey, Cyprus, and Egypt in the west. This empire lasted about two hundred years. A Persian ruler was called the King of Kings, or the Great King.

[1.] Identify the topic and the main events that relate to the topic. Quickly skim titles and headings to determine the topic of the passage. As you read the passage, write a list of significant events, individuals, or time periods related to the topic.

[2.] Note any dates and time words such as "before" and "after" that indicate the chronological order of events. Look through your list of events, individuals, or time periods and write down the date for each. This will give you information to apply absolute chronology by sequencing the events, individuals, or time periods. Remember that some events may have taken place over a number of months or years. Is your date the time when the event started or ended? Make sure to note enough details that you can remember the importance of the information. If no date is given, look for words such as "before" or "after" that can tell you where to place this event, time period, or individual compared to others on your list. This will allow you to apply relative chronology by sequencing the events, individuals, or time periods.

[3.] Determine the time range of the events. Place the events in chronological order on a timeline. Look for the earliest and latest events, individuals, or time periods on your list. The span of time between the first and last entries gives you the time range. To apply absolute chronology, sequence the entries by writing the date of the first event on the left side of a piece of paper and the date of the last event on the right side. Draw a line connecting the two events. This will be your timeline. Once you have drawn your timeline, put the events in order by date along the line. Label their dates. To apply relative chronology, sequence the significant individuals, events, or time periods on an undated timeline, in the order that they happened. You now have a clear image of the important events related to this topic. You can organize and interpret information from visuals by analyzing the information and applying absolute or relative chronology to the events. This will help you understand the topic better when you can see how events caused or led to other events. You will also be able to analyze information by developing connections between historical events over time.

Categorize

When you analyze information by categorizing, you create a system that helps you sort items into categories, or groups with shared characteristics, so that you can understand the information. Categorizing helps you see what groups of items have in common. What categories are shown on the chart below? Name at least one challenge you would list under each category. Then create your own chart following the steps below.

Foreign Policy Challenge	Economic Challenge

[1.] Identify similarities and differences among items you need to understand. You need to pay careful attention and sometimes do research to find the similarities and differences among the facts, topics, or objects that you need to understand. Scientists find groups, or categories, of related animals by analyzing the details of the animals' bodies. For example, insects with similar wings, legs, and mouthparts probably belong in the same category. Gather similar information about all the things you need to understand. For example, if you know the location of one thing, try to find the locations of all the things you are studying. If you have different types of information about your topics, you will not be able to group them easily.

[2.] Create a system to group items with common characteristics. Once you have gathered similar kinds of information on the items you need to understand, look for items that share characteristics or features. Create categories based on a feature shared by all of the facts, topics, or objects you need to understand. For example, if you have gathered information on the population and political systems of several countries, you could categorize them by the size of their population or their type of political system.

[3.] Form the groupings. Put each of the items that you are studying into one of the categories that you have created. If some items do not fit, you may need to make a new category or modify your categories. Label each category for the characteristic shared by its members. Examples of labels for categories might include "Countries with more than 100 million people," "Countries with fewer than 1 million people," "Democracies," or "Dictatorships."

Analyze Cause and Effect

When you analyze information by identifying cause-and-effect relationships, you find how one event leads to the next. It is important to find evidence that one event caused another. If one event happened earlier than another, it did not necessarily cause the later event. Understanding causes and effects can help you solve problems. Practice this skill as you read the text below. What words in the text indicate the causes of the end of communism in the Soviet Union and the eastern bloc? Which indicate effects?

> Economic stagnation, external pressure from the West, and internal dissent eroded the Soviet bloc. In the 1980s, the reformist Soviet leader Mikhail Gorbachev pushed both *perestroika*, a wide-ranging restructuring of political and economic life, and *glasnost*, a policy of openness where the Soviet government increased its tolerance of dissent and freedom of expression. The hunger for openness spread to the central European Soviet bloc countries. In 1989, the Polish reform party Solidarity competed in parliamentary elections, Hungarians enjoyed the freedom to visit Austria, and pro-democratic protests in East Germany led Communist governments to fold throughout the region.

[1.] Choose a starting point of observation. When trying to understand a historical event, choose the time of that event. If you are trying to understand a current event, you can work backward from a starting point in the present.

[2.] Consider earlier events to try to find connections to your starting point, including any language that signals causes. Put the evidence together to identify true causes. When reading, look for events that come before your starting point. Analyze whether these earlier events caused later events. Identify words that signal cause, such as "reason," "because," and "led to." Analyze the information by developing connections between historical events. Make sure that there is evidence showing that the earlier events caused the later events and did not just happen earlier.

[3.] Consider later events to try to find connections to your starting point, including any language that signals effects. Put the evidence together to determine true effects. Look for events that come after your starting point. Analyze the information in order to determine whether these later events are effects of earlier events. Identify words that signal effect, such as "led to," "so," and "therefore." Make sure that there is evidence showing that these later events were caused by earlier events and did not just happen later.

[4.] Summarize the cause-and-effect relationship and draw conclusions. Once you have identified the cause-and-effect relationships between different events, describe these relationships. Draw a diagram that develops the connections between the two historical events. Draw conclusions about any relationships that you see.

Compare and Contrast

When you analyze information by comparing and contrasting two or more things, you look for similarities and differences between them. This skill helps you understand the things that you are comparing and contrasting. It is also a skill that you can use in making choices. Practice this skill as you study the Venn diagram comparing socialism and communism. What words would you use to compare and contrast the two economic systems?

COMPARING AND CONTRASTING SOCIALISM AND COMMUNISM

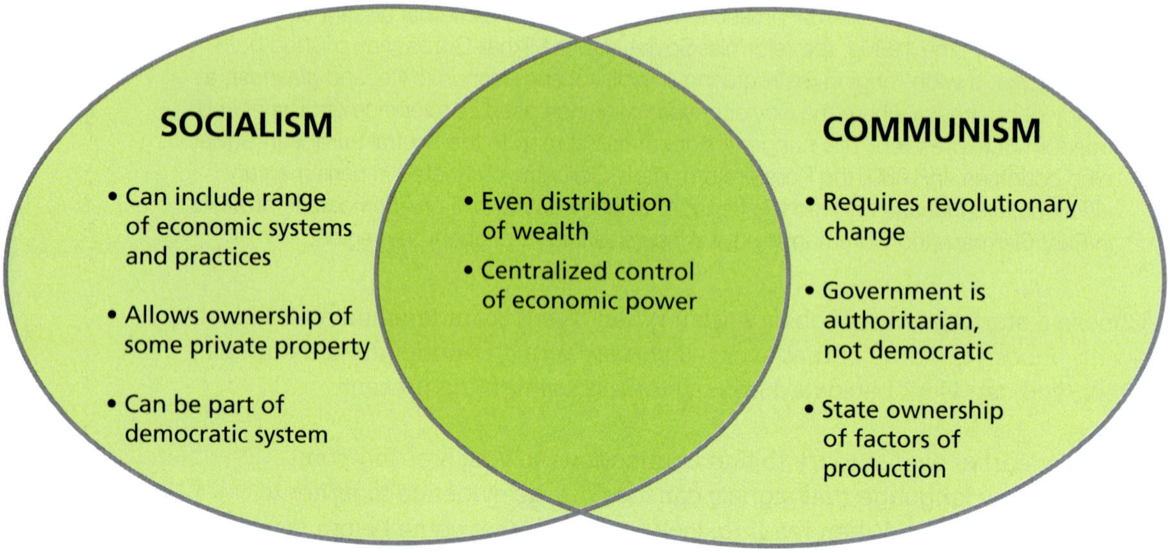

[1.] Look for related topics and characteristics that describe them. When you are looking for similarities and differences between two things, it can help to start by identifying relationships between them. What do the two things have in common? If two things have nothing in common, such as a dog and a piece of pie, it will be difficult to find similarities or differences. On the other hand, you can compare and contrast two countries or political systems. Look through the information you have on the things or topics you want to compare and contrast, and identify the characteristics, or features, that describe those things or topics.

[2.] Look for words that signal comparison ("both," "similar to," "also") or contrast ("unlike," "different," "instead"). Look for words that show comparison, or similarity, and those that show contrast, or difference. Take notes on these similarities and differences. This will make it possible to analyze information more quickly.

[3.] Identify similarities and differences in the topics, and draw conclusions about them. Look through your notes and analyze the ways in which your topics are similar and different. Usually, topics have both similarities and differences. Try to find patterns in these similarities and differences. For example, all the similarities between two countries might be related to climate, and all the differences might be related to economics. Draw conclusions based on these patterns. In this example, you might conclude that a country's economy does not depend on its climate. Identifying similarities and differences by comparing and contrasting two topics lets you draw conclusions that help you analyze both topics as well as other topics like them.

Identify Main Ideas and Details

You can analyze information in a selection by finding the main idea. A main idea is the most important point in a selection. Identifying the main idea will help you remember details, such as names, dates, and events, which should support the main idea. Practice this skill by reading the paragraph on this page. Find the main idea of this paragraph and the supporting details.

> During his first hundred days in office, which became known as the Hundred Days, Roosevelt proposed and Congress passed 15 major bills. These measures had three goals: relief, recovery, and reform. Roosevelt wanted to provide relief from the immediate hardships of the depression and achieve a long-term economic recovery. He also instituted reforms to prevent future depressions.

[1.] Scan titles, headings, and visuals before reading to see what the selection is about. Often, important ideas are included in titles, headings, and other special text. Special text may be primary sources, words that are highlighted, or ideas listed with bullet points. Also, take a look at visuals and captions. By analyzing these parts of the text, you should quickly get a sense of the main idea of the article.

[2.] Read the selection and then identify the main point of the selection, the point that the rest of the selection supports: this is the main idea. Read through the selection to identify the main idea. Sometimes, the main idea will be the first or second sentence of one of the first few paragraphs. Sometimes, it will be the last sentence of the first paragraph. Other times, no single sentence will tell you the main idea. You will have to come up with your own sentence answering the question, "What is the main point of this selection?"

[3.] Find details or statements within the selection that support or build on the main idea. Once you have identified the main idea, look for details that support the main idea. Many or most of the details should be related to the main idea. If you find that many of the details are not related to what you think is the main idea, you may not have identified the main idea correctly. Identify the main idea that the details in the selection support. Analyze the information in the text by finding the main idea and supporting details.

Summarize

When you analyze information by summarizing, you restate the main points of a passage in your own words. Using your own words helps you understand the information. Summarizing will help you understand a text and prepare for tests or assignments based on the text. Practice this skill by follow the steps to summarize the excerpt below.

> One of the most terrifying aspects of the Cold War was the arms race that began right after World War II. At first, the United States was the only nuclear power. By 1949, however, the Soviet Union had also developed nuclear weapons.
>
> Critics argued that a nuclear war would destroy both sides. Yet each superpower wanted to be able to deter the other from launching its nuclear weapons. Both sides engaged in a race to match each other's new weapons. The result was a "balance of terror." Mutually assured destruction—in which each side knew that the other side would itself be destroyed if it launched its weapons—discouraged nuclear war. Still, people around the world lived in constant fear of nuclear doom.

[1.] Identify and write down the main point of each paragraph in your own words. You may identify the main idea right at the beginning of each paragraph. In other cases, you will have to figure out the main idea. As you read each paragraph, ask yourself, "What is the point this paragraph makes?" The point the paragraph makes is the main idea. Write this idea down in your own words.

[2.] Use these main points to write a general statement of the overall main idea of the passage in your own words. Once you have written down the main idea for each paragraph, write down the main idea of the passage. Write the main idea in your own words. If you have trouble identifying the main idea of the passage, review the titles and headings in the passage. Often, titles and headings relate to the main idea. Also, the writer may state the main idea in the first paragraph of the passage. The main idea of a passage should answer the question, "What is the point this passage makes?"

[3.] Use this general statement as a topic sentence for your summary. Then, write a paragraph tying together the main points of the passage. Leave out unimportant details. Analyze the information in the passage by summarizing. Use the main idea of the passage as a topic sentence for your summary paragraph. Use the main ideas that you identified for each paragraph of the passage to write sentences supporting the main idea of the passage. Leave out details that are not needed to understand the main idea of the passage. Your summary should be in your own words, and it should be much shorter than the original passage. Once your summary is written, review it to make sure that it contains all the main points of the passage. If any are missing, revise your summary to include them. If the summary includes unimportant details, remove them.

PEARSON realize™
PearsonSchool.com/CASS
View Video Tutorials and other 21st Century Skills

Generalize

One good way to analyze materials about a particular subject is to make generalizations and predictions. What are the patterns and connections that link the different materials? What can you say about the different materials that is true of all them? Practice this skill by reading the following statements. What generalization can you make about how new thought and inventions change the economy and society?

- Beginning in the 1500s, profound changes took place in the sciences. These new understandings about the physical world became part of what is now called the Scientific Revolution. These startling discoveries radically changed the way Europeans viewed the physical world.
- The Industrial Revolution brought radical change to people's lives. Before industrialization, people lived in villages and farmed. The economy was based on farming and craftwork. By the late 1800s, the economy had shifted. Manufacturing by machine in factories and urbanization became commonplace.
- The invention of the computer in the twentieth century caused an unprecedented information revolution. It has helped spur development of the modern global economy and society. Few, if any, aspects of modern life remain untouched by computers.

[1.] Make a list. Listing all of the specific details and facts about a subject will help you find patterns and connections.

[2.] Generate a statement. From your list of facts and specific details, decide what most of the items listed have in common. Analyze your information by making generalizations and predictions.

[3.] Ensure your generalization is logical and well supported by facts. Generalizations can be valid or invalid. A generalization that is not logical or supported by facts is invalid.

Make Predictions

You can analyze information by making generalizations and predictions. Predictions are educated guesses about the future, based on clues you find in written material and information you already have. When you analyze information by making generalizations and predictions, you are thinking critically about the material you read. Practice this skill by analyzing the passage below and predicting the impact this epidemic might have on society and the economy.

> In the mid 1300s, a disease moved throughout Europe and North Africa. The bubonic plague, or Black Death, spread quickly. Boils erupted all over the body—a sign that the plague would likely claim more victims because the disease spread through contact. The plague brought terror and bewilderment, as people had no way to stop the disease. Entire villages were wiped out. It ravaged Europe: one in three people died.

[**1.**] Review the content. Read your material carefully and research any terms or concepts that are new to you. It's important to understand the material before analyzing the information to make a prediction.

[**2.**] Look for clues. Gathering evidence is an important part of making predictions. Look for important words, statements, and evidence that seem to support the writer's point of view. Ask questions about what you are reading, including who, what, where, when, why, and how. Look for and analyze clues to help you generalize and predict.

[**3.**] Consider what you already know. Use related prior knowledge and/or connect to your own experiences to help you make an informed prediction. If you have experience with the subject matter, you have a much better chance of making an accurate prediction.

[**4.**] Generate a list of predictions. After studying the content, list the clues you've found. Then use these clues, plus your prior knowledge, to form your predictions. List as many possible outcomes as you can based on clues in the material and the questions you have considered.

Draw Inferences

What is the author trying to tell you? To make a determination about the author's message, you analyze information by drawing inferences and conclusions. You consider details and descriptions included in the text, compare and contrast the text to prior knowledge you have about the subject, and then form a conclusion about the author's intent. Practice this skill by analyzing the primary source report below to infer the feelings of the crew towards Magellan.

> . . . Talking began amongst the crews about the old eternal hatred between the Portuguese and the Spaniards, and about Magellan's being a Portuguese. He, they said, could do nothing more glorious for his own country than to cast away this fleet, with so many men. Nor was it credible [believable] that he should wish to discover the Moluccas [a group of spice islands]. . . . Nor even had their course begun to turn towards those happy Moluccas, but rather to distant snow and ice, and to perpetual storms.
>
> Magellan, very much enraged by these sayings, punished the men, but rather more harshly than was proper for a foreigner, especially when commanding in a distant country.
> –Maximillianus Transylvanus, report to King Charles I of Spain

[**1.**] Study the image or text. Consider all of the details and descriptions included. What is the author trying to tell you? Look for context clues that hint at the topic and subject matter.

[**2.**] Make a connection. Use related prior knowledge to connect to the text or image. Analyze information by asking questions such as who, what, where, when, and how. Look for cause-and-effect relationships; compare and contrast. This strategy will help you think beyond the available surface details to understand what the author is suggesting or implying.

[3.] Form a conclusion. When you draw an inference, you combine your own ideas with evidence and details you found within the text or image to form a new conclusion. This action leads you to a new understanding of the material.

Draw Conclusions

When you analyze information by drawing inferences and conclusions, you connect the ideas in a text with what you already know in order to understand a topic better. Using this skill, you can "fill in the blanks" to see the implications or larger meaning of the information in a text. Practice this skill by reading the excerpt of text below. What conclusions can you draw based on the information in the passage?

> Indian merchants and Hindu priests filtered into Southeast Asia, slowly spreading their culture. Later, Buddhist monks and scholars introduced Theravada beliefs. Following the path of trade and religion came the influence of writing, law, government, art, architecture, and farming.
>
> In time, local Indian families exercised considerable power in Southeast Asia. Also, people from Southeast Asia visited India as pilgrims or students. As these contacts increased, Indian beliefs and ideas won widespread acceptance. Indian influence reached its peak between 500 and 1000.
>
> Long after Hinduism and Buddhism took root in Southeast Asia, Indians carried a third religion, Islam, into the region. By the 1200s, Muslims ruled northern India. From there, traders spread Islamic beliefs and Muslim culture throughout the islands of Indonesia and as far east as the Philippines. Today, Indonesia has the largest Muslim population of any nation in the world.

[1.] Identify the topic, main idea, and supporting details. Before reading, look at the titles and headings within a reading. This should give you a good idea of the topic, or the general subject, of a text. After reading, identify the main idea. The main idea falls within the topic and answers the question, "What is the main point of this text?" Find the details that the author presents to support the main idea.

[2.] Use what you know to make a judgment about the information. Think about what you know about this topic or a similar topic. For example, you may read that the English settlers of Jamestown suffered from starvation because many of them were not farmers and did not know how to grow food. Analyzing the information about their situation and what you know about people, you could draw the conclusion that these settlers must have had little idea, or the wrong idea, about the conditions that they would find in America.

PEARSON realize™

PearsonSchool.com/CASS
View Video Tutorials and other
21st Century Skills

[3.] Check and adjust your judgment until you can draw a well-supported conclusion. Look for details within the reading that support your judgment. Reading a little further, you find that these settlers thought that they would become rich after discovering gold or silver, or through trading with Native Americans for furs. You can use this information to support your conclusion that the settlers were mistaken about the conditions that they would find in America. By analyzing the information further, you might infer that the settlers had inaccurate information about America. To support your conclusions, you could look for reliable sources on what these settlers knew before they left England.

Interpret Sources

Outlines and reports are good sources of information. In order to interpret these sources, though, you'll need to identify the type of document you're reading, identify the main idea, organize the details of information, and evaluate the source for point of view and bias. Practice this skill by finding a newspaper or online report on a recent meeting between the President or Secretary of State and a foreign leader. What steps will you take to interpret this report?

[1.] Identify the type of document. Is the document a primary or secondary source? Determine when, where, and why it was written.

[2.] Examine the source to identify the main idea. After identifying the main idea, identify details or sections of text that support the main idea. If the source is an outline or report, identify the topic and subtopics; review the supporting details under each subtopic. Organize the information from the outline or report and think about how it connects back to the overall topic listed at the top of the outline or report.

[3.] Evaluate the source for point of view and bias. Primary sources often have a strong point of view or bias; it is important to analyze primary sources critically to determine their validity. Evaluating each source will help you interpret the information they contain.

Create Databases

Databases are organized collections of information which can be analyzed and interpreted. You decide on a topic, organize data, use a spreadsheet, and then pose questions which will help you to analyze and interpret your data. Practice this skill by creating a database of population statistics for five countries in the Middle East. Show information for each country for each decade from 1910 to 2010, then compare the statistics. What conclusions can you draw from your data?

[1.] Decide on a topic. Identify the information that you will convert into a table. This information may come from various sources, including textbooks, reference works, and Internet sites.

[2.] Organize the data. Study the information and decide what to include in your table. Only include data that is pertinent and available. Based on the data you choose, organize your information. Identify how many columns there will be and what the column headings will be. Decide the order in which you are going to list the data in the rows.

[3.] Use a spreadsheet. A spreadsheet is a computer software tool that allows you to organize data so that it can be analyzed. Spreadsheets allow you to make calculations as well as input data. Use a spreadsheet to help you create summaries of your data. For instance, you can compute the sum, average, minimum, and maximum values of the data. Use the graphing features of your spreadsheet program to show the data visually.

[4.] Analyze the data. Once all of your data is entered and you have made any calculations you need, you are ready to pose questions to analyze and interpret your data. Organize the information from the database and use it to form conclusions. Be sure to draw conclusions that can be supported by the data available.

Analyze Data and Models

Data and models can provide useful information about geographic distributions and patterns. To make sense of that information, though, you need to pose and answer questions about data and models. What does the data say? What does it mean? What patterns can you find? Practice this skill as you study the data below.

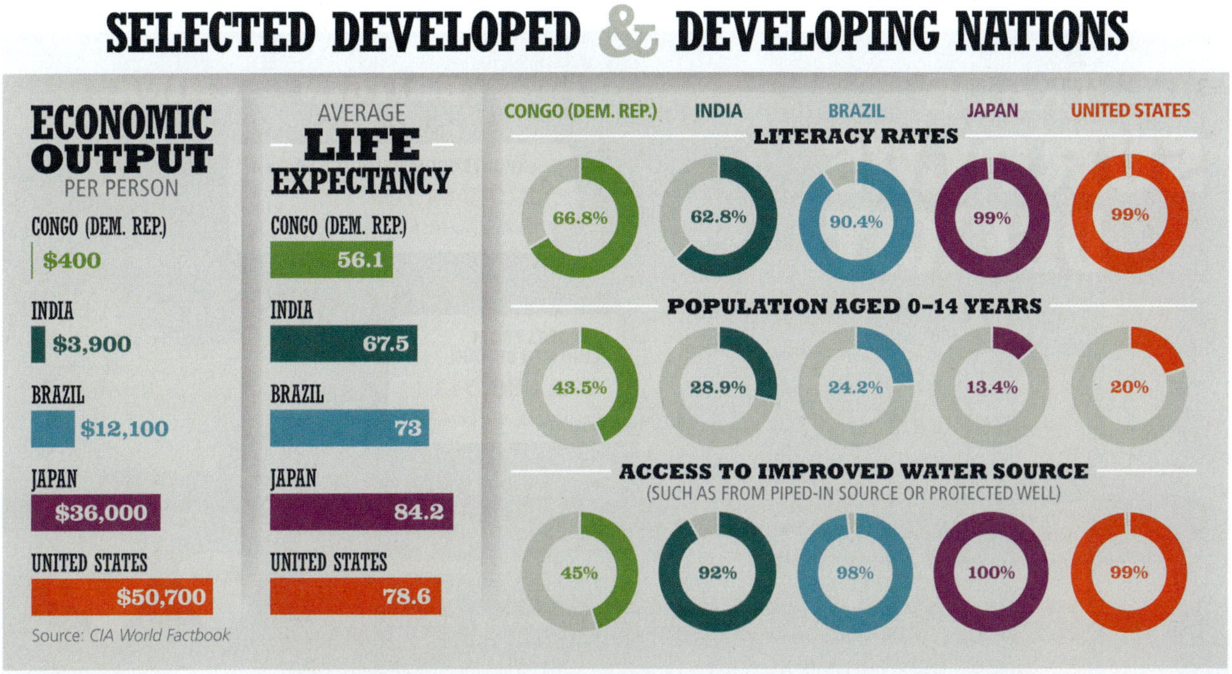

Source: *CIA World Factbook*

[1.] Read the title to learn the geographic distributions represented by the data set, graph, or model.

[2.] Read the data given. When reviewing a graph, read the labels and the key to help you comprehend the data provided. Pose and answer questions to further understand the material. For example, you might ask "Who could use this data?" or "How could this data be used?" or even "Why is this data presented in this particular format?" Thinking critically about the data presented will help you make predictions and comprehend the data.

[3.] Study the numbers, lines, and/or colors to find out what the graphs or data represent. Next, find similarities and differences between multiple models of the same data. Do any additional research to find out more about why the information in the models differs.

[4.] Interpret the graph, data set, or model. Look for interesting geographic distributions and patterns in the data. Look at changes over time or compare information from different categories. Draw conclusions.

Read Charts, Graphs, and Tables

If you pose and answer questions about charts, graphs, or tables you find in books or online, you can find out all sorts of information, such as how many calories are in your favorite foods or what the value of a used car is. Analyzing and interpreting the information you find in thematic charts, graphs, and tables can help you make decisions in your life. Practice this skill as you study the infographic below.

[1.] Identify the title and labels of a chart, graph, or table, and read the key, if there is one, to understand the information presented. The title often tells you the topic of the chart, graph, or table, or the type of information you will find. Make sure you understand how the graph shows information. A key or legend often appears in a small box near the edge of the graph or chart. The key will tell you the meaning of lines, colors, or symbols used on the chart or graph. Notice also the column and row headings, and use your reading skills to figure out the meanings of any words you don't know.

[2.] Determine consistencies and inconsistencies, to see whether there is a trend in a graph, chart, or table. Organize information from visuals such as charts and graphs and decide whether or not there is a trend or pattern in the information that you see. Evaluate the data and determine whether the trend is consistent, or steady. Remember that there could be some inconsistencies, or exceptions to the pattern. Try not to miss the overall pattern because of a couple of exceptions.

[3.] Draw conclusions about the data in a chart, graph, or table. Once you understand the information, try to analyze and interpret the information and draw conclusions. If you see a pattern, does the pattern help you to understand the topic or predict future events?

[4.] Create a chart or graph to make the data more understandable or to view the data in a different way. Does the data in the chart or graph help you answer questions you have about the topic or see any causes or effects? For example, you could use your mathematical skills to create circle graphs or bar graphs that visually organize the data in a different way that allows you to interpret the data differently.

[5.] Use the data or information in charts and graphs to understand an issue or make decisions. Use your social studies skills to make inferences, draw conclusions, and take a stand on the issue.

Create Charts and Maps

Thematic charts, graphs, and maps are visual tools for representing information. When you create a thematic chart, graph, or map you will start by selecting the type of data you want to represent. Then you will find appropriate data to include, organize your data, and then create symbols and a key to help others understand your chart, graph, or map. Practice this skill by creating a map of Asia showing which countries have a democratic government. Use computer software to generate the map, color the democratic countries, and create the key.

[1.] To create a chart or map, first select a region or set of data. Use a map to represent data pertaining to a specific region or location; use a chart to represent trends reflected in a set of data.

[2.] Research and find the data you would like to present in the chart or map. Your choice of data will be based on the theme you wish to explore. For example, a chart or map that explores the theme of changing demographics in Texas might include data about the location of different ethnic groups in Texas in the nineteenth, twentieth, and twenty-first centuries.

[3.] Organize the data according to the specific format of your chart or map.

[4.] Create symbols, a key (as needed), and a title. Create symbols to represent each piece of data you would like to highlight. Keep each symbol simple and easy to understand. After you have created the symbols, place them in a key. Add a title to your map or chart that summarizes the information presented. Your symbols and key will make it easier for others to interpret your charts and maps.

Analyze Political Cartoons

Political cartoons are visual commentaries about events or people. As you learn to analyze political cartoons, you will learn to identify bias in cartoons and interpret their meaning. You can start by carefully examining the cartoon and considering its possible meanings. Then you can draw conclusions based on your analysis. Practice this skill as you study the political cartoon below.

[1.] Fully examine the cartoon. Identify any symbols in the cartoon, read the text and title, and identify the main character or characters. Analyze the cartoon to identify bias and determine what each image or symbol represents. Conduct research if you need more information to decipher the cartoon.

[2.] Consider the meaning. Think about how the cartoonist uses the images and symbols in the cartoon to express his or her opinion about a subject. Try to interpret the artist's purpose in creating the image.

[3.] Draw conclusions. Use what you have gleaned from the image itself, plus any prior knowledge or research, to analyze, interpret, and form a conclusion about the artist's intentions.

Read Physical Maps

What mountain range is closest to where you live? What major rivers are closest to you? To find out, you would look at a physical map. You can use appropriate reading skills to interpret social studies information such as that found on different kinds of maps. Physical maps show physical features, such as elevation, mountains, valleys, oceans, rivers, deserts, and plains. Practice this skill as you study the map below.

The Indian Subcontinent: Physical Geography

[1.] Identify the title and region shown on a map. A map's title can help you to identify the region covered by the map. The title may also tell you the type of information you will find on the map. If the map has no title, you can identify the region by reading the labels on the map.

[2.] Use the map key to interpret symbols and colors on a map. A key or legend often appears in a small box near the edge of the map. The legend will tell you the meaning of colors, symbols, or other patterns on the map. On a physical map, colors from the key often show elevation, or height above sea level, on the map.

[3.] Identify physical features, such as mountains, valleys, oceans, and rivers. Using labels on the map and colors and symbols from the key, identify the physical features on the map. The information in the key allows you to interpret the information from visuals such as a map. Rivers, oceans, lakes, and other bodies of water are usually colored blue. Colors from the key may indicate higher and lower elevation, or there may be shading on the map that shows mountains.

[4.] Draw conclusions about the region based on natural resources and physical features. Once you understand all the symbols and colors on the map, try to interpret the information from the map. Is it very mountainous or mostly flat? Does it have a coastline? Does the region have lots of lakes and rivers that suggest a good water supply? Pose and answer questions about geographic distributions and patterns shown on the map. Physical maps can give you an idea of lifestyle and economic activities of people in the region.

Read Political Maps

What is the capital of your state? What countries border China? To find out, you could look at a political map. Political maps are colorful maps that show borders, or lines dividing states or countries. They also show capitals and sometimes major cities. Practice reading political maps by studying the map below.

Soviet-Controlled Countries, 1949

[1.] Identify the title of the political map and the region shown. A map's title can help you identify the region covered by the map. The title may also tell you the type of information you will find on the map. If the map has no title, you can identify the region by reading the labels on the map.

[2.] Use the map key to interpret symbols and colors on the map. A key or legend often appears in a small box near the edge of the map. The key will help you interpret information from visuals, including maps, by telling you the meaning of colors, symbols, or other patterns on the visual.

[3.] Identify boundaries between nations or states. Evaluate government data, such as borders, using the map. It is often easy to see borders, because each state or country will be a different color. If you cannot find the borders, check the key to find the lines used to mark borders on the map.

[4.] Locate capital cities. Look at the key to see how capital cities are shown on the map. They are often marked with a special symbol, such as a star.

[5.] Draw conclusions about the region based on the map. Once you understand all the symbols and colors on the map, use appropriate reading and mathematical skills to interpret social studies information, such as that shown on the map, in order to draw conclusions about the region. For example, are some countries very large with many cities? These countries are likely to be powerful and influential.

Read Special-Purpose Maps

Some maps show specific kinds of information. These special-purpose maps may show features such as climate zones, ancient trade routes, economic and government data, geographic patterns, or population. Locating and interpreting information from visuals, including special-purpose maps, is an important research skill. Practice this skill as you study this map.

PEARSON realize™
PearsonSchool.com/CASS
View Video Tutorials and other 21st Century Skills

World Oil Resources and Consumption

[1.] Identify the title and determine the purpose of a map. A map's title can help you identify the region covered by the map. The title may also tell you the purpose of the map. If the map has no title, see what information the map shows to determine its purpose.

[2.] Use the map key to make sense of symbols and colors on a map. A key or legend often appears in a small box near the edge of the map. The key will tell you the meaning of colors, symbols, or other patterns on the map. Special-purpose maps use these colors and symbols to present information.

[3.] Draw conclusions about the region shown on a map. Once you understand all the symbols and colors on the map, you can use appropriate skills, including reading and mathematical skills, to analyze and interpret social studies information such as maps. You can pose and answer questions about geographic patterns and distributions that are shown on maps. For example, a precipitation or climate map will show you which areas get lots of rainfall and which are very dry. You can evaluate government and economic data using maps. For example, a population map will show you which regions have lots of people and which have small, scattered populations. A historical map will show you the locations of ancient empires or trade routes. Thematic maps focus on a single theme or topic about a region. For example, you can interpret information from a thematic map representing various aspects of Texas during the nineteenth or twentieth century by studying the Great Military Map, which shows forts established in Texas during the nineteenth century, or by studying a map covering Texas during the Great Depression and World War II. By mapping this kind of detailed information, special-purpose maps can help you understand a region's history or geography.

Use Parts of a Map

If you understand how to organize and interpret information from visuals, including maps, you will be able to find the information you are looking for. Understanding how to use the parts of a map will help you find locations of specific places and estimate distances between different places. Practice this skill as you study the map below.

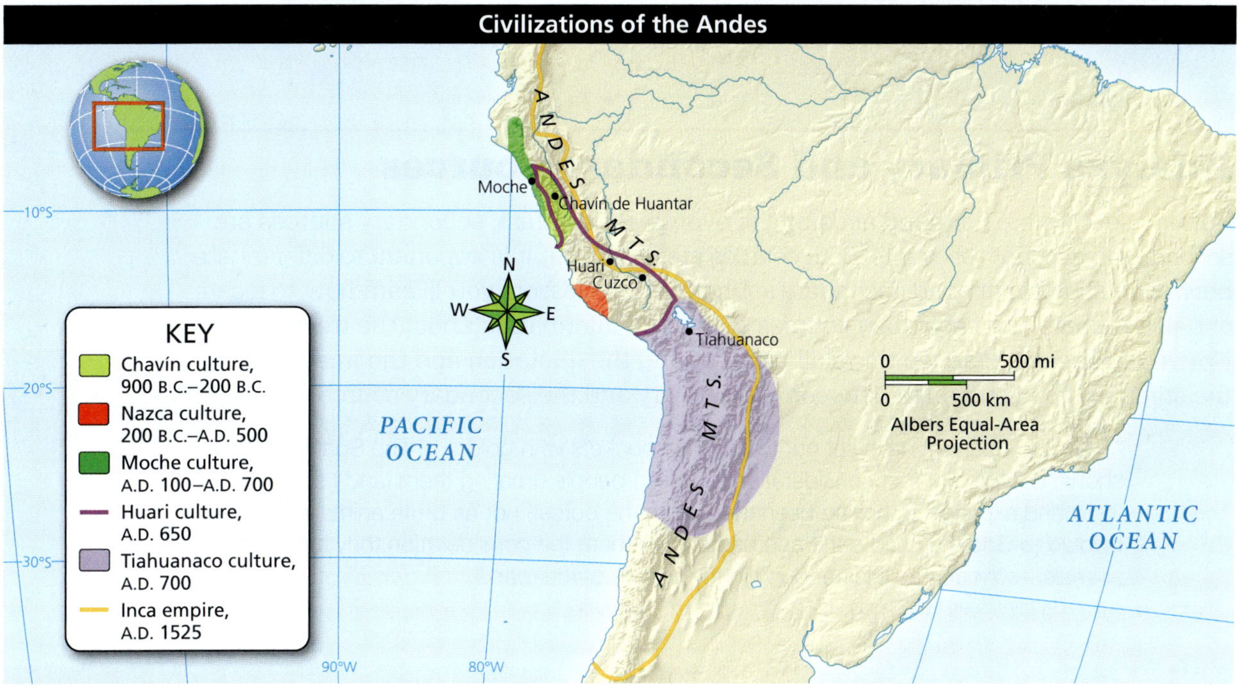

[1.] Identify the title and region of a map. Use appropriate reading skills to interpret social studies information such as map labels. A map's title can help you to identify the region covered by the map. The title may also tell you the type of information you will find on the map. If the map has no title, you can identify the region by reading the labels on the map.

[2.] Use the compass rose to determine direction. Although on most maps north is at the top of the map, you should always double check the compass rose. Often, on the compass rose, the first letter of each direction represents that direction. For example, "N" represents the direction "north." Some compass roses are as simple as an arrow pointing north.

[3.] Use the scale to estimate the distance between places. Use appropriate mathematical skills to interpret social studies information such as a map scale. The scale on a map shows how a measurement on the map compares to the distance on the ground. For example, if one inch on the map represents a mile, the number of inches between two places on the map is the distance in miles.

[4.] Use the key or legend on a map to find information about colors or symbols on a map. A key or legend often appears in a small box near the edge of the map. The legend will tell you the meaning of colors, symbols, or other patterns on the map.

[5.] Use the latitude and longitude grid to determine absolute locations. An absolute location is an exact description of a location on Earth's surface based on latitude and longitude. You can use the latitude and longitude lines on a map to find the absolute location of a place.

Analyze Primary and Secondary Sources

Primary sources are firsthand accounts of events. By contrast, secondary sources are secondhand accounts of events. Both sources are useful, but it is important to differentiate between valid primary and secondary sources. In this lesson, you'll learn how to locate and use primary and secondary sources to acquire information about the treatment of Native Americans. Practice this skill by analyzing the quotation and the image. Using the steps below, distinguish between the primary and the secondary source.

> "They [the Spanish] have set out to line their pockets with gold. . . . The Spaniards have shown not the slightest consideration for these people, treating them (and I speak from first-hand experience, having been there from the outset) not as brute animals—indeed, I would to God they had done and had shown them the consideration they afford their animals—so much as piles of dung in the middle of the road."
>
> –Bartolomé de Las Casas, 1542

[1.] Determine who created the source as well as when and why it was created. Determine whether it is a primary or secondary source. Identify the author of the document. Next, look for the date the document was written or the date when the document was first published. Most primary sources are written close to the date of the events described. Secondary sources are often written well after the events described. Firsthand observers or participants in an event create primary sources. People who did not witness an event create secondary sources. Primary sources record an event. Secondary sources analyze or draw conclusions about events. Secondary sources rely on both primary and secondary sources. Good research requires you to analyze and evaluate the validity of information, arguments, and counterarguments from a primary or secondary source for frame of reference.

[2.] Identify the main idea and supporting details, and determine whether they are facts or opinions. Read the text carefully and ask yourself, "What point is this text making?" This point is the main idea. Then reread the text and list details that support this main idea. Decide whether these details are facts or opinions. If the details are facts, it should be possible to confirm them in other sources. If the author uses emotional language that shows feelings, the supporting details are probably opinions. Carefully analyze and evaluate the validity of information, arguments, and counterarguments from primary and secondary sources for point of view.

[3.] Decide whether the source's information is biased or if it is accurate and credible. Check statements in the text against reliable sources, such as encyclopedias or books written by experts on the topic. If reliable sources agree with the text, it is probably fairly accurate. If most of the text seems to be opinions rather than facts, it is not an accurate source of information. Still, these opinions can teach you about the author's world. A writer who observed an exciting or scary event may use emotional language to describe the event, but the source may still be a reliable account. An important part of research is analyzing and evaluating the validity of the information, arguments, and counterarguments from primary and secondary sources for bias or propaganda.

Compare Viewpoints

When people disagree about a topic, they have different viewpoints. Knowing how to analyze and evaluate the validity of information, arguments, and counterarguments from both primary and secondary sources for point of view can help you to learn more about a topic. Practice this skill by reading the following quotes and comparing the viewpoints.

> "Dictatorship...involves costs which the American people will never pay: The cost of having our children brought up, not as free and dignified human beings, but as pawns...
>
> –Franklin Roosevelt, State of the Union Address, January 4, 1939

> "The [Nazi Party] has laid down the directive...we must insist that all organs of education...have to [fulfill] their duty towards the community...
>
> –Adolf Hitler, Speech delivered in German Reichstag on January 30, 1937

[1.] Identify the authors of texts presenting different points of view and identify each author's frame of reference. Frame of reference is a term that describes the experiences, values, and ideas that influence a person's opinions and actions. It can also be referred to as *point of view*. First, identify the group or individual that wrote each text. Determine if the source is primary or secondary. As you read, take note of any information about the author's experiences or background. Also, look for any signs of what the author thinks is important. These types of statements can help you analyze and evaluate the validity of information, arguments, and counterarguments from both primary and secondary sources for point of view.

[2.] Recognize any similarities and differences between the authors' frames of reference and identify the opinion of each author. Pay attention to any similarities and differences between the two authors' experiences, values, and ideas. Read carefully to identify the opinion of each author. In an article about a rock band, an author who played guitar in a band for ten years argues that Band A is the best band today because of its great guitarist. In a second article, another author who sang for many years argues that Band B is the best because of its lead singer. Notice how authors' arguments and counterarguments are shaped by their frame of reference, or point of view.

[3.] Draw conclusions about similarities and differences between authors' points of view. With some information about the point of view of each author, you can understand why they have different opinions. This helps you to analyze and evaluate the validity of the information, arguments, and counterarguments. In the example of the two authors writing about rock bands, each author stresses his or her own areas of expertise. You might decide to listen to the band recommended by the singer if you share an interest in vocals. If you are more interested in instrumentals, you might choose the band recommended by the guitarist.

Identify Bias

Being able to analyze and evaluate the validity of information, arguments, and counterarguments for bias helps you to determine whether primary or secondary sources you find online, in books, or in the media are reliable. When you are able to identify bias in written, oral, and visual material, you can see when someone is presenting only one side of an issue or basing an argument on emotion instead of facts. Use the Internet to locate an English-language newspaper in a foreign country. Practice identifying bias as you read an editorial or a political cartoon.

[1.] Identify the author of a source and the author's purpose. First, identify the author of the source. The author may be a group or an organization rather than a single person. The author may state his or her purpose very clearly in the source. If not, the type of source may give you an idea of the purpose. For example, the writer of an encyclopedia aims to summarize information about a subject. The author of a political Web site may want you to vote for a candidate.

[2.] Identify the main idea, and check whether the main idea is supported with facts or opinions. Read the document carefully and ask yourself, "What is the main point of this selection?" Your answer to this question is the main idea. Reread the document and list details that support this main idea. Decide whether these details are facts or opinions. To find out whether they are facts, check whether other reliable sources include the same information. If your source uses statements that shows feelings, those statements are probably opinions.

[3.] Look for the use of emotional language or one-sided opinions. Look for words that can show opinions such as "good" and "bad." Be aware of statements that make you feel angry, scared, or excited. Also, watch out for statements that only express one side of an issue. These are all signs of bias.

[4.] Draw conclusions about the author's bias, if any. Is the author using mostly emotional language with few facts to support his or her ideas? Are there insults or other very negative language in the source? If so, the source is probably biased. Similarly, if you notice that the author is presenting only one side of an issue, the source is probably not reliable. It is important to analyze and evaluate the information, arguments, and counterarguments in both primary and secondary sources for bias.

Evaluate Existing Arguments

When you evaluate existing arguments, you must evaluate and analyze the point of view and biases of your sources and their authors. Who is the author and what is he or she trying to accomplish? How valid are the arguments in your primary and secondary sources? If you master these skills, you will be able to analyze and interpret social studies information such as speeches. Practice this skill as you read and evaluate the excerpt below.

> There are two main ways in which those who have traveled to this part of the world pretending to be Christians have uprooted these pitiful peoples and wiped them from the face of the earth. First, they have waged war on them: unjust, cruel, bloody and tyrannical [using power unjustly] war. Second, they have murdered anyone and everyone who has shown the slightest sign of resistance. . . .
>
> The reason the [Spanish] have murdered on such a vast scale and killed anyone and everyone in their way is purely and simply greed. They have set out to line their pockets with gold. . . . The Spaniards have shown not the slightest consideration for these people, treating them (and I speak from first-hand experience, having been there from the outset) not as brute animals—indeed, I would to God they had done and had shown them the consideration they afford their animals—so much as piles of dung in the middle of the road. They have had as little concern for their souls as for their bodies. . . .
>
> —Bartolomé de Las Casas, *The Destruction of the Indies*, 1542

[1.] Identify the claim or thesis. What is the author or source claiming? The claim or thesis is usually found in the introduction and/or conclusion of a written or spoken argument.

[2.] Identify the reasons (claims to truth or facts) the author offers in support of his or her claim. What evidence does the author or source provide to support their claims? Make a list of the evidence provided to support each claim.

[3.] Evaluate the argument. Analyze and evaluate the validity of the evidence presented to support each claim. Use the appropriate skills to analyze and interpret social studies information, such as speeches. Research each claim to be sure that the author's statements are accurate. Carefully check for evidence of bias or propaganda. Be sure you understand the author's point of view and his or her frame of reference. Finally, check to be sure that the author's conclusions follow logically from the evidence presented. If the evidence is accurate, the author is free from bias, and conclusions follow logically from the evidence, the claims are probably valid.

Consider and Counter Opposing Arguments

Before you can effectively counter opposing arguments, you'll need to analyze possible counterarguments for frame of reference, bias, point of view, and propaganda. You'll plan your response ahead of time, collecting research and data. Then, you'll make a point of acknowledging the opposing view before presenting your counterarguments. To practice this skill, suppose you are preparing for a debate about whether the United States should take a more active role in promoting human rights in other parts of the world. Choose a side of the debate to support. What arguments will you use to support your side of the debate? What counterarguments will you anticipate the other side using? Why is it useful to anticipate the other side's arguments?

[1.] Fully understand your argument and the potential counter points. Do research as needed to find out more about other opposing views. Analyze and evaluate the validity of possible counterarguments from primary and secondary sources for frame of reference, bias, point of view, and propaganda.

[2.] Make predictions and outline a response to several of the opposing views. Continue researching as needed. Researching, analyzing, and evaluating the validity of opposing arguments will help you support and strengthen your own. Opposing arguments can consist of any reasons, conclusions, or claims that oppose yours. Outline your response to each opposing reason, conclusion, or claim.

[3.] To counter an opposing argument, first acknowledge the opposing view. This strategy shows that you have heard the opposing argument and are responding accordingly. Consider using statements such as "I understand your point, but you should also consider the following..." You can also respond by refuting facts, logic, etc. Be sure to respond to each opposing argument. Ignoring or dismissing a counterargument shows that your response is weak and unsupported.

Participate in a Discussion or Debate

When you participate in a discussion or debate, your goal is to explain, analyze, and defend a point of view–often related to a current political or economic issue. To be a successful debater, you'll do your research, present your position, and defend your point of view in a courteous manner. Use the steps below to prepare for a discussion on this question: Do you think the United States should act as a "global policeman?" Why or why not?

[1.] Research. Before participating in a discussion or debate, do research to gain knowledge of your subject so that you may be an informed and prepared participant. Take notes as needed to help you prepare. Jot down main points and any questions you may have. As you research, decide where you might stand on the issue. Be sure to gather research and sources that will allow you to explain, analyze, and defend your point of view.

[2.] Present your position. After you have organized your thoughts and decided where you stand, explain and defend your point of view. Be sure to stay focused on the topic and your line of argument. Ask questions that challenge the accuracy, logic, or relevance of opposing views.

[3.] During the discussion or debate, be patient and courteous. Listen attentively, be respectful and supportive of peers, and speak only when instructed to do so by the moderator. Be sure to allow others to express their views; do not monopolize the debate or discussion. Speak clearly and slowly.

Give an Effective Presentation

When you create a written, visual, and oral presentation, you teach, convince, or share information with an audience. Effective presentations use both words and visuals to engage audiences. Delivery is also important. For example, you can use the way you move, speak, and look at the audience to keep people interested. Use the steps below to prepare and deliver a presentation on the Silk Road.

[1.] Identify the purpose of your presentation and your audience. Think about the purpose of your written, visual, and oral presentation. If this is a research report, you will need facts and data to support your points. If you are trying to persuade your audience, look for powerful photos. Keep your audience in mind. Consider their interests and present your topic in a way that will engage them.

[2.] Write the text and find visual aids for your presentation. Look online and in books and magazines for information and images for your presentation. Organize the information and write it up carefully so that it is easy for your audience to understand. Diagrams can show complicated information in a clear way. Visuals also get people interested in the presentation. So choose large, colorful images that people in the back of the audience will be able to see.

[3.] Practice and work to improve your presentation. Keep practicing your oral presentation until you know the material well. Then, practice some more, focusing on improving your delivery.

[4.] Use body language, tone of voice, and eye contact to deliver an effective presentation. Answer questions if the audience has them. At the beginning of your oral presentation, take a breath, smile, and stand up tall. Speak more loudly and more clearly than you would in normal conversation. Also, try not to rush through the presentation. Glance at your notes but speak naturally, rather than reading. Look at people in the audience. If people are confused, pause to clarify. Finally, leave time for people in the audience to ask questions.

Write an Essay

There are four steps to writing an essay. You'll start by selecting a topic and research sources, then you'll write an outline and develop a thesis or point of view. After drafting your essay, you'll carefully proofread it to be sure you've used standard grammar, spelling, sentence structure, and punctuation. Finally, you'll revise and polish your work. To practice this skill, select a topic that interests you about the early history of Africa and develop a thesis. Then explain to a partner the steps you will take to write your essay.

[1.] Choose your topic and research sources. Check which types of sources you will need. Gather different types of reliable sources that support the argument you will be making.

[2.] Write an outline and generate a thesis. First write your topic at the top of the page then list all the points or arguments you want to make about the topic; also list the facts and examples that support these points. Your thesis statement will inform the reader of the point you are making and what question you will be answering about the topic. When writing your thesis, be as specific as possible and address one main idea.

[3.] Draft your essay. After finishing your research and outline, begin writing the body of your essay; start with the introduction then write a paragraph for each of your supporting points, followed by a conclusion. As you write, do your best to use standard grammar, spelling, sentence structure, and punctuation. Be sure any terminology is used correctly.

[4.] Revise. An important part of the writing process involves checking for areas in which information should be added, removed, or rewritten. Try to imagine that this paper belongs to someone else. Does the paper have a clear thesis? Do all of the ideas relate back to the thesis? Read your paper out loud and listen for awkward pauses and unclear ideas. Lastly, check for mistakes in standard grammar, spelling, sentence structure, punctuation, and usage.

Avoid Plagiarism

When you don't attribute ideas and information to source materials and authors, you are plagiarizing. Plagiarizing–claiming others' ideas and information as your own–is considered unethical. You can avoid plagiarizing by carefully noting down which authors and sources you'll be using, citing those authors and sources in your paper, and listing them in a bibliography. To practice this skill, suppose you have been assigned to write a research paper on the development of river valley civilizations. Name three types of sources you might use to help you gather information. Explain how you will avoid plagiarism when you use these sources.

[1.] Keep a careful log of your notes. As you read sources to gain background information on your topic, keep track of ideas and information and the sources and authors they come from. Write down the name of each source next to your notes from that particular source so you can remember to cite it later on. Create a separate section in your notes where you keep your own thoughts and ideas so you know which ideas are your own. Using someone else's words or paraphrasing their ideas does not make them yours.

[2] Cite sources in your paper. You must identify the source materials and authors you use to support your ideas. Whenever you use statistics, facts, direct quotations, or paraphrases of others' views, you need to attribute them to your source. Cite your sources within the body of your paper. Check your assignment to find out how they should be formatted.

[3.] List your sources in a bibliography at the end of your paper. List your source materials and authors cited in alphabetical order by author, using accepted formats. As you work, be sure to check your list of sources from your notes so that none are left out of the bibliography.

Solve Problems

Problem solving is a skill that you use every day. It is a process that requires an open mind, clear thinking, and action. Consider the fact that many of natural resources are in high demand around the world, and that some may be in danger of being depleted. Consider one source of power, such as natural gas, oil, or electricity, and use the steps below to solve the problem of conserving energy.

[1.] Understand the problem. Before trying to solve a problem, make sure that you gather as much information as possible in order to identify the problem. What are the causes and effects of the problem? Who is involved? You will want to make sure that you understand different perspectives on the problem. Try not to jump to conclusions or make assumptions. You might end up misunderstanding the problem.

[2.] Consider possible solutions and choose the best one. Once you have identified the problem and gathered some information, list and consider a number of possible options. Right away, one solution might seem like the right one, but try to think of other solutions. Be sure to consider carefully the advantages and disadvantages of each option. It can help to take notes listing benefits and drawbacks. Look for the solution whose benefits outweigh its drawbacks. After considering each option, choose the solution you think is best.

[3.] Make and implement a plan. Choose and implement a solution. Make a detailed, step-by-step plan to implement the solution that you choose. Write your plan down and assign yourself a deadline for each step. That will help you to stay on track toward completing your plan. Try to think of any problems that might come up and what you will do to address those problems. Of course, there are many things that you cannot predict. Stay flexible. Evaluate the effectiveness of the solution and adjust your plan as necessary.

Make Decisions

Everyone makes decisions. The trick is to learn how to make good decisions. How can you make good decisions? First, identify a situation that requires a decision and gather information. Then, identify possible options and predict the consequences of each option. Finally, choose the best option and take action to implement a decision. You know there are many issues in the world that affect children who are just like you. Some children face hunger, poverty, lack of schools or medical facilities, poor water supplies, or other challenges. What could you do to help? Practice this skill by following these steps to decide which issue you can best support and how you can help.

[1.] Determine the options between which you must decide. In some cases, like ordering from a menu at a restaurant, your options may be clear. In other cases, you will need to identify a situation that requires a decision, gather information, and identify the options that are available to you. Spend some time thinking about the situation and brainstorm a number of options. If necessary, do a little research to find more options. Make a list of options that you might choose.

[2.] Review the costs and benefits of each option. Carefully predict the consequences of each option. You may want to make a cost-benefit list for each option. To do this, write down the option and then draw two columns underneath it. One column will be the "pro" or benefit list. The other column will be the "con" or cost list. Note the pros and cons for each of your options. Try not to rush through this process. For a very important decision, you may even want to show your list to someone you trust. This person can help you think of costs and benefits that you had not considered.

PEARSON realize™ PearsonSchool.com/CASS View Video Tutorials and other 21st Century Skills

[3.] Determine the best option and act on it. Look through your cost-benefit lists. Note any especially serious costs. If an option has the possibility of an extremely negative consequence, you might want to cross it off your list right away. Look closely at the options with the most benefits and the fewest costs, and choose the one that you think is best. Once you have made a choice, take action to implement a decision. If necessary, make a detailed plan with clear steps. Set a deadline to complete the steps to keep yourself moving toward your goal.

Being an Informed Citizen

Informed citizens understand the responsibilities, duties, and obligations of citizenship. They are well informed about civic affairs, involved with their communities, and politically active. When it comes to issues they personally care about, they take a stand and reach out to others.

[1.] Learn the issues. A great way to begin to understand the responsibilities of citizenship is to first find topics of interest to you. Next, become well informed about civic affairs in your town, city, or country. Read newspapers, magazines, and articles you find online about events happening in your area or around the world. Analyze the information you read to come to your own conclusions. Radio programs, podcasts, and social media are also great ways to keep up with current events and interact with others about issues.

[2.] Get involved. Attend community events to speak with others who know the issues. Become well informed about how policies are made and changed. Find out who to speak to if you would like to take part in civic affairs and policy creation. There are government websites that can help direct you to the right person. These websites will also provide his or her contact details.

[3.] Take a stand and reach out. Write, call, or meet with your elected officials to become a better informed, more responsible citizen. Do research about candidates who are running for office to be an informed voter. Start your own blog or website to explore issues, interact with others, and be part of the community or national dialogue.

Political Participation

Political participation starts with an understanding of the responsibilities, duties and obligations of citizenship, such as serving the public good. When you understand your role as a political participant, you can get involved through volunteering for a political campaign, running for office, or interacting with others in person or online.

[1.] Volunteer for a political campaign. Political campaigns offer a wide variety of opportunities to help you become involved in the political process and become a responsible citizen by serving the public good. As a political campaign volunteer you may have the opportunity to attend events, make calls to voters, and explore your community while getting to know how other voters think about the responsibilities, duties, and obligations of citizenship.

[2.] Run for office in your school or community. A good way to become involved in your school or community is to run for office. Student council or community positions offer a great opportunity for you to become familiar with the campaign and election process.

[3.] Reach out to others. Start or join an interest group. Interest groups enable people to work together on common goals related to the political process. Write a letter or email to a public official. By contacting an elected official from your area, you can either support or oppose laws or policies. You can also ask for help or support regarding certain issues.

[4.] Interact online. Social networking sites and blogs offer a great way for people of all ages to interact and write about political issues. As you connect with others, you'll become more confident in your role as a citizen working for the public good.

Voting

Voting is not only a right. It is also one of the primary responsibilities, duties, and obligations of citizenship. Before you can legally vote, however, you must understand the voter registration process and the criteria for voting in elections. You should also understand the issues and know where different candidates stand on those issues.

[1.] Check eligibility and residency requirements. In order to vote in the United States, you must be a United States citizen who is 18 years or older, and you must be a resident of the place where you plan to vote.

PEARSON realize™

PearsonSchool.com/CASS
View Video Tutorials and other 21st Century Skills

[2.] Register to vote. You cannot vote until you understand the voter registration process. You can register at city or town election offices, or when you get a driver's license. You can also register by mail or online. You may also have the option of registering at the polls on Election Day, but this does not apply in all states. Make sure to find out what you need to do to register in your state, as well as the deadline for registering. You may have the option of declaring a political party when registering.

[3.] Learn the issues. As the election approaches, research the candidates and issues in order to be an informed voter. Watch televised debates, if there are any. You can also review the candidates' websites. By doing these things and thinking critically about what you learn, you will be prepared to exercise your responsibility, duty and obligation as a United States citizen.

[4.] Vote. Make sure to arrive at the correct polling place on Election Day to cast your ballot. Research to find out when the polls will be open. Advance voting, absentee voting, and voting by mail are also options in certain states for those who qualify.

Serving on a Jury

As an American, you need to understand the duties, obligations and responsibilities of citizenship; among these is the expectation that you may be required to serve on a jury. You will receive a written notice when you are summoned to jury duty and you'll receive instruction on the special duties and obligations of a juror. You'll follow the American code of justice which assumes that a person is innocent until proven guilty, and you'll follow instructions about keeping trial information confidential.

[1.] Wait to receive notification. If you are summoned to serve as a juror, you will be first notified by mail. If you are chosen to move on to the jury selection phase, lawyers from both sides will ask you questions as they select the final jury members. It is an honor to serve as a juror, as it is a responsibility offered only to American citizens.

[2.] Follow the law and remain impartial. Your job is to determine whether or not someone broke the law. You may also be asked to sit on the jury for civil cases (as opposed to criminal cases); these cases involve lawsuits filed against individuals or businesses for any perceived wrong doing (such as broken contracts, trespassing, discrimination, etc.). Be sure to follow the law as it is explained to you, regardless of whether you approve of the law or not. Your decision about the trial should not be influenced by any personal bias or views you may have.

PEARSON realize™
PearsonSchool.com/CASS
View Video Tutorials and other 21st Century Skills

[3.] Remember that the defendant is presumed innocent. In a criminal trial, the defendant must be proven guilty "beyond a reasonable doubt" for the verdict to be guilty. If the trial team fails to prove the defendant to be guilty beyond a reasonable doubt, the jury verdict must be "not guilty."

[4.] During the trial, respect the court's right to privacy. As a juror, you have specific duties, obligations, and responsibilities under the law. Do not permit anyone to talk about the case with you or in your presence, except with the court's permission. Avoid media coverage once the trial has begun so as to prevent bias. Keep an open mind and do not form or state any opinions about the case until you have heard all of the evidence, the closing arguments from the lawyers, and the judge's instructions on the applicable law.

Paying Taxes

Paying taxes is one of the responsibilities of citizenship. How do you go about figuring out how much you've already paid in taxes and how much you still owe? It's your duty and obligation to find out, by determining how much has been deducted from your pay and filing your tax return.

[1.] Find out how taxes are deducted from your pay. In the United States, payroll taxes are imposed on employers and employees, and they are collected and paid by the employers. Check your pay stub to find out how much money was deducted for taxes. Be sure to also save the W-2 tax form your employer sends to you. You will need this form later on when filing your tax paperwork. Also save any interest income statements. All this information will help you fulfill your obligation as an American taxpayer.

PEARSON realize™ PearsonSchool.com/CASS
View Video Tutorials and other 21st Century Skills

[2.] Check the sales taxes in your state. All but five states impose sales and use taxes on retail sale, lease, and rental of many goods, as well as some services. Sales tax is calculated as the purchase price times the appropriate tax rate. Tax rates vary widely from less than one percent to over ten percent. Sales tax is collected by the seller at the time of sale.

[3.] File your tax return. Filing your tax return is more than an obligation: it's also a duty and responsibility of citizenship. You may receive tax forms in the mail, or pick them up at the local Post Office or library. Fill the forms in and then mail or electronically send completed tax forms and any necessary payments to the Internal Revenue Service (IRS) and your state's department of revenue. The IRS provides free resources to help people prepare and electronically file their tax returns; go to IRS.gov to learn more. Note: certain things such as charitable donations and business expenses are tax deductible.

PEARSON realize™ PearsonSchool.com/CASS
View Video Tutorials and other
21st Century Skills

The United States: Political

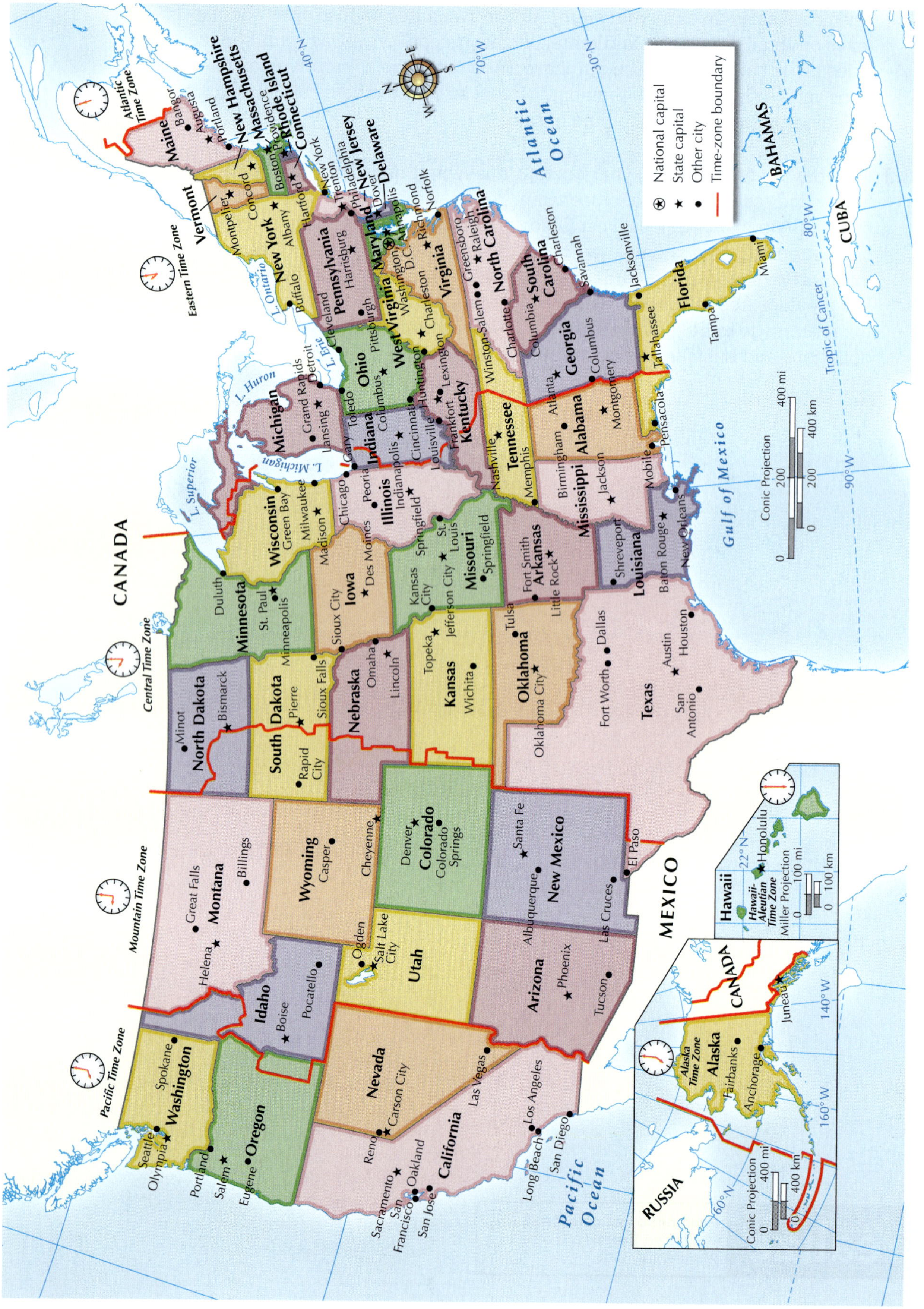

The United States: Physical

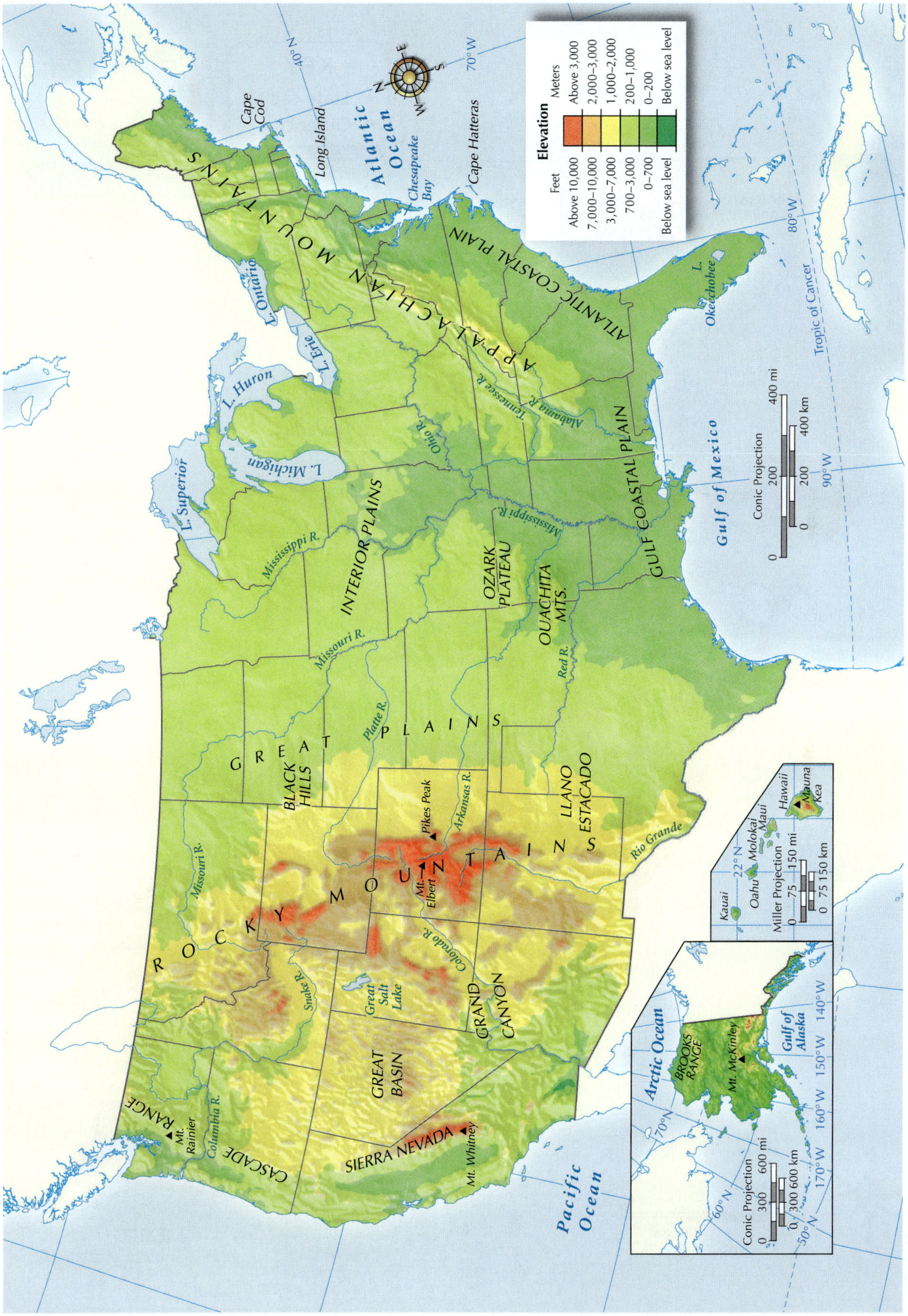

California: Political

California: Physical

The World: Political

Arctic Ocean
Arctic Circle
ICELAND
Greenland (Denmark)
EUROPE
RUSSIA
ASIA
KAZAKHSTAN
MONGOLIA
GEORGIA
AZER.
ARMENIA
UZBEK.
TURKMEN.
KYRGYZSTAN
TAJIKISTAN
Tehran
IRAN
AFGHAN.
IRAQ
ISRAEL
JORDAN
KUWAIT
BAHRAIN
QATAR
PAKISTAN
Karachi
U.A.E.
OMAN
SAUDI ARABIA
YEMEN
CHINA
Beijing
NORTH KOREA
SOUTH KOREA
Seoul
JAPAN
Tokyo
Shanghai
NEPAL
BHUTAN
New Delhi
INDIA
Mumbai
BANGLADESH
MYANMAR (BURMA)
TAIWAN (Claimed by China)
Hong Kong
LAOS
THAILAND
Bangkok
VIETNAM
CAMBODIA
PHILIPPINES
SRI LANKA
MALDIVES
BRUNEI
MALAYSIA
SINGAPORE
INDONESIA
Jakarta
TIMOR-LESTE
PAPUA NEW GUINEA
Pacific Ocean
MARSHALL ISLANDS
FEDERATED STATES OF MICRONESIA
KIRIBATI
NAURU
SOLOMON ISLANDS
TUVALU
OCEANIA
FIJI ISLANDS
VANUATU
New Caledonia (France)
AUSTRALIA
Sydney
NEW ZEALAND
MOROCCO
ALGERIA
LIBYA
Cairo
EGYPT
AFRICA
CHAD
SUDAN
ERITREA
DJIBOUTI
Addis Ababa
ETHIOPIA
SOUTH SUDAN
SOMALIA
CEN. AFR. REP.
CAMEROON
DEM. REP. OF THE CONGO
UGANDA
KENYA
RWANDA
BURUNDI
GABON
CONGO
SÃO TOMÉ AND PRÍNCIPE
TANZANIA
SEYCHELLES
COMOROS
ANGOLA
MALAWI
ZAMBIA
MOZAMBIQUE
MADAGASCAR
MAURITIUS
ZIMBABWE
BOTSWANA
NAMIBIA
SWAZILAND
LESOTHO
SOUTH AFRICA
Cape Town
see inset below
Atlantic Ocean
Indian Ocean
Southern Ocean
ANTARCTICA
Robinson Projection
0 1,000 2,000 mi
0 1,000 2,000 km
N S E W
80°N
60°N
40°N
20°N
0°
20°S
40°S
60°S
20°W 0° 20°E 40°E 60°E 80°E 100°E 120°E 140°E 160°E

Western Sahara (Morocco)
ALGERIA
MAURITANIA
MALI
NIGER
SENEGAL
GAMBIA
GUINEA-BISSAU
GUINEA
BURKINA FASO
BENIN
TOGO
SIERRA LEONE
LIBERIA
CÔTE D'IVOIRE
GHANA
NIGERIA
Lagos
Atlantic Ocean
Gulf of Guinea
EQUATORIAL GUINEA
Azimuthal Equidistant Projection
0 200 400 mi
0 200 400 km
20°W
20°N
10°N
0°

Barents Sea
Conic Projection
0 200 400 mi
0 200 400 km
SWEDEN
FINLAND
NORWAY
ESTONIA
LATVIA
LITHUANIA
RUSSIA
Moscow
North Sea
Baltic Sea
DENMARK
IRELAND
UNITED KINGDOM
NETHERLANDS
London
Berlin
POLAND
BELARUS
GERMANY
BELGIUM
LUX.
Paris
Kiev
UKRAINE
CZECH REP.
SLOVAKIA
LIECH.
SWITZ.
AUSTRIA
MOLDOVA
FRANCE
HUNGARY
SLOVENIA
CROATIA
ROMANIA
Atlantic Ocean
Bay of Biscay
ANDORRA
MONACO
ITALY
BOS. AND HERZ.
SERBIA
MONT.
BULGARIA
Black Sea
PORTUGAL
Madrid
SPAIN
Corsica (France)
SAN MARINO
Rome
ALBANIA
MAC.
Istanbul
Sardinia (Italy)
VATICAN CITY
GREECE
TURKEY
Gibraltar (U.K.)
Ceuta (Spain)
Melilla (Spain)
Balearic Islands (Spain)
Sicily (Italy)
MALTA
Mediterranean Sea
CYPRUS
SYRIA
LEBANON
Crete (Greece)
MOROCCO
ALGERIA
TUNISIA
60°N
50°N
40°E
50°E
70°N
20°W
10°W
0°
10°E
30°E
40°E

Africa: Political

Africa: Physical

Asia: Political

[Asia: Physical]

Europe: Political

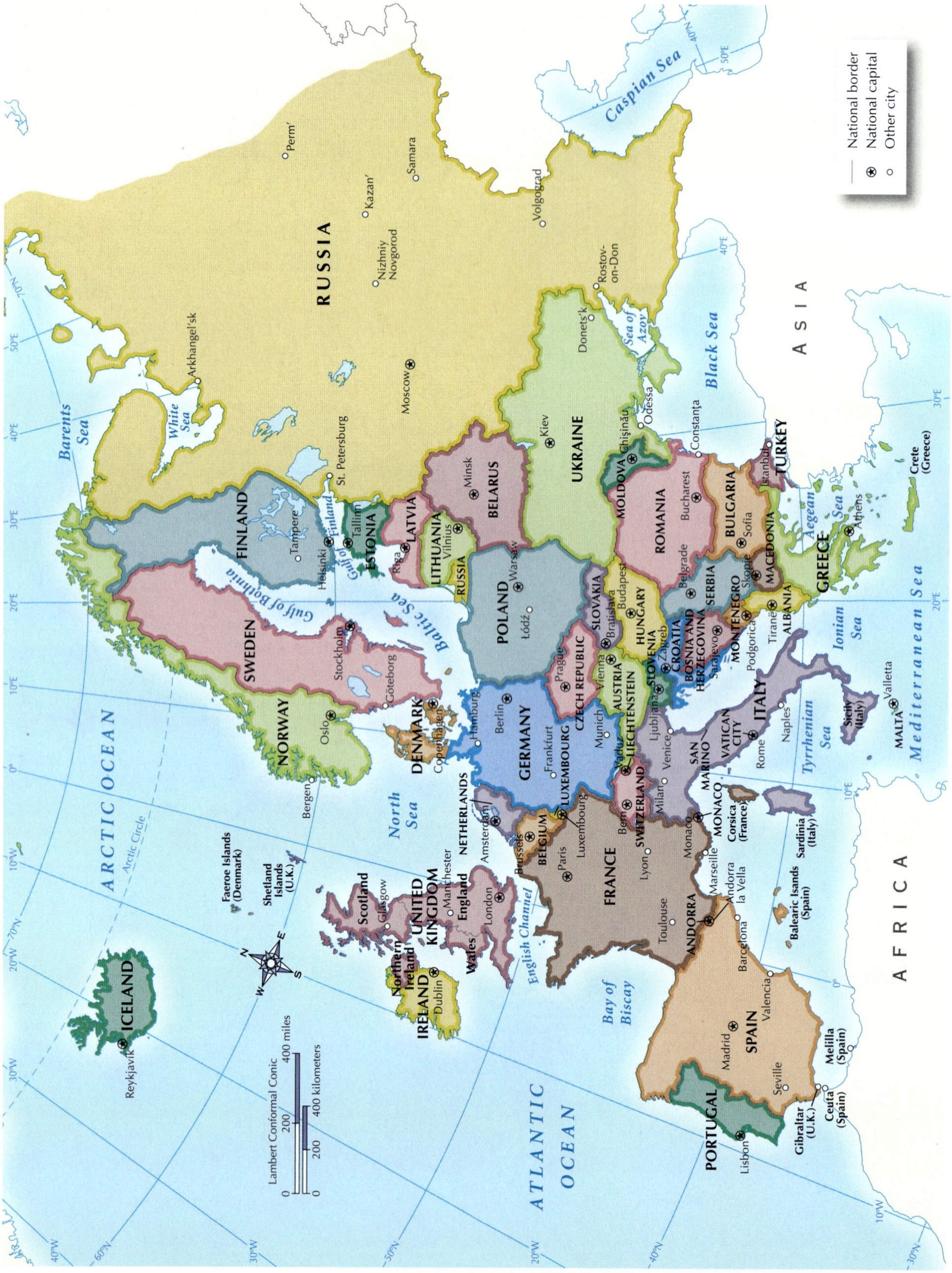

Europe: Physical

North and South America: Political

North and South America: Physical

Australia, New Zealand, and Oceania: Political-Physical

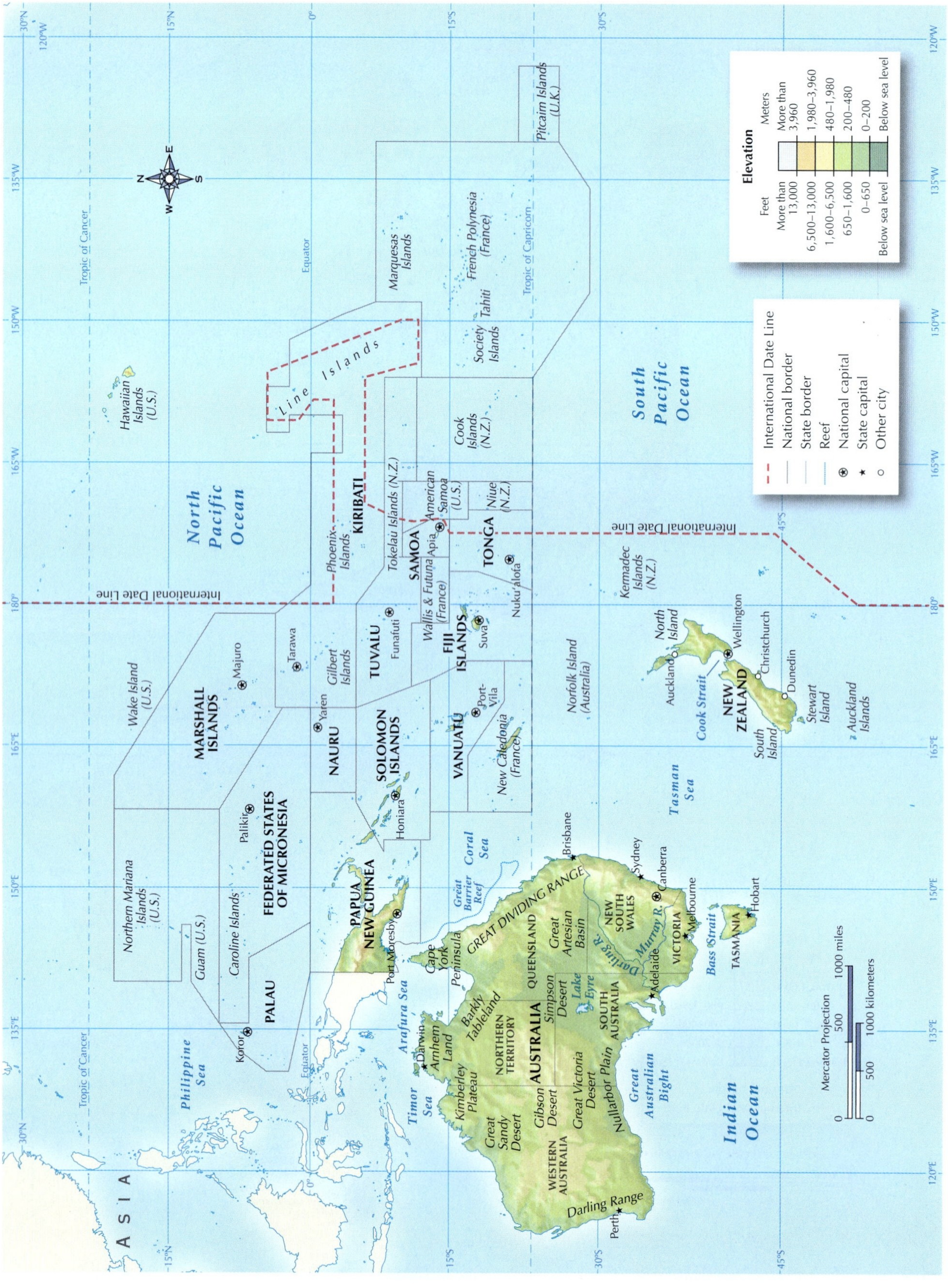

[The Arctic: Physical]

Elevation

Feet		Meters
More than 13,000		More than 3,960
6,500–13,000		1,980–3,960
1,600–6,500		480–1,980
650–1,600		200–400
0–650		0–200
Below sea level		Below sea level

— National border
- - International Date Line

[Antarctica: Physical]

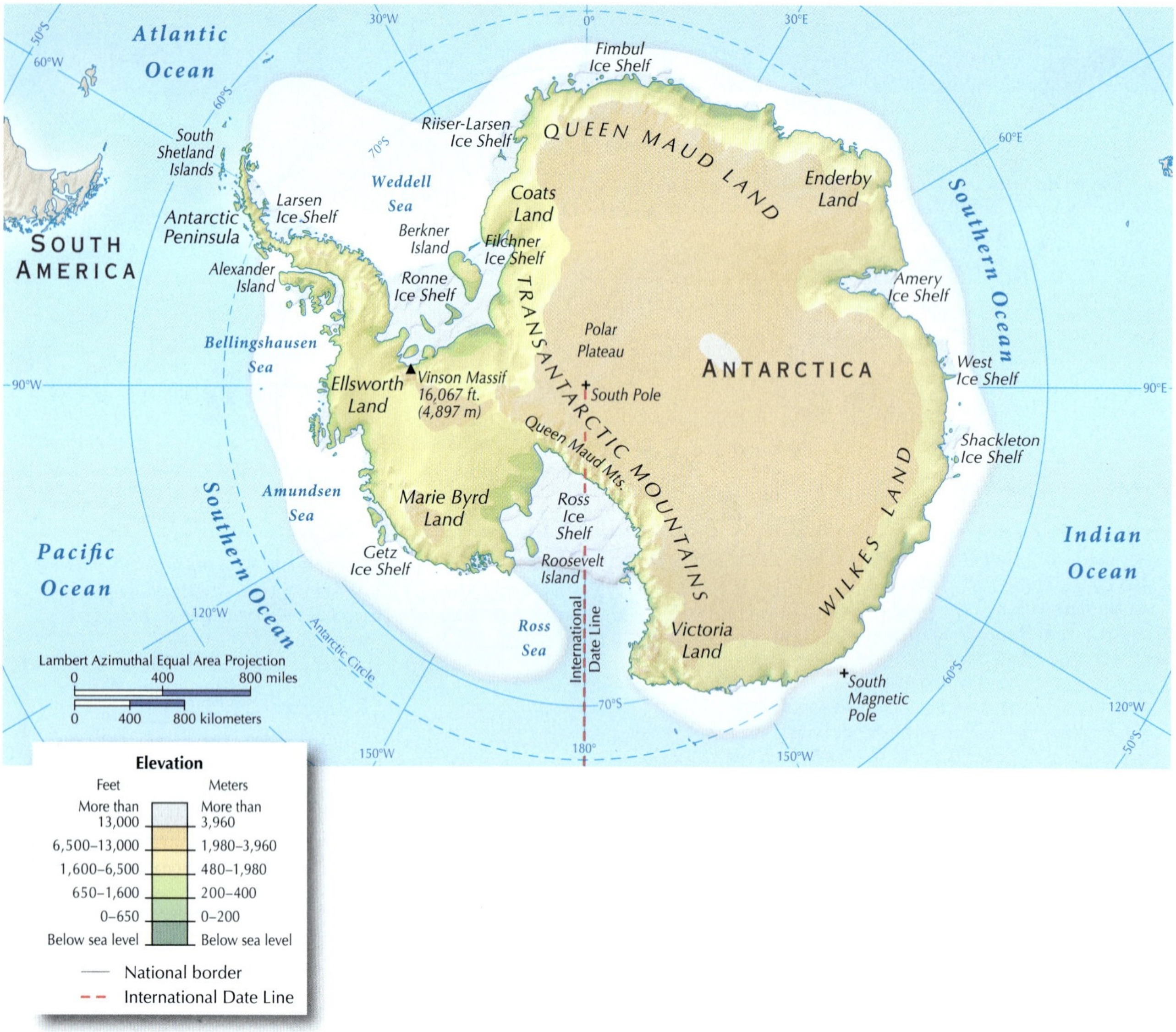

A

abacus a device used for counting and calculating by sliding small balls or beads along rods or in grooves

Abbas the Great, Shah Abbas the Great (1571–1629) was the shah of the Safavid dynasty from 1588 until his death. He drove Ottoman and Uzbek troops from Persia and sponsored a golden age of Persian arts and achievement.

Abbasid dynasty that ruled in Baghdad from 750 to 1258

abdicate give up or step down from power

abolition the campaign against slavery and the slave trade

Abraham According to Jewish tradition, Abraham is the ancestor of the Jewish people. From the city of Ur and the son of an idol merchant, Abraham made a special covenant with God. Abraham led his descendants to Canaan, which Jews consider their Promised Land.

absentee landlord one who owns a large estate but does not live there

absolute monarchy a form of government in which a ruler has complete authority over the government and lives of the people he or she governs

absolutism the belief of complete and unrestricted power in government

abstract art style of art composed of lines, colors, and shapes, sometimes with no recognizable subject matter at all

Abu Bakr Abu Bakr (573–634) was Muhammad's father-in-law and the first Muslim caliph, or leader, following Muhammad's death. An early convert to Islam, Abu Bakr advised Muhammad and traveled on the hijra with the prophet. He helped unite the Muslim people through his role as successor to Muhammad. Under his rule, the Muslim empire expanded.

acculturation the blending of two or more cultures

acid rain a form of pollution in which toxic chemicals in the air come back to Earth in the form of rain, snow, or hail

acropolis highest and most fortified point within a Greek city-state

acupuncture medical treatment, originated in ancient China, in which needles are inserted into the skin at specific points to relieve pain or treat various illnesses

Adenauer, Konrad Konrad Adenauer (1876–1967) served as the first chancellor of West Germany, from 1949 to 1963. He led West Germany during its recovery and reconstruction after World War II. His accomplishments included West Germany's entry into NATO and the founding of the European Economic Community.

adobe a mixture of clay and plant fibers that becomes hard as it dries in the sun and that can be used for building

Adulis strategic trading port of the kingdom of Axum

Afghanistan an Islamic country in Central Asia; invaded by the Soviet Union in 1979; later home to the radical Islamist Taliban and the terrorist group al Qaeda

Afonso I (born around 1460–died 1542), was the ruler of Kongo, a historical kingdom in west-central Africa, in the early 16th century. Afonso encouraged trade with Portugal, promoted European culture in his kingdom, and adopted Christianity as the state religion and as his own religion.

African National Congress (ANC) the main organization that opposed apartheid and pushed for majority rule in South Africa; later a political party

agribusiness giant commercial farm, often owned by a multinational corporation

ahimsa Hindu belief in nonviolence and reverence for all life

aircraft carrier ship that accommodates the taking off and landing of airplanes, and transports aircraft

Akbar Akbar (1542–1605) is considered by most to be the greatest of the Mughal emperors of India. He extended the empire over most of India, and maintained an efficient centralized government through policies that won the loyalty of non-Muslim subjects. His greatness was also built on his support of scholars, artists, and musicians, who made his court a center of culture.

Akhenaton Akhenaton was king of Egypt for 17 years. He abandoned traditional Egyptian polytheism and established a new cult dedicated to the Aton, the sun's disk. His attempt to start a new religion died with him in 1336 B.C.

al Qaeda a fundamentalist terrorist organization founded and led by Saudi Arabian Osama bin Laden until his death in 2011

al-Khwarizmi al-Khwarizmi (c. 780–c. 850) was a Muslim mathematician who developed groundbreaking concepts related to the study of algebra and introduced the term *algebra,* or *al-jabr.* Through his writings, he introduced Europeans to the study of this branch of mathematics. Working in the field of geography as well, al-Khwarizmi also supervised the production of one of the earliest maps of the world.

Albuquerque, Afonso de Afonso de Albuquerque (1453–1515) was a Portuguese admiral who helped found Portugal's trade empire in the East. He captured and built strategic forts at Goa, Calicut, Malacca, and Hormoz; reconstructed other forts; set up shipbuilding and other Portuguese industries in India; and built churches.

Alexander II Alexander II (1818–1881), son of emperor Nicholas I, became tsar in 1855. Alexander II assumed power in the middle of the Crimean War, which revealed Russia's backwardness. He instituted broad modernizing reforms, including emancipating the serfs in 1861. However, growing internal rebellion and increased revolutionary activity in Poland led Alexander to enact repressive measures. He was assassinated in 1881.

Alexander the Great Alexander the Great (356 B.C.–324 B.C.), Philip II's son and Aristotle's pupil, at age 20 became heir to Philip's territories. He conquered the Persian empire, founding new cities as his armies won victories in Asia Minor, Palestine, and Egypt, and then captured Babylon. Continuing eastward into India, his tired troops refused to go farther. Returned to Babylon, Alexander, age 32, died from a sudden fever.

Alexandria Alexandria, founded in 332 B.C. by Alexander the Great, became one of the greatest cities of the Mediterranean world. Located in Egypt on the sea lanes between Europe and Asia, Alexandria became known for its size, great markets, huge Pharos lighthouse, and the Museum, a learning center with a famous library.

Alighieri, Dante Dante Alighieri (1265–1321) was a philosopher, writer, and poet who was deeply involved in Italian politics, including the battles between the popes and monarchs of his time. He held political offices at different times throughout his life. Although he wrote many poems and other works, he is known best for *Divine Comedy.*

alliance formal agreement between two or more nations or powers to cooperate and come to one another's defense

alphabet writing system in which each symbol represents a single basic sound

Alsace and Lorraine region of northern Europe on the border between France and Germany, which was ceded to Germany after the Franco-Prussian War

Amon-Re Amon-Re was considered the king of the gods. He was present in the mythology and culture of the Egyptian people from their beginning.

Amritsar massacre an incident in 1919 in which British troops fired on an unarmed crowd of Indian protestors in the northern Indian town of Amritsar

anarchist a person who wants to abolish all government

ancien régime old order system of government in pre-revolutionary France

anesthetic drug that prevents pain during surgery

animism the belief that spirits and forces live within animals, objects, or dreams

annex add a territory to an existing state or country

Anschluss union of Austria and Germany

anthropology the study of the origins and development of people and their societies

anti-Semitism prejudice against Jews

apartheid a policy of rigid racial segregation in the Republic of South Africa

apostle leader or teacher of a new faith or movement

appeasement policy of giving in to an aggressor's demands in order to keep the peace

apprentice a young person learning a trade from a master

aqueduct in ancient Rome, underground or bridge-like stone structure that carried water from the hills into the city

Aquinas, Thomas Thomas Aquinas (1225–1274) was a philosopher, theologian, and monk who helped bridge the gap between medieval faith and the philosophy of reason promoted by Greek philosophy. He also explained the idea of natural law, that there are universal laws based on reason that are independent of laws passed by government.

Aquino, Benigno Benigno Aquino, Jr., (1932–1983) was the opposition leader during Ferdinand Marcos's dictatorship of the Philippines. His career in politics included terms as a provincial governor and senator, but when he planned to run for president in 1973, Marcos threw him in jail. Aquino spent eight years on death row but was then released to the U.S. to receive heart surgery. In 1983, Aquino returned to the Philippines and was assassinated at the Manila Airport. The military conspiracy against the popular politician led to support for his wife, Corazon Aquino, who proceeded to defeat Marcos in a presidential election.

Aquino, Corazon Corazon Aquino (1933–2009) was president of the Philippines, restoring democracy after Ferdinand Marcos's reign. Educated in the U.S., Aquino married politician Benigno Aquino and focused on raising their children. She accompanied her husband during his exile in the U.S., and when he was executed upon his return to the Philippines, people rallied behind her. She won in a presidential election against Marcos and soon after reestablished congress and appointed a team to write a new constitution. Though Aquino restored freedom to the Philippines, many of her policies were unpopular, and she lost the presidency to her defense secretary in 1992.

Arafat, Yasir Yasir Arafat (1929–2004) fought for Palestinian independence most of his life. He was a founder of Al-Fatah, a group that resisted Israel, and also of the Palestinian Liberation Organization (PLO). In 1969, he became chairman of the PLO. In the early 1990s, he reached a peace agreement with Israel. In 1994, together with Shimon Peres and Yitzhak Rabin, he won the Nobel Peace Prize. He then became the president of the newly created Palestinian Authority.

archaeology the study of people and cultures through material remains

Archimedes Archimedes (c. 287 B.C.–c. 212 B.C.), a famous Hellenistic mathematician and inventor from Syracuse, a Greek colony (now in Italy), is known for understanding the principle of levers, discovering the relation between the surface and volume of a sphere, and inventing the Archimedes screw, a device for raising water.

archipelago chain of islands

aristocracy government headed by a privileged minority or upper class

Aristotle Aristotle (384 B.C.–322 B.C.), a student of Plato, was a philosopher, writer about many branches of knowledge, founder of the Lyceum, and tutor of Alexander the Great.

armada fleet of ships

armistice agreement to end fighting in a war

artifact an object made by human beings

artificial satellite manmade object that orbits a larger body in space

artisan a skilled craftsperson

Asante kingdom kingdom that emerged in the 1700s in present-day Ghana and was active in the slave trade

Asantewaa, Yaa Yaa Asantewaa (c. 1850–c. 1920) was the queen mother of the Edweso tribe of the Asante, who led a revolt against British rule starting in 1900.

Asia Minor a peninsula in western Asia between the Black Sea and the Mediterranean Sea

Asoka Asoka, who died about 238 B.C., was the last major Mauryan emperor in India. A committed Buddhist, he helped to spread Buddhism throughout India. His rule was characterized by fairness, compassion, and the principles of right life, which he had inscribed on stone pillars erected throughout the empire.

assassination murder of a public figure, usually for political reasons

assembly line a production method that breaks down a complex job into a series of smaller tasks

assimilate absorb or adopt another culture

Atatürk Atatürk (1881–1938) is the name that Mustafa Kemal gave himself when he ordered all Turkish people to take on surnames. In 1920, he led Turkish nationalists in the fight against Greek forces trying to enforce the Treaty of Sèvres, establishing the borders of the modern Republic of Turkey. Once in power, he passed many reforms to modernize, Westernize, and secularize Turkey.

atheism belief that there is no god

Athens city-state in ancient Greece that evolved from a monarchy to a limited direct democracy and became famous for its great cultural achievements

Atlantic Charter agreement in which Franklin Roosevelt and Winston Churchill set goals for the defeat of Nazi Germany and for the postwar world

atman in Hindu belief, a person's essential self

atrocity horrible act committed against innocent people

Augustine Augustine (A.D. 364–A.D. 430) was a Christian scholar whose written works had long-lasting effects on the Christian religion. He studied in Roman Africa and went on to become a bishop.

Augustus (63 B.C.–14 A.D.) was the first Roman emperor of the newly established Roman empire. Augustus's rule began a long-lasting period of peace and wealth known as the *Pax Romana*.

Auschwitz a group of three German concentration camps and extermination camps in southern Poland, built and operated during the Third Reich

autocrat ruler who has complete authority

autocratic having unlimited power

autonomy self-rule

Axis powers group of countries led by Germany, Italy, and Japan that fought the Allies in World War II

Axum trading center and powerful ancient kingdom in northern present-day Ethiopia

ayllu in the Inca empire, a close-knit village

B

Babur Babur (1483–1530) was the founder of the Mughal Dynasty in India. He came from Turkish and Mongol heritages, a descendent of the great Mongol leader, Genghis Khan. His name is the Arabic word for "tiger," but he was as accomplished a poet as he was a warrior. His wise rule helped launch a powerful Muslim dynasty that had a permanent influence on northern India.

Bacon, Francis Francis Bacon (1561–1626) was a distinguished English philosopher, statesman, and lawyer. A man of many talents, he promoted rational thought. Bacon was held in high regard by philosophers and scientists in Europe as well as England.

Baghdad capital city of present-day Iraq; capital of the Muslim empire during Islam's golden age

balance of power distribution of military and economic power that prevents any one nation from becoming too strong

balance of trade difference between how much a country imports and how much it exports

Balfour Declaration statement issued by the British government in 1917 supporting the idea of a homeland for Jews in the Palestine Mandate

Balkan Peninsula triangular arm of land that juts from southeastern Europe into the Mediterranean

Bangladesh nation east of India that was formerly part of Pakistan

Bantu root language of West Africa on which some early African migration patterns are based

Barbarossa, Frederick Frederick Barbarossa (c. 1123–1190) was a German king who became Holy Roman Emperor in 1152. He fought hard against growing papal authority and led six expeditions into Italy in an attempt to increase his royal holdings. He died while on the Third Crusade.

baroque ornate style of art and architecture popular in the 1600s and 1700s

barter economy economic system in which one set of goods or services is exchanged for another

Bastille fortress in Paris used as a prison; French Revolution began when Parisians stormed it in 1789

Bataan Death March during World War II, the forced march of Filipino and American prisoners of war under brutal conditions by the Japanese military

battle of Tours battle in 732 in which the Christian Franks led by Charles Martel defeated the Muslim armies and stopped the Muslim advance into Europe

Bedouin a desert-dwelling Arab nomad

Beethoven, Ludwig van Ludwig van Beethoven (1770–1827) was a German composer trained in piano and violin by his father Johannes. At the age of 12, he published his first work and began playing viola in the symphony orchestra in Bonn, Germany. In 1792, he went to Vienna and began studying with Haydn. Beethoven remained in Vienna, where he wrote most of his symphonies, concertos, sonatas, and string quartets. Although he began to lose his hearing 1798, he continued to compose music he could hear only in his mind.

Benedictine Rule rules drawn up in 530 by Benedict, a monk, regulating monastic life. The Rule emphasizes obedience, poverty, and chastity and divides the day into periods of worship, work, and study

Bentham, Jeremy Jeremy Bentham (1748–1832) was a British philosopher and economist who advocated for utilitarianism, the belief that right and wrong can be measured by the greatest happiness of the greatest number of people. Bentham was trained in the law but did not become a practicing lawyer. Instead, he focused on legal reforms. Not content to simply suggest new laws, he also detailed plans for how to implement his proposals. His ideas were influential during his lifetime, and some of his reforms were enacted.

Bessemer, Henry Henry Bessemer (1813–1879) was a British inventor and engineer. His greatest invention was the Bessemer Converter, which could create high-quality steel quickly and inexpensively. In 1956 he patented his process for making steel. His process was essential to advances in transportation, construction, and defense. Today, steel is still made by a method based on the Bessemer process.

Biafra region of southeastern Nigeria that launched a failed bid for independence from Nigeria in 1966, resulting in a bloody war

biotechnology the application of biological research to industry, engineering, and technology

bishop high-ranking Church official with authority over a local area, or diocese

Bismarck, Otto von Otto von Bismarck (1815–1898) worked briefly as a civil servant before his career in government. He served as a diplomat to the German Federation, and he became chancellor of the German Empire in 1871, a position he held for 19 years.

Black Death an epidemic of the bubonic plague that ravaged Europe in the 1300s

Black Shirt any member of the militant combat squads of Italian Fascists set up under Mussolini

blitzkrieg lightning war

bloc a group of nations acting together in support of one another

Boer War (1899–1902) a war in which Great Britain defeated the Boers of South Africa

Boers Dutch farmers who settled in Cape Town, Africa, and eventually migrated inland

Bolívar, Simón Simón Bolívar (1783–1830) was a South American soldier and leader who was instrumental in the revolutions against Spain. He was born into wealth and educated in Spain. After France invaded Spain, he became involved in the resistance movement and played a key role in the Latin American fight for independence. He died in 1830 from tuberculosis.

Bonaparte, Napoleon Napoleon Bonaparte (1769–1821) was a huge figure in European history. He was a military genius who was elected consul for life. He later crowned himself France's emperor. His legal, educational, and militaristic reforms impacted French society for generations.

bourgeoisie the middle class

Boxer Uprising anti-foreign movement in China from 1898–1900

boyar landowning noble in Russia under the tsars

boycott refuse to buy

Boyle, Robert Robert Boyle (1627–1691) was one of the leading minds of the late 1600s. An English-Irish philosopher and writer, Boyle focused on chemistry, physics, and natural history. His work with pressurized air led to the development of Boyle's Law, which describes the relationship between pressure and the volume of gas. Boyle was one of the founders of the Royal Society of London.

Brahe, Tycho Tycho Brahe (1546–1601) was a Danish astronomer who produced the most accurate measurements and locations of the stars before the use of the telescope. His observation that a new star had appeared in an existing constellation challenged the belief that the stars were fixed and forever unchanging.

Brahman in the belief system established in Aryan India, a single spiritual power that resides in all things

Brezhnev, Leonid Leonid Brezhnev (1906–1982) led the Soviet Union from 1964, when he organized the removal of Nikita Khrushchev, until his death in 1982. He presided over the Soviet Union's last arms build-up and the economic stagnation that encouraged the reforms of Mikhail Gorbachev.

bureaucracy system of government through departments and subdivisions administered by officials who follow set rules

bushido code of conduct for samurai during the feudal period in Japan

Byron, Lord Lord Byron (1788–1824) was a member of the House of Lords, a political and social satirist, and one of the most memorable, fashionable, and captivating Romantic poets. He became the model for the Romantic hero and the embodiment of the movement. Byron believed in liberty, which he often focused on in both his works and deeds. Although Byron died before he completed his poem *Don Juan,* it is considered to be his masterpiece and one of England's great long poems.

C

cabinet parliamentary advisors to the king who originally met in a small room, or cabinet

Cabot, John John Cabot (c. 1450–c. 1499) had his early roots in Venice, Italy, working in a mercantile firm. He became a navigator and explorer who, during 1497–1498, claimed parts of Canada for Britain.

Caesar, Julius (c. 100 B.C.–44 B.C.) was a Roman general, master of political maneuvers, and a reformist. He advocated for the re-organization of Rome's government. In 47 B.C., he became dictator, and three years later was assassinated.

cahiers notebooks used in pre-revolutionary France to record grievances

Cahokia in Illinois, the largest earthwork of the Mississippian culture, c. A.D. 700

calculus a branch of mathematics in which calculations are made using special symbolic notations, developed by Isaac Newton

caliph successor to Muhammad as political and religious leader of the Muslims

calligraphy the art of producing beautiful handwriting

Calvin, John John Calvin (1509–1564) was a French theologian and lawyer. Influenced by the humanist philosophy of Erasmus, Calvin became involved with the Protestant movement while a student at the University of Paris. He later moved to Geneva, Switzerland, where he set up a theocracy and wrote *Institutes of the Christian Religion.* Calvin's interpretation of Christian doctrine is called Calvinism.

canon law body of laws of a church

canonize recognize a person as a saint

Cape Town the first permanent European settlement in Africa, established by the Dutch in 1652

capital money or wealth used to invest in business or enterprise

capital offense crime punishable by death

capitalism economic system in which the means of production are privately owned and operated for profit

Cárdenas, Lázaro Lázaro Cárdenas (1895–1970) joined the revolutionary forces when he was 18 and later became a general in the Mexican army. After the revolution, he served as governor of Michoacán and then as president of the PNR. In 1934, he was elected president of Mexico. During his presidency, Cárdenas worked to establish the social and economic reforms the revolutionaries had fought for, including the redistribution of land, the organization of confederations for both workers and peasants, and the nationalization of foreign-owned industries.

Carranza, Venustiano Venustiano Carranza (1859–1920) served as a leader in the Mexican Revolution in support of political, rather than social, reform. He was elected the first president after the revolution, and though he signed the Constitution of 1917, he did little to implement promised reforms. This reluctance led to social unrest and economic difficulties. When a rebellion began in April 1920, Carranza fled the capital and eventually went into hiding in the mountains. He was betrayed and murdered in May.

cartel a group of companies that join together to control the production and price of a product

Cartier, Jacques Jacques Cartier (1491–1557) is credited with naming Canada. He is also recognized for his limited exploration of the St. Lawrence River, stopped short by severe weather and hostile Iroquois Indians.

cartographer a person who makes maps

caste in traditional Indian society, an unchangeable social group into which a person is born

Castiglione, Baldassare Castiglione (1478–1529) was an Italian courtier, diplomat, and writer. His handbook, *The Book of the Courtier,* was widely read for its advice on the manners, skills, learning, and virtues that court members should display. He described an ideal courtier as well-mannered, well-educated, and multitalented.

Castro, Fidel Fidel Castro (b. 1926) served as leader of Cuba beginning in 1959, when he led the Cuban Revolution and installed a communist regime. During the Cold War, Castro's Cuba was allied with the Soviet Union and, therefore, at odds with the United States. His policies remained socialist after the fall of the Soviet Union. When his health began to fail in 2006, his brother, Raul, took over as the Cuban leader.

Çatalhüyük one of the world's first villages, established in modern-day Turkey around 7000 B.C.

cataract waterfall

Catherine the Great Catherine the Great (1729–1796) was the German-born empress of Russia (1762–1796) who led her country in becoming part of the political and cultural life of Europe.

caudillo military dictator in Latin America

Cavour, Camillo Camillo Cavour (1810–1861) was the second son of a noble family. After a brief career in the military, he decided that politics was his true strength. His ability to manipulate political situations to further the cause of Italian unification made him a valuable leader.

Ceausescu, Nicolae Nicolae Ceausescu (1918–1989) led the communist government in Romania from 1965 until his death in 1989. His regime was noted for its massive corruption, crippling economic conditions, and unchecked secret police. He was executed, along with his wife, Elena, after the coup that ended communist rule in Romania.

celadon porcelain made in Korea with an unusual blue-green glaze

censorship restriction on access to ideas and information

census population count

Cervantes, Miguel de Miguel de Cervantes (1547–1616), a Spanish novelist, playwright, and poet, was the most important figure in Spanish literature. His novel Don Quixote is his most well-known work.

Champlain, Samuel de Samuel de Champlain (1567–1635) was a French navigator and explorer who established the colony of Quebec in 1608. He became known as the "Father of New France" and was honored by the court of King Henry IV.

chancellor the highest official of a monarch, prime minister

characters written symbols in writing systems such as that of the Chinese

Charlemagne Charlemagne (747–814), (or "Charles the Great") king of the Franks, the Lombards, and emperor of the Romans, began as a warrior king seeking to conquer territory and distribute plunder in the Frankish tradition. But he also strove to unite and govern an increasingly diverse collection of conquered peoples as well as cope with threats from new invaders. He conducted a long series of successful military campaigns, made efforts to spread Christianity and implement religious reform, sought to make more effective inherited political institutions and procedures, and supported cultural renewal through a revival of learning.

Charles I Charles I (1600–1649) was the second Stuart king of England, Scotland, and Wales. His belief in the divine right of kings brought him into constant conflict with Parliament. This conflict eventually led to the English Civil War and Charles's defeat and execution for treason.

Charles V Charles V (1500–1558) was the Holy Roman emperor during the time of Martin Luther's reformation efforts. His immense empire included large areas of Europe. A staunch Catholic, he rejected Luther's doctrines. The Protestant upheaval, along with political pressures, led Charles to voluntarily give up his throne. He divided the empire between his son and his brother. Charles entered a Catholic monastery where he remained until his death.

charter in the Middle Ages, a written document that set out the rights and privileges of a town

Chaucer, Geoffrey Geoffrey Chaucer (1343–1400) was the first important poet of his time to write in English. At various times during his life he worked as a copywriter, member of Parliament, and justice of the peace. His keen observations of many different types of people was reflected in his famous work, *Canterbury Tales.*

Chavín a culture that thrived in the Andean region from about 900 to 200 B.C.

Chechnya a republic within Russia, where rebels have fought for independence

checks and balances system in which each branch of a government has the power to monitor and limit the actions of the other two

Cheka early Soviet secret police force

chinampa in the Aztec empire, an artificial island used to cultivate crops and made of mud piled atop reed mats that were anchored to the lake bed with willow trees

chivalry code of conduct for knights during the Middle Ages

Choson dynasty Korean dynasty that ruled from 1392 to 1910, the longest-lived of Korea's three dynasties

Christian Bible the sacred writings of the Christian religion

Churchill, Winston Winston Churchill (1874–1965) was born to British aristocracy and became prime minister of the British empire in 1940. Early on, he proclaimed the threats posed by Nazi Germany. His determination persuaded the country to defend itself against an encroaching enemy.

circumnavigate to travel completely around the world

citizen a native or resident of a town or city

city-state a political unit that includes a city and its surrounding lands and villages

civil disobedience the refusal to obey unjust laws

civil law branch of law that deals with private rights and matters

civil servants government officials

civil war a war fought between groups of people in the same nation

civilization an advanced stage of human society marked by a well-organized government and high levels of culture, science, and industry.

clan group of families with a common ancestor

clergy the body of people who conduct Christian services

Clovis Clovis (466–511) is known as the political and religious founder of the kingdom of the Franks. He ruled much of Gaul from the late fifth century until 511. His kingdom, which expanded south and west from what is present-day Belgium and northeastern France, was the most powerful in Gaul. He was also the most important ally of the Byzantine emperor Anastasius I. Born a pagan, Clovis corresponded with the powerful bishops of Gaul and, in 496 or perhaps later, became famous as one of the first Germanic kings to convert to Christianity.

coalition temporary alliance of various political parties

codify to arrange or set down in writing

Colbert, Jean-Baptiste Jean-Baptiste Colbert (1619–1683) served under King Louis XIV of France as controller general of finance (from 1665) and secretary of state for the navy (from 1668). He carried out economic programs that helped make France the strongest power in Europe.

Cold War state of tension and hostility between nations aligned with the United States on one side and the Soviet Union on the other that rarely led to direct armed conflict

collective large farm owned and operated by peasants as a group

collective security system in which a group of nations acts as one to preserve the peace of all

collectivization the forced joining together of workers and property into collectives, such as rural collectives that absorb peasants and their land

colony territory settled and ruled by people from another land

colossus giant

Columbian Exchange the global exchange of goods, ideas, plants and animals, and disease that began with Columbus's journey to the Americas

Columbus, Christopher Christopher Columbus (1451–1506) was an Italian explorer and navigator who went on Mediterranean and Africa expeditions, thought up a plan to sail west to reach India and China, and found support from the Spanish monarchs Ferdinand and Isabella. In 1492, he sailed west from Spain and reached the Caribbean Islands, which he mistakenly thought were the Indies of Asia. He made other voyages, but strained relations with the Spanish royal officials led to his arrest and dismissal as governor of the settlements on the island of Hispaniola.

comedy in ancient Greece, play that mocked people or social customs

Comintern Communist International, international association of communist parties led by the Soviet Union for the purpose of encouraging worldwide communist revolution

command economy system in which government officials make all basic economic decisions

Commercial Revolution A period of European economic expansion, colonialism, and mercantilism which lasted from about the 1500s until the early 1700s. It included the growth of capitalism, banking, and investing.

commissar Communist party official assigned to the army to teach party principles and ensure party loyalty during the Russian Revolution

commodity valuable product

common law a legal system based on custom and court rulings

communism form of socialism advocated by Karl Marx; According to Marx, class struggle was inevitable and would lead to the creation of a classless society in which all wealth and property would be owned by the community as a whole.

compact an agreement among people

compromise an agreement in which each side makes concessions; an acceptable middle ground

concentration camp detention center for civilians considered enemies of the state

Concert of Europe loose peacekeeping organization whose goal was to preserve the agreements set up by the Congress of Vienna

concession special economic right given to foreign companies or individuals

confederation unification

Confucius (551 B.C.–479 B.C.) is China's most famous philosopher. His teachings about the importance of education and public service influenced many eastern Asian civilizations. His ancestors, members of the aristocracy, were poor by the time of Confucius's birth. By the age of 15, Confucius was dedicated to the life of a scholar. Although his ideas about the proper way to live guided millions of people, Confucius's own life was simple and reflected a deep humility.

Congress of Vienna assembly of European leaders that met after the Napoleonic era to piece Europe back together; met from September 1814 to June 1815

conquistador "conqueror" in Spanish; a leader in the Spanish conquests of America, Mexico, and Peru in the sixteenth century

conscription "the draft," which required all young men to be ready for military or other service

consensus widespread agreement among all members of a group

Constantine Constantine (c. A.D. 280– A.D. 337) was the first Roman Emperor to become a Christian. During his reign, he prevented the persecution of Christians and helped to strengthen the early church.

Constantinople the capital of the eastern Roman empire; capital of the Byzantine and Ottoman empires, now called Istanbul

constitutional government government whose power is defined and limited by law

consul an official from the patrician class who supervised the government and commanded the armies

containment the U.S. strategy of limiting communism to the areas already under Soviet control

Continental System blockade designed by Napoleon to hurt Britain economically by closing European ports to British goods; ultimately unsuccessful

contra guerrilla who fought the Sandinistas in Nicaragua

contraband during wartime, military supplies and raw materials needed to make military supplies that may legally be confiscated by any belligerent

convoy group of merchant ships protected by warships

Copernicus, Nicolaus Nicolaus Copernicus (1473–1543) was a Polish astronomer who concluded that the sun is the center of the universe around which Earth and the other planets revolve. This contradicted the religious and scientific belief that Earth was the center of the universe. Although he did not suffer immediate challenges from the Church, his most important work did not appear in print until after his death.

corporation a business owned by many investors who buy shares of stock and risk only the amount of their investment

Cortés, Hernán Hernán Cortés (c. 1485–1547) was a Spanish landowner in Cuba and conquistador who in 1518 led an expedition to Mexico. Allied with some Native American groups, he conquered the Aztec empire, including its capital Tenochititlán in 1521. The Holy Roman Emperor Charles V in 1522 appointed him governor of New Spain, but Cortés was eventually removed from power and retired to Spain in 1540.

Council of Trent a group of Catholic leaders that met between 1545 and 1563 to respond to Protestant challenges and direct the future of the Catholic Church

coup d'état the forcible overthrow of a government

Courbet, Gustave Gustave Courbet (1819–1877) was a leading French painter in the Realist movement. While he more painted traditional subjects, such as seascapes, portraits, and landscapes, he also focused on representing daily life by painting the rural middle class and bohemian culture, as well as social issues by depicting the harsh lives of the poor.

covenant a binding agreement; specifically, in the Jewish tradition, the binding agreement God made with Abraham

Cranmer, Thomas Thomas Cranmer (1489–1556) was a Catholic theologian who strongly supported reform. When Henry VIII broke with the Roman Catholic Church, Cranmer became England's first Protestant archbishop of Canterbury. He distributed English language Bibles to parish churches and, later, developed the *Book of Common Prayer.* Cranmer also acted as an adviser to both Henry VIII and his son, Edward VI.

crematorium a place used to burn corpses

creole in Spanish colonial America, an American-born descendant of Spanish settlers

Crimean War war fought mainly on the Crimean Peninsula between the Russians and the British, French, and Turks from 1853–1856

criminal law branch of law that deals with offenses against others

Cromwell, Oliver Oliver Cromwell (1599–1658) was an English soldier and gentleman who led the forces against Charles I of England during the English Civil War. He made himself Lord Protector of England in 1653, leading the country as a republic until his death.

Crusades a series of wars from the 1000s through 1200s in which European Christians tried to win control of the Holy Land from Muslims

cult of domesticity idealization of women and the home

cultural diffusion the spread of ideas, customs, and technologies from one people to another

cultural nationalism pride in the culture of one's country

Cultural Revolution a Chinese Communist program in the late 1960s to purge China of nonrevolutionary tendencies that caused economic and social damage

culture the way of life of a society, which is handed down from one generation to the next by learning and experience

cuneiform in the ancient Middle East, a system of writing that used wedge-shaped marks

Curie, Marie Marie Curie (1867–1934) was born in Warsaw to Polish schoolteachers. She later moved to Paris, where she gained a formal education and met her husband Pierre Curie. The Curies conducted groundbreaking work on radioactivity, revolutionizing the fields of physics and chemistry. The first woman to win a Nobel Prize, Marie Curie also worked tirelessly to promote practical and medicinal applications of her work. She died in 1934, most likely from her many years of exposure to radioactive materials.

Cuzco capital city of the Inca empire

Cyrillic relating to the Slavic alphabet derived from the Greek and traditionally attributed to St. Cyril; in modified form still used in modern Slavic languages

D

D-Day code name for June 6, 1944, the day that Allied forces invaded France during WWII

da Vinci, Leonardo Leonardo da Vinci (1452–1519) was an Italian artist considered the ideal Renaissance man due to his varied talents. His interests included botany, anatomy, optics, music, architecture, and engineering. His sketches for flying machines and undersea boats resembled the later inventions of airplanes and submarines. Leonardo's paintings, such as the *Mona Lisa* and *The Last Supper,* remain famous today.

dada artistic movement in which artists rejected tradition and produced works that often shocked their viewers

Daguerre, Louis Louis Daguerre (1787–1851) was a French painter and physicist who invented photography. Before Daguerre invented the camera, he was a printmaker and painter. For years he had been experimenting with ways to capture detailed, photographic images. Finally, in 1839, he showed his process to the Académie des Sciences and the Académie des Beaux-Arts. He astounded everyone, and his invention revolutionized both the arts and the sciences.

dalit outcast or member of India's lowest caste

Dalton, John John Dalton (1766–1844) was an English teacher, lecturer, meteorologist, physicist, and chemist. His interest in the atmosphere led to his development of the Atomic Theory in 1803. His theory stated that atoms have mass, that elements are made up of atoms, and that chemical reactions could be explained by the combination and separation of atoms. Although parts of his theory have now been proved wrong, it remains the foundation of modern chemistry and physical science.

Dardanelles vital strait connecting the Black Sea and the Mediterranean Sea in present-day Turkey

Darfur a region in western Sudan where ethnic conflict threatened to lead to genocide

Darwin, Charles Charles Darwin (1809–1882) was an English naturalist who developed the theory of evolution through the process of natural selection. In 1831, he set sail on a five-year voyage around the world. While in the Galápagos Islands, Darwin observed that the four species of finches on the islands had different beaks and eating habits. He theorized that isolation, time, and adapting to local conditions, leads to new species. His observation and the samples he collected helped him develop his theory of evolution.

David As described in the Books of Samuel, 1 Kings, and 1 Chronicles, David was from the tribe of Judah and began his life as a shepherd in Bethlehem. Eventually, David became king of a united Israel. Jews and Christians also believe he edited the Book of Psalms.

Deák, Ferenc Ferenc Deák (1803–1876), also known as the Sage of the Country, was a Hungarian politician, reformer, and thinker. He is most famous for developing the concept of the Dual Monarchy and guiding that compromise to its final adoption.

decimal system system of numbers based on 10

decipher to figure out the meaning of

default fail to make payments

deficit gap between what a government spends and what it takes in through taxes and other sources

deficit spending situation in which the government spends more money than it takes in

deforestation the destruction of forest land

Delhi the third-largest city in India, capital of medieval India

delta triangular area of marshland formed by deposits of silt at the mouth of some rivers

demilitarized zone a thin band of territory across the Korean peninsula separating North Korean forces from South Korean forces; established by the armistice of 1953

democracy government in which the people hold ruling power

Deng Xiaoping Deng Xiaoping (1904–1997) was born in Sichuan province in China. As a young man, he studied in France and the Soviet Union. He became involved in the communist movement while in France. After the Communists took over China, he served in several high positions in the government, eventually becoming the most powerful policy maker in the nation. His policies are responsible for much of China's economic growth after the failures of the Cultural Revolution.

depopulation reduction in the number of people in an area

Descartes, René René Descartes (1596–1650) was a French philosopher, mathematician, and scientist. Descartes was one of the first to abandon traditional methods of thought based on Aristotle's teachings. Instead, he promoted a new science based on observation and experiments. For this, he has been called the father of modern philosophy.

desertification process by which fertile or semi-desert land becomes desert

détente the relaxation of Cold War tensions during the 1970s
developing world nations working toward development in Africa, Asia, and Latin America
development the process of building stable governments, improving agriculture and industry, and raising the standard of living
dharma in Hindu belief, the religious and moral duties of an individual
Diaspora the spreading of the Jews beyond their historic homeland
Díaz, Porfirio Porfirio Díaz (1830–1915) served as president of Mexico twice: 1877–1880 and 1884–1911. Díaz consolidated power in the central government and put wealth in the hands of a few by bringing in foreign investors to build infrastructure and dig mines. Because the wealth was not evenly distributed, discontent spread. By 1910, the economy was in a sharp decline, and workers and peasants were living in poverty or debt. In 1911, Díaz resigned and went into exile.
Dickens, Charles Charles Dickens (1812–1870) was an English author who began his writing career as a freelance reporter. In 1836, he began publishing installments of his first novel, *The Pickwick Papers,* which launched his career as a novelist. Dickens created some of literature's most famous and vivid characters. As a realist, Dickens was dedicated to depicting real life. He hoped to bring about reform, so his novels often focused on the problems of the poor to expose social ills.
dictator ruler who has complete control over a government
Dien Bien Phu small town and former French army base in northern Vietnam; site of the battle that ended in a Vietnamese victory, the French withdrawal from Vietnam, and the securing of North Vietnam's independence
Diet assembly or legislature
diet assembly or legislature
Diocletian (A.D. 245–A.D. 311) was a Roman general who became emperor. To make the government more effective, he divided the large empire into East and West and appointed a co-emperor.
direct democracy system of government in which citizens participate directly in the day-to-day affairs of government rather than through elected representatives
disarmament reduction of armed forces and weapons
discrimination unequal treatment or barriers
Disraeli, Benjamin Benjamin Disraeli (1804–1881) was a leading Conservative politician and spent seven years as prime minister. Along with other political leaders, Disraeli worked to expand suffrage and slowly transformed the British Parliament during the 1800s into a more democratic institution. His spearheading of the Second Reform Act of 1867, allowed more men to vote, including members of the working class. Disraeli also focused on other social reforms, including public health laws and recognition of workers' unions.
dissent ideas that oppose those of the government
dissenter Protestant whose views and opinions differed from those of the Church of England
divine right idea that a ruler's authority came directly from God
domesticate to tame animals and adapt crops so they are best suited to use by humans
dominion self-governing nation
domino theory the belief that a communist victory in South Vietnam would cause noncommunist governments across Southeast Asia to fall to communism, like a row of dominoes
dowry in some societies, payment a bride's family makes to the bridegroom and his family; payment a woman brings to a marriage
Dreyfus Affair a political scandal that caused deep divisions in France; it centered on the 1894 wrongful conviction for treason of Alfred Dreyfus, a Jewish officer in the French army.
Dual Monarchy the monarchy of Austria-Hungary
due process of law the requirement that the government act fairly and in accordance with established rules in all that it does
Duma elected national legislature in Russia
Dunkirk port in France from which 300,000 Allied troops were evacuated when their retreat by land was cut off by the German advance in 1940
Dürer, Albrecht Albrecht Dürer (1471–1528) was born in Nuremberg, Germany. A painter, draftsman, and writer, his greatest artistic impact was in engraving. He traveled to Italy, studied the Italian masters, and helped spread Renaissance ideas to northern Europe. Many of his famous works, such as *The Apocalypse,* and *Adam and Eve,* had religious themes.
Dutch East India Company a trading company established with full sovereign powers by the Netherlands in 1602 to protect and expand its trade in Asia
dynamo a machine used to generate electricity
dynastic cycle rise and fall of Chinese dynasties according to the Mandate of Heaven
dynasty ruling family

E

earthwork an embankment or other construction made of earth
East Timor a former Portuguese colony, seized by Indonesia, that gained independence in 2002
economic nationalism an emphasis on domestic control and protection of the economy
Edict of Nantes law issued by French king Henry IV in 1598 giving more religious freedom to French Protestants
Edison, Thomas Thomas Edison (1847–1931) applied for his first patent while working as a telegraph operator for Western Union. Although this first invention was a flop, Edison did not give up and went on to become one of the world's most prolific inventors. Throughout his life he patented 1,093 inventions and improvements in several industries, including telecommunications, electric power, mining, sound recording, automotive, military defense, and motion pictures.
Eightfold Path as taught by the Buddha, the path one must follow to achieve nirvana
Einstein, Albert Albert Einstein (1879–1955) was born into a middle-class Jewish family in Germany. He published his theories of relativity in 1905 and 1916, winning the Nobel Prize for Physics in 1921. These ideas challenged long-held beliefs regarding the nature of the universe. As German Nazis came to power, Einstein emigrated with his family to the United States in 1932 and became a citizen in 1940. During World War II, his work was used in the creation of the atomic bomb. As nuclear technology spread, Einstein advocated for international controls and limitations. He is widely considered the most influential physicist of the 20th century.

Eisenhower, Dwight Dwight Eisenhower (1890–1969) grew up poor and came from a hard-working family. During World War II, he was the American general who commanded the Allied forces in western Europe. "Ike" later served as the 34th president of the United States, from 1953–1961.

Eleanor of Acquitaine Eleanor of Aquitaine (1122–1204), was an heiress to the dukedom of Aquitaine. At age 15, she married the French royal heir, Louis VI, and became queen of France. Intelligent and energetic, she strongly influenced her husband and went with him on the Second Crusade. Her second marriage was to Henry Plantagenet, who became Henry II of England in 1154. While caring for five sons and three daughters, she actively helped administer England, managed her own domains—making the court at Poitiers a model of courtly life—and remained politically active into her 80s.

elector one of seven German princes who would choose the Holy Roman emperor

electorate body of people allowed to vote

elite upper class

Elizabeth Elizabeth Tudor (1533–1603) became Queen Elizabeth I of England upon the death of Queen Mary. Shifting politics made her early years quite hazardous. Elizabeth used her experiences to become a shrewd and powerful monarch. Under her reign, England became an important European power. England prospered both economically, and culturally. Her balanced handling of the English religious conflicts earned her the nickname Good Queen Bess.

emancipation granting of freedom to serfs or slaves

emigration movement away from one's homeland

émigré a person who flee his or her country for political reasons

empire a group of states or territories controlled by one ruler

enclosure the process of taking over and consolidating land formerly shared by peasant farmers

encomienda the right, granted by Spanish monarchs to conquistadors, to demand labor or tribute from Native Americans in a particular area

endangered species species threatened with extinction

engineering application of science and mathematics to develop useful structures and machines

English Bill of Rights series of acts passed in 1689 by the English Parliament that limited the rights of the monarchy and ensured the superiority of Parliament

engraving art form in which an artist etches a design on a metal plate with acid and then uses the plate to make multiple prints

enlightened despot absolute ruler who used his or her power to bring about political and social change

entente nonbinding agreement to follow common policies

enterprise business organization in such areas as shipping, mining, railroads, or factories

entrepreneur person who assumes financial risk in the hope of making a profit

Epic of Gilgamesh, The Mesopotamian narrative poem that was first recited in Sumer

epidemic outbreak of a rapidly spreading disease

Equiano, Olaudah (1745–1797) Olaudah Equiano was captured in West Africa when he was a boy of 11, sold into slavery, and transported to the Americas. Later, he found paying work and earned enough money to buy his freedom. In 1789, he wrote his autobiography, *The Interesting Narrative of the Life of Olaudah Equiano*. He died in London in 1797.

Erasmus Erasmus (c. 1466–1536) was a Dutch priest, writer, and scholar who promoted humanism. He wrote texts on various subjects and produced a new Greek edition of the Christian Bible. He also called for a translation of the Bible into the vernacular, or everyday language, to help spread learning, ideas, and education. He also wanted to reform Church corruption.

erosion the wearing away of land

estates social classes

Estates-General legislative body made up of the representatives of the three estates in pre-revolutionary France

ethics moral standards of behavior

Ethiopia ancient Greek term for Axumite kingdom; present-day country in East Africa

ethnic cleansing the killing or forcible removal of people of different ethnicities from an area by aggressors so that only the ethnic group of the aggressors remains

ethnic group large group of people who share the same language and cultural heritage

Etruscans a people who inhabited early Italy

euro common currency used by most member nations of the European Union

European Union (EU) an international organization made up of over two dozen European nations and dedicated to establishing free trade among its members, with a common currency and common policies and laws

excommunication exclusion from the Roman Catholic Church as a penalty for refusing to obey Church law

expansionism policy of increasing the amount of territory a government holds

extraterritoriality right of foreigners to be protected by the laws of their own nation

F

faction a group or clique within a larger group that has different ideas and opinions than the rest of the group

famine a severe shortage of food in which large numbers of people starve

Faraday, Michael Michael Faraday (1791–1867) was a British chemist and physicist who made significant contributions to the field of electricity. Some of his most important discoveries include electricity generation and transmission, the electric motor, and the chemical benzene. His discoveries have shaped the modern world.

fascism any centralized, authoritarian government system that is not communist, whose policies glorify the state over the individual and are destructive to basic human rights

federal republic government in which power is divided between the national, or federal, government and the states

Federal Reserve central banking system of the United States, which regulates banks

Ferdinand and Isabella Ferdinand III (1452–1516) and Isabella I (1451–1504) were the king of Aragon and the queen of Castile. Their marriage joined the two countries to become the country of Spain. Their military efforts were responsible for the final success of the Reconquista.

Ferguson, Miriam Miriam Ferguson (1875–1961), known to many as "Ma" Ferguson, was elected the first female governor of Texas in 1924. She ran when her husband, the politically disgraced Governor James E. Ferguson, was unable to secure a place on the ballot. Mrs. Ferguson was the first woman elected for the office in the United States but second to serve as governor because Wyoming's Nellie T. Ross was inaugurated upon the death of her husband. Mrs. Ferguson was reelected in 1932 for a second term.

Fertile Crescent region of the Middle East in which civilizations first arose

feudal contract exchange of pledges between lords and vassals

feudalism loosely organized system of government in which local lords governed their own lands but owed military service and other support to a greater lord

fief in medieval Europe, an estate granted by a lord to a vassal in exchange for service and loyalty

filial piety respect for parents

finance the management of money matters including the circulation of money, loans, investment, and banking

Firdawsi Firdawsi (c. 940–1020) was a Muslim poet most famous for the *Shah Namah,* or *Book of Kings,* which he wrote in Persian using Arabic script. Firdawsi wrote at a time when Persia, or Iran, was fairly free from the control of the Muslim empire and local leaders encouraged a flowering of Persian culture. The famed poet centered his writing on the stories of royalty and heroes, and many of the themes he introduced are still relevant today.

First Sino-Japanese War conflict between China and Japan in 1894–1895 over control of Korea

Five Ks Sikh articles of faith. The Five Ks are Kesh, which is uncut hair kept covered by a turban; the Kirpan (kir PAHN), a religious sword representing the responsibilities to fight oppression; the Kara (KEHR a), a metal bracelet; Kanga (KANG a), a comb; and the Kachera (kuh TSHERA), special underclothing.

Flanders a region that included parts of present-day northern France, Belgium, and the Netherlands; was an important industrial and financial center of northern Europe during the Middle Ages and Renaissance

flapper in the United States and Europe in the 1920s, a rebellious young woman

Florence a city in the Tuscany region of northern Italy that was the center of the Italian Renaissance

flying buttresses stone supports on the outside of a building that allowed builders to construct higher, thinner walls that contained large stained-glass windows.

Four Noble Truths as taught by the Buddha, the four basic beliefs that form the foundation of Buddhism

Fourteen Points list of terms for resolving WWI and future wars outlined by American President Woodrow Wilson in January 1918

Francis Joseph Francis Joseph (1830–1916) became emperor of Austria in 1848 after the abdication of Ferdinand I. After the creation of the Dual Monarchy in 1867, he also became king of Hungary. In 1879, Francis Joseph formed an alliance with Germany, which was led by the Prussians. His handling of relations with Serbia after the assassination of Archduke Francis Ferdinand, in 1914 was one of the catalysts for World War I.

Franco, Francisco Francisco Franco (1892–1975) was a Spanish military leader who came to power during the Spanish Civil War. He was dictator of Spain from 1939 to 1973, when he left his position as premier. He continued to be head of state until his death in 1975.

Franklin, Benjamin Benjamin Franklin (1706–1790) was a man of many talents. Born in 1706, Franklin was an author, inventor, and a statesman who helped persuade France to enter the Revolutionary War on the side of the Americans. He was actively involved in framing the Declaration of Independence.

Franks a Germanic tribe that conquered present-day France and neighboring lands in the 400s

Frederick II Frederick II (1712–1786) succeeded his father, Frederick William I, to serve as king of Prussia (1740–1786).

Frederick William I Frederick William I (1688–1740) was the second Prussian king who helped transform his country into a prosperous state.

free enterprise system an economic system, also known as capitalism, in which private businesses are able to compete with each other with little control by government. Products, prices, and services are driven by free market laws of supply and demand rather than government regulations.

free market market regulated by the natural laws of supply and demand

free trade trade between countries without quotas, tariffs, or other restrictions

French and Indian War war between Britain and France in the Americas that happened from 1754 to 1763; part of a global war called the Seven Years' War

French Indochina Western name for the colonial holdings of France on mainland Southeast Asia; present-day Vietnam, Laos, and Cambodia

fresco colorful painting completed on wet plaster

friar a medieval European monk who traveled from place to place preaching to the poor

fundamentalist religious leader who calls for a return to what he or she sees as the fundamental, or basic, values of his or her faith

G

Galileo Galileo Galilei (1564–1642) was an Italian astronomer and mathematician whose discoveries using a telescope supported the heliocentric universe theories of Copernicus. His discoveries challenged established scientific and religious thinking. Galileo was an important contributor to the development of the scientific method used by modern scientists.

Gama, Vasco da Vasco da Gama (c. 1460–1524) was a Portuguese explorer and navigator who in 1498 was the first person to directly reach India by sailing around Africa. He returned to India in 1502, fought Arab Muslim ships along the way, and established trading posts along the East African coast. After serving as an advisor to Portugal's king for 20 years, he returned to India in 1524 with the title of viceroy, but fell ill and died soon after arriving.

Gandhi, Indira Indira Gandhi (1917–1984) was a four-term prime minister of India. The daughter of Jawaharlal Nehru, Gandhi entered politics as part of the Congress Party, soon becoming its leader. After her father's death, she was elected India's prime minister. Gandhi stayed in power until 1977, when some of her authoritarian policies led to her popular defeat. In 1980, however, she was reelected to a fourth term as prime minister. After she ordered a military attack on a Sikh holy site, the Golden Temple, Gandhi was assassinated by her Sikh bodyguards.

Gandhi, Mohandas Mohandas Gandhi (1869–1948) was a mediocre student who went through a period of rebellion during his early teens. He married at age 13 and later was sent to England to attend law school. In 1891, Gandhi accepted a position in South Africa. Although he planned to be there only one year, he stayed until 1914, fighting for Indian rights. In 1919, Gandhi became active in the Indian independence movement and remained dedicated to the cause until his death. He was assassinated in 1948—just a few months after India won its independence.

Garibaldi, Giuseppe Giuseppe Garibaldi (1807–1882) was a nationalist soldier and military leader who effectively used guerilla tactics to win military victories throughout southern Italy. In his earlier years he was a member of Mazzini's Young Italy, where he began his involvement in the cause of Italian unity.

Garvey, Marcus Marcus Garvey (1887–1940) founded the Universal Negro Improvement and Conservation Association and African Communities League (UNIA) in Jamaica in 1914, with the goal of building a black-governed nation. Finding little support, Garvey moved to the United States and established the UNIA in Harlem. Garvey taught his followers about the African culture and preached the need for blacks to form a strong, independent economy. His adamant belief in separation of the races brought many enemies, and he was deported in 1927.

Gautama, Siddhartha Siddhartha Gautama (circa 563 B.C.–483 B.C.) was born a prince in India. Encounters with human suffering led him to leave his royal life to seek out the cause of suffering and sorrow. He sought answers from scholars and meditated until he developed a spiritual explanation for life. He became known as the "Buddha," and began teaching his beliefs to others. He taught the Four Noble Truths and encouraged the faithful to follow the Eightfold Path.

general strike strike by workers in many different industries at the same time

genetic engineering manipulation of living organism's chemical code in order to produce specific results

genetics a branch of biology dealing with heredity and variations among plants and animals

Geneva Swiss city-state that became a Calvinist theocracy in the 1500s; today a major city in Switzerland

Genghis Khan Genghis Khan (1162–1227) rose from poverty to unite the warring Mongol tribes. He imposed discipline, exacted loyalty, and then proceeded to build an army that conquered the vast areas of Central Asia and China and became the Mongol empire. He was known for both his fierceness and his generosity. The Mongol empire lasted long after his death during a military campaign. His descendants added to the empire until it became the largest empire in the world prior to the British empire.

genocide deliberate and systematic killing of people who belong to a particular racial, ethnic, or cultural group.

gentry wealthy, landowning class

George III George III (1738–1820) was the longest reigning monarch in British history, ruling at a time when Britain and France struggled to dominate Europe; he shared the blame for the loss of Britain's American colonies.

germ theory the theory that infectious diseases are caused by certain microbes

Gestapo secret police in Nazi Germany

Ghana early West African trading kingdom located in parts of present-day Mauritania and Mali

ghetto separate section of a city where members of a minority group are forced to live

Gladstone, William William Gladstone (1809–1898) Gladstone served as prime minister four separate times and was a leader of the Whigs, and later, the Liberal Party. He extended suffrage to farmworkers and most other men during the 1880s, most notably with the Representation of the People Act in 1884. Gladstone also strongly supported Irish home rule. Along with his chief rival, Benjamin Disraeli, Gladstone helped transform the British government into a parliamentary democracy.

glasnost "openness" in Russian; a Soviet policy of greater freedom of expression introduced by Mikhail Gorbachev in the late 1980s

global warming the increase in Earth's average surface temperature over time

globalization the process by which national economies, politics, cultures, and societies become closely linked with those of other nations around the world

Goa a coastal city seized in 1510 that became the commercial and military base of Portugal's India trade

golden age period of great cultural achievement

Golden Bull of 1222 charter that strictly limited royal power in Hungary

Golden Temple the most prominent Sikh house of worship

Good Friday Agreement an agreement to end the conflict in Northern Ireland signed in 1998 by Protestants and Catholics

Good Neighbor Policy policy in which American President Franklin Roosevelt promised that the United States would interfere less in Latin American affairs

Gorbachev, Mikhail Mikhail Gorbachev (b. 1931) was the leader of the Soviet Union from 1985 to 1991. He was responsible for introducing the reforms (glasnost and perestroika) that brought about the break up of the Soviet Union and the end of Soviet domination of Eastern Europe. He was driven from office by his popular rival, democratic advocate Boris Yeltsin, in 1991.

Gothic style type of European architecture that developed in the Middle Ages, characterized by flying buttresses, ribbed vaulting, thin walls, and high roofs

Gouges, Olympe de Olympe de Gouges (1745?–1793), author of the Declaration of the Rights of Women, railed against the treatment of women in France, addressing her concerns directly to Marie Antoinette.

Gracchus, Gaius (c. 154 B.C.–121 B.C.) was the brother of Tiberius and a plebeian political reformist who sought to limit senatorial power. He advanced checks and balances to minimize financial influence. Like his brother, he was murdered by thugs hired by the Roman Senate.

gravity force that pulls objects in Earth's sphere to the center of Earth

Great Depression a painful time of global economic collapse, starting in 1929 and lasting until about 1939

Great Leap Forward a Chinese Communist program from 1958 to 1960 to boost farm and industrial output that failed miserably

Great Schism the official split between the Roman Catholic and Byzantine churches that occurred in 1054; another event was the Great Western Schism, a period when rival popes fought for exclusive power and divided the Roman Catholic Church from 1378–1417

Great Zimbabwe powerful East African medieval trading center and city-state located in south-eastern present-day Zimbabwe

Greco, El El Greco (1541–1614) was a master of Spanish painting who also worked as a sculptor and architect during Spain's Golden Age.

Green Revolution the improved seeds, pesticides, mechanical equipment, and farming methods introduced in the developing world beginning in the 1950s

Gregory VII Gregory VII (c. 1025–1085) achieved success in his battle with the Holy Roman Emperor Henry IV on the matter of lay investiture. He greatly expanded papal power by claiming his supremacy over secular rulers.

griot professional storyteller in early West Africa

gross domestic product (GDP) the total value of all goods and services produced in a nation within a particular year

Guang Xu Guang Xu (1871–1908) was the ninth emperor of the Qing dynasty. When previous emperor Tongzhi died, his mother Ci Xi named Guang, her nephew, as new emperor. Ci Xi dominated his reign, influencing the government and making him ineffectual. During the Hundred Days of Reform, Guang attempted progressive reforms, angering conservatives. Ci Xi had Guang imprisoned. He died under suspicious circumstances.

Guangzhou coastal city in southeastern China, also known as Canton, where, during the Ming dynasty, the Dutch, English, and other Europeans could trade with Chinese merchants under the supervision of imperial officials, only during each year's trading season and only at Canton

guerrilla a soldier in a loosely organized force making surprise raids

guerrilla warfare fighting carried on through hit-and-run raids

guild in the Middle Ages, an association of merchants or artisans who cooperated to uphold standards of their trade and to protect their economic interests

guillotine device used during the Reign of Terror to execute thousands by beheading

Gulag in the Soviet Union, a system of forced labor camps in which millions of criminals and political prisoners were held under Stalin

Guomindang Nationalist party; active in China 1912 to 1949

Gutenberg, Johannes Gutenberg (c. 1400–1468) was born in Germany. He became a goldsmith, printer, and publisher. His pioneering invention of a printing press with moveable type changed the world. Around 1455, Gutenberg printed the first complete edition of the Christian Bible using his press.

H

habeas corpus principle that a person cannot be held in prison without first being charged with a specific crime

hacienda a large plantation

Hadrian (A.D. 76–A.D. 138) was a Roman Emperor from A.D. 117 to A.D. 138. Considered one of the "Five Good Emperors," he codified Roman law and traveled extensively, uniting the empire.

hajj one of the Five Pillars of Islam, the pilgrimage that all Muslims are expected to make at least once in their lifetime

Hammurabi (1792 B.C.–1750 B.C.) Hammurabi became the first king of the Babylonian empire. He inherited the power from his father, who extended Babylon's control across Mesopotamia. Hammurabi is known for writing the first code of law in recorded history.

hangul alphabet that uses symbols to represent the sounds of spoken Korean

Hapsburg empire Central European empire that lasted from the 1400s to the 1900s and at its height included the lands of the Holy Roman Empire and the Netherlands

Harappa large ancient city of the Indus civilization, located in present-day Pakistan

Harlem Renaissance an African American cultural movement in the 1920s and 1930s, centered in Harlem

Hatshepsut (Died 1458 B.C.) Queen Hatshepsut served for 20 years alongside her husband, Thutmose II, but after his death took the role of pharaoh and served as regent to Thutmose III. She is known for building temples and monuments and generally making Egypt flourish.

Havel, Václav Václav Havel (1936–2011) was a Czech playwright and human rights activist who became president of Czechoslovakia in 1989, after the Velvet Revolution. Because of his persecution during the later stages of communist rule in Czechoslovakia, Havel became a worldwide symbol of communist repression. After the division of Czechoslovakia, he served as the first president of the Czech Republic.

hejab headscarves and loose-fitting, ankle-length garments meant to conceal the body; traditionally worn by many Muslim women

heliocentric based on the belief that the sun is the center of the universe

Henry IV Henry IV (1050–1106) was a German king who became Holy Roman Emperor in 1084. His efforts to increase the power of the monarchy led him into conflict with Pope Gregory VIII over lay investiture. Gregory excommunicated Henry but later reinstated him in the church after Henry did penance.

Henry VIII Henry VIII (1491–1547) was the second Tudor king of England. Well-educated and athletic, he was initially a favorite of the English people. He lost much of that popularity with his constant involvement in wars. Henry's desire for a male heir was the catalyst for his eventual break with the Roman Catholic Church and the formation of the Church of England.

Henry, Prince Prince Henry (1394–1460) was a Portuguese prince and patron of explorers who helped his father capture the Moroccan city of Ceuta, became its governor, and sponsored voyages to the Madeira Islands and the West African coast. He raised money for expeditions and established a base for explorers in Sagres, later adding an arsenal, an observatory, and a school for studying geography. His support of cartography, advances in navigation, and exploration provided a foundation for Portugal's rise to international dominance and acquisition of its colonial empire in the sixteenth century.

heresy religious belief that is contrary to the official teachings of a church

Herodotus Herodotus (c. 484 B.C.–c. 425 B.C.), often called the "Father of History," traveled widely throughout the ancient Mediterranean world, collecting information for his chronicles of past events, including the Persian wars. In his writings, he noted bias and conflicting accounts in his sources.

Hidalgo, Father Miguel Father Miguel Hidalgo (1753–1811) was a Catholic priest in Mexico. He led Indians and mestizos in a revolution against the Spanish until he was captured and killed in 1811.

hierarchy system of ranking groups

hieroglyphics system of writing in which pictures called hieroglyphs represent objects, concepts, or sounds

hijra Muhammad's journey from Mecca to Medina in 622

Hippocrates Hippocrates (c. 460 B.C.–c. 375 B.C.), a Greek physician traditionally regarded as the father of medicine, who studied the causes of illnesses, seeking their cures. Many ancient medical writings are attributed to him, although he probably wrote few of them. He is honored for his Hippocratic oath that sets ethical standards for medical practice.

Hirohito Hirohito (1901–1989) became emperor in 1926 when his father died. Many believed he was a living god, descended from the sun goddess. Japanese military ultranationalists built a cult around the emperor, reviving ancient warrior values and suppressing most democratic freedoms. Although Hirohito was invested with supreme authority theoretically, he did little more than approve the policies presented by his ministers. He was more interested in marine biology, authoring several books on the subject. Hirohito was the longest reigning monarch in Japanese history, serving as emperor for an astonishing 63 years until his death in 1989.

Hiroshima city in Japan where the first atomic bomb was dropped in August 1945

historian a person who studies how people lived in the past

Hitler, Adolf Adolf Hitler (1889–1945) was chancellor of Germany from 1933 to 1945 and dictator of Nazi Germany from 1934 to 1945. After Hitler was appointed chancellor, he immediately transformed the Weimar Republic into the Third Reich. He wanted to establish a "New Order" and create more "living space" for what he believed was the superior Aryan race. Hitler aggressively invaded neighboring nations. which led to World War II. As Germany faced defeat in 1945, Hitler committed suicide to avoid capture by the Soviets.

Ho Chi Minh Ho Chi Minh (1890–1969) was born Nguyen That Thanh. He founded the Indochinese Communist Party and was the leader of the armed independence movement in Vietnam. Ho proclaimed Vietnam's independence in 1945 and became the leader of North Vietnam when the country was divided in 1954. He was the leader of North Vietnam until his death in 1969, and refused to negotiate an end to the war.

Hobbes, Thomas Thomas Hobbes (1588–1679) was an influential English political philosopher, best known for his work *Leviathan.* In it, Hobbes strongly advocated that only a powerful government was capable of protecting society. He believed that people entered into a social contract with their government to avoid the inevitable chaos and lawlessness of life in "the state of nature." Hobbes's political philosophy was foundational for later thinkers of the Enlightenment, including Locke, Rousseau, and Kant.

Holocaust the systematic genocide of about six million European Jews by the Nazis in World War II

Holy Land Jerusalem and other places where Christians believe Jesus had lived and preached

Holy Roman Empire empire of west central Europe from 962 to 1806, comprising present-day Germany and neighboring lands

home rule local self-government

Homer (c. 750 B.C.), according to tradition the author of the epic poems, the *Illiad* and the *Odyssey,* is thought to have traveled from village to village singing about heroic deeds of warriors during the Trojan War

homogeneous society society that has common culture and language

Huari a culture that thrived in the Andean region from about A.D. 600 to 1000

Hugo, Victor Victor Hugo (1802–1885) was a leading literary, intellectual, and political figure in France. His works were not only extremely popular—most notably *Notre Dame de Paris* and *Les Misérables* —but also highly influential and respected. Hugo believed in the cause of the common people and saw in them both strength and potential. He sought to portray both their virtues and their plights in his works. Although Hugo did not live in poverty, he associated with the lower class, and, according to his wishes, he had a pauper's funeral and grave

Huguenots French Protestants of the 1500s and 1600s

humanism an intellectual movement at the heart of the Renaissance that focused on education and the classics

humanities study of subjects such as grammar, rhetoric, poetry, and history that were taught in ancient Greece and Rome

Huns a nomadic people of central Asia

Hutus an ethnic group that forms the majority in Rwanda and Burundi

hyperinflation an extremely rapid and sharp rise in prices that causes money to lose value

hypothesis an unproved theory accepted for the purposes of explaining certain facts or to provide a basis for further investigation.

I

Ibn Khaldun Ibn Khaldun (1332–1406) was an Arab thinker who helped establish the principles of many branches of knowledge including history and economics. He is perhaps best known for the development of standards for studying and writing about history, which he explained in his landmark book, the *Muqaddimah.* He also introduced or refined many economic concepts relating to labor, profits, supply and demand, use of resources, production, and supply and demand.

Ibn Rushd Ibn Rushd (1128–1198), also known as Averroes, was a philosopher and scientist who lived in Córdoba and influenced European thought. As a philosopher, he placed a variety of subject matter under the scrutiny of reason and analysis and argued that humans were partially but not completely controlled by fate. In the field of science, Ibn Rushd contributed to the study of diseases.

Ibn Sina Ibn Sina (980–1037), also known as Avicenna, was a Persian physician who wrote the *Canon on Medicine,* which focused on past medical practices throughout the known world as well as his own procedures. This work features descriptions of anatomy, symptoms of diseases, and medicines and cures. Ibn Sina wrote on a variety of other topics as well, including philosophy, mathematics, and astronomy.

icon holy image of Christ, the Virgin Mary, or a saint venerated in the Eastern Orthodox Church

ideology system of thought and belief

Ignatius of Loyola Ignatius of Loyola (1491–1556) went from an early career as a Spanish nobleman soldier to become a theologian and an influential participant in the Catholic Reformation. While recovering from leg surgery, Ignatius read a book on the lives of the saints and decided that serving God was holy chivalry. From that time until his death, Ignatius studied, preached, and did missionary work as founder of the Society of Jesus, an order of religious men who came to be known as Jesuits.

illumination the artistic decoration of books and manuscripts

immunity resistance, such as the power to keep from being affected by a disease

imperialism domination by one country of the political, economic, or cultural life of another country or region

import substitution manufacturing goods locally to replace imports

impressionism school of painting of the late 1800s and early 1900s that tried to capture fleeting visual impressions

indemnity payment for losses in war

indigenous original or native inhabitants of a country or region

indigenous peoples term generally used to describe the descendants of the earliest inhabitants of a region

Indra in ancient India, the chief deity, the god of war

indulgence in the Roman Catholic Church, pardon for sins committed during a person's lifetime

Industrial Revolution period beginning in the 1700s in which production shifted from simple hand tools to complex machinery and sources of energy shifted from human or animal power to steam and electricity

inflation economic cycle that involves a rapid rise in prices linked to a sharp increase in the amount of money available

Innocent III, Pope Pope Innocent III (c. 1160–1216) was only 37 years old when he became pope and quickly extended the authority of the papacy over Rome and in Italy. When King John of England appointed the archbishop of Canterbury without Innocent's approval, the pope excommunicated John.

Inquisition A Church court set up to try people accused of heresy

insurgent rebel

intendant official appointed by French king Louis XIV to govern the provinces, collect taxes, and recruit soldiers

interchangeable parts identical components that can be used in place of one another in manufacturing

interdependence mutual dependence of countries on goods, resources, labor, and knowledge from other parts of the world

interdict in the Roman Catholic Church, excommunication of an entire region, town, or kingdom

International Space Station (ISS) an artificial structure built and maintained by a coalition of nations with the purpose of research

Internet a huge international computer network linking millions of users around the world

internment confinement during wartime

Inti the Inca sun god

intifada Palestinian Arab uprising against the Israeli occupation

Iroquois League political alliance of five Iroquois groups, known as the Five Nations, in the late 1500s

Isfahan capital of Safavid empire during the 1600s; located in present-day Iran

Isis Isis is the Egyptian god worshiped as the ideal mother and wife. She is known as the protector of the dead and goddess of children. She is usually portrayed as a woman, wearing a throne-shaped headdress.

Islamist a person who wants government policies to be based on the teachings of Islam

island-hopping during World War II, Allied strategy of recapturing some Japanese-held islands while bypassing others

Istanbul capital of the Ottoman empire, formerly called Constantinople when it was the center of the eastern Roman empire and also capital of the Byzantine empire

Ivan the Great Ivan the Great (1462–1505) was one of the most powerful Russian rulers. He consolidated his power by winning the voluntary allegiance of Russian princes and preventing further Mongol invasions.

Ivan the Terrible Ivan the Terrible (1530–1584) was the grandson of Ivan the Great. He continued to centralize power in his own hands, developing a brutal secret group that terrorized members of the hereditary nobility, or boyars. His eventual insanity contributed to his name "the Terrible."

J

Jacobin a member of a radical political club during the French Revolution

Jahan, Nur Nur Jahan (1577–1645) was a Persian widow with a small child who became the powerful wife of the Mughal emperor Jahangir. Her administrative, political, economic, and cultural skills so impressed Jahangir that she had virtual control over the empire until his death in 1627. Since women were not allowed to interact face to face with men in court, Nur Jahan relied on trusted men to act for her.

Jahan, Shah Shah Jahan (1592–1666) was the third son of the Mughal emperor Jahangir. With support from court nobles, he won succession to become emperor upon Jahangir's death. An effective and tolerant ruler, Shah Jahan was also an enthusiastic builder, involving himself in every detail of the building process. When his beloved wife Mumtaz Mahal died, he built the famous mausoleum called the Taj Mahal in her honor.

James I James I (1566–1625) was a king of Scotland who also became king of England and Ireland. He deeply believed in the divine right of kings to rule over all their subjects without interference from anyone. His views were in sharp contrast to Parliament, leading to constant conflict. He was also the author of the King James version of the Bible.

janizary a member of the elite forces of the Ottoman army

Jefferson, Thomas Thomas Jefferson (1743–1826) is known mainly as the primary author of the Declaration of Independence. Jefferson also served as minister to France and later as the third president of the United States.

Jericho the world's first village, established in the modern-day West Bank between 10,000 and 9000 B.C.

Jerusalem capital of the Jewish state of Judea in ancient times and capital of the modern state of Israel; city sacred to Jews, Muslims, and Christians

Jesus Jesus (c. 4 B.C.–A.D. 30) was the founder of Christianity. He is considered by most Christians to be the Son of God. Raised in a Jewish family, he began preaching a message of salvation and eternal life. He was put to death under Roman law. According to the Gospels, he rose from the dead. He is worshipped as a savior today by Christians around the world.

Jiang Jieshi Jiang Jieshi (1887–1975), also known as Chiang Kai-shek, was born to a merchant family in eastern China. Along with Sun Yixian, he formed the Nationalist Party, or Guomindang, and following Sun's death in 1925, Jiang took over control. After years of battling, Jiang joined forces with the Communists against the Japanese invaders. Jiang also led the Chinese military to assist the Allies in defeating Japan in World War II. Eventually, the Communists wrestled back control and Jiang fled to the island of Taiwan, which he ruled until his death in 1975.

Jinnah, Muhammad Ali Muhammad Ali Jinnah (1876–1948) was an Indian Muslim politician and leader of the Muslim League, which was founded in 1906 to protect Muslim interests in India. The League worked closely with the Indian Congress Party early on but later diverged from the Congress when Jinnah and other Muslims began to lobby for their own state. Jinnah helped found Pakistan in 1947 and was its first governor-general.

Johanson, Donald Born in 1942, anthropologist Donald Johanson found one of the most important early humans in history, a skeleton of a woman he called "Lucy." After studying her bones, Johanson concluded that Lucy walked upright and was about 4 feet tall.

John, King King John (c. 1166–1216) was a son of King Henry II. He seized control of the English throne when his brother, King Richard the Lionheart, was captured while on crusade. Conflicts with the English nobles led to John's forced signature to Magna Carta in 1215, which limited the power of the English kings.

joint family family organization in which several generations share a common dwelling

Joseph II Joseph II (1741–1790) ruled as Holy Roman Emperor in Austria and is considered the most radical of the enlightened despots. He continued many of the modernizing governmental reforms introduced by his mother, Maria Theresa, with the goal of equal treatment for all his subjects. He abolished serfdom and encouraged freedom of the press. Most notably, Joseph supported religious equality for Protestants and even Jews. He is also remembered for traveling among his subjects in disguise to learn about the everyday problems of the peasantry.

journeyman a salaried worker employed by a guild master

Juárez, Benito Benito Juárez (1806–1872) was a Mexican lawyer and politician. Coming from a Zapotec Indian heritage and peasant family background, he supported reforms to help oppressed people in Mexico. He helped start the La Reforma movement and became president of Mexico in 1861. He died while in office, but his reforms helped unite Mexico and bring mestizos into politics.

jury group of people with authority to make a decision in a legal case

Justinian Justinian (483–565) was born of peasant stock and adopted by his uncle Justin (emperor from 518). As the Byzantine emperor from 527 to 565, Justinian continued war with Persia and sought to win back former western Roman provinces from barbarian invaders. After riots and a major fire in 532, he rebuilt much of Constantinople in glorious style. He also instituted reforms to stop imperial corruption and promote justice for his subjects. His most influential achievement is Justinian's Code, a collection, organization, and revision of Roman laws.

Justinian's Code collection of Roman laws organized by the Byzantine emperor Justinian and later serving as a model for the Catholic Church and medieval monarchs

K

Kaaba the most sacred temple of Islam, located at Mecca

kaiser emperor of Germany

kamikaze Japanese pilot who undertook a suicide mission

kana in the Japanese writing system, phonetic symbols representing syllables

Karl Marx Karl Marx (1818–1883) was a German political thinker whose ideas became the foundation for communism. Marx trained as a lawyer and later studied philosophy, with plans to enter the academic world. His radical ideas, however, left him with few prospects, so he turned to writing. His most famous work was the *Communist Manifesto,* which criticized capitalism and predicted that alienated workers would rise up to overthrow the bourgeoisie. In the 1860s, Marx was an influential member of the International Working Men's Association.

karma in Hindu belief, all the actions that determine a person's fate in the next life

Kashmir a former princely state in the Himalayas claimed by both India and Pakistan, which have fought wars over its control

Katanga a province of the Democratic Republic of the Congo with rich copper and diamond deposits that tried to gain independence from Congo in 1960

Kellogg-Briand Pact an international agreement, signed by almost every nation in 1928, to stop using war as a method of national policy

Kennedy, John F. John F. Kennedy (1917–1963) was president of the United States from 1961 to 1963. A decorated naval commander in World War II, he was elected president at the age of 42. He was president during the communist revolution in Cuba and the Cuban Missile Crisis, and he increased U.S. involvement in Vietnam. On the domestic front, Kennedy's administration began the federal effort to enforce civil rights in the South. He was assassinated on November 22, 1963, by Lee Harvey Oswald.

Kenyatta, Jomo (1894–1978) was a nationalist and leader in the fight for Kenyan independence from Britain. In 1963, he became the country's first prime minister, and in 1964, the country's first president. He was president until his death.

Kepler, Johannes Johannes Kepler (1571–1630) was a German astronomer whose discoveries expanded on Copernicus's heliocentric universe. Kepler's research showed that the planets move in a particular orbit around the sun. His achievements included a correct description of how vision occurs, as well as how a telescope uses light.

Khan, Reza Reza Khan (1878–1944) joined the Iranian military at a young age. After leading the 1921 coup, Khan became the minister of war and then prime minister. Four years later, he was elected as shah and continued to radically reform both the government and nation. At the start of World War II, the Soviet Union and Britain occupied Iran. Khan abdicated, and his son became shah. The British exiled Khan to Mauritius and then Johannesburg, where he died.

Khayyám, Omar Omar Khayyám (1048–1131) is best known today as a poet who crafted many rubáiyáts, or quatrains. In his day, he was praised for his expertise in many areas. As a mathematician, he contributed to the development of algebra. As a astronomer, he carefully studied the sky to help improve the Muslim calendar. The Persian scholar also examined issues related to law, philosophy, and history.

Khmer Rouge a political movement and a force of Cambodian communist guerrillas that gained power in Cambodia in 1975

Khomeini, Ruhollah Ruhollah Khomeini (1902–1989) was a Shiite Muslim cleric (Ayatollah) who led the 1979 Islamic Revolution in Iran, which overthrew the Shah (Mohammed Reza). He was Iran's highest religious and political leader until his death 10 years later.

Khrushchev, Nikita Nikita Khrushchev (1894–1971) served in the Red Army during World War II as a lieutenant general and afterwards was a Communist Party official in Ukraine. He became part of the central party leadership in 1947 and rose to prominence after Stalin's death in 1953. As leader of the Soviet Union from 1955 to 1964, he introduced domestic reforms that made life in the Soviet Union less harsh, but he crushed rebellions in Eastern Europe. He was the Soviet leader during the Cuban Missile Crisis.

kibbutz a collective farm in Israel

Kiev capital of medieval Russia and of present-day Ukraine

Kim Il Sung Kim Il Sung (1912–1994) led the Democratic People's Republic of Korea (North Korea) from 1949 until his death in 1994. Supported by the Soviet Union during the Cold War, Kim established a totalitarian state with massive military budgets and virtually no political freedoms. In 1993, he declared that North Korea would withdraw from the Nuclear Nonproliferation Treaty.

King, Jr., Dr. Martin Luther Dr. Martin Luther King, Jr. (1929–1968), was an American minister and civil rights leader. He gained national prominence with his leadership of the Montgomery, Alabama, bus boycott in 1955. King helped organize the massive March on Washington in 1963, where he gave his famous "I Have a Dream" speech. He was assassinated on April 14, 1968.

kiva large underground chamber that the Anasazi used for religious ceremonies and political meetings

Klerk, F.W. de F.W. de Klerk (1936–) was a National Party member and the last president of South Africa under apartheid. With Nelson Mandela, he negotiated the transition of power from the white minority to majority rule, for which he and Mandela won the Nobel Peace Prize in 1993.

knight a European noble who served as a mounted warrior

Knossos city in ancient Crete, the principle center of Minoan civilization that dominated the Aegean between about 1600 B.C. and 1400 B.C. Excavations beginning in 1900 discovered a palace and surrounding buildings of a sophisticated culture.

Koch, Robert Robert Koch (1843–1910) was a German physician who was one of the founders of bacteriology, or the study of bacteria. Koch discovered the bacteria responsible for tuberculosis and cholera and determined the cycle of the anthrax disease. Koch also improved methods for studying bacteria, including cultivating pure cultures and staining bacteria to make them more visible and identifiable. In 1905 he was awarded the Nobel Prize for Physiology or Medicine.

Kolkata a large city in India, also known as Calcutta

Koryo dynasty Korean dynasty that ruled from 935 to 1392

Kossuth, Louis Louis Kossuth (1802–1894) was a Hungarian lawyer, journalist, politician and ruler of Hungary during the revolution of 1848–89.

Kublai Khan Kublai Khan (1215–1294) was the grandson of Genghis Khan and founded the Yuan dynasty, conquered the Song dynasty in the south to complete Mongol control of China, and proved a strong and intelligent ruler of the vast empire. Guided by Confucian Chinese advisors, he undertook reforms in his territories and politically reunited China, but also engaged in a series of costly and fruitless wars with neighboring kingdoms. He generally left Chinese life unchanged and, although religious, was known for his acceptance of various religious practices and for granting economic privileges to favored sects.

kulak wealthy peasant in the Soviet Union in the late 1930s

Kulturkampf Bismarck's "battle for civilization," intended to make Catholics put loyalty to the state above their allegiance to the Church

L

L'Ouverture, Toussaint Toussaint L'Ouverture (1743–1803) was born in Haiti as the son of an educated slave. He led an army of slaves, who he trained in guerrilla warfare, in a revolt against the French colonists. He was captured in 1802 by French forces and died in prison a year later.

La Reforma an era of liberal reform in Mexico from 1855 to 1876

labor union organization of workers who bargain for better pay and working conditions

Lafayette, Marquis de Marquis de Lafayette (1757–1834), a French noble, fought alongside the Americans in the Revolutionary War. Upon his return to France, Lafayette led the call for reform and in 1789 presented a draft of the Declaration of the Rights of Man to the National Assembly. He was hated by some for his moderate stance, and fled to Austria, but later returned.

laissez faire policy allowing business to operate with little or no government interference

Lalibela Ruler of Ethiopia who came to power in the 1200s. He built eleven Christian churches carved from ground level into the solid rock of the mountains below.

land reform break-up of large agricultural holdings for redistribution among peasants

Laozi Laozi means "Master Lao" or "Old Master" in the Chinese language. An old man when Confucius was a young scholar, Laozi was born in a small village in ancient China. He was appointed a historian in one of the Zhou dynasty courts. Laozi developed a philosophy of inner calm, purity of mind, and living in harmony with nature that is called Dao, or the way of the universe. His book, *The Way of Life,* had enormous influence on Chinese life.

Las Casas, Bartolomé de Bartolomé de Las Casas (c. 1474–July 17, 1566) was a Dominican priest and historian famed as an early advocate for human rights in the Americas. Knowing the evils suffered by Native Americans under the encomienda system, his vivid reports of abuses helped the passage of laws prohibiting enslavement and abuse in 1542. He spent the rest of his life fighting for the rights of peoples in the Americas.

laser a high-energy light beam that can be used for many purposes, including surgery, engineering, and scientific research

latifundia huge estates bought up by newly wealthy Roman citizens

Lawrence, T. E. Thomas Edward Lawrence, (1888–1935), also known as Lawrence of Arabia, was a British archaeologist, writer, and expert on Arabia who helped lead an Arab rebellion and guerilla war against the Ottoman Turks during World War I. In 1926, he published a memoir of his activities in those years, *The Seven Pillars of Wisdom.*

lay investiture appointment of bishops by anyone who is not a member of the clergy

Leakey, Louis (1903–1972) As an archaeologist, Louis Leakey, and his wife, Mary, searched for the remains of early humans in East Africa, finding many tools and bones that increased our understanding of early humans.

Leakey, Mary (1913–1996) Born in London, England, Mary Leakey traveled throughout Europe visiting numerous prehistoric sites, which increased her interest in archaeology and geology. She married Louis Leakey in 1936, and they spent 30 years digging for early humans in East Africa. Mary Leakey eventually found many remains that have increased our understanding of early hominids.

legion basic unit of the ancient Roman army, made up of about 5,000 soldiers

legislature lawmaking body

legitimacy principle by which monarchies that had been unseated by the French Revolution or Napoleon were restored

Lend-Lease Act act passed by the U.S. Congress in 1941 that allowed the president (FDR) to sell or lend war supplies to any country whose defense was considered vital to the United States

Lenin, V. I. V. I. Lenin (1870–1924) was a Russian communist revolutionary who led the Bolsheviks to victory in the Russian October Revolution. He served as the premier of the Soviet Union from 1922 until his death in 1924. He adapted the ideas of Karl Marx to create a type of communism known as Marxism-Leninism.

Leopold II Leopold II (1835–1909) was the king of Belgium who led the first Western efforts to develop and control the Congo basin. He ruled personally over the Congo Free State, which became part of Belgium in 1908.

levée morning ritual during which nobles would wait upon French king Louis XIV

libel knowing publication of false and damaging statements

liberation theology movement within the Catholic Church that urged the church to become a force for reform, social justice, and put an end to poverty

Liliuokalani Liliuokalani, born Lydia Kamakaeha (1838–1917), was the last Hawaiian sovereign before the islands were annexed by the United States in 1898. A princess during her brother's reign, Liliuokalani played an active role in Hawaii's government, improving education and meeting with foreign dignitaries. After her brother's death, she inherited the throne, becoming the first queen of Hawaii. In 1893, American planters, led by Sanford Dole, overthrew her.

limited monarchy government in which a constitution or legislative body limits the monarch's powers

Line of Demarcation line set by the Treaty of Tordesillas dividing the non-European world into two zones, one controlled by Spain and the other by Portugal

lineage a group claiming a common ancestor

Lister, Joseph Joseph Lister (1827–1912) was a Scottish surgeon who furthered medical knowledge by recognizing that the lack of cleanliness in hospitals directly correlated to deaths after surgeries. By studying the works of other scientists, he became convinced that microorganisms in the air entered the body through open wounds and caused infections that often led to death after surgery. He began using carbolic acid to clean patient wounds. He also began using an antiseptic liquid to treat dressings and later developed techniques to clean surgical instruments and keep wounds clean during surgery. He is known as the "Father of Antiseptic Surgery."

literacy the ability to read and write

literacy rate percentage of people who can read and write

Liverpool industrial city in northern Britain that was part of the first major railway line; it went from Liverpool to Manchester

Livingstone, David David Livingstone (1813–1873) was a Scottish missionary and explorer who influenced Western attitudes toward Africa.

Locke, John John Locke (1632–1704) grew up during the tumultuous era of the English Civil Wars. A prolific writer on political philosophy, Locke's works strongly influenced the U.S. Constitution and the development of American government. Locke proposed that people are born with certain natural rights that cannot be taken away, including life, liberty, and property. His radical ideas on government's responsibility to the people were fundamental to the leaders of the American Revolution.

loess fine windblown yellow soil

logic rational thinking

Long March epic march in which a group of Chinese Communists retreated from Guomindang forces by marching over 6,000 miles

longbow six-foot-long bow that could rapidly fire arrows with enough force to pierce most armor

Louis IX Louis IX (1214–1270) was King of France from 1226 to 1270. He was one of the most popular kings of France. He led the Seventh Crusade to the Holy Land and was canonized as a saint in recognition of his faith and services to the Church.

Louis Philippe Louis Philippe (1773–1850) was king of France from 1830 to 1848. He was known as the Citizen King because the people put him on the throne. He ultimately lost power because he did not support the working classes.

Louis XIV Louis XIV (1638–1715) served as king of France (1643–1715) and is considered the symbol of absolute monarchy.

Louis XVI Louis XVI (1754–1793) was king of pre-revolutionary France. He failed to support his ministers, who tried to reform France's finances and social institutions. Although he agreed in 1789 to summon the Estates-General, he resisted demands for reform by the National Assembly. He was later branded a traitor and executed in 1793.

Louisiana Purchase territory purchased by Thomas Jefferson from France in 1803

Luftwaffe German air force

Lusitania British liner torpedoed by a German submarine in May 1915

Luther, Martin Martin Luther (1483–1546) was a German monk and theologian who was the catalyst of the Protestant Reformation. Trained to become a lawyer, he changed his path, joined a strict order of Roman Catholic monks, and studied theology. Seeking to reform abuses within the Church, Luther challenged Church teachings with his 95 Theses. This led to his excommunication and the development of Lutheranism, the first of several Protestant sects.

M

Maathai, Wangari Wangari Maathai (1940–2011) was the founder of the Green Belt Movement as well as a human rights, AIDs prevention, and women's rights activist. She was elected to Kenya's national assembly in 2002 and won the Nobel Peace Prize in 2004.

Macao region of southeastern China made up of a peninsula and two islands; the Ming dynasty allowed the Portuguese to set up a trading post here

MacArthur, Douglas Douglas MacArthur (1880–1964) led the Allied assaults in the Southwest Pacific. He also commanded troops in World War I and the Korean War. He became a general and army chief of staff during the Depression.

Macartney, Lord Lord Macartney (1737–1806) Born to a Scots-Irish family in Ireland, Lord Macartney served as a member of the British Parliament, chief secretary for Ireland, and governor of several British colonies. King George III sent him on an unsuccessful mission to persuade Emperor Qianlong of China to allow British traders into northern port cities. He later became governor of the colony at the Cape of Good Hope.

Machiavelli, Niccoló Machiavelli (1469–1527) was born in Florence. He was a Renaissance political philosopher, statesman, and writer. His most famous work was a guide for rulers on how to gain and keep power. *The Prince* was realistic about political power. Machiavelli argued that the end justified the means in politics. The term "Machiavellian" is still used today to describe deceitful politics.

Madison, James James Madison (1751–1836) was a renowned U.S. statesman and fourth president of the United States. He is often called the "father of the Constitution" for the major role he played at the Constitutional Convention of 1789, which framed the federal Constitution.

Magellan, Ferdinand Ferdinand Magellan (1480–1521) was a Portuguese navigator and explorer who as a young man went on Portuguese expeditions to India and Africa, and later won Spanish support for his September 1519 expedition to sail west to reach the Moluccas. Beginning with five ships and a crew of 270, the long voyage through unknown waters encountered rough weather, scurvy, starvation, and eventual mutiny. Magellan was killed in 1521 during a battle in the present-day Philippines, and only one of his ships, carrying spices and 18 of the original crew, circumnavigated the world and at last returned to Spain in September 1522.

Maginot Line massive fortifications built by the French along their border with Germany in the 1930s to protect against invasion

Magna Carta The Great Charter approved by King John of England in 1215; it limited royal power and established certain rights of English freemen

Magyars an ethnic group centered in present-day Hungary

Mahdi a Muslim savior of the faith

maize corn

Malacca city located on the Malay Peninsula near the strategic Straits of Malacca

Mali medieval West African trading empire located in present-day Mali

Malinche Malinche (c. 1501–1550) was a young Indian woman, called Doña Marina by the Spanish, who spoke Maya and Aztec languages, learned Spanish, and served as Cortés's translator and advisor during his conquest of Mexico. Malinche converted to Christianity, later married one of Cortés's soldiers, and visited Spain, where she enjoyed a friendly reception at the Spanish court.

Malindi existing East African coastal city and hub of international trade, attacked in the 1400s by Portuguese explorers to expel the Arabs who control East African trade routes, and then take over those routes for themselves

Malthus, Thomas Thomas Malthus (1766–1834) was a British economist. He was born in Surrey to a wealthy family. After being educated at home, he attended college in Cambridge, where he earned a master's degree. His most well-known work is *An Essay on the Principle of Population.* In it, he argued that population increases would eventually use up the food supply, leading to poverty. He was a professor of history and political economy until his death.

Manchester industrial city in northern Britain that was part of the first major railway line; it went from Manchester to Liverpool

Manchuria historic province in northeastern China; rich in natural resources

Manchus people originally from Manchuria, north of China, who conquered the Ming dynasty and ruled China as the Qing dynasty from the mid-1600s to the early 1900s

mandate after World War I, a territory administered by a Western power

Mandela, Nelson Nelson Mandela (1918–2013) was a leader of the African National Congress and a freedom fighter during South Africa's apartheid era. He was jailed for 27 years and became the lightening rod for protests calling for an end to apartheid. He was freed from jail in 1990 and became South Africa's first black president in 1994, a post he held for only one term. Together with F.W. de Klerk he won the Nobel Peace Prize in 1993.

Mandelstam, Osip Osip Mandelstam (1891–1938?) grew up in St. Petersburg, Russia, in a Jewish household. Although Mandelstam is remembered as one of the foremost Russian poets of the 20th century, most of his work went unpublished during his lifetime. The Communists sent him into exile for a second time in 1938, and his wife, Nadezhda Khazina, received his last communication some months afterwards. He was never heard from again, but through the tireless efforts of his wife, the majority of Mandelstam's work was saved for future generations.

Manhattan Project code name for the project to build the first atomic bomb during WWII

Manifest Destiny American idea that the United States should stretch across the entire North American continent

manor during the Middle Ages in Europe, a lord's estate that included one or more villages and the surrounding lands

manor system also called manorial system; economic system during the Middle Ages in Europe that was built around large estates called manors, which included one or more villages and the surrounding lands

Mansa Musa Mansa Musa (died c. 1337) was a devoted Islamic ruler of Mali who came to the throne in 1312 and expanded Mali's borders to the Atlantic Ocean. He was one of the richest men of his era. His famous journey to Mecca was lavish and awakened the world to the riches of Mali.

Mao Zedong Mao Zedong (1893–1976) was born in central China to a peasant family. He helped form the Chinese Communist Party in 1921. After Jiang Jieshi launched "extermination campaigns" against the Communists, Mao led his army on the epic Long March. Mao briefly joined with the Guomindang to suppress Japanese aggression, but the partnership did not last after World War II ended. The People's Republic of China was established in 1949. Mao initiated drastic reforms, some of which had disastrous consequences. Mao's use of terror and intolerance of opposition became internationally notorious.

Maori the indigenous people of New Zealand

March on Rome planned march of thousands of Fascist supporters to take control of Rome; in response Mussolini was given the legal right to control Italy

Marconi, Guglielmo Guglielmo Marconi (1874–1937) was an Italian inventor who received the first patent for a wireless telegraphy system. In 1900, Marconi proved that wireless waves were not affected by Earth's shape when he transmitted a wireless signal across the Atlantic ocean for a distance of 2,100 miles. He continued to study waves, which resulted in a beam system for long distance communication, the first microwave radio, and the principles of radar. He received many honors and awards, including the Nobel Prize in Physics.

Marcos, Ferdinand Ferdinand Marcos (1917–1989) was the authoritarian leader of the Philippines from 1966–1986. Formerly a lawyer, Marcos won democratic presidential elections in the Philippines in 1965 and 1969. His reign became increasingly marked by corruption and human-rights incidents. In 1972, he declared martial law and persecuted his opponents. When exiled politician and Marcos critic Benigno Aquino, Jr., was assassinated, the majority of Filipinos threw their support behind his widow, Corazon, in the 1986 presidential election. After a contested loss, Marcos and his wife fled to exile in Hawaii.

Maria Theresa Maria Theresa (1717–1780) was the archduchess of Austria and queen of Hungary and Bohemia (1740–1780), wife and empress of the Holy Roman emperor Francis I (1745–1765) and mother of the Holy Roman emperor Joseph II (1765–1790).

Marie Antoinette Marie Antoinette's (1755–1793) frivolous ways, conduct, and various scandals helped discredit the monarchy. She told her husband, Louis XVI, to resist reform demands by the National Assembly. Like Louis, she was branded a traitor and executed.

Marseilles French port city; troops marched to a patriotic song as they left the city, the song eventually became the French national anthem

Marshall Plan massive aid package offered by the U.S. to Europe to help countries rebuild after World War II

Martel, Charles Charles Martel (688–741) served as mayor of the palace (the person who ruled in the name of the king) for the eastern part of the Frankish kingdom from 715 until 741. The illegitimate son of the former mayor, Martel seized power, eventually reunited, and then ruled the entire kingdom of the Franks. Since 711, Muslims had raided Frankish lands, and in 732 they reached Bordeaux. Called to help at the battle of Tours that year, Charles's cavalry halted this last great Muslim advance into Europe.

martyr a person who suffers or dies because of his or her beliefs

matrilineal kinship ties that are passed on through the mother's side of the family

Maurya, Chandragupta Chandragupta Maurya, who reigned from about 321 B.C. to 297 B.C., was the first Mauryan emperor. The son of a Mauryan chief, his family was left in poverty when his father died. After overcoming many challenges, Chandragupta learned military tactics and eventually formed a force strong enough to conquer most of India.

May Fourth Movement cultural movement in China that sought to reform China and make it stronger

means of production farms, factories, railways, and other large businesses that produce and distribute goods

Mecca a city in western Saudi Arabia; birthplace of Muhammad, viewed by Muslims as the prophet of Islam, and the most holy city for Islamic people

medieval referring to the Middle Ages in Europe or the period of history between ancient and modern times

Medina a city in western Saudi Arabia; a city where Muhammad preached

Meiji Restoration in Japan, the reign of emperor Meiji from 1868 to 1912 that was marked by rapid industrialization

Meir, Golda Golda Meir (1898–1978) was a founder and the first female prime minister of Israel (1969–1974). She was a founding member of the Israel Labour Party and had been foreign minister (1956–1966).

Menelik II Menelik II (1844–1913) was the emperor of Ethiopia who expanded his empire, modernized his country, and defeated the Italian invasion in 1896.

mercantilism policy by which a nation sought to export more than it imported in order to build its supply of gold and silver

mercenaries soldiers serving in a foreign army for pay

mercenary soldier serving in a foreign country for pay

Meroë capital of the ancient kingdom of Nubia

Mesa Verde the largest complex of Anasazi cliff-dwellings in the North American Southwest, built between A.D. 1150 and A.D. 1300

Mesoamerica region of North America, including Mexico and Central America, in which civilizations with common cultural features developed before Europeans entered the continent

Mesopotamia region within the Fertile Crescent that lies between the Tigris and Euphrates rivers.

messiah savior sent by God

mestizo in Spanish colonial America, a person of Native American and European descent

métis people of mixed Native American and French Canadian descent

Michelangelo Michelangelo Buonarroti (1475–1564) was an Italian painter also known for his sculpture, engineering, architecture, and poems. His famous marble statue, *David,* shows the influence of ancient Greek traditions on Renaissance artists. Michelangelo painted biblically themed ceiling murals for the Sistine Chapel in Rome. As an architect, he designed the dome of St. Peter's Cathedral in Rome, later a model for the U.S. Capitol in Washington D.C.

middle class a group of people, including merchants, traders, and artisans, whose rank was between nobles and peasants

Middle Passage the leg of the triangular trade route on which slaves were transported from Africa to the Americas

militarism glorification of the military

militia armed group of citizen soldiers

Milosevic, Slobodan Slobodan Milosevic (1941–2006) was a Serbian Socialist party leader, whose Serbian nationalist policies contributed to the breakup of the former Yugoslavia. He died in The Hague, Netherlands, while on trial at the UN's International Criminal Tribunal for the Former Yugoslavia (ICTY) for his role in the genocide in the Balkans.

minaret slender tower of a mosque, from which Muslims are called to prayer

Ming dynasty Chinese dynasty in which Chinese rule was restored; held power from 1368 to 1644

missionaries people sent to do religious work in a territory or foreign country

missionary someone sent to do religious work in a territory or foreign country

mobilize prepare military forces for war

Mobutu Sese Seko (1930–1997) was born Joseph-Desire Mobutu. He changed his name after he took control of Congo in 1965 in a military coup. He also renamed the country Zaire. Mobutu ruled Zaire as a dictator until he was overthrown by Laurent Kabila in 1997. He died of cancer a short time later.

Moche a culture that thrived in the Andean region from about 400 B.C. to A.D. 600

Moctezuma Moctezuma (Moctezuma II, 1466–c. June 30, 1520) was the last Aztec emperor, who mistakenly thought that the conquistador Cortés might be the god-king Quetzalcoatl. He was defeated by Cortés and forced to sign over his land and treasure. He was taken prisoner and killed as the Aztecs attempted to drive the Spanish from Tenochtitlán.

Mohenjo-Daro ancient city of the Indus civilization, located in present-day Pakistan

moksha in Hindu belief, the ultimate goal of existence, which is to achieve union with Brahman

Moluccas an island chain in present-day Indonesia, which Europeans in the 1400s called the Spice Islands because it was the chief source of spices

Mombasa established East African coastal city and hub of international trade, attacked in the 1400s by Portuguese explorers to expel the Arabs who controlled East African trade routes, so they could take over those routes for themselves

monarchy government in which a king or queen exercises central power

Monet, Claude Claude Monet (1840–1926) was one of the leading figures in the French Impressionist movement. Much like the Romantics, the Impressionists found inspiration in the outdoors and rejected traditional European artistic conventions. Monet sought to create an accurate depiction of nature through his use of color, tones, texture, and brush strokes. He often painted the same object or scene at different times of day to see how light and shadow changed its appearance. Two of his most famous series are the grain stacks and water lily pond.

money economy economic system in which goods or services are paid for through the exchange of a token of an agreed value

Mongkut Mongkut (1804–1868) was king of Siam (modern-day Thailand) from 1851–1868. Mongkut lived as a Buddhist monk while his older brother held the throne. Upon his brother's death, Mongkut's many influential friends helped him become king. The learned king was fond of Western philosophies and worked to modernize his kingdom. His educated children were able to further his progress after his death.

monopoly complete control of a product or business by one person or a group

monotheistic believing in one god

Monroe Doctrine American policy of discouraging European intervention in the Western Hemisphere

monsoon seasonal wind that regularly blows from a certain direction for part of the year

Montesquieu Baron de Montesquieu (1689–1755) was born Charles Louis de Secondat into a family of wealth and inherited the title Baron de Montesquieu from his uncle. Like many other reformers, he did not let his privileged status keep him from becoming a voice for democracy. His first book, titled *Persian Letters,* ridiculed the French government and social classes. In his work published in 1748, *The Spirit of the Laws,* he advanced the idea of separation of powers—a foundation of modern American democracy.

More, Sir Thomas Thomas More (1478–1535) was born in London. He became a lawyer, scholar, writer, and member of British parliament during the reign of Henry VIII. He wrote *Utopia,* describing an ideal society. The word *utopian* came to mean idealistic or visionary. In 1521, he was knighted.

Morelos, Father José Father José Morelos (1765–1815) was a Catholic priest who took command of the revolutionary movement after Father Miguel Hidalgo's death. He led the movement throughout southern Mexico, and in 1813, he called the Congress of Chilpancingo to form a government. In 1815 he was captured and executed as a traitor.

mosaic picture made of chips of colored stone or glass

Moses As described in the Hebrew Bible, Moses was a Jewish religious leader who led the Israelites out of Egyptian slavery back to Canaan. Jews believe that during the journey, or Exodus, God presented Moses with a set of religious and ethical laws for the Jewish people known as the Ten Commandments.

mosque Muslim house of worship

Mothers of the Plaza de Mayo a movement of women who protested weekly in a central plaza in the capital of Argentina against the disappearance or killing of relatives

Mughal Muslim dynasty that ruled much of present-day India from 1526 to 1857

Mughal empire Muslim empire that ruled most of northern India from the mid-1500s to the mid-1700s; also known as the Mogul empire

Muhammad Muhammad (c. 570–632) introduced the religion of Islam to southwestern Asia. According to Muslim belief, Muhammad heard the voice of the angel Gabriel instructing him to serve as a messenger for God. Muhammad spent the rest of his life spreading Islam. Muslims today honor Muhammad as God's final prophet.

Muhammad Ahmad Muhammad Ahmad (1844–1885) assumed the title and role of Mahdi in 1881, believing he was appointed by God to purify the Muslim religion and restore its greatness. Through his campaigns, he created a vast Islamic state in the Sudan region.

Muhammad al-Razi Muhammad al-Razi (865–925) was a renowned Muslim physician who pioneered the study of many diseases. In addition to a well-received book on measles and smallpox, he also wrote texts about the history of medicine and ways to advance the field. Al-Razi held the position of chief physician, first in the city of Rayy and then in Baghdad. Also a philosopher, al-Razi analyzed the works of Plato while presenting his own ideas.

Muhammad Ali Muhammad Ali (1769–1849) was the son of a military commander who died when Muhammad Ali was a young boy. He was appointed governor of Egypt by the Ottomans and seized power during the chaos of the civil war following Napoleon's invasion. Often called the "founder of modern Egypt," Muhammad Ali set in motion a number of economic, political, administrative, and military reforms. His reforms were intended to secure Egyptian independence and place Egypt on the road to becoming a major Middle Eastern power.

mujahedin Muslim religious warriors

mulatto in Spanish colonial America, a person of African and European descent

multiethnic made up of several ethnic groups

multinational corporation company with branches in many countries

Mumbai a large city in India, also known as Bombay

mummification the preservation of dead bodies by embalming and wrapping them in cloth

Mussolini, Benito Benito Mussolini (1883–1945) was born into a poor household in Italy. His father was a blacksmith and his mother a schoolteacher. Although Mussolini grew up in a socialist home and strongly advocated socialist policies as a young man, he formed the Fascist party in Italy after returning from fighting in World War I. Using terror and fear tactics together with the Black Shirts, Mussolini created and ruled Italy as a totalitarian state. After Italy invaded Ethiopia in 1935, Mussolini and Hitler made an alliance and, with Japan, fought against the Allies in World War II.

mutiny revolt, especially of soldiers or sailors against their officers

Mutsuhito Mutsuhito (1852–1912) was declared emperor Meiji in 1868 following the death of his father, the emperor Kōmei. Emperor Meiji embodied a blend of Western and Japanese ideals, seeking out foreign examples as models for his country. He initiated major political, economic, and cultural reforms that led to an era of rapid modernization.

mutual-aid society self-help group to aid sick or injured workers

mystic person who devotes his or her life to seeking direct communication with the divine

N

Nagasaki Japanese city; on an island in its harbor, the Tokugawa shoguns in the 1600s permitted one or two Dutch ships to trade with Japan each year

Nanak, Guru Guru Nanak (1469–c. 1539) was the founder of Sikhism. According to Sikh beliefs, Nanak entered a trance while swimming and experienced a spiritual revelation. He preached a message of equality and opportunity, and of one God for all humanity. His teachings, and those of his successors, shaped the core beliefs of Sikhism.

Napoleon III Napoleon III (1808–1873) was the nephew of Napoleon Bonaparte. He was president of the Second Republic (1850–1852), then emperor of the Second Empire of France (1852–1870). Napoleon III built France's economic and political power, but his foreign policies were unsuccessful. He was deposed in 1870 after France's defeat in the Franco-Prussian War.

Napoleonic Code body of French civil laws introduced in 1804; served as a model for many nations' civil codes

Napoleonic Wars a series of wars from 1804 to 1805 that pitted Napoleon's French empire against the major powers of Europe

Nasser, Gamal Abdel Gamal Abdel Nasser (1918–1970) was the president of Egypt (1956–1970). He nationalized the Suez Canal, was a leader of the Pan Arab movement, and allied Egypt with the Soviet Union during the Cold War. He led his country to war with Israel in 1956 and 1967.

Nationalism a strong feeling of pride and devotion to one's country

nationalization takeover of property or resources by the government

natural law unchanging principle, discovered through reason, that governs human conduct

natural rights rights that belongs to all humans from birth, such as life, liberty, and property

Nazca a culture that thrived in the Andean region from about 200 B.C. to A.D. 600

Nazi-Soviet Pact agreement between Germany and the Soviet Union in 1939 in which the two nations promised not to fight each other and to divide up land in Eastern Europe

Nebuchadnezzar (634 B.C.–562 B.C.) Nebuchadnezzar was king of the Babylonian empire from 605 B.C. to 562 B.C. He led several military campaigns, which expanded the empire to Aramea, Judah, and other cities. He rebuilt the city of Babylon and is credited with the construction of the famous Hanging Gardens.

Necker, Jacques Jacques Necker (1732–1804) was director of the French treasury before the revolution, Necker attempted to reform the country's finances, although he also tried to finance France's participation in the American Revolution through heavy borrowing, while trying to conceal the country's huge deficit. Later, his calls for reform were thwarted by Louis XVI.

négritude movement movement in which writers and artists of African descent expressed pride in their African heritage

Nehanda Nehanda (c. 1840–1898) was a spiritual leader of the Shona people in southern Africa and the inspiration for a revolt against the British South Africa Company's colonization of the territory that is now Zimbabwe. She was eventually captured and executed by the British.

Nehru, Jawaharlal Jawaharlal Nehru (1889–1964) was the first prime minister of independent India. Educated in England, Nehru returned to India to practice law. He joined the Indian National Congress, an independence movement led by Mohandas Gandhi. Named Gandhi's successor, Nehru led the Congress until India achieved independence from Great Britain. As prime minister, Nehru focused on industrialization, socialist economic policies, and neutrality in the Cold War.

Neolithic Period the final era of prehistory, which began about 9000. B.C.; also called the New Stone Age

Neolithic Revolution the period of time during which the introduction of agriculture led people to transition from nomadic to settled life

neutrality policy of supporting neither side in a war

Neutrality Acts a series of acts passed by the U.S. Congress from 1935 to 1939 that aimed to keep the U.S. from becoming involved in WWII

New Deal a massive package of economic and social programs established by Franklin Delano Roosevelt to help Americans during the Great Depression

New France French possessions in present-day Canada from the 1500s to 1763

New Stone Age the final era of prehistory, which began about 9000 B.C.; also called the Neolithic Period

Newton, Isaac Isaac Newton (1642–1727) was one of the most important figures of the Scientific Revolution. An English mathematician and physicist, Newton's three laws of motion form the basic principles of modern physics and led to the formulation of the universal law of gravity. His 1687 book, *Mathematical Principles of Natural Philosophy,* is considered one of the most important works in the history of modern science.

Nightingale, Florence Florence Nightingale (1820–1910) was a nurse in the British military hospital in Crimea. When she arrived at the hospital in 1854, she was shocked by the state of the hospital and the rate at which the men were dying. She fought to have the barracks cleared, latrines dug, laundry washed, and the sick cared for. Six months after her arrival, the death rate dropped from 60 percent to 2 percent. When she returned to Britain, she pressured the government to reform hospitals to improve sanitation and care.

nirvana in Buddhist belief, union with the universe and release from the cycle of rebirth

Nkrumah, Kwame (1909–1972) fought to make Ghana (then Gold Coast) independent from Britain. He then became the first president of independent Ghana, which he led from 1957 until he was forced from office during a military coup. He spent the rest of his life in Guinea.

no-fly zone in Iraq, area where the United States and its allies banned flights by Iraqi aircraft after the 1991 Gulf War

Nobel, Alfred Alfred Nobel (1833–1896) was a Swedish chemist, inventor, engineer, business man, and author. Although dynamite is his most well-known invention, he holds 355 patents. In 1895, Nobel bequeathed most of his fortune to create the Nobel Prize in order to honor men and women for important achievements in physics, chemistry, medicine, literature, and peace.

nomad person who moves from place to place in search of food

nonalignment political and diplomatic independence from both Cold War powers

North Atlantic Treaty Organization (NATO) a military alliance between several North Atlantic states to safeguard them from the presumed threat of the Soviet Union's communist bloc; countries from other regions later joined the alliance

Northern Ireland the northeastern portion of the island of Ireland, a part of the United Kingdom that has had a long religious conflict

Nubia ancient kingdom of northeastern Africa, also called Kush

nuclear family family unit consisting of parents and children

Nuremberg Laws laws approved by the Nazi Party in 1935, depriving Jews of German citizenship and taking some rights away from them

Nuremberg Trials series of war crimes trials held in Germany after WWII

O

Old Stone Age the era of prehistory that lasted from 2 million B.C. to about 9000 B.C.

Olduvai Gorge Located in eastern Africa, the gorge is made up of numerous sedimentary layers of ash and lava deposited over millions of years. It has provided archaeologists with a geological yardstick for measuring the age of early stone tools and hominid bones excavated at the site.

oligarchy government in which ruling power belongs to a few people

Olmec the earliest American civilization, located along the Gulf Coast of Mexico from about 1200 B.C. to 400 B.C.

one-child policy a Chinese government policy limiting urban families to a single child

Open Door Policy American approach to China around 1900, favoring open trade relations between China and other nations

Opium War war between Great Britain and China over restrictions to foreign trade

oracle bone in Shang China, animal bone or turtle shell used by priests to predict the future

Organization of American States (OAS) a group formed in 1948 to promote democracy, economic cooperation, and human rights in the Americas

Osiris Osiris is the Egyptian god identified as the god of the afterlife. He is often depicted as a green-skinned man with a pharaoh's beard, partially mummy-wrapped at the legs wearing a crown with ostrich feathers, holding a symbolic crook.

ostracism practice used in ancient Greece to banish or send away a public figure who threatened democracy

Ottoman a member of a Turkish-speaking nomadic people who migrated from Central Asia into northwestern Asia Minor

outpost a distant military station or a remote settlement

outsourcing the practice of sending work to outside enterprises in order to save money or increase efficiency

overproduction condition in which production of goods exceeds the demand for them

Owen, Robert Robert Owen (1771–1858) set up a model community in New Lanark, Scotland based on Utopianism. At New Lanark, Owen established revolutionary changes by limiting the age for children workers and providing a school for all children. In 1824, he invested in an experimental community in America called New Harmony. He became a leader in the labor movement in England and continued his involvement in the movement until his death.

Oyo empire Yoruba people formed this state in present-day southwestern Nigeria in the 1600s. This empire used wealth from trade, including slave trading, to maintain a trained army and to eventually conquer the neighboring Dahomey kingdom. The Yoruba people then traded with European merchants from Dahomey's ports.

P

Pachacuti Inca Yupanqui Pachacuti Inca Yupanqui (1438–1471) was a skilled warrior growing up. He expanded the Inca empire to what is now Peru and Ecuador. His capital was Cuzco, and he is credited with developing its city plan.

Pacific Rim vast region of nations, including countries in Southeast Asia, East Asia, and the Americas, that border the Pacific Ocean

pacifism opposition to all war

paddy rice field

pagoda multi-storied Buddhist temple with eaves that curve up at the corners

Paleolithic Period the era of prehistory that lasted from at least 2 million B.C. to about 9000 B.C.; also called the Old Stone Age

Pan-Africanism movement which began in the 1920s that emphasized the unity and strength of Africans and people of African descent around the world

Pan-Arabism movement in which Arabs sought to unite all Arabs into one state

Panama Canal manmade waterway connecting the Atlantic and Pacific oceans

pandemic spread of a disease across a large area, country, continent, or the entire world

papal supremacy the claim of medieval popes that they had authority over all secular rulers

papyrus plant used to make a paper-like writing material in ancient Egypt

Parliament the legislature of England, and later of Great Britain

parliamentary democracy a form of government in which the executive leaders (usually a prime minister and cabinet) are chosen by and responsible to the legislature (parliament), are also members of it

Parthenon the chief temple of the Greek goddess Athena on the Acropolis in Athens, Greece

partition a division into pieces

partnership a group of merchants who joined together to finance a large-scale venture that would have been too costly for any individual trader

pasha provincial ruler in the Ottoman empire

Pasternak, Boris Boris Pasternak (1890–1960) grew up in an well-educated Jewish family. His father was an artist and professor, while his mother was an accomplished concert pianist. Pasternak is best remembered for his epic novel *Doctor Zhivago,* which helped him to win the Nobel Prize for Literature in 1958. The accolades and publicity from the West only created problems for Pasternak at home in the Soviet Union. He was expelled from the Union of Soviet Writers and died in poverty. Pasternak's literary masterpiece remained banned in the Soviet Union until the mid-1980s.

Pasteur, Louis Louis Pasteur (1822–1895) was a French chemist and one of the founders of microbiology. Pasteur developed the germ theory of disease and identified the causes of many diseases, including rabies, anthrax, small pox, and chicken cholera. By discovering the causes of these diseases, Pasteur determined that they could be prevented by vaccines. He helped develop several vaccines, including the rabies vaccine. He also invented the process of pasteurization for wine, beer, milk, and vinegar.

paternalistic the system of governing a country as a father would a child

patriarch in the Roman and Byzantine empires, the highest church official in a major city

patriarchal relating to a society in which men hold the greatest legal and moral authority

patrician a member of the land-holding upper class

patrilineal kinship ties that are passed on through the father's side of the family

patron a person who provides financial support for the arts

Paul Paul (c. 4 B.C.–A.D. 64) was an early opponent of Christianity who, after having a vision, was converted to the teachings of Jesus. He became a missionary to spread the teachings of Jesus.

Peace of Westphalia series of treaties that ended the Thirty Years' War

Pedro, Dom Dom Pedro (1825–1891) was the second and final emperor of Brazil. Pedro II turned Portugese-speaking Brazil into an emerging power. He created political stability and sought to protect freedom of speech and civil rights. Dom Pedro's government was a parliamentary monarchy. Under his leadership, Brazil experienced significant economic growth. His reign ended in 1889 after a military coup took control of the government and forced him into exile in Europe.

penal colony place where people convicted of crimes are sent

peninsular in Spanish colonial America, a person born in Spain

peon a worker forced to labor for a landlord to pay off a debt that is impossible to pay off in his or her lifetime, which is incurred by food, tool, or seeds the landlord has advanced to him or her

peonage system by which workers owe labor to pay their debts

perestroika a Soviet policy of democratic and free-market reforms introduced by Mikhail Gorbachev in the late 1980s

Pericles (495 B.C.–429 B.C.) was an Athenian statesman in the 400s B.C. who led Athens during its golden age of cultural achievement under democratic government

Perón, Juan Juan Perón (1895–1974) was first elected president of Argentina in 1946. He ruled with the help of his wife, Eva, who was popular with Argentinians. Perón established an authoritarian government and instituted broad reforms, but his government was plagued with corruption. He was overthrown in a coup in 1955. His supporters, known as Peronists, continued to fight for control of the government, and Perón returned to power in the 1970s. His third wife, Isabel, became president upon her husband's death in 1974. She was overthrown by the military in 1976.

Perry, Matthew Matthew Perry (1794–1858) was a successful officer in the U.S. Navy. He led a naval expedition to Japan in an effort to establish diplomatic and trade relations after centuries of Japanese isolation. The overwhelming military presence opened the way for U.S. trading privileges in Japan, with other Western powers soon to follow.

perspective artistic technique used to give paintings and drawings a three-dimensional effect

Peter the Great Peter the Great (1672–1725), tsar of Russia, reigned jointly with his half-brother Ivan V (1682–1696) and alone (1696–1725). He was proclaimed emperor in 1721. He was one of Russia's greatest statesmen, organizers, and reformers.

Petrarch Francesco Petrarch (1304–1374) lived in Florence and was an early Renaissance humanist, poet, and scholar. He assembled a library of Greek and Roman manuscripts gathered from monasteries and churches, helping to preserve these classic works for future generations.

phalanx in ancient Greece, a massive tactical formation of heavily armed foot soldiers

pharaoh title of the rulers of ancient Egypt

Philip II Philip II (359 B.C.–336 B.C.), restored internal peace to Macedonia, built an effective army, and then formed alliances with many Greek city-states or conquered them. After defeating the united forces of Athens and Thebes at Chaeronea, all of Greece came under his control. Assassination ended his aim to conquer Persia.

Philippines a country in southeastern Asia made up of several thousand islands; seized by the Spanish in the 1500s; became an important link in Spain's overseas trading empire as the destination of silver fleets sent from the Americas

philosophe French for "philosopher"; French thinker who desired reform in society during the Enlightenment

philosopher someone who seeks to understand and explain life; a person who studies philosophy

philosophy system of ideas

Piankhi Piankhi was king of Kush from around 750 to 719 B.C. He was known for his military prowess throughout North Africa. A very conservative ruler, Piankhi sought to strengthen some of Egypt's declining institutions.

pictograph a simple drawing that looks like the object it represents

Pilgrim English Protestants who rejected the Church of England

Pisan, Christine de Christine de Pisan (c. 1364–1430) was the daughter of a physician and astronomer in the French court. Highly educated, de Pisan spoke several languages. After being widowed at 25, she began to write poetry and then comment on social issues.

Pizarro, Francisco Francisco Pizarro (c. 1476–June 26, 1541) was born into a very poor Spanish family and in 1513 joined Balboa's expedition to discover the "South Sea." In 1532, he arrived in Peru with his brothers, deposed the Incan ruler Atahualpa, conquered Peru, founded Lima in 1535, and was later assassinated by Spanish rivals.
plantation large estate run by an overseer and worked by laborers who live there
plateau raised area of level land
Plato Plato (437 B.C.–347 B.C.), a student of Socrates, was an Athenian thinker, writer of philosophical dialogues, and founder of the Academy in Athens.
plebeian a members of the class that included farmers, merchants, artisans, and traders
plebiscite a ballot in which voters have a direct say on an issue
pogrom violent attack on a Jewish community
Pol Pot Pol Pot (1925–1998) was the leader of the Khmer Rouge, a communist guerrilla army that took over Cambodia in 1975. Under his rule, roughly two million of his nation's people died from murder, starvation, and disease. In 1979, Pol Pot was driven from power. He was captured in 1997, tried, and sentenced to life imprisonment. He died of natural causes while under house arrest.
polis city-state in ancient Greece
Polo, Marco Marco Polo (c. 1254–1324) was a traveler, merchant, and adventurer from Venice who journeyed from Europe to Asia in 1271–95, spending 17 years serving the Mongol emperor Kublai Khan. Polo dictated the account of his travels, *The Travels of Marco Polo* (originally iii *Il Milione* in Italian), to a fellow prisoner while imprisoned during a war with Genoa. His book proved a great success, but few readers believed it was true. Evidence outside his book that he journeyed so far to the east has not been found; however, during the centuries since his death, others have confirmed the accuracy of most of what he described.
polytheistic believing in many gods
pope head of the Roman Catholic Church; in ancient Rome, bishop of Rome who claimed authority over all other bishops
popular sovereignty limited government based on the separation of powers and a system of checks and balances
potlatch among Native American groups of the Northwest Coast, ceremonial gift-giving by people of high rank and wealth
predestination Calvinist belief that God long ago determined who would gain salvation
prehistory the period of time before writing was invented
premier prime minister
price revolution period in European history when inflation rose rapidly
prime minister the chief executive of a parliamentary government
privateer Dutch, English, and French pirates who preyed on treasure ships from the Americas in the 1500s, operating with the approval of European governments
Prohibition a ban on the manufacture and sale of alcohol in the United States from 1920 to 1933
proletariat working class
proliferate to multiply rapidly
propaganda spreading of ideas to promote a cause or to damage an opposing cause
prophet spiritual leader who interprets God's will
protectionism the use of tariffs and other restrictions to protect a country's home industries against competition
protectorate country with its own government but under the control of an outside power
Prussia area of eastern and central Europe which came under Polish and German rule in the Middle Ages and from 1701 was ruled by the German Hohenzollern dynasty
psychoanalysis a method of studying how the mind works and treating mental disorders
Ptolemy Ptolemy (A.D. 100–A.D. 170) was a Roman astronomer, mathematician, and geographer who incorrectly theorized that Earth is the center of the universe. He lived in Alexandria, Egypt, where he studied the planets and stars and developed a system to explain their movements.
pueblo Native American village of the North American Southwest
Pueblo Bonito the largest Anasazi pueblo, built in New Mexico in the A.D. 900s
Punjab state in northwestern India with a largely Sikh population
purdah isolation of women in separate quarters
Puritan member of an English Protestant group who wanted to "purify" the Church of England by making it more simple and more morally strict
Pusan Perimeter a defensive line around the city of Pusan, in the southeast corner of Korea, held by South Korean and United Nations forces in 1950 during the Korean War; marks the farthest advance of North Korean forces
Putin, Vladimir Vladimir Putin (b. 1952) served as president of Russia (1999–2008, 2012–). He began his career with the Soviet KGB (Committee for State Security) and also served as Russia's prime minister (1999, 2008–2012).
putting-out system system developed in the 18th century in which tasks were distributed to individuals who completed the work in their own homes; also known as cottage industry
Pythagoras Pythagoras (570 B.C.–c. 490 B.C.), a Greek philosopher and mathematician who studied the meaning of numbers and their relationships. He formulated principles that influenced the thinking of Plato and Aristotle, and also established an academy in Croton (now in Italy). Today he is best known for deriving the Pythagorean Theorem, a formula to calculate the relationship between the sides of a right triangle.

Q

Qajar a member of the dynasty that ruled present-day Iran from the late 1700s until 1925
Qianlong Qianlong (1711–1799) was a Chinese emperor who expanded the size of China's empire to include Tibet and much of central Asia, creating a multiethnic state that included Han Chinese, Mongols, Tibetans, and Manchus. Qianlong saw himself as a "Universal Monarch" both within and beyond the Chinese empire. He patronized the arts, commissioned great literary works, and formed China's national palace museum with art collections that remain important today.
Qing dynasty established by the Manchus in the mid-1600s that lasted until the early 1900s; China's last dynasty
quipu knotted strings used by Inca officials for record-keeping
Quran the holy book of Islam

R

Rabin, Yitzhak Yitzhak Rabin (1922–1995) was born in Jerusalem and served as an important military leader both before and after the creation of Israel. He served as prime minister twice, from 1974 to 1977 and from 1992 to 1995. In the 1990s, he reached a peace agreement with the PLO, for which he shared the Nobel Peace Prize with Shimon Peres and Yasir Arafat. Rabin was assassinated in 1995 by a Jewish extremist.

racism belief that one racial group is superior to another

radical one who favors extreme changes

rajah in ancient India, the elected warrior chief of an Aryan tribe

Ramses II (1292 B.C.–1190 B.C.) Ramses II is known for his building programs and for the wars he waged with the Hittites and Libyans. He reigned for more than 66 years and is known for the construction of Egypt's most famous monuments and architecture.

Raphael Raphael (1483–1520) was a Renaissance painter who blended Christian and classical styles. His famous paintings include one of the Madonna, the mother of Jesus, and *School of Athens,* showing an imaginary gathering of great thinkers, scientists, and artists including Michelangelo, Leonardo, and himself.

realism 19th-century artistic movement whose aim was to represent the world as it is

Realpolitik realistic politics based on the needs of the state

recession period of reduced economic activity

Reconquista During the 1400s, the campaign by European Christians to drive the Muslims from present-day Spain

refugee a person who flees from home or country to seek refuge elsewhere, often because of political upheaval or famine

regionalism loyalty to a local area

Reich German empire

Reign of Terror time period during the French Revolution from September 1793 to July 1794 when people in France were arrested for not supporting the revolution and many were executed

reincarnation in Hindu belief, the rebirth of the soul in another bodily form

reparation payment for war damage or damage caused by imprisonment

repeal cancel

republic system of government in which officials are chosen by the people

revenue money taken in through taxes

Rhee, Syngman Syngman Rhee (1875–1965) was president of the Republic of Korea (South Korea) from its founding in 1949 until 1960. He was elected to four terms of office, but accusations of election fraud in 1960 led to student-led protests and demands for his resignation from the National Assembly and the U.S. government. He resigned and went into exile in Hawaii.

rhetoric art of skillful speaking

Ricci, Matteo Matteo Ricci (1552–1610) was an Italian scholar and Jesuit priest who traveled to China. In 1589, Ricci began to teach Chinese scholars European mathematical ideas. Later he lived in Nanjing, where he worked on mathematics, astronomy, and geography. He became famous in China for his knowledge of astronomy, writing books in Chinese, and his talents as a painter.

Richelieu, Cardinal Cardinal Richelieu (1585–1642) considered one of the greatest politicians in history, he played an important role in France's history while serving as chief minister to Louis XIII.

Robespierre, Maximilien Maximilien Robespierre (1758–1794) was a French revolutionary elected to the Estates-General in 1789. He later became an important member of the Jacobin club and a member of the Committee of Public Safety. As a member of the Committee he began the Reign of Terror. He was later arrested and executed by the revolution's leaders.

rococo personal, elegant style of art and architecture made popular during the mid-1700s that featured designs with the shapes of leaves, shells, and flowers

romanticism 19th-century artistic movement that appealed to emotion rather than reason

Romero, Oscar Oscar Romero (1917–1980) was a Roman Catholic archbishop in El Salvador who became an outspoken critic of human rights abuses in his country and an advocate for the poor. He frequently came into conflict with the Salvadoran government for his criticism of the regime, and he was assassinated in 1980 while performing mass in a hospital chapel, most likely by Salvadoran death squads.

Rommel, Erwin Erwin Rommel (1891–1944) was a career military officer and one of Hitler's most successful generals. He took his own life after a failed attempt to assassinate Hitler.

Roosevelt, Franklin Delano Franklin D. Roosevelt (1882–1945) was the longest serving American president, elected to the office four times. Roosevelt was born into a wealthy family in New York and was a distant cousin of the early president Theodore Roosevelt. Elected in 1932, his first term as president focused on lifting America out of the Great Depression. He successfully passed legislation, crafting a massive package of economic and social programs, called the New Deal. During his third term, Roosevelt inspired many through his strong leadership during the Japanese attack on Pearl Harbor and America's subsequent entry into World War II. He was elected to a fourth term in 1944, but his health deteriorated as the war came to an end. Roosevelt died in April 1945.

Rosetta Stone stone monument that includes the same passage carved in hieroglyphics, demotic script, and Greek and that was used to decipher the meanings of many hieroglyphs

Rosie the Riveter popular name for women who worked in war industries during WWII

rotten borough rural town in England that sent members to Parliament despite having few or no voters

Rousseau, Jean-Jacques Jean-Jacques Rousseau (1712–1778) was a Swiss-born philosopher and writer whose works inspired leaders of the French Revolution. He revolutionized thought in politics and ethics, had an impact on how parents educated their children, and even influenced people's taste in music and in other arts.

Roy, Ram Mohun Ram Mohun Roy (1772–1833) was a founder of Hindu College in Calcutta, which provided an English-style education to Indians. While Roy wanted to reform some parts of traditional Indian and Hindu culture, he also revived India's pride in its culture. He is considered the founder of Indian nationalism.

Ruhr Valley coal-rich industrial region of Germany

russification Stalin's policy of imposing Russian culture on the Soviet Union

Russo-Japanese War conflict between Russia and Japan in 1904–1905 over control of Korea and Manchuria

S

Sabbath a holy day for rest and worship

sacrament sacred ritual of the Roman Catholic Church

Sadat, Anwar Anwar Sadat (1918–1981) was president of Egypt (1970–1981). He signed a peace treaty with Israel, the Camp David Accords, which was brokered by the U.S. He was assassinated by Muslim extremists in 1981.

Saddam Hussein Saddam Hussein (1937–2006) was a member of the Ba'ath Party and spent several years in prison when the Ba'athists were not in power. In 1968, he participated in a coup where the Ba'athists took over the government, and by 1979 he had total control of the government. Hussein was the dictator of Iraq until the 2003 Iraq War. In 2006, he was convicted in an Iraqi court of crimes against humanity and executed shortly afterward.

Safavid Shiite Muslim dynasty that ruled much of present-day Iran from the 1500s into the 1700s

Sahara largest desert in the world, covering almost all of North Africa

St. Francis of Assisi St. Francis of Assisi (1181?–1226) came from a wealthy family and had been a fun-loving and worldly young man. He gave up his wealth to "walk in the footsteps" of Jesus. The first Franciscan friars were his followers, and together they lived a life of service to the poor and sick. Francis regarded all nature as the mirror of God, and called animals his brothers and sisters. Famous stories tell of him preaching to the birds and convincing a wolf to stop attacking townspeople, if they, in turn, would feed the wolf. The Church made him a saint in 1228.

St. Petersburg a port city in northwestern Russia founded in 1703 by Peter the Great

St. Teresa of Avila St. Teresa of Avila (1515–1582) gained renown as the author of several books on spiritual matters. She was a key influence during the Catholic Reformation. As a Carmelite nun, she dedicated herself to a simple religious life built on quiet reflection. Teresa dedicated most of her life to the reform of the Carmelite order, founding many convents throughout Spain.

salon informal social gathering at which writers, artists, *philosophes,* and others exchanged ideas

samurai member of the warrior class in Japanese feudal society

San Martín, José de José de San Martín (1778–1850) was born in Argentina and educated in Spain. He helped lead the revolutions against Spanish rule in Argentina, Chile, and Peru. He became protector of Peru after its liberation from Spain but resigned in 1822 after conflict with Simón Bolívar. He lived in exile in Europe after his resignation.

Sandinista a socialist political movement and party that held power in Nicaragua during the 1980s

sans-culottes members of the working class who made the French Revolution more radical; called such because men wore long trousers instead of the fancy knee breeches that the upper class wore

Sapa Inca the title of the Inca emperor

Sargon The exact dates of King Sargon's birth and death are unknown, but according to Sumerian historians, he reigned from 2334 B.C. to 2279 B.C. He is known for creating the first empire in Mesopotamia.

sati custom that called for a widow to join her husband in death by throwing herself on his funeral pyre

satirize make fun of

savanna grassy plain with irregular patterns of rainfall

schism a split or divide

scholasticism in medieval Europe, the school of thought that used logic and reason to support Christian belief

scientific method careful, step-by-step process used to confirm findings and to prove or disprove a hypothesis

scribe in ancient civilizations, a person specially trained to read, write, and keep records

secede withdraw

secret ballot votes cast without announcing them publicly

sect a subgroup of a major religious group

secular having to do with worldly, rather than religious, matters; nonreligious

segregation forced separation by race, sex, religion, or ethnicity

Sejong, King King Sejong (1397–1450), Korea's most celebrated ruler and known as the Great, in 1443 he replaced the complex Chinese system of writing with hangul. His numerous cultural and intellectual accomplishments have led historians to call his reign the Korean Golden Age.

selective borrowing adopting or adapting some cultural traits but discarding others

self-determination right of people to choose their own form of government

sepoy Indian soldier who served in an army set up by the French or English trading companies

Septimius Severus Septimius Severus was born around A.D. 145 in what is today Tripoli. Before his death in 211, he was the emperor who converted the Roman government into a military monarchy. His reign set the stage for other Roman rulers.

serf in medieval Europe, a peasant bound to the lord's land

shah king

Shaka Shaka (1787–1828) was a Zulu chief and founder of southern Africa's Zulu empire.

Shakespeare William Shakespeare (1564–1616), born in England, became a famous poet and playwright during the reign of Queen Elizabeth I. Between 1590 and 1613, he wrote 37 plays that are still performed around the world. He invented words and phrases still used today. Like other Renaissance writers, he took a humanist approach to his characters.

shantytown slum of flimsy shacks

Sharia body of Islamic law that includes interpretation of the Quran and applies Islamic principles to everyday life

Sharpeville a black township in South Africa where the government killed anti-apartheid demonstrators in 1960

Shi Huangdi (about 259 B.C.–210 B.C.) was originally named Zhao Zheng. He was the son of the king of the Qin territory. At age 13, Zhao became the king of Qin. He proclaimed himself Shi Huangdi, or "First Emperor." Using spies, loyal generals, and bribery, he removed the leaders of six other surrounding states to create a unified China under his authoritarian rule. However, the unified China he created was too dependent on Shi Huangdi. The Qin dynasty collapsed four years after his death.

Shiite a member of one of the two major Muslim sects; believe that the descendants of Muhammad's daughter and son-in-law, Ali, are the true Muslim leaders

Shikibu, Murasaki Muraski Shikibu (c. 973–c. 1014 or 1025) was a lady-in-waiting in the Heian Court. Historians credit her with writing the world's first full-length novel, *The Tale of Genji,* written between A.D. 1000 and 1008.

Shinto principal religion in Japan that emphasizes the worship of nature

shrine altar, chapel, or other sacred place

Sikh member of an Indian religious minority

Sikhism monotheistic religion founded in the late 1400s by Guru Nanak in the Punjab region of India

Silla dynasty Korean dynasty that ruled from 668 to 935

Sino-Japanese War war between China and Japan in which Japan gained Taiwan

smelt melt in order to get the pure matter away from its waste matter

Smith, Adam Adam Smith (1723–1790) was a Scottish economist most remembered for his masterpiece, *An Inquiry into the Nature and Causes of the Wealth of Nations.* His argument for free markets with minimal government interference has helped shape productive economies around the world for more than 200 years. He has been called the father of modern economics and remains one of the most influential economic philosophers in history.

social contract an agreement by which people gave up their freedom to a powerful government in order to avoid chaos

social democracy political ideology in which there is a gradual transition from capitalism into socialism instead of a sudden, violent overthrow of the system

social gospel movement of the 1800s that urged Christians to do social service

social mobility the ability to move in social class

social welfare programs provided by the state for the benefit of its citizens

socialism system in which the people as a whole rather than private individuals own all property and operate all businesses

socialist realism artistic style whose goal was to promote socialism by showing Soviet life in a positive light

Socrates Socrates (469 B.C.–399 B.C.) was an Athenian stonemason and philosopher who sought truth by questioning, as described in dialogues written by Plato.

Solidarity a Polish labor union and democracy movement

Solomon In Jewish tradition, Solomon was the son of David, known for building the Temple in Jerusalem. He was also famous for his wisdom. After his death, the Kingdom of Israel was divided into two parts.

Song dynasty Chinese dynasty from 960 to 1279

Songhai medieval West African kingdom located in present-day Mali, Niger, and Nigeria

sovereign having full, independent power

soviet council of workers and soldiers set up by Russian revolutionaries in 1917

Spanish-American War conflict between the United States and Spain in 1898 over Cuban independence

Sparta city-state in ancient Greece settled by the Dorians and built as a military state

sphere of influence area in which an outside power claims exclusive investment or trading privileges

stalemate deadlock in which neither side is able to defeat the other

Stalin, Joseph Joseph Stalin (1879–1953) (real name: Iosif Vissarionovich Dzhugashvili) adopted the name Stalin, meaning "man of steel," after he joined the Bolshevik underground. He was the sole ruler of the Soviet Union for 33 years. Stalin stood his ground against Hitler and refused to leave Moscow. He eventually forced the Germans into retreat.

Stalingrad now Volgograd, a city in SW Russia that was the site of a fierce battle during WWII

Stamp Act law passed in 1765 by the British Parliament that imposed taxes on items such as newspapers and pamphlets in the American colonies; repealed in 1766

standard of living the level of material goods and services available to people in a society

Stanley, Henry Henry Stanley (1841–1904) was a British explorer of central Africa, famous for the rescue of Dr. David Livingstone and discoveries in the region of the Congo River.

Stanton, Elizabeth Cady Elizabeth Cady Stanton (1815–1902) was an author, lecturer, and activist who played a major role in the women's right movement. She drafted speeches and many of the movement's important documents, including the women's "Declaration of Rights." Stanton helped plan and lead the 1848 Seneca Falls Convention. Later in life, she began to focus more on social reforms, including child care, divorce laws, and temperance. Stanton died 18 years before women were granted the right to vote.

stela in the ancient world, a tall, commemorative monument that was often decorated

steppe sparse, dry, treeless grassland

stipend a fixed salary given to public office holders

stock shares in a company

Stolypin, Peter Peter Stolypin (1862–1911) was a Russian statesman under Tsar Nicholas II. He served as minister of the interior and president of the Council of Ministers. Although he instituted agricultural reforms that improved the lives of the peasantry, he made enemies on both sides of the political spectrum. He was assassinated in 1911.

strait narrow water passage

stupa large domelike Buddhist shrine

subcontinent large landmass that juts out from a continent

suburbanization the movement to build up areas outside of central cities

Sudetenland a region of western Czechoslovakia

Suez Canal a canal in Egypt linking the Red Sea and the Indian Ocean to the Mediterranean Sea, which also links Europe to ports in Asia and East Africa

suffrage right to vote

Sufi Muslim mystic who seeks communion with God through meditation, fasting, and other rituals

Suharto Suharto (1921–2008) was a highly ranked Indonesian military official who became the country's second president. Suharto fought against the Dutch in Indonesia's independence movement and achieved a distinguished rank in the new country's government. When Sukarno, the country's first president, started to institute communist policies, the anti-communist military rebelled. Suharto led purges against communists and a violent coup against Sukarno. Taking power in 1967, he worked to modernize and stabilize the country.

Sukarno Sukarno (1901–1970) was a freedom fighter and Indonesia's first president. Involved in the independence movement against the Dutch, Sukarno spent some time jailed or exiled. During World War II, Japan invaded the Indies, and Sukarno cooperated with the new regime. The collapse of Japan at the end of the war enabled Indonesia's independence, despite Dutch attempts to regain power. As the new country's president, Sukarno dismantled the parliamentary government and instituted communist policies. A violent coup led by General Suharto deposed Sukarno in 1967.

Suleiman Suleiman (1494–1566) was a sultan of the Ottoman Empire who ruled from 1520 to 1566. During this time he brought bureaucracy and stability to the empire and advanced the arts, law, and architecture. His military campaigns greatly expanded the scope of the empire.

sultan Muslim ruler

Sumer site of the world's first civilization, located in southeastern Mesopotamia

Sun Yixian Sun Yixian (1866–1925), also known as Sun Yat-sen, was the son of poor farmers in a small village. He left a career in medicine to revolt against the Qing government. After a failed uprising, Sun was forced into exile in Japan. In 1911, delegates elected Sun as provisional president of the newly established Republic of China. In 1921, Sun established a Nationalist government in South China and allied with the communists to defeat the warlords.

Sundiata Sundiata was a West African ruler who was responsible for laying the groundwork for Mali to be a rich and powerful kingdom. He died in 1255.

Sunni a member of one of the largest Muslim sects; believe that inspiration came from the example of Muhammad as recorded by his early followers

superpower a nation stronger than other powerful nations

surplus an amount that is more than needed; excess

surrealism artistic movement that attempts to portray the workings of the unconscious mind

Suryavarman II, King Suryavarman II was a famous king of Cambodia, who died in 1150 A.D. He built the world's largest religious structure at Angkor Wat and conquered much of what is now Thailand and Vietnam. He made the capital, Angkor, into one of the great cities of the world at that time.

sustainability development that balances people's needs today with the need to preserve the environment for future generations

sustainable development development that meets the needs of the present without compromising the ability of future generations to meet their own needs

Suu Kyi, Aung San Aung San Suu Kyi (1945–) is a human rights leader and Nobel Peace Prize recipient from Myanmar. The daughter of the leader of independent Burma and an ambassador to India, Suu Kyi was inspired to fight for peace and freedom against the military oppressors who had ruled Burma since 1962. She helped to found the independence movement the National League for Democracy, which won a democratic election in 1990 but was silenced by the military. In 2010, Suu Kyi was released from house arrest and won a seat in the legislature. She continues to lead the opposition to the authoritarian rulers and is expected to run for the country's presidency.

Swahili an East African culture that emerged about A.D. 1000; also a Bantu-based language, blending Arabic words and written in Arabic script.

T

Taíno Native American group encountered by Columbus when he first arrived in the West Indies

Taiping Rebellion peasant revolt in China

Taj Mahal a tomb built by Shah Jahan for his wife

Taliban Islamist fundamentalist faction that ruled Afghanistan for nearly ten years until ousted from power by the United States in 2002

Tang dynasty Chinese dynasty from 618 to 907

Tang Taizong Tang Taizong (598–649) was an accomplished general, government reformer, historian, Confucian scholar, and artist. These qualities and skills helped him to become China's most admired emperor.

tariff tax on imported goods

technology the skills and tools people use to meet their basic needs

Tehran capital of the Qajar dynasty and present-day Iran

temperance movement campaign to limit or ban the use of alcoholic beverages

tenant farmer someone who would pay rent to a lord to farm part of the lord's land

tenement multistory building divided into crowded apartments

Tennis Court Oath famous oath made by on a tennis court by the Third Estate in pre-revolutionary France

Tenochtitlán capital city of the Aztec empire, on which modern-day Mexico City was built

Teotihuacán city that dominated the Valley of Mexico from about A.D. 200 to A.D. 750 and that influenced the culture of later Mesoamerican peoples

Teresa, Mother Mother Teresa (baptized 1910, died 1997) was the Romanian-born founder of the Order of the Missionaries of Charity, a Roman Catholic group of women dedicated to helping the poor, especially those in India. She won the Nobel Peace Prize in 1979 and was also honored for her work by the Indian government. She was beatified, or named a blessed one, by the Roman Catholic Church in 2003 for her lifetime of commitment to those in need.

terrorism deliberate use of random violence, especially against civilians, to achieve political goals

Tet Offensive a massive and bloody offensive by communist guerrillas against South Vietnamese and American forces on Tet, the Vietnamese New Year, 1968; helped turn American public opinion against military involvement in Vietnam

Thatcher, Margaret Margaret Thatcher (1925–2013) was Britain's first female prime minister, serving from 1979 to 1990. Thatcher was a conservative and an avowed opponent of socialism, seeing it as anti-British because it eroded self-reliance. Under Thatcher, the British government sold nationalized industries to private firms. Thatcher also led the country during the Falklands War (1982) with Argentina.

theocracy government run by religious leaders

Theodora Theodora (497–548) was the wife of the emperor Justinian and was his most trusted advisor. Known for her powerful intelligence and shrewd political insight, Theodora exerted decisive influence in Byzantine political affairs. She is mentioned by name in almost every law passed during Justinian's reign. Theodora used her position and power to advance her interests, including pioneering efforts for women's rights. She supported strong laws to end the traffic in young women and revised divorce laws in favor of more benefits to women.

Third Reich official name of the Nazi party for its regime in Germany; held power from 1933 to 1945

38th parallel an imaginary line marking 38 degrees of latitude, particularly the line across the Korean Peninsula, dividing Soviet forces to the north and American forces to the south after WWII

Thutmose III (1504 B.C.–1426 B.C.) Thutmose III shared power with his aunt Queen Hatshepsut before becoming pharaoh. He battled to regain Egyptian rule of Syria and Palestine and created Egypt's largest dynasty.

Tiahuanaco a culture that thrived in the Andean region from about A.D. 200 to 1000

Tiananmen Square a huge public plaza at the center of China's capital, Beijing

Tiberius (c. 163 B.C.–133 B.C.) was a Roman plebeian who became a tribune and lobbied for government reform. He was killed in 133 B.C. by gangs hired by Roman senators.

Tojo, Hideki Hideki Tojo (1884–1948) was born in Tokyo and was a career military man. He was a general of the Imperial Japanese Army and the 40th prime minister of Japan during most of World War II, from 1941 to 1945. He was directly responsible for the attack on Pearl Harbor, and was arrested and sentenced to death for Japanese war crimes.

Tokugawa shoguns, descended from Tokugawa Ieyasu (1542–1616) who were supreme military leaders; ruled Japan from 1603 through 1869; reunified Japan and reestablished order following a century of civil war and disturbance

Tokyo capital of Japan

Torah the most sacred text of the Hebrew Bible, includes the first five books

total war channeling of a nation's entire resources into a war effort

totalitarian state government in which a one-party dictatorship regulates every aspect of citizens' lives

Touré, Samori Samori Touré (c. 1830–1900) was a Muslim military leader who founded a powerful West African kingdom in the Niger River region and fought against French forces.

tournament a mock battle in which knights would compete against one another to display their fighting skills

trade deficit situation in which a country imports more than it exports

trade surplus situation in which a country exports more than it imports

traditional economy undeveloped economic systems that rely on custom and tradition

tragedy in ancient Greece, a play about human suffering often ending in disaster

Treaty of Paris treaty of 1763 that ended the Seven Years' War and resulted in British dominance of the Americas

Treaty of Tordesillas treaty signed between Spain and Portugal in 1494, which divided the non-European world between them

triangular trade colonial trade routes among Europe and its colonies, the West Indies, and Africa in which goods were exchanged for slaves

tribune an official elected by the plebeians to protect their interests

tributary state independent state that has to acknowledge the supremacy of another state and pay tribute to its ruler

tribute payment that conquered peoples may be forced to pay their conquerors

Trojan War military conflict around 1250 B.C. between Mycenae and Troy, a rich trading city in present-day Turkey, described in Homer's epic poems, the *Illiad* and the *Odyssey*

troubadour a wandering poet or singer of medieval Europe

Truman Doctrine United States policy, established in 1947, of trying to contain the spread of communism

Truman, Harry Harry Truman (1884–1972) was the vice president of the United States when Roosevelt died and became the 33rd president upon his death. After being in office for only a few months, Truman made the decision to drop atomic bombs on Japan.

Truth, Sojourner Sojourner Truth (1797–1883) was one of the most well-known African American women during the 19th century. She was born a slave, and when she earned her freedom in 1826, she changed her name to Sojourner Truth. In 1843, she began travelling the country to spread the truth about injustice and to preach for human rights. Truth was an important figure in several movements—including the women's rights movement, temperance, racial equality, and prison reform—and she was not afraid to petition the government for reform.

tsunami a very large wave caused by an earthquake or very strong wind

Tudor, Mary Mary Tudor (1516–1558) was the first queen to rule England in her own right. The daughter of Henry VIII and his first wife, Catherine of Aragon, Mary was a staunch Catholic who failed to turn back the tide of the Protestant Reformation in England. Her vigorous persecution of Protestants earned her the nickname "Bloody Mary."

turnpike private road built by entrepreneurs who charged a toll to travelers to use it

Tutsis the main ethnic minority group in Rwanda and Burundi

Tutu, Desmond Desmond Tutu (1931–) is an archbishop of the Anglican church and was a leader in the fight against apartheid in South Africa. In 1984 he won the Nobel Peace Prize for his efforts.

Tutu, Osei Osei Tutu was born around 1660 and died in the early 1700s. He was a founder and first ruler of the Asante empire in present-day Ghana. He started as the chief of the small state of Kumasi. But he realized that small separate Asante kingdoms needed to unite in order to protect themselves from powerful Denkyera neighbors.

Twenty-One Demands list of demands given to China by Japan in 1915 that would have made China a protectorate of Japan

tyrant in ancient Greece, ruler who gained power by force

U

U-boat German submarine

ultimatum final set of demands

ultranationalist extreme nationalist

Umayyad Sunni dynasty of caliphs that ruled from 661 to 750

United Nations (UN) an international organization formed in 1945 at the end of World War II. Since then, its global role has expanded to include economic and social development, human rights, humanitarian aid, and international law.

universal manhood suffrage right of all adult men to vote

untouchable in India, a member of the lowest caste

Urban II, Pope Pope Urban II (1042–1099) was the leader of the Roman Catholic church at the time the Seljuk Turks were threatening the Byzantine empire. He convened the Council of Clermont, where he launched the First Crusade to win the Holy Land from the Muslims.

urban renewal the process of fixing up the poor areas of a city

urbanization movement of people from rural area to cities

Usman dan Fodio Usman dan Fodio (1754–1817) was a Fulani revolutionary leader, mystic, and philosopher. He led a revolt (1804–1808) to create a new Muslim state, the Fulani empire, in what is now northern Nigeria.

usury the practice of lending money at interest

utilitarianism idea that the goal of society should be to bring about the greatest happiness for the greatest number of people

utopian idealistic or visionary, usually used to describe a perfect society

V

V-E Day Victory in Europe Day, May 8, 1945, the day the Allies won WWII in Europe

Valley of Mexico valley in Mexico in which the numerous Mesoamerican civilizations, including the Aztecs, arose

van Gogh, Vincent Vincent van Gogh (1853–1890) was an artist for only ten years, yet he produced more than 2,000 drawings, sketches, and paintings. Early on, the Impressionists greatly influenced his style. Van Gogh later moved to Arles, France. While there he had a breakdown and committed himself to an asylum. During this time, he began to use more vibrant colors, wide brushstrokes, movement in form and line, and thick layers of paint. He was released in May 1890 and died two months later.

vanguard group of elite leaders

vassal in medieval Europe, a lord who was granted land in exchange for service and loyalty to a greater lord

Vedas a collection of prayers, hymns, and other religious teachings developed in ancient India beginning around 1500 B.C.

veneration special regard

vernacular everyday language of ordinary people

Versailles royal French residence and seat of government established by King Louis XIV

veto block a government action

viceroy representative of the king of Spain who ruled colonies in his name

Vichy city in central France where a puppet state governed unoccupied France and the French colonies

Victoria, Queen Queen Victoria (1819–1901) reigned from 1837 until 1901, the longest reign in British history. She symbolized British life during the period now known as the Victorian age. Queen Victoria set a tone of moral respectability and strict social manners. A trend-setter for the growing middle class, she introduced customs such as displaying a Christmas tree (a German practice) and wearing a white wedding gown.

Viet Cong communist rebels in South Vietnam who sought to overthrow South Vietnam's government; received assistance from North Vietnam

Vikings Scandinavian peoples whose sailors raided Europe from the 700s through the 1100s

Virgil Virgil (70 B.C–19 B.C.) was a Roman poet who wrote the *Aeneid* in 30 B.C. He studied mathematics and other subjects in Rome and Naples and was inspired by Greek poets

vizier chief minister who supervised the business of government in ancient Egypt

Voltaire Voltaire (1694–1778) was born François-Marie Arouet, but was known as Voltaire. He was an impassioned poet, historian, essayist, and philosopher who wrote with cutting sarcasm and sharp wit. Voltaire was sent to the Bastille prison twice due to his criticism of French authorities and was eventually banned from Paris. When he was able to return to France, he wrote about political and religious freedom. Voltaire spent his life fighting what he considered to be the enemies of freedom, such as ignorance, superstition, and intolerance.

W

Walesa, Lech Lech Walesa (b. 1943) helped found and direct the Polish independent trade union, Solidarity, at the Lenin Shipyards in Gdansk, where he was an electrician. After the Polish government crackdown on Solidarity in 1981, he was imprisoned for nearly a year. Walesa was awarded the Nobel Peace Prize in 1983. After the fall of the communist regime in Poland, Walesa was elected president of Poland, serving from 1990 to 1995.

War of the Austrian Succession series of wars in which various European nations competed for power in Central Europe after the death of Hapsburg emperor Charles VI

warlords local military rulers

warm-water port port that is free of ice year round

Warsaw Pact mutual-defense alliance between the Soviet Union and seven satellites in Eastern Europe set up in 1955

Washington, George George Washington (1732–1799) was a wealthy Virginia planter before becoming the commander of American forces during the Revolutionary War and first president of the United States. He owned a vast estate named Mount Vernon. Using his skill as a politician, negotiator, and general, Washington was able to keep the American cause of liberty alive during and after the revolution.

Watt, James James Watt (1736–1819) of Scotland invented the steam engine. James Watt first developed an interest in building models and measuring instruments in the workshop of his father, who built houses and ships. Watt apprenticed with a maker of mathematical instruments. In 1765, Watt worked on his steam engine. It had a separate condenser that helped keep steam from escaping. Later in life, he worked as a land surveyor and then returned to inventing and perfecting machines, until his retirement in 1800.

weapon of mass destruction (WMD) nuclear, biological, or chemical weapon

welfare state a country with a market economy but with increased government responsibility for the social and economic needs of its people

westernization adoption of western ideas, technology, and culture

Whitney, Eli Eli Whitney (1765–1825) showed mechanical and engineering skill at a young age. After he graduated from Yale College, he headed south where plantation owners learned of his mechanical skill and asked for his help. The cost of the labor to process cotton was too high. In response, Whitney invented the cotton gin, which revolutionized the textile industry and helped the South's economy. Unfortunately, Whitney did not profit from his invention. He left the South in debt but continued to design new inventions until his death.

William II William II (1859–1941) was the last German emperor and king of Prussia. He ruled the German empire and the kingdom of Prussia from 1888 to 1918. He led Germany into World War I. An ineffective military leader, he lost the support of his army and fled to exile in the Netherlands in November 1918.

William the Conqueror William the Conqueror (1028–1087) became the Duke of Normandy at age 7 and was knighted at age 15. He pressured King Edward of England to name him heir to the throne. Upon Edward's death, William invaded England and won the throne after the Battle of Hastings in 1066.

Wittenberg a city in northern Germany, where Luther drew up his 95 Theses

women's suffrage right of women to vote

Wordsworth, William William Wordsworth (1770–1850) was instrumental in launching Romanticism and wrote some of Western literature's most influential poems. While touring Europe, he encountered the French Revolution, which sparked in him an interest in the plight of the "common man." His sympathy for people and recognition of societal ills—particularly in urban areas—served as an inspiration for his work and his strong focus on emotion. It also inspired his view of the poet's role in society and his political ideals.

World Trade Organization (WTO) international organization set up to facilitate global trade

Wright, Orville and Wilbur Orville (1871–1948) and Wilbur (1867–1912) Wright were bicycle mechanics who used their knowledge of science and their experience in mechanics to create the first flying machine. After nearly 1,000 flights in gliders and testing in wind tunnels, the brothers built a powered plane. On December 17, 1903, the brothers tested their machine at Kitty Hawk, North Carolina. The first flight lasted 12 seconds; the longest flight that day lasted 59 seconds.

Wudi (156 B.C.–87 B.C.) was given the name Liu Che at birth. As the eleventh son of the Han emperor Jingdi, he would not have been destined to rule. However, the influence of his relatives changed this and he became emperor in 141 B.C. Determined to expand his dynasty's rule, he succeeded, though it came at a high cost to his soldiers and people. Liu Che made Confucianism the state religion. He was given the title Wudi (Martial Emperor) upon his death.

Y

Yalta Conference meeting between Churchill, Roosevelt, and Stalin in February 1945 where the three leaders made agreements regarding the end of World War II

Yathrib final destination of Muhammad's hijra and the home of the first community of Muslims; later renamed Medina; located in the northwest of present-day Saudi Arabia

Yorktown, Virginia location where the British army surrendered in the American Revolution

Yuan dynasty Chinese dynasty ruled by the Mongols from 1279 to 1368; best-known ruler was Kublai Khan

Z

zaibatsu since the late 1800s, powerful banking and industrial families in Japan

Zapata, Emiliano Emiliano Zapata (1879–1919) grew up a peasant. In 1897, he began a long struggle against the hacienda system to regain peasant land. After Francisco Madero lost the election to Porfirio Díaz, Zapata joined the revolution and fought for social reform. Zapata built up a strong following and played an essential role in ousting Victoriano Huerta in 1914. After Venustiano Carranza was elected president, he turned on Zapata. Zapata's revolutionaries went to war with the moderates who supported Carranza. In 1919, Carranza's army ambushed and killed Zapata.

zemstvo local elected assembly set up in Russia under Alexander II

Zen the practice of meditation; a school of Buddhism in Japan

zeppelin large gas-filled balloon

Zheng He Zheng He (c. 1371–1433) was an admiral in the Ming Chinese navy and diplomat who made his first voyage in 1405 to Vietnam, India, and Africa to both explore and trade. His huge fleet of hundred of junks (Chinese ships) and thousands of sailors carried silk, porcelain, and lacquerware to trade for pearls, spices, ivory, and timber. Zheng He made seven voyages in all, exploring, trading successfully, and thereby motivating Chinese merchants to establish trade centers in Southeast Asia and India.

ziggurat in ancient Mesopotamia, a large, stepped platform thought to have been topped by a temple dedicated to a city-state's chief god or goddess

Zionism a movement devoted to rebuilding a Jewish state in the ancient homeland

Zoroaster (about 628 B.C.–551 B.C.) Zoroaster was an Iranian religious reformer and founder of Zoroastrianism. He emphasized individual freedom to choose right or wrong and individual responsibility for one's actions. Zoroaster's ideas influenced the early development of philosophy.

A

abacus > ábaco Artefacto que sirve para contar y calcular al deslizar pequeñas bolas o cuentas a lo largo de varillas o muescas.

Abbas the Great, Shah > Abbas el Grande, sah Abbas el Grande (1571–1629) fue el sah de la dinastía Safávida desde 1588 hasta su muerte. Expulsó a las tropas otomanas y uzbekas de Persia y patrocinó una era de oro de las artes y los logros persas.

Abbasid > Abasí Dinastía que gobernó Bagdad de 750 a 1258.

abdicate > abdicar Renunciar a un puesto de poder.

abolition > abolición Campaña contra la esclavitud y contra el tráfico de esclavos.

Abraham > Abraham Según la tradición judía, Abraham es el ancestro del pueblo judío. Hijo de un mercader de ídolos de la ciudad de Ur, Abraham hizo una alianza especial con Dios. Llevó a sus descendientes a Canaán, que los judíos consideran su Tierra Prometida.

absentee landlord > dueño ausente Dueño de una gran propiedad que no vive en ella.

absolute monarchy > monarquía absoluta Forma de gobierno en la cual el gobernante tiene autoridad completa sobre el gobierno y las vidas de las personas a las que dirige.

absolutism > absolutismo Creencia de un poder total y sin restricciones en el gobierno.

abstract art > abstracto Estilo de arte compuesto de líneas, colores y formas, que a veces no tiene un tema reconocible.

Abu Bakr > Bakr, Abu Abu Bakr (573–634) fue el suegro de Mahoma y el primer califa musulmán, o líder, después de la muerte de Mahoma. Convertido al islam, Abu Bakr aconsejó a Mahoma e hizo un viaje llamado hégira con el profeta. En su papel de sucesor de Mahoma, ayudó a unir al pueblo musulmán. Bajo su gobierno, el imperio musulmán se expandió.

acculturation > aculturación Mezcla de dos o más culturas.

acid rain > lluvia ácida Forma de contaminación en la que los productos químicos tóxicos que se encuentran en el aire vuelven a la tierra en la lluvia, nieve o granizo.

acropolis > acrópolis El punto más alto y fortificado de una ciudad-estado griega.

acupuncture > acupuntura Tratamiento médico, originado en la antigua China, en el cual se insertan agujas en puntos específicos de la piel para aliviar el dolor o tratar diferentes enfermedades.

Adenauer, Konrad > Adenauer, Konrad Konrad Adenauer (1876–1967) fue el primer canciller de Alemania Occidental, de 1949 a 1963. Gobernó Alemania Occidental durante su recuperación y reconstrucción después de la Segunda Guerra Mundial. Sus logros incluyeron la entrada de Alemania Occidental en la OTAN y la fundación de la Comunidad Económica Europea.

adobe > adobe Mezcla de arcilla y fibras vegetales que se endurece cuando se seca al sol y que se usa para la construcción.

Adulis > Adulis Puerto comercial estratégico del reino de Aksum.

Afghanistan > Afganistán País islámico en Asia central; invadido por la Unión Soviética en 1979; más tarde hogar de los radicales islamistas talibán y de los terroristas de al-Qaeda.

Afonso I > Afonso I Afonso I (nacido alrededor de 1460–muerto en 1542) fue gobernador de Kongo, un reino histórico de África centro-occidental, a principios del siglo XVI. Afonso fomentó el comercio con Portugal, promovió la cultura europea en su reino y adoptó el cristianismo como su religión y la del estado.

African National Congress (ANC) > Congreso Nacional Africano (CNA) Principal organización que se oponía al apartheid y abogaba por un gobierno de mayoría en Sudáfrica; más tarde se convirtió en un partido político.

agribusiness > agroindustria Inmensa granja comercial generalmente administrada por una corporación multinacional.

ahimsa > ahimsa Creencia hindú en la no violencia y el respeto a todas las formas de vida.

aircraft carrier > portaaviones Buque dotado de las instalaciones necesarias para el transporte, despegue y aterrizaje de aparatos de aviación.

Akbar > Akbar Akbar (1542–1605) es considerado por la mayoría como el más grande de los emperadores mogoles de India. Amplió su imperio por la mayor parte de India, y mantuvo un gobierno eficiente a través de políticas que se ganaron la lealtad de los súbditos no musulmanes. Su grandeza creció también por su apoyo a eruditos, artistas y músicos que hicieron de su corte un centro de cultura.

Akhenaton > Aknatón Aknatón fue rey de Egipto durante 17 años. Abandonó el tradicional politeísmo egipcio y estableció un nuevo culto dedicado a Atón, el disco del sol. Su intento de comenzar una nueva religión murió con él en 1336 a. C.

al Qaeda > al-Qaeda Grupo terrorista establecido y dirigido por el saudita Osama bin Laden hasta su muerte en 2011.

al-Khwarizmi > al-Khwarizmi al-Khwarizmi (alrededor del año 780–alrededor del año 850) fue un matemático musulmán que desarrolló conceptos básicos relacionados con el estudio del álgebra e introdujo el término *álgebra,* o *al-jabr.* Por medio de sus escritos, introdujo a los europeos al estudio de esta rama de las matemáticas. Al trabajar en el campo de la geografía, al-Khwarizmi también supervisó la producción de uno de los primeros mapas del mundo.

Albuquerque, Afonso de > Albuquerque, Afonso de Afonso de Albuquerque (1453–1515) fue un almirante portugués que ayudó a fundar el imperio comercial de Portugal en el este. Capturó y construyó fuertes estratégicos en Goa, Calicut, Malaca y Hormoz; reconstruyó otros fuertes; estableció la construcción de barcos y otras industrias portuguesas en India y construyó iglesias.

Alexander II > Alejandro II Alejandro II (1818–1881), hijo del emperador Nicolás I, llegó a ser zar en 1855. Alejandro II asumió el poder en medio de la Guerra de Crimea, la cual reveló el retraso de Rusia. Instituyó amplias reformas de modernización, incluyendo la emancipación de los siervos en 1861. Sin embargo, las crecientes rebeliones internas y el aumento de la actividad revolucionaria en Polonia llevó a Alejandro a tomar medidas represivas. Fue asesinado en 1881.

Alexander the Great > Alejandro Magno Alejandro Magno (356 a. C.–324 a. C.), hijo de Filipo II y alumno de Aristóteles, se convirtió a los 20 años en el heredero de los territorios de su padre. Conquistó el imperio Persa, fundando nuevas ciudades a medida que sus ejércitos lograban victorias en Asia Menor, Palestina y Egipto, y luego tomó Babilonia. Continuó hacia el este de India, pero sus tropas cansadas se negaron a seguir adelante. De regreso en Babilonia, Alejandro, murió de una fiebre repentina a los 32 años de edad.

Alexandria > Alejandría Alejandría, fundada en el año 332 a. C. por Alejandro Magno, se convirtió en una de las mayores ciudades del mundo mediterráneo. Ubicada en Egipto en las rutas marítimas entre Europa y Asia, Alejandría fue conocida por su tamaño, grandes mercados, el enorme faro de la isla de Faro y el Museo, un centro de enseñanza con una famosa biblioteca.

Alighieri, Dante > Alighieri, Dante Dante Alighieri (1265–1321) fue un filósofo, escritor y poeta que participó activamente en la política italiana, incluyendo las batallas entre los papas y los monarcas de su época. Ocupó varios cargos en diferentes momentos de su vida. Aunque escribió muchos poemas y otras obras, es más conocido por *La Divina Comedia.*

alliance > alianza Acuerdo formal de cooperación y defensa mutua entre dos o más naciones o potencias.

alphabet > alfabeto Sistema de escritura en el que cada símbolo representa un sonido básico único.

Alsace and Lorraine > Alsacia-Lorena Región del norte de Europa en la frontera entre Francia y Alemania que fue cedida a Alemania después de la Guerra Franco-Prusiana.

Amon-Re > Amón (Ra) Amón (Ra) era considerado el rey de los dioses. Estuvo presente en la mitología y cultura del pueblo egipcio desde sus comienzos.

Amritsar massacre > masacre de Amritsar Incidente ocurrido en 1919 en el que tropas británicas abrieron fuego contra una multitud de manifestantes indios desarmados en la ciudad de Amritsar, al norte de India.

anarchist > anarquista Persona que quiere abolir toda forma de gobierno.

ancien régime > ancien regime Antiguo sistema de gobierno en la Francia prerrevolucionaria.

anesthetic > anestesia Fármaco que suprime el dolor durante la cirugía.

animism > animismo Creencia de que el mundo estaba lleno de espíritus y fuerzas que podían residir en los animales, objetos o sueños.

annex > anexar Agregar un territorio a un estado o país existente.

Anschluss > Anschluss Unión de Alemania y Austria en 1933.

anthropology > antropología Campo de estudio relacionado con los orígenes y el desarrollo de las personas y sus sociedades.

anti-Semitism > antisemitismo Prejuicio contra los judíos.

apartheid > apartheid Política de estricta separación racial en la República de Sudáfrica.

apostle > apóstol Líder o maestro de una nueva fe o movimiento.

appeasement > apaciguamiento Política de otorgar concesiones para mantener la paz.

apprentice > aprendiz Persona joven que aprende un oficio de un maestro.

aqueduct > acueducto En la antigua Roma, estructura de piedra parecida a un puente que llevaba agua desde las colinas hasta la ciudad

Aquinas, Thomas > Aquino, Tomás de Tomás de Aquino (1225–1274) fue un filósofo, teólogo y monje que ayudó a cerrar la brecha entre la fe medieval y la filosofía de la razón que promovía la filosofía griega. También explicó la idea de la ley natural, es decir que hay leyes universales basadas en la razón, y que son independientes de las leyes que aprueben los gobiernos.

Aquino, Benigno > Aquino, Benigno Benigno Aquino, Jr., (1932–1983) fue el líder de la oposición durante la dictadura de Ferdinand Marcos en Filipinas. Su carrera en la política incluyó periodos como gobernador provincial y senador, pero cuando planeaba postularse para presidente en 1973, Marcos lo encarceló. Aquino pasó ocho años en el corredor de la muerte pero fue liberado para ser operado en los Estados Unidos de una cirugía de corazón. En 1983, Aquino regresó a Filipinas y fue asesinado en el aeropuerto de Manila. La conspiración militar contra el popular político llevó el apoyo a su esposa, Corazón Aquino, quien continuó hasta derrotar a Marcos en una elección presidencial.

Aquino, Corazon > Aquino, Corazón Corazón Aquino (1933–2009) fue presidenta de Filipinas, restaurando la democracia después del gobierno de Ferdinand Marcos. Educada en los Estados Unidos, Aquino se casó con el político Benigno Aquino y se centró en la crianza de sus hijos. Acompañó a su esposo durante el exilio en los Estados Unidos y cuando él fue ejecutado en su regreso a Filipinas, la gente se unió apoyándola. Ganó una elección presidencial en contra de Marcos y poco después reestableció el congreso y nombró a un equipo para escribir una nueva constitución. Aunque Aquino restauró la libertad en Filipinas, muchas de sus políticas fueron impopulares y perdió la presidencia ante su secretario de defensa en 1992.

Arafat, Yasir > Arafat, Yasir Yasir Arafat (1929–2004) luchó por la independencia palestina la mayor parte de su vida. Fue el fundador de Al-Fatah, un grupo que resistía a Israel, y también de la Organización para la Liberación de Palestina (OLP). En 1969 fue nombrado presidente de la OLP. A principios de la década de 1990, llegó a un acuerdo de paz con Israel. En 1994, junto con Shimon Peres y Yitzhak Rabin, ganó el Premio Nobel de la Paz. Luego fue el presidente de la recién creada Autoridad Palestina.

archaeology > arqueología Estudio de los pueblos y culturas pasados mediante sus restos materiales

Archimedes > Arquímedes Arquímedes (c. 287 a. C.–212 a. C.), un famoso matemático e inventor helenístico de Siracusa, una colonia griega (ahora en Italia), es conocido por entender el principio de las palancas, descubriendo la relación entre la superficie y el volumen de una esfera, e inventar el tornillo de Arquímedes, un aparato para elevar agua.

archipelago > archipiélago Cadena de islas.

aristocracy > aristocracia Gobierno encabezado por una minoría provilegiada o de clase alta.

Aristotle > Aristóteles Aristóteles (384 a. C.–322 a. C.), alumno de Platón, fue un filósofo y escritor sobre muchas ramas del conocimiento, fundador del Liceo y tutor de Alejandro Magno.

armada > armada Flota de barcos.

armistice > armisticio Acuerdo para dejar de luchar en una guerra.

artifact > artefacto Objeto fabricado por los seres humanos.

artificial satellite > satélite artificial Objeto artificial que gira en el espacio alrededor de un cuerpo más grande.

artisan > artesano Trabajador cualificado que hace objetos a mano.

Asante kingdom > reino Asante Reino que surgió en el siglo XVIII en el actual territorio de Ghana y tuvo un activo comercio de esclavos.

Asantewaa, Yaa > Asantewaa, Yaa Yaa Asantewaa (c. 1850–c. 1920) fue la reina madre de la tribu edweso de los asante y lideró una rebelión en contra del gobierno británico que comenzó en 1900.

Asia Minor > Asia Menor Península en Asia occidental entre el mar Negro y el mar Mediterráneo.

Asoka > Asoka Asoka, que murió aproximadamente en 238 a. C., fue el último gran emperador Maurya de India. Budista comprometido, ayudó a difundir el budismo a través de India. Su gobierno se caracterizó por la justicia, la compasión y los principios de la vida recta que él había inscrito en pilares de piedra que mandó erigir por todo el imperio.

assassination > magnicidio Asesinato de una figura pública, generalmente por razones políticas.

assembly line > línea de montaje Método de producción que distribuye un trabajo complejo en una serie de pequeñas tareas.

assimilate > asimilar Absorber o adoptar otra cultura.

Atatürk > Atatürk Atatürk (1881–1938) es el nombre que Mustafa Kemal se dio a sí mismo cuando ordenó a todo el pueblo turco que adoptara apellidos. En 1920 lideró a los nacionalistas turcos en la lucha contra del ejército griego, que trataba de hacer cumplir el Tratado de Sèvres, el establecer las fronteras de la moderna República de Turquía. Una vez en el poder, aprobó muchas reformas para modernizar, occidentalizar y secularizar Turquía.

atheism > ateísmo Creencia de que no existe dios.

Athens > Atenas Ciudad-estado de la antigua Grecia que evolucionó de una monarquía a una democracia directa limitada y se hizo famosa por sus grandes logros culturales.

Atlantic Charter > Carta del Atlántico Acuerdo en el que Franklin Roosevelt y Winston Churchill fijaron los objetivos para la derrota de la Alemania nazi y para el mundo de la posguerra.

atman > atman En la creencia hindú, naturaleza de una persona.

atrocity > atrocidad Acto brutal cometido en contra de inocentes.

Augustine > Agustín Agustín (364 d. C.–430 d. C.) fue un erudito cristiano cuyas obras escritas tuvieron efectos duraderos en la religón cristiana. Estudió en la África romana y llegó a ser obispo.

Augustus > Augusto Augusto (63 a. C.–14 d. C.) fue el primer emperador romano del recién establecido Imperio Romano. El gobierno de Augusto comenzó un largo periodo de paz y riqueza conocido como la Pax Romana.

Auschwitz > Auschwitz Grupo de tres campos de concentración y campos de exterminio alemanes al sur de Polonia, construidos y operados durante el Tercer Reich.

autocrat > autócrata Gobernante que tiene poder ilimitado.

autocratic > autocrático Que tiene poder ilimitado.

autonomy > autonomía Autogobierno

Axis powers > Potencias del Eje Grupo de países liderado por Alemania, Italia y Japón que luchó contra los Aliados en la Segunda Guerra Mundial.

Axum > Aksum Centro de comercio y poderoso reino antiguo del norte situado en lo que actualmente es Etiopía.

ayllu > ayllu En el Imperio Inca, una aldea que se mantenía estrechamente unida.

B

Babur > Babur Babur (1483–1530) fue el fundador de la dinastía Mogol en India. Tenía herencia turca y mongola, descendiente del gran líder mongol, Genghis Khan. Su nombre es la palabra árabe para "tigre", pero era tan buen poeta como guerrero. Su sabio gobierno ayudó a lanzar una poderosa dinastía musulmana que tuvo una influencia permanente en el norte de India.

Bacon, Francis > Bacon, Francis Francis Bacon (1561–1626) fue un distinguido filósofo, estadista y abogado inglés. Hombre de muchos talentos, promovió el pensamiento racional. Bacon fue muy reconocido por filósofos y científicos de Europa, así como de Inglaterra.

Baghdad > Bagdad Capital del actual Iraq; capital del Imperio Musulmán durante la época dorada del islam.

balance of power > equilibrio de poder Distribución del poder militar y económico que evita que una nación se vuelva demasiado fuerte.

balance of trade > balanza comercial Diferencia entre lo que importa y exporta un país.

Balfour Declaration > Declaración Balfour Declaración hecha por el gobierno británico en 1917 en la que apoyaba la constitución de un estado judío en Palestina.

Balkan Peninsula > península de los Balcanes Extensión triangular de tierra que sobresale del sureste de Europa hasta el Mediterráneo.

Bangladesh > Bangladesh País al este de India que antiguamente formaba parte de Pakistán.

Bantu > bantú Lengua madre de África occidental en la que están basados algunos patrones migratorios africanos.

Barbarossa, Frederick > Barbarroja, Federico Federico Barbarroja (c. 1123–1190) fue un rey alemán que llegó a ser emperador del Sacro Imperio Romano en 1152. Luchó contra la creciente autoridad papal y dirigió seis expediciones a Italia en un intento de aumentar sus territorios. Murió en la Tercera Cruzada.

baroque > barroco Estilo artístico y arquitectónico elaborado que se dio en los siglos XVII y XVIII.

barter economy > economía de trueque Sistema económico en el que un conjunto de bienes o servicios se intercambia por otro.

Bastille > Bastilla Fortificación en París usada como prisión; la Revolución Francesa empezó cuando los parisinos la asaltaron en 1789.

Bataan Death March > marcha de la muerte de Bataan Durante la Segunda Guerra Mundial, la marcha forzada de prisioneros de guerra estadounidenses y filipinos bajo condiciones brutales impuestas por los militares japoneses.

battle of Tours > Batalla de Tours Batalla en 732 en la que los francos cristianos liderados por Charles Martel derrotaron al ejército musulmán y detuvieron el avance árabe en Europa.

Bedouin > beduino Nómada árabe que vive en el desierto.

Beethoven, Ludwig van > Beethoven, Ludwig van Ludwig van Beethoven (1770–1827) fue un compositor alemán que aprendió a tocar el piano y el violín con su padre Johannes. A la edad de 12 años, publicó su primera obra y comenzó a tocar la viola en la orquesta sinfónica de Bonn, Alemania. En 1792, fue a Viena y comenzó a estudiar con Haydn. Beethoven permaneció en Viena, donde escribió la mayoría de sus sinfonías, conciertos, sonatas y cuartetos de cuerda. Aunque comenzó a perder el oído en 1798, siguió componiendo la música que él podía oír en su mente.

Benedictine Rule > regla benedictina En el año 530, reglas establecidas por Benedicto, un monje, para regular la vida monástica. La regla enfatiza la obediencia, pobreza y castidad, y divide el día en períodos de adoración, trabajo y estudio.

Bentham, Jeremy > Bentham, Jeremy Jeremy Bentham (1748–1832) fue un filósofo y economista británico que defendía el utilitarismo, la creencia de que se podía medir el bien y el mal por la máxima felicidad del mayor número de personas. Bentham estudió leyes pero no ejerció como abogado. En lugar de eso, se centró en las reformas legales. No contento con simplemente sugerir nuevas leyes, también detalló planes sobre cómo implementar sus propuestas. Sus ideas influyeron durante su vida y algunas de sus reformas fueron aprobadas.

Bessemer, Henry > Bessemer, Henry Henry Bessemer (1813–1879) fue un inventor e ingeniero británico. Su mayor invento fue el convertidor Bessemer, que podía crear acero de alta calidad rápidamente y de forma económica. En 1956 patentó su proceso para fabricar acero. Su proceso fue esencial para lograr avances en el transporte, la construcción y la defensa. Hoy en día, el acero todavía se fabrica siguiendo un método basado en el proceso Bessemer.

Biafra > Biafra Región del sureste de Nigeria que lanzó un fallido intento de independizarse de Nigeria en 1966, y por el que se desató una cruenta guerra.

biotechnology > biotecnología Aplicación de la investigación biotecnológica en la industria, ingeniería y tecnología.

bishop > obispo Funcionario de alto rango de la Iglesia con autoridad sobre una zona local, o diócesis.

Bismarck, Otto von > Bismarck, Otto von Otto von Bismarck (1815–1898) trabajó brevemente como funcionario civil antes de hacer carrera en el gobierno. Fue diplomático de la Federación Alemana y llegó a ser canciller del Imperio Alemán en 1871, un cargo que ocupó durante 19 años.

Black Death > Muerte Negra Epidemia de la peste bubónica que arrasó Europa en el siglo XIV.

Black Shirt > Camisa Negra Cualquier miembro de las escuadras militantes de combate de los fascistas italianos que estableció Mussolini.

blitzkrieg > blitzkrieg Guerra relámpago.

bloc > bloque Grupo de naciones que actúan conjuntamente en apoyo mutuo.

Boer War > guerra de los bóers (1899–1902) guerra en la que Gran Bretaña venció a los Bóers de Sudáfrica.

Boers > bóers Neerlandeses establecidos en Ciudad del Cabo, África, que con el tiempo emigraron hacia el interior.

Bolívar, Simón > Bolívar, Simón Simón Bolívar (1783–1830) fue un soldado y líder sudamericano que fue esencial en las revoluciones en contra de España. Nació en el seno de una familia acaudalada y culta en España. Después de que Francia invadiera España, participó en el movimiento de resistencia y desempeñó un papel clave en la lucha latinoamericana por la independencia. Murió de tuberculosis en 1830.

Bonaparte, Napoleon > Bonaparte, Napoleón Napoleón Bonaparte (1769–1821) fue una figura importante en la historia europea. Fue un genio militar que fue electo cónsul de por vida. Más tarde se coronó él mismo emperador de Francia. Sus reformas legales, educativas y militares impactaron la sociedad francesa por generaciones.

bourgeoisie > burguesía Clase media.

Boxer Uprising > Rebelión de los bóxers Movimiento en contra de los extranjeros ocurrido en China de 1898 a 1900.

boyar > boyardo En la época de los zares, noble terrateniente ruso.

boycott > boicot Negarse a comprar.

Boyle, Robert > Boyle, Robert Robert Boyle (1627–1691) fue una de las mentes destacadas de finales del siglo XVII. Fue un filósofo y escritor inglés-irlandés que se centró en la química, física e historia natural. Su trabajo con el aire presurizado llevó al desarrollo de la ley de Boyle, que describe la relación entre la presión y el volumen del gas. Boyle fue uno de los fundadores de la Real Sociedad de Londres.

Brahe, Tycho > Brahe, Tycho Tycho Brahe (1546–1601) fue un astrónomo danés que produjo las medidas y ubicaciones más precisas de las estrellas antes de usar el telescopio. Su observación de que una nueva estrella había aparecido en una constelación existente desafió la creencia de que las estrellas estaban fijas y eran inmutables.

Brahman > brahmán En el sistema de creencias establecido en la India aria, el único poder espiritual que reside en todas las cosas.

Brezhnev, Leonid > Brezhnev, Leonid Leonid Brezhnev (1906–1982) gobernó la Unión Soviética desde 1964, cuando organizó la destitución de Nikita Khrushchev, hasta su muerte en 1982. Presidió la última acumulación de armas de la Unión Soviética y el estancamiento económico que fomentó las reformas de Mijail Gorbachov.

bureaucracy > burocracia Sistema de gobierno mediante departamentos y subdivisiones administrados por funcionarios que siguen un conjunto de reglas.

bushido > bushido Código de conducta de los samuráis durante el periodo feudal japonés.

Byron, Lord > Byron, Lord Lord Byron (1788–1824) fue miembro de la Cámara de los Lores, satírico político y social y uno de los poetas románticos más sobresalientes, novedosos y cautivadores. Llegó a ser el modelo del héroe romántico y la personificación del movimiento. Byron creía en la libertad, que él a menudo reflejaba en sus obras y hazañas. Aunque Byron murió antes de haber terminado su poema *Don Juan,* este es considerado su obra maestra y uno de los grandes poemas de Inglaterra.

C

cabinet > gabinete Consejeros parlamentarios del rey que originalmente se reunían en un pequeño cuarto o gabinete.

Cabot, John > Caboto, Juan Juan Caboto (alrededor de 1450–alrededor de 1499) tuvo sus primeras raíces en Venecia, Italia, trabajando en una empresa mercantil. Llegó a ser un navegante y explorador, que durante los años 1497 y 1498, reclamó partes de Canadá para Gran Bretaña.

Caesar, Julius > César, Julio Julio César (alrededor del año 100 a. C.–44 a. C.) fue un general romano, maestro de las maniobras políticas y un reformista. Defendió la reorganización del gobierno de Roma. En el año 47 a. C. se nombró dictador, y tres años más tarde fue asesinado.

cahiers > memorándum Cuaderno usado durante la Francia prerrevolucionaria para anotar los agravios.

Cahokia > Cahokia En Illinois, el mayor terraplén de la cultura de los misisipianos, construido alrededor del año 700 d. C.

calculus > cálculo Rama de las matemáticas en la que los cálculos se hacen con notaciones simbólicas especiales; fue desarrollado por Isaac Newton.

caliph > califa Sucesor de Mahoma como líder religioso y político de los musulmanes.

calligraphy > caligrafía Arte de producir una bella escritura a mano.

Calvin, John > Calvino, Juan Juan Calvino (1509–1564) fue un abogado y teólogo francés. Influenciado por la filosofía humanista de Erasmo, Calvino llegó a participar en el movimiento protestante mientras estudiaba en la Universidad de París. Más tarde se trasladó a Ginebra, Suiza, donde estableció una teocracia y escribió *Institutos de la Religión Cristiana.* La interpretación de Calvino de la doctrina cristiana se llama calvinismo.

canon law > ley canónica Serie de leyes de una iglesia.

canonize > canonizar Reconocer a una persona como un santo.

Cape Town > Ciudad del Cabo El primer asentamiento permanente europeo en África, establecido por los neerlandeses en 1652.

capital > capital Dinero o bienes que se usan para invertir en negocios o empresas.

capital offense > delito capital Crimen que puede castigarse con la muerte.

capitalism > capitalismo Sistema económico en el que los medios de producción son propiedad privada y se administran para obtener beneficios.

Cárdenas, Lázaro > Cárdenas, Lázaro Lázaro Cárdenas (1895–1970) se unió a las fuerzas revolucionarias cuando tenía 18 años y más tarde llegó a ser general del ejército mexicano. Después de la revolución, fue gobernador de Michoacán y luego presidente del PNR. En 1934, fue electo presidente de México. Durante su presidencia, Cárdenas trabajó para establecer las reformas sociales y económicas por las que habían luchado los revolucionarios, entre ellas la redistribución de la tierra, la organización de las confederaciones para trabajadores y campesinos, y la nacionalización de las industrias propiedad de extranjeros.

Carranza, Venustiano > Carranza, Venustiano Venustiano Carranza (1859–1920) fue un líder de la Revolución Mexicana en apoyo de una reforma política, más que social. Fue electo el primer presidente después de la revolución, y aunque firmó la Constitución de 1917, hizo poco para implementar las reformas prometidas. Esa renuencia llevó a disturbios sociales y dificultades económicas. Cuando en abril de 1920 comenzó una rebelión, Carranza huyó de la capital y finalmente se fue a esconder a las montañas. Fue traicionado y asesinado en mayo.

cartel > cartel Asociación de grandes corporaciones formada para controlar la producción y el precio del producto.

Cartier, Jacques > Cartier, Jacques Jacques Cartier (1491–1557) recibe el crédito de haber dado nombre a Canadá. También es reconocido por su exploración limitada del río San Lorenzo, detenida al poco tiempo por las severas condiciones del clima y la hostilidad de los indígenas iroqueses.

cartographer > cartógrafo Persona que hace mapas.

caste > casta Grupo social en la sociedad tradicional de India en el que una persona nace y del que no se puede cambiar.

Castiglione, Baldassare > Castiglione, Baldassare Castiglione (1478–1529) fue un cortesano, diplomático y escritor italiano. Su manual, *El Cortesano,* fue muy leído por sus consejos sobre buenos modales, habilidades, aprendizaje y virtudes que los miembros de la corte debían mostrar. Describía al cortesano ideal como bien educado, de buenas costumbres y con muchos talentos.

Castro, Fidel > Castro, Fidel Fidel Castro (n. 1926) fue líder de Cuba desde 1959, cuando dirigió la Revolución Cubana e instaló un régimen comunista. Durante la Guerra Fría, la Cuba de Castro se alió con la Unión Soviética y, por consiguiente, en desacuerdo con los Estados Unidos. Sus políticas siguieron siendo socialistas después de la caída de la Unión Soviética. Cuando su salud comenzó a fallar en 2006, su hermano, Raúl, quedó a cargo como el líder cubano.

Çatalhüyük > Çatalhüyük Una de las primera aldeas del mundo, establecida en la Turquía actual alrededor del año 7000 a. C.

cataract > catarata Cascada; caída de agua.

Catherine the Great > Catalina la Grande Catalina la Grande (1729–1796) fue una emperatriz de Rusia nacida en Alemania (1762–1796) que llevó a su país a formar parte de la vida cultural y política de Europa.

caudillo > caudillo Dictador militar en América Latina.

Cavour, Camillo > Cavour, Camillo Camillo Cavour (1810–1861) fue el segundo hijo de una familia noble. Después de una breve carrera en el ejército, decidió que la política era su verdadera fortaleza. Su capacidad para manipular situaciones políticas con el fin de impulsar la causa de la unificación italiana hizo de él un valioso líder.

Ceausescu, Nicolae > Ceausescu, Nicolae Nicolae Ceausescu (1918–1989) dirigió el gobierno comunista en Rumania desde 1965 hasta su muerte en 1989. Su régimen fue notorio por su corrupción masiva, devastadoras condiciones económicas y una policía secreta desenfrenada. Fue ejecutado, junto con su esposa, Elena, después del golpe de estado que terminó con el gobierno comunista en Rumania.

celadon > celadon Porcelana hecha en Corea con brillo azulverdoso poco común.

censorship > censura Restricción en el acceso a ideas o información.

census > censo Conteo de población.

Cervantes, Miguel de > Cervantes, Miguel de Miguel de Cervantes (1547–1616), novelista, dramaturgo y poeta español, fue la figura más importante de la literatura española. Su novela Don Quijote es su obra más conocida.

Champlain, Samuel de > Champlain, Samuel de Samuel de Champlain (1567–1635) fue un navegante y explorador francés que estableció la colonia de Quebec en 1608. Se le conoció como el "Padre de la Nueva Francia" y fue honrado en la corte del rey Enrique IV.

chancellor > canciller Oficial con mayor rango dentro de una monarquía; primer ministro.

characters > caracteres Símbolos escritos de algunos sistemas de escritura como la de los chinos.

Charlemagne > Carlomagno Carlomagno (747–814), (o "Carlos el Grande") rey de los francos, los lombardos y emperador de los romanos, comenzó como un rey guerrero que buscaba conquistar territorios y distribuir el botín siguiendo la tradición de los francos. Pero también luchó por unir y gobernar una creciente diversidad de pueblos conquistados, además de tratar con las amenazas de nuevos invasores. Dirigió una larga serie de campañas militares exitosas, realizó esfuerzos para difundir el cristianismo e implementar una reforma reliigiosa, buscó hacer más eficaces las instituciones y los procedimientos políticos, y apoyó la renovación cultural mediante un resurgimiento de la enseñanza.

Charles I > Carlos I Carlos I (1600–1649) fue el segundo rey Estuardo de Inglaterra, Escocia y Gales. Su creencia en el derecho divino de los reyes lo puso en un conflicto continuo con el Parlamento. Finalmente este conflicto llevó a la Guerra Civil inglesa, a la derrota de Carlos y a su ejecución por traición.

Charles V > Carlos V Carlos V (1500–1558) fue emperador del Sacro Imperio Romano durante la época de la reforma de Martín Lutero. Su inmenso imperio incluía grandes zonas de Europa. Como católico devoto, rechazó las doctrinas de Lutero. La revuelta protestante, junto con las presiones políticas, llevó a Carlos a dejar voluntariamente el trono. Dividió el imperio entre su hijo y su hermano y entró a un monasterio católico donde permaneció hasta su muerte.

charter > cédula En la Edad Media, documento escrito que establecía los derechos y privilegios de un pueblo.

Chaucer, Geoffrey > Chaucer, Geoffrey Geoffrey Chaucer (1343–1400) fue el primer poeta importante de su tiempo que escribió en inglés. En diversos momentos trabajó como redactor, miembro del Parlamento y juez de paz. Sus agudas observaciones de muchos tipos diferentes de personas se reflejaron en su famosa obra, *Cuentos de Canterbury.*

Chavín > chavín Cultura que tuvo su apogeo en la región andina, aproximadamente desde el año 900 a. C. al año 200 a. C.

Chechnya > Chechenia República dentro del territorio ruso en la que grupos rebeldes lucharon por su independencia.

checks and balances > controles y equilibrios Sistema en el que cada poder del estado tiene la facultad para monitorear y limitar las acciones de los otros dos.

Cheka > Cheka Una de las primeras fuerzas policiales secretas soviéticas.

chinampa > chinampa En el Imperio Azteca, una isla artificial que se usaba para cultivar las cosechas y estaba fabricada de lodo apilado encima de bases de juncos que estaban anclados al lecho del lago con sauces.

chivalry > Código de Caballería Durante la Edad Media, código de conducta para los caballeros.

Choson dynasty > dinastía Choson Dinastía coreana que gobernó de 1392 a 1910; la que más perduró de las tres dinastías coreanas.

Christian Bible > Biblia cristiana Escrituras sagradas de la religión cristiana.

Churchill, Winston > Churchill, Winston Winston Churchill (1874–1965) nació en la aristocracia inglesa y fue primer ministro del Imperio Británico en 1940. Desde el principio avisó de la amenaza que suponía la Alemania nazi. Su determinación convenció al país de defenderse a sí mismo contra el enemigo invasor.

circumnavigate > circunnavegar Viajar alrededor del mundo.

citizen > ciudadano Nativo o residente de un pueblo o ciudad.

city-state > ciudad-estado Unidad política que incluía una ciudad y las tierras y aldeas que la rodean.

civil disobedience > desobediencia civil Práctica de renuencia pacífica a obedecer las leyes injustas.

civil law > derecho civil Rama del derecho acerca de los derechos y los asuntos privados.

civil servants > siervos civiles Funcionarios del gobierno.

civil war > guerra civil Guerra en la que luchan dos grupos de personas de una misma nación.

civilization > civilización Orden social complejo y sumamente organizado.

clan > clan Grupo de familias con un ancestro común.

clergy > clero Aquellos que dirigen los servicios religiosos cristianos.

Clovis > Clodoveo Clodoveo (466–511) es conocido como el fundador político y religioso del reino de los francos. Gobernó gran parte de la Galia desde finales del siglo V hasta el año 511. Su reino, que se expandió al sur y al oeste de lo que hoy en día es Bélgica y el noreste de Francia, fue el más poderoso de la Galia. También fue el aliado más importante del emperador bizantino Anastasio I. Nacido pagano, Clodoveo correspondió con los poderosos obispos de la Galia y, en el año 496 o quizá más tarde, se hizo famoso como uno de los primeros reyes germanos en convertirse al cristianismo.

coalition > coalición Alianza temporal de varios partidos políticos.

codify > codificar Organizar o dejar por escrito.

Colbert, Jean-Baptiste > Colbert, Jean Baptiste Jean Baptiste Colbert (1619–1683) fue, bajo el rey Luis XIV de Francia, controlador general de finanzas (desde 1665) y secretario de estado para la armada (desde 1668). Llevó a cabo programas que ayudaron a hacer de Francia la potencia más fuerte de Europa.

Cold War > Guerra Fría Después de la Segunda Guerra Mundial, largo periodo de intensa rivalidad y hostilidad entre las naciones alineadas con los Estados Unidos, por un lado, y la Union Soviética, por el otro, que rara vez llevó a un conflicto armado directo.

collective > granja colectiva Granja grande que pertenece a campesinos que la administran en grupo.

collective security > seguridad colectiva Sistema por el que un grupo de naciones actúa como una para preservar la paz común.

collectivization > colectivización Unión forzada de trabajadores y propiedad en colectivos, como colectivos rurales que absorben a campesinos y sus tierras.

colony > colonia Territorio ocupado y gobernado por personas de otro territorio.

colossus > coloso Gigante

Columbian Exchange > intercambio colombino Intercambio global de bienes, ideas, plantas, animales y enfermedades entre Europa, Africa y las Americas posterior al primer viaje trasatlántico de Colón en 1492.

Columbus, Christopher > Colón, Cristóbal Cristóbal Colón (1451–1506) fue un explorador y navegante italiano que realizó expediciones por el Mediterráneo y África, estableció un plan para navegar por el oeste hasta llegar a India y China, y contó con el apoyo de los reyes de España, Fernando e Isabel. En 1492, navegó hacia el oeste desde España y llegó a las islas del Caribe, las cuales creyó equivocadamente como las Indias de Asia. Hizo otros viajes, pero las tensas relaciones con los oficiales reales españoles lo llevaron a su arresto y dimisión como gobernador de los asentamientos de la isla de La Española.

comedy > comedia En la antigua Grecia, obra de teatro humorística que se burló de las personas o de las costumbres sociales.

Comintern > Comintern Internacional Comunista, asociación internacional de partidos comunistas liderada por la Unión Soviética con el propósito de extender por el mundo una revolución comunista.

command economy > economía dirigida Sistema en el que los funcionarios del gobierno toman todas las decisiones económicas básicas.

Commercial Revolution > Revolución Comercial Un periodo de expansión económica, colonialismo y mercantilismo en Europa que duró desde el siglo XVI hasta principios del siglo XVIII. Incluye el crecimiento del capitalismo, la banca y las inversiones.

commissar > comisario Funcionario del partido comunista asignado al ejército para enseñar los principios del partido y asegurar la lealtad al mismo durante la Revolución Rusa.

commodity > bien de consumo Producto valioso.

common law > derecho consuetudinario Sistema legal basado en la costumbre y en las sentencias de los tribunales.

communism > comunismo Forma de socialismo defendida por Karl Marx; según Marx, la lucha de clases era inevitable y llevaría a la creación de una sociedad sin clases en la que toda la riqueza y la propiedad pertenecería a la comunidad como un todo.

compact > pacto Acuerdo entre personas.

compromise > compromiso Acuerdo en el que cada parte hace concesiones; un término medio aceptable.

concentration camp > campos de concentración Campos usados por los nazis para encarcelar a miembros "indeseables" de la sociedad.

Concert of Europe > Concierto de Europa Organización de conservación de la paz cuyo objetivo era preservar los acuerdos establecidos por el Congreso de Viena.

concession > concesión Derechos económicos especiales que se dan a un poder extranjero.

confederation > confederación Unificación

Confucius > Confucio Confucio (551 a. C.–479 a. C.) es el filósofo más famoso de China. Sus enseñanzas sobre la importancia de la educación y el servicio público influyeron en muchas civilizaciones asiáticas. Sus ancestros, miembros de la aristocracia, eran pobres cuando Confucio nació. A la edad de 15 años, se dedicó a la vida de erudito. Aunque sus ideas sobre el camino apropiado para vivir guiaron a millones de personas, su vida fue sencilla y reflejaba una profunda humildad.

Congress of Vienna > Congreso de Viena Asamblea de líderes europeos que se reunió después de la era napoleónica para reconstruir Europa; se realizó de septiembre de 1814 a junio de 1815.

conquistador > conquistador Líder en las conquistas españolas de America, México y Perú, en el siglo XVI.

conscription > conscripción Llamado a filas que exigía que todos los hombres jóvenes estuvieran listos para el servicio militar u otro servicio.

consensus > consenso Acuerdo general entre todos los miembros de un grupo.

Constantine > Constantino Constantino (alrededor del año 280 d. C.–alrededor del año 337 d. C.) fue el primer emperador romano en hacerse cristiano. Durante su reinado, impidió la persecución de los cristianos y ayudó a fortalecer la iglesia de los primeros tiempos.

Constantinople > Constantinopla Capital del Imperio Romano Oriental; capital de los imperios bizantino y otomano, en la actualidad llamada Estambul.

constitutional government > gobierno constitucional Gobierno cuyo poder está definido y limitado por las leyes.

consul > cónsul Funcionario de la clase de los patricios que supervisaba el gobierno y comandaba los ejércitos.

containment > política de contención Estrategia de los Estados Unidos para mantener el comunismo dentro de las áreas que ya estaban dentro del control soviético.

Continental System > sistema continental Bloqueo diseñado por Napoleón para dañar a Gran Bretaña económicamente al cerrar los puertos europeos a los productos británicos; con el tiempo no tuvo éxito.

contra > contras Grupo guerrillero que luchó contra los sandinistas en Nicaragua.

contraband > contrabando Durante el tiempo de guerra, provisiones militares y materias primas necesarios para fabricar artículos militares, y que pueden ser confiscados legalmente por cualquiera de las partes beligerantes.

convoy > convoy Grupo de buques mercantes que navegan juntos bajo la protección de buques de guerra.

Copernicus, Nicolaus > Copérnico, Nicolás Nicolás Copérnico (1473–1543) fue un astrónomo polaco que concluyó que el Sol es el centro del universo alrededor del cual giraban la Tierra y los otros planetas. Esto contradecía la creencia religiosa y científica de que la Tierra era el centro del universo. Aunque no sufrió retos inmediatos de la Iglesia, su trabajo más importante no fue publicado hasta después de su muerte.

corporation > corporación Empresa de varios inversionistas que comparten acciones y riesgos con base en lo que invirtió cada uno de sus miembros.

Cortés, Hernán > Cortés, Hernán Hernán Cortés (alrededor de 1485–1547) fue un terrateniente de Cuba y conquistador que en 1518 lideró una expedición a México. Aliado con algunos grupos indígenas americanos, conquistó el Imperio Azteca, incluyendo su capital, Tenochtitlán, en 1521. En 1522, el emperador del Sacro Imperio Romano, Carlos V, lo nombró gobernador de la Nueva España, pero Cortés fue finalmente retirado del poder y enviado a España en 1540.

Council of Trent > Concilio de Trento Grupo de líderes católicos que se reunió entre 1545 y 1563 para responder a los retos protestantes y dirigir el futuro de la Iglesia católica.

coup d'état > golpe de estado Derrocamiento obligado de un gobierno.

Courbet, Gustave > Courbet, Gustave Gustave Courbet (1819–1877) fue un destacado pintor francés del movimiento realista. Aunque pintaba temas más tradicionales como vistas del mar, retratos y paisajes, también se centró en representar la vida diaria al pintar la clase media rural y la cultura bohemia, así como temas sociales al representar la difícil vida de los pobres.

covenant > alianza Acuerdo vinculante; específicamente, en la tradición judía, el acuerdo vinculante que Dios hizo con Abraham.

Cranmer, Thomas > Cranmer, Thomas Thomas Cranmer (1489–1556) fue un teólogo católico que apoyó fuertemente la reforma. Cuando Enrique VIII rompió con la Iglesia católica, Cranmer se convirtió en el primer arzobispo protestante de Canterbury, Inglaterra. Distribuyó biblias escritas en inglés a las parroquias y, más tarde, desarrolló el *Book of Common Prayer*. Cranmer fue consejero de Enrique VIII y de su hijo, Eduardo VI.

crematorium > crematorio Lugar donde se queman los cadáveres.

creole > criollo En las colonias españolas de América, descendiente de colonos españoles nacido en América.

Crimean War > Guerra de Crimea Guerra librada principalmente en la península de Crimea entre los rusos y los británicos, franceses y turcos entre 1853 y 1856.

criminal law > derecho penal Rama del derecho que trata de los delitos contra los demás.

Cromwell, Oliver > Cromwell, Oliver Oliver Cromwell (1599–1658) fue un soldado y caballero inglés que dirigió los ejércitos en contra de Carlos I de Inglaterra durante la Guerra Civil inglesa. Se nombró a sí mismo Lord Protector de Inglaterra en 1653, gobernando el país como una república hasta su muerte.

Crusades > Cruzadas Serie de guerras entre el siglo XI y el siglo XIII en las que los cristianos europeos intentaron ganar el control sobre los musulmanes de la Tierra Santa.

cult of domesticity > culto a lo doméstico Idealización de las mujeres y del hogar.

cultural diffusion > difusión cultural Expansión de las ideas, costumbres y tecnologías de un pueblo a otro.

cultural nationalism > nacionalismo cultural Orgullo por la cultura del país propio.

Cultural Revolution > Revolución Cultural Programa de la China comunista a finales de la década de 1960 que pretendía eliminar de China todas las tendencias no revolucionarias y que causó daños económicos y sociales.

culture > cultura Forma de vida de una sociedad, que pasa de una generación a la siguiente por el aprendizaje y la experiencia.

cuneiform > cuneiforme En el antiguo Oriente Medio, sistema de escritura cuyos caracteres tenían forma de cuña.

Curie, Marie > Curie, Marie Marie Curie (1867–1934) nació en Varsovia en una familia de maestros polacos. Más tarde se trasladó a París, donde obtuvo educación formal y conoció a su esposo Pierre Curie. Los Curie fueron pioneros en los estudios sobre la radioactividad, revolucionando los campos de la física y la química. Fue la primera mujer en ganar un Premio Nobel. Marie Curie trabajó incansablemete para promover las aplicaciones prácticas y médicas de su trabajo. Murió en 1934, probablemente a causa de sus muchos años de exposición a materiales radioactivos.

Cuzco > Cuzco Capital del imperio Inca.

Cyrillic > cirílico relativo al alfabeto eslavo derivado del griego y atribuido por tradición a San Cirilo; en forma modificada todavía se utiliza en lenguas eslavas modernas.

D

D-Day > Día D Nombre clave para el 6 de junio de 1944, el día en que los Aliados desembarcaron en las playas de Normandía, Francia, durante la Segunda Guerra Mundial.

da Vinci, Leonardo > da Vinci, Leonardo Leonardo da Vinci (1452–1519) fue un artista italiano considerado el hombre ideal del Renacimiento debido a su variedad de talentos. Sus intereses incluían la botánica, anatomía, óptica, música, arquitectura e ingeniería. Sus bocetos de máquinas voladoras y de botes submarinos recuerdan los inventos posteriores de aviones y submarinos. Las pinturas de Leonardo, como la iii Mona Lisa y iii La última cena, siguen siendo famosas hoy en día.

dada > dadaísmo Movimiento artístico en el que los artistas rechazaban la tradición y producían obras que a menudo sorprendían a su público.

Daguerre, Louis > Daguerre, Louis Louis Daguerre (1787–1851) fue un pintor y físico francés que inventó la fotografía. Antes de que inventara la cámara, fue grabador y pintor. Durante años había estado experimentando con formas de captar imágenes fotográficas detalladas. Finalmente, en 1839, mostró su proceso a la Académie des Sciences y la Académie des Beaux-Arts. Sorprendió a todo el mundo y su invento revolucionó las artes y las ciencias.

dalit > dalit Marginado; miembro de la casta más baja de India

Dalton, John > Dalton, John John Dalton (1766–1844) fue un profesor, conferencista, meteorólogo, físico y químico inglés. Su interés en la atmósfera le llevó al desarrollo de su teoría atómica en 1803. Su teoría establecía que los átomos tienen masa, que los elementos están formados de átomos y que las reacciones químicas podían explicarse por la combinación y separación de los átomos. Aunque ahora se ha comprobado que partes de su teoría están equivocadas, sigue siendo la base de la química y la física modernas.

Dardanelles > Dardanelos Estrecho de vital importancia que conecta el mar Negro y el mar Mediterráneo en la actual Turquía.

Darfur > Darfur Región occidental de Sudán donde un conflicto étnico amenazó con provocar un genocidio.

Darwin, Charles > Darwin, Charles Charles Darwin (1809–1882) fue un naturalista inglés que desarrolló la teoría de la evolución mediante el proceso de la selección natural. En 1831, se embarcó en un viaje de cinco años alrededor del mundo. Mientras estaba en las islas Galápagos, Darwin observó que cuatro especies de pinzones de las islas tenían diferentes picos y hábitos de alimentación. Promulgó la teoría de que el aislamiento, el tiempo y la adaptación a las condiciones locales lleva a nuevas especies. Su observación y las muestras que recolectó le ayudaron a desarrollar su teoría de la evolución.

David > David Como se describe en los Libros de Samuel, 1 Reyes y 1 Crónicas, David pertenecía a la tribu de Judá y comenzó su vida como pastor en Belén. Finalmente, David se convirtió en el rey de un Israel unido. Los judíos y cristianos creen también que editó el Libro de los Salmos.

Deák, Ferenc > Deák, Ferenc Ferenc Deák (1803–1876), también conocido como el Sabio del País, fue un político, reformador y pensador húngaro. Es conocido por desarrollar el concepto de la monarquía dual y guiar ese compromiso hasta su adopción final.

decimal system > sistema decimal Sistema numérico basado en el 10.

decipher > descifrar Averiguar el significado de algo.

default > cese de pagos Imposibilidad de realizar pagos.

deficit > déficit Diferencia entre los gastos de un gobierno y las recaudaciones por impuestos y otras fuentes de ingresos.

deficit spending > déficit de gastos Práctica de las naciones que gastan más de lo que reciben por ingresos.

deforestation > deforestación Destrucción de tierras forestales.

Delhi > Delhi Tercera ciudad más grande de India; capital de la India medieval.

delta > delta Zona triangular pantanosa que se forma por depósitos de cieno en la desembocadura de algunos ríos.

demilitarized zone > zona desmilitarizada Estrecha franja de tierra que cruza la península de Corea y que separa las fuerzas de Corea del Norte y las fuerzas de Corea del Sur; establecida por el armisticio de 1953.

democracy > democracia Forma de gobierno en el que la soberanía reside en el pueblo.

Deng Xiaoping > Deng Xiaoping Deng Xiaoping (1904–1997) nació en la provincia de Sichuan en China. De joven, estudió en Francia y en la Unión Soviética. Se involucró con el movimiento comunista mientras estaba en Francia. Después de que los comunistas tomaran el poder en China, ocupó diversos cargos en el gobierno, llegando a ser finalmente el político más poderoso de la nación. Sus políticas son responsables de gran parte del crecimiento económico de China después de los fracasos de la Revolución Cultural.

depopulation > despoblación Reducción del número de la población en una zona.

Descartes, René > Descartes, René René Descartes (1596–1650) fue un filósofo, matemático y científico francés. Descartes fue uno de los primeros en abandonar los medios tradicionales de pensamiento basado en las enseñanzas de Aristóteles. En su lugar, promovió una nueva ciencia basada en la observación y los experimentos. Por eso, se le ha llamado el padre de la filosofía moderna.

desertification > desertización Proceso por el que la tierra fértil o semifértil se convierte en desierto.

détente > distensión Relajamiento de las tensiones de la Guerra Fría en los años 70.

developing world > mundo en desarrollo Naciones de África, Asia y América Latina que trabajan para lograr el desarrollo.

development > desarrollo Proceso de establecer gobiernos estables, mejorar la agricultura, la industria y las condiciones de vida.

dharma > dharma Según la creencia hindú, deberes personales religiosos y morales.

Diaspora > diáspora Diseminación de los judíos más allá de su patria histórica.

Díaz, Porfirio > Díaz, Porfirio Porfirio Díaz (1830–1915) fue presidente de México dos veces: 1877–1880 y 1884–1911. Díaz consolidó el poder en el gobierno central y puso la riqueza en manos de unos pocos al llevar inversores extranjeros para construir infraestructuras y explotar las minas. Como la riqueza no estaba repartida equitativamente, el descontentó se generalizó. Para 1910, la economía iba en grave declive, y los trabajadores y campesinos vivían en la pobreza o sumidos en deudas. En 1911, Díaz renunció y salió al exilio.

Dickens, Charles > Dickens, Charles Charles Dickens (1812–1870) fue un escritor inglés que comenzó su carrera como reportero independiente. En 1836, comenzó a publicar capítulos de su primera novela, *The Pickwick Papers,* que impulsó su carrera como novelista. Dickens creó algunos de los personajes más famosos y vívidos de la literatura. Como realista, Dickens se dedicó a representar la vida real. Esperaba llevar a cabo una reforma, así que sus novelas a menudo se enfocaban en los problemas de los pobres para exponer desgracias sociales.

dictator > dictador Gobernante que tiene control total sobre un gobierno.

Dien Bien Phu > Dienbienphu Pequeño pueblo y antigua base del ejército francés en el norte de Vietnam; lugar de la batalla que terminó con la victoria vietnamita, la expulsión de los franceses de Vietnam y la obtención de la independencia de Vietnam del Norte.

Diet > dieta Asamblea o cuerpo legislativo.

diet > dieta Asamblea o cuerpo legislativo.

Diocletian > Diocleciano Diocleciano (245 d. C.–311 d. C.) fue un general romano que llegó a ser emperador. Para hacer el gobierno más eficaz, dividió el gran imperio en Oriente y Occidente y nombró un coemperador.

direct democracy > democracia directa Sistema de gobierno en el que los ciudadanos participan directamente, en lugar de hacerlo a través de representantes, en los asuntos diarios del gobierno.

disarmament > desarme Reducción del ejército y del armamento.

discrimination > discriminación Tratamiento desigual o barreras.

Disraeli, Benjamin > Disraeli, Benjamin Benjamin Disraeli (1804–1881) fue un político conservador destacado y primer ministro durante siete años. Junto con otros líderes políticos, Disraeli trabajó para expandir el sufragio y transformó lentamente el Parlamento Británico durante el siglo XIX para convertirlo en una institución más democrática. Su vehemente defensa de la Ley de la Segunda Reforma de 1867, permitió que más hombres votaran, entre ellos los miembros de la clase trabajadora. Disraeli también se enfocó en otras reformas sociales, incluyendo leyes de salud pública y el reconocimiento de los sindicatos de los trabajadores.

dissent > disensión Ideas que se oponen a las del gobierno.

dissenter > disidente Protestante cuyos puntos de vista y opiniones diferían de los de la Iglesia de Inglaterra.

divine right > derecho divino Creencia de que la autoridad de un gobernante proviene directamente de Dios.

domesticate > domesticar Amansar animales y adaptar cosechas para que sean más adecuados para el uso de los seres humanos.

dominion > dominio Nación que se gobierna a sí misma.

domino theory > efecto dominó Creencia de que una victoria comunista en Vietnam del Sur podría causar que los gobiernos no comunistas del sureste de Asia cayeran bajo dominio del comunismo, como una fila de fichas de dominó.

dowry > dote En algunas sociedades, pago de la familia de la novia al novio y a su familia; pago que una mujer proporciona a su matrimonio.

Dreyfus Affair > Caso Dreyfus Escándalo político que causó divisiones profundas en Francia entre los realistas, liberales y republicanos; basado en la injusta condena en 1894 de Alfred Dreyfus, un oficial judío del ejército francés.

Dual Monarchy > monarquía dual Monarquía de Austria-Hungría

due process of law > garantías procesales debidas Requisito para que el gobierno actúe justamente y en concordancia con las normas establecidas en todo lo que hace.

Duma > Duma En Rusia, asamblea legislativa nacional electa.

Dunkirk > Dunkirk Puerto de Francia desde donde fueron evacuadas 300,000 tropas aliadas en 1940 al ser bloqueada su retirada terrestre por el avance del ejército alemán.

Dürer, Albrecht > Durero, Alberto Alberto Durero (1471–1528) nació en Nuremberg, Alemania. Fue pintor, dibujante y escritor; su mayor impacto artístico fue en el grabado. Viajó a Italia, estudió con los maestros italianos y ayudó a difundir las ideas del Renacimiento al norte de Europa. Muchas de sus obras famosas, como *El Apocalipsis* y *Adán y Eva,* eran de temas religiosos.

Dutch East India Company > Compañía Neerlandesa de las Indias Orientales Compañía de comercio con poder soberano y absoluto establecida por los Países Bajos en 1602 para proteger y aumentar su comercio con Asia.

dynamo > dínamo Máquina que se usa para generar electricidad.

dynastic cycle > ciclo dínastico Florecimiento y caída de las dinastías chinas de acuerdo con el Mandato del Cielo.

dynasty > dinastía Familia gobernante.

E

earthwork > bancal Muros de contención u otro tipo de construcciones hechos de tierra.

East Timor > Timor Oriental Antigua colonia portuguesa, ocupada por Indonesia, que obtuvo su independencia en 2002.

economic nationalism > nacionalismo económico Énfasis en el control nacional y en la protección de la economía.

Edict of Nantes > Edicto de Nantes Ley promulgada por el rey francés Enrique IV en 1598 en la que se concedía mayor libertad religiosa a los protestantes franceses.

Edison, Thomas > Edison, Thomas Alva Thomas Alva Edison (1847–1931) solicitó su primera patente mientras trabajaba como operador de telégrafos para la Western Union. Aunque su primer invento fue un fracaso, Edison no abandonó el esfuerzo, y continuó hasta convertirse en uno de los inventores más prolíficos del mundo. Durante su vida patentó 1,093 inventos y mejoras en varias industrias, entre ellas de telecomunicaciones, energía eléctrica, minería, registro de sonidos, automotriz, defensa militar y películas de cine.

Eightfold Path > Óctuple Sendero Según las enseñanzas de Buda, el camino que uno debe seguir para lograr el nirvana.

Einstein, Albert > Einstein, Albert Albert Einstein (1879–1955) nació en Alemania, en el seno de una familia judía de clase media. Publicó sus teorías de la relatividad en 1905 y 1916, ganando el Premio Nobel de Física en 1921. Estas ideas cambiaron las creencias sostenidas por mucho tiempo respecto a la naturaleza del universo. Cuando los nazis llegaron al poder en Alemania, Einstein emigró a los Estados Unidos en 1932 y se nacionalizó en 1940. Durante la Segunda Guerra Mundial, se usó su trabajo en la creación de la bomba atómica. A medida que la tecnología nuclear se expandía, Einstein estuvo a favor de controles y limitaciones internacionales. Es ampliamente considerado como el físico más influyente del siglo XX.

Eisenhower, Dwight > Eisenhower, Dwight Dwight Eisenhower (1890–1969) creció en una familia pobre muy trabajadora. Durante la Segunda Guerra Mundial, fue el general estadounidense que comandó las fuerzas aliadas en Europa occidental. Más tarde, "Ike" fue el 34° Presidente de los Estados Unidos, de 1953 a 1961.

Eleanor of Acquitaine > Aquitania, Leonor de Leonor de Aquitania (1122–1204) fue una heredera al ducado de Aquitania. A la edad de 15 años, se casó con el heredero al trono francés, Luis VI, y fue reina de Francia. Inteligente y tenaz, influyó fuertemente en su esposo y fue con él a la Segunda Cruzada. Su segundo matrimonio fue con Henry Plantagenet, quien se convirtió en Enrique II de Inglaterra en 1154. Mientras cuidaba de cinco hijos y tres hijas, ayudó activamente a administrar Inglaterra, gestionó sus propios dominios —haciendo de la corte en Poitiers un modelo de vida cortesana— y permaneció políticamente activa ya cumplidos los 80 años.

elector > elector Uno de los siete príncipes germanos que elegían al emperador del Sacro Imperio Romano.

electorate > electorado Conjunto de personas a quienes se permite votar.

elite > élite Clase alta.

Elizabeth > Isabel I Isabel Tudor (1533–1603) llegó a ser la reina Isabel I de Inglaterra después de la muerte de la reina María. Los cambios políticos hicieron que su infancia fuera bastante peligrosa. Isabel usó sus experiencias para convertirse en una monarca poderosa y astuta. Bajo su reinado, Inglaterra se convirtió en una potencia europea importante. Inglaterra prosperó, tanto económica como culturalmente. Su equilibrado manejo de los conflictos religiosos ingleses le ganaron el apodo de la Buena Reina Isabel.

emancipation > emancipación Concesión de libertad a esclavos o siervos.

emigration > emigración Trasladarse de su propio país a otro.

émigré > exiliado Persona que deja su país por razones políticas.

empire > imperio Grupo de estados o territorios controlados por un gobernante.

enclosure > cercamiento Proceso de apropiarse y consolidar una tierra que anteriormente compartían campesinos.

encomienda > encomienda Derecho que los monarcas españoles otorgaban a los conquistadores para exigir tributos o trabajo a los indígenas americanos en una zona determinada.

endangered species > especie en vías de extinción Especie amenazada de extinción, es decir, de desaparición.

engineering > ingeniería Aplicación de la ciencia y las matemáticas para desarrollar estructuras y máquinas.

English Bill of Rights > Declaración de Derechos inglesa Serie de leyes aprobadas por el parlamento inglés en 1689 que limitaba los derechos de la monarquía y establecía la primacía del Parlamento.

engraving > grabado Forma de arte en la que un artista graba un diseño en una placa de metal y después la usa para producir múltiples impresiones.

enlightened despot > déspota ilustrado Gobernante absoluto que usaba su poder para precipitar cambios políticos y sociales.

entente > entente Acuerdo no vinculante de seguir normas comunes.

enterprise > empresa Entidad empresarial en áreas como transportes, minería, ferrocarriles o fábricas.

entrepreneur > empresario Persona que asume riesgos financieros con la esperanza de obtener beneficios.

Epic of Gilgamesh, The* > *Epopeya de Gilgamesh Poema narrativo de Mesopotamia que se contó por primera vez en Sumeria.

epidemic > epidemia Brote de una enfermedad que se extiende rápidamente.

Equiano, Olaudah > Equiano, Olaudah Olaudah Equiano (1745–1797) fue capturado en África occidental cuando era un niño de 11 años, vendido como esclavo y enviado a las Américas. Más tarde, encontró un trabajo pagado y ganó dinero suficiente para comprar su libertad. En 1789, escribió su autobiografía, *Interesante relato de la vida de Olaudah Equiano.* Murió en Londres en 1797.

Erasmus > Erasmo Erasmo (c. 1466–1536) fue un sacerdote, escritor y erudito holandés que promovió el humanismo. Escribió textos sobre varios temas y produjo una nueva edición griega de la Biblia cristiana. También pidió la traducción de la Biblia a un lenguaje vernáculo, o cotidiano, para ayudar a difundir las enseñanzas, las ideas y la educación.También quería reformar la corrupción de la Iglesia.

erosion > erosión El desgaste paulatino de la tierra.

estates > estado Clase social.

Estates-General > Estados Generales Cuerpo legislativo formado por representantes de los tres estados en la Francia prerevolucionaria.

ethics > ética Estándares morales de comportamiento.

Ethiopia > Etiopía Antiguo término griego para el reino de Axumite; también es un país actual del este de África.

ethnic cleansing > limpieza étnica La matanza o expulsión forzosa de personas de diferentes grupos étnicos de una zona, llevadas a cabo por agresores para que su grupo étnico tenga permanencia exclusiva.

ethnic group > grupo étnico Grupo grande de personas que comparten el mismo idioma y herencia cultural.

Etruscans > etruscos Pueblo que habitó en la Italia antigua.

euro > euro Moneda común usada por la mayoría de las naciones que pertenecen a la Unión Europea.

European Union (EU) > Unión Europea (UE) Organización internacional formada por más de dos docenas de naciones europeas y dedicada a establecer el libre comercio entre las naciones miembros, con una moneda común y leyes y políticas comunes.

excommunication > excomunión Exclusión de la Iglesia católica romana como castigo por negarse a obedecer la ley de la Iglesia.

expansionism > expansionismo Política de aumentar el territorio que posee un gobierno.

extraterritoriality > extraterritorialidad Derecho de los extranjeros a que las leyes de su propia nación los protejan.

F

faction > facción Un grupo o camarilla dentro de un grupo más grande que tiene diferentes ideas y opiniones que el resto del grupo.

famine > hambruna Escasez severa de alimentos por la que perece gran número de personas.

Faraday, Michael > Faraday, Michael Michael Faraday (1791–1867) fue un químico y físico británico que hizo contribuciones importantes en el campo de la electricidad. Algunos de sus descubrimientos más importantes incluyen la generación y transmisión de electricidad, el motor eléctrico y el benceno químico. Sus descubrimientos han dado forma al mundo moderno.

fascism > fascismo Cualquier sistema de gobierno autoritario centralizado no comunista, cuya política glorifica al estado por encima del individuo y que destruye los derechos humanos fundamentales.

federal republic > república federal Gobierno en el que el poder se divide entre el gobierno nacional o federal y los estados.

Federal Reserve > Reserva Federal Sistema central de banca de los Estados Unidos, el cual regula los bancos.

Ferdinand and Isabella > Fernando e Isabel Fernando III (1452–1516) e Isabel I (1451–1504) fueron el rey de Aragón y la reina de Castilla. Su matrimonio unió los dos países para convertirse en la nación de España. Sus campañas militares fueron responsables del éxito final de la Reconquista.

Ferguson, Miriam > Ferguson, Miriam Miriam "Ma" Ferguson (1875–1961), conocida por muchos como "Ma" Ferguson, fue electa la primera gobernadora de Texas en 1924. Se postuló cuando su esposo, el políticamente deshonrado gobernador James E. Ferguson, fue incapaz de asegurar un lugar en la votación. La Sra. Ferguson fue la primera mujer electa para el cargo en los Estados Unidos pero la segunda en ser gobernadora porque Nellie T. Ross de Wyoming fue investida después de la muerte de su esposo. La Sra. Ferguson fue reelecta en 1932 para un segundo periodo.

Fertile Crescent > Creciente Fértil Región de Oriente Medio en la cual surgieron las primeras civilizaciones.

feudal contract > contrato feudal Intercambio de garantías entre los señores y los vasallos.

feudalism > feudalismo Sistema de gobierno poco organizado en el que los señores gobernaban sus propias tierras, pero debían servicio militar y otras formas de apoyo a un superior.

fief > feudo En la Europa medieval, estado que un señor otorga a un vasallo a cambio de sus servicios y lealtad.

filial piety > amor filial Respeto hacia los padres.

finance > finanzas Gestión de los asuntos monetarios incluyendo la circulación de dinero, préstamos, inversiones y banca.

Firdawsi > Firdusi Firdusi (c. 940–1020) fue un poeta musulmán famoso por el *Shah Namah,* o *Libro de los Reyes,* que escribió en persa usando grafía árabe. Firdusi escribió en una época en la que Persia, o Irán, era bastante libre del control del Imperio Musulmán y los líderes locales fomentaban un florecimiento de la cultura persa. El afamado poeta centró sus escritos en historias de realeza y héroes, y muchos de los temas que introdujo siguen siendo relevantes hoy en día.

First Sino-Japanese War > Primera guerra sino-japonesa Conflicto entre China y Japón de 1894 a 1895 por el control de Corea.

Five Ks > Cinco K Artículos sijes de la fe. Las cinco K son Kesh, o cabello sin cortar siempre cubierto por un turbante; Kirpan, espada religiosa que representa las responsabilidades de combatir la opresión; Kara, pulsera de metal; Kanga, peine; y Kachera, ropa interior especial.

Flanders > Flandes Región que incluye partes de los actuales norte de Francia, Bélgica y Países Bajos; fue un importante centro industrial y financiero del norte de Europa durante la Edad Media y el Renacimiento.

flapper > *flapper* En los Estados Unidos y Europa, mujer joven de la década de 1920 que desafiaba las reglas tradicionales de conducta y atuendo.

Florence > Florencia Ciudad de la región de Toscana en el norte de Italia que fue el centro del Renacimiento italiano.

flying buttresses > contrafuertes flotantes Soportes de piedra en la parte exterior de un edificio que permitía a los constructores construir paredes más finas y más altas que contenían ventanas con vidrieras.

Four Noble Truths > Cuatro Nobles Verdades Según las enseñanzas de Buda, las cuatro creencias básicas que forman la base del budismo.

Fourteen Points > Los Catorce Puntos Lista de condiciones planteada por el presidente estadounidense Woodrow Wilson en enero de 1918 para resolver la Primera Guerra Mundial y guerras futuras.

Francis Joseph > Francisco José Francisco José (1830–1916) fue emperador de Austria en 1848 después de la abdicación de Fernando I. Después de la creación de la monarquía dual en 1867, también fue rey de Hungría. En 1879, Francisco José formó una alianza con Alemania, que fue dirigida por los prusianos. Su manejo de las relaciones con Serbia después del asesinato del archiduque Francisco Fernando en 1914 fue uno de los catalizadores de la Primera Guerra Mundial.

Franco, Francisco > Franco, Francisco Francisco Franco (1892–1975) fue un líder militar español que llegó al poder durante la Guerra Civil española. Fue dictador de España de 1939 a 1973, cuando dejó su cargo como jefe de gobierno. Siguió siendo jefe del estado hasta su muerte en 1975.

Franklin, Benjamin > Franklin, Benjamin Benjamin Franklin (1706–1790) fue un hombre de muchos talentos. Nacido en 1706, Franklin fue un autor, inventor y estadista que ayudó a convencer a Francia de que entrara a la Guerra de Independencia del lado de los estadounidenses. Participó activamente en la redacción de la Declaración de Independencia.

Franks > francos Tribu germánica que conquistó la actual Francia y las tierras colindantes en el siglo V.

Frederick II > Federico II Federico II (1712–1786) heredó de su padre, Federico Guillermo I, el trono como rey de Prusia (1740–1786).

Frederick William I > Federico Guillermo I Federico Guillermo I (1688–1740) fue el segundo rey prusiano; ayudó a transformar su país en un estado próspero.

free enterprise system > sistema de libre empresa Sistema económico, también conocido como capitalismo, en el que las empresas privadas son capaces de competir entre sí con poco control del gobierno. Productos, precios y servicios son impulsados por las leyes del libre mercado de la oferta y la demanda en lugar de las regulaciones del mercado.

free market > libre mercado Mercado regulado por las leyes naturales de la oferta y la demanda.

free trade > libre comercio Comercio entre países, sin cuotas, tasas u otras restricciones.

French and Indian War > Guerra contra la Alianza Franco- Indígena Guerra entre Gran Bretaña y Francia en las Américas, que ocurrió de 1754 a 1763; fue parte de una guerra global que se conoció como la Guerra de los Siete Años.

French Indochina > Indochina francesa Nombre occidental para las colonias de Francia en el sureste asiático continental. Actualmente es Vietnam, Laos y Camboya.

fresco > fresco Pinturas de acuarela sobre yeso húmedo.

friar > fraile Monje de la Europa medieval que viajaba de un lugar a otro predicando a los pobres.

fundamentalist > fundamentalista Líder religioso que aboga por el retorno de los que considera que son los valores fundamentales, o básicos, de sus creencias.

G

Galileo > Galileo Galileo Galilei (1564–1642) fue un astrónomo y matemático italiano cuyos descubrimientos con el telescopio apoyaron las teorías heliocéntricas del universo de Copérnico. Sus descubrimientos desafiaron el pensamiento religioso y científico establecido. Galileo contribuyó de manera importante al desarrollo del método científico usado por los científicos modernos.

Gama, Vasco da > Gama, Vasco da Vasco da Gama (c. 1460–1524) fue un explorador y navegante portugués que en 1498 fue la primera persona en llegar directamente a India navegando alrededor de África. Regresó a India en 1502, luchó contra barcos árabes musulmanes en el camino y estableció puestos de comercio a lo largo de la costa de África oriental. Después de servir al rey de Portugal durante 20 años, regresó a India en 1524 con el título de virrey, pero enfermó y murió poco después de llegar.

Gandhi, Indira > Gandhi, Indira Indira Gandhi (1917–1984) fue primer ministro de India durante cuatro periodos. Hija de Jawaharlal Nehru, Gandhi entró en la política como parte del Partido del Congreso, convirtiéndose pronto en su líder. Después de la muerte de su padre, fue electa primera ministra de India. Gandhi permaneció en el poder hasta 1977, cuando algunas de sus políticas autoritarias llevaron a su derrota popular. Sin embargo, en 1980, fue reelecta para un cuarto periodo como primera ministra. Después de que ordenara un ataque militar al Templo Dorado, un lugar sagrado para los sijs, Gandhi fue asesinada por sus guardaespaldas sijs.

Gandhi, Mohandas > Gandhi, Mohandas Mohandas Gandhi (1869–1948) fue un estudiante mediocre que pasó por un periodo de rebelión durante su adolescencia. Se casó a los 13 años y más tarde fue enviado a Inglaterra a la escuela de leyes. En 1891, Gandhi aceptó un cargo en Sudáfrica. Aunque planeaba estar solo un año, permaneció hasta 1914, luchando por los derechos de los indios. En 1919, Gandhi comenzó a ser activo en el movimiento de independencia de India y se dedicó a la causa hasta su muerte. Fue asesinado en 1948, solo unos cuantos meses después de que India ganara su independencia.

Garibaldi, Giuseppe > Garibaldi, Giuseppe Giuseppe Garibaldi (1807–1882) fue un soldado nacionalista y líder militar que usó eficazmente tácticas de guerrilla para obtener victorias militares por el sur de Italia. En su juventud fue miembro de la Joven Italia de Mazzini, donde comenzó a involucrarse con la causa de la unidad italiana.

Garvey, Marcus > Garvey, Marcus Marcus Garvey (1887–1940) fundó la Asociación Universal para el Progreso de la Raza Negra y la Liga de Comunidades Africanas (UNIA) en Jamaica en 1914, con la intención de construir una nación gobernada por negros. Al descubrir que tenía poco apoyo, Garvey se trasladó a los Estados Unidos y estableció la UNIA en Harlem. Garvey enseñaba a sus seguidores sobre la cultura africana y predicaba la necesidad de que los negros formaran una economía fuerte e independiente. Su creencia firme en la separación de las razas le trajo muchos enemigos y fue deportado en 1927.

Gautama, Siddhartha > Gautama, Siddhartha Siddhartha Gautama (alrededor del año 563 a. C.–483 a. C.) nació siendo un príncipe de India. Su encuentro con el sufrimiento humano le llevó a dejar su vida de realeza para buscar la causa del sufrimiento y la pena. Buscó respuestas de los eruditos y meditó hasta que desarrolló una explicación espiritual de la vida. Llegó a ser conocido como "Buda" y comenzó a enseñar sus creencias a los demás. Enseñó las Cuatro Nobles Verdades y fomentó la fe de seguir el Óctuple Sendero.

general strike > huelga general Huelga de trabajadores de muchas industrias diferentes al mismo tiempo.

genetic engineering > ingeniería genética Alteración del código genético que portan todas las formas de vida con el fin de producir resultados específicos.

genetics > genética Rama de la biología que trata sobre la herencia y las variaciones entre sí de los animales y las plantas.

Geneva > Ginebra Ciudad-estado suiza que se convirtió en una teocracia calvinista en el siglo XVI; en la actualidad es una de las principales ciudades de Suiza.

Genghis Khan > Gengis Kan Gengis Kan (1162–1227) surgió de la pobreza para unir a las guerreras tribus mongolas. Impuso disciplina, exigió lealtad y luego procedió a formar un ejército que conquistó las amplias áreas de Asia central y China y que se convirtieron en el Imperio Mongol. Fue conocido por su ferocidad y su generosidad. El Imperio Mongol duró largo tiempo después de que él muriera durante una campaña militar. Sus descendientes aumentaron el imperio hasta que llegó a ser el imperio más grande del mundo antes del Imperio Británico.

genocide > genocidio Intento deliberado de destruir la totalidad de un grupo religioso o étnico.

gentry > clase alta Clase adinerada, terrateniente.

George III > Jorge III Jorge III (1738–1820) fue el monarca reinante que más tiempo estuvo en el trono en la historia británica; gobernó en una época en la que Gran Bretaña y Francia luchaban por dominar Europa; compartió la culpa por la pérdida de las colonias americanas de Gran Bretaña.

germ theory > teoría de los gérmenes Teoría de que las enfermedades infecciosas son causadas por ciertos microbios.

Gestapo > Gestapo Policía secreta de la Alemania nazi.

Ghana > Ghana Antiguo reino comerciante de África occidental ubicado en partes de las actuales Mauritania y Malí.

ghetto > gueto Área separada de una ciudad donde se obliga a vivir a los miembros de una minoría.

Gladstone, William > Gladstone, William William Gladstone (1809–1898) fue primer ministro cuatro veces por separado, líder de los Whigs y más tarde del Partido Liberal. Amplió el sufragio a los campesinos y a la mayoría de los demás hombres durante la década de 1880, muy especialmente con la Ley de Representación del Pueblo de 1884. Gladstone también fue un firme defensor de la autonomía gubernamental irlandesa. Junto con su principal rival, Benjamin Disraeli, Gladstone ayudó a transformar el gobierno británico en una democracia parlamentaria.

glasnost > glásnost Término ruso para "nueva apertura", una política en la Unión Soviética en la década de 1980 para garantizar mayor libertad de expresión.

global warming > calentamiento global Aumento de la temperatura de la superficie terrestre a través del tiempo.

globalization > globalización Proceso por el cual las economías nacionales, la política, las culturas y las sociedades se relacionan con las de otras naciones en todo el mundo.

Goa > Goa Ciudad costera tomada en 1510 que se convirtió en la base comercial y militar de la India de Portugal.

golden age > época dorada Periodo de grandes logros culturales.

Golden Bull of 1222 > Bula de Oro de 1222 Carta constitucional que limitaba rigurosamente el poder de la realeza en Hungría.

Golden Temple > Templo Dorado Santuario de mayor peso sagrado en la religión sij.

Good Friday Agreement > Acuerdo del Viernes Santo Acuerdo firmado por protestantes y católicos en 1998 para poner fin al conflicto en Irlanda del Norte.

Good Neighbor Policy > Política del Buen Vecino Política con la que el presidente estadounidense Franklin Roosevelt prometió que los Estados Unidos interferirían menos en los asuntos de America Latina.

Gorbachev, Mikhail > Gorbachov, Mijaíl Mikhail Gorbachev (n. 1931) fue el líder de la Unión Soviética de 1985 a 1991. Fue responsable de introducir las reformas (glasnost y perestroika) que llevaron a la división de la Unión Soviética y al fin del dominio soviético en Europa Oriental. Fue relevado del cargo por su rival popular, el defensor democrático, Boris Yeltsin, en 1991.

Gothic style > estilo gótico Tipo de arquitectura europea que se desarrolló en la Edad Media, caracterizada por contrafuertes flotantes, bóvedas estriadas, paredes finas y techos altos.

Gouges, Olympe de > Gouges, Olympe de Olympe de Gouges (1745?–1793), autora de la Declaración de los Derechos de la Mujer, clamó contra el trato que recibían las mujeres en Francia, abordando sus asuntos directamente con María Antonieta.

Gracchus, Gaius > Graco, Cayo Cayo Graco (alrededor del año 154 a. C.–121 a. C.) fue hermano de Tiberio y un reformista político plebeyo que buscó limitar el poder del Senado. Propuso un equilibrio de poderes para minimizar la influencia financiera. Al igual que su hermano, fue asesinado por matones contratados por el Senado Romano.

gravity > gravedad Fuerza que atrae los objetos dentro de la esfera terrestre al centro de la Tierra.

Great Depression > Gran Depresión Periodo difícil de colapso económico global entre 1929 y 1939.

Great Leap Forward > Gran Salto Adelante Programa de la China comunista de 1958 a 1960 para aumentar la producción agrícola e industrial, el cual fracasó estrepitosamente.

Great Schism > Gran Cisma División oficial entre las iglesias católica romana y bizantina ocurrida en 1054; otro caso fue el Gran Cisma occidental, un periodo en el cual los papas rivales lucharon por el poder exclusivo y en el que se dividió la Iglesia católica romana desde 1378 hasta 1417.

Great Zimbabwe > Gran Zimbabue Poderoso centro de comercio medieval de África oriental y ciudad estado ubicada en el sureste del actual Zimbabue.

Greco, El > Greco, El El Greco (1541–1614) fue un maestro de la pintura española que también trabajó como escultor y arquitecto durante el Siglo de Oro de España.

Green Revolution > Revolución verde La introducción, en los países en vías de desarrollo durante la década de 1950, de semillas, pesticidas, equipo mecánico y métodos de agricultura mejorados.

Gregory VII > Gregorio VII Gregorio VII (alrededor de 1025–1085) logró el éxito en su batalla contra el emperador del Sacro Imperio Romano Enrique IV por la cuestión de la investidura. Expandió mucho el poder papal al reclamar su supremacía sobre los gobernantes seculares.

griot > griot Antiguo narrador profesional de historias en África occidental.

gross domestic product (GDP) > producto interno bruto (PIB) Valor total de todos los productos y servicios producidos en una nación en un determinado año.

Guang Xu > Guang Xu Guang Xu (1871–1908) fue el noveno emperador de la dinastía Qing. Cuando murió el emperador anterior Tongzhi, su madre Ci Xi nombró a Guang, su sobrino, como nuevo emperador. Ci Xi dominó su reino, influyendo en el gobierno y haciéndole inútil. Durante los Cien Días de Reforma, Guang intentó reformas progresistas, enojando a los conservadores. Ci Xi encarceló a Guang. Murió en circunstancias sospechosas.

Guangzhou > Guangzhou Ciudad costera del sureste de China, también conocida como Cantón, donde, durante la dinastía Ming, los neerlandeses, británicos y otros europeos, podían comerciar con mercaderes chinos bajo la supervisión de funcionarios imperiales, sólo durante la temporada comercial de cada año y sólo en Canton.

guerrilla > guerrilla Pequeños grupos de soldados pertenecientes a una fuerza poco organizada que despliega ataques por sorpresa.

guerrilla warfare > guerra de guerrillas Método de combate no tradicional.

guild > gremio En la Edad Media, asociación de mercaderes o artesanos que cooperaban para mantener los valores de sus oficios y para proteger sus intereses económicos.

guillotine > guillotina Aparato usado durante el Terror para decapitar a miles de personas.

Gulag > *Gulag* En la Unión Soviética, un sistema de campos de trabajo forzado donde millones de criminales y prisioneros políticos fueron detenidos durante el gobierno de Stalin.

Guomindang > Guomindang Partido nacionalista, activo en China entre 1912 y 1949.

Gutenberg, Johannes > Gutenberg, Johannes Gutenberg (c. 1400–1468) nació en Alemania. Fue herrero, impresor y editor. Su invento vanguardista de una imprenta con tipos movibles cambió el mundo. Alrededor de 1455, Gutenberg imprimió la primera edición completa de la Biblia cristiana usando su prensa.

H

habeas corpus > hábeas corpus Garantía constitucional que evita arrestos y encarcelamientos injustos o sin cargos específicos.

hacienda > hacienda Plantación grande.

Hadrian > Adriano Adriano (76 d. C.–138 d. C.) fue emperador romano desde el año 117 d. C. hasta el año 138 d. C. Considerado uno de los "Cinco emperadores buenos", codificó la ley romana y viajó mucho, uniendo al imperio.

hajj > *hajj* Uno de los Cinco Pilares del islam, la peregrinación a La Meca que se espera hagan todos los musulmanes por lo menos una vez en la vida.

Hammurabi > Hammurabi Hammurabi (1792 a. C.–1750 a. C.) fue el primer rey del Imperio Babilónico. Heredó el poder de su padre, quien extendió el control de Babilonia por Mesopotamia. Hammurabi es conocido por escribir el primer código de leyes de la historia escrita.

hangul > hangul Alfabeto que usa símbolos para representar gráficamente los sonidos del idioma coreano.

Hapsburg empire > Imperio Habsburgo Imperio centroeuropeo que duró desde el siglo XV hasta el siglo XX, y que en su plenitud abarcó los territorios del Sacro Imperio Romano y los Países Bajos.

Harappa > Harappa Antigua gran ciudad de la civilización del Indo, ubicada en el presente Pakistán.

Harlem Renaissance > Renacimiento de Harlem Movimiento cultural afroamericano durante las décadas de 1920 y 1930, centrado en Harlem.

Hatshepsut > Hatshepsut (Murió en 1458 a. C.) La reina Hatshepsut sirvió durante 20 años junto con su esposo, Tutmosis II, pero después de la muerte de éste tomó la función de faraona y actuó como regente de Tutmosis III. Es conocida por haber construido templos y monumentos y, en general, por una época de prosperidad en Egipto.

Havel, Václav > Havel, Václav Václav Havel (1936–2011) fue un dramaturgo checo y activista de los derechos humanos que llegó a ser presidente de Checoslovaquia en 1989, después de la Revolución de Terciopelo. Debido a que fue perseguido durante las últimas etapas del gobierno comunista en Checoslovaquia, Havel llegó a ser un símbolo mundial de represión comunista. Después de la división de Checoslovaquia, fue el primer presidente de la República Checa.

hejab > hejab Velos, pañuelos y prendas de vestir amplias y hasta los tobillos cuya finalidad es ocultar el cuerpo; lo visten por lo general las mujeres musulmanas.

heliocentric > heliocéntrico Sistema basado en la creencia de que el Sol es el centro del universo.

Henry IV > Enrique IV Enrique IV (1050–1106) fue un rey alemán que llegó a ser emperador del Sacro Imperio Romano en 1084. Sus esfuerzos para aumentar el poder de la monarquía le llevaron a entrar en conflicto con el papa Gregorio VIII sobre la investidura. Gregorio excomulgó a Enrique pero más tarde lo readmitió en la iglesia después de que Enrique hiciera penitencia.

Henry VIII > Enrique VIII Enrique VIII (1491–1547) fue el segundo rey Tudor de Inglaterra. Bien educado y atlético, al principio fue un favorito del pueblo inglés. Perdió gran parte de su popularidad debido a su costante participación en guerras. El deseo de Enrique de tener un heredero varón fue el catalizador de su ruptura final con la Iglesia Católica Romana y la formación de la Iglesia de Inglaterra.

Henry, Prince > Enrique el Navegante, príncipe El príncipe Enrique (1394–1460) fue un príncipe portugués y patrón de exploradores que ayudó a su padre a capturar la ciudad marroquí de Ceuta; fue gobernador y patrocinó viajes a las islas Madeira y la costa de África occidental. Reunió dinero para las expediciones y estableció una base de exploradores en Sagres, añadiendo más tarde un arsenal, un observatorio y una escuela para estudiar geografía. Su apoyo a la cartografía, avances en la navegación y la exploración proporcionó una base para el surgimiento del dominio internacional de Portugal y la adquisición de su imperio colonial en el siglo XVI.

heresy > herejía Creencia religiosa en contra de las enseñanzas oficiales de una Iglesia.

Herodotus > Herodoto Herodoto (484 a. C.–425 a. C.), a menudo llamado el "Padre de la Historia", hizo numerosos viajes por todo el mundo mediterráneo, recopilando información para sus crónicas de eventos pasados, entre ellos las guerras persas. En sus escritos, observó prejuicios y relatos opuestos a sus fuentes.

Hidalgo, Father Miguel > Hidalgo, padre Miguel El padre Miguel Hidalgo (1753–1811) fue un sacerdote católico de México. Dirigió a indígenas y mestizos en una revolución en contra de los españoles hasta que fue capturado y asesinado en 1811.

hierarchy > jerarquía Sistema que clasifica a las personas de una sociedad.

hieroglyphics > jeroglíficos Sistema de escritura en el que dibujos llamados jeroglifos representan objetos, conceptos o sonidos.

hijra > hégira Viaje de Mahoma desde La Meca hacia Medina en el año 622.

Hippocrates > Hipócrates Hipócrates (c. 460 a. C.–375 a. C.) fue un médico griego considerado tradicionalmente como el padre de la medicina; estudió las causas de las enfermedades y buscó sus curas. Se le atribuyen muchos escritos médicos antiguos, aunque probablemente escribió pocos de ellos. Es honrado por su juramento hipocrático que fija los estándares éticos para la práctica médica.

Hirohito > Hirohito Hirohito (1901–1989) fue emperador en 1926 cuando murió su padre. Muchos creían que era un dios vivo, descendiente de la diosa del sol. Los ultranacionalistas militares japoneses construyeron un culto alrededor del emperador, reviviendo antiguos valores guerreros y suprimiendo la mayoría de las libertades democráticas. Aunque Hirohito fue investido teóricamente con la autoridad suprema, no hizo más que aprobar las políticas que le presentaban sus ministros. Estaba más interesado en la biología marina y escribió varios libros sobre el tema. Hirohito fue el monarca que más tiempo reinó en la historia de Japón, siendo emperador durante la increíble cantidad de 63 años, hasta su muerte en 1989.

Hiroshima > Hiroshima Ciudad de Japón donde fue lanzada la primera bomba atómica en agosto de 1945.

historian > historiador Persona que estudia cómo vivía la gente en el pasado.

Hitler, Adolf > Hitler, Adolf Adolf Hitler (1889–1945) fue canciller de Alemania de 1933 a 1945 y dictador de la Alemania nazi de 1934 a 1945. Después de ser nombrado canciller, transformó inmediatamente la República de Weimar en el Tercer Reich. Quería establecer un "Nuevo Orden" y crear más "espacio para vivir" para la raza aria, la cual creía que era superior. Hitler invadió agresivamente las naciones vecinas, lo que llevó a la Segunda Guerra Mundial. Cuando Alemania se enfrentó a la derrota en 1945, Hitler se suicidó para evitar que lo capturaran los soviéticos.

Ho Chi Minh > Ho Chi Minh Ho Chi Minh (1890–1969); su nombre fue Nguyen That Thanh. Fundó el Partido Comunista Indochino y fue el líder del movimiento armado de independencia en Vietnam. Ho proclamó la independencia de Vietnam en 1945 y se convirtió en el líder de Vietnam del Norte cuando el país quedó dividido en 1954. Fue el líder de Vietnam del Norte hasta su muerte en 1969 y se negó a negociar el fin de la guerra.

Hobbes, Thomas > Hobbes, Thomas Thomas Hobbes (1588–1679) fue un influyente filósofo político inglés, mejor conocido por su obra *Leviathan.* En ella, Hobbes defiende fuertemente que solo un gobierno poderoso es capaz de proteger a la sociedad. Creía que las personas entraban en un contrato social con su gobierno para evitar el caos inevitable y la anarquía de la vida en el "estado natural". La filosofía política de Hobbes fue fundamental para los pensadores posteriores de la Ilustración, incluyendo a Locke, Rousseau y Kant.

Holocaust > Holocausto Genocidio sistemático de aproximadamente seis millones de judíos europeos por parte de los nazis.

Holy Land > Tierra Santa Jerusalén y otros lugares donde los cristianos creen que Jesús vivió y predicó.

Holy Roman Empire > Sacro Imperio Romano Imperio de la Europa central occidental desde 962 a 1806, que comprendía la actual Alemania y las tierras aledañas.

home rule > autogobierno Autogobierno local.

Homer > Homero Homero (c. 750 a. C.) según la tradición es el autor de poemas épicos, la *Ilíada* y la *Odisea;* se cree que viajó de aldea en aldea cantando sobre las hazañas heroicas de los guerreros de la Guerra de Troya.

homogeneous society > sociedad homogénea Sociedad que tiene un lenguaje y una cultura en común.

Huari > huari Cultura que tuvo su apogeo en la región andina, aproximadamente desde el año 600 d. C. al año 1000 d. C.

Hugo, Victor > Hugo, Víctor Víctor Hugo (1802–1885) fue una destacada figura literaria, intelectual y política de Francia. Sus obras no solo fueron extremadamente populares, siendo las más notables *Nuestra Señora de París* y *Los miserables,* sino que también fueron muy influyentes y respetadas. Hugo creía en la causa de la gente común y veía en ella fuerza y potencial. Trató de representar en sus obras tanto sus virtudes como sus preocupaciones. Aunque Victor Hugo no vivió en la pobreza, se asociaba con la clase baja y, según sus deseos, tuvo un funeral y una tumba pobres.

Huguenots > hugonotes Protestantes franceses de los siglos XVI y XVII.

humanism > humanismo Movimiento intelectual durante el auge del Renacimiento que se centraba en la educación y los clásicos.

humanities > humanidades Estudio de asignaturas como la gramática, la retórica, poesía e historia que se enseñaban en las antiguas Grecia y Roma.

Huns > hunos Pueblo nómada del centro de Asia.

Hutus > hutus Grupo mayoritario de Ruanda y Burundi.

hyperinflation > hiperinflación Aumento rápido y brusco de los precios que hace que el dinero pierda su valor.

hypothesis > hipótesis Teoría sin probar, aceptada con el propósito de explicar determinados hechos o de proveer una base para investigaciones posteriores.

I

Ibn Khaldun > Abenjaldún Abenjaldún (1332–1406) fue un pensador árabe que ayudó a establecer los principios de muchas ramas del conocimiento, entre ellas la historia y la economía. Quizá sea más conocido por el desarrollo de estándares para estudiar y escribir sobre historia, mismos que explicó en su obra maestra, el *Muqaddimah.* También introdujo o refinó muchos conceptos económicos relacionados con el trabajo, las ganancias, la oferta y la demanda, el uso de los recursos y la producción.

Ibn Rushd > Ibn Rushd Ibn Rushd (1128–1198), también llamado Averroes, fue un filósofo y científico que vivió en Córdoba e influyó en el pensamiento europeo. Como filósofo, puso una variedad de temas bajo el escrutinio de la razón y el análisis y argumentó que los seres humanos estaban parcial, pero no completamente, controlados por el destino. En el campo de la ciencia, Ibn Rushd contribuyó al estudio de las enfermedades.

Ibn Sina > Ibn Sina Ibn Sina (980–1037), también llamado Avicena, fue un médico persa que escribió el *Canon de Medicina,* que se enfocaba en prácticas médicas antiguas de todo el mundo conocido así como en sus propios procedimientos. Esta obra presenta descripciones de anatomía, síntomas de enfermedades, medicinas y curas. Ibn Sina también escribió sobre una variedad de otros temas, entre ellos filosofía, matemáticas y astronomía.

icon > ícono Imagen sagrada de Cristo, la Virgen María o de un santo venerado por la Iglesia ortodoxa oriental.

ideology > ideología Sistema de pensamiento y creencias.

Ignatius of Loyola > Ignacio de Loyola Ignacio de Loyola (1491–1556) pasó de una temprana carrera de soldado noble español a teólogo y participante influyente en la Reforma Católica. Mientras se recuperaba de una herida en una pierna, Ignacio leyó un libro sobre la vida de los santos y decidió que servir a Dios era una hidalguía santa. Desde ese momento hasta su muerte, Ignacio estudió, rezó y realizó trabajo misionero como fundador de la Sociedad de Jesús, una orden de hombres religiosos que fue conocida como los jesuitas.

illumination > iluminación Decoración artística de libros y manuscritos.

immunity > inmunidad Resistencia, como la facultad de evitar ser afectado por una enfermedad.

imperialism > imperialismo Dominio político, militar y económico de naciones poderosas sobre territorios más débiles.

import substitution > sustitución de importaciones Producción local de bienes para reemplazar su importación.

impressionism > impresionismo Escuela de pintura de finales del siglo XIX y principios del siglo XX que trataba de captar impresiones visuales fugaces.

indemnity > indemnización Compensación como pago por pérdidas de guerra.

indigenous > Indígena Originario o nativo de un país o región.

indigenous peoples > pueblos indígenas Término generalmente usado para describir a los descendientes de los primeros habitantes de una región.

Indra > Indra En la antigua India, dios de la guerra, la deidad principal.

indulgence > indulgencia Perdón por los pecados cometidos en vida concedido por la Iglesia católica romana.

Industrial Revolution > Revolución Industrial Periodo que comienza en el siglo XVIII en el cual la producción pasó de utilizar sencillas herramientas manuales a máquinas complejas, y las fuentes de energía cambiaron de usar energía humana y animal a vapor y, más tarde, electricidad.

inflation > inflación Ciclo económico caracterizado por una rápida subida de los precios ligada a un aumento rápido del dinero disponible.

Innocent III, Pope > Inocencio III, papa El papa Inocencio III (c. 1160–1216) tenía solo 37 años cuando fue nombrado papa y rápidamente extendió la autoridad del papado sobre Roma e Italia. Cuando el rey Juan de Inglaterra nombró al arzobispo de Canterbury sin la aprobación de Inocencio, el Papa le excomulgó.

Inquisition > Inquisición Tribunal de la Iglesia establecido para juzgar a la gente acusada de herejía.

insurgent > insurgente Rebelde

intendant > intendente Funcionario nombrado por el rey francés Luis XVI para gobernar las provincias, recaudar impuestos y reclutar soldados.

interchangeable parts > repuestos intercambiables Componentes idénticos que pueden usarse unos en lugar de otros en el proceso de producción.

interdependence > interdependencia Dependencia mutua de los países con los de otras partes del mundo en cuanto a productos, recursos, mano de obra y conocimientos.

interdict > interdicto En la Iglesia católica romana, excomunión de una región, pueblo o reino.

International Space Station (ISS) > Estación Espacial Internacional Estructura artificial construida y mantenida por una coalición de naciones con el fin de llevar a cabo investigaciones.

Internet > Internet Inmensa red internacional de computadoras que une a millones de usuarios en todo el mundo.

internment > campo de internamiento Confinamiento durante tiempos de guerra.

Inti > Inti Dios sol inca.

intifada > intifada Levantamiento de árabes palestinos en contra de Israel.

Iroquois League > Liga Iroquesa Alianza política de cinco grupos iroqueses, conocida como las Cinco Naciones, de finales del siglo XVI.

Isfahan > Isfahan Capital del Imperio Safávida durante el siglo XVII, situada en el actual Irán.

Isis > Isis Isis es la diosa egipcia adorada como la madre y esposa ideal. Es conocida como la protectora de los muertos y diosa de los niños. Por lo general se la representa como una mujer que viste un tocado en forma de trono.

Islamist > islamista Persona que desea que las políticas del gobierno tengan su fundamento en las enseñanzas del islam.

island-hopping > salto entre islas Estrategia durante la Segunda Guerra Mundial que involucraba apoderarse de islas selectas que mantenía Japón en el Pacífico a la vez que se evitaban otras.

Istanbul > Estambul Nombre usado comunmente para referirse a la capital del Imperio Otomano, la ciudad también se conoció como Constantinopla (lo cual comenzó cuando era el centro del Imperio Romano oriental) y Bizancio (cuando fue la capital del Imperio Bizantino).

Ivan the Great > Iván el Grande Iván el Grande (1462–1505) fue uno de los gobernantes rusos más poderosos. Consolidó su poder al ganar la lealtad voluntaria de los príncipes rusos e impedir más invasiones mongolas.

Ivan the Terrible > Iván el Terrible Iván el Terrible (1530–1584) fue el nieto de Iván el Grande. Siguió centralizando el poder en sus manos, desarrollando un grupo secreto brutal que atrerrorizaba a los miembros de la nobleza hereditaria, o boyardos. Su locura contribuyó a su nombre "el Terrible".

J

Jacobin > jacobino Miembro de un club político radical durante la Revolución Francesa.

Jahan, Nur > Jahan, Nur Nur Jahan (1577–1645) fue una viuda persa con un hijo pequeño. Jahan se convirtió en la poderosa esposa del emperador mogol Jahangir. Sus habilidades administrativas, políticas, económicas y culturales impresionaron tanto a Jahangir que ella tuvo prácticamente el control sobre el imperio hasta su muerte en 1627. Dado que no se permitía a las mujeres interactuar cara a cara con los hombres en la corte, Nur Jahan dependía de que hombres confiables actuaran en su nombre.

Jahan, Shah > Jahan, sah El sah Jahan (1592–1666) fue el tercer hijo del emperador mogol, Jahangir. Con el apoyo de los nobles de la corte, ganó la sucesión y se convirtió en emperador tras la muerte de Jahangir. Gobernante tolerante y eficaz, el sah Jahan fue también un constructor entusiasta, participando personalmente en cada detalle del proceso de construcción. Cuado su amada esposa Mumtaz Mahal murió, construyó en su honor el famoso mausoleo llamado Taj Mahal.

James I > Jacobo I Jacobo I (1566–1625) fue rey de Escocia que también llegó a ser rey de Inglaterra e Irlanda. Creía profundamente en el derecho divino de los reyes a gobernar sobre todos sus súbditos sin interferencia de nadie. Sus puntos de vista discrepaban con los del Parlamento, lo que llevó a conflictos constantes. También fue el autor de la versión de la Biblia del rey Jacobo.

janizary > jenízaro Miembro de la élite del ejército otomano.

Jefferson, Thomas > Jefferson, Thomas Thomas Jefferson (1743–1826) es conocido principalmente como el autor principal de la Declaración de Independencia. También sirvió como ministro ante Francia y más tarde como el tercer Presidente de los Estados Unidos.

Jericho > Jericó La primera aldea del mundo, establecida en la actual Cisjordania entre los años 10,000 y 9000 a. C.

Jerusalem > Jerusalén Capital del estado judío de Judea en la antigüedad, y capital del actual estado de Israel; ciudad sagrada para los judíos, musulmanes y cristianos.

Jesus > Jesús (c. 4 a. C.–30 d. C.) Fue el fundador del cristianismo. Es considerado por la mayoría de los cristianos como el hijo de Dios. Criado en una familia judía, comenzó a predicar un mensaje de salvación y vida eterna. Fue condenado a muerte bajo la ley romana. Según los evangelios, resucitó de entre los muertos. En la actualidad, es venerado como un salvador por los cristianos de todo el mundo.

Jiang Jieshi > Chiang Kai-chek Chiang Kai-chek (1887–1975) nació en el seno de una familia comerciante en el este de China. Junto con Sun Yixian, formó el Partido Nacionalista, o Guomindang; después de la muerte de Sun en 1925, Chiang tomó el control. Después de años de batallas, Chiang unió fuerzas con los comunistas en contra de los invasores japoneses. Chiang también lideró el ejército chino para ayudar a los Aliados a derrotar a Japón en la Segunda Guerra Mundial. Finalmente, los comunistas volvieron a luchar para recuperar el control y Chiang huyó a la isla de Taiwán, la cual gobernó hasta su muerte en 1975.

Jinnah, Muhammad Ali > Jinnah, Muhammad Ali Muhammad Ali Jinnah (1876–1948) fue un político indio musulmán y líder de la Liga Musulmana, que fue fundada en 1906 para proteger los intereses musulmanes en India. Al principio la Liga trabajó de cerca con el Partido del Congreso Indio pero más tarde se separó del Congreso cuando Jinnah y otros musulmanes comenzaron a cabildear a favor de su propio estado. Jinnah ayudó a fundar Pakistán en 1947 y fue su primer gobernador general.

Johanson, Donald > Johanson, Donald Nacido en 1942, el antropólogo Donald Johanson encontró los restos más importantes de uno de los primeros seres humanos de la historia, el esqueleto de una mujer a la que él llamó "Lucy". Después de estudiar sus huesos, Johanson concluyó que Lucy caminaba erguida y que medía aproximadamente 4 pies de altura.

John, King > Juan, rey El rey Juan (alrededor de 1166–1216) fue hijo del rey Enrique II. Se hizo del control del trono de Inglaterra cuando su hermano, el rey Ricardo Corazón de León, fue capturado mientras estaba en una cruzada. Los conflictos con los nobles ingleses hicieron que se viera obligado a firmar la Carta Magna en 1215, que limitaba el poder de los reyes ingleses.

joint family > familia extensa Organización familiar en la cual conviven diferentes generaciones en una misma vivienda.

Joseph II > José II José II (1741–1790) gobernó como emperador del Sacro Imperio Romano en Austria y es considerado el más radical de los déspotas ilustrados. Siguió muchas de las reformas de modernización gubernamental introducidas por su madre, María Teresa, con el objetivo de alcanzar el mismo trato para todos sus súbditos. Abolió la servidumbre y fomentó la libertad de prensa. Lo más destacado es que José apoyó la igualdad religiosa para los protestantes e incluso los judíos. También es recordado por viajar entre sus súbditos disfrazado para conocer los problemas cotidianos de los campesinos.

journeyman > oficial trabajor Empleado asalariado por el maestro del gremio.

Juárez, Benito > Juárez, Benito Benito Juárez (1806–1872) fue un abogado y político mexicano. Proveniente de una familia de herencia indígena zapoteca y campesina, apoyó las reformas para ayudar a los oprimidos de México. Ayudó a comenzar el movimiento de la Reforma y fue nombrado presidente de México en 1861. Murió en el cargo, pero sus reformas ayudaron a unir a México y a introducir a los mestizos en la política.

jury > jurado Grupo de ciudadanos con autoridad para emitir un veredicto final en un tribunal.

Justinian > Justiniano Justiniano (483–565) nació de linaje campesino y fue adoptado por su tío Justino (emperador desde 518). Como emperador bizantino de 527 a 565, Justiniano siguió la guerra contra Persia y buscó recuperar las provincias romanas occidentales de los invasores bárbaros. Después de disturbios y de un importante incendio en el año 532, reconstruyó gran parte de Constantinopla con un estilo majestuoso. También instituyó reformas para detener la corrupción imperial y promover la justicia para sus súbditos. Su logro más influyente es el Código Justiniano, una recopilación, organización y revisión de las leyes romanas.

Justinian's Code > Código de Justiniano Recopilación de leyes romanas organizada por el emperador bizantino Justiniano y que luego sirvió como modelo para la iglesia católica y los monarcas medievales.

K

Kaaba > Kaaba El templo más sagrado del islam, ubicado en La Meca.

kaiser > káiser Emperador de Alemania.

kamikaze > kamikaze Piloto japonés que tomaba misiones suicidas.

kana > kana En el sistema japonés de escritura, símbolos fonéticos que representan sílabas.

Karl Marx > Marx, Karl Karl Marx (1818–1883) fue un pensador político alemán cuyas ideas llegaron a ser la base del comunismo. Marx estudió para abogado y más tarde estudió filosofía, con planes para entrar en el mundo académico. Sin embargo, sus ideas radicales le dejaron con pocas posibilidades, así que se dedicó a escribir. Su obra más famosa fue el *Manifiesto Comunista,* el cual criticaba el capitalismo y predecía que los trabajadores alineados se levantarían para derrotar a la burguesía. En la década de 1860, Marx fue un miembro influyente de la Asociación Internacional de Hombres Trabajadores.

karma > karma Según la creencia hindú, todas las acciones que afectan el destino de una persona en la próxima vida.

Kashmir > Cachemira Antiguo estado principesco de los Himalayas, reclamado tanto por India como Pakistán, y por cuyo control han librado varias guerras.

Katanga > Katanga Provincia de la República Democrática del Congo con ricos depósitos de cobre y diamantes, que intentó independizarse del Congo en 1960.

Kellogg-Briand Pact > Pacto de Kellogg-Briand Acuerdo internacional firmado por casi todas las naciones en 1928 para erradicar el uso de la guerra como un método de política nacional.

Kennedy, John F. > Kennedy, John F. John F. Kennedy (1917–1963) fue presidente de los Estados Unidos de 1961 a 1963. Comandante naval condecorado en la Segunda Guerra Mudial, fue electo presidente a los 42 años de edad. Fue presidente durante la revolución comunista en Cuba y la crisis de los misiles de Cuba y aumentó la participación de los Estados Unidos en Vietnam. En el frente doméstico, la administración de Kennedy comenzó el esfuerzo federal por hacer cumplir los derechos civiles en el Sur. Fue asesinado el 22 de noviembre de 1963 por Lee Harvey Oswald.

Kenyatta, Jomo > Kenyatta, Jomo Jomo Kenyatta (1894–1978) fue un nacionalista y líder de la lucha de independencia keniana de Gran Bretaña. En 1963, se convirtió en el primer ministro del país, y en 1964, en el primer presidente del país, cargo que ocupó hasta su muerte.

Kepler, Johannes > Kepler, Johannes Johannes Kepler (1571–1630) fue un astrónomo alemán cuyos descubrimientos ampliaron la idea del universo heliocéntrico descrita por Copérnico. La investigación de Kepler mostró que los planetas se mueven en una órbita particular alrededor del Sol. Sus logros incluyeron una descripción correcta de cómo ocurre la visión, así como la forma en que un telescopio usa la luz.

Khan, Reza > Khan, Reza Reza Khan (1878–1944) se unió de joven al ejército iraní. Después de liderar el golpe de estado de 1921, Khan fue ministro de guerra y luego primer ministro. Cuatro años más tarde, fue electo sah y siguió reformando radicalmente el gobierno y la nación. A principios de la Segunda Guerra Mudial, la Unión Soviética y Gran Bretaña ocuparon Irán. Khan abdicó y su hijo fue designado sah. Los ingleses exiliaron a Khan a Mauricio y luego a Johannesburgo, donde murió.

Khayyám, Omar > Khayyám, Omar Omar Khayyám (1048–1131) es más conocido hoy en día como un poeta que creó muchos rubáiyáts, o cuartetos. En sus días, fue elogiado por su experiencia en muchas áreas. Como matemático, contribuyó al desarrollo del álgebra. Como astrónomo, estudió cuidadosamente el cielo para ayudar a mejorar el calendario musulmán. El erudito persa también examinó los temas relacionados con la ley, la fillosofía y la historia.

Khmer Rouge > Jemeres Rojos Movimiento político y fuerza guerrillera comunista de Camboya que llegó al poder en ese país en 1975.

Khomeini, Ruhollah > Jomeini, Ruhollah Ruhollah Jomeini (1902–1989) fue un clérigo musulmán chiíta (ayatolá) que lideró en 1979 la Revolución Islámica en Irán, la cual derrocó al sah (Mohammed Reza). Fue el mayor líder político y religioso hasta su muerte 10 años más tarde.

Khrushchev, Nikita > Jruschov, Níkita Níkita Jruschov (1894–1971) sirvió en el Ejército Rojo durante la Segunda Guerra Mundial como teniente general y después fue funcionario del Partido Comunista oficial de Ucrania. Llegó a formar parte del liderazgo del partido central en 1947 y se destacó después de la muerte de Stalin en 1953. Como líder de la Unión Soviética de 1955 a 1964, introdujo reformas domésticas que hicieron menos difícil la vida en la Unión Soviética, pero aplastó las rebeliones en Europa oriental. Fue el líder soviético durante la crisis de los misiles de Cuba.

kibbutz > kibbutz En Israel, granja comunitaria.

Kiev > Kiev Capital de la Rusia medieval y de la actual Ucrania.

Kim Il Sung > Kim Il Sung Kim Il Sung (1912–1994) gobernó la República Popular Democrática de Corea (Corea del Norte) desde 1949 hasta su muerte en 1994. Apoyado por la Unión Soviética durante la Guerra Fría, Kim estableció un estado totalitario con presupuestos enormes para el ejército y prácticamente ninguna libertad política. En 1993, declaró que Corea del Norte se retiraría del Tratado de No Proliferación Nuclear.

King, Jr., Dr. Martin Luther > King, Jr., Dr. Martin Luther Dr. Martin Luther King, Jr. (1929–1968) fue un ministro y líder de los derechos civiles estadounidense. Se destacó a nivel nacional con su liderazgo del boicot al autobús de Montgomery, Alabama, en 1955. King ayudó a organizar la marcha masiva a Washington en 1963, donde dio su famoso discurso "Yo tengo un sueño". Fue asesinado el 14 de abril de 1968.

kiva > kiva Gran habitación subterránea que los anasazi usaban para ceremonias religiosas y reuniones políticas.

Klerk, F.W. de > Klerk, F.W. de F.W. de Klerk (1936–) fue miembro del Partido Nacional y el último presidente de Sudáfrica bajo el apartheid. Junto con Nelson Mandela, negoció la transición del poder de la minoría blanca al gobierno de la mayoría, por lo cual él y Mandela ganaron el Premio Nobel de la Paz en 1993.

knight > caballero Noble europeo que servía como guerrero montado.

Knossos > Cnosos Antigua ciudad de la isla de Creta, centro principal de la civilización minoica que dominó el mar Egeo aproximadamente entre los años 1600 a. C. y 1400 a. C. Las excavaciones que comenzaron en 1900 descubrieron un palacio y edificios aledaños de una cultura sofisticada.

Koch, Robert > Koch, Robert Robert Koch (1843–1910) fue un médico alemán y uno de los fundadores de la bacteriología, o el estudio de las bacterias. Koch descubrió las bacterias responsables de la tuberculosis y el cólera y determinó el ciclo de la enfermedad del ántrax. También mejoró métodos para estudiar las bacterias, entre ellos el cultivo de cepas puras y el teñido de las bacterias para hacerlas más visibles e identificables. En 1905 recibió el Premio Nobel de Fisiología o Medicina.

Kolkata > Calcuta Ciudad grande de India.

Koryo dynasty > dinastía Koryo Dinastía coreana que gobernó desde 935 a 1392.

Kossuth, Louis > Kossuth, Louis Louis Kossuth (1802–1894) fue un abogado, periodista, político y gobernante húngaro durante la revolución de 1848–89.

Kublai Khan > Kublai Khan Kublai Khan (1215–1294) fue nieto de Gengis Kan y fundó la dinastía Yuan, conquistó la dinastía Song del sur para completar el control absoluto de los mongoles en China, y demostró ser un gobernante fuerte e inteligente del vasto imperio. Guiado por consejeros chinos confucionistas, llevó a cabo reformas en sus territorios y reunificó políticamente a China, pero también participó en una serie de costosas e infructuosas guerras con los reinos vecinos. Por lo general, no cambió la vida china y, aunque religioso, fue conocido por aceptar diversas prácticas religiosas y por otorgar privilegios económicos a las sectas preferidas.

kulak > kulak Campesino adinerado de la Unión Soviética a finales de la década de 1930.

Kulturkampf > Kulturkampf "Batalla por la civilización" de Bismarck, cuyo objetivo era que los católicos pusieran la lealtad al estado por encima de la lealtad a la Iglesia.

L

L'Ouverture, Toussaint > L'Ouverture, Toussaint Toussaint L'Ouverture (1743–1803) nació en Haití, hijo de un esclavo educado. Dirigió un ejército de esclavos, que entrenó en la guerra de guerrillas, en una revuelta en contra de los colonos franceses. El ejército francés lo capturó en 1982 y murió en prisión un año más tarde.

La Reforma > La Reforma Era de reforma liberal en México de 1855 a 1876.

labor union > sindicato Organización de trabajadores que negocian por mejores pagas y condiciones de trabajo.

Lafayette, Marquis de > Lafayette, marqués de El marqués de Lafayette (1757–1834), un noble francés, luchó en las Américas en la Guerra de Independencia. Tras su regreso a Francia, Lafayette dirigió la petición de reforma en 1789 y presentó un boceto de la Declaración de los Derechos del Hombre a la Asamblea Nacional. Odiado por algunos debido a su actitud moderada, huyó a Austria, pero regresó después.

laissez faire > ***laissez faire*** Política que permite a los negocios y empresas operar con poca o ninguna interferencia del gobierno.

Lalibela > Lalibela Gobernante de Etiopía que llegó al poder en el siglo XIII. Construyó once iglesias cristianas excavadas desde el nivel del suelo en la roca sólida de las montañas.

land reform > reforma agraria División de grandes propiedades dedicadas a la agricultura para distribuirlas entre los campesinos.

Laozi > Laozi (o Lao Tsé) Laozi significa "Maestro Lao" o "Viejo Maestro" en el idioma chino. Ya un hombre anciano cuando Confucio era un joven erudito, Laozi nació en una pequeña aldea en la antigua China. Fue nombrado historiador en una de las cortes de la dinastía Zhou. Laozi desarrolló una fiolosofía de calma interna, pureza de mente y vida en armonía con la naturaleza que se llama Dao (o Tao), o el camino del universo. Su libro, *El camino de la vida,* tuvo una enorme influencia en la vida china.

Las Casas, Bartolomé de > Las Casas, Bartolomé de Bartolomé de Las Casas (c. 1474–17 de julio de 1566) fue un sacerdote e historiador dominico, famoso por ser uno de los primeros defensores de los derechos humanos en las Américas. Al conocer los males que sufrían los indígenas americanos bajo el sistema de encomiendas, sus vívidos informes sobre los abusos ayudaron en 1542 a la aprobación de leyes que prohibieron la esclavitud y el maltrato. Pasó el resto de su vida luchando por los derechos de los pueblos de las Américas.

laser > láser Haz luminoso de alta energía que puede ser usado para muchos fines, entre ellos la cirugía, la ingeniería y la investigación científica.

latifundia > latifundio Grandes propiedades adquiridas por los ciudadanos romanos que se habían vuelto ricos recientemente.

Lawrence, T. E. > Lawrence, T.E. Thomas Edward Lawrence, (1888–1935), también conocido como Lawrence de Arabia, fue un arqueólogo inglés, escritor y experto en Arabia que ayudó a dirigir una rebelión árabe y una guerrilla en contra de los turcos otomanos durante la Primera Guerra Mundial. En 1926, publicó una memoria de sus actividades en esos años, *Los siete pilares de la sabiduría.*

lay investiture > investidura Nombramiento de obispos por cualquiera que no sea miembro del clero.

Leakey, Louis > Leakey, Louis (1903–1972) Como arqueólogo, Louis Leakey y su esposa, Mary, buscaron los restos de los primeros seres humanos en el este de África, encontrando muchas herramientas y huesos que aumentaron nuestros conocimientos sobre los primeros seres humanos.

Leakey, Mary > Leakey, Mary (1913–1996) Nacida en Londres, Inglaterra, Mary Leakey viajó por Europa visitando numerosos sitios prehistóricos, lo cual aumentó su interés por la arqueología y la geología. En 1936, se casó con Louis Leakey y pasaron 30 años cavando en busca de los primeros seres humanos en el este de África. Finalmente Mary Leakey encontró muchos restos que han aumentado nuestros conocimientos sobre los primeros homínidos.

legion > legión Unidad militar básica del ejército romano que incluía aproximadamente 5,000 soldados.

legislature > cuerpo legislativo Organismo que hace o establece leyes.

legitimacy > legitimidad Principio por el que las monarquías que habían sido derrocadas por la Revolución Francesa o por Napoleón fueron restituidas.

Lend-Lease Act > Ley de Préstamo y Arriendo Decreto aprobado por el Congreso de los Estados Unidos en 1941 que permitió al presidente (FDR) vender o arrendar materiales de guerra a cualquier país cuya defensa fuese considerada de vital importancia para los Estados Unidos.

Lenin, V. I. > Lenin, V.I. V. I. Lenin (1870–1924) fue un revolucionario comunista ruso que llevó a los bolcheviques a la victoria en la Revolución de Octubre rusa. Fue jefe de gobierno de la Unión Soviética de 1922 hasta su muerte en 1924. Adaptó las ideas de Karl Marx para crear un tipo de comunismo conocido como marxismo-leninismo.

Leopold II > Leopoldo II Leopoldo II (1835–1909) fue el rey de Bélgica que lideró los primeros esfuerzos de Occidente para desarrollar y controlar la cuenca del Congo. Gobernó personalmente sobre el Estado Libre del Congo, el cual llegó a formar parte de Bélgica en 1908.

levée > recepción matutina Ritual de la mañana en el que los nobles esperaban al rey Luis XIV.

libel > difamación Publicación de declaraciones falsas y perjudiciales.

liberation theology > teología de la liberación Movimiento dentro de la Iglesia católica que urgía a la iglesia a liderar un llamamiento a favor de la reforma, la justicia social y el fin de la pobreza.

Liliuokalani > Liliuokalani Liliuokalani, nacida Lydia Kamakaeha (1838–1917), fue la última soberana hawaiana antes de que se anexaran las islas a los Estados Unidos en 1898. Durante el reinado de su hermano, la princesa Liliuokalani desempeñó un papel activo en el gobierno de Hawái, mejorando la educación y recibiendo a dignatarios extranjeros. Después de la muerte de su hermano, heredó el trono y se convirtió en la primera reina de Hawái. En 1893, plantadores estadounidenses, liderados por Sanford Dole, la derrocaron.

limited monarchy > monarquía limitada Gobierno en el que la constitución o el cuerpo legislativo limitan los poderes de la monarquía.

Line of Demarcation > Línea de demarcación Línea establecida por el Tratado de Tordesillas que dividía el mundo fuera de Europa en dos zonas: una controlada por España y otra por Portugal.

lineage > linaje Grupo que reivindica un antepasado en común.

Lister, Joseph > Lister, Joseph Joseph Lister (1827–1912) fue un cirujano escocés que amplió el conocimiento médico al reconocer que la falta de limpieza en los hospitales estaba directamente relacionada con las muertes ocurridas después de las cirugías. Al estudiar las obras de otros científicos, se convenció de que los microorganismos del aire entraban en el cuerpo por las heridas abiertas y provocaban infecciones que a menudo llevaban a la muerte después de la cirugía. Comenzó a usar ácido carbólico para limpiar las heridas de los pacientes. También empezó a usar un líquido antiséptico para tratar los vendajes y más tarde desarrolló técnicas para limpiar los instrumentos quirúrgicos y mantener las heridas limpias durante las cirugías. Es conocido como el "padre de la cirugía antiséptica".

literacy > alfabetismo Conocimiento básico de la lectura y la escritura.

literacy rate > tasa de alfabetización Porcentaje de personas que pueden leer y escribir.

Liverpool > Liverpool Ciudad industrial y uno de los puertos más grandes de Inglaterra que fue parte de la línea principal de ferrocarril; unió Liverpool con Manchester en 1830.

Livingstone, David > Livingstone, David David Livingstone (1813–1873) fue un misionero y explorador escocés que influyó en las posturas occidentales hacia África.

Locke, John > Locke, John John Locke (1632–1704) creció durante la tumultuosa época de las Guerras Civiles inglesas. Prolífico escritor sobre filosofía política, las obras de Locke influyeron fuertemente en la Constitución de los Estados Unidos y el desarrollo del gobierno estadounidense. Locke proponía que las personas nacían con ciertos derechos naturales que no podían serles arrebatados, entre ellos la vida, la libertad y la propiedad. Sus ideas radicales sobre la responsabilidad del gobierno para con el pueblo fueron fundamentales para los líderes de la Guerra de Independencia.

loess > loes Fina arena amarilla que transporta el viento.

logic > lógica Pensamiento racional.

Long March > Larga Marcha Marcha épica en la que un grupo de comunistas chinos marcharon en retirada de las fuerzas del Guomindang por más de 6,000 millas.

longbow > arco largo Arco de seis pies de largo que podía disparar rápidamente flechas con suficiente fuerza como para agujerear una armadura.

Louis IX > Luis IX Luis IX (1214–1270) fue rey de Francia de 1226 a 1270. Fue uno de los reyes más populares de Francia. Dirigió la Séptima Cruzada a Tierra Santa y fue canonizado como santo en reconocimiento a su fe y servicios a la Iglesia.

Louis Philippe > Luis Felipe Luis Felipe (1773–1850) fue rey de Francia de 1830 a 1848. Fue conocido como el "rey ciudadano" porque el pueblo le puso en el trono. Finalmente perdió el poder porque no apoyó a las clases trabajadoras.

Louis XIV > Luis XIV Louis XIV (1638–1715) fue rey de Francia (1643–1715) y es considerado el símbolo de la monarquía absoluta.

Louis XVI > Luis XVI Louis XVI (1754–1793) fue rey de la Francia prerrevolucionaria. No logró apoyar a sus ministros, quienes trataron de reformar las finanzas y las instituciones sociales de Francia. En 1789, aunque estuvo de acuerdo en convocar los Estados Generales, se resisitió a las demandas de reforma de la Asamblea Nacional. Más tarde fue acusado de traidor y ejecutado en 1793.

Louisiana Purchase > Compra de Luisiana Territorio comprado por Thomas Jefferson a Francia en 1803.

Luftwaffe > Luftwaffe Fuerza aérea alemana.

Lusitania > Lusitania Trasatlántico británico hundido por un submarino alemán en mayo de 1915.

Luther, Martin > Lutero, Martín Martín Lutero (1483–1546) fue un monje y teólogo alemán que fue el catalizador de la Reforma Protestante. Formado como abogado, se unió a una orden estricta de monjes católicos romanos y estudió teología. Buscando reformar los abusos dentro de la Iglesia, Lutero desafió las enseñanzas de la Iglesia con sus 95 tesis. Esto le llevó a la excomunión y al desarrollo del luteranismo, la primera de varias sectas protestantes.

M

Maathai, Wangari > Maathai, Wangari Wangari Maathai (1940–2011) fue la fundadora del Movimiento del Cinturón Verde así como una activista de los derechos humanos, prevención del SIDA y derechos de las mujeres. Fue electa para la Asamblea Nacional de Kenya en 2002 y ganó el Premio Nobel de la Paz en 2004.

Macao > Macao Región al sudeste de China formada por una península y dos islas; la dinastía Ming permitió a los portugueses instalar un puesto comercial aquí.

MacArthur, Douglas > MacArthur, Douglas Douglas MacArthur (1880–1964) dirigió los ataques aliados en el sureste del Pacífico. También comandó las tropas en la Primera Guerra Mundial y en la Guerra de Corea. Fue general y jefe del ejército durante la Depresión.

Macartney, Lord > Macartney, Lord Lord Macartney (1737–1806) nacido en una familia escocesa-irlandesa en Irlanda, fue miembro del Parlamento británico, secretario en jefe de Irlanda y gobernador de varias colonias británicas. El rey Jorge III le envió a una misión que no tuvo éxito para convencer al emperador Qianlong de China para que permitiera a los comerciantes británicos operar en las ciudades portuarias del norte. Más tarde fue gobernador de la colonia del Cabo de Buena Esperanza.

Machiavelli, Niccoló > Maquiavelo, Nicolás Maquiavelo (1469–1527) nació en Florencia. Fue un filósofo político, estadista y escritor. Su obra más famosa fue una guía para los gobernantes sobre cómo ganar y mantener el poder. *El príncipe* era realista sobre el poder político. Maquiavelo argumentaba que en la política el fin justifica los medios. El término "maquiavélico" todavía se usa actualmente para describir políticas engañosas.

Madison, James > Madison, James James Madison (1751–1836) fue un renombrado estadista estadounidense y cuarto Presidente de los Estados Unidos. A menudo se le llama el "padre de la Constitución" por el papel destacado que desempeñó en la Convención Constitucional de 1789, que dio el marco de la Constitución federal.

Magellan, Ferdinand > Magallanes, Fernando de Fernando de Magallanes (1480–1521) fue un navegante y explorador portugués que de joven fue en expediciones portuguesas a India y África, y más tarde obtuvo el apoyo de España para su expedición de septiembre de 1519 de navegar hacia el oeste para llegar a las Molucas. Comenzó con cinco barcos y una tripulación de 270 hombres; en la larga travesía por aguas desconocidas se enfrentó a aguas revueltas, el escorbuto, hambre y a un motín. Magallanes fue asesinado en 1521 durante una batalla en lo que hoy es Filipinas, y solo uno de sus barcos, llevando especias y 18 hombres de la tripulación original, circunnavegó el globo y regresó por fin a España en septiembre de 1522.

Maginot Line > Línea Maginot Grandes fortificaciones construídas por los franceses a lo largo de su frontera con Alemania en la década de 1930 para protegerse contra invasiones.

Magna Carta > Carta Magna Carta constitucional aprobada por el rey Juan de Inglaterra en 1215; limitó el poder del rey y estableció ciertos derechos a los ciudadanos ingleses.

Magyars > magiares Grupo étnico establecido en la actual Hungría.

Mahdi > Mahdi Salvador musulmán de la fe.

maize > mais Maíz.

Malacca > estrecho de Malaca Uno de los primeros centros de comercio de especias; tomado por los portugueses en 1511.

Mali > Malí Imperio comercial medieval de África occidental ubicado en el actual Malí.

Malinche > Malinche Malinche (alrededor de 1501–1550) fue una joven indígena, llamada Doña Marina por los españoles, que hablaba maya y azteca, aprendió español y fue la intérprete y consejera de Cortés durante su conquista de México. Malinche se convirtió al cristianismo y se casó después con uno de los soldados de Cortés; visitó España donde disfrutó de una cálida recepción en la corte española.

Malindi > Malindi Pueblo costero de África oriental y eje del comercio internacional; fue atacado en el siglo XV por los exploradores portugueses para expulsar a los árabes que controlaban las rutas comerciales de África oriental, y luego tomar ellos mismos el control de esas rutas.

Malthus, Thomas > Malthus, Thomas Thomas Malthus (1766–1834) fue un economista británico. Nació en Surrey en una familia acomodada. Después de recibir su educación en casa, asistió a la universidad en Cambridge, donde obtuvo un título de maestro. Su obra más conocida es *Ensayo sobre el principio de la población*. En ella, argumentaba que el aumento de la población finalmente agotaría el suministro de alimentos, llevando a la pobreza. Fue catedrático de historia y economía política hasta su muerte.

Manchester > Manchester Ciudad industrial del norte de Inglaterra que fue parte de la primera línea de ferrocarril importante que unía Manchester con Liverpool.

Manchuria > Manchuria Provincia histórica en el noreste de China rica en recursos naturales.

Manchus > manchú Personas originalmente de Manchuria, al norte de China, que derrotaron a la dinastía Ming y gobernaron como la dinastía Chin desde mediados del siglo XVII hasta prinicipios del siglo XX.

mandate > mandato Territorio administrado por un poder occidental después de la Primera Guerra Mundial.

Mandela, Nelson > Mandela, Nelson Nelson Mandela (1918–2013) fue un líder del Congreso Nacional Africano y un luchador de la libertad durante la época del apartheid en Sudáfrica. Fue encarcelado durante 27 años y se convirtió en la antorcha de las manifestaciones que pedían el fin del apartheid. Fue liberado en 1990 y en 1994 se convirtió en el primer presidente negro de Sudáfrica, un cargo que ocupó durante solo un periodo. En 1993 ganó el Premio Nobel de la Paz junto con F.W. de Klerk.

Mandelstam, Osip > Osip, Mandelstam Osip Mandelstam (1891–1938?) creció en San Petersburgo, Rusia, en un hogar judío. Aunque es recordado como uno de los principales poetas rusos del siglo XX, la mayor parte de su trabajo quedó sin publicar durante su vida. Los comunistas le enviaron al exilio una seguda vez en 1938, y su esposa, Nadezhda Khazina, recibió su última comunicación unos meses más tarde. Nunca se volvió a saber de él, pero gracias a los incansables esfuerzos de su esposa, la mayor parte de la obra de Mandelstam fue salvada para las generaciones futuras.

Manhattan Project > Proyecto Manhattan Nombre en clave del proyecto para la fabricación de la primera bomba atómica durante la Segunda Guerra Mundial.

Manifest Destiny > Destino Manifiesto Idea estadounidense que establecía que los Estados Unidos debían expandirse a través de todo el norte del continente americano.

manor > feudo En la Europa medieval, estado de un señor que incluye una o más villas y las tierras aledañas.

manor system > feudo También llamado sistema feudal; sistema económico durante la Edad Media en Europa que se construía alrededor de grandes estados llamados feudos que incluían uno o más pueblos y sus terrenos adyacentes.

Mansa Musa > Mansa Musa Mansa Musa (murió alrededor del año 1337) fue un devoto gobernante islámico que llegó al trono en 1312 y expandió las fronteras de Malí hasta el océano Atlántico. Fue uno de los hombres más ricos de su época. Su famoso viaje a la Meca fue espléndido y dio a conocer al mundo las riquezas de Malí.

Mao Zedong > Mao Zedong Mao Zedong (1893–1976) nació en el centro de China en una familia campesina. Ayudó a formar el Partido Comunista Chino en 1921. Después de que Chiang Kai-chek lanzara sus "campañas de exterminación" en contra de los comunistas, Mao llevó su ejército a la épica Larga Marcha. Mao se unió brevemente con el Guomindang para suprimir la agresión japonesa, pero su asociación no duró después de que terminara la Segunda Guerra Mundial. La República Popular de China se estableció en 1949. Mao inició reformas drásticas, algunas de las cuales tuvieron consecuencias desastrosas. El uso del terror de Mao y la intolerancia a la oposición fueron notorios a nivel internacional.

Maori > maoríes Pueblo indígena de Nueva Zelanda.

March on Rome > marcha hacia Roma Marcha planeada por miles de simpatizantes fascistas sobre Roma para tomar su control; en respuesta a ella a Mussolini se le concedió el derecho legal del control de Italia.

Marconi, Guglielmo > Marconi, Guglielmo Guglielmo Marconi (1874–1937) fue un inventor italiano que recibió la primera patente de un sistema de telégrafos sin cable. En 1900, Marconi demostró que las ondas transmitidas sin cables no se veían afectadas por la forma de la Tierra cuando transmitió una señal inalámbrica por el océano Atlántico a una distancia de 2,100 millas. Siguió estudiando las ondas, lo cual resultó en un sistema de rayos para la comunicación de larga distancia, el primer radio de microondas y los principios del radar. Recibió muchos honores y premios, entre ellos el Premio Nobel de Física.

Marcos, Ferdinand > Marcos, Ferdinand Ferdinand Marcos (1917–1989) fue el líder autoritario de Filipinas de 1966 a 1986. Anteriormente abogado, Marcos ganó las elecciones presidenciales democráticas en Filipinas en 1965 y 1969. Su gobierno estaba cada vez más marcado por la corrupción y los incidentes de derechos humanos. En 1972, declaró la ley marcial y persiguió a sus opositores. Cuando Benigno Aquino, Jr., un político exiliado y crítico de Marcos fue asesinado, la mayoría de los filipinos apoyaron a su viuda, Corazón, en la elección presidencial de 1986. Después de perder, Marcos y su esposa se exiliaron en Hawái.

Maria Theresa > María Teresa María Teresa (1717–1780) fue archiduquesa de Austria y reina de Hungría y Bohemia (1740–1780), emperatriz y esposa del emperador del Sacro Imperio Romano Francisco I (1745–1765) y madre del emperador del Sacro Imperio Romano José II (1765–1790).

Marie Antoinette > María Antonieta Los modales, la conducta y los diversos escándalos de María Antonieta (1755–1793) ayudaron al descrédito de la monarquía. Dijo a su esposo, Luis XVI, que se resistiera a las demandas de la Asamblea Nacional. Al igual que Luis, fue acusada de traición y ejecutada.

Marseilles > Marsella Ciudad portuaria francesa; las tropas que marcharon al ritmo de una canción patriótica mientras abandonaban esta ciudad inspiraron que la canción posteriormente llegara a ser el himno nacional francés.

Marshall Plan > Plan Marshall Cuantioso paquete de ayuda que ofrecieron los Estados Unidos a los países de Europa occidental después de la Segunda Guerra Mundial.

Martel, Charles > Martel, Carlos Carlos Martel (688–741) sirvió como mayordomo de palacio (la persona que gobernaba en nombre del rey) para la zona oriental del reino franco desde el año 715 hasta el año 741. Hijo ilegítimo del mayordomo principal, Martel se fortaleció con el poder, y finalmente reunificó y gobernó todo el reino de los francos. Desde el año 711, los musulmanes saquearon las tierras francas y en el año 732 llegaron a Burdeos. Requerida para ayudar en la batalla de Tours ese año, la caballería de Carlos detuvo este gran avance musulmán en Europa.

martyr > mártir Persona que sufre o muere por sus creencias.

matrilineal > matrilineal Organización familiar en la que los lazos de parentesco se siguen a través de la madre.

Maurya, Chandragupta > Maurya, Chandragupta Chandragupta Maurya, que reinó aproximadamente desde el año 321 a. C. al año 297 a. C., fue el primer emperador maurya. Era hijo de un jefe maurya, y su familia quedó en la pobreza cuado su padre murió. Después de superar muchos retos, Chandragupta aprendió tácticas militares y finalmente formó un ejército lo suficientemente fuerte como para conquistar la mayor parte de India.

May Fourth Movement > Movimiento del Cuatro de Mayo Movimiento cultural en China que se centró en reformar China para fortalecerla.

means of production > medios de producción Granjas, fábricas, ferrocarriles y otros grandes negocios que producen y distribuyen mercancías.

Mecca > Meca Ciudad en el oeste de Arabia Saudita; lugar de nacimiento del profeta Mahoma, visto por los musulmanes como el profeta, y ciudad sagrada para los creyentes islámicos.

medieval > medieval Se refiere a la Edad Media en Europa, es decir, el período de la historia entre la edad antigua y la edad moderna.

Medina > Medina Ciudad en el oeste de Arabia Saudita; ciudad donde predicó Mahoma.

Meiji Restoration > restauración Meiji En Japón, reino del emperador Meiji desde 1868 a 1912 que fue marcado por la rápida modernización e industrialización.

Meir, Golda > Meir, Golda Golda Meir (1898–1978) fue fundadora y la primera mujer que ocupó el cargo de primer ministro de Israel (1969–1974). Fue miembro fundador del Partido Laborista de Israel y también fue ministra de asuntos exteriores (1956–1966).

Menelik II > Menelik II Menelik II (1844–1913) fue el emperador de Eitopía que expandió su imperio, modernizó su país y derrotó la invasión italiana de 1896.

mercantilism > mercantilismo Política por la que una nación trataba de exportar más de lo que importaba para aumentar sus reservas de oro y plata.

mercenaries > mercenarios Soldado que sirve en un ejército extranjero a cambio de dinero.

mercenary > mercenario Soldado que sirve en un ejército extranjero a cambio de dinero.

Meroë > Meroe Capital del antiguo reino de Nubia.

Mesa Verde > Mesa Verde El mayor complejo de viviendas anasazi construidas en acantilados en el sudeste de los Estados Unidos, entre alrededor de 1150 d. C. y 1300 d. C.

Mesoamerica > Mesoamérica Región de América del Norte, que incluye a México y América Central, en la cual se desarrollaron, antes de la llegada de los europeos al continente, civilizaciones con características en común.

Mesopotamia > Mesopotamia Región del Creciente Fértil que se encuentra entre los ríos Tigris y Éufrates.

messiah > mesías Rey ungido enviado por Dios.

mestizo > mestizo En las colonias españolas de América, descendiente de indígenas americanos y europeos.

métis > métis Pueblo de descendientes con mezcla de indígenas americanos y franceses canadienses.

Michelangelo > Miguel Ángel Miguel Ángel Buonarroti (1475–1564) fue un pintor italiano también conocido por sus esculturas, obras de ingeniería, arquitectura y poemas. Su famosa estatua de mármol, *David,* muestra la infuencia de las antiguas tradiciones griegas en los artistas del Renacimiento. Miguel Ángel pintó temas bíblicos en los murales del techo de la Capilla Sixtina en Roma. Como arquitecto diseñó el domo de la catedral de San Pedro en Roma, que después sería el modelo para el Capitolio de los Estados Unidos en Washington D. C.

middle class > clase media Grupo de personas, incluyendo mercaderes, comerciantes y artesanos, cuyo rango estaba entre los nobles y los campesinos.

Middle Passage > Travesía Intermedia El tramo de la ruta del comercio triangular en la cual los esclavos eran transportados desde África a las Américas.

militarism > militarismo Glorificación de lo militar.

militia > milicia Cuerpo organizado de voluntarios armados.

Milosevic, Slobodan > Milosevic, Slobodan Slobodan Milosevic (1941–2006) fue un líder del Partido Socialista serbio, cuyas políticas nacionalistas contribuyeron a la ruptura de la antigua Yugoslavia. Murió en La Haya, Países Bajos, mietras estaba en juicio en el Tribunal Criminal Internacional de la ONU para la Antigua Yugoslavia (ICTY) por su papel en el genocidio de los Balcanes.

minaret > minarete Torre esbelta de una mezquita desde la que se convoca a los musulmanes a la oración.

Ming dynasty > dinastía Ming Dinastía china en la que se restauró el gobierno chino; se mantuvo en el poder desde 1368 hasta 1644.

missionaries > misioneros Personas enviadas a hacer trabajo religioso en un territorio o país.

missionary > misionero Persona enviada para hacer trabajos religiosos en un territorio u otro país.

mobilize > mobilizar Preparar las fuerzas militares para la guerra.

Mobutu Sese Seko > Mobutu Sese Seko Mobutu Sese Seko (1930–1997) recibió al nacer el nombre de Joseph Desire Mobutu. Cambió su nombre después de hacerse con el control de Congo en 1965 en un golpe de estado militar. También renombró al país como Zaire. Mobutu gobernó Zaire como dictador hasta que fue derrocado por Laurent Kabila en 1997. Murió de cáncer poco después.

Moche > moche Cultura que tuvo su apogeo en la región andina, desde alrededor de 400 a. C. a 600 d. C.

Moctezuma > Moctezuma Moctezuma (Moctezuma II, 1466–alrededor del 30 de junio de 1520) fue el último emperador azteca, que por error confudió al conquistador Cortés con el rey dios Quetzalcoatl. Fue derrotado por Cortés y obligado a renunciar a su tierra y sus tesoros. Fue hecho prisionero y asesinado cuando los aztecas trataron de expulsar a los españoles de Tenochtitlán.

Mohenjo-Daro > Mohenjo-Daro Antigua ciudad de la civilización del Indo, ubicada en el actual Pakistán.

moksha > moksha En la creencia hindú, objetivo final de la existencia, que es alcanzar la unión con el brahmán.

Moluccas > Molucas Grupo de islas en el este de la actual Indonesia, la cual fue llamada por los europeos la isla de las Especias en el s. XV por ser la fuente principal de especias.

Mombasa > Mombasa Ciudad costera establecida al este de África y centro del comercio internacional; fue atacada en el s. XV por exploradores portugueses para expulsar a los árabes que controlaban las rutas comerciales del este de África, con el fin de obtener el control de esas rutas.

monarchy > monarquía Gobierno en el que el poder reside en el rey o la reina.

Monet, Claude > Monet, Claude Claude Monet (1840–1926) fue una de las figuras más destacadas del movimiento impresionista francés. De forma muy similar a los románticos, los impresionistas se inspiraban en el exterior y rechazaban las tradiciones convencionales artísticas de Europa. Monet trató de crear una representación precisa de la naturaleza mediante su uso del color, los tonos, la textura y las pinceladas. A menudo pintaba el mismo objeto o escena en diferentes momentos del día para ver cómo la luz y la sombra cambiaban su apariencia. Dos de sus series más famosas son montones de grano y nenúfares.

money economy > economía monetaria Sistema económico en el que los bienes y servicios se pagan mediante el intercambio de una ficha que tiene un valor acordado.

Mongkut > Mongkut Mongkut (1804–1868) fue rey de Siam (hoy Tailandia) de 1851 a 1868. Mongkut vivió como un monje budista mientras su hermano mayor ocupaba el trono. Después de la muerte de su hermano, los muchos amigos influyentes de Mongkut le ayudaron a ser rey. El rey instruido era aficionado a las filosofías occidentales y trabajó para modernizar su reino. Después de su muerte, sus hijos, también instruidos, pudieron continuar sus avances.

monopoly > monopolio Control total de un producto o negocio por una persona o grupo.

monotheistic > monoteísta Que cree en un solo dios.

Monroe Doctrine > Doctrina Monroe Política estadounidense para desalentar la intervención europea en el hemisferio Occidental.

monsoon > monzón Viento estacional que sopla regularmente desde una dirección determinada durante parte del año.

Montesquieu > Montesquieu El barón de Montesquieu (1689–1755) nació como Charles Louis de Secondat en una famiia acaudalada y heredera del título de barón de Montesquieu de su tío. Al igual que muchos otros reformadores, no dejó que su estatus privilegiado le impidiera ser una voz de la democracia. Su primer libro, titulado *Cartas persas,* ridiculizaba al gobierno francés y las clases sociales. En su obra publicada en 1748, *El espíritu de las leyes,* avanzó la idea de la separación de poderes, la base de la democracia estadounidense moderna.

More, Sir Thomas > Moro, Tomás, sir Tomás Moro (1478–1535) nació en Londres. Fue abogado, erudito, escritor y miembro del parlamento británico durante el reinado de Enrique VIII. Escribió *Utopía,* que describía una sociedad ideal. La palabra *utópico* llegó a significar idealista o visionario. En 1521, fue nombrado caballero.

Morelos, Father José > Morelos, padre José El padre José Morelos (1765–1815) fue un sacerdote católico que tomó el mando del movimiento revolucionario después de la muerte del padre Miguel Hidalgo. Dirigió el movimiento por el sur de México y en 1813 llamó al Congreso de Chilpancingo a formar un gobierno. En 1815 fue capturado y ejecutado como traidor.

mosaic > mosaico Dibujos hechos de teselas de piedra o cristal coloreado.

Moses > Moisés Según lo describe la Biblia hebrea, Moisés fue un líder religioso judío que sacó a los israelitas de la esclavitud egipcia de regreso a Canaán. Los judíos creen que durante el viaje, o Éxodo, Dios presentó a Moisés un conjunto de leyes éticas y religiosas que el pueblo judío conoce como los Diez Mandamientos.

mosque > mezquita Templo musulmán.

Mothers of the Plaza de Mayo > Madres de la Plaza de Mayo Movimiento de mujeres que se reunía semanalmente en una céntrica plaza de la capital de Argentina para protestar por la desaparición o asesinato de sus familiares.

Mughal > Mogol Dinastía musulmana que gobernó gran parte de la India actual de 1526 a 1857.

Mughal empire > Imperio Mogol Imperio musulmán que gobernó la mayor parte del norte de India desde mediados del siglo XVI hasta mediados del siglo XVIII; también se conoce como Imperio Mogol.

Muhammad > Mahoma Mahoma (alrededor de 570–632) introdujo la religión del islam al suroeste de Asia. Según la creencia musulmana, Mahoma oyó la voz del ángel Gabriel instruyéndole a servir como mensajero de Dios. Mahoma pasó el resto de su vida difundiendo el islam. Actuamente, los musulmanes honran a Mahoma como el profeta final de Dios.

Muhammad Ahmad > Muhammad Ahmad Muhammad Ahmad (1844–1885) asumió el título y el papel de Mahdi en 1881, creyendo que había sido designado por Dios para purificar la religión musulmana y restaurar su grandeza. Mediante sus campañas, creó un vasto estado islámico en la región de Sudán.

Muhammad al-Razi > Muhammad al-Razi Muhammad al-Razi (865–925) fue un renombrado médico musulmán, pionero en el estudio de muchas enfermedades. Además de haber escrito un libro que tuvo buena acogida sobre el sarampión y la viruela, también escribió textos sobre la historia de la medicina y formas de avanzar en el campo. Al-Razi ocupó el cargo de médico jefe, primero en la ciudad de Rayy y luego en Bagdad. También fue filósofo y analizó las obras de Platón mientras presentaba sus propias ideas.

Muhammad Ali > Muhammad Ali Muhammad Ali (1769–1849) fue el hijo de un comandante militar que murió cuando él era un niño. Fue nombrado gobernador de Egipto por los otomanos y se apoderó del poder durante el caos de la guerra civil que siguió a la invasión de Napoléon. A menudo llamado "el padre del Egipto moderno", Muhammad Ali puso en marcha una serie de reformas económicas, políticas, administrativas y militares. Sus reformas trataron de asegurar la independencia de Egipto y colocar a Egipto en el camino para ser una potencia de Oriente Medio.

mujahedin > muyahidín Guerrero religioso musulmán.

mulatto > mulato En las colonias españolas de América, descendiente de africanos y europeos.

multiethnic > multiétnico Formado por diferentes grupos étnicos.

multinational corporation > corporación multinacional Empresas que producen y venden sus productos y servicios en todo el mundo.

Mumbai > Bombay Ciudad grande de India.

mummification > momificación Preservación de los cadáveres al embalsamarlos y envolverlos en tela.

Mussolini, Benito > Mussolini, Benito Benito Mussolini (1883–1945) nació en una familia pobre en Italia. Su padre era herrero y su madre, maestra. Aunque Mussolini creció en un hogar socialista y de joven defendía fuertemente las politicas socialistas, formó un partido fascista en Italia cuando regresó de luchar en la Primera Guerra Mundial. Usando el terror y las tácticas de miedo junto con los Camisas Negras, Mussolini creó y gobernó Italia como un estado totalitario. Después de que Italia invadiera Etiopía en 1935, Mussolini y Hitler firmaron una alianza y, con Japón, lucharon en contra de los Aliados en la Segunda Guerra Mundial.

mutiny > motín Revuelta, especialmente de soldados o marineros contra sus oficiales.

Mutsuhito > Mutsuhito Mutsuhito (1852–1912) fue declarado emperador Meiji en 1868 después de la muerte de su padre, el emperador Kōmei. El emperador Meiji personificaba una mezcla de ideales occidentales y japoneses, tratando de encontrar ejemplos extranjeros como modelos para su país. Inició reformas políticas, económicas y culturales importantes que llevaron a una época de rápida modernización.

mutual-aid society > sociedades de ayuda mutua Grupos de apoyo establecidos para ayudar a los trabajadores enfermos o heridos en accidentes laborales.

mystic > místico Persona que dedica su vida a buscar la comunión directa con las fuerzas divinas.

N

Nagasaki > Nagasaki Ciudad japonesa; en una isla y su puerto, los sogún Tokugawa permitieron que uno o dos barcos neerlandeses comerciaran con Japón cada año en el s. XVII.

Nanak, Guru > Nanak, Guru (1469–c. 1539) Fue el fundador del sijismo. Según las creencias sijs, Nanak entró en trance mientras nadaba y experimentó una revelación espiritual. Predicó un mensaje de igualdad y oportunidad, y de un solo Dios para toda la humanidad. Sus enseñanzas y las de sus sucesores dieron forma a las creencias fundamentales del sijismo.

Napoleon III > Napoleón III Napoleón III (1808–1873) fue sobrino de Napoleón Bonaparte, presidente de la Segunda República (1850–1852) y luego emperador del Segundo Imperio de Francia (1852–1870). Napoleón III construyó el poder económico y político de Francia, pero sus políticas extranjeras no tuvieron éxito. Fue depuesto en 1870 después de la derrota de Francia en la Guerra Franco-Prusiana.

Napoleonic Code > Código Napoleónico Cuerpo de las leyes civiles francesas presentadas en 1804, que sirvieron como modelo para los códigos civiles de muchos países.

Napoleonic Wars > Guerras Napoleónicas Serie de guerras libradas de 1804 a 1805 que enfrentaron al Imperio Francés de Napoléon contra las principales potencias de Europa.

Nasser, Gamal Abdel > Nasser, Gamal Abdel Gamal Abdel Nasser (1918–1970) fue presidente de Egipto (1956–1970). Nacionalizó el canal de Suez, fue líder del movimiento panárabe y se alió con la Unión Soviética durante la Guerra Fría. Dirigió a su país a la guerra contra Israel en 1956 y 1967.

Nationalism > nacionalismo Fuerte sentimiento de orgullo y devoción hacia el país propio.

nationalization > nacionalización Apropiación de propiedades o recursos por parte del gobierno.

natural law > ley natural Principio inmutable, descubierto por la razón, que rige la conducta humana.

natural rights > derechos naturales Derecho que pertenece a todos los humanos desde el nacimiento, como la vida, la libertad y la propiedad.

Nazca > Nazca Cultura que tuvo su apogeo en la región andina desde alrededor de 200 a. C. a 600 d. C.

Nazi-Soviet Pact > Pacto nazi-soviético Acuerdo en 1939 entre Alemania y la Unión Soviética mediante el cual las dos naciones prometen no atacarse mutuamente y dividirse entre sí el territorio de Europa del Este.

Nebuchadnezzar > Nabucodonosor (634 a. C.–562 a. C.) Nabucodonosor fue rey del Imperio Babilónico desde el año 605 a. C. al año 562 a. C. Dirigió muchas campañas que expandieron el imperio a Aramea, Judá y otras ciudades. Reconstruyó la ciudad de Babilonia y se le acredita la construcción de los famosos Jardines Colgantes.

Necker, Jacques > Necker, Jacques Jacques Necker (1732–1804) fue director de la tesorería francesa antes de la revolución. Necker intentó reformar las finanzas del país, aunque también intentó financiar la participación de Francia en la Guerra de Independencia mediante préstamos sólidos, a la vez que intentaba ocultar el enorme déficit del país. Más tarde, sus llamadas por la reforma fueron frustradas por Luis XVI.

négritude movement > movimiento de la negritud Movimiento en el que escritores y artistas descendientes de africanos expresaban su orgullo por su herencia africana.

Nehanda > Nehanda Nehanda (alrededor de 1840–1898) fue una líder espiritual del pueblo Shona al sur de África y la inspiración de una revuelta en contra de la colonización de la Compañía Inglesa de Sudáfrica del territorio que ahora es Zimbabue. Finalmente fue capturada y ejecutada por los británicos.

Nehru, Jawaharlal > Nehru, Jawaharlal Jawaharlal Nehru (1889–1964) fue el primer ministro de la India independiente. Educado en Inglaterra, Nehru regresó a India para practicar la abogacía. Se unió al Congreso Nacional Indio, un movimiento de independencia liderado por Mohandas Gandhi. Nombrado sucesor de Gandhi, Nehru lideró el Congreso hasta que India logró la independencia de Gran Bretaña. Como primer ministro, Nehru se enfocó en la industrialización, las políticas económicas socialistas y la neutralidad en la Guerra Fría.

Neolithic Period > periodo neolítico Era final de la prehistoria que empezó hacia el 9000 a. C; también llamado Nueva Edad de Piedra.

Neolithic Revolution > revolución neolítica Periodo durante el cual el comienzo de la agricultura llevó a la gente a la transición de la vida nómada a la vida sedentaria.

neutrality > neutral Política que no apoya a ninguna de las partes en una guerra.

Neutrality Acts > Leyes de Neutralidad Serie de decretos aprobados por el Congreso de los Estados Unidos de 1935 a 1939 con el fin de evitar la implicación del país en la Segunda Guerra Mundial.

New Deal > Nuevo Trato Paquete de programas económicos y sociales establecidos por Franklin D. Roosevelt para ayudar a los estadounidenses durante la Gran Depresión.

New France > Nueva Francia Posesiones francesas en el actual Canadá del siglo XVI a 1763.

New Stone Age > Nueva Edad de Piedra Era final de la prehistoria que empezó aproximadamente hacia el 9000 a. C. ; también llamado periodo neolítico.

Newton, Isaac > Newton, Isaac Isaac Newton (1642–1727) fue una de las figuras más importantes de la Revolución Científica. Matemático y físico inglés, las tres leyes del movimiento de Newton forman los principios básicos de la física moderna y llevaron a la formulación de la ley universal de la gravedad. Su libro de 1687, *Principios Matemáticos de la Filosofía Natural,* es considerado una de las obras más importantes de la historia de la ciencia moderna.

Nightingale, Florence > Nightingale, Florence Florence Nightingale (1820–1910) fue enfermera en el hospital militar británico en Crimea. Cuando llegó al hospital en 1854, quedó conmocionada por el estado del hospital y la velocidad con la que los hombres morían. Luchó para que tuvieran las barracas limpias, cavaran letrinas, la ropa estuviera lavada y los enfermos cuidados. Seis meses después de su llegada, la tasa de mortalidad bajó de 60 por ciento a 2 por ciento. Cuando regresó a Gran Bretaña, presionó al gobierno para que reformara los hospitales y mejoraran la higiene y los cuidados.

nirvana > nirvana Según la creencia budista, unión con el universo y liberación del ciclo de muerte y renacimiento.

Nkrumah, Kwame > Nkrumah, Kwame Kwamw Nkrumah (1909–1972) luchó por la independencia de Ghana (entonces Costa de Oro) de Gran Bretaña. Luego se convirtió en el primer presidente de la Ghana independiente, a la cual lideró desde 1957 hasta que se vio obligado a dejar el cargo durante un golpe militar. Pasó el resto de su vida en Guinea.

no-fly zone > zona de exclusión aérea En Iraq, área en la que los Estados Unidos y sus aliados prohibieron los vuelos de la aviación iraquí después de la guerra del Golfo, en 1991.

Nobel, Alfred > Nobel, Alfred Alfred Nobel (1833–1896) fue un químico, inventor, ingeniero, hombre de negocios y escritor sueco. Aunque la dinamita es su invento más conocido, registró 355 patentes. En 1895, Nobel legó la mayor parte de su fortuna para crear el Premio Nobel con el fin de honrar a los hombres y las mujeres que tuvieran logros importantes en física, química, medicina, literatura y paz.

nomad > nómada Persona que se traslada de un lugar a otro en busca de alimentos.

nonalignment > sin alineación Independencia política y diplomática de ambas potencias de la Guerra Fría.

North Atlantic Treaty Organization (NATO) > Organización del Tratado del Atlántico Norte (OTAN) Alianza militar entre varios estados del Atlántico Norte para salvaguardarlos de la presunta amenaza del bloque comunista de la Unión Soviética; países de otras regiones más tarde se unieron a la alianza.

Northern Ireland > Irlanda del Norte Parte norte de la isla de Irlanda y territorio del Reino Unido, que ha sufrido un conflicto religioso durante mucho tiempo.

Nubia > Nubia Antiguo reino del noreste africano, también llamado Kush.

nuclear family > núcleo familiar Hogar ideal o típico con un padre, una madre y niños.

Nuremberg Laws > Leyes de Nuremberg Leyes aprobadas por el Partido Nazi en 1935 que negaban la ciudadanía alemana a los judíos y los privaban de otros derechos.

Nuremberg Trials > juicios de Nuremberg Serie de juicios de crímenes de guerra llevados a cabo en Alemania después de la Segunda Guerra Mundial.

O

Old Stone Age > Antigua Edad de Piedra Era de la prehistoria que duró desde aproximadamente dos millones de años a. C. hasta el 9000 a. C.

Olduvai Gorge > garganta de Olduvai Ubicado en el este de África, el desfiladero está formado por numerosas capas sedimentarias de ceniza y lava depositadas durante millones de años. Ha proporcionado a los arqueólogos un criterio para medir la edad de las primeras herramientas de piedra y de huesos de homínidos excavados en el lugar.

oligarchy > oligarquía Gobierno en el que el poder está en manos de unas pocas personas.

Olmec > olmeca La primera civilización americana, ubicada a lo largo de la costa del Golfo de México, desde alrededor de 1200 a. C. a 400 a. C.

one-child policy > política de hijo único Política del gobierno chino que limita a las familias urbanas a tener únicamente un hijo.

Open Door Policy > Política de puertas abiertas Acercamiento estadounidense a China alrededor de 1900, que favorecía el libre comercio entre China y otras naciones.

Opium War > Guerra del opio Guerra librada entre Gran Bretaña y China por las restricciones sobre el comercio exterior.

oracle bone > huesos oraculares En la China Shang, los sacerdotes usaban huesos de animales o caparazones de tortugas para predecir el futuro.

Organization of American States (OAS) > Organización de los Estados Americanos (OEA) Grupo formado en 1948 con el fin de promover la democracia, la cooperación económica y los derechos humanos en las Américas.

Osiris > Osiris Osiris es el dios egipcio identificado como el dios de la vida después de la muerte. A menudo es representado como un hombre de piel verde con barba de faraón y con las piernas parcialmente envueltas en vendas; lleva una corona de plumas de avestruz y un báculo simbólico.

ostracism > ostracismo Práctica de la antigua Grecia de prohibir o apartar a una figura pública que amenazara la democracia.

Ottoman > otomano Miembro de un pueblo nómada de habla turca que emigró de Asia Central al noroeste de Asia Menor.

outpost > fuerte fronterizo Estación militar distante o asentamiento lejano.

outsourcing > subcontratación Práctica empresarial de enviar trabajo a compañías de países en vías de desarrollo con el fin de ahorrar dinero o aumentar el rendimiento.

overproduction > superproducción Condición en la que la producción de mercancías excede la demanda.

Owen, Robert > Owen, Robert Robert Owen (1771–1858) estableció un modelo de comunidad en Nueva Lanark, Escocia, basada en el utopismo. Allí, Owen estableció cambios revolucionarios al limitar la edad de los niños trabajadores y dar escuela a todos los niños. En 1824, invirtió en una comunidad experimental en los Estados Unidos llamada Nueva Armonía. Llegó a ser un líder en el movimiento sindicalista de Inglaterra y siguió participando en el movimiento hasta su muerte.

Oyo empire > Imperio Oyo Los Yoruba crearon este imperio en el siglo XVII en la actual Nigeria. Este imperio utilizó la riqueza del comercio, incluido el comercio de esclavos, para mantener un ejército entrenado y conquistar finalmente el reino vecino Dahomey. El pueblo Yoruba negociaba con los comerciantes europeos de los puertos de Dahomey.

P

Pachacuti Inca Yupanqui > Pachacuti Inca Yupanqui Pachacuti Inca Yupanqui (1438–1471) fue de joven un hábil guerrero. Expandió el Imperio Inca a lo que hoy en día es Perú y Ecuador. Su capital fue Cuzco y recibe el crédito de haber desarrollado el plan de su ciudad.

Pacific Rim > Cuenca del Pacífico Vasta región de naciones, que incluye los países del sureste y este asiático y de las Américas, que limitan con el océano Pacífico.
pacifism > pacifismo Oposición a las guerras.
paddy > arrozal Campo de arroz.
pagoda > pagoda Templo budista de varios pisos con aleros que se curvan en las esquinas.
Paleolithic Period > periodo paleolítico Era de la prehistoria que duró desde aproximadamente dos millones de años a. C. hasta el 9000 a. C.; también llamado la Antigua Edad de Piedra.
Pan-Africanism > panafricanismo Movimiento que empezó en la década de 1920 que se centraba en la unidad y fuerza de los africanos y personas con ascendencia africana en todo el mundo.
Pan-Arabism > panarabismo Movimiento en el que los árabes pretendían unir a todos los árabes en un sólo estado.
Panama Canal > Canal de Panamá Vía fluvial artificial que une los océanos Atlántico y Pacífico.
pandemic > pandemia Propagación de una enfermedad a una gran área, país, continente o al mundo entero.
papal supremacy > supremacía papal Demanda de los papas medievales de que ellos tenían autoridad sobre todos los gobernantes laicos.
papyrus > papiro Planta que se usaba en el antiguo Egipto para hacer un material para escribir parecido al papel.
Parliament > Parlamento Asamblea legislativa de Inglaterra, y más tarde de Gran Bretaña.
parliamentary democracy > democracia parlamentaria Forma de gobierno en la que la dirección ejecutiva (normalmente un primer ministro y el gabinete) es elegida por la asamblea legislativa (parlamento) y controlada por la misma, además de formar parte de ella.
Parthenon > Partenón Templo principal de la diosa griega Atenea, situado en la Acrópolis de Atenas, Grecia.
partition > partición División en partes.
partnership > sociedad Grupo de mercaderes que se unen para financiar una empresa más grande que hubiera sido demasiado costosa para un solo comerciante.
pasha > bajá Gobernante provincial del Imperio Otomano.
Pasternak, Boris > Pasternak, Boris Boris Pasternak (1890–1960) creció en una familia judía bien educada. Su padre era artista y profesor, mientras que su madre era una destacada concertista de piano. Pasternak es muy conocido por su novela épica *Doctor Zhivago,* que le ayudó a ganar el Premio Nobel de Literatura en 1958. Los premios y la publicidad que recibió del occidente solo le crearon problemas en la Unión Soviética. Fue expulsado de la asociación de Escritores de la Unión Soviética y murió en la pobreza. La obra maestra literaria de Pasternak estuvo prohibida en la Unión Soviética hasta mediados de la década de 1980.
Pasteur, Louis > Pasteur, Louis Louis Pasteur (1822–1895) fue un químico francés y uno de los fundadores de la microbiología. Pasteur desarrolló la teoría de los gérmenes de las enfermedades e identificó las causas de muchas enfermedades, entre ellas, la rabia, el ántrax, la varicela y el cólera. Al descubrir las causas de estas enfermedades, Pasteur determinó que podían prevenirse con vacunas. Ayudó a desarrollar varias vacunas, incluyendo la vacuna contra la rabia. También inventó el proceso de pasteurización para el vino, la cerveza, la leche y el vinagre.
paternalistic > paternalista Sistema de gobernar un país como un padre lo hace con su hijo.
patriarch > patriarca En los imperios Romano y Bizantino, el funcionario de rango más alto en la iglesia de una ciudad importante.
patriarchal > patriarcal Relativo a una sociedad en la que los hombres ostentan la máxima autoridad legal y moral.
patrician > patricio Miembro de la clase alta terrateniente.
patrilineal > patrilineal Organización familiar en la que los lazos de parentesco se siguen a través del padre.
patron > mecenas Persona que proporciona apoyo financiero a las artes.
Paul > san Pablo San Pablo (alrededor del año 4 a. C.–64 d. C.) fue un opositor al cristianismo, quien después de tener una visión, se convirtió a las enseñanzas de Jesús. Se hizo misionero para difundir las enseñanzas de Jesús.
Peace of Westphalia > Paz de Westfalia Serie de tratados por los que se puso fin a la Guerra de los Treinta Años.
Pedro, Dom > Pedro, Dom Dom Pedro (1825–1891) fue el segundo y último emperador de Brasil. Pedro II convirtió al Brasil de habla portuguesa en una potencia emergente. Creó estabilidad política y buscó proteger la libertad de expresión y los derechos civiles. El gobierno de Dom Pedro fue una monarquía parlamentaria. Bajo su liderazgo, Brasil experimentó un importante crecimiento económico. Su reinado terminó en 1889 después de que un golpe militar tomara el control del gobierno y le obligara a exiliarse en Europa.
penal colony > colonia penal Lugar al que se manda a los condenados por crímenes.
peninsular > peninsular En las colonias españolas de América, persona nacida en España.
peon > peón Trabajador forzado a trabajar para un terrateniente con el fin de pagar una deuda que es imposible de saldar durante su vida, en la cual incurrió por alimento, herramientas o semillas que el terrateniente le adelantó.
peonage > peonaje Sistema en el que los trabajadores deben trabajar como pago por sus deudas.
perestroika > perestroika Política soviética de reformas democráticas y de libre mercado que introdujo Mikhail Gorbachev a finales de la década de 1980.
Pericles > Pericles Pericles (495 a. C.–429 a. C.) fue un estadista ateniense del siglo V a. C. que lideró Atenas durante la época dorada de logros culturales bajo un gobierno.
Perón, Juan > Perón, Juan Juan Perón (1895–1974) fue electo por primera vez presidente de Argentina en 1946. Gobernó con la ayuda de su esposa, Eva, quien fue popular entre los argentinos. Perón estableció un gobierno autoritario e instituyó amplias reformas, pero su gobierno estaba plagado de corrupción. Fue destituido en un golpe de estado en 1955. Sus partidarios, llamados peronistas, siguieron luchando por el control del gobierno, y Perón regresó al poder en la década de 1970. Su tercera esposa, Isabel, llegó a ser presidenta después de la muerte de su esposo en 1974. Fue derrocada por los militares en 1976.
Perry, Matthew > Perry, Matthew Matthew Perry (1794–1858) fue un exitoso oficial de la Marina de los Estados Unidos. Dirigió una expedición naval a Japón en un intento de establecer relaciones diplomáticas y comerciales después de siglos de aislamiento japonés. La abrumadora presencia militar abrió el camino con privilegios comerciales entre los Estados Unidos y Japón, que otras potencias occidentales se apresuraron a seguir.
perspective > perspectiva Técnica artística usada para lograr el efecto de tercera dimensión en dibujos y pinturas.

Peter the Great > Pedro el Grande Pedro el Grande (1672–1725), zar de Rusia, reinó junto con su medio hermano Iván V (1682–1696) y luego solo (1696–1725). Fue proclamado emperador en 1721. Fue uno de los mayores estadistas, organizadores y reformadores de Rusia.

Petrarch > Petrarca Francesco Petrarca (1304–1374) vivió en Florencia y fue uno de los primeros humanistas, poetas y eruditos del Renacimiento. Recopiló una biblioteca de manuscritos griegos y romanos reunidos de monasterios e iglesias, lo que ayudó a conservar estas obras clásicas para las generaciones futuras.

phalanx > falange En la antigua Grecia, sólida formación táctica de soldados de infantería pesada.

pharaoh > faraón Título de los gobernantes del antiguo Egipto.

Philip II > Filipo II Filipo II (359 a. C.–336 a. C.) restauró la paz en Macedonia, construyó un ejército eficaz y luego formó alianzas con muchas ciudades-estado griegas o las conquistó. Después de derrotar a los ejércitos unidos de Atenas y Tebas en Queronea, toda Grecia quedó bajo su control. Su asesinato terminó con el objetivo de conquistar Persia.

Philippines > Filipinas País al sureste de Asia formado por varios miles de islas. Invadido por los españoles en el s. XVI, llegó a ser un importante vínculo comercial internacional al que llegaron flotas con cargas de plata proveniente de las Américas.

philosophe > *philosophe* Palabra francesa que significa "filósofo"; pensador francés que abogaba por reformas en la sociedad durante la Ilustración.

philosopher > filósofo Alguien que busca entender y explicar la vida; persona que estudia filosofía.

philosophy > filosofía Sistema de ideas.

Piankhi > Piye Piye fue rey de Kush desde alrededor del año 750 al año 719 a. C. Fue conocido por su destreza militar en todo el norte de África. Gobernante muy conservador, Piye buscó fortalecer algunas de las instituciones egipcias en declive.

pictograph > pictografía Dibujo sencillo que se parece al objeto que representa.

Pilgrim > peregrinos Protestantes ingleses que rechazaron la Iglesia de Inglaterra.

Pisan, Christine de > Pisan, Christine de Christine de Pisan (c. 1364–1430) fue la hija de un médico y astrónomo de la corte francesa. Altamente educada, de Pisan hablaba varios idiomas. Después de enviudar a los 25 años de edad, comenzó a escribir poesía y luego a comentar cuestiones sociales.

Pizarro, Francisco > Pizarro, Francisco Francisco Pizarro (alrededor de 1476–26 de junio de 1541) nació en el seno de una familia española muy pobre y en 1513 se unió a la expedición de Balboa para descubrir el "mar del Sur". En 1532, llegó a Perú con sus hermanos, depuso al gobernador inca Atahualpa, conquistó Perú, fundó Lima en 1535 y más tarde fue asesinado por rivales españoles.

plantation > plantación Gran propiedad administrada por un dueño o capataz y cultivada por trabajadores que viven en ella.

plateau > meseta Área elevada del terreno llano.

Plato > Platón Platón (437 a. C.–347 a. C.), alumno de Sócrates, fue un pensador ateniense, escritor de diálogos filosóficos y fundador de la Academia en Atenas.

plebeian > plebeyo Granjeros, mercaderes y artesanos que conformaban la mayor parte de la población.

plebiscite > plebiscito Votación en la que los votantes expresan su opinión sobre un tema en particular.

pogrom > pogromo Ataque violento a una comunidad judía.

Pol Pot > Pol Pot Pol Pot (1925–1998) fue el líder de los Jemeres Rojos, una guerrilla comunista que tomó el control de Camboya en 1975. Bajo su gobierno, casi 2 millones de personas de su nación murieron asesinadas o murieron de hambre y enfermedades. En 1979, Pol Pot fue retirado del poder. Fue capturado en 1997, juzgado y sentenciado a prisión de por vida. Murió por causas naturales mientras estaba en arresto domiciliario.

polis > polis Ciudad-estado de la antigua Grecia.

Polo, Marco > Polo, Marco Marco Polo (alrededor de 1254–1324) fue un viajero, mercader y aventurero de Venecia que hizo la travesía de Europa a Asia en 1271–95, pasando 17 años al servicio de emperador mongol Kublai Khan. Polo dictó el relato de sus viajes, *Los viajes de Marco Polo* (originalmente *Il Milione* en italiano), a un compañero de prisión mientras estuvo encarcelado durante la guerra con Génova. Su libro demostró ser un gran éxito, pero pocos lectores creyeron que era verdad. Aparte de su libro, no se ha encontrado evidencia de que viajara tan lejos hacia el este; sin embargo, durante siglos después de su muerte, otros han confirmado la precisión de la mayor parte de lo que describió.

polytheistic > politeísta Creencia en muchos dioses.

pope > papa Cabeza de la Iglesia católica romana; en la antigua Roma, obispo de Roma que afirmaba tener la autoridad sobre los otros obispos.

popular sovereignty > soberanía popular Gobierno limitado basado en la separación de poderes y un sistema de controles y equilibrios.

potlatch > potlatch Entre los grupos de indígenas americanos de la costa noroeste, ceremonias en las que personas de alto rango y riquezas ofrecían regalos.

predestination > predestinación Creencia calvinista de que Dios decidió hace mucho tiempo quién conseguiría la salvación.

prehistory > prehistoria Largo periodo antes de que el ser humano inventara la escritura.

premier > premier Primer ministro.

price revolution > revolución de los precios Periodo en la historia europea en el que la inflación aumentó rápidamente.

prime minister > primer ministro Jefe del ejecutivo de un gobierno parlamentario.

privateer > corsario Piratas neerlandeses, ingleses y franceses que apresaban los barcos que llevaban los tesoros desde las Américas en el siglo XVI y que operaban con la aprobación de los gobiernos europeos.

Prohibition > Ley Seca Prohibición total de la venta y consumo de alcohol en los Estados Unidos, de 1920 a 1923.

proletariat > proletariado Clase trabajadora.

proliferate > proliferar Multiplicarse rápidamente.

propaganda > propaganda Divulgación de ideas para promover cierta causa o para perjudicar una causa opuesta.

prophet > profeta Líder espiritual a quien se le atribuye la interpretación de la voluntad de Dios.

protectionism > proteccionismo Uso de aranceles y otras medidas restrictivas para proteger a las empresas de un país frente a la competencia.

protectorate > protectorado País con su propio gobierno pero que está bajo el control de una potencia exterior.

Prussia > Prusia Zona de Europa oriental y central, que estuvo bajo el dominio polaco y alemán en la Edad Media y desde 1701 fue gobernada por la dinastía alemana Hohenzollern.

psychoanalysis > psicoanálisis Método que estudia el funcionamiento de la mente y trata los trastornos mentales.

Ptolemy > Ptolomeo Ptolomeo (100 d. C.–170 d. C.) fue un astrónomo, matemático y geógrafo romano que expuso erróneamente la teoría de que la Tierra era el centro del Universo. Vivió en Alejandría, Egipto, donde estudió los planetas y desarrolló un sistema para explicar sus movimientos.

pueblo > pueblos Aldeas de los indígenas norteamericanos del Suroeste de América del Norte.

Pueblo Bonito > Pueblo Bonito El mayor poblado anasazi, construido en Nuevo México en el siglo X.

Punjab > Punjab Estado del noroeste de India de población mayoritariamente sij.

purdah > purdah Aislamiento de las mujeres en recintos separados.

Puritan > puritanos Miembros de un grupo de protestantes ingleses que querían "purificar" la Iglesia de Inglaterra, haciéndola más sencilla y moralmente más estricta.

Pusan Perimeter > Perímetro de Pusan Línea defensiva alrededor de la ciudad de Pusan, en el sudeste de Corea, custodiada por Corea del Sur y las fuerzas de las Naciones Unidas en 1950 durante la Guerra de Corea; marca el mayor avance de las fuerzas de Corea del Norte.

Putin, Vladimir > Putin, Vladimir Vladimir Putin (b. 1952) fue presidente de Rusia (1999–2008, 2012–). Comenzó su carrera con la KGB soviética (Comité para la Seguridad del Estado) y también fue primer ministro de Rusia (1999, 2008–2012).

putting-out system > sistema de trabajo a domicilio Sistema desarrollado en el siglo XVIII en el que las tareas se distribuían a individuos que completaban el trabajo en sus hogares; tambien se conoce como industria familiar.

Pythagoras > Pitágoras Pitágoras (570 a. C.–490 a. C.) fue un filósofo y matemático griego que estudió el significado de los números y sus relaciones. Formuló principios que influyeron en el pensamiento de Aristóteles y Platón, y también estableció una academia en Croton (hoy en día en Italia). Actualmente es más conocido por derivar el teorema de Pitágoras, una fórmula para calcular la relación entre los lados de un triángulo rectángulo.

Q

Qajar > Qajar Miembro de la dinastía que gobernó la zona del actual Irán desde fines del siglo XVIII hasta 1925.

Qianlong > Qianlong Qianlong (1711–1799) fue un emperador chino que amplió el tamaño del imperio de China para incluir Tíbet y gran parte de Asia central, creando un estado multiétnico que incluía chinos Han, tibetanos y manchús. Qianlong se veía a sí mismo como un "monarca universal", tanto dentro como fuera del Imperio Chino. Patrocinó las artes, comisionó grandes obras literarias y formó un museo palacio nacional de China con colecciones de arte que siguen siendo importantes hoy en día.

Qing > Chin Dinastía establecida por los manchús a mediados del siglo XVII que duró hasta principios del siglo XX; fue la última dinastía china.

quipu > quipu Cuerdas con nudos que usaban los funcionarios incas para guardar sus registros.

Quran > Corán El libro sagrado del islam.

R

Rabin, Yitzhak > Rabin, Yitzhak Yitzhak Rabin (1922–1995) nació en Jerusalén y fue un importante líder militar antes y después de la creación de Israel. Fue dos veces presidente, de 1974 a 1977 y de 1992 a 1995. En la década de 1990, llegó a un acuerdo de paz con la OLP, por lo que compartió el Premio Nobel de la Paz con Shimon Peres y Yasir Arafat. Rabin fue asesinado en 1995 por un extremista judío.

racism > racismo Creencia de que un grupo racial es superior a otro.

radical > radical Persona que quiere hacer cambios extremos.

rajah > rajah Jefe guerrero electo de una tribu aria en la antigua India.

Ramses II > Ramsés II Ramsés II (1292 a. C.– 1190 a. C.) es conocido por sus programas de construcción y por las guerras que declaró a los hititas y los libios. Reinó por más de 66 años y es conocido por la construcción de los monumentos y la arquitectura más famosos de Egipto.

Raphael > Rafael Rafael (1483–1520) fue un pintor renacentista que fusionó los estilos clásico y cristiano. Sus famosas pinturas incluyen una de la Madonna, la madre de Jesús, y *Escuela de Atenas,* que muestra una reunión imaginaria de grandes pensadores, científicos y artistas, entre ellos Miguel Ángel, Leonardo y él mismo.

realism > realismo Movimiento artístico del siglo XIX cuyo objetivo era representar el mundo tal como es.

Realpolitik > realpolitik Política realista basada en necesidades concretas del estado.

recession > recesión Contracción económica prolongada.

Reconquista > Reconquista Durante el siglo XV, campaña por parte de cristianos europeos para expulsar a los musulmanes de la actual España.

refugee > refugiado Persona que abandona su hogar o país en busca de refugio en otro lugar, a menudo como consecuencia de inestabilidad política o hambruna.

regionalism > regionalismo Lealtad a un área local.

Reich > Reich Imperio alemán.

Reign of Terror > el Terror Periodo durante la Revolución Francesa de septiembre de 1793 a julio de 1794, en el que la gente en Francia era arrestada por no apoyar la revolución y mucha fue ejecutada.

reincarnation > reencarnación Según la creencia hindú, renacimiento del alma en otra forma corporal.

reparation > reparación Pago de los daños causados por la guerra.

repeal > derogar Cancelar

republic > república Sistema de gobierno en el cual los funcionarios son elegidos por el pueblo.

revenue > renta Dinero que se recauda por impuestos.

Rhee, Syngman > Rhee, Syngman Syngman Rhee (1875–1965) fue presidente de la República de Corea (Corea del Sur) desde su fundación en 1949 hasta 1960. Fue electo para cuatro periodos en el cargo, pero las acusaciones de fraude electoral en 1960 llevaron a manifestaciones estudiantiles y demandas de renuncia por parte de la Asamblea Nacional y el gobierno de los Estados Unidos. Renunció y se fue al exilio en Hawái.

rhetoric > retórica Arte de hablar con habilidad.

Ricci, Matteo > Ricci, Matteo Matteo Ricci (1552–1610) fue un erudito italiano y sacerdote jesuita que viajó a China. En 1589, Ricci comenzó a enseñar a los eruditos chinos ideas matemáticas europeas. Más tarde vivió en Nanjing, donde trabajó en matemáticas, astronomía y geografía. Se hizo famoso en China por sus conocimientos de astronomía, escrituras en chino y su talento como pintor.

Richelieu, Cardinal > Richelieu, cardenal El cardenal Richelieu (1585–1642) es considerado uno de los más grandes políticos de la historia; desempeñó un papel importante en la historia de Francia como primer ministro de Luis XIII.

Robespierre, Maximilien > Robespierre, Maximilien Maximilien Robespierre (1758–1794) fue un revolucionario francés electo para los Estados Generales en 1789. Más tarde llegó a ser un miembro importante del club jacobino y miembro del Comité de Seguridad Pública. Como miembro del comité comenzó su reinado de terror. Más tarde fue arrestado y ejecutado por los líderes de la revolución.

rococo > rococó Estilo de arte y arquitectura elegante y personal que se hizo popular a mediados del siglo XVIII y que incluía diseños con formas de hojas, conchas y flores.

romanticism > romanticismo Movimiento artístico del siglo XIX que apelaba a la emoción más que a la razón.

Romero, Oscar > Romero, Óscar Óscar Romero (1917–1980), un arzobispo católico romano de El Salvador, fue un crítico franco de los abusos de los derechos humanos en su país y defensor de los pobres. Con frecuencia, entraba en conflicto con el gobierno salvadoreño por su crítica del régimen. Fue asesinado en 1980 mientras daba misa en la capilla de un hospital, probablemente por escuadras de la muerte salvadoreñas.

Rommel, Erwin > Rommel, Erwin Erwin Rommel (1891–1944) fue un militar de carrera y uno de los generales más exitosos de Hitler. Se suicidó después de un intento fallido de asesinar a Hitler.

Roosevelt, Franklin Delano > Roosevelt, Franklin Delano Franklin D. Roosevelt (1882–1945) fue el presidente estadounidense que más tiempo ocupó el cargo, ya que fue elegido cuatro veces. Roosevelt nació en una familia acomodada de Nueva York y era primo lejano del presidente Theodore Roosevelt. Elegido en 1932, su primer periodo como presidente se centró en sacar a los Estados Unidos de la Gran Depresión. Pasó con éxito leyes, creando un paquete masivo de programas económicos y sociales, llamado el Nuevo Trato. Durante su tercer periodo, Roosevelt inspiró a muchos a través de su fuerte liderazgo durante el ataque japonés a Pearl Harbor y la consiguiente entrada de los Estados Unidos en la Segunda Guerra Mundial. Fue elegido para un cuarto periodo en 1944, pero su salud se deterioró conforme se acercaba el final de la guerra. Roosevelt murió en abril de 1945.

Rosetta Stone > piedra de Rosetta Piedra arquitectónica que incluye el mismo pasaje con caracteres jeroglíficos, demóticos y en escritura griega que se usó para descifrar el significado de muchos jeroglíficos.

Rosie the Riveter > Rosita la Remachadora Nombre popularmente dado a las mujeres que trabajaban en las fábricas de armamento durante la Segunda Guerra Mundial.

rotten borough > "distrito podrido" En Inglaterra, ciudad rural que enviaba miembros al parlamento a pesar de no tener o tener pocos votantes.

Rousseau, Jean-Jacques > Rousseau, Jean-Jacques Jean-Jacques Rousseau (1712–1778) fue un filósofo y escritor nacido en Suiza cuyos trabajos inspiraron a líderes de la Revolución Francesa. Su pensamiento revolucionario en política y ética tuvo un impacto en cómo los padres educaban a sus hijos e incluso influyó en el gusto de las personas por la música y por otras artes.

Roy, Ram Mohun > Roy, Ram Mohun Ram Mohun Roy (1772–1833) fue fundador del Colegio Hindú de Calcuta, que daba educación al estilo inglés a los indios. Aunque Roy quería reformar algunas partes de la cultura tradicional india e hindú, también revivió el orgullo de India por su cultura. Es considerado el fundador del nacionalismo indio.

Ruhr Valley > Valle del Ruhr Región industrial alemana rica en carbón.

russification > rusificación Política de Stalin para imponer la cultura rusa a la Unión Soviética.

Russo-Japanese War > Guerra ruso-japonesa Guerra entre Japón y Rusia durante 1904–1905 por el control de Corea y Manchuria.

S

Sabbath > sabbat Día sagrado para descansar y rendir culto.

sacrament > sacramento Ritual sagrado de la Iglesia católica romana.

Sadat, Anwar > Sadat, Anwar Anwar Sadat (1918–1981) fue presidente de Egipto (1970–1981). Firmó un tratado de paz con Israel, los Acuerdos de Camp David, moderado por los Estados Unidos. En 1981 fue asesinado por extremistas musulmanes.

Saddam Hussein > Saddam Hussein Saddam Hussein (1937–2006) fue miembro del Partido Baas y pasó siete años en prisión cuando los baasistas no estaban en el poder. En 1968, participó en un golpe de estado en el que los baasistas se apoderaron del gobierno, y para 1979 él tenía el control total del gobierno. Hussein fue el dictador de Iraq hasta la Guerra de Iraq de 2003. En 2006, fue condenado en un tribunal iraquí por crímenes contra la humanidad y poco después fue ejecutado.

Safavid > safávida Imperio musulmán chiíta que gobernó la mayor parte del actual Irán desde el siglo XVI hasta el siglo XVIII.

Sahara > Sahara Desierto más grande del mundo que cubre casi todo el norte de África.

St. Francis of Assisi > san Francisco de Asís San Francisco de Asís (1181?–1226) provenía de una familia acaudalada y fue un joven cosmopolita. Abandonó su riqueza para "caminar tras las huellas de Jesús". Los primeros frailes franciscanos fueron sus seguidores, y juntos llevaron una vida de servicio a los pobres y enfermos. Francisco consideraba a toda la naturaleza como un reflejo de Dios, y llamaba a los animales sus hermanos y hermanas. Relatos famosos cuentan que él predicaba a las aves y convencía al lobo de que dejara de atacar a los aldeanos si ellos, a cambio, daban de comer al lobo. La Iglesia lo nombró santo en 1228.

St. Petersburg > San Petersburgo Capital portuaria del noroeste de Rusia fundada en 1703 por Pedro el Grande.

St. Teresa of Avila > santa Teresa de Jesús Santa Teresa de Jesús (1515–1582) obtuvo fama como autora de varios libros sobre temas espirituales. Fue una influencia clave durante la Reforma Católica. Como monja carmelita, se dedicó a la sencilla vida religiosa basada en la tranquila reflexión. Teresa dedicó gran parte de su vida a la reforma de la orden de las carmelitas, fundando muchos conventos por toda España.

salon > salón Reuniones sociales informales en las que escritores, artistas, *philosophes* y otros intercambiaban ideas.

samurai > samurái Miembro de la clase guerrera en la sociedad japonesa feudal.

San Martín, José de > San Martín, José de José de San Martín (1778–1850) nació en Argentina y fue educado en España. Ayudó a liderar las revoluciones en contra del gobierno español en Argentina, Chile y Perú. Se convirtió en protector de Perú después de su liberación de España pero renunció en 1822 después de un conflicto con Simón Bolívar. Vivió en el exilio en Europa después de su renuncia.

Sandinista > sandinista Partido y movimiento político socialista que gobernó Nicaragua durante la década de 1980.

sans-culottes > sans culottes Miembros de la clase obrera que hicieron la Revolución Francesa más radical; llamados así porque los hombres llevaban pantalones largos en vez de los pantalones ajustados a la rodilla, como los que llevaba la clase alta.

Sapa Inca > Sapa Inca Título del emperador inca.

Sargon > Sargón Las fechas exactas del nacimiento y muerte de Sargón no se conocen, pero según los historiadores sumerios, reinó desde el año 2334 a. C. hasta el año 2279 a. C. Es conocido por crear el primer imperio de Mesopotamia.

sati > sati Costumbre que requería que la esposa se uniera a su marido en la muerte arrojándose a su pira funeraria.

satirize > satirizar Hacer burla de algo o alguien.

savanna > sabana Planicie con pastizales cuyo régimen de lluvias es irregular.

schism > cisma División o ruptura.

scholasticism > escolástica En la Edad Media europea, escuela de pensamiento que usaba la lógica y el razonamiento para apoyar las creencias cristianas.

scientific method > método científico Proceso cuidadoso y de varios pasos que se usa para confirmar descubrimientos y para aprobar o desaprobar una hipótesis.

scribe > escriba En las civilizaciones antiguas, persona especialmente educada para leer, escribir y mantener registros.

secede > separarse Retirarse

secret ballot > voto secreto Votos que se dan sin hacerlos públicos.

sect > secta Subgrupo de un grupo religioso importante.

secular > laico Que tiene que ver más con asuntos mundanos que religiosos; no religioso.

segregation > segregación Separación forzada por razón de raza, sexo, religión o etnia.

Sejong, King > Sejong, rey El rey Sejong (1397–1450), el gobernante más famoso de Corea y conocido como el Grande, reemplazó en 1433 el complejo sistema chino de escritura con el hangul. Sus numerosos logros culturales e intelectuales han llevado a los historiadores a llamar a su reinado la Edad de Oro de Corea.

selective borrowing > préstamo selectivo Adoptar o adaptar algunos rasgos culturales y descartar otros.

self-determination > autodeterminación Derecho de los pueblos a elegir su propia forma de gobierno.

sepoy > cipayo Soldado indio que sirvió en un ejército establecido por las compañías de comercio francesas o inglesas.

Septimius Severus > Septimio Severo Septimio Severo nació alrededor del año 145 d. C. en lo que hoy es Trípoli. Antes de morir en el año 211, fue el emperador que convirtió el gobierno romano en una monarquía militar. Su reinado fijó la organización para otros gobernantes romanos.

serf > siervo En la Europa medieval, campesino vinculado a las tierras del señor.

shah > sah Rey

Shaka > Shaka Shaka (1787–1828) fue un jefe zulú y fundador del Imperio Zulú de África.

Shakespeare > Shakespeare William Shakespeare (1564–1616), nacido en Inglaterra, fue un famoso poeta y dramaturgo durante el reinado de Isabel I. Entre 1590 y 1613 escribió 37 obras de teatro que todavía se representan en todo el mundo. Inventó palabras y frases que todavía se usan en la actualidad. Al igual que otros autores del Renacimiento, adoptó un enfoque humanista en sus personajes.

shantytown > barrio de chabolas Barrios muy pobres de casuchas endebles.

Sharia > sharia Ley canónica del islam que incluye la interpretación del Corán y que aplica los principios islámicos a la vida diaria.

Sharpeville > Sharpeville Municipio sudafricano habitado por personas de raza negra donde el gobierno mató a decenas de manifestantes antiapartheid en 1960.

Shi Huangdi > Shi Huang Shi Huang (alrededor del año 259 a. C.–210 a. C.) se llamaba originalmente Zhao Zheng. Fue hijo del rey del territorio Quin. A los 13 años de edad, Zheng fue el rey de Qin. Se proclamó a sí mismo Shi Huang, o "Primer Emperador". Con espías, generales leales y sobornos, retiró a los otros seis líderes de los estados de alrededor para crear una China unificada bajo su gobierno autoritario. Sin embargo, la China unificada que él creó era demasiado dependiente de Shi Huang. La dinastía Qin colapsó cuatro años después de su muerte.

Shiite > chiíta Miembro de una de las dos sectas musulmanas principales; creyente de que los descendientes de la hija y el yerno de Mahoma, Alí, son los verdaderos líderes musulmanes.

Shikibu, Murasaki > Shikibu, Murasaki Murasaki Shikibu (alrededor de 973–alrededor de 1014 o 1025) fue dama de compañia en la corte Heian. Los historiadores le otorgan el crédito de haber escrito la primera novela larga del mundo, *La historia de Genji,* escrita entre los años 1000 y 1008 d. C.

Shinto > sintoísmo Principal religión de Japón que enfatiza la adoración a la naturaleza.

shrine > santuario Altar, capilla u otro lugar sagrado.

Sikh > sij Miembro de una minoría religiosa de India.

Sikhism > sijismo Religión monoteísta fundada a finales del siglo XV por Gurú Nanak en la región Punjab de India.

Silla dynasty > dinastía Silla Dinastía coreana que gobernó de 668 a 935.

Sino-Japanese War > Primera guerra sino-japonesa Guerra entre China y Japón en la cual Japón adquirió Taiwán.

smelt > refinar Fundir mineral para separar el mineral puro de las impurezas.

Smith, Adam > Smith, Adam Adam Smith (1723–1790) fue un economista escocés recordado por su obra maestra, *An Inquiry into the Nature and Causes of the Wealth of Nations.* Su argumento a favor del libre mercado con interferencias mínimas del gobierno ha ayudado a determinar las economías productivas en todo el mundo durante más de 200 años. Se le ha llamado el padre de la economía moderna y sigue siendo uno de los filósofos de la economía más influyentes de la historia.

social contract > contrato social Acuerdo mediante el cual el pueblo cede sus libertades a un gobierno poderoso para evitar el caos.

social democracy > democracia social Ideología política en la que hay una transición gradual del capitalismo al socialismo en vez de un derrocamiento violento y repentino del sistema.

social gospel > evangelio social Movimiento del siglo XIX que urgía a los cristianos a que hicieran servicios sociales.

social mobility > movilidad social Capacidad de cambiar de clase social.

social welfare > bienestar social Programas ofrecidos por el estado para el beneficio de sus ciudadanos.

socialism > socialismo Sistema en el que el pueblo como un todo, en vez de los individuos, es dueño de todas la propiedades y controla todos los negocios.

socialist realism > realismo socialista Estilo artístico cuyo objetivo era promover el socialismo mostrando la vida en la Unión Soviética desde un perspectiva positiva.

Socrates > Sócrates Sócrates (469 a. C.–399 a. C.) fue un cantero y filósofo ateniense que buscaba la verdad mediante el cuestionamiento, como lo describen los diálogos escritos por Platón.

Solidarity > Solidaridad Sindicato laboral y movimiento democrático polaco.

Solomon > Salomón En la tradición judía, Salomón fue el hijo de David, conocido por la construcción del Templo de Jerusalén. También fue famoso por su sabiduría. Después de su muerte, el reino de Israel se dividió en dos partes.

Song dynasty > dinastía Song Dinastía china que gobernó de 960 a 1279.

Songhai > Songay Reino medieval de África occidental ubicado en el presente Malí, Níger y Nigeria.

sovereign > soberanía Tener poder total e independiente.

soviet > sóviet Consejo de trabajadores y soldados establecido por los revolucionarios rusos en 1917.

Spanish-American War > Guerra Hispano-Estadounidense Conflicto entre los Estados Unidos y España en 1898 por la independencia de Cuba.

Sparta > Esparta Antigua ciudad-estado en Grecia establecida por los dorios y construida como un estado militar.

sphere of influence > esfera de influencia Área sobre la que un poder exterior se reserva privilegios comerciales o la exclusividad de realizar inversiones.

stalemate > estancamiento Punto muerto en una confrontación, en el que ninguna de las partes puede vencer a la otra.

Stalin, Joseph > Stalin, Joseph Joseph Stalin (1879–1953) (nombre real: Iosif Vissarionovich Dzhugashvili) adoptó el nombre Stalin, que significa "hombre de acero", después de unirse a los bolcheviques clandestinos. Fue el único gobernante de la Unión Soviética durante 33 años. Stalin se mantuvo firme en contra de Hitler y se negó a dejar Moscú. Finalmente obligó a los alemanes a retirarse.

Stalingrad > Stalingrado Actualmente Volgogrado; ciudad del suroeste de Rusia donde se libró una encarnizada batalla durante la Segunda Guerra Mundial.

Stamp Act > Ley del Timbre Ley promulgada en 1765 por el Parlamento Británico, la cual imponía gravámenes a artículos como diarios y panfletos en las colonias americanas; revocada en 1766.

standard of living > estándar de vida Nivel de bienes materiales y de servicios disponibles en una sociedad.

Stanley, Henry > Stanley, Henry Henry Stanley (1841–1904) fue un explorador británico de África central, famoso por el rescate del Dr. David Livingstone y sus descubrimientos en la región del río Congo.

Stanton, Elizabeth Cady > Stanton, Elizabeth Cady Elizabeth Cady Stanton (1815–1902) fue una escritora, conferencista y activista que desempeñó un papel importante en el movimiento de los derechos de la mujer. Esbozó discursos y muchos de los documentos importantes del movimiento, incluyendo la "Declaración de derechos" de las mujeres. Stanton ayudó a planear y dirigió la Convención de Seneca Falls de 1848. Más adelante, comenzó a enfocarse más en las reformas sociales, incluyendo el cuidado infantil, las leyes de divorcio y la templanza. Stanton murió 18 años antes de que las mujeres obtuviera el derecho al voto.

stela > estela En el mundo antiguo, altos monumentos conmemorativos que a menudo estaban decorados.

steppe > estepa Tierra de pastos secos.

stipend > estipendio Salario fijo de los funcionarios públicos.

stock > acciones Títulos o valores de una compañía.

Stolypin, Peter > Stolypin, Peter Peter Stolypin (1862–1911) fue un estadista ruso bajo el zar Nicolás II. Fue ministro del interior y presidente del Consejo de Ministros. Aunque instituyó reformas agrícolas que mejoraron la vida de los campesinos, hizo enemigos a ambos lados del espectro político. Fue asesinado en 1911.

strait > estrecho Vía marítima angosta.

stupa > stupa Gran altar budista en forma de cúpula.

subcontinent > subcontinente Gran masa continental que sobresale de un continente.

suburbanization > suburbanización Proceso de construcción en áreas fuera del centro de la ciudad.

Sudetenland > Sudetes Región occidental de la antigua Checoslovaquia.

Suez Canal > canal de Suez Canal de Egipto que une el mar Rojo y el océano Índico con el mar Mediterráneo, que a la vez une Europa con puertos en Asia y África oriental.

suffrage > sufragio Derecho al voto.

Sufi > sufí Místico musulmán que busca la comunión con Dios mediante la meditación, el ayuno y otros rituales.

Suharto > Suharto Suharto (1921–2008) fue un oficial militar indonesio de alto rango que se convirtió en el segundo presidente del país. Suharto luchó contra los neerlandeses en el movimiento de independenca de Indonesia y logró un rango distinguido en el gobierno del nuevo país. Cuando Sukarno, el primer presidente del país, comenzó a instituir políticas comunistas, el ejército anticomunista se rebeló. Suharto llevó a cabo purgas en contra de los comunistas y un violento golpe de estado en contra de Sukarno. Habiendo tomado el poder en 1967, trabajó para modernizar y estabilizar el país.

Sukarno > Sukarno Sukarno (1901–1970) fue un luchador de la libertad y primer presidente de Indonesia. Participó en el movimiento de independencia en contra de los neerlandeses, y pasó algún tiempo encarcelado o exiliado. Durante la Segunda Guerra Mundial, Japón invadió las Indias y Sukarno cooperó con el nuevo régimen. El colapso de Japón al final de la guerra permitió la independencia de Indonesia, a pesar de los intentos neerlandeses de recuperar el poder. Como el nuevo presidente de Indonesia, Sukarno desmanteló el gobierno parlamentario e instituyó políticas comunistas. Un violento golpe de estado liderado por el general Suharto depuso a Sukarno en 1967.

Suleiman > Solimán Solimán (1494–1566) fue un sultán del Imperio Otomano que gobernó de 1520 a 1566. Durante este tiempo llevó burocracia y estabilidad al imperio y fomentó las artes, las leyes y la arquitectura. Sus campañas militares ampliaron mucho el alcance del imperio.

sultan > sultán Gobernante musulmán.

Sumer > Sumeria Lugar de la primera civilización del mundo, ubicada en el sureste de Mesopotamia.

Sun Yixian > Sun Yixian (también llamado Sun Yat-Sen) Sun Yixian (1866–1925) fue hijo de unos campesinos pobres de una pequeña aldea. Dejó la carrera de medicina para participar en una revuelta en contra del gobierno Qing. Después de un levantamiento fallido, Sun se vio obligado a exiliarse en Japón. En 1911, los delegados eligieron a Sun como presidente provisional de la recién establecida República de China. En 1921, Sun estableció un gobierno nacionalista en el sur de China y se alió con los comunistas para derrotar a los señores de la guerra.

Sundiata > Sundiata Sundiata fue un gobernante de África occidental que fue el responsable de poner las bases para que Malí se convirtiera en un reino rico y poderoso. Murió en 1255.

Sunni > suní Miembro de una de las dos sectas musulmanas principales; los sunitas creen que la inspiración proviene del ejemplo de Mahoma según fue registrada por sus primeros seguidores.

superpower > superpotencia Una nación más fuerte que otras naciones poderosas.

surplus > superávit Cantidad que rebasa lo necesario; exceso.

surrealism > surrealismo Movimiento artístico que trata de mostrar el funcionamiento del inconsciente.

Suryavarman II, King > Suryavarman II, rey Suryavarman II fue un famoso rey de Camboya, que murió en 115 d. C. Construyó la estructura religiosa más grande del mundo en Angkor Wat y conquistó gran parte de lo que ahora es Tailandia y Vietnam. Hizo de la capital, Angkor, una de las grandes ciudades del mundo de esa época.

sustainability > sostenibilidad Desarrollo que equilibra las necesidades actuales de las personas con la necesidad de conservar el medio ambiente para las generaciones futuras.

sustainable development > desarrollo sostenible Desarrollo que cubre las necesidades del presente sin perjudicar la capacidad de las generaciones futuras de cubrir sus necesidades.

Suu Kyi, Aung San > Suu Kyi, Aung San Aung San Suu Kyi (1945–) es una líder de los derechos humanos de Myanmar y Premio Nobel de la Paz. Hija del líder de la Birmania independiente y embajador en India, Suu Kyi estaba motivada para luchar por la paz y la libertad en contra de los opresores militares que habían gobernado Birmania desde 1962. Ayudó a fundar el movimiento de independencia de la Liga Nacional por la Democracia, la cual ganó la elección democrática en 1990 pero fue callada por los militares. En 2010, Suu Kyi fue liberada de su arresto domiciliario y obtuvo un escaño en la Cámara de Diputados. Sigue liderando la oposición a los gobernantes autoritarios y se espera que se postule para la presidencia del país.

Swahili > suajili Cultura del este de África que emergió alrededor del año 1000 d. C.; también un idioma basado en el bantú, que mezcla palabras árabes y usa la escritura árabe.

T

Taíno > taínos Grupo indígena americano que encontró Colón cuando llegó por primera vez a las Indias Occidentales.

Taiping Rebellion > Rebelión Taiping Revuelta campesina en China.

Taj Mahal > Taj Mahal Tumba construida por Sah Jahan para su esposa.

Taliban > talibán Facción fundamentalista islámica que controló la mayor parte de Afganistán durante diez años hasta que los Estados Unidos la removió del poder en 2002.

Tang dynasty > dinastía Tang Dinastía china que gobernó de 618 a 907.

Tang Taizong > Tang Taizong Tang Taizong (598–649) fue un consumado general, reformador del gobierno, historiador, erudito de la sabiduría de Confucio y artista. Estas cualidades y habilidades le ayudaron a ser el emperador más admirado de China.

tariff > arancel Impuesto a mercancías importadas.

technology > tecnología Habilidades y herramientas que las personas usan para satisfacer sus necesidades básicas.

Tehran > Teherán Capital de la dinastía Qajar y del actual Irán.

temperance movement > movimento por la templanza Movimiento encausado a eliminar el abuso del alcohol y los problemas que éste genera.

tenant farmer > granjero arrendatario Alguien que paga renta a un señor para cultivar parte de la tierra del señor.

tenement > vecindad Edificios de varios pisos divididos en apartamentos para alojar a tantos residentes como sea posible.

Tennis Court Oath > Juramento del juego de pelota Famoso juramento hecho en una cancha de frontón por los miembros del Tercer Estado en la Francia prerrevolucionaria.

Tenochtitlán > Tenochtitlán Capital del Imperio Azteca sobre la cual se construyó la actual Ciudad de México.

Teotihuacán > Teotihuacán Ciudad que dominó el valle de México desde alrededor del año 200 d. C. hasta el año 750 d. C.; influyó en la cultura de los pueblos mesoamericanos posteriores.

Teresa, Mother > Teresa, Madre La Madre Teresa (bautizada en 1910, murió en 1997) fue la fundadora de origen rumano de la Orden de las Misioneras de la Caridad, un grupo católico romano dedicado a ayudar a los pobres, especialmente a los de India. Ganó el Premio Nobel de la Paz en 1979, y también fue honrada por su trabajo por el gobierno indio. Fue beatificada, o nombrada bendita, por la Iglesia católica romana en 2003 por toda una vida comprometida con aquellos que sufren necesidades.

terrorism > terrorismo Uso deliberado de la violencia indiscriminada, especialmente en contra de civiles, para lograr fines políticos.

Tet Offensive > ofensiva del Tet Ofensiva masiva y sangrienta de las guerrillas comunistas contra las fuerzas estadounidenses y las de Vietnam del Sur durante el Tet, el año nuevo vietnamita, en 1968. Influyó a que la opinión pública estadounidense se opusiera a la intervención militar en Vietnam.

Thatcher, Margaret > Thatcher, Margaret Margaret Thatcher (1925–2013) fue la primera mujer en ocupar el cargo de primera ministra en Gran Bretaña, de 1979 a 1990. Thatcher era conservadora y una firme opositora al socialismo, al que consideraba como antibritánico porque erosionaba la autoconfianza. Bajo Thatcher, el gobierno británico vendió las industrias nacionalizadas a empresas privadas. Thatcher también lideró al país durante la Guerra de las Malvinas (1982) contra Argentina.

theocracy > teocracia Gobierno administrado por líderes religiosos.

Theodora > Teodora Teodora (497–548) fue la esposa del emperador Justiniano y su más leal consejera. Conocida por su poderosa inteligencia y astuta perspectiva política, Teodora ejerció una influencia decisiva en los asuntos políticos bizantinos. Su nombre se menciona en casi todas las leyes aprobadas durante el reinado de Justiniano. Ella usó su posición y poder para sus intereses, entre ellos ser una pionera en los esfuerzos a favor de los derechos de las mujeres. Respaldó sólidas leyes para terminar el tráfico de mujeres jóvenes y revisó las leyes de divorcio a favor de más beneficios para las mujeres.

Third Reich > Tercer Reich Nombre oficial del partido nazi durante su mandato en Alemania; mantuvo el poder de 1933 a 1945.

38th parallel > paralelo 38 Línea imaginaria que marca los 38 grados de latitud, en particular la línea que cruza la península coreana, que dividía las fuerzas soviéticas al norte y las fuerzas estadounidenses al sur, después de la Segunda Guerra Mundial.

Thutmose III > Tutmosis III (1504 a. C.–1426 a. C.) Tutmosis III compartió el poder con su tía la reina Hatshepsut antes de ser faraón. Luchó contra Siria y Palestina para recuperar el gobierno egipcio y creó la mayor dinastía de Egipto.

Tiahuanaco > Tiahuanaco Cultura preincaica que tuvo su apogeo en la región andina desde alrededor de 200 d. C. a 1000 d. C.

Tiananmen Square > Plaza de Tiananmen Inmensa plaza pública en el centro de Beijing, la capital de China.

Tiberius > Tiberio Tiberio (alrededor de 163 a. C.–133 a. C.) fue un plebeyo romano que llegó a ser tribuno y cabildeó para lograr una reforma del gobierno. Fue asesinado en el año 133 a. C. por matones contratados por los senadores romanos.

Tojo, Hideki > Tōjō, Hideki Hideki Tōjō (1884–1948) nació en Tokio y fue militar de carrera. Fue general del ejército del Imperio Japonés y el 40° primer ministro de Japón durante la mayor parte de la Segunda Guerra Mundial, de 1941 a 1945. Fue directamente responsable del ataque a Pearl Harbor, y fue arrestado y sentenciado a muerte acusado de crímenes de guerra japoneses.

Tokugawa > Tokugawa Los sogún, descendientes de Tokugawa Ieyasu (1542–1616), eran líderes militares supremos; gobernaron Japón de 1603 a 1869; reunificaron Japón y establecieron el orden después de un siglo de guerra civil y disturbios.

Tokyo > Tokio Capital de Japón.

Torah > Tora El texto más sagrado de la Biblia hebrea que incluye sus cinco primeros libros.

total war > guerra total Tipo de guerra en la que todos los objetivos son atacados, incluidos los civiles y las líneas de suministro.

totalitarian state > estado totalitario Gobierno en el que una dictadura de partido único regula todos los aspectos de la vida de los ciudadanos.

Touré, Samori > Touré, Samori Samori Touré (c. 1830–1900) fue un líder militar musulmán que fundó un poderoso reino en África occidental, en la región del río Nilo y luchó contra el ejército francés.

tournament > torneo Batalla simulada en la que los caballeros competían entre ellos para lucir sus destrezas de lucha.

trade deficit > déficit comercial Situación en la que un país importa más de lo que exporta.

trade surplus > superávit comercial Situación en la cual las exportaciones de bienes y servicios de un país son más altas que las importaciones.

traditional economy > economía tradicional Sistema económico que depende del hábito, la costumbre o los rituales y tiende a no cambiar con el tiempo.

tragedy > tragedia En la antigua Grecia, obra de teatro sobre el sufrimiento humano que termina, por lo general, en un desastre.

Treaty of Paris > Tratado de París Tratado de paz de 1763 que finalizó la Guerra de los Siete Años y culminó con el dominio británico de las Americas.

Treaty of Tordesillas > Tratado de Tordesillas Tratado firmado por España y Portugal en 1494 por el que se dividían entre ellos el mundo fuera de Europa.

triangular trade > comercio triangular Ruta colonial de comercio entre Europa y sus colonias en las Indias Occidentales y África, en donde las mercancías se cambiaban por esclavos.

tribune > tribuno Funcionario elegido por los plebeyos para proteger sus intereses.

tributary state > estado tributario Estado independiente que debe reconocer la supremacía de otro estado y pagar tributo a su gobernante.

tribute > tributo Pago que los conquistadores podían obligar a pagar a los pueblos conquistados.

Trojan War > Guerra de Troya Conflicto militar que surgió alrededor del año 1250 a. C. entre Micenas y Troya, una rica ciudad comercial en lo que hoy es Turquía; descrito en los poemas épicos de Homero, la *Ilíada* y la *Odisea*.

troubadour > trovador Poeta o cantante itinerante de la Europa medieval.

Truman Doctrine > Doctrina Truman Promesa del presidente Truman de ayudar a las naciones en lucha contra los movimientos comunistas.

Truman, Harry > Truman, Harry Harry Truman (1884–1972) era vicepresidente de los Estados Unidos cuando Roosevelt murió y se convirtió en el 33° Presidente después de la muerte de Roosevelt. Después de estar en el cargo durante solo unos cuantos meses, Truman tomó la decisión de lanzar las bombas atómicas sobre Japón.

Truth, Sojourner > Truth, Sojourner Sojourner Truth (1797–1883) fue una de las mujeres afroamericanas más conocidas del siglo XIX. Nació esclava y cuando ganó su libertad en 1826, cambió su nombre a Sojourner Truth. En 1843, comenzó a viajar por el país para difundir la verdad sobre la injusticia y abogar por los derechos humanos. Truth fue una figura importante en varios movimientos —entre ellos el movimiento de los derechos de las mujeres, la templanza, la igualdad racial y la reforma de las prisiones— y no temía pedir reformas al gobierno.

tsunami > tsunami Ola enorme y destructiva causada por un terremoto o vientos muy fuertes.

Tudor, Mary > Tudor, María María Tudor (1516–1558) fue la primera reina en gobernar Inglaterra por derecho propio. Hija de Enrique VIII y de su primera esposa, Catalina de Aragón, María fue una devota católica que no logró acabar con la oleada de la Reforma Protestante en Inglaterra. Su activa persecución contra los protestantes le valieron el apodo de "María la Sanguinaria".

turnpike > camino de peaje Camino construido por una compañía privada que cobra una cuota por su uso.

Tutsis > tutsis Principal grupo étnico minoritario de Ruanda y Burundi.

Tutu, Desmond > Tutu, Desmond Desmond Tutu (1931–) es un arzobispo de la Iglesia Anglicana y fue líder de la lucha en contra del apartheid en Sudáfrica. En 1984 ganó el Premio Nobel de la Paz por sus esfuerzos.

Tutu, Osei > Tutu, Osei Osei Tutu nació alrededor de 1660 y murió a principios del siglo XVIII. Fue fundador y primer gobernante del Imperio Asante en lo que hoy en día es Ghana. Comenzó como el jefe del pequeño estado de Kumasi, pero se dio cuenta de que los pequños reinos asantes independientes tenían que unirse para protegerse de los poderosos vecinos Denkiera.

Twenty-One Demands > Veintiuna Exigencias Lista de exigencias dadas por Japón a China en 1915 por las que, si hubiera estado de acuerdo, China se habría convertido en un protectorado de Japón.

tyrant > tirano En la antigua Grecia, gobernante que obtenía el poder por la fuerza.

U

U-boat > U boot Submarino alemán.

ultimatum > ultimátum Serie final de exigencias.

ultranationalist > ultranacionalista Nacionalista extremo.

Umayyad > omeyas Miembros de la dinastía sunita de califas que gobernó de 661 a 750.

United Nations (UN) > Organización de las) Naciones Unidas (ONU) Organización internacional fundada en 1945 al final de la Segunda Guerra Mundial. Desde entonces, su rol global ha crecido e incluye economía y desarrollo social, derechos humanos, ayuda humanitaria y derecho internacional.

universal manhood suffrage > sufragio universal masculino Derecho de todos los hombres adultos a votar.

untouchable > intocable Marginados o miembros de la casta más baja de India.

Urban II, Pope > Urbano II, papa El papa Urbano II (1042–1099) fue el líder de la Iglesia católica romana en la época en la que los turcos selyúcidas amenazaban el Imperio Bizantino. Convocó el Concilio de Clermont, donde lanzó la Primera Cruzada para liberar Tierra Santa a los musulmanes.

urban renewal > renovación urbana Programas gubernamentales para el desarrollo de las áreas urbanas.

urbanization > urbanización Movimiento de personas de las áreas rurales a las ciudades.

Usman dan Fodio > Usman dan Fodio Usman dan Fodio (1754–1817) fue un líder revolucionario, místico y filósofo fulani. Lideró una revuelta (1804–1808) para crear un nuevo estado musulmán, el Imperio Fulani, en lo que ahora es el norte de Nigeria.

usury > usura Práctica de prestar dinero a interés.

utilitarianism > utilitarismo Idea de que el objetivo de la sociedad debería ser lograr la mayor felicidad para el mayor número de personas.

utopian > utópico Idealista o visionario; normalmente se usa para describir una sociedad perfecta.

V

V-E Day > Día V-E Día de la Victoria en Europa, el 8 de mayo de 1945, fecha en que los Aliados vencieron en Europa durante la Segunda Guerra Mundial.

Valley of Mexico > valle de México Valle en México en el cual se desarrollaron numerosas civilizaciones mesoamericanas, incluyendo los aztecas.

van Gogh, Vincent > van Gogh, Vincent Vincent van Gogh (1853–1890) fue un artista durante solo diez años, pero produjo más de 2,000 dibujos, bocetos y pinturas. Desde el principio, los impresionistas influyeron mucho en su estilo. Más tarde se trasladó a Arles, Francia. Mientras estaba allí tuvo un colapso nervioso y él mismo pidió que le internaran en un hospital psiquiátrico. Durante este tiempo, comenzó a usar colores más llamativos, pinceladas amplias, movimiento en formas y líneas y gruesas capas de pintura. Fue dado de alta en mayo de 1890 y murió dos meses más tarde.

vanguard > vanguardia Grupo de líderes de la élite.

vassal > vasallo Durante la Edad Media, señor a quien se le cedía un terreno a cambio de servicio y lealtad al señor más importante.

Vedas > Vedas Conjunto de oraciones, himnos y otras enseñanzas religiosas desarrolladas en la antigua India a partir de alrededor del siglo XVI a. C.

veneration > veneración Consideración especial.

vernacular > vernáculo Lenguaje diario de la gente común.

Versailles > Versalles Residencia de la realeza francesa y sede de gobierno establecidos por el rey Luis XIV.

veto > veto Bloqueo a la acción de un gobierno.

viceroy > virrey Representante del rey de España que gobernaba las colonias en su nombre.

Vichy > Vichy Ciudad en el centro de Francia desde donde un gobierno títere dirigió la Francia no ocupada y las colonias francesas.

Victoria, Queen > Victoria, reina La reina Victoria (1819–1901) reinó de 1837 a 1901, el reinado más largo de la historia de Inglaterra. Simbolizó la vida inglesa durante el periodo conocido como la época victoriana. Fijó un tono de respetabilidad moral y estrictos modales sociales. Iniciadora de las tendencias entre la creciente clase media, introdujo costumbres como poner el árbol de Navidad (una costumbre alemana) y llevar un vestido de boda blanco.

Viet Cong > Vietcong Rebeldes comunistas sudvietnamitas que hicieron guerra de guerrillas que buscó derrocar al gobierno de Vietnam del Sur; recibió ayuda de Vietnam del Norte.

Vikings > vikingo Pueblo escandinavo cuyos marineros asaltaron Europa durante los siglos VIII al XII.

Virgil > Virgilio Virgilio (70 a. C.–19 a. C.) fue un poeta romano que escribió la *Eneida* en el año 30 a. C. Estudió matemáticas y otros temas en Roma y Nápoles y se inspiró en los poetas griegos.

vizier > visir Primer ministro que supervisaba los asuntos de gobierno en el antiguo Egipto.

Voltaire > Voltaire Voltaire (1694–1778) al nacer recibió el nombre de François-Marie Arouet, pero fue conocido como Voltaire. Fue un apasionado poeta, historiador, ensayista y filósofo que escribió con mordaz sarcasmo y aguda inteligencia. Voltaire fue enviado a la prisión de La Bastilla dos veces debido a sus críticas a las autoridades francesas y finalmente fue expulsado de París. Cuando pudo regresar a Francia, escribió sobre libertad política y religiosa. Voltaire pasó su vida luchando contra aquellos que consideraba enemigos de la libertad, como la ignorancia, la superstición y la intolerancia.

W

Walesa, Lech > Walesa, Lech Lech Walesa (n. 1943) ayudó a fundar y dirigir el sindicato independiente polaco, Solidaridad, en el Astillero Lenin en Gdansk, donde era electricista. Después de las enérgicas medidas que el gobierno polaco tomó sobre Solidaridad en 1981, fue encarcelado durante casi un año. Walesa fue premiado con el Premio Nobel de la Paz en 1983. Después de la caída del régimen comunista en Polonia, Walesa fue electo presidente de Polonia desde 1990 hasta 1995.

War of the Austrian Succession > Guerra de Sucesión Austriaca Serie de guerras en las que diversos países europeos lucharon por la hegemonía en Centroeuropa después de la muerte de Carlos IV, emperador Habsburgo.

warlords > señores de la guerra Gobernantes militares locales.

warm-water port > puerto de aguas templadas Puerto en el que sus aguas nunca se congelan a lo largo del año.

Warsaw Pact > Pacto de Varsovia Alianza de mutua defensa establecida en 1955 entre la Unión Soviética y siete estados satélite en Europa del Este

Washington, George > Washington, George George Washington (1732–1799) fue un acaudalado hacendado de Virginia antes de ser el comandante del ejército americano durante la Guerra de Independencia y primer Presidente de los Estados Unidos. Poseía una gran propiedad llamada Mount Vernon. Usando sus habilidades como político, negociador y general, Washington pudo mantener viva la causa americana de la libertad durante y después de la guerra.

Watt, James > Watt, James James Watt (1736–1819) de Escocia inventó la máquina de vapor. Desarrolló primero un interés por construir modelos y medir instrumentos en el taller de su padre, que construía casas y barcos. Watt fue aprendiz con un fabricante de instrumentos matemáticos. En 1765, trabajó en su máquina de vapor. Tenía un condensador independiente que ayudaba a impedir que se escapara el vapor. Más tarde, trabajó como topógrafo y luego volvió a inventar y perfeccionar máquinas, hasta su retiro en 1800.

weapon of mass destruction (WMD) > arma de destrucción masiva Arma nuclear, biológica o química.

welfare state > estado de bienestar Un país con una economía de mercado, pero con una mayor responsabilidad del gobierno hacia las necesidades sociales y económicas de su pueblo.

westernization > occidentalización Adopción de ideas, tecnología y cultura occidentales.

Whitney, Eli > Whitney, Eli Eli Whitney (1765–1825) mostró tener habilidades mecánicas y de ingeniería desde temprana edad. Después de graduarse de la Universidad de Yale, se dirigió hacia el sur donde los propietarios de plantaciones supieron de su habilidad mecánica y le pidieron ayuda. El costo de la mano de obra para procesar el algodón era demasiado alto. En respuesta,Whitney inventó la desmotadora, que revolucionó la industria textil y ayudó a la economía del Sur. Lamentablemente, Whitney no sacó beneficios de su invento. Dejó el Sur lleno de deudas pero siguió diseñando inventos hasta su muerte.

William II > Guillermo II Guillermo II (1859–1941) fue el último emperador alemán y rey de Prusia. Gobernó el Imperio Alemán y el reino de Prusia de 1888 a 1918. Llevó a Alemania a la Primera Guerra Mundial. Fue un líder militar ineficaz y perdió el apoyo de su ejército; en noviembre de 1918 huyó al exilio en los Países Bajos.

William the Conqueror > Guillermo el Conquistador Guillermo el Conquistador (1028–1087) fue duque de Normandía a los 7 años de edad y nombrado caballero a los 15. Presionó al rey Eduardo de Inglaterra para que lo nombrara heredero del trono. Después de la muerte de Eduardo, Guillermo invadió Inglaterra y ganó el trono después de la batalla de Hastings en 1066.

Wittenberg > Wittenberg Ciudad al norte de Alemania donde Lutero redactó sus 95 tesis.

women's suffrage > sufragio femenino Derecho de las mujeres a votar.

Wordsworth, William > Wordsworth, William William Wordsworth (1770–1850) fue decisivo en el surgimiento del Romanticismo y escribió algunos de los poemas más influyentes de la literatura occidental. Mientras viajaba por Europa, se encontró con la Revolución Francesa, que despertó en él un interés en las preocupaciones del "hombre común". Su simpatía por la gente y el reconocimiento de las desgracias sociales, particularmente en las zonas urbanas, le sirvieron de inspiración para su obra y su fuerte enfoque en las emociones. También inspiró su punto de vista del papel del poeta en la sociedad y sus ideales políticos.

World Trade Organization (WTO) > Organización Mundial del Comercio (OMC) Organización internacional formada para estimular el comercio mundial.

Wright, Orville and Wilbur > Wright, Orville y Wilbur Orville (1871–1948) y Wilbur (1867–1912) Wright fueron mecánicos de bicicletas que usaron sus conocimientos de ciencia y su experiencia como mecánicos para crear la primera máquina voladora. Después de casi 1,000 vuelos en planeadores y pruebas en túneles de viento, los hermanos construyeron un avión a motor. El 17 de diciembre de 1903, los hermanos probaron su máquina en Kitty Hawk, Carolina del Norte. El primer vuelo duró 12 segundos; ese día el vuelo más largo duró 59 segundos.

Wudi > Wudi Wudi (156 a. C.–87 a. C.) recibió al nacer el nombre de Liu Che. Fue el onceavo hijo de Jingdi, el emperador Han y, por tanto, no hubiera estado destinado a gobernar. Sin embargo, la influencia de sus parientes cambió esto y fue nombrado emperador en el año 141 a. C. Determinado a ampliar el gobierno de su dinastía, tuvo éxito, aunque a un gran costo de soldados y gente. Liu Che hizo de la doctrina de Confucio la religión de estado. Después de su muerte recibió el título de Wudi (Emperador Marcial).

Y

Yalta Conference > Conferencia de Yalta Reunión entre Roosevelt, Churchill y Stalin realizada en febrero de 1945 en la que los tres líderes llegaron a acuerdos para finalizar la Segunda Guerra Mundial.

Yathrib > Yathrib Destino final de la hégira de Mahoma y hogar de la primera comunidad de musulmanes; posteriormente rebautizada como Medina; ubicada en el noroeste de la actual Arabia Saudita.

Yorktown, Virginia > Yorktown, Virginia Lugar donde el ejército británico se rindió en la Guerra de Independencia.

Yuan dynasty > dinastía Yuan Dinastía china gobernada por los mongoles de 1279 a 1368; su gobernante más conocido fue Kublai Khan.

Z

zaibatsu > zaibatsu Familias japonesas de banqueros e industriales poderosos desde finales del siglo XIX.

Zapata, Emiliano > Zapata, Emiliano Emiliano Zapata (1879–1919) creció como campesino. En 1897 comenzó una larga lucha contra el sistema de haciendas para recuperar la tierra a los campesinos. Después de que Francisco Madero perdiera las elecciones frente a Porfirio Díaz, Zapata se unió a la revolución y luchó a favor de la reforma social. Zapata formó un fuerte grupo de seguidores y desempeñó un papel esencial en la derrota de Victoriano Huerta en 1914. Después de que Venustiano Carranza fuera electo presidente, este se volvió contra Zapata. Los revolucionarios de Zapata fueron a la guerra con los moderados que apoyaban a Carranza. En 1919, el ejército de Carranza emboscó y mató a Zapata.

zemstvo > zemstvos Asamblea local electa que se estableció en Rusia en la época de Alejandro II.

Zen > zen Práctica de meditación; escuela del budismo en Japón.

zeppelin > zepelín Dirigible, globo grande lleno de gas.

Zheng He > Cheng Ho Cheng Ho (c. 1371–1433) fue un diplomático y almirante de la Marina china de los Ming que hizo su primer viaje en 1405 a Vietnam, India y África para explorar y comerciar. Su enorme flota de cientos de juncos (barcos chinos) y miles de marineros llevaron seda, porcelana y artesanías lacadas para intercambiar por perlas, especias, marfil y madera. Cheng Ho hizo en total siete viajes, explorando y comercializando con éxito y, por tanto, motivando a los mercaderes chinos a establecer centros de comercio en el sureste de Asia e India.

ziggurat > zigurat Templo piramidal de la antigua Mesopotamia dedicado al dios o diosa principal de una ciudad-estado.

Zionism > sionismo Movimiento dedicado a la reconstrucción del estado judío en Palestina.

Zoroaster > Zaratustra Zaratustra (alrededor del año 628 a. C.–551 a. C.) Zaratustra fue un reformador religioso iraní y fundador del zaratustrismo. Enfatizó la libertad individual para elegir lo correcto de lo incorrecto y la responsabilidad individual de las acciones de cada uno. Las ideas de Zaratustra influyeron en los primeros tiempos de la filosofía.

A

B

G

H

I

J

M

N

O

P

Q

R

S

U

V

W

Y

Z

Photography

CVR: Andrew Marriott/Moment/Getty Images; **iii:** Fotomak/Shutterstock; **v:** Goodluz/Shutterstock; **vii:** Fuse/Getty Images; **viii:** The Print Collector/Alamy; **x:** Larry Lilac/Alamy Stock Photo; **xi:** Scala/Art Resource, NY; **xii:** World History Archive/Alamy; **xiii:** Stuart Forster/Alamy; **xiv:** Derek Bayes/Lebrecht Music & Arts/Lebrecht Music & Arts/Corbis; **xv:** Susan Law Cain/Shutterstock; **xvi:** Chronicle/Alamy Stock Photo; **xvii:** Bettmann/Corbis; **xviii:** Robert Maass/Corbis; **xix:** Daniel Irungu/EPA/Newscom; **xx:** Massimo_g/Fotolia; **xxx:** North Wind Picture Archives/Alamy Stock Photo; **xxxi:** Pearson Education Ltd.; **xxxii:** Derek Bayes/Lebrecht Music & Arts/Lebrecht Music & Arts/Corbis; **xxxiiiB:** Bibliotheque des Arts Decoratifs, Paris, France/Archives Charmet/Bridgeman Images; **xxxiiiT:** Everett Collection Historical/Alamy Stock Photo; **xxxiT:** National Geographic Image Collection/Alamy Stock Photo; **xxxiv:** AP Images; **xxxvB:** NataliaBratslavsky/Shutterstock; **xxxvi:** zimmytws/Fotolia; **xxxvii:** Bettmann/Corbis; **xxxvT:** Chronicle/Alamy Stock Photo; **000–001:** Larry Lilac/Alamy Stock Photo; **002L:** SuperStock/Alamy Stock Photo; **002R:** Lordprice Collection/Alamy Stock Photo; **003:** GlowImages/Alamy Stock Photo; **004:** Chris Howes/Wild Places Photography/Alamy Stock Photo; **008:** SuperStock/Alamy Stock Photo; **014:** Mary Evans Picture Library/Alamy Stock Photo; **015T:** DeaPicture Library/De Agostini Editore/Age Fotostock; **015B:** Dinodia Photos/Alamy Stock Photo; **016T:** DINODIA/Age Fotostock; **016B:** Pitchaya Thammasamisorn/Alamy Stock Photo; **021:** Dorling Kindersley Ltd/Alamy Stock Photo; **022:** Jess Kraft/Shutterstock; **025:** Richard A. Cooke/Corbis; **026:** Peter Phipp/Travelshots.com/Alamy Stock Photo; **027T:** De Agostini Picture L/Age Fotostock; **027B:** Ancient Art & Architecture Collection Ltd/Alamy Stock Photo; **029:** Erich Lessing/Art Resource, NY; **031:** RMN-Grand Palais/Art Resource, NY; **032:** North Wind Picture Archives/Alamy Stock Photo; **034:** Erich Lessing/Art Resource, NY; **035T:** Alan Williams/Dorling Kindersley; **035B:** Hemis/Alamy Stock Photo; **037:** Gianni Dagli Orti/The Art Archive at Art Resource, NY; **038:** Private Collection/Index/Bridgeman Images; **043:** North Wind Picture Archives/The Image Works; **045:** North Wind Picture Archives/Alamy; **046T:** Oronoz/Album/Superstock; **046B:** De Agostini Picture Library/Getty Images; **047:** Vadim kozlovsky/Shutterstock; **049T:** Corbis; **049B:** Kristina Postnikova/Shutterstock; **051:** The Trustees of the British Museum/Art Resource, NY; **052:** Universal Images Group/Art Resource, NY; **060T:** André Held/akg-images; **060B:** The Art Archive/Alamy Stock Photo; **061:** John Warburton Lee/Superstock; **062:** DeAgostini/Superstock; **064T:** British Library/Robana via Getty Images; **064B:** Werner Forman/Art Resource, NY; **067T:** Rick Browne/Photo Researchers, Inc.; **067B:** Peter Horree/Alamy Stock Photo; **068T:** Cristiano Burmester/Alamy Stock Photo; **068B:** Culver Pictures, Inc./Superstock; **070:** Gianni Dagli Orti/The Art Archive/Alamy Stock Photo; **072:** WorldPhotos/Alamy Stock Photo; **073:** Antiquarian Images/Alamy Stock Photo; **075:** akg-images/The Image Works; **077:** North Wind Picture Archives/Alamy Stock Photo; **078:** Mary Evans Picture Library/Alamy Stock Photo; **080:** Album/Art Resource, NY; **085:** De Agostini Picture Library/Getty Images; **088:** Jess Kraft/Shutterstock; **091:** Peter Brown/KRT/Newscom; **096–097:** Scala/Art Resource, NY; **098T:** Erich Lessing/Art Resource, NY; **098B:** Gianni Dagli Orti/The Art Archive/Art Resource, NY; **099:** Granger, NYC/Alamy Stock Photo; **100:** Erich Lessing/Art Resource, NY; **101:** Reich, Jacques/Copyright by Lea Brothers & Company/Library of Congress; **102T:** Paul M.R. Maeyaert/akg-images; **102B:** akg-images; **104:** Peter Horree/Alamy Stock Photo; **105T:** akg-images; **105B:** Gianni Dagli Orti/The Art Archive at Art Resource, NY; **107T:** Forget Patrick/SAGAPHOTO.COM/Alamy Stock Photo; **107B:** Jose Ignacio Soto/Shutterstock; **108:** North Wind Picture Archives/Alamy Stock Photo; **109:** De Agostini/Getty Images; **111:** De Agostini Pict.Lib./M. Seemuller/akg-images; **112:** Dea/G. Dagli Orti/De Agostini/Getty Images; **113T:** Sovfoto/Universal Images Group/Getty Images; **113B:** Image Asset Management Ltd/Superstock; **114T:** The Art Gallery Collection/Alamy Stock Photo; **114B:** akg-images; **115T:** State Central Navy Museum/St. Petersburg/Bridgeman Images; **115B:** akg-images; **118:** akg-images; **119T:** Glasshouse Images/Alamy Stock Photo; **119B:** Lebrecht Music and Arts Photo Library/Alamy Stock Photo; **120:** Copley, John Singleton (1738–1815)/Boston Public Library, Boston, Massachusetts, USA/Bridgeman Images; **121T:** Ernest Crofts/The Bridgeman Art Library/Getty Images; **121B:** akg-images; **123:** Universal History Archive/Getty Images/Universal Images Group/Getty Images; **125:** Balthasar Nebot/Getty Images; **126:** The Print Collector/Alamy Stock Photo; **128:** National Geographic Image Collection/Alamy Stock Photo; **129:** Stefano Bianchetti/Corbis; **131:** Tate, London/Art Resource, NY; **132:** North Wind Picture Archives/Alamy Stock Photo; **133:** SuperStock/Superstock; **134:** Pictorial Press Ltd/Alamy; **135:** Fine Art Images/Age Fotostock; **136:** Peter Horree/Alamy Stock Photo; **137:** GL Archive/Alamy Stock Photo; **138:** North Wind Picture Archives/Alamy Stock Photo; **140:** akg-images; **141:** Everett Collection Inc/Alamy Stock Photo; **142T:** UniversalImagesGroup/Universal History Archive/Getty Images; **142B:** Onur ERSIN/Shutterstock; **144:** Lebrecht Music and Arts Photo Library/Alamy Stock Photo; **146:** Mary Evans Picture Library/Alamy Stock Photo; **147T:** RMN-Grand Palais/Art Resource, NY; **147B:** Thomas Naudet/Getty Images; **149:** Stefano Bianchetti/Corbis; **150:** Gianni Dagli Orti/The Art Archive/Art Resource, NY; **151:** Hulton Archive/Getty Images; **152T:** The Gallery Collection/Corbis; **152B:** akg-images; **154:** akg-images; **155:** The Gallery Collection/Corbis; **157:** Mary Evans Picture Library/Age Fotostock; **159:** The Art Gallery Collection/Alamy Stock Photo; **160:** Classic Vision/Age Fotostock/Superstock; **162:** Nick Hanna/Alamy; **164:** Laurent Lecat/akg-images; **165:** The Print Collector/Alamy Stock Photo; **167T:** The Gallery Collection/Corbis; **167B:** SuperStock/Alamy Stock Photo; **168T:** Prisma Archivo/Alamy Stock Photo; **168B:** The Print Collector/Alamy Stock Photo; **169:** Mary Evans Picture Library/Alamy Stock Photo; **172:** Gianni Dagli Orti/The Art Archive/Art Resource, NY; **174:** World History Archive/Newscom; **175:** GL Archive/Alamy Stock Photo; **178–179:** World History Archive/Alamy Stock Photo; **180T:** North Wind Picture Archives/Alamy Stock Photo; **180B:** Eileen Tweedy/The Art Archive/Art Resource, NY; **181:** Album/Art Resource; **182:** Everett Collection/Superstock; **183:** American School, (19th century)/Private Collection/Ancient Art and Architecture Collection Ltd./Bridgeman Images; **184:** North Wind Picture Archives/Alamy Stock Photo; **187T:** Doughty, C.L. (1913–85)/Private Collection/Look and Learn/Bridgeman Images; **187B:** ClassicStock.com/Superstock; **189:** Glasshouse Images/Alamy Stock Photo; **190:** Pantheon/Superstock; **192:** Niday Picture Library/Alamy Stock Photo; **193:** Corbis; **194:** Everett Collection Inc/Alamy Stock Photo; **195:** GL Archive/Alamy Stock Photo; **196T:** The Print Collector/Alamy Stock Photo; **196B:** North Wind/North Wind Picture Archives; **197:** Austrian Archives/Corbis; **199:** Everett Collection Inc/Alamy Stock Photo; **200:** Pictorial Press Ltd/Alamy Stock Photo; **201:** Archive Pics/Alamy Stock Photo; **202:** The Art Archive/Alamy Stock Photo; **204:** akg-images/The Image Works; **205:** Keystone-France/Gamma-Keystone/Getty Images; **206:** akg-images/The Image Works; **208:** Library of Congress/Photri Images/Alamy; **209:** Oote Boe 1/Alamy; **210:** Archive Pics/Alamy; **211:** Science and Society/Superstock; **212:** The Print Collector/Alamy; **213T:** Underwood & Underwood/Corbis; **213B:** The Art Gallery Collection/Alamy; **214:** V&A Images/Alamy Stock Photo; **215T:** Peter Horree/Alamy; **215B:** akg-images; **216T:** Michael Freeman/Alamy; **216B:** ArtPix/Alamy Stock Photo; **217:** Album/Art Resource, NY; **218:** Archive Pics/Alamy; **221:** BLM Collection/Alamy Stock Photo; **224–225:** Stuart Forster/Alamy Stock Photo; **226L:** Interfoto/Alamy Stock Photo; **226R:** Snark/Art Resource, NY; **227:** 19th era/Alamy; **228:** World History Archive/Alamy Stock Photo; **229T:** Pearson Education Ltd.; **229B:** Album/Prisma/Album/SuperStock; **231:** Gianni Dagli Orti/The Art Archive/Alamy Stock Photo; **232:** French School, (19th century)/Musee de la Ville de Paris, Musee Carnavalet, Paris, France/Bridgeman Images; **234:** Album/Art Resource, NY; **237:** Album/Oronoz/Album/SuperStock; **239T:** Mary Evans Picture Library/The Image Works; **239B:** Embleton, Ron (1930–88)/Private Collection/Look and Learn/Bridgeman Images; **240:** Gianni Dagli Orti/The Art Archive/Art Resource, NY; **242:** SuperStock/Superstock; **244:** Niday Picture Library/Alamy Stock Photo; **245:** Interfoto/Alamy Stock Photo; **246T:** Interfoto/Alamy Stock Photo; **246B:** World History Archive/Alamy; **247T:** akg-images; **247B:** S.M./SZ Photo/The Image Works; **248:** Interfoto/Alamy; **249:** Interfoto/Alamy; **250T:** Interfoto/Alamy; **250B:** De Agostini Picture Lib./A. De Gregorio/akg-images; **251:** The Cartoon Collector/Print Collector/Getty Images; **252:** Collection Dagli Orti/The Art Archive/Alamy; **253:** The Art Archive/Alamy Stock Photo; **254:** English School, (19th century)/London Metropolitan Archives, City of London/Bridgeman Images; **255T:** GL Archive/Alamy Stock Photo; **255B:** Scala/White Images/Art Resource, NY; **256:** North Wind Picture Archives/Alamy Stock Photo; **257T:** World History Archive/Alamy Stock Photo; **257B:** North Wind Picture Archives/Alamy Stock Photo; **258:** Everett Collection Historical/Alamy Stock Photo; **259:** 19th era/Alamy Stock Photo; **261:** Tarker/Corbis; **262:** Gianni Dagli Orti/The Art Archive/Alamy Stock Photo; **263T:** akg-images; **263B:** Interfoto/Alamy; **264:** akg-images; **265:** French Photographer, (20th century)/Musee National de l'Education, Rouen, France/Archives Charmet/Bridgeman Images; **266:** Library of Congress; **268T:** Glasshouse Images/Alamy Stock Photo; **268B:** Kurz and Allison (fl.1880–98)/Collection of the New-York Historical Society, USA/Bridgeman Images; **271:** Library of Congress; **273:** Alfredo Dagli Orti/The Art Archive/Art Resource, NY; **274:** World History Archive/Alamy; **276:** DeAgostini/Superstock; **277:** Pantheon/Superstock; **278T:** HIP/Art Resource, NY; **278B:** akg-images/The Image Works; **279T:** Snark/Art Resource, NY; **279B:** Russian Photographer, (20th century)/Private Collection/Calmann & King Ltd/Bridgeman Images; **280:** Collection Dagli Orti/The Art Archive/Alamy Stock Photo; **282:** Mary Evans Picture Library/Alamy Stock Photo; **284:** Keystone-France/Gamma-Keystone/Getty Images; **285:** Caran D'Ache, Emmanuel Poire; **288–289:** Derek Bayes/Lebrecht Music & Arts/Lebrecht Music & Arts/Corbis; **290L:** Glasshouse Images/Alamy Stock Photo; **290R:** Everett Collection Inc/Alamy Stock Photo; **291:** Getty Images; **292:** RMN-Grand Palais/Art Resource, NY; **293:** Isaac Holden & Sons' Alston, Bradford, United Kingdom/Universal History Archive/UIG/The Bridgeman Art Library; **294:** PhotoQuest/Getty Images; **295:** Schuler, Jules Theophile (1821–78) (after)/Private Collection/Bridgeman Images; **296:** Bibliotheque des Arts Decoratifs, Paris, France/Archives Charmet/Bridgeman Images; **297:** RMN-Grand Palais/Art Resource, NY; **298:** DEA picture library/Getty Images; **299T:** Classic Image/Alamy Stock Photo; **299B:** Bojan Brecelj/Corbis; **300:** English School, (19th century)/Private Collection/Bridgeman Images; **302:** Universal Images Group/Superstock; **303:** Prisma Archivo/Alamy Stock Photo; **304:** Popperfoto/Getty Images; **305:** The Art Gallery Collection/Alamy Stock Photo; **307:** Thomas Nast/CartoonStock; **308:** English Photographer, (19th century)/Private Collection/Bridgeman Images; **309:** Hulton Archive/Stringer/Getty Images; **310:** The Print Collector/Alamy Stock Photo; **311T:** Pictorial Press Ltd/Alamy Stock Photo; **311B:** British Library/Robana/Hulton Fine Art Collection/Getty Images; **312:** Haig, Axel (1835–1921)/British Library, London, UK/Bridgeman Images; **314:** Hulton-Deutsch Collection/Corbis; **315:** De Agostini Picture Library/The Bridgeman Images; **316:** The Art Archive/Art Resource, NY; **318T:** Everett Collection Historical/Alamy Stock Photo; **318B:** Snark/Art Resource, NY; **319:** Everett Collection Inc/Alamy Stock Photo; **320:** Popperfoto/Getty Images; **321:** Glasshouse Images/Alamy Stock Photo; **322:** Toyohara Chikanobu; **324T:** Rykoff Collection/Corbis; **324B:** Apic/Hulton Archive/Getty Images; **325:** Michelle Gilders/Alamy Stock Photo; **326:** The Castle of Batavia, as Seen from Kali Besar West, c.1656 (oil on canvas), Beeckman, Andries (fl.1651)/Rijksmuseum, Amsterdam, The Netherlands/Bridgeman Images; **328:** Naval Battle, (oil on canvas), Tyler, James Gale (1855–1931)/Private Collection/Photo © Christie's Images/Bridgeman Images; **329:** akg-images/Newscom; **330:** Lindsey Talbert/Alamy Stock Photo; **331:** Alinari Archives/Getty Images; **332:** Interim Archives/Getty Images; **333:** Dea/G Dagli Orti/Getty Images; **334:** World History Archive/Alamy Stock Photo; **336:** Bettmann/Corbis; **337T:** H.N. Rudd/Historical/Corbis; **337B:** Settler's Log House, 1856 (oil on canvas), Krieghoff, Cornelius (1815–72)/Art Gallery of Ontario, Toronto, Canada/Bridgeman Images; **340:** Isaac Holden & Sons' Alston, Bradford, United Kingdom/Universal History Archive/UIG/The Bridgeman Art Library, NY; **346–347:** Susan Law Cain/Shutterstock; **348T:** Bettmann/Corbis; **348B:** The Image Works; **349:** Comando Supremo, Italian Army/National Geographic Society/Corbis; **350:** Bettmann/Corbis; **351T:** DIZ Muenchen GmbH/Sueddeutsche Zeitung Photo/Alamy Stock Photo; **351B:** Mary Evans Picture Library/Alamy Stock Photo; **353:** Bettmann/Corbis; **354T:** S&M/ANSA/UIG/Getty Images; **354B:** General Photographic Agency/Getty Images; **356:** The Print Collector/Alamy; **358T:** Hulton-Deutsch Collection/Corbis; **358B:** Hulton-Deutsch Collection/Corbis; **359:** Comando Supremo, Italian Army/National Geographic Society/Corbis; **361:** akg-images/Alamy Stock Photo; **362:** Imperial War Museum/The Art Archive/Art Resource,NY; **363T:** akg-images/The Image Works; **363B:** Pictorial Press Ltd/Alamy Stock Photo; **364:** Photos 12/Alamy Stock Photo; **365T:** akg-images/Alamy Stock Photo; **365B:** Robert Hunt Library/Mary Evans/The Image Works; **368:** WW/Alamy Stock Photo; **370:** Bettmann/Corbis; **371:** Bettmann/Corbis; **373:** Hulton Archive/Stringer/Getty Images; **374:** Fine Art Images/Heritage Images/The Image Works;375: World History Archive/Alamy Stock Photo; **376:** Fine Art Images/Agefotostock; **378:** Everett Collection Historical/Alamy Stock Photo; **380:** akg-images/The Image Works; **386–387:** Chronicle/Alamy Stock Photo; **388T:** RIA Novosti/Alamy Stock Photo; **388B:** Interfoto/Alamy Stock Photo; **389:** Heritage Image Partnership Ltd/Alamy; **390:** Corbis; **391T:** Historic Collection/Alamy; **391B:** Agencia el Universal/El Universal de Mexico/Newscom; **393T:** Daniel Leclair/X00162/Reuters/Corbis; **393B:** AP Images; **395:** Emiliano Rodriguez/Alamy; **396:** FPG/Getty Images; **398T:** Sophie Bassouls/Sygma/Corbis; **398B:** Peter Horree/Alamy Stock Photo; **399T:** DIZ Muenchen GmbH/Sueddeutsche Zeitung Photo/Alamy Stock Photo; **399B:** Bettmann/Corbis; **401:** Hulton-Deutsch Collection/Corbis; **403:** Dinodia/Age Fotostock; **404T:** Yvan Travert/akg-images; **404B:** GandhiServe/Archiv Peter Rhe/akg-images; **405:** Dinodia/Age Fotostock; **407:** Interfoto/Alamy Stock Photo; **409:** Hulton Archive/Stringer/Getty Images; **410:** Age fotostock/Alamy Stock Photo; **412:** Pictorial Press Ltd/Alamy Stock Photo; **413T:** Underwood & Underwood/Corbis; **413B:** SOTK2011/Alamy; **415:** Interfoto/Alamy Stock Photo; **416:** Bettmann/Corbis; **417:** DIZ Muenchen GmbH, Sueddeutsche Zeitung Photo/Alamy; **418:** Keystone Pictures USA/Alamy Stock Photo; **419T:** Everett Collection Historical/Alamy Stock Photo; **419B:** Dennis Van Tine/LFI/Photoshot/Newscom; **420:** Painting/Alamy Stock Photo; **421T:** Mark Burnett/Alamy Stock Photo; **421B:** Hulton Archive/Stringer/Getty Images; **422:** Bettmann/Corbis; **423:** Private Collection/Peter Newark Military Pictures/Bridgeman Images; **426:** Interfoto/Alamy Stock Photo; **427:** Hulton-Deutsch Collection/Corbis; **428:** Leemage/UIG/Getty Images; **429:** Hulton-Deutsch Collection/Corbis; **430:** Stefano Bianchetti/Corbis; **431:** Hulton-Deutsch Collection/Corbis; **433T:** Fine Art Images/Heritage Images/The Image Works; **433B:** akg-images; **434:** Heritage Image Partnership Ltd/Alamy Stock Photo; **436:** Heritage Image Partnership Ltd/Alamy Stock Photo; **437:** Planet News Archive/SSPL/Getty Images; **439:** Mary Evans Picture Library/Alamy Stock Photo; **440:** SSPL/The Image Works; **441:** Interfoto/History/Alamy; **442:** SZ Photo/Scherl/The Image Works; **443:** Interfoto/Alamy Stock Photo; **446:** Corbis; **448:** Fine Art Images/Heritage Images/The Image Works; **449:** akg-images/Archiv Peter Rhe/Newscom; **452–453:** Bettmann/Corbis; **454T:** AP Images; **454B:** Roger Viollet/Getty Images; **455:** AP Images; **456:** FPG/Archive Photos/Getty Images; **457T:** David Low/British Cartoon Archive, University of Kent/Solo Syndication; **457B:** Bettmann/Corbis; **458L:** Bettmann/Corbis; **458C:** AP Images; **458R:** Everett Collection; **459T:** Robert Capa/International Center of Photography/Magnum Photos; **459B:** AP Images; **460T:** Interfoto/akg-images; **460B:** AP Images; **461:** De Agostini Picture Library/Bridgeman Images; **462:** IBL Collections/Mary Evans/Everett Collection; **464T:** The National Archives/SSPL/Getty Images; **464B:** Courtesy Everett Collection; **465:** Berliner Verlag/Archiv/picture-alliance/dpa/AP Images; **467:** Interfoto/Alamy Stock Photo; **468:** US National Archives/Alamy Stock Photo; **470:** Anne Frank Fonds Basel/Getty Images; **471:** akg-images; **473:** JIM HOLLANDER/epa/Corbis; **474:** Anne Frank Fonds Basel/Getty Images; **476:** Hulton-Deutsch Collection/Corbis; **478:** AP Images; **481:** Lightroom Photos/Alamy Stock Photo; **482:** AP Images; **484T:** Interfoto/Alamy Stock Photo; **484B:** Bettmann/Corbis; **485:** Roger Viollet/Getty Images; **486T:** Corbis; **486B:** Pictorial Press Ltd./Alamy Stock Photo; **489:** Natalia Bratslavsky/Shutterstock; **492:** IBL Collections/Mary Evans/Everett Collection; **498–499:** Robert Maass/Corbis; **500T:** Thomas Hoepker/Magnum Photos; **500B:** Library of Congress, Prints & Photographs Division, drawing by Edmund S. Valtman, LC-DIG-ppmsc-07958; **501:** Sovfoto/UIG/Getty Images; **502:** AP Images; **503:** Hulton-Deutsch Collection/Corbis; **504:** Walter Sanders/Life Magazine/The LIFE Picture Collection/Getty Images; **507:** MPI/Stringer/Getty Images; **508:** Sovfoto/UIG/Getty Images; **509:** Universal Images Group Limited/Education Images/Alamy; **511:** Bert Morgan/Getty Images; **512:** Bettmann/Corbis; **513T:** Elliott Erwitt/Magnum Photos; **513B:** AP Images; **516:** AP Images; **517T:** John Florea/The LIFE Picture Collection/Getty Images; **517B:** Jerry Cooke/Corbis; **519:** Keystone/Getty Images; **520:** Keystone-France/Gamma-Keystone/Getty Images; **521T:** AFP/Getty Images; **521B:** Edmund S. Valtman/Library of Congress; **523:** Jason Reed/Reuters/Corbis; **524:** AP Images; **525:** Horst Faas/AP Images; **527T:** JP Laffont/Sygma/Corbis; **527B:** AFP/Getty Images; **528:** Bettmann/Corbis; **529:** Sovfoto/UIG/Getty Images; **530:** Scott Stewart/AP Images; **532T:** Fabian Cevallos/Sygma/Corbis; **532B:** AP Images; **533:** MIKE PERSSON/AFP/Getty Images; **534:** Brennan Linsley/AP Images; **535:** Scott Stewart/AP Images; **538:** TM and Copyright 20th Century Fox Film Corp. All rights reserved./Courtesy Everett Collection; **540:** Imagebroker/Alamy Stock Photo; **541:** Martyn Goddard/Corbis; **544–545:** Daniel Irungu/Epa/Newscom; **546T:** Dinodia Photos/Alamy Stock Photo; **546B:** Bettmann/Corbis; **547:** Stuart Forster/Alamy; **548:** Dinodia Photos/Alamy Stock Photo; **549:** Bettmann/Corbis; **550T:** RIA Novosti/Alamy Stock Photo; **550B:** Interfoto/Alamy Stock Photo; **552T:** David Edwards/National Geographic Society/Corbis; **552B:** Mike Goldwater/Alamy Stock Photo; **553:** AP Images; **554:** Homer W Sykes/Alamy Stock Photo; **555:** Bettmann/Corbis; **556:** Stringer/Reuters/Corbis; **557:** Homer W Sykes/Alamy Stock Photo; **559:** Bettmann/Corbis; **560:** Tommy Trenchard/Alamy; **562:** Bettmann/Corbis; **563:** Bettmann/Corbis; **564:** Gallo Images/Alamy Stock Photo; **565T:** Stuart

Forster/Alamy Stock Photo; **565B:** Eddie Gerald/Alamy Stock Photo; **567:** Bettmann/Corbis; **569:** Dbimages/Alamy Stock Photo; **571T:** Bettmann/Corbis; **571B:** David S. Boyer/Bettmann/Corbis; **572T:** Art Directors & TRIP/Alamy Stock Photo; **572B:** Bettmann/Corbis; **573T:** Claudia Wiens/Alamy Stock Photo; **573B:** Stefano Politi Markovina/Alamy Stock Photo; **575T:** AVI Pictures/Alamy Stock Photo; **575B:** Claudia Wiens/Alamy Stock Photo; **577:** Peter Jordan/Alamy Stock Photo; **579:** AFP/Getty Images; **580:** Bernard Bisson/Sygma/Corbis; **584:** Dinodia Photos/Alamy Stock Photo; **587:** Farooq Khan/EPA/Newscom; **590–591:** massimo_g/Fotolia; **592T:** Greg Marinovich/Africa Media Online/The Image Works; **593:** Thakala/Fotolia; **594:** Thakala/Fotolia; **596:** Dinodia Photos/Alamy Stock Photo; **597:** National Geographic Image Collection/Alamy Stock Photo; **599:** Greg Marinovich/Africa Media Online/The Image Works; **600:** Baileys Archive/africanpictures/The Image Works; **601:** Hutchison Archive/Eye Ubiquitous/Alamy Stock Photo; **603T:** Micheline Pelletier/Corbis; **603B:** Thelma Sanders/Eye Ubiquitous/Alamy Stock Photo; **605:** Greg Marinovich/Africa Media Online/The Image Works; **607:** Jane Sweeney/Corbis; **608:** Reuters/Corbis; **609:** jeremy sutton-hibbert/Alamy Stock Photo; **610:** Madeleine Jettre/dbimages/Alamy Stock Photo; **611:** Tim Graham/Alamy Stock Photo; **612:** epa european pressphoto agency b.v./Alamy Stock Photo; **614T:** Stephen Bisgrove/Alamy Stock Photo; **614B:** Horacio Villalobos/Corbis; **615:** Alain Keler/Sygma/Corbis; **616:** Peter Turnley/Corbis; **617T:** Les Stone/The Image Works; **617B:** Bettmann/Corbis; **618:** Micheline Pelletier/Sygma/Corbis; **619:** leeyiutung/Fotolia; **622:** Epa european pressphoto agency b.v./Alamy Stock Photo; **627:** Dinodia Photos/Alamy Stock Photo; **630:** Dereje Belachew/Alamy Stock Photo; **631T:** Greg Balfour Evans/Alamy Stock Photo; **631B:** David Hoffman Photo Library/Alamy Stock Photo; **632:** Werli Francois/Alamy Stock Photo; **634:** Irene Abdou/Alamy; **635T:** FPG/Getty Images; **635B:** Bryan Denton/Corbis; **636T:** Joerg Boethling/Alamy Stock Photo; **636B:** Jeff Greenberg/Alamy Stock Photo; **637T:** Imagebroker/Superstock; **637B:** US Coast Guard Photo/Alamy Stock Photo; **638:** BrazilPhotos.com/Alamy Stock Photo; **640:** FPG/Getty Images; **642:** AP Images; **643T:** Caren Firouz/Reuters/Corbis; **643B:** Rafael Ben Ari/Fotolia; **644:** AP Images; **645:** Patrick Robert/Corbis; **646:** Dacology/Alamy Stock Photo; **647:** AP Images; **648:** Interfoto/Alamy Stock Photo; **649:** NASA Photo/Alamy Stock Photo; **650:** Pictorial Press Ltd/Alamy; **652:** dieKleinert/Alamy Stock Photo; **654:** DeAgostini/Superstock; **658:** Stock Connection Blue/Alamy Stock Photo; **696:** Bill Schorr/Cagle Cartoons, Inc

[Text Acknowledgments]

A.S. Kline, The Aeneid. Copyright © A.S. Kline; **ABC-CLIO,** U.S. Foreign Policy: A Documentary and Reference Guide by Akis Kalaitzidis and Gregory W. Streich, 2011. Copyright © ABC-CLIO, 2011; **ABC-CLIO LLC,** Genghis Khan: Founder of the Mongol Empire by David W Del Testa from Government Leaders, Military Rulers and Political Activists. Copyright © Dover Publications, Inc. Used by permission; **Agence Global,** Is the World Really Safer Without the Soviet Union? by Mikhail Gorbachev from The Nation, January 6–19, 2012. Copyright © Agence Global. Used by permission; **Alfred A. Knopf,** "The Negro Speaks of Rivers" and "My People" from THE COLLECTED POEMS OF LANGSTON HUGHES by Langston Hughes, edited by Arnold Rampersad with David Roessel, Associate Editor, copyright © 1994 by the Estate of Langston Hughes. Used by permission of Alfred A. Knopf, an imprint of the Knopf Doubleday Publishing Group, a division of Random House LLC. All rights reserved; **Allen & Unwin, Ltd.,** The Massacre of Saint Bartholomew by Henri Nogueres. Copyright © 1962. Allen & Unwin; **Amereon Limited,** Genghis Khan: The Emperor of All Men by Harold Lamb. Copyright © Amereon Limited; **American Heritage,** The Age of Napoleon by J. Christopher Herold (ed.). Copyright © 2002 American Heritage; **American Journal of Public Health,** Cummings SR, Ling X, Stone K. Consequences of foot binding among older women in Beijing, China. American Journal of Public Health 1997; 87(10):1677–1679; Author Solutions, The Truth of Nanak and the Sikhs, 2004. Copyright © Author Solutions; **Barbara Levy Literary Agency,** Copyright Siegfried Sassoon by kind permission of the Estate of George Sassoon; **Basil Blackwell Ltd.,** Power and Faction in Louis XIV's France by R. Mettam. Copyright © 1988 Oxford: Basil Blackwell; **Beacon Press,** The Pentagon Papers, Gravel Edition, 1971. Copyright © Beacon Press; **Bloomsbury Publishing Plc,** Mao's Great Famine: The History of China's Most Devastating Catastrophe, 1958–62 by Frank Dikötter, 2010. Copyright © Bloomsbury; **Bolchazy-Carducci Publishers,** The Complete Hitler: A Digital Desktop Reference to His Speeches and Proclamations 1932–1945 by Max Domarus. 2007. Copyright © Bolchazy-Carducci Publishers; **Boundless,** US History, Volume II: 1865—present, 2013. Copyright © Boundless; **Brill Academic Publishers,** The True Dates of the Chinese Maritime Expeditions in the Early Fifteenth Century by Jan Julius Lodewijk Duyvendak. Copyright © 1959 Brill Academic Publishers; **C.T. Evans,** C.T. Evans, "Notes on the Cold War and Dominos," http://novaonline.nvcc.edu/eli/evans/his242/notes/dominos. html; **Cambridge University Press,** CORPUS OF EARLY AFRICAN SOURCES FOR WEST AFRICAN HISTORY. edited by N. Levtzion, edited and translated by J. F. P. Hopkins. Copyright © 1981 University of Ghana, International Academic Union and Cambridge University Press. Reprinted with the permission of Cambridge University Press; **Cengage Learning,** Paul Brians, Reading About the World. Boston, MA: Cengage, 1999; **Christian Classics Ethereal Library (CCEL),** History of the Christian Church by Phillip Schaff. Copyright © 2005 Christian Classics Ethereal Library; **Christopher L.C.E. Witcombe,** Sacredness of Teotihuacan, Mexico. Copyright © Christopher L.C.E. Witcombe; **Cohen, Michael,** Peace in the Post-Cold War World by Michael Cohen from The Atlantic, December 15, 2011. Copyright © Michael Cohen. Used by permission; **Columbia University Press,** "Reading and Keeping the Books" by Boncompagno de Signa from Books, Banks, Buttons: And Other Inventions from the Middle Ages by Chiara Frugoni and William McCuaig (trans). Copyright © 2005 Columbia University Press; **Columbia University Press,** God's Playground: A History of Poland, Vol. 1: The Origins to 1795 by Norman Davies. Copyright 2005 Columbia University Press; **Columbia University Press,** Traditional Japanese Literature: An Anthology, Beginnings to 1600 by Haruo Shirane, 2008. Copyright © Columbia University Press; **Cornell University Press,** "Part II: The Ascendancy of Islam, 711–1031" from A History of Medieval Spain by Joseph F. Callaghan. Copyright © Cornell University Press; **Crabtree Publishing Company,** The Sapa Inca by Hazel Richardson from Life in Ancient South America, 2005. Copyright © the Crabtree Publishing Company; **D C Books,** Quotable Quotes by Saraswathy. Copyright © by D C Books; **David & Charles,** William Pressey quoted in People at War 1914– 1918 by Michael Moynihan (ed.). Copyright © 1988 David & Charles; **DEMCO, Inc,** Sundiata: An Epic Of Old Mali by D.T. Niane, 1995. Copyright © Demco Media; **Doubleday,** Excerpts from "Diary of a Young Girl: The Definitive Edition" by Anne Frank, edited by Otto H. Frank and Mirjam Pressler, translated by Susan Massotty, translation copyright © 1995 by Doubleday, a division of Random House LLC. Used by permission of Doubleday, an imprint of the Knopf Doubleday Publishing Group, a division of Random House LLC. All rights reserved; **Dover Publications,** How the Other Half Lives by Jacob Riis. Copyright © Dover Publications; **Dover Publications, Inc.,** The Fifteen Decisive Battles of the World: From Marathon to Waterloo by Edward Shepherd Creasy. Copyright © Dover Publications. Used by permission; **Encyclopedia Britannica, Inc.,** John P. Rafferty, "Donald C. Johanson" Encyclopædia Britannica, 2014. Reprinted with permission from Encyclopædia Britannica, © 2014 by Encyclopædia Britannica, Inc.; **Encyclopedia Britannica, Inc.,** Dame Kathleen Mary Kenyon, "Jericho," Encyclopædia Britannica, 2014; **Encyclopedia Britannica, Inc.,** Unknown, "Catalhüyük," Encyclopædia Britannica, 2014. Reprinted with permission from Encyclopædia Britannica, © 2014 by Encyclopædia Britannica, Inc.; **Encyclopedia Britannica, Inc.,** The Editors of Encyclopædia Britannica, "Olduvai Gorge," Encyclopædia Britannica, 2014. Reprinted with permission from Encyclopædia Britannica, © 2014 by Encyclopædia Britannica, Inc.; **Encyclopedia Britannica, Inc.,** The Editors of Encyclopædia Britannica, "Mary Douglas Leakey," Encyclopædia Britannica, 2014. Reprinted with permission from Encyclopædia Britannica, © 2014 by Encyclopædia Britannica, Inc.; **Encyclopedia Britannica, Inc.,** The Editors of Encyclopædia Britannica, "Iceman," Encyclopædia Britannica, 2014. Reprinted with permission from Encyclopædia Britannica, © 2014 by Encyclopædia Britannica, Inc.; **Encyclopedia Britannica, Inc.,** Unknown, "Cahokia," Encyclopædia Britannica, 2014. Reprinted with permission from Encyclopædia Britannica, © 2014 by Encyclopædia Britannica, Inc.; **Encyclopedia Britannica, Inc.,** Unknown, "Inca Religion," Encyclopædia Britannica, 2014; **Encyclopedia Britannica, Inc.,** Marco Polo, The book of Ser Marco Polo, the Venetian, concerning the kingdoms and marvels of the East. (Henry Yule, tr.) London: J. Murray, 1871; **Encyclopedia Britannica, Inc.,** Unknown, "Tsunami," Encyclopædia Britannica, 2014; **Encyclopedia Britannica, Inc.,** J O'Connor and E F Robertson, "Cheng Dawei." http://www-history.mcs.

Britannica, Inc., Joseph Hsing-san Shih, S.J., "Matteo Ricci," Encyclopædia Britannica, 2014; **Encyclopedia Britannica, Inc.,** The Editors of Encyclopædia Britannica, "Middle Passage," Encyclopædia Britannica, 2014. Reprinted with permission from Encyclopædia Britannica, © 2014 by Encyclopædia Britannica, Inc.; **Encyclopedia Britannica, Inc.,** Michael Sullivan, "Chinese Painting," Encyclopædia Britannica, 2014; **Encyclopedia Britannica, Inc.,** The Editors of Encyclopædia Britannica, "George Macartney, Earl Macartney, Viscount Macartney of Dervock, Baron of Lissanoure, Baron Macartney of Parkhurst and of Auchinleck, Lord Macartney," Reprinted with permission from Encyclopædia Britannica, © 2014 by Encyclopædia Britannica, Inc.; **Encyclopedia Britannica, Inc.,** Ludwig von Mises, Human Action. Ludwig Von Mises Institute, 1949. Copyright © Ludwig Von Mises Institute; **Encyclopedia Britannica, Inc.,** Agnus Ullmann, "Louis Pasteur," Encyclopædia Britannica, 2014. Reprinted with permission from Encyclopædia Britannica, © 2014 by Encyclopædia Britannica, Inc.; **Encyclopedia Britannica, Inc.,** William Loren Katz, "Toussaint L'Ouverture and the Haitian Revolution," 2014. http://people.hofstra.edu/alan_j_singer/CoursePacks/ToussaintLOuvertureandtheHaitianRevolution.pdf. Copyright © Hofstra University; **Encyclopedia Britannica, Inc.,** The Editors of Encyclopædia Britannica, "Pogrom," Encyclopædia Britannica, 2014. Reprinted with permission from Encyclopædia Britannica, © 2014 by Encyclopædia Britannica, Inc.; **Encyclopedia Britannica, Inc.,** Unknown, "Hidalgo's Call for Mexican Independence," 2014. Copyright © Mexico History Directory; **Encyclopedia Britannica, Inc.,** Paul Brians, Reading About the World. Boston, MA: Cengage, 1999; **Encyclopedia Britannica, Inc.,** Luigi Villari, The Awakening of Italy: The Fascista Regeneration. London, 1924, pp. 171–188; **Encyclopedia Britannica, Inc.,** Adolph Hitler, Mein Kampf. London. Hurst and Blackett, Ltd., 1939; **Encyclopedia Britannica, Inc.,** The Editors of Encyclopædia Britannica, "Venustiano Carranza," Encyclopædia Britannica, 2014; **Encyclopedia Britannica, Inc.,** Unknown, "Winston Churchill: calling for a United States of Europe", European Commission, 2014. http://europa.eu/about-eu/eu-history/founding-fathers/pdf/winston_churchill_ en.pdf; **Encyclopedia Britannica, Inc.,** Ronald Francis Hingley, "Joseph Stalin," Encyclopædia Britannica, 2014; **Encyclopedia Britannica, Inc.,** The Editors of Encyclopædia Britannica, "Bataan Death March," Encyclopædia Britannica, 2014. Reprinted with permission from Encyclopædia Britannica, © 2014 by Encyclopædia Britannica, Inc.; **Encyclopedia Britannica, Inc.,** Michael Berenbaum, "Holocaust," Encyclopædia Britannica, 2014; **Encyclopedia Britannica, Inc.,** The Editors of Encyclopædia Britannica, "The Munich Agreement," Encyclopædia Britannica, 2014. Reprinted with permission from Encyclopædia Britannica, © 2014 by Encyclopædia Britannica, Inc.; **Encyclopedia Britannica, Inc.,** The Editors of Encyclopædia Britannica, "Allied Powers," Encyclopædia Britannica, 2014; **Encyclopedia Britannica, Inc.,** The Editors of Encyclopædia Britannica, "Neville Chamberlain," Encyclopædia Britannica, 2014. Reprinted with permission from Encyclopædia Britannica, © 2014 by Encyclopædia Britannica, Inc.; **Encyclopedia Britannica, Inc.,** The Editors of Encyclopædia Britannica, "Bataan Death March," Encyclopædia Britannica, 2014. Reprinted with permission from Encyclopædia Britannica, © 2014 by Encyclopædia Britannica, Inc.; **Encyclopedia Britannica, Inc.,** The Editors of Encyclopædia Britannica, "Nagasaki," Encyclopædia Britannica, 2014. Reprinted with permission from Encyclopædia Britannica, © 2014 by Encyclopædia Britannica, Inc.; **Encyclopedia Britannica, Inc.,** C.T. Evans, "Notes on the Cold War and Dominos," http://novaonline.nvcc.edu/eli/evans/his242/notes/dominos.html; **Encyclopedia Britannica, Inc.,** The Editors of Encyclopædia Britannica, "Solidarity," Encyclopædia Britannica, 2014; **European Commission, Unknown,** "Winston Churchill: calling for a United States of Europe", European Commission, 2014. http://europa.eu/about-eu/eu-history/founding-fathers/pdf/winston_churchill_en.pdf; **Foreign Languages Press,** "The Chinese People Have Stood Up, September 21, 1949" from Selected Works of Mao Tse-Tung by Mao Tse-Tung. Copyright © 1965 Foreign Languages Press; **Foundation for Economic Education,** Lenin: A Biography, by Yuri Maltsev from Ideas of Liberty, March 2002. Copyright © Foundation for Economic Education. Used by permission; **Franz Steiner Verlag,** Conspiracy Encyclopedia by Thom Burnett, 2006. Copyright © Franz Steiner Verlag; **George Allen and Unwin,** Class Structure and Economic Growth: India & Pakistan since the Moghuls by Angus Maddison. Copyright © 1971 George Allen & Unwin Limited; **George Spindler,** A History of the African People, Fifth edition by Jomo Kenyatta. Copyright © n.d. George Spindler; **Georgetown University Press,** "I ACCUSE…!" Open Letter to the President of the French Republic by Emile Zola and Shelley Temchin and Jean-Max Guieu (trans.). Copyright © 2011 Shelley Temchin and Jean-Max Guieu, Georgetown University; **Globe Pequot Press,** 48 Hours of Kristallnact: Night of Destruction/Dawn of the Holocaust by Michael Goeffrey Bard. Copyright © 2008 Globe Pequot; **Greenwood Press, Inc.,** Chapter 6: Building Communism: 1921–1953 from The History of Russia by Charles E. Ziegler. Copyright © Greenwood Press; **Gyan Publishing House,** Freedom Fighters of India by M G Agrawal, 2008. Copyright © Gyan Publishing House; **Hachette UK (brand under Lagardère Group),** Marco Polo, The book of Ser Marco Polo, the Venetian, concerning the kingdoms and marvels of the East. (Henry Yule, tr.) London: J. Murray, 1871; **Harold Ober Associates,** The Collected Poems of Langston Hughes by Langston Hughes edited by Arnold Rampersad with David Roessel, Associate Editor. Copyright © 1994 by the Estate of Langston Hughes. Used by permission of Harold Ober Associates Incorporated; **Harper Collins Publishers,** The French and Indian War. by Walter R. Borneman. Copyright © 2007 Harper Collins; **HarperCollins Publishers,** The French and Indian War by Borneman, Walter R. Copyright © 2007 by HarperCollins; **Harvard University Press,** Natural History by Pliny the Elder and D.E. Eicholz (trans.). Copyright © 1967 Harvard University Press; **Harvard University Press,** "Marcus Tullius" by Cicero from Cicero: De re Publica (On the Republic), Clinton W. Keyes (trans.). Copyright © 1928 Harvard University Press; **Harvard University Press,** Apostles and Agitators: Italy's Marxist Revolutionary Tradition by Richard Drake, 2009. Copyright © Harvard University Press; **Hendrickson Publishers,** Holy Bible: King James Version, 1611 Edition. Copyright © 2006 by Hendrickson Publishers; **Hendrickson Publishers,** Josephus Describes the Mass Suicide at Masada. Copyright © Hendrickson Publishers; **Henry Holt & Company,** "Livy, The History of Rome" from The Classical Roman Reader: New Encounters with Ancient Rome by Kenneth J. Atchity (ed.). Copyright © 1998 Oxford University Press; **Hofstra University,** William Loren Katz, "Toussaint L'Ouverture and the Haitian Revolution," 2014. http://people.hofstra.edu/alan_j_singer/CoursePacks/ToussaintLOuvertureandtheHaitianRevolution.pdf. Copyright © Hofstra University; **Houghton Mifflin Harcourt,** "How Masha Secured Her Freedom" in Memoirs of a Revolutionist by Peter Kropotkin and Georg Brandes. Copyright © 2009 Houghton Mifflin Harcourt; **Houghton Mifflin Harcourt Publishing Company,** Silent Spring by Rachel Carson. Copyright © Houghton Mifflin Harcourt; **Human Security Research Group,** Overview of the Human Security Report 2009/2010: The Cause of Peace and the Shrinking Costs of War. Copyright © The Human Security Research Group; **HURST AND BLACKETT LTD,** Adolph Hitler, Mein Kampf. London. Hurst and Blackett, Ltd., 1939; **Immanuel Kant,** "Of National Characteristics, so far as they Depend on the Distinct Feeling of the Beautiful and the Sublime," 1764; **Independent,** The Historical Notes: God and England Made the Irish Famine by Brendan Graham. Copyright © The Independent. Used by permission; **Independent,** No Need to Apologise for the Potato Famine by Ruth Dudley Edwards. Copyright © The Independent. Used by permission; **Institute of Islamic Knowledge,** English Translation of the Meaning of Al-Qur'an: The Guidance for Mankind translated by Muhammad Farooq-i-Azam Malik. Copyright © 1997 The Institute of Islamic Knowledge. Used by permission; **J.J. O'Connor,** J O'Connor and E F Robertson, "Cheng Dawei." http://wwwhistory. mcs.st-and.ac.uk/Biographies/Cheng_Dawei.html; **John Benjamins Publishing Company,** Dialectics and Revolution, Volume 2 by DeGrood, David H Copyright © 1978 by John Benjamins Publishing; **Longman Publishing Group,** Christine de Pisan from Sources of the West, Volume 1: From the Beginning to 1715 by Mark Kishlansky and Daniel Gordon (trans.). Copyright © 2011 Pearson; **Lucent Books, Inc.,** "The Fall of Constantinople" from The Age of Feudalism by Geoffrey Villehardouin and Timothy L. Biel (ed.). Copyright © 1994 Lucent Books; **Lucent Books, Inc.,** "The Growing Challenge" by Martin Luther from The Reformation by Sarah Flowers. Copyright © 1995 Lucent Books; **Lucent Books, Inc.,** Life on an African Slave Ship by Joseph Kleinman & Eileen Kurtis-Kleinman. Copyright © 2000 Lucent Books; **Macmillan Press Ltd.,** Arms for Empire by Edward Douglas Leach. Copyright © 1973 Macmillan; **Macmillan Press Ltd.,** Life in Ancient Athens: The Social and Public Life of a Classical Athenian from Day to Day by T.G. Tucker. Copyright © Macmillan Press, Ltd; **Macmillan Press Ltd.,** Arms for Empire by Douglas Edward Leach. Copyright © 1973 by MacMillan Publishers; **Macmillan Publishing Company,** "Political

MacMillan Publishers; **Macmillan Publishing Company,** "Political Authority" by Denis Diderot from Diderot's Selected Writings by Lester G. Crocker (Ed.) and Derek Coltman (Trans.). Copyright © 1966 Macmillan; **Macmillan Publishing Company,** Clemenceau and the Third Republic by J. Hampden Jackson. Copyright © 1979 Macmillan; **Macmillan Publishing Company,** Excerpt from History of the Arabs: From the Earliest Times to the Present by Philip K Hitti. Copyright © Macmillan; **Methuen Publishing, Ltd.,** Luigi Villari, The Awakening of Italy: The Fascista Regeneration. London, 1924, pp. 171–188; **Mexico History Directory,** Unknown, "Hidalgo's Call for Mexican Independence," 2014. Copyright © Mexico History Directory; **Military Heritage Press,** a division of Marboro Books Corporation, "The Making of Peace" from The Thirty Years War by Geoffrey Parker. Copyright © 1997 Military Heritage Press; **Michigan Publishing,** University of Michigan Library, "Slave Trade," by Louis Jaucourt, The Encyclopedia of Diderot & d'Alembert Collaborative Translation Project, translated by Stephanie Noble, 2007, originally published in 1765, Paris, France; **Monthly Review Magazine,** The Great Irish Famine: A Crime of Free Market Economics by John Newsinger from The Monthly Review, April 1996. Copyright © The Monthly Review. Used by permission; **National Council of Churches,** Matthew 5:5–9 from The Holy Bible with the Apocrypha. Copyright © 1994 National Council of the Churches of Christ; **National Council of Churches,** "I Corinthians, Chapter 13" from Holy Bible: With the Apocryphal. Copyright © 1989 National Council of Churches of Christ; **Navajivan Trust,** Passive resistance is a method. Copyright © The Navajivan Trust. Used by permission; **Navajivan Trust,** India Home Rule by Mohandas Gandhi. Copyright © Navajivan Trust; **New York University Press,** Ireland: Contested Ideas of Nationalism and History by Hugh F Kearney. Copyright © New York University Press; **NuVision Publications,** LLC., The Code of Hammurabi by King, L. W. Copyright © 1999 by NuVision Publications; **Orion,** Age of Revolution 1789–1848 by Eric Hobsbawm. Copyright © 2010 by Orion Publishing Group Ltd; **Oxbow Books (UK),** William the Conqueror by David Bates. Copyright © 2001 Tempus Pub Limited; **Oxford University Press (US),** C. Suetonius Tranquillus. 2008. Lives of the Caesars. Catharine Edwards (trans). Oxford University Press; **Oxford University Press (US),** "Introduction" from Islam and the West by Bernard Lewis. Copyright © Oxford University Press; **Oxford University Press (US),** Everyday Life in Ancient Greece by C.E. Robinson. Copyright © Oxford University Press; **Oxford University Press (US),** Everyday Life in Ancient Greece by C.E. Robinson. Copyright © Oxford University Press; **Oxford University Press (US),** Rethinking the Soviet Experience: Politics and History Since 1917 by Stephen F. Cohen. Copyright © Oxford University Press; **Palgrave Macmillan,** A History of Ireland by Mike Cronin. Copyright © Palgrave Macmillan; **Panorama of Russia,** The Memoirs of Stalin's Former Secretary by Boris Bazhanov, 1992. Copyright © Panorama of Russia; **Pearson Education,** Letters to a Law Student: A Guide to Studying Law at University by Nicolas McBride. Copyright © Pearson. Used by permission; **Penguin Books, Ltd. (UK),** "Freedom from Fear" from FREEDOM FROM FEAR AND OTHER WRITINGS, REVISED EDITION by Aung San Suu Kyi, edited by Michael Aris, copyright © 1991, 1995 by Aung San Suu Kyi. Used by permission of Viking Penguin, a division of Penguin Group (USA) LLC; **Penguin Books, Ltd. (UK),** The Canterbury Tales. Copyright © Penguin Books, Ltd. (UK); **Penguin Group USA,** "Bulgarian Statesman interviewed by Leon Trotsky" from The Balkans, 1804–1999 by Marsha Glinny (ed.). Copyright © 2001 Penguin; **Pennsylvania State University Press,** Locke, John. 2005. The Wealth of Nations. Pennsylvania State University; **Periplus Publishing Group,** The Tale of Genji by Murasaki Shikibu, 2006. Copyright © Tuttle Publishing; **Popular Press,** A Pillar of Fire to Follow: American Indian Dramas, 1808–1859 by Priscilla Sears, 1982 Copyright © Popular Press; **Praeger Publishers,** Excerpts from Chapter 19 of The Great Armies of Antiquity by Richard A Gabriel. Copyright © Praeger Publishers; **Prentice-Hall (Pearson Prentice-Hall) 2005,** "Democracy and Dictatorship: The Western World in Crisis, German War Letter: 'One Blood-Soaked, Corpse-Strewn Field'" from Aspects of World Civilization: Problems and Sources in History, Volume 2 by Perry M. Rogers. Copyright © 2002 Prentice Hall; **Princeton University,** The Roman Empire Lasted a Lot Longer... by Peter Brown. Copyright © Princeton University; **Progress Publishers,** Lenin's Testament 1922 by Vladimir Lenin from Lenin, Collected Works, Vol. 36. Copyright © Progress Publishers; **Quercus Publishing Plc,** 50 Political Ideas You Really Need to Know by Ben Dupre, 2011. Copyright © Quercus; **Random House, Inc.,** All Quiet on the Western Front by Erich Maria Remarque, 2010. Copyright © Random House; **Read How You Want,** Germinal: Easyread Comfort Edition by Emile Zola, 2006. Copyright © ReadHowYouWant.com; **Routledge Publishers,** Ibn Battuta: Travels in Asia and Africa 1325–1354 by Ibn Battua and H.A.R. Gibb (trans.). Copyright © 1986 Routledge; **Routledge, Ltd.,** A History of Ireland: From Earliest Times to 1922 by Edmund Curtis. Copyright © Routledge; **Routledge, Ltd.,** "Chapter 3: The Economic and Social Impact of Colonial Rule in India" by Angus Maddison from Class Structure and Economic Growth: India & Pakistan Since the Moghuls. Copyright © Routledge, Ltd; **Schocken Books,** "The Solitude of Self," January 18, 1892 by Elizabeth Cady Stanton from The Elizabeth Cady Stanton–Susan B. Anthony Reader: Correspondence, Writings, Speeches by Ellen Carol DuBois and Gerda Lerner. Copyright © 1987 Schocken Books; **Stephanie Noble,** "Slave trade." By Jaucourt, Louis, Chevalier de. The Encyclopedia of Diderot & d'Alembert Collaborative Translation Project. Translated by Stephanie Noble. Michigan Publishing, University of Michigan Library, 2007. Copyright © Stephanie Noble; **Taylor & Francis Books, Ltd** (Routledge: Military and Strategic Studies), The Secret History of the Mongols: The Life and Times of Chinggis Khan by Urgunge Onon. Copyright © Taylor and Francis; **The Bruce Publishing Company,** "Apprenticeship in the Weaving Industry" from A Source Book for Medieval Economic History by Roy C. Cave and Herbert H. Coulson. Copyright © 1965 The Bruce Publishing Company; **The Churchill Society,** "Address to the House of Commons, June 4, 1940" from Wartime Speeches by Winston Churchill. Copyright © n.d. The Churchill Society; **The McGraw-Hill Companies,** "Secret Memorandum to Tsar Alexander I, 1820" by Clemens von Metternich in Western Civilization: Sources, Images, Interpretations, from the Renaissance to the Present by Dennis Sherman (ed.). Copyright © 2003 McGraw-Hill; **The National Center for Public Policy Research,** "Magna Carta or, The Great Charter of King John Granted June 15, 1215." Copyright © The National Center; **The New York Times Company,** "Like Taking the Napoleon Chapters Out of War and Peace by Simon Karlinsky from The New York Times, April 25, 1976. Copyright © The New York Times; **The Washington Post,** The Era of His Ways; In Which We Choose The Most Important Man of the Last Thousand Years from The Washington Post, December 31, 1995. Copyright © The Washington Post. Used by permission; **The Yale Law School,** Declaration of the Rights of Man, 1789. Copyright © Lillian Goldman Law Library; **Thomas Nelson, Inc.,** Ghana: The Autobiography of Kwame Nkrumah by Kwame Nkrumah. Copyright © Thomas Nelson, Inc.; **Turkish Times,** Adana Çiftçileriyle Konusma by Talat S. Halman, December 1, 1995. Copyright © The Turkish Times; **University of California Museum of Paleontology, Berkeley,** Monoculture and the Irish Potato Famine: Cases of Missing Genetic Variation from Understanding Evolution. Copyright © University of California Berkeley Museum of Paleontology. Used by permission; **University of Chicago Press Books,** Plutarch's Life of Tiberius Gracchus. Copyright © University of Chicago Press Books; **University of Hawaii Press,** Tea in Japan: Essays on the History of Chanoyu by H. Paul Varley and Isao Kumakura, 1989. Copyright © University of Hawaii Press; **University of Iowa Press,** Memoirs of a Revolutionary by Victor Serge, 2002. Copyright © University of Iowa Press; **University of North Carolina Press,** From THE POEMS OF PHILLIS WHEATLEY edited and with an introduction by Julian D. Mason Jr. Copyright © 1966 by the University of North Carolina Press, renewed 1989. Used by permission of the publisher. www.uncpress.unc.edu; **University of Pennsylvania Museum of Archaeology and Anthropology,** Philadelphia, University of Pennsylvania. Dept. of History: Translations and Reprints from the Original Sources of European History (Philadelphia, University of Pennsylvania Press [1897?–1907?]), Vol 4, 1, pp. 28–30. This text is in the public domain; **University of Pennsylvania Press,** Fulcher of Chartres. Chronicle of the First Crusade by Martha Evelyn translated by McGinty. Copyright © 1941 University of Pennsylvania Press; **Vintage Books,** The Discoverers by Daniel J. Boorstein. Copyright © 1983 Vintage Books; **Vital Speeches of the Day,** Glory and Hope Speech by Nelson Mandela, May 11, 1994. Copyright © Vital Speeches of the Day; **W.W. Norton & Company, Inc.,** the Feminine Mystique by Betty Friedan. Copyright © W.W. Norton & Company; **Western Pennsylvania Conservancy,** A Building Should Grace its Environment Rather than Disgrace it from Western Pennsylvania Conservancy. Copyright © Western Pennsylvania Conservancy; **Wikimedia Foundation,** Realpolitik in Europe and

Britain. Copyright © Wikimedia Foundation; **Wikimedia Foundation,** Pan-Slavism: Origins. Copyright © Wikimedia Foundation; **Writers House LLC,** "I Have a Dream" by Martin Luther King. Copyright © 1963 Dr. Martin Luther King, Jr. Copyright © 1991 Coretta Scott King. Used by permission; **Writers House LLC,** "Letters From a Birmingham Jail" by Martin Luther King. Copyright © 1963 Dr. Martin Luther King, Jr. Copyright © renewed 1991 Coretta Scott King. Used by permission; **Yale Center for the Study of Globalization,** The History of Zero. Copyright © Yale Center for the Study of Globalization; **Yale University Press,** A Source Book for Russian History, Vol. 2. 1972. G. Vernadsky (trans.) New Haven: Yale University Press; **Yale University Press,** "Catherine the Great, Decree on Serfs" from A Source Book for Russian History translated by G. Vernadsky. Copyright © 1972 by the Yale University Press; **Yale University Press,** Philotheos, quoted in "Tsar and People: Studies in Russian Myths" by Michael Cherniavsky. Copyright © 2011 Yale University Press; **Yale University Press,** The Suggestive Portrait of Shah 'Abbas: Prayer and Likeness in a Safavid Shahnama by Kishwar Rizvi. Copyright © Yale University Press.